Early Modern Catholicism makes available in modern spelling and punctuation substantial Catholic contributions to literature, history, political thought, devotion, and theology in the sixteenth and early seventeenth centuries. Rather than perpetuate the usual stereotypes and misinformation, it provides a fresh look at Catholic writing long suppressed, marginalized, and ignored. The anthology gives back voices to those silenced by prejudice, exile, persecution, or martyrdom while attention to actual texts challenges conventional beliefs about the period.

The anthology is divided into eight sections entitled CONTROVERSIES, LIVES AND DEATHS, POETRY, INSTRUCTIONS AND DEVOTIONS, DRAMA, HISTORIES, FICTION, and DOCUMENTS, and includes seventeen black and white illustrations from a variety of Early Modern sources. Amongst the selections are texts which illuminate the role of women in recusant community and in the Church; the rich traditions of prayer and mysticism; the theology and politics of martyrdom; the emergence of the Catholic Baroque in literature and art; and the polemical battles fought within the Church and against its enemies. *Early Modern Catholicism* also provides a context that redefines the established canons of Early Modern England, including such figures as Edmund Spenser, John Donne, John Milton, William Shakespeare, and Ben Jonson.

1. Durante Alberti, 'The Martyrs Picture', 1583. The Blessed Trinity is depicted with two martyrs, St Thomas of Canterbury (1118–70) on the left and St Edmund of East Anglia (849–69) on the right. Christ's blood falls on the British Isles and erupts in flame. The text is the College motto, *Ignem veni mittere in terram* (I have come to bring fire to the earth) (Luke 12:49). The painting forms the centrepiece for the martyr frescoes memorialized in Johannes Baptista de Cavalleriis' *Ecclesiae Anglicanae Trophaea* (1584). Seminarians today still sing the *Te Deum* around the painting to honour English martyrs.

EARLY MODERN CATHOLICISM

An Anthology of Primary Sources

ROBERT S. MIOLA

OXFORD

UNIVERSITY PRESS

OXFORD
UNIVERSITY PRESS

Great Clarendon Street, Oxford OX2 6DP

Oxford University Press is a department of the University of Oxford.
It furthers the University's objective of excellence in research, scholarship,
and education by publishing worldwide in

Oxford New York

Auckland Cape Town Dar es Salaam Hong Kong Karachi
Kuala Lumpur Madrid Melbourne Mexico City Nairobi
New Delhi Shanghai Taipei Toronto

With offices in

Argentina Austria Brazil Chile Czech Republic France Greece
Guatemala Hungary Italy Japan Poland Portugal Singapore
South Korea Switzerland Thailand Turkey Ukraine Vietnam

Oxford is a registered trade mark of Oxford University Press
in the UK and in certain other countries

Published in the United States
by Oxford University Press Inc., New York

British Library Cataloguing in Publication Data

Data available

Library of Congress Cataloging in Publication Data

Data available

Typeset by SPI Publisher Services, Pondicherry, India
Printed in Great Britain
on acid-free paper by
Antony Rowe Ltd., Chippenham

ISBN 978–0–19–925985–4
ISBN 978–0–19–925986–1 (Pbk.)

1 3 5 7 9 10 8 6 4 2

ACKNOWLEDGEMENTS

I record permission to reprint texts and illustrations in the Textual Notes.

Thanks first go to Thomas M. McCoog, SJ, who shared with me the resources of the Jesuit archives on Farm Street as well as his rich knowledge of the period; and to David Bevington, who read drafts with shrewd judgement for general concept as well as a sharp eye for detail. I am grateful to many other friends and colleagues who have read selections or discussed the project with me over the years: Arthur Marotti, Peter Milward, SJ, Paul Voss, R. V. Young, Gerard Kilroy, Donna B. Hamilton, Dennis Taylor, Alison Shell, and Phebe Jensen. John W. O'Malley, SJ, Vincent Carey, D. R. Woolf, F. J. Levy, and H. R. Woudhuysen answered queries and made helpful suggestions. Heather Wolfe and Laetitia Yeandle gave expert assistance with manuscript readings; Frank Romer carefully checked my translations of Mariana and Bellarmine. Gen Rafferty transformed early modern texts into modern typefaces. I am also grateful to my teachers (especially John Olin and Paul Memmo at Fordham University) and to my students.

The project could not have come to fruition without institutional support, especially from Loyola College of Maryland, its Gerard Manley Hopkins Chair of English, sabbaticals, summer grants, and library, including a timely investment in digital databases such as Early English Books Online. I am also indebted to the Knott Foundation and the Catholic Studies Program at Loyola (Paul Bagley) for funding a semester's leave. The National Endowment for the Humanities and the Folger Shakespeare Library also supported research through grants. I am grateful to libraries and their staffs, again the Folger Shakespeare Library (Gail Kern Paster, Richard Kuhta, and Betsy Walsh), The New York Public Library, the Biblioteca Apostolica Vaticana, the Venerable English College, Rome (Sister Mary Joseph), the Bodleian at Oxford, and the British Library. Other institutions, associations, and gracious individuals provided opportunities to speak and collegial forums: the Lancaster Shakespeare Conference (Richard Dutton), Wheaton College (Beatrice Batson), St Peter's College (James Loughran, SJ), Cornell University (Carol Kaske), the University of Alabama at Tuscaloosa (Gary Taylor), the University of Massachusetts at Amherst (Arthur Kinney), the Centro di Alti Studi di San Bruno, Segni (Sister Maria del Fiat), the International Shakespeare Conference in Stratford (Peter Holland), the Recusant Society, The Renaissance Society of America, the Shakespeare Association of America, and Villa Le Balze, Florence (Michael Collins and Georgetown University). Steven Miola gave expert technical help with the illustrations. Diligent student assistants worked well over the years: Rachel Miola, Kate Barker, Ashley St Thomas, and John Wixted.

The personal debts are beyond telling, especially those to my daughters at home, Rose, Karen, and Michele, and my son Daniel. If it were appropriate to dedicate an anthology, this one would belong to Timothy S. Healy, SJ, whose edition of Donne's *Ignatius his Conclave* first started me thinking about these issues; the memory of his voice, laughing and growling, has been a constant companion. I hope this book is worthy of him and its many benefactors.

CONTENTS

POETRY

INSTRUCTIONS AND DEVOTIONS

DRAMA

(Dates record composition or first performance.)

HISTORIES

FICTION

DOCUMENTS

LIST OF ILLUSTRATIONS

NOTE ON BIBLE VERSIONS

For references to the Bible I have used throughout the Douay-Rheims version (with the Challoner revisions, 1749–52). This version differs from most Protestant ones in its inclusion of the seven Deuterocanonical books (Tobias, Judith, Wisdom, Ecclesiasticus, Baruch, 1 and 2 Machabees), and some additions to Esther and Daniel. The numbering of psalms also differs slightly: 10–146 here corresponds roughly to 11–147 there (113–14 sometimes appears as 115–16). Protestant Bibles call the four books of Kings 1 and 2 Samuel, 1 and 2 Kings respectively. Similarly, 1 and 2 Paralipomenon become there 1 and 2 Chronicles; 2 Esdras, Nehemiah; Canticles, the Song of Solomon or Song of Songs; Jonas, Jonah; and Apocalypse, Revelation.

INTRODUCTION

By any other name?

This anthology makes available in modern spelling and punctuation substantial Catholic contributions to literature, history, and theology in the sixteenth and early seventeenth centuries. Featuring some essential medieval and Continental works, *Early Modern Catholicism* aims to recover the Catholic origins and expressions of the English Renaissance (*c*.1520–1640). The term 'Catholic' (from *katholicos*, 'universal') names the Western Latin church loyal to Rome, as it did originally in the work of St Cyprian (*c*.252). This term, of course, is fraught with complexities. The Eastern schism (1054) established a rival Catholic structure with a patriarch in Constantinople. The Roman Church experienced severe internal divisions as it struggled to balance temporal and spiritual concerns and to lead a far-flung collection of powerful, autonomous kingdoms. Church authorities, moreover, often suspected their own: Savonarola was burned for heresy; the works of Erasmus and St Ignatius Loyola made the Index of Prohibited Books; St Teresa of Ávila and St John of the Cross appeared before the Inquisition; Mary Ward and her order (and later the Jesuits) endured papal suppression.

Some, moreover, protested that the Roman Church was not Catholic at all, not the universal church Christ had established on earth, but rather the corrupt kingdom of Antichrist. John Jewel, bishop of Salisbury and defender of the Elizabethan settlement, discoursed lengthily on 'the Roman religion, which of late hath been accounted Catholic' (*A Reply unto M. Harding's Answer*, 1565, title-page). Speaking for many, John Philpot, archdeacon of Winchester, argued that the Roman Church could not be considered Catholic because it had never gained acceptance in Asia and Africa, because it departed from the Bible in matters of doctrine and sacraments, and because it had a corrupt leadership. Before being burned for heresy he declared, 'I acknowledge one, holy, Catholic, and apostolic Church, whereof I am a member (I praise God) and I am of that Catholic faith of Christ, whereinto I was baptized' (*The Examination of the Constant Martyr of Christ, John Philpot*, 1556, sig. D8).

John Foxe, influential historian and polemicist, likewise corrected the error of all who thought the false Church of Rome 'the right Catholic mother' (*Acts and Monuments*, 1610, sig. ¶3ᵛ). Thinkers such as these generally called the Roman Church 'papist', often in combination with abusive epithets, rather than 'Catholic'. Still, even as it became a flashpoint for debates on history, the visibility of church, the nature of apostolic succession, the status of early Christian communities, the primacy of Scripture, and the authority of the pope, the term 'Catholic' prevailed to name the traditional Latin church in the West.

To designate the various movements initiated by Luther and others in opposition to the Roman Catholic Church I use the term 'Protestant'. This sense of 'Protestant' originated at the Holy Roman Emperor's assembly at Speyer (1529), when princes who supported Martin Luther and Ulrich Zwingli issued a *protestatio* announcing that they would not tolerate Catholicism within their borders. The term became part of German imperial politics in the sixteenth century and later designated a military alliance against Roman Catholic states, the *Protestantische Union* (1608–21). The English religious movements came to be called 'Protestant' because the name suggested affinities with the European movements and a common protest against Rome. Some new sects, however, preferred to be called 'Evangelical', from *evangelium*, 'good news', because this name asserted the primacy of the Gospel. Many other names arose to identify specific Protestant communities, often as terms of reproach—Lutherans, Calvinists, Zwinglians, Anabaptists, Familists, and Puritans. This last, appearing in the 1560s, has an especially rich and complicated history in England, generally nominating all those who wanted further purification—doctrinal and organizational—of the English Church. Before railing against Catholics, John Norden rose to an insight that neither he nor many on either side could maintain: 'it is not the name or title of a Protestant, Christian, or Catholic, but the true imitation of Christ that maketh a Christian' (*A Mirror for the Multitude*, 1586, title-page.).

Late and reluctantly, I abandoned my original title for this collection, *The Catholic Renaissance*, for *Early Modern Catholicism*. Both 'Renaissance' and 'Early Modern' are chronologically indeterminate, capable of flexible definition. But 'Renaissance' ('rebirth'), first coined by the French historian Jules Michelet in the 1850s, perpetuates the traditional historical schematics I hope to challenge, as it signifies discontinuity with the medieval past and the Protestant future. *The Catholic Renaissance*, moreover, could easily be taken to mean merely a rebirth in the precincts of Catholicism, on analogy to the Italian Renaissance, the Dutch Renaissance, the Harlem Renaissance, and so on. I wish to advance a much broader thesis, namely that the period we used to call the Renaissance is importantly Catholic in its origins and expressions. Hence I take issue with Jacob Burckhardt's seminal *Die Kultur der Renaissance in Italien* ('The Civilization of the

Renaissance in Italy', 1860) in so far as it portrayed the Church as an outdated medieval institution, governed by corrupt popes, over and against which the Renaissance occurred. To be sure, Burckhardt took notice of such learned churchmen as Pope Nicholas V, but he characterized Humanism as essentially a pagan, oppositional movement. And yet, Church traditions supported the New Learning, and some Catholics became its leading figures: Lorenzo Valla, for example, whose exposure of the Latin 'Donation of Constantine' as a forgery demolished papal claims for temporal power and won for him the position of Apostolic Secretary; Cardinal Ximénez de Cisneros, who founded the University of Alcalá and published the remarkable Complutensian Polyglot Bible; Desiderius Erasmus, textual critic and translator of the New Testament, who thought of himself as continuing the work of St Jerome; and, in England, Thomas More, who welcomed correction of the Vulgate and translation of the Bible into the vernacular.

Since Burckhardt's essay, moreover, the rise of social history has shifted focus from the papacy and institutional Church and redefined Catholicism in the process. In 1929 Lucien Febvre and Marc Bloch founded *Annales d'histoire économique et sociale*, a French journal that revolutionized the study of the past by emphasizing geographical, economic, and social factors. That year Febvre also rejected the conventional understanding of the 'Reformation' as 'une question mal posée' (a badly posed question): he argued that simple revulsion over abuses did not precipitate the changes but rather a deep shift in religious sentiment, a new hunger for the divine which the old forms, created in different economic and social environments, could not accommodate. 'To the degree Febvre was correct,' writes John W. O'Malley, 'he shot the foundation out from under standard church history of the sixteenth century and, hence, out from under the standard categories of interpret-ations—like Catholic Reform and Counter Reformation' (*Trent and all that*, 2000: 97). And 'Renaissance', too, at least as Burckhardt conceived the period and the Catholic Church. For the French social historians, and those in Italy (Giuseppe De Luca and Gabriele De Rosa), Catholicism in this period best reveals itself 'from below', not in the history of great figures and ecclesiastical politics but in devotional literature and in the pious practices of local communities.

So it is that important modern historians avoid the old terms, particularly 'Renaissance', and their assumptions altogether, often taking a much broader chronological perspective: Jean Delumeau writes *Catholicism between Luther and Voltaire* and his masterwork *Sin and Fear: The Emergence of a Western Guilt Culture, 13th–18th Centuries*. He sees Protestantism and Catholicism as related confessional responses to the same deep religious anxiety. John Bossy explores *The English Catholic Community, 1570–1850*, not the 'English Catholic Church', and *Christianity in the West, 1400–1700*. Like Delumeau, with whom he has substantial disagreements, Bossy sees Catholicism and Protestantism in the larger context of Christianity as it evolved in response to specific cultural pressures. Accordingly, regional and local history has now assumed great significance as such 'microhistory' records spiritual realities manifested in concrete cultural particulars. Studying an Inquisition register, Emmanuel Le Roy Ladurie brilliantly reconstructs life in fourteenth-century Montaillou, a village in the Pyrenees. Reviewing a single priest's parochial accounts from 1520 to 1574, Eamon Duffy studies the monumental religious changes of half a century writ small in Morebath.

Given these developments, despite the attractive sense of energy and creativity in the phrase 'The Catholic Renaissance', I have finally come round to John W. O'Malley's suggested 'Early Modern Catholicism'. Despite (or perhaps because of) its blandness, the descriptor 'early modern' encourages a fresh look at the evidence. More capacious than 'Renaissance', 'early modern' has also the advantage of reconceiving that past period as the beginning of our own. This underscores the relevance of the writers here presented and, more important, challenges the predominant view of Catholicism in this period as moribund, soon to be overtaken by a distinctly Protestant modernity. This is the view implicit in Burckhardt and in another seminal essay, Max Weber's *Die protestatische Ethik und der 'Geist' des Kapitalismus* ('The Protestant Ethic and the Spirit of Capitalism', 1905), which located the origins of capitalist acquisitiveness and productivity in Protestant teaching about work and duty.

Visions and Revisions

Throughout this volume I reject the standard label 'Reformation' as prejudicial. In this period Catholics such as William Bishop (*A Reformation of a Catholic Deformed*, 1604) and Lawrence Anderton (pseud. John Brereley, *The Reformed Protestant*, 1621) saw deformation not reformation. Furthermore, Catholics insisted that the term 'Reformation' misrepresented the essential disunity of the Protestant movements. An Ashmolean woodcut, 'The Protestants' Pedigree', reprinted in Frederick Staphylus, *Apology* (1565), shows a tree branching off into many subsections from the original arch-heretics—Luther (depicted with his wife, Katherine Bora), Zwingli, Melanchthon, and Rotman (head of Anabaptists) (see Fig. 2). After reviewing the civil conflicts of Protestant Europe, *Adelphomachia, or the wars of Protestantcy* (1636) catalogues Protestant theological disputes under some forty headings. Clearly, a polemical purpose drove Catholic emphasis on Protestant disunity: so many opposing sects could not claim to be the *one*, holy, Catholic, and apostolic church. Yet any historian would be hard-pressed to ignore the essential diversity of the Protestant revolution. The disagreements of Luther, Carlstadt, and Zwingli on the

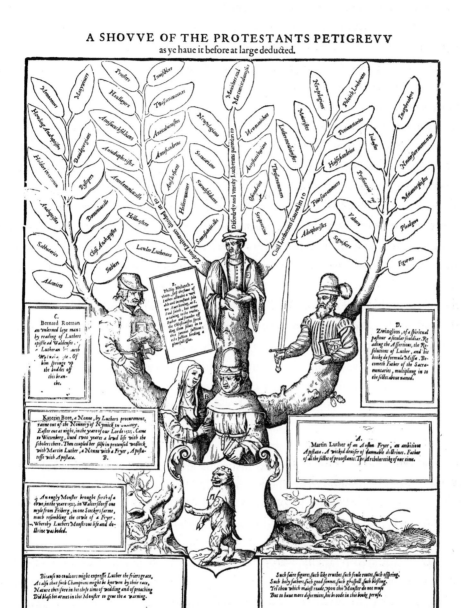

2. Frederick Staphylus, 'A Show of the Protestants' Pedigree', *The Apology*, tr. Thomas Stapleton, 1565, between Gg4 and Hh1. The monstrous creature below Luther and the toads on the roots represent Protestant innovation as deformities.

nature of the Eucharist soon hardened into dogma with the *Consensus Tigurinus* (1549) and the Heidelberg Catechism (1563). (Ironically, historians now sometimes distinguish between Lutheranism and 'Reformed Protestantism'.) Calvin's emphasis on predestination provoked widespread dissension. Furthermore, the religious movements of Luther, Zwingli, Calvin, and others existed in sometimes violent opposition to what George Huntston Williams calls 'the Radical Reformation', 'loosely interrelated congeries of reformations and restitutions which, besides the Anabaptists of various types, included Spiritualists and spiritualizers of varying tendencies, and the Evangelical Rationalists, largely Italian in origin' (*The Radical Reformation*, 1992: p. xxix). In England disagreements between the episcopacy and those who wanted further purification (Puritans) festered and finally exploded into civil war.

What is more, to view the separatist Protestant movements of Luther, Calvin, Henry VIII, and others as 'the Reformation' misrepresents Catholicism as well as Protestantism. This perspective assumes a simple, binary opposition between a uniform Catholicism—static and corrupt—and a uniform Protestantism—dynamic and purifying. It thus depicts the Catholic Church as a kind of Hegelian thesis over which reformation (and modernity) eventually triumph. John Foxe and his many descendants propounded this view, including John Strype, who compiled *Ecclesiastical Memorials* in the eighteenth century to show that religion 'met with so many remarkable changes and struggles till at last by the good providence of God overruling the counsels and contrivances of men, the Church of England was purged from many gross errors in doctrine and inveterate superstitions in worship, and a happy reformation at length effected' (1822: i. p. vi).

This self-flattering caricature of Catholicism ignores large historical realities. The seven deadly sins, to be sure, flourished among the popes and the clergy, particularly in the noisome practices of simony, nepotism, lust, and greed. But considerable reform movements stirred within the hierarchical Church, at least since Pope Gregory VII (*r.* 1073–85) sought to correct abuses and improve the clergy. William Durandus at the Council of Vienne (1311–12) coined the phrase 'reformatio in capite et in membris' (reform in the head and members) (*Catholic Reformation*, ed. J. C. Olin, 1969, pp. xix–xx), which echoed through the Council of Constance (1414–18) and the conciliar movement. In the fifteenth century Cardinal Capranica recommended more careful examination and education of clergy; Nicolaus of Cusa (1400–64) sought to transform all Christians, beginning with the pope, into the 'forma Christi' (likeness of Christ). At the Fifth Lateran Council (1512–17) two Camoldolese monks, Tommaso Giustiniani and Vincenzo Quirini, proposed a series of changes, including better preparation of clergy, extirpation of superstition, translation of the Bible, reorganization of religious orders, and revision of canon law. In 1537 a papal committee led by Cardinal Contarini presented Pope Paul III with *Consilium de emendanda ecclesia*, which recommended reform of the papacy and swift correction of rampant abuses. The great reform Council of Trent met from 1545 to 1563 to clarify doctrine, especially that of justification, and to effect improvements in Church institutions.

The Catholic impulse for reform resulted in spiritual, as well as institutional, renewal. Originating in the Netherlands and spreading through Europe, the *Devotio moderna* inspired its followers—clergy and, significantly, laity—to follow Christ and practise piety. De-emphasizing ritual, members prayed, meditated, and cultivated a fervent interior life. The movement produced one spiritual masterpiece, Thomas à Kempis's *The Imitation of Christ*, and influenced Nicolaus of Cusa, Erasmus, Jacques Lefèvre, and, probably, Ignatius Loyola. The emphasis on lay spirituality in the *Devotio moderna* found expression elsewhere, notably in the many confraternities such as the Oratory of Divine Love. Other illuminist movements, such as that of the *alumbrados* in Spain, stressed the interior life and mental prayer as preparation for the experience of unity with God. Established religious orders experienced reinvigoration. New orders and institutions flourished: the Capuchins (from the Observant Franciscans), Theatines, Barnabites, Somaschi, Lazarists, Brothers Hospitallers, Oratorians, Piarists, and, most important, the Society of Jesus. Educated, disciplined, zealous, Jesuits dispensed sacraments, preached, founded schools and missions. New female orders, often arousing the suspicion and hostility of the Church hierarchy, compiled an impressive record of charity and service to the poor: the Angelics of San Paolo, the Ursulines, the Visitadines, and the English sisters of the extraordinary Mary Ward (see LIVES AND DEATHS).

Though not well recognized, all this reform and rebirth has been well documented for some time, at least since Wilhelm Maurenbrecher's *Geschichte der katholischen Reformation* ('History of the Catholic Reformation', 1880). In 1946 Hubert Jedin, the modern historian of the Council of Trent, distinguished between internal reform (*Katholische Reformation*, 'Catholic Reformation'), and the Church's concerted defence against its enemies (*Gegenreformation*, 'Counter-Reformation'). In the wake of Jedin's essay many modern scholars have adopted the term 'Reformation' to designate reform movements within, not merely against, the Catholic Church. But if 'Reformation' in its popular Protestant sense is prejudicial and passé then so must be its derivative 'Counter-Reformation', coined in 1776 by a Lutheran lawyer, Johann Pütter (*Gegenreformation*) to designate the political, diplomatic, and military measures of German Catholic princes against Lutherans. Since then the term has referrred to many diverse aspects of Catholicism in the early modern period—baroque art, Ignatian Spirituality, the Inquisition, the rise of new orders, the Council of Trent, and the centralization of power in the papacy. Its widespread use has promoted a vision of Catholicism as the threatened and threatening Church Militant, clad often in distinctively Spanish rather than Roman armour, jealously protecting its privileges, ruthlessly suppressing dissent. H. Outram Evennett's classic *The Spirit of the Counter-Reformation* (1951; pub. 1968), which explored the resurgent spirituality that inspired works of charity and piety throughout Europe, considerably broadened perspective. And yet, the term 'Counter-Reformation' has never quite escaped the taint of its sectarian origins. Inevitably it defines an age of Catholicism solely as a reaction to Protestantism—a precise reversal of the historical actuality. It also characterizes Catholicism as 'anti-Reformation', in other words, as opposed to the reform and renewal that it so energetically, and on so many levels, embraced.

To promote a broader understanding and encourage a new perspective, *Early Modern Catholicism* presents a variety of Catholic primary sources. In its work of revision this anthology continues the long labours of past historians: Henry More, Christopher Grene, and Henry Foley, early chroniclers of the Society of Jesus; Bishop Richard Challoner, who compiled memoirs of missionary priests in 1741; Hugh Tootel (pseud. Charles Dodd), who reprinted many documents for his *The Church History of England* (1737–42); nineteenth-century historians such as John Morris, Dom Bede Camm, and Joseph Gillow, and the Catholic lay periodical, *The Rambler* (founded 1848). Though at times hagiographical in perspective, this early work preserved manuscript and print records. At the turn of the century J. S. Hansom and others founded The Catholic Record Society (1904) with the motto, 'colligite fragmenta ne pereant' (collect the fragments so they do not perish). The premier Catholic historical society in the United Kingdom, CRS has published a remarkable series of monographs, occasional publications, records (registers of baptisms, marriages, burials, etc.), and a scholarly journal, *Recusant History* (1951–present). Two of its leaders, A. F. Allison and D. M. Rogers, compiled a two-volume bibliography of Catholic writings, *The Contemporary Printed Literature of the English Counter-Reformation between 1558 and 1640* (1989, 1994), and reprinted many Catholic texts in the *English Recusant Literature* series (394 vols.).

Spurred by new perspectives and many recovered documents, modern scholars have begun the massive work of reappraising Catholicism in early modern England. To name just a few here, J. J. Scarisbrick has examined wills and the role of Marian priests and argued for the vitality of Catholic practices. Christopher Haigh has envisioned a piecemeal reformation, forced upon a largely unwilling populace. Eamon Duffy has explored Catholic piety and the devastation of traditional worship. Collectively scholars like these have begun to dismantle the Whig vision of blessed Protestant Brittania, cleansed of popish corruption, rising in the godly Reformation morning. Instead they portray a conflicted United Kingdom, wherein factions fought, compromised, and responded to political pressures. Their England includes Catholics as part of a divided, struggling population, not as a lunatic fringe or treasonous minority. It also includes Catholicism, not as a dying institution, but as a vital, dynamic, pluralistic, and learned confession that could inspire both heroism and holiness. Such historical revision has naturally prompted literary re-evaluation. R. V. Young and others have dethroned regnant assumptions about 'Protestant poetics'; Alison Shell has learnedly and suggestively reconsidered early modern poetry and drama. A host of other studies revise accepted views on genres and figures, both major and minor. (See FURTHER READING.)

Catholicism in Rome

Though early modern Catholicism comprises varied practices in different locales, Catholics always recognized the authority of the pope and looked to Rome, sometimes with distrust, for spiritual leadership. Catholics located the origins of the papacy in Christ's address to Peter (inscribed around the dome of Saint Peter's Basilica): 'Thou art Peter and upon this rock I will build my church, and the gates of hell shall not prevail against it. And I will give to thee the keys of the kingdom of heaven. And whatsoever thou shalt bind on earth it shall be bound also in heaven, and whatsoever thou shalt loose on earth, it shall be loosed also in heaven' (Matt. 16: 18–19). Feared and revered, the papacy was not, by any means, the Church, though sometimes it acted as if it were to the detriment of its members and the delight of its enemies. Still, the pope defined doctrines and ruled the bureaucracy of the Church, the Roman Curia, i.e. the many congregations, tribunals, and offices that govern the Church Universal.

Eighteen popes reigned from 1520 to 1640, each charged with (and sometimes overwhelmed by) the burdens of spiritual leadership and temporal survival. The papacy in this period inherited responsibility for territories surrounding Rome, the papal states, and functioned partly as a civil government. On papal shoulders also rested responsibility for the care and conversion of souls in the new missions—India, the Philippines, Japan, China, and the Americas—and also for the devastation which others, despite papal protest, wreaked upon native peoples. Among many challenges, popes had to contend with the rival patriarch in Constantinople; the rebellion of Luther, Calvin, and other Protestants; continually warring Italian republics, duchies, and the Kingdom of Naples to the south; the powerful Holy Roman Empire; France, which controlled its own clerical offices and major benefices, and which endured a succession crisis at the end of the sixteenth century; Spain, where the 'most Catholic King' Philip II (r. 1556–98) exercised even greater control over religious doctrine and practice; the menace of the Turks; and the perceived threat from Jews, who were shamefully mistreated by Catholics and Protestants alike. Popes countenanced the expulsion of Jews from various countries, submitted *conversos* to the Inquisition, and created the ghetto. In *On the Jews and their Lies* (1543) Martin Luther advised Christians to burn all synagogues, raze Jewish homes, confiscate the Talmud and Jewish wealth, abolish safety for Jews on highways, reduce them to servile labour, and, finally, to expel them from Germany. Neither Catholics nor Protestants, it must be said, brought the good news of Christ's Gospel to Jews, to Muslims, to the massacred Indians of the Americas, or to each other.

Among early modern popes, Pope Clement VII (1523–34) proved himself inadequate to the great changes sweeping across Europe—the centralization of governments in hands of strong leaders, the Protestant rebellions in Germany and Switzerland, the war between the Valois and the Habsburgs, the troubles brewing in England. In 1527 imperial troops under Charles V, the Holy Roman Emperor, sacked Rome, looting, murdering, pillaging. After his return to power, Pope Clement refused Henry VIII's petitions for divorce from Catherine of Aragon, aunt of the conqueror Charles V.

The Church was not fortunate in the next occupants of the Holy Seat. The zealot Cardinal Caraffa became Pope Paul IV (1555–9) and initiated a series of repressive measures: he increased Inquisition activities, herded Jews into ghettos, imprisoned revered clerics, suspended the Council of Trent, and introduced the Roman Index of Prohibited Books. His one positive legacy is the establishment of the Theatines, a religious order dedicated to reforming the clergy and edifying the laity. Pope Pius V (1566–72) was a better priest but not a better leader. A rigorous ascetic, he fasted, prayed, washed the feet of the poor, and took lepers in his arms, but he propagated the infamous bull, *Regnans in excelsis* (1570), which excommunicated Queen Elizabeth and absolved her subjects from obedience (see DOCUMENTS). Pope Gregory XIII (1572–85), who sent Robert Persons and Edmund Campion on the English Mission (1580), attempted to palliate the damage caused by declaring the bull non-binding on English Catholics, 'rebus sic stantibus' (as things stand now). But that clause, read as an ominous portent of future action, only made matters worse. Notoriously, Gregory XIII struck a medal and commissioned paintings to celebrate the St Bartholomew's Day Massacre (24 August 1572), in which thousands of French Protestants (Huguenots) were savagely slaughtered (see Fig. 16).

Some popes ruled to better effect. Pope Sixtus V (1585–90) undertook an extensive rebuilding campaign in Rome, making the city the architectural and artistic centre of world Christianity. The saintly Clement VIII (1592–1605) revivified devotions and reformed educational and charitable institutions. He acknowledged Henri Navarre King of France, thus ending years of war, and accepted the Edict of Nantes (1598), which granted toleration to Protestants in France. Pope Gregory XV (1621–3) established the Congregation for the Propagation of the Faith to oversee missions, lessened penalties for witchcraft, and canonized four early modern figures—Teresa of Ávila, Ignatius Loyola, Francis Xavier, and Philip Neri. Pope Urban VIII (1623–44) patronized baroque art, especially that of Bernini, but squandered money in nepotism, pursued ineffective foreign policies, and forced Galileo to abjure the Copernican system. At the end of his reign, the papacy, mired in debt, sunk to a low ebb of power, prestige, and authority.

The papacy in this period featured reformers and repressors, saints and sinners, as Eamon Duffy put it, often in the same persons. Though important, their story (and that of the ecclesiastical hierarchy) does not constitute the history of Catholicism in Rome, let alone the whole Church. During this period a powerful spirit of renewal transformed the faithful and the city. Hundreds of men and women joined the new orders and lived holy lives of service to the poor and sick. Lay people practised their faith in parishes as well as confraternities, lay associations, and oratories, extra-parochial organizations for prayer and the mass. Archbishop Charles Borromeo (1538–84) transformed the Baths of Diocletian into a Carthusian monastery, restored churches including Santa Prassede (where today is the table he used to distribute food to the poor), and revised the breviary. Borromeo promoted pilgrimages and encouraged the formation of charitable organizations. Philip Neri (1515–95), living on bread and water, visited hospitals, markets, and warehouses, transforming his listeners with the simple message of God's mercy and love. He founded the Confraternity of the Most Holy Trinity for pilgrims and convalescents and organized visits to the seven Basilical churches of Rome. Throughout the city and the world Dominicans and Jesuits revitalized the 'artes praedicandi' (the arts of preaching).

As the activities of Borromeo and Neri suggest, the city of Rome functioned as a sacramental centre of the Roman Catholic faith. The relics of the saints, often on elaborate and ceremonial display, established kinship with the early Christian Church, while providing lessons in holy living and dying as well as a means to make contact with the sacred. Enemies regarded the city as a sink of pagan idolatry and worldly corruption, still subscribing to the old reading of ROMA as an anagram for 'Radix Omnium Malorum Avaritia' (Avarice is the root of all evils). Some Protestants denounced the 'whore of Babylon' in apocalyptic indignation. After accepting the hospitality of the Venerable English College at Rome and returning home to bear witness against Edmund Campion, Anthony Munday sought to profit from his Roman sojourn with *The English Roman Life* (1582), marketed as an inside account of life in the unholy city, brimming with sedition and superstition, with pilgrimages and 'paltry relics' (title-page). But Catholics and non-Catholics still flocked to the city and its 366 churches. The young Catholic Sir Charles Somerset wrote a detailed description of his visit to Roman churches, holy monuments, and relics in 1612. Writing of his conversion to Catholicism, another seventeenth-century traveller, Toby Matthew, eloquently recorded the powerful effect of the physical city on his imagination: 'I must confess in the presence of God that the sight of those most ancient crosses, altars, sepulchres, and other marks of Catholic religion, having been planted there in the persecution of the primitive Church (which might be more than fifteen hundred years ago and could not be less than thirteen hundred), did strike me with a kind of reverent awe' (see LIVES AND DEATHS). Guidebooks for tourists and pilgrims proliferated then as now, combining histories, architectural information, and devotional instructions. One such guidebook is *Roma Sancta* (1581) by the English translator of the Rheims New Testament, Gregory Martin. The first part of *Roma Sancta* portrays the devotion of the city, its array of churches and chapels, the preaching in church and in the streets, the pilgrimages, relics, liturgies, and hymns. The second part records the charitable institutions of Rome, the monasteries, hospitals, hospices, and lay companies that relieved the poor and ministered to the needy. Martin concludes the work as he began it, with an allusion to Matthew 5: 14: 'A city set upon a hill cannot be hid.'

Everywhere in Rome a surging religious energy manifested itself in the production of artistic masterpieces—paintings, sculptures, and churches. The achievements of the Renaissance and Baroque age, of Fra Angelico, Raphael, Michelangelo, Bernini, and others, remain today on glorious display (see Figs. 3, 7). The Council of Trent's ratification of the image inspired new artistic forms and expressions. In 1582 Niccolò Circignani painted frescoes of the early Christian martyrdoms for the German-Hungarian College, today Santo Stefano Rotondo. He then went on to paint a similar sequence in the English College at Rome, depicting the gruesome deaths of ancient and modern English martyrs (see, as printed by de Cavalleriis, Figs. 8, 14). Art inspired moral heroism as students returned to native countries to face prejudice and persecution.

The energy and programme of the Catholic Reformation also shaped directly Il Gesù, the baroque mother church of the Jesuits (see Fig. 3). To symbolize Jesuit commitment to active involvement in the world, Ignatius chose to locate the church near the pope and the Campidoglio (seat of city government), in the heart of a vital neighbourhood populated by rich and poor, Christians and non-Christians. The great portal in the calm façade invites the world to enter. The Latin-cross floorplan, developed by several architects including Michelangelo, consists of a large central nave with side chapels and a dome over the intersection of the nave and transepts. Clear glass for reading replaces the traditional stained glass. With no columns or side aisles, the nave sweeps forward to the altar, a theatrical stage for the celebration of the Eucharist, surmounted by a sunburst with IHS (the first letters of the name of Jesus in Greek). The architecture thus proclaims visually the doctrine of the Real Presence of Christ in the sacrament. The monogram IHS appears above as well as at the centre of Gaulli's swirling and dazzling fresco above the nave, which depicts humanity floating on clouds to Christ while the cardinal sins plummet to darkness.

3. Giacomo della Porta, Interior of the Gesù, Rome, 16th century. The elevted pulpit is just visible on the left; the IHS (first letters of 'Jesus' in Greek) above the altar affirms the real presence of Christ in the Eucharist.

The pulpit appears not by the altar but in an elevated position at the centre of the nave on the left side, thus reflecting the new emphasis on homiletics. Sculptural groups celebrate the Society of Jesus, and the triumph of faith over idolatry and heresy. The church affirms the central position of Mary against Protestant attack, both in the Chapel of the Madonna della Strada, which preserves the image of Mary from a church given to Ignatius in 1540, and in the dome fresco, where the Virgin and Jesus intercede for humanity in the midst of angels and the communion of saints. Progressing forward, the paired side chapels represent the Church in pilgrimage (the saints and apostles), the mystery of redemption (the Holy Family and the Passion), and a vision of glory (angels and Holy Trinity). The chapel and tomb of St Ignatius on the left, richly resplendent in lapis lazuli and marble, and that of St Francis Xavier on the right, both preserve the remains of the saints, relics to move the faithful to wonder and virtue. Illustrating the power of art and architecture to teach and delight, Il Gesù became an important model for Jesuit churches throughout the world.

Catholicism in England

Few people today doubt that the institutional Catholic Church in medieval and early modern England, despite its problems, ministered vigorously and well to its various apostolates. Devotions, fasts, feast days, and seasonal rituals ordered life into a sequence of rhythm, beauty, and meaning. Approximately 100 days in the year were days of fast (one meal only) or abstinence from meat; people attended mass irregularly, depending on its (and their) availability. They communicated once a year, wore *Agnus Deis* (discs of wax impressed with the figure of a lamb and a cross and blessed by the pope), prayed the rosary, kissed the pax (a tablet with a sacred image), and gathered together for a small meal after services. They relied on priests and sacraments for protection against harm and forgiveness of sins. Ceremonies gave meaning to the great times of transition in human life—births, baptisms, weddings, funerals. Catholics worshipped and worked together in parishes and related organizations. The living and the dead belonged to the same mystical body of Christ and communication was possible through the offices of indulgences, prayers for the souls in purgatory, and good works (see Garnet, CONTROVERSIES).

   The religious changes in England shook these beliefs and practices to their foundations, abolishing many feast days, devotional practices, and communal celebrations. In Morebath, for example, the state religion put out the candles and condemned as vanities the revered statues and images in the church—the Virgin and St George by the altar, the Sunday Christ (Jesus pierced by tools), St Loy (St Eligius), patron of smiths and carters,

St Anthony, healer of men and animals, St Anne, Mary weeping over the dead Christ in her lap, and St Sidwell, a local saint whom the priest, Sir Christopher Trychay, and the villagers cultivated with pride and sacrifice. It prohibited Sir Christopher's black vestments and the community's church ales, i.e. banquets that raised parish funds by selling beer, usually held in a church alehouse, a building for community meetings and celebrations.

These changes in England arose from a grass-roots protest against abuses in selling indulgences and clerical power, from an insular, well-founded distrust of foreign Catholic powers in Spain, France, and Italy, and from an unholy desire for Church lands, wealth, and power. Historians disagree about the relative importance of these motivations: Catholics tend to underestimate the first, but protests such as Simon Fish's *A Supplication for the Beggars* (1529) struck a national nerve in its depiction of clerical greed and the consequences for the poor. The rejection of a foreign papal bureaucracy, associated with the Spanish threat, also exerted a powerful national appeal. Protestants tend to underestimate the third but many non-Catholics lamented the wholesale depredation and desecration. Thomas Becon, for example, condemned those who 'abhor the names of monks, friars, canons, nuns, etc., but their goods they greedily gripe'; instead of using Church property to build schools, hospitals, housing for the poor, English spoliators proved themselves to be 'right brothers of Cain, which had rather slay his brother Abel than he should have any part with him of worldly possessions' (*The Jewel of Joy*, 1550, sigs. hii^v, hii). One thing seems clear: the changes, at least initially, were top-down. A long, oscillating series of royal statutes, commissions, requirements, oaths, and penalties outlawed the Catholic religion. A powerful local machinery identified offenders and levied penalties. J. C. H. Aveling (*Northern Catholics*, 1966: 13 ff.) described this machinery as a broad-based pyramid with the Privy Council and archbishops at the top, followed by sheriffs, clerks of peace, and justices in the middle, and, finally, at the base, underlings and private citizens.

Dubbed 'Defender of the Faith' for his refutation of Luther, *Assertio septem sacramentorum* (1521), Henry VIII (r. 1509–47) began a revolution that was primarily political and jurisdictional rather than doctrinal and devotional. Frustrated by the pope's refusal to annul his marriage to Catherine of Aragon in order to clear the way for a marriage to Anne Boleyn and, he hoped, a male heir, the king declared independence from Rome. The 1533 Act in Restraint of Appeals broke juridical ties with the Catholic Church, and the 1536 Act of Supremacy pronounced the king supreme head of the Church of England. Thomas Cromwell, Vicar General, and Thomas Cranmer, archbishop of Canterbury, set about the work of revolution. Several acts for the Suppression of Monasteries, purportedly for their 'manifest sin, vicious, carnal, and abominable living', refurbished the royal exchequer by delivering Church property to the crown (*The Tudor Constitution*, ed. G. R. Elton, 1982: 383). In some sixty years over a quarter of the landed property in England changed hands and some 11,000 clergy suffered displacement or destitution. Henry promised to free the English Church from the burden of papal taxation but 'the act for the First Fruits and Tenths of 1534 would bring to him perhaps as much as ten times the amount per annum which English churchmen had paid to Rome before he liberated them' (J. J. Scarisbrick, *Henry VIII*, 1968: 509). The king partially reversed doctrinal direction at the end of his reign. He promulgated the conservative Six Articles (1539) which affirmed the Catholic doctrine of the real presence of Christ in the Eucharist, as well as the Catholic practices of clerical celibacy and auricular confession. His government executed Anne Askew for denying the doctrine of transubstantiation (1546).

Henry's successor, the short-lived Edward VI (*r.* 1547–53), with powerful advisers further changed doctrine and religious practices. The young Josiah stripped churches, prohibited processions and the rosary, destroyed images, and deposed bishops such as Edmund Bonner (London) and Stephen Gardiner (Winchester). Nurtured by Continental theologians, particularly Jean Calvin in Geneva and Heinrich Bullinger in Zürich, the king and his ministers forged an iconoclastic Protestantism with an important component of common worship (see Fig. 4). Clerics preached official homilies; the laity worshipped out loud from an official Book of Common Prayer (1549). The second edition of this text (1552), sometimes prefaced by Parliamentary decree, furnished English services for three centuries. Altering the first edition, it omitted exorcism, anointing, and triple immersion from the baptismal service, prayers for the dead and the psalms from the burial service. The famous new 'black rubric' pointedly denied the Catholic doctrine of transubstantiation, though this was omitted in the 1559 version and in subsequent editions. Edward's reign also initiated another long-running religious practice. In 1549 Thomas Sternhold published a metrical psalter, ancestor of the 'Sternhold and Hopkins' psalters that enabled the powerful communal singing of psalms for many generations.

Reaction against the changes occurred with the accession of Mary I (*r.* 1553–8), who, with Cardinal Reginald Pole, repealed statutes and set about reconciling England to Rome. Pole, a papal legate, emphasized peaceful reconciliation, administrative improvement, and a high standard of education for clergy until an old enemy, Caraffa, became Pope Paul IV and in 1557 deprived him of his authority. Across the nation in Mary's reign rood screens, vestments, copes, chalices, and icons came out of hiding as Catholics returned to power. Many, like poet and polemicist Miles Huggard, celebrated the restoration. In order to win support, Mary largely ignored the dissolutions, conceding the Church lands and possessions to the nobility; she did, however, grant benefactions for six new religious houses. She ignored also national sentiment against her intended marriage to Philip of Spain, which ignited armed protest in Wyatt's rebellion (1554). Mary passed An Act for the Punishment of Heresies (1554), and with Edmund Bonner, again bishop of London, initiated a notorious series of persecutions and

The Ship of the Romish Church.
Burning of images.
Ship over your trinkets & be packing you papists.
The Temple well purged.
The Papists packing away their Paltry.
The Comu nion Table.

4. John Foxe, 'Edwardian Revolution: Iconoclasm and Purgation', *Acts and Monuments*, 1576: 1257. The top panel portrays the burning of images and the packing off of papists and their 'trinkets'; the bottom panels show Protestant services as a return to the Bible and to orderly worship, centring on the communion table and baptismal font.

public burnings. Between February 1555 and November 1558 almost 300 persons were executed for heresy, including respected Protestant divines Thomas Cranmer, Hugh Latimer, and Nicholas Ridley; more died in prison. Despite attempts at exculpation and extenuation by Catholic historians, Marian persecution was an atrocity that aroused permanent hostility to Rome and all things Roman. While attempting to restore the Catholic faith, the queen, ironically, confirmed the Protestant one: 'what had appeared to be a discredited and ineffectual movement had become a cause that brave men would die for, and testify to in the face of death' (D. Loades, *The Reign of Mary Tudor*, 1991: 275).

Elizabeth I acceded to the throne in 1558, despite the Second Succession Act (1536, 28 Henry VIII c. 7) which had declared her illegitimate and excluded; this statute was never repealed but simply ignored by the Third Succession Act (1544). In a precarious legal and political position Elizabeth I (*r.* 1558–1603) reversed Mary's policies and returned the country to Protestantism with the Act of Supremacy (1559) and the Act of Uniformity (1559). Though she famously walked out of a Christmas mass before the elevation of the host (1558), Elizabeth practised a doctrinally moderate Protestantism, as evident in the Thirty-Nine Articles (1563), at least partly from necessity. Product of the papally unsanctioned marriage between Henry VIII and Anne Boleyn, the queen sought support from the Protestant base at home while keeping open the possibility of alliances, both personal and political, with Catholic powers abroad. Her pragmatic, *via media* Protestantism, uncomfortable with clerical marriage, tolerant of some ceremony, and receptive to the idea of Christ's spiritual presence in the Eucharist, consistently rankled many who thought she had not gone far enough. But the so-called Elizabethan settlement of religion, promoted by ardently anti-Catholic Secretaries Francis Walsingham and William Cecil, and defended by such learned divines as Matthew Parker, John Jewel, and Richard Hooker, aimed to destroy Catholicism in England. Legislation eventually made it a crime to say or sing mass, to administer Catholic sacraments, to speak against the state religion, and to ignore state services. The penalties included stiff fines, forfeiture of land and goods, imprisonment, and execution for treason. Pius V's 1570 bull excommunicating Elizabeth incited harsher statutes and increased prosecutions as did the Irish rebellion (1579) and arrival of the missionary priests Edmund Campion and Robert Persons (1580). In 1587 Elizabeth executed the chief Catholic claimant to the throne and an anointed sovereign, Mary, Queen of Scots (see Fig. 6).

Catholics in England hoped for better days with the accession of James I (*r.* 1603–25) and the Hampton Court Conference (1604), wherein the new king rejected most of the Puritan agenda. They were soon disappointed. James did not grant the toleration for which Catholics yearned. The discovery of the Gunpowder Plot, an alleged Catholic conspiracy to blow up the Houses of Parliament, spurred new measures: An Act for Better Repressing of Popish Recusants (1606) mandated communion, empowered the government to seize two-thirds of the property of recusants instead of the former monthly fine of twenty pounds, and required all office holders to swear a new Oath of Allegiance. In later years, as political and personal alliances shifted, James showed himself to be more tolerant. He accepted and advanced Catholics at court. The Book of Sports legislation (1618) defended village practices and local ceremonies against severe sabbatarians. James's queen, Anne of Denmark, converted to Catholicism as did the countess of Buckingham, mother of his favourite. James entertained the idea of a Spanish match for his second son and heir, Charles, and an alliance with Spain. There was a clandestine suspension of the penal laws in the 1620s.

Charles I (*r.* 1625–40) belonged to the High Church party, which stressed the Prayer Book and the importance of rituals. He married a Catholic, Henrietta Maria of France, who urged toleration and, with her expanding Catholic circle at court, conspicuously supported priests and attended masses in hope of reclaiming England to the faith. Parliament complained about the lax enforcement of penal laws but local officials continued persecution, especially fines and imprisonments. The real threat came not from the right but from the left, not from Catholics but from Puritans, who grew increasingly disturbed by the resurgence of Catholicism and Charles's High Church policies. These policies in part found support in William Laud, archbishop of Canterbury (1633–45), who affirmed the importance of good works, questioned the Calvinist doctrine of predestination, and revered sacrament and ceremony. Laud, however, was no friend to Catholicism: he opposed toleration and lenient administration of the Oath, destroyed the devotional articles at St Winifred's Well, a popular shrine, and burned copies of Francis de Sales's *A Devout Life*. Still, in 1637 Scottish Presbyterians rejected Laud's revised Book of Common Prayer as popish; they ignited smouldering antagonisms that eventually led to the rise of Oliver Cromwell, the civil war, and the executions of both Laud and Charles himself.

Throughout this period institutional Catholicism survived in early modern England with minimal structure. Rome continued to appoint bishops to vacant sees in Ireland—though they were unable to take possession of them—and thus created a hierarchy that shadowed the official Church structure. But there were no similar appointments in England and, consequently, after the Marian bishops died out no Catholic hierarchy existed to adjudicate disputes, grant dispensations, or administer sacraments such as confirmation. The Society of Jesus coordinated some activities through the Superior of the Jesuits in England, but England was officially an anomalous 'mission', only becoming a regular province belatedly in 1623. Henry Garnet served well as Superior from 1586 to 1606, when he was tried and executed for involvement in the Gunpowder Plot. Cardinal William Allen exercised general jurisdiction over the English mission until his death in 1594, when he was succeeded by Robert Persons. Much of the administrative work *per force* fell into the hands of local organizers such as Richard Holtby, SJ, who built an efficient northern network that covered several counties.

At the end of the century tensions grew as the secular English clergy in Wisbech Castle and in the Venerable English College of Rome increasingly wished to distance themselves from Jesuits such as Persons, who favoured military intervention in England. In 1598 Cardinal Cajetan, cardinal-protector of England, named George Blackwell archpriest of England, head of the secular clergy, but instructed him to consult with the Jesuits on all important matters. Rejecting Blackwell as a Jesuit puppet, dissatisfied secular priests, the 'Appellants', protested the appointment in Rome; they were promptly imprisoned, and then forbidden to return to England. Such high-handed treatment incensed many who distrusted the Jesuits, and the 'Appellant' controversy, as it came to be known, generated a wave of Catholic loyalist, anti-Spanish, and anti-Jesuit writing by secular priests such as Thomas Bluet, Christopher Bagshaw, and William Watson. Watson's story provides ironies worth pondering: after attacking Jesuit treachery and sedition in *A Decacordon of Ten Quodlibetical Questions* (1602), Watson joined the Bye Plot, a conspiracy to kidnap King James and force toleration of Catholics, for which he was executed as a traitor the very next year, 1603.

In the early seventeenth century the Gunpowder Plot (1604) and its aftermath created new divisions among Catholics. James's mandatory Oath of Allegiance, which called the deposing power of the pope 'impious', 'heretical', and 'damnable' doctrine, forced Catholics to declare loyalty to their country by declaring disloyalty to the papacy (*The Stuart Constitution*, ed. J. P. Kenyon, 1986: 170). Robert Bellarmine, Robert Persons, and Francisco Suárez asserted papal prerogatives against the Oath, which was in turn defended by James I himself and Catholics such as George Blackwell, Richard Sheldon, William Barclay, William Barret, and William Warmington. As intended, the Oath confused, divided, and weakened the Catholic clergy and laity in England. By and large, restrictions on Catholics in England eased after the Gunpowder furore, though there were invasion scares in the 1620s. In 1623 the pope appointed William Bishop as bishop of Chalcedon, with episcopal authority over the Catholics in England and Scotland. He died the next year, before he could effect any changes, and his ineffectual successor Richard Smith earned the enmity of the Jesuits and the denunciation of the Catholic gentry. Having largely established itself as the religion of the realm, Protestantism now focused on the problems of internal division and government. Catholicism, despite its internal divisions and lack of external structure, survived and made quiet gains.

English Catholics

Surveying institutional Catholicism in England through the Tudor and Stuart reigns, one can easily lose sight of what matters most, the people. Here are two London Catholics in 1593, John Craddock and Bridget Strange, both imprisoned for recusancy, i.e. refusal to attend the mandated church service based on the Protestant Book of Common Prayer:

John Craddock, aged 38 years. He is by trade a singing man, and was imprisoned by Master Secretary Walsingham six years past. And he saith [he] will not go to church, nor will not have conferences with any, nor will not take any oath. And [he] is prisoner in the Marshalsea.

Bridget Strange, wife of Thomas Strange. She is aged 50 years and she saith [she hath] not been at church these 30 years. And being demanded whether she would go to the church, she answereth she should be mad if she should go to the church. And she is [in] prison in the Gatehouse.   (*Recusant Documents from the Ellesmere Manuscripts*, ed. A. G. Petti, 1968: 86–7)

Tucked away among similar examination reports, these brief notices conjure real people: the 38-year-old singing man John Craddock, now silent, for some reason imprisoned by the powerful Master Secretary himself, refusing to take conference with any, refusing to swear the Oath of Allegiance, enduring since age 32 the deprivations of Marshalsea. Resisting the collective power of the state and church for thirty years, the 50-year-old wife Bridget Strange flings defiance at her persecutors, saying she 'should be mad' to conform, accepting instead imprisonment in the dank Gatehouse. Committed? Cantankerous? Crazy? There is plenty of tragedy (and comedy too), here, defeat and victory, all in the poignant drama of early modern religious struggle.

As the stories above illustrate, English Catholics who openly resisted Protestantism have always been most visible to later generations, for better and for worse. They represent only the most convicted (in both senses) edge of Catholic presence in England; many more, doubtless, chose external conformity or outright dissimulation. Still, civic and legal documents identify thousands of recusants who suffered fines, confiscations, loss of land, imprisonment, or execution. The story of Bridget Strange, particularly, calls attention to the large role of Catholic women in recusancy. In the recusant rolls for 1593–4 more than half of the estreated convictions for recusancy (i.e. those entered with an abstract including a statement of the fine) in twenty counties name women (489 of 895), with some very lopsided individual tallies (Lancashire, 44 women of 72 convictions; Monmouthshire, 58 of 60; Oxfordshire, 29 of 39; Staffordshire, 112 of 187). Archbishop Matthew's recusant list for Yorkshire, 1615, names 811 females to 426 males (B. Sheils, *English Catholics of Parish and Town*, ed. M. Rowlands, 1999: 133). Recusant women such as these opened their homes to refugee priests, collected prohibited Catholic books, and stood fast in their convictions despite imprisonment and persecution. Dorothy Vavasour harboured priests in York; Dorothy Lawson set up a chapel for mass in her Tyneside home. In a letter dated 12 April 1606 Luisa de Carvajal, an extraordinary lay Spanish missionary to England, tells of the legendary Anne Vaux, imprisoned for sheltering Henry Garnet:

And they said Mistress Anne has lived in sin with Master Farmer, who is Father Garnet, and they said as much to her, and she, even though she was imprisoned there in the Tower, laughed loudly two or three times (for she really is quite funny and very lively), and she said, 'You come to me with this child's play and impertinence? A sign that you have nothing of importance with which to charge me.' And she laughed bravely at them, making a great joke of their behaviour in that business. They asked her whether she had known about the Gunpowder Plot. She said of course she had known, for, since she was a woman, how could anything possibly happen in England without her being told of it?   (*This Tight Embrace*, ed. E. Rhodes, 2000: 239)

After being released, Anne Vaux opened a school for the children of Catholic gentry at Stanley Grange, a centre for Jesuit activities in England. Margaret Clitherow's neighbor, Grace Babthorpe endured five years in prison and, widowed, became a nun in 1617; in the next hundred years or so her family produced five Jesuit priests and eight nuns. Three women died for their faith in Elizabeth's reign: Margaret Clitherow, Margaret Ward, and Anne Line, who is perhaps remembered in Shakespeare's *The Phoenix and Turtle*.

Other tallies tell a grimmer story of recusancy, imprisonment, and execution. Numerous Catholics served time for recusancy: the Jesuit William Weston spent seventeen years in prison; the gentleman Francis Tregian, over twenty years; the lay brother Thomas Pounde, thirty years. About 130 priests from Mary's reign suffered imprisonment, and approximately thirty of them, aged and sickly, died during confinement. About 100 Catholic lay persons, men and women, died in Elizabethan prisons. Of 471 seminary priests who came to England during Elizabeth's reign, 285 suffered capture and incarceration (P. McGrath and J. Rowe, *Recusant History*, 1991: 416). Between 1535 and 1603, 239 Catholics suffered death for treason. (The exception to the rule is the Franciscan friar, John Forest, who alone was executed for heresy in 1538.) The government of Queen Elizabeth put to death 189 Catholics; that of James I, 25 Catholics; that of Charles I, 24 Catholics (G. F. Nuttall, *Journal of Ecclesiastical History*, 1971). Subject to such penalty, Catholicism survived largely in secret and in suspicion, dependent on fugitive, sometimes heroic ministers who wore disguises and hid in priest-holes, some contrived by the ingenious Nicholas Owen. For many English Catholics, the discovery of St Priscilla's catacombs in 1578 confirmed their place in the Church Universal and their solidarity with the ancient persecuted Christians 'who were wont to lie hidden and secret from their enemies', enduring persecution and danger. The catacombs ratified 'Catholic religion' as well as 'Catholic rites and observances', especially icons, images, and reverence for saints. The past attackers were Roman soldiers, the present, those who 'presume to deface' pictures 'and throw them out of holy temples' (Gaspare Loarte, *The Exercise of a Christian Life*, 1579, sigs. EEvi^v–EEviii).

Many Catholics who ventured out of the catacombs soon found themselves incarcerated in prisons—national (the Tower, Fleet, Marshalsea, King's Bench), county, municipal, or ecclesiastical (inherited from earlier times). In his prison diary (1580–5), the priest John Hart names eleven London prisons where Catholics suffered seven different forms of torture (*A Tudor Journal*, ed. Bryan A. Harrison, 2000: 35–6). Chief Justice Popham's brief, a list of seventeen putative examples of Catholic sedition, ranging from the Northern Rebellion (1569) to incidents in the 1580s, reveals the strategy used to convict Catholics who were being tried for unrelated charges (*Unpublished Documents Relating to the English Martyrs*, ed. J. H. Pollen, 1908: 289–95). Kept in jails or private castles, subject to widely variant treatment and surveillance, incarcerated Catholics remained active in the faith. Records, letters, and autobiographical accounts attest to the creation of a literary prison culture within Elizabethan Catholicism. George Cotton, imprisoned from 1577 to 1589, translated Diego de Estella; Philip Howard translated Lanspergius and wrote a meditation. In Fleetwood Stephen Vallenger, who had copied Campion's writing for manuscript circulation, had a library of 101 volumes in six languages. In Marshalsea William Hartley sold Catholic devotions (1585–6). The imprisoned Thomas Wright published two books before his release in 1600. Permitted books and a clerk in a Dublin jail, Henry Fitzsimon wrote a polemic against John Rider (1608). The imprisoned Thomas Preston wrote a response to Bellarmine (1611) that attracted the favourable attention of James I. Francis Tregian (the Younger) passed his time in prison (1608–19) by copying and compiling over 2,000 pieces of music into what became known as the *Fitzwilliam Virginal Book*.

In places of relatively easy restriction, Wisbech castle, for example, prisoners practised their faith openly; in places of stricter punishment they went to remarkable lengths to console and support each other. In the Tower, for example, an Anglo-Scottish priest, John Ingram (executed 1591) bequeathed beads, medals, and crosses to fellow Catholic prisoners, as well as Latin verses inscribed on the walls with a blunt knife. Surviving in autograph manuscript, one verse exhorts others to martyrdom; another vividly expresses very human fears:

> Aeternos si vis cum Christo ducere soles
> Incipe mundanos spernere corde dies.
> (If thou wouldst with Christ spend eternal days,
> Begin to scorn in heart the days of earth.)

> Altera sanguineae mors est cunctatio mortis,
> Quae ridet veteres tincta cruore comas.
> (The expectation of a bloody death is another death
> Which grins at me, her grey hairs steeped in gore.)
> (*Unpublished Documents*, ed. J. H. Pollen, 1908: 273, 278).

Philip Howard likewise left inscriptions in the prison cell he occupied for nearly ten years, including these words of encouragement: 'sicut peccati causa vinciri opprobrium est, ita e contra pro Cristo custodiae vincula sustinere maxima gloria est' (Just as to be bound because of sin is a disgrace, so, in contrast, to suffer the chains of imprisonment for Christ is the greatest glory) (*Philip Howard*, ed. J. H. Pollen, W. MacMahon, 1919: 354). Many wrote poems and meditations. The Benedictine Benet Canfield (William Fitch) and the Jesuit Robert Southwell wrote consolations, as did John Fisher in two letters to his sister, and Thomas More. More's famous Tower works deeply meditate on the passion of Christ, and compare the wide world to a prison and all mortal life to capital punishment (see *Consolations*, INSTRUCTIONS AND DEVOTIONS). Catholics formed faith communities in prison itself: Ben Jonson remembered converting to Catholicism while in prison, under the influence of a priest (perhaps Thomas Wright) who visited him there.

The Jesuit John Gerard has left behind a vivid account of Catholic life in Elizabethan prisons. He visited Bridewell and the starved and beaten Oxford musician John Jacob, still wearing a hairshirt though covered with lice. Captured in 1594, he faced the sadistic, threatening Topcliffe: 'I will hang you up in the air and will have no pity on you; and then I shall watch and see whether God will snatch you from my grasp'; 'You can do nothing unless God allows it', Gerard replied calmly (tr. P. Caraman, 1951: 70). After being tortured, Gerard moved to another prison, the Clink, a 'translation from Purgatory to Paradise' (78) because of the community of Catholics incarcerated there. Gerard said masses, heard confessions, reconciled many to the Church, set up a chapel, and led six prisoners in the Ignatian Spiritual Exercises. Transferred to the Tower and further torture in 1597, he took comfort at finding the name of another Jesuit, Henry Walpole, scratched on the walls, alongside the names of the angels, Mary, and Jesus in Latin, Greek, and Hebrew letters. 'It was a great comfort to me to find myself in a place sanctified by this great and holy martyr, and in the room where he had been tortured so many times—fourteen in all' (105). (For an eyewitness account of Walpole's death, see LIVES AND DEATHS.) Gerard's memoir, ending in exciting escape, illuminates the culture of Catholicism in captivity, highlighting particularly the courage of many imprisoned recusants and their capacity for communal ritual, sacrifice, and survival.

Additionally, records identify those who opposed Protestantism from a distance, especially from exile abroad. Some clustered around Catholic aristocrats and courts; others went to schools and universities. Oxford and Cambridge lost many of their best and brightest Catholics to the University at Louvain, which became a centre of English Catholic activity and scholarship. Some English academics in the period went to different European universities, while seminarians journeyed to English schools founded by William Allen, Robert Persons, and others in Douai, Rheims, Saint-Omer, Rome, Valladolid, Seville, and elsewhere. Thomas Goldwell, bishop of St Asaph, migrated to Italy; Queen Mary's attendant, Jane Dormer, became the duchess of Feria in Spain. Talented Catholics took up service in royal courts (that of Philip of Spain, e.g., who was generous with pensions) or great ducal households (those of Parma, Savoy, and Guise); less talented ones became menials or mercenaries. The convent at Cambrai attracted Gertrude More and others. English men and women tasted the salt bread of exile, in Dante's phrase (*Par.* 17. 58–9), with grace and courage, but Robert Peckham's poignant epitaph in San Gregorio, Rome, reminds us of the price some paid: 'Here lies Robert Peckham, Englishman and Catholic, who, after England's break with the Church, left England because he could not live in his country without the Faith and, having come to Rome, died there because he could not live apart from his country' (*The Other Face*, ed. P. Caraman, 1960: 141). In a letter to the Privy Council, exiled priests spoke of 'this hard and heavy sentence of exile, which is a certain kind of civil death, or rather a languishing and continual dying' (*Petition apologetical*, 1604, sig. Eiv). The English at home regarded the exiles with suspicion and kept tabs on them through a network of informers and spies.

Early modern Catholics who chose rebellion over recusancy, imprisonment, or exile also remain conspicuous to the modern eye. In 1536 some 40,000 northern Catholics of Yorkshire and Lincolnshire and other counties revolted in protest over the closing of monasteries and a new tax, rallying around a banner that displayed the five wounds of Christ. The government promised a general pardon but then massacred the insurgents. In 1549 parishioners from Devon and Cornwall rejected the mandated English prayerbook. In the resulting Western Rebellion farmers united under a nobleman, Humphrey Arundell, and met government forces, composed largely of foreign mercenaries, who killed some 4,000, armed and unarmed alike. In 1569 the Northern Rebellion sought the release of Mary, Queen of Scots, and the restoration of Catholicism. The government again conquered the insurgents and executed hundreds as admonitory examples. Mary, Queen of Scots, a Catholic claimant for the English throne, remained the focus of conspiracies national and international. Foreign invasion, supported by the papacy, threatened. Italian and Spanish forces joined Gerald Fitzgerald, earl of Desmond, in Smerwick (1579) and suffered treachery and defeat; from 1595 to 1603 the earl of Tyrone led a bloody rebellion in Ireland (see O'Sullivan-Beare's account, HISTORIES). In 1588 the Spanish Armada went down to bad weather and courageous English forces, an event that proved to many Protestants that God was on their side. Cardinal William Allen's broadside, prepared for distribution after Spanish victory, outlines ruthless procedures for reconverting England (see CONTROVERSIES).

Despite a long tradition of self-congratulation and flattering comparison with Germany and France, the English did not achieve religious uniformity peacefully, honourably, or bloodlessly. Things could have been far worse, to be sure, and some credit for relative stability must go to the thousands of local Protestant neighbours, officials, and citizens who adopted a policy of *de facto* toleration despite urgent paranoia and pressure. This toleration occasionally extended to the upper reaches of society, where flourished outright Catholics such as the brilliant lawyer Edmund Plowden, the musician William Byrd, and 'crypto'- Catholic nobles such as Henry Howard, the earl of Northampton, in James's reign. Credit too must go to the many Catholics who remained loyal to their country and to their faith, choosing to endure persecution for their religious beliefs. These Catholics Southwell represented in *An Humble Supplication* (1591, pr. 1600–1), which asserted Catholic patriotism and begged for leniency. And these Catholics assumed important names and faces in 1585 when Thomas Tresham, Lord William Vaux, and Sir John Arundell presented Elizabeth with a declaration of allegiance and a request for the exercise of some religious freedom in their households. Hoping to prevent legislation that would make it treason to harbour priests, these lords promised to turn in any priest who presumed to hint at sedition. The nobles repeated this request without success to James in *A Petition Apologetical* (1604), on behalf of important Catholic families—the Howards, Percies, Pagets, Throckmortons, Windsors, Salisburys, and Habingtons.

Such declarations demonstrate an important aspect of English Catholicism, its persistence among the English gentry. John Bossy famously argued that Elizabethan Catholicism could exist only where there were supporting social institutions, i.e. where public authority remained virtually in private hands. This meant that the survival of Elizabethan Catholicism depended largely on geography and became *per force* 'seigneurial', that is, centred in the relatively inaccessible and independent noble households. 'This assumption,' writes Bossy elsewhere, 'might be demonstrated almost by statistics alone: from the Recusant rolls of Elizabeth to the Returns of the Papists of the later eighteenth century, every attempt to count Catholics reveals them as coagulated in local groups at the centre of which a gentleman's household will usually be found' (*The English Catholic Community*, 1975: 175). In addition to the noble families mentioned above, there was Francis Tregian of Cornwall, the Gages of Surrey, the Stonors of Oxfordshire, the Bedingfields of Norfolk, the Rookwoods of Suffolk, and others.

How many English were Catholics in this period? This question remains impossible to answer with any precision, despite repeated attempts. Almost everyone was Catholic in the early 1530s; by the end of the century Catholics were a distinct minority, which John Bossy puts at about 40,000 out of a population of about 5 million, in 1603 (1975: 192), or less than 1 per cent. By 1640, however, 20 per cent of the peerage were Catholic; 750 priests, an increase from 300 at the beginning of James's reign, served 60,000 Catholics (R. Lockyer, *Early Stuarts*, 1999: 198, 201). Deriving largely from recusancy data, these figures may considerably underrepresent the Catholic population. Pastorally speaking, recusancy was a counsel of perfection, an ideal of conduct officially encouraged but, as causists and confessors well recognized, beyond the reach of many ordinary, compromising, less ideologically committed Catholics. Condemned to die with Campion in 1581, for example, the secular priest John Hart recanted, then subsequently repented, and eventually suffered the milder punishment of banishment. As Michael Questier has observed, early modern Catholicism existed 'as a larger, inclusive and more flexible quantity of which absolute recusancy (unmoderated noncomformity) and moderate or moderated recusancy (partial or occasional nonconform-ity) were both expressions' (*Conformity and Orthodoxy*, ed. M. Questier, P. Lake, 2000: 257). In 1614 the Spanish ambassador Gondomar reported to Philip III that out of some 3.5 million English people, a twelfth were committed Catholics, two-twelfths committed but outwardly conforming to the law, and three-twelfths favourably inclined to Catholicism; in other words, half the population was Catholic or potentially Catholic (Lockyer, *Early Stuarts*, 201–2). Though this is probably an overestimate it well reminds us that Catholics in early modern England came in all sizes and shapes—conspicuous recusants, martyrs, theologians, scholars, historians, and poets, to be sure, but also, more numerously and less visibly, lukewarm sentimentalists, superstitious traditionalists, conflicted undecideds, and Church papists, who attended mandated services for a variety of reasons. As Alexandra Walsham (*Church Papists*, 1993) has well shown, Church papists represent a large and uncountable part of the population; some conformed as a harmless exercise of civic duty, some out of doctrinal confusion or indifference, some with gritted teeth to avoid penalty, and some few, like John Harley who read aloud from the Latin primer during service in 1577, as subversive witnesses against the false religion on display. Whatever their motivations, most maintained the faith quietly, striking precarious balances between the dictates of conscience and crown. After several citations for recusancy in York, Margaret Raines finally attended services and communicated but was caught leaving with the sacramental bread hidden in her hand. (For the Catholic debate on Church papistry see Langdale's response to Persons, CONTROVERSIES.)

Furthermore, the question of how many Catholics lived in early modern England is another question *mal posée* because it requires the respondent to define one religion exclusively against the other in the population at large. Exhibiting the polarizing mentality of early modern polemic, this question oversimplifies the complex realities of religious experience and identity in early modern England. Tessa Watt's study of the ballads, broadsides, tables, pamphlets, and chapbooks that constituted popular devotion (*Cheap Print and Popular Piety*, 1993), replaces this confrontational model with a vision of religious accommodation and interchange. Despite the iconophobia, Catholics and Protestants alike still looked at walls decorated with woodcut Christs and biblical scenes. They still heard about Susannah, Tobias, Dives and Lazarus, and the Prodigal Son; they still read warnings against vanity, bawdry, usury, and so on. Alexandra Walsham (*Providence in Early Modern England*, 1999) likewise recognizes continuities, shared beliefs, and common practices: both Catholics and Protestants pointed to Providence to explain monstrous births, strange occurrences, and unusual deaths; they both perceived visible sermons, though not always the same message, in public calamities and disasters. Both confessions believed in an omniscient all-powerful God, feared the devil and witchcraft, and lived by homespun bromides that promised punishment for the wicked and reward for the good. Accordingly, Peter Lake envisions 'a cultural terrain strewn with the wreckage of partially disrupted belief systems, sets of assumptions about how the world worked and where the holy was to be found and how it might be approached, invoked, and manipulated' (*Companion to Shakespeare*, ed. D. Kastan, 1999: 78). Catholics and Protestants variously mixed, matched, appropriated, glossed, and reified available cultural materials, producing a 'creative bricolage' (79).

This view of the English religious landscape, consonant with that of confessional historians such as Delumeau and Bossy, offers some revealing insights. For one thing it explains why, despite the incessant din of condemnation, Protestants read and published Catholic devotional works. Augustine and Thomas à Kempis remained standards. The Yorkshire minister Edmund Bunny sold several modified editions of Robert Persons's *Christian Directory* as a perfectly orthodox Protestant text. Thomas Rogers published Diego de Estella's reflections on the vanity of the world (*A Method unto Mortification*, 1586), complete with several indexes of omitted Catholic 'errors'. Giles Randall's *A Bright Star* (1646) included parts of Benet Canfield's *Rule of Perfection* (1609). Daniel Powel published *The Redemption of Lost Time* (1608), an unacknowledged translation of Andrés de Soto. The Catholic Rheims translation of the Bible, finally, played a large and unacknowledged role in the majestic phrasing of the Authorized, or King James, Version (1611).

Moreover, this view provides a plausible cultural context for the large-scale phenomenon of conversion in the period. Edmund Campion, Francis Walsingham (namesake kinsman to the Secretary of State), and Toby Matthew famously converted to Catholicism; to Protestantism, John Donne, Christopher Perkins (an ex-Jesuit who helped frame the Jacobean Oath of Allegiance), Thomas Gage (an ex-Dominican who became vicar of Deal), Thomas Bell and Thomas Clark (who both wrote public recantations), and most of England. Both sides moved quickly to exploit converts. Preachers and pamphlets published the scaffold confession of John Dudley, duke of Northumberland, who in 1553 stunned the assembled throngs by repudiating Protestantism and declaring himself a Catholic. James I employed Richard Sheldon and another Catholic, William Warmington, as theological writers. Members of both confessions prayed, struck balances, stood fast, and yielded, often (like Ben Jonson and William Alabaster) changing their minds and hearts several times during one lifetime. Marcantonio de Dominis, the archbishop of Spaleto (now in Croatia), sensationally converted to the Church of England in 1616, became dean of Windsor, and took part in the consecration of English bishops, only to convert back to Catholicism and face the rigours of the Inquisition. The spectacle of conversion and reconversion, as Michael Questier concludes in an important study, 'tells us that instability was as much a defining characteristic of English religion in this unsettled period as the placid acquiescent conformity for which some historians have argued, or, as others have it, a stubborn conservative adherence to the values and practice of the past in opposition to Protestant novelty...flux in religion was the norm rather than the exception in religious experience' (*Conversion, Politics, and Religion in England*, 1996: 205–6).

The view of early modern England as characterized by confessional common ground and fluid interchange, finally, turns us from inconclusive head counting to a recognition of pluralities, to notice of the different kinds and expressions of Catholicism in the period. Doctrinal and legal canons defined religious identity in the period but so did the shifting vagaries of personal choice and interior experience, insusceptible to enumeration. Arthur Marotti has well called attention to the 'great muddled middle in English Christianity' (*Theatre and Religion*, eds. Richard Dutton *et al.*, 2003: 219). What religion did Catholics such as William Bishop and William Barclay practise when they, speaking for many countrymen, denied the power of the pope to depose Elizabeth? What religion did John Donne, dean of St Paul's, practise when he remembered his Catholic upbringing, hung paintings of the Virgin Mary in his deanery, and composed poetry in her praise? How about those churchgoers who looked to a patron saint for healing and comfort? Who yearned for the cleansing ritual of pilgrimage, who longed to lift eyes up to a God-made-flesh in the Eucharist, who remembered the light and warmth of a Candlemas ceremony in the dead of English winter? Any assessment of Catholicism in the period has to be flexible enough to accommodate pluralities; it must be inclusive rather than exclusive in order to represent the ordinary as well as the extraordinary, the lukewarm, hidden, and halfway believers who lived beneath official notice.

Catholic Publication

Catholicism in early modern England, no less than Protestantism, was a ministry of the word. And, in addition to the oral media, words circulated in manuscript and in print. People conducted business in manuscript, producing millions of handwritten papers for personal, civic, legal, ecclesiastical, military, and commercial affairs. They kept diaries, composed letters, bought property, made wills, recorded infractions, registered names, produced poetry and polemic in manuscript. The state, at times, exercised control over manuscripts, and stationers and booksellers sometimes offered them for sale. An army of clerks and scriveners kept the quills moving and the world turning.

Denied access to licensed printing presses as well as their own voice in public and private, Catholics naturally created and circulated manuscripts, some of which are printed for the first time in this volume. Replying to Persons's published work, Alban Langdale argued in manuscript that Catholics could go to state services without fear of scandal or mortal sin. Thomas Pounde circulated Edmund Campion's letter to the Privy Council (his 'Brag'), and Catholics passed around handwritten accounts of Campion's Tower debates which contradicted the official Protestant version, *A True Report of the Disputation* (1583). One such account passed from the home of the recusant printer William Carter to the raiding Richard Topcliffe, to the martyrologist John Foxe, to the ecclesiastical historian John Strype, and finally to the librarian Humphrey Walney, who in 1709 purchased it for Robert Harley (MS Harley 422). Watching Alexander Rawlins and Henry Walpole die at Tyburn in 1585, an anonymous bystander scribbled an account of their executions. The tattered pages sit in a small folder at the Venerable English College, Rome. Edmund Plowden published in manuscript a potentially explosive treatise on Mary, Queen of Scots, meticulously demonstrating her eligibility for the throne of England. Copies survive in the Bodleian and British Library.

Many of the most important Catholic writings in the period reached contemporaries in manuscript: Philip Howard's letter to the queen explaining his intended flight from England, Persons's *Memorial for the Reformation of England*, Southwell's poetry and prose, Donne's religious poems, Persons's four-volume *Certamen Ecclesiae Anglicanae*. Peter Mowle's miscellany, presently in manuscript at St Mary's College, Oscott, contains the Jesus Psalter, Vaux's catechism, works by Robert Southwell and William Alabaster, prayers, and other items for the East Anglian faithful. Such works, along with newsletters, broadsides, letters, and other ephemera, passed from hand to hand through back channels of personal contacts, such as the network Nancy Pollard Brown discovered for Southwell's work leading from the countess of Arundel's house in Spitalfields to the country. Gerard Kilroy has linked the transmission of Campion manuscripts to Sir John Harington and the Sidney circle, including Lady Penelope Riche. He has also brought to light the Brudenell manuscript, a two-volume Catholic compendium by Sir Thomas Tresham that contains first-hand accounts of exorcisms and executions as well as theological discussion. A great number of other Catholic manuscripts await rediscovery.

Many Catholic manuscripts, of course, sooner or later, naturally and unnaturally, found their way into early modern print. William Roper's hagiographical biography of Thomas More (composed 1553–8) circulated widely in manuscript before its belated publication in 1626. The Catholic pamphlet popularly known as *Leicester's Commonwealth* also enjoyed a full life as a manuscript both before and after its print publication in 1584; Justice Popham complained of some 500 copies. Manuscripts and print could exist in an uneasy relationship, sometimes in a tense symbiosis. Robert Southwell wrote a consolatory letter to the imprisoned Philip Howard which he later 'could not but condescend' to publish as *An Epistle of Comfort*, at the request of 'divers', though it cost 'no small labour in altering the style' (1587, sig. A2). Cardinal DuPerron's confidential handwritten letter to Isaac Casaubon, urging him to persuade King James to return England to Catholicism, appeared in print with errors and heresies; the embarrassed cardinal printed a copy of the original (*A Letter written from Paris*, 1612) to replace the unauthorized versions.

Sometimes symbiosis became open opposition as enemies published Catholic writing to expose its errors and dangers. Polemical works habitually provided block quotations from Catholic treatises for point-by-point refutation, thus providing summaries of the very heresies they sought to extirpate. After a wide circulation in manuscript, Chidiock Tichborne's prison lament, 'My prime of youth is but a frost of cares', oddly appeared in *Verses of Praise and Joy* (1586), a book that celebrates the foiling of Babington's plot; a companion poem parodically moralizes Tichborne's death as just deserts for his treasonous popery. The Appellant priests published Southwell's *An Humble Supplication* in 1600–1 to discredit Jesuits. In this cause they found ready allies in London authorities, who allowed publication of their books under fictitious foreign imprints. In 1690 Edward Gee published Persons's *Memorial for the Reformation of England* as *The Jesuit's Memorial for the Destruction of the Church of England* because, he said, it more eloquently exposed Jesuit perfidy than any book he had written.

Orality, manuscript, and print, moreover, often intersected in complicated triangulation. Protest songs and ballads lifted the spirits of Catholics in secret gatherings and in manuscript anthologies, such as Constance Aston Fowler's book, Huntington 904, Cotton Vespasian A-25, Additional MS 15,225, and sporadically in print. In the early 1620s a running series of multimedia debates between Protestants and Catholics occurred in person, manuscript, and print. Published disagreements led to a series of conferences and debates. King James himself became involved, first as a debater, then as a writer who delivered a manuscript raising nine questions to the Jesuit John Percy, alias Fisher. Percy answered the King in a manuscript which drew print rebuttals from Francis White and Archbishop Laud, which in turn evoked further print responses from Percy and his fellow Jesuit John Floyd.

These examples demonstrate that manuscript and print coexisted in the early modern period as competing and complementary forms of Catholic publication. Sometimes the publication process reversed its usual direction, going instead from print to script: scribes regularly made manuscript copies of Catholic books from the Continent to achieve a wider circulation. The facts and scope of Catholic publication contradict the pervasive depiction of a literate, modern Protestantism artfully deploying the word against an illiterate, medieval Catholicism. This depiction, we should recall, originated in the propagandistic traditions of Lutheran hagiography. A woodcut in the Pepys collection (*c.*1550) shows Luther protecting a farmer by wielding a pen against the abashed and triple-crowned pope, sword in hand, a cardinal bearing a pardon by his side (T. Watt, *Cheap Print and Popular Piety,* 1991: pl. 12). The timely invention of print, naturally, fitted well into the evolving mythology, as polemicists such as John Foxe hailed Gutenberg's invention as a Providentially delivered Protestant weapon. An anonymous writer in 1662 spoke for many before and after when he boasted that the press had given the church of Rome 'such a wound as she will never be able to cure' (*The Uses of Script and Print,* ed. J. Crick and A. Walsham, 2004: 3). As usual, sectarian propaganda codified into a historical understanding that is evident today in a score of studies on print and Protestantism. But the Fifth Lateran Council (1512–17) had officially recognized and embraced the new power of the press: 'Ars imprimendi libros temporibus potissimum nostris divino favente numine, inventa seu aucta et perpolita' (The art of printing books [has been] chiefly discovered, or rather enlarged and perfected in our time by divine favour, below, DOCUMENTS). And well before Luther English Catholics devoured printed primers, indulgences, and images. Benedictines stocked their libraries with printed books and at St Albans and Canterbury the monks sponsored presses. Surveying the wide expanses of Catholic publication, historical revisionists such as Alexandra Walsham have largely dismantled the impacted cluster of simplification and misconception: Protestantism 'had no monopoly on religious publishing and Tridentine Catholicism too was a religion of the printed book' (*Cambridge History of the Book in Britain,* iv, ed. John Barnard *et al.,* 2002: 44).

Where did these printed books come from? Rarely did English publishers and printers with Catholic sympathies or a shrewd eye for the market take a chance on a Catholic book per se: Gabriel Cawood hired John Wolfe to print Robert Southwell's *Mary Magdalen's Funeral Tears* (1591) and James Roberts for Southwell's *Saint Peter's Complaint, with other poems* (1595). The latter has a title-page that displays eucharistic symbols and IHS. Whether from prudence or ignorance, the collection does not contain Southwell's more politically or doctrinally Catholic poems, 'Decease Release', for example, on the death of Mary, Queen of Scots, or 'Of the Blessed Sacrament of the Altar'. Other editions, such as

William Barrett's 1620 collection of Southwell's verse and prose, show more careful presentation and expurgation for Protestant readers. The English Catholic editions of Southwell are exceptions that prove the rule. Catholics printed books normally issued from foreign presses as well as from twenty-one secret presses in England. From 1608 to 1642 the Jesuit press at Saint-Omer published over 300 titles in English. Allison and Rogers's bibliography of Catholic works printed between 1558 and 1640 identifies 932 titles in English and an additional 1,619 in Latin and other languages. These impressive numbers do not include publications from mainstream presses, non-religious books by Catholics, or books by Catholics written during periods of apostasy. In *The Foot out of the Snare* (1624) John Gee claimed to know of a Jesuit who had more books crammed into two or three large rooms of his Savoy chamber than any stationer had in a warehouse at St Paul's (sig. S4^v). Reflecting on forty years in the book trade, Michael Sparke recalled his time as an apprentice early in James's reign, when his master in Staffordshire ran a lively illegal trade in 'popish books, pictures, beads, and such trash' (*Second Beacon*, 1652, sig. 3^v). He laments Catholic success at publication despite prohibitions: 'yet so many pass and such multitudes printed' (sig. A3). Devout readers and risk-taking profiteers created a thriving black-market business in Catholic publication, sustained by a local network of agents and merchants as well as figures abroad such as Richard Verstegan, who coordinated the flow of European news and information from Antwerp for three decades, 1589–1620.

Both Gee and Sparke call upon the authorities to suppress Catholic, and therefore seditious, publication. In early modern England a complicated machinery of licensing and authorization existed just for that purpose. The London Company of Stationers, the printers at Oxford and Cambridge, and the crown exercised a monopoly on printing. The Stationers' Company granted individual members the rights to print but members had to acquire a licence from them for every individual title. In addition to obtaining the licence, the stationer had also to get 'authorization' for the work from the High Commission, an ecclesiastical body headed by the archbishop of Canterbury and the bishop of London. When Sparke complained in an earlier pamphlet that there was 'more punishment for selling a quarto bible with notes than one hundred mass books in the High Commission' (*Scintilla*, 1641, sig. A3), he invoked the primary agency responsible for safeguarding the republic from popery. Royal proclamations and Privy Council orders could also suppress certain books but not declare felonies or treasons. Periodically the government responded to perceived threats by parliamentary statutes that redefined the rules and adjusted the controls over printed texts. In Elizabeth's reign eleven treason statutes protected the monarch by prohibiting all imputation of heresy, question of her right to rule, and the like; six of these specifically referenced Catholic texts. The statutes in James's reign expanded the motives of control from simple suppression to stricter regulation of discourse. James suppressed several books on his own, including Francisco Suárez's *Defensio Catholicae Fidei* in 1613, which was publicly burned at St Paul's.

In this culture of suppression and book burning publishers routinely used pseudonyms, false imprints, and other subterfuges. Catholic publishers, printers, and booksellers lived in constant danger of detection. Operator of two secret presses in the 1590s, Henry Garnet, SJ, published St Peter Canisius's *A Sum of Christian Doctrine* (1592–6), but apologized for rushing the book into print without the supplement on service and prayer advertised in the table of contents: 'by reason of the continual wars in this country and the manifold difficulties which all those that live here about do feel, I have been constrained to finish this work without full accomplishment of my promise and purpose' (sig. *4). Catholic manuscripts that made it into print sometimes never made it to a reader. The informer William Udall claimed to have arranged for the interception of 10,000 books in the early years of James's reign, and to have exposed numerous suppliers and distributors. His investigations led to the confiscation of 700 copies of the scurrilous *Prurit-anus* (1609), a Latin work that particularly galled the king. *Prurit-anus* ('Itchy arse') consisted of questions ludicrously answered by misquotations of Scripture, a device intended to parody Protestant methods of argument. Udall also engineered a raid at the Venetian ambassador's residence in July 1609, where authorities found bales of Catholic books under twenty-five separate titles stashed in the cellar by the embassy priest and other employees. Such raids were common occurrences, as the antiquary John Stow, subjected to search and seizure in 1569, could have testified. In a letter to Richard Verstegan, Robert Southwell describes the procedure vividly:

Their manner of searching is to come with a troop of men to the house as though they come to fight a-field. They beset the house on every side, then they rush in and ransack every corner— even women's beds and bosoms—with such insolent behaviour that their villainies in this kind are half a martyrdom. The men they command to stand and to keep their places; and whatsoever of price cometh in their way, many times they pocket it up, as jewels, plate, money and such like ware, under pretense of papistry.... When they find any books, church stuff, chalices, or other like things, they take them away, not for any religion that they care for but to make a commodity. (*Letters and Dispatches*, ed. A. G. Petti, 1959: 7–8)

Catholics who wrote, published, printed, imported, read, or disseminated Catholic books risked serious punishment. In 1579 Stephen Brinkley located his secret press at Greenstreet House, East Ham, London, then after some time moved it to Francis Browne's house in Southwark, London, and finally to Stonor House near Henley. Authorities seized the press on 8 August 1581 and imprisoned Brinkley for two years. In 1582 they convicted Stephen Vallenger of writing *A True Report* of Campion's death, cut off his ears, and imprisoned him until his death in 1591. The government executed the courageous if foolhardy John

Felton for tacking a copy of Pius V's bull to the bishop of London's gate. William Carter, who printed at least twenty-two titles from two secret presses in London (1575–81), aroused the wrath of John Aylmer, bishop of London, and Richard Topcliffe, who imprisoned him in 1579 and executed him in 1584. The verdict rested on dubious interpretation of a passage from one of Carter's books, Gregory Martin's *A Treatise of Schism* (1578), which exhorted women to imitate the biblical Judith, slayer of Holofernes. Martin stressed Judith's constancy in adversity but authorities naturally saw an incitement to assassinate Elizabeth. For distributing some five hundred copies of William Allen's *A True, Sincere, and Modest Defence* (1584), Thomas Alfield and Thomas Webley met their deaths at Tyburn in 1585. After several convictions for possessing and distributing Catholic books, James Duckett also suffered capital punishment in 1601.

That so many texts survived the prohibitions, confiscations, and punishments testifies to the strength of a religious conviction translated into driving market demand. What books were Catholics taking such risks to write, read, and publish? Gee's catalogue of 156 popish books in London (1624) includes authors medieval (Bede and Augustine) as well as contemporary (Bellarmine, Richard Smith), Continental (Granada, Canisius, Puenta) as well as English (More, Persons, Brereley). A host of translators brought the wide world of Catholic thought and culture home to English readers: Anthony Batt, Thomas Everard, John Fen, Henry Garnet, Richard Gibbons, John and Thomas Hawkins, John Heigham, Richard Hopkins, William Kinsman, Toby Matthew, and John Wilson. Gee lists controversial works, histories, translations of the Bible, catechisms, devotional works, prayer-books including primers and offices, and saints' lives.

Notice of such instructional and devotional works certainly contradicts received wisdom about early modern religious publication, reflected, for example, in Elizabeth Eisenstein's considered judgement: 'In marked contrast to Catholic policy, vernacular Bibles, prayer books and catechisms were adopted by all reforming churches' (*The Printing Press as an Agent of Change*, 1979: 349). On the matter of biblical translation, initial impetus, of course, came from Protestants but Catholic versions soon competed in the marketplace. Gee's list begins with Catholic translations of the Old Testament and two separate editions of the Rheims New Testament (1582). Sparke rails against such translations as well as the 'wicked designs' of the papists 'cunningly to usher in popery by introducing pictures to the Holy Bible' (*Second Beacon*, 1652, title-page). Winding up the peroration, he fulminates against all 'poisonous popish pictures' (sig. B2).

Sparke here calls attention to an underappreciated aspect of Catholic publication, its use of illustrations. Gennings's account of his brother's life and death uses twelve engravings. Johannes Baptista de Cavalleriis's *Ecclesiae Anglicanae Trophaea* (1584), based on the frescoes in the Venerable English College, and Richard Verstegan's *Theatrum crudelitatum haereticorum* (1587) feature graphic copperplate engravings depicting the horrible torture and deaths of Catholic martyrs, the burnings, disembowellings, dismemberments; the latter achieved eight editions in Latin and French before 1609 (see Figs. 6, 8, 9, 14). Protestants used the same devices, of course, if not the same woodcuts and engravings, and also did a booming business in antipapal cartoons. But as champions of the image against iconoclasts and iconophobes, Catholics naturally used illustrations for polemical, devotional, and educational purposes. The French Jesuit Louis Richeôme published pictures to prepare the soul for reception of the Eucharist. John Bucke provided a fold-out picture to illustrate his instructions on the rosary. Since most printed works assumed a relatively high level of literacy, Catholics provided illustrations for the unlearned. Petrus Frarinus's *Oration against the unlawful insurrections of the Protestants* (1566) contains thirty-six woodcuts depicting the Protestant outrages. *Godly Contemplations for the unlearned* (1575) consists of sixty small woodcuts that depict scenes from the Old and New Testaments. Bellarmine's *A Short Catechism* (1614) appeared in various languages with illustrations of the Creed, Ave Maria, Ten Commandments, works of mercy, sins, and virtues.

Conclusion

The outmoded picture of a decaying, foreign, seditious, backward, and oral Catholicism reformed by a vital, popular, loyalist, modern, and literate Protestantism still persists today in popular and academic discourse, in authoritative histories, standard surveys, and ubiquitous anthologies. *The New Cambridge Modern History* devotes its entire second volume to the *Reformation* and one chapter (twenty-seven pages) in the third volume to 'The Papacy, Catholic Reform, and the Christian Mission'. In *The Tudor Constitution* G. R. Elton discusses anti-Catholic legislation under the heading, 'The Catholic Threat'; in *The Stuart Constitution* J. P. Kenyon employs the similar heading, 'The Catholic Problem'. Previous legislation 'ought to have been sufficient to eliminate them', Kenyon complains, calling the survival of Catholicism 'exasperating and alarming' and putting the 'blame' for it upon 'strangely reluctant' and 'amateur' local officials (1986: 166). Inertia and ignorance continue to distort the reality of Catholic presence and to silence Catholic voices, warping understanding of early modern English literature and culture. C. S. Lewis's influential *English Literature of the Sixteenth Century, Excluding Drama* (1954) employs the terms 'Papist' and 'Reformed' throughout (though with a disclaimer); Lewis rechristens Thomas Harding John in the text (299) and index; he makes no mention of Robert Persons and Thomas Stapleton, even in a chapter that purports to treat 'Religious Controversy and Translation'. (One of the greatest and most prolific polemicists of the age, Persons earns only one passing reference in Douglas Bush's following volume on the seventeenth century.) The eighth edition of *The Norton Anthology of English Literature* (2006) disproportionately represents the Protestant side in its *Faith in Conflict* section: one page from Thomas More's *Dialogue concerning Heresies* stands against selections from William Tyndale, John Calvin, Anne Askew, John Foxe, the Book of Common Prayer, the Book of Homilies, and Richard Hooker. Robert Southwell appears here, but not among the other English lyric poets, and only in one poem (his anthology piece), 'The Burning Babe'. David Cressy and Lori Anne Ferrell present an even more Protestantized version of history in an anthology that manifestly fails to live up to its title, *Religion & Society in Early Modern England: A Sourcebook*; they include only three Catholic selections among forty-six primary sources in the first edition (1996), and the same three selections among sixty-eight primary sources in the second edition (2005).

Since relatively few Catholic writers are available in individual modern editions or collections such as Louise Imogen Guiney's *Recusant Poets* (1938, only vol. i published) and A. C. Southern's *Recusant Prose* (1951), both long out of print, such neglect in the anthologies maintains old prejudices. To begin to remedy that neglect, *Early Modern Catholicism* presents Catholic writing under eight related headings: CONTROVERSIES, LIVES AND DEATHS, POETRY, INSTRUCTIONS AND DEVOTIONS, DRAMA, HISTORIES, FICTION, and DOCUMENTS, along with ILLUSTRATIONS. Most writers here excerpted affirm Church beliefs and traditions against the dominant theological and cultural imperatives of the day. Their voices need to be heard. Early modern England now, as it did then, should include Margaret Clitherow as well as the ubiquitous Anne Askew, Nicholas Sander as well as John Jewel, the Council of Trent as well as the Book of Common Prayer, Robert Bellarmine as well as Jean Calvin, Robert Persons and Thomas Stapleton as well as John Foxe, Robert Southwell as well as George Herbert, the traditions of Catholic meditative prayer, and, of course, baroque artists such as Henry Hawkins and Richard Crashaw. This anthology also takes notice of extraordinary English Catholic women—Jane Owen, polemicist; Gertrude More, poet; Elizabeth Cary, versatile author; Lady Lumley, dramatist; Mary Ward, religious activist, and others. Such figures challenge regnant clichés about Protestant emancipation and empowerment, reminding us that Catholic women traditionally held office in the guilds and confraternities, followed vocations to communal religious life, and gave varied, courageous witness to their faith while actively reshaping its ministries.

The selections below also aim to reflect the essential diversity of Catholicism in the period. The landmark 'Recusant' collections of Guiney and Southern as well as the 'Counter-Reformation' bibliography of Allison and Rogers define early modern Catholicism in opposition to English Protestantism. On a deep epistemological level, such works replicate the categorical assumptions of the Tudor–Stuart propaganda machine, which depicts Catholicism as monolithically other and insists on the alien nature of its legal and religious identity. Such assumptions enable a certain tidiness in taxonomy but distort historical realities. Some Catholic writers interrogate or deny official Church positions. Erasmus mocks clerical venality and the abuses of relics and shrines. Alban Langdale justifies the practice of external conformity, or 'Church papistry'. Many express views and beliefs that are doctrinally neutral, acceptable to Protestants and non-Christians alike. To represent early modern Catholicism in its actual fullness a collection must go beyond the litmus test of recusancy and the stance of opposition. It must tolerate a certain degree of untidiness and be inclusive rather than exclusive. Early modern Catholics opposed Protestants and variously shared common ground with them; they contested the dominant cultural institutions of their day and variously accepted them.

Early modern Catholic writing, finally, provides a context that redefines the established canons and literary culture of early modern England. English drama, as has long been known, owes its deep structure to Catholic liturgy and theatrical forms, the medieval moral and mystery plays. The English lyric, particularly the sonnet sequence and poems of praise, springs from deep roots in Dante's *dolce stil novo* and Petrarch, and, deeper still, in Marian devotion. Bringing silenced Catholic voices again into audible range, moreover, enables us to hear anew familiar voices. The elegant poet laureate Edmund Spenser, for example, set about colonizing the 'barbarous' Irish, profited from the military occupation, and idealized the ruthless Lord Grey as Artegal, who most certainly did not represent Justice to those he massacred at Smerwick. And yet, Book I of the *Faerie Queene* reconstitutes a medieval saint's life and the epic has surprising moments and touches that qualify the shrill anti-Catholic polemic. William Shakespeare's biographical links to Catholicism, though largely indirect and circumstantial, open new vistas on his poems and plays. And, more fruitfully, commentators have begun to discern in his plays a complicated and positive response to England's Catholic cultural heritage. John Donne's lyrics and satires, often conflicting with the sermons, show the impress of a Catholic upbringing and formation. A professed Catholic for the most productive years of his career, Ben Jonson's poetry and plays variously reflect his recusancy and religious convictions. The revered genius John Milton needs to have his prejudices reexamined, clearly evident in his poetry and *Areopagitica*; despite its canonization as a classic argument for freedom of speech, for example, the essay calls for extirpation of 'popery and open superstition' (*Prose Selections*, ed. M. Hughes, 1947: 264). Prefacing Southern's anthology, H. O. Evennett's comment over a half-century ago remains all too true: 'there is a great harvest waiting to be reaped in the literary and other aspects of Recusant history—and, indeed, in the whole story of Catholicism in modern England' (p. vii).

CONTROVERSIES

Catholic writing in this period, regardless of genre, is at its heart controversial: it denounces sin and preaches the Gospel; it attacks heresy and defends its own beliefs. Sometimes the gaze turns inward and exposes corruption within the Church. The pardoner and friar in Heywood's play illustrate clerical greed and the abuse of indulgences; Erasmian satire pillories the misuse of petitionary prayer and profiteering at holy shrines. More often, however, the target is without, i.e. the great European movements of religious redefinition. Robert Southwell's poetic 'Saint Peter's Complaint' (1595) defends the sacraments of Penance and the Eucharist by illustrating Tridentine teaching about contrition and transubstantiation. Anthony Copley's poem, *A Fig for Fortune* (1596), responds to Spenser's Protestant epic by depicting a New Jerusalem with Catholic priests, nuns, and sacraments. Recording individual witnesses to the faith, Catholic biographies, autobiographies, conversion accounts, and martyrologies preserve individual memories against erasure and inspire others to holiness. Catholic histories, such as those of Nicholas Sander and Robert Persons, provide counter-narratives to the national myths of godly reformation. Instructional and devotional works educate the faithful in Catholic prayer and practices.

Engaging specifically in the great theological and political disputes of early modern Europe, Catholics produced a vast, multilingual corpus of controversial writing. The preferred language of learned debate, of course, was Latin. Some of the most important Catholic books achieved circulation throughout Europe but did not appear in contemporary English translation: Nicholas Sander's defence of the Church, *De visibili monarchia ecclesiae* (1571); John Gibbons's account of martyrs, *Concertatio ecclesiae Catholicae in Anglia* (1583); Robert Bellarmine's polemical masterwork, *Disputationes de Controversiis* (1586–9); and Philip O'Sullivan-Beare's indignant history of Ireland, *Historiae Catholicae Iberniae Compendium* (1621).

At once political and theological, controversial writing illustrates the learning, power, and eloquence of the best Catholic minds in Europe. The Jesuit Juan de Mariana, for example, cogently justifies tyrannicide. The majority of disputants represented here defend the faith against Protestant attack. Erasmus argues against Luther for the freedom of the will. Thomas More excoriates Tyndale's translation of the New Testament as inaccurate and heretical. Answering the challenge of Archbishop John Jewel, Nicholas Sander distinguishes Catholic veneration of images from pagan idolatry. Having endured capture, imprisonment, and torture, Edmund Campion dramatically confronts Protestant adversaries in the Tower on the visibility of the Church. Henry Garnet defends the granting of indulgences and the practice of equivocation. On one side of the stylistic spectrum Edmund Plowden writes a legal brief on Mary Stuart's right to the throne, rich in philosophical implication. On the other, Jane Owen contributes a discussion of purgatory late in the period, including an imaginative dream vision of a dying Catholic who might have been saved, he realizes, had he only read *An Antidote against Purgatory* by Jane Owen.

Though they usually defended the faith against Protestants, Catholic controversialists in this period often disagreed significantly among themselves. Erasmus collated the earliest Greek texts, consulted the Latin manuscripts, and wanted to make Scripture accessible to everyone through translation. Gregory Martin thought many of the Greek texts corrupt and based his English New Testament (1582) on the Latin Vulgate; he offered it reluctantly, as a corrective to the errors of other translations. Three other debates divided Catholics through the period. Responding to the official Church position on recusancy as articulated by Robert Persons, Alban Langdale contended that Catholics could practise an outward conformity in time of persecution to save their property and their lives. To reclaim England from heresy the most radical Catholic thinkers, Cardinal William Allen and Robert Persons, advocated rebellion against Elizabeth and Spanish intervention. Most English Catholics rejected these expedients, including the Appellant priest William Watson, who condemned Allen and Persons as traitors to their country and to their faith. In much intramural Catholic dispute the central issue of contention is the papacy, specifically, the origins of its authority and the limits of its power. Arguing against fellow Catholic William Barclay, Robert Bellarmine claimed that the pope's spiritual responsibility for his flock necessarily conferred an indirect authority in matters temporal.

Whether speaking out on important issues, disputing Protestants, or arguing against each other, the Catholic controversial voices here represented make audible some of the most urgent national and international conversations in early modern England.

DESIDERIUS ERASMUS

Great Dutch humanist, scholar, and priest, Desiderius Erasmus (1459–1536) applied new philological methods to biblical texts, producing the *Novum Instrumentum* in 1516, an annotated Greek text of the New Testament with a revision of the Vulgate (the standard Latin translation by St Jerome). Erasmus diligently revised this work, finding many supporters in the Church, and many opponents, notably Gregory Martin, later translator of the Rheims *New Testament* (1582). Moreover, contributing to the great controversy over Luther's doctrine of predestination, Erasmus affirmed the freedom of the will in *De libero arbitrio* (*On Free Will*, 1524) and *Hyperaspistes* (1526). He wrote schoolbooks for Europe and urged reform of the clergy and of church practices (see FICTION).

In the first selections Erasmus argues that his *Novum Instrumentum* continues the work of St Jerome, originally commissioned by Pope Damasus to preserve the sacred texts from error. Erasmus advocates the study of languages, careful collation of texts, and scrupulous attention to possible variations. The *Paraclesis* or *Exhortation* (as it was translated in 1529) argues that Scripture should be made available in vernacular translation to everyone— women, pagans, the ploughman at his plough, the weaver at his loom. In the selection from *On Free Will* Erasmus contends that the doctrine of predestination renders all scriptural exhortation meaningless. He further asserts that human will (a secondary cause) cooperates with divine grace (the primary cause) in every act of virtue or vice. (See the similar formulations of the Council of Trent, the Decree concerning Justification, Sixth Session, 1543.)

On the New Testament, 1516

[Knowledge of Languages and Jerome's Translation]

Now, regarding the knowledge of letters, which we may more easily attain for our support, the first concern should be the learning of three languages—Latin, Greek, and Hebrew—since it is agreed that all sacred Scripture is handed down from these. Now do not immediately recoil from this, dear reader, because of the difficulty of the task, as if struck with a spike. If one can find a teacher and a little courage, these three 5 languages may be learned with barely more trouble than the wretched chatter of one half language today—all because of the incompetence of teachers. Nor do we require that you

ON THE NEW TESTAMENT Contrast Erasmus' views here with those of Gregory Martin, who felt obliged to undertake his translation of the *New Testament* (1582) 'for due preservation of this divine work from abuse and profanation' (sig. aiii).

advance yourself to a miraculous level of eloquence; it is enough to advance to some middle level of refinement and elegance, which may suffice for making judgements. For even as we pass over all other human disciplines, you can by no means understand what is written if you are ignorant of the language in which it is written. I think, then, we must not listen to those people, who, persisting in sophistical nonsense until they decay into a decrepit senility, always say 'The translation of Jerome is good enough for me!'

For this is the usual response of those who take so little trouble to learn Latin that for them Jerome has made his translation in vain. For now I pass over the question, important to many discussions, whether one should draw from the same fountains or from whatsoever pools are available. For are there not idioms in language that certainly cannot be rendered in another language in such a way that they retain the same light, native grace, and the connotations? What about those nuances that cannot be precisely captured in translation, which everywhere divine Jerome himself notes and laments? What about the many corrections made by Jerome which the toll of time has destroyed, just as is the case of the Gospels themselves which he emended according to the Greek truth? What about those alterations introduced by scribes, either by error or audacity, which at one time corrupted the texts which are now today corrupted throughout? Finally, what about the fact that the texts that enabled Jerome to produce his translations are not understood today, since you cannot read the languages of his copy texts?

If Jerome's translation was sufficient once and for all, why was it important that pontifical decrees advised that the truth of the Old Instrument was to be sought in Hebrew volumes, and that of the New Instrument in Greek sources? Certainly, Jerome had already completed his translation by then. Finally, if this work was sufficient, which afterwards was done, how have so many first-rank theologians fallen into obvious and shameful errors? This fact is so evident that it cannot be denied or dissimulated.

[Revision of the Text]

Now the point which is not debated among the learned but certainly among the ignorant, reiterated in many of their books, is that my edition of the New Testament is substantially not that of Jerome. This rumour persists, though we have neither battered nor slandered the book in any way, whatsoever its kind or whosoever its author. We have restored only so many readings as had been corrupted by the fault of time or scribes

10

15

20

25

30

35

---

13. translation of Jerome St Jerome (*c.*340–420) produced a revised and corrected Latin translation of Scripture, which came to be known as the Vulgate. The Vulgate achieved a hallowed status as a biblical text, though humanist scholars such as Lorenzo Valla noted that it contained many errors and did not always embody Jerome's corrections. **16–17. same fountains . . . pools** i.e. original languages . . . other languages. Erasmus here passes over the question of whether one should attempt any translation at all, even one into Latin. **22–23. Greek truth** i.e by collation with the earliest Greek manuscripts. Again contrast Gregory Martin, who took the Vulgate as his copy-text, believing that Greek manuscripts had been lost and that surviving ones were corrupt: 'Most of the ancient heretics were Grecians and therefore the Scriptures in Greek were more corrupted by them' (sig. biii^v). **28. pontifical decrees** probably the decrees of Clement V (*r.* 1304–14). **Instrument**: Erasmus preferred 'instrumentum' (a written document) to 'testamentum' (a will or covenant that might or might not be written); the Scriptures are 'instrumenta', he argued, because they describe the Hebrew and Christian covenants, or 'testamenta'.

(having noted these emendations in passing), readings which were ambiguous or which the translator rendered inattentively. (For me it is a religious offence to speak imprecisely, even if Jerome did not fear that in several places.) We did not emend with a light hand, so to speak, nor rashly, but first from consultation of the Canon, and then after from examination of the Latin manuscripts to establish their fidelity to the Greek originals, not trusting in a small number or random sampling. Lorenzo Valla testifies that he followed seven reliable manuscripts. We based our first revision on four Greek codices, our next on five. Afterwards, we then consulted the Latin manuscripts which were the oldest and corrected. Not content with this, we explored and examined the most approved authors and noted attentively their citations, sources, emendations, and interpretations. Having performed these tasks with all possible vigilance and the greatest fidelity, and after having compared and weighed all possibilities, we determined which readings were best, adopted and published them so that each reader might profit through use of his own judgement.

[The Necessity of Comparison]

And so, dear reader, when you come upon one of our innovations, please do not reject it immediately for the taste and flavour of the familiar reading, and condemn it, as if every change were necessarily evil, in one stroke cheating me of my due praise and yourself of the fruits of my labour. But first compare our translation with the Greek text, which (to make the task easier) we have placed on a facing page. Judge if I have not expressed the sense more faithfully, more clearly, and more expressively than the old translator. Let none drag me back here to court if word does not correspond exactly with word, as this kind of translation is simply impossible to achieve, even if one tries with all his might. If they hold it a crime ever to depart at all from letters and syllables, why has the old translator throughout dared to do so, sometimes for no reason, neither forced by necessity nor encouraged by advantage, but just as in a sport or stage play, frisking and yawning. If variation then is permissible—and it certainly is permissible—and if you judge that I have translated the text more accurately than that man did, do not condemn what is new but embrace what is more correct.

If the comparison does not satisfy you, do not stop and make a quick judgement; consult our annotations, which perhaps may give you satisfaction by the authority of the witnesses or the reasons adduced. It happens sometimes that one's preferred reading is different or that the same words may produce different meanings. We propose no more than one single reading, for we are not able to do otherwise. In the annotations, however, we have recorded variants, either indicating which seems best to us or leaving to your

43. **Lorenzo Valla** Italian humanist (1407–57), who exposed as a forgery the supposed Donation of Constantine (upon which some claims for papal temporal power rested), and applied humanist philology to sacred texts to correct the Vulgate. He was appointed papal secretary to Nicholas V in 1448. Erasmus published Valla's comparison of the Vulgate with Greek manuscripts of the New Testament under the title of *Adnotationes* (1505). **44. first revision ... next** Two revisions of the Vulgate preceded the 1516 publication of the New Testament, which Erasmus later characterized famously as 'praecipitatum est verius quam editum' (rushed rather than edited) (qtd. Jerry H. Bentley, *Humanists and Holy Writ*, 1983: 122).

judgement which you prefer to follow. In several places our Vulgate edition or the Ambrosiana is better attested than the Greek manuscripts. And though it used to be thought impossible to change anything when all the Greek manuscripts were in accord, we have, nevertheless, adapted according to the Latin, lest there should be a discrepancy 75 when they are compared. As for other matters, we discuss them in the notes.

I find, moreover, that certain things have been added to the text from sacred practices, such as that flourish added to the Lord's Prayer ['for thine is the kingdom, the power, and the glory'], just as we have added the 'Glory be to the Father' to the end of the psalms. We have not deleted these from their context, but we have noted in the commentary that 80 they are additions. Another common but less serious error is the insertion from other places of words missing in a similar thought elsewhere. But of this also we have taken care to give warning. Therefore, we do not provide a text in which all readings are certain and above question, but one which can greatly profit the attentive and vigilant reader who carefully examines our emendations and annotations. Many points may seem trivial or 85 frivolous and, therefore, worthy of dismissal. But in truth the reader who makes comparisons, weighs carefully, treats, and translates sacred Scripture will find that such small matters have large importance. And anyone will easily pardon such attentiveness to minutiae who recalls that scholars of the first rank dashed themselves against stones of this kind and sometimes fell into shameful error, notably, Hilarius, Augustine, and, more 90 recently, the most learned Thomas Aquinas, to name just a few.

An Exhortation to the Diligent Study of Scripture

Insomuch that the sun is not more common and indifferent to all men than this doctrine of Christ, she forbiddeth no man at all, except he abstain willingly, envying his own profit. And truly I do greatly dissent from those men which would not that the Scripture of Christ should be translated into all tongues that it might be read diligently of the 95 private and secular men and women; other, as though Christ had taught such dark and insensible things that they could scant be understood of a few divines; or else as though the pith and substance of the Christian religion consisted chiefly in this, that it be not known. Peradventure it were most expedient that the counsels of kings should be kept secret, but Christ would that his counsels and mysteries should be spread abroad as much 100 as is possible.

I would desire that all women should read the Gospel and Paul's epistles and I would to God they were translated into the tongues of all men so that they might not only be read and known of the Scots and Irishmen, but also of the Turks and Saracens. Truly, it is one degree to good living, yea, the first (I had almost said the chief) to have 105

73. **Ambrosiana** Latin documents falsely attributed to St Ambrose, consisting of commentaries on Paul's epistles and a collection of questions on the Old and New Testaments (Yves Delègue, ed. *Érasme: Les Préfaces au Novum Testamentum (1516)*, 1990: 142–3 n.). 90. **Hilarius** St Hilary of Poitiers (315–67), scholar, bishop, doctor of the Church. 92. **indifferent** impartial. 93. **she forbiddeth** the sun (as the teaching of Christ) keeps at a distance (*arcet*). **envying** begrudging. 96. **other** and from others. 97. **insensible** unintelligible. 99. **Peradventure** perhaps. 104. **Saracens** generic term for Arabs, Muslims, and non-Christians. 105. **degree** step (*gradus*).

a little sight in the Scripture, though it be a gross knowledge and not yet consummate, be it in case that some would laugh at it, yea, and that some should err and be deceived. I would to God the ploughman would sing a text of the Scripture at his plough beam and that the weaver at his loom with this would drive away the tediousness of time. I would the wayfaring man with this pastime would expel the weariness of his journey. And, to be short, I would that all the communication of the Christian should be of the Scripture, for in a manner such are we ourselves as our daily tales are.

[...]

We cannot call any man a Platonist unless he have read the works of Plato, yet call we them Christian, yea, and divines, which never have read the Scripture of Christ. Christ saith, 'He that loveth me doth keep my sayings' [John 14: 23]; this is the knowledge and mark which he hath prescribed. Therefore if we be true Christian men in our hearts, if we believe unfeignedly that he was sent down from heaven to teach us such things as the wisdom of the philosophers could never attain, if faithfully we trust or look for such things of him as no worldly prince (be he never so rich) can give unto us, why have we anything in more reverence and authority than his Scripture, word, and promise, which he left here among us to be our consolation? Why recount we anything of gravity or wisdom which dissenteth from his doctrine? Why in this heavenly and mystical learning do we counter and descant, running more at riot than the common and profane interpreters in the civil law or books of physic, winding ourselves in it as in a trifling game or matter of small substance, commenting, tossing, and wresting it, even as it cometh to our tongues' end? We apply and draw this heavenly and unspotted doctrine unto our life, and measure it after our vain conversation according unto the manner of the Lydians, which bend their rule to the fashion of their stone or timber and cut not their stone and timber to the rule. And because we will not be seen ignorant in anything but rather that we have read and know much, we do I dare not say corrupt these fruitful springs, but (that no man can deny) we appropriate unto a few men that thing which Christ would have most common.

And this kind of philosophy doth rather consist in the affects of the mind than in subtle reasons. It is a life rather than a disputation; it is an inspiration rather than a science, and rather a new transformation than a reasoning. It is a seldom thing to be a well-learned man, but it is lawful for every man to be a true Christian. It is lawful for every man to live a godly life, yea, and I dare be bold to say it is lawful for every man to be a pure divine. How doth every man's mind incline unto that which is wholesome and expedient for his nature, and what other thing is this doctrine of Christ which he calleth

110

115

120

125

130

135

140

106. consummate complete. 107. be it in case that although. 108. plough beam central, longitudinal timber of a plough. Contrast Gregory Martin again, who believed that commoners should not meddle with the 'hard and high mysteries and places of greater difficulty. The poor ploughman could then in labouring the ground sing the hymns and psalms either in known or unknown languages, as they heard them in the holy Church' (sigs. aiii–aiiiᵛ). In later editions Erasmus advised due caution in reading Scriptures. 124. counter and descant oppose and comment on. 128–30. according . . . rule The translator interpolates this definition of the Lydian rule, a flexible leaden instrument used to model curves and other irregularities. 134. affects inclinations.

the new regeneration [Matt. 19: 28] but a restoring or repairing of our nature, which in his first creation was good.

On Free Will, 1524

By 'free will' here we understand a power of the human will by which man may be able to direct himself towards, or turn away from, what leads to eternal salvation.
[...]

But what point is there in quoting a few passages of this kind when all Holy Scripture is full of exhortations like this: 'Turn back to me with all your heart' [Joel 2: 12]; 'Let every man turn from his evil way' [Jonas 3: 8]; 'Come back to your senses, you transgressors' [Isa. 46: 8]; 'Let everyone turn from his evil way, and I will repent the ill that I have thought to do them on account of the evil of their endeavours'; and 'If you will not listen to me, to walk in my law' [Jer. 26: 3–4]. Nearly the whole of Scripture speaks of nothing but conversion, endeavour, and striving to improve. All this would become meaningless once it was accepted that doing good or evil was a matter of necessity; and so too would all the promises, threats, complaints, reproaches, entreaties, blessings, and curses directed towards those who have amended their ways, or those who have refused to change: 'As soon as a sinner groans at his sin' [Ezek. 18: 27; Isa. 30: 15]; 'I have seen that this is a stubborn people' [Exod. 32: 9]; 'Oh my people, what have I done to you?' [Mic. 6: 3]; 'They have rejected my laws' [Ezek. 20: 13]; 'Oh, that my people had listened to me, that Israel had walked in my ways!' [Ps. 80: 14]; 'He who wishes to see good days, let him keep his tongue from evil' [Ps. 33: 13–14] The phrase 'he who wishes to see' speaks of free will.

Since such phrases are frequently encountered, does it not immediately occur to the reader to ask, 'why promise conditionally what is entirely dependent on your will? Why complain of my behaviour, when all my actions, good or bad, are performed by you in me regardless of my will? Why reproach me, when I have no power to preserve the good you have given me, or keep out the evil you put into me? Why entreat me, when everything depends on you, and happens as it pleases you? Why bless me, as though I had done my duty, when whatever happens is your work? Why curse me, when I sinned through necessity?' What is the purpose of such a vast number of commandments if not a single person has it at all in his power to do what is commanded? For there are some who believe that man, albeit justified by the gift of faith and charity, cannot fulfil any of God's commandments, but rather that all good works, because they are done 'in the flesh', would lead to damnation were not God in his mercy to pardon them on account of the merit of our faith.

Yet the word spoken by God through Moses in Deuteronomy [30: 11–14] shows that what he commands is not merely within our power, but that it demands little effort. He says: 'The commandment that I lay upon you this day is not beyond you, nor is it far

away. It is not in heaven, that you might say, "Which one of us is strong enough to go up   35
to heaven and bring it back to us, that we may hear and fulfil it?" Neither is it beyond the
sea, that you should make excuses, and say, "Who among us can cross the sea and bring it
back to us, that we may hear what is commanded?" No, the word is very near to you, on
your lips and in your heart, that you may do it.'

Yet here he is speaking of the greatest commandment of all: 'that you turn back to   40
the Lord your God with all your heart and with all your soul' [Deut. 30: 10]. And what is
the meaning of 'but if you will listen', 'if you will keep the commandments', 'if you will
turn back', if none of this is in our power at all? I will not attempt to quote an extensive
selection of such texts, for the books of both testaments are so full of them wherever you
look that anyone attempting to search them out would simply be 'looking for water in the   45
sea', as the saying goes. And so, as I said, a considerable amount of Holy Scripture will
obviously become meaningless if you accept the last opinion discussed above, or the
previous one.

[. . .]

We listen with equanimity, however, to our opponents' boundlessly exalting faith in,
and love of, God, for we are of the opinion that the corruption of Christian life   50
everywhere by so many sins has no other cause than the coldness and drowsiness of
our faith, which gives us a merest verbal belief in God: a faith on the lips only, whereas
according to Paul 'man is justified by believing from the heart' [Rom. 10: 10]. Nor will I
particularly take issue with those who refer all things to faith as their ultimate source,
even though I believe that faith is born from and nurtured by charity, and charity in turn   55
born from and nurtured by faith. Charity certainly feeds faith, just as the light in a
lantern is fed by oil, for we more readily trust the person we ardently love: and there is no
dearth of people who contend that faith is the beginning, rather than the completion, of
salvation. But our argument does not concern these matters.

Yet here we should beware of being so absorbed in enlarging on the praises of faith that   60
we subvert the freedom of the will; and once it has been denied I do not see how the
problem of the justice and mercy of God can be resolved. When the ancient authors
found they could not extricate themselves from these difficulties, some were forced to
posit two Gods: one of the Old Testament who they argued was only just, not good; and
one of the New Testament who they argued was only good, not just. Tertullian   65
adequately refuted their wicked fabrication. Manichaeus, as we said, dreamed up the
notion of two natures in man, one which could not avoid sinning and one which could
not avoid doing good. Pelagius, concerned for God's justice, attributed too much to free
will. There is little difference between him and those who attribute so much to human

47–8. last opinion . . . one those of Luther and Carlstadt respectively, which both denied free will. 59. these matters
Erasmus here alludes to Luther's doctrine of salvation *ex fide sola*, 'by faith alone'. 65. Tertullian (*c*.155–220), an important
early Christian theologian and polemicist, who refuted this heresy in *Adversus Marcionem*. 66. Manichaeus actually Mani
(216–77), whose followers were Manicheans; he taught that two opposing principles, one of light and goodness, the other of
darkness and evil, struggled against each other in the universe and in human life. 68. Pelagius fifth-century heretic who
denied the Catholic doctrine of original sin and asserted that the human will is capable of good once grace has been granted,
not merited.

will as to say that through our natural powers, by morally good works, it can merit the   70
supreme grace by which we are justified. They seem to me to have wanted to urge man to
moral effort by holding out a good hope of obtaining salvation, just as Cornelius, because
of his prayers and almsgiving, deserved to be taught by Peter, and the eunuch by Philip
[Acts 10: 1–43; 8: 26–38], and Saint Augustine, who assiduously sought Christ in Paul's
letters, deserved to find him. Here we can placate those who believe that man cannot do   75
any good deed which he does not owe to God by saying that the whole work is no less
due to God, without whom we could achieve nothing; that the contribution of free will is
very small indeed; and that our very ability to direct our mind to the things that pertain
to salvation, or to cooperate with grace, is itself a gift of God. As a result of the
controversy with Pelagius, Augustine reached a less favourable view of free will than he   80
had previously held. In the opposite way Luther, who previously attributed something to
free will, has been carried so far by the heat of his defence as to remove it altogether. Yet
I believe that among the Greeks Lycurgus is blamed for having had the vines cut down
because he hated drunkenness, whereas by bringing the sources of water closer he could
have prevented drunkenness without abolishing wine-drinking.   85

   In my opinion free will could have been established in such a way as to avoid that trust
in our own merits and the other harmful consequences which Luther avoids, as well as
those which we mentioned above, yet so as not to destroy the benefits which Luther
admires. This I believe is achieved by the opinion of those who ascribe entirely to grace
the impetus by which the mind is first aroused, and only in the succeeding process   90
attribute something to human will in that it does not resist the grace of God. Since there
are three parts to everything—beginning, continuation, and completion—they ascribe
the first and last to grace and allow that free will has an effect only in the continuation, in
so far as in a single, indivisible act there are two causes, divine grace and human will,
working together. However, grace is the principal cause and will the secondary cause,   95
unable to do anything without the principal cause, whereas the principal cause is
sufficient in itself. Just so the power inherent in fire burns, yet the principal cause is
God acting at the same time through the fire, a cause which would be sufficient in itself,
and without which fire would have no effect if that cause were to withdraw itself.

   On this moderate view man must ascribe his salvation entirely to the grace of God; for   100
what free will accomplishes in this is very insignificant indeed, and what it can accomplish is itself due to divine grace, which first created free will, then freed and healed it.
And this will appease (if they can be appeased) those who believe that there is no good in
man which he does not owe to God. Owe it he does, but in a different way and for a
different reason, as an inheritance falling to children in equal shares is not called   105
benevolence, since it comes to them all in the ordinary course of law. (It is called
liberality if one or other of them has been given something over and above his legal
due.) Yet children are indebted to their parents even on account of an inheritance.

83. **Lycurgus** king of Edoni in Thrace, who banned the cult of Dionysus, god of wine.

THOMAS MORE

Humanist and martyr, Thomas More (*c.*1477–1535), Lord Chancellor of England, stands as a towering figure in early modern Catholicism. He wrote polemical works, Latin poetry, the brilliantly satirical *Utopia*, and deep spiritual works composed in the Tower (see *Consolations*, INSTRUCTIONS AND DEVOTIONS). More defended Erasmus's biblical scholarship and vernacular translation of the Bible. He suppressed Protestant writing and executed Protestants for heresy. Opposing King Henry VIII's divorce, remarriage, and break with Rome, he suffered imprisonment and public execution (see LIVES AND DEATHS).

The historical Thomas More does not always resemble the tight-lipped figure of Holbein's famous portrait, or the saintly man for all seasons of popular memory. In controversy the fighting Lord Chancellor freely deploys the rhetoric of outrage. Luther, More writes, ought to lick with his 'beshitted tongue . . . the very posterior of a pissing she-mule'; Tyndale's invocation of 'certain circumstances' to justify his translation evokes this scorn: 'For so he may translate the world into a football if he join therewith certain circumstances . . . then say it is on this round rolling football that men walk upon and ships sail on' (*Works*, Toronto edn., v. 181; vi. 166). In *A Dialogue Concerning Heresies* (1529) below, More criticizes Tyndale's translation of the New Testament (1525) as bad Latin and worse theology. He adduces the Peasants' Wars to illustrate the results of unchecked Lutheranism and to justify the use of force against heretics. Tyndale responded in *An Answer unto Sir Thomas More's Dialogue* (1531).

A Dialogue Concerning Heresies, 1529

[Why Tyndale's New Testament was burned]

But now, I pray you, let me know your mind concerning the burning of the New Testament in English which Tyndale lately translated and, as men say, right well, which maketh men much marvel of the burning.

It is, quod I, to me great marvel that any good Christian man, having any drop of wit in his head would anything marvel or complain of the burning of that book if he know   5
the matter. Which whoso calleth the New Testament calleth it by a wrong name, except they will call it Tyndale's Testament or Luther's Testament, for so had Tyndale after Luther's counsel corrupted and changed it from the good and wholesome doctrine of Christ to the devilish heresies of their own that it was clean a contrary thing.

---

1. **burning** There was a burning of Tyndale's New Testament (1525) in 1526 and several times thereafter. 4. **quod** quoth, said.

That were marvel, quod your friend, that it should be so clean contrary. For to some that read it, it seemed very like.

It is, quod I, nevertheless contrary, and yet the more perilous, for like as to a true silver groat a false copper groat is nevertheless contrary though it be quicksilvered over, but so much the more false in how much it is counterfeited the more like to the truth, so was the translation so much the more contrary in how much it was craftily devised like, and so much the more perilous in how much it was to folk unlearned more hard to be discerned.

Why, quod your friend, what faults were there in it?

To tell you all that, quod I, were in a manner to rehearse you all the whole book, wherein there were found and noted wrong and falsely translated above a thousand texts by tally.

I would, quod he, fain hear some one.

He that should, quod I, study for that should study where to find water in the sea. But I will show you for ensample two or three such as every one of the three is more than thrice three in one.

That were, quod he, very strange except ye mean more in weight, for one can be but one in number.

Surely, quod I, as weighty be they as any lightly can be. But I mean that every one of them is more than thrice three in number.

That were, quod he, somewhat like a riddle.

This riddle, quod I, will soon be read. For he hath mistranslated three words of great weight and every one of them is, as I suppose, more than thrice three times repeated and rehearsed in the book.

Ah, that may well be, quod he, but that was not well done. But, I pray you, what words be they?

The one is, quod I, this word 'priest'. The other, the 'church'. The third, 'charity'. For priests, wheresoever he speaketh of the priests of Christ's church, he never calleth them 'priests', but always 'seniors'. The church he calleth always the 'congregation', and charity he calleth always 'love'. Now do these names in our English tongue neither express the things that be meant by them, and also there appeareth, the circumstances well considered, that he had a mischievous mind in the change. For, first, as for priests and priesthood, though that of old they used commonly to choose well elderly men to be priests and therefore in the Greek tongue priests were called *presbuteroi*, as we might say, 'elder men', yet neither were all priests chosen old, as appeareth by Saint Paul writing to Timotheus, 'nemo iuventutem tuam contemnat' [1 Tim 4: 12] (Let no man condemn thy youth), nor every elder man is not a priest. And in our English tongue this word 'senior' signifieth nothing at all, but is a French word used in English more than half in mockage when one will call another 'my lord' in scorn. And if he mean to take the Latin word *senior*, that word in the Latin tongue never signified a priest but only an elder man. By

13. **groat** small coin. 21. **fain** gladly. 23. **ensample** example. 27. **as weighty...be** as serious as any error can easily be. 46. **mockage** mockery.

which name of elder men, if he would call the priests Englishly, then should he rather signify their age than their office. And yet the name doth in English plainly signify the aldermen of the cities and nothing the priests of the Church. And thus may we perceive that rather than he would call a priest by the name of a priest he would seek a new word he neither wist nor cared what.

Now where he calleth the Church always the 'congregation' what reason had he therein? For every man well seeth that though the Church be indeed a congregation, yet is not every congregation the Church, but a congregation of Christian people, which congregation of Christian people hath been in England always called and known by the name of the Church. Which name, what good cause or colour could he find to turn into the name of congregation, which word is common to a company of Christian men or a company of Turks?

Like wisdom was there in the change of this word charity into 'love'. For though charity be always love, yet is not, ye wot well, love always charity.

The more pity, by my faith, quod your friend, that ever love was sin. And yet it would not be so much so taken if the world were no more suspicious than they say that good Saint Francis was, which when he saw a young man kiss a girl once in way of good company, kneeled down and held up his hands into heaven, highly thanking God that charity was not yet gone out of this wretched world.

He had, quod I, a good mind and did like a good man that deemed all thing to the best.

So say I too, quod he. But how far be folk fallen from the good mind now. Men be nowadays waxen so full of mistrust that some man would in faith ween his wife were naught if he should but find her in bed with a poor friar.

Forsooth, ye be a wanton, quod I. But yet, in earnest, how like you the change of these words?

Surely, quod he, very naught. And that it was not well nor wisely done, there will, I trow, no good wise man deny. But yet whether Hitchens had in the translation thereof any malicious purpose or not, therein will I, till I see further, play Saint Francis' part and judge the man no worse than the matter requireth.

First, quod I, would ye that the book should go forth and be read still in that fashion?

Nay, in good faith, quod he, that would I not if he use it so very often.

With that word, quod I, ye hit the nail on the head. For surely if he changed the common known word into the better, I would well allow it; if he changed it into as good, I would suffer it; if somewhat into worse, so he did it seld, I would wink at it. But now when he changeth the known usual names of so great things into so far the worse, and that not repeateth seldom but so often and so continually inculketh that almost in the whole book his lewd change he never changeth, in this manner could no man deem other but that the man meant mischievously, scant such a good silly soul as would ween all were

---

51. **aldermen** officials. 53. **wist** knew. 62. **wot** know. 70. **waxen** grown. **ween** think. 71. **naught** wicked. 74. **very naught** not at all. 75. **trow** think. **Hitchens** Tyndale's ancestors used the name 'Hutchins' and he sometimes went by 'Hychyns'. 82. **seld** seldom. 84. **inculketh** inculcates, repeats. 86. **scant** except.

well when he found his wife where ye said right now. If ye called charity sometime by the bare name of love, I would not stick thereat. But now whereas charity signifieth in Englishmen's ears not every common love but a good, virtuous, and well-ordered love, he that will studiously flee from that name of good love and always speak of love, and always leave out good, I would surely say that he meaneth naught.

In good faith, quod he, so is it not unlikely.

Then, quod I, when ye see more ye shall say it is much more than likely. For now it is to be considered that at the time of this translation, Hitchens was with Luther in Wittenberg and set certain glosses in the margent, framed for the setting forth of the ungracious sect.

By Saint John, quod your friend, if that be true that Hitchens were at that time with Luther, it is a plain token that he wrought somewhat after his counsel and was willing to help his matters forward here. But whether Luther's matters be so mad as they be made for, that shall we see hereafter.

Very true, quod I. But as touching the confederacy between Luther and him is a thing well known and plainly confessed by such as have been taken and convicted here of heresy, coming from thence and some of them sent hither to sow that seed about here and to send word thither from time to time how it sprang.

But now the cause why he changed the name of charity, and of the Church, and of priesthood is no very great difficulty to perceive. For sith Luther and his fellows, among other their damnable heresies, have one that all our salvation standeth in faith alone and toward our salvation nothing force of good works, therefore it seemeth that he laboureth of purpose to minish the reverent mind that men bear to charity, and therefore he changeth that name of holy, virtuous affection into the bare name of love, common to the virtuous love that man beareth to god and to the lewd love that is between fleck and his make. And for because that Luther utterly denyeth the very Catholic Church in earth and saith that the Church of Christ is but an unknown congregation of some folk here two and there three (no man wot where) having the right faith, which he calleth only his own new forged faith. Therefore Hitchens in the New Testament cannot abide the name of the Church but turneth it into the name of congregation, willing that it should seem to Englishmen either that Christ in the Gospel had never spoken of the Church, or else that the Church were but such a congregation as they might have occasion to say that a congregation of some such heretics were the Church that God spake of.

90

95

100

105

110

115

---

88. **stick** object. 95. **margent** margin (of the Bible Luther translated). 98. **a . . . counsel** obvious he worked under his influence. 106. **sith** since. 108. **nothing force of** there is no validity to. Tyndale responded: 'Our deeds are but thanksgiving to God to help our neighbours at their need, for which our neighbours and each of them owe us as much again at our need. So that the testament of forgiveness of sins is built upon faith in Christ's blood and not on works' (*Answer*, 1531, sig. Q7). 109. **minish** diminish. 111–12. **fleck and his make** a worthless man and his lover. 119. **Church . . . of** Tyndale declared that Scripture originally used 'church' 'for the whole multitude of all them that receive the name of Christ to believe in him and not for the clergy only'. Since a corrupt clergy had appropriated this name for themselves, 'and with their false and subtle wiles had beguiled and mocked the people and brought them into the ignorance of the word', he returned to the true meaning with 'congregation' (*Answer*, 1531, sigs. A6–A6^v).

Now as touching the cause why he changed the name of priest into senior, ye must understand that Luther and his adherents hold this heresy, that all Holy Order is nothing and that a priest is nothing else but a man chosen among the people to preach. And that by that choice to that office he is priest by and by without any more ado and no priest again whensoever the people choose another in his place, and that a priest's office is nothing but to preach. For as for saying mass and hearing of confession and absolution thereupon to be given—all this he saith that every man, woman, and child may do as well as any priest. Now doth Hitchens, therefore, to set forth this opinion withal after his master's heresy put away the name of priest in his translation as though priesthood were nothing. Wheresoever the Scripture speaketh of the priests that were among the Jews, there doth he in his translation call them still by the name of priests. But wheresoever the Scripture speaketh of the priests of Christ's Church, there doth he put away the name of priest in his translation because he would make it seem that the Scripture did never speak of any priests different from laymen among Christian people. And he saith plainly in his book of *Obedience* that priesthood and all Holy Orders among Christian people be but feigned inventions, and that priests be nothing but officers chosen to preach, and that all the consecration whereby they be consecrate is nothing worth. And for this cause in all his translation wheresoever he speaketh of them the name of priest, which to us in our own tongue hath always signified an anointed person and with Holy Orders consecrated unto God, he hath changed into the name of senior, no word of our language but either used half in mockage when we speak French in sport, *Dieu vous garde, seigneur*, or at the furthest nothing betokening but elder. So that it is easy to see what he meant in the turning of these names.

In good faith, quod your friend, it seemeth verily that he meant not well.

Surely, quod I, ye would well say so if you saw all the places which I shall cause you to see when ye will, and ye shall soon judge them yourself. For it were too long to rehearse them all now. Nor these have I not rehearsed you as for the chief but for that they came first to mind. For else I might shortly rehearse you many things more as far out of tune as these be. For he changeth commonly the name of grace into this word 'favour', whereas every favour is not grace in English, for in some favour is there little grace. Confession he translateth into 'knowledging', penance into 'repentance'. A contrite heart he changeth into a 'troubled heart'. And many more things like and many texts untruly translated for the maintenance of heresy, as I shall show you some when we look in the book. Which things we shall not now reason upon for they be not worthy to be brought into question. But I tell you this much only for this cause, that ye may perceive that he hath thus used himself in his translation to the intent that he would set forth Luther's heresies and his

120
125
130
135
140
145
150
155

134. book of *Obedience* **The** *Obedience of a Christian Man* (Antwerp, 1528). **140.** *Dieu...seigneur* God keep you, sir. **141.** **what he meant** Tyndale accepted More's argument against 'senior' but defended 'elder' on philological grounds by citing Scripture, and on theological grounds: 'And I say, moreover, that their anointing is but a ceremony borrowed of the Jews, though they have somewhat altered the manner, and their shaving borrowed of the heathen priests, and that they be no more of their priesthood than the oil, salt, spittle, taper, and chrism cloth of the substance of baptism' (*Answer*, 1531, sig. B2). **149–51. Confession...'troubled heart'** Tyndale hereby denied the Catholic sacrament of Penance.

own thereby. For first he would make the people believe that we should believe nothing but plain Scripture, in which point he teacheth a plain, pestilent heresy. And then would he with his false translation make the people ween further that such articles of our faith as he laboureth to destroy, and which be well proved by Holy Scripture were in Holy Scripture nothing spoken of, but that the preachers have all this fifteen hundred year   160
misreported the Gospel and Englished the Scripture wrong to lead the people purposely out of the right way.

[The Peasants' Revolt]

Now was this doctrine in Almaine of the common uplandish people so pleasantly hard that it blinded them in the looking upon the remnant and could not suffer them to consider and see what end the same would in conclusion come to. The temporal lords   165
were glad also to hear this gear against the clergy and the people as glad to hear it against the clergy, and against the lords too, and against all their governors of every good town and city. And, finally, so far went it forward that at the last it began to burst out and fall to open force and violence. For intending to begin at the feeblest, there gathered them together for the setting forth of these ungracious heresies a boisterous company of   170
that unhappy sect, and first rebelled against an abbot and after against a bishop, wherewith the temporal lords had good game and sport and dissembled the matter, gaping after the lands of the spirituality till they had almost played, as Aesop telleth of the dog, which to snatch at the shadow of the cheese in the water let fall and lost the cheese that he bare in his mouth. For so was it shortly after that those uplandish Lutherans took   175
so great boldness and so began to grow strong that they set also upon the temporal lords. Which had they not set hand thereto the sooner while they looked for other men's lands, had been like shortly to lose their own. But so quit they themselves that they slew upon the point of seventy thousand Lutherans in one summer, and subdued the remnant in that part of Almaine to a right miserable servitude. Howbeit in the meanwhile many   180
mischievous deeds they did.

And yet in divers other parts of Almaine and Switzerland, this ungracious sect by the negligence of the governors in great cities is so far forth grown that finally the common people have compelled the rulers to follow them, whom, if they had taken heed in time, they might have ruled and led.   185

And now is it too piteous a sight to see the dispiteous despites done there in many places to God and all good men with the marvellous change from all face and fashion of Christendom into a very tyrannous persecution not only of all good Christian people,

---

156–7. nothing . . . Scripture a reference to the Protestant doctrine, *sola Scriptura*, which Catholics rejected, asserting also the validity of Church traditions. **163. doctrine in Almaine** Luther's denial of papal and, by extension, civil authority in Germany. More blamed Luther and his followers for the Peasants' Rebellion (1523–5), a popular uprising in Germany. Thus heresy, in More's view, destroyed bodies and souls. **uplandish** rustic. **166. gear** business. **173–4. Aesop . . . dog** This fable of Aesop, the Greek storyteller (6th c. BC) is known as 'The Dog and the Shadow'. **178. quit** requited. **178–9. upon the point of** very nearly. **181. they** Lutherans. **186. dispiteous despites** merciless outrages.

quick and dead, but also of Christ himself. For there shall ye see now the goodly
monasteries destroyed, the places burned up, the religious people put out and sent to   190
seek their living or in many cities the places yet standing with more despite to God than if
they were burned up to ashes. For the religious people—monks, friars, and nuns—be
clean drawn and driven out, except such as would agree to forsake their vows of chastity
and be wedded, and the places dedicate to cleanness and chastity left only to these
apostates and brothels to live there in lechery. Now the parish churches in many places   195
not only defaced, all ornaments withdrawn, the holy images pulled down and either
broken or burned, but also the Holy Sacrament cast out and the abominable beasts
(which abhorreth me to think on) not abhorred in despite to file in the pyxes and use in
many places continually the churches for a common siege. And that in so despiteful wise
that when a stranger of other places where Christ is worshipped resorteth to these cities,   200
some of those unhappy, wretched citizens fail not, as it were, for courtesy and kindness to
accompany them in walking abroad to show them the pleasures and commodities of the
town, and then bring them to no place lightly but only the churches to show them in
derision what uses the churches serve for.

EDMUND PLOWDEN

A scholar at the Middle Temple and a steadfast Catholic, Edmund Plowden (1518–85)
revolutionized the practice of law by providing thorough, detailed accounts of various
legal arguments in his *Commentaries* (1571). Plowden enjoyed relative immunity from
persecution as a Catholic because of his membership in the close-knit Inns of Court and
his outstanding abilities. Plowden wrote his *Treatise on Mary, Queen of Scots* (1566) in
response to John Hales's manuscript tract (early 1560s) denying the claims of Catholic
Mary, Queen of Scots, to the English throne. Plowden dismisses the common-law
argument that prohibits inheritance by aliens. He articulates, perhaps for the first time,
the important doctrine of the king's two bodies, the body natural with which he is born,
mortal and defective, and the body politic which he acquires with succession, deathless
and incorruptible. Analysing the politically explosive topic with learning and relentless
logic, Plowden ends with a prayer for Queen Elizabeth's long life and many children.
His *Treatise*, extant only in manuscript, supplied later pro-Marian writings, including
John Leslie's similar *Defence* (1569) and the popular pamphlet *Leicester's Commonwealth*
(1586), as well the arguments for unifying Scotland and England at the end of the century.
Mary, of course, did not succeed to the throne but was executed by Queen Elizabeth for

198. **file** defile. **pyxes** containers for the consecrated host. 199. **siege** seat.

treason in 1587 (see Fig. 6). Plowden here provides a moderate Catholic response to the reign of a Protestant queen and the succession question, one entirely consonant with British law.

A Treatise on Mary, Queen of Scots, 1566

A recapitulation of the whole contents of this treatise

Now at length, sithence, as I think, I have sufficiently proved the matter taken in hand, to wit, that the Queen of Scots is not by her birth disabled to receive by descent the crown of England, if none other obstacle were to the contrary, I will make an end with recital for reviving of your memory of the contents of the whole treatise

Divided into two parts, as in the prologue is recited and before in the whole work doth appear, the first point or step of the first part thereof setteth forth the two bodies that the law of this realm doth adjudge in the king, to wit, the body natural and the body politic, whereof they consist, and how they are created, what number they have, and their several degrees and qualities, and the several offices and actions that the law doth ascribe and appoint to them.

The second step setteth forth the conjunction of the two bodies and the making of an union of them both, and one body indivisible, and how in this consolidation the body politic, being the worthier, draweth unto him the name, and that name includeth both the bodies and receiveth and departeth with other additions.

The third step showeth that the conjunction of the two bodies in one confoundeth not the several capacities, but the capacity of each body remaineth to retain things before acquired and to bring in newly two ways.

The fourth step showeth that the acts of the body politic, which is the more precious, is not unblemished by this conjunction of the body natural, being the more base, and how the body politic, being the greater, attaineth the superiority, and draweth unto him all the effects, according to his property.

The fifth step showeth how the natural body is extolled by his conjunction with the body politic, and altereth in quality and in use touching things enjoined in the capacity of the body natural, and how he is participate of the prerogatives and the state royal, and hath ampleness and fullness of power and liberty, and how he is by means of the body politic magnified.

The sixth step setteth forth how the privies in blood and disabled in law by causes criminal may receive the crown by descent or by acquisition. And how by the access of the

---

1. **sithence** since. 3. **recital** summary of pertinent facts (a legal term). 7. **adjudge** judge to be. **body natural . . . politic** The **body natural** refers to the physical person of the king, the human being; the **body politic** refers to the corporate official self, a legal fiction. 13. **draweth . . . name** takes precedence over the body natural. 17. **newly two ways** things newly acquired to both the body natural and the body politic. 27. **privies in blood** those who are blood relations.

body politic to the body natural, the body natural is purged and discharged of all criminal offences and cannot be disabled by causes sufficient to disable other natural bodies.   30

The seventh step showeth foreign birth to be no disability to receive the crown by descent or acquisition and two objections against it. The confutation of the first, which is, he born beyond the sea cannot be known to be descended of English blood.

The eighth step showeth that the second objection, that is, to wit, born in the ligeance of others, is allowed against inferior persons to the crown, and who shall be accounted so   35
born, and who not. The exposition of the act made in the 25th year of King Edward III of those born beyond the sea and of *prerogativa regis ca: 12*, how far aliens be disabled and the reasons why they be disabled, which cannot take place in the crown and then sithence the law for subjects and the reasons extendeth not to the crown. There is none other law special that foreign birth is a disability to receive the crown and concludeth therefore that   40
foreign birth holdeth no place in this case of the crown.

The ninth step showeth that the ligeance of this natural body after he is king is discharged against him to whom the natural body did before owe ligeance or obedience and showeth causes why and examples.

The tenth step showeth that if the foreign born be subject to none other, then it is clear   45
he is not disabled to receive the crown of England.

The eleventh point or article confuteth the assertion that the maxim of foreign birth extendeth to the crown because it is a body politic and showeth that the maxims of the common law, which extend but to bodies natural only, cannot be applied to the bodies politic, and showeth examples thereof, and of foreign birth to be none impediment from   50
receipt of that that maketh a body to be a body politic, and containeth the conclusion that foreign birth is no disability to the next of blood wheresoever he were born to receive by descent the crown of England.

And touching the second part of this treatise, the first thereof showeth that the Scots nor Scotland be not out of the ligeance of England, and that the subjects of Scotland owe   55
an immediate ligeance to the King of Scots and a mediate ligeance to the King of England, and all the Scots by their king do service to the King of England for the realm of Scotland, and that, therefore, they born there be not disabled in this realm.

The second step thereof showeth that the Queen of Scots is not out of the ligeance of the crown of England, albeit it were granted that the subjects of Scotland were, and that   60
the Queen of Scots is an immediate homager to the crown of England.

---

31. **foreign birth** Mary was born in Scotland. 34. **ligeance** allegiance (a legal term), meaning jurisdiction. 36. **the act** John Leslie likewise explains that the law (25 Edward III, c. 12) does not exclude children of kings and that Scotland is not out of allegiance of England (*Defence*, 1569, sigs. hi–ivi). 37. *prerogative regis ca: 12* the rights of the monarch according to this statute. 49. **common law** the body of customary law, based on judicial decisions. Plowden argues that this law cannot apply to the king. Cf. John Leslie, 'The title of the crown of this realm is not subject to the rules and principles of the common law of this realm as to be ruled and tried after such order and course as the inheritance of private persons is by the same' (*Defence*, 1569, sig. gviii^v). 61. **homager** one who owes homage or fealty.

The third step showeth the opinion of King Henry VII touching the commodities or discommodities that this realm should have if it descended to the crown of Scotland and which I have done by the provocation of the author of the printed book.

Fourthly and lastly I have made this recapitulation of the whole contents of this   65
treatise for reviving your memory therein. And this I make an end of the whole matter, praying to God he will bless our sovereign Queen Elizabeth with long life and many children and that she and they and their issues by lineal descent may inherit and continue this kingdom, *et nunc et semper et in saecula saeculorum, Amen*, and make frustrate all this my disceptation upon this point. And if not, then I pray God to settle the kingdom there   70
where of right it ought to be.

NICHOLAS SANDER

In the first wave of Catholic exiles under Elizabeth, Nicholas Sander (1530–81) became a priest and professor of theology at Louvain. He wrote a weighty defence of the Church, *De visibili monarchia ecclesiae* (Louvain, 1571), as well as a Catholic account of the changes in religion in England, *De schismate Anglicano* (Cologne, 1585) (see HISTORIES). His *A Treatise of the Images of Christ* (1566) defended Catholic beliefs and practices against Protestant iconoclasm, specifically against the attack of Bishop Jewel, *A Reply unto M. Harding's Answer* (1565), who condemned Catholic veneration of images as idolatry (see also Foxe's depiction, Fig. 4). In the selections below Sander recalls with horror the Lutheran desecration of Catholic icons in Antwerp. When Catholics venerate images of God, Sander explains, they venerate the spiritual truths that the images represent not the images themselves. *Latria*, the honour due to God, belongs to God alone. Sander adduces the Incarnation itself to ratify the principle of representing divine nature in human form and distinguishes in detail between pagan idols and Catholic images.

A Treatise of the Images of Christ and of his Saints, 1566

[Iconoclasm at Antwerp]

Would God they had only abstained from keeping holy her [Mary's] feast, but they are so far from sanctifying her memory that they profaned it most horribly. For the 20th day of

---

64. printed book *Allegations against the Surmised Title of the Queen of Scots* (1565).   **69.** *et... Amen* 'now and always, forever and ever, Amen', a liturgical formula.   **70. disceptation** disputation, discussion.
TREATISE OF THE IMAGES   **1. her feast** the Assumption, 15 August.

August, whiles the octaves of the said feast was yet a-celebrating by those blessed generations who account Christ's Mother holy and blessed, these new gospellers came into our Lady's church at Antwerp about five of the clock after dinner. The beginning of their purposed mischief was committed to a boy, who with a wand, coming into the chapel of our Lady, struck her image, saying, 'Mary, thou must come down.' At which voice, as it were at a watchword, the false brethren approached near. Those that were set to keep the chapel cried out; others called the chief magistrate, whose request and commandment these new gospellers no more regarded than they do the word of God, which biddeth them, 'Obey the king and the officers whom he sendeth' (1 Pet. 2: 13–14).

Neither can it serve for their excuse as though the officer forbidding them to spoil the church willed them to do against the commandment of God, sithence it is also against the commandment of God to steal, to spoil, to injury, or hurt any private or public treasure against their wills to whom it belongeth. And certainly the goods of the Church even by the common law of nations are holy and sacred. So that it is no common theft to lay hands upon them wrongfully.

Which notwithstanding, these fresh followers of this new preaching threw down the graven and defaced the painted images, not only of our Lady but of all others in the town. They tore the curtains, dashed in pieces the carved work of brass and of stone, brake the altars, spoiled the clothes and corporesses, wrested the irons, conveyed away or brake the chalices and vestiments, pulled up the brass of the gravestones, not sparing the glass windows and seats which were made about the pillars of the churches for men to sit in.

What shall I speak of the Blessed Sacrament of the altar, which they trod under their feet and (horrible it is to say!) shed also their stinking piss upon it, as though, if it were not Christ's own body, it were not by their own doctrine a mystical figure of his body. Or if it be not so, yet at the least a creature of God, which of purpose ought not to be spitefully ordered. A greater fault, in truth, cannot be named than this was. But to them who esteem the tremend mysteries for profane idols, it seemeth more grievous that these false brethren burned and rent not only all kind of Church books, but, moreover, destroyed whole libraries and books of all sciences and tongues, yea, the Holy Scriptures, and the ancient fathers, and tore in pieces the maps and charts of the descriptions of countries.

[On *latria*, or honour due to God]

As the making of images for this end, that they should be taken for gods, is absolutely forbidden, so is the worshipping of them with that honour which is proper to God

---

3. **octaves** celebratory period of eight days after a feast day. 6. **purposed mischief** Bishop Jewel and others defended iconoclasm: 'Neither doth God throughout all his holy Scriptures anywhere condemn image-breakers but expressly and everywhere he condemneth image-worshippers and image-makers. God saith, "They are snares to catch the ignorant" (Wisd. 14: 11). He knoweth the inclination of the heart of man and therefore he saith, "Accursed be he that leadeth the blind out of his way" (Deut. 27: 18); and, "Accursed be he that layeth a stumbling block to overthrow the blind" (Lev. 19: 14)' (*Reply*, 1565, sig. Xx3ᵛ). 8. **watchword** signal to begin an attack. 12. **spoil** despoil, plunder. 13. **sithence** since. 14. **injury** injure. 19. **graven** sculptured or carved. 21. **corporesses** linen cloths used with the consecrated bread and wine. 22. **vestiments** clerical garb. 29. **tremend** tremendous.

absolutely forbidden. But as images might be made by the authority of Moses or of the governors of God's people (this only provided, that they be not taken for gods), so may they likewise be worshipped by the authority of God's Church, this only proviso being made, that God's own honour be not given to them. For God, perceiving well that when the images of honourable personages are made honour is naturally due unto them, because their images might be set forth for honourable (as the image of Jupiter or of Mars) who were not indeed honourable, and, again, because though the persons were honourable (as Moses or Elijah), the weak Jews, who were in knowledge like children and in faith or spirit like bondmen, might give too much honour to the images of these men—for these causes God commanded that neither any image should be made by private authority, nor any adored with *latria*, which is the honour peculiarly due to God.

'Non adorabis ea', saith God, 'neque coles' (thou shalt not adore them, nor give them the worship which is due to God alone, Exod. 20: 5).

For albeit the word which signifieth adoration be indifferent to God or to honourable creatures, yet the words *neque coles* do in Greek betoken the peculiar honour of God, μὴ λατρεύσεις, 'nor thou shalt not give them that honour which is due unto God'.

And surely, howsoever we name or call this or that honour, if indeed there be no difference between honour, and honour when God biddeth us 'honour' our father and mother (Exod. 20: 12), or when St Peter biddeth us 'honour the king' (1 Pet. 2: 17), it must be meant that we should give them God's own proper honour. But seeing it is absurd to give unto creatures the honour due unto the Creator, we must confess a difference between honour due to God and honour due to his friends or ministers.

Now for so much as the proven duty of honouring God is (by such instruments of the Holy Ghost as have written in Greek or Latin) most commonly named *latria*, we must think that when we are forbidden to make any image and to give it such honour as is described by the word *latria*, that then we are only forbidden to give godly honour to any artificial image, which thing may well appear by the circumstance of the place where the commandment is written.

For whereas it is said in the beginning of the commandments, 'I am the Lord thy God', and afterward, 'thou shalt not have strange gods before me', and thirdly, whereas he had said, 'thou shalt not make an idol' (for so the seventy interpreters did translate it into Greek), and whereas it followeth, 'thou shalt not make the similitude of anything', and yet again, whereas it is afterward added, 'thou shalt not adore them, nor give them

---

39–47. Sander outlines two reasons for the prohibition of images in Exodus: the possibility of setting up unworthy figures for honour (Jupiter or Mars), the possibility of excessive, improper devotion to worthy figures (Moses or Elijah). **44. bondmen** slaves. **46–7.** *latria*...**God** In contradistinction to 'latria' (adoration), Catholics used 'doulia' (veneration) to describe the honour due to images. Bishop Jewel scoffed at the distinction: 'But what if the simple people understand no Greek and cannot so learnedly discern *latria* from *doulia* but take the one adoration for the other? Verily, as it now fareth in the Church of Rome they use them both universally without difference.... Do you by this distinction anything abate idolatry?' (*Reply,* 1565, sig. Xx2ᵛ). **67. seventy interpreters** the seventy-two legendary translators of the Old Testament from Hebrew to Greek (3rd century BC), who produced the Septuagint.

latria', that is to say, 'God's own honour', and, last of all, whereas immediately after it doth follow, 'Ego sum Dominus Deus tuus, fortis, zelotes' (Exod. 20: 5), 'I am the Lord, thy God, strong, jealous' (the which words import that God will have no creature to be made his companion in honour), it may well appear by all that goeth before and followeth after that God mindeth to forbid the worship of false gods and of all such idols as are made and used to be worshipped as either being themselves true gods, or as being the representation of such creatures which are taken for true gods. For by all means we are forbidden to think either any creature to be God, or that God his own divine substance and incomprehensible nature may be represented by any artificial image.

It is a much sweeter contemplation to consider that, whereas our bodily and imperfect nature would needs covet always to worship God by some bodily image or other, God the Father's own natural image and Son took of the Virgin Mary our natural flesh to the end we might not lack some corporal truth of body and flesh, wherein we might boldly worship the divine substance.

After then that this manhood was assumed, seeing the shape of man may be lawfully showed by an artificial image, we, making the image of Christ who was man, do not make any such idol or similitude as God forbade the Jews to make, but we make a similitude of an honourable truth, whereas no idol doth represent a truth.

Again, we give not unto Christ's artificial image any godly honour, albeit we, being provoked by the sight thereof, do give godly honour to Christ, who is immediately adored by the warning of the artificial image.

images compared to human body [marginal note]

[The image of Christ in the Incarnation]

An artificial image is only the image of the person or rather of the personal shape of every man whom it signifieth, and not at all the image of his nature. Howbeit we are brought into remembrance of the nature also by the mean of seeing the person represented.

This much being confessed, it is easy to answer their argument who say that, 'an image of Christ cannot be made, except it be a lying image, because his godhead cannot be represented in an image, which yet is the most excellent part of him'. I answer that, although Christ had been only a man, yet his image would not have represented, no, not so much as his human nature, but only by a consequent. Much less any man should require to have Christ's divine nature represented and set forth in an image or else to

---

82. corporal truth physical manifestation or representation. **88–90.** Compare the similar formulation of the Council of Trent on images, Session 25, 1563: 'the honour which is shown them is referred to the prototypes which those images represent; in such wise that by the images which we kiss, and before which we uncover the head, and prostrate ourselves, we adore Christ' (*Canons and Decrees of the Council of Trent*, tr. J. Waterworth, 1848: 235). **90. warning** representation. **91. artificial** manufactured, produced by human effort. **98. consequent** consequence (of imaginative sympathy). Sander argues that an image merely reproduces externals and, therefore, cannot truly represent the nature, or substance, of any human person. Therefore, it is folly to expect images to represent the divine nature, intangible and incomprehensible anyway. Images can, however, represent external accidents truly and put us in mind of substances human and divine.

account it a lying image. For an artificial image setteth forth only the outward shape and form of everything and not also the inward substance. How then can it be a lying image which representeth such an external shape of Christ as he had indeed?

For albeit he had not a mortal and human person, but assumed and united the true nature of man to his only divine person, yet, as Saint Paul testifieth, 'Formam servi accipiens in similitudinem hominum factus, habitu inventus (est) ut homo' (Phil. 2: 7. Taking the shape of a servant and made to the likeness of men, he was found in clothing as man). That shape which Christ took, that similitude which he bare walking on the earth, that figure or clothing which he was found in, if any man represent by art, his image cannot be a lying image. For although it express not all that was in Christ, yet that which it representeth is true.

As, therefore, when he lived in the world and was seen and touched of his apostles, the only shape of man was seen, and not either the person of man, which he had not, or the naked substance of man (which is not seen but by his accidents), or the godhead (which hath no such form at all as is able to be seen of mortal men), so now by his image the same only shape of man is expressed, and not either his godhead, or his human substance, or any person of man. On the other side, as when he lived, by the shape of his manhood the faithful were led to his true manhood, and thence to his divine nature and person. So in his image we are put in mind first of his human shape and figure, and thence we are also carried up to the remembrance of his human nature, and so upward to his divine nature and person.

If then we paint as much as the apostles saw, our image is no more a lying image than their sight was a lying sight. But as they might lawfully see the only shape of man, believing all the rest according as they were taught, so may we lawfully paint the only shape of Christ's manhood, leaving the rest to be supplied by faith and by the preaching of wise and learned men.

[Pagan idols vs. Catholic images]

The differences between the idols of the gentiles and our images are briefly these:

1. First, some kind of idols had no truth at all in nature but were feigned monsters; all our images have that essential truth extant in the world, which they represent.
2. All their idols were without truth concerning faith and religion; all our images contain such a truth as belongeth to Christ's faith and religion.
3. Sacrifice was done to their idols; not so to our images, but only to God.
4. Their idols belonged many times to very wicked men; our images, which we worship, belong always to blessed saints.

---

113. godhead divine nature or substance. **126. gentiles** pagans. Against Harding's assertion that God first created images, Jewel argued, 'But learned and wise men think that the invention hereof came first from the heathens and infidels that knew not God' (*Reply*, 1565, sig. Tt5ᵛ).

5. Some of the gentiles professed themselves to adore the unsensible wood or stone; we do not profess or teach any such thing but rather the contrary.   135

6. Other of the gentiles thought a certain substance of God to lie privy in the idol; we make our images only remembrances of holy things, and not to contain any godhead.

7. The wisest of the gentiles adored by the image of Juno or of Vulcanus unreasonable creatures as the earth or the fire, and by them certain gods who governed   140 those creatures; we adore by our images no unreasonable creature but only blessed souls and one God, their maker.

8. The devils ruled their idols; the same devils fear our images, which are set up in a right faith.

9. The devils maintained their idols; the same covet to throw down our images.   145

10. To be short, their idols were dedicated by infidels to an heathenish purpose; our images be dedicated to a virtuous intent.

Therefore, our images, being so far different from the heathenish idols, are injuriously by Master Jewel and such other called idols. And the convenient worship which we give to them is slanderously called idolatry. And where in the Bible mention is made of idols,   150 they are falsely translated into English by the name of images.

EDMUND CAMPION

Silver-tongued Oxford scholar, Edmund Campion (1540–81) left his university and Church of England deaconate for Ireland and the Catholic faith. He went to the seminary at Douai and then to Rome to enter the Society of Jesus in 1573. After teaching at Prague and writing Latin dramas, he returned home for the English Mission, the attempt to support oppressed Catholics and reclaim the country to the faith. Campion wrote *Rationes decem* (1581), 'Ten Reasons' to accept Roman Catholicism over Protestantism. He suffered capture, torture, and eventually execution at Tyburn in 1581 (see LIVES AND DEATHS; Fig. 8).

The selections below illustrate Campion as polemicist—spirited, erudite, adept at the cut-and-thrust of contemporary argument. The letter to the Privy Council, Campion's 'Brag', defines his mission as spiritual not political and challenges the best Protestant

134. **unsensible** incapable of sensation. 136. **privy** hidden. 139–40. **unreasonable** incapable of reason. 149. **convenient** fitting, appropriate.

divines in England to a debate. After Campion's arrest (1581), the government answered the call in its own fashion, setting teams of Protestant theologians against the debilitated and bookless prisoner. The official report of Protestant victory, *A True Report of the Disputation* (1583), asserted that Campion had 'much waste speech, which, being impertinent, is now omitted' (*Epistle*, before the second day). Catholic versions of the debate, however, circulated in manuscript, from which the excerpt below recounts an exchange on the nature and visibility of the Church. At issue here is the oft-repeated Catholic challenge, 'Where was your church before Luther?' Campion argues that the Roman Church, by virtue of its very existence and visibility through the ages, must be the only true Church.

A Letter to the Privy Council, 1580

Right Honourable,

Whereas I came out of Germany and Boemeland, being sent by my superiors, and ventured myself into this noble realm, my dear country, for the glory of God and the benefit of souls, I thought it like enough that in this busy, watchful, and suspicious world, I should either sooner or later be intercepted and stopped of my course. Wherefore, providing for all events and uncertain what may become of me when God shall haply deliver my body into durance, I supposed it needful to put this writing in a readiness, desiring your Lordships to give it the reading and to know my cause. This doing, I trust I shall ease you of some labour, for that which otherwise you must have sought by practice of wit, I do now lay into your hands by plain confession. And to the end the whole matter may be conceived in order, and so the better both understood and remembered, I make thereof these nine points or articles, directly, truly, and resolutely opening my full enterprise and purpose.

1. I confess that I am (albeit unworthy) a priest of the Catholic Church, and through the great mercy of God vowed now these eight years into the religion of the Society of Jesus, and thereby have taken upon me a special kind of warfare under the banner of obedience, and eke resigned all my interest and possibility of wealth, honour, pleasure, and other worldly felicity.

2. At the voice of our General Provost, which is to me a warrant from heaven and an oracle of Christ, I took my voyage from Prague to Rome (where our said General

Privy Council chief advisory body to the crown. **2. Boemeland** Bohemia, central Europe, formerly the Austrian empire. Campion refers to his sojourn in Prague. **3–4. for…souls** Campion cites the Jesuit motto, *ad maiorem Dei gloriam et bonum animarum*, 'for the greater glory of God and the good of souls'. **5. I…course** Campion had strong premonitions of martyrdom. **7. durance** imprisonment. **17. eke** also. **19. General Provost** Everard Mercurian, Jesuit General (1573–80).

Father is always resident) and from Rome into England, as I might or would have done joyously into any part of Christendom or heathenesse, had I been thereto assigned.

3. My charge is of free cost to preach the Gospel, to minister the sacraments, to instruct the simple, to reform sinners, to refute errors, and, in brief, to cry alarm 25 spiritual against foul vice and proud ignorance, wherewith my poor countrymen are abused.

4. I never had mind, and am straitly forbidden by our Father that sent me, to deal in any respect with matters of state or policy of this realm, as those things that appertain not to my vocation, and from which I do gladly restrain and sequester my 30 thoughts.

5. I ask to the glory of God, with all humility and under your correction, three sorts of indifferent and quiet audiences: the first before Your Honours, where I will discourse of religion so far as it toucheth the commonweal and your nobilities; the second, whereof I make most account, before the doctors and masters and chosen 35 men of both the universities, wherein I undertake to avow the faith of our Catholic Church by proofs innumerable—Scriptures, councils, fathers, histories, natural and moral reasons; the third before the lawyers, spiritual and temporal, wherein I will justify the said faith by the common wisdom of laws standing yet in force and practice. 40

6. I would be loath to speak anything that might sound of any insolent brag or challenge, especially being now as a dead man to this world and willing to put my head under every man's foot, and to kiss the ground they tread upon. Yet, have I such a courage in the advancing the majesty of Jesus my king, and such affiance in his gracious favour, and such assurance in my quarrel, and my evidence so impregnable, 45 that because I know perfectly none of the Protestants living, nor any sect of our adversaries (howsoever they face men down in pulpits and overrule us in their kingdom of grammarians and unlearned ears), can maintain their doctrine in disputation. I am to sue most humbly for the combat with them all, and every of them, and the most principal that may be found, protesting that in all this trial the better furnished they 50 come, the more welcome they shall be to me.

---

22. **heathenesse** heathendom, non-Christian lands. **28. straitly** strictly. Mercurian ordered the Jesuits to advance Catholics in the faith and prohibited them from mixing in affairs of state (*Non se immisceant negotiis statuum*), from even speaking against the queen or tolerating such speech in others (*Letters and Memorials of Father Robert Persons, SJ*, ed. Leo Hicks, 1942: 316–21, 318). **33. indifferent** impartial. **36. avow** justify. **38. lawyers, spiritual** i.e. canon lawyers. **44. affiance** confidence.

7. And because it hath pleased God to enrich the Queen, my sovereign Lady, with noble gifts of nature, learning, and princely education, I do verily trust that—if her Highness would vouchsafe her royal person and good attention to such a conference as I in the second part of my fifth article have mentioned and requested, or to a few   55
sermons which in her or your hearing I am to utter—such a manifest and fair light by good method and plain dealing may be cast upon those controversies that possibly her zeal of truth and love of her people shall incline her noble Grace to disfavour some proceedings hurtful to the realm and procure towards us oppressed more equity.   60

8. Moreover, I doubt not but your honourable Council, being of such wisdom and drift in cases most important, when you shall have heard these questions of religion opened faithfully, which many times by our adversaries are huddled up and confounded, will see upon what substantial grounds our Catholic faith is builded, and how feeble that side is which by sway of the time prevaileth against us, and at the   65
last for your own souls and many thousand souls that depend upon government will discountenance error when it is bewrayed, and hearken to those that would spend the best blood in their bodies for your salvation. Many innocent hands are lifted up to heaven for you daily and hourly by those English students, whose posterity shall not die, which beyond the seas, gathering virtue and sufficient knowledge for the   70
purpose, are determined never to give you over, but either to win you heaven or to die upon your pikes. And touching our Society, be it known unto you that we have made a league—all the Jesuits in the world, whose succession and multitude must overreach all the practices of England—cheerfully to carry the cross that you shall lay upon us and never to despair your recovery, while we have a man left to enjoy your   75
Tyburn, or to be racked with your torments, or to be consumed with your prisons. The expense is reckoned, the enterprise is begun; it is of God, it cannot be withstood. So the faith was planted, so it must be restored.

9. If these my offers be refused and mine endeavours can take no place, and that I, having run thousands of miles to do you good, shall be rewarded with rigour,   80
I have no more to say but to recommend your case and mine to almighty God, the searcher of hearts, who, send us of his grace and set us at accord before the day of payment, to the end at the last we may be friends in heaven, when all injuries shall be forgotten.

---

62. drift purpose. **67. discountenance** turn from, disfavour. **bewrayed** revealed. **72. pikes** spears. **76. Tyburn** place of public execution. **82. send...set** may he send, and may he set.

The Tower Debates, 1581

Second Day: Whether the Church Militant be visible always or no

So after some variance in exposition of that place, whether visibility were the Scriptures, etc., Master Doctor Goade began his argument out of the New Testament as followeth:

GOADE In the time of our Saviour Christ the scribes and Pharisees sat in Moses' chair, yet the Church rested in our Saviour Christ. *Ergo*, the Church was not then visible, as 5 you have said.

CAMPION You make an argument for me. Although the Church were then beginning, yet Christ preaching openly in the temple, there were a number that believed, as Mary the Virgin, Mary Magdalene, Joseph of Arimathea, St John the Evangelist, and many others that stood about the cross, which either openly or secretly acknowledged the 10 true religion and were known one to another.

GOADE You said before that the property of a visible church is to have a place of resort, wherein the sacraments may be ministered, which could not be done at that time, nor afterwards in the time of persecution under Diocletian, when Christians were kept in prison and martyred, and had no public place for resort for service and 15 sacraments.

CAMPION I do not say that the Church should always be in pomp and prosperity, yet I doubt not but the members of the same were known one to another, and known also to them that did persecute them, howbeit they believed not as they did. For in the time of persecution under Diocletian certain escaped the prison, as Sylvester and others, as 20 in time of Queen Mary many did, and in this Queen's time do.

GOADE You meddle too much with the state of this time.

CAMPION I mean as well Queen Mary's time as this present time.

GOADE Whereas you say that the Church is so visible that one member knoweth another, that cannot be; for the faithless do not know the faithful, according to the 25 saying of St John, 'The world doth not know us' [1 John 3: 1].

CAMPION I answer that the faithless do know the faithful, although not to their salvation, even as I do know you to be a Protestant, and you me to be a Catholic. And for the

Second Day The excerpt here comes from the second debate, 18 September 1581. Campion acquitted himself so well in the first debate (31 August 1571), that the authorities changed the opponents and the venue, reduced the audience, and excluded fellow Catholic prisoners. **Church Militant** the Church on earth, struggling against the powers of evil. **1. visibility** i.e. visibility of the Church. Catholics argued that Christ established the Roman Church and that the institution and its followers were visible through the ages; Protestants argued that the true Church consisted in the invisible fellowship of the elect. **2. Goade** Roger Goade (1538–1610), Cambridge scholar and administrator. **14. Diocletian** Roman emperor (245–313) who persecuted Christians. **20. Sylvester** Saint Sylvester, pope (*r*. 314–35). **21. Queen Mary** Catholic Mary Tudor (*r*. 1553–8), a period of persecution for Protestants. **22.** Goade's response differs in *A True Report* (1583): 'Surely you make evil and untrue comparisons. You have no such cause to complain of bloody persecutions in the time of our gracious queen, and do not well to compare Her Highness's peaceable and mild government with those tyrannical persecutions' (sig. J1).

place of St John, it is to be intended, as I said before, *non sciunt eos, ut oportet, per fructum* [they know them not, as is proper, by their fruit].   30

GOADE   *Deus tantum noverit qui sunt eius* [God alone knows who are his own].

CAMPION   True it is that *Deus tantum noverit qui sunt eius*, that is, 'God alone knoweth by election who are his.' And seeing you yourselves do call your church a congregation of the faithful, and the angels in heaven cannot be called a congregation of the faithful because they are in heaven, but must be a company in earth, as your meaning is, and so   35 visible. *Ergo*, you mean the Church visible.

FULKE   What! Is all the Church visible?

CAMPION   Not all at one time by one man in one place, as it is not possible for me, being in this chamber, to see all men or all Catholics in all places. But yet it is possible for a man being in Spain to see Catholics there, and so there the Church is visible.   40

FULKE   The Church is a congregation of the elected.

CAMPION   Can you say any one man to be elected? This man or that man? Which if you cannot say, then cannot you show any one man to be of your church. How then, I pray you, answer you the Scripture, or can you say with the Scriptures, 'dic ecclesiae' [tell it to the Church, Matt. 18: 17]?   45

Whereupon Master Goade somewhat pausing, Master Campion said:

CAMPION   Master Doctor Fulke, help him with an answer if you can.

FULKE   What then? Another time shall serve, for it is not your part to oppose.

And thereupon Master Goade proceeded as followeth.

GOADE   I will urge you with an argument which is taken upon the strongest place of your   50 own side to prove your opinion, which is out of the 5th of Matthew, 'vos estis', etc. [you are the light of the world, 14].

CAMPION   I can show you a stronger; the place you mean is very good.

GOADE   If you will refuse this, I will take yours.

CAMPION   No, I will not refuse it, but sithence as we come hither for the glory of God   55 and the sifting out of his truth rather than for victory in argument, it were good we should have in question the most forcible text, whereby the truth might be the sooner

---

29–30. **non…fructum** Campion alludes to Matt. 7: 16, 20: 'By their fruits ye shall know them.' **32–3. *Deus*…his** Goade interprets the sentence to mean that God alone can see the Church, invisible to mortal eyes; Campion reinterprets it to mean that God alone can see into the future and know who will attain eternal salvation. **35. must** i.e. the Church must. Here citing the faithful angels in heaven as a counter-example, Campion attacks the Protestant definition of church as a congregation of the faithful. His point is that the Church must consist of earthly beings and, therefore, be visible. **37. Fulke** William Fulke (1538–89), Puritan scholar and polemicist. **41. elected** those chosen by God for eternal happiness; Campion uses the term 'election' above (**33**) but without the Protestant significance of predestination. **46. Goade somewhat pausing** In *A True Report* (1583) Goade answers more cogently: 'When the Church is gathered and may retain a face, when it doth execute government and hath a consistory to hear matters, then it ought to be done; but this cannot be always had, being often hindered by persecution' (sig. Ki^v). **48. your part** The debate format prohibited Campion from introducing arguments.

debated and discussed. Also, the place which I would show you is literal and plain and so more familiar to the audience. And yours, although it is very good, yet is it allegorical.   60

GOADE Then bear witness, my masters, that he refuseth the place which Hosius and others of his side do esteem as most strong.

CAMPION No, you cannot witness that, for I will admit it lest we should lose our argument. And, therefore, frame your argument and you shall be answered.

GOADE The place above mentioned of St Matthew hath these words, 'non potest civitas   65 supra montem posita abscondi' [a city placed on a mountain cannot be hidden, 5: 14]. You say this is intended as spoken of the whole Church, and we affirm that it was only meant of the apostles.

CAMPION It was spoken of them in two degrees, as well in respect that they were of the faithful, as in respect that they were apostles in their function. And this is not particularly   70 spoken unto them in respect of their function only, wherefore not like other places of Scripture, which import a special reference to their function, as 'ite et baptizate' [go forth and baptize, Matt. 28: 19], and many other places which is only proper to their function. But the circumstance of this place and the plain words of the text do evidently prove these words above mentioned to pertain to them in both the degrees, as I have already said. For   75 mark the words precedent spoken to the apostles in the same chapter, 'vos estis sal terrae et lux mundi' [you are the salt of the earth and the light of the world, Matt. 5: 13–14], meaning by this word *sal* the apostles, and by *terrae* the rest of the Church, likewise meaning by *lux* the apostles, and by *mundi* the rest of the Church. Howbeit by these words the apostles and the Church are severed; yet in the text immediately following it is   80 said, *non potest civitas*, etc., wherein the apostles are considered in both the respects, as I have said above. As oftentimes by naming the principal of anything, the inferior parts be included. As for example, in this word *paterfamilias* [head of the family] is included the whole family. Even so, speaking in this place to the apostles as the chief of the faithful, he included the remnant, having no other words to prove he spake severally of the apostles,   85 as he did in the other places before, so that it is evident by the circumstance of the text that Christ meant the whole Church.

GOADE I will urge you with two doctors, which are Chrysostom and Jerome, which do expound this place to be meant of the apostles, as I have alleged.

And because Master Goade could not readily turn to the places, it was appointed they   90 should be prepared against after dinner.

CAMPION I would, Master Goade, that you and I might shake hands together of St Jerome his religion, that we might meet together with him in heaven.

60 allegorical figurative. **61. Hosius** Stanislaus Hosius (1504–79), Polish bishop and Catholic polemicist. **68. meant...
apostles** Goade amplifies the point in *A True Report* (1583): 'For the drift and scope of the place is only to set forth the apostles' doctrine and conversation, and you violently wrest it to the whole Church. The life of the ministry is, as it were, set upon an high stage; the light of their conversation is looked unto of all. What is this to the visibility of the whole Church?' (sig. Jiv^v). **91. against** for.

GOADE I will not be of man's religion further than he is of Christ's.

CAMPION Therein do you well, for we must not be of Paul, Cephas, or Apollo further   95
than they are of Christ.

And having thus ended, Master Campion wished that he might urge the other place
before by him mentioned, which he said was a stronger.

GOADE Although it be contrary to the order of disputation and to our appointed
conference, yet I will admit it; wherefore, show the place.   100

CAMPION It is taken out of the 18th of Matthew, where it is said, 'si peccaverit in te frater
tuus, corripe eum, sic si te non audierit, dic ecclesiae,' [if your brother trespass against
you, reprove him, and if he will not hear you, tell it to the Church, 15, 17]. Whereupon
thus I reason: seeing these words, *dic ecclesiae*, are always to be executed in the Church
of God, *ergo*, it must be always visible.   105

GOADE I will distinguish of your antecedent, for it must be executed when there is a
visible face of the Church, but not always when the members thereof are afflicted and
the congregation unknown.

CAMPION This was a remedy for all ages; then, seeing the malady is continual, the
remedy must be in like manner continual. As for example, offence betwixt brother and   110
brother do continually chance, whereupon he must exhort him privately and after,
'show the Church', as by this text he is counselled. *Ergo*, the remedy in all ages must be
executed. And I pray you, before Luther his time, whither or to what pastor should one
resort for this continual remedy, seeing for many hundred years there was none at all
known of this religion?   115

GOADE It cannot be had in persecution.

CAMPION In vain was it then of Christ commanded that this remedy should be always
executed, seeing it cannot be put in execution in time of persecution. For although
persecution be in one place, yet this complaint may be done in other places. As for
example, the Protestants in Queen Mary's time being persecuted in England, yet they   120
might have this remedy in Germany where their religion was used. And although
everyone cannot attain to this remedy, yet the remedy is in being as good and available.
As for example, if a man make a feast for all comers, yet two or three being restrained
by imprisonment or otherwise may die for hunger, and yet the remedy in being and to
be had, although not to them.   125

FULKE The remedy may be good although not applied, as a remedy in a pothecary's
shop may be good, although it be not used.

CAMPION That proveth the remedy to be in being to all such as could come by it.

95–6. we...Christ Campion paraphrases Paul identifying the true leader of the early Christian community at Corinth,
not Paul himself, Cephas or Peter, or Apollo, a wealthy and learned Jew, but Christ: 'Now this I say, that every one of you
saith: "I indeed am of Paul; and I am of Apollo; and I of Cephas; and I of Christ." Is Christ divided? Was Paul then
crucified for you? Or were you baptized in the name of Paul?' (1 Cor. 1: 12–13). 106. distinguish...antecedent qualify
your antecedent, i.e. the premise on which your proof depends, namely, the assumption that one must always resort to the
Church.

And thus having in manner ended the forenoon's disputation, Master Fulke said after divers intercourse of speech that *ecclesia* is sometimes taken for 'coetus fidelium' [assembly of the faithful]: 130

CAMPION *Ecclesia* is never taken for the Church invisible only.

FULKE Yes, for to believe in the Church is an article of our faith; and faith is invisible; *ergo*, the Church is invisible.

CAMPION Although faith be invisible, yet 'obiectum fidei' [object of faith] is *visibile*. 135 And to believe in Christ is an article of our faith. Will you conclude, therefore, that Christ could not be seen when he was here on earth in his natural body?

Master Campion urging them to reply against these answers, Master Fulke and Master Goade said that he vaunted himself too much and hath deceived them of the opinion of modesty which they conceived and heard of him. Whereunto Master Campion replied 140 that for humility he said he would be contented to kiss their feet; 'but in the truth of Christ I must not by humility give you place; for the Scripture saith, "non sis humilis in sapientia tua"' [be not humble in your wisdom, Ecclus. 13: 11], and uttered other texts to that purpose, saying that he must not betray the truth by using too much humility. And thus they ended, declaring what should be their question for the afternoon, namely, 145 'Whether the Church Militant of Christ may err in matters of faith.'

ALBAN LANGDALE

The Act of Uniformity (1559) stipulated harsh penalties for those who refused to attend Church of England services: first offence, forfeiture of one year's profit of benefices and six months' imprisonment; second offence, deprivation and one year's imprisonment; third offence, deprivation and imprisonment for life. For those not beneficed, the first offence brought imprisonment for one year; the second offence, for life (1 Elizabeth I, c. 2). The Church strongly urged recusancy, however, and Robert Persons, SJ articulated the official position in *A Brief Discourse containing Certain Reasons why Catholics refuse to go to Church* (1580). (On Persons see HISTORIES.) Persons argued that attendance at state services brought danger of infection, gave scandal, assented to a sign distinctive between the religions, fostered schism, signalled participation in a forbidden rite, dissimulated in a matter of conscience, accepted heresies and blasphemies, removed one from the benefits of Catholicism, and ran counter to the example even of infidels and heretics who absented themselves from proscribed services.

130. **intercourse** exchange. 139. **deceived them of** proved false to them.

Resident priest to the Montague household in Sussex, Alban Langdale disagreed. Contending contrarily that 'circumstances alter cases', Langdale recalled biblical precedents and argued that Catholics might, with no danger of mortal sin, attend Church of England services out of a proper regard (*ex iusto metu*) for their lives. His pamphlet dared to articulate what many ordinary Catholics thought, and it offered clear justification for the weekly or monthly compromises that many made.

Reasons why Catholics may go to Church, 1580

Ob. [Naaman would have committed a sin by going to pagan services, had not the prophet Elisha excused him.]

R. And it is plain that the prophet allowed his doings for otherwise he would plainly and directly have said that it was not lawful and that if he do not forthwith dispatch himself of that service, in vain it were for him either to worship or to build an altar in the   5
honour of the God of Israel. Thus we see that Naaman in that place might exhibit his service to the king, that in his fact he was no idolater nor committed mortal sin, and so by a consequent, it appeareth that the bare, local abiding in the profane temple at their time of service was not of itself a mortal sin. Now compare the act of him whom we speak of with Naaman from point to point, etc., and though he be in the church of Protestants, as   10
Naaman was with idolaters, yet his profession is known, he seemeth not to dissimule. By his own acts he uttereth himself evidently, and that he doth is not to any evil end nor with intention to deceive insomuch as he abstaineth from their works and to everyone which asketh he is ready and with firm mind determined to confess his faith; he is not pertinacious nor contemptuous against any law or authority. To the contrary, he con-   15
fesseth his faith, he avoideth all scandal as much as he may, etc. And it is to little purpose it is objected Naaman was a novice, or no scandal or little was to be given there in Syria where all were idolaters, for the bare act of being in such a place is here in question. And if it be of itself a mortal sin his novice-ship is no excuse, and the scandal is an accident. Then, that taken away, the thing is not unlawful yet his servants might take scandal, etc.,   20
'ut supra dicitur' [as is said above].

Ob. It is not to be denied that many of the faithful martyrs and confessors in time of persecution have utterly refused to come into the churches of Protestants and temples of idolaters, and did so abhor from every manner of conversing with them as when they

---

1. **Naaman** Naaman was a Syrian general whom Elisha, a prophet of Israel, cured of leprosy. After declaring his belief in the God of Israel, Naaman asked Elisha to beg God's pardon for him when he accompanied his master to the temple of the pagan god Remmon and bowed down with him. Elisha told him to go in peace (4 Kings 5). Langdale uses the story to justify religious conformity that is motivated by political obedience and expediency. (The format here is *Ob.* [objection] and *R.* [reply].) 4. **dispatch** rid. 7. **fact** deed. 8. **consequent** necessary conclusion. 11. **profession** i.e. Catholicism. **dissimule** dissemble. 12. **uttereth** reveals. **doth** i.e. attends Protestant service. 15. **pertinacious** stubborn. 17. **novice** new convert. 19. **novice-ship** status as a new convert. 20. **yet** even if.

were to suffer death with idolaters and Protestants at any place of execution, they would   25
as they might ever there go about to be separated from them, because they would not
seem to die of one profession with them, and this their act is worthily commended.

  R. Even if it is commendable in them which utterly refused (as many did) to come to
their churches, but this allegation 'ex gestis prorsum praesumpta' [assumed directly from
these deeds] proveth not against the case before set down. For it seemeth no good   30
consequent in every case: good men and martyrs did this, *ergo*, this not to do or otherwise
to do is Protestantism or mortal sin. For good men and martyrs in time of persecution
have gone amongst Protestants and idolaters and sometimes to their churches and
temples without grudge of conscience and were not defiled with their works of Protestantism or idolatry. And thus they did as circumstances moved them for circumstances do   35
alter cases. And that good men and martyrs in times of persecution have not forbidden
the bare and naked going to churches and conferences of them, and that without
blemish, it appeareth by the examples of many, whereof some are hereafter set down.

  We read that the apostles were mixed amongst the wicked Jews in the temple and there
prayed amongst them, though not with them, nor such prayers as the Jews prayed, who   40
could not brook the name of Christ, and they observed the same times of prayer. And this
they did after they had received their commission to preach the gospel and after they had
received the Holy Ghost. This proveth that the bare going and naked corporate presence
with Protestants or idolaters in their church at times of prayer without further circumstances is neither Protestantism nor mortal sin. Now compare this with our man's doing: 45
every Jew had, as it were, a freehold or interest in the temple for to come and pray. The
apostles did keep their possession, were in the temple among the Jews which crucified
Christ, and there prayed in the form which was to them commended, namely, 'in
nomine Patris, et Filii, et Spiritus Sancti' [in the name of the Father, and of the Son,
and of the Holy Spirit], though not with them, nor their prayers, which indeed could not   50
brook the name of Christ. This man likewise whom I speak of keepeth his possession in
the church ordained for the prayers of faithful, there remaineth, prayeth in the form set
forth by the faithful. Add hereunto the other circumstances set down in the case, I see not
any matter of reprehension in his bare coming more than it of the apostles.

  Gamaliel was a disciple of Christ and a companion with the apostles, yet neither did   55
he bewray himself to the Jews nor forbear the fellowship of the Pharisees, but to the end
he might pacify their fury he remained among them, even in their consultation as well
touching the law of God as touching their civil policy.
  [. . .]

  Ob. There must be *signum distinctivum* between Catholics and Protestants, and now the
going and not going is made a sign distinctive between Catholicism and Protestantism,   60

---

29. allegation i.e. that all must do likewise. **34. grudge** murmuring, discontent. **46. freehold** lifelong grant. **47. keep
their possession** retain what was properly their own. **55. Gamaliel** A Pharisee who advised fellow members of the
Sanhedrin not to put to death Peter and the apostles (Acts 5: 34–5). Church traditions portrayed Gamaliel as a secret
Christian who remained a member of the Sanhedrin to help other Christians. **56. bewray** reveal. **59. *signum distinctivum***
a distinguishing mark. Langdale here replies directly to Persons's argument that 'the going to church is in the realm of

therefore each man is now bound to keep his mark lest refusing that he seem thereby to deny his profession. And he must follow the example of the Christian soldiers which would not wear the garlands on their heads as the infidels did to the honour of their false gods, but in their hands they did hold them for a mark and distinction from the infidels, for which they are commended.   65

R. The going and not going is not made a sign distinctive between Catholicism and Protestantism for Puritans refuse to go to the churches of Protestants. Again the Protestants do not account it a special mark for they know that there be many Catholics which go to the church of Protestants, and many Catholics there be which would be so accepted and ready to die for their faith, which, nevertheless, go to the church of   70 Protestants and make it not a special mark. Further, in the case set down there be special marks enough and a plain profession; if I pray not with them, if I sit when they kneel, if I refuse their communion, etc., be not these *signa distinctiva* and do not these facts show a dissent as well as express words? But it is not to be neglected that this is made *signum distinctivum* between a true subject and a rebel, and, therefore, if the bare going be but in   75 his own nature a thing indifferent, let every wise man weigh his own case. And for example of the garland, mark that they did yet bear the garland in their hands though not on their heads, and so they did wear the garland though not to the honour of the idol. [...]

Ob. [Augustine says that consent to sin causes corruption.]

R. Saith he, a consent to the fact, which the man whom we spake of doth not, but   80 utterly abhorring from all consent, doth but 'ex iusto metu' [from a proper fear] or for avoiding of temptation give a bare corporal presence, and seeketh for his part a means to mollify the wrath of the persecutor, which in every age wise and good men have done, and never was it more needful than now. For seeing the outward face of religion, etc., is through God's permission for our sins taken away by the civil magistrate, folly it were for   85 a man to seek to exulcerate that which he cannot heal. And it is not every man's lot to purge the Church of chaff. And for a matter which might be made indifferent, to stir trouble is not the best course to quietness. A man which dwelleth among the wicked must lament the state and providently avoid the peril of temptation and as much as he may must withdraw himself from trouble as a peaceable child of the Church, not seeking   90 unnecessarily to provoke ire. [...]

Ob. All open professors of Protestantism or known here are to be eschewed. In their prayers and sermons their profession is manifest, *ergo*, then specially we must abstain

England a plain and apparent sign of a schismatic, that is to say, of a conformable man (as they call him) to the Protestants' proceedings' (Persons, *A Brief Discourse*, Douai, 1580, sigs. Bviii–Bviii^v). **62. example...soldiers** Citing Tertullian's *De Corona*, Persons recalled the story of Christian soldiers who refused to wear the emperor's garland because it signified a denial of their faith (sig. Ci^v). **75. true...rebel** After dismissing the religious significance of conformity, Langdale here shrewdly focuses on the civil significance in contemporary circumstances. **81. 'ex iusto metu'** i.e. a proper regard for self-preservation. **82. temptation** a severe or painful trial. **85. taken away** controlled. **86. exulcerate** cause ulcers in.

from them 'quia participare in Protestantis divinibus etiam Catholice grave peccatum est' [because to participate in Protestant prayers for a Catholic is a grave sin].   95

    R. That is answered before but note: many parishes in England there be where neither the curate nor parishioners are open professors of Protestantism nor known Protestants but dissembling Catholics. For that one sort is bound by word and the other by power to withstand. Therefore, herein every man is to ask of his own conscience what scandal he giveth and therefore note that as it is much material with what mind a man doth a thing   100 for that God doth more regard the will and intention of the doer than the deed itself. Even so the manner of doing altereth a case. For if it be not done rightly and agreeably to charity it is a sin though otherwise very good and indifferent.

William Allen

Cardinal William Allen (1532–94), helped found the English Colleges at Douai, Rome, and Valladolid and emerged as a leader of English Catholics during Elizabeth's reign. In *A True, Sincere, and Modest Defence of English Catholics* (1584) Allen argues that the English torture and murder Catholics for religious not political reasons; he describes the Catholic plight in vivid detail, including the use of 'bloody questions' designed to trap defendants into declaring loyalty to the pope or the crown. Outraged by the continued oppression of Catholics, Allen later joined Robert Persons to plot Elizabeth's overthrow and the invasion of the Spanish Armada in 1588. He wrote *An Admonition to the Nobility and People of England* (1588), which appeared, condensed, as a broadside, *A Declaration of the Sentence and Deposition of Elizabeth* (1588), to be distributed after the Spanish victory. Here Allen recapitulates the case against Elizabeth, reviews the suffering of English Catholics, and outlines some chilling procedures for the country's reconversion. This resort to force, seasoned with the promise of a plenary indulgence for actions that almost everyone regarded as treasonous, confirmed Protestant fears and drew condemnation from both sides of the aisle. William Watson (1559?–1603), for example, a seminary priest who spent much time in and out of prison, strongly protested his loyalty and vilified Allen and Persons in *A Decacordon of Ten Quodlibetical Questions* (1602). Though Allen persuasively criticized government policy and championed Catholic rights, he seriously underestimated Catholic popular loyalty to the government and country.

---

100. **material** pertinent.

A True, Sincere, and Modest Defence of English Catholics, 1584

[Bloody Questions]

1. Whether the bull of Pius Quintus against the Queen Majesty be a lawful sentence and ought to be obeyed by the subjects of England?

2. Whether the Queen Majesty be a lawful queen and ought to be obeyed by the subjects of England, notwithstanding the bull of Pius Quintus or any other bull or sentence that the pope hath pronounced or may pronounce against Her Majesty? 5

3. Whether the pope have or had power to authorize her subjects to rebel or take arms against her or to invade her dominions, and whether such subjects so doing do lawfully therein?

4. Whether the pope have power to discharge any of Her Majesty's subjects or the subjects of any Christian prince from their allegiance or oath of obedience to Her 10 Majesty or to their prince for any cause?

5. Whether Doctor Sander in his book *Of the Visible Monarchy of the Church* and Doctor Bristow in his book of *Motives* (writing in allowance, commendation, and confirmation of the said bull of Pius Quintus) have therein taught, testified, or maintained a truth or a falsehood? 15

6. If the pope do by his bull or sentence pronounce Her Majesty to be deprived and no lawful queen, and her subjects to be discharged of their allegiance and obedience unto her, and after, the pope or any other by his appointment and authority do invade this realm, which part would you take, or which part ought a good subject of England to take? 20

Wherein if you say nothing or refuse to answer somewhat in contempt or derogation of the See Apostolic, then are you judged no good subject but a traitor; whereby let all princes and people Christian bear witness of our miseries and unjust afflictions who are

---

Defence This work responds to Lord Burlegh's *The Execution of Justice in England* (1583, rev. 1584), the official, widely circulated justification of Campion's execution and the persecution of Catholics. **1. bull** Pius V's infamous *Regnans in excelsis* (1570), which excommunicated Elizabeth and absolved Catholics from obedience to her (see DOCUMENTS). The use of the Bloody Questions to secure convictions was legally dubious. In a brief to the Privy Council (20 July 1588) two lawyers for the crown, William Fleetwood and Thomas Egerton, advised that if Catholics did not answer, pleaded ignorance, or claimed that they ought not be examined on things in the future, 'then upon such manner of answer made by them, they are not comprehended directly within the compass of the law for any proceeding to be had against them in case of treason or felony' (*Unpublished Documents Relating to the English Martyrs*, ed. J. H. Pollen, 1908: 151). **12. Doctor Sander** Louvain exile, Nicholas Sander (1530–81) wrote *De visibili monarchia ecclesiae* (1571), a powerful defence of Catholicism. **13. Doctor Bristow** Richard Bristow (1538–81), popular Catholic polemicist, whose *Motives* first appeared in 1574. **22. See Apostolic** papal authority. **traitor** Burlegh maintained, contrarily, that those who affirmed the pope's supremacy in the Church or denied the queen's supremacy over bishops might incur penalty but not the charge of capital treason, which applied only to those who 'did obstinately maintain the contents of the pope's bull' (*Execution*, 1584, sig. Bii^v).

enforced to suffer death for our only cogitations and inward opinions, unduly sought out
by force and fear, and yet not condemned by any Christian school in the world, nor 25
uttered by us but upon forcing interrogatories, we having committed nothing by word or
deed against our prince or laws but doing all acts of honour and homage unto her, and
suffering meekly what punishment soever she would lay upon us for our religion. For so
most part of all sorts of Catholics have done both in England and Ireland for this twenty-
five years' space, only a very few nobles of both countries taking once arms for their 30
defence in all this long time of intolerable affliction. The like patience you shall hardly
find in Protestants, as their furious rebellions against their sovereigns in France, Flanders,
and Scotland do testify. Our nobles and gentlemen, having borne all those anguishes of
body and mind with loss of honours, country, lands, and liberty for so long time, have
both at home and abroad obeyed her with such loyalty as subjects ought to do their 35
sovereign; never took arms in all England upon the bull of Pius Quintus, nor any time
since the publication thereof (contrary to the deceitful division of those times, things,
and actions set down by the Libeller, placing that after, which was done before the bull
was published), but have shown themselves in all cases as serviceable as before.

A Declaration of the Sentence and Deposition
of Elizabeth, 1588 *Condensed fr. longer, but also a little sanitized*

Sixtus the Fifth, by God's providence the universal pastor of Christ's flock, to whom by
perpetual and lawful succession appertaineth the care and government of the Catholic
Church, seeing the pitiful calamities which heresy hath brought into the renowned
countries of England and Ireland, of old so famous for virtue, religion, and Christian
obedience, and how at this present through the impiety and perverse government of 5
Elizabeth, the pretensed Queen, with a few of her adherents, those kingdoms be brought
not only to a disordered and perilous state in themselves but are become as infected
members, contagious and troublesome to the whole body of Christendom, and not
having in those parts the ordinary means which by the assistance of Christian princes he
hath in other provinces to remedy disorders and keep in obedience and ecclesiastical 10
discipline the people, for that Henry the Eighth, late king of England, did of late years by
rebellion and revolt from the See Apostolic violently separate himself and his subjects
from the communion and society of the Christian commonwealth; and Elizabeth, the
present usurper, doth continue the same with perturbation and peril of the countries
about her, showing herself obstinate and incorrigible in such sort that without her 15

---

24. **only** mere. 37. **deceitful division** Burlegh blamed the Northern Uprising in 1569, led by the earls of Westmoreland and Northumberland, on the papal bull that appeared in 1570 (*Execution*, 1584, sigs. Biii–Biii^v). 38. **Libeller** Lord Burleigh.

DECLARATION William Watson delivered his hostile verdict of the work: 'great pity it was that the books and the burner, the worthless work and the wretched father, were not both made a burnt sacrifice or offering combust together' (*Decacordon*, 1602, sig Q8^v). 1. **Sixtus the Fifth** (r. 1585–90). 6. **pretensed** pretended. 15. **sort** kind.

deprivation and deposition there is no hope to reform those states, nor keep Christendom in perfect peace and tranquillity; therefore our Holy Father, desiring, as his duty is, to provide present and effectual remedy, inspired by God for the universal benefit of his Church, moved by the particular affection which himself and many his predecessors have had to these nations, and solicited by the zealous and importunate instance of sundry the 20
most principal persons of the same, hath dealt earnestly with divers princes, and specially with the mighty and potent King Catholic of Spain, for the reverence which he beareth to the See Apostolic, for the old amity between his house and the crown of England, for the special love that he hath showed to the Catholics of those places, for the obtaining of peace and quietness in his countries adjoining, and for the augmenting and increase of 25
the Catholic faith, and finally for the universal benefit of all Europe, that he will employ those forces which almighty God hath given him to the deposition of this woman and correction of her complices, so wicked and noisome to the world, and to the reformation and pacification of these kingdoms, whence so great good and so manifold public commodities are like to ensue. 30

And to notify to the world the justice of this act, and give full satisfaction to the subjects of those kingdoms and others whosoever, and finally to manifest God's judgements upon sin, His Holiness hath thought good, together with the declaratory sentence of this woman's chastisement, to publish also the causes which have moved him to proceed against her in this sort. First, for that she is an heretic and schismatic, excom- 35
municated by two His Holiness's predecessors, obstinate in disobedience to God and the See Apostolic, presuming to take upon her, contrary to nature, reason, and all laws both of God and man, supreme jurisdiction and spiritual authority over men's souls. Secondly, for that she is a bastard, conceived and born by incestuous adultery and, therefore, uncapable of the kingdom as well by the several sentences of Clement the Seventh and 40
Paul the Third of blessed memory, as by the public declaration of King Henry himself. Thirdly, for usurping the crown without right, having the impediments mentioned, and contrary to the ancient accord made between the See Apostolic and the realm of England, upon reconciliation of the same after the death of Saint Thomas of Canterbury in the time of Henry the Second, that none might be lawful king or queen thereof without the 45
approbation and consent of the supreme Bishop; which afterward was renewed by King John and confirmed by oath as a thing most beneficial to the kingdom at request and instance of the Lords and Commons of the same. And, further, for that with sacrilege and impiety she continueth violating the solemn oath made at her coronation to maintain and defend the ancient privileges and ecclesiastical liberties of the land; for many and 50

21. **dealt earnestly** decided. 23. **old amity** Philip II was married to Queen Mary of England from 1554 to 1558. 28. **complices** associates. 39. **bastard** Elizabeth was born of Henry VIII and Anne Boleyn, whose union was not recognized as a marriage by the Catholic Church. 40. **Clement the Seventh** (r. 1523–34). 41. **Paul the Third** (r. 1534–49). **public declaration** The Second Succession Act (28 Henry VIII c. 7) secured the crown to the issue of Jane Seymour and declared all previous issue illegitimate. The statute was ignored, but not revoked, by the Third Succession Act (1544). 44. **Thomas of Canterbury** St Thomas Becket, martyred in 1170. 46–7. **King John** John (r. 1199–1216), after suffering excommunication, conceded to the pope spiritual leadership of the English Church and the right to appoint bishops. 48. **instance** urging.

grievous injuries, extortions, oppressions, and other wrongs done by her and suffered to
be done against the poor and innocent people of both countries; for stirring up to
sedition and rebellion the subjects of other nations about her against their lawful and
natural princes to the destruction of infinite souls, overthrow and desolation of most
goodly cities and countries; for harbouring and protecting heretics, fugitives, rebels, and   55
notorious malefactors, with great injury and prejudice of divers commonwealths, and
procuring for the oppression of Christendom and disturbance of common peace to bring
in our potent and cruel enemy, the Turk; for so long and barbarous persecution of God's
saints, afflicting, spoiling and imprisoning the sacred bishops, tormenting, and pitifully
murdering numbers of holy priests and other Catholic persons; for the unnatural and   60
unjust imprisonment and late cruelty used against the most gracious Princess Mary,
Queen of Scotland, who under promise and assurance of protection and succour came
first into England; for abolishing the true Catholic religion, profaning holy sacraments,
monasteries, churches, sacred persons, memories of saints, and what else soever might
help or further to eternal salvation; and in the commonwealth disgracing the ancient   65
nobility, erecting base and unworthy persons to all the civil and ecclesiastical dignities,
selling of laws and justice, and finally exercising an absolute tyranny with high offence to
almighty God, oppression of the people, perdition of souls, and ruin of those countries.

Wherefore, these things being of such nature and quality that some of them make her
unable to reign, others declare her unworthy to live, His Holiness, in the almighty power   70
of God and by apostolical authority to him committed, doth renew the sentence of his
predecessors Pius Fifth and Gregory the Thirteenth touching the excommunication and
deposition of the said Elizabeth, and further anew doth excommunicate and deprive her
of all authority and princely dignity, and of all title and pretension to the said crown and
kingdoms of England and Ireland, declaring her to be illegitimate, and an unjust usurper   75
of the same, and absolving the people of those states and other persons whatsoever from
all obedience, oath, and other band of subjection unto her or to any other in her name.
And, further, doth straightly command, under the indignation of almighty God and pain
of excommunication, and the corporal punishment appointed by the laws, that none of
whatsoever condition or estate, after notice of these presents, presume to yield unto her   80
obedience, favour, or other succours, but that they and every of them concur by all means
possible to her chastisement. To the end that she which so many ways hath forsaken God
and his Church, being now destitute of worldly comfort and abandoned of all, may
acknowledge her offence, and humbly submit herself to the judgements of the Highest.

Be it therefore notified to the inhabitants of the said countries and to all other persons   85
that they observe diligently the premises, withdrawing all succour public and private
from the party pursued and her adherents after they shall have knowledge of this present.
And that forthwith they unite themselves to the Catholic army conducted by the most

61–2. **Mary, Queen of Scotland** Mary Stuart, Catholic claimant to the English throne whom Elizabeth held as prisoner
and executed in 1587 (see Fig. 6). **72. Pius Fifth** (*r.* 1566–72). **Gregory the Thirteenth** (*r.* 1572–85). **80. presents**
contents.

noble and victorious prince, Alexander Farnesius, Duke of Parma and Piacenza, in name
of His Majesty, with the forces that each one can procure to help and concur as is   90
aforesaid (if need shall be) to the deposition and chastisement of the said persons, and
restitution of the holy Catholic faith, signifying to those which shall do the contrary or
refuse to do this here commanded that they shall not escape condign punishment.

Moreover, be it known that the intention of His Holiness, of the King Catholic, and
the Duke His Highness in this enterprise is not to invade and conquer these kingdoms,   95
change laws, privileges, or customs, bereave of liberty or livelihood any man (other than
rebels and obstinate persons), or make mutation in anything, except such as by common
accord between His Holiness, His Catholic Majesty, and the states of the land shall be
thought necessary for the restitution and continuance of the Catholic religion and
punishment of the usurper and her adherents. Assuring all men that the controversies   100
which may arise by the deprivation of this woman or upon other cause, either between
particular parties or touching the succession to the Crown, or between the Church and
commonwealth, or in other wise whatsoever, shall be decided and determined wholly
according to justice and Christian equity without any injury or prejudice to any person.
And there shall not only due care be had to save from spoil the Catholics of these   105
countries, which have so long endured, but mercy also showed to such penitent persons
as submit themselves to the Captain General of this army. Yea, for so much as information is given that there be many which only of ignorance or fear be fallen from the faith
and yet, notwithstanding, are taken for heretics. Neither is it purposed presently to
punish any such persons but to support them with clemency till by conference with   110
learned men and better consideration, they may be informed of the truth, if they do not
show themselves obstinate.

To prevent also the shedding of Christian blood and spoil of the country which might
ensue by the resistance of some principal offenders, be it known by these presents that it
shall not only be lawful for any person public or private (over and besides those which   115
have undertaken the enterprise) to arrest, put in hold, and deliver up unto the Catholic
part the said usurper, or any of her complices, but also holden for very good service and
most highly rewarded, according to the quality and condition of the parties so delivered.
And in like manner all others which heretofore have assisted or hereafter shall help and
concur to the punishment of the offenders and to the establishment of Catholic religion 120
in these provinces shall receive that advancement of honour and estate which their good

---

89. Alexander Farnesius (1545–92), governor-general of the Netherlands under Philip II, leader of an invasion force with
the Spanish Armada in 1588. **92. signifying** giving notice. **94. King Catholic** Philip II of Spain (r. 1556–98). **113 ff.** In
response to this call for Catholic assistance in the coup Watson asserted the loyalty of Catholic nobles and commoners:
'For of the Lord Dacres and sundry others as well of the clergy as laity, it is well known they were ever most opposite to
those traitorous practices and therefore most mightily persecuted by Persons and his confederates; notwithstanding, they
still held and do hold out as loyal English subjects 'usque ad sanguinem' [ever unto blood], and as obedient Catholic
children 'usque ad aras' [ever unto altars, i.e. sacrificial altars], and as serviceable in heart to both God and man, pope and
prince, and to the Catholic Roman Church and the English commonwealth, as soul and body in one person can afford, or
faith and fealty, religion and loyalty, divine love and natural affection can expect or demand at their hands' (*Decacordon*,
1602, sig. R1ᵛ).

and faithful service to the commonwealth shall require; in which, respect shall be used to preserve the ancient and honourable families of the land, inasmuch as is possible. And, finally, by these presents free passage is granted to such as will resort to the Catholic camp to bring victuals, munition, or other necessaries, promising liberal payment for all such 125 things, as shall be received from them for service of the army. Exhorting withal and straightly commanding that all men according to their force and ability be ready and diligent to assist herein, to the end no occasion be given to use violence or to punish such persons as shall neglect this commandment.

Our said Holy Father, of his benignity and favour to this enterprise, out of the spiritual 130 treasures of the Church committed to his custody and dispensation, granteth most liberally to all such as assist, concur, or help in any wise to the deposition and punishment of the above named persons, and to the reformation of these two countries, plenary indulgence and pardon of all their sins, being duly penitent, contrite, and confessed, according to the law of God and usual custom of Christian people. 135
    Laus Deo.

see below. This is huge!

HENRY GARNET

Henry Garnet (1555–1606) entered the Society of Jesus in Rome (1575) and lectured in Hebrew, mathematics, and metaphysics. Named superior of the English Mission in 1586, he organized the clergy, administered sacraments, ran printing presses, wrote polemical and devotional works, and evaded authorities for nearly two decades. On 25 July 1605, in confession and under its seal, Garnet heard of a plot against parliament from the Jesuit Oswald Tesimond. Though Garnet unsuccessfully tried to prevent this and any Catholic attempt at violence, the discovery of the plot led to his arrest, torture, and execution for complicity, 3 May 1606.

In his writings Garnet addresses some major controversies of his time. He argues against church papistry in *An Apology against the Defence of Schism* (1593) and *A Treatise of Christian Renunciation* (1593) (see Langdale above). Adding an appendix to his translation of Peter Canisius's *The Sum of Christian Doctrine* (1592–6), excerpted below, he clearly explains the Church position on indulgences, much reviled, caricatured, and misunderstood. Only God can forgive sin, he affirms, and only the truly contrite and confessed can receive this forgiveness. Granting indulgences and pardons, the Church draws upon the treasury of

126. **withal** in addition. 130–1. **spiritual treasures** the spiritual 'treasury' of the Church, i.e. the merits of Christ and the saints. 134. **plenary indulgence** a remission of all the temporal punishment due to sin. 134–5. **penitent, contrite, and confessed** Prerequisites for any indulgence are the penitent's true contrition and confession. 136. *Laus Deo* Praise be to God.

merit created by Christ and the saints to remit merely the temporal punishment or penance remaining for those already contrite, confessed, and forgiven. Properly administered, indulgences reform the will of the sinner by encouraging almsgiving, strengthen the communion of saints (those in heaven, the faithful on earth, and the penitent in purgatory, who could receive pardons), and benefit the Church Militant on earth.

In the selection from his notorious *A Treatise of Equivocation* (*c*.1598), Garnet defends equivocation, the telling of partial truths, including the practice of *oratio mixta* and mental reservation, the denial or qualification of a spoken proposition by an unspoken one. The practice of equivocation has been roundly condemned as lying, drawing ridicule from all sides, including even Shakespeare, whose Porter in *Macbeth* probably alludes to Garnet when he welcomes to hell an equivocator, 'who committed treason enough for God's sake, yet could not equivocate to heaven' (2. 3. 9–11). But originally titling the work 'A Treatise against lying and fraudulent dissimulation', Garnet here addresses a very specific problem, namely, whether a Catholic under oath could dissimulate knowledge of a priest's whereabouts. Since revealing the priest would expose him to imprisonment, torture, and death, and deprive the flock of its clergy, Garnet follows Continental theologians such as Martin Azpilcueta to answer in the affirmative and justify the deception. That such deception needed justification at all (who would not lie to protect a human life he or she thought unjustly endangered?) testifies to the rigours of Jesuit formation by Church teaching against mendacity (especially Augustine's treatises), the daily Ignatian examen of conscience, and the study of casuistry (the application of general moral principles to specific cases). Fully expounding the doctrine of equivocation with reference to Scripture, the Church Fathers, and English law, Garnet warns that the practice needs to have 'certain fit limitations' and 'convenient moderation' without which 'neither God would be pleased, nor the link and conjunction of human societies, either civil or ecclesiastical and spiritual, could be duly maintained' (53–4).

Of Indulgences or Pardons, 1592–6

What is the ground and foundation of pardons?

First we must call to mind that which hath been showed above out of Scriptures and Fathers: that sins committed after baptism, although in respect of the fault and disgrace of God and guilt of everlasting pain and damnation they be fully remitted through the merits only of Christ's Passion in the sacrament of Penance, do, notwithstanding, leave

---

4. **merits…Passion** These merits constitute the primary satisfaction for sin, accomplished by Christ in his death and resurrection. The secondary or temporal satisfaction consists of penitential actions, 'those things which the priest when he gave absolution enjoined', or the 'worthy fruits of penance' performed 'of our own accord' (sig. O), or suffering in purgatory.

most ordinarily behind them (if the contrition be not the greater) a debt of temporal 5
punishment. And that by such temporal punishment satisfaction is to be made unto
God's justice either in this world by works of penance enjoined in the sacrament, or
voluntarily undertaken, or in the other life in the fire of purgatory.

Now, therefore, as almighty God hath left in his Church authority and jurisdiction to
bind such penitents as have recourse to the sacrament for help unto a convenient 10
satisfaction answerable to his divine justice and decree, so likewise, he being always
more prone to mercy than to justice and his grace superabounding where sin aboundeth
(Rom. 5: 10), it necessarily followeth that he hath given as great a power to his pastors in
the one as in the other. And, therefore, as they may impose so they may release penance;
as they are executioners of his justice to punish, so they are also dispensers of his mercy to 15
remit and pardon. Finally, as the power of his keys do extend to bind so they do also
extend to loose whatsoever is bound or loosed in heaven (Matt. 16: 19), which shall be
more largely showed hereafter.

What is an indulgence or pardon?

Then may we hereby plainly see what is an indulgence or pardon, which being well
understood and duly considered, we shall not need any long discourse for the proof and 20
defence of the same. An indulgence, therefore, or pardon is the remission of the temporal
punishment due unto sin already forgiven, granted by the pastors of the Church for just
and convenient cause unto him which is in God's grace and favour. Hence it followeth
that whosoever will be partaker of an indulgence granted, first he must be in grace, and
then perform that which is in the grant of the indulgence required, as fasting or prayer or 25
alms. And so he shall enjoy the fruit thereof.

How many things are necessary to obtain a pardon?

But if we will consider all the whole chain of things concurring and necessarily required
in this matter, we may the better conceive the malicious slanders and cavils of our
adversaries herein.

First, therefore, he that will gain an indulgence must be heartily sorry for his sins. 30
Secondly, he must have a full and resolute purpose to amend his life and never to fall into
any mortal sin. Thirdly, he must make a diligent search of his conscience, calling exactly
to mind (so far as the frailty of man's memory can reach) all the particulars of his
thoughts, words, and deeds offensive unto God. Fourthly, he must humbly and sincerely
lay them open before the priest who in God's stead is to judge thereof. Fifthly, he is to 35
accept that penance which is imposed upon him. And all this is so necessary for remission

---

10. **convenient** fitting. **16. power of his keys** Christ's donation of the keys, the power to bind and loose sin (Matt. 16: 19),
is the foundation for the Catholic doctrines concerning penance and pardons. **28. conceive** understand. **30–46.** The
six prerequisites for an indulgence or pardon articulate the three traditional parts of the sacrament of Penance: the first
two (sorrow and a purpose to amend) define Contrition; the second two (examination of conscience and revelation to
a priest), Confession; the third two (performing of penance enjoined by the priest or the grant of indulgence), Satisfaction.

of sins that if there want but one of them—either sorrow, or purpose, or due examination, or pure confession, or fulfilling the penance enjoined—or at the least in the three
last a full intent to execute them in due time, no man can obtain the grace of God, much
less such pardons as we speak of, which are not, nor can be, imparted but to those only   40
which are in God's blessed favour. Now if there happen any opportunity of indulgence or
remission of this penance enjoined or of that which by the ancient canons of the Church
or by God's secret and most just judgement should in rigour be enjoined (for ordinarily
the penance in our age enjoined in confession is not equal unto that which the ancient
canons of the Church and God's own determination hath allotted), then, sixthly, there is   45
required the fulfilling of that work unto which the indulgence is annexed.

The right and authority of God's Church in giving pardons
is largely proved

Christ hath left in his Church the keys of the kingdom of heaven (Matt. 16: 19), authority
to remit sins (John 20: 23), the word of reconcilement (2 Cor. 5: 19), dispensers of his
mysteries (1 Cor. 4: 1), feeders of his sheep (John 21: 15–17), stewards of his family to give
everyone meat in due season (Matt: 24: 45). But in every one of these is without any   50
limitation contained everything belonging to those several offices of government, feeding, and remitting, and consequently the remission of temporal chastisement and
correction. Most certainly, therefore, hath God left the same in his Church. But such
authority cannot be executed in the sacrament of Penance, which, as we supposed, is only
ordained to remit the offence of God, always in as much as it hath in itself, leaving a   55
temporal punishment. Therefore, it is to be executed out of the sacrament, which is the
very indulgence which we defend.

   Secondly, St Paul in the person of Christ and at the request of the Corinthians
pardoneth the incestuous person, remitting him (as Theodosius expoundeth and the
words do manifestly impart) part of his deserved penance (2 Cor. 2: 10). But what   60
authority Christ gave unto St Paul, the same hath he left in his Church until we meet all
into the unity of faith and knowledge of the son of God into a perfect man, that is, even
unto the world's end (Eph. 4: 13). Therefore doth there now remain in the pastors the
same authority. See here the very word of pardoning if the heretics have not left it out or
altered it in their Bible. Where also is to be noted that St Paul executed this lenity in the   65
person of Christ and so do our pastors, always using this phrase, 'Mercifully in our Lord
we release.' Of which our Saviour hath left us sundry examples in divers offenders,
particularly in the [. . .], whose temporal punishment he released.

   Thirdly, the first Council of Nicaea unto some which had fallen in persecution and
whom the Council calleth unworthy of mercy yet determineth to show humanity and,   70
imposing them penance, yet giveth liberty to the bishop upon the fruit of their

---

58. **person** Garnet writes in a note 'The heretics falsely translate in the "sight" of Christ'. (See e.g. the Geneva Bible, 1599).
The Greek *prosōpōi* admits both readings. **69. Council...Nicaea** a general Church council held in 325 to combat
Arianism, a heresy that denied the divinity of Christ.

repentance and demonstration of a sorrowful mind to deal yet more gently (Can. 11). But what is this but a pardon?

The like authority is given to bishops in the Anciran Council before the Nicaean Council concerning deacons, which in persecution for fear did sacrifice unto idols, and 75 towards others also, that they may *humanius agere*, 'deal more favourably' (Can. 2).

Divers canons (Can. 75, 76, 77, 79) we have also in the fourth Council of Carthage, where St Augustine was present, of the speedy or slow reconciling of penitents. Which is nothing else but to remit them their temporal punishment, which they at that time fulfilled, as now also sometimes is done, in the Church before reconciliation by the 80 sacrament of Penance.

Fourthly, St Cyprian in divers epistles (*Lib.* 1, *ep.* 3; *Lib.* 3, *ep.* 14, 18, etc., *de lapsis*) complaineth of those which over easily did give peace unto penitents. For so he calleth that which we now call pardons, and he writeth unto the holy confessors of Christ then in prisons to request them not to exceed herein. For those which for some faults were in the 85 number of penitents ordinarily had recourse unto those which for Christ's sake did suffer torments or imprisonment, and by their letters commended to their bishops were for their sakes released. Of which custom Tertullian also is a notable witness, exhorting the martyrs to peace amongst themselves because they obtained peace for many, which otherwise had not peace in the Church (*Lib. ad Mart.*). 90

Fifthly, the penitential canons of the Church were made and decreed by the Church and by the same they have been released, as we have showed. But to release the punishments of this world and to leave men with the debt of more bitter punishment in the other were not to provide carefully for the welfare of Christ's flock. Therefore, the continual practice of the Fathers hath been in remitting the penances enjoined to remit 95 all the desert of chastisement even in the other world.

Divers illations out of the premises concerning the nature of pardons

To conclude this whole treatise of indulgences we may gather out of that which is said, first, that although a pardon be principally and properly an absolution from the debt of punishment given by the virtue of the keys, yet is it also a kind of compensation withal. For the prelate granting a pardon doth so absolve the penitent that he maketh out of the 100 treasure of the Church an equal payment unto almighty God for the whole debt, paying in the head and in other members that which should without his sacred authority have been paid by the party himself. Or thus more plainly for the capacity of the simpler sort: a pardon is a merciful release in respect of the penitent but in respect of God's justice an equal payment, made by the merits of others, applied for a recompense of the penitent 105 his sins. And herein we may see how this absolution differeth from the sacramental

77. **Council of Carthage** This African synod met in 419. 82. **St Cyprian** 3rd-c. bishop and martyr. 88. **Tertullian** (*c*.155–220) early Christian moralist and theologian.

ILLATIONS conclusions. 99. **withal** in addition. 101. **treasure of the Church** the merits of Christ and the saints, conceived of as an infinite treasure which the Church can dispense on behalf of deserving penitents for the remission of the temporal punishment due to sin. 102. **in the head ... members** by the agency of Christ and the other members of his mystical body, i.e. the communion of saints.

absolution in penance. For there is applied only the merits of Christ and not of his saints, whereas their merits could not reach unto the taking away of the sins themselves, nor of the everlasting pain due unto the same. But here the merits also of the saints, in as much as they are satisfactorious, do take place. God having so disposed that according to the sweet government of his Church, his members do in the course of their justification and delivery from all punishments what they are able, they being able by the concourse of his spirit now dwelling within them to satisfy for temporal pain. Besides, in Penance the whole everlasting pain is taken away but here not always the whole temporal correction, but so much only as it pleaseth the giver, according to the proportion of the cause. Finally, the sacrament is an instrument of Christ's eternal priesthood, in which he himself remitteth sins by the instrumentary ministry of his priest. But in indulgences the prelate is properly the worker by his authority received from Christ.

Of pardons for the dead

Finally, we hence infer that pardons may be granted unto the dead who in the unity of Christ's body have departed this life; and that in as infallible a manner (if the cause be sufficient) as unto those which are alive, yet not by way of absolution but by way of suffrage, which we will forthwith expound. For it is to be understood that the souls departed out of this world and in purgatory suffering the chastisement of God may, as above hath been showed out of St Augustine, be holpen by those which are alive three ways: first, by the holy sacrifice of the mass, which is undoubtedly propitiatory for the quick and the dead; secondly, by the prayers of the Church and of other devout Christians; thirdly, by alms or any other penal work done for them.

A Treatise of Equivocation, c.1598

And we may say with the logicians that there be four kinds of propositions. The first is a mental position, only conceived in the mind, and not uttered by any exterior signification, as when I think with myself these words, 'God is not unjust.' The second is a vocal proposition, as when I utter those words with my mouth. The third is a written proposition, as if I should set the same down in writing. The last of all is a mixed proposition, when we mingle some of these positions (or parts of them) together, as in our purpose, when being demanded whether John at Style be in such a place, I, knowing that he is there indeed, do say nevertheless 'I know not'—reserving or understanding within myself these other words 'to th' end for to tell you.' Here is a mixed proposition containing all this, 'I know not to th' end for to tell you.' And yet part of it is expressed, part reserved in the mind.

110. **satisfactorious** able to serve for satisfaction of temporal punishment. 115. **giver** i.e. priest (who assigns penance). 122. **suffrage** intercessory prayers, especially for the departed. 124. **holpen** helped. 126. **quick** living.

TREATISE OF EQUIVOCATION 9. **mixed proposition** Garnet's version of *oratio mixta* ('mixed discourse'), discourse containing a mix of verbal, written, and mental propositions.

Now unto all these propositions it is common that then they are true when they are conformable to the thing itself, that is, when they so affirm or deny as the matter itself in very deed doth stand. Whereof we infer that this last sort of proposition, which partly consisteth in voice and partly is reserved in the mind, is then to be adjudged true, not when that part only which is expressed or the other only which is reserved is true, but 15 when both together do contain a truth. For as it were a perverse thing in that vocal proposition, 'God is not unjust', to say that position is false because if we leave out the last word the other three contain a manifest heresy (as if we affirmed God were not at all), the truth of every vocal proposition being to be measured not according to some parts but according to all together; even so that other proposition of which we spake, being a 20 mixed proposition, is not to be examined according to the variety of the part expressed alone, but according to the part reserved also, they both together compounding one entire proposition.

Herein, therefore, consisteth the difficulty and this will we endeavour to prove: that whosoever frameth a true position in his mind and uttereth some part thereof in words, 25 which of themselves being taken several from the other part reserved, were false, does not say false or lie before God, howsoever he may be thought to lie before men or otherwise commit therein some other sin. For yet we will not clear this party of sin herein, whereof we will speak hereafter, but only at this present we defend him not to have lied.

JUAN DE MARIANA

A Spanish Jesuit, Juan de Mariana (1536–1624) taught theology in Rome and Paris and wrote an influential history of Spain, *Historiae de rebus Hispaniae* (1592). Though he frequently clashed with civil and ecclesiastical authorities, Spanish royalty supported the publication of Mariana's most controversial work, *De Rege et Regis Institutione* (Toledo, 1599), which contained advice on raising a true Christian prince and, notoriously, some chapters defending tyrannicide. These chapters caused concern among Jesuit authorities and, after the assassination of Henri IV (1610), an outcry of condemnation in France: by government order the public executioner burned the book. In the selection below Mariana argues that kings who act as tyrants forfeit their right to rule and that anyone may depose or kill them if there is no other remedy and if the will of the people so mandate. Echoing resistance arguments articulated by Protestants such as the Scottish George Buchanan and the French monarchomachs (François Hotman, Theodore Beza, Philippe du Plessis-Mornay), Mariana fearlessly pushes the argument to its logical extreme and serves it up with rhetorical flair.

On the King and the Education of the King, 1599

[Whether it is right to destroy a tyrant]

These are the defences of each side, and after they have been carefully considered, it will not be difficult to set forth what must be decided about the proposed question. For certainly I see that the philosophers and theologians agree in this matter, that the prince who has taken possession of a republic by force and arms and, moreover, with no right and no public consent of the citizens can be killed by anyone and be deprived of his 5 life and dominion. Because he is a public enemy and oppresses his country with all evils, and because he truly and properly puts on the name and nature of a tyrant, he may be removed by any method and he may put off his power as violently as he took possession of it. (With this merit, then, Ehud, having insinuated himself into the graces of Eglon, King of the Moabites, slew him with a dagger plunged into the stomach; he 10 snatched his people from the hard servitude which had oppressed them for eighteen years.)

For if the prince holds power by the consent of the people or by hereditary right, his vices and lusts must be borne until he neglects those laws of honour and virtue by which he is bound. For princes must not be changed easily lest the republic 15 fall into greater evils and serious disturbances arise, as was set down in the beginning of this disputation. But if, in truth, he destroys the republic, considers public and private fortunes as his own booty, holds public laws and sacred religion in contempt, and if he makes a virtue out of pride, brazenness, and impiety against heaven—this cannot be dissembled. One must consider carefully, however, what method of reject- 20 ing his prince should be taken, lest evil be piled upon evil and crime be avenged with crime.

And the readiest and safest way is to debate what must be decided by common consent, if the opportunity for a public meeting may be given, and to ratify and validate what has been decided by the common opinion. In which matter one may 25 proceed by these steps: first, the prince will have to be warned and summoned back to sanity; if he regulates his conduct, makes satisfaction to the republic, and corrects the faults of his past life, the process must be halted, I think, and no harsher remedies attempted. If he spits out the medicine, however, and no hope of sanity is left, it will be permissible for the republic by a declared sentence first to reject his sovereignty. 30 And since war necessarily will be provoked, it will then be permissible to make plans for driving him out, to bring forth arms, to raise money from the people for the

---

4. **by force and arms** Mariana describes the tyrant in entrance (*ex defectu tituli*, 'from defect of title'), the ruler who unlawfully seizes power. Below (17–20) he will describe the tyrant in practice (*ex parte exercitii*, 'from the part of practice'), the ruler who abuses his power. 9. **Ehud** For the Old Testament story of Ehud, Eglon, and the freeing of the Israelites, see Judges 3: 12–4: 1.

costs of war, and if the matter requires and if the republic cannot be protected otherwise, by its same right of defence and in truth by its better and proper authority, to declare the prince a public enemy and to slay him with a sword. Let there be the same opportunity for any private citizen whatsoever who, with all hope of impunity tossed aside and his own safety ignored, wishes to step forward in the attempt to help the republic.

You may ask what must be done if the opportunity to hold a public meeting will have been taken away, as often can happen. The same, certainly, in my opinion, will be the judgement when the republic is oppressed by the tyranny of a prince, when the capacity for public meeting has been taken away from the citizens, when the will is not lacking to destroy the tyranny, to avenge manifest and intolerable crimes of the prince, and to crush his destructive efforts, so that if the sacred fatherland should fall into ruins and attract public enemies into the province, I shall think that the man who, heeding the people's prayers, tries to kill the tyrant, has in no way acted as an enemy. And this is sufficiently confirmed by those arguments which are placed against the tyrant later in this disputation.

So the question of fact in this controversy is, 'Who is properly considered to be a tyrant?' The question of law is clear, that it will be right to kill a tyrant. There is no danger that many by this example will rage against the lives of princes as though they were tyrants; for we place the matter in the private will neither of any one citizen, nor of many, unless the public voice of the people is present, and serious and learned men are brought together in council. Things would turn out very well in human affairs if many men of strong heart were found for the liberty of their country to be contemptuous of life and health; but the contrary desire for safety often holds back many in great endeavours. So, from such a great number of tyrants as have existed in ancient times, it is possible to reckon that only a few perished by the sword of their own people. In Spain scarcely one or two, although one should attribute this to the loyalty of the subjects and the clemency of princes who received sovereignty with the best right and exercised it modestly and humanely. Nevertheless, it is a salutary reflection that it may be impressed upon princes, if they oppress the republic and are intolerable because of their vices and foulness, that they live in such a condition that they may be killed, not only by right but also with praise and glory. Perhaps this fear will hinder someone, lest he allow himself to be deeply corrupted by vices and praises; it will put reins on madness. This is the main point, that it be impressed upon the prince that the authority of the whole republic is greater than that of one man, and that he not believe the worst men affirming something different in their desire to please him, which is a great wickedness.

There was not sufficient cause for David to kill King Saul, it used to be objected, since David was able to reach safety by flight. If he, using this logic to save himself, were to slay

---

69 ff. The story of King Saul and David appears in 1 Kings 16–2 Kings 1.

a king especially established by God, it would have been impiety, not love of the republic. For Saul was not so depraved in morals that he was oppressing his subjects in tyranny, that he was overturning divine and human laws, that he was treating the citizens as spoil. The rights of rule certainly were transferred to David so that he might succeed the dead king, not, however, so that he might seize the life and power from the living one. Moreover, Augustine (*Contra Adimantum*, ch. 17) says this, namely that David did not wish to kill Saul, but that it would have been permissible. It is not necessary to go on about the Roman emperors: by the blood and suffering of the pious the foundations of the Church's greatness were laid out precisely to the very ends of the earth. And it was the greater miracle that the oppressed Church was growing and, diminished in number, was gaining greater increments day by day. And in truth, the Church was not free according to its doctrines in that time, nor even in this time, to do all the things which had been granted to it by right and laws. Thus, the famous historian Sozomen (Book 6, chapter 2) says that if a soldier happened to have killed the Emperor Julian, since at that time they were actually accusing him specifically, he would have done so by right and with honour.

Finally, we think that upheavals in the republic must be avoided. Care must be taken lest joy from the expulsion of tyrants run wild in a brief moment and turn out to be empty; and all remedies for restoring a prince to health must be tried before it comes to this last and most serious measure. But if it is the case that every hope has been taken away and the public safety and the holiness of religions are called into danger, who will be so poor in counsel as not to avow that it is allowable to strike at the tyrant by right, by law, and by arms? One, perhaps, would move to this extreme position of denial because the following proposal was rejected by the Fathers at the Council of Constance in the 15th session, 'A tyrant can and ought to be killed by any subject, not only by open force but also through plotting and deceit.' But, in truth, I do not find that conciliar decree approved by the Roman Pope Martin V, nor by Pope Eugene or his successors, by whose consent the holiness of ecclesiastical councils stands.

[. . .]

It is pleasing to conclude this disputation with the words of the Tribune Flavius, who, convicted of conspiracy against Domitius Nero, in the midst of the questions about why he had acted oblivious to his oath of allegiance: 'I hated you,' he said, 'but no soldier was more faithful to you while you deserved to be loved; I began to hate you after you became the murderer of your own mother and wife, a charioteer and actor, and an arsonist.' A spirit soldierly and brave, according to Tacitus, Book 15.

75

80

85

90

95

100

77. it . . . permissible not merely for self-preservation, that is, but under certain circumstances. 83. Sozomen Christian lawyer in Constantinople who compiled a church history for the period 324–439. 84. Julian Julian the Apostate was a Roman emperor (361–3) and an enemy of Christianity. 93. Council of Constance the sixteenth ecumenical council of the Church (1414–18), which settled rival claims to the papacy, combated heresy, and initiated some reforms. 95. that conciliar decree i.e. the rejection of the proposition above, namely, that a subject can kill a tyrant. 99. Domitius Nero fifth Roman emperor (54–68), infamous for debauchery and the persecution of Christians.

[Whether it is licit to kill a tyrant with poison]

A wicked mind has unfathomable internal torments and the conscience of a tyrant is his own executioner. So even if no external adversary approaches, depravity of life and morals makes every joy and liberty of life bitter. For what condition of life, and how miserable, is it to singe off the beard and hair with burning coals for fear of the barber, as Dionysius the Tyrant used to do? What pleasure was there to him who hid himself in the citadel like a snake in the time of quiet and sleep, as Clearchus, the Pontic tyrant, was accustomed to do? What fruit of rule enjoyed Argive Aristodemus, who used to conceal himself in a garret by means of a hanging door with a ladder added and removed? Or could there be greater unhappiness than to trust no one, not even friends and family? To quake at any noise and shadow as if rebellion had broken out and the spirits of all were enraged against him? He clearly lives a miserable life whose life is such that the one who slays him will have great gratitude and praise.

It is a glorious thing to exterminate all of this pestilent and deadly species from the human community. For in truth certain limbs are cut off if they are rotten lest they infect the rest of the body; so the monstrosity of a beast in this likeness of a man ought to be removed from the republic as from a body and cut out with a blade. Certainly the tyrant who spreads terror ought to fear; but the terror he arouses is not greater than the fear he endures. There is not so much protection in military strength, arms, and troops as there is danger in the people's hatred, whence destruction threatens. All orders busy themselves to remove a monster conspicuous for his abominations of villainy and his sordid deeds of cowardice. After hatreds have grown daily, either insurrection breaks out and there is a rush to open force when the people have taken up arms (which admirable spirit of nature we ought to restore to our country, by which means not a few tyrants have perished by open force!), or else with greater caution, by fraud and plotting, tyrants perish by one or a few individuals gathering secretly and working to regain safety for the republic at their own peril. But if they succeed, they are regarded in every station of life as great heroes; if it should fall out otherwise, they fall as sacrifices pleasing to heaven and pleasing to men, famous to all posterity for their noble attempt.

105

110

115

120

125

130

ROBERT BELLARMINE

Italian cardinal and Doctor of the Church, Robert Bellarmine (1542–1621) taught theology at Louvain and Rome, wrote a Hebrew grammar and catechisms, and emerged as the leading Catholic voice against Protestants with his *Disputationes de Controversiis* (1586–93).

Whether... poison Mariana will answer the title question in the negative, arguing, remarkably, that such a method of assassination puts the victim's soul at risk, implicating him in a kind of suicide. **108. Dionysius the Tyrant** ruthless tyrant of Syracuse (r. 405–367 BC). **109. Clearchus** severe Spartan governor of Byzantium (r. 411–401 BC). **110. Aristodemus** tyrant of Cumae, early 6th century BC.

He defended the papacy against the attacks of Martin Luther, John Bale, and the many Protestants who considered the pope to be the Antichrist. Bellarmine clashed famously, moreover, with William Barclay, a Scottish Catholic jurist, on the nature and limits of papal power. Barclay's *De potestate papae* (1609) affirmed the temporal sovereignty of kings, characterized papal intervention as a cause of war, schism, and ruin to the Church, and argued prophetically for the limitation of papal authority and the separation of church and state. Contrarily, Bellarmine asserted that the pope had incontestable and supreme superiority in spiritual matters and that this superiority conferred an 'indirect' power in temporal matters, in so far as they were instrumental to the spiritual good, *in ordine ad bonum spirituale* (*Disputationes*, Cologne, 1628: 234). In the treatise excerpted below, *Tractatus de potestate summi pontificis in rebus temporalibus adversus Gulielmum Barclaeum* (1610), Bellarmine inserts the following imaginary dialogue between the Pope and the People to explicate regnant Catholic doctrine on the origins and prerogatives of papal power.

On the Authority of the Pope against William Barclay, 1610

PEOPLE Holy Father, you are in no way superior to our king in temporal matters, and, therefore, you are not able to interfere with the temporal submission which we offer to him.

POPE When your eternal salvation is brought into danger because of the temporal submission which you offer to the king, then I am in every way superior to your   5 king in temporal matters; for my duty is to direct him as well as you to eternal life and to remove from your path all obstacles which impede this journey.

PEOPLE Why do you prohibit us to do that which God commands us to do?

POPE Not so; I do not prohibit this, but, contrarily, prohibit you from doing what God forbids you to do. I am made your shepherd by Christ, who is lord of the flock. You,   10 the people, are little sheep, your kings are rams. Therefore, while your kings continue to be rams, I allow them to rule and lead you; but if they turn into wolves, will it be right to allow the sheep of my Lord to be led by wolves? Thus, rightly I forbid you to follow those, for even God forbids this, since there is too great a danger when little sheep are ruled by wolves.   15

14. **even God forbids** A crucial point of disagreement with Barclay, who bases his argument on the contention that God grants power to kings and thus requires obedience from subjects: 'The Scripture itself witnesseth that kings and emperors receive power from God, whose vicegerents they are therein, as said Lyranus upon that of Wisdom 6: [4]: "Power is given to you from the Lord and virtue from the Highest, who will inquire into your works." Why then should not a man use a dilemma out of Bellarmine against Bellarmine? The pope can one way or other, that is, directly or indirectly, take away kingdoms and empires from kings and emperors and give them to others or he cannot. If he can, he is in some manner greater than God because he takes away that which God hath given' (*Of the Authority of the Pope*, London, 1611, sig. E3).

PEOPLE And this is because it is your business to interpret the will of God as expressed in divine law and the Scriptures?

POPE You have spoken truly.

PEOPLE But that interpretation, however, must not be applied which completely nullifies the law, destroying altogether and dissolving its command. 20

POPE What law of God have we, either my predecessors or I, ever destroyed or dissolved with our interpretation?

PEOPLE If something is doubtful or obscure in divine law, then to the seat of Peter, that is, to the seat which you now hold, we flee for refuge, ready to accept the truth of your interpretation; that which is clear and plain in itself, however, needs no light of 25 interpretation.

POPE So what, then?

PEOPLE Since Our Lord and Saviour bids us to render unto Caesar the things which are Caesar's and to God those things which are God's [Matt. 22: 21; Mark 12: 17; Luke 20: 25], and, thereafter, through the apostle to be subject to princes and earthly powers and 30 to obey the law [Rom. 13: 1], then it is your duty to declare to us which things are Caesar's, that is, which things we owe to our king, and which things are God's, so that we may render to each his own. And in this distinction we shall gladly listen to your voice; but when you say do not render anything unto Caesar, or to your prince, you contradict Christ and, therefore, we do not listen to your voice. 35

POPE When Our Lord said, 'Render unto Caesar the things which are Caesar's', He commanded that a tax be given to him who then was ruling and who was not forcing the Jews to idolatry; nor at this point had the king been deposed by any legitimate authority. Which same thing many years before through the prophet Jeremiah God ordered to be done to Nebuchadnezzar, king of Babylon, for the same reason [Jer. 27: 40 6–8]; but in the time of the Machabees, when King Antiochus was turning the people from faith and divine religion, God did not command that they continue to have him as a king, but inspired Matthias and his sons, very powerful and holy men, to gather an army and wage war against Antiochus as against an enemy and liberate the people [1 Mach. 2]. Accordingly, therefore, will you, Christian people, render due obedience to 45 a legitimate king who does not turn you from the law of God and the Catholic religion (and who, on account of this, is loved as a son by me, the vicar of Christ) in those things he orders that are not contrary to the law of God and the Catholic faith. But you will not accept as a king one who, whether by threats, or flatteries, or another method, tries to turn you from the path that leads to life, one who has by my sentence 50 been ejected from the flock of the faithful and deprived of his royal authority. But you will show due civil obedience to the other king who will have legitimately succeeded to

23. **seat of Peter** the *sancta sedes*, or 'holy chair' of Peter, i.e. the position as God-appointed, supreme ruler of the church.
41. **time . . . Machabees** 175–135 BC, when the Machabees family led the Jewish people's struggle for liberty; Catholics accept two of the Machabees books as canonical; Protestants reject all four.

his place. Furthermore, you will render unto God which things are God's when you worship God in faith, hope, and charity, and you do not, because of the fear or love of any man, allow yourself to be separated from the fear and love of God. And so never will you hear me say, 'Don't render anything to Caesar or to your prince'; but you will hear me say, 'Don't be misled so that you consider as Caesar and your prince a man who, in truth, has ceased to be Caesar and prince.' 55

PEOPLE We confess, certainly, and profess that there is a place in the observance of divine law for the exposition and interpretation of Your Holiness; but we declare that what makes natural and divine law a mockery and something wholly condemned is not to be admitted, just as we shall not stray from our starting point: we are commanded to obey princes and earthly powers. And we gladly embrace as obedient sons your explications and restrictions in the observance of this mandate, which do not in any way extinguish the mandate itself; just as when you say that there arises no obligation to obey kings except in those matters which fall under their temporal jurisdiction, and that all spiritual matters must be reserved for the vicar of Christ and the Church. Likewise, when you advise that a king is not to be obeyed in that command which he orders contrary to divine or natural law, or which is otherwise contrary to good morals. But when simply and absolutely you teach that we should not obey our legitimate prince, or his counsels, commands, and laws in any fashion, we are not able to obey your teaching, because this is not to interpret the mandates of God, which is conceded to be proper to Your Holiness, but wholly to reject and to abrogate them, which in no way can you do. 60 65 70

POPE In excessive speaking, error will not be absent; for you seem to have come from the school of some Barclay so long as you multiply so many words without reason. You sin more gravely, however, when you presume to teach your teacher and give law to your legislator; but you very seriously miss the point and err when you lay it to the charge of the vicar of Christ that he makes natural and divine law into a mockery and that he wishes to reject and abrogate God's command concerning the obedience owed to princes. For never did I or my predecessors, simply and absolutely (as you say), teach that a legitimate prince, and his counsels, mandates, and laws, should in any way be disobeyed. These are the calumnies and deceits of your Doctor Barclay. For what we say and teach is this, that to a prince who has been excommunicated and deposed by the Church with its public authority (who, consequently, has ceased to be a legitimate prince) no obedience thereafter is owed. This, in truth, conflicts with no divine mandate for the divine mandate does not hold that to him who ceases to be a legitimate prince obedience should be rendered. But attend and consider carefully whether you owe it to your father, the vicar of Christ, and your mother, the Church, to have greater faith in them or in one false brother who misleads you and makes it that you, contrary to the command of God, do not obey your father and mother, so long as you wish to have zeal for royal obedience without understanding. 75 80 85 90

PEOPLE When Christ handed over to Peter the keys to the heavenly kingdom [Matt. 16: 18–19], He did not give to him the power to make a sin not a sin.

POPE You know not what you say, since, in a good sense, Christ gave to Peter the power   95
of making a sin not a sin, and something not a sin a sin. For it is a sin to enter into matrimony in a prohibited state, not to fast during Lent, to work slavishly on a feast day, and, nevertheless, all these things and many more of this kind by Peter's dispensation and by the authority of the keys given to him cease to be sins; on the contrary, indeed, Peter can add a new grade of consanguinity and relation, a new fast   100
day, a new feast day, and from these actions sins will be made if anyone in that added grade should contract a marriage, or not fast, or abstain from servile labour on the added days—which things, nevertheless, before this had not been sins. So, therefore, to obey such a king, or even to disobey him, would be a sin and, nevertheless, if by the keys of Peter a king like that should be declared a heretic, excommunicated, and   105
deposed, then it will not be a sin to disobey him. It is true, however, that the keys of Peter do not extend to this power, that the high pope can declare a sin not to be a sin or something not a sin to be a sin; for that would be to call evil good and good evil, which practice is very far (and always was and always will be) from the teaching of that man who presides over the Church, which is the pillar and prop of truth.   110

PEOPLE We, then, shall follow the common doctrine of the canonists in this part, who hold that a papal mandate must not be obeyed either if it is unjust or if from it many evils should arise, being either an actual inducement for others to sin in the future or a disturbance to the condition of the Church and the republic; as, for example, if the pope should order something for the religious which goes against the substance of   115
their order, that is, which contradicts the rule professed by them [cites references]. How much less, therefore, should the subjects of kings listen to the pope if he tries to draw them from the obedience owed to their king by natural and divine law and sanctified by the strictest oath?

POPE What is the common judgement not only of canonists, but also of theologians,   120
and those experienced in civil law, nay, and even of the sacred councils themselves, you will be able to learn from the prolegomena of this book, where it is affirmed by common consent that a king may lawfully be excommunicated and deposed for just cause by the high pope, and his subjects freed from the bond of all obedience and fidelity. And it is not believable that all the canonists disagree with each other. When,   125
therefore, some canonists say that the pope is not to be obeyed when his command is unjust, or the cause of scandals or perturbation, first, they do not speak of the pope teaching the universal Church, *ex cathedra*; furthermore, they do not speak absolutely

---

93. **the keys** Christ's handing of the 'keys' to Peter stood for Catholics as the establishment of the papacy as the supreme office of the Church with the authority to forgive or retain sins. 100. **grade of consanguinity** category of blood-relationship (thus affecting eligibilities for marriage). 104. **obey... disobey** In this somewhat muddled passage Bellarmine argues that to obey or disobey a king *qua* king after he has been declared excommunicate by the pope is wrong because both obedience and disobedience assume sovereignty in the deposed. 111. **canonists** experts in ecclesiastical law. 128. *ex cathedra* 'from the chair' of Peter, i.e. with the supreme authority of the papal office. Pronouncements on faith and morals

but conditionally, that is, if it should be the case, if by chance it should happen, that the pope were to command some particular man to do something contrary to the law 130 of God. For at that point the teaching of St Peter is generally known (Acts 5: 29): 'It is more necessary to obey God than men.' But when my predecessor popes, as Gregory VII, Innocent IV, and others wished to excommunicate and depose great princes and to liberate their subjects from obedience to them, they did so *ex cathedra*, and in council, with public ceremony, acting from the authority of God, and of the holy 135 apostles Peter and Paul, communicated from heaven to them. Therefore, he who says it is not necessary to obey the vicar of Christ when he teaches in this way condemns the universal Church, and ought to be called not a canonist but a corrupter of canon law; and although we think that no good canonist has fallen into this error, nevertheless, if one were to fall so, the faithful and prudent Christian would surely be able to place the 140 makers of canon law before one or another canonist. What you say, however—that by divine and natural law obedience is owed to kings—is true regarding legitimate kings and those not yet deposed by the sentence of a judge, and since from these so deposed and not from those others, do we draw you back from obedience, consequently, either you impute to us something false or complain about us in vain. 145

JANE OWEN

Jane Owen of Oxfordshire (d. *c*.1625) published posthumously *An Antidote against Purgatory* (1634), which includes partial translation of Cardinal Bellarmine's *De gemitu columbae* (1617). The Council of Trent (Session 25, 1563) defined purgatory as the place or state of purgation where souls after death render the temporal satisfaction due to sin. The Council also affirmed that the living too can make purgatorial satisfaction for their sins or the sins of others through good works. Dante's *Commedia* bequeathed to the world the fullest, most evocative depiction of purgatory (see Fig. 5). Protestants uniformly and vehemently rejected the doctrine of purgatory. The controversies in England started with Simon Fish's *Supplication for the Beggars* (1529), which implored the king to stop the corrupt traffic in pardons and indulgences that originated in the doctrine of purgatory. Representing 'lepers, and other sore people, needy, impotent, blind, and lame, and sick,

---

ex cathedra are held to be infallible. **132–3. Gregory VII, Innocent IV** Pope Gregory VII (d. 1085) excommunicated Henry IV of Germany in 1076 and released subjects from obedience to him; Innocent IV (d. 1254) did likewise to Frederick II of Germany in 1245. **134. to liberate...subjects** Barclay took a very different view of the historical effects of excommunication: 'Did not all these princes not only not acknowledge but also condemn and laugh to scorn that same papal imperiousness, carried beyond the bounds of a spiritual jurisdiction, as mere arrogation and an usurped domination? For the two last popes [Clement VII and Pius V], I dare be bold to affirm upon a clear ground (for the matter is known to all the world) that they were the cause that religion was lost in England for that they took upon them to usurp and practise so odious and so large a jurisdiction over the prince and people of that kingdom' (sig. Y2ᵛ).

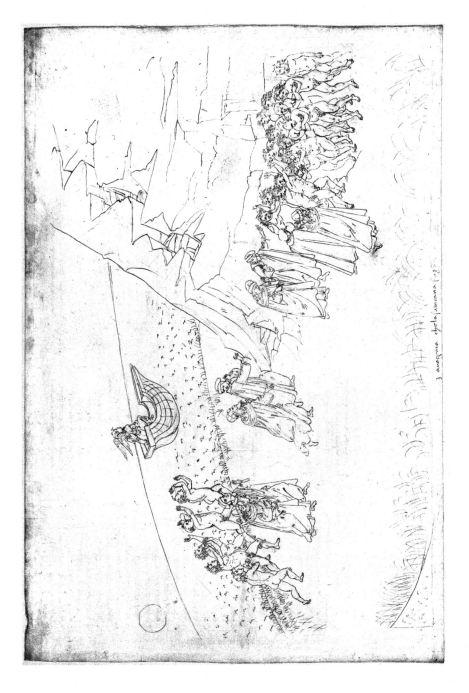

5. Sandro Botticelli (1444–1510), 'Dante's Purgatorio III: The Excommunicated', Staatliche Museen zu Berlin. Here Dante and Vergil approach the mountain of Purgatory and confront the excommunicated outside, apart from the faithful in death as in life; they wait for *l'etterno amore* (134, the eternal love) and *buon prieghi* (141, 'good prayers' from the living) to return them to the body of Christ.

that live only by alms', Fish cited learned men who thought purgatory 'a thing invented by the covetousness of the spirituality only to translate all kingdoms from other princes unto them' (fos. 1ʳ, 6).

Owen uses the doctrine of purgatory to commend the performance of good works and almsgiving as the 'antidote', the chief remedy for pain in the afterlife, vividly described. Among such good works Owen suggests specifically the financing of English Catholics abroad at schools and religious institutions, the paying of recusancy fines, and the relief of imprisoned Catholics at home. The selections below end with the fantastic lament of a reader who, facing death, repents his misspent life and inattention to such worthy books as *An Antidote against Purgatory.*

An Antidote against Purgatory, 1634

On the pains of purgatory

Three things do concur as well to grief or pain as to joy, to wit, 'potentia' [power], 'obiectum' [object], and 'coniunctio unius cum altero' [union of one with the other], as St Thomas (*ST* II q. 31 a. 5) saith: an intelligent or at least a sentient power or faculty, a convenient object to that power, and an union or conjunction of the object with the power.　　　　　　　　　　　　　　　　　　　　　　　　　　　　　　　　　　　　5

Now as concerning the power, doubtlessly 'potentia rationalis', (a rational power or faculty), is more capable of pain or grief than 'potentia animalis' (a sensible faculty or function). For if we respect apprehension or knowing, the understanding in a rational soul is, as it were, a main fountain, the sense but a small river. So far as concerneth the appetite or desire, the will of a rational soul is a main fountain also; the appetite, being　10 inferior to it, is but like a small river. Seeing, therefore, the naked soul itself is immediately tormented, the grief thereof ought to be the greatest in respect of the patient. For there in this life not so much the soul as the body is tormented, and by reason of the pains of the body some grief and dolour passeth into the soul.

Now concerning the object: the fire of purgatory must be far more violent, horrible,　15 and intense than the fire in this world is, seeing that fire is created and instituted as an instrument of God's justice, who would show his power in the creation of it.

Lastly, touching the conjunction of the power with the object: the conjunction of the soul with the fire in purgatory shall be most strait and, as it were, intrinsical. For here in this world, where all things are corporal and bodily, there is no conjunction made but　20 only by the touch of the extremities or utmost parts of the bodies, and the superficies of

---

6–7. Aristotle (*De anima*), and others after including Aquinas, distinguished between the rational power of the soul (capable of intellectual activity) and the animal power (dependent on the senses). **8. respect** consider. **14. dolour** suffering. **19. strait** severe. **instrinsical** pervasive. **21. superficies** outer surfaces.

things; whereas in purgatory the torments and fire thereof shall penetrate most inwardly the very soul itself.

How to avoid or mitigate the pains of purgatory

Now, to begin with the testimonies of God's Holy Writ, we first read thus therein: 'Eleemosyna ab omni peccato & a morte liberat, & non patitur animam ire in tenebras' 25 (Tob. 4: 11, Alms-deeds free a man from sin and death, and suffer not the soul to descend into darkness). And in another place we read, 'Sicut aqua extinguit ignem, ita Eleemosyna extinguit peccatum' (Ecclus. 3: 33. As water doth extinguish the fire, so do alms-deeds extinguish sins). Yea, alms-deeds and good works are so powerful as that our Saviour, after he had charged the Pharisees with divers great sins, yet thus concludeth, 30 'Verum tamen date Eleemosynas, & ecce omnia munda sunt vobis' (Luke 11: 41, But, notwithstanding, do you give alms, and behold, all things are clean unto you).

And, which is more, God's holy word extendeth the virtue of alms-deeds even to the gentiles and heathens, for thus we find it said to Nebuchadnezzar, who was a pagan, 'Hear my counsel, O King, and redeem thy sins with alms and thy iniquities with works 35 of mercy' (Dan. 4: 24).

Now if good works of charity and alms-deeds performed even by heathens and wicked livers be so much respected by God, much more, then, good works of Christians and good livers are accepted of God, not only for the preventing the pains of eternal damnation, but also, which is less, of the temporal pains of purgatory. 40 [. . .]

Another point wherein we may well follow the steps of our adversaries is this: the Protestant gentlemen, though of very great worth and rank, do often send their younger sons to our English universities, providing that they may become fellows of the houses; whose *terminus ad quem*, as I may say, is finally to become ministers, and thereby to be promoted to great and rich ecclesiastical livings, in which store and abundance England 45 exceedeth all nations in Christendom. Now to be emulous of our adversaries' proceeding herein: if Catholic parents would seriously ponder this point, no doubt they would be more careful and willing to send over their younger sons to Catholic colleges beyond the seas than they are, not to become scholars only thereby to be advanced to spiritual livings (an over unworthy allective), but to become priests, that through shedding of their blood 50 even after an apostolical manner, they may labour to reduce their own country to its former ancient Catholic and Roman faith.
[. . .]

And here by digression I will touch a little upon the daughters of Catholic gentlemen. Here in England divers of them, as well as the daughters of Protestants, take, through a blind affection often cast upon some base man or other, a most unworthy course to the 55 unutterable grief of their parents and overthrow of their temporal state. And if they be

---

26. Alms-deeds acts of charity, especially to the poor. This section ratifies the contested Catholic doctrine of good works.
44. *terminus ad quem* purpose, object. **50. allective** inducement. **51. reduce** lead back.

placed in marriage with their parents' consent answerably to their degree, yet if either the husbands prove unkind or in course of life vicious, or their children untoward and licentious, what a vexation is it then to the parents? And how do they languishingly spend their days in inconsolable sighs and sorrow?   60

But now if the said daughters, being in their virginal, tender, and innocent age, be brought up in places of religion, and that through the special grace of God and means of their daily education they proceed and become religious women in the Church of God, how ineffable a comfort may this be to their Catholic parents? Since they then by these means, freeing themselves from all illaqueations and worldly entanglements, shall bestow   65 the greatest part both of day and night in performing and singing hymns of praises to His Divine Majesty for the good of themselves and their friends.

A reader faces death and disputes with his soul

'True it is, I thank God of his most infinite and boundless mercy, that as a straying sheep I am at length brought into Christ's sheepfold, and I hope to die through the benefit of our Saviour's passion and of the holy sacraments his servant and in state of grace, and finally   70 to enjoy the interminable joys of heaven. But, alas, though the guilt of eternal damnation, incurred by my long former schismatical life and by my many other infinite sins, as I hope, through God's infinite mercy be remitted, yet temporal punishment due for all my former said sins in most inexplicable torments of purgatory doth expect me.

'My poor soul must continue in those burning flames (how many years, His Divine   75 Majesty only knoweth) for the expiating of my said sins before I can arrive to heaven. When I was in health, enjoying my temporal state in all fullness, how easily with a voluntary relinquishing of a reasonable part thereof to pious and religious uses, could I have avoided (at least mitigated) these now imminent and unavoidable torments! Good God! Where then were my wits? The very ploughman provides for the time of winter;   80 yea, the ant, to the which we are sent by God's word (Prov. 6: 6–8) to be instructed, hoards grains of corn for his after sustenance. And have I so negligently carried myself as to lay up beforehand no provision against this tempestuous and rugged future storm? Oh, beast that I was! Sweet Jesus, how far distant were my former course of life and daily actions from ever thinking of this unavoidable danger? I have lived many years in fullness   85 of state. I have been labouring in laying out good sums of silver to heap land to land for my children to inherit. I have lived, perhaps, in a most profuse or wasteful manner. I have spent too much to gain the deceitful favour of the world in sumptuous apparel exceeding my state, in keeping an over-wasteful house, and in over-great and unnecessary attendance about me. By means of some or all of these extravagant courses I have spent much.   90 And yet, not once did I ever think to bestow the twentieth part of those superfluous charges to pious uses for the preventing of those flames which within few days, perhaps, few hours, my poor soul must suffer.

65. illaqueations entrapments. 72. schismatical heretical. 74. inexplicable inexpressible. expect await.

'Oh, wretch that I am, that have thus senselessly so neglected this fearful day! Here now my former pleasures and jollity are come to their last end and period. God's justice   95 must and will be satisfied, since nothing defiled and contaminated, except all the rust thereof be afore filed away, can enter into the kingdom of heaven. Whither, then, now, being encompassed on each side with such thorns of danger and anxiety, shall I turn myself? To the world and my former pleasures thereof? Oh, God, the remembrance of them is most nauseous and distasteful to me, since the fruition of them is a great cause of   100 my future pains. To my former greatness and fullness of my temporal state? Oh, that I had been so happy as to have made true benefit in time of that mammon of iniquity, my wasteful spending, whereof must give fuel to that fire! And we are taught that "Divitiae non proderunt in die ultime" [Prov. II: 4, Riches will not profit on the last day]. To my friends, kindred, and former familiar acquaintance, which I shall leave behind me in the   105 world? Woe is me, they are as wholly negligent of their own souls' danger concerning this point as myself have been. How then can I expect them to be solicitous and careful of mine?

'To thee then alone, most merciful and heavenly Father, who art "Pater misericordiarum" [2 Cor. I: 3, Father of mercies], and who dost crown us "in misericordia et   110 miserationibus" [Ps. 102: 4, with mercy and compassion], I do fly, who tookest mercy of the woman of Canaan [Matt. 15: 22–8], of Mary Magdalen, of the publican [Luke 18: 10–14], and of the thief hanging upon the cross. Between the arms of thy ineffable compassion I cast myself. Lessen, oh, lessen for thy own honour's sake and the bitter passion of thy most dear Son, my Saviour Jesus Christ, these temporal pains which now   115 wait for me. Let my present compunction and contrition of all my former sins through thy mercy and Son's precious death arrive to that ascent and height as that my Saviour may say to me with the good thief, "Today thou shalt be with me in Paradise" [Luke 23: 43]. So shall thy mercy thereby overbalance thy justice. For to speak in the Church's dialect, "Plus potes dimittere quam ego committere" [You can forgive more than I can   120 commit]. And it is my comfort that I read in Holy Writ, "Suauis est Dominus universis, & miserationes eius super omnia opera eius" (Ps. 144: 9, Our Lord is sweet to all, and his mercy is above all his works).

'Oh, that I had been so happy as to have followed the wholesome advice given to me by way of presage in a little treatise entitled *An Antidote against Purgatory*. I then did read   125 it but with a certain curiosity, as thinking it nothing to belong to me. But, alas, I now find it to be a true sibyl or prophet of my future calamitous state.

---

97. afore before. 102. mammon idol of riches (see Matt 6: 24; Luke 16: 9–13). III–14. Here the sinner echoes the *Oratio praeparatoria ad confessionem sacramentalem*, the prayer before confession from the Roman sacramentary or missal, which lists these same figures. 120. "Plus…committere" another phrase from the *Oratio praeparatoria*: 'si mortuus et sepultus sum, potes me resuscitare; quia maior est misericordia tua quam iniquitas mea: maior est pietas tua quam impietas mea; plus potes dimittere quam ego committere, et plus parcere quam ego peccator peccare' (If I am dead and buried, you can bring me back to life; for greater is your mercy than my iniquity, greater is your piety than my impiety; you can forgive more than I can commit, and spare more than I, a sinner, can sin) (online database, *Thesaurus Precum Latinarum*). 125. presage forewarning.

'Well, then, seeing my own hourglass is almost run out, let me turn my speech to you, dear Catholics, in my health my chiefest familiars, and with whom I did most consociate in my former pleasures. There is no difference between you and me but the time present and the time to come. You all must once be forced to this bed of sorrow and be brought to your last sickness. To you, then, and to all others who are negligent in providing against this day, I do direct this my charitable admonition. You are yet in health and perhaps as improvident in laying up spiritual riches against this fearful day as myself have been. Oh, change your course while there is time! Let my present state preach to you, and suffer these my last dying words to give life to your future actions, since they preach feelingly whose pulpit is their deathbed. Be not in the number of those senseless creatures who are buried so deep in earth as that they have no taste or feeling of things to come: "Nolunt intelligere ut bene agant" [Ps. 35: 4, They do not understand that they might do well].

'Do now, therefore, dear friends, do now what you can. Now while you have time, heap up together that spiritual wealth which will buy out all ensuing pains and turn the current of your former superfluous charges into the fair stream of pious works, that so it may afford you water for the quenching of those raging flames. Consider how you shall be convented before the severe Judge, from whom nothing can be hidden, of whom the prophet saith: "Tu cognovisti omnia, novissima & antiqua" [Ps. 138: 5, You know all things, most new and old]. He is not appeased with gifts nor admitteth excuses, who out of his boundless mercy remitteth to us upon our true repentance the pains of eternal damnation, but yet chastiseth us with temporal punishment to satisfy his justice: "Misercordia & veritas obviaverunt sibi, iustitia & pax osculati sunt" [Ps. 84: 11, Mercy and truth have met each other; justice and peace have kissed]. Therefore, now begin to spread yourselves in works of piety. Lessen your temporal pomp, descend in outward comportment under yourselves, and let your sparing charges by this means saved serve to redeem you from those horrid flames which are hereafter to invade you.'

To these and the like disconsolate and tragical lamentations in the inward reflex of thy soul, my dear Catholic, shalt thou in thy last sickness be driven if thou seek not to prevent the danger in time. Therefore, remember that he is truly wise who laboureth to be such in his health as he wisheth to be found in God's sight at the hour of his death.

129. **consociate** associate with. 145. **convented** gathered together.

LIVES AND DEATHS

Two great spiritual autobiographies tower over the period, Augustine's *Confessions* and Teresa of Ávila's *Vida*. Augustine demonstrates for subsequent ages the power of sin and the miracle of God's love; Teresa of Ávila provides a new and mystical model for religious experience. In the 1620 translation of the *Confessions* excerpted here Augustine's work takes on topical meaning as it confutes Protestant doctrines and practices. The translator, Toby Matthew, also contributes his own story of conversion below, telling of his eventful trip to Rome, his conflict with English authorities, and his eventual acceptance as a Catholic in England. Another early modern autobiography, that of the Jesuit exorcist William Weston, records the struggles of a missionary amidst a flock that constantly fears detection and believes in demonic possession. Weston's life story illuminates the religious and cultural history of the period as well as its literature, especially Shakespeare's *King Lear*.

The selections pertaining to Thomas More, Edmund Campion, Margaret Clitherow, Alexander Rawlins, and Henry Walpole all tell stories of death, specifically of martyrdom. Despite official prohibitions and punishments, early modern Catholics avidly wrote and read stories of martyrs. In addition to providing moral instruction, such stories contested the master narrative of Protestantism suffering and triumphant in its own martyrs through God's grace. This narrative began in Europe with Jean Crespin and Ludwig Rabe, and continued in England with William Tyndale, John Bale, and John Foxe. Accounts of Catholic martyrs also contradicted the official accounts of the deaths as executions for treason, evident in Tudor–Stuart statutes, court proceedings, and government propaganda. The government version of the story appears throughout these accounts themselves in the various voices of magistrates, prosecutors, and crowds.

In every sense unique, the story of Mary Stuart, Queen of Scots, showed the same struggle to control the meaning of Catholic death (see Fig. 6). Though convicted of treason, Mary Stuart wore an *Agnus Dei*, rosaries, and a red bodice (the liturgical colour of martyrdom), and declared herself a martyr: 'know that I am settled in the ancient Catholic

and Roman religion and in defence thereof, by God's grace, I mind to spend my blood'
(Robert Wingfield, *A Circumstantial Account*, Edinburgh, 1752: 259). Replete with personal
and political ambivalences, Mary's story calls attention by contrast to the many Catholic
English women who led simpler lives of prayer and charity—the butcher's wife Margaret
Clitherow, for example, her neighbour Grace Babthorpe, or Lady Magdalen, Viscountess
Montague, whose virtues circulated in a Latin *Vita* (1609, tr. 1627) by Richard Smith,
bishop of Chalcedon. Clitherow died a martyr's death in York; Lady Magdalen turned her
home into a centre for Catholic sacraments and community. Some Catholic women
engaged in broader social ministries. Mary Ward founded the Institute of the Blessed
Virgin Mary, an international network of Catholic schools for girls. Battling social
prejudice, Jesuit distrust, and Church censure, Ward blazed new paths for women,
expanding their possible sphere of action beyond the family and cloister into the wide
world.

The lives and deaths in this section are, of course, extraordinary: six figures have been
canonized as saints (Augustine of Hippo, Teresa of Ávila, Thomas More, Edmund
Campion, Margaret Clitherow, Henry Walpole), and one, Alexander Rawlins, has been
nominated 'Blessed'. But in many senses the early modern figures are representative. The
few martyrs here stand for the many who died for the faith, whose stories have been
assiduously compiled by Nicholas Sander (1585), Christopher Grene, SJ (d. 1697), Bishop
Challoner (1741), John Morris (1874–7), John Hungerford Pollen (1908), and many others.
The conversion story of Toby Matthew likewise affords insight into the lives of
many others who changed faiths in order to cope with opposing political and religious
exigencies. Finally gaining acceptance and, indeed, 'more honour and advantage' than
conformity would have merited, Matthew provides a counter-narrative to early modern
stories of Catholic recusancy, suffering, and martyrdom. Living in a bewildering world of
shifting definitions and boundaries, Catholics continually struggled to balance witness
and accommodation, resistance and retreat. The stories of extraordinary Catholics and
converts afford glimpses into the more ordinary English Catholics, those Alban Langdale
speaks for (see CONTROVERSIES), seeking to live at peace with their neighbours and
government, aspiring to moderate virtue, adopting the occasional compromise.

Narratives of Catholic lives and deaths construct in a revealing way the history of early
modern England. The individuals here struggle not merely against death but also against
the extinction mandated by a national programme of erasure, manifested in the defacing
of images, the appropriation of Church properties and prerogatives, the enforcing of
conformity, and the control of the press and publication. In this culture, writing Catholic
lives and deaths defiantly asserts individual rights and communal identity, linking past,
present, and future generations in a shared witness and vision.

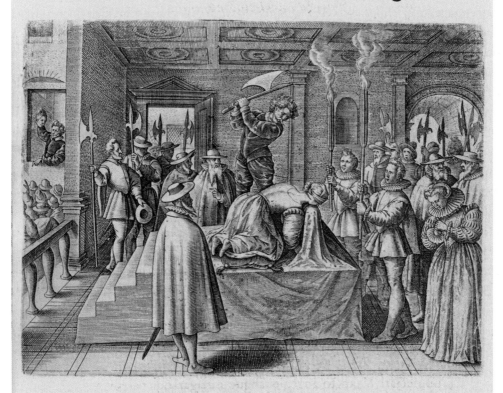

Persecutiones aduersus Catholicos à Prote-
stantibus Caluiniftis excitæ in Anglia.

Poft varias clades miferorum, & cædis aceruos
Jnfontum, comes exornat fpectacula mater
Supplicio, & regum foror & fidißima coniux.
Jlla Caledonijs diademate claruit oris,
Sed micat in cœlo fulgentior, inde corona
Sanguinis, infandaq, manet vindicta fecuris.

L 3   NOMI-

6. Richard Verstegan, 'The Execution of Mary, Queen of Scots', *Theatrum crudelitatum haereticorum*, 1587, sig. L3. Verstegan portrayed Mary's death as a martyrdom and the culminating outrage against Catholics in England. He demanded requital in the form of a European crusade against Elizabeth.

AUGUSTINE OF HIPPO

Saint Augustine of Hippo (354–430) adapted classical thought to Christian doctrine and in various writings, including *De civitate Dei*, established the foundations for medieval and modern Christian theology. Born in north Africa, Augustine started out as a teacher, orator, and worldly man. He took a concubine for some years and had a son, Adeodatus. He fell in with the Manicheans, who believed that good and evil, light and darkness, were equal powers in conflict with each other. In 386, two years after taking the prestigious chair in rhetoric at Milan, Augustine experienced the conversion to Christ for which his mother Monica had long and fervently prayed. After giving up his post and his plans for marriage, Augustine became a priest and then bishop of Hippo (in Algeria today) until his death.

Augustine's *Confessions*, as the Latin *confessio* implies, both relate sin and praise God. Written when he was 43 and ailing, they present a highly selective narrative of the youthful sinner lost in earthly pleasures and delusions until blessed with salvific illumination and mystical communion. The *Confessions* have become a beloved, classic account of a soul's journey to God. In this translation Toby Matthew presents 'both Catholics and Protestants' with a work 'which may extraordinarily serve to the setting out of man's extreme misery and the manifesting of God's unspeakable mercy' (sig. a1). This translation, however, also aims to confute Protestant heresy, specifically the doctrine of predestination and the enslaved will, as excerpts below illustrate. (On Toby Matthew, see the autobiography below and POETRY.)

Confessions, wr. 397, trans. 1620

How he took fruit out of another man's orchard

Thy law indeed, O Lord, doth punish theft [Exod. 20: 15], and this law is written in the hearts of men [Rom. 2: 14–15], which sin itself cannot blot out. For what thief will endure another man that is a thief? Nay, a rich thief will not excuse another man that steals, though he be urged by want. Yet I would needs commit a theft and I performed it, not being constrained by any misery or penury, but through a weariness of doing well and by   5
an abundance of iniquity. For I stole that of which I had at home both in great plenty and much better; neither cared I to enjoy that which I stole, but I took pleasure in the very theft and sin itself.

1. ff. The theft of the pears, linked metaphorically to the story of the forbidden fruit in Genesis, illustrates the gratuitous nature of evil. Augustine echoes Sallust's description of the Roman traitor Catiline to present himself as a traitor to God.

A pear tree there was near our vineyard, heavy loaded with fruit which tempted not greatly either the sight or taste. To the shaking and robbing thereof certain most wicked youths (whereof I was one) went late at night, for till then, according to our lewd custom, we had drawn our sports and play into length. We carried away huge burdens of fruit from thence, not for our own eating, but to be cast before the hogs; and if we did taste thereof at all, it was not for any reason so much as because we would do that which was not lawful.

Behold my heart, O my God, behold my heart, whereof thou hadst mercy, whilst yet it was even in the bottom of hell! Behold, let now my heart confess to thee what it meant to seek in this theft whilst I was wicked to no purpose and there was no other cause of this malice but the malice itself. It was deformed and yet I loved it; I loved to perish. I loved the sin, not that which I obtained by the same, but I loved the sin itself, of my deformed soul. And springing or starting off from thy firm protection, I was abandoned to a total ruin, not desiring anything which was comely, but thirsting even after shame itself.

How he carried himself when he first went to Carthage

I came to Carthage where there were, as if it had been a frying pan full, flagitious loves which crackled round about me on every side. I was not yet immersed in love but I desired to be so; and with a profound kind of poverty I hated myself for not being poor enough. I was in search of somewhat that I might affect and I despited to live in safety or to travel in any way wherein there were no difficulties to be encountered, because my soul was even famished for want of that spiritual food which is thyself, O God. For want of that food I was not hungry, but I was without all appetite of incorruptible nourishment; not that I had been full fed therewith but because, by how much the more empty so much the more was my stomach queasy and fastidious. For this reason my soul fell sick and broke forth as it were by ulcers, being miserably greedy to be eased by the solace of sensible creatures, which yet if they had not life could not deserve to be beloved. It was a dear thing for me to love and to be beloved, and the more if I arrived to enjoy the person which I pretended to. I troubled, therefore, the water of friendship with the dirt of unclean appetite, and I obscured the brightness thereof with hellish lust. And yet even when I was thus ugly and unclean, I would needs be counted for a choice and civil

9. **pear tree** sometimes thought a metaphor for the sexual temptations that figure so largely in Augustine's life. 13. **cast...hogs** Cf. Jesus's warning not to cast pearls before swine (Matt. 7: 6), and the Prodigal Son's feeding of the pigs (Luke 15: 15). 22. **Carthage** a leading city of the 4th-c. Roman Empire, also, the place of Aeneas's love affair with Dido, a dangerous distraction in his journey to Rome. **frying pan** an accurate translation of *sartago*, also 'cauldron'. **flagitious** wicked. 24. **profound...poverty** *secretiore indigentia*, i.e. a 'deeper need', mistakenly directed to sensible objects and human beings. **not...poor enough** Matthew translates the Latin to suggest that Augustine hated himself more for his lack of spiritual poverty, i.e. for not recognizing his true need of God. But Augustine says that he hated *me minus indigentem*, 'myself needing less', i.e. the idea of himself as less needy of worldly love. In Carthage Augustine is unwilling to surrender his passions and the delusive dream of earthly desire. 25. **somewhat...affect** someone or something to love. **despited** refused contemptuously. 26. **difficulties** 'snares' (*muscipulis*) in the original; cf. Wis. 14: 11; Ps. 90: 3. 28. **appetite of** desire for. 32. **life** i.e. soul (*animam*). Augustine means that the immortal soul in lovers attracted him, but he was distracted by their bodies and incapable of rising above sensual love. 33–4. **arrived...pretended to** achieved sexual intercourse (*amantis corpore fruerer*) with my false love.

person, with a superlative kind of vanity. I rushed upon those affections whereby I desired to be taken. O my God, O thou who art my mercy (Ps. 58: 15), with how much gall didst thou sprinkle these delights of mine, and how good wert thou to me in doing so! For when I grew to obtain my unchaste desires, in the midst of my jollity I was tied by   40 miserable chains that so I might be beaten with the burning rods of jealousy, suspicions, fears, angers, and brawls. About that time was I much carried away with spectacles represented upon the stage, which were full of images wherein mine own miseries were expressed, and they served as fuel to my fire

All beauty proceeds from God, who is to be praised in all things

'O God of power, convert us towards thee; show us thy face and we shall be safe' [Ps. 79: 8];   45 for which way soever the soul of man turneth itself otherwise than towards thee, it is fixed to pain, although it be fastened upon such delightful creatures as are both out of thee and out of themselves, and which yet would be nothing unless they were of thee. These things have their spring and fall: when they spring they begin to be and grow towards their perfection and, being perfected, they grow old and die, for all things grow old and all   50 things die. When, therefore, they spring and grow, how much the more speedily they grow to be, so much the more do they hasten not to be. Such is their nature and so much thou hast given them, for they are but parts of things which consist not all together but by departing and succeeding do all constitute one whole whereof they are the parts. In the selfsame manner is our speech delivered by words spoken, for a whole speech will   55 never be made if one word depart not when the sound is past that another may succeed.

Let my soul praise thee for them [Ps. 145: 2], O God, thou Creator of all things, but let it not be fastened to them with the glue of inordinate affection by the senses of my body. These creatures go on whither they were going towards a not-being, and so they slice the soul with pestiferous desires. For the soul desires to be and would feign repose in those   60 things which it loveth; but in those things it cannot repose for instead of remaining they fly away. And who is he that can follow them with the sense of flesh and blood? Yea, or who can overtake them even when they are near at hand? For the sense of the flesh is slow and the nature of it is such. It is able to attain another end, for which it is made, but it arriveth not so far as that it can entertain and arrest things as they pass from the just   65 beginning to the very end. For in thy Word, by which they are created, there it is that they receive their commission both of whence they must come and how far they are to go.

---

41. **burning rods** instruments of torture in Roman courts. **45 ff.** The death of a friend spurs this meditation on transience. 47. **delightful creatures** Augustine wrote *in pulchris*, 'in beautiful things', thus continuing his meditation on beauty, which originates in God, causes delight, and, properly perceived, brings the beholder to love God the Creator, not the ephemeral creation. 57. **God . . . things** a quotation of Ambrose's hymn, *Deus Creator Omnium*, one of Augustine's favourites. 59. **not-being** state of non-existence (*ut non sint*, 'so that they might not be'). 64. **another end** mere sensation. 65. **entertain . . . things** delight and repose in things (even for the duration of their temporal existence). Sensual pleasure is merely momentary.

How he continued in his sensualities

In the meantime my sins were multiplied, and a certain woman, with whom I used to defile myself, being torn, as it were, from my side as the impediment of my disposing myself to marriage, my heart, where formerly it had cloven to her, grew to be sliced and 70 wounded in such sort as that the very blood did follow. She was returned into Africa and had made a vow unto thee that she would never more know man, having left with me a son whom I had unlawfully begotten by her. But I, miserable man, who had not the courage so much as to imitate a woman, and being impatient of two years' delay, by which time another whom I was named to in the way of marriage was to grow of years, 75 I, who was indeed not so much a lover of marriage as a slave to lust, did procure yet another concubine, by whom that disease of my soul (which, if it were not incurable, it was at least much increased) might be entertained and guarded on, as by the safe conduct of my ill custom still continuing, till I should arrive in the kingdom of marriage. Neither yet was that wound cured which had been made in me by cutting off the former, but 80 rather, after an extreme inflammation and affliction, it did putrefy and pain me, though in some sort more dully, yet after a more desperate and dogged manner.

Free will is the cause of sin

But howsoever that I did firmly believe and declare that thou wert pure and inviolable and wholly immutable, O thou our Lord and true God (who didst create not only our souls but our bodies also, and not only our souls and our bodies but all men and all 85 things), yet, nevertheless, I understood not what was the explicit and clear cause of evil. But whatsoever that were, I resolved that so it was to be sought as that I must not thereby oblige myself to believe that the immutable God was subject to mutability, lest myself should become the very thing which I was going to seek. Therefore, now I did securely search after it, being certain that it was not true which they said, from whom I fled with 90 my whole heart, because whilst I was seeking whence sin proceeded, I found them to be full of all sinfulness, whereby they pronounced that even thy substance did rather endure ill than that their own did commit ill.

I did, therefore, bend myself to understand the thing whereof I had heard, 'That the free disposition of the will was the cause of our doing ill, as thy just judgment was the 95 cause of our suffering ill.' But I was not able clearly to see this truth and, therefore, endeavouring to draw the eye of my mind out of that deep darkness, I was again and again plunged into it. That which raised me towards thy light was the knowing that I had

---

68. certain woman lower-class woman with whom Augustine lived from 370/1 to 385, mother of his son Adeodatus. **69–70. impediment ... marriage** legal block to his contraction of marriage with another, a social equal and heiress. **70. cloven** clung. **78. entertained ... on** indulged and protected. **83 ff.** Here Augustine struggles to understand the origins of evil as well as the relation between his own free will and his sinfulness. **89. the very thing** i.e. 'the cause of evil' (Matthew's note). **90. they** Manicheans. **95. free ... will** 'See how blasphemous Calvin is in making God withhold his grace and make us sin to the end that afterward he may damn us for it, according to his first counsel (*Calv. Instit.* lib. 3. c. 23. sect. 6 & cap. 24. sect. 12, 13, 14, 15), where he saith that we sin by necessity' (Matthew's note). The quotation in Augustine's text represents a general topic of discussion, appearing, for example, in Plotinus and in Ambrose's sermons.

such a will, as well as I was sure that I did live. And, therefore, when I did will anything or not will it, I was most certain that there was no mystery in the matter but only that I willed   100
or not willed it; and I did even already observe that the cause and root of my sin lay there.

But whatsoever I did willingly I saw that I did rather suffer than do; and I esteemed not that to be a fault but a punishment, and I quickly confessed (when I remembered how just thou wert) that I was punished not unjustly.

But yet again I said, 'Who is it that made me? Is it not my God, who is not only good   105
but even goodness itself? Whence, therefore, come I thus to will that which is evil and not to will that which is good, by means whereof I may grow to be justly punished? Who placed this power in me? And who engrafted upon my stock this branch of bitterness [Heb. 12: 15], since I was all made by my God most sweet. If the devil be the author of it, whence is that very devil? And if even myself of a good angel that I was am become a devil   110
by this perverse will of mine, whence grew this will to be wicked in me, whereby I might turn devil, since the whole angel was made good by that excellent Creator?' By these cogitations I was again depressed and even suffocated; but I was not laid so low as that hell of error where no man shall confess to thee [Ps. 6: 6], who believeth that thou dost rather suffer ill than man commit it.   115

He reflecteth upon himself

But thou, O Lord, whilst he was speaking to me, didst turn me inward upon myself, taking my soul from behind me, where I may be said to have placed it whilst I marked it not, and thou didst set it before my face [Ps. 49: 21] that so I might see how filthy, how deformed, and how full of hateful spots and sores it was. I saw and withal I abhorred myself; nor was there any place whither I could fly from that odious spectacle. And if   120
I endeavoured at any time to cast mine eye some other way, yet he proceeded in his discourse, and thou didst again oppose me unto myself, and didst fasten mine eyes upon my sins to the end that I might know and hate them; or rather I had already known them, but I dissembled and connived and procured again to forget them. But now the more ardently I loved those two of whose excellent resolution I had heard in giving themselves   125
wholly over to be cured by thee, so much the more detestably did I hate myself, being compared with them. For some twelve years had now passed since in the nineteenth of mine age I was first stirred up to the desire of wisdom by reading the *Hortensius* of Cicero, and yet I delayed to condemn temporal happiness for the search thereof, whose not only finding, but even the very seeking, was to have been preferred before treasures and   130
kingdoms of this world, and before the most prosperous carnal pleasures that could be thought of. But I, being a miserable and most miserable creature, even in the beginning of

---

115. that thou ... it i.e. that God allows and ordains sin rather than that man freely chooses and commits sin. This 'hell of error' Matthew's note again identifies with the doctrine of the 'most wicked Calvin'.   **116. he** Ponticianus, an Imperial agent who has just told Augustine how a visit to the Egyptian monks and the story of their founder, Saint Anthony, moved two of his colleagues to forsake the world and dedicate themselves to Christ.   **119. withal** at the same time.   **127–8. nineteenth of mine** i.e. 372/3; twelve years later is 384/5.   **128. Hortensius** a lost exhortation to philosophy by Cicero (106–43 BC).

my youth had begged chastity at thy hands, and thus I said, 'Give me chastity and continence, O Lord, but do not give it yet.' For I was afraid lest thou wouldst hear me and instantly deliver me from the disease of concupiscence, which I rather wished might 135 be satisfied and glutted than otherwise quenched. And I went by crooked ways with a sacrilegious superstition and (though not as one resolved of the truth thereof), yet I preferred it before other things, after which I did not piously enquire, but with the mind of an enemy oppose unto.

And I conceived that I deferred from day to day [Ecclus. 5: 8] to condemn the world 140 and to follow thee alone because I thought I was not sure enough by which way I was to direct my course. But now the time was come wherein I was set naked before myself, and my conscience did thus reproach me: 'Where is that tongue of thine which said that thou wert not to cast away the certain pleasure of vanity for the obtaining of a happiness which was uncertain? At least thou mightst see and feel that the burden of sin doth certainly and 145 heavily oppress thee whilst others have gotten wings to fly nimbly from under it, who yet were neither so overwrought with curious enquiries, nor took they, as thou hast done, the time of more than ten years to think upon it.'

Thus was I inwardly fretted or fed upon and vehemently even confounded with a horrible shame, whilst Ponticianus related to me the things aforesaid. But that speech 150 being ended with the cause for which he came, away went he and I came home into myself. What did I not then say for my greater confusion? With what scourges of forcible reason did I not whip on my soul that it might follow me than endeavouring to go after thee? But still it was held back and it refused, though it knew not how to excuse itself. For now all the arguments which I was wont to bring were solved, and there remained only a 155 kind of speech trembling; and it feared, even as death itself, to be restrained from the course and flux which it had long taken towards sin, whereby it was daily pining away and growing nearer to destruction [John 11: 4].

He was miraculously called

As soon as a deep consideration had drawn up out of the hidden bottom of my heart the whole heap of my misery and laid it together before the sight of my mind, there rose a 160 tempestuous storm, which brought forth a huge shower of tears. And that I might send them out with such exclamations as became them best, I rose from Alypius. That business of weeping I thought would better be dispatched by my being alone. And I went so far off as that even his presence might not be of trouble to me. So was I made at that time, and what he thought thereof I cannot tell though I think I had said somewhat 165 whereby it might appear that the sound of my voice was great with tears and would gladly

---

153. **than** instead of. 156. **speech trembling** i.e. silent trembling (*muta trepidatio*). 159 ff. This famous garden scene recounts Augustine's miraculous conversion in 386; he presented himself to Saint Ambrose for baptism in 387. 162. **Alypius** Augustine's friend, later bishop of Thagaste.

be delivered of them. In this sort I rose, and he remained where formerly we sat together, too much amazed.

I did cast myself, I know not how, upon the ground under a certain fig tree, and I gave all liberty to my tears, which brake like rivers through mine eyes, an acceptable sacrifice   170 unto thee, O Lord [Ps. 50: 19]. Not perhaps in these words but to this effect I cried out to thee at large, 'And thou, O Lord, how long, how long, O Lord? Wilt thou be angry with me forever? Remember not, Lord, mine old iniquities' [Ps. 6: 4]. For I found that I was still detained by them and, therefore, I cast out these lamentable exclamations: 'How long, how long, tomorrow and yet tomorrow? Why not even now? Why even at this   175 instant is there not an end made of my uncleanness?' This did I say, and I wept in the most bitter sorrow of my heart.

And behold I heard a voice, as if it had been of some boy or girl from some house not far off, uttering and often repeating these words in a kind of singing manner, 'Take up and read, take up and read.' And instantly with another countenance and with entire   180 attention, I began to consider whether children in some play of theirs had not used to sing some such thing; nor did it occur unto me that ever I had heard the like. And, therefore, moderating the course of my tears, I rose up, conceiving that I was only required from heaven to read that chapter which the first opening of the book should lead me to. For I had heard of Anthony that by reading of the Gospel (to the hearing   185 whereof he came once by accident), he held himself to be admonished, as if that which was read had been particularly meant for him: 'Go, and sell all that thou hast, and give it to the poor, and thou shalt have treasures in Heaven, and come, thou, and follow me' [Matt. 19: 21]. By which oracle he was instantly converted to thee [Ps. 50: 15], O Lord.

Therefore, I went hastily thither where Alypius sat, for there I had laid the apostolical   190 book. I took it quickly into my hand; I opened it and I read of that chapter in silence, which first mine eyes were cast upon. 'Not in surfeiting and drunkenness, not in carnality and uncleanness, not in strife and emulation, but put you on the Lord Jesus Christ, and take not care to fulfil the concupiscences of the flesh' [Rom 13: 13–14]. Neither would I read any further; neither was there any cause why I should, for instantly with the end of   195 this sentence, as by a clear and constant light infused into my heart, the darkness of all former doubts was driven away.

Then shutting the book though interposing my finger or some other such thing between the leaves, I declared to Alypius all that had happened with a quiet countenance. And he did also in this following manner discover to me that which had passed in his   200 heart, whereof I knew nothing. He demanded to see what I had read; I showed it and he went on further, and I was ignorant of what followed, which yet was this: 'But take unto you him who is weak in faith' [Rom. 14: 1], which he applied to himself, and so he told me. And by this admonition he was strengthened and he joined himself without any

---

167. sort condition. **169. fig tree** Citing various scriptural parallels (including Matt. 21: 19, John 1: 48), commentators have read the fig tree as symbolic of fallen man and the flesh in need of redemption. **185. Anthony** Saint Anthony, 3rd–4th c.

troublesome or perplexed delay to that good purpose and election which was most   205
agreeable to his condition, wherein he did ever infinitely differ from me to the better.

From thence we went to my mother. We told her what we meant to do; she most
cordially rejoiced. We declared to her in what manner all things passed; she exulted, and
triumphed, and blessed thee, O Lord, who art able to do beyond that which we can either
ask or think [Eph. 3: 20]. Because now she saw that thou hadst given her more   210
concerning me than she was wont to beg of thee by her miserable and lamenting groans.
For thou didst so convert me to thee as that I did neither desire a wife, nor had I any
ambitious care of any worldly thing. Thou didst place me in that line and rule of faith
wherein thou hadst revealed unto her so many years before that I should stand. And thou
didst convert her sorrow into joy of heart [Ps. 29: 12] much more plentifully than she   215
wished and much more dearly and more chastely than she could have found it in the
children of my body.

He striveth to conceive what kind of thing God is

O Lord, I love thee. Thou hast struck my heart through with thy Word, and I have loved
thee; yea, behold, the heavens and the earth with all that is in them proclaim to me on
every side that I ought to love thee, and they publish the same to all men to the end that   220
they may be inexcusable [Rom. 1: 20]. But thou shalt more profoundly have mercy upon
whom thou wilt have mercy, and thou shalt perform more mercy towards them to whom
thou hast showed mercy [Rom. 9: 15], for else, the heaven and the earth do but sing thy
praises to deaf persons. But yet when I love thee, what kind of thing is it that I love? Not
the beauty of bodies, not the order of time, not the clearness of this light which our eyes   225
are so glad to see, not the harmony of sweet songs in music, not the fragrancy of flowers,
and other unctuous and aromatical odours, not manna, nor anything of sweet and
curious taste, not carnal creatures which may delightfully be embraced by flesh and
blood. They are not these things which I love in loving God. And yet I love a kind of
light, a kind of voice, a kind of odour, a kind of food, and a kind of embracing, when   230
I love my God—the light, the voice, the odour, the food, and the embracing of my
inward man, where that shines to my soul which is not circumscribed by any place, that
sounds to mine ear which is not stolen and snatched away by time, that yieldeth smell
which is not scattered by air, that savours in taste which is not consumed by our eating,
that remains enjoyed which is not divorced by satiety. This is that which I love when   235
I love my God.

---

208. cordially fervently. **213–14. Thou . . . stand** Monica had dreamt that Augustine would one day stand on the 'rule'
[wooden measuring rod], i.e. submit to the rule of faith (*Confessions* 3. 11). **217. children . . . body** Monica had tried to
arrange a lawful marriage for her son (ibid. 6. 13). **218 ff.** A sublime passage wherein Augustine approaches the invisible
and incorporeal God by means of visible and material creations. The mystical idea of the spiritual senses here had already
been developed by another Church Father, Origen, in the 3rd century.

He bewaileth his time past and lost

Too late am I come to love thee, O thou who art beauty itself, both so ancient and yet withal so fair and fresh; too late I am come to love thee. And, behold, thou wert within me when I went looking for thee abroad and I did in a deformed manner cast myself away upon thy creatures, which yet thou hadst made fair. Thou were with me but   240
I remained not with thee. Those things withheld me from thee which yet, if they had not their being in thee, would not be at all. Thou didst call and cry out, and so didst break through my deafness. Thou didst shine and lighten, and so didst chase away my blindness. Thou didst breathe upon me, and I drew it inward, and, behold, I do even pant towards thee. I tasted of thee and I still hunger and thirst for more. Thou didst but   245
touch me and I do even burn with a desire to enjoy thee.

Teresa of Ávila

Teresa of Ávila (1515–82), a Carmelite nun, experienced a rare state of mystical union with God. Although contemporary Catholic reform movements encouraged mental prayer and the private experience of illumination, Teresa's visions aroused scepticism and opposition. At the request of her superiors Teresa recounted her spiritual experiences in her *Vida*, or 'Life' (1562, revised several times), which the Inquisition impounded until 1586, distrustful of a woman's claim to such unusual (and unregulated) manifestations. Teresa went on to found a number of convents in Spain, received canonization in 1622, and became a doctor of the Church in 1970.

In her *Vida* Teresa advocates the practice of 'mental prayer', a personal conversation with God that grows in intimacy and richness over time. Her humility and honesty make credible her story, particularly her relation of supernatural pleasures and pains in mystical visions. In ecstatic trance Teresa see Christ's beautiful face and experiences transverberation, i.e. the piercing of her heart with a seraph's dart. Teresa's account of the transverberation, excerpted below, inspired some crowning glories of the Catholic baroque—Bernini's sculpture, dramas by Lope de Vega and other Spanish playwrights, and Richard Crashaw's poem, 'The Flaming Heart' (see Fig. 7, and Crashaw, POETRY). Her *Vida*, moreover, 'became the single most important work of mysticism in early modern Catholicism and served as the exemplum for the shaping and writing of the religious life of women' (R. Po-Chia Hsia, *The World of Catholic Renewal*, 1998: 139).

237 ff. Fusing images from the Song of Songs and Neoplatonism, Augustine passionately and poetically expresses his love for God, source of all beauty and goodness. This justly celebrated passage redirects the impulse and language of eros to its proper end. **238. withal** besides.

7. Gian Lorenzo Bernini, 'Ecstasy of St Teresa of Ávila', Coronaro Chapel, Santa Maria della Vittoria, Rome, 1645–52. Teresa receives the dart of divine love.

The Life of Mother Teresa of Jesus, wr. 1562, tr. 1611

I have gone far from my purpose for I was about to declare the causes by which we may see that it is no imagination, for we might by our care represent to ourselves the humanity of Christ, contriving with our imagination his great beauty. And for this no little time were needful, if it were to be like him in anything. We may well represent him before our imagination, and continue beholding him for some space, and what figures he hath, and his fairness, and so perfect it by little and little, and commit that image to our memory. Who can hinder this since that we may frame it with our understanding? But there is no remedy to do this in that which we treat of but we must behold it when our Lord will represent it, and how he will, and what he will; neither can we add, nor diminish, or use any means for it how much soever we endeavour, nor see it when we will, nor yet leave seeing it. If we will behold anything in particular, we presently lose Christ.

For the space of two years and a half God did me this favour very ordinarily; now there are more than three past that he hath taken this continual use of it from me by giving another more high, as peradventure I will declare afterward. And though I did see him speak with me and I beheld that great beauty and the sweetness with which he speaketh those words by that most beautiful and divine mouth, and other times with rigour, and though I desired extremely to perceive the colour of his eyes or of what bigness they were that I might be able to tell it, I never deserved to see it. Neither doth it help me to procure it, but rather by this I lose the vision altogether. Although sometimes I see him behold me benignly, but this sight is of such force that the soul cannot endure it, and the soul remaineth in so high a rapt, that for to enjoy the whole more she loseth this beautiful sight. So that here it helpeth not neither to desire or not to desire; it appeareth plainly that our Lord will have nothing but humility and confusion, and that we take that which is given us and praise the giver.

This is so in all visions, without excepting any, for we can do nothing; neither doth our diligence help or hinder us to see more or less. Our Lord will have us see very clearly that this is not our work but the work of His Majesty, for we can much less be proud but rather it maketh us humble and fearful, seeing that as our Lord taketh from us the power to see what we would, he can likewise take from us these favours and his grace so that we remain spoiled altogether, and that we may always walk in fear so long as we live in this banishment.

Always in a manner our Lord was represented unto me in this manner after his resurrection, and in the host in like sort, if it were not sometimes to strengthen me if

5

10

15

20

25

30

---

2. **it … imagination** The image of Christ seen in Teresa's visions is not a product of her own imagination or intellect. 5. **figures** lineaments, dimensions. 7. **frame** construct. 8. **remedy** possibility. 11. **will behold** wish to see. 15. **peradventure** perhaps. 20. **procure it** labour to attain the vision. 22. **rapt** rapture. 31. **spoiled** deprived. 33–4. **in this … resurrection** as he appeared after the resurrection. 34. **host** Eucharist. **if … not** unless.

I were in tribulation, for then sometimes he showed me his wounds upon the cross, and 35
in the Garden, and more seldom with his crown of thorns, and carrying his cross also
sometimes, in respect of my necessities, as I say, and those of others, but always with his
flesh glorified.

I have had much confusion and trouble in declaring these things, and many fears and
many persecutions. It seemed so certain to be the devil that some would have exorcized 40
me; of this I made little account, but I was grieved when I did see my confessors afraid
to hear my confession, or when I knew that they said anything to them. Notwithstanding, I could never be sorry for having seen these celestial visions, and I would not
have changed the having of them only once for all the goods and delights of the world.
I always held it for a great favour of our Lord, and it seemeth to me an exceeding 45
great treasure, and our Lord himself secured me many times. I saw myself increase very
much in loving him; I complained to him of all these troubles; I always departed
with comfort and new forces from my prayer. I durst not contradict them because
I saw that it made matters but worse, for it seemed to them little humility. I conferred
with my confessarius; he always comforted me much when he saw me afflicted. 50

The visions increasing, one of those which did help me before, with whom I was wont
to confess sometimes when the vice-rector could not attend it, began to say that it was
manifestly the devil. They commanded me that since there was no remedy to resist,
that I should always bless myself when I did see any vision, and set it at naught, for
I might certainly believe that it was the devil, and that in this sort he would not come, 55
and that I should not fear for God would defend me and deliver me from him. This was
a great pain to me, for since that I could not believe but that it was God, it was a terrible
thing for me. Neither could I, as I have said, desire to have it taken from me, but finally
I did all that they commanded me. I beseeched God much to deliver me from being
deceived (this I did always, and that with many tears), and likewise Saint Peter and Saint 60
Paul, for our Lord told me (it being upon their day that he first appeared to me) that
they would defend me from being deceived; and so many times I did see them at my
left hand very plainly, though not with any imaginary vision; these glorious saints were
my very good lords.

That setting it at naught vexed me exceedingly when I did see this vision of our Lord. 65
For when I did see him present, if they had pulled me in pieces, I could not have believed
that it was the devil, and so it was a very great penance for me. And not to stand blessing
myself so often, I took a cross in my hand. This I did ever almost; the setting at naught
I used not so continually, for I was much afflicted with it. I remembered the injuries
which the Jews had done him and I beseeched him to pardon me, since that I did it to 70

---

37. **in respect of** taking into account. 42. **they** others. 46. **secured** assured. 48. **forces** strength. 50. **confessarius**
confessor, at this time Baltasar Álvarez, a young Jesuit. 51. **one** Gonzalo de Aranda. 54. **set it at naught** consider it
nothing. The Spanish reads *dar higas*, 'to make the fig or *fico*', a gesture of contempt which consisted of a fist with
the thumb between the index and third fingers. 55. **in this sort** in this way, i.e. with these precautions having been taken.
61. **their day** their feast day, 29 June.

obey him whom I held in his place, and that he would not blame me since that they were his officers, whom he had placed in his church. He willed me not to care for it, that I did well in obeying, but that he would cause the truth to be understood. When they took away my prayer, methought he was angry. He bade me tell them that it was tyranny. He gave me reasons to understand that it was no devil. I will declare some of them afterward.   75

One time while I held the cross in my hand, which hung at my rosary, he took it in his and when he gave it me again it was of four great precious stones, much more precious than diamonds without comparison, for there is none in a manner to that which we see supernaturally. The diamond seemeth a counterfeit and imperfect thing in respect   80
of the stones which are seen there. They had the five wounds very artificially engraven. He told me that I should see it so after that time, and so I did, for I did not see the wood of which it was but these stones. But none did see them besides myself.

When they commanded me to make these trials and resist, the increase of the favours was much greater when I would divert myself. I could never desist from prayer (me-   85
thinks I was in prayer even while I slept!), for here my love increased, and I made great complaints to our Lord, and I could not endure it. Neither was it in my power, although I would, and procured greatly not to think upon it. Notwithstanding, I obeyed as much as I could, but I could little or nothing in this. And our Lord did never take it from me, but although he willed me to do it, he assured me on the other side and   90
taught me what I should say to them, and so he doth still, and he gave me such sufficient reasons that they caused me all security.

Not long after His Majesty began, as he had promised me, to declare more that it was he, so great a love of God increasing in me that I knew not who caused it in me, for it was very supernatural and I procured it not. I felt myself die with the desire of seeing   95
God, and I knew not where I should seek for this life, if it were not with death. I had some great impulsions of this love, which, though they were not so intolerable as others that I have spoken of before nor of such value, I knew not what to do for nothing did satisfy me. Neither could I contain myself but in very truth my soul seemed to depart out of my body. Oh, sovereign art of our Lord! What delicate invention didst thou use   100
with thy miserable slave! Thou didst hide thyself from me, and increase thy love in me with such a delightful death that the soul would never be rid of it.

He that hath not proved these so great impulses cannot possibly understand them, for it is not any disquietness of our heart nor certain devotions which we have many times which seem to choke our spirit so that it cannot contain itself. This is a more base   105
prayer, and we must take away those precipitations by procuring sweetly to recollect

---

79. in a manner like. 81. five wounds the stigmata, the five wounds of Christ on the cross. artificially artfully. 82. it the cross. 87–8. Neither…would I could not stop seeing visions, though I tried. 90. it visionary prayer. it their instructions. 97. impulsions stirrings. 98. spoken of before In a preceding passage (ch. 20) Teresa described the commingled pain and pleasure in her former visions. 103. proved experienced. 105. This i.e. these devotions. 106. precipitations impulses experienced during these devotions.

them within ourselves and to bring our souls into a calm. For this is like to certain children that have certain precipitate cryings that seem to choke them, and by giving them drink that excessive molestation ceaseth; so here reason must pull in the reins for it may be that nature itself causeth it in part; let consideration be used, fearing lest that all be not perfect but that a great part of it may be sensual. And let it still this child by cherishing it lovingly so that it be moved sweetly to love and not with blows, as they say, so that this love be recollected inwardly, and not like a pot that seetheth too fast because the fire is made without discretion, and so it runneth all over. But let us moderate the cause which we gave to this fire and procure to put out the flame with sweet tears and not painful, as those of these commotions are and do much harm. I had them sometimes in the beginnings and they had almost spoiled my head and wearied my spirit in such sort that for the next day and longer I was not fit to return to prayer. Wherefore great discretion is necessary at the beginning that all may proceed sweetly and the spirit may be taught to work inwardly. The exterior is to be avoided with great care.

These other impulses are exceeding different. We lay not on the wood ourselves but it seemeth that the fire being already made, they cast us in with speed that we may be burnt. The soul procureth not that this wound of our Lord's absence should grieve her, but they fix a dart in her very entrails and heart sometimes, so that the soul knoweth not what she aileth, or what she would have. She understandeth well that she would have God, and that the arrow seemeth to bring an herb with it, which causeth to abhor herself for the love of this Lord, and she would willingly lose her life for his sake. The manner with which God draweth the soul to him cannot be expressed nor declared, nor what pain it causeth her, making her not know herself, but this pain is so delightful that there is no delight in the world that giveth more contentment. The soul, as I have said, would always lie dying of this sickness.

This pain and glory together astonished me for I could not understand how it could be. Oh, what is it to see a soul wounded (for, as I say, she is conceived, so far as can be declared, to be wounded) for so excellent a cause; and she seeth clearly that the motion from whence this love came to her proceeded not from herself; but it seemeth that this spark which setteth her all on a fire fell suddenly upon her from that great love which our Lord beareth her. Oh, how many times do I remember when I am in this taking that verse of David, 'Quemadmodum desiderat ceruus ad fontes aquarum' [Ps. 41: 2, As the hart panteth after the fountains of water [so my soul panteth after thee, O God]], for methinks I see it literally fulfilled in myself.

When it is not very extreme, the soul seemeth to be somewhat appeased (at least she seeketh some remedy for she knoweth not what to do) with certain penances, which are no more felt, nor the shedding of blood causeth any more pain, than if the body were

108. precipitate sudden. 110. nature human nature, as opposed to divine agency. 111. perfect i.e. wholly caused by God. sensual from the sensory portion of the soul, i.e. self-induced. it reason or consideration. 120. exterior feelings exterior to those produced by the true mystical experience of God. 121. These other impulses true mystical feelings. 125. she aileth hurts her. 137. taking rapture. 141. it this thirst.

dead. She seeketh ways and devices to do part of that which she feeleth for the love of God, but the first pain is so great that I know not what corporal torment could take it   145
away. For the remedy not being there, these medicines are very base for so high a sickness. It is somewhat appeased and part of it passeth away by asking of God the remedy for her malady; and she seeth none but death, for with this she thinketh that she shall wholly enjoy her good. Other times it is so extreme that she can neither do this nor anything else, for it lameth, as it were, her whole body so that she can neither move foot nor hand;   150
but if she did stand, she sitteth down as one transported for she cannot so much as breathe. Only she fetcheth some sighs, not very great because she cannot, but they are great in their cause.

   Our Lord vouchsafed to let me see in this occasion this vision sometimes: I did see an angel not far from me toward my left hand in corporal form, which I am not wont to   155
see but very seldom (although I have angels often represented unto me, it is without seeing them but as the former vision, which I spake of before). In this vision it pleased our Lord to let me see him so: he was not great but little, very beautiful, his face so glorious that he seemed to be one of the higher angels which seem to be all inflamed. Perhaps they are those which are called Seraphim, for they tell me not their names, but   160
I see plainly that in heaven there is so great difference between some angels and other, and between these again and other, that I am not able to declare it. I did see in his hand a long dart of gold, and at the end of the iron head it seemed to have a little fire. This he seemed to pass through my heart sometimes, and that it pierced to my entrails, which methought he drew from me when he pulled it out again, and he left me wholly   165
inflamed in great love of God. The pain was so great that it made me complain grievously, and the sweetness was so excessive, which this exceeding great pain causeth, that I could not desire to have it taken away. Neither is the soul contented with less than with God; neither is it any corporal but a spiritual pain, although the body hath some, yea, a great, part of it. It is so sweet an intercourse which passeth betwixt the soul and   170
God that I beseech his goodness to give them to taste of it who think that I lie.

   The days that this continued I was like a fool. I desired neither to see nor speak but to embrace my pain, which for me was a greater glory than any which is to be found in creatures. I had this sometimes when it pleased our Lord that these so great rapts should come upon me, so that even being among others I could not resist them. But to my great   175
grief they began to be published. Since I have these rapts I feel not this pain so much but that which I spake of somewhere before (I remember not in what chapter), which is very different in many things and more to be esteemed. Yea, when this pain of which I now speak beginneth, our Lord seemeth to elevate my soul, and he putteth

---

146. there in corporal penance. 154. vouchsafed granted. 157. the former vision Earlier (ch. 27) Teresa described a vision wherein she felt divine presences around her but did not see them with the 'eye of her soul', or imagination. 160. Seraphim highest order of angels, associated with fire. Teresa originally wrote Cherubim but P. Domingo Bañez, her Dominican editor, made this correction in a marginal note. 162. declare explain. 172. fool (1) speechless simpleton; (2) infant. 176. published made public. Later, in 1726, Pope Benedict XIII appointed a festival and office for the Transverberation, observed 27 August.

her in an *extasis*, and so there is no space to have pain, nor to suffer, for joy presently   180
succeedeth. Blessed be he forever who doth so many favours to one that giveth him so evil
correspondence for so great benefits.

Thomas More

Thomas More (*c*.1477–1535) lived as a brilliant polemicist and Lord Chancellor of
England but died for refusing to assent to the Act of Supremacy, which declared King
Henry VIII Supreme Head of the Church in England (see CONTROVERSIES). According
to an act of Parliament (1534: 26 Henry VIII, c. 13), such refusal constituted high treason.
Recounting the trial and execution, William Roper, his son-in-law, depicts Thomas
More as a new kind of martyr, as one who died for the unity of the Catholic faith.
Largely ignoring the Lord Chancellor who burned books and heretics, Roper's account
energetically counters the emergent Protestant martyrology created by John Bale and John
Foxe. His Thomas More, loyal first to God then king, is fit to join St Thomas the Apostle
and St Thomas Becket in the holy triumvirate of the *Tres Thomae*, 'three Thomases'
(T. Stapleton, Douai, 1588). The selections below show More's conviction and equanimity,
his flashes of wit and learning, and his profound humility in the service of God. Such
qualities have made his story a mixture of high tragedy, saint's life, and myth, compelling
from its beginnings up through modern times in Robert Bolt's moving adaptation, *A Man
for All Seasons*.

William Roper, *The Life of Sir Thomas More*, wr. 1557

As Sir Thomas More in the Tower chanced on a time, looking out of his window, to
behold one Master Reynolds, a religious, learned, and virtuous father of Sion, and three
monks of the Charterhouse for the matters of the matrimony and Supremacy going out
of the Tower to execution, he, as one longing in that journey to have accompanied them,

---

180. *extasis* ecstasy. 182. **correspondence** return.

LIFE OF SIR THOMAS MORE 1. **in the** **Tower** Protestant historians emphasized More's persecution of heretics and his
disloyalty to the king. Recalling the burnings of John Frith, John Tewkesbery, Thomas Hitton, Richard Bayfield, and
'divers other good saints', John Foxe delivered this verdict: More was 'recounted a man both witty and learned, but
whatsoever he was beside, a bitter persecutor he was of good men and a wretched enemy against the truth of the
gospel. . . . [And] such a blind devotion he bare to the Pope-holy See of Rome, and so wilfully stood in the Pope's quarrel
against his own prince, that he would not give over till he had brought the scaffold of the Tower Hill, axe and all, upon his
own neck' (*Acts and Monuments*, 1610, sigs. Aaaaa4–4ᵛ) 2. **Reynolds** Richard Reynolds, member of the Bridgettine
monastery at Sion. 3. **Charterhouse** a Carthusian monastery in London where More spent four years.

said unto my wife, then standing there besides him: 'Lo, dost thou not see, Meg, that 5
these blessed fathers be now as cheerfully going to their deaths as bridegrooms to their
marriage? Wherefore thereby mayst thou see, mine own good daughter, what a great
difference there is between such as have in effect spent all their days in a strait, hard,
penitential, and painful life religiously, and such as have in the world, like worldly
wretches, as thy poor father hath done, consumed all their time in pleasure and ease 10
licentiously. For God, considering their long-continued life in most sore and grievous
penance, will no longer suffer them to remain here in this vale of misery and iniquity,
but speedily hence taketh them to the fruition of his everlasting deity. Whereas thy silly
father, Meg, that like a most wicked caitiff hath passed forth the whole course of his
miserable life most sinfully, God, thinking him not worthy so soon to come to that 15
eternal felicity, leaveth him here yet still in the world, further to be plunged and
turmoiled with misery.'
[...]

When Sir Thomas More had continued a good while in the Tower, my Lady his wife
obtained licence to see him; who at her first coming, like a simple, ignorant woman and
somewhat worldly too, with this manner of salutation bluntly saluted him: 20

'What the goodyear, Master More,' quoth she, 'I marvel that you that have been
always hitherto taken for so wise a man will now so play the fool to lie here in this
close, filthy prison, and be content thus to be shut up amongst mice and rats, when you
might be abroad at your liberty, and with the favour and good will both of the king and
his Council, if you would but do as all the bishops and best learned of this realm have 25
done. And seeing you have at Chelsea a right fair house, your library, your books,
your gallery, your garden, your orchard, and all other necessaries so handsome about
you, where you might in the company of me, your wife, your children, and household
be merry, I muse what a' God's name you mean here still thus fondly to tarry.'

After he had a while quietly heard her, with a cheerful countenance he said unto her: 30
'I pray thee, good Mistress Alice, tell me, tell me one thing.'

'What is that?' quoth she.

'Is not this house', quoth he, 'as nigh heaven as mine own?'

To whom she, after her accustomed homely fashion, not liking such talk, answered,
'Tilly-vally, tilly-vally!' 35

'How say you, Mistress Alice,' quoth he, 'is it not so?'

'*Bone deus, bone deus*, man, will this gear never be left?' quoth she.

'Well then, Mistress Alice, if it be so,' quoth he, 'it is very well. For I see no great cause
why I should much joy either of my gay house or of anything belonging thereunto, when,
if I should but seven years lie buried under the ground and then arise and come thither 40
again, I should not fail to find some therein that would bid me get me out of doors, and

---

13. **silly** foolish. 14. **caitiff** wretch. 17. **turmoiled** troubled. 21. **What...goodyear** an expression of impatience and
frustration, like 'What the devil!' 23. **close** enclosed. 29. **muse** wonder. **a' God's name** in God's name. **fondly** foolishly.
35. **Tilly-vally** 'Nonsense!' 37. *Bone deus* 'Good God!' **gear** nonsense.

tell me it were none of mine. What cause have I then to like such an house as would so soon forget his master?'

So her persuasions moved him but a little.

Not long after came there to him the Lord Chancellor, the dukes of Norfolk and   45
Suffolk, with Master Secretary, and certain other of the Privy Council, at two several times, by all policies possible procuring him either precisely to confess the Supremacy or precisely to deny it. Whereunto, as appeareth by his examinations in the said great book, they could never bring him.

Shortly hereupon, Master Rich (afterwards Lord Rich), then newly made the King's   50
Solicitor, Sir Richard Southwell, and one Master Palmer, servant to the Secretary, were sent to Sir Thomas More into the Tower to fetch away his books from him. And while Sir Richard Southwell and Master Palmer were busy in the trussing-up of his books, Master Rich, pretending friendly talk with him among other things of a set course, as it seemed, said thus unto him: 55

'Forasmuch as it is well known, Master More, that you are a man both wise and well-learned, as well in the laws of the realm as otherwise, I pray you, therefore, sir, let me be so bold as of good will to put unto you this case. Admit there were, sir,' quoth he, 'an act of Parliament that all the realm should take me for king. Would not you, Master More, take me for king?'   60

'Yes, sir,' quoth Sir Thomas More, 'that would I.'

'I put case further,' quoth Master Rich, 'that there were an act of Parliament that all the realm should take me for pope. Would not you, then, Master More, take me for pope?'

'For answer, sir,' quoth Sir Thomas More, 'to your first case: the Parliament may well, Master Rich, meddle with the state of temporal princes. But to make answer to your   65
other case, I will put you this case: Suppose the Parliament would make a law that God should not be God. Would you, then, Master Rich, say that God were not God?'

'No, sir,' quoth he, 'that would I not, sith no Parliament may make any such law.'

'No more,' said Sir Thomas More, as Master Rich reported of him, 'could the Parliament make the king Supreme Head of the Church.'   70

Upon whose only report was Sir Thomas More indicted of treason upon the statute whereby it was made treason to deny the king to be Supreme Head of the Church. Into which indictment were put these heinous words, 'maliciously, traitorously, and diabolically'.

When Sir Thomas More was brought from the Tower to Westminster Hall to answer   75
the indictment, and at the King's Bench bar before the judges thereupon arraigned, he openly told them that he would upon that indictment have abiden in law but that he

---

45. Norfolk Sir Thomas Howard, 2nd earl of Surrey. **46. Suffolk** Charles Brandon (1484–1545). **Master Secretary** Thomas Cromwell (1485?–1540), chief architect of the Protestant revolution in England. **47. procuring** inducing. **48–9. said great book** perhaps an official court register **50. Master Rich** Richard Rich (1496–1567), created Baron Rich in 1547. **53. trussing-up** tying-up. **54. set course** predetermined plan. **68. sith** since. **71. only** single. **77. abiden in law** abided by the law.

thereby should have been driven to confess of himself the matter indeed, that was the denial of the King's Supremacy, which he protested was untrue. Wherefore he thereto pleaded not guilty, and so reserved unto himself advantage to be taken of the body 80 of the matter, after verdict, to avoid that indictment. And, moreover, added that if those only odious terms, 'maliciously, traitorously, and diabolically' were put out of the indictment, he saw therein nothing justly to charge him.

And for proof to the jury that Sir Thomas More was guilty of this treason, Master Rich was called forth to give evidence unto them upon his oath, as he did. Against whom thus 85 sworn, Sir Thomas More began in this wise to say:

'If I were a man, my lords, that did not regard an oath, I needed not (as it is well known) in this place at this time nor in this case to stand here as an accused person. And if this oath of yours, Master Rich, be true, then pray I that I never see God in the face, which I would not say, were it otherwise, to win the whole world.' Then recited he to the 90 court the discourse of all their communication in the Tower according to the truth and said, 'In good faith, Master Rich, I am sorrier for your perjury than for mine own peril. And you shall understand that neither I nor no man else to my knowledge ever took you to be a man of such credit as in any matter of importance I or any other would at any time vouchsafe to communicate with you. And I, as you know, of no small while have 95 been acquainted with you and your conversation, who have known you from your youth hitherto. For we long dwelled both in one parish together, where, as yourself can tell (I am sorry you compel me so to say), you were esteemed very light of your tongue, a great dicer, and of no commendable fame. And so in your house at the Temple, where hath been your chief bringing-up, were you likewise accounted. 100

'Can it, therefore, seem likely unto your honourable Lordships that I would in so weighty a cause so unadvisedly overshoot myself as to trust Master Rich, a man of me always reputed for one of so little truth, as your Lordships have heard, so far above my sovereign Lord, the King, or any of his noble counsellors, that I would unto him utter the secrets of my conscience touching the King's Supremacy—the special point and only 105 mark at my hands so long sought for? A thing which I never did, nor never would, after the statute thereof made, reveal either to the King's Highness himself, or to any of his honourable counsellors, as it is not unknown to your Honours, at sundry, several times sent from His Grace's own person unto the Tower unto me for none other purpose. Can this in your judgements, my lords, seem likely to be true? 110

'And yet, if I had so done indeed, my lords, as Master Rich hath sworn, seeing it was spoken but in familiar, secret talk, nothing affirming, and only in putting of cases without other displeasant circumstances, it cannot justly be taken to be spoken "maliciously". And where there is no malice there can be no offence. And, over this, I can

80–1. **advantage...matter** the possibility of confuting the charge. 82. **those only** only those. **put out** dismissed as non-applicable (because More was speaking only hypothetically). 96. **conversation** conduct. 99. **fame** reputation. 100. **Temple** the Middle Temple, one of the Inns of Court, where students studied law. 106. **mark** objective. 114. **over this** moreover.

never think, my lords, that so many worthy bishops, so many honourable personages, and so many other worshipful, virtuous, wise, and well-learned men, as at the making of that law were in the Parliament assembled, ever meant to have any man punished by death in whom there could be found no malice—taking *malitia* [malice] for *malevolentia* [evil-wishing]. For if *malitia* be generally taken for "sin", no man is there then that can thereof excuse himself. "Quia si dixerimus quod peccatum non habemus, nosmet ipsos seducimus, et veritas in nobis non est" [1 John 1: 8, Because if we say we have no sin we deceive ourselves and the truth is not in us]. And only this word "maliciously" is in the statute material, as this term "forcible" is in the statute of forcible entries. By which statute, if a man enter peaceably, and put not his adversary out forcibly, it is no offence. But if he put him out forcibly, then by that statute it is an offence, and so shall he be punished by this term "forcibly".'

'Besides this, the manifold goodness of the King's Highness himself, that hath been so many ways my singular good lord and gracious sovereign, that hath so dearly loved and trusted me even at my very first coming into his noble service with the dignity of his honourable Privy Council vouchsafing to admit me, and to offices of great credit and worship most liberally advanced me, and finally with that weighty room of His Grace's high Chancellor (the like whereof he never did to temporal man before), next to his own royal person the highest officer in this noble realm, so far above my merits or qualities able and meet therefore, of his incomparable benignity honoured and exalted me, by the space of twenty years and more, showing his continual favour towards me. And until at mine own poor suit it pleased His Highness, giving me licence with His Majesty's favour, to bestow the residue of my life for the provision of my soul in the service of God, of his especial goodness thereof to discharge and unburden me, most benignly heaped honours continually more and more upon me. All this His Highness's goodness, I say, so long thus bounteously extended towards me, were in my mind, my lords, matter sufficient to convince this slanderous surmise by this man so wrongfully imagined against me.'

Master Rich, seeing himself so disproved and his credit so foully defaced, caused Sir Richard Southwell and Master Palmer, that at that time of their communication were in the chamber, to be sworn what words had passed between them. Whereupon Master Palmer upon his deposition said that he was so busy about the trussing-up of Sir Thomas More's books in a sack that he took no heed to their talk. Sir Richard Southwell, likewise, upon his deposition said that because he was appointed only to look unto the conveyance of his books, he gave no ear unto them.

After this were there many other reasons (not now in my remembrance) by Sir Thomas More in his own defence alleged to the discredit of Master Rich's aforesaid evidence, and proof of the clearness of his own conscience. All which notwithstanding,

---

116. **worshipful** reputable. 123. **material** relevant. 131. **weighty room** important office. 132. **temporal** secular. 141. **convince** overturn. 145. **chamber** More's room in the Tower.

the jury found him guilty. And incontinent upon their verdict the Lord Chancellor (for that matter chief commissioner), beginning to proceed in judgement against him, Sir Thomas More said to him, 'My Lord, when I was toward the law, the manner in such case was to ask the prisoner before judgement why judgement should not be given against him.' Whereupon the Lord Chancellor, staying his judgement, wherein he had partly proceeded, demanded of him what he was able to say to the contrary. Who then in this sort most humbly made answer: [155]

'Forasmuch as, my lord,' quoth he, 'this indictment is grounded upon an act of Parliament directly repugnant to the laws of God and his holy Church, the supreme government of which, or of any part whereof, may no temporal prince presume by any law to take upon him, as rightfully belonging to the See of Rome, a spiritual pre-eminence by the mouth of our Saviour himself, personally present upon the earth, only to St Peter and his successors, bishops of the same See, by special prerogative granted, it is, therefore, in law amongst Christian men insufficient to charge any Christian man.' [160] [165]

And for proof thereof like as, among divers other reasons and authorities, he declared that this realm, being but one member and small part of the Church, might not make a particular law disagreeable with the general law of Christ's universal Catholic Church, no more than the city of London, being but one poor member in respect of the whole realm, might make a law against an act of Parliament to bind the whole realm. So farther showed he that it was contrary both to the laws and statutes of our own land yet unrepealed, as they might evidently perceive in Magna Carta: 'Quod Ecclesia Anglicana libera sit et habeat omnia jura sua integra, at libertates suas illaesas' [That the English Church may be free, and that it may have all its laws whole and its liberties unviolated]. And also contrary to that sacred oath which the King's Highness himself and every other Christian prince always with great solemnity received at their coronations, alleging, moreover, that no more might this realm of England refuse obedience to the See of Rome than might the child refuse obedience to his own natural father. For as St Paul said of the Corinthians, 'I have regenerated you, my children in Christ' [1 Cor. 3: 1], so might St Gregory, Pope of Rome (of whom by St Augustine, his messenger, we first received the Christian faith) of us Englishmen truly say, 'You are my children, because I have given to you everlasting salvation, a far higher and better inheritance than any carnal father can leave to his child, and by regeneration made you my spiritual children in Christ.' [170] [175] [180] [185]

Then was it by the Lord Chancellor thereunto answered that, seeing all the bishops, universities, and best learned of this realm had to this act agreed, it was much marvelled that he alone against them all would so stiffly stick thereat, and so vehemently argue there against.

---

153. **incontinent upon** immediately after. 155. **toward** practising. 163. **See** ecclesiastical territory (from Latin *sedes*, 'seat'). 166. **it** i.e. the act of Parliament. 174. **Magna Carta** charter of liberties granted by King John in 1215. 181. **children in Christ** only this phrase appears in Paul. **St Gregory** Gregory the Great (*r.* 590–604). 182. **St Augustine** Saint Augustine of Canterbury, apostle of the English (*d.* 604), not the more familiar St Augustine of Hippo. (See Bede, Persons in HISTORIES; Fig. 14.) 188. **stiffly stick** obstinately refuse.

To that Sir Thomas More replied saying, 'If the number of bishops and universities be so material as your Lordship seemeth to take it, then see I little cause, my lord, why that thing in my conscience should make any change. For I nothing doubt but that, though not in this realm, yet in Christendom about, of these well-learned bishops and virtuous men that are yet alive, they be not the fewer part that be of my mind therein. But if I should speak of those which already be dead (of whom many be now holy saints in heaven), I am very sure it is the far greater part of them that, all the while they lived, thought in this case that way that I think now. And, therefore, am I not bound, my lord, to conform my conscience to the Council of one realm against the general Council of Christendom.'

Now when Sir Thomas More for the avoiding of the indictment had taken as many exceptions as he thought meet, and more reasons than I can now remember alleged, the Lord Chancellor, loath to have the burden of that judgement wholly to depend upon himself, then openly asked the advice of the Lord Fitz-James, then the Lord Chief Justice of the King's Bench and joined in commission with him, whether this indictment were sufficient or not. Who, like a wise man, answered, 'My lords all, by St Julian' (that was ever his oath), 'I must needs confess that if the act of Parliament be not unlawful, then is not the indictment in my conscience insufficient.' Whereupon the Lord Chancellor said to the rest of the lords, 'Lo, my lords, lo, you hear what my Lord Chief Justice saith', and so immediately gave he judgement against him.

After which ended, the commissioners yet further courteously offered him, if he had anything else to allege for his defence, to grant him favourable audience. Who answered, 'More have I not to say, my lords, but that like as the blessed apostle St Paul, as we read in the Acts of the Apostles [7: 57–9], was present and consented to the death of St Stephen, and kept their clothes that stoned him to death, and yet be they now both twain holy saints in heaven, and shall continue there friends forever, so I verily trust and shall therefore right heartily pray that though your lordships have now here in earth been judges to my condemnation, we may yet hereafter in heaven merrily all meet together to our everlasting salvation.'

Thus much touching Sir Thomas More's arraignment, being not thereat present myself, have I by the credible report partly of the right worshipful Sir Anthony Saint Leger, knight, and partly of Richard Heywood, and John Webb, gentlemen, with others of good credit at the hearing thereof present themselves, as far as my poor wit and memory would serve me, here truly rehearsed unto you.

Now after this arraignment departed he from the bar to the Tower again, led by Sir William Kingston, a tall, strong, and comely knight, Constable of the Tower and his very dear friend, who, when he had brought him from Westminster to the Old Swan towards the Tower, there with an heavy heart, the tears running down by his cheeks, bade him farewell. Sir Thomas More, seeing him so sorrowful, comforted him with as good

207. Lo behold. 213. twain two.

words as he could, saying, 'Good Master Kingston, trouble not yourself, but be of good cheer. For I will pray for you, and my good lady, your wife, that we may meet in heaven together, where we shall be merry for ever and ever.' 230

Soon after, Sir William Kingston talking with me of Sir Thomas More, said, 'In good faith, Master Roper, I was ashamed of myself that at my departing from your father I found my heart so feeble and his so strong that he was fain to comfort me, which should rather have comforted him.'

When Sir Thomas More came from Westminster to the Tower-ward again, his 235 daughter, my wife, desirous to see her father, whom she thought she should never see in this world after, and also to have his final blessing, gave attendance about the Tower wharf, where she knew he should pass by before he could enter into the Tower, there tarrying for his coming home. As soon as she saw him, after his blessings on her knees reverently received, she, hasting towards him and without consideration or 240 care of herself, pressing in among the midst of the throng and company of the guard that with halberds and bills were round about him, hastily ran to him, and there openly in the sight of them all embraced him, took him about the neck, and kissed him. Who, well liking her most natural and dear daughterly affection towards him, gave her his fatherly blessing and many goodly words of comfort besides. 245

From whom after she was departed she, not satisfied with the former sight of him and like one that had forgotten herself, being all ravished with the entire love of her dear father, having respect neither to herself nor to the press of the people and multitude that were there about him, suddenly turned back again, ran to him as before, took him about the neck, and divers times together most lovingly kissed him, and at last with a full 250 heavy heart was fain to depart from him. The beholding whereof was to many of them that were present thereat so lamentable that it made them for very sorrow thereof to mourn and weep.

So remained Sir Thomas More in the Tower more than a seven-night after his judgement. From whence, the day before he suffered he sent his shirt of hair, not willing 255 to have it seen, to my wife, his dearly beloved daughter, and a letter, written with a coal, contained in the foresaid book of his works, plainly expressing the fervent desire he had to suffer on the morrow in these words following: 'I cumber you, good Margaret, much, but I would be sorry if it should be any longer than tomorrow. For tomorrow is St Thomas's Even and the Utas of St Peter and therefore tomorrow long I to go to 260 God. It were a day very meet and convenient for me, etc. I never liked your manner towards me better than when you kissed me last. For I like when daughterly love and dear charity hath no leisure to look to worldly courtesy.'

232. father father-in-law. 233. fain obliged. 242. halberds and bills pole-axes and broadswords. 247. entire perfect. 255. shirt of hair shirt made of hair or coarse fabric, worn next to the skin as penance. 258. cumber trouble. 260. Even…Utas Eve…Octave (eighth day after a feast), i.e. 6 July 1535. More was sentenced on 1 July, so Roper misremembers the intervening period as 'more than a seven-night', 254). 261. meet fit.

And so upon the next morrow, being Tuesday, St Thomas's Even and the Utas of
St Peter in the year of our Lord one thousand five hundred thirty and five, according as   265
he in his letter the day before had wished, early in the morning came to him Sir Thomas
Pope, his singular friend, on message from the king and his Council that he should
before nine of the clock the same morning suffer death, and that therefore forthwith he
should prepare himself thereunto.

'Master Pope,' quoth he, 'for your good tidings I most heartily thank you. I have been   270
always much bounden to the King's Highness for the benefits and honours which he hath
still from time to time most bountifully heaped upon me. And yet more bound I am
to His Grace for putting me into this place, where I have had convenient time and
space to have remembrance of my end. And so help me God, most of all, Master Pope,
am I bound to His Highness that it pleaseth him so shortly to rid me out of the miseries   275
of this wretched world. And, therefore, will I not fail earnestly to pray for His Grace
both here and also in another world.'

'The King's pleasure is further,' quoth Master Pope, 'that at your execution you shall
not use many words.'

'Master Pope,' quoth he, 'you do well to give me warning of His Grace's pleasure, for   280
otherwise I had purposed at that time somewhat to have spoken, but of no matter
wherewith His Grace or any other should have had cause to be offended. Nevertheless,
whatsoever I intended, I am ready obediently to conform myself to His Grace's
commandments. And I beseech you, good Master Pope, to be a mean unto His Highness
that my daughter Margaret may be at my burial.'   285

'The King is content already,' quoth Master Pope, 'that your wife, children, and other
friends shall have liberty to be present thereat.'

'Oh how much beholden, then' said Sir Thomas More, 'am I to His Grace that unto
my poor burial vouchsafeth to have so gracious consideration.'

Wherewithal Master Pope, taking his leave of him, could not refrain from weeping.   290
Which Sir Thomas More perceiving, comforted him in this wise, 'Quiet yourself,
good Master Pope, and be not discomforted. For I trust that we shall, once in heaven,
see each other full merrily, where we shall be sure to live and love together in joyful bliss
eternally.'

Upon whose departure Sir Thomas More, as one that had been invited to some   295
solemn feast, changed himself into his best apparel. Which Master Lieutenant espying,
advised him to put it off, saying that he that should have it was but a javel.

'What, Master Lieutenant,' quoth he, 'shall I account him a javel that shall do me this
day so singular a benefit? Nay, I assure you, were it cloth-of-gold I would account it well
bestowed on him, as St Cyprian did, who gave his executioner thirty pieces of gold.' And   300
albeit at length through Master Lieutenant's importunate persuasion he altered his

---

267. **singular** special. 284. **mean** means. 297. **javel** worthless fellow. Executioners customarily received the clothes of their
victims. 300. **St Cyprian** 3rd-c. bishop and martyr.

apparel, yet after the example of that holy martyr, St Cyprian, did he of that little money that was left him send one angel of gold to his executioner.

And so was he by Master Lieutenant brought out of the Tower and from thence led towards the place of execution. Where, going up the scaffold, which was so weak   305 that it was ready to fall, he said merrily to Master Lieutenant, 'I pray you, Master Lieutenant, see me safe up, and for my coming down, let me shift for myself.'

Then desired he all the people thereabout to pray for him, and to bear witness with him that he should now there suffer death in and for the faith of the holy Catholic Church. Which done, he kneeled down, and after his prayers said, turned to the   310 executioner and with a cheerful countenance spake thus to him:

'Pluck up thy spirits, man, and be not afraid to do thine office. My neck is very short. Take heed, therefore, thou strike not awry, for saving of thine honesty.'

So passed Sir Thomas More out of this world to God upon the very same day in which himself had most desired.   315

Soon after whose death came intelligence thereof to the Emperor Charles, whereupon he sent for Sir Thomas Elyot, our English ambassador, and said unto him, 'My Lord Ambassador, we understand that the King, your master, hath put his faithful servant and grave, wise counsellor, Sir Thomas More, to death.' Whereunto Sir Thomas Elyot answered that he understood nothing thereof.   320

'Well,' said the emperor, 'it is too true. And this will we say, that if we had been master of such a servant, of whose doings ourself have had these many years no small experience, we would rather have lost the best city of our dominions than have lost such a worthy counsellor.'

Which matter was by Sir Thomas Elyot to myself, to my wife, to Master Clement and   325 his wife, to Master John Heywood and his wife, and unto divers others his friends accordingly reported.

EDMUND CAMPION

The Jesuit Edmund Campion (1540–81) and his companions comprised the first wave of the English Mission, the attempt to support suppressed Catholics and to reclaim the country to Catholicism (see CONTROVERSIES). Months after arriving in Dover on the morning of 25 June 1580, disguised as a jewel merchant, Campion wrote the letter reprinted below. It gives a vivid sense of his life on the run, the solidarity of the

303. **angel** an English coin. 313. **saving…honesty** preserving your reputation. 316. **Charles** Charles V (r. 1519–56), Holy Roman Emperor. 317. **Thomas Elyot** (1490–1546), English diplomat and scholar. 326. **John Heywood** Catholic playwright and poet (see DRAMA), who married Thomas More's niece, Joan Rastell.

underground Catholic community, and his courage in the face of imminent death. Next, recounting his holy demeanour at execution, the address from the cart, and the final prayer for Elizabeth, Thomas Alfield portrays Campion's death as a martyrdom for the faith. Like William Allen's *A True, Sincere, and Modest Defence of English Catholics* (1584, see CONTROVERSIES) and Circignani's martyr fresco in the English College of Rome, subsequently published by de Cavalleriis (see Fig. 8), Alfield's account thus contradicts Lord Burlegh's *The Execution of Justice in England* (1583, rev. 1584), the official government report of the death as punishment for treason.

Letter to Mercurian, 1580

Right Reverend Father,

Having now passed by God's great mercy five months in these places, I thought it good to give you intelligence by my letters of the present state of things here, and what we may of likelihood look for to come. For I am sure, both for your common care of us all and special love to me, you long to know what I do, what hope I have, how I proceed.   5
Of other things that fell before I wrote from Saint-Omer; what have sithence happened now I will briefly recount unto you.

It fell out, as I construe it, by God's special provision that, tarrying for wind four days together, I should at length take sea the fifth day in the evening, which was the feast of St John Baptist, my peculiar patron, to whom I had often before commended my   10
cause and journey. So we arrived safely at Dover the morrow following very early, my little man and I together. There we were at the very point to be taken, being by commandment brought before the mayor of the town, who conjectured many things, suspected us to be such as indeed we were—adversaries of the new heretical faction, favourers of the old fathers' faith, that we dissembled our names, had been abroad for   15
religion, and returned again to spread the same. One thing he especially urged, that I was Allen, which I denied, proffering my oath if need were for the verifying thereof.

At length, he resolveth (and that so it should be, he often repeated) that with some to guard me I should be sent to the council. Neither can I tell who altered his determination, saving God to whom underhand I then humbly prayed, using St John's interces-   20
sion also, by whose happy help I safely came so far. Suddenly cometh forth an old man—God give him grace for his labour! 'Well,' quoth he, 'it is agreed you shall be dismissed.

1. **Father** Everard Mercurian, the General of the Society of Jesus (1573–80). 3. **intelligence** news. 6. **Saint-Omer** a town near Calais in France that served as a centre for expatriate English Catholics, later home of a Jesuit College. **sithence** since then. 10. **peculiar** particular. 12. **little man** Brother Ralph Emerson (1550–81), who suffered severe torture before execution with Campion. **we . . . taken** After the ill-fated papal military expedition to Ireland earlier that year, which the English routed at Smerwick, port authorities were especially vigilant. (See O'Sullivan-Beare, HISTORIES.) 17. **Allen** William Allen, by this time, feared and hated in England for his support of the Spanish invasion. 20. **underhand** secretly.

Roman Mannovist

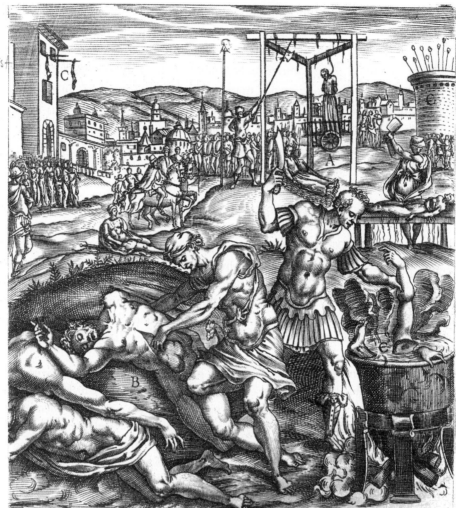

A. *Edmundus Campianus focietatis Iesu sub patibulo concionatur, statimq, cum Alexandro Brianto Rhemensis, et Rodulpho-Sheruiño huius Collegij alumno suspenditur.*

B. *Illis adhuc tepentibus cor et uiscera extrahuntur, et in ignem proijciuntur.*

C. *Eorundem membra feruenti aqua elixantur, tum adurbis turres et portas appenduntur, regnante Elizabetha Anno M.D.LXXXI. die prima Decebris. Horum constanti morte aliquot hominum millia ad Romanam Ecclesiam conuersa sunt.*

33

8. Giovanni Baptista de Cavalleriis, 'The Martyrdom of Edmund Campion, Alexander Briant, and Ralph Sherwin', *Ecclesiae Anglicanae Trophaea*, 1584, pl. 33. The A section depicts the hanging; B, the disembowelling and burning of body parts to prevent the creation of relics; C, the hanging of heads and limbs from towers and gates as a proclamation and warning.

Fare you well.' And so we go apace. The which things considered and the like that daily befall unto me, I am verily persuaded that one day I shall be apprehended, but that then when it shall most pertain to God's glory and not before. 25

Well, I came to London and my good angel guided me unwitting into the same house that had harboured Father Robert before. Whither young gentlemen came to me; on every hand they embrace me, reapparel me, furnish me, weapon me, and convey me out of the city. I ride about some piece of the country every day. The harvest is wonderful great. On horseback I meditate my sermon; when I come to the house, I polish it. Then 30 I talk with such as come to speak with me, or hear their confessions. In the morning after mass I preach. They hear with exceeding greediness and very often receive the sacraments.

For the ministration whereof we are ever well assisted by priests whom we find in every place, whereby both the people is well served and we much eased in our charge. The 35 priests of our country, themselves being excellent for virtue and learning, yet have raised so great an opinion of our Society that I dare scarcely touch the exceeding reverence all Catholics do unto us. How much more is it requisite that such as hereafter are to be sent for supply, whereof we have great need, be such as may answer all men's expectation of them. Specially let them be well trained for the pulpit. I cannot long escape the 40 hands of the heretics; the enemies have so many eyes, so many tongues, so many scouts and crafts.

I am in apparel to myself very ridiculous. I often change it and my name also. I read letters, sometimes myself that in the first front tell news, 'That Campion is taken'. Which, noised in every place where I come, so filleth mine ears with the sound thereof 45 that fear itself has taken away all fear. 'My soul is in my own hands ever' [Ps. 118: 109]. Let such as you send for supply premeditate and make count of this always.

Marry, the solaces that are ever intermeddled with these miseries are so great that they do not only countervail the fear of what punishment temporal soever, but by infinite sweetness make all worldly pains, be they never so great, seem nothing. A conscience 50 pure, a courage invincible, zeal incredible, a work so worthy, the number innumerable— of high degree, of mean calling, of the inferior sort, of every age and sex. Here even amongst the Protestants themselves that are of milder nature it is turned into a proverb, that he must be a Catholic that payeth faithfully that he oweth. Insomuch that if any Catholic do injury, everybody expostulateth with him as for an act unworthy of men 55 of that calling.

25. **to God's glory** In the original Latin version of the letter, which William Allen reprints along with this translation in *A Brief History of the Glorious Martyrdom of XII Reverend Priests* (1582), Campion here uses the Jesuit motto, *ad maiorem Dei gloriam*, 'to the greater glory of God'. 27. **Father Robert** Robert Persons, SJ, brilliant polemicist and Campion's immediate superior, who, disguised as a soldier, had arrived earlier and prepared contacts for Campion in London. 40. **trained...pulpit** Campion was a superb preacher, and Jesuits, prizing rhetoric and debate, cultivated the art of the homily. 44. **myself...news** that on the first page tell news of me. 47. **make count of** take into account. 48. **Marry** a mild oath ('By Mary', originally).

To be short, heresy heareth ill of all men. Neither is there any condition of people commonly counted more vile and impure than their ministers. And we worthily have indignation that fellows so unlearned, so evil, so derided, so base should in so desperate a quarrel overrule such a number of noble wits as our realm hath. 60

Threatening edicts come forth against us daily. Notwithstanding, by good heed, and the prayers of good men, and which is the chief of all, by God's special gift we have passed safely through the most part of the island. I find many neglecting their own security to have only care of my safety.

A certain matter fell out these days by God's appointment unlooked for. I had set 65 down in writing by several articles the causes of my coming in, and made certain demands most reasonable. I professed myself to be a priest of the Society, that I returned to enlarge the Catholic faith, to teach the Gospel, to minister the sacraments, humbly asking audience of the queen and the nobility of the realm, and proffering disputations to the adversaries. One copy of this writing I determined to keep with me, that if I should 70 fall into the officers' hands it might go with me. Another copy I laid in a friend's hand, that when myself with the other should be seized on, the other might thereupon straight be dispersed.

But my said friend kept it not close long but divulged it, and it was read greedily. Whereat the adversaries were mad, answering out of their pulpits that themselves 75 certes would not refuse to dispute, but the queen's pleasure was not that matters should be called to question, being already established. In the meanwhile they tear and sting us with their venomous tongues, calling us seditious, hypocrites, yea, heretics too, which is much laughed at. The people hereupon is ours. And that error of spreading abroad this writing hath much advanced the cause. If we be commanded and may have safe conduct, 80 we will into the court.

But they mean nothing less, for they have filled all the old prisons with Catholics, and now make new, and, in fine, plainly affirm that it were better to make a few traitors away than so many souls should be lost. Of their martyrs they brag no more now. For we surpass them in the cause, number, dignity, and reputation of all. For it is now come to 85 pass that for a few apostates and cobblers of theirs burned we have bishops, lords, knights, the old nobility, patterns of learning, piety, and prudence, the flower of the youth, noble matrons, and of the inferior sort innumerable either martyred at once or by consuming prisonment dying daily. At the very writing hereof the persecution rageth

57. heareth ill of is reported as bad by. **65 ff.** Campion here recounts the circumstances of his famous 'Letter to the Privy Council' (CONTROVERSIES). **71. friend** lay brother Thomas Pounde (1538–1612), who later passed Campion's paper to fellow prisoners at Marshalsea in Southwark, where it eventually came to the authorities. Pounde, a writer himself, spent nearly thirty years in prison for his Catholicism (see POETRY). **76. certes** certainly. **84–5. For…all** Allen omits this sentence in his translation. **86. few…burned** Like many before and after, Campion fails to acknowledge the sins of his own side, here dismissing the victims of Marian persecution. The contrast between the 'cobblers' and the 'patterns of learning' illustrates the larger Catholic tendency to deny martyr status to the Marian victims because of their supposed ignorance of doctrine (see Persons, HISTORIES).

most cruelly. The house where I am is sad; no other talk but of death, flight, prison, or   90
spoil of their friends. Nevertheless, they proceed with courage.

Very many even at this present being restored to the Church, new soldiers give up their
names while the old offer up their blood. By which holy hosts and oblations, God will be
pleased and we shall, no question, by him overcome.

You see now, therefore, Reverend Father, how much need we have of your prayers and   95
sacrifices, and other heavenly help to go through with these things. There will never want
in England men that will have care of their own salvation, nor such as shall advance other
men's. Neither shall this Church here ever fail so long as priests and pastors shall be found
for the sheep, rage man or devil never so much. But the rumour of present peril causeth
me here to make an end. 'Arise, God; His enemies, avoid' [Ps. 67: 2]. Fare you well.   100

Thomas Alfield, *A True Report*, 1582

The divers and contrary reports falsely and maliciously bruited and published of
Master Everard Hanse, directly executed for cause of religion, after his late martyrdom
gave just fear of the like practice towards those three glorious martyrs, learned, meek,
stout, and constant priests, Master Edmund Campion, Jesuit, Master Ralph Sherwin,
and Master Alexander Briant, priests, who upon the first day of December last past were   5
under pretence of high treason most injuriously to the great lamentation generally of all
good men martyred for the Catholic faith and religion. Upon which occasion many good
Catholic gentlemen, desirous to be eyewitnesses of that which might happen in the
speech, demeanour, and passage of those three rare patterns of piety, virtue, and
innocency, presented themselves at the place of execution, and myself, a Catholic priest,   10
pressed to that bloody spectacle (no doubt a lively sacrifice unto God and a sweet savour
unto his angels) with mind upon occasion to refer sincerely and truly to my power this
tragedy, with such accidents as did happen, in the manner, course, and end thereof. Since
which time, upon request of some of my fellows and brethren, I wrote those dealings to
answer and satisfy our adversaries generally, and to content and comfort our persecuted   15
brethren specially, and in part to diminish those sinister rumours which are raised against
these good men by a notable and most infamous libel, entitled *An Advertisement and
Defence for Truth against her Backbiters.*
[. . .]

100. **avoid** be gone.

A TRUE REPORT 1. **bruited** rumoured. 2. **Everard Hanse** priest, martyred 31 July 1581. 4–5. **Master Ralph . . . Briant**
fellow missionaries executed with Campion. 6. **pretence . . . treason** Burlegh printed supposedly incriminating evidence in
the form of a letter 'taken about one of their complices immediately after Campion's death'. Recovered after the sentence
had been carried out, the document is Gregory XIII's *rebus sic stantibus* provision, which actually declares Pius's bull non-
binding on English Catholics, 'as things stand now' (*Execution*, 1584, sigs. Biv^v–Ci^v). 11. **savour** scent (as from a sacrifice
or incense). 12. **with . . . refer** intending on this occasion to tell. 17–18. ***An . . . Backbiters*** an anonymous pamphlet (1581,
STC 153.7) that portrayed Campion and his companions as seditious traitors.

What he [Campion] spake openly, that my meaning is to set down truly, myself being present and very near, as hard by Sir Francis Knollys, the Lord Howard, Sir Henry Lee, and other gentlemen then gathered there to see and hear him. And here I will omit, though it be very much material, his usage in time of imprisonment, his constant patience in his rackings, and after his condemnation, by report of some very near to him, his five days' fast from temporal and bodily sustenance, his abstinence from sleep and ordinary rest, which was before his death by credible report of some, continued two nights, bestowed in meditation and prayer. Who, after many conflicts and agonies joyfully coming to receive his reward and crown, the kingdom of heaven, an inheritance certain to such who in this life refuse the world, things worldly, and themselves for Christ's sake, after some small pause in the cart with grave countenance and sweet voice stoutly spake as followeth:

'Spectaculum facti sumus Deo, angelis, et hominibus' (1 Cor. 4: 9), saying, 'these are the words of Saint Paul, Englished thus, "We are made a spectacle or a sight unto God, unto his angels, and unto men," verified this day in me, who am here a spectacle unto my Lord God, a spectacle unto his angels, and unto you men.'

And here, going forward in this text, was interrupted and cut off by Sir Francis Knollys and the sheriffs, earnestly urging him to confess his treason against Her Majesty and to acknowledge himself guilty. To whom he answered, saying, 'You have now what you do desire. I beseech you to have patience and suffer me to speak a word or two for discharge of my conscience.'

But being not suffered to go forward, gave answer to that point they always urged, that he was guiltless and innocent of all treason and conspiracy, craving credit to be given to this answer as to his last answer, made upon his death and soul, adding that, touching this point, both the jury might be deceived and more also put in the evidence than was true. Notwithstanding, he forgave as he would be forgiven, desiring all them to forgive him whom he had confessed upon the rack.

Further, he declared the meaning of a letter sent by himself in time of his imprisonment out of the Tower, in which he wrote he would not disclose the secrets of some houses where he had been entertained, affirming on his soul that the secrets he meant in that letter were not, as some misconstrued them, treason or conspiracy, or any matter else any way intended against Her Majesty or the state, but saying of mass, hearing of confession, preaching, and such like duties and functions of priests. This he protested to be true as he would answer before God.

20. Sir Francis Knollys militant Protestant (1514–96), active in persecuting Catholics. **Lord Howard** Charles Howard (1536–1624), later Lord Admiral of England against the Armada. **Sir Henry Lee** another Protestant (1532–1611), active against Catholics in the north. **23. rackings** sessions of torture on the rack, a wooden frame which stretched its victims. **29. cart** wagon in which the condemned rode to execution. **35. cut off** 'They would not suffer him to speak in religion lest he should have persuaded the people' (William Allen, *A Briefe Historie*, 1582, sig. d). **45. whom . . . rack** 'Upon the commissioners' oaths that no harm should come unto them, he uttered some persons with whom he had been' (Allen, *Briefe Historie*, sig. di^v). Much controversy exists over the alleged confessions of Campion; see James V. Holleran, *A Jesuit Challenge* (1999), 36–41. **46. letter** to Thomas Pounde, also captive in the Tower.

Then he desired Sir Francis Knollys and some other of nobility to hear him touching one Richardson, condemned about a book of his, and earnestly besought them to have consideration of that man, saying he was not that Richardson which brought his book, 55 and this he affirmed with vehement protestation upon his death.

Then one Hearne, a schoolmaster, as I learned after, read the new advertisement openly with loud voice unto the people, published only to colour so manifest and express injury, Master Campion all the time of his reading devoutly praying. Notwithstanding which advertisement or defence of theirs, as well because they distrusted their own policy in 60 publication thereof as that they did also desire some better colour or faster vizard for their proceedings, pressed him to declare his opinion of Pius Quintus' Bull concerning the excommunication of our sovereign and queen. To which demand he gave no answer. But being asked whether he renounced the pope, said he was a Catholic, whereupon one inferred, saying, 'In your Catholicism—I noted the word—all treason is contained.' In 65 fine, preparing himself to drink his last draught of Christ his cup, was interrupted in his prayer by a minister, willing him to say, 'Christ have mercy upon me,' or such like prayer with him. Unto whom he, looking back with mild countenance, humbly said, 'You and I are not one in religion; wherefore, I pray you, content yourself. I bar none of prayer, only I desire them of the household of faith to pray with me and in mine agony to say one Creed.' 70

Some also called on him to pray in English, to whom he answered that he would pray in a language that he well understood. At the upshot of this conflict he was willed to ask the queen forgiveness and to pray for her. He meekly answered, 'Wherein have I offended her? In this I am innocent. This is my last speech; in this give me credit. I have and do pray for her.' Then did the Lord Charles Howard ask of him for which queen he prayed, 75 whether for Elizabeth Queen. To whom he answered, 'Yea, for Elizabeth, your queen and my queen, unto whom I wish a long, quiet reign with all prosperity.' And so he meekly and sweetly yielded his soul unto his Saviour, protesting that he died a perfect Catholic.

MARGARET CLITHEROW

Still remembered today as 'the Pearl of York', Margaret Clitherow (1556?–86) converted to Catholicism in 1574 and led a life of joyful devotion and humble service. Wife of the Protestant butcher, John Clitherow, Margaret Clitherow, like so many Catholic women,

54. **Richardson** Laurence Richardson, a secular priest on the mission, executed 30 May 1582. 57. **advertisement** a proclamation asserting Campion's treachery. 61. **faster vizard** more secure mask. 62. **Pius Quintus' Bull** Pope Pius V's infamous bull, *Regnans in excelsis* (1570), excommunicated Elizabeth I and absolved Catholic subjects from obedience (see DOCUMENTS). 65. **inferred** broke in. 70. **I...faith** Catholics were not permitted to pray with Protestants. **Creed** either the Apostles' Creed or the Nicene Creed. Campion prays the Creed 'For a signification that he died for the confession of the Catholic faith therein contained' (William Allen, *Briefe Historie*, sig. dii), and not for the alleged treason. 76–7. **Yea...prosperity** Prayers for Elizabeth at the gallows, perhaps sincere, publicly confuted the charge of treason. See also Clitherow below. 78. **protesting** showing.

acted on the conviction that she was in her 'necessary duty to God . . . no whit inferior' to her husband (ed. J. Morris, *Troubles of our Catholic Forefathers*, 1877: iii. 382). She turned their home into a refuge for priests and a centre of Catholic liturgy and fellowship; she emerged as a religious leader in York, which had a vital recusant community. Indicted for harbouring priests, Margaret Clitherow refused trial and, despite her possible pregnancy, received the sentence of *peine forte et dure*, i.e. pressing to death by stones. She fasted, prayed, and, dressed in white linen, preparing for death as for a banquet and marriage. She sent her hat to her husband 'in sign of her loving duty to him' and her hose and shoes to her eldest daughter, Anne, 'signifying that she should serve God and follow her steps of virtue' (ed. Morris, 432).

    A True Report of the Life and Martyrdom of Mrs. Margaret Clitherow circulated in manuscript in York from 1586 and in an abstracted printed version (1619), excerpted below. Clitherow's confessor, John Mush, presents here a Catholic saint's life to counter the Protestant canonization of Anne Askew. Another influential account of Margaret Clitherow as martyr appears in Richard Verstegan's *Theatrum crudelitatum haereticorum* (1587) (see Fig. 9).

John Mush, *A True Report of the Life and Martyrdom of Mrs. Margaret Clitherow*, 1619

The name of this virtuous and holy martyr was Mistress Margaret Clitherow, the wife of Master John Clitherow, citizen of York, the head city of the kingdom of England next unto London, enjoying privileges equally with it in having a Lord Mayor with the sword carried before him, sheriffs, and aldermen, as London hath. She was the daughter of one Master Middleton, a man of good wealth, and estimation, who had been   5 sheriff in the same city, an office next in place and credit unto the Lord Mayor. She was about some 18 years of age when she was married, her breeding giving her knowledge of no other religion than of that was publicly taught within the kingdom. But years ripening her judgement, and she, finding nothing but froth and dross in the Protestant faith, began to search after the truth, which she followed with such labour and care as that   10 within two or three years after her marriage she became a true member of the Catholic Church. There were two motives amongst others that drew her to this consideration:

---

1. **martyr** Some Catholics, notably Robert Persons, excluded Clitherow from the ranks of Catholic martyrs because she was unlearned. She here falls victim to Persons's argument with Foxe on many Protestant martyrs, who, he claimed, were simply ignorant and did not understand the religious doctrines for which they died (see Persons, HISTORIES). 3–4. **Lord Mayor . . . him** The mayor in certain large towns had the honorific title of 'Lord Mayor' and walked behind a drawn sword in civic processions. In 1586 the Lord Mayor was Henry May, Margaret's stepfather. 4. **aldermen** chief officers of wards. 5. **estimation** reputation.

Perfecutiones aduerfus Catholicos à Prote-
ftantibus Caluiniftis excitæ in Anglia.

Et tua femineum commendat gloria fexum,
Dura nec in fummis animo demiffa virago
Supplicijs, tenerámque tui non pondera molem
Corporis, iniecti non turbauere molares:
Quin, ait, his totos membris imponite montes,
Spiritus innocua tranfcendet ad aftra ruina.

K 3   PRES-

9. Richard Verstegan, 'The Martyrdom of Margaret Clitherow', *Theatrum crudelitatum haereticorum*, 1587, sig. K3. The A section presents Clitherow's execution; B, the torture of a priest; C and D, the prisons where Catholics died of disease.

the one was the regular lives of Catholics compared with the irregularity of the Protestants; the other, the persecution that priests and laymen patiently and constantly suffered for the Catholic and apostolic faith, with the loss of goods, liberty, and life.   15

There were not above twelve years between her conversion and her martyrdom, during which time she so perfected herself in virtue and strictness of life as that she was rather a spectacle for others than truly imitated. For she was truly humble, truly charitable to God and her neighbours, truly obedient unto her spiritual and temporal superiors, a diligent observer and follower of others' virtues, and a true condemner of the world.   20 She had a mind full of peace and tranquillity, full of spiritual joy and comfort; her abstinence was great, her pilgrimages many, and her fervour and zeal unto Catholic religion such, and her desire so great to frequent the sacraments, as continually she maintained priests for the spiritual comfort of herself and others to the daily hazard of her life.   25

All these virtues did perfectly shine in her. But as humility and charity are the fundamental virtues that do give life unto the rest, so these by God's especial favour were very truly inoculated in her, for she was so humble as she preferred all others before herself. Her most devout actions seemed base in her own sight, and she was so far from delighting in her own praises as that she desired (so far forth as charity would give her   30 leave) to be ill thought of by others. She took it ever well to have her faults told her, were it done by her ghostly father, friend, or stranger. She was jealous of her actions, pensive when she heard her own praises, and at quiet when she heard herself dispraised.

If her good desires took not effect, she imputed the cause unto her own unworthiness, yielding all honour unto God and not regarding the judgement of men. Answer she   35 would for herself to wipe out ill imputations laid on her, but rather for the good of others than in respect for herself. The basest works of her house were her task, ennobling them with this saying: 'God forbid I should command that unto others which myself will refuse.' They that grudge at these things do not go to the way of perfect humility.

Her ghostly father, writing of her life, says that the humility, contrition, and loath-   40 someness which he saw in her of herself did make a deep impression in him of his estate. What shall I say? She was so resigned up unto God as all fortunes were indifferent unto her, in herself ever preferring those things wherein God's honour might be most advanced. Insomuch as being many times calumniated for her virtue by Catholics and such of them as were by courtesies obliged unto her, she would rejoice concerning   45 herself, but be very pensive to see others run themselves on so dangerous a shipwreck. No opportunity was let slip by her wherein she might help her neighbour, she, wishing God's favour and graces to shine as well that way as on herself, being never better pleased than in the well doing of others.

All distressed Catholics in prison or at liberty she would relieve by all the means that   50 lay in her power. She continually sought the conversion of souls. Beginners in the

---

28. inoculated imbued.   **32. ghostly** spiritual, i.e. her confessor John Mush.   **jealous** vigilant.   **33. pensive** sad, thoughtful.

Catholic faith she would encourage and with deep sighs bewail the sins of others. She was much delighted to hear the lives of holy saints related, bewailing that she was so far from their perfection. She had ever a strong resolution against sinning and an extraordinary contrition for those she had committed, accompanied with a vehement desire to suffer 55
for them, insomuch as when she was afflicted, she exceedingly rejoiced, being never more pensive or more doubtful of God's favour unto her than when she enjoyed any relaxation. Such was her love unto God, which ruled all her actions as for him she abandoned all fear of persecution, and in the end she gave her life for him.

Humility and charity begat in her such obedience as all her actions were squared by 60
the advice of her ghostly father, and they bred in her such a respect unto priests as that she reverenced all without respect of persons.

They begat in her such devotion as few in a religious cloister lived more strictly, for besides her prayers morning and evening at each time for the space of an hour or two, with certain meditations on the passion of our Saviour, the benefices of God, and such 65
like, and besides the keeping of priests in her own house for her own spiritual comfort and abroad for the good of others, all her actions were directed to the honour of God. And if at any time she did anything without an actual intention that way, upon the first reflection she would much reprove herself. They begat also in her a life of so great abstinence as four times in the week she fasted and upon every Friday used discipline if 70
she had leave, the other days feeding on the grossest meats, excusing herself from feasts all that she could for fear of excess, bestowing that time in prayer and meditation in which she could keep herself from them.

All these virtues, meeting within the centre of her soul, made indivisible from God and nothing unto herself by her resignation unto him, did prepare her way after many 75
persecutions unto a most glorious martyrdom, as will appear.
[...]

After her examination she was put into a secret place under ground, and her husband into another, but about seven of the clock at night she was conveyed into the castle and there committed close prisoner, and her husband also about some hour after.

Four days she remained there before she came to her trial, during which time she never 80
spake with her husband but once, and that in the presence of the jailer, after which time she could never be admitted to see him or speak with him, notwithstanding all the suit she and her friends could make, unless she would do something against her conscience and contrary to the rules of a good Roman Catholic.

During her imprisonment in the Castle she gave herself unto more strictness in 85
abstinence and prayer. And it being reported to her that the boy had accused her for harbouring and maintaining divers priests, but of two officially by name, to wit, Master

60. squared by conformed to. **70. discipline** beating or whipping of oneself. **78. castle** York Castle, which was used for a prison. **79. close** secluded. **86. the boy** a student, aged 10–12, who had been receiving instruction in the house when the pursuivants broke in. Stripped naked and threatened with rods, he revealed the hidden priest chambers. The story is told in a manuscript account (ed. J. Morris, *Troubles of our Catholic Forefathers*, 1877: iii. 410–11).

Francis Ingleby and Master John Mush, and that, according to a law newly in force, she was to suffer death for the same, she was much pleased with the news and, smiling, thanked the messenger, wishing she had some good thing to give him, but, wanting   90
better means, having a fig in her hand, she gave him that for a reward.
[...]

The judge demanded how she would be tried. 'Having not offended,' quoth she, 'I need no trial.' Answer was made that she had offended the statute made against the maintenance of priests and therefore she must have her trial, urging her to say how she would be tried. 'If you say,' quoth she, 'that I have offended and that I must be tried, then   95
I will be tried by none but by God and your own consciences.'

One of the judges told her that they would admit no such answer for that they sat there to see justice executed and to give judgement according unto the verdict delivered unto them and therefore she must be tried by the country. But still she appealed to God and their consciences.   100

Hereupon the judges commanded to be brought forth the two chalices, divers pictures, and some vestments with other ornaments of the altar in use in the Catholic Church. These sacred ornaments were by way of derision put on two fellows' backs, who with twenty antic faces made themselves apes to please the judges and the multitude, and, holding up some wafer breads, said to the martyr, 'Behold thy God, in whom thou   105
believest.' They asked her how she liked the vestments. 'I like them well,' quoth she, 'if they were on their backs that know how to use them unto God's honour.'

The judge, Clinch, asked her in whom she believed. 'I believe,' quoth she, 'in God.' He demanded in what God. 'I believe,' quoth she, 'in God the Father, in God the Son, and in God the Holy Ghost, in three persons and one God, and that by the passion, death, and   110
mercy of Christ Jesus I must be saved.' The judge told her she said well and he, having paused a while, demanded of her again if she were contented to be tried by God and the country, the which she refused. Hereupon the judge bid her to consider well what she did. 'For,' quoth he, 'if you refuse to be tried by the country, you make yourself guilty of your own death. For we cannot try you but by order of law, and you need not fear this   115
kind of trial, for I do think the country cannot find you guilty upon the bare evidence of a child.' Yet this trial she still refused, and her reason was, as it hath been reported, for that she saw they intended to have her blood, whereof she would not have the child to be guilty, being brought to accuse her for fear of whipping, as is before declared.
[...]

'If then,' quoth the judge to the martyr, 'you will not put yourself on the country, hear   120
your judgement. You shall return unto the place from whence you came, and there in the lower part of the prison be stripped stark naked, laid down on your back to the ground, and so much weight laid on you as you are able to bear, and thus you shall continue

88. **Francis Ingleby** (1551–86), priest and Yorkshire martyr. **John Mush** (1551–1612?), Yorkshire priest, author of the present narrative, and later an Appellant, one who protested the appointment of George Blackwell as archpriest of England. 104. **apes** mimicking clowns. 113. **and the country** i.e. and by a jury of peers.

for three days without any other food than a little barley bread and puddle water, and the third day you shall have a sharp stone put under your back, and your hands and feet shall be tied unto posts that, more weight being laid upon you, you may be pressed to death.' 125

The martyr, not dismayed with the sentence, told the judge that if this judgement were according to his conscience, she prayed God to send him a better judgement in the later day, and so gave humble thanks unto God for that which was done against her. [...]

From the time that this holy martyr was committed again to prison unto her death, 130 which was some nine or ten days, she never wore any linen next unto her skin and her diet was water-pottage, rye bread, and small ale, the which she took once in the day but in a very little quantity. And from the time that she had certain notice that she should die she took no food at all.
[...]

Thus was this innocent lamb delivered up into the butcher's hands. Some of the 135 Council and divers ministers at several times repaired unto her, and pressed her going unto their church for the saving of her life, wherein she constantly resisted them. They also demanded of her many questions concerning religious priests resorting unto her house and of some particularly by name, but she, aiming at their ill intentions, by her discreet answers frustrated their hopes. Wherefore, hopeless to draw her unto their desires or to get 140 anything from her to the prejudice of others, they resorteth no more unto her, but resolved she should die according to the judgement given against her. And the better to colour her death under the show of justice, they raised of her many false and slanderous reports.

And now the 25th of March being come, and no word sent from the judge to stay execution, she had word brought to her by the sheriff that she must prepare herself to die, 145 telling the day and hour. The night before her death she spake unto the man's wife that had the custody of her to have some women watch with her that night. 'Not that I fear death,' quoth she, 'for that is comfort; but the flesh is frail.' The woman told her that the jailer had locked the door and was gone to bed and, therefore, none could be had. But the woman herself, being ready to go to bed, put on her clothes again and sat by her until 150 towards midnight, the martyr spending her time in prayer. About midnight the woman went unto her rest, and within some hour after the martyr rose up from her prayers, put off her apparel, and put on a linen habit which she had made of purpose for her martyrdom. In this habit without any other garment she betook herself again unto her prayers on her knees until three of the clock, at which time she came unto the fireside 155 and laid herself flat down upon the stones a quarter of an hour and so went to bed, where she lay until six in the morning.

126. pressed to death Upon hearing of Margaret's sentence, John Clitherow wept until blood came from his nose and exclaimed, 'Alas! Will they kill my wife?' (ed. Morris, iii. 418). 129. later day i.e. at the Last Judgement. 132. water-pottage thin soup. small ale weak beer. 136. divers ministers Edmund Bunney, who attempted to browbeat her with scriptural quotation and argument; Giles Wiggington, the Puritan who had objected to the use of the boy witness at court (ed. Morris, iii. 416, 420 ff.). 136-7. pressed...unto urged her to go to. 143. false and slanderous reports the standard accusation of harlotry with priests (ed. Morris, iii. 414).

Then, preparing for death, she entreated this Yoward's wife that had the custody of her to see her die, wishing she might be accompanied by some Catholics in that time of her agony to put her in mind of God. 160

Yoward's wife denied to be present at so cruel a death, but proffered to procure some friend to lay on store of weight to put her quickly out of her pain, the which the martyr absolutely refused.

About eight of the clock the sheriff came, who found her ready, expecting this rich banquet prepared for her. With the linen habit on her arm and some inckle which 165 she had provided to tie her feet and hands, she went barefoot and bare-legged, and her gown loose about her, but her headgear was decently put on, and so she went cheerfully unto her marriage, as she called it.

The place of execution was the toll-booth some twenty foot distant from the prison, and she must of necessity come into the street to go unto this place. The street was full of 170 people, insomuch as she could hardly pass. Yet as she went, she dealt her alms. The sheriff hastened her to come away, to whom she answered merrily, 'Good Master Sheriff, let me deal my poor alms before I go. I have but a short time in this world.'

There were admitted into the room where she suffered no more but the two sheriffs, one gentleman, one minister, four women, three or four men, four sergeants, and those 175 the sergeants had hired to do the execution.

The martyr, coming into the room, kneeled down and prayed unto herself. The officers and standers-by bid her pray with them and they would pray with her, which she denied, saying she would not so much as say 'Amen' unto their prayers, nor willingly should they do unto hers. 180

Then they willed her to pray for the queen, whereupon the martyr in the hearing of them all began as followeth:

'I do pray for the Catholic Church, for the Pope's Holiness and Cardinals, for all such as have care of souls, and for all Christian princes in the world.' At which words the officers interrupted her, and commanded her not to put the Queen's Majesty amongst 185 that company. Yet the martyr proceeded. 'And for Elizabeth, Queen of England. And I humbly beseech God to turn her to the Catholic faith that after this mortal life she may enjoy the joys of heaven, unto whose soul I do wish as much joy as unto mine own.'

One of the sheriffs, called Gibson, moved with compassion towards her, withdrew himself unto the door, and stood weeping. The other, nameth Fawcett, commanded her 190 to put off her apparel, saying she must die naked, according to the judgement given against her. She fell down on her knees, and the rest of the women with her, requesting him, for the honour of womankind, that she might not be seen naked, but be suffered to die in her smock, which he would not grant.

---

162. **store** abundant supply. 165. **inckle** tape or linen yarn. 167. **headgear** Since respectable women appeared in public with headcoverings of some kind, Margaret probably fashioned something with her linen or inkle. 169. **toll-booth** the custom house on the bridge over the river Ouse. 186–8. **And . . . own** Clitherow's prayer for Elizabeth confutes the charge of treason.

Then she requested that the women might unclothe her, and that they would turn their   195
faces from her during the time of her unclothing, which was granted. And the women put
upon her the long linen habit which she had brought with her, and so was quickly laid
down upon the ground, a sharp stone being laid upon her back. Her face was covered with
a handkercher, her secret parts with the linen habit, and all the rest of her body left naked.

When the boards that were joined together in the fashion of a broad door were laid on   200
her to bear the weight, she raised up her hands toward her face and joined them together,
which the sheriff seeing, commanded two of the sergeants to part them and to tie them
unto two posts set there for that purpose; which was done with the inckle she brought
with her, and so her arms extended and her body made a perfect cross.

Then they called on her again to ask the Queen's Majesty forgiveness and to pray for   205
her. And when the martyr replied she had prayed for her, they willed her to ask her
husband forgiveness. 'If ever I have offended him,' said the martyr, 'I do ask him
forgiveness from the bottom of my heart.' After this they laid weight on her, which
when she felt, she cried out, 'Jesu, Jesu, Jesu, have mercy upon me!', which were the last
words that were heard to come from her. She was dying about one quarter of an hour.   210
They laid on her about seven or eight hundred weight, which did not only break her ribs
but caused them to break through her skin.

And this was the end of this virtuous and glorious martyr, the proto-martyr of her sex
in the kingdom of England, since heresy infected it in these later times.

The day of her death was the 25th of March, on which day she ever was desirous to   215
offer up her soul, which is very remarkable, being a day that she did highly honour in
regard of the general opinion that the world was made on that day and that our Saviour
was then incarnate in the womb of the Blessed Virgin.

WILLIAM WESTON

'If I spoke with the tongue of Father Campion', declared a popular saying recorded in a
Valladolid archive, 'and wrote with the pen of Father Persons, and led the austere life of
Father Weston, and yet had not charity, it would avail me nothing' (P. Caraman, ed.,
Autobiography from the Jesuit Underground, 1955: p. xvi). Called to the English Mission
from Seville, the Jesuit William Weston (1550–1615) sold the horse he was given for
the journey, donated the money to the poor, and walked to Paris. In 1584 he began
his extraordinary activities of the next two decades, converting souls, ministering the
sacraments, and enduring long periods of imprisonment. Exiled to the Continent in 1603,

---

199. handkercher handkerchief.   **213. proto-martyr** first martyr.   **215. 25th of March** 'Lady Day', the feast of the Annunciation.

Weston taught Greek and Hebrew in the English College of Rome and then returned to Seville, where in 1611 he recorded his English experiences.

The following selections from this record illustrate Weston's controversial involvement with demonic possession in 1585–6, when he and others performed a spectacular series of exorcisms. Sceptics then as now dismiss the entire affair as papist trickery, among them Samuel Harsnett, whose *Declaration of Egregious Popish Impostures* (1603), starring William Weston, supplied Shakespeare's *King Lear*. Others explain away the phenomenon in medical or psychological terms. But Weston's account clearly reveals early modern belief in Satan and portrays exorcism as a practical, compassionate response to pastoral urgencies. Below, William Cecil himself and his agents betray their fear of the devil. And Weston listens to a tormented sinner's claims of demonic possession without assent or denial; referring always to God's power and mercy, he administers the sacraments to bring the dying man comfort and peace.

Autobiography, 1611

In those days there were many persons, even Catholics, tormented with an evil spirit who caused terrible molestation to the people with whom they dwelt, whom it was difficult, nevertheless, to relieve by exorcisms because of the loud and vehement shriekings, vociferations, and howlings which they are accustomed to raise during such ceremonies. Notwithstanding this, the deliverance of those who laboured under so grievous an affliction 5 and compassion towards those who had such persons in their houses seemed to demand that something should be tried and that the care of them should not be neglected, seeing that God might be pleased to assist the sufferers and grant them the desired relief. This indeed he did clearly; for out of many persons the devils were cast, not without the manifest interference of heaven and to the incredible admiration of those who looked on. Persons 10 were cured and set free from those monsters when I was myself present and beheld that which passed. At the time when the matter was fresh I wrote in letters many details concerning it which I could not now remember; neither would they perhaps belong exactly to my present undertaking. Still a few words upon the subject will not be out of place.

In the service of the elder Cecil there was a young Catholic gentleman who had been a 15 witness of these exorcisms, for it was in the house of a relation of his that many were used and upon divers persons. When, therefore, the matter became notorious and the rumour of it reached as far as the Court and the ears of the Queen's Counsellors, Cecil conversed upon the subject with the above-mentioned young man, and in talking of

10. **incredible admiration** disbelieving astonishment. 12. **letters** At least one such letter has survived, Stonyhurst MSS, *Anglia* i, no. 28. 15. **elder Cecil** Sir William Cecil, Lord Burghley (1520–98), Lord Treasurer, militant anti-Catholic, principal adviser to Elizabeth. 18. **Counsellors** members of the Privy Council, chief advisory body to the king.

these possessed persons and the exorcisms, he raised various questions and desired the youth to report to him clearly as to the truth of what was in everyone's mouth respecting the possessed, and whether the narrations concerning them were realities that deserved to be believed.

The young man, having received permission from his lord (whom he knew to be a persecutor of the faith and of all good men), related to him what he had seen and heard, which amounted to something so marvellous that it could hardly be described. Cecil laughed at everything as being probably a fraud and a series of impositions devised by priests to deceive. Then the young man swore a solemn oath to the truth of his assertions. 'Apart from other awful things,' he said, 'you could see the devils gliding about and moving under the skin in immense numbers in visible form, like fishes swimming.' 'Go along with you,' said Cecil, 'great knave that you are! Never see me again or come near my house any more.' Knowing that he was wrong, vexed by the evidence of the thing and still more by his own conscience, he could not endure to learn any further for he was afraid, I think, lest such a striking testimony of the truth should compel him to open his eyes and assent to it, or lest it should increase the remorse of his conscience that was uneasy.

Here, likewise, it may not be unsuitable to narrate that some pursuivants with warrants to search came to that very house where the demoniacs were with an intention of discovering what might be going on and who were present so that they might arrest any priests or suspected persons whom they might find. They chose the time that seemed most likely for the celebration of Mass and exorcisms. They knocked a long time at the door for that house was a large one and surrounded with a lofty wall; otherwise they would have rushed in at any visible entrance and have taken all unawares. On being required to show their authority, they produced the warrants with which they were furnished, and named the magistrates by whom they had been sent, and at last were admitted into the house. Just within the threshold they met with one of the victims of possession. It was a girl, and as soon as she saw them she looked and ground her teeth and declared that one of them (a man whom she named) had a thousand devils hanging on the buttons of his dress. At this the pursuivants were so scared that they forgot all the furious temper with which they had come. In their excessive fright they seemed half dead and became perfectly gentle. They not only showed no violence but did not so much as touch a thing in the whole house, either because they had no will to do so or because they durst not. They did not search any corner or room but went only where they were taken. However, when they went away they asked the lady of the house to give security for her appearance within a certain time before the Privy Council. There were, nevertheless, various priests at the time in that house, and some of them actually saying mass when they came. Everything was finished before the rogues were admitted into the house, and the priests had concealed themselves in the different hiding-places.

37. **pursuivants** officials authorized to search and arrest. 54. **give security** guarantee.

This also I am inclined to mention. After the lapse of nearly a year, when I had been taken and had fallen into the power of the heretics, a secret examiner was sent, who came 60 to me into the prison to take information. Being an inquisitive man, he inquired with much minuteness about those events, but turned them all into ridicule, saying that he had seen the same kind of things performed by the tricks of juggling for the astonishment of the simple. In order to put down his insolence, I informed him of some of the events that were then passing, and I said that I wished that the queen herself had been present or 65 some of her counsellors to view those spectacles or else that they could have taken place in public. I had no doubt but that many persons, on witnessing and recognizing the power and majesty of the keys of the Church when used against those furies and monsters and easily discerning the difference of power between the two religions, would yield the palm of victory to the Catholic faith. He then swore with a great oath that he would not 70 by any means have liked to have been present at scenes so terrific; so little strength is there in an evil conscience when it is in the smallest degree touched by the weapon of God's majesty or by the root of things which are divine.

[...]

It is not without reason that I mention these details, however unimportant they may seem, for they helped to obtain for me not only the presence and sight of Father 75 Robert Southwell and a long interview with him and the means of visiting other illustrious personages, but they enabled me to supply comfort to a certain soul that was labouring in extreme sorrow and to afford it a remedy for its salvation. For there lay in a certain heretical house a Catholic, who with the consent of his keeper had come to London for the completion of some urgent business. He had been committed to a prison 80 in the country, a good way out of London. He was seized, however, and overpowered by a long sickness, which brought him near to death. The woman who nursed him, being a Catholic, had diligently searched the whole city through to find a priest but in vain; she then sent word to me of the peril of that person and entreated me, if it could be contrived, to come to his assistance as he was almost giving up the ghost. I went 85 to him when the little piece of gold obtained for me the liberty to do so. I explained that I was a priest (for I was dressed like a layman), and that I had come to hear his confession.

'If that is the reason why you have come, it is in vain,' he said; 'the time for it is passed away.' 90

---

63. juggling deception. **68. keys...Church** i.e. power to forgive sins (Matt. 16: 19), here a broader symbol of divinely granted authority. **70. palm of victory** Catholics and Protestants viewed the exorcisms as a powerful incentive to conversion to Catholicism. Samuel Harsnett branded all of the exorcisms 'Daemono-poiia, or devil-fiction', stage shows to deceive onlookers (*Declaration*, 1603, sig. V3ᵛ). James I went so far as to argue that the devil permitted exorcisms to ensnare the innocent, 'thereby to obtain the perpetual hurt of the souls of so many that by these false miracles may be induced or confirmed in the profession of that erroneous religion' (*Daemonologie*, 1597, sig. K4ᵛ). **71. terrific** terrifying. **74. these details** Preceding this story, Weston recalls the increased suspicion against Catholics in 1588 and his payment of a gold coin (**95**) to his prison guard, John Sheppard at the Clink, so that he could have some free hours. **76. Robert Southwell** Jesuit missionary and poet (see POETRY, INSTRUCTIONS AND DEVOTIONS).

I said to him: 'What! Are you not a Catholic? If you are, you know what you have to do. This hour, which seems to be your last, has been given you that by making a good and sincere confession you may while there is time wash away the stains of your past life, whatever they are.'

He answered: 'I tell you that you have come too late; that time has gone by. The judgement is decided; the sentence has been pronounced; I am condemned and given up to the enemy; I cannot hope for pardon.' 95

'That is false,' I answered, 'and it is a most fearful error to imagine that a man still in life can assert that he is already deprived of God's goodness and abandoned by his grace in such a way that even when he desires and implores mercy it should be denied him. Since your faith teaches you that God is infinitely merciful, you are to believe with all certitude that there is no bond so straitly fastened but the grace of God can unloose it, no obstacle but grace has power to surmount it.' 100

'But do you not see,' he asked me, 'how full of evil spirits this place is, where we are? There is no corner or crevice in the walls where there are not more than a thousand of the most dark and frightful demons, who with their fierce faces, horrid looks, and atrocious words threaten perpetually that they are just going to carry me into the abyss of misery. Why, even my very body and entrails are filled with these hateful guests, who are lacerating my body and torturing my soul with such dreadful cruelty and anguish that it seems as if I were not so much on the point merely of going there as that I am already devoted and made over to the flames and agonies of hell. Wherefore it is clear that God has abandoned me forever and has cast me away from hope of pardon.' 105

110

When I had listened in trembling to all these things and to much more of a similar kind, and saw at the same time that death was coming fast upon him, and that he would not admit of any advice or persuasion, I began to think within myself in silence and anxiety what would be the wisest course to choose. There entered into my mind through the inspiration, doubtless, of God, the following most useful plan and method of dealing with him. 'Well, then,' I said, 'if you are going to be lost, I do not require a confession from you; nevertheless, recollect yourself just for a moment and with a quiet mind answer me in a few words, either yes or no, to the questions that I put to you. I ask for nothing else and put upon you no other burden.' Then I began to question him and to follow the order of the Commandments, first, whether he had denied his faith. 'See,' I said, 'do not worry yourself; say just those simple words, yes or no.' As soon as he had finished either affirming or denying anything, I proceeded through four or five commandments, whether he had killed anyone, stolen anything, or fornicated, etc. When he had answered with tolerable calmness I said to him: 'What are the devils doing now? What do you feel or suffer from them?' 115

120

125

He replied: 'They are quieter with me; they do not seem to be so furious as they were before.'

102. **straitly** tightly. 107. **just** now. 111. **devoted** consigned.

'Lift up your soul to God,' I said, 'and let us go on to the rest.' In the same fashion and   130
order I continued to question him about other things; then I enquired again, saying,
'How is it now?'

He replied: 'Within I am not tormented; the devils stand at a distance; they throw
stones, they make dreadful faces at me and threaten me horribly; I do not think that
I shall escape.'   135

Going forward as before, I allured and encouraged the man by degrees till every
moment he became more reasonable and at last made an entire confession of all his sins;
after which I gave him absolution and asked him what he was suffering from his cruel and
harassing enemies.

'Nothing,' he said; 'they have all vanished; there is not a trace of them. Thanks be to   140
God.'

Then I went away, after strengthening him by a few words and encouraging him
beforehand against temptations which might return. I promised at the same time that
I would be with him on the morrow, and meant to bring the most sacred body of Christ
with me, and warned him to prepare himself diligently for the receiving of so excellent a   145
banquet. The whole following night he passed without molestation from the enemy and
on the next day he received with great tranquillity of mind the most Holy Sacrament,
after which, at an interval of a few hours, without disturbance he breathed forth his soul
and quietly gave it up to God. Before he died I asked the man what cause had driven him
into such desperation of mind.   150

He answered me thus: 'I was detained in prison many years for the Catholic faith;
nevertheless, I did not cease to sin and to conceal my sins from my confessor, being
persuaded by the devil that pardon must be sought for from God rather by penances and
severity of life than by confession. Hence I either neglected my confessions altogether or
else made insincere ones, and so I fell into that melancholy of mind and that state of   155
tribulation which has been my punishment.'

How extraordinary may be the effects produced by a mind in the agitations of terror
and consciousness of wrong may in truth be well gathered from those events narrated
above.

ALEXANDER RAWLINS AND HENRY WALPOLE

Reprinted below is an anonymous letter from the archives of the Venerable English
College, Rome, an important seminary since 1579. The letter describes the execution
of two priests, Alexander Rawlins (1555?–95) and Henry Walpole, SJ (1558–95). Rawlins
worked as an English missionary, suffered imprisonment, and consoled himself and
others with the thought of God's justice and mercy, 'Deus iustus est, iudex, patiens,

multum misericors, et in fine reddet unicuique secundum opera sua' (God is a just judge, patient, pitying much, and in the end he shall render to each according to his works) ('Some Papers of Bl. Alexander Rawlins,' *The Venerabile*, 8, 1937, 216). Henry Walpole converted to Catholicism while witnessing Campion's execution in 1581, when, legend has it, the blood of the martyr—drawn, quartered, and decapitated—spurted upon him. Walpole seems to recall the incident in his poem on Campion's death, where he testifies, at least figuratively, to the mystical power of the martyr's blood:

> We cannot fear a mortal torment, we;
> This martyr's blood hath moistened all our hearts;
> Whose parted quarters when we chance to see,
> We learn to play the constant Christian's parts.
> His head doth speak and heavenly precepts give,
> How we that look should frame ourselves to live.
>
> (T. Alfield, *A True Report*, 1582, sig. F)

The poem circulated in manuscripts as a song, meditation, and sacred memorial. Walpole subsequently entered the Venerable English College, then the Jesuits, became a chaplain to the Spanish forces in the Netherlands, and endured several years of imprisonment and torture.

The following eyewitness account of the double execution reports the spectators' questions as well as the victims' answers regarding loyalty to the queen and the acceptable form of prayer. Remembering the merciful gentleman on horseback who let Rawlins die before he was quartered as well as the words of the gallows debate, the unidentified Catholic vividly recreates the scene in York, 7 April 1595.

Anonymous, *Letter to Holtby*, 1595?

To Master Ducket

Jesus

  Master Alexander, when he was come so high on the ladder as he was to go, began to turn his back to the ladder, but before he had done it turned again his face to the ladder and made both on it and the halter the sign of the cross and kissed them, at which, some 5 of the beholders began to jest. After this done, he turned his face as before he intended

---

1. **Ducket** Richard Holtby, SJ (1552–1640), master organizer and servant of the Catholics in north-east England. For his account of the persecutions in the north see J. Morris, ed., *Troubles of our Catholic Forefathers*, 1877: iii. 103–230. 2. **Jesus** an invocation and salutation. 5. **halter** noose. **kissed them** 'as the happy instruments which were to send him to heaven' (R. Challoner, *Memoirs*, 1924: 218).

and with a good, loud voice uttered these words: 'It hath pleased almighty God to bring me to this place to make a confession of my faith: I am a Catholic priest.' At which word those that were to see him executed willed him not to talk of these matters, and asked him what he thought of the Queen's Majesty.   10

'I acknowledge her,' saith he, 'for my lawful prince, and if I did know myself to have offended her, I would make what satisfaction I were able. I forgive all the world, and those who think themselves to have given me right cause to think them my enemies, let them assure themselves I take them for my best friends after this word.'

For aught I remember he prayed quietly with his hands lifted up together. They   15 urged him to pray with them, which he refused. And so shortly after he was cast from the ladder where, hanging a little space, one made to have him cut down, but a gentleman that sat on horseback by the head sheriff said, 'No let him alone.' After that again he made to have him cut down, saying his judgement was to be cut down afore he was dead. Yet the gentleman (God make him a good man) said, 'No let him alone.' And so, as   20 I remember, said the head sheriff, so that he hung till he was dead. At which time one going up the ladder to cut the rope, this foresaid gentleman bade him take hold of the rope and stay him that he fall not down, and so he did. Others took hold of his legs till he was down and after carried him a little off where he was quartered. This is as much as I can remember that was said and done to him.   25

After this Father Walpole went up the ladder, and after he had turned his back to the ladder very gravely, he made the sign of the cross, repeating the words with his actions that all might see and hear. That done, he said, 'I am come hither to die, not knowing myself any other cause but for being a priest and of the Society of Jesus.' They willed him not to speak of those things and asked him what he thought of his prince.   30

'I acknowledge her,' saith he, 'for my lawful prince not in that manner as you do, head of the church, but in all temporal causes.'

'What do you think,' said they, 'of the excommunication?'

'I speak directly, if you will credit me, that notwithstanding any excommunication that I know of, I acknowledge her for my lawful prince.'   35

'You have heard,' said they, 'of the excommunication.'

'I have,' saith he, 'but yet notwithstanding any that I know of, I acknowledge her for my lawful prince.'

Then said one, 'Bring a minister. You ground your faith on the pope with prayers to saints and such like things. You should rely on the Scriptures.' To this effect was his words   40 as I remember.

---

16. which he refused Catholics were forbidden to pray with Protestants. **16–17. cast...ladder** i.e. thrown from the gallows with the noose around his neck. **17. one...down** so that he could be disembowelled while still alive. **23. stay** support. **33. excommunication** Pope Pius V's bull (1570) excommunicated Elizabeth and absolved Catholic subjects from obedience (see DOCUMENTS). **37. notwithstanding...of** Walpole could be equivocating here, denying any knowledge of the bull; or he could simply be asserting his loyalty to the crown.

Then said Father Walpole, 'I rely my faith on such things as are decreed by General Councils, which all Christians are bound to believe. I speak not of provincial councils but of General Councils in which the pope is one or head' (I remember not whether he said). 45

'No,' said King, 'you should rely only on the Scripture.'

Father Walpole said, 'The Scriptures expounded by the Catholic Church doth either directly or consequently defend whatsoever we hold.' Next after this, as I remember, he began to pray and said, 'Veni, Creator Spiritus, mentes tuorum visita, imple superna gratia quae tu creasti pectora' [Come, Holy Spirit, visit the minds of your 50 people, and fill with eternal grace the hearts you have made], and no more of the hymn. This he said with a loudable voice that all might hear and after it the *Pater noster*, to the end to which Master King said, 'Amen.' But the father went on and said *Ave, Maria*, at which Master King and others began to trouble him. But he, not minding them, said it to the end; but to that Master King said not 'Amen.' After *Ave*, the father 55 said *Gloria patri* to the end, and to that Master King said 'Amen.'

Then said Master King, 'Master Walpole, why pray you not in English? You do not edify the people.'

Then Father Walpole: 'God knoweth what I say, and I understand it myself and those that are members of the Catholic Church are partakers with me, of which Church Jesus 60 make you all members.' At which word he blessed the company, for out of that Church there is no salvation.

Master King said again, 'Master Walpole, we have more charity than you for we pray with you, but you will not with us.'

Father Walpole: 'You do well, but I may not for that charity lose unity.' 65

King: 'If we do well, why will you not join with us?'

Father Walpole, as one half hour taken, began to stir himself a little. 'You do well,' saith he, 'in that it is good for all men to have recourse to God; but I that am of another communion may not join with you in prayer.' And then as I remember, he, praying quietly to himself, some urged him to speak. And he said, 'With all my heart I would 70 speak and, I pray you, give me leave and I will speak at length. Loath I am to offend any by my speeches.' But some said no. Then said he, 'I will commend myself to God and so leave you.'

---

42. **rely** place. 42–3. **General Councils** legally convened meetings of Church officials and theologians to regulate matters of ecclesiastical dogma and practice. 43. **provincial councils** regional meetings of local bishops and others. 44–5. **whether he said** if he spoke further. 48. **consequently** indirectly. 49. **Veni, Creator Spiritus** a popular hymn and invocation of the Holy Spirit, perhaps by Rabanus Maurus (776–856), used at Vespers, Pentecost, the dedication of a church, and other solemn occasions. 52. **loudable** loud. 54. **trouble him** bother him, because the *Ave, Maria*, 'Hail, Mary', seemed idolatrous. A. Jessopp published another account of Walpole's death from a Stonyhurst manuscript, perhaps by Richard Holtby, in which the offended officials hung Walpole before he could finish the prayer (*One Generation of a Norfolk House*, 1879: 279–82). 57. **in English** The important theological debates concerning Latin and the vernacular, and the correct forms of prayer, frequently recur during executions. See Campion above. 65. **for…unity** for the sake of fellowship pray with you, thereby committing heresy and harming the unity of the Catholic Church. 67. **taken** had passed.

Master King said, 'Master Walpole, will you accept of the prince's laws and you may have favour.' 75

Father Walpole: 'I own fully wherein these disagree not with God's laws.'

King: 'You should think that these agree with God's laws. I pray God,' said King, 'I may find such favour as now is offered you, but for that cause I trust never to need it. But what say you, Master Walpole, will you accept of the prince's laws?'

Father Walpole: 'I own fully wherein these disagree not with God's laws for I must 80 obey God rather than man.'

King: 'Then Lord have mercy on you.'

And the Father, saying, 'In manus tu—' [Luke 23: 46, into your hands—] but before he had said it they cast him off the ladder. And before he was cut down I was gone, so what was done to him after I know not, but I heard he was dead or he was cut down and 85 after that quartered, as the other was before him. It may be that in this I have set somewhat before that was after said, but as I can remember it so have I set it down.

TOBY MATTHEW

Son of the archbishop of York, a Protestant divine noted for severe anti-Catholicism, Toby Matthew (1577–1655) defied his father's wishes and travelled to Italy in 1604, where he converted to Catholicism. Upon returning home, he endured interrogation, disputation, and imprisonment in 1607. Matthew gained release from prison through the intercession of Francis Bacon and Robert Cecil, and eventually took orders in 1614. After several years of exile (1619–22), Matthew found himself in favour with James I, who employed him to promote the marriage of Prince Charles and the Spanish Infanta. After being knighted by James, Matthew attained a position of respect in the court of Charles I as well, where he worked for the Catholic cause until the civil war of 1640. Matthew translated Bacon's essays into Italian and many religious works into English, including Augustine's *Confessions* (1620) (see above).

Among Toby Matthew's miscellaneous English works is some verse (see POETRY) and an account of his own life and conversion. Since conversion to and from Catholicism recurs so frequently in the period, Matthew's articulate account illuminates a vital early modern religious and political experience. Matthew portrays his conversion as the operation of grace on the human will, and as a movement of both the intellect and the heart. The selections below show the powerful effect of Rome—its churches, art, and architecture—on

76. **own** accept. 83. **'In manus tu—'** 'Into your hands [I commend my spirit]' Jesus' last words on the cross (Luke 23: 46). 87. **somewhat** something.

one English traveller. They also reveal the various difficulties Catholics faced in the early Stuart period and the shift to greater toleration later.

A True Historical Relation of the Conversion of Sir Toby Matthew, wr. 1640

[Sojourn in Rome]

[Cardinal Pinelli's] answer was to this effect: that welcome was due to me as a stranger, but that as I was an Englishman I might expect and should receive a double welcome, both because that country had been formerly one of the dearest children of God's Church, as also for that it had not forsaken the Catholic faith out of heresy and election, but only by the imposition and power of temporal princes who had misguided them- 5
selves; that so long as I would converse there without scandal, I might promise myself the same security which I could expect at home in any house of mine own; that if danger should be coming towards me (which yet, he said, could not arrive without his privity), he would be sure to enable me with means how to avoid it; that if in the meanwhile I would pass any part of my time with him either within doors or abroad, his palace 10
should be ever open to me and his coach ever ready to attend me; that although he would oblige me to nothing, yet he would make one request to me for mine own sake—namely, that, since I was a stranger and a traveller and had suffered my curiosity to lead me thither, I would be careful not only to view the antiquities of the old, decayed Roman Empire but also of the not-decayed Catholic Roman Church, which were there to be 15
read in a fair letter and in a large volume; that if men should endeavour to conceal the antiquity and excellency of that Church the very stones might serve for preachers, and not only the buildings above ground but even the very vaults and caves under it; and in conformity hereof, he recommended to me very particularly those of St Sebastian and St Pancras, to which I went soon after with an extraordinary kind of curiosity. 20

So as I did in that what I desired, and I must confess in the presence of God that the sight of those most ancient crosses, altars, sepulchres, and other marks of Catholic religion, having been planted there in the persecution of the primitive Church (which might be more than fifteen hundred years ago and could not be less than thirteen hundred), did strike me with a kind of reverent awe and made me absolutely resolve 25
to repress my insolent discourse against Catholic religion ever after.

But for the present I did reverence to the cardinal and gave him most humble and entire thanks for the nobleness and favour of his proceeding towards me; and so

1. **Cardinal Pinelli** (1541–1611) Chief of the Congregation of the Inquisition. **8. privity** knowledge. **9. enable** provide. **16. fair letter** clear, legible script. **18. vaults and caves** catacombs, where ancient Christians met and buried their dead. **18–19. in conformity hereof** accordingly. **19–20. St Sebastian…St Pancras** San Sebastiano fuori le Mure is a basilica dedicated to St Sebastian, 3rd-c. martyr, built on the site of catacombs. San Pancrazio is a church dedicated to St Pancras, 4th-c. martyr, built on the site of a cemetery.

I departed for that time and waited upon him often afterward, according to the occasion. And, finally, I took my leave of him when I went away, and still he continued towards me in the self-same way of civility, only he asked me if I had done what he had desired by visiting the holy places aforesaid, and whether I went not out of Rome with better thoughts of the religion which was professed there than I had brought thither. I told him that I had done what he commanded and, for the rest, that I was better informed of some things than I had formerly been, and that I would carry my heart open to the inspirations which it should please God to send me. In the meantime I professed myself to be extremely obliged to His Lordship for his great favour and I humbly prayed him to behold me as a most faithful servant of his. And so we parted.

But the memory of his proceeding passed not from me when I considered, as I do still, that many a High Commissioner or Justice of the Peace in England would perhaps, and even without perhaps, have looked upon a better man than myself, if he had been a stranger and of a strange religion and liable to his jurisdiction, after a much more severe and surly manner. For the cardinal would never speak to me till I had put on my hat as soon as he, nor till I sat down in as good a chair as his. And whensoever I parted from him, he accompanied me two or three rooms from his own and with a countenance, if it were possible, which even made the sauce better than the meat. By this means I had procured to make it most perfectly safe for me to stay as long as I would in Rome, from whence, when my occasions should call me (which was not likely to be during three months at least), I intended to go towards Florence to make a much longer residence there.

In the meantime during my stay at Rome my pleasures and vain curiosities took up the greatest part of my time, though yet such hours as I could spare I was glad to bestow upon Father Persons, whom I thanked in most particular manner for the address which he had given me to the cardinal, wherein he also rejoiced. And daily he procured to put new courtesies and civilities upon me, and desired (upon my profession) that I would requite the good will which he had to serve me by casting an eye at idle hours upon such a Catholic book as he would send me by the same friend of mine, Master Sweet, who was a great dependent of his and to whom I had much obligation from much of his good company at that time. Now this book is one of them which Master William Rainoldes wrote, and it is called, as I remember, his *Reprehension of Dr. Whitaker*. I promised to read both that and whatsoever else Father Persons should recommend to me, though my idle and worse courses made me slack in my performance at that time.

41. **High Commissioner** member of the ecclesiastical court that exercised jurisdiction in religious cases. **44–5. put...he** Matthew had taken off his hat as a sign of respect and the cardinal humbly treated him as an equal. **47. sauce...meat** The cardinal's gracious expression and behaviour, presumably his sadness at the parting, made the leave-taking all the more pleasant. **54. Father Persons** prolific Jesuit (1546–1610), missionary to England (see HISTORIES). **address** access. **56. profession** request. **58. Master Sweet** John Sweet, SJ (1570/1–1632), educated at the English College, Rome. **60. William Rainoldes** A convert from the Church of England, Rainoldes (1544–94) refuted William Whitaker's attack on the Rheims New Testament in *A Refutation of Sundry Reprehensions* (1583).

Yet, to keep my negligence from his knowledge my custom was at the instant (whensoever I went to visit the good Father) to open the book which he had lent me in three or four several places, thereby to enable myself to propound some few questions or doubts that so he might conceive I was not wholly careless of what he advised. And thus I hoped that I had only circumvented him, though I quickly found afterward that it was myself whom I had deceived most. For besides the hurt which I did myself in order to mine own soul, it deprived me for a time of reading one of the most excellent books even for wit and good discourses that ever I saw, and especially in respect of the Preface, which is both very large and perfect in the proof of that to which it drives; and I wish that the world would so peruse it as thereby to make it wholly their own.

But the shift which then I made to cozen me even of myself could not long serve my turn against such a man as Father Persons was in such a cause as his. And so in after conferences (for by that time he was grown to speak clearly to me), he convinced my understanding in many things, wherein yet I profess that I do not so much as mean to praise him much or to flatter him at all. For the truth and certainty of Catholic doctrine is such that I hold it at this day the greatest miracle of the whole world that a man who is in any way of a judgement and will which is not mightily depraved can forbear to subscribe entirely to the truth of Catholic doctrine and to acknowledge his obedience to the holy Catholic Church, upon that kind of conference and proof which he may easily hear thereof within the space of a very few hours from any Catholic learned man.

But now the Father proved to me by a most evident demonstration out of St Thomas (as evident as it is that two and two make four, though at the first it may perhaps seem to some but a kind of impossible and ridiculous paradox), that whosoever believes not all the points of Catholic doctrine hath no supernatural faith at all in any one of them. Because such a person wants the true and formal reason of faith, which only is and only can be the revelation of God's truth, propounded by the Catholic Church to be believed; which Church, if it teach two doctrines or twenty or two-hundred, if a man will not believe any one of all that number, it is evident that he believes not any of the rest, upon the said formal reason of faith, which is the revelation of God, propounded by that Church which Christ our Lord hath instituted and established, since the same authority extends alike to all the other articles which she propounds. But he doth it either upon the discourse of his own reason or spirit, which perhaps he will miscall the Holy Ghost; or upon his own idle interpretation of Holy Scripture, which he will not stick to call the Word of God; or else upon the credit which he gives to some modern sectary or other, which he will needs conceive to be, forsooth, the congregation of the elect or

---

70. **order** respect. 72. **Preface** Rainoldes's *Preface to the Reader*, written for 'reducing to the fold of Christ's Catholic Church the souls of our poor countrymen, so miserably seduced' (sig. a2), presents in ninety-one pages a well-informed conspectus of Catholic arguments against Protestant doctrine. Noting the variations in English religious statutes as well as the different beliefs and practices in Protestant countries, Rainoldes rehearses arguments about the sacraments, papal supremacy, the authenticity of the Roman Church, and other matters. **perfect** accomplished. 74. **shift** evasion. **cozen** cheat. 96. **stick** hesitate. 97. **sectary** member of a heretical or schismatic sect.

faithful; or, in a word, upon some such fallible and false motive as one of those, which is a foundation so slippery or so sandy as no article of faith (which must needs be certain or otherwise it can be no true faith at all) is ever to be established thereupon.

In the second place he showed me out of the Fathers of the first four hundred years after Christ our Lord (which I knew to be within that time wherein the English Protestants confess the Church to have been incorrupt) that prayers to saints, prayers and sacrifice for the dead, *limbus patrum*, justification by faith and works, the preferring of virginity before matrimony, the necessity of baptism, the sacrifice of the body and blood of Christ our Lord, which is the mass, the Catholic canon of Holy Scripture, the lawfulness and frequent use of vows, and the other doctrines which are controverted at this day between Catholics and Protestants were all embraced and believed by the Catholics of those times, as they are now by them of these.

And here he gave me also a most excellent rule: that whensoever any writer or Father (either by way of expounding Scripture, or else by way of recommending or declaring the practice of the Church of his time, or upon any other occasion whatsoever) did set on foot any doctrine which was contrary to the ancient tradition and judgement of the holy Catholic Church of his time, he was presently rebuked and confuted by the other Fathers of that present age. And this proposition he exemplified in the persons of Tertullian, St Cyprian, and the most learned Origen. And he showed that whensoever any doctrine was affirmed by any of the Fathers which was not contradicted or controlled by any other of the same or the next succeeding age, it might serve us for an assurance that the said doctrine was no innovation or particular opinion of that private Father, but expressed by him upon such occasions as then were ministered in the sense and spirit of the holy Catholic Church of Christ our Lord. Nay, it is not only so, as he said, whensoever one of the Fathers hath differed from another in any point of doctrine, but even when they have earnestly varied in the interpretation of some important part of Scripture. For they were not then wont to fail to express home enough what they thought; and therein, said he, let that serve for good proof which occurred between St Jerome and St Augustine about the reprehensibleness of St Peter by St Paul.

He represented to me also then in a third place how the Fathers of the aforesaid ages did not only agree with the present Catholics in those articles which are received at this day by the Protestants, and which I have already pointed out, but did also condemn all heretics in general as incapable of salvation, and consequently all such persons as either in ancient or any other times did obstinately profess any one of those or any other heresy at all. And to prove that assertion he showed me (besides the practice of those ancient Fathers) their express authorities also, which are plentifully set forth in many of their

---

102. Fathers important early teachers of the Church. **105.** *limbus patrum* 'limbo of the fathers', abode where the souls of the just who died before Christ waited for admission to heaven. **117.** Tertullian...Origen Church Fathers from the 2nd and 3rd centuries. **118.** controlled modified. **126–7.** which occurred...St Paul Jerome thought Paul's account of his rebuking Peter (Gal. 2: 11–14) a false report, made out of a sense of duty in the interest of religion; defending the veracity of Scripture, Augustine accepted the account as true.

writings, to prove that not only heretics but even schismatics also (who only refuse 135
Church discipline) can never be saved except they do penance for that sin, although they
should sell and dispose of all their substance to the poor, yea, and sacrifice their very lives
for the exaltation and honour of the name of Christ our Lord, in contradiction of the
impiety of the pagans. And he showed me also divers catalogues, and namely those of
St Epiphanius and St Augustine, wherein the heresies both of those and of the former 140
times were set down, amongst which there are divers which are held by Protestants at this
day, whereas yet St Augustine declares that whosoever holds any one is not so much as a
Christian and, therefore, that without repentance he cannot possibly be saved.

[Conclusion]

You must therefore be content to consider that unspeakable kind of mercy, wherewith it
pleased almighty God to overshadow me after my conversion, even in all temporal 145
respects also as well as others, that so you may discern how gracious and good a master
God almighty is, and how worthy he is to be served by the whole world since he
vouchsafes to deal so tenderly with them who, by his holy grace (without which they
cannot think a good thought), proceed not mechanically and upon conditions and
capitulations with him, but cast themselves totally and even, as it were, blindfold and 150
bound hand and foot into the arms of his protection and good pleasure. For you have
seen how it stood with me in the beginning, and how the enemy of mankind, taking
the advantage of mine own corrupt nature, sought to stay me from being converted to
the holy Catholic religion upon many fears and frights which he laid before me. And here
you may see also how the mercy of almighty God vouchsafed, as a man may say, to 155
reward himself, for it was only his great goodness which enabled me to overcome the
difficulties which threatened me.

My parents grew kind towards me, yea, and careful of me, and bountiful to me, and
expressed not only their love but such a particular kind of respect as was very extraordinary for parents to show towards a son. And though it grew at length to be less tender 160
in my mother than formerly it had been, I impute it but to the craft of certain persons,
who, distracting her mind from me by other motives, sought to fasten that wound upon
my person for the hatred which they bore to my religion.

That great man who had formerly borne a most particular hatred against me when
I was of the same religion with himself grew to be of the noblest and greatest friends that 165
I ever had in my whole life, upon my being a Catholic declared. And particularly I
conceive that almighty God was pleased to allow me unexpected comfort in these two
kinds because they were my greatest temptations, and his mercy made me able to
overcome them.

---

140. St Epiphanius…Augustine Epiphanius of Salamis (310–403) wrote *Panarion*, 'The Medicine-Chest', which listed
eighty heresies and remedies for them. Augustine (354–430) wrote *De haeresibus* (429), a catalogue of errors to avoid.
164. great man Robert Cecil (1563–1612), earl of Salisbury, chief minister of Elizabeth and James I.

It is true that my temporal means was lessened almost to the one half by a very hasty 170
sale which I was fain to make thereof for fear of worse, but yet still, that which was left
was abundant, and afterwards my parents themselves gave also good supplies. Yea, and
formerly I had received some such light from a certain Catholic in the sale of some lands,
as it is probable I should have wanted in Protestancy. I acknowledged that kindness in
him who did me the courtesy with much bounty, though afterwards he fell into some 175
miseries, whereby he was loaded with wants which kept him from being so constant in
acknowledging my kindness to him as I had showed myself for his to me. And upon the
whole matter I can without vanity and may with much gratitude to God affirm that
I have never been either in want or near it, but my hands have always been full of money,
and my fortune far superior to my expense, and so my mind at ease. And, in fine, I have 180
been ever the more able to lend my friends my service in that kind than obliged to expect
it from them.

My country I lost many years, which yet God gave me life and health to expect, and he
also raised me friends whereby I recovered it and amongst whom I enjoy it with as
much honour and advantage of many kinds as any man of my poor condition hath 185
received, yea, and in my conscience I think with more than I should have been admitted
to if I had been a Protestant. So that these things may well be able to teach that part of
the world which shall hereafter come to understand of my little story how they are to
cast themselves headlong into the hands of God, and especially to instruct myself that
I am ever to be kept in fresh memory of how infinitely I have been obliged to his 190
Divine Majesty, and how carefully I am bound to serve him all the days of my life.

Mary Ward

One year before Margaret Clitherow's execution, her neighbours in York celebrated the
birth of Mary Ward (1585–1645). Ward received training in the faith from strong women
around her, especially her grandmother, Ursula Wright, who spent fourteen years in
prison, and her cousin, Grace Babthorpe, one of Clitherow's friends. These women created
a strong community of prayer, faith, and charity. After trying several religious orders,
Mary Ward in 1611 received a visionary message, 'Take the same of the Society', which
she interpreted as a command to imitate the Society of Jesus in its mixing of contemplation and action. Despite the strong protests of the Jesuits, the Church, which mandated
the cloister for religious women, and early modern society, Mary Ward created an
international Institute that promoted virtue, performed good works, and educated girls.

183. **expect** await.

She walked to Rome several times for official recognition and support but in 1625 and 1631 papal decrees suppressed her houses and seven schools; in 1631 the Inquisition condemned and imprisoned her. Later, Ward returned to England to find her work in ruins, but she persisted in good works and her faith until death.

The selections below, excerpted from fragments, letters, memorials, and an early biography record pivotal moments in Mary Ward's life. The Church finally confirmed the Institute of the Blessed Virgin Mary in 1877, and rehabilitated Mary Ward as foundress in 1909; the Jesuits approved the granting of the Institute their Constitutions in 1978. In 2003 the Institute of the Blessed Virgin Mary officially became the Congregation of Jesus, at last fulfilling Mary Ward's original hope and vision. Today Mary Ward's successors sponsor schools and ministries in twenty-four countries throughout five continents.

Autobiography, wr. 1617–26

[Her Grandmother]

She was noted and esteemed for her great virtue. She had in her younger years suffered imprisonment for the space of fourteen years together, in which times made profession of her faith before the president of York, Huntingdon, and other officers, etc. She was once for her speeches to the said Huntingdon, tending to exaltation of the Catholic religion and contempt of heresy, thrust into a common prison or dungeon amongst 5 thieves, where she stayed not long because, being much spoken of, it came to the hearing of her kindred, who procured her speedy removal to the prison where she was before. At her entrance into this dungeon the malefactors judged she had been committed for theft or murder (for such were all that came to that place), said unto her that she must either give six pence into the common purse, as the custom of all that came there at their first 10 entrance was, or else she would not eat of their common meat, which was that which good people of charity would give, all sorts of meat put together in one vessel and so given them at the prison door. To these their words my grandmother made no other reply than that she would willingly give them six pence, and so she did.

When I came unto her, she had been released for a few years and had come to live at 15 home. I remained with them near five years, the most of the time I lodged with herself, for the house being great, she was very careful lest by idle or ill company I should be drawn to offend God. And although my grandfather was living yet, for holy respect they

AUTOBIOGRAPHY Manuscript copies of Mary Ward's autobiographical writings, covering the years 1585–1609, are housed in the archives of the Institute of the Blessed Virgin Mary at Munich. These consist of fragments in English and a longer section (28 quarto pages) in Italian, probably dictated to her secretary, Elizabeth Cotton. **3. Huntingdon** Henry, earl of Huntingdon, anti-Catholic president of the Council of the North. **15. When . . . her** 1590, at age 5. Mary stayed with her grandparents, Robert and Ursula Wright of Ploughland Hall, East Riding of Yorkshire until 1595.

lodged in separate chambers. And so great a prayer she was that I do not remember in
that whole five years that ever I saw her sleep, nor did I ever awake when I perceived her   20
not to be at her prayers. She used to provide much alms to Catholic prisoners, which she
gave them secretly and several times of the year.

Once I heard her give order amongst other things for the killing of certain poultry,
some of which I called and accounted mine, coaxing them as children will such toys. I was
sorry but made no sign to have understood of any such things. Soon after I asked my   25
grandmother (which appeared as a sign of devotion) when she should send any alms to
the prison. She bid me to tell why I asked. I answered because I was desirous such poultry
which she had before given me should be so bestowed. This seemed to please her much,
and I said it only to gain her esteem.

[The Gloria Vision in England, 1609]

One morning, making my meditation coldly and not at all to my satisfaction, at the end   30
of it I resolved to assist a person to be accepted in some convent, who much desired to
become a nun but, wanting a portion, could not otherwise enter. And then, going to
dress myself according to the fashion of the country and other circumstances, whilst
I adorned my head at the mirror, something very supernatural befell me, similar to that
already related on the day of St Athanasius, but more singular, and as it appears to me,   35
with greater impetuosity, if greater there could be. I was abstracted out of my whole
being, and it was shown to me with clearness and inexpressible certainty that I was not to
be of the Order of St Teresa, but that some other thing was determined for me, without
all comparison more to the glory of God than my entrance into that holy religion. I did
not see what the assured good thing would be, but the glory of God which was to come   40
through it showed itself inexplicably and so abundantly as to fill my soul in such a way
that I remained for a good space without feeling or hearing anything, but the sound,
'Glory, glory, glory!' By accident I was then alone; therefore, what external changes
this and similar things cause I cannot say, but from the internal feeling and bodily
disturbance they must be remarkable. My knowledge fails as to their continuance; all   45
appears to last but a moment, even at those times when afterwards I made a computation
and found it to have been about two hours.

On this occasion a good deal of time passed before I recovered. But returning to
myself, I found my heart full of love for this thing, accompanied by such glory that not
yet can I comprehend what it was. And seeing for certain that I was not to be of the Order   50
of St Teresa, remembering also the vow which I had made, being of that order if my
confessor should command me, I felt great fear of offending God in these two contraries

---

32. wanting a portion lacking a dowry. **35. day…Athanasius** 2 May 1609, the day Mary had a vision which convinced her
that she was not to belong to the Franciscan mendicant order of St Clare. **36. impetuosity** force. **38. Order of St Teresa**
reformed, contemplative branch of the Carmelites. **39. religion** order. **43. Glory…glory** emphasis on the glory of God
looks ahead to Mary's embracing of Ignatian spirituality and the Jesuit ideal, *ad maiorem Dei gloriam* (to the greater glory
of God).

or of adhering to one or the other side. To resist that which now had been operated in me I could not, and to have a will in opposition to the vow I ought not. In this conflict, giving myself to prayer, I protested to God so liberal that I had not and would not admit   55
on this occasion any other will than his. As a testimony and sign that my mind and will were totally to do his without exception, I put on a haircloth, which I have forgotten for how long a time I wore, but I believe for some continuance, for I well recollect through this and other corporal penances, done for this end during the months that I remained in England, I did no little injury to my health, especially being occupied at that time with   60
some fervour in winning and aiding others, observing (according to my knowledge) the circumstances requisite and suitable to the said business and to my condition. Such a labour is only too honourable but, nevertheless, painful enough if not undertaken for him to whom we owe all, and through the help of whose grace alone it is fitly and perseveringly feasible.   65

Letter to Monsignor Albergati, 1620

[The Founding Vision of the Institute]

About this time, in the year 1611, I fell sick in great extremity, being somewhat recovered by a vow made to send myself in pilgrimage to our Blessed Lady of Sichem, being alone in some extraordinary repose of mind, I heard distinctly, not by sound of voice but intellectually understood, these words, 'Take the same of the Society', so understood as that we were to take the same both in matter and manner, that only excepted which   5
God by diversity of sex hath prohibited. These few words gave so great measure of light in that particular Institute, comfort and strength, and changed so the whole soul, as that impossible for me to doubt but that they came from him, whose words are works.

My confessor resisted; all the Society opposed. Divers Institutes were drawn up by several persons, some of which were approved and greatly commended by the last bishop,   10
Blasius of Saint-Omer, our so great friend, and some other divines. These were offered us and, as it were, pressed upon us. There was no remedy but to refuse them, which caused infinite troubles. Then would they needs that at least we should take the name of some order confirmed or some new one or any we could think of, so not that of Jesus. This the fathers of the Society urged exceedingly (and do still every day more than other), telling   15
us that to any such name we may take what Constitutions we will, even theirs in

---

55. **liberal** freely. 57. **haircloth** undergarment made of hair or rough material, worn for penance and mortification. 59–60. **months . . . England** Shortly after her vision in London late in 1609, Mary left for Saint-Omer and, with her companions, began to educate girls. 65. **perseveringly feasible** possible to persevere in.

ALBERGATI the papal representative in Lower Germany. 1. **sick** Mary contracted the measles. 2. **our . . . Sichem** another name for our Lady of Montaigu, near Louvain. 8. **as that impossible** so that it was impossible. 9. **confessor** Richard Holtby, SJ (1552–1640). 11. **Blasius** James Blaise, bishop of Saint-Omer (1601–18), a Franciscan supporter of Mary Ward's Institute.

substance, if otherwise we will not be satisfied. But by no means will they that we observe that form in which their constitutions and rules are written, which, they say, are not essential or needful.

The neglect of their offers did and does cause extreme troubles, especially for the first 20 seven years while my confessarius (whom I had tied myself to obey) lived, they urging him in many things to say as they said, though against his own judgement and knowledge, as after I understood. Neither could he yield unto them in all; one time in particular they urged him so much about the name as that he made answer to divers grave fathers that if their case were his, they durst not urge any change. Concerning the name, 25 I have twice in several years understood, in as particular a manner as these other things I have recounted, that the denomination of these must be of Jesus. And thrice, I think more often, of the inconveniences would happen to both parts if ours should have any dependence of the fathers of the Society.

The Memorial to Pope Paul V, 1616

We propose to follow a mixed kind of life, such a life as we hold Christ our Lord and Master to have taught his disciples, such a life as his Blessed Mother seems to have lived and to have left to those following her, such a life as appears to have been led by Saints Mary Magdalen, Martha, Praxedes, Pudentiana, Thecla, Cecilia, Lucy, and many other holy virgins and widows; and this most especially in these times (in which as in early 5 times the Church is sorely oppressed in our country), that by this means we may more easily instruct virgins and young girls in piety, Christian morals, and the liberal arts, that they may afterwards, according to their respective vocations, profitably embrace either the secular or the religious state.

It is necessary, therefore, that whoever wishes to serve God in this least family should 10 well understand the end of this our vocation and the proper or right means by which it may be obtained.

Our end, then, is to work constantly at the perfection of our own souls under the Standard of the Cross, both by the acquirement of all virtues, by abnegation of all self-will, and by diligent extirpation of self-love. Virtue, indeed, we would have so highly 15 valued in all those who would embrace our manner of life that anyone wanting in it is to be judged unfit for our state, no matter what may be her other talents and endowments;

MEMORIAL This memorial presented the official plan of the Institute to Pope Paul V (r. 1605–21). **1. mixed** i.e. of contemplation and action. **4. Mary Magdalen...Lucy Mary Magdalen** the penitent sinner who witnessed the crucifixion and resurrection. **Martha** the busy sister who received Christ (Luke 10: 38–42), a symbol of the active life. **Praxedes** and **Pudentiana** 2nd-c. women who helped the poor and died martyrs. **Thecla** 8th-c. Benedictine abbess. **Cecilia**, 4th-c. virgin martyr. **Lucy** 3rd-c. virgin martyr. **14. Standard of the Cross** In the *Spiritual Exercises* (2nd week, 4th day), Ignatius proposes meditation on the two standards, i.e. military flags: the standard of Christ urges poverty, humility, and love; the opposing one of Lucifer rallies its followers to riches, honour, and pride (see INSTRUCTIONS AND DEVOTIONS).

much more does this same want of virtue disqualify a person for the task of government and for the discharge of any other important office in the Institute.

Besides attending to our own perfection, we desire in the second place to devote ourselves with all diligence and prudent zeal to promote or procure the salvation of our neighbours by means of the education of girls, or by any other means that are congruous to the times, or in which it is judged that we can by our labours promote the greater glory of God and in any place further the propagation of our Holy Mother, the Catholic Church.

It is necessary that all of ours should know on entering on this manner of life that they are not called to a manner of life in which they can devote themselves only to themselves, but that, having divine love alone in view, they are to prepare themselves to undertake any labour whatsoever in the education of virgins and young girls; in the first place by instructing them generally in their duties towards God, that is to say, in those things to the knowledge of which all Christians are bound, moving all by example and by prayer to embrace the Catholic faith with the utmost zeal. Secondly, all those among whom ours labour are to be specially recommended to approach the holy sacraments frequently, to recite the Divine Office, and to be present at sermons; they are also to be taught the method of mental prayer and examen of conscience, and they are likewise to be trained to the use of other spiritual exercises, according to each one's attraction and capacity. With all diligence and charity they are in like manner to be assisted and encouraged to enter those religious orders to which they seem to be called by God. Yet, as all are not so happy as to be called to the religious state, the virgins who have not this vocation are to be no less carefully instructed in the manners and virtues necessary to a praiseworthy Christian life in the world. Always and everywhere keeping in view the greater glory of God, each one of ours should be ready to perform, according to the commands of holy obedience, any works of charity and humility.

All should understand that they should ever be most ready, without any choice but with all diligence and alacrity, to learn and to execute any duty, office, or employment to which the Superior may think fit to apply them to the greater glory of God, the common good of our Congregation, or for the service of our neighbour. And as far as in us lies, each one should for her greater mortification, abnegation, and spiritual profit voluntarily seek for duties or employments that are considered vile or abject, or to which she has great natural repugnance, remembering the humility of our Lord.

Not only the Chief Superior, but all those, moreover, who are appointed to govern, should ever have before their eyes the burning charity of Christ our Lord, the profound and illimitable humility of the Blessed Virgin, and the example of all the saints, and to this model they should as far as possible conform themselves in all their actions.

---

34. Divine Office official Catholic regimen of daily prayer. **35. mental prayer** various forms of meditation. **examen** examination. In the *Spiritual Exercises* Ignatius recommends daily and detailed examination of conscience as a means of rooting out sin and growing in grace. **46. Superior** One of Mary Ward's controversial innovations was the appointment of a female Chief Superior on the Jesuit model, answerable only to the pope, not to a male counterpart.

As an exercise of humility, which can never be sufficiently praised, and as a means of   55
considerably promoting discipline and religious observance, it is expedient that all the
subjects of the Congregation should be bound to obey not only the Mother Chief
Superior, in whose person they chiefly recognize Christ our Lord and see him, as it
were, present, and that they should render her all due reverence, but that they should also
obey the other superiors and intermediate officials in all things that fall under their   60
authority.

A Conference on Fervour and Verity, 1617

Mr Sackville said: 'It is true whilst they are in their first fervour, but fervour will decay,
and when all is done, they are but women!' I would know what you all think he meant by
this speech of his, 'but women', and what 'fervour' is.

Fervour is a will to do good, that is, a preventing grace of God and gift given *gratis* by
God, which we could not merit. It is true fervour doth many times grow cold, but what is   5
the cause? Is it because we are women? No, but because we are imperfect women. There is
no such difference between men and women. Therefore, it is not because we are women
but, as I have said before, because we are imperfect women, we love not verity, but seek
after lies. 'Veritas Domini manet in aeternum' [Ps. 116: 2] (the verity of our Lord
remaineth forever). It is not *veritas hominis*, verity of men, nor verity of women, but   10
veritas Domini, and this verity women may have as well as men. If we fail it is for want of
this verity and not because we are women. . . . Divers religious, both men and women,
have lost their fervour, because they have been unmindful of this preventing truth, which
is a gift of God and a sign of predestination, as you have often heard (I am sure I have) of
those that are wiser than I.   15

Fervour is not placed in feelings but in a will to do well, which women may have as
well as men. There is no such difference between men and women that women may not
do great things, as we have seen by example of many saints who have done great things.
And I hope in God it will be seen that women in time to come will do much. I beseech
you all for God's love to love verity and true dependence, and not adhere too much to the   20
Superior, to this father, or this creature for affection, so that if they be lost all is
lost. . . . This is verity, to do what we have to do well. Many think it nothing to do
ordinary things. But for us it is. To do ordinary things well, to keep our constitutions,
and all other things that be ordinary in every office or employment, whatsoever it be, to
do it well, this is for us, and this by God's grace will maintain, fervour.   25

CONFERENCE This and other meetings took place in Saint-Omer in late 1617. **1. Mr Sackville** Thomas Sackville,
a prominent English Catholic, bearer of Mary Ward's Memorial to Pope Paul V. In other versions it is a clergyman who
makes the remark 'they are but women'. **4. preventing** coming before. **23. it is** i.e. it is something.

I would to God that all men understood this verity, that women if they will, be perfect, and if they would not make us believe we can do nothing and that we are 'but women', we might do great matters. What can it profit you to tell you you are but women, weak and able to do nothing, and that fervour will decay? I say what doth it profit you but bring you to dejection and without hope of perfection? All are not of this opinion.   30

This is all I have to say at this time, that you love verity and truth.

Mary Poyntz and Winifred Wigmore, *A Brief Relation... Mary Ward, c.*1647–57

[Imprisonment in the Anger Convent, 1631]

All that could be said or done to make her seem horrid or criminal to the religious was done—her prison the room that had been used for all desperate and infectious diseases; the ceiling one might reach with one's hand; two little windows which looked upon the graves and yet those boarded up, saving the space of one's hand to give a little light through the glass; her door with double locks and chained; so many to watch by   5
turns and others allotted to come into her, and none but such, and none at all to speak to her; the abbess commanded under pain of excommunication to let none of hers to converse with her by word or letter. The religious, all in horror and amazement expecting to receive (according to the cipher was given) this monstrous heretic, found themselves in a strange surprise of reverence and devotion, beholding they knew not what of divine in   10
her presence, which they found so humble, meek, peaceful, and courageous, which made some of them, one in particular, go to their prayers. She was an ancient religious and of noted sanctity, who, returning to the Mother abbess, said: 'How are we misinformed! This is a holy servant of God and our house happy in receiving her. Let me have the happiness at the door to see her, though I speak not.' Which at her extreme importunity   15
the Mother granted, and was no small admiration to our dear Mother to see that dumb show, a venerable religious woman in the door on her knees with her hands up, not knowing what it meant. But this and much more we had from the religious themselves, as also the precise following words, 'God forbid Christian ears should hear what was ordained them to do with her.'   20

But to return to our blessed prisoner, the disposition of her mind, which she so candidly and serenely recounted herself. Thus locked up and chained, etc., there was no

A BRIEF RELATION On 13 January 1631 Pope Urban VIII signed the Bull of Suppression, which shut down the Institute and accused its founders of presuming to found a new order in opposition to the decrees of the Councils of the Lateran (1214) and Lyons (1274), which authorized four established rules (those of St Basil, St Augustine, St Benedict, and St Francis). Mary Ward was arrested on 7 February that year and remained incarcerated until 15 April. After her release from prison Ward spent her remaining years until her death fighting for recognition of her Institute. **7. abbess** Catherine Bernardin. **9. cipher** notice that. **16. admiration** wonder. **Mother** Mary Ward. **16–17. dumb show** show without words, often emblematical of larger action. **21–2. which...herself**. Mary wrote secret letters to her companions in lemon-juice.

other appearance than death, not only in regard of the condition of her health and the quality of the place, but also that it seemed impossible that man that had wit should proceed so far and let her ever again appear abroad. She knew full well the persons and actors of the business, making an act of resignation and oblation of herself to God, finding an unspeakable content, peace, and joy of mind in the hope she had that now was come that long wished-for time where she might have nothing to do but to think of God, love him, and depend upon him, with confidence he would have care of hers. In this disposition she went to her bed, hoping to rest very quietly, all labours being now taken out of her hands. But in all these her contents she found, as it were, a suspension of the grant from above, and rather something that had of the check that she should think it enough to suffer and not labour. She did not murmur but had a little inclination to dispute, but resolved to do neither then but sleep, and this notwithstanding the condition of her mind and the extreme smell of the bedstead and walls of spit and such like, as contagious and dying people do ordinarily leave. The exterior she soon overcame, but in her mind grew a strong force and threat if she did not resolve to labour in defence of her own and hers their innocency, and consequently her own delivery; which at length she promised to do and so fell asleep, which till this resolution made she by no means could do, and so slept well according to her sleeps. But what can express the sensibilities hers were left in, considering the state of her health? The power and violence of her enemies seemed to shut up all recourse but to God, to whom they betook themselves night and day without ceasing.

31. **contents** contentments. 32. **of the check** a reproof. 38. **hers their** her company's. 40. **sleeps** usual slumbers. 42. **they** her company.

POETRY

Though such early modern Catholics as Thomas Lodge and Jasper Heywood wrote noteworthy non-religious verse, the selections below present Catholic religious poetry from the period. These selections comprise only a sampling of the riches, extant in print and manuscript, that await rediscovery. (One thinks of Miles Huggard, William Forest, Thomas, Lord Vaux, Richard Gwyn, Richard Stanihurst, and Kenelm Digby.) Despite the occasional oppositional stance towards Protestantism, many of the poems here are generally Christian, completely acceptable to Protestants as well. Catholics and Protestants shared many beliefs, prayed some of the same devotions, and admired each other's art. Catholics read and appreciated George Herbert; Protestants read and published Robert Southwell and Richard Crashaw.

What is Catholic about Catholic poetry in this period? Some of the selections below respond polemically to specific political and cultural circumstances. Robert Southwell's 'Decease, release' laments the execution of Mary, Queen of Scots; John Beaumont imagines her triumphant in heaven. Some pointedly rewrite Protestant history and mythology. The ballad 'From Winter Cold into Summer Hot' catalogues the changes in religion as deformation not reformation, especially the devaluation of fasting, prayer, and good works, the dishonouring of saints and Mary, the loss of unity and the sacraments. Anthony Copley recasts Spenser's epic to depict Queen Elizabeth as the wicked Doblessa, not the Fairy Queen. Thomas Pounde mocks the 'rabble rout' of martyrs in John Foxe's 'brainsick' book and encourages persecuted Catholics. William Alabaster also writes a sonnet against Foxe's pseudomartyrs. James's accession prompts Ben Jonson to protest the destruction of churches by government decree. John Beaumont writes against Protestant moralization of the 'Fatal Vesper', the 1623 collapse of a floor that killed nearly a hundred Catholics at services.

Throughout the period the legislated persecution of Catholics gives rise to recurrent expressions of protest, suffering, and resistance. The verses on Walsingham lament the destruction of Mary's shrine and the replacement of hymn-singing pilgrims by owls, toads, and serpents. Sighting Dover cliffs from Calais, Toby Matthew expresses the pain of exile. There are also prison poems, notably Chidiock Tichborne's 'My prime of life is but a frost of cares', written several days before his execution, and Francis Tregian's poignant verse letters. The ballad 'Calvary Mount is my Delight' sounds a more defiant note, inviting torture and death, yearning for union with Christ in bloody martyrdom. Throughout the period the prophetic books and psalms take on new life: William Byrd provides magnificent musical settings to voice the anguish of recusant communities and offer consolation (see INSTRUCTIONS AND DEVOTIONS). Richard Verstegan publishes *Odes in Imitation of the Seven Penitential Psalms* (1601), and his translations reappear in Elizabeth Grymeston's *Miscellanea* (1604). Those who live under the shadow of Calvary continually look to the heavenly Jerusalem. Copley envisions the Temple of Peace there, surrounded by flowers and precious gems, featuring priests, nuns, and Catholic sacraments. The ballad 'Jerusalem, my Happy Home' depicts a similarly Paradisal setting of saints and heavenly choirs.

Some Catholic poetry defends contested doctrines and practices. The five great hymns of St Thomas Aquinas on the Eucharist, written to celebrate the newly established Feast of Corpus Christi, circulate in Latin and in new translations by Henry Garnet, Robert Southwell, and Richard Crashaw (see INSTRUCTIONS AND DEVOTIONS). Henry Constable writes a sonnet to the sacrificed Lamb in the Blessed Sacrament, and others that defend Catholic beliefs. The extraordinary Literature of Tears, a genre that expatiates upon the sorrows of famous figures, often sinners, arises directly from Catholic teaching about the sacrament of Penance and its three constituent parts—Contrition, Confession, and Satisfaction (see Canons and Decrees of the Council of Trent, Fourteenth Session). Robert Southwell's popular 'St Peter's Complaint' shows Peter shedding copious tears as a sign of his true contrition and as partial satisfaction. Southwell's similar prose work, *Mary Magdalen's Funeral Tears*, features the penitent sinner who appears throughout Catholic poetry on the Continent and in England, below in a sonnet by Henry Constable and in Richard Crashaw's extravagant 'The Weeper'.

Catholic doctrines and devotions inspire other poems. Ben Jonson alludes approvingly to the doctrine of good works in 'The New Cry', for example, and John Donne envisions a Virgin immaculately conceived in 'The Litany'. Catholic poetry often features the Virgin Mary, *Theotokos* 'Mother of God', Queen of heaven, merciful mediatrix, prime target of Protestant iconoclasm and prime object of Catholic veneration. Catholics in the period still sing medieval hymns (*Salve, Regina, O Gloriosa Domina, Stabat Mater Dolorosa*), and say traditional prayers (the rosary, *Ave, Maria*, the Litany of Loreto). Many of these appear in the influential *Primer* of Richard Verstegan (see Prayers and Hymns, INSTRUCTIONS AND DEVOTIONS), who also presents below a Marian lullaby. Robert Southwell writes a moving sequence of poems rehearsing events in the lives of Mary and Christ. The rough bricklayer Ben Jonson also sings poems in Mary's praise. John Beaumont celebrates the Assumption (a doctrine rejected by the Church of England), as does Richard Crashaw, who venerated Mary throughout his life and art. A Laudian such as Anthony Stafford might also praise Mary in *The Female Glory* (1635), but such exceptions prove the general rule. Mary functions as the archetypal *donna angelica* for English Catholics, as she did for Dante, whose pilgrim finally gazes on the face that gazes on Christ, and for Petrarch, whose last poem in the *Rime sparse* abjures love of Laura for love of Mary. Through Dante, Petrarch, and others Marian devotion eventually passed into secular European lyric and generated the familiar early modern rhetoric of praise and pain. Some of this great movement remains visible in the works of William Alabaster and Henry Constable, both of whom write secular and sacred sonnets.

Two well-known authors, not traditionally considered as Catholic poets, deserve reconsideration. A professed Catholic for over a decade, Ben Jonson wrote plays and poetry that reflect his experience of the forbidden faith. Catholicism inflects the anti-Puritan satire of the plays as well as individual poems of praise and blame. Jonson's verse epistle to the Lady Aubigny depicts the recusant world that he, she, and many others experienced as daily life. 'The Sinner's Sacrifice' draws upon well-established meditative traditions. Raised as a Catholic, John Donne repudiated his faith to become an Anglican divine. Secular poems, nevertheless, frequently bear the imprint of Donne's origins, while the Marian devotions he forbade from the pulpit empower 'The Litany', 'La Corona', and the praise of Elizabeth Drury in *An Anatomy of the World*. The techniques of Ignatian meditation structure some holy sonnets and the 'Hymn to God, my God, in my Sickness'. Catholicism provided both Jonson and Donne with a circle of friends and acquaintances, time-honoured authority, long traditions of learning, ceremony, and sacrifice, and a range of beliefs as well as evocative devotional practices.

Two additional developments mark Catholic poetry at the end of the early modern period. First, a new concern with mysticism and a receptivity to Continental writers on the subject generate poems of extraordinary intensity and spiritual insight. Gertrude More expresses infinite longings in verse and Richard Crashaw, likewise, explores the rapturous state of mystical union with God. Teresa of Ávila, her heart enflamed with the seraphic dart, becomes a central symbol of Catholic mystical poetry. Second, Emblem literature, the *Partheneia sacra* of the Jesuit Henry Hawkins, for example (see INSTRUCTIONS AND DEVOTIONS), inspires devotional poems that develop themes by symbolic meditation. Poets employ the visual and the literary through use of extended analogy and profuse variation; they explore metaphorical, moral, allusory, and other levels of meaning. Meditating on the Passion for twelve books, John Beaumont's neglected *The Crown of Thorns* well illustrates this type of verse, as does the mature work of the baroque master, Richard Crashaw.

A Lament and Some Ballads

These poems are of uncertain origin and authorship but express popular Catholic sentiments in the Tudor and Stuart periods. The 'Lament' mourns the 1538 destruction of the priory at Walsingham in Norfolk, site of a beloved shrine of Mary for generations of pilgrims. (Compare the contrary, cynical account of Erasmus, FICTION). 'Winter Cold into Summer Hot' humorously and indignantly chronicles the deterioration of religious life in England under Protestantism. More seriously, 'Calvary Mount is my Delight' identifies the suffering of persecuted Catholics with that of Christ. Probably written by a priest to encourage his oppressed flock, the ballad expresses a fervent wish for martyrdom. In 'Jerusalem, my Happy Home' English Catholics, forced to hide in their native country or live abroad, express longing for their true home, the heavenly Jerusalem.

From 'A Lament for our Lady's Shrine at Walsingham'

> In the wracks of Walsingham
>   Whom should I choose,
> But the queen of Walsingham
>   To be guide to my muse.
> Then thou, prince of Walsingham,   5
>   Grant me to frame
> Bitter plaints to rue thy wrong,
>   Bitter woe for thy name.
> Bitter was it so to see
>   The silly sheep   10
> Murdered by the ravening wolves,
>   While the shepherds did sleep.
> Bitter was it, oh, to view
>   The sacred vine,
> Whiles the gardeners played all close,   15
>   Rooted up by the swine.
> Bitter, bitter, oh, to behold

LAMENT   In July 1538 Henry VIII's men removed the statue of Mary, confiscated the gold and silver, and tore down the priory at Walsingham. **1. wracks** ruins. **3. queen** Mary. **5. prince** Christ. **7. plaints** complaints. **15. gardeners** Prior Richard Vowell and his monks assented to the destruction in exchange for pensions. **played all close** (1) managed all in secret; (2) played nearby.

The grass to grow,
Where the walls of Walsingham
    So stately did show.   20
Such were the works of Walsingham,
    While she did stand,
Such are the wracks as now do show
    Of that holy land!
Level, level with the ground   25
    The towers do lie,
Which with their golden, glittering tops
    Pierced once to the sky.
Where were gates no gates are now,
    The ways unknown,   30
Where the press of peers did pass,
    While her fame far was blown.
Owls do screech where the sweetest hymns
    Lately were sung
Toads and serpents hold their dens,   35
    Where the palmers did throng.
Weep, weep, O Walsingham,
    Whose days are nights,
Blessings turned to blasphemies,
    Holy deeds to despites.   40
Sin is where our Lady sat,
    Heaven turned is to hell,
Satan sits where our Lord did sway,
    Walsingham, oh, farewell.

From 'Winter Cold into Summer Hot'

Winter cold into summer hot
    Well changèd now may be;
For things as strange do come to pass,
    As we may plainly see:
England priests which honoured hath   5
    So many hundred years,

---

31. **press of peers** crowds of visitors, common and noble. 32. **blown** spread. 36. **palmers** pilgrims. 40. **despites** outrages.
'WINTER COLD INTO SUMMER HOT' 2. **Well** easily. 5. **England . . . hath** England, which hath honoured priests.

Doth hang them up as traitors now,
　　Which causeth many tears.

She doth condemn her elders all,
　　As all the world beside,　　　　　　　　　　10
Religion old, which long hath been
　　In lands both far and wide.
A gospel new she hath found out,
　　A bird of Calvin's brood,
Abandoning all memory　　　　　　　　　　　15
　　Of Christ his holy rood.

Abstinence is Papistry,
　　As this new error saith;
Fasting, prayer, and all good works
　　Avoid, for only faith　　　　　　　　　　　20
Doth bring us all to heaven straight—
　　A doctrine very strange,
Which causeth men at liberty
　　Of vice and sin to range.

From angels honour taken is,　　　　　　　　25
　　From saints all worship due;
The mother of our living God—
　　A thing most strange yet true!—
Comparèd is by many a Jack
　　Unto a saffron bag,　　　　　　　　　　　30
To a thing of naught, to a paltry patch,
　　And to our vicar's hag!

Unity is clean exiled,
　　For preachers do agree
As do our clocks when they strike noon,　　35
　　Now one, now two, now three,
But all together never jump;
　　When as our elders all,
Of faith and doctrine did accord

---

14. **bird . . . brood** offshoot of Calvinism. 16. **rood** cross. 17. **Abstinence** refusal to take food and drink during prescribed periods, a Catholic exercise of penance and mortification. 20. **only faith** *sola fides*, a Protestant doctrine that denied the propitiatory value of good works. 29. **Jack** common, worthless fellow. 30. **saffron bag** Hugh Latimer, in a sermon preached at St Paul's, 18 January 1548, compared the Virgin Mary to a saffron bag: 'as the saffron bag that hath been full of saffron or hath had saffron in it doth ever after savour and smell of the sweet saffron that it contained, so our Blessed Lady, which conceived and bare Christ in her womb, did ever after resemble the manners and virtues of that precious babe' (*A Notable Sermon*, 1548, sig. Aiiii). The metaphor denies Mary's intrinsic worth and holiness. 31. **paltry patch** insignificant material cover. 37. **jump** agree precisely.

In points both great and small.   40

   .   .   .   .   .

Contrition a trash is called,
   Confession scoffed and scorned,
And so is Satisfaction,
   Purgatory pains forlorned.
Which causeth fear of sin to flee,   45
   Where sole faith doth suffice
To amend all that is amiss—
   But none thinks so that's wise.

They deem themselves predestinates,
   Yet reprobates indeed;   50
Free will they will not have; good works
   With them are void of need.
Which points of doctrine do destroy
   Each commonwealth and land;
Religion old in order due   55
   Makes kingdoms long to stand.

From 'Calvary Mount is my Delight'

Cavalry Mount is my delight,
   A place I love so well,
Cavalry Mount, oh, that I might
   Deserve on thee to dwell.
Oh, that I might a pilgrim go,   5
   That sacred mount to see,
Oh, that I might some service do,
   Where Christ died once for me!

   .   .   .   .   .

Might there my dwelling be, no force
   Nor fear should me remove,   10
To meditate with great remorse
   Upon my Saviour's love.

41–3. Catholics believed that the sacrament of Penance consisted of three parts: Contrition, or sorrow for sin, Confession to a priest, and Satisfaction, the performance of penitential or charitable actions as payment of the temporal punishment due to sin. **44. forlorned** abandoned. Protestants rejected the doctrine of purgatory. **49. predestinates** The Calvinist doctrine of predestination held that God had already decided for all time who was to be saved (the elect) and who condemned for all eternity (the reprobate); this belief denied the doctrine of free will (see Erasmus, CONTROVERSIES). **52. void of need** unnecessary.

'CALVARY MOUNT'   **10. remove** prevent.

No Herod nor Herodian
   Should cause me thence to flee;
No Pilate, Jew, nor soldier   15
   Should move me till I die,
Nor all the help that they would have
   From Calvin's cursèd crew.
There would I make my tomb and grave,
   And never wish for new.   20
No pursuivant I would esteem,
   Nor crafty catchpole fear;
Of jail nor jailer nothing deem,
   If I might harbour there.

No rope nor cruel torture then   25
   Should cause my mind to fail;
Nor lewd device of wicked men
   Should cause my courage quail.
On rack in tower let me be led,
   Let joints at large be stretched;   30
Let me abide each cruel braid,
   Till blood from veins be fetched.

And if they can devise worse ways
   To utter things untrue,
Let them proceed by all assays   35
   To frame inventions new;
Let all distress to me befall
   To do my country good,
And let the thirst of tyrants all
   Be quenchèd in my blood.   40

Let me be falsely condemnèd;
   Let sheriff on me take charge;
With bows and bills let me be led,
   Lest I escape at large;
Let me from prison pass away   45
   On hurdle hard to lie,

---

13. **Herod nor Herodian** Herod the Great (73–4 BC) was the Judaean tyrant responsible for the slaughter of the Holy Innocents. **Herodian** was an anti-Christian supporter of Herodian dynasty in Palestine in the first century AD. 15. **Pilate** Pontius Pilate, prefect of Judaea (AD 26–36), presided at the trial of Christ and gave the order for the execution. 21. **pursuivant** a citizen empowered to search and arrest, used extensively in the apprehension of Catholics. 22. **catchpole** petty officer. 27. **lewd** evil. 28. **quail** fail. 31. **braid** twist. 35. **assays** attempts. 43. **bows and bills** i.e. weapons. The bow is used for shooting arrows; the bill is a blade attached to a long handle. 46. **hurdle** frame on which traitors were dragged to execution.

To Tyburn drawn without delay,
    In torments there to die.

Let me be hanged and yet for doubt
    Lest I be dead too soon,   50
Let there some devilish spirit start out
    In haste to cut me down;
Let bowels be burnt, let paunch be fried
    In fire ere I be dead!
O London bridge, a pole provide,   55
    Thereon to set my head!

O London, let my quarters stand
    Upon thy gates to dry;
And let them bear the world in hand
    I did for treason die.   60
Let crows and kites my carcass eat,
    Let ravens their portion have,
Lest afterwards my friends entreat
    To lay my corpse in grave.

Sweet Jesu, if it be thy will,   65
    Unto my plaints attend:
Grant grace I may continue still
    Thy servant to the end,
Grant, blessed Lord, grant, Saviour sweet,
    Grant, Jesu, king of bliss,   70
That in thy love I live and die,
    Sweet Jesu, grant me this.

From 'Jerusalem, my Happy Home'

Jerusalem, my happy home,
    When shall I come to thee?
When shall my sorrows have an end,
    Thy joys when shall I see?

47. **Tyburn** London site of the Middlesex gallows, which were used for the execution of traitors. **49–54.** The poet accurately describes the customary practice of disembowelling hanged prisoners before their death and burning the body parts. **55. pole** Heads of traitors were mounted on poles at London bridge to serve as warnings. **57. quarters** the four parts of the body, usually cut up and hung for display after execution. **59. bear...hand** advertise to the world.

'JERUSALEM' **1. Jerusalem** The heavenly, as distinct from the earthly, Jerusalem, i.e. heaven: see Heb. 12: 22: 'But you are come to mount Sion and to the city of the living God, the heavenly Jerusalem, and to the company of many thousands of angels.'

O happy harbour of the saints,   5
   O sweet and pleasant soil,
In thee no sorrow may be found,
   No grief, no care, no toil.

In thee no sickness may be seen,
   No hurt, no ache, no sore;   10
There is no death nor ugly devil,
   There is life for evermore.

    ·   ·   ·   ·   ·   ·

Thy houses are of ivory,
   Thy windows crystal clear,
Thy tiles are made of beaten gold,   15
   O God, that I were there!

Within thy gates nothing doth come
   That is not passing clean;
No spider's web, no dirt, no dust,
   No filth may there be seen.   20

Ay, my sweet home, Jerusalem,
   Would God I were in thee;
Would God my woes were at an end,
   Thy joys that I might see!

Thy saints are crowned with glory great,   25
   They see God face to face;
They triumph still, they still rejoice,
   Most happy is their case.

We that are here in banishment
   Continually do mourn;   30
We sigh and sob, we weep and wail,
   Perpetually we groan.

Our sweet is mixed with bitter gall,
   Our pleasure is but pain,
Our joys scarce last the looking on,   35
   Our sorrows still remain.

But there they live in such delight,
   Such pleasure, and such play,
As that to them a thousand years
   Doth seem as yesterday.   40

Thy vineyards and thy orchards are
   Most beautiful and fair,

Full furnishèd with trees and fruits,
    Most wonderful and rare.

Thy gardens and thy gallant walks   45
    Continually are green;
There grows such sweet and pleasant flowers
    As nowhere else are seen.

There is nectar and ambrosia made,
    There is musk and civet sweet;   50
There many a fair and dainty drug
    Are trodden under feet.

There cinnamon, there sugar grows,
    There nard and balm abound.
What tongue can tell or heart conceive   55
    The joys that there are found?

Quite through the streets with silver sound
    The flood of life do flow;
Upon whose banks on every side,
    The wood of life doth grow.   60

There trees for evermore bear fruit,
    And evermore do spring;
There evermore the angels sit,
    And evermore do sing.

There David stands with harp in hand,   65
    As master of the choir;
Ten thousand times that man were blest
    That might this music hear.

Our Lady sings *Magnificat*,
    With tune surpassing sweet,   70
And all the virgins bear their parts,
    Sitting about her feet.

Te Deum doth Saint Ambrose sing,
    Saint Augustine doth the like;
Old Simeon and Zachary   75
    Have not their songs to seek.

---

49. nectar and ambrosia mythical drink and food of the gods. **50. musk and civet** fragrant substances. **54. nard and balm** aromatic ointments. **55–6.** an echo of Paul's words on heaven, 1 Cor. 2: 9. **65. David** composer of the Psalms. **69. *Magnificat*** Mary's declaration of joy to Elizabeth (Luke 1: 46–55). **73. *Te Deum*** well-known hymn of praise to God, traditionally credited to Ambrose and Augustine. **75. Simeon and Zachary** New Testament figures whose praises of God became canticles (sacred songs) in Roman Catholic ritual (Luke 2: 29–32; 1: 68–79).

There Magdalen hath left her moan,
    And cheerfully doth sing,
With blessèd saints whose harmony
    In every street doth ring.   80

Jerusalem, my happy home,
    Would God I were in thee;
Would God my woes were at an end,
    Thy joys that I might see!

CHIDIOCK TICHBORNE

Born into a noble Catholic family, Chidiock Tichborne (1558?–86) joined the 1586 Babington plot to assassinate Elizabeth and put Mary Stuart on the throne, for which he was executed on 20 September 1586. Tichborne repented on the gallows and left behind a moving letter to his wife and several verses, including the poignant lament below. This admired poem, ironically, first appeared to the public in a pamphlet celebrating the foiling of the plot and the execution of the conspirators, *Verses of Praise and Joy written upon Her Majesty's Preservation* (1586). Facing Tichborne's poem is a parodic response by T.K., beginning 'Thy prime of youth is frozen with thy faults, | Thy feast of joy is finished with thy fall,' and ending, 'Thy glory and thy glass are timeless run, | And this, O Tichborne, hath thy treason done' (sig. Aiii). The poem has found more sympathetic readers through the ages, appearing in numerous anthologies and some musical settings.

'Tichborne's Verses made by Himself not Three Days before his Execution', 1586

My prime of youth is but a frost of cares,
My feast of joy is but a dish of pain,
My crop of corn is but a field of tares,
And all my good is but vain hope of gain.
    The day is gone and yet I saw no sun,   5
    And now I live and now my life is done.

The spring is past and yet it hath not sprung,
The fruit is dead and yet the leaves are green,
My youth is gone and yet I am but young,
I saw the world and yet I was not seen.   10

77. **Magdalen** Mary Magdalen became a symbol of penitence to later ages. **3. tares** weeds. The line refers to the parable of the wheat and tares (Matt. 13: 25–30).

My thread is cut and yet it was not spun,
And now I live and now my life is done.

I sought my death and found it in my womb,
I looked for life and saw it was a shade,
I trod the earth and knew it was my tomb,   15
And now I die and now I am but made.
    The glass is full and now the glass is run,
And now I live and now my life is done.

FRANCIS TREGIAN

For sheltering Cuthbert Mayne, future martyr, and for his Catholicism, Francis Tregian (1548–1608) was the first Catholic under Elizabeth to lose all his lands and goods for his faith; he also lost his freedom, suffering over twenty years in prison. In 1625 English Catholics in Lisbon exhumed Tregian's body and reburied it standing up in honour of his long resistance to Elizabeth and her government. While in prison from 1579 to 1601 Tregian composed verses with a pin and candle snuff. The 'Letter from Prison' voices his anguish and his hope for salvation. The 'Letter' to his wife Mary advises her to pray and bids poignant farewell. Tregian's son, also Francis (1574–1619), became a composer and, while in prison for recusancy, compiled the Fitzwilliam Virginal Book, a primary source of keyboard music for the period.

From 'A Letter from Prison'

I am become as pelican
    That doth in desert dwell,
And as the night crow in his nest,
    Whom other birds expel,
My foes revile me day by day.   5
    Incensed through rage they fret,
Wherefore my drink is mixed with tears,
    I ashes eat for meat.
The want of worldly wealth, O Lord,

---

11. **thread** The thread of life, woven, spun, and cut by the three fates of Greek mythology. 13. **womb** i.e. his Catholic upbringing, which led to his execution. 17. **glass** hourglass, filled with sand to mark the passing of time.
'A LETTER FROM PRISON' 1. **pelican** not the water fowl but the 'the pelican of the wilderness' (Ps. 101: 7), a generic designation for a bird living apart from civilization. 7–8. See Ps. 101: 10: 'For I did eat ashes like bread, and mingled my drink with weeping.'

Thou seest I do sustain,   10
And how that fury with great force,
   Is poured on me amain.
What should I show thee one by one,
   The causes of my grief?
Thou seest my wrack, thou knowst my lack,   15
   Thou canst give me relief.
The which if so thy pleasure be,
   I humbly ask of thee,
For will of thine, not will of mine,
   O Lord, fulfillèd be.   20
But if thy doom hath so decreed
   I shall be scourgèd more,
Grant yet at least I never lack
   A plaster for each sore.
As is thy holy ghost, O Lord,   25
   I pray that thou wouldst spare
The workers of my web of woe,
   The causers of my care.
I humbly thee beseech, O Lord,
   E'en by thy blessèd blood,   30
Forgive their guilt, forgive their ill,
   And send them all much good.
Turn not, O Lord, thy face from me,
   Although a wretched wight,
But let me joy in thee all day,   35
   Rejoice in thee all night.
And in all chances of this life,
   By sea and eke by land,
Let me always protected be,
   By thy almighty hand.   40
Preserve, O Lord, my shaking ship,
   From pirates, spoils, and knocks,
From gulfs, from shelves, from sinking sands,
   From rending on the rocks,
That after stirring storms are stayed,   45
   And surging seas do cease,
I may with mirth cast anchor in,
   The pleasant port of peace.

12. **amain** with full force. 13. **What** why. 24. **plaster** medicated bandage. 25. **As ... ghost** As your holy mind is merciful. 34. **wight** person. 38. **eke** also. 43. **shelves** sandbars or underwater reefs.

From 'A Letter to his Wife'

My wont is not to write in verse,
    You know, good wife, iwis,
Wherefore you may well bear with me,
    Though now I write amiss.
For lack of ink the candle coal,   5
    For pen a pin I use,
The which also I may allege
    In part of my excuse.
For said it is of many men,
    And such as are no fools,   10
A workman is but little worth
    If he do want his tools.

            .   .   .   .   .   .

What I should send I know not well,
    But sure I am of this,
The doleful mind restored to mirth   15
    By perfect prayer is.
Let prayer be your practice, wife,
    Let prayer be your play,
Let prayer be your staple of trust,
    Let prayer be your stay.   20
Let prayer be your castle strong,
    Let prayer be your fort,
Let prayer be your place of rest,
    Let prayer be your port.

            .   .   .   .   .   .

My keeper knocks at door, who comes   25
    To see his hawks in mew;
Wherefore, good wife, I must make short,
    Farewell, sweet spouse, adieu.
Farewell, the anchor of my hope,
    Farewell, my stay of life,   30
Farewell, my poor Penelope,
    Farewell, my faithful wife.
Bless in my name my little babes,

2. **iwis** certainly. 4. **amiss** poorly. 16. **prayer** disyllabic. 19. **staple** chief component 26. **mew** confinement. 31. **Penelope** Odysseus' faithful wife.

God send them all good hap,
And bless withal that little babe   35
   That lieth in your lap.

    .   .   .   .   .

Farewell again, thou lamp of light,
   Vicegerent of my heart.
He that takes leave so oft, I think,
   He likes not to depart.   40
And yet depart we must, of force,
   To my no little grief,
God send us well to meet again,
   God send us still relief,
And well to run our restless race,   45
   Though rough and full of pain,
That through the blessèd blood of Christ,
   True glory we may gain.

THOMAS POUNDE

Personal servant of Queen Elizabeth, Thomas Pounde (1538–1613) left court in 1551 and became a Catholic and active missionary in England. Accepted as a Jesuit lay brother in 1578, Pounde circulated Campion's *A Letter to the Privy Council* in manuscript (see CONTROVERSIES), and wrote a challenge of his own. He spent at least thirty years of his life in various prisons for his faith. About 1582 Pounde sent to Francis Tregian a manuscript poem that contrasts true Catholic martyrs with Protestant pseudomartyrs, 'A Challenge unto Foxe' (for another rebuttal of Foxe, see Persons, HISTORIES). The second part of this poem, based on Robert Persons's *De persecutione Anglicana* (1581), offers comfort to all afflicted Catholics.

'A Challenge unto Foxe', 1582

Come forth, fond Foxe, with all the rabble rout
Of monstrous martyrs in thy brainsick book;
Compare them to this glorious martyr stout,

---

38. **Vicegerent** appointed ruler.
'A CHALLENGE' 1. **fond** foolish. **Foxe** John Foxe (1516–87), whose *Acts and Monuments* (1563) rehearsed the atrocities of Mary's persecution and created a national mythology of Protestant martyrs. **rabble rout** low-class band. 3. **this glorious martyr** Peter Elcius a Spanish Catholic executed in Morocco memorialized by F. Zara (Cologne, 1582).

And thou shalt see how loathly foul they look.
  For black and white comparèd somewhat near,   5
  Will cause them both the better to appear.

This blessèd man, of God's professèd foes
With deep despite in ruthful sort was slain;
What time himself a Catholic he shows,
And in that faith he hoped to obtain   10
  The endless empire of eternal bliss,
Who prayed the saints to help and pray for this.

[On Foxe's false martyrs]

For 'tis not pain that doth a martyr make,
Nor glorious sort in which he seems to die,
But faith the cause, which thine did them forsake,   15
When from Christ's spouse they would so fondly fly.
  Where truth doth want, to utter wrack they fall,
  Not martyrs made, but most accursed of all.

    .   .   .   .

For if that he a glorious martyr be,
Which spite herself for shame cannot deny,   20
Then every man which is not blind may see
In what bad state thy monsters mad did die.
  For where the day appeareth fair and bright,
  There is no place for ugly shade of night.

On altars God and Dagon cannot hold,   25
Our Christ and Belial needs must be at jar;
For wolves and lambs agree not in one fold,
No more than peace can live at ease with war.
  If, therefore, he in endless bliss do reign,
  The state of thine is ever during pain.   30

Call in, therefore, thy loathsome lump of lies,
With humble mind make suit to God for grace;
That He may ope thy blind and blearèd eyes
Thereby to see, and purchase thee a place.
  Whereas thy masters could not enter in,   35
  Because they were so deeply drowned in sin.

Which, that thou mayst, with all my heart I pray,
And that is all the hurt I wish to thee,

14. **sort** manner. 15. **faith the cause** Catholics, recalling Augustine, frequently argued that true faith, not punishment, makes the martyr. 16. **Christ's spouse** the Church. 19. **he** Peter Elcius 25. **Dagon** god of the Philistines. 26. **Belial** a devil. **jar** conflict. 30. **during** lasting. 31. **Call in** revoke. 35. **masters** (1) Protestant leaders; (2) false martyrs.

That we in peace may meet another day
In bliss, which here on earth could not agree.   40
   And so, farewell, from thee I turn my style,
   To comfort Christian Catholics awhile.

[handwritten note: Broadly Christian, not specifically English]

[Christ's speech of comfort]

'Discomfort not, whate'er your foes do threat;
Reck not of racks, their torments are but toys;
The more they do upon your bodies set,   45
The more with me they shall increase your joys.
   Yea, and the greater that your torments be,
   The greater comfort shall you have of me.

[handwritten note: what a list!]

'Recount what tortures martyrs old did feel,
As stones, and whips, hooks, plummets, clubs, and chains,   50
Saws, swords, shafts, darts, the cross, the rack, and wheel,
Frost, water, fire, the axe, and sundry pains.
   Some choked with stink, some famished, wanting meat,
   And some were flung to brutish beasts to eat.

'And some by them were likewise drawn in twain,   55
Some piecemeal hewn, some strippèd of their skin,
Some boiled, some broiled, and some with bodkins slain,
And some hot oil and lead were dippèd in.
   And each of these of comfort had such store,
   As all did wish their torments had been more.   *[handwritten note: really?]*   60

'Peruse their lives and use their virtues rare,
And then of what estate soever thou be,
Their mildness may your Christian minds prepare
With them to take all griefs and cares in gree.
   For no estate upon the earth doth dwell   65
   Which with my saints may not be suited well.

.   .   .   .

'You likewise may record how many ills
All foolish worldlings daily do endure
For health, for wealth, for pleasure's poisoned pills,
In which their banes oftimes they do procure.   70
   And let not these for shame take greater pain
   To purchase hell, than you the heav'ns to gain.

---

41. **turn my style** change the subject (from *stylus*, a writing instrument). 44. **Reck not of** heed not. 50. **plummets** lead weights for pressing to death. 57. **bodkins** knives. 64. **in gree** graciously.

'My word is past, my promise may not fail,
Conform yourselves, I will confirm your grace;
Hell gates shall not against your faith prevail,   75
Though these as rods we use now for a space.
    But in the end they shall be endless fire,
    And you with joy shall reap your earnèd hire.

'And as the dandling nurse with babe doth play,
Which, puling long, hath wept and cried for woe,   80
Even so will I with you, and wipe away
The tears which down your leers have trickled so.
    Meantime, cheer each his mate, to praying fall,   *Social*
    And I will be the cheerer of you all.'

[Conclusion]

Here with our Saviour's speech I will conclude,   85
And you, renowned confessors, do request
In humble sort, my homely metres rude
To take in gree, and construe to the best.
    For zeal, not skill, did make me take my pen,
    To stir myself by stirring other men.   90

For as the trumpeter whose limbs be lame,
To battle's broils encouraging the knight,
Some comfort takes, partaking of the fame,
If foes he foil and gain the spoil by fight,
    So I in hope that you of prey right sure,   95
    Will help with prayers my lamèd lines to cure.

HENRY CONSTABLE

Born into a noble family and educated at Cambridge, Henry Constable (1562–1613) served the government in Europe, numbering among his acquaintances kings, statesmen, and intellectuals. A committed Protestant early on, he wrote against Cardinal William Allen, defended Protestant doctrine, attacked papal authority, and condemned rebellion. In 1589 Constable's *Examen pacifique de la Doctrine des Huguenots* defended French Protestants but adopted the viewpoint of a moderate Catholic. About 1590 Constable officially became a

76. **these as rods** these persecutors as rods of penance. 80. **puling** crying. 82. **leers** cheeks. 94. **he** the knight. 95. **of . . . sure** of the rewards of martyrdom very sure.

Catholic but he always remained, as did many, loyal to the government and distrustful of Jesuits. For his faith he suffered periodic imprisonment, loss of his inheritance, and exile.

Constable's secular sonnets first appeared in *Diana* (1592), and thereafter with additions. Ardent and skilful, his love poetry reflects Continental traditions and writers, especially the works of Petrarch and Desportes. A religious sensibility appears in these secular sonnets (excerpted below), as Constable alludes to punishment for pride, the seven deadly sins, the stigmata of St Francis, and the veneration of relics. But the treatment is playful and metaphorical. *The Spiritual Sonnets*, written sometime after the conversion, more seriously develop religious themes and articulate Catholic doctrines. The first below philosophically explores the mystery of the Trinity. The others affirm the contested beliefs and practices recently ratified by the Council of Trent: the real presence of Christ in the Eucharist, the importance of contrition and penance, the validity of devotion to the saints and to Mary as mediatrix. In these poems Constable sings with a small but thoughtful and lyrical Catholic voice.

Diana, 1592

'Mine eye with all the deadly sins is fraught'
Mine eye with all the deadly sins is fraught:
1. First, *proud*, sith it presumed to look so high,
A watchman being made, stood gazing by;
2. And *idle*, took no heed till I was caught;
3. And *envious*, bears envy that my thought   5
Should in his absence be to her so nigh.
To kill my heart mine eye let in her eye,
4. And so consent gave to a *murder* wrought;
5. And *covetous*, it never would remove
From her fair hair (gold so doth please his sight);   10
6. *Unchaste*, a bawd between my heart and love;
7. A *glutton* eye, with tears drunk every night.
These sins procurèd have a goddess' ire,
Wherefore my heart is damned in love's sweet fire.

---

1. **deadly sins** pride, envy anger, sloth, avarice (or covetousness), gluttony, and lust, though numbers and names varied (see Aquinas, e.g. *ST* II q. 1 a. 84 ad 4). 2. **sith** since. 3. **watchman** guard. 6. **Should...nigh** The eye envies thoughts, which can be near the lady anytime. 7. **let in** The beloved's eyes are imagined as shooting darts through the lover's eyes into his heart. 8. *murder* **wrought** Not named, the deadly sin here is anger. 13. **goddess** the beloved.

'My lady's presence makes the roses red'

My lady's presence makes the roses red,
Because to see her lips they blush for shame.
The lilies' leaves for envy pale became,
And her white hands in them this envy bred.
The marigold the leaves abroad doth spread,   5
Because the sun's and her power is the same;
The violet of purple colour came,
Dyed in the blood she made my heart to shed.
In brief, all flowers from her their virtue take;
From her sweet breath their sweet smells do proceed;   10
The living heat which her eyebeams doth make
Warmeth the ground and quickeneth the seed.
The rain wherewith she watereth the flowers
Falls from mine eyes, which she dissolves in showers.

'Sweet hand, the sweet but cruel bow thou art'

Sweet hand, the sweet but cruel bow thou art,
From whence at me five ivory arrows fly;
So with five wounds at once I wounded lie,
Bearing in breast the print of every dart.
Saint Francis had the like yet felt no smart,   5
Where I in living torments never die;
His wounds were in his hands and feet, where I
All these five helpless wounds feel in my heart.
Now, as Saint Francis, if a saint am I,
The bow that shot these shafts a relic is;   10
I mean the hand, which is the reason why
So many for devotion thee would kiss.
And some thy glove kiss as a thing divine,
Thy arrows' quiver and thy relics' shrine.

'MY LADY'S PRESENCE' Constable's most famous sonnet. **3. leaves** now the white petals of her flower. **5. the leaves...spread** gives forth blossoms. **9. virtue** individual quality of excellence. **11. eyebeams** The eye was supposed to emit glances like beams of light. **12. quickeneth** brings to life.

'SWEET HAND' **2. five ivory arrows** metaphorically, her five fingers, the sight of which wounds the lover. **5.** Saint Francis of Assisi (1182–1226) bore the mystical stigmata, the five wounds of Christ impressed on feet, hands, and side. For poetic purposes Constable alters the facts, as St Francis and all stigmatics suffer from the wounds. **10. relic** some tangible part of a saint or holy person left behind (a body part or article of clothing).

Spiritual Sonnets

'To God the Father'

Great God, within whose simple essence we
Nothing but that which is thyself can find,
When on thyself thou didst reflect thy mind,
Thy thought was God, which took the form of thee.
And when this God thus borne thou lov'st, and he   5
Loved thee again with passion of like kind,
(As lovers' sighs which meet become one wind),
Both breathed one Sprite of equal deity.
Eternal Father, whence these two do come,
And whilst the title of my father have,   10
An heavenly knowledge in my mind engrave,
That it thy Son's true image may become;
And 'cense my heart with sighs of holy love,
That it the temple of the Sprite may prove.

'To the Blessed Sacrament'

When thee, O holy sacrificèd Lamb,
In severed signs I white and liquid see,
As on thy body slain I think on thee,
Which pale by shedding of thy blood became.
And when again I do behold the same,   5
Veiled in white to be received of me,

'TO GOD THE FATHER' The poem is a serious reflection on the doctrine of the Trinity, i.e. the belief that God contains three distinct persons, Father, Son (Jesus Christ), and Holy Spirit, who are all united, coeternal, coequal, uncreated, and omnipotent. **1. simple essence** Essence is 'that whereby a thing is what it is, an equivalent of the *to ti en einai* of Aristotle (*Metaph.* 7. 7).' 'The Supreme Being has—or rather is—a unique and utterly simple essence, free from all composition, whether physical or metaphysical' (*New Catholic Encyclopedia*, 'Essence'). Creatures have an essence that, compounded with matter, becomes manifest in their existence; pure and incorporeal, God's essence and existence are one. **3. reflect** turn. **3–4.** Constable reflects Catholic theology on the creation of the Son, coeternal and coequal with the Father and Holy Spirit. According to Aquinas (*ST* I q. 34 a. 1), the divine generation is analogous to the act by which the created intellect produces a concept or word, *logos* (John 1: 1); thus the Son proceeds from the Father by an act of intellect, by the Father's action of knowing himself, or in Constable's formulation, 'When on thyself thou didst reflect thy mind' (3). **8. Sprite** the Holy Spirit. The Holy Spirit proceeds not as an act of intellect but as an act of divine will; loving himself, God breathes forth this person (Augustine, *De Trinitate*; Aquinas, *ST* I q. 36 a. 3; q. 37 a. 1). **10. have** you have. **13. 'cense** burn incense to. **14. temple . . . Sprite** 'Or know you not that your members are the temple of the Holy Ghost, who is in you, whom you have from God, and you are not your own?' (1 Cor. 6: 19).

'TO THE BLESSED SACRAMENT' **1. sacrificèd Lamb** Catholics affirmed mass to be a true sacrifice, not a commemoration (Council of Trent, Session 22). Christ is the sacrificial lamb, *agnus dei* (lamb of God) (John 1: 29). **2. severed signs** the signs of Christ's real presence, i.e. bread and wine, which retain their external accidents (the external characteristics of whiteness and liquidity respectively), while their internal being, or substance, has been changed to the body and blood of Christ.

Thou seemest in thy sindon wrapped to be,
Like to a corpse, whose monument I am.
Buried in me, unto my soul appear,
Prisoned in earth and banished from thy sight,   10
Like our forefathers who in limbo were.
Clear thou my thoughts as thou didst give the light,
And as thou others freed from purging fire,
Quench in my heart the flames of bad desire.

'To St Mary Magdalen'
For few nights' solace in delicious bed,
Where heat of lust did kindle flames of hell,
Thou nak'd on naked rock in desert cell
Lay thirty years, and tears of grief did shed.
But for that time thy heart there sorrowèd,   5
Thou now in heaven eternally dost dwell,
And for each tear which from thine eyes then fell,
A sea of pleasure now is renderèd.
If short delights entice my heart to stray,
Let me by thy long penance learn to know,   10
How dear I should for trifling pleasures pay;
And if I virtue's rough beginning shun,
Let thy eternal joys unto me show
What high reward by little pain is won.

'To our Blessed Lady'
Sweet queen, although thy beauty raise up me
From sight of baser beauties here below,
Yet let me not rest there but higher go,
To him who took his shape from God and thee.
And if thy form in him more fair I see,   5

---

7. **sindon** shroud. **11. limbo** the temporary place where the souls of the just resided until freed by Christ's ascension into heaven. (Cf. the fifth article of the Creed, 'he descended into hell', i.e. limbo.) **12–14.** For Catholics the Eucharist has the power to strengthen virtue and preserve the recipient from sin (see Aquinas, *ST* III q. 79 a. 6).

'TO ST MARY MAGDALEN' This saint became an important Catholic Reformation symbol of contrition (see Crashaw below). **1. delicious** delightful. **4. thirty years** According to a French tradition, Magdalen left the Holy Lands for France after the Resurrection. After converting the whole of Provençe, she retired to a hill, La Sainte-Baume, and lived a life of penance for thirty years. **9. short** brief.

'TO OUR BLESSED LADY' **1–4.** Constable articulates the Neoplatonic notion that love of heavenly beauty purges the soul from its attachment to earthly beauties and elevates it to contemplation of God, the source of all beauty. **5.** Mary's beauty is but a form or manifestation of the infinite beauty of God.

What pleasure from his deity shall flow,
By whose fair beams his beauty shineth so,
When I shall it behold eternally.
Then shall my love of pleasure have his fill,
When Beauty's self, in whom all pleasure is,   10
Shall my enamoured soul embrace and kiss,
And shall new loves and new delights distil,
Which from my soul shall gush into my heart,
And through my body flow to every part.

ROBERT SOUTHWELL

Brilliant and well born, Robert Southwell (1561–95) joined the Society of Jesus in 1578, and in 1586 he returned to England to minister to Catholics, including Philip Howard, imprisoned for his faith. He wrote an *An Epistle of Comfort* (1587) to all persecuted Catholics (see Consolations, INSTRUCTIONS AND DEVOTIONS), and other works, notably *Mary Magdalen's Funeral Tears* (1591), and a plea for tolerance, *An Humble Supplication to Her Majesty* (1595, pub. 1600–1). Southwell endured capture, imprisonment, and torture before his execution in 1595.

Southwell's poetry circulated in manuscript and, remarkably, in print, enjoyed by Catholics and Protestants (albeit in expurgated editions). Below 'The Virgin's Salutation', 'The Nativity of Christ', 'Christ's Bloody Sweat', and others bring the human actors of the divine drama to life. Fusing mystical vision and metaphysical wit, 'The Burning Babe' portrays Christ's sacrifice with daring imagery and immediacy. Southwell's longest poem, 'St Peter's Complaint' (132 six-line stanzas) ratifies the Catholic sacrament of Penance through an extraordinary series of conceits on Christ's and Peter's eyes. His translation of St Thomas Aquinas's *Lauda, Sion,* celebrates the doctrine of real presence (see Prayers and Hymns, INSTRUCTIONS AND DEVOTIONS). 'What Joy to Live?' turns Petrarchan conventions inward to depict a moment of spiritual desolation; it urges Christians, especially persecuted Catholics, to sacrifice the momentary pleasures of this world for the eternal joys of the next. The poetry of Robert Southwell displays the ingenuity, paradox, and playfulness characteristic of the best early seventeenth-century verse.

---

11. **enamoured soul** The idea of God as husband-lover of the soul-bride appears in the writings of St Bonaventure and St Bernard, and in the commentaries on the *Canticle of Canticles.*

'The Virgin's Salutation'

Spell 'Eva' back and 'Ave' shall you find,
The first began, the last reversed our harms;
An angel's witching words did Eva blind,
An angel's 'Ave' disenchants the charms.
    Death first by woman's weakness entered in;   5
    In woman's virtue life doth now begin.

O Virgin's breast, the heavens to thee incline,
In thee they joy and sovereign they agnize;
Too mean their glory is to match with thine,
Whose chaste receipt God more than heaven did prize.   10
    Hail, fairest heaven, that heaven and earth do bless,
    Where virtue's star, God's sun of justice, is.

With haughty mind to godhead man aspired,
And was by pride from place of pleasure chased;
With loving mind our manhood God desired,   15
And us by love in greater pleasure placed.
    Man, labouring to ascend, procured our fall;
    God, yielding to descend, cut off our thrall.

'The Nativity of Christ'

Behold, the father is his daughter's son;
The bird that built the nest is hatched therein;
The old of years an hour hath not outrun;
Eternal life to live doth now begin.
    The Word is dumb, the mirth of heaven doth weep;   5
    Might feeble is and force doth faintly creep.
O dying souls, behold your living spring;

'THE VIRGIN'S SALUTATION' the greeting of Mary by the angel Gabriel (Luke 1: 28), 'Ave, gratia plena' ('Hail, full of grace'), announcing that she was to be the mother of God. **2. reversed our harms** Catholics praised Mary as the woman who reversed Eve's sin by bringing the Saviour into the world. **3.** The fallen angel Lucifer, as a serpent, tempted Eve to eat the forbidden fruit (Gen. 3). **8. agnize** recognize. **10. receipt** act of receiving, i.e. assent to the angel's invitation and the will of God. **18. thrall** bondage, misery.
'THE NATIVITY OF CHRIST' **1. daughter's** i.e. Mary's. **3. old of** aged in. The timeless God is not even an hour old, another paradox of the Incarnation. **5. Word is dumb** The *logos*, or 'word' (John 1: 1), the ordering principle of the universe incarnate in Jesus Christ, is now a baby unable to speak. **7. living spring** See John 4: 10–11; 7: 38.

O dazzled eyes, behold your sun of grace;
Dull ears, attend what word this Word doth bring;
Up, heavy hearts, with joy your joy embrace.   10
   From death, from dark, from deafness, from despairs,
   This life, this light, this Word, this joy repairs.

Gift better than himself God doth not know;
Gift better than his God no man can see.
This gift doth here the giver given bestow;   15
Gift to this gift let each receiver be.
   God is my gift, himself he freely gave me;
   God's gift am I and none but God shall have me.

Man altered was by sin from man to beast;
Beast's food is hay, hay is all mortal flesh;   20
Now God is flesh and lies in manger pressed
As hay, the brutest sinner to refresh.
   O happy field, wherein this fodder grew,
   Whose taste doth us from beasts to men renew!

'Christ's Return out of Egypt'

When death and hell their right in Herod claim,
Christ from exile returns to native soil,
There with his life more deeply death to maim
Than death did life by all the infants' spoil.
   He showed the parents that the babes did moan   5
   That all their lives were less than his alone.

But hearing Herod's son to have the crown,
The impious offspring of the bloody sire,
To Nazareth (of heaven beloved) town,
Flower to a flower he fitly doth retire.   10
   For he is a flower and in a flower he bred,
   And from a thorn now to a flower he fled.

8. sun spelled 'sonne' in the text, the usual son/sun pun. **12. repairs** restores, recovers (us). **15. the giver given** the giver as given, i.e. as a gift. **17–18.** These lines depart from the stanzaic pattern (ababcc) with their repetition of the b rhyme (ababbb), thus emphasizing the relevance of the Nativity to 'me', the speaker. **21–4.** The metaphor here equates flesh to hay and turns on the idea that the infant Christ lay in hay (**in manger pressed**); as hay, i.e. as a mortal, he became food for humanity in the Eucharist, thus changing humans, altered by sin into beasts, back to humans again. **22. brutest** most bestial.

'CHRIST'S RETURN OUT OF EGYPT' See Matt. 2: 13–23 for the story of Herod's slaughter of the Holy Innocents, Christ's escape into Egypt, and return. **3.** There to harm death more deeply with his life. **7. son** Archelous. **10. flower** St Jerome suggested that 'Nazareth' signifies 'flower'. Christ was the flower of the tree of Jesse (Isaiah 11: 1).

And well deserved this flower his fruit to view,
Where he invested was in mortal weed,
Where first into a tender bud he grew,   15
In virgin branch unstained with mortal seed.
    Young flower, with flowers, in flower well may he be,
    Ripe fruit he must with thorns hang on a tree.

'The Burning Babe'

As I in hoary winter's night
    Stood shiv'ring in the snow,
Surprised I was with sudden heat,
    Which made my heart to glow.

And lifting up a fearful eye   5
    To view what fire was near,
A pretty Babe all burning bright
    Did in the air appear.

Who, scorchèd with excessive heat,
    Such floods of tears did shed,   10
As though his floods should quench his flames,
    Which with his tears were fed.

'Alas!' quoth he, 'but newly born,
    In fiery heats I fry,
Yet none approach to warm their hearts   15
    Or feel my fire but I!

'My faultless breast the furnace is,
    The fuel, wounding thorns;
Love is the fire and sighs the smoke,
    The ashes, shames and scorns.   20

'The fuel Justice layeth on,
    And Mercy blows the coals;
The metal in this furnace wrought
    Are men's defilèd souls.

---

14. **invested ... weed** was clothed in earthly attire, i.e. flesh.

'THE BURNING BABE' The poem combines Ignatian meditative methods, the Petrarchan imagery of burning, melting, and dying, and emblem traditions to celebrate the birth of Christ the redeemer. Published in couplets of fourteen syllables, several MS versions present the poem in ballad meter, i.e. quatrains alternating lines of eight and six syllables, rhyming *abab*. Ben Jonson said that 'so he had written' this poem, 'he would have been content to destroy many of his' (*Ben Jonson*, ed. Herford and Simpsons, 11 vols., 1925–52: i. 137). 1. **hoary** grey or white. 23. **wrought** made, moulded.

'For which, as now on fire I am 25
    To work them to their good,
So will I melt into a bath
    To wash them in my blood.'

With this he vanished out of sight
    And swiftly shrunk away, 30
And straight I callèd unto mind
    That it was Christmas day.

'Christ's Bloody Sweat'

Fat soil, full spring, sweet olive, grape of bliss
That yields, that streams, that pours, that dost distil,
Untilled, undrawn, unstamped, untouched of press,
Dear fruit, clear brooks, fair oil, sweet wine at will.
    Thus Christ unforced prevents in shedding blood 5
    The whips, the thorns, the nail, the spear, and rood.

He pelican's, he phoenix's fate doth prove,
Whom flames consume when streams enforce to die,
How burneth blood, how bleedeth burning love.
Can one in flame and stream both bathe and fry? 10
    How would he join a phoenix's fiery pains
    In fainting pelican's still bleeding veins?

Elias once to prove God's sovereign power,
By prayer procured a fire of wondrous force,
That blood and wood and water did devour, 15
Yea, stones and dust, beyond all nature's course.
    Such fire is love that, fed with gory blood,
    Doth burn no less than in the driest wood.

O sacred fire, come show thy force on me
That sacrifice to Christ I may return. 20
If withered wood for fuel fittest be,
If stones and dust, if flesh and blood will burn,
    I withered am, and stony to all good,
    A sack of dust, a mass of flesh and blood.

'CHRIST'S BLOODY SWEAT' See Luke 22: 44: 'And his sweat became as drops of blood, trickling down upon the ground.' **3. press** Southwell varies the conventional image of the Old Testament wine press (Isa. 63: 2–3), which here becomes the wine of salvation in blood of the Eucharist; this wine is unpressed because Christ gives it freely. **5. prevents** anticipates. **7–12.** This stanza turns on the common identification of two birds with Christ, the pelican, thought to feed its young with its own blood, and the phoenix, thought to rise reborn from its own funeral pyre. **13. Elias** Elijah, who triumphed over the priests of Baal by evoking the Lord's wondrous fire (3 Kings 18: 37–9). **16. course** capacity.

'Decease Release'

Dum morior orior

The pounded spice both taste and scent doth please,
In fading smoke the force doth incense show,
The perished kernel springeth with increase,
The loppèd tree doth best and soonest grow.

God's spice I was and pounding was my due,   5
In fading breath my incense savoured best,
Death was my mean my kernel to renew,
By lopping shot I up to heavenly rest.

Some things more perfect are in their decay,
Like spark that going out gives clearest light;   10
Such was my hap, whose doleful dying day,
Began my joy and termèd fortune's spite.

Alive a queen, now dead I am a saint;
Once Mary called, my name now martyr is;
From earthly reign debarrèd by restraint,   15
In lieu whereof I reign in heavenly bliss.

My life my grief, my death hath wrought my joy;
My friends my foil, my foes my weal procured;
My speedy death hath shortened long annoy;
And loss of life an endless life assured.   20

My scaffold was the bed where ease I found,
The block a pillow of eternal rest;
My headman cast me in a blissful swoon,
His axe cut off my cares from cumbered breast.

Rue not my death, rejoice at my repose;   25
It was no death to me but to my woe.
The bud was opened to let out the rose,
The chains unloosed to let the captive go.

'DECEASE RELEASE' The poem is written from the viewpoint of Mary Stuart, Queen of Scots (1542–87), Elizabeth's chief rival for the throne and the focus of Catholic political hopes and conspiracies. Elizabeth held her captive for eighteen years and had her executed (see Fig. 6) One copy substitutes 'Anna' for 'Mary' (**14**), perhaps referring to Anne of Denmark, abandoned by her husband King James. *Dum morior orior* 'while I die, I rise'. **7. mean** means. **11. hap** fortune. **12. termèd** ended. **15. debarrèd by restraint** prohibited by captivity. **17. My . . . grief** My life has wrought my grief. Southwell uses the same inverted syntax with the delayed verb throughout the poem. **18. foil** misery. **weal** happiness. **23. headman** executioner. Mary was beheaded.

A prince by birth, a prisoner by mishap,
From crown to cross, from throne to thrall I fell;   30
My right my ruth, my titles wrought my trap;
My weal my woe, my worldly heaven my hell.

By death from prisoner to a prince enhanced,
From cross to crown, from thrall to throne again;
My ruth my right, my trap my style advanced,   35
From woe to weal, from hell to heavenly reign.

England = hell ?

'What Joy to Live?'

I wage no war yet peace I none enjoy.
  I hope, I fear, I fry in freezing cold.
I mount in mirth still prostrate in annoy,
  I all the world embrace yet nothing hold.
All wealth is want where chiefest wishes fail;   5
Yea, life is loathed where love may not prevail.

For that I love I long but that I lack,
  That others love I loathe and that I have,
All worldly freights to me are deadly wrack,
  Men present hap, I future hopes do crave.   10
They, loving where they live, long life require,
To live where best I love, death I desire.

Here love is lent for loan of filthy gain,
  Most friends befriend themselves with friendship's show,
Here plenty peril, want doth breed disdain,   15
  Cares common are, joys faulty, short, and few.
Here honour envied, meanness is despised,
Sin deemed solace, virtue little prized.

Here beauty is a bait that swallowed chokes,
  A treasure sought still to the owner's harms,   20

31. **ruth** ruin. 33. **enhanced** raised. 35. **my trap...advanced** the trap that caught me advanced my **style**, i.e. the ceremonial designation of a sovereign; in other words, my downfall on earth made me a true queen in heaven.

'WHAT JOY TO LIVE?' This is a poem of desolation, which St Ignatius defined as the spiritual state of darkness and separation from God, characterized by emotional tumult, sadness, and loss of faith, hope, and love (see INSTRUCTIONS AND DEVOTIONS). 1–4. Southwell's poem begins by translating the first few lines of Petrarch's celebrated *Pace non trovo* (*Rime*, 134) ('I find no peace'), which describes the miserable state of the unrequited lover suffering contrary passions (laughing and weeping, burning and freezing). He alters the lover's lament, 'in questo stato son, donna, per vui' (I am in this state, lady, because of you) to a Christian 'contemptus mundi' (contempt for the world); one can only find salvation, the poem implies, in Christ. 3. **prostrate in annoy** laid low in trouble. 7. **For that** for that which. 9. **wrack** ruin, shipwreck. 10. **Men...hap** Men crave good fortune now. 17. **meanness** low birth or humble condition.

A light that eyes to murd'ring sights provokes,
    A grace that souls enchants with mortal charms,
A luring aim to Cupid's fiery flights,
A baleful bliss that damns where it delights.

Oh, who would live so many deaths to try,   25
    Where will doth wish that wisdom doth reprove,
Where nature craves that grace must needs deny,
    Where sense doth like that reason cannot love,
Where best in show in final proof is worst,
Where pleasure's upshot is to die accursed?   30

'The Virgin Mary to Christ on the Cross'

What mist hath dimmed that glorious face,
What seas of grief my sun doth toss?
The golden rays of heavenly grace
Lies now eclipsèd on the cross.

Jesus, my love, my son, my God,   5
Behold thy mother washed in tears.
Thy bloody wounds be made a rod
To chasten these my latter years.

You cruel Jews, come work your ire
Upon this worthless flesh of mine,   10
And kindle not eternal fire
By wounding him which is divine.

Thou messenger that didst impart
His first descent into my womb,
Come help me now to cleave my heart,   15
That there I may my son entomb.

You angels all that present were,
To show his birth with harmony,
Why are you now not ready here,
To make a mourning symphony?   20

22. **souls enchants** enchants souls. **25–30.** The poem and its pessimistic conclusion fits with a group of poems in the manuscripts which are meant to comfort persecuted Catholics by turning them away from worldly pleasure.

'THE VIRGIN MARY TO CHRIST ON THE CROSS' This poem belongs to the tradition of the *Stabat mater dolorosa* ('the sorrowful mother was standing'), a beloved 13th-c. hymn that reflects on Mary's suffering at the crucifixion. (See Crashaw below.) Southwell, innovatively, gives Mary her own voice.

The cause I know: you wail alone,
And shed your tears in secrecy,
Lest I should movèd be to moan,
By force of heavy company.

But wail, my soul, thy comfort dies,   25
My woeful womb, lament thy fruit,
My heart, give tears unto my eyes,
Let sorrow string my heavy lute.

From 'Saint Peter's Complaint'

Launch forth, my soul, into a main of tears,
Full fraught with grief, the traffic of thy mind.
Torn sails will serve, thoughts rent with guilty fears.
Give care the stern; use sighs in lieu of wind,
    Remorse the pilot, thy misdeed the card,   5
    Torment thy haven, shipwreck thy best reward.

Shun not the shelf of most deservèd shame;
Stick in the sands of agonizing dread;
Content thee to be storms' and billows' game,
Divorced from grace, thy soul to penance wed.   10
    Fly not from foreign evils, fly from thy heart;
    Worse than the worst of evils is that thou art.

Give vent unto the vapours of thy breast
That thicken in the brims of cloudy eyes;
Where sin was hatched, let tears now wash the nest,   15
Where life was lost, recover life with cries.
    Thy trespass foul, let not thy tears be few,
    Baptize thy spotted soul in weeping dew.

21. **cause** reason for the angels' absence. 28. **heavy** mournful.

'SAINT PETER'S COMPLAINT' Peter laments his triple denial of Jesus, a betrayal recounted in all the gospels (e.g. Matt. 26: 69–75). Based on Luigi Tanzillo's *Lacrime di San Pietro*, this poem combines the Continental fashion of 'tear' poetry with the native complaint. 1. **main** sea. The sea and boat imagery of the opening is appropriate for Peter the fisherman (see John 21: 1–7). 2. **traffic** merchandise, cargo. 4. **Give...stern** Let care steer the ship. 5. **card** nautical map. 7. **shelf** reef. 10. **penance** The poem and Peter's tears illustrate his contrition and stand as exercises in Satisfaction, the performance of the temporal punishment for the forgiveness of sin. 13–14. Tears were thought to arise from the condensation of chest vapours. 18. **Baptize** The tears have a sacramental agency, namely to cleanse the soul of sin. 'Baptism' comes from the Greek verb βαπτίζω, 'I immerse' or 'wash'.

[On Christ's eyes]

O sacred eyes, the springs of living light,
The earthly heavens, where angels joy to dwell,   20
How could you deign to view my deathful plight,
Or let your heav'nly beams look on my hell?
   But those unspotted eyes encount'red mine,
   As spotless sun doth on the dunghill shine.

Sweet volumes stored with learning fit for saints,   25
Where blissful choirs imparadise their minds,
Wherein eternal study never faints,
Still finding all, yet seeking all it finds.
   How endless is your labyrinth of bliss,
   Where to be lost the sweetest finding is?   30

Ah, wretch, how oft have I sweet lessons read
In those dear eyes, the registers of truth!
How oft have I my hungry wishes fed,
And in their happy joys redressed my ruth!
   Ah, that they now are heralds of disdain,   35
   That erst were ever pitiers of my pain.

You flames divine that sparkle out your heats,
And kindle pleasing fires in mortal hearts,
You nectared aumbries of soul-feeding meats,
You graceful quivers of love's dearest darts,   40
   You did vouchsafe to warm, to wound, to feast
   My cold, my stony, my now famished breast.

The matchless eyes, matched only each by other,
Were pleased on my ill-matchèd eyes to glance.
The eye of liquid pearl, the purest mother,   45
Broched tears in mine to weep for my mischance.
   The cabinets of grace unlocked their treasure,
   And did to my misdeed their mercies measure.

These blazing comets, lightning flames of love,
Made me their warming influence to know;   50
My frozen heart their sacred force did prove,
Which at their looks did yield like melting snow.

---

21. **deign** condescend. 26. **imparadise** bring into paradise or rapture. 34. **redressed my ruth** remedied my sorrow. 39. **aumbries** cupboards for sacramental vessels and vestments. 41. **vouchsafe** grant as a favour. 45. **mother** mother of pearl, the shining, iridescent substance found inside many shells. 46. **Broched** raised, as a design of silver or gold on fabric.

> They did not joys in former plenty carve,
> Yet sweet are crumbs where pinèd thoughts do starve.

> O living mirrors, seeing whom you show,   55
> Which equal shadows' worths with shadowed things,
> Ye make things nobler than in native hue,
> By being shaped in those life-giving springs.
>   Much more my image in those eyes was graced,
>   Than in myself whom sin and shame defaced.   60

> All-seeing eyes, more worth than all you see,
> Of which one is the other's only price,
> I worthless am. Direct your beams on me,
> With quick'ning virtue cure my killing vice.
>   By seeing things you make things worth the sight,   65
>   You, seeing, salve, and being seen, delight.

> O pools of Hesebon, the baths of grace,
> Where happy spirits dive in sweet desires,
> Where saints rejoice to glass their glorious face,
> Whose banks make echo to the angels' choirs,   70
>   An echo sweeter in the sole rebound
>   Than angels' music in the fullest sound.

[On Peter's tears]

> But, oh, how long demur I on his eyes,
> Whose look did pierce my heart with healing wound,
> Lancing impostumed sore of perjured lies,   75
> Which these two issues of mine eyes hath found,
>   Where run it must till death the issues stop,
>   And penal life hath purged the final drop.

> Like solest swan that swims in silent deep,
> And never sings but obsequies of death,   80
> Sigh out thy plaints and sole in secret weep,
> In suing pardon spend thy perjured breath.
>   Attire thy soul in sorrow's mourning weed,
>   And at thine eyes let guilty conscience bleed.

53. **carve** apportion, serve. 55–60. The stanza turns on a physiological fact dear to metaphysical poets, namely that the surface of an eye mirrors what it sees. 56. Which make the reflections (**shadows**) equal in worth to the things reflected. The next lines assert that the reflections in Christ's eyes are more valuable than the things themselves. 64. **quick'ning** animating, vivifying. 66. **salve** (1) save (from *salvare*); (2) anoint, heal. 67. **pools of Hesebon** springs in Hesebon, near Jerusalem. 'Thy eyes like the fishpools in Hesebon' (Cant. 7: 4). 69. **glass . . . face** reflect the glorious face of Christ, by gazing lovingly on God. 71. **sole rebound** one echo. 75. **impostumed** swollen with infection. 76–7. Peter's tears have found the sore of his sinful denial of Christ and must run till death in order to drain sin from the infected heart. 78. **penal life** The poem shifts in focus from Christ's eyes to the penitential agency of Peter's tears, cleansing him of sin. 79–80. According to legend, the solitary swan sang only before its death, thus performing its own obsequy or funeral ritual.

Still in the limbeck of thy doleful breast,   85
These bitter fruits that from thy sins do grow;
For fuel self-accusing thoughts be best,
Use fear as fire, the coals let penance blow.
   And seek none other quintessence but tears,
   That eyes may shed what entered at thine ears.   90

Come sorrowing tears, the offspring of my grief,
Scant not your parent of a needful aid;
In you I rest the hope of wished relief,
By you my sinful debts must be defrayed.
   Your power prevails, your sacrifice is grateful,   95
   By love obtaining life to men most hateful.

Come good effects of ill deserving cause,
Ill-gotten imps yet virtuously brought forth,
Self-blaming probates of infringèd laws,
Yet blamèd faults redeeming with your worth.   100
   The signs of shame in you each eye may read,
   Yet while you guilty prove, you pity plead.

O beams of mercy, beat on sorrow's cloud,
Pour suppling showers upon my parchèd ground,
Bring forth the fruit to your due service vowed,   105
Let good desires with like deserts be crowned,
   Water young blooming virtue's tender flower;
   Sin did all grace of riper growth devour.

Weep balm and myrrh, you sweet Arabian trees,
With purest gums perfume and pearl your rind;   110
Shed on your honey drops, you busy bees.
I, barren plant, must weep unpleasant brine;
   Hornets I hive, salt drops their labour plies,
   Sucked out by sin and shed by show'ring eyes.

If David night by night did bathe his bed,   115
Esteeming longest days too short to moan,
Inconsolable tears if Anna shed,
Who in her son her solace had forgone,

85. **Still in the limbeck** distil in the alembic, a vessel used in chemical and alchemical processes. Alchemy supplies the conceit of the stanza, wherein sin's bitter fruits are heated in the limbeck of Peter's breast to extract the **quintessence (89)**, or divine 'fifth essence', here Peter's tears. 90. **what . . . ears** the sound of his own denials of Jesus. 95. **grateful** pleasing. 98. **imps** children. 99. **probates** proofs, testimonies. 104. **suppling** softening. 108. Sin cancelled out previous graces and merits. 110. **pearl your rind** adorn as with pearl your bark. 111. **Shed on** continue shedding. 113. **Hornets I hive** I have hornets and the stings of remorse within (and therefore drop bitter, salty tears). **plies** yields. 115. **David** author of the Psalms, e.g. 'Every night I will wash my bed; I will water my couch with my tears' (Ps. 6: 7). 117–18. The story of the inconsolable Anna, mother of a missing son, appears in Tobias 10: 1–7 (a book not accepted by Protestants as canonical).

Then I to days and weeks, to months and years,
Do owe the hourly rent of stintless tears.

120

Anthony Copley

Born into a Catholic family, Robert Southwell's kinsman, Anthony Copley (1567–1609?), studied at the English College in Rome (1584–6) and then entered the service of the king of Spain. After returning to England in 1590, he suffered several imprisonments. Later protesting the appointment of pro-Jesuit George Blackwell as Archpriest of England, he published letters (1601, 1602) supporting the seminary priests against the Jesuits, whom he considered to be dangerous and immoral interlopers. Upon the accession of James I, Copley became involved in the Bye plot to seize King James and force him to grant toleration to Catholics. After making a full confession and giving damning evidence against other conspirators, Copley received a full pardon.

Anthony Copley published jokes and humorous tales in *Wits, Fits, and Fancies* (1595, see FICTION), as well as a Catholic poetic response to Book I of Spenser's *The Faerie Queen* (1590), entitled *A Fig for Fortune* (1596). In this poem Copley's quester, like Spenser's Redcrosse Knight, battles Despair (cf. *FQ* I. 9), reveres a figure of Queen Elizabeth, and progresses through repentance to holiness and a vision of the celestial city. In the selection below the quester finally reaches Mount Zion, which (unlike Spenser's New Jerusalem, *FQ* I. 10) features Catholic priests, nuns, and sacraments.

A Fig for fortune, 1596

[Mount Zion]

Ah, now I want the Muse of Solomon
To tell you a temple-tale, a tale of truth,
All of the architect and frame of Zion,
To tell you of her age and of her youth,
   And of her reverend reign and regiment,
   And how Doblessa rues her high achievement.

5

---

120. **stintless** unceasing.

A FIG FOR   The phrase signals contemptuous dismissal. **1. Solomon** Solomon built the magnificent Temple of Jerusalem (3 Kgs 5 ff.). **3. architect** architecture. **Zion** originally one of the hills of Jerusalem, representing heaven and the true home of the faithful. On Mount Zion the quester enters the Temple of Peace, a Catholic version of Spenser's House of Holiness (*FQ* I. 10). **6. Doblessa** the Church of England and Elizabeth, Copley's refashioning of Duessa, Spenser's sinister

The ground was Faith; the mean work, Charity,
The top, a Hopeful apprehension
Of heaven's attain. All was of unity,
A solid metal hewn out of Christ his passion.   10
  Yea, Christ himself was fundamental stone,
  And all the solder was devotion.

There shined the ruby and the chrysolite,
The sparkling diamond and the emerald green,
Each sapphire in their several delight;   15
There was the happy jacinth to be seen,
  The topaz, onyx, and many a fair gem.
  Coral, amber, and agates were trash among them.

Which, such bright rough-cast over all encrusted,
'Twas heaven to see what rainbow rays it yielded,   20
Whiles every gem ambitiously contended
T'outstare each other's starry neighbourhood.
  It was enough t'illumine all the world,
  But for the mists that false Doblessa hurled.

Roses and flowers of all coloured kinds,   25
The mary bush and pleasant eglantine,
The honeysuckle in her twisted twines,
In-mixed with ivy and the grapeful vine,
  Did all grow up that starry spanglement,
  Spousing her splendour with their spicèd scent.   30

Below these heaven a-mounting suavities,
Grew over all the temple green beside
Sweet gillyflowers and primroses,
The pink, and gerisole (the sun's dear bride),
  The moly, violet, and the pleasant daisy,   35
  Balm, marjoram, and sweet costmary.

There grew the lofty cedar and the pine,
The peaceful olive and the martial fir,
The verdant laurel in her shady-shine,

---

enchantress who represents Roman Catholicism. **7. mean work** middle part. **9. attain** attainment. **unity** one substance (unlike the different Protestant sects). **11. fundamental** foundational. **13. chrysolite** the name of several green gems. **16. jacinth** a yellow or orange gem. **18. agates** variegated, multicoloured gems. **19. rough-cast** plaster. **26. mary** rosemary. **eglantine** sweet-briar. **29. that starry spanglement** to that glittering sky. **30. Spousing** wedding. **31. heaven … suavities** sweetnesses rising to heaven. **33. gillyflowers** pink flowers scented like cloves. **34. pink** general name for a garden plant with pink, white, red, and variegated blossoms. **35. moly** a magic herb, sometimes identified as garlic. **36. costmary** a flavouring herb. **39. shady-shine** the bright, smooth leaves of the laurel, which also give shade.

The patient palm and penitential myrrh,   40
   The elm, the poplar, and the cypress tree,
   And all trees else that pleasant are to see.

All kinds of fruits were there perpetual,
The date, the almond, and the sauceful citron,
The fig, the orange, and pomegranate royal,   45
The quince, the apricot, and the musk-melon,
   The plum, the cherry, and the pleasant pear,
   The filbert and the mulberry grew there.

Amid these trees, these fruits, these flowery sweets,
Ran in a maze-like wile a crystal stream   50
Of heavenly nectar; in whose sweet floods and fleets,
Swam schools of fishes, every fish's gleam
   Brighter than Titan in his southern stage.
   This stream was strong against prime guilt's enrage.

[The Temple of Peace; Doblessa]

There on my knees my heart was full of fire,   55
Fire of the grace of God, dear grace of God,
Which strong bemettled my zeal's aspire
To view the glory of that shone abode.
   It was a pigeon from the temple top,
   Which all that frame and glory did up-prop.   60

A pigeon whiter than the whitest pigeon,
Solely subsistent of his own pure *esse*,
His *posse* was sanctification,
And grace's bounteous liberality.
   What Jesus erst had planted with his blood,   65
   This pigeon gave it graceful livelihood.

The beams which issued from his brightsome breast
Were such as none but Zion ever saw,
Nor ever could Doblessa's dreary mist
Endarken, or resemble, or withdraw: 70

40. **patient palm** Pilgrims carried palms on long journeys, and so the plant became associated with the virtue of patience. **penitential myrrh** The attribute 'penitential' may derive from the supposed healing properties of this aromatic gum. 44. **citron** an acidic yellow tree fruit. The name refers as well to lemons and limes. 50. **wile** pattern. 51. **fleets** ebbs. 53. **Titan...stage** the sun at its hottest. 54. **prime...enrage** the destructive fury caused by original sin. 57. **bemettled...aspire** strengthened my zealous wish. 58. **shone** shining. 59. **pigeon** dove, symbolizing the Holy Spirit. 60. **up-prop** support. 62–4. Employing scholastic Latin terms (*esse*, 'to be'; *posse*, 'to be able'), Copley here defines the Holy Spirit as pure, self-subsistent being (*esse*) whose function (*posse*) is to sanctify, i.e. to bestow the grace that enables and strengthens holiness. In this way the Holy Spirit completes the work of Jesus Christ (65–6). 67. **brightsome** bright.

Love, peace, and magnanimity in good,
Patience, and prudence above all flesh and blood,

Justice, and temperance, and benignity,
Zeal and internal consolation,
Pity and hopeful longanimity,   75
Obedience and brotherly correction,
    Devotion and mortification,
    And firm affiance in our Lord's salvation.

Such were the pigeon's rays from the temple top,
Which like a heaven of light illumined all,   80
It being thereto a more secure up-prop,
Than any lime and stone, or brazen wall.
    O Zion, Zion, happy city, thou,
    So Holy-Ghosted against all overthrow!

Then, looking down unto the residue,   85
I might discern a reverend ministry
Of men and angels, chanting unto Jesu
Incessant hymns of praise and jubilee,
    The high Sacrificator at the altar,
    Victiming with holy rites his Maker.   90

What shall I say of all the majesty,
Of all the reverend rites and ceremonies,
The rich adorn, the heavenly melody,
The lustre and the precious suavities
    That there I saw, felt, heard, and understood?   95
    Oh, they transcended far poor flesh and blood!

For what the goodness and the power of God
In their immensity could jointly do
Was there in force *sans* bound or period;
His grace and glory both did tend thereto.   100
    The meanest object there unto my sense,
    Was more than all the world's magnificence.

There saw I sacred imposition
Of hands and grace abundantly imparted,

71–8. Peace, patience, benignity, longanimity (long-suffering), and affiance (faith) are five of the traditional twelve gifts of the Holy Spirit (Gal. 5: 22–3); the other virtues named here are classical and Christian. **78. affiance** trust. **84. Holy-Ghosted** guided by the Holy Spirit (**112**). There is also perhaps an allusion to Jesus' promise of the abiding presence of the Holy Spirit (John 14: 16–17; 26), an important biblical passage used to authenticate the historical Catholic Church against Protestantism. **89. Sacrificator** sacrificer, priest. Copley here (**89–90**) represents the mass in explicitly Catholic terms: a priest celebrates a sacrifice (not a mere ceremony) which re-enacts (not commemorates) the death and resurrection of Jesus Christ, actually (not symbolically) present in the Eucharist. **93. adorn** adornment. **103–6.** The quester sees three Catholic

Chrism and authentic sanctification,   105
And exorcism of such as were possessed.
    Their credence and their language was alike,
    All Babel-biblers they did dead dislike.

There was no scambling for the Gospels' bread,
But what a public unity deliverèd,   110
The same a prompt credulity receivèd.
Their humbleness was so beholy-Ghosted,
    As pride had not the power to entice
    The wisest of them all to a new device.

Casting my eye aside, I might descry   115
Selected troops of people from the rest,
Dooming themselves with great austerity,
Both men and women in discoloured vest.
    They were the people of vows and high aspire,
    Endued with grace's more especial fire.   120

On no hand could I cast my liquorish eye
From heavenly miracles and mysteries.
Some schooled their pupils' frail infirmity,
Dispensing them God's sacramental graces;
    Some raised the dead and some expulsed the devil,   125
    Yet nought could make Doblessa see her evil.

How many Zionites of choice esteem,
Brave men of wonders, have been sent from thence
To teach Doblessa, Error's dreary queen,
Their temple's sanctimony and innocence?   130
    How many worthies have dispensed their blood,
    To do th'unkind Doblessa so much good?

But she, oh, she, accursèd sorceress,
Would never yet believe, nor gree their grace,
But still persisteth in her wretchedness,   135
Warfaring with bloody broil this happy place.

practices emphatically rejected by Protestants: the imposition of hands, by which a priest actually or symbolically confers some favour; the use of chrism, an oil made of olives and balsam; the rite of exorcism. **108. Babel-biblers** A reference to the profusion of Bibles, in various and conflicting vernacular translations, produced by Protestants. **109. scambling** scrambling (by individual interpreters of the Bible), as opposed to the single authoritative teaching of the Church (110). **111. credulity** readiness to believe. **112. beholy-Ghosted** guided by the Holy Spirit. **115. descry** perceive. **117. Dooming themselves** practising severe penances. **118. discoloured vest** dull clothing, i.e. the habits of religious orders, including, notably, Catholic nuns. **121. On no hand** in no direction. **liquorish** desirous. **129. Error's...queen** Compare Spenser's Error, the serpent woman of the dark wood, who vomits Catholic polemics (*FQ* I. 1). **131. worthies** contemporary martyrs. **134. gree** accept.

Yea, had she might according to her malice,
Zion had been a ruin long ere this.

She was a witch and queen of all the desert
From Babel Mount unto the pit of hell;   140
She forced nor God nor any good desert;
She could do anything save doing well.
　　Her law was liberty, her lust was pride,
　　And all good awe and order she defied.

　　　　.　　.　　.　　.　　.　　.　　.　　.

For she could quaintly mask in Zion's guise,   145
And suck out venom from the flow'r of life,
And so retail it with her subtleties
For purest honey—such was her deed of strife.
　　Her wolfish nature in a lambly hue
　　She could disguise and seem of Zion's crew.   150

Like ensigns she opposed to Zion's ensigns,
Like her pretence of grace and God's high honour,
Like grapes she did contend grew up her vines,
And as good gold as Zion's seemed her copper.
　　It was but seeming so, not so indeed;   155
　　Her seeming flower was a very weed.

For why, the spirit which she did pretend,
Was not authentic from the Holy Ghost.
On no authority she did depend,
Nor had she certain being in any coast.   160
　　Her own behest she did idolatrize,
　　And hydra-like renewed her fallacies.

She had no altar, nor no sacrament,
No ceremony, nor oblation;
Her school was cavil and truthless babblement,   165
Riot her reign, her end damnation.
　　This was the haggard Whore of Babylon,
　　Whose cup envenomed all that drunk thereon.

---

141. forced cared about. **145. quaintly mask** cleverly disguise herself. **147. retail** sell. **151. ensigns** military banners. **157. For why** as for the reason. **160.** a gibe at the diversity and disunity of reformist religions. **161. behest** whim. **idolatrize** make into an idol. The line refers to the royal appropriation of Church authority and prerogatives. **162. hydra-like** The hydra was a mythical snake whose many heads grew as fast as they were cut off. **167. Whore of Babylon** Copley concludes this attack on Protestantism, its denial of traditions, authority, sacrament, and ritual (163–4), with this reference to the Whore of Babylon (Apoc. 17), a symbol of idolatry often applied by Protestants to Roman Catholicism.

Richard Verstegan

Educated at Oxford, Richard Verstegan (1548–1636) had a varied career in England and on the Continent as a Catholic writer, translator, and publisher. His first important work, *Theatrum crudelitatum, haereticorum nostri temporis* (1587), depicted the martyrdoms of English Catholics in graphic copperplate engravings (see Figs. 6, 9). From Antwerp Verstegan served as writer, publisher, and coordinator of news for Catholics in England. He published the principal Catholic prayer-book for the next century, *The Primer, or Office of the Blessed Virgin Mary* (1599), and wrote a pioneering historical work, *A Restitution of Decayed Intelligence in Antiquities* (1605) (see INSTRUCTIONS AND DEVOTIONS and HISTORIES). Verstegan also wrote an accomplished book of poetry, *Odes in Imitation of the Seven Penitential Psalms* (1601), which features a Marian lullaby, skilful translations of psalms, and other poems.

Odes in Imitation of the Seven Penitential Psalms, 1601

From 'Our Blessed Lady's Lullaby'

My babe, my bliss, my child, my choice,
My fruit, my flower, and bud,
My Jesus and my only joy,
The sum of all my good.
   Sing lullaby, my little boy,   5
   Sing lullaby, my life's joy.

My sweetness and the sweetest most
That heaven could earth deliver,
Soul of my love, spirit of my life,
Abide with me forever.   10
   Sing lullaby, my little boy,
   Sing lullaby, my life's joy.

Live still with me and be my love,
And death will me refrain,
Unless thou let me die with thee,   15
To live with thee again.

13. **still** ever. The line echoes Marlowe's popular verse, 'Come live with me and be my love.'   14. **refrain** avoid.

Sing lullaby, my little boy,
Sing lullaby, my life's joy.

'In imitation of the sixth penitential psalm
De profundis clamavi ad te Domine

Ev'n from the depth of woes
Wherein my soul remains,
To thee in supreme bliss,
O Lord that highest reigns,
    I do both call and cry.   5
'Tis deep heart-sorrow's force
That moves me thus to wail,
'Tis pity, Lord, in thee,
Must make it to avail;
    Thine ears, therefore, apply.   10

If strictly, thou, O Lord,
Observèd hast my sin,
Alas, what shall I do?
What case then am I in,
    If rigour thou extend?   15
But well, O Lord, I know,
Sweet mercy dwells with thee,
And with thy justice then,
It must expected be,
    And I, therefore, attend.   20

My soul doth wait on thee,
Thy grace confirms my trust,
My warrant is thy word,
Thou keepest promise just;
    Keep me, O Lord, secure.   25
Let thy afflicted flock
Comfort in thee retain,
From dawning day to night,
From night to day again,
    Let still their hope endure.   30

SIXTH PENITENTIAL PSALM Psalms 129 (130 in some numerations). The Psalms are a collection of prayers and songs composed throughout Israel's history; the early Church called seven psalms (6, 31, 37, 50, 101, 129, 142) penitential, because they sounded notes of contrition and sorrow. Verstegan contributes to the flourishing subgenre of Psalms translation, which includes the Sternhold-Hopkins Psalter and Sir Philip Sidney. *De...Domine* (From the depths I have cried unto thee, O Lord), the Vulgate rendering of the Hebrew first line. **11. strictly** closely, with insistence on due punishment. **20. attend** wait.

> There is with our good God
> Much mercy still in store,
> Redemption doth remain
> With him forever more,
>   Abundant is his grace.   35
> His people he affects,
> He will not leave distressed,
> The thrallèd he will free,
> With ease of their unrest,
>   And all their faults deface.   40

WILLIAM ALABASTER

Educated at Cambridge University, William Alabaster (1567–1640) started life as a literate anti-Catholic. His *Elisaeis*, a Latin panegyric to Queen Elizabeth, modelled on the *Aeneid*, features Satan persuading the pope to promote the Catholic cause in England. In 1597, however, Alabaster converted to Catholicism through the offices of a Catholic priest, Thomas Wright, and the reading of William Rainoldes's defence of the Rheims New Testament, *A Refutation of Sundry Apprehensions* (1583), as he recalls in a memoir. Subsequently, Alabaster gave evidence against pro-Spanish Catholics abroad, revolted from the Catholic faith, recanted, and wavered back and forth several times before his death. As a new Catholic in 1597–8, Alabaster prepared himself for martyrdom and wrote religious verse in what was to become the new metaphysical style of Donne and his followers. Employing paradox and conceit, the sonnets below use biblical image and allegory to convey the poet's fearful struggles and the inexpressible mysteries of sin and redemption.

'Over the brook of Cedron Christ is gone'

> Over the brook of Cedron Christ is gone,
> To entertain the combat with his death,
> Where David fled beforetime, void of breath,
> To scape the treacheries of Absalom.
> Go, let us follow him in passion   5
> Over this brook, this world that walloweth,

---

36. affects loves. **38. thrallèd** imprisoned. **40. deface** blot out.

'OVER THE BROOK' **1. brook of Cedron** brook near Jerusalem, which Christ crossed to enter Gethsemane and begin the Passion (John 18: 1), and which King David had crossed, fleeing his rebellious son Absalom (2 Kgs. 15: 23). **2. entertain** conduct. **6. walloweth** (1) rolls with waves; (2) delights in sensual pleasure.

A stream of cares that drown our thoughts beneath,
And wash away all resolution.
Beyond the world he must be passèd clear
That in the world for Christ will troubles bear.   10
Leave we, oh, leave we then this miry flood,
Friends, pleasures, and unfaithful good.
Now we are up, now down, but cannot stand,
We sink, we reel—Jesu, stretch forth thy hand!

''Tis not enough over the brook to stride'

'Tis not enough over the brook to stride
By scorn of fear and pleasures put to flight,
Unless we likewise follow Christ aright,
Up to Mount Olivet as he did guide;
For they whose spirits are not deified   5
In height of purest love and heaven's delight,
For Christ's dear sake with death to enter fight,
Go not to die with him but stray aside.
In vain they do that act and monument,
The death of heretics, with rubric red,   10
Whom just desert cut off by punishment,
As barren branches from the vine are shred.
For though they seem beyond the brook to get,
Yet never come they to Mount Olivet.

'Upon the Crucifix'

Now I have found thee, I will evermore
Embrace this standard where thou sitst above.
Feed, greedy eyes, and from hence never rove,
Suck, hungry soul, of this eternal store,

---

9. **he** anyone. 10. **That** who.

''TIS NOT ENOUGH' 1. **brook** symbol of worldly desire. 4. **Mount Olivet** the hill near Jerusalem beyond the brook of Cedron, which Jesus frequented during his final days. 9. **do** celebrate. **act and monument** Alluding to John Foxe's *Acts and Monuments* (1563), this phrase, appositive to 'the death of heretics', reveals that the poem attacks the Protestant martyrs as 'pseudomartyrs,' heretics who falsely claim to 'follow Christ aright' (3). 10. **rubric red** Foxe distinguished some of his martyrs with red lettering.

'UPON THE CRUCIFIX' Cf. Donne's 'The Cross' below. 2. **standard** flag or military symbol, here, the crucifix.

Issue, my heart, from thy two-leaved door, 5
And let my lips from kissing not remove.
Oh, that I were transformèd into love,
And as a plant might spring up in his flower,
Like wandering ivy or sweet honeysuckle!
How would I with my twine about it buckle, 10
And kiss his feet with my ambitious boughs,
And climb along upon his sacred breast,
And make a garland for his wounded brows.
Lord, so I am if here my thoughts might rest.

'Away, fear, with thy projects!'

Away, fear, with thy projects! No false fire
Which thou dost make can aught my courage quail,
Or cause me backward come or strike my sail.
What if the world do frown at my retire,
What if denial dash my wished desire, 5
And purblind pity do my state bewail,
And wonder cross itself and free speech rail,
And greatness take it not and death show nigher?
Tell them, my soul, the fears that make me quake,
The smothering brimstone and the burning lake, 10
Life feeding death, death ever life devouring,
Torments not moved, unheard, yet still roaring,
God-lost, hell-found, ever, never begun—
Now bid me into flame from smoke to run!

'A Preface to the Incarnation'

I sing of Christ, oh, endless argument!
Profaner thoughts and ears, begone, begone,
Lest thunder push down your presumption.

---

5. **two-leaved door** the two parts of the door, its hinged subsections, here a symbol for the lips. 10. **twine** shoots. **buckle** cling, attach. 11. **ambitious** eager. 14. **so I am** I am so transformed.

'AWAY, FEAR, WITH THY PROJECTS!' Some editors title this poem 'Of his Conversion'. 1. **projects** projections. 2. **aught...quail** make faint my courage at all. 6. **purblind** totally blind. 7. **cross itself** make the sign of the cross (in awe). 12. **not moved** everlasting. 13. **ever...begun** always new, never ending. 14. **smoke** the mere smoke of worldly disapproval.

'A PREFACE TO THE INCARNATION' The speaker imagines himself a choir here, singing praises to the incarnate Christ.

I sing of Christ. Let many worlds be lent
To enrobe my thoughts with all their ornament,   5
And tongues of men and angels join in one,
To show the riches of invention
Before the eyes of all the firmament.
The temple where I sing is heaven, the choir
Are my soul's powers, the book's a living story.   10
Each takes his time but with a low retire,
That modesty may after reach his glory;
And let the humble bass beneath begin,
To show when he descended for our sin.

'O wretched man, the knot of contraries'

O wretched man, the knot of contraries,
In whom both heaven and earth doth move and rest,
Heav'n of my mind, which with Christ's love is blest,
Death of my heart, which in dull languor lies.
Yet doth my moving will still circulize   5
My heaven about my earth with thought's unrest,
Where reason as a sun from east to west
Darteth his shining beams to melt this ice.
And now with fear it southward doth descend,
Now between both is equinoctial,   10
And now to joys it higher doth ascend,
And yet continues my sea glacial.
What shall I do but pray to Christ the Son:
'In earth as heaven, Lord, let thy will be done.'

8. firmament heaven. 10. book's . . . story The song book is the living story of Christ's life and death. 11. time musical time also, as one MS reading, 'tune', suggests. low retire humble withdrawal or retreat. 12. reach his glory relate the glorious story of Christ. 13–14. The musical descent to the lower bass tones echoes the descent of Christ from heaven to earth, from God to human form, for our sin.

'O WRETCHED MAN' 1. knot of contraries mixture of spirit and body, good and evil, heavenly aspirations and earthly desires. 3–4. Alabaster here associates heaven (and eternal life) with the mind or rational part of man, and death and earth (6) with the heart, or source of dull desire. 5. moving inconstant. still circulize ever cause to circle. 8. ice the ice of the cold heart, fixed on worldly pleasure. 9–11. Developing the 'reason as sun' conceit, Alabaster traces the solar movements through the winter solstice (the time of the sun's lowest descent), the equinox (the time it crosses the equator), and the summer solstice (the time of its highest ascent). 13. Son with a culminating pun on 'sun', the poet having found at last his true sun, Christ.

Toby Matthew

Toby Matthew (1557–65) converted to Catholicism and experienced subsequent trials and triumphs (see LIVES AND DEATHS). He wrote a poetic panegyric to the Virgin Mary in Anthony Stafford's *The Female Glory* (1635) and twenty-nine sonnets, devotional and personal, which are preserved in a manuscript commonplace book. The sonnet below expresses poignant grief at the common Catholic experience of exile.

'Upon the Sight of Dover Cliffs from Calais'

Better it were for me to have been blind,
Than with sad eyes to gaze upon the shore
Of my dear country, but now mine no more,
Which thrusts me thus, both of sight and mind.
Better for me to have in cradle pined,   5
Than live thus long to choke upon the core
Of his sad absence, whom I still adore
With present heart, for hearts are not confined.
Poor heart, that dost in so high tempest sail
Against both wind and tide of thy friend's will,   10
What remedy remains that can avail,
But that thou do with sighs the sails fulfil,
Until they split and if the body die,
'Tis well employed; the soul shall live thereby.

John Donne

Descended from Thomas More, the Heywoods, and the Rastells, John Donne (1572–1631) grew up Catholic amidst the ancient Catholic nobility—the Percies, Stanleys, and Howards. Donne wrote that he had his 'first breeding and conversation with men of a suppressed and afflicted religion, accustomed to the despite of death and hungry of an imagined martyrdom' (*Biathanatos*, 1648, sig. C). Meditation on martyrdom, inspired by his family and upbringing, he said elsewhere, kept him 'ever…awake' (*Pseudo-martyr*, 1610, sig. ¶1). The earliest

'UPON THE SIGHT OF DOVER CLIFFS FROM CALAIS' Matthew was exiled three times (1608, 1618, and 1640). The sonnet probably records his first experience. **4. of** out of. **7. his sad absence** separation from George Gage, the Catholic friend to whom Matthew entrusted the sonnets.

portrait of Donne, featuring him with a cross earring under the Spanish motto, 'Antes muerto que mudado' (better dead than changed), may reflect a defiant, self-conscious Catholicism. Donne attended Oxford University, converted to the state religion (*c.*1597), fought with Essex against the Spanish, and eventually received ordination in the Church of England (1615). He circulated poetry in manuscript and print, wrote polemical and devotional works, preached brilliantly, and died in 1631. His poetry appeared in posthumous collections, 1633 and 1635.

Donne's formation in Elizabethan Catholicism coloured his entire life and work. To be sure, Doctor Donne eventually preached sermons against the Roman Church, supported the Oath of Allegiance, and satirized the founder of the Jesuits in *Ignatius his Conclave* (1611). Yet, even as late as 1610–11, Donne's *Catalogus Librorum Aulicorum* gibes at Topcliffe, the sadistic priest-hunter, and John Foxe. Recording his doubts and struggles, Donne's poetry often draws upon the potent images, beliefs, and devotions of his family's faith. His poetry does not present a coherent Catholic vision, like that of Robert Southwell, for example, who united the art and life; in contrast, Donne's Catholicism ranges from playful metaphor to serious remembrance, consisting largely of unexpected resonances, fluid manoeuvrings, and transformed devotions, often presented in a spirit of restless enquiry. The secular lyrics variously adapt Catholic discourse about pilgrimages, saints, and angels (witness 'Song, The Canonization', 'A Letter to the Lady Carey and Mrs Essex Rich', and 'Air and Angels'). Below, 'The Relic' turns the discourse of miracles and relics into a poetry of praise. Like 'The Funeral' this poem mocks 'Catholic superstition, only to replace it with something which is both Catholic and superstitious' (John Carey, *John Donne*, 1981: 45). Contesting Puritan iconoclasts, 'The Cross' affirms the validity of the Catholic image and the symbolic imagination. The forbidden doctrines and practices of Marian devotion supply 'The Litany', 'La Corona', 'Good Friday, 1613. Riding Westward', and *An Anatomy of the World*. In such poems the poet reveals a devotion to Mary that the preacher denied, though Dr Donne hung pictures of the Virgin in his deanery. A late poem, 'A Hymn to God, my God, in my Sickness' deploys the Ignatian practice of meditation evident earlier in many holy sonnets ('At the round earth's imagined corners', 'Spit in my face', 'What if this present were the world's last night'). As we might expect, there are few certainties offered by so complex a poet, who memorably described the search for religious conviction as continual struggle:

> On a huge hill,
> Cragged and steep, Truth stands, and he that will
> Reach her about must and about must go,
> And what the hill's suddenness resists, win so.
>
> (*Satire 3*)

But Donne's Catholicism informs that struggle and enriches his poetry with possibilities.

'The Relic'

When my grave is broke up again,
Some second guest to entertain,
(For graves have learned that womanhead
To be to more than one a bed),
    And he that digs it spies   5
A bracelet of bright hair about the bone,
    Will he not let us alone,
And think that there a loving couple lies,
Who thought that this device might be some way
To make their souls at the last busy day   10
Meet at this grave and make a little stay?

If this fall in a time or land
Where mis-devotion doth command,
Then he that digs us up will bring
Us to the bishop and the king   15
    To make us relics; then
Thou shalt be a Mary Magdalen and I,
    A something else thereby.
All women shall adore us, and some men;
And since at such times miracles are sought,   20
I would have that age by this paper taught
What miracles we harmless lovers wrought.

First, we loved well and faithfully,
Yet knew not what we loved, nor why;
Difference of sex no more we knew   25
Than our guardian angels do;
    Coming and going, we

1. grave . . . again Graves were periodically emptied of corpses and reused for new ones. 3. that womanhead the behaviour characteristic of women (on analogy with maidenhead or virginity). Graves, like women, host more than one in bed. 6. bracelet . . . hair lock of blond hair on the dead man's wrist, given as a friend's gift or lover's token. 9. device scheme. 10. last . . . day Judgement Day, when souls reunite with bodies. 13. mis-devotion erroneous belief and practice. 16. make us relics execute us for heresy. Relics are holy remains of saints and martyrs, venerated by Catholics. 17. Mary Magdalen a saint much admired by 17th-c. Catholics, often depicted with long, golden hair. The poem is probably addressed to a friend, Magdalen Herbert. 20. at such times i.e. in times of 'mis-devotion'. Protestants claimed that the age of miracles had passed, but belief in miracles enables the poem, especially its concluding assertions. 21. this paper the poem. 26. guardian angels tutelary spirits, thought to be incorporeal and asexual.

Perchance might kiss, but not between those meals;
    Our hands ne'er touched the seals
Which nature, injured by late law, sets free.   30
These miracles we did; but now, alas,
All measure and all language I should pass,
Should I tell what a miracle she was.

'The Cross'

Since Christ embraced the cross itself, dare I,
His image, th'image of his cross deny?
Would I have profit by the sacrifice,
And dare the chosen altar to despise?
It bore all other sins, but is it fit   5
That it should bear the sin of scorning it?
Who from the picture would avert his eye,
How would he fly his pains who there did die?
From me no pulpit, nor misgrounded law,
Nor scandal taken shall this cross withdraw;   10
It shall not for it cannot; for the loss
Of this cross were to me another cross.
Better were worse, for no affliction,
No cross is so extreme as to have none.
Who can blot out the cross which th'instrument   15
Of God dewed on me in the sacrament?
Who can deny me power and liberty
To stretch mine arms and mine own cross to be?
Swim, and at every stroke thou art thy cross;
The mast and yard make one where seas do toss.   20

29–30. **seals . . . free** restrictions on love, which did not exist in the original state of nature, but came about as a result of late laws. These two friends, enjoying an ideal, spiritual love, never transgressed these restrictions.

'THE CROSS' The cross and crucifix were major targets of Puritan iconoclasm. In 1604 James rejected Puritan demands for the abolition of the sign of the cross in baptism. Appropriating traditional Catholic arguments, Donne affirms the value of the symbolic imagination and that of the cross as symbol. **2. His image** (1) the poet, made in the image of God; (2) the memory of Christ on the cross; (3) God made visible in Christ. **4. altar** the cross on which Christ was sacrificed. **9–10.** The speaker defies the attempts of Puritans to ban the cross by preaching against it from the pulpit, by enacting prohibitive laws, and by equating veneration of the cross with the scandal of idolatry. **12. another cross** another affliction. The poem plays with the various senses of cross: the instrument of Christ's crucifixion, the religious artefact, any affliction, or anything joined at right angles. **13. Better . . . worse** it would be better to suffer worse punishments. **15. instrument** agent, i.e. the priest. **16. dewed** let fall as dew, poured. **sacrament** baptism. Catholic theology taught that baptism conferred an indelible mark on the soul (see Council of Trent, Session 7, canon 9). **17–24.** Early Christian writers compiled similar lists of crosses in nature and everyday life, which Lipsius collected in *De Cruce* (1595) (Donne, *Divine Poems*, ed. Helen Gardner, 1952, rev. 1978: 155). **20. yard** yard-arm, a beam perpendicular to the upright mast of a ship.

Look down, thou spiest out crosses in small things;
Look up, thou seest birds raised on crossèd wings.
All the globe's frame and spheres is nothing else
But the meridians crossing parallels.
Material crosses, then, good physic be,   25
And yet spiritual have chief dignity.
These for extracted chemic medicine serve,
And cure much better, and as well preserve.
Then are you your own physic or need none,
When stilled or purged by tribulation,   30
For when that cross ungrudged unto you sticks,
Then are you to yourself a crucifix.
As, perchance, carvers do not faces make,
But that away, which hid them there, do take,
Let crosses so take what hid Christ in thee,   35
And be his image, or not his, but he.
But as oft alchemists do coiners prove,
So may a self-despising get self-love,
And then, as worst surfeits of best meats be,
So is pride issued from humility;   40
For 'tis no child, but monster. Therefore, cross
Your joy in crosses, else 'tis double loss,
And cross thy senses, else both they and thou
Must perish soon and to destruction bow.
For if th'eye seek good objects and will take   45
No cross from bad, we cannot 'scape a snake.
So with harsh, hard, sour, stinking, cross the rest,
Make them indifferent, call nothing best.
But most the eye needs crossing that can roam

23–4. The earth and heavenly spheres move in circular orbits (**meridians**) that continually cross **parallels**, i.e. the planes perpendicular to the north–south axes that mark degrees of latitude. **25. Material crosses** (1) plants with upright stalks and perpendicular branches, also *Cruciferae*, plants with their four petals in the shape of a cross; (2) physical ailments, sometimes thought to purge the body. **physic** medicine. **26. spiritual** spiritual crosses or afflictions. **27. extracted chemic medicine** the quintessence of a medicine, according to the practice of Paracelsus, who held that diseases could be cured by the application of antagonistic chemical essences. Donne is praising the curative power of affliction and its ability to preserve us from sin. **30. stilled** distilled. **31. ungrudged** accepted willingly. **33. carvers** sculptors. **34. that away** take that away (**take** is postponed to the line's end). **36. but he** Through affliction the sufferer can become one with Christ. **37–8.** Just as alchemists, who strive to make pure gold, can be corrupted into becoming mere counterfeiters (**coiners**), so can a willingness to humble oneself and suffer affliction be corrupted into a kind of spiritual pride. Puritans who professed humility and self-contempt were commonly charged with arrogant self-love and pride. See Jonson's devastating portraits, DRAMA. **39. surfeits** excesses. **41–2. cross … crosses** check your delight in afflictions. **42. double loss** first in the suffering itself, and then in failing to achieve any spiritual reward from the suffering. **46. a snake** entrapment by apparent beauty (alluding to the outwardly beautiful serpent in the Garden of Eden). **47.** So mortify your other senses with things repugnant to them. **48. Make … best** Make your senses indifferent to pleasure or pain; have no preferences. Donne echoes the Ignatian prescription of 'indifference' (see INSTRUCTIONS AND DEVOTIONS). **49–50.** Visual delights most need

And move; to th'others th'objects must come home.   50
And cross thy heart, for that in man alone
Points downwards and hath palpitation.
Cross those dejections when it downward tends,
And when it to forbidden heights pretends.
And as thy brain through bony walls doth vent   55
By sutures, which a cross's form present,
So when thy brain works, ere thou utter it,
Cross and correct concupiscence of wit.
Be covetous of crosses; let none fall;
Cross no man else but cross thyself in all.   60
Then doth the cross of Christ work fruitfully
Within our hearts, when we love harmlessly
That cross's pictures much, and with more care
That cross's children, which our crosses are.

From *La Corona*: 'Annunciation'

Salvation to all that will is nigh.
That All, which always is all everywhere,
Which cannot sin and yet all sins must bear,
Which cannot die yet cannot choose but die,
Lo, faithful Virgin, yields himself to lie   5
In prison in thy womb; and though he there
Can take no sin, nor thou give, yet he'll wear,
Taken from thence, flesh, which death's force may try.
Ere by the spheres time was created thou

checking and frustration since one can easily direct one's gaze to beautiful things; the other senses more passively receive impressions. **52.** Inclines towards earthly things and experiences anticipation and hope. Aristotle noted that man is practically the only animal whose heart jumps because he has hope and anticipates future joys (Donne, *Divine Poems*, ed. Gardner, 93–4). **53. dejections** jumps or impulses. **it** the heart. **54. pretends** aspires. **55–6.** Donne reflects the Aristotelian idea that the brain is formed by ventilation through **sutures**, i.e. the seams of human skull bones that, in fact, form a cross on the top of the human head. **58. concupiscence of wit** any sinful idea or utterance. **59. fall** escape your attention. **63. pictures** images, including tangible representations such as crucifixes.

LA CORONA 'The crown', consisting of seven interlinked sonnets, derives from the Italian poetic form, *Corona di sonnetti*, and from a Catholic devotion, the Bridgettine Rosary, 'The Corona of Our Lady', divided into seven parts (Louis Martz, *The Poetry of Meditation*, 1954, rev. 1962: 105–8; see Jonson's 'The Garland' below). Donne probably composed *La Corona* in 1611. **Annunciation** Gabriel's announcement to Mary that she would bear a son (Luke 1: 26–35). (See Fig. 11.) The first and last lines are italicized because they repeat, respectively, in the lines immediately preceding and following the sonnet. **2. All** Christ, sometimes designated Pan ('all' in Greek). **7. nor thou give** Donne articulates the Catholic doctrine of Mary's Immaculate Conception (i.e. that she was conceived without original sin), which Protestants firmly rejected. **8. try** attempt to conquer. **9. spheres** concentric celestial circles thought to revolve around the earth; their motion, in the view of Aristotle and others, created time.

Wast in his mind, who is thy son and brother,   10
Whom thou conceiv'st, conceived; yea, thou art now
Thy Maker's maker and thy Father's mother,
Thou'st light in dark and shutst in little room
Immensity cloistered in thy dear womb.

From *The Litany*: 'The Virgin Mary'

For that fair, blessèd mother-maid,
Whose flesh redeemed us, that she-cherubin
  Which unlocked Paradise, and made
One claim for innocence, and disseized sin,
  Whose womb was a strange heav'n, for there   5
  God clothed himself and grew,
Our zealous thanks we pour. As her deeds were
Our helps, so are her prayers; nor can she sue
In vain, who hath such titles unto You.

'Good Friday, 1613. Riding Westward'

Let man's soul be a sphere, and then in this
Th'intelligence that moves, devotion is,
And as the other spheres, by being grown
Subject to foreign motions, lose their own,
And being by others hurried every day,   5

10. **son and brother** for similar paradoxes see Southwell's 'The Nativity of Christ', above. 11. **Whom...conceived** He whom you conceive conceived you. 13. **Thou'st** thou hast. 14. *cloistered...womb* The phrase echoes the Catholic matins hymn for feasts of the Blessed Virgin, which sings of Mary's cloister (*claustrum Mariae*) bearing the Lord of earth, sea, and heavens (Donne, *Divine Poems*, ed. Gardner, 60).

THE LITANY From Greek λιτανεία, 'prayer or supplication', usually organized as a responsive repetition. This selection expresses a very Catholic devotion to Mary. Probably composed in 1608–9, 'The Litany' appeared in several manuscripts with the Catholic title, 'Our Lady'. 2. **redeemed us** i.e. by producing the Saviour, but Donne adopts a formulation specifically offensive to Protestants, who denied Mary any special status or active role in the Redemption. 2–3. **she-cherubin...Paradise** Contrast the Protestant position of Donne's sermons: 'God forbid that any should say that the Virgin Mary concurred to our good as Eve did to our ruin...The Virgin Mary had not the same interest in our salvation as Eve did in our destruction; nothing that she did entered into that treasure, that ransom that redeemed us' (Donne, *Divine Poems*, ed. Gardner, 84). 4. **One claim** Mary's one or singular claim for innocence suggests Catholic belief in the Immaculate Conception. **disseized** dispossessed. 8–9. Mary appears in the familiar role of mediatrix, emphatically rejected by Protestants. 9. **titles unto** claims upon.

'GOOD FRIDAY, 1613.'In 1613 Good Friday fell on 2 April. 1. **soul...sphere** The opening conceit equates man's soul to a sphere (a planet) and devotion to the angelic intelligence supposed to move the spheres in perfectly circular orbits to give praise to God. 2. **intelligence** i.e. the angel. 4. **foreign motions** external influences. **lose their own** vary their proper orbit, their **natural form** (6). Just as such influences disturb proper orbits, so pleasure and business interfere with the proper devotions.

Scarce in a year their natural form obey,
Pleasure or business so our souls admit
For their first mover, and are whirled by it.
Hence is't that I am carried towards the west
This day, when my soul's form bends toward the east.   10
There I should see a sun by rising set,
And by that setting endless day beget.
But that Christ on this cross did rise and fall,
Sin had eternally benighted all.
Yet dare I almost be glad I do not see   15
That spectacle of too much weight for me.
Who sees God's face, that is self life, must die;
What a death were it then to see God die?
It made his own lieutenant, Nature, shrink;
It made his footstool crack and the sun wink.   20
Could I behold those hands which span the poles
And tune all spheres at once pierced with those holes?
Could I behold that endless height which is
Zenith to us and our antipodes,
Humbled below us? Or that blood which is   25
The seat of all our souls, if not of his,
Made dirt of dust, or that flesh which was worn
By God for his apparel ragg'd, and torn?
If on these things I durst not look, durst I
Upon his miserable mother cast mine eye,   30
Who was God's partner here, and furnished thus
Half of that sacrifice which ransomed us?
Though these things as I ride be from mine eye,
They're present yet unto my memory,
For that looks towards them, and thou lookst towards me,   35
O Saviour, as thou hangst upon the tree.

7. admit accept. 8. first mover (1) God, the prime mover or first cause; (2) also the *primum mobile*, the tenth sphere beyond the nine planets that caused motion in the spheres. 10. form proper devotional course. 11. sun The pun on sun and Son (Christ) drives the whole poem, as Christ set in the west by dying on the cross and rose in the east by his resurrection. 14. benighted put into darkness. 17. self itself. The line alludes to Exod. 33: 20: 'And again he said: "Thou canst not see my face, for man shall not see me and live."' 19. lieutenant deputy. Nature serves God and recoiled in horror at Christ's death: 'And behold, the veil of the temple was rent in two from the top even to the bottom, and the earth quaked and the rocks were rent. And the graves were opened and many bodies of the saints that had slept arose' (Matt. 27: 51–2). 20. footstool the earth: 'Thus saith the Lord: Heaven is my throne, and the earth my footstool' (Isa. 66: 1). 22. tune Some manusripts and editors read 'turn' here. 24. Zenith...antipodes the highest point to us and to those dwelling on the other side of the world. 26. seat Some thought blood to be the seat or residence of the soul; Christ's blood is the proper seat of all souls. if...his even if Christ's soul did not reside in his blood, in his human form. 27. Made...dust (1) mingled with dust; (2) made vilest of the vile. 30. miserable pitiable. 31–2. an explicit statement of the theological position that Donne as Protestant preacher denied (see above *Litany* 2–3 n.). Mary participates in the redemption of mankind by furnishing half of that sacrifice, i.e. the flesh and blood of the incarnate God.

I turn my back to thee but to receive
Corrections, till thy mercies bid thee leave.
Oh, <u>think me worth thine anger, punish me,</u>
<u>Burn off my rusts and my deformity,</u>   40
Restore thine image so much by thy grace
That thou mayst know me, and I'll turn my face.

From *An Anatomy of the World*

When that rich soul which to her heaven is gone,
Whom all they celebrate who know they have one—
For who is sure he hath a soul unless
It see and judge and follow worthiness,
And by deeds praise it? He who doth not this   5
May lodge an inmate soul but 'tis not his—
When that queen ended here her progress time,
And as t'her standing house to heaven did climb,
Where, loath to make the saints attend her long,
She's now a part both of the choir and song,   10
This world in that great earthquake languishèd,
For in a common bath of tears it bled,
Which drew the strongest vital spirits out.

    .   .   .   .

Thus man, this world's vice-emperor, in whom
All faculties, all graces are at home   15
(And if in other creatures they appear,
They're but man's ministers and legates there,
To work on their rebellions and reduce
Them to civility and to man's use),
This man, whom God did woo, and loath t'attend   20
Till man came up, did down to man descend,

38. **Corrections** punishments. **leave** cease. 41. **Restore thine image** (1) make me mindful of your suffering on the cross; (2) restore me to a proper image of you.

AN ANATOMY OF THE WORLD This poem laments the death of Elizabeth Drury and satirizes the world she left behind, now bereft of its most virtuous inhabitant and animating principle. Also called 'The First Anniversary', it evokes the Catholic practices of celebrating saints' days and offering prayers for the dead. 2. **all...one** all celebrate who know they have a soul (and are therefore capable of virtuous action). 4. **see...judge...follow** The actions correspond to the three faculties of the soul—memory, understanding, and will. 6. **inmate** guest. 7. **progress** royal procession. 8. **standing house** chief royal residence. 9. **attend** await. 10. **choir and song** She now joins the heavenly choir in praise and is praised herself in song. 12–13. Weeping into a common bath of tears, the world lost its 13. **vital spirits**, which supply natural heat and sustain life. 14. **vice-emperor** God's regent on earth with dominion over creation (Gen. 1: 26 ff.). 17. **legates** servants. 18. **reduce** lead back. 20. **t'attend** to wait.

This man so great that all that is, is his,
Oh, what a trifle and poor thing he is!
If man were anything, he's nothing now.
Help, or at least some time to waste, allow   25
T'his other wants, yet when he did depart
With her whom we lament, he lost his heart.
She of whom th'ancients seemed to prophesy,
When they called virtues by the name of 'she',
She in whom virtue was so much refined,   30
That for allay unto so pure a mind
She took the weaker sex, she that could drive
The poisonous tincture and the stain of Eve
Out of her thoughts and deeds, and purify
All by a true religious alchemy,   35
She, she is dead, she's dead. When thou knowest this,
Thou knowest how poor a trifling thing man is,
And learnst thus much by our anatomy:
The heart being perished, no part can be free.

'Hymn to God, my God, in my Sickness'

Since I am coming to that holy room,
    Where, with thy choir of saints for evermore,
I shall be made thy music, as I come
    I tune the instrument here at the door,
    And what I must do then think now before.   5

Whilst my physicians by their love are grown
    Cosmographers, and I their map, who lie
Flat on this bed, that by them may be shown

25–6. Help…wants even if one grants help to man's other deficient faculties or concedes that there remains some time before they waste entirely away. **26. depart** part. **29.** Greek and Latin nouns naming virtues are feminine in gender. **31. allay** alloy, admixture with a less pure element. **33.** the stain caused by original sin. **Tincture** means 'colouring' and also the alchemical quintessence, or spiritual principle in material things. The hyperbole derives from Marian devotions, which honour Mary as the second Eve, i.e. the second woman born without original sin, who reversed evil caused by the first (see above, *The Litany*, 2–3 n.; Southwell, 'The Virgin's Salutation'). **38. anatomy** analysis.

'HYMN TO GOD, MY GOD, IN MY SICKNESS' Donne wrote the poem either in 1623 or in 1631, before he died. Louis L. Martz explicates it as the 'epitome' of the art of Ignatian meditation (*Anchor Anthology*, 1969: pp. xxx–xxxvi). The formal preparation and composition of place occur in the first stanza, wherein the speaker places himself in the presence of God. The poet employs his memory and understanding in the second part, the elaborate cosmographical conceit (stanzas 2–4), wherein analysis leads to the realization that 'death doth touch the Resurrection'. He closes in impassioned colloquy, praying that Christ's blood may redeem his soul, that his impending death may lead to eternal life (see Ignatius, INSTRUCTIONS AND DEVOTIONS). **1. that holy room** heaven. **4. tune the instrument** (1) prepare my soul; (2) write this poem. **7. Cosmographers** map makers or readers, who pore over the sick speaker as if he were a map.

That this is my south-west discovery,
    Per fretum febris, by these straits to die,   10
I joy that in these straits I see my west,
    For though their currents yield return to none,
What shall my west hurt me? As west and east
    In all flat maps—and I am one—are one,
    So death doth touch the Resurrection.   15
Is the Pacific sea my home? Or are
    The eastern riches? Is Jerusalem?
Anyan, and Magellan, and Gibraltar?
    All straits, and none but straits, are ways to them,
    Whether where Japhet dwelt, or Cham, or Shem.   20
We think that Paradise and Calvary,
    Christ's cross and Adam's tree, stood in one place;
Look, Lord, and find both Adams met in me:
    As the first Adam's sweat surrounds my face,
    May the last Adam's blood my soul embrace.   25
So in his purple wrapped, receive me, Lord;
    By these his thorns, give me his other crown;
And as to others' souls I preached thy word,
    Be this my text, my sermon to mine own:
    'Therefore that he may raise, the Lord throws down.'   30

9. this...south-west discovery The sickness is the discovery of his south-west, i.e. of his death through fever. The south is the hot zone and the west is the zone of the setting sun. There is also the suggestion that the south-west discovery is the revelation of a new world. 10. *Per fretum febris* 'through the straits of fever'. straits (1) sufferings; (2) channels. 11. west death. 12. yield return flow back towards the east and enable return. 13–14. As...one On a flat map the ends representing west and east, which appear furthest apart, are actually contiguous places, as is apparent when the map is folded around a globe. 15. So our end is our beginning, our death merely a prelude to new life in the Resurrection. 16–17. These lines name exotic places of peace and serenity. The earthly Jerusalem suggests the heavenly Jerusalem that is the speaker's real destination. 18. Anyan...Magellan...Gibraltar Three straits, the first legendary: Anyan supposedly dividing America from Asia, connects the Atlantic and Pacific oceans; Magellan, dividing South America from Tierra del Fuego, connects the Atlantic and Pacific oceans; Gibraltar, dividing Africa and Europe, connects the Atlantic Ocean and the Mediterranean sea. 19. none but straits only sufferings. 20. Japhet...Cham...Shem sons of Noah whose descendants populated the three continents of the known world; Japhet's progeny settled in Europe, Ham's in Africa, Shem's in Asia (Gen. 10). 21–2. The idea that the Tree of Knowledge and the Cross of Christ stood in one place is well attested in Catholic iconography. 23. both Adams Christ is the second Adam. 26. purple i.e. red, here (1) the speaker's feverish flush; (2) Christ's royal cloak; (3) Christ's blood. 27. thorns i.e. the speaker's suffering. other crown heavenly reward. 29. mine own my soul. 30. The text is not exactly scriptural but rehearses a common idea and a central paradox for Donne (see also Holy Sonnet 14, 'Batter my heart').

BEN JONSON

Cranky, learned, satirical, and brilliant, Ben Jonson (1572–1637) is one of the most distinguished poets and playwrights of the Renaissance. He wrote court masques, influential 'humours' comedy, satirical dramas, critical prefaces, and poems, much admired and imitated. According to his own testimony (*Conversations with Drummond*, 1. 205), Jonson was Catholic during the period of his greatest productivity, converting in 1598 through the ministrations of a priest who visited him in prison, and remaining as such until 1610. In 1604 Jonson's first version of the play *Sejanus* occasioned charges of popery and treason; in 1605, after the Gunpowder Plot, he used his connections in Catholic circles to assist the government; in 1606 the Consistory Court asked for certification of his attendance at church and communion, indicted him as 'a seducer of youth to the popish religion', and required him to engage in theological disputation with learned Protestants. Several times he paid recusancy fines. Jonson maintained relations with Catholics like Thomas Wright (a priest), Hugh Holland, and important patrons, Sir Kenelm Digby and Esmé Stuart. He certainly echoed anti-Catholic discourse in his poetry and plays, but he paid penalties for his Catholicism and took considerable risks to maintain it. The reconversion to Anglicanism in 1610 elicited harsh judgement from at least one of his eulogists, Thomas Willford: 'The last act did disgrace the first; | His part he played exceeding well, | A Catholic, until he fell | To sects and schisms' (*Ben Jonson*, ed. Herford and Simpsons, 11 vols., 1925–52: xi. 493).

Jonson is primarily a secular poet and Catholicism does not pervasively enable and condition his art as it does that of Robert Southwell and Richard Crashaw, for example. And yet, Jonson's Catholicism certainly shapes 'Panegyre' (1604), wherein the goddess Themis offers the newly crowned King James a Catholic perspective on the Henrician revolution, when 'acts gave licence to impetuous lust | To bury churches in forgotten dust'. Recalling Jonson's satires on Puritans (see DRAMA), 'The New Cry' attributes all the popular anti-Catholicism of the day to ignorant, callow frauds. Jonson's professed Catholicism affords insight into other non-religious poems as well. It explains, for example, the references to Luther's beer and to Poley and Parrot in 'Inviting a friend to Supper', and the allusion to the doctrine of good works in 'Of Life and Death'. Like passages in *Sejanus*, the verse epistle praising Lady Aubigny recognizes the plight and courage of a recusant house in England. Jonson's Catholicism appears more overtly and traditionally in his surprising devotion to Mary, evident in the poem on his daughter's death and in 'The Garland of the Blessed Virgin Mary' (1635), which draws upon the Litany of Loreto. Jonson's mature poetic collection, *The Underwood* (published in 1641), begins with three neglected devotional poems, the first of which, 'The Sinner's Sacrifice', embodies the meditative techniques of St Bernard and St Ignatius. Clearly, Catholicism offered substantial gifts to the poet throughout his career.

From 'Panegyre', 1604

She then remembered to his thought the place
Where he was going, and the upward race
Of kings preceding him in that high court;
Their laws, their ends, the men she did report,
And all so justly as his ear was joyed   5
To hear the truth, from spite or flattery void.
She showed him who made wise, who honest acts,
Who both, who neither; all the cunning tracts
And thriving statutes she could promptly note;
The bloody, base, and barbarous she did quote;   10
Where laws were made to serve the tyrant will,
Where sleeping they could save, and waking kill,
Where acts gave license to impetuous lust
To bury churches in forgotten dust,
And with their ruins raise the pander's bowers;   15
When public justice borrowed all her powers
From private chambers, that could then create
Laws, judges, counsellors, yea, prince and state.
All this she told and more with bleeding eyes,
For right is as compassionate as wise.   20

'Of Life and Death'

The ports of death are sins, of life, good deeds,
Through which our merit leads us to our meeds.

'PANEGYRE' A panegyre is a poem of praise; this one celebrated the entrance of King James to his first session of Parliament, 19 March 1603. **1. She** Themis, goddess of justice, order, and peace. **his thought** the mind of James, whom she is introducing to his new kingdom. **12. sleeping...waking** unenforced...enforced. **13–14.** 'Written in Jonson's Catholic days', Herford and the Simpsons tersely comment (x. 393). These lines reflects a Catholic view of the Protestant revolution as a politically mandated plunder of Church property, resulting in the ruination of churches across the land. **15. pander's bowers** the bedchamber of the procurer or pimp. The change to Protestantism resulted not in reformation, Jonson declares with this striking metaphor, but in the institutional gratification of sinful lusts and desires. **19. bleeding** weeping.

'OF LIFE AND DEATH' **1. ports** gates. **2. meeds** rewards. Jonson stresses the efficacy of good works, a doctrine pointedly denied by Protestants.

How wilful blind is he, then, that would stray,
　　And hath it in his powers to make his way!
This world death's region is, the other, life's,   5
　　And here it should be one of our first strifes
So to front death, as men might judge us past it,
　　For good men but see death, the wicked taste it.

'The New Cry'

Ere 'Cherries ripe!' and 'Strawberries!' be gone,
　　Unto the cries of London I'll add one:
'Ripe statesmen, ripe!'—they grow in every street—
　　'At six-and-twenty, ripe!' You shall 'em meet,
And have 'em yield no savour but of state.   5
　　Ripe are their ruffs, their cuffs, their beards, their gait,
And grave as ripe, like mellow as their faces.
　　They know the states of Christendom, not the places;
Yet have they seen the maps and bought 'em too,
　　And understand 'em, as most chapmen do.   10
The counsels, projects, practices they know,
　　And what each prince doth for intelligence owe,
And unto whom; they are the almanacs
　　For twelve years yet to come, what each state lacks.
They carry in their pockets Tacitus,   15
　　And the *Gazetti*, or *Gallo-Belgicus*,
And talk reserved, locked up, and full of fear,
　　Nay, ask you how the day goes in your ear,
Keep a Star-Chamber sentence close twelve days,
　　And whisper what a proclamation says.   20
They meet in sixes and at every mart,
　　Are sure to con the catalogue by heart;

3. **wilful** perversely. 6. **strifes** strivings. 7. **front** confront. **past it** over death, reconciled completely to it. 8. **taste it** Compare Jesus' saying, 'If any man keep my word, he shall not taste death forever' (John 8: 52).

'THE NEW CRY' The street-vendor's cry furnishes this satire (wr. 1611?) on the new breed of statesman in London, young, pretentious, and ignorant. 6–7. Fashionable gallants wore **ruffs** (broad collars of starched linen or muslin) and **cuffs** (ornamented sleeves), trimmed their beards stylishly, and walked with affected gait and serious expression. 7. **like** as. 8. **states** political conditions. 10. **chapmen** workmen (who have only superficial knowledge). 12. **intelligence owe** information own. 13. **almanacs** popular books of tables, containing calendars, astronomical data, notice of ecclesiastical and other anniversaries, used for reference and prediction. They appeared annually, hence Jonson's joke, 'for twelve years yet to come' (14). 15–16. The new statesman carries indiscriminately the Roman historian **Tacitus**, news bulletins from Italy (*Gazetti*), and the European register of news (*Mercurii Gallo-Belgici*). 19. **Star-Chamber** a powerful, autonomous royal court presided over by the King's Council. **close** secret. 22. **con . . . heart** commit some register to memory.

Or every day someone at Rimee's looks,
    Or Bill's, and there he buys the names of books.
They all get Porta for the sundry ways   25
    To write in cipher, and the several keys
To ope the character. They've found the sleight
    With juice of lemons, onions, piss, to write,
To break up seals and close 'em. And they know,
    If the States make peace, how it will go   30
With England. All forbidden books they get,
    And of the Powder Plot they will talk yet;
At naming the French king their heads they shake,
    And at the pope and Spain slight faces make,
Or 'gainst the bishops for the Brethren rail,   35
    Much like those Brethren, thinking to prevail
With ignorance on us, as they have done
    On them; and, therefore, do not only shun
Others more modest but condemn us too,
    That know not so much state, wrong, as they do.   40

'Inviting a Friend to Supper'

Tonight, grave sir, both my poor house and I
    Do equally desire your company;
Not that we think us worthy such a guest,
    But that your worth will dignify our feast
With those that come, whose grace may make that seem   5
    Something, which else could hope for no esteem.
It is the fair acceptance, sir, creates
    The entertainment perfect, not the cates.

23–4. **Rimee's . . . Bill's** the shops of James Rimee and John Bill, two London booksellers. **24. names** (1) books to use for name-dropping, not for reading; (2) title-pages, sold separately. **25. Porta** Giovanni Battista della Porta, who wrote a book on secret writing, *De Furtivis Literarum Notis* (1563). **26. cipher** secret. **27. ope . . . character** decode the letters or symbols. **sleight** trick. The listed liquids (28) made invisible ink. **29. To . . . 'em** to open a seal (a wax impressure used on folded letters) in order to read someone else's mail and then to close it again. **30. States** The States General of the Low Countries (now Holland, Belgium, and Luxembourg) began negotiating with England's enemy, Spain, in 1604 and agreed to a truce in 1609. **32. Powder Plot** The plot, allegedly of Catholic extremists, to blow up the Houses of Parliament on 5 November 1605. **33. French king** Henri IV (1589–1610), who famously converted to Catholicism (1593), and issued the Edict of Nantes (1598), which made Catholicism the official religion of France and granted toleration to Protestants. **34. pope** Paul V (1605–21), who urged toleration of loyal Catholic subjects and condemned James's Oath of Allegiance in two Briefs (1606, 1607). The new statesmen exhibit fashionably anti-Catholic prejudices and fears. **35. bishops . . . Brethren** Anglicans . . . radical Puritans. See also Jonson's portrayal of Puritans in DRAMA. **40. state** statecraft.
'INVITING A FRIEND' Martial's invitations to supper (5. 78, 10. 48, 11. 52), featuring a list of appetizing foods and entertainments, inspire this adaptation. **5. whose** you whose. **7–8. creates . . . perfect** perfects the entertainment. **8. cates** cakes.

Yet shall you have, to rectify your palate,
    An olive, capers, or some better salad   10
Ush'ring the mutton, with a short-legged hen,
    If we can get her, full of eggs, and then
Lemons and wine for sauce; to these, a coney
    Is not to be despaired of for our money,
And though fowl now be scarce, yet there are clerks,   15
    The sky not falling, think we may have larks.
I'll tell you of more and lie, so you will come,
    Of partridge, pheasant, woodcock (of which some
May yet be there), and godwit, if we can,
    Knat, rail, and ruff, too. Howsoe'er, my man   20
Shall read a piece of Virgil, Tacitus,
    Livy, or of some better book to us,
Of which we'll speak our minds amidst our meat.
    And I'll profess no verses to repeat;
To this, if aught appear, which I not know of,   25
    That will the pastry, not my paper, show of.
Digestive cheese and fruit there sure will be;
    But that which most doth take my Muse and me
Is a pure cup of rich Canary wine,
    Which is the Mermaid's now but shall be mine,   30
Of which, had Horace or Anacreon tasted,
    Their lives as do their lines till now had lasted.
Tobacco, nectar, or the Thespian spring
    Are all but Luther's beer to this I sing.
Of this we will sup free but moderately.   35
    And we will have no Poley or Parrot by;
Nor shall our cups make any guilty men,
    But at our parting we will be as when
We innocently met. No simple word

9. **rectify** refine (by means of appetizers). 13. **coney** rabbit. 15. **clerks** shopkeepers. 16. Jonson humorously inverts the proverb, 'If the sky falls, we shall have larks.' 18–20. **partridge...ruff** game birds. 20. **Knat** knot, or sandpiper. **Howso'er** in any case. 25–6. In addition, if anything else appears, and I don't know if anything will, it will be a pastry from the chef rather than a poem from me. 29. **Canary wine** a light, sweet wine from the Canary islands. 30. **Mermaid's** The Mermaid was a famous tavern in Cheapside. 31. **Horace...Anacreon** two classical poets who wrote in praise of wine. 33–4. Exotic beverages—**Tobacco** (considered a drink), **nectar** (drink of the gods), and the **Thespian spring** (a mythological spring, sacred to the Muses)—are all weak beer to the wine that will be served. Jonson's association of weaker, Continental beer with Martin Luther gibes at the arch-reformer and his doctrine, a diluted, inferior form of Catholicism. 36. **Poley or Parrot** Robert Poley, a government spy who betrayed the Catholic Thomas Babington in 1586; Henry (?) Parrot, another spy, who once gave evidence against a Benedictine monk Mark Barkworth. 37–42. The references to anti-Catholic spies above condition the conventional ending, which promises that no unguarded words will cause unpleasant consequences (see Martial, 10. 48). Spies often infiltrated Catholic banquets and social occasions to gather evidence against the participants.

That shall be uttered at our mirthful board   40
   Shall make us sad next morning, or affright
The liberty that we'll enjoy tonight.

From 'Epistle to Katherine, Lady Aubigny'

'Tis only that can time and chance defeat,
   For he that once is good is ever great.
Wherewith, then, madam, can you better pay
   This blessing of your stars than by that way
Of virtue which you tread? What if alone,   5
   Without companions? 'Tis safe to have none.
In single paths dangers with ease are watched;
   Contagion in the press is soonest catched.
This makes that wisely you decline your life
   Far from the maze of custom, error, strife,   10
And keep an even and unaltered gait,
   Not looking by or back (like those that wait
Times and occasions to start forth and seem);
   Which, though the turning world may disesteem,
Because that studies spectacles and shows,   15
   And after varied, as fresh, objects goes,
Giddy with change and, therefore, cannot see
   Right the right way. Yet must your comfort be
Your conscience, and not wonder if none asks
   For truth's complexion, where they all wear masks.   20
Let who will follow fashions and attires,
   Maintain their liegers forth for foreign wires,
Melt down their husbands' land to pour away
   On the close groom and page on New Year's Day,
And almost all days after while they live   25
   (They find it both so witty and safe to give).
Let 'em on powders, oils, and paintings spend
   Till that no usurer nor his bawds dare lend
Them or their officers, and no man know

KATHERINE, LADY AUBIGNY In 1604 and for a period of five years thereafter, Jonson lodged with Esmé Stuart, Lord Aubigny, a Catholic relative of the king. The poem celebrates the impending birth of Lady Aubigny's first son in April 1612. **1. that** virtue. **3. Wherewith** with what. **8. Contagion ... press** disease in a crowd. **9. decline** turn away. **12. by** around. **wait** await. **14–20.** The language of this section, describing the solitary path of virtue and conscience in a world giddy with change, had special resonance for English Catholics. **22. leigers forth** agents abroad. **wires** frames used to support the hair or ruff. **24. close groom** secret servant. **27. paintings** cosmetics.

Whether it be a face they wear, or no.   30
Let 'em waste body and state, and after all,
   When their own parasites laugh at their fall,
May they have nothing left whereof they can
   Boast but how oft they have gone wrong to man,
And call it their brave sin. For such there be   35
   That do sin only for the infamy,
And never think how vice doth every hour
   Eat on her clients and someone devour.
You, madam, young have learned to shun these shelves,
   Whereon the most of mankind wrack themselves,   40
And, keeping a just course, have early put
   Into your harbour, and all passage shut
'Gainst storms or pirates that might charge your peace.
For which you worthy are the glad increase
   Of your blest womb, made fruitful from above,   45
To pay your lord the pledges of chaste love,
   And raise a noble stem to give the fame
To Clifton's blood that is denied their name.

'On My First Daughter'

Here lies, to each her parent's ruth,
Mary, the daughter of their youth.
Yet, all heaven's gifts being heaven's due,
It makes the father less to rue.
At six months' end she parted hence   5
With safety of her innocence,
Whose soul heaven's queen (whose name she bears),
In comfort of her mother's tears,
Hath placed amongst her virgin train;
Where while that severed doth remain,   10
This grave partakes the fleshly birth,
Which cover lightly, gentle earth.

35. brave fine (said sarcastically). **39. shelves** sandbanks or rocks under water. **45.** The language echoes the *Ave, Maria* and one of its sources, Elizabeth's greeting: 'Blessed art thou among women, and blessed is the fruit of thy womb' (Luke 1: 42). **47. stem** main line of descent. **48. Clifton's blood** Katherine was the daughter of Sir Gervase Clifton of Nottinghamshire.

FIRST DAUGHTER Mary, born 1598, died 6 months later. Ben Jonson's first son, Benjamin, died of the plague at age 7 in 1603 and occasioned the companion poem of grief, 'On my First Son' (*Epigrams* 45). **1. ruth** sorrow. **7. heaven's queen** the Virgin Mary, here imagined in Catholic terms as a queen attended by a virgin train, a comforter of the distressed. (See also Jonson's *Underwood* 66). **10. that severed** the soul apart in heaven **11. partakes** receives. **12. cover lightly** a classical formula ('sit tibi terra levis'); see Martial 5. 24, 9. 29, 11. 14 (*Ben Jonson*, ed. Ian Donaldson, 1985: 649–50).

'The Garland of the Blessed Virgin Mary', 1635

Here are five letters in this blessèd name,
Which, changed, a fivefold mystery design:
The 'M' the myrtle, 'A' the almonds claim,
'R', rose, 'I', Ivy, 'E', sweet eglantine.

These form thy garland. Whereof myrtle green,   5
The gladdest ground to all the numbered five,
Is so implexèd and laid in between
As love here studied to keep grace alive.

The second string is the sweet almond bloom,
Ymounted high upon Selinus' crest,   10
As it alone, and only it, had room,
To knit thy crown and glorify the rest.

The third is from the garden called the rose,
The eye of flowers, worthy for his scent
To top the fairest lily now that grows,   15
With wonder on the thorny regiment.

The fourth is humble ivy intersert,
But lowly laid as on the earth asleep,
Preservèd in her antique bed of vert;
No faith's more firm or flat than where 't doth creep.   20

But that which sums all is the eglantine,
Which of the field is cleped the sweetest briar,
Inflamed with ardour to that mystic shine
In Moses' bush, unwasted in the fire.

Thus love and hope and burning charity,   25
Divinest graces, are so intermixed,

'THE GARLAND' Herford and the Simpsons (xi. 159–60) make persuasive arguments in favour of Jonson's authorship; some contest the ascription. This poem by 'B.I.' prefaces Anthony Stafford's *The Female Glory* (1635), a Laudian tribute to the Virgin Mary. The poem may gloss an emblem or the pendant on the Bridgettine rosary, which consisted of seven meditative sections, each corresponding to a verse, as Paul Cubeta suggests ('Ben Jonson's Religious Lyrics', *Journal of English and German Philology*, 62, 1963: 96–110; see Donne's *La Corona* above). 2. **design** reveal. The acronym, in which each of the letters in a name stands for something else, is a traditional meditative device. 5. **myrtle** symbol of joyous love, occupying the base (**ground, 6**) of the garland. 7. **implexèd** entwined. 9. **almond** symbol of hope. 10. **Ymounted** mounted (archaic form). **Selinus** a mountain in Sicily. (This description of the almond derives from Spenser's *The Faerie Queene*, 1. 7. 32). 13. **rose** symbol of beauty. (See Hawkins, INSTRUCTIONS AND DEVOTIONS.) 14. **eye** choicest. 15. **lily** symbol of purity. 16. **regiment** array. 17. **ivy** symbol of humility and fidelity. **intersert** inserted. 19. **vert** green foliage. 20. **flat** absolute. 21. **eglantine** symbol of poetry and love. 22. **cleped** called. 24. **Moses' bush** God spoke to Moses through a burning bush, miraculously unconsumed by the fire (Exod. 3). The poet here associates this bush with Mary, mother and virgin.

With od'rous sweets and soft humility,
As if they adored the head whereon they're fixed.

The Reverse on the back side

These mysteries do point to three more great,
On the reverse of this your circling crown,   30
All pouring their full show'r of graces down,
The glorious trinity in union met.

Daughter, and mother, and the spouse of God,
Alike of kin to that most blessèd trine
Of persons, yet in union one divine.   35
How are thy gifts and graces blazed abroad!

Most holy and pure virgin, blessèd maid,
Sweet tree of life, King David's strength and tower,
The house of gold, the gate of heaven's power,
The morning star whose light our fall hath stayed.   40

Great queen of queens, most mild, most meek, most wise,
Most venerable, cause of all our joy,
Whose cheerful look our sadness doth destroy,
And art the spotless mirror to man's eyes.

The seat of sapience, the most lovely mother,   45
And most to be admirèd of thy sex,
Who mad'st us happy all in thy reflex,
By bringing forth God's only son, no other.

Thou throne of glory, beauteous as the moon,
The rosy morning, or the rising sun,   50
Who like a giant hastes his course to run,
Till he hath reached his twofold point of noon.

How are thy gifts and graces blazed abroad,
Through all the lines of this circumference,
T'imprint in all purged hearts this virgin sense   55
Of being daughter, mother, spouse of God!

The Reverse on the back side These verses ornament the other side of the imagined emblem or pendant; poetically, they are described as appearing on the reverse of Mary's crown (30). **29. mysteries** those virtues suggested by the name Marie, revealed by the flowers of her garland or **circling crown** (30). **32. trinity** i.e. Mary's threefold nature, her coincident roles as God's daughter, mother, and spouse. **34. trine** Trinity, the threefold existence of God in the persons of Father, Son, and Holy Spirit. **36. blazed abroad** proclaimed everywhere. **37–45.** Jonson draws these epithets from the Litany of Loreto, a traditional Catholic intercessory prayer (see Prayers and Hymns, INSTRUCTIONS AND DEVOTIONS). Jonson's lines translate the Latin advocations to Mary, *Turris davidica* (Tower of David), *Domus aurea* (House of gold), *Janua coeli* (Gate of heaven), *Stella matutina* (Morning star), *Causa nostra laetitiae* (Cause of our joy), *Sedes sapientiae* (Seat of wisdom), *Mater amabilis* (Mother most lovable), *Mater admirabilis* (Mother most admirable). **44. mirror** perhaps a reminiscence of another epithet, *Speculum Iustitiae* (Mirror of justice). **47. reflex** reflection. **52. twofold . . . noon** the high point of his journey, i.e. the time when the two hands of the clock point upright. **54. circumference** (1) the garland she wears; (2) the garland of the present poem of praise; (3) the garland of the rosary. **55. virgin sense** unique status.

'The Sinner's Sacrifice'
To the Holy Trinity

O holy, blessèd, glorious Trinity
Of persons, still one God in unity,
The faithful man's believèd mystery,
    Help, help to lift
Myself up to thee, harrowed, torn, and bruised   5
By sin and Satan; and my flesh misused,
As my heart lies in pieces, all confused,
    Oh, take my gift.
All-gracious God, the sinner's sacrifice,
A broken heart thou wert not wont despise,   10
But 'bove the fat of rams or bulls to prize
    An off'ring meet
For thy acceptance. Oh, behold me right
And take compassion on my grievous plight.
What odour can be, than a heart contrite,   15
    To thee more sweet?
Eternal Father, God who didst create
This all of nothing, gavest it form and fate,
And breath'st into it life and light with state
    To worship thee;   20
Eternal God the Son, who not denied'st
To take our nature, becam'st man, and died'st
To pay our debts upon thy cross, and cried'st
    'All's done in me';
Eternal Spirit, God from both proceeding,   25
Father and Son, the Comforter in breeding
Pure thoughts in man, with fiery zeal them feeding
    For acts of grace:

'THE SINNER'S SACRIFICE' The triple rhymes honour the trinity. (See also Constable's 'To God the Father' above.) Cubeta (1963: 103–7), moreover, observes that the poem is divided into three parts that correspond to the meditative model of St Bernard of Clairvaux. Lines 1–16 portray the speaker's *humilitas*, the recognition of his sinfulness; lines 7–36 portray *compassio*, love, of fellow man usually, here directed to the triune God; lines 37–48 portray *contemplatio*, the longed-for union with God. These divisions correspond to the three steps in the mystical journey, Purgation, Illumination, and Union, and also to the Ignatian emphasis on memory (of past sins), understanding (of God's great gifts), and will (finally turned to God alone). **9–16.** See Ps. 50: 18–19: 'For if thou hadst desired sacrifice, I would indeed have given it; with burnt offerings thou wilt not be delighted. A sacrifice to God is an afflicted spirit, a contrite and humbled heart, O God, thou wilt not despise.' **19. with state** ready. **24.** See John 19: 30 'It is consummated.'

Increase those acts, O glorious Trinity
Of persons, still one God in unity, 30
Till I attain the longed-for mystery
      Of seeing your face,
Beholding one in three, and three in one,
A Trinity, to shine in union!
The gladdest light dark man can think upon, 35
      Oh, grant it me!
Father, and Son, and Holy Ghost—you three
All coeternal in your majesty,
Distinct in persons, yet in unity,
      One God to see. 40
My Maker, Saviour, and my Sanctifier,
To hear, to meditate, sweeten my desire
With grace, with love, with cherishing entire.
      Oh, then how blest,
Among thy saints elected to abide, 45
And with thy angels placed side by side,
But in thy presence truly glorified,
      Shall I there rest!

JOHN BEAUMONT

Born to a Catholic family at Grace-Dieu, a former priory, John Beaumont (1584–1627), brother of the more famous playwright Francis Beaumont, married Elizabeth Fortescue, also a Catholic, and suffered financial penalties for recusancy. Beaumont wrote a clever mock-epic panegyric, *The Metamorphosis of Tobacco* (1602), a court entertainment, *The Theatre of Apollo* (1625), and poetry. In 1629 his son published a collection of Beaumont's poetry, *Bosworth Field* (1629), which shows a flair for drama and metaphysical conceit as well as a facility with rhyming couplets. The verses below on the Assumption and on the accident in Blackfriars, censored from all extant copies of *Bosworth Field*, display Beaumont respectively as Catholic lyricist and apologist. Beaumont's greatest work, *The Crown of Thorns* (wr. 1620–5), is extant only in manuscript. This long poem meditates on Christ's passion in the manner of contemporary emblematists such as the Jesuit Henry Hawkins (see INSTRUCTIONS AND DEVOTIONS), who develop themes by logical analysis and free metaphorical association. Focusing on the circle as symbol, Beaumont draws parallels from nature, science (including mathematics), medieval symbolism, Scripture, and

41. Here begins the final colloquy, or direct conversation with God.

Neoplatonic philosophy to reform sinners and promote holy living. The selections below end with praise of Mary, Queen of Scots.

'Upon the two great feasts of the Annunciation and Resurrection falling on the same day, March 25, 1627'

Thrice happy day, which sweetly dost combine
Two hemispheres in th'equinoctial line,
The one debasing God to earthly pain,
The other raising man to endless reign!
Christ's humble steps declining to the womb,   5
Touch heav'nly scales erected on his tomb.
We first with Gabriel must this prince convey
Into his chamber on the marriage day;
Then with the other angels clothed in white,
We will adore him in this conq'ring night.   10
The Son of God, assuming human breath,
Becomes a subject to his vassal Death,
That graves and hell, laid open by his strife,
May give us passage to a better life.
See for this work how things are newly styled: 15
Man is declared almighty, God, a child;
The Word made flesh is speechless, and the light
Begins from clouds and sets in depth of night.
Behold the sun, eclipsed for many years,
And ev'ry day more dusky robes he wears,   20
Till after total darkness, shining fair,
No moon shall bar his splendour from the air.
Let faithful souls this double feast attend
In two processions: let the first descend
The temple's stairs and with a downcast eye   25
Upon the lowest pavement prostrate lie;

UPON THE TWO GREAT FEASTS Compare Donne's poem, 'Upon the Annunciation and Passion Falling upon one Day'. **2. th'equinoctial line** the equator, where the north and south hemispheres meet. The coincidence of the two feasts provides a similar meeting of the divine and human spheres. **3. debasing** lowering. **6. scales** ladders. **7–8.** See Luke's account of the angel Gabriel greeting Mary and announcing that she has been chosen to bear Jesus into the world (1: 26–35). (See also Fig. 11.) **8. his chamber** i.e. Mary's womb. **9. angels...white** Luke (24: 4) and John (20: 12) tell of two angels clothed in white at Jesus' tomb. **13.** The opening of the graves looks ahead to the Last Judgement, when souls will be reunited with their bodies; the opening of hell refers to Christ's descent to limbo just before the Resurrection to free the virtuous souls imprisoned there. **16–18.** Compare the similar paradoxes in Robert Southwell's 'Nativity' poem above. **19. sun** with the usual sun/son pun. **20.** an allusion to the idea that humans continue to fall.

In creeping violets, white lilies, shine
Their humble thoughts and ev'ry pure design.
The other troop shall climb with sacred heat
The rich degrees of Solomon's bright seat;   30
In glowing roses fervent zeal they bear,
And in the azure fleur-de-lis appear
Celestial contemplations, which aspire
Above the sky up to th'immortal choir.

'Of the Assumption of our Blessed Lady'

Who is she that ascends so high,
   Next the heavenly king,
Round about whom angels fly,
   And her praises sing?

Who is she that adorned with light,   5
   Makes the sun her robe;
At whose feet the queen of night,
   Lays her changing globe?

To that crown direct thine eye,
   Which her head attires;   10
There thou mayst her name descry,
   Writ in starry fires.

This is she in whose pure womb,
   Heav'n's prince remained;
Therefore in no earthly tomb   15
   Can she be contained.

Heaven she was which held that fire,
   Whence the world took light;
And to heav'n doth now aspire
   Flames with flames to unite.   20

She that did so cleanly shine
   When our day begun,

27–8. The processing faithful celebrating the Annunciation carry violets, symbol of humility, and lilies, symbol of pure intentions. **30. Solomon's bright seat** symbol of earthly achievement, a high point from which to contemplate heaven. 'And Solomon sat on the throne of the Lord as king instead of David his father, and he pleased all, and all Israel obeyed him' (1 Paralipomenon 29: 23). **31–3.** The group celebrating the Resurrection carries roses, symbol of zeal, and the blue fleur-de-lis, symbol of contemplation. **33. aspire** rise.

'OF THE ASSUMPTION' The veneration of Mary in this poem probably caused its removal from all extant copies of *Bosworth Field*. **11. descry** perceive.

See how bright her beams decline,
Now she sits with the sun.

'On the death of many good people slain by the fall of a floor at a Catholic sermon in Blackfriars'

Man hath no safe defence, no place of rest,
Between the earth and mansion of the blest.
Raise him on high yet still he downward falls,
Depressing death our heavy bodies calls
To his low caves. No soul can pierce the skies, 5
But first the flesh must sink with hope to rise.
See here the trophies of that rig'rous hand,
Whose force no worldly mixture can withstand,
For it united elements divides,
And parts their friendly league to diff'rent sides. 10
In this most doleful picture we display
The gen'ral ruin on the Judgement Day.
Thrice happy they whom that last hour shall find,
So clearly watching in such ready mind
As was this blessèd flock, who filled their ears 15
With pious counsels and their eyes with tears,
Whose hearts were ravished with a sacred bell
And heavenly trumpet when the chamber fell.
And that the preacher's words might more prevail
When he describes this life, unsure and frail, 20
God by his death would confirmation give,
To make impression in our breasts that live.
Rest safe, dear saints, and may this fun'ral song
Become a charm to ev'ry serpent's tongue.

23. **decline** shine down.
'ON THE DEATH' Like the preceding, this poem was cancelled from all extant copies of *Bosworth Field*. The poem recalls an accident which came to be known as 'The Fatal Vesper', which occurred at the London house of the French ambassador on 26 October 1623, or in the New Style, 5 November, the anniversary of the Gunpowder Plot. Though the audience included some of their confession, Protestants seized upon the incident and resulting death of about a hundred persons as God's punishment of Catholics. Catholics such as John Beaumont and John Floyd, *A Word of Comfort* (1623, STC 11118), offered other explanations and consolation (see T. Harmsen, ed., *John Gee's Foot out of the Snare*, 1992: 49–56). **4. Depressing** (1) conquering; (2) lowering (by force). **8. worldly mixture** living being, made of spirit and flesh. **13. Thrice happy they** Compare John Floyd: 'Then were these men most happy whom the last hour, yea, moment of life, found in the noblest act of the divine service, hearing his holy word, with great content and devotion of soul' (*Word*, 1623, sig. G1). **19. the preacher's words** The preacher was Robert Drury, SJ, who was preaching not on the uncertainty of mortal life, as Beaumont suggests below, but on 'the precept of charity, persuading his devout auditors to love their enemies, to forgive injuries, to root revenge and rancour clean out of their heart' (*Word*, 1623, sig. D4ᵛ). The text was the parable of the unforgiving servant (Matt. 18. 23–35). **24. serpent's tongue** the detractors who moralized the incident as God's judgement on the Catholics.

From *The Crown of Thorns*

I sing of thorns transformed in bloody springs
To pearls, and raised above all earthly things,
Which, having dwelt below, dare now aspire
To crown his forehead whom the heav'ns admire.
My hand through forests hews mine entrance plain   5
To narrow gates which spacious joys contain.
Eternal, boundless, undependent might,
Whose palace is beyond access or sight,
Thou life of creatures, to whose piercing eye
Entangled thickets smooth and open lie,   10
Since thou with human nature wouldst combine
The heavenly lustre of thy rays divine,
Let fiery drops of thy redeeming blood
Secure my pace through this shady wood,
Where I have ventured from the prickly thorn   15
To gather flowers which yet no muse hath worn.

> .   .   .   .

Let lovesick poets wreaths of myrtle twine,
Let ivy cool the brow which sweats with wine,
Let him be crowned with never fading bays,
Whose lofty quill the sound of war displays,   20
Let those their smooth and dainty forehead bind,
With tender twigs blown off by every wind.
Give me a garland got and worn with pain,
Whose piercing points cleave fast into my brain,
Whose deep engraven prints far longer stand   25
Than lines which worldlings paint or write in sand.
Let rosy crowns the Thespian sisters please,
My soaring flight condemns untiring ease.
My muse with mountain's thorns her bosom fills,
Despising flowers which grow on lesser hills;   30
She aims at chaplets of a nobler kind,
Which more than Delphian fillets stir my mind.

---

1. **bloody springs** Christ's wounds. **5–6. My…gates** The poet's hand through the action of writing brings him to the heavenly gates. **13–14.** The drops of Christ's blood guide the poet through the earthly forest. **19. bays** the laurel wreath, ancient reward and symbol for accomplishment. **27. Thespian sisters** the Muses, goddesses of the arts. **31. chaplets** wreaths of flowers. **32. Delphian fillets** headbands from Delphi, here a symbol of pagan antiquity.

[Invocation]

You powerful spirits moving heavenly spheres,
Whose equal circles guide the sliding years,
You sirens whom the springs of light inspire,   35
Whose songs keep time with every dancing fire,
Whom sitting on their orbs each planet feels,
Whose music drives their ever-turning wheels,
Whom rude antiquity could blindly view,
And when the eightfold course of heaven she knew,   40
Conceiving some ninth power, whose general might
Should rule the choir and keep the concord right.
Or adding to those eight celestial strings
The ninth base sphere of sublunary things,
She hence the nine Aonian sisters made   45
Of your nine orders an unperfect shade.
From your high seats some quick'ning influence send,
Which, falling on my heart, may it extend
Beyond all forms which sides and corners bound,
And cast my thoughts into a spacious round,   50
To see my Saviour in this sphere divine,
And trace the Son in his ecliptic line.
The wise gymnosophists undazzled gaze
On Titan's face, and in the fiery blaze
Of his brave circle wondrous secrets find.   55
Oh, teach me then to fix my fervent mind,
Like true-born eagles, on this radiant sun,
And not prove bastard when his sight I shun.
Teach me to draw back to the eternal round
The knowledge of celestial circles drowned   60
In curious deeps, choked with erroneous thorns,
Exposed in fables to contempts and scorns.

33. **spheres** crystalline paths encircling the earth, through which angels were thought to move the planets and stars to celestial music. This world-view, the Ptolemaic conception of the universe, furnishes central metaphors for the poem. 35. **sirens** not the mythological temptresses but here the angelic singers who move the planets and stars in their orbits. 40. **eightfold course** the eight heavenly spheres of the Ptolemaic world-view. **she** i.e. rude antiquity. 41. **ninth power** the *primum mobile*, or ninth sphere, which turned the other eight. 43–4. **Or . . . things** an alternative reckoning to make up the nine spheres of the cosmos, the adding of earth instead of the *primum mobile*. 45. **nine Aonian sisters** the Muses. 47. **quick'ning** animating. 49. Unlike the circle, other shapes are imperfect because they have sides and corners (see below, 86–9). 52. **ecliptic line** the great orbit of the sun, a metaphor for the Son's life and death. 53. **gymnosophists** ancient, ascetic Hindu philosophers. 54. **Titan's face** the sun. 61. **deeps . . . thorns** the delusions and vanities of earthly life.

[Meditations on the Crown of Thorns]

Our God who thus to dazzled eyes appears,
Who guides the circles and contains the spheres,
Is truly in a circle here enclosed, 65
Upon his forehead for our sakes imposed.
O happy crown, which canst his brows enfold,
Whose wond'rous might no shape nor place can hold!
How could my mind to thy perfection reach
With dark'ned knowledge, did not faith me teach, 70
That he who in the Virgin's womb first lay,
And barred himself nine months from sight of day,
Whose godhead fills all things and is true light,
He for our sakes immured, and the bright
Effusions of his beams, which had no bound, 75
Now know their limits moving in this round.
Time measures his creator, place confines
Th'almighty, and revolves his endless lines;
To narrow compass he vouchsafes to draw
His spacious crown, which keeps the world in awe, 80
To make our garlands of an ample size,
That from his one may infinite arise.

.   .   .   .

A circle aptly may his head enclose,
Who fears no end and no beginning knows;
His purity and simple essence shine 85
In this fair round, which with a single line
The nimble hand by revolution draws,
But is in cornered forms constrained to pause.
This figure holds more bodies than the rest,
By which his wondrous glory is expressed, 90
Who can above the heavens man's nature raise,
And in his palm the world contains and sways.
Straight lines with new increase still forward run,
But circles, closed, their perfect course have done,
Admitting no addition. Hence we learn 95
Our Saviour's high perfection to discern,
Whose motions keep one journey and detest

70. **dark'ned** earthly and hence imperfect. 74. **immured** enclosed (in flesh). 82. **infinite** the innumerable garlands of suffering that good Christians wear for Christ.

Distracted paths which aim not at the best.
He to his servants doth this course prefix,
Since squares and trigons with confusion mix. 100
But every of these nobler forms repines
To traffic with another circle's lines:
They cross but in two points and touch in one,
Not willing to confound their limits known.
The lower spheres in higher orbs contained, 105
Are by this figure in firm union chained,
To show with what strict love and circling grace
The arms of God the sons of man embrace.
All other moving forms except a sphere
Leave empty spaces where the corners were, 110
But this, inclining to an endless race,
May ever move and never change the place,
To teach that God all things can always fill,
Unmoved can move, and labour resting still.
This form with equal height preserves the heart, 115
The root, the centre, in the lowest part,
And hence we learn our humble souls to keep
From all temptations when we fix them deep.
The lines run even hence to every side,
This shape endures no swelling length of pride. 120

[The four crowns]

In this our globe with several circles crowned,
The perfect fabric of the sphere is found.
Four crowns to them who strive in holy wars
Are due—of flowers, of thorns, of clouds, of stars.
The first is given to those whom God invites 125
To fervent love by insensible delights:
Th'approaching sun when from his tropics moves
To greet his spouse whom he entirely loves,
And now to parched and frozen grounds will bring

---

100. trigons triangles. **101. repines** shows discontent. **103.** Circles cross other circles only at two points and touch tangentially at one. **105–8.** The concentric circles of the spheres, surrounded by the *primum mobile*, represent God's encircling love for humanity. **112.** i.e. by rotation. **119.** Every radius in a circle is equal. **121 ff.** This section describes the various celestial crowns those who suffer for Christ may symbolically wear. The first, that of flowers, is the orbit of the sun; the second, of thorns, is the equinox, supposed to be the special solar orbit which makes night equal to day; the third, of clouds, is made of the orbits that pass around the desolate ends of the earth; the fourth, of stars, is the zodiac or belt of visible stars, divided into twelve parts or signs, based on constellations. **126. insensible delights** delights in non-sensory things.

The autumn's fruits and beauties of the spring.   130
The second garland Christ is pleased to make
For those who of his pains a part will take:
Them Phoebus in his equinoctial stays,
And makes the darkness even with the days.
Our thoughts must then be equally resigned,   135
As well to sorrows as to joys inclined.
The third is theirs whom desolation tries,
That virtue to a constant state may rise,
While they imagine in this depth of grief
That heaven is shut and yields them no relief,   140
And though our Saviour sees and aids their fight,
Yet show'rs of tears obscure them from his light.
The cold, straight wreaths which bind such pressèd souls,
Are like the circles nearest to the poles.
The fourth eternal crown twelve stars contains,   145
With this the spouse of Christ forever reigns;
The sun within this zodiac never leaves
The soul, which such a blessèd gift receives.

     .   .   .   .

Hence we behold the radiant milky way,
Where chainèd fires their mutual light display;   150
Whose mingled rays, which joined more powerful are,
Th'entangled points of piercing thorns declare.
And in some places this bright knot of beams
Divides itself, as into several streams,
And takes large islands from the heavenly main.   155
So when these boughs the head of Christ contain,
We find some empty spaces in the folds,
Through which the eye his sacred brow beholds.
See how his splendour parts the azure sky,
And shines the brighter, having darkness by;   160
So when swift ships the dusky sea divide,
They make white, frothy furrows as they slide.
See how the spacious world is compassed round
With one clear circle, where poor souls are found.
This plain and trodden way is soon descried   165
Among green fields, which lie on either side.

---

133. Them . . . stays The sun stops them at the time of the equinoxes. **144. poles** north and south extremities of the earth. The zodiac rolls a course oblique to those of the others, on a different axle and with different poles. **149 ff.** The crown of thorns here becomes transfigured into earth's celestial crown, the Milky Way. **165. descried** perceived.

This is the crown which heaven in triumph wears,
When full of golden spangles it appears.

[Mary, Queen of Scots]

Among those queens who deck their royal stems
On earth with pearls, in heaven with richer gems,   170
Shall we forget one glory of the north,
Triumphant Mary, who, dispersing forth
Her beams from snowy Caledonian hills,
This happy isle with princely offspring fills,
While two large realms, united in her son,   175
Laments the wrongs which they to her have done.
When Scotland closed in walls her free-born breath,
And England stood astonished at her death.
The blood which she from kingly veins received
Confirmed that faith to which her parents cleaved.   180
The miners of God's house destroyed this wall,
And joined her murder to our Church's fall.
But he who firmness to his rock imparts,
Erects new temples in religious hearts,
As he hath changed her short and earthly reign   185
For heavenly crowns, which no foul hand can stain,
So though with us material churches fail,
Devotion lives and shall at last prevail.

WILLIAM HABINGTON

Born into a recusant family in the Catholic stronghold of Hindlip Hall, William Habington (1605–54) received his education in Paris and Saint-Omer. He wrote a tragicomedy, *The Queen of Aragon* (1640), and some prose, notably *The History of Edward IV* (1640). Habington married Lucy Herbert, for whom he wrote his principal work, *Castara* (1634), a series of love poems, which, furnished by Catholic devotions to Mary and Teresa, show

169 ff. On the death of Mary, Queen of Scots, Catholic hope for the throne of England, see Fig. 6. 173. **Caledonian** Scottish. 175. **her son** James VI of Scotland and James I of England. Earlier Beaumont expressed hope for James's restoration of Catholicism: 'Pull up these roots of schism, let none divide | The married realms from Christ's unspotted bride' (fo. 134ᵛ). The poem ends with the hope that Charles I's mariage to Catholic Henrietta Maria, 'our second Marie', will restore Catholicism to England. 180. Like Mary herself and many others, Beaumont sees the execution as a martyrdom for the Catholic faith. 183. An allusion to Matt. 16: 18, a central text for Catholics who read it as God's institution of their Church on earth under the pope: 'And I say to thee that thou art Peter, and upon this rock I will build my church, and the gates of hell shall not prevail against it.'

lyrical elegance and a capacity for sudden shifts and surprise. The 1640 edition of *Castara* includes religious poetry, particularly powerful meditations on the Psalms and mutability.

'To Roses in the Bosom of Castara'

Ye blushing virgins happy are
In the chaste nunn'ry of her breasts,
For he'd profane so chaste a fair,
Whoe'er should call them Cupid's nests.

Transplanted thus, how bright ye grow,   5
How rich a perfume do ye yield!
In some close garden cowslips so
Are sweeter than i'th'open field.

In those white cloisters live secure
From the rude blasts of wanton breath,   10
Each hour more innocent and pure,
Till you shall wither into death.

Then that which living gave you room,
Your glorious sepulchre shall be.
There wants no marble for a tomb,   15
Whose breast hath marble been to me.

'To Castara: A Vow'

By those chaste lamps which yield a silent light
To the cold urns of virgins, by that night
Which, guilty of no crime, doth only hear
The vows of recluse nuns and th'anch'rite's prayer,
And by thy chaster self, my fervent zeal,   5
Like mountain ice which the north winds congeal
To purest crystal, feels no wanton fire.
But as the humble pilgrim, whose desire
Blest in Christ's cottage's view (by angels' hands

'TO ROSES' **2. nunn'ry** convent. **7. close** enclosed, secret. **cowslips** fragrant yellow flowers. **15. wants** lacks.

'TO CASTARA: A VOW' **4. recluse** cloistered. **anch'rite** person who has withdrawn from the world, usually for devotion to prayer and contemplation. **9. Blest ... view** Blessed in the sight of Christ's cottage. This and the next lines refer to the house of the Virgin and, subsequently, of the Holy Family. Legend has it that angels miraculously transported the house from Nazareth (not Bethlehem, 10) to Loreto in Italy at the end of the thirteenth century. The *Santa Casa di Loreto* has been a shrine for Catholic pilgrims ever since.

Transported from sad Bethl'em), wond'ring stands   10
At the great miracle, so I at thee,
Whose beauty is the shrine of chastity.
Thus my bright muse in a new orb shall move,
And even teach religion how to love.

'To Castara: Looking upon him'

Transfix me with that flaming dart,
I'th'eye, or breast, or any part,
So thou, Castara, spare my heart.

The cold Cimmerian, by that bright
Warm wound i'th'darkness of his night,   5
Might both recover heat and light;

The rugged Scythian gently move,
I'th'whisp'ring shadow of some grove
That's consecrate to sportive love;

December see the primrose grow,   10
The rivers in soft murmurs flow,
And from his head shake off his snow;

And crooked age might feel again
Those heats of which youth did complain,
While fresh blood swells each withered vein.   15

For the bright lustre of thy eyes,
Which but to warm them would suffice,
Would burn me to a sacrifice.

'Universum stratum eius versasti in infirmitate eius. David'

My Soul! When thou and I
Shall on our frighted death-bed lie,
Each moment watching when pale death
Shall snatch away our latest breath,

13. **orb** sphere, world.

'TO CASTARA: LOOKING UPON HIM' I. **flaming dart** A favourite Catholic image, the flaming dart derives
from classical traditions concerning Cupid's arrow, neo-Platonic lore about love, and mystical writings, especially those of
St Teresa of Ávila (see LIVES AND DEATHS; Fig. 7; Crashaw, POETRY). Here it is a glance from Castara's eyes. **4. Cimmerian** a
member of the tribe fabled to live in perpetual darkness (see Homer, *Od.* 11. 14). **7. Scythian** a member of the rugged, ancient
nomadic tribe that wandered over present-day Russia.

'UNIVERSUM STRATUM' The title comes from Ps. 40: 4, a line about God's sustaining care of the infirm, 'thou hast
turned all his couch in his sickness', i.e. made his bed, attended to his needs.

And between two long-joined lovers force   5
    An endless sad divorce,

    How wilt thou then, that are
My rational and nobler part,
Distort thy thoughts? How wilt thou try
To draw from weak philosophy   10
Some strength, and flatter thy poor state,
    'Cause 'tis the common fate?

    How will thy spirits pant
And tremble when they feel the want
Of th'usual organs, and that all   15
The vital powers begin to fall,
When 'tis decreed that thou must go,
    Yet whither, who can know?

    How fond and idle then
Will seem the mysteries of men?   20
How like some dull, ill-acted part,
The subtlest of proud human art?
How shallow e'en the deepest sea,
    When thus we ebb away?

    But how shall I (that is   25
My fainting earth) look pale at this,
Disjointed on the rack of pain?
How shall I murmur, how complain,
And craving all the aid of skill,
    Find none but what must kill?   30

    Which way so e'er my grief
Doth throw my fight to court relief,
I shall but meet despair, for all
Will prophesy my funeral.
The very silence of the room   35
    Will represent a tomb.

    And while my children's tears,
My wife's vain hopes but certain fears,
And counsels of divines advance
Death in each doleful circumstance,   40
I shall even a sad mourner be
    At my own obsequy.

5. two...lovers i.e. soul and body. 9. Distort twist and turn. 19. fond foolish. 42. obsequy funeral.

> For by examples I
> Must know that others' sorrows die
> Soon as ourselves, and none survive   45
> To keep our memories alive.
> Even our false tombs, as loath to say
> We once had life, decay.

GERTRUDE MORE

Great-great-granddaughter of Thomas More, Gertrude More (née Helen) (1604–33) inherited the family faith, Catholicism, its intellectual traditions, and its practice of educating women. Gertrude's father, Cresacre More, founded the English Benedictine convent at Cambrai and sent Gertrude there, along with her sister and two cousins. Under the spiritual direction of the great contemplative Dom Augustine Baker (see INSTRUCTIONS AND DEVOTIONS), More studied St Augustine as well as mystics such as St John of the Cross, St Teresa of Ávila, St Gertrude, and Walter Hilton. She wrote two prose works, *The Holy Practices of a Divine Lover* (1657) and *The Spiritual Exercises* (1658), both of which contain mystical poetry—poetry that charts the journey of the human soul to love and praise of God. In the selections below she stretches language to compass the infinite, and to express the ineffable; she employs powerful, elemental images (fire, light, darkness), paradoxes, and mystical symbolism (the seraphic dart, the wound of love, Christ as spouse).

'The Spiritual Exercises', 1658

'Frontispiece'
> Renownèd More, whose bloody fate
> England ne'er yet could expiate,
> Such was thy constant faith, so much
> Thy hope, thy charity was such
> As made thee twice a martyr prove,   5
> Of faith in death, in life of love.
> View here thy grandchild's broken heart,

---

47. **false tombs** memorials made from the sorrows of others.
FRONTISPIECE The poem appears opposite a portrait of Gertrude More in habit. **1. More** Thomas More.

Wounded with a seraphic dart,
Who, while she lived mortals among,
Thus to her spouse divine she sung: 10
'Mirror of beauty in whose face
The essence lives of every grace!
True lustre dwells in thy sole sphere;
Those glimmerings that sometimes appear
In this dark vale, this gloomy night,   15
Are shadows tipped with glowworm light.
Show me thy radiant parts above,
Where angels unconsumèd move,
Where amorous fire maintains their lives,
As man by breathing air survives.   20
But if, perchance, the mortal eye
That views thy dazzling looks must die,
With blind faith here I'll kiss them, and desire
To feel the heat before I see the fire.'

From 'Cantum Cygnaeum' (Swan Song)

My heart shall only this desire,
    That thou, my Lord, dispose,
Even as thou pleasest in all things,
    Till these mine eyes thou close
By death, which I so much desire,   5
    Because it will procure
Me to enjoy my God, my all,
    Where I shall be secure
That none from me can take my Lord;
    But for eternity,   10
I shall enjoy my only good,
    And to him ever be
United by a knot of love,
    Which nothing shall untie,

8. **seraphic dart** The arrow of a seraph, one of the seraphim, the highest order of angels. St Teresa, among others, envisioned the seraphic dart as an instrument that inflames the soul with love (see LIVES AND DEATHS; Fig. 7). 10. **spouse divine** Mystics such as St Teresa and St John of the Cross employ the metaphor of 'mystical marriage' to describe the total union with God that is the highest condition attainable by a human soul in this life. 11. **Mirror of beauty** Since God is the source of all beauty and humans know God indirectly by various reflections, he is sometimes imagined as a divine mirror. 'We see now through a glass and in a dark manner, but then face to face' (1 Cor. 13: 12). 21–2. Citing Exod. 33: 20, 'Man shall not see me, and live', St Thomas Aquinas articulated the Catholic belief that no human in this life can see the essence of God (*ST* Iq. 12 a.11).
'CANTUM CYGNAEUM' Dom Augustine Baker gave this title to these lines. 13. **knot of love** the mystical union of the contemplative soul and God. More wrote elsewhere, 'Never was there or can be imagined such a love as is between an humble soul and Thee' (sig. A⁵).

But will remain as permanent   15
   As his divinity.
O happy hour, when wilt thou come
   And set my spirit free,
That I may love and praise my God
   For perpetuity,   20
Contemplating his glorious face,
   With all that him adore,
Singing with them his sweetest praise,
   Forever and ever more!

'To Saint Augustine'

O glorious saint, whose heart did burn
   And flame with love divine,
Remember me, most sinful wretch,
   Who, hunger-starved, doth pine,
For want of that which thou enjoy'st   5
   In such abundant measure;
It is my God that I do mean,
   My joy and all my treasure.
Thy words, O saint, are truly sweet,
   Because thou dost address   10
Them unto him who's only meet
   Our mis'ries to redress.

'If we would die unto ourselves'

If we would die unto ourselves,
   And all things else but thee,
It would be natural to our souls
   For to ascend and be
United to our centre dear,   5
   To which our souls would hie,
Being as proper then to us,
   As fire to upwards fly.
Oh, let us, therefore, love my God,
   For love pertains to him,   10

'TO SAINT AUGUSTINE' untitled in the text. More introduced the poem by thanking God for the saints 'to whom thou hast given charge of me, and to whom I fly when my sins affright me, amongst whom next after thy dear mother, the queen of mercy, is my beloved St Augustine' (sig. Avii).

'IF WE WOULD DIE UNTO OURSELVES' This is the concluding section of a prayer/poem, 'which whosoever practiseth, shall find a spiritual internal life so easy, sweet, secure, and void of all questions' and will walk 'with a heavenly peace and security' (sig. Cii^v). 5. The poem describes here Union, i.e. the third and final stage of mystical progress, after Purgation and Illumination. (Compare Crashaw's 'Prayer' below.) 6. hie hasten.

And let our souls seek nothing else
    But in this love to swim,
Till we, absorbed by his sweet love,
    Return from whom we came,
Where we shall melt into that love,   15
    Which joyeth me to name.
And never can I it too much
    Speak of, or it desire,
Since that my God, who's love itself,
    Doth only love require.   20
Come, therefore, all, and let us love,
    And with a pure aspect,
Regard our God in all we do,
    And he will us protect.
Oh, that all things upon the earth   25
    Re-echoed with thy praise,
My everlasting glorious God,
    The ancient of days!
And it I wish with all my soul
    Incessantly to sing,   30
But seeing this I cannot do,
My sighs to heav'n shall ring.
Yea, if I writ out all the sea,
    Yet could I not express
The joy and comfort I do feel   35
    In what thou dost possess,
No gifts, or grace, nor comforts here,
    How great so e'er they be,
Can satiate my longing soul,
    While I possess not thee.   40
For thou art all my heart's desire,
    Yea, all that I do crave,
In earth or heaven, now and ever,
    Thou art all that I would have.
And I do wish with all my soul,   45
    That to thee I could pray,
With all my heart and all my strength,

15. melt...love The metaphor follows that of swimming (12) and suggests the transformation of self in divine love. 22. aspect gaze. 34–5. While the speaker lives time bound on earth, the mystical rapture of union remains unspeakable. 37–44. The entire poem and, specifically, this section arises from St Augustine's famous saying, 'Fecisti nos ad te et inquietum est cor nostrum donec requiescat in te' (Thou hast made us for thyself and our heart is troubled till it rests in thee, *Confessions* I. I).

Ten thousand times a day.
Let peoples, tribes, and tongues confess
    Unto thy majesty,   50
And let us never cease to sing
    '*Sanctus, Sanctus*' to thee.

'A Short Oblation'

My God, to thee I dedicate
    This simple work of mine,
And also with it heart and soul,
    To be forever thine.
No other motive will I have,   5
    Than by it thee to praise,
And stir up my poor frozen soul,
    By love itself to raise.
Oh, I desire neither tongue nor pen,
    But to extol God's praise,   10
In which excess I'll melt away
    Ten thousand, thousand ways,
And as one that is sick with love
    Engraves on every tree
The name and praise of him she loves,   15
    So shall it be with me.

RICHARD CRASHAW

Son of an anti-Catholic preacher who died in 1626, Richard Crashaw (1612–49) in 1635 became a fellow of Peterhouse College, centre of Laudianism (High Church Anglicanism) or, as the Puritans charged, popery. He contributed money and wrote poems to support the restoration of the Peterhouse chapel in Roman style. From 1639 he also held the curacy at Little St Mary's, a church adjoining Peterhouse. Crashaw's Catholic predilections, particularly his love of iconic adornment and the Virgin, aroused the ire of Puritans. Invoking the act against 'monuments of superstition or idolatry' (28 August 1643), Parliamentary commissioners in 1643 ransacked both of Crashaw's churches, tearing

---

49–50. **confess Unto** proclaim. **52.** *Sanctus, Sanctus* 'Holy, holy', the first part of the angelic hymn from Isa. 6: 3, which concludes the Eucharistic preface in the mass: 'Holy, holy, holy, Lord God of hosts, the heavens and earth are full of your glory, Hosanna in the highest. Blessed is he who comes in the name of the Lord, Hosanna in the highest.'

'A SHORT OBLATION' Oblation offering. The rest of the introduction reads 'of this small work by the writer-gatherer thereof to our most sweet and merciful God'. **13–15.** More transforms to divine ends one of the conventional expressions of love-sickness. (See Orlando's homage to Rosalind, *As You Like It*, 3.2.1–10.)

down pictures, inscriptions, and crucifixes. Crashaw left Cambridge and some time before 1646 formally entered the Roman Catholic church. Months before his death in 1649 he became a canon at the cathedral of the Santa Casa di Loreto, believed to be the house in which the Virgin Mary was born and received the Annunciation.

Though technically a Catholic only for the last few years of his life (when most of his poetry was published), Richard Crashaw has been rightly viewed (and wrongly dismissed) as a Catholic poet on the grounds of doctrine, devotion, and style. Crashaw translated six great hymns of the medieval Church, including two by Aquinas on the real presence in the Eucharist (see INSTRUCTIONS AND DEVOTIONS). His poetry reflects a life-long devotion to the Virgin Mary, evident below in the translation of *Stabat Mater Dolorosa*. Crashaw also venerates the saints, especially Mary Magdalen and Teresa of Ávila, two favourites of the European Catholic Reformation. He illustrates the nature of contrition in his tribute to Magdalen, 'The Weeper', an exercise in the literature of tears. Among the poems written to honour Teresa of Ávila, 'The Flaming Heart' explores the erotic wounding and self-annihilation of mystical experience, as does the 'Ode' in a prayer-book (compare Bernini's depiction of Teresa in mystical ecstasy, Fig. 7). The final chorus from the 'Holy Nativity' celebrates lyrically the birth of Christ. 'The Hymn to the Name above every Name, the Name of Jesus', a symphonic masterpiece, moves from meditation on biblical texts to a vision of the Last Judgement. Frequently adapting Jesuit models, combining the natural and supernatural, the erotic and the sacred, fusing the arts of sacred music and poetry, Crashaw's work stands as an exemplary achievement of the Catholic baroque—profuse in imagery, abundant in theatrical emotion, and rich in intellectual energy.

From 'Upon the Ensuing Treatises', 1635

> Be it enacted then,
> By the fair laws of thy firm-pointed pen,
> God's services no longer shall put on
> A sluttishness for pure religion;
> No longer shall our churches' frighted stones   5
> Lie scattered like the burnt and martyred bones
> Of dead devotion, nor faint marbles weep
> In their sad ruins, nor Religion keep

'UPON THE ENSUING TREATISES' This poem, prefacing Robert Shelford's Laudian *Five Pious and Learned Discourses* (1635), endorsed the use of church ornament and the practice of charity, while denying that the pope was the Antichrist. 2. **thy** i.e. that of Religion, who arises to her former splendour in the beginning of the poem. 4. **sluttishness...religion** slovenliness in the name of true worship. The line attacks Puritans for purging churches of their proper architecture and ornaments.

A melancholy mansion in those cold
Urns. Like God's sanctuaries they looked of old;
Now seem they temples consecrate to none,   10
Or to a new god, Desolation.
No more the hypocrite shall th'upright be
Because he's stiff, and will confess no knee;
While others bend their knee, no more shalt thou,
Disdainful dust and ashes, bend thy brow,   15
Nor on God's altar cast two scorching eyes,
Baked in hot scorn, for a burnt sacrifice,
But for a lamb, thy tame and tender heart,
New struck by love, still trembling on his dart,
Or for two turtle doves it shall suffice   20
To bring a pair of meek and humble eyes.
This shall from henceforth be the masculine theme
Pulpits and pens shall sweat in to redeem
Virtue to action, that life-feeding flame
That keeps Religion warm, not swell a name   25
Of faith, a mountain word made up of air,
With those dear spoils that wont to dress the fair
And fruitful Charity's full breasts (of old),
Turning her out to tremble in the cold.
What can the poor hope from us when we be   30
Uncharitable ev'n to charity?
Nor shall our zealous ones still have a fling
At that most horrible and hornèd thing,
Forsooth, the pope; by which black name they call
The Turk, the devil, furies, hell, and all,   35
And something more: oh, he is Antichrist!
Doubt this and doubt, say they, that Christ is Christ.
Why, 'tis a point of faith. Whate'er it be,
I'm sure it is no point of charity.
In sum, no longer shall our people hope   40
To be a true Protestant is but to hate the pope.

12. **shall . . . be** shall be considered upright. 13. **confess no knee** refuse to kneel. 14–19. **no . . . dart** No longer will the Puritan offer scorn to the altar but, now awed by the beauty of restored churches, he will offer a heart new struck by love. 17. **for** as. 22. **This** proper devotional activity, including works of charity. 23–4. **redeem Virtue to** recover virtue in. 25. **swell a name** make a show. 26. **mountain word** word made into a mountain. Crashaw criticizes the Protestant doctrine of *sola fides* (faith alone), which denied the salvific value of good works. 27–9. No longer will Puritans attribute to faith alone the benefits (**spoils**) that used to be properly attributed to charity, who now, abandoned, trembles in the cold. 27. **wont** i.e. were wont, used to. 28. **full breasts** an iconographical attribute of Charity.

From 'A Pathetical Descant upon the Devout Plainsong of *Stabat Mater Dolorosa*'

In shade of death's sad tree
   Stood doleful she.
Ah, she! Now by none other
Name to be known, alas, but sorrow's mother.
   Before her eyes   5
Hers and the whole world's joys,
Hanging all torn she sees, and in his woes
And pains her pangs and throes.
Each wound of his from every part,
All more at home in her own heart.   10

   What kind of marble, then,
   Is that cold man
   Who can look on and see,
Not keep such noble sorrows company?
   Sure, e'en from you,   15
   My flints, some drops are due,
To see so many unkind swords contest
   So fast for one soft breast,
While with a faithful, mutual, flood
Her eyes bleed tears, his wounds weep blood.   20

.   .   .   .

   Shall I set there
   So deep a share,
   Dear wounds, and only now
In sorrows draw no dividend with you?
   Oh, be more wise   25
   If not more just, mine eyes!
Flow, tardy founts, and into decent show'rs
   Dissolve my days and hours.

PATHETICAL . . . PLAINSONG a sorrowful musical accompaniment, with variations, to the melody, *Stabat Mater Dolorosa*, 'The mother of sorrows was standing', one of the greatest Latin hymns, based on the prophecy that a sword of sorrow would pierce Mary's heart (Luke 2: 35). Crashaw freely transforms the stately, mournful Latin into an emotional dramatic scene. See Southwell's 'The Virgin Mary to Christ on the Cross' above. **1 ff.** The hymn begins 'Stabat mater dolorosa, | Iuxta crucem lacrymosa, | Dum pendebat filius. | Cuius animam gementem, | Contristantem et dolentem, | Pertransivit gladius' (At the cross her station keeping, stood the mournful mother weeping, close to Jesus at the last. Through her heart, his sorrow sharing, all his bitter anguish bearing, now at length the sword has passed, tr. traditional.) **1. tree** the cross. **16. flints** stones, proverbial for hardness, here the eyes of the poet. **22. share** portion, with a commercial meaning picked up in **dividend** (24) below. The speaker, claiming his share in the redemption, urges himself in the following lines to share also in Christ's suffering. **27. decent** fitting.

And if thou yet, faint soul, defer
To bleed with him, fail not to weep with her.   30

    Rich queen, lend some relief,
    At least an alms of grief,
    To a heart who, by sad right of sin,
Could prove the whole sum (too sure) due to him.
    By all those stings   35
    Of love, sweet bitter things,
Which these torn hands transcribed on thy true heart,
    Oh, teach mine too the art
To study him so, till we mix
Wounds, and become one crucifix.   40

    Oh, let me suck the wine
    So long of this chaste vine,
    Till, drunk of the dear wounds, I be
A lost thing to the world, as it to me.
    O faithful friend   45
    Of me and of my end!
Fold up my life in love and lay't beneath
    My dear Lord's vital death.
Lo, heart, thy hope's whole plea! Her precious breath
Poured out in prayers for thee, thy Lord's in death.   50

Intercessor Mary

From 'Saint Mary Magdalen, or The Weeper'

31. relief i.e. some portion of your sorrow. Metaphorically the speaker is a beggar and Mary is rich in sorrow. **34. prove...him** merit all the sorrow caused by human sin. **37. torn hands** the nailed hands of Christ (which transcribed the sorrows in Mary's heart). **42. vine** Christ is the vine that gives the blood/wine of eternal life. **48. vital** life-giving. **49–50**. The poem closes with an image of Mary as intercessor, praying that the speaker, at the time of his death, may belong totally to the Lord.

Lo where a wounded heart with bleeding eyes conspire,
Is she a flaming fountain or a weeping fire?

> Hail, sister springs!
> Parents of silver-footed rills,
> Ever bubbling things,
> Thawing crystal, snowy hills,
> Still spending, never spent! I mean   5
> Thy fair eyes, sweet Magdalen!

> Heavens thy fair eyes be,
> Heavens of ever-falling stars;
> 'Tis seed-time still with thee,
> And stars thou sow'st, whose harvest dares   10
> Promise the earth to counter-shine
> Whatever makes heav'n's forehead fine.

> But we're deceivèd all.
> Stars, indeed, they are too true,
> For they but seem to fall,   15
> As heav'n's other spangles do.
> It is not for our earth and us
> To shine in things so precious.

> Upwards thou dost weep.
> Heav'n's bosom drinks the gentle stream.   20
> Where the milky rivers creep,
> Thine floats above and is the cream.
> Waters above th'heav'ns, what they be,
> We're taught best by thy tears and thee.

> .   .   .   .

> 'Twas his well-pointed dart   25
> That digged these wells and dressed this vine,
> And taught the wounded heart
> The way into these weeping eyne.
> Vain loves avaunt! Bold hands forbear!
> The Lamb hath dipped his white foot here.   30

'SAINT MARY MAGDALEN' The Catholic Reformation especially revered this saint for her thirty years of penance after Christ's death. (See Southwell's 'St Peter's Tears' above and Lodge's *Prosopopeia*, **Fiction**.) **2. rills** streams. **9–12.** The conceit depicts the tears as stars that fall to the ground as seeds and promise a harvest of more stars. (The next stanzas correct the conceit by noting that the tears fall upwards.) **11. counter-shine** shine against (the stars above). **21. milky rivers** the Milky Way, a path to heaven. **25. his** Christ's. **28. eyne** eyes. **29. avaunt** begone! The God-inspired tears purify the weeper from all earthly loves.

And now where'er he strays
Among the Galilean mountains
Or more unwelcome ways,
He's followed by two faithful fountains,
Two walking baths, two weeping motions,   35
Portable and compendious oceans.

 . . . . . .

Say, the bright brothers,
The fugitive sons of those fair eyes,
Your fruitful mothers!
What make you here? What hopes can 'tice   40
You to be born? What cause can borrow
You from those nests of noble sorrow?

Whither away so fast?
For sure the sordid earth
Your sweetness cannot taste,   45
Nor does the dust deserve your birth.
Sweet, whither haste you then? Oh, say
Why you trip so fast away?

'We go not to seek
The darlings of Aurora's bed,   50
The rose's modest cheek,
Nor the violet's humble head,
Though the field's eyes too weepers be,
Because they want such tears as we.

'Much less we mean to trace   55
The fortune of inferior gems,
Preferred to some proud face,
Or perched upon feared diadems.
Crowned heads are toys. We go to meet
A worthy object, our Lord's feet.'   60

34–6. The **fountains** suggest contrition arising from the heart of the sinner; the **baths**, the purgation of sin; the **motions**, the vigour of the penance; the **oceans**, the magnitude of sorrow (Crashaw, *Complete Poetry*, ed. G. Williams, 1970: 133). **37 ff.** These stanzas, which conclude the poem, comprise a dialogue between the speaker and the tears. **40.** 'tice entice. **50. Aurora** goddess of dawn. The tears reply that they do not wish to be drops of dew or (in the next stanza) gems. **57. Preferred** presented.

From 'The Flaming Heart'

O heart! The equal poise of love's both parts,
Big alike with wounds and darts,
Live in these conquering leaves, live all the same,
And walk through all tongues one triumphant flame.
Live here, great heart, and love and die and kill,　　　　5
And bleed and wound and yield and conquer still.
Let this immortal life where e'er it comes
Walk in a crowd of loves and martyrdoms.
Let mystic deaths wait on't, and wise souls be
The love-slain witnesses of this life of thee.　　　　10
O sweet incendiary! Show here thy art
Upon this carcass of a hard, cold heart;
Let all thy scattered shafts of light that play
Among the leaves of thy large books of day,
Combined against this breast at once break in,　　　　15
And take away from me myself and sin.
This gracious robbery shall thy bounty be,
And my best fortunes such fair spoils of me.
O thou undaunted daughter of desires!
By all thy dower of lights and fires,　　　　20
By all the eagle in thee, all the dove,
By all thy lives and deaths of love,
By thy large draughts of intellectual day,
And by thy thirsts of love more large than they,
By all thy brim-filled bowls of fierce desire,　　　　25
By thy last morning's draught of liquid fire,
By the full kingdom of that final kiss
That seized thy parting soul and sealed thee his,
By all the heav'ns thou hast in him,
Fair sister of the seraphim,　　　　30
By all of him we have in thee,
Leave nothing of myself in me.

'THE FLAMING HEART' One of Crashaw's three poems to Saint Teresa (see her account of the transverberation above, LIVES AND DEATHS, and Fig. 7). **1. heart** Teresa's heart, on fire with God's love for her and her love for God. **poise... parts** balance of love's active and passive qualities, i.e. the capacity to wound and be wounded. **3. leaves** pages (of Teresa's *Vida*). **11. incendiary** fire starter. **14. day** intellectual or spiritual light. **18. spoils** ruins. The speaker hopes for such ruination as his best fate. **20. dower** dowry, as Christ's bride. **21. eagle... dove** The eagle suggests wisdom and power, the dove, love and gentleness. **23. draughts** swallows. **30. seraphim** highest order of angels, associated with fire.

> Let me so read thy life that I
> Unto all life of mine may die.

From 'Prayer: An Ode which was Prefixed to a Little Prayer Book Given to a Young Gentlewoman'

Delicious deaths, soft exhalations
Of soul, dear and divine annihilations,
   A thousand unknown rites
Of joys and rarefied delights,
A hundred thousand goods, glories, and graces,   5
   And many a mystic thing
   Which the divine embraces
Of the dear spouse of spirits with them will bring,
   For which it is no shame
That dull mortality must not know a name   10
   Of all this store
Of blessings and ten thousand more.
   If when He come
   He find the heart from home,
   Doubtless, he will unload   15
   Himself some other where,
   And pour abroad
   His precious sweets
On the fair soul whom first he meets.
O fair, O fortunate, O rich, O dear,   20
O happy and thrice happy she,
   Selected dove,
   Whoe'er she be,
   Whose early love
   With wingèd vows   25
Makes haste to meet her morning spouse,
And close with his immortal kisses.
Happy, indeed, who never misses
To improve that precious hour,

PRAYER BOOK The Book of Common Prayer. Inspired by St Teresa's writings, this ode depicts the mystical progress of the soul through Purgation and Illumination to Union with God. This section expresses the rapture of the final stage. (Compare G. More, 'If we should die', above.) **8. spouse** The image of the soul as the bride and Christ as bridegroom, venerable in Christian traditions, especially the commentaries on Canticles. **10.** Mystics continually affirm the incapacity of language to convey the sublime experience. **27. close with** encounter. **29. improve** profit from.

And every day   30
    Seize her sweet prey,
All fresh and fragrant as he rises,
Dropping with a balmy shower
A delicious dew of spices.
Oh, let the blissful heart hold fast   35
Her heav'nly armful; she shall taste
At once ten thousand paradises;
    She shall have power
    To rifle and deflower
The rich and roseal spring of those rare sweets, 40
Which with a swelling bosom there she meets,
    Boundless and infinite,
    Bottomless treasures
Of pure, inebriating pleasures.
Happy proof! She shall discover   45
    What joy, what bliss,
How many heav'ns at once it is
To have her God become her lover.

From 'Hymn in the Holy Nativity'

[Final chorus]

Welcome all wonders in one sight!
Eternity shut in a span,
    Summer in winter, day in night,
Heaven in earth, and God in man.
    Great little one, whose all-embracing birth   5
Lifts earth to heaven, stoops heaven to earth.

    Welcome, though nor to gold nor silk,
To more than Caesar's birthright is.
    Two sister-seas of virgin milk,
With many a rarely-tempered kiss,   10
    That breathes at once both maid and mother,
Warms in the one, cools in the other.

40. **roseal** roseate. **45. proof** conclusion.
'HYMN IN THE HOLY NATIVITY'   The first of Crashaw's three Christmas hymns (followed by 'Circumcision Hymn' and 'Epiphany Hymn'), and sung by the shepherds; 'And the shepherds returned, glorifying and praising God for all the things they had heard and seen, as it was told unto them' (Luke 2: 20). **8. Caesar's birthright** an allusion to Jesus' saying, 'Render therefore to Caesar the things that are Caesar's, and to God, the things that are God's' (Matt. 22: 21). **12.** Mary's breast grows warm as she is a nursing mother, but remains cool as she is a chaste maid. The paradox signals her unique status.

Welcome, though not to those gay flies,
Gilded i'th' beams of earthly kings,
   Slippery souls in smiling eyes,   15
But to poor shepherds, home-spun things,
   Whose wealth's their flock, whose wit, to be
Well read in their simplicity.

   Yet when young April's husband, show'rs,
Shall bless the fruitful Maia's bed,   20
   We'll bring the first-born of her flow'rs
To kiss thy feet and crown thy head.
   To thee, dread lamb, whose love must keep
The shepherds, more than they the sheep.

   To thee, meek majesty, soft king   25
Of simple graces and sweet loves,
   Each of us his lamb will bring,
Each his pair of silver doves,
   Till burnt at last in fire of thy fair eyes,
Ourselves become our own best sacrifice.   30

From 'To the Name above Every Name, the Name of Jesus: A Hymn'

I sing the name which none can say,
But touched with an interior ray,
The name of our new peace, our good,
Our bliss and supernatural blood,
The name of all our lives and loves.   5
Hearken and help, ye holy doves!
The high-born brood of day, you bright
Candidates of blissful light,
The heirs elect of love, whose names belong

13. **flies** courtiers. 20. **Maia** Roman earth goddess, associated with spring and fertility, eponym for the month of May, here made fruitful by her husband, April rain.

'TO THE NAME' Devotion to the Holy Name of Jesus has a long and venerable history in the Church, including St Bernard, many popes from the Middle Ages on, and St Bernardino of Siena. The Jesuits adopted IHS (the first three letters of Jesus in Greek) as the emblem of their society and titled their mother church in Rome Santissimo Nome di Gesù, 'The Holy Name of Jesus' (see Fig. 3). Written to celebrate the Feast of the Holy Name (second Sunday after Epiphany), the poem is an extended meditation on Philippians 2: 9–10: 'For which cause God also hath exalted him and hath given him a name which is above all names: That in the name of Jesus every knee should bow, of those that are in heaven, on earth, and under earth.' Psalm 56, which praises God, is also a central text. **1. none can say** Hebrew traditions considered the name of God unspeakable. The poem never actually says the name of Jesus. **2. But touched** but those touched. **ray** the light of conscience or divine grace. **8. Candidates** those clothed in white robes (from *candidatus*), i.e. souls or angels in heaven.

Unto the everlasting life of song, 10
All ye wise souls, who in the wealthy breast
Of this unbounded name build your warm nest.
Awake, my glory. Soul, if such thou be,
And that fair word at all refer to thee,
   Awake and sing, 15
   And be all wing!
Bring hither thy whole self, and let me see
What of thy parent heav'n yet speaks in thee.
   Oh, thou art poor
   Of noble powers, I see, 20
And full of nothing else but empty me,
Narrow and low and infinitely less
Than this great morning's mighty business.
   One little world or two,
   Alas, will never do. 25
   We must have store.
Go, soul, out of thyself and seek for more.
   Go and request
Great nature for the key of her huge chest
Of heav'ns, the self-involving set of spheres, 30
Which dull mortality more feels than hears;
   Then rouse the nest
Of nimble art, and traverse round
The airy shop of soul-appeasing sound,
And beat a summons in the same 35
   All-sovereign name
To warn each several kind
And shape of sweetness, be they such
   As sigh with supple wind,
   Or answer artful touch, 40
That they convene and come away,
To wait at the love-crowned doors of
   This illustrious day.
Shall we dare this, my soul? We'll do't and bring
No other note for't but the name we sing. 45

12. This line ends the first part of the Ignatian meditation, the proposal of subject and introductory prayer. The second part, the preliminary self-address extends through line 45 (L. Martz, *The Poetry of Meditation*, 1954, rev. 1962: 337–41). 21. The speaker realizes his own sinfulness and turns to others for help. 24. **One little world** i.e. himself. 26. **store** abundance. 30. **self-involving...spheres** rotating spheres of the Ptolemaic universe, thought to produce celestial harmonies inaudible to mortals. 37. **several kind** separate kind of musical instrument.

Wake, lute and harp,
And every sweet-lipped thing
That talks with tuneful string;
Start into life and leap with me
Into a hasty fit-tuned harmony.   50
Nor must you think it much
T'obey my bolder touch;
I have authority in love's name to take you,
And to the work of love this morning wake you.
Wake, in the name   55
Of him who never sleeps, all things that are,
Or, what's the same,
Are musical!
Answer my call,
And come along,   60
Help me to meditate mine immortal song.
Come, ye soft ministers of sweet, sad mirth,
Bring all your household stuff of heav'n on earth;
Oh, you, my soul's most certain wings,
Complaining pipes and prattling strings,   65
Bring all the store
Of sweets you have, and murmur that you have no more.
Come near to part,
Nature and art,
Come and come strong   70
To the conspiracy of our spacious song.
Bring all the powers of praise
Your provinces of well-united worlds can raise,
Bring all your lutes and harps of heav'n and earth,
Whate'er cooperates to the common mirth,   75
Vessels of vocal joys,
Or you, more noble architects of intellectual noise,
Cymbals of heav'n or human spheres,
Solicitors of souls or ears.
And when you're come with all   80
That you can bring or we can call,
Oh, may you fix
Forever here, and mix

---

46. Here begins the address to all creatures to ask for assistance, followed by the address to the speaker himself (**88–104**) (Martz, *Meditation*, 341–5). **50. fit-tuned** tuned to a song. **71. conspiracy** (1) group; (2) breathing together (from *conspirare*).

Yourselves into the long
And everlasting series of a deathless song.   85
Mix all your many worlds above,
And lose them into one of love.
  Cheer thee, my heart,
  For thou too hast thy part
  And place in the great throng   90
Of this unbounded, all-embracing song.
  Powers of my soul, be proud!
  And speak aloud
To all the dear-bought nations this redeeming name,
And in the wealth of one rich word proclaim   95
New similes to nature.
  May it be no wrong,
Blest heav'ns, to you and your superior song,
That we, dark sons of dust and sorrow,
  A while dare borrow   100
The name of your delights and our desires,
And fit it to so far inferior lyres.
Our murmurs have their music too,
Ye mighty orbs, as well as you.

         .   .   .   .

Oh, that it were as it was wont to be!   105
When thy old friends of fire, all full of thee,
Fought against frowns with smiles, gave glorious chase
To persecutions, and against the face
Of death and fiercest dangers durst with brave
And sober pace march on to meet a grave.   110
On their bold breasts about the world they bore thee,
And to the teeth of hell stood up to teach thee;
In centre of their inmost souls they wore thee,
Where racks and torments strived in vain to reach thee.
  Little, alas, thought they   115
Who tore the fair breasts of thy friends,
  Their fury but made way
For thee, and served them in thy glorious ends.
What did their weapons but with wider pores
Enlarge thy flaming-breasted lovers,   120

105. Before this line the omitted sections of the poem invoke and celebrate the name, engaging love, the will, and the affections. This section begins the conclusion, which contrasts the faith of the ancient martyrs with the 'sons of shame' who do not kneel before the holy name of Jesus. 118. them i.e. the martyrs. 119. pores openings.

More freely to transpire
    That impatient fire
The heart that hides thee hardly covers?
What did their weapons but set wide the doors
For thee? Fair, purple doors of love's devising,   125
The ruby windows which enriched the east
    Of thy so oft-repeated rising,
Each wound of theirs was thy new morning,
And re-enthroned thee in thy rosy nest,
With blush of thine own blood thy day adorning.   130
It was the wit of love o'erflowed the bounds
Of wrath, and made thy way through all those wounds.
Welcome dear, all-adorèd name!
    For sure there is no knee
    That knows not thee.   135
Or if there be such sons of shame,
    Alas, what will they do
    When stubborn rocks shall bow,
And hills hang down their heav'n-saluting heads
    To seek for humble beds   140
Of dust, where in the bashful shades of night,
Next to their own low nothing they may lie,
And couch before the dazzling light of thy dread majesty.
They that by love's mild dictate now
    Will not adore thee,   145
Shall then with just confusion bow
    And break before thee.

121. **transpire** breathe forth. **125–30.** The profusion of images here describes the martyrs' wounds, which, like daybreak, manifest Christ again and again to the world. **131. wit** knowledge. **138 ff.** Crashaw here uses scriptural imagery (Isa. 40: 4; 64: 1–3) to depict the Last Judgement. **143. couch** lie down.

INSTRUCTIONS AND DEVOTIONS

Early modern Catholic instructions and devotions retain important continuities with the patristic and medieval past. St Augustine, St Benedict, St Francis of Assisi, and St Bernard of Clairvaux cast giant shadows over early modern Europe. Their rules, series of prescriptions for monastic living, working, and praying, organize the lives of traditional religious orders, reformed branches, and lay affiliates. Hagiographies also proliferate in the early modern period, the *Legenda Aurea* of Jacobus de Voragine (thirteenth century), spawning many subsequent lives of saints and reports of their miracles. John Falconer, for example, translates the life of the seventh-century St Winifred to illuminate the darkness of Great Britain ten centuries later. The great medieval synthesis of St Thomas Aquinas continues to find devotional expression in his beautiful hymns celebrating the Eucharist, here represented by early modern translations of the *Pange, lingua, Lauda, Sion*, and *Adoro te*. The stringent piety of the *Devotio moderna*, a late fourteenth-century reform movement, lives on in numerous translations of Thomas à Kempis's *Imitation of Christ*. Medieval prayers remain potent—the translated, annotated, and revised psalters, liturgical sequences, primers, and daily offices. The faithful everywhere pray traditional hymns and devotions. Reciting the 'Prayer unto the wounds of Christ', an emotional meditation on the suffering of Jesus, the average Elizabethan Catholic or Protestant probably would have been surprised to learn that those five wounds served as an emblem for the Pilgrimage of Grace, a rebellion against Henry VIII in 1536, and also for the Northern Rebellion against Elizabeth in 1569. Devotional traditions arising from centuries of belief had a deeply resonant and affective power that transcended political or confessional appropriation.

Forces of continuity and change contest each other also in the devotional traditions concerning Mary, *stella maris* (star of the sea), *regina caeli* (queen of heaven), *mater dolorosa* (sorrowful mother). Mary occupies a central place in early modern Catholic devotion as the accessible human mother who reversed the sin of Eve and made possible the Incarnation through a profound gesture of humility and acceptance. Mary's response to Gabriel's message furnishes many meditations (see John Bucke below) and artistic representations of the Annunciation, among them Fra Angelico's magnificent fresco in San Marco, Florence (see Fig. 11). The beautiful young virgin, arms folded in a gesture of submission, emptied of her own desires (*kenosis*), opens herself to God's will, her eyes alone expressing, perhaps, a trace of sadness at the Passion to come. The line of her gaze moves out from the bare earth-toned arcade in which she sits, past the colourful angel, to the green garden and forest beyond the fence, the promise of new life and redemption.

The Office of the Virgin Mary (based on the medieval *Horae*), moreover, along with such prayers as the *Obsecro te*, and hymns as the *Salve, regina* and *Stabat mater dolorosa*, supplies early modern Catholic worship. Iconoclasts could tear down the 'image of our Blessed Lady' lamenting over Christ in the Church at Long Melford, but they could not obliterate the power of the image in the minds and hearts of parishioners such as Roger Martin. Marian devotion takes on new life and new forms in poetry (see Robert Southwell and Richard Crashaw) and also in prose, in Henry Hawkins's extraordinary *Partheneia Sacra*, a fusion of patristic, medieval, iconographical, and scriptural traditions, organized into an emblematic homage to Mary the *hortus conclusus*, 'enclosed garden'. Hawkins presents a ninefold exegesis on various aspects of the metaphor, combining artistic creativity and moral exhortation into a bravura display of traditional learning and metaphysical wit.

Penalized for open ceremony, Catholics naturally developed those traditions that turned the gaze inwards to meditation or 'mental prayer', as it was called. Continental writers such as Antonio de Molina, Luis de Granada, and Gaspare Loarte wrote public manuals for meditation, outlining methods for quieting the mind from distractions and for turning it to God by consideration of a biblical passage or event. As John Bucke makes clear, the most maligned Catholic devotion, the rosary, is actually a meditative sequence of prayers centring on the Mysteries of Redemption for use by individuals as well as sodalities and confraternities. Ignatius of Loyola, founder of the Jesuits, introduces other influential meditative techniques in his *Spiritual Exercises*, wherein prayers, contemplations, imaginative reconsideration of Gospel moments, and colloquies with God proceed in an ordered sequence to transform the fallen retreatant. Adapted by Robert Persons into *The Christian Directory* (1582, many times emended, reprinted, and even transformed into a Protestant version), Ignatius and his methods guided many ordinary sinners to a life of virtue. In this aim Ignatius has a companion in St Francis de Sales, whose *A Devout Life* (1613) encourages internal reformation and tutors erring souls in holy living and dying.

Three final examples of Catholic instruction and devotion are particularly noteworthy. The pressures of persecution give rise to an important subgenre of catechesis, the consolation. John Fisher, Thomas More, and Robert Southwell, all martyrs, leave behind starkly moving reflections on the purpose of life and on the possibilities after. Next, the

Catholic William Byrd composes sacred music that incorporates previous traditions while giving voice to the joys, sorrows, and hopes of the recusant community. There can be no substitute for hearing Byrd's music, of course, but the brief textual selections below suggest the doctrinal content of his extraordinary ministry. Finally, drawing on the works of Continental and English mystics, Dom Augustine Baker's *Sancta Sophia* (1657) encourages the lay person to try the prayer of contemplation, or mystical union, without use of discrete thoughts or images. The end of this prayer is 'wonderful stillness', the total, affective, inflamed, and reposeful union with God. The consoler, the musician, and the mystic all seek to bring the sublime experience of God within the reach of the common person—the ordinary listener or prayerful member of the Catholic community.

Prayers and Hymns

Most Catholic prayers and hymns appeared in a prayer book known as the Primer, which derived from the Divine Office (monastic prayers recited at certain hours of the day) but soon incorporated the Little Office or Hours of the Virgin Mary, including psalms, the Litany of the Saints, the Office of the Dead. Richard Verstegan's translation of the Primer in 1599 (excerpted below) achieved forty-two editions in the following century. There meditations on the Passion envision Jesus as both suffering brother and divine redeemer. The *Fifteen Oes* (from an earlier text) unites scriptural, liturgical, patristic, and iconic traditions to form a deeply affective and richly doctrinal plea for salvation. Mary also figures largely in the Primer and in Catholic devotions, appearing as a heavenly queen and mediator, but also as a human being who rejoices in the Incarnation and grieves at the Passion. Catholics sang traditional hymns, especially those of Thomas Aquinas, originally written in Latin to celebrate the newly instituted Feast of Corpus Christi (1264); in early modern English translation these Eucharistic hymns reaffirm the doctrine of transubstantiation.

Prayers and Hymns, Eleventh to Sixteenth centuries

'A prayer unto the wounds of Christ', fourteenth century
I beseech thee, O Lord Jesu, by those thy health-bringing wounds which thou suffered upon the cross for our salvation, out of the which flowed that precious blood wherewith

'A PRAYER UNTO THE WOUNDS' Late medieval Europe showed great devotion to the wounds of Christ, which become a focus for affective meditation.

we are redeemed, wound this my sinful soul, for which thou also vouchsafed to die; wound it with the fiery and most forcible weapon of thy abundant charity. Pierce my heart with the dart of thy love that my soul may say to thee, 'I am wounded with thy charity,' in such sort that from the same wound of thy love most abundant tears may flow from me day and night. Strike, O Lord, strike, I beseech thee, this my most hard heart with the holy and forcible prick of thy love, and pierce it more deeply into the inner parts with thy mighty force, who livest and reignest world without end. Amen.

'Of the seven words which Christ spake hanging on the cross', fourteenth century

O Lord Jesu Christ, Son of the living God, which, hanging upon the cross, said, 'Father, forgive them for they know not what they do,' grant that I for the love of thee may pardon all that do me harm. And thou which said unto the thief, 'This day thou shalt be with me in paradise,' grant me so to live that in the hour of my death thou may say to me, 'This day shalt thou be with me in paradise.' And thou which said unto thy mother, 'O woman, behold thy son,' and forthwith to the disciple, 'Behold thy mother,' grant that thy love and thy true charity may associate me unto thy mother. And thou which said, 'Eli, Eli, lama sabachthani,' that is to say, 'My God, my God, why has thou forsaken me?', grant me to say in all my tribulation, and anguish, 'My father, my lord, have mercy on me a sinner, and help me, my king and my God, which did redeem me with thy precious blood.' And thou which said, 'I thirst,' grant that I may always thirst after thee, the fountain of living water. And thou which said, 'Father, into thy hands I commend my spirit,' receive me returning unto thee. And thou which said, 'It is ended,' grant that I may deserve to hear that most sweet voice of thine, to wit, 'Come, my lover, my dear, my spouse, come that thou may ascend with me, my angels, and saints to banquet in my kingdom, to be made merry and to dwell with me world without end.' Amen.

From 'The Fifteen Oes of St Bridget', fourteenth century

O Jesu, endless sweetness of loving souls, O Jesu, ghostly joy passing and exceeding all gladness and desires, O Jesu, health and tender lover of all repentant sinners that likest to dwell, as thou said thyself, with the children of men. For that was the cause why thou were incarnate and made man in the end of the world.
[. . .]

---

6. **sort** fashion.
'OF THE SEVEN WORDS' This popular prayer assembles from the Gospel accounts the seven final sayings of Jesus on the cross. **1–2. Father . . . do** Luke 23: 34. **3–4. This . . . paradise** Luke 23: 43. **5–6. O woman . . . mother** John 19: 26–7. **8. Eli . . . sabachthani** Matt. 27: 46; Mark 15: 34 (a quotation from Ps. 21: 2). **11. I thirst** John 19: 28. **12–13. Father . . . spirit** Luke 23: 46. **13. It . . . ended** John 19: 30.
'THE FIFTEEN OES OF ST BRIDGET' 'An unrivalled epitome of late medieval English religion at its most symbolically resonant' (E. Duffy, *The Stripping of the Altars*, 1992: 250), this prayer turns meditation on the passion into pleas for mercy. **St Bridget** of Sweden (1303–73) founded the Brigittines, especially devoted to the Passion and Mary. **1. ghostly** spiritual.

O blessed Jesu, lovable king and friend in all things, have mind of the sorrows that thou   5
had when thou hangest naked despiteously on the cross. And all thy friends and
knowledge stood against thee, of whom thou found no comfort but only thy blessed
mother, standing with thee faithfully and truly all the time of thy bitter passion when
thou commandest to thy disciple Saint John, saying to her, 'Lo, woman, thy son.' For
mind of this passion, namely for that sword of sorrow that which that time pierced the   10
soul of thy mother, I beseech thee, blessed Jesu, have compassion of my tribulations and
affections, bodily and ghostly, and give me comfort in all my diseases. Amen. *Pater
Noster. Ave, Maria, gratia.*
[. . .]
   O blessed Jesu, beginning and ending, life and strength in every middle, have mind
that from the top of thy head to the sole of thy foot thou suffered for us to be drowned in   15
the water of thy painful passion; for mind of this great pain and namely for deepness of
thy wounds, I beseech thee, blessed Jesu, that am drowned in all foul sin, teach me thy
large precept and commandment of thy love. Amen. *Pater Noster. Ave, Maria, gratia.*
[. . .]
   O blessed Jesu, deepness of thy endless mercy, I beseech thee for the deepness of thy
wounds that went through thy tender flesh, also thy bowels and the marrow of thy bones,   20
that thou would vouchsafe to draw me out of sin and hide me ever after in the holes of
thy wounds from the face of thy wrath unto the time, Lord, that the dreadful doom be
passed. Amen. *Pater Noster. Ave, Maria, gratia.*
[. . .]
   O blessed Jesu, very and true plenteous vine, have mind of thy passion and abundant
shedding of blood that thou sheddest most piteously as if it had been thrust out of a ripe   25
cluster of grapes, when they pressed thy blessed body as a ripe cluster upon the pressure of
the cross, and gave us drink both blood and water out of thy body pierced with a knight's
spear. So that in thy blessed body was not left a drop of blood nor water. Then at the last
as a bundle of myrrh thou hangest on the cross on height where thy tender flesh changed
his colour because the liquor of thy bowels and the marrow of thy bones were dried up.   30
For mind of this bitter passion, sweet Jesu, wound my heart that my soul may be fed
sweetly with water of penance and tears of love both night and day. And, good Jesu, turn
me wholly to thee that my heart may be ever to thee a dwelling place, and that my living
may be ever pleasant and acceptable, and that the end of my life may be so commendable
that I may perpetually deserve to praise thee with all saints in bliss. Amen. *Pater Noster.*   35
Ave, Maria, gratia. Credo.

---

5. This 'O', celebrating Mary's devotion, was omitted in a Protestant reprinting of the prayer, 1578 (H. White, *Tudor Books of Private Devotion*, 1971: 223). 6. **despiteously** cruelly 9. **Lo . . . son** At the crucifixion Jesus says this to Mary before commending her to St John's care (John 19: 26–7). 10–11. **sword . . . mother** Cf. Luke 2: 35. 22. **dreadful doom** Last Judgement. 24 **ff.** This last 'O' turns on the image of Christ as winepress (Isa. 63; John 15: 1–8). 27. **drink** to drink.

Marian Prayers and Hymns

Salve, regina, eleventh century

All hail, O queen, mother of mercy, life, sweetness, and our hope, all hail! We exiled the sons of Eve do cry unto thee. To thee we sigh, groaning and weeping in this vale of tears. Therefore, O thou, our advocate, turn those thy merciful eyes unto us. And show unto us after this exile blessed Jesus, the fruit of thy womb. O clement, O pitiful, O sweet Virgin Mary.   5

    v. Pray for us, O holy mother of God.
    r. That we may be made worthy the promises of Christ.

Obsecro te, twelfth century

I beseech thee, O holy lady Mary, mother of God, most full of pity, the daughter of the highest king, mother most glorious, mother of orphans, the consolation of the desolate, the way of them that go astray, the safety of all that trust in thee, a virgin before child-bearing, a virgin in child-bearing, and a virgin after child-bearing, the fountain of mercy, the fountain of health and grace, the fountain of consolation and pardon, the fountain of   5
piety and gladness, the fountain of life and forgiveness.

By that holy, unspeakable gladness by the which thy spirit did rejoice in that hour wherein the Son of God was unto thee by the angel Gabriel declared and conceived, and by that holy, unspeakable humility in which thou did answer the archangel Gabriel, 'Behold the handmaid of our Lord; be it unto me according unto thy word,' and by that   10
divine mystery which the Holy Ghost as then did work in thee, and by that unspeakable grace, pity, mercy, love, and humility by the which thy son, our Lord Jesus Christ, came down to take human flesh in thy most venerable womb, and by the most glorious joys which thou had of thy son, our Lord Jesus Christ.

And by that holy and most great compassion and most bitter grief of thy heart, which   15
thou had whenas thou did behold thy son, our Lord Jesus Christ, made naked before the cross and lifted up upon the same, hanging, crucified, wounded, thirsting, and the most bitter drink of gall and vinegar put unto his mouth. Thou heard him cry 'Eli', and did see him die. And by those five wounds of the same thy son, and by the sore shrinking

SALVE, REGINA One of the most celebrated anthems to the Virgin Mary, this antiphon was sung throughout the liturgical year in church, at guild meetings, feasts, and processions. Some perceived idolatry in the hymn: Luther objected; John Hollybush wrote a confutation and a revision that substituted Christ for Mary throughout Hollybush (*An Exposition upon the song of the Blessed Virgin Mary called Magnificat*, STC 16979.7, 1538).

OBSECRO TE An important summation of Marian devotion, this prayer appeared in virtually every primer. It invokes Mary as mother of mercy, hope, and consolation for suffering humanity, and celebrates the joy of her role in the Incarnation. The prayer then recounts Mary's sorrows and begs her to help the petitioner lead a virtuous, peaceful life in accordance with Church teaching. **10. Behold . . . word** Luke 1: 38. **15. compassion** suffering.

together of thy inward parts through the extreme grief of his wounds, and by the sorrow   20
which thou had when thou did behold him wounded, and by the fountains of his blood,
and by all his passion, and sorrow of thy heart, and by the fountains of thy tears, that
thou would come with all the saints and elect of God and hasten unto my help and my
counsel in all my prayers and petitions, in all my distresses and necessities. As also in all
those things wherein I am to do anything, speak, or think, all the days and nights, hours   25
and moments of my life.

  And obtain for me, thy servant of thy beloved son, our Lord Jesus Christ, the
accomplishment of all virtues with all mercy and consolation, all counsel and aid, all
benediction and sanctification, all salvation, peace, and prosperity, all joy and gladness,
also abundance of all spiritual good things, and sufficiency of corporal, and grace of the   30
Holy Ghost, which may well dispose me in all things, and may guard my soul, govern
and protect my body, stir up my mind, order my manners, approve my acts, suggest holy
cogitations, pardon my evils past, amend things present, and moderate things to come.
Bestow on me an honest and chaste life; grant me faith, hope, and charity; make me
firmly to believe the articles of the faith and to observe the precepts of the law; rule and   35
protect the senses of my body; and evermore deliver me from mortal sins, and defend me
to my life's end, that he may graciously and meekly hear and receive this prayer, and give
me life everlasting. Hear and make intercession for me, most sweet Virgin Mary, mother
of God and mercy. Amen.

From 'The Litany of Loreto', twelfth to sixteenth centuries

Mater Christi,	[Mother of Christ,
R. ora pro nobis.	R. pray for us.
Mater divinae gratiae,	Mother of divine grace,
R. ora pro nobis.	R. pray for us.
Mater purissima,	Mother most pure,
R. ora pro nobis.	R. pray for us.
Mater castissima,	Mother most chaste,
R. ora pro nobis.	R. pray for us.
Mater inviolata,	Mother inviolate,
R. ora pro nobis.	R. pray for us.
Mater intemerata,	Mother undefiled,
R. ora pro nobis.	R. pray for us.
Mater amabilis,	Mother most lovable,
R. ora pro nobis.	R. pray for us.

5

10

22. **that** (I pray) that.   33. **cogitations** thoughts and prayers.

'THE LITANY OF LORETO' An antiphonal series of invocations to Mary, this litany became popular at Loreto, Italy, site
of a famous Marian shrine and her transported house. Deriving from medieval litanies, the version reprinted here won
official Church approval in 1587. The invocations principally honour Mary as mother, virgin, vessel, mediatrix, and queen.

Mater admirabilis,	Mother most admirable,	15
R. ora pro nobis.	R. pray for us.	
Mater Creatoris,	Mother of our Creator,	
R. ora pro nobis.	R. pray for us.	
Mater Salvatoris,	Mother of our Saviour,	
R. ora pro nobis.	R. pray for us.	20
Virgo prudentissima,	Virgin most prudent,	
R. ora pro nobis.	R. pray for us.	
Virgo veneranda,	Virgin most venerable,	
R. ora pro nobis.	R. pray for us.	
Virgo praedicanda,	Virgin most renowned,	25
R. ora pro nobis.	R. pray for us.	
Virgo potens,	Virgin most powerful,	
R. ora pro nobis.	R. pray for us.	
Virgo clemens,	Virgin most merciful,	
R. ora pro nobis.	R. pray for us.	30
Virgo fidelis,	Virgin most faithful,	
R. ora pro nobis.	R. pray for us.	
Speculum iustitiae,	Mirror of justice,	
R. ora pro nobis.	R. pray for us.	
Sedes sapientiae,	Seat of wisdom,	35
R. ora pro nobis.	R. pray for us.	
Causa nostra laetitiae,	Cause of our joy,	
R. ora pro nobis.	R. pray for us.	
Vas spirituale,	Spiritual vessel,	
R. ora pro nobis.	R. pray for us.	40
Vas honorabile,	Vessel of honour,	
R. ora pro nobis.	R. pray for us.	
Vas insigne devotionis,	Singular vessel of devotion,	
R. ora pro nobis.	R. pray for us.	
Rosa mystica,	Mystical rose,	45
R. ora pro nobis.	R. pray for us.	
Turris Davidica,	Tower of David,	
R. ora pro nobis.	R. pray for us.	
Turris eburnea,	Tower of ivory,	
R. ora pro nobis.	R. pray for us.	50

35. **Sedes sapientiae** This ancient title honours Mary as mother to incarnate wisdom, and as wise herself in assenting to God's plan. 45. **Rosa mystica** Alluding to Cant. 2 and several other biblical texts, this invocation praises Mary's beauty and virtue. 47. **Turris Davidica** Alluding to Cant. 4 and the tower which David built on the walls of Jerusalem, the invocation celebrates Mary as protector. 49. **Turris eburnea** Alluding to Cant. 7, the invocation celebrates Mary's beauty and power to protect the faithful.

Domus aurea,	House of gold,
R. ora pro nobis.	R. pray for us.
Foederis arca,	Ark of the Covenant,
R. ora pro nobis.	R. pray for us.
Ianua caeli,	Gate of heaven,
R. ora pro nobis.	R. pray for us.
Stella matutina,	Morning star,
R. ora pro nobis.	R. pray for us.]

55

Aquinas's Eucharistic Hymns, 1264

Pange, lingua, tr. Henry Garnet, SJ?
Of Christ his body glorious,
Sing, my tongue, the mystery,
And also of his precious blood,
Which the world's price to be,
The king of nations did shed forth,   5
Fruit of noble womb was he.

On us bestowed and for us born,
Of a maid untouched, indeed,
Conversant upon the earth,
Sowing of his word the seed,   10
And of his time of being here,
Strangely he the end decreed.

The night he with his brethren sat,
And his supper last did make,
In full observance of the law,   15
Law-assignèd meats did take;
Himself food to apostles twelve
With his hands he did betake.

---

53. **Foederis arca** Alluding to Noah's ark (Gen. 6–8), which saved humanity from destruction, and the Ark of the Covenant (Exod. 25–7), the chest that contained the holy artefacts of the Jews, the invocation recognizes Mary's role in salvation history as the one who carried Christ within her.

PANGE, LINGUA This hymn, adapting a Roman triumphal march, summarizes the Catholic doctrine of transubstantiation in concise phrases. The probable translator, Henry Garnet, was head of the Jesuit missions in England from 1586 to 1606 (see CONTROVERSIES). **4. price** payment for sin, ransom. **9. Conversant upon** having lived on (*conversatus*). **12. Strangely** marvellously (*miro ordine*). **15.** Notice of Jewish dietary laws sets the scene for Christ's departure from tradition in the institution of the Eucharist, in the giving of himself as food (17). **18. betake** deliver.

The Word now being flesh become,
So very bread flesh by the word,   20
And wine the blood of Christ is made;
Though our sense it not afford,
But this in heart sincere to fix,
Faith sufficeth to accord.

Wherefore a sacrament so great,   25
Humbly prostrate we adore,
And unto rites begun of late,
Saws must yield that were before,
And where our sense is seen to fail,
There must faith supply restore.   30

Unto the Father and the Son,
Joy and praise ascribèd be,
And saving health, honour, and power,
As also *Benedicite*,
And to him that from both proceeds,   35
Praises like acknowledge we. Amen.

Lauda, Sion, tr. Robert Southwell, SJ
Praise, O Zion, praise thy Saviour,
Praise thy captain and thy pastor,
With hymns and solemn harmony.
What power affords perform indeed,
His works all praises far exceed,   5
No praise can reach his dignity.

A special theme of praise is read,
A living and life-giving bread,
Is on this day exhibited,
Within the supper of our Lord,   10
To twelve disciples at his board,
As doubtless 'twas deliverèd.

Let our praise be loud and free,
Full of joy and decent glee,
With mind's and voice's melody,   15

19–21. Verbal antitheses and paradoxes struggle to express the sacred mystery in these famous lines: 'Verbum caro panem verum | Verbo carnem efficit, | Fitque sanguis Christi merum' (The Word-made-flesh changes true bread into his flesh by a word [the words of the consecration], and wine becomes the blood of Christ). 22. **sense...afford** understanding fails (an awkward rendering of *sensus deficit*). 24. **accord** settle the matter. 27–36. These verses alone (*Tantum ergo*) are often used for benedictions and processions. 27. **rites...late** the sacrament of the Holy Eucharist, instituted at the Last Supper. 28. **Saws** laws, decrees, i.e. the old Law with its sacrifices. 30. **restore** restoration. 34. **Benedicite** 'Bless you!', i.e. blessings. 35. **him** the Holy Spirit.

LAUDA, SION 1. **Zion** one of the hills of Jerusalem, site of the city of David, hence, Israel, and by transference here, the Christian Church. 7. **is read** we celebrate. 11. **board** table. 14. **decent** fitting.

For now solemnize we that day,
Which doth with joy to us display
The prime use of this mystery.

At this board of our new ruler,   20
Of new law, new paschal order,
The ancient rite abolisheth;
Old decrees by new annulled,
Shadows are in truth fulfilled,
Day former darkness finisheth.

That at supper Christ performed,   25
To be done, he straitly charged,
For his eternal memory.
Guided by his sacred orders,
Bread and wine upon our altars,
To saving host we sanctify.   30

Christians are by faith assured
That to flesh the bread is changed,
The wine to blood most precious;
That no wit nor sense conceiveth,
Firm and grounded faith believeth,   35
In strange effects not curious.

Under kinds two in appearance,
Two in show but one in substance,
Be things beyond comparison.
Flesh is meat, blood, drink most heavenly,   40
Yet is Christ in each kind wholly,
Most free from all division.

None that eateth him do chew him;
None that takes him doth divide him;
Received, he whole persevereth,   45

18. **prime use** first celebration at the Last Supper (*institutio*). 20. **new law** the dispensation of the New Testament, which replaces the Old. **new paschal order** The Jews in Egypt sacrificed the paschal lamb to save themselves from death (Exod. 12); Christ is the new paschal lamb, who shed his blood to save the world from eternal death. The new order abolishes the **ancient rite** (21), or law of the Old Testament. 25. **That** that which. 26. He strictly ordered us to do this (consecrate bread and wine) in the future. 36. Not anxious or inquisitive about supernatural things (*praeter rerum ordine*). 37–60. Articulating the Roman Catholic doctrine of transubstantiation, these lines were omitted in editions of Southwell's poetry from 1620 on (*The Poems of Robert Southwell*, ed. J. H. McDonald and N. P. Brown, 1967: 130). 37–8. **Under . . . substance** These lines summarize the doctrine of the Real Presence, asserting that bread and wine retain their outward appearances without their underlying subject (*accidentia sine subjecto*), and that their substance is changed to the body and blood of Christ. 41–2. **wholly . . . division** a statement of the doctrine called the Totality of the Presence, which affirms that the sacrament contains Christ in his entirety, body, soul, and divinity. This stanza affirms the spatially unlimited, spiritual existence of Christ's eucharistic body (*existentia corporis ad modum spiritus*), therefore not subject to physical diminishment and capable of simultaneous existence in many places (*multilocatio*).

Be there one or thousands houseled,
One as much as all received.
He by no eating perisheth.

Both the good and bad receive him,
But effects are divers in them,   50
True life or true destruction,
Life to the good, death to the wicked.
Mark how both alike received
With far unlike conclusion.

When the priest the host divideth,   55
Know that in each part abideth
All that the whole host coverèd;
Form of bread not Christ is broken,
Not of Christ but of his token,
Is state or stature alterèd.   60

Angels' bread made pilgrims' feeding,
Truly bread for children's eating,
To dogs not to be offerèd,
Signed by Isaac on the altar,
By the lamb and paschal supper,   65
And in the manna figurèd.

Jesu, food and feeder of us,
Here with mercy feed and friend us,
Then grant in heaven felicity;
Lord of all whom here thou feedest,   70
Fellow heirs, guests with thy dearest,
Make us in heav'nly company.

   Adoro te, tr. Richard Crashaw
With all the powers my poor heart hath
Of humble love and loyal faith,
Thus low (my hidden life!) I bow to thee,

---

46. houseled communicated (having received the Eucharist). **59. token** sign, outward appearance. **61. Angel's . . . feeding**
The experience of Christ in heaven which directly feeds and sustains the angels spiritually now is available in the Eucharist
to pilgrims on earth. *Panis angelicus* (angelic bread) also refers to the manna which fed the wandering Israelites (Exod. 16)
and which prefigured the Eucharist (**66**). **63. dogs** unworthy persons. **64. Signed** prefigured or prophesied. **Isaac** beloved
son of Abraham, whom God commanded to be sacrificed (Gen. 22). **69. in heaven** So Southwell translates *in terra
viventium*, 'in the land of the living' (Ps. 26: 13), which might equally mean 'on earth'.

ADORO TE Reflecting his newly declared Catholicism, Crashaw changed the title from 'A Hymn to our Saviour by the
faithful receiver of the Sacrament' (1648) to 'The Hymn of Saint Thomas in adoration of the Blessed Sacrament' (1652).
Article 28 of the Church of England's Thirty-nine Articles expressly forbade worship of the sacrament.

Whom too much love hath bowed more low for me.
Down, down, proud sense! Discourses, die!   5
Keep close, my soul's enquiring eye!
Nor touch nor taste must look for more,
But each sit still in his own door.

Your ports are all superfluous here,
Save that which lets in faith, the ear.   10
Faith is my skill. Faith can believe
As fast as love new laws can give.
Faith is my force. Faith strength affords
To keep pace with those powerful words.
And words more sure, more sweet than they,   15
Love could not think, truth could not say.

Oh, let thy wretch find that relief
Thou didst afford the faithful thief!
Plead for me, love! Allege and show
That faith has farther here to go   20
And less to lean on because then,
Though hid as God, wounds writ thee man.
Thomas might touch, none but might see
At least the suff'ring side of thee;
And that too was thyself which thee did cover,   25
But here ev'n that's hid too which hides the other.

Sweet, consider, then, that I
Though allowed not hand nor eye
To reach at thy loved face, nor can
Taste thee God or touch thee man   30
Both yet believe and witness thee
My Lord too and my God, as loud as he.
Help, Lord, my faith, my hope increase,
And fill my portion in thy peace.
Give love for life, nor let my days   35
Grow but in new powers to thy name and praise.

---

6. soul's enquiring eye intelligence. 8. each...door Each sense must rest quietly when confronted with the spiritual mystery of the Eucharist. 10. ear The sense of hearing alone can be useful because it can receive the word of God. 14. those powerful words The words of the consecration, 'This is my body', etc. (Matt. 26: 26–9; Mark 14: 22–5; Luke 22: 19–20). 18. the faithful thief the repentant thief to whom the crucified Jesus said, 'Amen, I say to thee; this day thou shalt be with me in paradise' (Luke 23: 43). 20–1. farther...less The speaker prepares for the extended comparison with Thomas Didymus, the doubting apostle, who would not believe in the Resurrection until he put his fingers in the wounds of the risen Jesus (John 20: 24–9). 24. the suff'ring side the body of Jesus, symbolizing his human nature. 25. that too the blood of Jesus, also symbolizing his human nature. 26. The blood is no longer visible (not even in the sacrament), nor is the human nature of Jesus, which hid his divine essence. 32. Thomas finally declared his faith in the risen Jesus by saying, 'My Lord and my God' (John 20: 28). 34. portion span of life.

O dear memorial of that death
Which lives still and allows us breath!
Rich, royal food! Bountiful bread!
Whose use denies us to the dead,   40
Whose vital gust alone can give
The same leave both to eat and live.
Live ever, bread of loves, and be
My life, my soul, my surer self to me.

O soft, self-wounding pelican,   45
Whose breast weeps balm for wounded man!
Ah, this way bend thy benign flood
To a bleeding heart that gasps for blood.
That blood, whose least drops sovereign be
To wash my worlds of sins from me.   50
Come, love! Come, Lord! And that long day
For which I languish, come away,
When this dry soul those eyes shall see,
And drink the unsealed source of thee,
When glory's sun faith's shades shall chase,   55
And for thy veil give me thy face. Amen.

ROBERT, PRIOR OF SHREWSBURY

Hagiography, or the writing of saints' lives, constitutes a popular form of early modern
instruction and devotion. Compiled in the twelfth century by Robert of Shrewsbury, *The
Life of St Winifred* tells the story of the seventh-century patroness of Wales, beheaded for
refusing the advances of the pagan Prince Cradocus. Winifred miraculously regains her life
(and her head) through the intercession of her uncle, St Beuno. A sacred fountain springs
up at the place of the miracle. Winifred devotes the rest of her days to prayer, contemplation, and good works.

St Winifred's Well became a celebrated shrine for pilgrimage and healing, a local 'point
of intersection of the timeless | With time', as T. S. Eliot put it ('The Dry Salvages'), and
also a site of folklore and superstition. As such, it stands with other regional shrines—those,
for example, described by Nicholas Roscarrock in his work on the saints in Cornwall and

37. **memorial** The speaker addresses the Eucharist. 41. **gust** taste. 45. **pelican** traditional iconographic symbol of Christ,
because supposed to feed her young with her own blood. 48. a typically emotive and Crashavian expansion of *me immundum*
('me unclean'). 51. **that long day** union with God after death for eternity. 54. **unsealed source** ever-flowing spring.

Devon (1590) and, of course, the famous national shrine to Mary at Walsingham (see *Lamentation*, POETRY; Erasmus, FICTION). The well continued to attract pilgrims even after being 'lamentably defaced' (sig. *5) by Henry VIII's iconoclasts in 1540. In 1635 John Falconer, SJ, translated the Latin *Life of St Winifred* to reveal the saint again, 'a bright morning star...in this late darkness overwhelming our country' (sigs. *3ᵛ–*4). Despite Protestant scepticism and ridicule, Falconer declared, the story of St Winifred's life and miracles manifest 'God's wisdom and power' and 'will by devout Catholics be piously believed' (sigs. S1ᵛ–S2).

The Life of St Winifred, 1130

How St Winifred was raised from death to life and her head reunited to her body by St Beuno's prayers, with a small white circle remaining in the place of her neck where it was cut, and other wonders gracing still the place of her martyrdom.

After the holy man had ended his mass and the people their prayers, lifting up his hands towards heaven, he prayed in this manner: 'O Lord Jesus Christ, for whose sake this holy virgin condemned the world and coveted heavenly things, vouchsafe by the tender bowels of thy mercy, love, and bounty to grant us the effect of our vows now made and prayers offered here humbly unto thee. And albeit we are fully persuaded that this 5
godly virgin, who lived holily and died constantly for thee, be now highly exalted in heaven also with thee, wanting no more the society of us mortal and miserable creatures, yet to manifest thine omnipotency and that supreme dominion which thou hast over souls and bodies, never dead to thy power of raising and reuniting them, for the greater merit also of her soul whose body here lieth before us, we crave a new life for her, and that 10
she may return after a long and plentiful harvest of new merits here gained more enriched and divinely beautified unto thee, the beloved of her heart and eternal spouse, who with the Father and the Holy Ghost dost rule in earth and reign in heaven forever and ever.'

And when the people had cried with great devotion, 'Amen', unto his prayer, the virgin as newly wakened from sleep wiped her eyes and face, besmeared with sweat and dust 15
before as having tumbled on the ground, filling all present and her parents there amongst them with joy and admiration; observing also, as they more fixedly beheld her, a pure white circle no bigger than a small thread to remain in her fair neck, showing the place where it had been cut off before and was miraculously then to her body conjoined; which because it ever afterwards remained conspicuously seen after the same manner, Brewa, 20
her name before, is said to have been changed by the people's great veneration and love towards her into Winifred by *wen*, which doth signify 'white' in the old British tongue, added unto it and two letters thereof for better sound quite altered. And in many

---

1. holy man St Beuno, 7th-c. abbott of Clynnog. **4. bowels** heart (figuratively). **22. old British** Welsh. **23. letters** syllables.

apparitions of her to men and women after her second corporal death authentically recounted, this white circle in her neck conspicuously appeared to give worldly souls thereby to understand the particular glory which she had received of her heavenly spouse for suffering that wound so constantly for him.

And whereas the valley where she was martyred had been called ever before a dry or barren bottom, it was for the crystal fountain of pure waters breaking miraculously out of the ground where her head first fell called afterwards in memory of this miracle, *finhon*, which in old Welsh doth signify a 'fountain or well'. And, indeed, as this fountain was wonderful in the first origin thereof, so did the same by miraculous cures of men and beasts either bathed in that water or drinking thereof become famously afterwards renowned.

In memory likewise that store of the virgin's pure blood had been spilt in that place, and to signify withal how sweet a sacrifice was offered there by her, the stones of the well are either dyed or spotted all over with drops, as it were, of blood, and the moss growing about it is as with musk yet to this day sweetly perfumed.

The miracle of her raising from death to life divulged in those parts gained to St Beuno so great a fame of his singular sanctity and power with God to obtain anything, that multitudes thereupon of Gentile people in those days for their instruction in the Christian faith and Baptism repaired unto him, whose famous acts and St Winifred's holy life after her being raised shall in the rest of this book be briefly declared.

Of daily cures done upon sick children thrown into the stream of St Winifred's Well, and of others also cured miraculously of agues and hot fevers by drinking of the same water.

In process of time this sacred fountain, the trophy and triumphant sign of St Winifred's martyrdom, became so famously renowned for miraculous cures done by the waters thereof that mothers were usually wont to throw their young children, sick of any disease, into the stream running from the same, who became presently cured by the touch of those waters.

Such also as had agues or hot burning fevers in any part of the country were wont for a certain and present remedy thereof either to drink a draught of that pure fountain water or, if they had it not at hand, to put in some one of the bloody stones taken out of the well into a draught of any other water, and became thereby presently cured. In like manner such as had any swelling or sore about them were accustomed to bathe the part affected with the said water and found present remedy thereby.

The first use of which remedies for all sorts of sores and diseases is said to have been taught by the holy virgin-martyr herself, who, visibly after her death appearing to many who in dangerous sickness devoutly called upon her, willed them to apply the water and stones of her well in manner aforesaid for their perfect and speedy recovery, almighty God continuing

---

35. **withal** in addition. 40. **Gentile** non-Christian. 43. **trophy** memorial. 48. **agues** ailments characterized by fever or chills.

still to grace this glorious monument of his dear spouse's death by affording help thereby to such as either devoutly repair unto it or faithfully seek remedies from it, according to St Beuno his holy prediction, when before his departure from those parts he sat upon a stone   60 with St Winifred herself near to the well's side and foretold the miraculous cures which should through her merits and prayers be at the same afterwards performed.

Thomas à Kempis

Thomas à Kempis (1380–1471) joined the *Devotio moderna* (new devotion) movement, which created radical Christian communities of poverty, chastity, and obedience. After ordination in 1413, Thomas spent most of his life as a monk at Mount St Agnes, where he wrote some three dozen religious works. Of these *The Imitation of Christ* (composed 1420–7) stands as the most widely read devotional work ever written (excepting the Bible), admired by Thomas More, Ignatius of Loyola, John Wesley, Thomas Merton, and many others. It achieved several early translations from Latin to English, including that of William Atkinson and Margaret Beaufort, mother of Henry VII (1504), and that of Richard Whitford (1530, excerpted below), remarkable for its freshness and easy grace.

Throughout *The Imitation of Christ* Thomas à Kempis sees the world with uncompromising clarity. He unsettles the comfortable pieties of modernity, wherein we assume we will be saved unless we commit some terrible sin; Thomas assumes that we will all be damned unless we reform. The work also challenges the current gospel of self-fulfilment with a summons to self-sacrifice; few preachers, teachers, psychologists, or corporations today echo Thomas's fourfold prescription for bringing 'peace into the soul': 'Study, my son, rather to fulfil another man's will than thine own. Choose always to have little worldly riches than much. Seek also the lowest place and desire to be under rather than above. And covet always and pray that the will of God be wholly done in thee' (fo. 83). As the selection below illustrates, Thomas's challenging message begins and ends with the cross of Christ, which summons everyone to a life of suffering, patience, and eternal glory.

The Imitation of Christ, 1420–7

Of the way of the cross and how profitable patience is in adversity

The words of our Saviour be thought very hard and grievous when he saith thus: 'Forsake yourself, take the cross, and follow me' [Matt. 16: 24]. But much more grievous shall it be to hear these words at the last day of Judgement: 'Go ye from me, ye cursed people, into the fire that ever shall last' [Matt. 25: 41]. But those that now gladly hear and follow the words of Christ, whereby he counseleth them to follow him, shall not then need to dread for hearing those words of everlasting damnation. The sign of the cross shall appear in heaven when our Lord shall come to judge the world, and the servants of the cross who conformed themselves here in this life to Christ crucified on the cross shall go to Christ their judge with great faith and trust in him. Why dost thou then dread to take this cross sith it is the very way to the kingdom of heaven and none but that? In the cross is health, in the cross is life, in the cross is defence from our enemies, in the cross is infusion of heavenly sweetness, in the cross is the strength of mind, the joy of spirit, the highness of virtue, and the full perfection of all holiness. And there is no health of soul nor hope of everlasting life but through virtue of the cross.

Take, therefore, the cross and follow Jesus, and thou shalt go into the life everlasting. He hath gone before thee bearing his cross, and died for thee upon the cross, that thou shouldst in like wise bear with him the cross of penance and tribulation, and that thou shouldst be ready likewise for his love to suffer death if need require, as he hath done for thee. If thou die with him, thou shalt live with him; and if thou be fellow with him in pain, thou shalt be with him in glory. Behold, then, how in the cross standeth all, and how in dying to the world lieth all our health, and that there is no other way to true and inward peace but the way of the cross and of deadly mortifying of the body to the spirit. Go whither thou wilt, and seek what thou list, and thou shalt never find above thee nor beneath thee, within thee nor without thee, more high, more excellent, nor more sure way to Christ than the way of the holy cross.

Dispose everything after thy will, and thou shalt never find but that thou must of necessity somewhat suffer, either with thy will or against thy will, and so shalt thou always find the cross; for either thou shalt feel pain in thy body, or in thy soul thou shalt have trouble of spirit. Thou shalt be sometime as thou were forsaken of God. Sometime thou shalt be vexed with thy neighbour, and, that is yet more painful, thou shalt sometime be grievous to thyself. And thou shalt find no mean to be delivered but that it behoveth thee to suffer till it shall please almighty God of his goodness otherwise to dispose for thee; for he will, that thou shalt learn to suffer tribulation without consolation, that thou mayest thereby learn wholly to submit thyself to him and by tribulation to be made more meek than thou were at the first. No man feeleth the passion of Christ so effectuously as he that feeleth like pain as Christ did. This cross is always ready, and everywhere it abideth thee, and thou mayest not flee nor fully escape it, wheresoever thou come; for in what place soever thou art, thou shalt bear thyself about with thee, and so always shalt thou find thyself. Turn thee where thou wilt—above thee, beneath thee, within thee, and without thee—and thou shalt find this cross on every side, so that it shall be necessary for thee that thou always keep thee in patience;

---

10. **sith** since. 14. **virtue** means. 27. **somewhat** something. 31. **mean** means. 32. **behoveth thee** is necessary for you. 36. **effectuously** deeply. 37. **abideth** awaits.

and that it behoveth thee to do, if thou wilt have inward peace and deserve the perpetual crown in heaven.

If thou wilt gladly bear this cross, it shall bear thee and bring thee to the end that thou desirest, where thou shalt never after have anything to suffer. And if thou bear this cross 45 against thy will, thou makest a great burden to thyself, and it will be the more grievous to thee, and yet it behoveth thee to bear it. And if it happen thee to put away one cross, that is to say, one tribulation, yet surely another will come, and haply more grievous than the first was. Trowest thou to escape that never yet any mortal man might escape? What saint in this world hath been without this cross and without some trouble? Truly, our 50 Lord Jesu was not one hour without some sorrow and pain as long as he lived here, for it behoved him to suffer death and to rise again and so to enter into his glory. And how is it, then, that thou seekest any other way to heaven than this plain, high way of the cross?

All the life of Christ was cross and martyrdom, and thou seekest pleasure and joy. Thou errest greatly if thou seek any other thing than to suffer, for all this mortal life is full 55 of miseries and is all beset about and marked with crosses. And the more highly that a man profiteth in spirit, the more painful crosses shall he find, for by the soothfastness of Christ's love, wherein he daily increaseth, daily appeareth unto him more and more the pain of this exile. But, nevertheless, a man thus vexed with pain is not left wholly without all comfort, for he seeth well that great fruit and high reward shall grow unto him by the 60 bearing of his cross. And when a man freely submitteth himself to such tribulation, then all the burden of tribulation is suddenly turned into a great trust of heavenly consolation. And the more the flesh is punished with tribulation, the more is the soul strengthened daily by inward consolation. And sometime the soul shall feel such comfort in adversities that for the love and desire that it hath to be conformed to Christ crucified, it would not 65 be without sorrow and trouble; for it considereth well that the more that it may suffer for his love here, the more acceptable shall he be to him in the life to come.

But this working is not in the power of man but through the grace of God, that is to say, that a frail man should take and love that which his bodily kind so much abhorreth and flieth. For it is not in the power of man gladly to bear the cross, to love the cross, to 70 chastise the body, and to make it obedient to the will of the spirit, to flee honours, gladly to sustain reproofs, to despise himself, and to covet to be despised, patiently to suffer adversities with all displeasures thereof, and not to desire any manner of profit in this world. If thou trust in thyself thou shalt never bring this matter about; but if thou trust in God, he shall send thee strength from heaven, and the world and the flesh shall be made 75 subject to thee. Yea, and if thou be strongly armed with faith and be marked with the cross of Christ as his household servant, thou shalt not need to fear thy ghostly enemy for he shall also be made subject to thee so that he shall have no power against thee.

---

42. that i.e. practising patience. **48. haply** by chance. **49. Trowest thou** do you think. **that** that which. **56. beset about** besieged. **57. soothfastness** truthfulness. **69. bodily kind** human nature. **77. ghostly enemy** spiritual enemy, i.e. the devil, who (along with the world and flesh) opposes humanity.

Purpose thyself, therefore, as a true, faithful servant of God manfully to bear the cross of thy Lord Jesu, that for thy love was crucified on the cross. Prepare thyself to suffer all 80 manner of adversities and discommodities in this wretched life, for so shall it be with thee wheresoever thou hide thee, and there is no remedy to escape but that thou must keep thyself always in patience. If thou desire to be a dear and well-beloved friend of Christ, drink effectuously with him a draught of the chalice of his tribulation. As for consolations, commit them to his will, that he order them as he knoweth most expedient for thee. But as 85 for thyself and for as much as in thee is, dispose thee to suffer, and when tribulations come take them as special consolations, saying with the Apostle thus: 'The passions of this world be not worthy of themselves to bring us to the glory that is ordained for us in the life to come' [Rom. 8: 18], yea, though thou thyself mightest suffer as much as all men do.

When thou comest to that degree of patience that tribulation is sweet to thee and for 90 the love of God is savoury and pleasant in thy sight, then mayest thou trust that it is well with thee and that thou art in good estate, for thou hast found paradise in earth. But as long as it is grievous to thee to suffer and thou seekest to flee, so long it is not well with thee; neither art thou in the perfect way of patience. But if thou couldst bring thyself to that estate that thou shouldst be at, that is, to suffer gladly for God and to die fully to the 95 world, then should it shortly be better with thee and thou shouldst find great peace. But yet, although thou were rapt with Paul into the third heaven [2 Cor. 12: 2], thou shouldst not, therefore, be sure without all adversity; for our Saviour, speaking of Saint Paul after he had been rapt into heaven, said thus of him: 'I shall show him how many things he shall suffer for me' [Acts 9: 16]. To suffer, therefore, to thee remaineth if thou wilt love thy 100 Lord Jesu and serve him perpetually. Would to God that thou were worthy to suffer somewhat for his love. Oh, how great joy should it be to thee to suffer for him! What gladness to all the saints of heaven! And how great edifying to thy neighbour! All men commend patience and yet few men will suffer. Righteously thou oughtest to suffer some little thing for God, that sufferest much more for the world. 105

And know this for certain, that after this bodily death thou shalt yet live, and the more that thou canst die to thyself here, the more thou beginnest to live to God. No man is apt to receive the heavenly reward but he have first learned to bear adversities for the love of Christ, for nothing is more acceptable to God nor more profitable to man in this world than to be glad to suffer for Christ. Insomuch that if it were put in thy election, thou shouldst rather 110 choose adversity than prosperity, for then by the patient suffering thereof thou shouldst be more like to Christ, and the more conformed to all his saints. Our merit and our perfection of life standeth not in consolations and sweetness, but rather in suffering of great grievous adversities and tribulations. For if there had been any nearer or better way for the health of man's soul than to suffer, our Lord Jesu would have showed it by words or by examples. But 115 for there was not, therefore, he openly exhorted his disciples that followed him, and all other

---

79. **Purpose thyself** resolve. 87. **passions** sufferings. 97. **third heaven** God's abode, also called Paradise (2 Cor. 12: 4), located above the aerial heaven where birds fly and the starry heaven. 105. **that** you who. 110. **election** choice.

that desired to follow him, to forsake their own will and to take the cross of penance, and follow him, saying thus: 'Whoso will come after me, forsake he his own will, take he the cross, and follow he me' [Matt. 16: 24]. Therefore, all things searched and read, be this the final conclusion, that by many tribulations it behoveth us to enter into the kingdom of   120 heaven. To the which bring us, our Lord Jesu. Amen.

IGNATIUS LOYOLA

A worldly soldier recovering from a wound in 1521, Ignatius of Loyola (1491–1556) read saints' lives and turned his life to Christ. Undertaking a regimen of penance, study, and prayer, he attracted a small group of followers who became the Society of Jesus (the Jesuits) in 1540, founded 'ad maiorem Dei gloriam et bonum animarum' (for the greater glory of God and the good of souls). The Society differed from other orders in its long period of formation, its refusal of ecclesiastical dignities for members, its lack of a habit and rule, and its constitutional commitment to active ministries (preaching, teaching, retreats, schools), the sacraments, and works of mercy (in hospitals, prisons, and orphanages). Because they originated in Spain, gave allegiance to the pope, and had such members as Robert Persons, who advocated Elizabeth's deposition, the Jesuits aroused hostility. In 1585 An Act against Jesuits and Others stipulated that any Jesuit found in England was *ipso facto* guilty of high treason (27 Elizabeth I, c. 2).

The foundational text of Jesuit spirituality is Ignatius's *Spiritual Exercises*, one of the world's most famous and least understood books. The *Exercises* are actually a guide for a spiritual director, a teacher's manual of drills and meditations meant to guide a retreatant in election, the making of a choice of life, and perfection, the surrender of self to love of God. Focusing on the movements of the heart and intellect in four stages or 'weeks', they enable a personal and profound experience of Jesus Christ. Adopted by Protestants (in modified form), the *Exercises* are a pre-eminent document of the Catholic Reformation, one that echoes throughout early modern poetry (see Donne, POETRY) and culture.

The Spiritual Exercises, 1521–2

First Principle and Foundation

Man was created to praise, do reverence to, and to serve God, our Lord, and thereby to save his soul. And the other things on the face of the earth were created for man's sake,

FIRST PRINCIPLE This is the starting point of the *Exercises* and, it may be said, their ending point, as the retreatant must come to a deep realization of God's presence and the purpose of human life.

and to help him in the following out of the end for which he was created. Hence it follows that man should make use of creatures so far as they do help him towards his end, and should withdraw from them so far as they are a hindrance to him in regard of that end. Wherefore it is necessary to make ourselves indifferent to all created things—in all that is left to the liberty of our free will and is not forbidden it—so that we on our part should not wish for health rather than sickness, for riches rather than poverty, for honour rather than ignominy, for a long life rather than a short life, and so in all other matters, solely desiring and choosing those things which may better lead us to the end for which we were created.

The Examen of our Conscience

The examen of our conscience, that it may be done well, must consist in the five points following here briefly declared. The first is to give thanks unto almighty God for the benefits received at his most liberal hand; to wit, for that he hath created, redeemed, and conserved us, and hath made us Christians, and chiefly for those which he hath done unto us in particular, for which we owe unto such a most liberal Lord special gratitude.

The second is to ask of His Divine Majesty light and grace to know and amend the faults committed against him that day.

The third is to bethink ourselves and diligently to examine from hour to hour, since the morning we did rise until that present time, all our thoughts, words, and deeds, what we have done, spoken, or hath passed in our mind.

The fourth is to render hearty thanks unto God our Lord for all the good which we shall perceive to have done, not attributing unto ourselves (being so bad as we are) any good thing of those which we have done, but unto God who moved us to do them.

The fifth and last is to be sorry with all our heart for the offences we shall discover in ourselves, committed against so good a Lord, craving pardon for them. And so finally (firmly proposing through the assistance of his divine grace to amend), let us repeat this Act of Contrition to obtain pardon for our sins.

O my Lord Jesus Christ, true God and man, my Creator and Redeemer, thou being whom thou art and for that I love thee above all things, I am sorry with all my heart that I have offended thee. And here I firmly purpose never to sin any more, and to avoid all

---

3. **end . . . created** Robert Persons glosses this text as follows: 'If the merchant factor, which I spake of before, after many years spent beyond the seas returning home to give accounts to his master, should yield a reckoning of so much time spent in singing, so much in dancing, so much in courting, and the like, who would not laugh at his accounts? But being further asked by his master what time he bestowed on his merchandise which he sent him for, if he should answer, none at all, nor that he ever thought or studied upon that matter, who would not think him worthy of all shame and punishment? And surely with much more shame and confusion shall they stand at the day of Judgement, who, being placed here to so great a business as is the service of almighty God and the gaining of his eternal kingdom of heaven, have, notwithstanding, neglected the same' (*The First Booke of the Christian Exercise*, Rouen, 1582, sig. C3). **6. indifferent to** Indifference is a key principle of Ignatian spirituality, meaning the ordering of one's affections and desires to God and the freeing of oneself from worldly affections and attachments (*indiferentes á*).

EXAMEN Ignatian spirituality is characterized by daily self-examination. Particular exercises aim at rooting out individual sins; the General Examination here aims at self-purification and preparation for confession. **17. His Divine Majesty** one of Ignatius's favourite expressions for God. **19. bethink** reflect upon.

occasions of offending thee, as also purpose to confess and fulfil the penance enjoined me for the same. And in satisfaction thereof I offer up unto thee thine own sacred Passion, the merits of thy blessed mother, the Virgin Mary, and of all the saints, and all my works, labours, and pains, yea, and my whole life. And I trust in thy infinite goodness and mercy 35 that by the merits of thy most precious blood and passion thou wilt forgive me all my sins and bestow upon me such plenty of thy grace as therewith I may be able to lead a holy life and perfectly to serve thee unto the end.

First Exercise: A Meditation on Sin

The preparatory prayer is to ask grace of God our Lord that all my intentions, actions, and operations may be directed purely to the service and praise of His Divine Majesty. 40

The first prelude is a composition, seeing the place. Here it is to be observed that in contemplation, or visible meditation, as contemplating Christ our Lord, who is visible, the composition will be to see with the eye of the imagination the corporeal place where there is found the object which I wish to contemplate. By corporeal place I mean, for instance, a temple or mountain where Jesus Christ is found, or our Lady, according as I 45 wish to contemplate. In meditation of the invisible, as here of sins, the composition will be to see with the eye of the imagination and consider my soul imprisoned in this corruptible body, and my whole compound self in this vale of tears as in banishment among brute animals. I mean the whole compound of soul and body.

The second prelude is to ask of God our Lord that which I wish and desire. The 50 petition ought to be according to the subject matter: that is to say, if the contemplation is on the Resurrection, to ask for joy with Christ rejoicing; if it is on the Passion, to ask for pains, tears, and torment with Christ tormented. Here it will be to ask for shame and confusion at myself, seeing how many have been damned for one mortal sin, and how often I have deserved to be damned eternally for those many sins of mine. 55

Before all contemplations and meditations there ought always to be made the preparatory prayer without change and the two above-mentioned preludes, changing them from time to time according to the subject matter.

The first point will be to carry the memory over the first sin, which was that of the angels, and then the understanding over the same, reasoning; then the will, seeking to 60 remember and understand it all that I may the more blush and be confounded, bringing into comparison with the one sin of the angels those many sins of mine, and seeing that they for one sin have gone to hell, how often I have deserved it for so many. I say, to bring into memory the sin of the angels, how having been created in grace, and then refusing to

FIRST EXERCISE This beginning exercise, like all those of the first week, brings the retreatant to a realization of sin in the world and self by using the three powers of the soul—memory, intellect or understanding, and will. The exercise focuses first on the sins of the angels and Adam to establish the context of salvation history and aims at purification or purgation. **39. preparatory prayer** Ignatius thought this an important first step in all meditations. **40. operations** mental activities (*operaciones*). **41. composition . . . place** Ignatius frequently directs the retreatant to imagine concretely scenes from the Bible, especially from Christ's life. **42. visible meditation** meditation on a visible thing. **50. that . . . desire** Ignatius constantly focuses on the heart, on wants and desires, in order to make the retreatant realize that true desire can only be for eternal life in Christ and not for the false goods of riches, pleasures, or honours.

help themselves by the aid of their liberty to pay reverence and obedience to their Creator   65
and Lord, coming to pride, they were changed from grace to malice and cast down from
heaven to hell; and so consequently to discourse more in detail with the understanding,
and thereupon more to stir the affections by the will.

The second, to do as much again, that is to say, to carry the three powers over the sin of
Adam and Eve, bringing into memory how for that sin they did such long penance, and   70
what great corruption has come over mankind, so many men going to hell. I say, to bring
into memory the second sin, that of our parents, how after Adam had been created in the
plain of Damascus and placed in the earthly paradise and Eve had been formed from his
rib, being forbidden to eat of the Tree of Knowledge, they ate and thereby sinned. And
afterwards, clad in frocks of skins and cast out of paradise, they lived without the original   75
justice which they had lost, all their life in many travails and much penance; and
thereupon to discourse with the understanding more in detail and use the will, as has
been said.

The third, in like manner to do as much again over the third particular sin, of one
individual, who for one mortal sin has gone to hell, and many others without number for   80
fewer sins than I have committed. I say, to do as much again over the third particular sin,
bringing into memory the grievousness and malice of that sin against the man's Creator
and Lord; to discourse with the understanding how in sinning and acting against infinite
goodness he has justly been condemned for ever; and to conclude with acts of the will, as
has been said.   85

Colloquy. Imagining Christ our Lord present and placed on the cross, to make a
colloquy, how of being Creator he has come to make himself man, and pass from eternal
life to temporal death, and so to die for my sins. In like manner, looking at myself, what I
have done for Christ, what I am doing for Christ, what I ought to do for Christ; and so
seeing him in such condition and so fastened on the cross, to think over what shall occur.   90

The colloquy is made, properly speaking, just as one friend speaks to another or a
servant to his master, now asking for some favour, now reproaching oneself for some evil
done, now telling out one's affairs and seeking counsel in them. And say one Our Father.

Rules for the Discernment of Spirits

The third, of spiritual consolation: I call it 'consolation' when there is set up in the soul
some inward motion, whereby the soul begins to be on fire with the love of her Creator   95
and Lord, and, consequently, when she can love no created thing on the face of the earth
in itself but only in the Creator of them all. Likewise, when she bursts forth into tears out
of love of her Lord, be it for grief over her sins, or over the Passion of Christ our Lord, or
over other matters directly ordered to his service and praise. In short, I call 'consolation'

---

86. *Colloquy* Ignatius ends each exercise with a colloquy or 'conversation,' here with Christ himself.

DISCERNMENT OF SPIRITS the discrimination between good spirits (God and the angels) and evil spirits (Lucifer and
the devils) as they cause motions in the soul. **94. consolation** not sensory pleasures, ephemeral feelings of happiness, self-
satisfactions, or good feelings, but the deep inner peace of Christ's love that increases compassion and charity in the human heart.

any increase of hope, faith, and charity, and any inward joy that calls and attracts   100
to heavenly things and to the salvation of one's own soul, rendering her restful and
pacifying her in her Creator and Lord.

The fourth, of spiritual desolation: I call 'desolation' everything that is contrary to
the third rule—as a darkening of the soul, trouble of mind, movement to base and
earthly things, restlessness of various agitations and temptations, moving to distrust, loss   105
of hope, loss of love; when the soul feels herself thoroughly apathetic, tepid, sad, and, as
it were, separated from her Creator and Lord; because as consolation is contrary to
desolation in the same way the thoughts that spring from consolation are contrary to the
thoughts that spring from desolation.

The fifth: in time of desolation one ought never to make a change but to stand firm   110
and steady in the resolutions and determination in which one was on the day previous to
such desolation, or in the determination in which one was in the previous consolation;
because as in consolation the good spirit rather leads us and directs us by his counsel, so
in desolation does the evil spirit, by whose counsels we cannot find the way to any right
resolve.   115

The sixth: though in desolation we ought not to change our previous purposes, it
is very helpful heartily to change ourselves in the direction contrary to the said desolation—for instance, by insisting more on prayer, meditation, much examination, and
putting out our strength in some suitable manner of doing penance.

The seventh: let him who is in desolation consider how God is leaving him by way of   120
probation to his natural powers that he may stand out against the various agitations and
temptations of the enemy; for he can stand out with the divine aid, which ever attends
upon him although he does not manifestly feel it, because the Lord has withdrawn from
him his high fervour, strong love, and intense grace, yet leaving him grace enough for
eternal salvation.   125

The eighth: let him who is in desolation labour to hold on in patience, such patience as
makes against the vexations that harass him. Let him consider that soon he shall be
consoled, using diligent efforts against such desolation, as is enjoined in the sixth rule.

The ninth: there are three chief causes why we find ourselves in desolation. The first is
by reason of our being tepid, indolent, or negligent in our spiritual exercises, and so for   130
our faults spiritual consolation goes away. The second, to prove us, what we are worth
and how far we will hold on in his service and praise without so much remuneration of
consolations and ample graces. The third, to give us a true knowledge and understanding
whereby we may inwardly feel that it is not in our power to bring on or maintain a flood
of devotion, intense love, tears, nor any other spiritual consolation, but that it is all a gift   135
and grace of God our Lord; and that we may not build our nest in another man's house,

---

103. **desolation** not mere sadness, or pain, but the deep alienation from God and the service of self or Satan, 'the fell of dark not day' as Gerard Manley Hopkins put it. 121. **probation** trial. **stand out** resist. 136. **build ... house** take credit for something not our own.

lifting up our intellect to some pride or vain glory, attributing to ourselves devotion or other parts of spiritual consolation.

The tenth: let him who is in consolation think how he shall carry himself in the desolation that will come on afterwards, gathering new strength for that time.   140

The eleventh: let him who is in consolation take care to humble and abase himself as much as he can, thinking how little he is worth in time of desolation, without such grace or consolation. On the other hand, let him who is in desolation think that he can do much with the grace that he has, sufficient to withstand all his enemies, taking strength in his Creator and Lord.   145

A Meditation on Two Standards

The usual preparatory prayer.

The first prelude is the history. Here it will be how Christ calls and wishes for all men under his standard, and Lucifer contrariwise under his.

The second, the composition, seeing the place. It will be here to see a great plain, taking in all that region of Jerusalem, where is the Captain-General-in-Chief of the good,   150
Christ our Lord; another plain in the region of Babylonia, where is the bandit-chief of the enemies, Lucifer.

The third, to ask for what I want, and it will be here to beg a knowledge of the machinations of the evil bandit-chief and aid to be on my guard against them; and a knowledge of the true life which the sovereign and true captain shows forth, and grace to   155
imitate him.

The first point is to imagine the bandit-chief of all the enemies in that great plain of Babylonia, seated, as it were, in a sort of big chair of fire and smoke—a horrid and terrible figure.

The second, how he calls a convocation of countless demons, and how he scatters   160
them, these to such a city and those to another, and so all the world over, leaving out no provinces, places, states, nor any private individuals.

The third, to consider the address that he makes them, and how he urges them to cast nets and chains so that they should tempt men first with the desire of riches, as is his wont in most cases, to the end that they may more easily come on to the vain honour of the   165
world, and thence to swollen pride. Thus the first stage is to be that of riches, the second of honours, the third of pride. And from these three stages he leads on to all the other vices.

In like manner contrariwise we must exercise the imagination on the sovereign and true captain, who is Christ our Lord.   170

The first point is to consider how Christ our Lord takes his stand in a great plain of that region of Jerusalem, in a lowly place, fair and gracious.

TWO STANDARDS Standards (*banderas*) are flags or banners around which followers and soldiers rally. The celebrated meditation depicts human life as the scene of a stark struggle between Christ and Lucifer. No mere superstition, the devil had a real presence in the early modern world (see Weston, LIVES AND DEATHS).

The second, to consider how the Lord of the whole world chooses ever so many persons, apostles, disciples, etc., and sends them all the world over, spreading his sacred doctrine through all sorts and conditions of men.   175

The third, to consider the address which Christ our Lord delivers to all his servants and friends whom he sends on the said expedition, commending to them to be ready to help all, leading them first to the highest spiritual poverty, and—if it shall please His Divine Majesty and he shall will to choose them—not less to actual poverty; secondly, to the desire of reproaches and affronts, because out of these two things ensues humility.   180 Thus there are three stages: the first, poverty against riches; the second, reproach or affront against worldly honour; the third, humility against pride. And by these three stages they are to lead men on to all the other virtues.

A colloquy with our Lady, to obtain for me grace from her son and our Lord that I may be received under his standard; and first, in the highest spiritual poverty, and—if it shall   185 please His Divine Majesty and he shall will to choose and receive me—not less in actual poverty; secondly, in enduring insults and injuries, the better to imitate him therein, provided I can bear them without sin of any person or displeasure of His Divine Majesty. And thereupon a Hail Mary.

To ask the same of the Son, that he may obtain it for me from the Father, and   190 thereupon say *Anima Christi*.

To ask the same of the Father, that he would grant it to me, and say an Our Father.

A Contemplation to attain Love

First it is desirable to note two things.

The first is that love ought to be placed rather in works than in words.

The second, love consists in mutual interchange on either side, that is to say, in the   195 lover giving to and sharing with the loved one that which he has or can attain; and so, conversely, the loved one doing the like for the lover, so that if one has science, he gives to the other who has it not, if honours, if riches, and so, one to another.

The usual prayer.

First prelude is a composition, which is here to see how I stand before God our Lord,   200 the angels, the saints interceding for me.

---

178. spiritual poverty purification of self from all attachment to worldly goods. **180. humility** submission of self to God, a virtue arising from awareness of one's weakness and imperfections. In the exercises for the second week, Ignatius distinguishes between three degrees of humility: (1) the abasement of self for God; (2) the indifference to self for God; (3) the wish to suffer poverty and reproaches with Christ. The degrees distinguish between suppression of desire, cessation of desire, and transformation of desire. **191. *Anima Christi*** 'Soul of Christ', a 14th-c. prayer, often mistakenly attributed to Ignatius: 'Soul of Christ, sanctify me. Body of Christ, save me. Blood of Christ, inebriate me. Water from the side of Christ, wash me. Passion of Christ, strengthen me. O good Jesus, hear me. Within your wounds hide me. Do not allow me to be separated from you. From the malevolent enemy defend me. In the hour of my death call me and bid me come unto you, that with your saints I may praise you forever and ever. Amen.'

CONTEMPLATION TO ATTAIN LOVE This culminating meditation increases the retreatant's love of God by increasing awareness of God's love and presence in all things.

The second, to ask for that which I want. It will be here to ask for an inward knowledge of so much good received in order that I, being fully grateful for the same, may in all things love and serve His Divine Majesty.

The first point is to bring into memory the benefits received of creation, redemption, and particular gifts, pondering with much affection how much God our Lord has done for me, and how much he has given me of what he has, and, further, the same Lord desires to give himself to me so far as he can according to his divine ordinance; and therewithal to reflect within myself, considering with much reason and justice what I ought on my part to offer and give to His Divine Majesty, to wit, all my possessions and myself with them, as one who offers with much affection: 'Take, O Lord, and receive all my liberty, my memory, my understanding, and all my will, all I have and possess. You have given it me; to you, Lord, I return it; all is yours, dispose of it entirely according to your will. Give me your love and grace, because that is enough for me.'

The second, to look how God dwells in creatures, in the elements giving being, in the plants giving vegetation, in the animals giving sensation, in men giving understanding, and so in me, giving me being, life, sensation, and making me understand; likewise making of me a temple, as I am created to the likeness and image of His Divine Majesty; in the same way reflecting on myself in the manner mentioned in the first point, or in some other way which I may deem better. In the same manner it shall be done over each point that follows.

The third, to consider how God works and labours for me in all things created on the face of the earth—that is, he holds himself as one who labours—as in the heavens, elements, plants, fruits, flocks, etc., giving being, conservation, vegetable, and sensitive life, etc.; then to reflect on myself.

The fourth, to look how all good things and gifts descend from above, as my limited powers from that power sovereign and infinite above, and so justice, goodness, pity, mercy, etc., as from the sun come down the rays, from the spring the waters, etc. Then to conclude, reflecting on myself, as has been said. To end with a colloquy and an Our Father.

CONSOLATIONS

Comforting the suffering and dying, ancients like Cicero, Seneca, Pliny, and Plutarch created a genre of philosophical consolation that found late representation in Boethius's medieval *De consolatione philosophiae*. Christian writers inflected the genre with a biblical

---

211–14. 'Take...me' the *Suscipe*, Ignatius's prayer of total surrender and dedication to God. **215. God...creatures** Ignatian spirituality modifies the *contemptus mundi* (contempt of the world) of other religious traditions by recognizing God's presence in creation and abiding care for all things.

contemptus mundi, a belief in providence, and hopeful anticipation of the next life. Both traditions mingle in early modern England, where over seventy consolations circulated in the Tudor period alone. The three consolations excerpted below offer comfort to Catholics suffering persecution. Imprisoned in the Tower for opposing Henry VIII's divorce and new church, Bishop John Fisher's (1469–1535) *A Spiritual Consolation* (1534) shocks readers to repentance by presenting the lament of a sinner facing death. Also awaiting execution in the Tower at the same time (see LIVES AND DEATHS), Thomas More wrote *A Dialogue of Comfort against Tribulation* (1534), which addresses compellingly the problems of human freedom and death. Robert Southwell's *An Epistle of Comfort* (1588; see also POETRY) inspires the persecuted to the crown of martyrdom. These works stand worthily with other consolations in the period, including those of the Huguenot Philippe de Mornay (*Excellent Discours de la Vie et de la Mort*, 1577, often translated) and the poet/minister John Donne (*Devotions upon Emergent Occasions*, 1624; *Death's Duel*, 1632).

John Fisher, *A Spiritual Consolation*, 1534

For if it shall please my Lord God that I might any longer live, I would otherwise exercise myself than I have done before. Now I wish that I may have time and place but righteously I am denied, for when I might have had it I would not well use it. And, therefore, now when I would well use it, I shall not have it. O ye, therefore, that have and may use this precious time in your liberty, employ it well and be not wasteful thereof, lest, peradven- 5
ture, when you would have it, it shall be denied you likewise as now it is to me.

But now I repent me full sore of my great negligence, and right much I sorrow that so little I regarded the wealth and profit of my soul, but rather took heed to the vain comforts and pleasures of my wretched body. O corruptible body, O stinking carrion, O rotten earth to whom I have served, whose appetites I have followed, whose desire I have 10
procured! Now dost thou appear what thou art in thy own likeness. That brightness of thy eyes, that quickness in hearing, that liveliness in thy other senses by natural warmness, thy swiftness and nimbleness, thy fairness and beauty—all these thou hast not of thyself. They were but lent unto thee for a season, even as a wall of earth that is fair painted without for a season with fresh and goodly colours and also gilt with gold, it 15
appeareth goodly for the time to such as consider no deeper than the outward craft thereof. But when at the last the colour faileth and the gilting falleth away, then appeareth it in his own likeness. For then the earth plainly showeth itself.

In like wise my wretched body for the time of youth it appeareth fresh and lusty, and I was deceived with the outward beauty thereof, little considering what naughtiness was 20

---

7. **full sore** grievously. 15. **without** on the outside. 16. **craft** art. 19. **wise** manner.

covered underneath. But now it showeth itself. Now, my wretched body, thy beauty is faded, thy fairness is gone, thy lust, thy strength, thy liveliness—all is gone, all is failed. Now art thou then returned to thine own earthly colour. Now art thou black, cold, and heavy, like a lump of earth. Thy sight is darkened, thy hearing is dulled, thy tongue faltereth in thy mouth, and corruption issueth out of every part of thee. Corruption was 25 thy beginning in the womb of thy mother and corruption is thy continuance. All thing that ever thou receivest, were it never so precious, thou turnest into corruption, and naught came from thee at any time but corruption, and now to corruption thyself returnest.

Thomas More, *A Dialogue of Comfort Against Tribulation*, 1534

Of imprisonment and comfort thereagainst

ANTHONY Yet forgat I, cousin, to ask you one question.

VINCENT What is that, uncle?

ANTHONY This, lo: If there be two men kept in two several chambers of one great castle, of which two chambers the one is much more large than the other, whether be they prisoners both or but the one that hath the less room to walk in?　　5

VINCENT What question is it, uncle, but that they be prisoners both, as I said myself before, although the one lay fast locked in the stocks and the other had all the whole castle to walk in.

ANTHONY Methinketh, verily, cousin, that you say the truth. And that if prisonment be such a thing as yourself here agree it is, that is, to wit, but a lack of liberty to go whither 10 we list, now would I fain wit of you what any one man you know that is at this day out of prison?

VINCENT What one man, uncle? Marry, I know almost none other. For surely, prisoner am I none acquainted with that I remember.

ANTHONY Then, I see well you visit poor prisoners seld.　　15

VINCENT No, by troth, uncle, I cry God mercy. I send them sometime mine alms, but, by my troth, I love not to come myself where I should see such misery.

ANTHONY In good faith, cousin Vincent, though I say it before you, you have many good conditions, but surely, though I say it before you too, that condition is none of them. Which condition, if you would amend, then should you have yet the more good 20 conditions by one and, peradventure, the more by three or four. For I assure you it is

---

DIALOGUE Imitating in part the Platonic dialogues, More stages a conversation between two Hungarians under threat of invasion by the Turks, Anthony (the wise uncle) and Vincent (the naive nephew). **1. cousin** kinsman. **3. several** separate. **7. stocks** device of wooden slats that immobilized a prisoner's head and hands. **11. list** wish. **fain wit** gladly know. **13. Marry** by Mary (an oath). **15. seld** seldom. **16. troth** truth. **cry God mercy** an expression of exasperation and impatience. **19. conditions** virtues. **that condition** the virtue of mercy. **21. peradventure** by chance.

hard to tell how much good to a man's soul the personal visiting of poor prisoners doth.

But now, sith ye can name me none of them that are in prison, I pray you, name me some one of all them that you be, as you say, better acquainted with, men, I mean, that are out of prison; for I know, methinketh, as few of them as you know of the other.

VINCENT That were, uncle, a strange case. For every man is, uncle, out of prison that may go where he will, though he be the poorest beggar in the town. And in good faith, uncle, because you reckon imprisonment so small a matter of itself, the poor beggar that is at his liberty and may walk where he will is, as me seemeth, in better case than is a king kept in prison, that cannot go but where men give him leave.

ANTHONY Well, cousin, whether every way-walking beggar be by this reason out of prison or no, we shall consider further when you will. But in the meanwhile I can by this reason see no prince that seemeth to be out of prison. For if the lack of liberty to go where a man will be imprisonment, as yourself say it is, then is the great Turk, by whom we so fear to be put in prison, in prison already himself, for he may not go where he will. For an he might, he would into Portingale, Italy, Spain, France, Almaine, and England, and as far on another quarter too, both Prester John's land and the Grand Cam's too.

Now the beggar that you speak of: if he be, as you say he is, by reason of his liberty to go where he will, in much better case than a king kept in prison, because he cannot go but where men give him leave, then is that beggar in better case not only than a prince in prison but also than many a prince out of prison too. For I am sure there is many a beggar that may without let walk further upon other men's ground than many a prince at his best liberty may walk upon his own. And as for walking out abroad upon other men's, that prince might hap to be said nay and holden fast, where that beggar with his bag and his staff should be suffered to go forth and hold on his way.

But, forasmuch, cousin, as neither the beggar nor the prince is at free liberty to walk where they will, but that if they would walk in some place neither of them both should be suffered but men would withstand them and say them nay, therefore, if imprisonment be (as you grant it is) a lack of liberty to go where we list, I cannot see but, as I say, the beggar and the prince whom you reckon both at liberty be by your own reason restrained in prison both.

[. . .]

ANTHONY Consider, then, cousin, whether this thing seem any sophistry to you that I shall show you now, for it shall be such as seemeth in good faith substantial true to me. And if it so happen that you think otherwise, I will be very glad to perceive which

---

30. **me seemeth** it seems to me. 37. **an** if. **Portingale** Portugal. **Almaine** Germany. 38. **quarter** part (i.e. the east). **Prester John** legendary ruler of India or Ethiopia. 38–9 **Grand Cam** i.e. Grand Khan, legendary ruler of China or the Mongols. 44. **let** hindrance. 46. **hap . . . nay** chance to be denied. **holden** held, stopped. 47. **hold** continue.

of us both is beguiled. For it seemeth to me, cousin, first, that every man coming into this world here upon earth, as he is created by God, so cometh he hither by the providence of God. Is this any sophistry first or not?

VINCENT Nay, verily, this is very substantial truth.   60

ANTHONY Now take I this also for very truth in my mind: that there cometh no man nor woman hither into the earth but that ere ever they come quick into the world out of the mother's womb, God condemneth them unto death by his own sentence and judgement for the original sin that they bring with them, contracted in the corrupted stock of our forefather, Adam. Is this, think you, cousin, verily thus or not?   65

VINCENT This is, uncle, very true indeed.

ANTHONY Then seemeth this true further unto me: that God hath put every man here upon the earth under so sure and under so safe keeping that of all the whole people living in this wide world there is neither man, woman, nor child—would they never so far wander about and seek it—that possibly can find any way whereby they may 'scape   70 from death. Is this, cousin, a fond, imagined fantasy or is it very truth indeed?

VINCENT Nay, this is none imagination, uncle, but a thing so clearly proved true that no man is so mad to say nay.

ANTHONY Then need I no more, cousin, for then is all the matter plain and open evident truth which I said I took for truth. Which is yet more a little now than I told you   75 before, when you took my proof yet but for a sophistical fantasy and said that, for all my reasoning that every man is a prisoner, yet you thought that except these whom the common people call prisoners, there is else no man a very prisoner indeed. And now you grant yourself again for very substantial, open truth that every man is here (though he be the greatest king upon earth), set here by the ordinance of God in a place (be it   80 never so large), a place, I say, yet (and you say the same) out of which no man can escape, but that therein is every man put under sure and safe keeping to be readily set forth when God calleth for him, and that then he shall surely die. And is not then, cousin, by your own granting before, every man a very prisoner when he is put in a place to be kept to be brought forth when he would not, and himself wot not whither?   85

VINCENT Yes, in good faith, uncle, I cannot but well perceive this to be so.

ANTHONY This were, you wot well, true, although a man should be but taken by the arm and in fair manner led out of this world unto his judgement. But now while we well know that there is no king so great but that all the while he walketh here, walk he never so loose, ride he with never so strong an army for his defence, yet himself is very sure—   90 though he seek in the mean season some other pastime to put it out of his mind—yet is he very sure, I say, that escape can he not. And very well he knoweth that he hath already sentence given upon him to die, and that, verily, die he shall, and that himself, though he hope upon long respite of his execution, yet can he not tell how soon, and, therefore (but if he be a fool), he can never be without fear that either on the morrow   95

---

62. ere before.   71. fond foolish.   85. wot know.   90. loose freely.   91. mean season meanwhile.   95. but except.

or on the self-same day the grisly, cruel hangman Death, which from his first coming in hath ever hovered a-loose, and looked toward him, and ever lien in a wait on him shall, amid all his royalty and all his main strength, neither kneel before him, nor make him any reverence, nor with any good manner desire him to come forth, but rigorously and fiercely grip him by the very breast and make all his bones rattle, and so by long and divers sore torments strike him stark dead in this prison; and then cause his body to be cast into the ground in a foul pit within some corner of the same, there to rot and be eaten with the wretched worms of the earth, sending yet his soul out further unto a more fearful judgement, whereof at his temporal death his success is uncertain; and, therefore, though by God's grace not out of good hope, yet for all that in the meanwhile in very sore dread and fear and, peradventure, in peril inevitable of eternal fire too.

Methinketh, therefore, cousin, that (as I told you) this keeping of every man in this wretched world for execution of death is a very plain imprisonment indeed. And that (as I say) such, that the greatest king is in this prison in much worse case in all his wealth than many a man is by the other imprisonment that is therein sore and hardly handled, for where some of those lie not there attainted nor condemned to death, the greatest man of this world and the most wealthy in this universal prison is laid in to be kept undoubtedly for death.

Robert Southwell, *An Epistle of Comfort*, 1588

Tribulation best agreeth with the place and condition of this life

But though this example of Christ and the title of a Christian were not so forcible motives to suffer adversity as they be, yet, considering where we are, what state we stand in, the dangers that hang over us, and our ordinary misses and wants, we shall find that our whole life is so necessarily joined with sorrows that it might rather seem a madness to live in pleasure than odious to live in pain.

Consider, O man, saith St Bernard, from whence thou comest, and blush whither thou goest, and fear where thou livest, and lament. We are begotten in uncleanness, nourished in darkness, brought forth with throbs and throes. Our infancy is but a dream, our youth but a madness, our manhood a combat, our age a sickness, our life misery, our death horror. If we have anything that delighteth us, it is in so many hazards that more is the fear of losing it than the joy of the use of it. If we have anything that annoyeth us, the aggrievance thereof increaseth with the doubt of as evil or worse that may straight ensue after it.

97. **a-loose** around freely. **lien** lay. 98. **main** great. 112. **attainted** convicted. 113. **laid in** confined.
EPISTLE This work originated in a letter Southwell wrote to comfort Philip Howard, 1st earl of Arundel, imprisoned in the Tower for his faith. 11. **aggrievance** burden. 12. **doubt** fear.

Which way can we cast our eyes but that we shall find cause of complaint and heaviness? If we look up towards heaven, from thence we are banished. If we look towards earth, we are there imprisoned. On the right hand we have the saints, whose steps we have not followed; on the left hand the wicked, whose course we have pursued. Before us we have our death ready to devour us; behind us our wicked life ready to accuse us; above us God's justice ready to condemn us; under us hell-fire ready to swallow us into endless and everlasting torments.

And, therefore, St Damascene most fitly compareth us to a man that, pursued by an enraged unicorn, while he was swiftly fleeing from it, fell into a well, and in the falling got hold by a little tree, and settled his feet on a weak stay, and thus thought himself very secure. But looking a little better about him, he espied two mice, one white and another black, that continually lay gnawing asunder the root of the tree which he held by, underneath him a terrible dragon with open jaws ready to devour him. At the stay of his feet he found four adders that issued out of the wall. And after all this, lifting up his eye, he espied upon one of the boughs of the tree a little honey. He, therefore, unmindful of all his dangers, not remembering that above the unicorn waited to spoil him, that beneath the fiery dragon watched to swallow him, that the tree was quickly to be gnawn asunder, that the stay of his feet was slippery and not to trust unto—not remembering, I say, all these perils, he only thought how he might come by that little honey.

The unicorn is death; the pit, the world; the tree, the measure and time of our life; the white and black mice, the day and night; the stop borne up by four adders, our body framed of four brittle and contrary elements; the dragon, the devil; the honey, worldly pleasure. Who, therefore, would not think it a madness in so many dangers rather to be eager of vain delight than fearful and sad with consideration of so manifold perils? O blindness of worldlings, that 'love vanity and seek lies' (Ps. 4: 3), that 'rejoice when they have done evil and triumph in the baddest things' (Prov. 2: 14), that have no fear of God before them. 'A nation without counsel or prudence. Oh, that they would be wise, understand, and provide for their last things' (Deut. 32: 28–9), lest it fare with them as Job saith: 'They hold the drum and cithern, and rejoice at the sound of the organ; they pass their days in pleasure and in a moment they descend into hell' (Job 21: 12–13).

MEDITATIONS

Arising from Scripture, patristic writing, and early Christian practice, the traditions of Catholic meditation or 'mental prayer' are rich and deep. Early modern manuals and handbooks by such writers as Antonio de Molina and Gaspare Loarte, provide instructions

20. **St Damascene** John of Damascus, 8th-c. Church Father. **22. stay** support. **34. four...elements** earth, air, fire, and water, supposed the basic elements of creation. **41. cithern** wire-strung instrument.

for beginner and advanced students. The practice of Catholic, like Protestant, meditation entails careful self-examination and the contemplation of biblical passages; it enlists the imagination and understanding to move the heart in order to reform the will. The meditant aims at transforming a life enslaved to sin to one animated by grace and the indwelling Word.

The Catholic Church everywhere encouraged and taught meditation. Below, Luis de Granada, an influential Spanish Dominican, offers a sample meditation on the Scourging at the Pillar. Next John Bucke gives instructions on praying the rosary, a beloved and much misunderstood meditative practice, consisting of prayers correlated to a string of beads. Dismissed as merely mechanical repetition, the rosary actually provides ordered access to the fifteen traditional mysteries of redemption—Joyful (Annunciation, Visitation, Nativity, Presentation, Finding in the Temple), Sorrowful (Agony in the Garden, Scourging at the Pillar, Crowning with Thorns, Carrying the Cross, Crucifixion), and Glorious (Resurrection, Ascension, Descent of Holy Spirit, Assumption, Coronation of Mary). (Pope John Paul II added five Luminous mysteries.) Below John Bucke focuses on the Annunciation (Luke 1: 26–38), a moment signally important to the Catholic imagination, celebrated in churches, art, and literature throughout all Christendom (see Fra Angelico's fresco, Fig. 11).

Luis de Granada, *Of Prayer and Meditation*, 1582

The Scourging at the Pillar

This is one of the greatest and most wonderful sights that ever was seen in the world. Who would ever have thought that whips and lashes should have been laid upon the shoulders of almighty God? The prophet David saith that 'The place of thy habitation, O Lord, is most high', and that 'there shall none evil approach near unto thee'. He saith that 'there shall no whip be felt in thy tabernacle' (Ps. 90). Now what thing is farther 5 from the high majesty and glory of almighty God than to be villainously whipped and scourged? This is surely a punishment rather for bondslaves and thieves. Yea, it was accounted generally so vile and infamous that in case the offender were a citizen of Rome, though his offence were never so heinous, he was thereby quit and exempted from that most slavish and villainous kind of punishment. All which notwithstanding, behold here 10 how the lord of the heavens, the creator of the world, the glory of the angels, the wisdom, power, and glory of the living God vouchsafeth for our sakes to be punished with whips and scourges! Certainly I do believe that all the orders of angels were wholly amazed and

---

1. **wonderful** astonishing. 12. **vouchsafeth** grants.

11. Fra Angelico (1387–1455). 'The Annunciation', San Marco, Florence. The angel Gabriel greets Mary with the news that she is to give birth to Jesus Christ (Luke 1: 26–38).

astonished when they beheld this so strange and wonderful sight, and that they adored
and acknowledged the unspeakable goodness of almighty God, which was very mani-   15
festly discovered unto them in this act (Luke 2). Wherefore, if they filled the air with
high lauds and praises upon the day of his nativity, when as yet they had seen nothing
else but only the swaddling clouts and the manger where he was laid, what did they now,
trow ye, when they beheld him so villainously and most cruelly whipped and scourged at
the pillar? Consider thou, therefore, O my soul, unto whom this business appertaineth   20
much more than to the angels, consider, I say, how much more oughtest thou to be
inwardly moved in thy very heart with this so wonderful and most pitiful, doleful sight of
thy sweet Saviour, and to acknowledge unto him much more humble thanks and praise
for his so passing great love showed hereby unto thee.

Go now, therefore, and enter with thy spirit into Pilate's consistory and carry with thee   25
great store of tears in a readiness, which in that place shall be very needful to bewail such
things as there thou shalt both hear and see. Consider on the one side with what rudeness
those cruel and bloody tormentors do strip our Saviour of his garments. And see on the
other side with what humility he suffereth himself to be stripped by them, never so much
as once opening his mouth or answering one word to so many despiteful scoffs and   30
blasphemous speeches as they uttered there against him. Consider also what haste they
make to bind that holy body to a pillar, that being fast bound they might fetch their full
strokes more at pleasure and strike him where and how they list. Consider how the lord
of angels standeth their post alone among so many cruel tormentors, having on his part
neither friend nor acquaintance to entreat or defend him from injury, no, not so much as   35
eyes to take compassion upon him. Mark now with what furious cruelty they begin to
discharge their whips and scourges upon his most tender flesh, and how they lay on lashes
upon lashes, strokes upon strokes, and wounds upon wounds.

There mightest thou see that sacred body swollen with wheals, all black and blue, the
skin rented and torn, the blood gushing out and streaming down on every side throughout   40
all parts of his body.

But above all this, what a pitiful sight was it to behold that so great and deep open
wound that was given him upon the shoulders, where chiefly all their lashes and strokes
did light! Verily, I am persuaded that that wound was so large and deep that if they had
laid on a little longer, they had discovered the white bones between the bloody flesh and   45
made an end of his holy life at the pillar before he had come to the cross. To be short, they
so struck and rent that most amiable and beautiful body, they so bound him and laid on
such load of stripes and lashes upon him, they so tormented and filled his blessed body
with most cruel strokes and wounds, that he had now clean lost the form and shape he
had before. Yea, and to say further, they so foully disfigured him that he scarcely seemed   50
to have the shape of a man. Consider now, O my soul, in what a doleful plight that

---

18. **clouts** cloths. **19. trow ye** do you think. **24. passing** surpassing. **25. consistory** council-chamber. **30. despiteful**
contemptuous. **39. wheals** welts.

goodly and bashful young man stood there, being as he was in that pitiful case so evil entreated, so reproachfully used, and set out so nakedly to the utter shame of the world. Behold how that most tender and beautiful flesh, yea, even the flower of all flesh, is there most cruelly rent and torn in all parts of it. 55

The law of Moses commanded that malefactors should be beaten with whips and that according to the quality of their offences so should the number of the lashes be, howbeit with this condition, that they should never pass forty lashes, to the end (saith the law) that thy brother fall not down before thee, foully torn and mangled, seeming to the lawmaker that to exceed this number was a kind of punishment so cruel that it could not 60 stand with the laws of brotherly love (Deut. 25). But against thee, O good Jesus, that didst never break the law of justice, were broken all the laws of mercy. Yea, and that in such sort that instead of forty lashes, they gave thee five thousand and above, as many holy fathers do testify. If then a body would seem so foully berayed, being scourged not passing with forty stripes, in what plight was thy body, my sweet Lord and Saviour, being 65 scourged with above five thousand stripes? O joy of the angels and glory of the saints, who hath thus disfigured thee? Who hath thus defiled thee with so many spots, being the very glass of innocency? Certain it is, O Lord, that they were not thy sins but mine, not thy robberies but mine that have thus evil entreated thee. It was even love and mercy that compassed thee about and caused thee to take upon thee this so heavy a burden. 70 Love was the cause why thou didst bestow upon me all thy benefits, and mercy moved thee to take upon thee all my miseries. Wherefore, if love and mercy have caused thee to enter into these so cruel and terrible conflicts, who can now stand in doubt of thy love? If the greatest testimony of love be to suffer pains for the beloved, what else are each one of thy pains but a several testimony of thy love? 75

What else are all these wounds of thine but, as it were, certain heavenly voices that do all preach and proclaim unto me thy love and require me to love thee again? And if the testimonies be so many as the stripes and blows were that thou suffered for my sake, who can then put any doubt in the proof, being as it is so plainly avouched and proved by so many witnesses? What meaneth, then, this incredulity of mine that is not yet convinced 80 with so manifold and so great arguments? Saint John the Evangelist wondered at the incredulity of the Jews for that our Lord wrought so many miracles among them for confirmation of his doctrine and they, nevertheless, would not believe in him (John 12). O holy Evangelist, wonder no more at the incredulity of the Jews but rather at mine. For so much as to suffer pains is no less argument to cause me to believe the love of Christ 85 than is the working of miracles to cause me to believe in Christ. If, then, it be a great wonder that after so many miracles wrought by our Saviour Christ his words are not yet believed, how much more wonderful is it that, having suffered for our sakes above five thousand stripes, we believe not yet that he loveth us?

---

52. **bashful** modest. 53. **entreated** treated. 63. **sort** fashion. 64. **berayed** disfigured. 68. **glass** mirror. 75. **several** multiple.

But what shall we say if to all these strokes and wounds which he received for us at the pillar, we add, moreover, all the other pains and travails of his whole life, all which proceeded of love? What brought thee down, O Lord, from heaven unto the earth but only love? What thing pulled thee out of thy Father's bosom and laid thee in thy mother's womb? What thing caused thee to take the garment of our frail nature upon thee and to become partaker of our miseries but only love? What thing placed thee in an ox stall, and swaddled thee in a manger, and chased thee into strange countries but only love? What thing made thee to carry the yoke of our mortality for the space of so many years but only love? What thing made thee to sweat, to travail, to watch, to continue waking all the long night, and to pass over both sea and land seeking after lost souls but only love? What thing bound Sampson hand and foot, shaved his hair, spoiled him of all his force, and caused him to be mocked and scorned of his enemies but only the love of his spouse Dalila (Judg. 16)? And what thing hath bound thee, our true Sampson, and shaved thee and spoiled thee of thy force and strength, and given thee into thine enemies' hands to be reproachfully laughed, spitted, and scoffed at but only the love that thou bearest unto thy spouse, the Catholic Church, and unto each one of our souls? Finally, what thing hath brought thee to be crucified upon the tree of the cross, there to stand so cruelly tormented from top to toe, thy hands nailed, thy side opened, thy members racked one from another, thy body all of a gore blood, thy veins exhausted and void of blood, thy lips pale and wan, thy tongue bitter, to be short, all thy body wholly rent and torn? What thing could have wrought such a most cruel, foul mangling and butchery of thee as this was but only love? O passing great love! O gracious love! O love, seemly for the great unspeakable mercy and infinite goodness of him who is infinitely good and loving, yea, wholly love.

Having, therefore, so great and so many testimonies of thy love (O my sweet Lord and Saviour) as these be, how can I but believe that thou lovest me, sith it is most certain that thou hast not changed that most charitable, loving heart, being now in heaven, which thou hadst when thou didst walk here upon earth. Thou art not like that cup-bearer of King Pharaoh, who, when he saw himself in prosperity, forgat his poor friends that he had left in prison (Gen. 40). But rather the prosperity and glory that thou dost now enjoy in heaven moveth thee to have greater pity and compassion upon thy children whom thou hast left here in earth. Now, then, sith it is certain that thou lovest me so much, as I see very evidently thou dost, why do not I love thee again? Why do not I put my whole trust and affiance in thee? Why do not I esteem myself very happy and rich, having even almighty God himself so constant and loving a friend unto me? It is undoubtedly a great wonder that anything in this life doth make me careful and heavy, having on my side so rich and so mighty a lover, through whose hands all things do pass.

108. **all...blood** all covered with blood. 115. **sith** since. 123. **affiance** confidence.

John Bucke, *Instructions for the Use of the Beads*, 1589

The first Joyful Mystery or secret is the Annunciation of the Blessed Virgin Mary. Therefore, when you take your beads and have advisedly commended yourself to God, blessing yourself with, 'In nomine Patris et Fili et Spiritus Sancti, Amen' [In the name of the Father, and of the Son, and of the Holy Spirit, Amen], then may you first set before the eyes of your soul the Annunciation of our Blessed Lady, and imagine in your   5
mind that you behold the angel Gabriel presenting himself before that blessed virgin with his heavenly salutation, 'Ave, Maria', and declaring to her his message from the Council of the Trinity.

And with that imagination still kept in mind, say the first *Pater noster* and ten *Ave Maria*s following (which is the first part of the beads) attentively, distinctly, and devoutly.   10
There let these cogitations following run through your mind a while before you go any further.

First, think how the angel found her at prayer and here admonish yourself how nigh unto you your good angel standeth in time of prayer, and how apt you are then to receive heavenly comfort and good motions, and that in consideration hereof it is good to pray   15
ever, more or less.

Secondly, mark with what modest silence she gave ear to the message, not uttering any idle or curious speech, and study you to follow that example.

Thirdly, note her zeal to keep her maidenhood and virginity, vowed and promised to God, and so think to keep your Christian vow made at your baptism.   20

Fourthly, consider her present faith in believing the words of the angel, passing all natural reason that she, being a virgin, should bear a child, and here learn faithfully to believe the promises of God.

Fifthly, behold her humble obedience, and resigned will to the disposition of almighty God. And when you have thus occupied your mind some little time, then prepare   25
yourself to the second Joy.

Beads The rosary consisted of decades, groups of ten beads for ten recitations of the *Ave, Maria,* and preliminary and intermediary beads for other prayers. **24. humble . . . will** Gaspare Loarte dilates upon this point: 'Thou shalt never want matter, meditating the things that took effect presently after the queen of heaven had given her consent, saying, "Fiat mihi secundum verbum tuum", (Be it done unto me according to thy word: Luke 1: 38). Sith in that very instant the most sacred body of Jesus was by virtue of the Holy Ghost formed of the most pure blood of the Blessed Virgin Mary; and in the self-same instant was his glorious soul created and infused in his body; and in the same instant was his most holy humanity united with the eternal word of God in one self-same person. And thenceforth was the Blessed Virgin mother of God, queen of angels and men, full of grace, replenished with all the gifts and prerogatives meet for so incomparable a dignity. O *Fiat* most puissant and effectual! With another *Fiat* God did erst make the heavens, earth, and all the creatures of the world (Gen. 1). Yet were there far greater and more important matters made with this *Fiat*, seeing that by means of this *Fiat*, the same God made himself man and man was made God, with all the other right wonderful works that proceed out of this change and most miraculous metamorphosis' (*Instructions and Advertisements: How to Meditate the Misteries of the Rosarie* [tr. John Fen], 1597, sigs. Bvii–Bvii^v). **26. second Joy** the second Joyful Mystery, the Visitation of Mary to her cousin Elizabeth, mother of John the Baptist (Luke 1: 39–57).

ROGER MARTIN

Roger Martin (1527?–1615) experienced the turmoil of the Protestant revolution in Long Melford, a town in Suffolk. During the reign of Queen Mary (1553–8) he became churchwarden and worked to revive Catholic ceremonies and traditions. Later, he suffered several indictments for recusancy, financial penalties, and imprisonments. In an extraordinary memoir Martin recalls the Catholic church, chapels, and services of his youth—the processions, liturgies, and festivals that once ordered life and gave it meaning. He also remembers the gilt sculptures, stained glass, icons, and paintings later destroyed by iconoclasts. At the end of his narrative Martin hopes that his descendants, 'when time serve, shall repair, place there, and maintain all these things again'. Though this wish was never realized, Martin's memoir brings to brief but vivid life the English Catholic Church in operation, its deft and daily interweaving of devotional ritual, charitable work, and communal celebration.

Memories of Long Melford, c.1590

At the back of the high altar in the said church there was a goodly mount made of one great tree, and set up to the foot of the window there, carved very artificially with the story of Christ's Passion, representing the horsemen with their swords and the footmen, etc., as they used Christ on the mount of Calvary, all being fair gilt and lively and beautifully set forth. To cover and keep clean all the which, there were very fair and   5
painted boards, made to shut to, which were opened upon high and solemn feast days, which then was a very beautiful show. Which painted boards were set up again in Queen Mary's time. At the north end of the same altar there was a goodly tilt tabernacle, reaching up to the roof of the chancel in the which there was one large, fair, gilt image of the Holy Trinity, being patron of the church, besides other fair images. The like   10
tabernacle was at the south end.

   There was also in my aisle, called 'Jesus Aisle', at the back of the altar, a table with a crucifix on it, with the two thieves hanging, on every side one, which is in my house decayed, and the same I hope my heirs will repair and restore again one day. There was also two fair tilt tabernacles from the ground up to the roof, with a fair image of Jesus   15
in the tabernacle at the north end of the altar, holding a round ball in his hand,

---

1. **mount** mounted wooden sculpture. 2. **artificially** artfully. 4. **lively** lifelike. 8. **tilt tabernacle** carved or constructed frame, covered by a canopy, for storing and showing holy objects. 9. **chancel** altar area, set off from the congregation space by a screen. 12. **my aisle** aisle in front of the Martin family chapel. 13. **every** each. **in my house** In 1559 an injunction expressly forbade the keeping of such artefacts in private homes.

signifying, I think, that he containeth the whole round world. And in the tabernacle at the south end there was a fair image of our Blessed Lady having the afflicted body of her dear son as he was taken down off the cross lying along on her lap, the tears, as it were, running down pitifully upon her beautiful cheeks, as it seemed bedewing the said sweet 20
body of her son, and therefore named the image of Our Lady of Pity.

There was a fair rood loft with the rood, Mary and John of every side, and with a fair pair of organs standing thereby; which loft extended all the breadth of the church, and on Good Friday a priest then standing by the rood sang the Passion. The side thereof towards the body of the church, in twelve partitions in boards was fair painted with 25
the images of the twelve apostles. All the roof of the church was beautified with fair gilt stars. Finally, in the vestry where there were many rich copes and suits of vestments there was a fair press with fair large doors to shut to, wherein there were made devices to hang on all the copes without folding or frumpling of them, with a convenient distance the one from the other. In the choir was a fair painted frame of timber, to be set up about 30
Maundy Thursday, with holes for a number of fair tapers to stand in before the sepulchre and to be lighted in service time. Sometimes it was set overthwart the choir before the altar, the sepulchre being always placed and finally garnished at the north end of the high altar between that and Master Clopton's little chapel there, in a vacant place of the wall, I think upon a tomb of one of his ancestors. The said frame with the tapers 35
was set near the steps going up to the said altar. Lastly, it was used to be set up all along by Master Clopton's aisle with a door made to go out of the rood loft into it.

Upon Palm Sunday the Blessed Sacrament was carried in procession about the churchyard under a fair canopy borne by four yeomen. The procession coming to the church gate went westward, and they with the Blessed Sacrament went eastward; and 40
when the procession came against the door of Master Clopton's aisle, they with the Blessed Sacrament and with a little bell and singing approached at the east end of Our Lady's Chapel, at which time a boy with a thing in his hand pointed to it, signifying a prophet as I think, sang, standing on the turret, that is, on the said Master Clopton's aisle door, 'Ecce, Rex tuus venit', etc., and then all did kneel down, and then rising up 45

21. **Lady of Pity** the Pietà (see Michelangelo's famous sculpture; Crashaw, POETRY); the sorrowing Mary, *mater dolorosa*, was an extremely affective and popular devotional image. **22. rood loft** platform on top of the screen dividing the nave and chancel of the church, on or over which was a large crucifix (**rood**). On either side of the cross were the figures of Mary and St John (cf. John 19: 25–6). **23. pair** probably two parts of one organ. **24. side thereof** i.e. of the screen. **27. vestry** dressing room. **copes and suits** A cope is a semicircular cloak, often decorated, worn by priest; suits were either matching vestments for the priest or for the priest and his concelebrants, a deacon and sub-deacon. **28. press** cupboard or closet. **29. frumpling** wrinkling. **31. Maundy Thursday** Holy Thursday. **number…tapers** Normally between fifteen and twenty-five candles provided light in the church and were used in *tenebrae* (darkness) services during Holy Week, during which they were ceremoniously extinguished. **sepulchre** the Easter sepulchre, on the north side of the chancel. The Blessed Sacrament was placed there on Good Friday and restored to the main altar in celebration on Easter. **32. overthwart** crosswise. **34. Master Clopton's…chapel** John Clopton (d. 1497), who presided over the rebuilding of the church, built an aisle with brasses of his family ('Clopton's chapel') and a chantry (worship space with altar) at the end of it. **38. Palm Sunday** the Sunday before Holy Week, on which the Melford congregation commemorated Christ's triumphant entrance into Jerusalem before distributing palms. **39. yeomen** attendants. **43. Our Lady's Chapel** large chapel at the east end of the church. **44. turret** a high, brick tower and look-out post on the north wall, where the boy, dressed as a prophet, sang 'Behold, your king, comes' and other texts to signal the fulfilment of prophecies.

went and met the sacrament, and so then went singing together into the church. And coming near the porch, a boy or one of the clerks did cast over among the boys flowers and singing cakes, etc.

On Corpus Christi day they went likewise with the Blessed Sacrament in procession about the church green in copes, and I think also they went in procession on St Mark's day about the said green, with handbells ringing before them, as they did about the bounds of the town in Rogation Week, on the Monday one way, on the Tuesday another way, on the Wednesday another way, praying for rain or fair weather as the time required, having a drinking and a dinner there upon Monday, being fast day; and Tuesday, being a fish day, they had a breakfast with butter and cheese, etc., at the parsonage and a drinking at Master Clopton's by Kentwell at his manor of Lutons near the ponds in the park, where there was a little chapel, I think of St Anne, for that was their longest perambulation. Upon Wednesday, being fasting day, they had a drinking at Melford Hall. All the choir dined there three times in the year at least, namely, St Stephen's day, mid-Lent Sunday, and I think upon Easter Monday. On St James's day, mass being sung then by note, and the organs going in St James's Chapel (which were brought into my house with the clock and bell that stood there, and the organs that stood upon the rood loft) that was then a little from the road, which chapel had been maintained by my ancestors. And therefore I will that my heirs, when time serve, shall repair, place there, and maintain all these things again. There were also fair stools on either side, such as are in the church, which were had away by John King's means, who was Sir William Cordell's bailiff; about which chapel there was paled in round about a convenient piece of the green for one to walk in.

On St James's Even there was a bonefire, and a tub of ale and bread then given to the poor, and before my door there was made three other bonefires, namely, on Midsummer Even, on the Even of St Peter and St Paul, when they had the like drinkings, and on St Thomas's Even, on which, if it fell not on the fish day, they had some long pies of mutton and peasecods, set out upon boards with the aforesaid quantity of bread and ale. And in all these bonefires, some of the friends and more civil poor neighbours were called in, and sat at the board with my grandfather, who had at the lighting of the bonefires wax tapers with balls of wax, yellow and green, set up all the breadth of the hall, lighted then

48. singing cakes breads or baked goods given as a reward to the choir. **49. Corpus Christi day** feast of the Blessed Sacrament, observed on a Thursday about eight weeks after Easter, sometimes celebrated with pageants and sacred plays. **50. church green** large expanse of common land used for civic and church functions. **50–1. St Mark's day** 25 April. **51. handbells** rung to discourage evil spirits. **52. Rogation Week** week before Ascension Day, when people walked the boundaries of the parish (about 21 miles) and prayed for good weather and for avoidance of plague and pestilence. **54–5. fast day...fish day** On a fast day one abstained from meat, fish, and animal products and ate lightly; on a fish day one abstained from meat but could eat fish in light meals. **60. St Stephen's Day** 26 December. **St James's Day** 25 July. **61. St James's Chapel** a small church, which stood nearly opposite to Martin's house, dismantled by Protestants. **66. John King** A bailiff (administrative officer), King removed the benches in King James's Chapel as part of the state-ordered purge. **67. paled** fenced. **69. St James's Even** 24 July. **bonefire** outdoor fire, subsisting chiefly on animal bones. **70–1. Midsummer Even** 24 June. **71. Even...St Paul** 28 June. **72. St Thomas's Even** 20 December. **76. hall** main living area of the house, heated by a hearth.

and burning there before the image of St John the Baptist. And after they were put out, a watch candle was lighted, and set in the midst of the said hall upon the pavement, burning all night.

WILLIAM BYRD

A devout Catholic his whole life, William Byrd (1543–1623) was the most accomplished and prolific musician of his time. Writing for the Church of England and for Catholic services, he revolutionized the use of keyboard, popularized the madrigal, and excelled in Latin sacred music. Byrd wrote *Cantiones Sacrae* (1575), *Psalms, Sonnets, & Songs of Sadness & Piety* (1588), contributed to *The Fitzwilliam Virginal Book* (1612–19), and composed motets as well as voice and consort music.

William Byrd's *Gradualia ac Cantiones Sacrae* (1605, etc.) consists primarily of music for the Catholic mass, i.e. the introit (opening), gradual (psalm), tract or Alleluia, offertory, and communion. This music enabled Catholic worship, officially prohibited, in private households, and provided comfort to recusants. In his choice of texts Byrd follows the reforms recommended by the Council of Trent. Moreover, he writes music for the feasts that aroused especially contentious theological debate, those dedicated to the Blessed Virgin Mary, All Saints Day, and Corpus Christi (for which he set to music Aquinas's eucharistic hymns). Throughout, he shows himself keenly aware of biblical text and church tradition as he celebrates Catholic liturgy and gives hope to the persecuted. Fully to appreciate the achievement, one must hear Byrd's glorious music, readily available today in a variety of formats.

Gradualia, 1605

Recusant music

Plorans plorabit, et deducet oculus meus lachrimas, quia captus est grex Domini. Dic regi et dominatrici: Humiliamini, sedete, quoniam descendit de capite vestro corona gloriae vestrae. [Jer. 13: 17–18]

---

78. **watch candle** a vigil candle that burned in front of an image on the eve of a feast.

1. **Plorans plorabit** This lamentation offers comfort to a captured people. Philip Brett, ed. *Works: The Byrd Edition* (1970–), observes, 'the low clefs isolate the soprano as effectively as the legislation of the 1580s and 1590s was meant to isolate the Jesuits, seminary priests, and those who harboured them' (vol. via, p. viii). **oculus** 'eye'; the Vulgate reads *anima* (soul).
2–3. Jeremiah's protest against the throne gives voice to Catholic anger and frustration.

[Weeping, my eye will weep ever and bring forth tears because the flock of the Lord has
been captured. Tell the king and the queen, 'Be humbled, be seated, for the crown of   5
your glory has fallen from your head.']

[. . .]

Timete Dominum, omnes sancti eius, quoniam nihil deest timentibus eum. [Ps. 33. 10]

Versus: Inquirentes autem [Dominum non deficient omni bono. Alleluia. Ps. 33. 11]

Versus: Venite ad me, omnes qui laboratis et onerati estis, et ego reficiam vos. Alleluia.
[Matt. 11: 28].   10

[Fear the Lord, all his saints, for nothing is denied those who fear him.

Verse: Those who seek the Lord, indeed, will not want any good thing. Alleluia.

Verse: Come to me, all you who labour and are burdened, and I shall refresh you.
Alleluia.]

Marian music

Gaude, Maria Virgo, cunctas haereses sola interemisti.   15

[Versus:] Quae Gabrielis Archangeli dictis credidisti.

[Versus:] Dum Virgo Deum et hominem genuisti, et post partum, Virgo, inviolata
permansisti.

[Versus:] Dei genitrix, intercede pro nobis.

[Rejoice, Virgin Mary, you alone have destroyed all heresies.   20

Verse: You who believed the words of the Archangel Gabriel.

Verse: While a virgin you gave birth to God and man, and after the birth, O Virgin,
you remained ever inviolate.

Verse: Mother of God, intercede for us.]

Francis de Sales

Admired preacher and doctor of the Church, Francis de Sales (1567–1622) founded the
Institute of the Visitation (a religious order for women) and a congregation of priests now
known as the Oblates of St Francis de Sales. Among his writings is *An Introduction to a
Devout Life* (tr. 1613), which broke with previous practice by addressing not religious but

7. **Timete Dominum** sung as a gradual at the All Saints Mass. Brett comments: 'the tenor, on its only top B flat in the
piece, clashes wildly with the superius's adjacent B natural at the elaborate cadence on C depicting "onerati estis" ('you who
are burdened').' Educated contemporary listeners, Brett continues, would naturally consider contemporary saints,
especially 'the sufferings of the many Jesuits and seminary priests who had indeed carried a great burden and had been
hunted down and often put to death' (ibid. pp. vii–viii). 15. **Gaude, Maria** This is the tract (or Alleluia verse) for the votive
mass of the Blessed Virgin Mary sung for nine weeks before Easter. **haereses** 'heresies'. Mary traditionally protected the
faith against heresy. 17. **inviolata** 'inviolate'. Catholics believe in the perpetual virginity of Mary. 19. **Dei genitrix,
intercede** 'Mother of God, intercede.' The Council of Ephesus (431) declared Mary *theotokos* (Mother of God); she appears
in her traditional and contested role as intercessor here and in the *Salve, Regina* (see *Prayers and Hymns* above).

common people, 'such as by the obligation of their estate are bound to take a common course of life' (sig. A7). The selections below illustrate the special spiritual gifts of St Francis de Sales, his gentleness and meekness, here presented as attainable virtues for the common person along with practical remedies for the contrary vice of anger.

An Introduction to a Devout Life, 1613

Of meekness and gentleness towards our neighbours and remedies against anger

The holy chrism, which by apostolical tradition we use in the church of God for confirmations and consecrations, is composed of oil of olives mingled with balm, which beside other things representeth unto us the two dear and lovely virtues which shined in the sacred person of our Lord, and which he most particularly did commend unto us as if by them our heart were especially to be consecrated to his service and applied   5
to his imitation. 'Learn of me,' saith he, 'for I am meek and humble of heart.' Humility perfecteth us to Godward and mildness or meekness towards our neighbour. The balm, which, as I said before, sinketh to the lowest place in all other liquors, representeth humility. And the oil of olives, which swimmeth always above other liquors, signifieth mildness and affability, which among all virtues is most excellent and of delightfullest   10
appearance, as being the flower of charity. For charity, according to St Bernard, is then most perfect when it is not only patient but mild also and courteous.

But take heed, Philotheus, that this mystical chrism, composed of meekness and humility, be indeed within thy heart, for it is one of the greatest subtleties of the devil to make many a man very curiously study to make a show of these two virtues in words   15
and exterior compliments, who, not examining thoroughly their inward affections, esteem themselves humble and meek whereas in deed they be nothing so; which we may well perceive because, for all their ceremonious mildness and humility, at the least cross word given them, at the very least injury proffered them, they puff and swell like toads with marvellous arrogancy and impatience. They say that those who have taken   20
the preservative commonly called the grace of St Paul swell not at all by the biting and stinging of vipers, provided that the preservative be not counterfeit. In like manner, when humility and mildness are true and unfeigned, they preserve us from the burning sores and swelling humours which injuries are wont to raise in men's hearts. But if being stung and bit by the slanderous and malicious tongues of our enemies, we swell   25
with fierceness, spite, and rage, it is an evident sign that our humility and meekness is not frank and free but artificially counterfeited.

---

1. **chrism** ointment used in administering sacraments. 2. **balm** aromatic, resinous substance. 7. **to Godward** towards God. 13. **Philotheus** 'lover of God', a name that represents the common people St Francis addresses in the book. 15. **curiously** carefully.

That holy and illustrious patriarch Joseph, sending back his brethren from Egypt to his father, gave them this only advice: 'Be not angry by the way' [Gen. 45: 24]. I say the selfsame to thee, Philotheus. This wretched life is but a way to the happy life of heaven. 30 Let us not be angry one with another in this way but march with the troop of our brethren and companions sweetly, peaceably, and lovingly. And I mean we should do so roundly without all exception. Be not angry at all, if it be possible. Take no occasion or pretext, whatsoever be offered, to open the gate of your heart to anger, for St James tells us very briefly and without any distinction or reservation, 'The anger of man worketh not 35 the justice of God' [James 1: 20].

We must indeed resist the evil and suppress the vices of them that are under our charge constantly and stoutly but yet mildly and peaceably. Nothing so soon tameth the elephant, being angered, than the sight of a little lamb; nothing breaketh so easily the force of cannon shot as soft wool. We esteem not so much the correction that proceeds from passion, 40 though it be accompanied with never so much reason, as that which hath no other cause or beginning but reason. For the soul of man, being naturally subject to the rule of reason, is never subject to passion but tyrannically; and, therefore, when reason is accompanied with passion she maketh herself odious, her just government being abased and vilified by the fellowship of the tyrant passion. Princes do honour and comfort their people exceedingly 45 when they visit them with a peaceable train; but when they come guarded with armed troops, though it be for the good of the commonwealth, their coming is always displeasing and damageable. For let them keep military discipline never so rigorously among their soldiers, yet they can never bring it so to pass but some disorder will always chance whereby the good poor man is injured. Even so, as long as reason ruleth and exerciseth sweetly 50 and mildly the chastisements, corrections, and reprehensions due to offences, although they be inflicted exactly and with rigour, every man loveth and liketh of it. But when she brings with her those armed passions of wrath, choler, spite and rage, taunts and frowning (which St Austin calleth the soldiers of reason), she maketh herself more dreaded than loved and even her own heart becomes thereby afflicted and ill handled. 55

Better it is (saith the same glorious saint writing to his friend Profuturus) to deny the entry to anger, be it never upon so just and reasonable a cause, than to receive it, be it never so little, into our hearts; for being once admitted, it is hardly got out a-doors again. For it entereth like a little branch and in a moment waxeth a great tree [Letter 38]. And if it can but gain the night of us that the sun do but set upon our anger, which the 60 Apostle forbiddeth [Eph. 4: 26], converting itself into hatred and rancour, there is almost no remedy to be freed from it. For it nourisheth itself with a thousand surmises and false persuasions because never was there yet any angry man that thought his anger to be causeless or unjust. It is better, then, and easier to learn and accustom ourselves to live without choler than to use our choler and anger moderately and discreetly. But if through 65

33. **roundly** thoroughly. 46. **train** escort. 48. **damageable** injurious. 53. **choler** anger, thought to be caused by an excess of bile. 54. **Austin** Augustine.

imperfection and frailty we find ourselves surprised and overtaken therewith, it is better to chase it away speedily than to stand dallying and, as it were, coping with it. For give it never so little leave and it will be mistress of the fort and like the serpent which can easily draw in his whole body where he can once get in his head.

But thou wilt say, 'How shall I repress and refrain my anger once heated and inflamed?' Thou must, Philotheus, at the first assault of choler speedily assemble thy forces together, reflecting upon that which thou hast in hand, not rudely nor violently but mildly and gently, though seriously and in all earnest. For as we see in the audiences and assemblies of the senates or courts, the ushers with crying of peace make more noise a great deal than those whom they bid to be silent, so it happeneth many times that, endeavouring with impetuosity and many forces to assuage our choler, we stir up more perturbation and trouble in ourselves than the motion itself of choler had done before, so that the heart, being thus troubled, is no more master of itself.

Secondly, after this soft and sweet straining of thy powers to reflect upon themselves, practise the advice which St Austin, being now old, gave unto the young bishop Auxilius: 'Do', saith he, 'that which a man should do. If that bechance thee which the man of God said in the psalm, "My eye is troubled for anger,' have recourse unto God crying, "Have mercy upon me, O Lord!" [Ps. 30: 10] that he may stretch forth his right hand to repress thy choler' [Letter 250]. I mean that we should invoke the assistance of God when we perceive ourselves shaken with choler, imitating the apostles when they were tossed with winds and tempest upon the waters. For he will command our passions to cease and cause a quiet calm to ensue. But I admonish thee that always the prayer which thou makest against this passion of anger which then possesseth and presseth thee be exercised meekly, leisurely, and calmly, not violently, hastily, or turbulently, and this self-same rule must be observed in all remedies which are applied against this passion of anger.

Thirdly, so soon as thou perceivest that thou hast done some act of choler, repair and redress the fault immediately with another contrary act of mildness, exercised promptly and sweetly towards the same person against whom thou wast angry. For as it is a sovereign remedy against lying to unsay it and go back from the lie even in the very place where thou toldest it, so is it an excellent salve against anger to apply suddenly and out of hand a contrary act of mildness and courtesy, for green wounds, they say, are easiest to be cured.

Fourthly, when thou art at repose and tranquillity and without any occasion or subject of choler, make great store and provision, as they say, of meekness and gentleness, speaking all thy words, and working all thy actions, and using all thy behaviour in the sweetest, softest, and mildest manner thou canst, calling to mind that the spouse in the Canticles had honey not only in her lips but also under her tongue (that is, in her breast), nor honey only but milk too; for so we must not only have sweet and courteous words to our neighbour, but they must proceed also from the bottom of our heart. Neither must

we have this honey-sweet mildness, which is pleasant and odoriferous, in our conversation
with strangers and foreigners abroad, but with all the milk-sweet behaviour and fatherly   105
or brotherly carriage also within doors amongst our domestical friends and near neighbours; wherein they are greatly to seek who in the street be like angels and within their
house seem almost devils.

HENRY HAWKINS

Born Catholic in Kent, Henry Hawkins (1577?–1646) joined the Society of Jesus in 1615,
suffered imprisonment and exile, and returned to labour pastorally in London for about
twenty-five years. He translated religious works, saints' lives, the Jesuit emblem book, *Le
Cœur Devot*, and published *Partheneia Sacra* (1633). *Partheneia Sacra* is an extraordinary
fusion of emblem book and devotional manual, organized by the controlling metaphor of
Mary as *Hortus Conclusus*, 'enclosed garden' (Cant. 4: 12). Its twenty-four chapters
expatiate on related Marian attributes and symbols, the rose, lily, bee, star, and nightingale,
for example. Drawing upon biblical, ecclesiastical, patristic, and secular traditions, the
book explicates these symbols with poetic lyricism and erudition. In its intellectual energy,
metaphysical wit, sensuous fullness, and interdisciplinarity, *Partheneia Sacra* recalls other
baroque achievements in art and literature, especially the poetry of Richard Crashaw.

Partheneia Sacra, 1633

The Rose

The Devise

106. **carriage** demeanour. 107. **seek** practise.

THE DEVISE The Devise consists of an engraved plate and a motto. This motto, *casto perfusa rubore* (suffused with a
chaste blush), describes Mary's supposed reaction to the Annunciation, but the phrase does not appear in Luke (1: 26–38).
The Character offers definitions and expansions of the image; the Morals explains the motto.

The Character

The rose is the imperial queen of flowers, which all do homage to as to their princess, she being the glory and delight of that monarchy. She is herself a treasury of all sweets, a cabinet of musks, which she commends to none to keep but holds them folded in her leaves, as knowing well how little conscience is made of such stealths. If any have a will to seek diamonds among flowers, he may seek long enough ere he find them; but if a ruby he seeks for, the rose is a precious ruby. It is the darling of the garden nymphs and the cause sometimes perhaps of much debate between them, while each one strives to have it proper to herself, being made for all, and is verily enough for all. It is the palace of the flowery *numens*, environed round with a court-of-guard about her that stand in a readiness with javelins in hand and the '*Qui va la?*' in the mouth, with whom is but a word and a blow, or rather whose words are blows that fetch the blood. It is the metropolis of the Graces, where they hold their commonwealth, and where the senate of all odoriferous spices keep their court. It is the chiefest grace of spouses on their nuptial days and the bride will as soon forget her fillet as her rose. It is the masterpiece of nature in her garden works, and even a very spell to artisans to frame the like, for though perhaps they may delude the eye, yet by no means can they counterfeit the odour, the life, and spirit of the rose. When Flora is disposed to deliciate with her minions, the rose is her Adonis, bleeding in her lap; the rose, her Ganymede, presenting her cups full of the nectar of her sweets. It is even the confectionary box of the daintiest conserves which nature hath to cherish-up herself with when she languisheth in autumn; the cellar of the sweetest liquors, either wine or water, her wines being nectars and her waters no less precious than they whose dried leaves are the empty bottles. In a word, the rose for beauty is a rose, for sweetness a rose, and for all the graces possible in flowers, a very rose, the quintessence of beauty, sweets, and graces, all at once, and all as epitomized in the name of rose.

The Morals

Casto perfusa rubore [suffused with a chaste blush]. It is a common saying, 'the honest bridegroom and the bashful bride'. For so when Rebecca first was brought to the youthful Isaac as a spouse, she put her scarf or veil before her eyes [Gen. 24: 65]. So Rachel did and many others. Lucretia the Chaste chose rather to wallow in her blood than to survive her shame, wherein she blushed indeed, but yet without cause; for yet still she remains in all men's mouths, 'the chaste Lucretia'. The heart and cheeks have their intelligences together, and the purest blood is messenger between them. The heart is put into a

---

3. musks perfumes. **4. conscience … stealths** guilt is felt by those who steal such scents. **9.** *numens* divinities. **court-of-guard** i.e. thorns. **10.** *Qui va la?* Who goes there? (a watchman's cry). **12. Graces** sister-goddesses who bestowed beauty and charm. **14. fillet** headband. **17. Flora** goddess of spring. **deliciate** take pleasure. **18. Adonis** Greek god, wounded by a boar while escaping the amorous goddess Aphrodite. **Ganymede** boy cup-bearer of Zeus. **19. conserves** medicinal preparation of a plant, preserved with sugar. **20. cherish-up** gladden. **28. Rachel** daughter of Laban, wife of Jacob (Gen. 29). **29. Lucretia the Chaste** legendary heroine (6th c. BC) who, after suffering rape, committed suicide to purge herself of shame and restore her honour. **31. intelligences** communications.

fright; the obsequious blood comes in anon and asks, 'What ails you, sir? Go, get you up and mount to the turret of the cheeks, my only friend, and call for help.' The blood obeys and makes the blush that raiseth such alarms in tender virgins most especially.   35
What fears the virgin when she blushes so? The wrack of her honour, you will say. How so? Is honour in the body or the mind? If in the mind, the mind is a citadel impregnable, not subject to violence, nor to be betrayed but by itself. Then blush not, virgin, for the matter; thy hold is sure enough and thou in safety, if thou wilt thyself. But this of all other virtues never is safe and secure enough; this of all others fears the very   40
shadows themselves and trembles like an aspen leaf at the least motions. Now looks she pale like a very clout; and now through modesty the colour mounts into her cheeks and there sets up his ruddy standard as if the fort were his, till fear, again prevailing, plucks it down. And these were the vicissitudes our sacred Virgin had when her glorious paranymph discovered his embassage to her in her secret closet, presenting her a shadow   45
only, seeming opposite to her chaste vow, whereat she trembled in his sight, *casto perfusa rubore*.

The Essay

Behold here the princess of flowers, the pearl of roses, with all its varieties: the damask rose, the musk rose, the red, the cinnamon, the carnation, the province, the white, the savage rose (which grows in the eglantines), and lastly the golden rose, fair indeed to   50
behold but not so sweet. The rose grows on a speckled thorn, swelling into sharp or pointed buttons somewhat green, which rives by little and little, and opens at last, then unbuttons and discloses its treasure. The sun unfolds it and opens the lights and leaves, making it display itself and take life, so affording it the last draught of beauty to its scarlet; and now, having perfumed it, and made the infusion of rose-water thereinto, in   55
the midst appears as in a cup certain golden points and little threads of musk or saffron, sticking in the heart of the rose. But to speak of the fires of its carnation, the snow of the white satin, the fine emeralds cut into little tongues round about to serve as a train to wait upon it; of the balm and ambergris that breathes from this little crop of gold which is in the midst; of the sharpness of the thorns that guard it from the little thieves that would be   60
nibbling it away with their beaks; of the juice and substance which, being squeezed, embalms all round about it with its favour of a hundred hidden virtues, as to fortify the heart, to clear the crystal of the eyes, to banish clouds, to cool our heats, to stir up the appetite, and a thousand the like were a world to deal with. But I hasten to the Mistress-flower herself, who mysteriously sits in this goodly economy of sweets and   65
beauties as in her bower, wherein she delights to shroud herself.

---

39. **wilt** will be. 42. **clout** cloth or rag. 43. **ruddy standard** red flag (of the blush). 45. **paranymph** one who woos for another, here the angel Gabriel wooing Mary for the Holy Spirit. **secret closet** private room.

THE ESSAY The Essay meditates poetically on the image. 50. **eglantines** sweet-briar plants. 52. **buttons** buds. **rives** comes apart. 56. **threads** stamina, the filaments or stalks of the interior blossom that support pollen sacs. 57. **carnation** red colour. 59. **ambergris** wax-like substance used in perfumes. 65. **economy** household.

The Discourse

Two things in the rose chiefly do I note: what inwardly it contains, and what virtue and quality the rose outwardly gives forth. It is strange the same should be hot and cold together—cold in the leaves, hot in the seed—so as passions proceeding of excessive heat it allays and qualifies with its leaves, and with the heat and vigour of its seeds it quickens 70 and virifies the frigid and melancholy affections of the body. Some men are tepid, yea, cold in the love of God; they are so dull and stupid in divine things that they cannot raise up the mind from terrene and earthly cogitations to sublimer thoughts, being immured with base affections. But our mystical rose, with the seed of grace in her wherewith she was replenished, inflames their hearts to the love of God. Oh, seed of our 75 rose! 'She shall not fear her house for the colds of the snows, for all her household are clothed double' (Prov. 31: 21). This snow so cold is a frigidity of mind, but against this cold she clothes her devotees with double suits of charity, to God and their neighbour. Some also are hot and most desperately inflamed with the fires of concupiscence; these heats she tempers and extinguishes with the dews of her refrigerating grace, as with the 80 leaves or mantle, as it were, of her gracious protection.

The rose, the more it is wrung or pressed, the sweeter odour it sends forth, and yields such a redolent fragrancy withal that all are wonderfully taken with the odoriferous breath it gives. And this our rose, the more she was wrung and pressed with the cruel finger of tribulations and afflictions, the greater her sanctity appeared. Being banished 85 into Egypt, she gave forth a most fragrant odour of patience, wherewith she embalmed all Egypt and fructified afterwards into an infinite race of devotees to her and her Son; witness the Pauls, the Anthonies, the Hilarions, the Macarians of Egypt. In the Passion of her Son, transfixed with the sword of sorrow, she yielded a sweet perfume of perfect faith. In other afflictions and tribulations she imparted the communicative odour of 90 compassion. For the torments which he suffered of the Jews, she sent up the fragrancy of thanksgiving to the heavenly Father from the thurible of her heart. And in the desolation she felt after his Ascension for the absence of her beloved, she poured forth incense of her holy desires and incomparable devotion. After all which odours, oh, give me leave, most sweet and odoriferous rose, through desires and devotion to run after thee, or do thou 95 but draw me after thee unto the odour of thy ointments (Cant. 1).

The rose grows on thorns but puts not on their nature; the thorns are churlish and rough while the rose is sweet and gentle. And our rose, sprung indeed from the

THE DISCOURSE The Discourse surveys theological meanings. **70. qualifies** moderates. **70–1. quickens and virifies** animates and strengthens. **74. mystical rose** a traditional title of the Virgin Mary, found, for example, in the Litany of Loreto (see *Prayers and Hymns* above). **76. fear** fear for. **88. Pauls...Macarians** St Paul founded early Christian communities in Greece, Asia Minor, and the Middle East; St Anthony, St Hilarion, and Macarius the Egyptian were 4th-c. ascetics and founders of monastic communities. **90. communicative** generous. **92. thurible** vessel for burning incense.

thorny stock of the Jewish race but yet took nothing of the condition of thorns
with her. The Jews were proud and haughty, she most humble; they full of vices,   100
she fully replenished with grace; the Jews, we see, are infidels, she the pattern and
mirror of faith; the Jews covetous of earthly and terrene things, and she most
thirsting after celestial. She sprung likewise from the thorny Eva but yet took not
after her nature. 'O thou Virgin,' saith St Bernard, 'most flourishing rod of Jesse
[Isa. 11: 1], through whom was recovered in the branch what had perished in the root!'   105
Eva was a branch of bitterness, Mary a branch of eternal sweetness. An admirable
and most profound dispensation of the divine wisdom, that such a rod should grow
from such a root, such a daughter from such a mother, such a free-born from such
a bond-slave, such an empress from such a captive, from so dry a thorn so flourishing
a rose!   110

What the rose gives outwardly forth are the objects of three principal senses: of seeing,
smelling, and touching. And for the first, who sees not that hath the benefit of eyes how
gorgeous the rose is among all the flowers of the garden, alluring and attracting the eyes
of all that enter into it? So our incomparable rose was exceeding fair and with incredible
beauty seemed gracious and amiable to the eyes of all (Esther 2). She was a glad 'spectacle   115
unto God, men, and angels' [1 Cor. 4: 9]: to God because so specious to her Son, her
spouse, her God. 'The King desires thy beauty' [Ps. 44: 12] and says therefore, 'Show me
thy face, for thy face is comely' [Cant. 2: 14]. Unto men she was so admirable for beauty
and grace that St Denis, that great light of the militant Church, beholding her,
acknowledged himself to have been dazzled and nigh transported from himself. And   120
for the angels, hear what the prophet says, 'All the rich of the people shall implore thy
countenance' [Ps. 44: 13]. And who are these rich but the angels, who beyond others
enjoy the riches of the heavenly kingdom? Whence she is said to be the glory of
Jerusalem, the gladness of Israel, the honour of her people.

As for the odour she gave forth of her sanctity, it is said, the odour of thy garments,   125
which is of her outward virtues, being as the odour of incense (Cant. 4), a grateful
sacrifice to God, which recreates those that are edified therewith.

And for the sense of touching in the rose, it is understood in a spiritual sense. Hear St
Bernard: 'Why fears human frailty to approach to Mary? You shall find nothing terrible;
she is wholly sweet and gentle and, being so sweet, is therefore to be sought-for and   130
embraced through devotion. Take her then, and she shall exalt thee; when thou shalt
embrace her, thou shalt be glorified by her.'

98–103. This passage reflects the current and shameful prejudices against Jews evident in Catholics and Protestants alike. 104. St Bernard Bernard of Clairvaux, 12th-c. Benedictine monk. rod of Jesse branch from the genealogical tree of Jesse, father of David. The prophecy in Isaiah predicts the birth of Jesus Christ from this family line. 116. specious beautiful (Lat. speciosus). 119. St Denis 3rd-c. missionary to Paris and martyr. militant Church church on earth in conflict with evil.

The Emblem

The Poesy

The Virgin sprung even from the barren earth,
A pure white rose was in her happy birth
Conceived without a thorn. This only flower   135
The Father raised by his almighty power.
When th'angel said she should conceive a son,
She blushed, and asked how it should be done.
The Holy Ghost inflamed, and so the white
By him was made a damask fiery bright.   140
Lastly her son made her purple red,
When on the cross his precious blood was shed.
No faith of mortals then but had a stain,
Excepting hers, for she was dyed in grain.

The Theories

Contemplate first a gallant and odoriferous rose, growing on a prickly and thorny stem,   145
and men with admiration to stand pointing at it, saying to one another, 'What is that
there, so shot-up, so beautiful to behold, from so ragged, sharp, and harsh a thorn?' And
then ponder how the angels stood amazed, seeing so our mystical rose transplanted from
Jericho into the heavenly paradise, or ascending rather, so flourishing, from the desert,
when there was like questioning amongst them at her glorious Assumption, asking, 'Who   150
it was that ascended, flowing with delights?' (Cant. 8: 5).

THE EMBLEM   The three roses represent the Trinity: the Hebrew letters signify 'Yahweh'; the dove, the Holy Spirit; and the
five wounds, Christ. The emblem thus depicts the mystery of the Trinity as incarnated in Jesus Christ through the mystical
rose, Mary. The motto is *pulchra es speciosa et macula non est in te* (adapted from Cant. 4: 7: You are beautiful, fair one, and there
is no spot in thee.)

THE POESY   140. **damask** i.e. damask rose, a pink or red variety.   144. **dyed in grain** dyed red ineradicably.

THE THEORIES   The Theories recollects ideas and extends consideration.   150. **Assumption** the transporting of Mary's
body into heaven at her death, one of the five Glorious Mysteries of the rosary.

Consider then the rose, while it grows in the garden and flourisheth as it were alive, how it cheers and glads the eyes of all with its glorious presence, and how, after it is cropped from its stem also, which is the death of the said rose, what an odour it hath with it, even after it hath been persecuted with fire in the furnace of the still, as well in the   155
water as in the cake; and then think what a mirror and pattern of sanctity our Lady was during her abode here in the garden of the world, and how she multiplied her favours to mankind especially after she was translated thence and had been proved and exercised with infinite tribulations, leaving an unspeakable odour behind of miracles and graces; witness the innumerable votes that hang on her temples and chapels throughout the   160
world.

Ponder lastly that of roses are made sometimes electuaries, sometimes oils, sometimes plasters, and conserves very sovereign and medicinal for many diseases, namely four: for first, the rose fortifies the stomach and comforts the heart; secondly, it stops the flux of the venter; thirdly, it clarifies the eyes; and finally, heals the headache. So our mystical   165
rose comforts the heart in affording it the charity of God; restrains the flux of sins through the fear of God, which she gives to eschew sins withal; clarifies the eye of the understanding by imparting to it the knowledge of divine things; and cures the head, which is hope, being 'the helmet of health' (1 Thess. 5), when she raiseth our tepid hope to desire celestial things, and therefore saith, 'I am the mother of fair dilection, of fear, of   170
knowledge, and of holy hope' (Ecclus. 24: 24).

The Apostrophe

Flower of flowers, O rose of roses, O flower of roses, O rose of flowers! Shore me up with flowers because I languish for love of thy love, Jesus, the bud of thee, O rose, little in thy womb, greater in thine arms, and then fairest of all when opened thoroughly and displayed on the cross. By that precious bud of thine, I beseech thee, and the shedding   175
of his most precious blood, thou wouldst change my thorns into roses, and present me as a rose of sweet odours to thy Son, and not as thorns for fuel of the fire of his indignation. O grant me this, I beseech thee, and here do I present thee in honour of thee, the mystical rose, and thy Son, thy sovereign bud, the hymn that follows:

Salve, Christi sacra parens,   180
    Flos de spina, spina carens,
    Flos, spineti gloria.
Nos spinetum, nos peccati
    Spina sumus cruentati,
    Sed tu spinae nescia.   185

155–6. **fire . . . cake** The passage describes the operation of a distillation device (**still**) to extract perfume from roses; first one heats the roses and then condenses the vapours into a liquid that cools to form an aromatic residue (**cake**). 158. **proved** tested. 160. **votes** votive offerings. 162. **electuaries** salves. 164–5. **flux . . . venter** outpourings . . . stomach. 170. **dilection** charity. 176. **thou** that thou. 180–5. a hymn to Mary by Adam of St Victor, a 12th-c. French monk.

[Hail, sacred parent of Christ, flower from thorn, without a thorn, flower, glory of the thorn-hedge. We are a thorn-hedge, bloody from the thorn of sin; but you know no thorn.]

AUGUSTINE BAKER

A Welsh convert to Catholicism, Augustine Baker (1575–1641) joined the Benedictines in Padua (1605) and produced (with others) *Apostalatus Benedictinorum in Anglia* (1626), a scholarly history of the order in Great Britain. Baker spent nine years (1624–33) in Cambrai (NE France) as spiritual adviser to Benedictine nuns, including Gertrude More (see POETRY). There he wrote over forty spiritual treatises, later digested and published by Father Serenus Cressy as *Sancta Sophia*, 'Holy Wisdom' (1657), a guidebook to prayer now recognized as a classic of mystical theology. Drawing upon many previous writers, *Sancta Sophia* teaches the prayer of mystic contemplation. In this sublime prayer, the soul, without thoughts or images, experiences God directly as infinite and incomprehensible truth and goodness (cf. Crashaw's 'The Flaming Heart' and 'Ode', POETRY). The selection below outlines the means by which the devout soul can ascend beyond perception and reason to mystic contemplation.

Sancta Sophia, 1657

Of Contemplation

Hitherto the exercises of a devout soul have been exceedingly laborious, in which she hath been obliged to use force and constraint, more or less, upon herself to elevate the will above all created things and to apply it unto God. She hath struggled through terrible oppositions of the devil and corrupt nature, the instability of the imagination, tumultuousness of passions, etc., all which would hinder her perseverance in her   5 recollections. But notwithstanding all this, pursuing them still sometimes in light and sometimes in darkness, sometimes allured by sweetness and again sometimes afflicted (but not discouraged) with desolations, in the end God crowns her courage and patience by exalting her to a new, more perfect, and divine exercise of the Prayer of Union or Contemplation.   10

Contemplation, in the accepted general notion of the word, signifies a clear, ready, mental seeing and quiet regarding of an object, being the result and effect of a precedent,

---

9–10. **Prayer...Contemplation** This prayer represents the highest state of mystical union with God.

diligent, and laborious enquiry and search after the nature, qualities, dependences, and other circumstantial conditions of it.

Now according to the nature of the object contemplated, and the disposition or end of the person contemplating, there are several sorts of contemplations, at least, so-called. For in the first place, anciently there was a certain kind of false contemplation, which we may call philosophical, practised by some learned heathens of old and imitated by some in these days, which hath for its last and best end only the perfection of knowledge and a delightful complacency in it. Others there were (and it is to be feared, are still) that contented themselves with an airy, vain renown which they hoped to gain by their knowledge. So that whatsoever was the object of their contemplation (whether things natural, moral, yea, or even divine, as far as by wit and subtlety or tradition they could be known), self-love and pride was the utmost end of all these contemplators. Yea, to this rank of philosophical contemplators may be referred those scholastic wits which spend much time in the study and subtle examination of the mysteries of faith, and have not for their end the increasing of divine love in their hearts. Nay, these are indeed more imperfect and culpable (saith Albertus Magnus, *lib. De Adhaer. Deo*) inasmuch as they offend against a greater and supernatural light.

Yea, and those among them that do truly intend as their last and principal end the glory of God and seeking his divine love (which is the best sort of scholastic contemplatives), yet since their chief employment consists in much internal discourse and reasoning, which cannot be practised without various and distinct sensible images by which to represent God, etc., the knowledge which they attain to is not properly contemplative, and the highest degree of prayer that they arrive unto is only a perfect kind of meditation.

In the second place there is a mystic contemplation which is indeed truly and properly such, by which a soul without discoursings and curious speculations, without any perceptible use of the internal senses or sensible images, by a pure, simple, and reposeful operation of the mind, in the obscurity of faith, simply regards God as infinite and incomprehensible verity, and with the whole bent of the will rests in him as her infinite, universal, and incomprehensible good. This is true contemplation indeed. And as rest is the end of motion, so is this the end of all other both internal and external exercises. For, therefore, by long discourse and much practice of affection, the soul enquires and tends to a worthy object that she may quietly contemplate it and, if it deserve affection, repose with contentment in it.

So it is in prayer: the soul, aspiring to a perfect union with God, as yet absent, begins with enquiry by meditation. For as St Augustine saith, 'Intellectus cogitabundus principium omnis boni', that is, 'All good proceeds from the understanding as its first

---

25. scholastic wits Church intellectuals from 5th to 15th c., often disparaged for their excessive rationalism and sterile theological and philosophical subtleties. **28. Albertus Magnus** 13th-c. Dominican bishop and philosopher. **38. curious** ingenious. **39. internal senses** thoughts and feelings. **40. obscurity of faith** darkness wherein faith operates. **48. meditation** the first and least perfect degree of internal prayer, consisting of discursive thought and images.

principle.' By meditation the soul labours to represent this divine object with all the sensible advantages and motives of admiration and of love that it can invent to the end the will by pure love may rest in him. But this being done, the will, being not yet at free liberty to dispose of itself, is forced with some violence to untwine and withdraw its adhesion from creatures that it may elevate itself and be firmly fixed to this her only good. And at last by long custom, the force by little and little diminishing, the object begins to appear in its own perfect light, and the affections flow freely but yet with a wonderful stillness to it. And then such souls are said to be arrived to perfect mystical union or contemplation.

This is properly the exercise of angels, for their knowledge is not by discourse, but by one simple intuition all objects are represented to their view at once with all their natures, qualities, relations, dependences, and effects. But man, that receives all his knowledge first from his senses, can only by effects and outward appearances with the labour of reasoning collect the nature of objects, and this but imperfectly. But his reasoning being ended, then he can at once contemplate all that is known unto him in the object.

Now in Holy Scripture our chiefest happiness and perfection is said to consist in this, that we shall be like unto angels both in our knowledge and love [Matt. 22: 30], for we shall (as they) have a perfect view and contemplation of God as he is, not by any created forms and representations. And so beatifical shall that contemplation be that it will forever engulf all our affections. But in this life our perfection will consist in approaching as near as may be to such an angelical contemplation of God, without sensible forms, and as he is indeed proposed by faith, that is, not properly represented, but as obscure notions imprinted in our minds concerning him, by which we do perceive that he is not anything that we can perceive or imagine but an inexhaustible ocean of universal being and good, infinitely exceeding our comprehension. The which being and good, whatsoever it is in itself, we love with the whole possible extension of our wills, embracing God beyond the proportion of our knowing him. But yet, even such a contemplation and love in this life, by reason of our bodily weakness and necessities, cannot be without many descents and interruptions.

This mystic contemplation or union is of two sorts: (1) active and ordinary, being indeed an habitual state of perfect souls by which they are enabled, whensoever fit occasion shall be, to unite themselves actively and actually to God by efficacious, fervent, amorous, and constant, yet withal silent and quiet, elevations of the spirit; (2) passive and extraordinary, the which is not a state but an actual grace and favour from God, by which he is pleased at certain times according to his free, good pleasure to communicate a glimpse of his majesty to the spirits of his servants after a secret and wonderful manner. And it is called passive, not but that therein the soul doth actively contemplate God, but she can neither when she pleases dispose herself thereto nor yet refuse it when that God thinks good to operate after such a manner in the soul and to represent himself unto her

---

54. **adhesion** affection. 63. **collect** apprehend. 68. **beatifical** full of blessings. 71. **proposed** intuited. 86. **not but** not denying.

by a divine, particular image, not at all framed by the soul but supernaturally infused into her. The which grace is seldom if ever afforded but to souls that have attained to the former state of perfect active union. Concerning this passive union and the several kinds of it, we shall speak more hereafter. 90

As for the former sort, which is active contemplation, of which we have already treated in gross in this chapter, we read in mystic authors, Thaulerus, Harphius, etc., that he that would become spiritual ought to practise the drawing of his external senses inwardly into 95 his internal, there losing and, as it were, annihilating them. Having done this, he must then draw his internal senses into the superior powers of the soul and there annihilate them likewise. And those powers of the intellectual soul he must draw into that which is called their unity, which is the principle and fountain from whence those powers do flow and in which they are united. And lastly that unity, which alone is capable of perfect 100 union with God, must be applied and firmly fixed on God. And herein, say they, consists the perfect divine contemplation and union of an intellectual soul with God.

Now whether such expressions as these will abide the strict examination of philosophy or no, I will not take on me to determine. Certain it is that by a frequent and constant exercise of internal prayer of the will, joined with mortification, the soul comes to operate 105 more and more abstracted from sense, and more elevated above the corporal organs and faculties, so drawing nearer to the resemblance of the operations of an angel or separated spirit.

Yet this abstraction and elevation perhaps is not to be understood as if the soul in these pure operations had not use at all of the internal senses or sensible images, for the schools 110 resolve that cannot consist with the state of a soul joined to a mortal body. But surely her operations in this pure degree of prayer are so subtle and *intime*, and the images that she makes use of so exquisitely pure and immaterial, that she cannot perceive at all that she works by images. So that spiritual writers are not much to be condemned by persons utterly unexperienced in these mystic affairs, if delivering things as they perceived 115 by their own experience, they have expressed them otherwise than will be admitted in the schools.

Now to this kind of purely intellectual operations doth a soul begin to arrive after a sufficient exercise of immediate acts of the will. And having attained thereto, they do grow more and more spiritual and sublime by the exercise of aspirations and blind 120 elevations without all limit.

I call them pure intellectual operations in opposition to actuations imaginative, produced by mean of gross sensible images, and not as if the said operations were in the intellect or understanding. For on the contrary, they are exercised in a manner wholly by the will. For in proper aspirations the soul hath no other use of the understanding but 125

---

94. in gross at large. **Thaulerus ... Harphius** Johannes Tauler (1300–61), a Dominican ... Hendrik Herp (Harphius, 1410–78), a Franciscan. **95. external senses** the sensory faculties of perception. **96. internal** thoughts and feelings. **97. superior powers** rational faculties of soul, as opposed to vegetative and animal. **112. *intime*** intimate (Fr.). **122. actuations** impulses.

only antecedently to propose an object, which is no other but a general, obscure, confused notion of God, as faith darkly teaches, and this rather virtually than directly and expressly, the main business being to elevate the will and unite it to God so presented.

In which union, above all particular images, there is neither time nor place, but all is 130 vacuity and emptiness, as if nothing were existent but God and the soul. Yea, so far is the soul from reflecting on her own existence that it seems to her that God and she are not distinct but one only thing. This is called by some mystic authors the state of nothingness, by others the state of totality, because therein God is all in all, the container of all things. And the prayer proper to this state is thus described by a holy hermit in Cassian 135 (*Collat*. x. c. ii): 'Ita ad illam orationis incorruptionem mens nostra perveniat', etc., that is, 'So will the mind ascend to that pure simplicity of prayer, the which is freed from all intuition of images, undistinguished with any prosecution of words or senses, but uttered internally by an inflamed intention of the mind, by an unutterable excess of affection and inconceivable quickness and alacrity of spirit. The which prayer the spirit, being 140 abstracted from all senses and sensible objects, doth pour forth unto God by sighs and groans that cannot be expressed.'

127. **virtually** indirectly. 135. **Cassian** St John Cassian, 5th-c. monk. 138. **prosecution** exercise.

DRAMA

Catholic rituals and traditions are inherently dramatic and deeply inform Western drama. From the early Middle Ages on, the faithful understood the mass as sacred drama with prescribed costume, dialogue, and action. The Church produced Latin plays that elaborated certain liturgies, the Christmas and Easter morning services especially. Communities staged various pageants, festivals, and enactments to commemorate the feasts or seasons of the Church year. Towns, for example, performed mystery play cycles—dramatizations of events from the Old and New Testaments. The movement of the cycle from the Old Testament to the New, through Christ's Passion to his Resurrection, like the sequence of the Church year, articulated a deep comedic structure for later literatures, an archetypal progression from death to rebirth, from sin to redemption. Morality plays featured a representative lead, Everyman, who normally succumbed to an attractive figure of temptation—Vice, Iniquity, or Sin—but repented before death. These plays created enduring character types and patterns for later drama. Saints plays, finally, dramatized the exemplary lives and deaths of St George, Mary Magdalen, and others. All forms of religious drama contested and blended with secular dramatic traditions.

And yet, some dramatists produced works that could specifically lay claim to Catholic identity. A member of Thomas More's charmed circle, John Heywood, wrote *The Pardoner and the Friar*, which presents two hypocritical hucksters in an unholy scramble for money. His vivid characterization and broad humour recall the best traditions of medieval satire (Geoffrey Chaucer, especially), while featuring the dramatic innovation of simultaneous speeches. A learned Catholic noblewoman, Jane Lumley, produced the first extant translation of a Greek tragedy in English, Euripides' *Iphigeneia at Aulis* (1555?). Lumley imbued the mythological sacrifice with Christian values, however, obliquely reflecting the culture of Catholic martyrdom. Jesuits wrote Latin dramas for performance (sometimes in large civic spectacles) in order to educate their students, combat heresy, and proclaim the Gospel. In the seventeenth century at least one hundred thousand Jesuit dramas played on European stages (mostly in schools), influencing many major writers, including de Vega, Calderòn, Goldoni, Tasso, Molière, and Voltaire. In the selection below, Jacob Bidermann, SJ, richly refashions *Everyman* into *Cenodoxus* ('vainglory'). Drawing upon Ignatian spiritual exercises, particularly the meditations on Satan and hell, he presents a frightening spectacle of sin and damnation.

Of major early modern dramatists, Ben Jonson professed Catholicism for twelve years (1598–1610), the period of his greatest literary productivity. Though the significance of this profession to Jonson's strained relations with political, spiritual, and literary authority remains unclear, it left some impress on his drama. Cited for 'popery and treason' in its own day, *Sejanus* reflects the world of spies, betrayal, oppression, and danger that Catholics well knew. *The Alchemist* and *Bartholomew Fair* portray Puritans as self-serving hypocrites who spout the official line of anti-Catholic bigotry. Jonson's greater contemporary, William Shakespeare, scholars now recognize, grew up in a Catholic family in a region that maintained many ties to the old faith. Though Shakespeare's personal beliefs remain a mystery, his plays clearly appealed to people of various religious persuasions. With increasing conviction scholars have recently explored his biographical Catholicity (family connections, Stratford schoolteachers, the Lancaster connections), literary Catholicity (portraits of clerics and Roman rituals in plays and poems), and cultural Catholicity (response to embedded Catholic beliefs, controversies, and practices). The selections here show Shakespeare working apart from the official party line and drawing upon Catholic doctrine and beliefs.

Finally, Philip Massinger and James Shirley, two possibly Catholic Caroline playwrights, deserve at least passing notice because they variously express Catholic sympathies in their works. Denying audiences the usual comic ending in *The Maid of Honour* (1626), Massinger has his heroine choose religious life as a nun instead of marriage. In *The Renegado* (1624) he endorses Catholic views of the sacraments and, astonishingly, portrays a Jesuit as a wise and good spiritual leader. At the end of our period, James Shirley reworks the medieval saints play in his *St Patrick in Ireland* (1639–40). Producing the play for Thomas Wentworth, the Protestant regent of Ireland, however, Shirley eschews serious moral instruction for flashy shows and *coups de théâtre*. His play represents the decadence rather than culmination of a great religious tradition.

JOHN HEYWOOD

Singer, musician, court entertainer, and playwright, John Heywood (1497–1575) belonged to Thomas More's circle and remained a Roman Catholic through the tumultuous changes of his long life. Both his sons, Ellis and Jasper, became priests: Ellis wrote a reminiscence of Thomas More in Italian, *Il Moro*; and Jasper, a Jesuit, translated Seneca and led the English Mission from 1581 until his imprisonment in 1583. John Heywood wrote epigrams, a religious allegory, *The Spider and the Fly*, and, most important, interludes—comic satiric verse dialogues. In *The Pardoner and the Friar* below Heywood presents two conmen: the Pardoner, a layman licensed to sell relics and indulgences, and the Friar, a mendicant priest. Blustering and preaching, both frauds hawk spiritual gifts for material gain. Innovatively Heywood presents their two rhyming spiels simultaneously. Underlying the roistering comic action are serious controversies regarding papal power, the sale of relics and indulgences, and the sacrament of penance. Like Erasmus's dialogues (see FICTION), the play harks back to medieval satires on church abuses and shows a capacity for religious self-scrutiny and laughter.

*The Pardoner and the Friar, c.*1530

[*The* FRIAR *enters*]

FRIAR Beware how ye despise the poor friars,
 Which are in this world Christ's ministers,
 But do them with an hearty cheer receive,
 Lest they happen your houses for to leave,
 And then God will take vengeance in his ire.   5
 Wherefore, I now, that am a poor friar,
 Did enquire where any people were
 Which were disposed the word of God to hear.
 And as I came hither, one did me tell
 That in this town right good folk did dwell,   10
 Which to hear the word of God would be glad.
 And as soon as I thereof knowledge had,
 I hither hied me as fast as I might,
 Intended by the grace of God almight,
 And by your patience and supportation,   15
 Here to make a simple collation.
 Wherefore I require all ye in this presence
 For to abide and give due audience.
 But first of all,
 Now here I shall   20

---

1. **friars** probably Dominicans, the *ordo praedicatorum*, 'order of preachers'. 13. **hied** hurried. 14. **Intended** led.
15. **supportation** assistance. 16. **collation** (1) collection of money; (2) homily; (3) light meal.

To God my prayer make,
To give ye grace
All in this place,
His doctrine for to take.

And then kneeleth down the Friar, saying his prayers, and in the meanwhile entereth the
PARDONER *with all his relics, to declare what each of them be and the whole power and*
virtue thereof.

PARDONER God and Saint Leonard, send ye all his grace,   25
As many as be assembled in this place!

. . . .

Lo, here my bulls, all and some!
Our liege lord's seal here on my patent
I bear with me, my body to warrant,
That no man be so bold, be he priest or clerk,   30
Me to disturb of Christ's holy work,
Nor have no disdain nor yet scorn
Of these holy relics which saints have worn.
First, here I show ye of a holy Jew's sheep
A bone. I pray you, take good keep   35
To my words and mark them well:
If any of your beasts' bellies do swell,
Dip this bone in the water that he doth take
Into his body, and the swelling shall slake.
And if any worm have your beasts stung,   40
Take of this water and wash his tongue,
And it will be whole anon; and, furthermore,
Of pox and scabs and every sore,
He shall be quite whole that drinketh of the well
That this bone is dipped in. It is truth that I tell!   45
And if any man that any beast oweth,
Once in the week ere that the cock croweth,
Fasting, will drink of this well a draught,
As that holy Jew hath us taught,
His beasts and his store shall multiply.   50
And, masters all, it helpeth well,
Though a man be foul in jealous rage,

---

25. Saint Leonard St Leonard of Limousin (11th c.), revered throughout Europe for effecting cures, exorcisms, and other miracles. **27–74.** These lines follow closely Chaucer's Prologue to 'The Pardoner's Tale', 335–88. **27. bulls** papal pronouncements with leaden seals. **all and some** the whole sum. **28. liege lord** the king. **patent** permission. **29. body to warrant** to give authority to my presence here. **30. clerk** any ecclesiastic, including deacons. **34. a holy Jew** probably a figure from Scripture such as Jacob. **40. worm** insect. **46. oweth** owns.

Let a man with this water make his potage,
And nevermore shall he his wife mistrust,
Though he in sooth the fault by her wist,   55
Or had she be take with friars two or three.
Here is a mitten eke, as ye may see:
He that his hand will put in this mitten,
He shall have increase of his grain
That he hath sown, be it wheat or oats.   60
So that he offer pence or else groats.

.   .   .   .

Wherefore, to these relics now come crouch and creep.
But look that ye offering to them make,
Or else can ye no manner profit take.
But one thing, ye women all, I warrant you: 65
If any wight be in this place now
That hath done sin so horrible that she
Dare not for shame thereof shriven be,
Or any woman, be she young or old,
That hath made her husband cuckold,   70
Such folk shall have no power nor no grace,
To offer to my relics in this place.
And who so findeth herself out of such blame,
Come hither to me, on Christ's holy name!
And because ye   75
Shall unto me
Give credence at the full,
Mine authority
Now shall ye see:
Lo, here the pope's bull!   80

.   .   .   .

[*They speak simultaneously.*]
FRIAR **What, should ye give aught to prating pardoners?**
PARDONER What should ye spend on these flattering liars,
FRIAR **What, should ye give aught to these bold beggars?**
PARDONER As be these babbling monks and these friars,
FRIAR **Let them hardily labour for their living.**   85
PARDONER Which do nought daily but babble and lie,
FRIAR **It much hurteth them, good men's giving,**

---

53. potage soup. **55. sooth** truth. **fault** sin (of infidelity). **wist** knows. **56. take** caught (in sexual activity). **57. eke** also. **61. groats** small coins. **62. creep** advance on your knees, a ritual gesture of respect to the cross. **65. warrant** guarantee. **66. wight** person. **68. shriven** absolved. **81. aught** anything.

PARDONER And tell you fables dear enough a fly,

FRIAR **For that maketh them idle and slothful to work,**

PARDONER As doth this babbling friar here today!   90

FRIAR **That for none other thing they will cark.**

PARDONER Drive him hence, therefore, in the twenty-devil way!

FRIAR **Hardily, they would go both to plow and cart,**

PARDONER On us pardoners hardily do your cost,

FRIAR **And if of necessity once they felt the smart.**   95

PARDONER For why? Your money never can be lost;

FRIAR **But we friars be not in like estate,**

PARDONER For why, there is in our fraternity,

FRIAR **For our hands with such things we may not maculate;**

PARDONER For all brethren and sisteren that thereof be,   100

FRIAR **We friars be not in like condition,**

PARDONER Devoutly sung every year,

FRIAR **We may have no prebends nor exhibition,**

PARDONER As he shall know well that cometh there,

FRIAR **Of all temporal service are we forbid,**   105

PARDONER At every of the five solemn feasts,

FRIAR **And only bound to the service of God,**

PARDONER A mass and *dirige* to pray for the good rest

FRIAR **And therewith to pray for every Christian nation,**

PARDONER Of the souls of the brethren and sisteren all,   110

FRIAR **That God witsafe to save them from damnation.**

PARDONER Of our fraternity in general,

FRIAR **But some of you so hard be of heart,**

PARDONER With a hearse there standing, well arrayed and dight,

FRIAR **Ye cannot weep, though ye full sore smart,**   115

PARDONER And torches and tapers about it burning bright,

FRIAR **Wherefore some man must ye hire needs,**

PARDONER And with the bells eke solemnly ringing,

FRIAR **Which must entreat God for your misdeeds.**

PARDONER And priests and clerks devoutly singing.   120

FRIAR **Ye can hire no better in mine opinion**

PARDONER And, furthermore, every night in the year,

FRIAR **Than us, God's servants, men of religion.**

---

88. dear...fly not worth a fly. 91. cark be anxious, fret. 92. in...way in the name of the devil many times over. 93. Hardily surely. 94. hardily...cost confidently put your money. 97. estate condition. 99. maculate get dirty. 103. prebends stipends from church. exhibition pension or salary. 106. five solemn feasts probably the immovable feasts, Christmas, Circumcision, Epiphany, Purification, and Annunciation. 108. *dirige* dirge, derived from the first word of the Latin antiphon, *Dirige, Domine*, 'Direct O Lord, my God, my way in thy sight' (Ps. 5: 9), used in the funeral service. 111. witsafe grant. 114. hearse frame which carried candles over the bier. dight properly.

PARDONER Twelve poor people are receivèd there,

FRIAR **And specially God heareth us poor friars,**   125

PARDONER And there have both harbour and food,

FRIAR **And is attentive unto our desires,**

PARDONER That for them is convenient and good.

FRIAR **For the more of religion, the more heard of our Lord,**

PARDONER And, furthermore, if there be any other,   130

FRIAR **And that it so should, good reason doth accord,**

PARDONER That of our fraternity be sister or brother,

FRIAR **Therefore, doubt not, masters, I am even he,**

PARDONER Which hereafter hap to fall in decay,

FRIAR **To whom ye should part with your charity.**   135

PARDONER And if he then chance to come that way,

FRIAR **We friars be they that should your alms take,**

PARDONER Nigh unto our foresaid holy place,

FRIAR **Which for your souls' health do both watch and wake.**

PARDONER Ye shall there tarry for a month's space.   140

FRIAR **We friars pray, God wot, when ye do sleep,**

PARDONER And be there found of the place's cost.

FRIAR **We for your sins do both sob and weep,**

PARDONER Wherefore, now, in the name of the Holy Ghost,

FRIAR **To pray to God for mercy and for grace,**   145

PARDONER I advise you all that now here be

FRIAR **And thus do we daily with all our whole place.**

PARDONER For to be of our fraternity.

FRIAR **Wherefore, distribute of your temporal wealth,**

PARDONER Fie on covetise! Stick not for a penny,   150

FRIAR **By which ye may preserve your soul's health.**

PARDONER For which ye may have benefits so many!

FRIAR **I say, wilt thou not yet stint thy clap?**

  Pull me down the pardoner with an evil hap!

PARDONER Master Friar, I hold it best,   155

  To keep your tongue while ye be in rest.

FRIAR **I say, one pull the knave off his stool!**

PARDONER Nay, one pull the friar down like a fool!

---

124. Twelve poor people charitable orders and institutions often provided for twelve indigents in remembrance of the twelve apostles. **129. For...lord** The greater the number of religious, the more likely God will hear them. **131. And...accord** And that it should be so is very reasonable. **134. hap** chance. **141. wot** knows. **142. found** provided. **150. Stick** hesitate. **153. stint thy clap** stop your noise. **154. Pull...hap** Pull down the Pardoner from his stool and bad luck to him! **156. in rest** free (from my attack).

FRIAR Leave thy railing and babbling of friars,
    Or, by Jeez, I sha' lug thee by the sweet ears!   160
PARDONER By God, I would thou durst presume to it!
FRIAR By God, a little thing might make me to do it!

    .   .   .   .

[*They fight.* PARSON *and* PRAT *enter*]

PRAT [*to the Pardoner*] Nay, I am once charged with thee:
    Wherefore, by Saint Johan, thou shalt not escape me,
    Till thou hast scoured a pair of stocks.   165
PARSON Tut, he weeneth all is but mocks!
    Lay hand on him. And come ye on, Sir Friar,
    Ye shall of me hardily have your hire!
    Ye had none such this seven year,
    I swear by God and by our Lady dear.   170
FRIAR Nay, Master Parson, for God's passion,
    Entreat not me after that fashion,
    For, if ye do, it will not be for your honesty!
PARSON Honesty or not, but thou shall see
    What I shall do by and by.   175
    Make no struggling; come forth soberly,
    For it shall not avail thee, I say.
FRIAR Marry, that shall we try even straightway!
    I defy thee, churl priest, an there be no more than thou,
    I will not go with thee, I make God a vow!   180
    We shall see first which is the stronger.
    God hath sent me bones, I do thee not fear.
PARSON Yea, by thy faith, wilt thou be there?
    Neighbour Prat, bring forth that knave!
    And thou, Sir Friar, if thou wilt algates rave—   185
FRIAR Nay, churl, I thee defy,
    I shall trouble thee first!
PARSON Thou shalt go to prison by and by.
    Let me see now, do thy worst!
    PRAT [*fights*] with the PARDONER, *and the* PARSON *with the* FRIAR.
PARSON Help, help, neighbour Prat, neighbour Prat!   190
    In the worship of God, help me somewhat!

---

160. **lug** pull. 163. **once charged with** responsible to arrest. 165. **scoured** sat in. 166. **weeneth** thinks. **mocks** jokes. 173. **be . . . honesty** be good for your reputation. 185. **algates** always. 189 ff. The violence of the conclusion illustrates the sinful and destructive nature of avarice or 'covetise'.

PRAT Nay, deal as thou canst with that elf!
  For why, I have enough to do myself.
  Alas, for pain I am almost dead!
  The red blood so runneth down about my head!   195
  Nay, an thou canst, I pray thee, help me!
PARSON Nay, by the mass, fellow, it will not be,
  I have more tow on my distaff than I can well spin.
  The cursed friar doth the upper hand win!
FRIAR Will ye leave, then, and let us in peace depart?   200
PARSON and PRAT Yea, by our Lady, even with all our heart.
FRIAR and PARDONER Then, adieu, to the devil, till we come again!
PARSON and PRAT And a mischief go with you both twain!

JANE LUMLEY

Jane Lumley (1537?–1577?), Catholic noblewoman, left behind in manuscript Isocrates translated into Latin, two Latin letters, and *Iphigeneia at Aulis* (1555?), the first extant rendering of a Greek tragedy into English. Probably consulting the Greek original along with Erasmus's Latin translation, her primary source, Lumley strips the Euripidean action to its bare bones, omits the choruses and lyric flights, and produces a redactive but powerful paraphrase. Christianizing the terms and meaning of the ancient drama, she transforms the alien pagan sacrifice into a contemporary martyrdom. In the selections below Iphigeneia, unlike Euripides' tragic hero, suffers her misfortune 'patiently' and ends in 'heaven'. Like Jasper Heywood, Catholic translator of Seneca, Jane Lumley played an important role in the early modern rediscovery of classical drama.

---

192. **elf** tricky, malicious person. 198. **I...spin** proverbial for 'I have more trouble than I can handle' (the metaphor derives from spinning unworked fibre on a distaff, or cleft rod). 202. **to the devil** i.e. 'I commend you to the devil', reversing the formula of *adieu*, 'I commend you to God'.

Iphigeneia at Aulis, c.1555

[*The* CHORUS, IPHIGENEIA, CLYTEMNESTRA, ORESTES, *and* AGAMEMNON *are on stage.*]

CHORUS It is meet, O Agamemnon, that you should follow your wife's counsel, for it is not lawful that a father should destroy his child.

IPHIGENEIA Now, O father, I, kneeling upon my knees and making most humble suit, do most earnestly desire you to have pity upon me, your daughter, and not to slay me so cruelly, for you know it is given to all mortal men to be desirous of life. Again, 5 remember that I am your daughter, and how you seemed ever to love me best of all your children, insomuch that you were wont ever to desire that you might see me married to one worthy of my degree. And I did ever wish again that I might live to see you an old man that you might have much joy both of me and also of your other children. And will you now consent to my death, forgetting both that which you were 10 wont to say and also what pain you and my mother took in bringing me up, knowing no cause in me worthy of death? For what have I to do with Helena? But now, father, seeing you are nothing moved with my lamentation, I will call hither my young brother Orestes, for I know he will be sorry to see his sister slain. And again, you cannot choose but you must needs have pity either of him or else of me, considering 15 what a lawful request we do desire, for you know that all men are desirous of life and there is no wise man but he will choose rather to live in misery than to die.

AGAMEMNON I know in what things I ought to show pity and wherein I ought not, and I love my children as it becometh a father, for I do not this of myself, nor yet for my brother's sake, but rather by compulsion of the host. For the gods have answered that 20 they cannot pass the sea without your death, and they are so desirous to go thither that they care not what trouble and misery they suffer so that they may see it. Wherefore it lieth not in my power to withstand them, for I am not able to make any resistance against them. I am, therefore, compelled, daughter, to deliver you to them.   [*Exit*]

CLYTEMNESTRA Alas, daughter, into what misery are both you and I driven, seeing that 25 your own father will consent to your death?

IPHIGENEIA Alas, mother, this the last day that ever I shall see you! O unhappy Troy, which hast nourished and brought up that wicked man Paris! O unfortunate Venus,

---

IPHIGENEIA AT AULIS Ready to sail against Troy for Helen, Agamemnon and the Greek forces at Aulis discover that Artemis (Diana) requires first a sacrifice, namely, Iphigeneia, Agamemnon's eldest daughter. Agamemnon promises Iphigeneia in marriage to Achilles in order to trick his wife Clytemnestra into bringing the girl to Aulis. Iphigeneia begs for her life. **1. meet** proper. **12. Helena** wife of Agamemnon's brother, Menelaus. Paris abducted Helena to Troy, thus beginning the Trojan war. **14. Orestes** Present as a young child on stage, Orestes will avenge his father's death by slaying his mother Clytemnestra and her lover Aegisthus. **20. compulsion...host** Lumley simplifies both the Greek original and Latin intermediary here, which both adduce the desire that burns in Greeks to avenge the rape of Greek wives, and the importance of establishing the supremacy of Greece over the barbarians. **21. they** the Greeks. **pass** pass over. **28–9. Venus...him** This alludes to the mythic Judgement of Paris: Paris had to decide who was preferable— Hera (Juno), Athena (Minerva), or Aphrodite (Venus). He chose Aphrodite (Venus) because she had promised him

which didst promise to give Helena to him, for you have been the cause of my destruction, though, indeed, I through my death shall purchase the Grecians a glorious victory. Alas, mother, in what an unlucky time was I born that mine own father, which hath consented unto my death, doth now forsake me in this misery. I would to god that the Grecians had never taken in hand this journey. But methinks, mother, I see a great company of men coming hither. What are they, I pray you?   30

CLYTEMNESTRA   Truly, yonder is Achilles.   35

IPHIGENEIA   Let me, then, I pray you, go hence that I may hide my face for I am ashamed.

CLYTEMNESTRA   What cause have you to do so?

IPHIGENEIA   Truly, because it was said that I should have been his wife.

CLYTEMNESTRA   Daughter, you must lay away all shamefastness now, for you may use no niceness but rather prove by what means you may best save your life.   40

[*Enter* AGAMEMNON, SOLDIERS, *and* NEW MEMBERS OF THE CHORUS]

CHORUS   Alas, Clytemnestra, how unhappy art thou, for truly there is great talking of thee in the whole city.

CLYTEMNESTRA   Whereof, I pray you?

CHORUS   Of your daughter, how she shall be slain.   45

CLYTEMNESTRA   You have brought me very evil news. But tell me, I pray you, doth nobody speak against it?

ACHILLES   Yes, I myself have been in danger of my life because I took your daughter's part.

CLYTEMNESTRA   Who, I pray you, dare hurt you?

ACHILLES   Truly, the whole host.   50

CLYTEMNESTRA   Do not your own countrymen of Myrmidon help you?

ACHILLES   No, truly, for even they also did speak against me, saying that I was in love with her and therefore I did prefer my own pleasure above the commodity of my country.

CLYTEMNESTRA   What answer then made you unto them?

ACHILLES   I said that I ought not to suffer her to be slain, which was reported by her own father that she should have been my wife.   55

CLYTEMNESTRA   You said well, indeed, for Agamemnon sent for her from Greece, feigning that it was for that purpose.

ACHILLES   But though I could not prevail against such a multitude of people, yet I will do as much as shall lie in my power for you.   60

CLYTEMNESTRA   Alas, then you alone shall be compelled to strive against many.

ACHILLES   Do you not see a great company of harnessed men?

in exchange the most beautiful woman, Helena. **40. shamefastness** (1) shame; (2) modesty. **41. niceness** scrupulosity, fastidiousness. **prove** try. **(SD)** [stage direction] Lumley imagines here the entrance of some new choral members, who bring news and join the women already on stage. **51. Myrmidon** region in Thessaly that supplied Achilles with his followers. **53. commodity** interests. This pithy summary owes more to Erasmus' Latin than to Euripides: 'Meque dicebant amore vincier connubii, | Proin parum consuler Graium copiarum commodis' (*Hecuba et Iphigenia in Aulide*, Vienna, 1511, sigs. L5ᵛ–L6: They were saying that I was vanquished by love of a wife so that I cared less for the interests of the Greek troops'. **55. which** who. **62. harnessed** armed.

CLYTEMNESTRA   I pray god they be your friends.

ACHILLES   Yes, truly, that they be.

CLYTEMNESTRA   Then, I hope my daughter shall not die.   65

ACHILLES   No, that she shall not if I can help her.

CLYTEMNESTRA   But will there come anybody hither to slay her?

ACHILLES   Yea, truly, Ulysses will be here anon with a great company of men to take her
away.

CLYTEMNESTRA   Is he commanded to do so, or doth he it but of his own head?   70

ACHILLES   No, truly, he is not commanded.

CLYTEMNESTRA   Alas, then, he hath taken upon him a wicked deed, seeing he will defile
himself with the danger and death of my daughter.

ACHILLES   Truly, but I will not suffer him.

CLYTEMNESTRA   But if he go about to take my daughter away with strong power, what   75
shall I do then?

ACHILLES   You were best to keep her by you, for the matter shall be driven to that point.

IPHIGENEIA   Hearken, O mother, I pray you, unto my words, for I perceive you are
angry with your husband, which you may not do. For you cannot obtain your purpose
by that means and you ought rather to have thanked Achilles because he so gently hath   80
promised his help, which may happen to bring him into a great mischief. I would
counsel you, therefore, to suffer this trouble patiently, for I must needs die and will
suffer it willingly. Consider, I pray you, mother, for what a lawful cause I shall be slain.
Doth not both the destruction of Troy and also the wealth of Greece, which is the most
fruitful country of the world, hang upon my death? And if this wicked enterprise of the   85
Trojans be not revenged, then truly the Grecians shall not keep neither their children
nor yet their wives in peace. And I shall not only remedy all these things with my death
but also get a glorious renown to the Grecians forever. Again, remember how I was not
born for your sake only but rather for the commodity of my country. Think you,
therefore, that it is meet that such a company of men, being gathered together to   90
revenge the great injury which all Greece hath suffered, should be let of their journey
for my cause. Surely, mother, we cannot speak against this, for you do not think it to
be better that I should die than so many noble men to be let of their journey for one
woman's sake? For one noble man is better than a thousand women. Besides this,
seeing my death is determined amongst the gods, truly no mortal man ought to   95
withstand it. Wherefore I will offer myself willingly to death for my country, for by this
means I shall not only leave a perpetual memory of my death, but I shall cause also the

---

68. Ulysses Odysseus, shrewd king of Ithaca and ally of Agamemnon.   **78–99.** Iphigeneia's reversal here drew Aristotle's
famous criticism of her as inconsistent, 'since the girl who beseeches bears no resemblance to her later self' (*Poetics*
1454[a]26).   **82. suffer…patiently** Lumley departs from the Greek to introduce here the Christian virtue of
patience.   **87. remedy…death** E. V. Beilin (*Redeeming Eve*, 1987: 314) contrasts this line with the Greek, ταῦτα πάντα
κατθανοῦϲα ῥύϲομαι (1383: (By dying I shall protect all things) and notes a Christian resonance, perhaps deriving from
Erasmus, 'Haec profecto cuncta redimam morte (si cadem), mea (Iphigenia', 1511, sig. M1: If I should fall, I shall truly
redeem this whole state of affairs with my death).   **93. let** prevented.

Grecians to rule over the barbarians, which doth, as it were, properly belong to them, for the Grecians by nature are free like as the barbarians are born to bondage.

CHORUS Surely you are happy, O Iphigeneia, that you can suffer so patiently all this 100
trouble!

ACHILLES Truly, I would count myself happy if I might obtain thee, O Iphigeneia, to be my wife. And I think thee, O Greece, to be very fortunate because thou hast nourished such a one. For you have spoken very well in that you will not strive against the determination of the gods. Wherefore I, being not only moved with pity for that I see 105
you brought into such a necessity, but also stirred up more with love towards you, desiring to have you to my wife, will promise you faithfully to withstand the Grecians, as much as shall lie in my power, that they shall not slay you.

IPHIGENEIA Surely I have spoken even as I thought indeed. Wherefore I shall desire you, O Achilles, not to put yourself in danger for my cause but suffer me rather to save 110
all Greece with my death.

ACHILLES Truly, I wonder greatly at the boldness of your mind. And because you seem to be so willing to die, I cannot speak against you. Yet, nevertheless, I will promise to help you still lest you should happen to change your mind.   [*Exit*]

IPHIGENEIA Wherefore, mother, do you hold your peace, lamenting so within your- 115
self?

CLYTEMNESTRA Alas, I, wretched creature, have great cause to mourn.

IPHIGENEIA Be of good comfort mother, I pray you, and follow my counsel, and do not tear your clothes so.

CLYTEMNESTRA How can I do otherwise, seeing I shall lose you? 120

IPHIGENEIA I pray you, mother, study not to save my life, for I shall get you much honour by my death.

CLYTEMNESTRA What, shall not I lament your death?

IPHIGENEIA No, truly you ought not, seeing that I shall both be sacrificed to the goddess Diana and also save Greece. 125

CLYTEMNESTRA Well, I will follow your counsel, daughter, seeing you have spoken so well. But tell me, what shall I say to your sisters from you?

IPHIGENEIA Desire them, I pray you, not to mourn for my death.

CLYTEMNESTRA And what shall I say unto the other virgins from you?

IPHIGENEIA Bid them all farewell in my name and, I pray you, for my sake bring up my 130
little brother Orestes till he come to man's age.

CLYTEMNESTRA Take you leave of him for this is the last day that ever you shall see him.

100–1. The Greek choral comment, τὸ μὲν cόν, ὦ νεᾶνι, γενναίως ἔχει· | τὸ τῆς τύχης δὲ καὶ τὸ τῆς θεοῦ νοcεῖ. (1402–3: The part you play, maiden, is a noble one. But fate and the goddess—that is where the sickness lies), suggests a deep malaise in the divine order; Erasmus shifted the emphasis: 'beata es tam uirile pectore, at | Ex parte sortis, ac deae felix parum' (*Iphigenia*, 1511, sig. M1ᵛ): You are blessed in your manly heart, but less fortunate in your fate and in the goddess). Lumley again emphasizes the virtue of patience in worldly misfortune.

IPHIGENEIA Farewell, my well-beloved brother, for I am even, as it were, compelled to love you because you were so glad to help me.

CLYTEMNESTRA Is there any other thing that I may do for you at Greece?   135

IPHIGENEIA No, truly, but I pray you not to hate my father for this deed, for he is compelled to do it for the wealth and honour of Greece.

CLYTEMNESTRA If he hath done this willingly, then truly he hath committed a deed far unworthy of such a noble man as he is.

IPHIGENEIA Who is this that will carry me hence so soon?   140

CLYTEMNESTRA I will go with you, O daughter.

IPHIGENEIA Take heed, I pray you, lest you happen to do that which shall not become you. Wherefore, O mother, I pray you, follow my counsel and tarry here still, for I must needs go to be sacrificed unto the goddess Diana.

CLYTEMNESTRA And will you go away, O daughter, leaving me your mother here?   145

IPHIGENEIA Yea, surely, mother, I must go from you unto such a place from whence I shall never come again, although I have not deserved it.

CLYTEMNESTRA I pray you, daughter, tarry, and do not forsake me now.

IPHIGENEIA Surely I will go hence, mother, for if I did tarry, I should move you to more lamentation. Wherefore I shall desire all you women to sing some song of my death,   150
and to prophesy good luck unto the Grecians, for with my death I shall purchase unto them a glorious victory. Bring me, therefore, unto the altar of the temple of the goddess Diana, that with my blood I may pacify the wrath of the gods against you.

CHORUS O Queen Clytemnestra of most honour, after what fashion shall we lament, seeing we may not show any token of sadness at the sacrifice?   155

IPHIGENEIA I would not have you to mourn for my cause for I will not refuse to die.

CHORUS Indeed, by this means you shall get yourself a perpetual renown forever.

IPHIGENEIA Alas, thou sun, which art comfort to man's life! O thou light, which dost make joyful all creatures! I shall be compelled by and by to forsake you all and to change my life.   [*Exit with soldiers*]   160

CHORUS Behold, yonder goeth the virgin to be sacrificed with a great company of soldiers after her, whose beautiful face and fair body anon shall be defiled with her own blood. Yet happy art thou, O Iphigeneia, that with thy death thou shalt purchase unto the Grecians a quiet passage, which, I pray god, may not only happen fortunately unto them, but also that they may return again prosperously with a glorious victory.   165

[*Enter* MESSENGER]

MESSENGER Come hither, O Clytemnestra, for I must speak with you.

CLYTEMNESTRA Tell me, I pray you, what would you with me that you call so hastily? Is there any more mischief in hand that I must hear of?

---

134. **glad** eager. 135. **Greece** Argos, actually, a region in the central Peloponnesus around Mycenae, Agamemnon's city. 150. **some song** the ritual *threnos* or sung lamentation. 151–2. **with . . . victory** Lumley omits Euripides' description of a Greek sacrifice, replete with baskets, barley, and ritual movement.

MESSENGER I must tell you of a wonder which hath happened at the sacrificing of you daughter.   170

CLYTEMNESTRA Show me, I pray you, quickly what it is!

MESSENGER As we went unto the place where the sacrifice should be and passed through the pleasant fields where the whole host waited for your daughter, Agamemnon, seeing her brought unto her death, began to lament and weep. But she, perceiving what moan her father made, said unto him these words: 'O father, I am come hither to   175 offer my body willingly for the wealth of my country. Wherefore, seeing that I shall be sacrificed for the commodity of all Greece, I do desire you that none of the Grecians may slay me privily, for I will make no resistance against you.' And when she had spoken these words, all they that were which were present were wonderfully astonied at the stoutness of her mind. So after this Achilles with the rest of the whole host began to   180 desire the goddess Diana that she would accept the sacrifice of the virgin's blood and that she would grant them a prosperous success of their journey. And when they had made an end, the priest, taking the sword in his hand, began to look for a place convenient where he might slay your daughter. Suddenly there chanced a great wonder, for although all the people heard the voice of the stroke, yet she vanished   185 suddenly away. And when all they, marvelling at it, began to give a great screech, then there appeared unto them a white hart lying before the altar, struggling for life. And Calchas, being then present and seeing what had happened, did wonderfully rejoice, and told the captains that this hart was sent of the goddess because she would not have her altar defiled with the blood of your daughter. Moreover, he said that this was a   190 token of good luck, and that their journey should chance prosperously unto them. Wherefore he willed that they should tarry no longer here. And when this was so finished, Agamemnon willed me to show all these things unto you, because that I myself was present there. Wherefore I shall desire you to think no unkindness in the king, your husband, for surely the secret power of the gods will save them whom they   195 love, for this day your daughter hath been both alive and dead.   [*Exit*]

CHORUS Surely, O Clytemnestra, you ought to rejoice of this news that your daughter is taken up into heaven.

CLYTEMNESTRA But I am in doubt whether I should believe that thou, O daughter, art amongst the gods, or else they have feigned it to comfort me.   200

CHORUS Behold, yonder cometh Agamemnon, who can tell the truth of all this matter.

[*Enter* AGAMEMNON]

AGAMEMNON Truly, wife, we are happy for our daughter's sake for surely she is placed in heaven. But now I think it best that you go home, seeing that we shall take our journey

---

178. privily secretly. Iphigeneia demands the public ceremony of ritual sacrifice. **179. astonied** astonished. **185. voice** sound. **188. Calchas** seer who originally proclaimed that Artemis (Diana) required the sacrifice of Iphigeneia. **198. up into heaven** Lumley substitutes the Christian ascent into heaven here and below (202–3) for the Greek πρὸς θεοὺς (1608: to the gods) and ἐν θεοῖς (1622: among the gods).

so shortly unto Troy. Wherefore now, fare you well. And of this matter I will commune more at my return, and in the mean season I pray god send you well to do and your   205 heart's desire.

CHORUS O happy Agamemnon, the goddess grant thee a fortunate journey unto Troy and a most prosperous return again!   [*Exeunt all*]

JACOB BIDERMANN

Jacob Bidermann (1578–1639) entered the Society of Jesus in 1594, taught at the Jesuit university in Dillingen, and served as theologian of the Society. He wrote a wide range of works in Latin—epigrams, hymns, a novel (*Utopia*), an epic (*Herodias*), devotional and philosophical treatises, and, most important, plays. Mingling scenes of comedy and tragedy, these plays well represent the important genre of Jesuit drama, which delighted audiences throughout Europe and educated them in Catholic doctrines and perspectives.

Bidermann's most famous play, *Cenodoxus* (1602), dramatizes the life and death of the apparently saintly doctor of Paris, whose corpse cried out a different phrase on three successive days: 'I stand accused,' 'I am sentenced,' and, finally, 'I am condemned.' Shocked bystanders included the future St Bruno, who thereupon retreated to the wilderness and founded the Carthusians. Bidermann converts the Doctor into Cenodoxus (vainglory), an Everyman who freely chooses worldly over heavenly praise. In this *comico-tragoedia* humorous vice scenes set up the chilling final spectacle of judgement, wherein Christ condemns the sinner to hell-fire and mocking demons. Worthy of comparison with Marlowe's *Doctor Faustus*, *Cenodoxus* moved its large public audience in Munich (1609): they witnessed the conclusion in stunned silence; fourteen members subsequently asked to perform the Ignatian Spiritual Exercises; the actor who played Cenodoxus joined the Jesuits and lived a holy life (*innocenter ac sancte vixit*); the play accomplished more than a hundred sermons (*centenae conciones, Ludi Theatrales*, 1666, sigs. +8ᵛ−++1).

---

205. **well to do** good fortune.

Cenodoxus, 1602

2. 6 [Cenodoxus' home]

NAVEGUS   Be mindful of your lot,
    And pity mine. Then everlasting God
    With equal clemency will spare your sins
    And give you grace.
CENODOXUS   You dare, you shameless wretch,
    Compare yourself to me? Suggest that I   5
    Have been a sinner, whom the world proclaims
    Stainless and sinless? Who am known by all
    To have won the hearts of men with my good works
    And glorious deeds? My probity a model
    For all posterity? You think this man   10
    A sinner who is punishable like you?
    You wretch! Get out! I'll have you put to death
    If ever I set eyes on you again.
HYPOCRISY Quite right and proper. Doing good is pointless
    When there's no audience to approve your virtue.   15
NAVEGUS [Aside] Is this his marvellous generosity?
    His kindness? Then may all the gods destroy
    Benevolent and kind men such as this.
    Instead of cash they'd rather box your ears.
    I'll get no pittance here to ease my want.   20
—Goodbye.   [He begins to leave]

[Enter BRUNO, HUGO, EXORISTUS, PTOCHUS]

CENODOXUS Here Bruno and Hugo come at last.
    Greetings!
BRUNO   Do we disturb you, Cenodoxus?
CENODOXUS Disturb me? Never! I was strolling here
    Alone, relaxing with some music, waiting   25
    Till I should see you.
HUGO   We have hurried here
    To talk to you.

2. 6 Here Navegus, survivor of a shipwreck, pleads with Cenodoxus for alms. Hypocrisy is visible and audible only to Cenodoxus and to the audience. A boy servant, Dama, is also present. [SD] **Bruno** a nobleman (1030–1101), later St Bruno, founder of the abstemious Carthusian order of monks. **Hugo**, another nobleman. **Exoristus** (banished) and **Ptochus** (cringer or beggar) are two captives.

CENODOXUS   Laudwinus and the others,
Do they decline to come?
BRUNO   They're on their way,
And will be here quite soon.
CENODOXUS   Let's wait for them
Inside. And you, boy, go and set out chairs   30
So we can sit in comfort and converse.   [*Exit Dama*]
EXORISTUS By your good fortune, by your life, I beg
Your Excellence to pity us poor men.
PTOCHUS Squalid captivity and barbarous chains,
Outlawed, we suffered long, and now seek alms   35
To buy our freedom.
EXORISTUS   See our rotting limbs
Covered with filth; bring back to light of day
Men racked with famine and the dungeon's night.
HUGO Desist now, do not trouble this great man.
EXORISTUS Our stomachs should desist from troubling us.   40
HYPOCRISY They're watching; don't delay, give bounteously;
This will procure for you most bounteous glory.
CENODOXUS Far be it from me to find the meanest man
A trouble to me. But whose captive bonds
Confined you?
PTOCHUS   Captured by a barbarous foe   45
Ten years ago, our country occupied,
Our wives and children lost, we both were led
To spend a captive's life in foreign lands.
CENODOXUS Here are three golden coins for each of you.
Remember me and in your prayers to God   50
Pray for me always.
EXORISTUS, PTOCHUS May salvation's self
Preserve you, sir, most generous of men.
NAVEGUS [*Aside*] I didn't sacrifice, when I got up,
To Lady Luck. She favours him, shuns me.
Starvation eggs me on to beg again.   55
—Am I alone denied your alms? Have pity,
Be just as generous to wretched me.
Though you have put me off, don't let it seem
You've totally denied me.

---

27. Laudwinus another noble, friend of Cenodoxus.

HYPOCRISY   You're being watched.
  Mind what you do and give him something.
CENODOXUS   I   60
  Denied, rejected you, my man?
NAVEGUS   Just now.
CENODOXUS Forgive me, friends, I did not know he'd asked.
NAVEGUS Shipwrecked, I asked for alms, and do again.
BRUNO Immersed in thought, perhaps you didn't notice?
CENODOXUS Take heart, and ask: you'll find me generous.   65
NAVEGUS Whatever your generosity will give.
CENODOXUS Here, take two sovereigns.
NAVEGUS   God preserve your grace.
CENODOXUS I've learned above all else to love the poor
  And care for them.
HUGO   Such liberality
  I've never seen.
HYPOCRISY   Virtue deserves its place   70
  On such a stage.
CENODOXUS   We'll go then?
BRUNO   Certainly.   [*All leave except Navegus*]
NAVEGUS How much it matters, who asks what, and when!
  Men change so suddenly: yesterday's miser
  Today in one brief hour becomes a prodigal.
  I should tell fortunes, and take up astrology;   75
  In a few days of begging I'd get rich.

5. 5 [*The third and final session of the heavenly tribunal*]

[*Enter* CHRIST, JUDGES, SPIRIT OF CENODOXUS, PANURGUS]

CHRIST Summon the sinner back, that final judgement
  May be pronounced on him: that he shall burn
  For all succeeding ages.
ALL   Long enough
  His sins have gone unpunished.
CHRIST   Sinner, stay!
  Receive your evil doings' just deserts.   5
SPIRIT OF CENODOXUS Oh, spare your wrath, most merciful of judges.
CHRIST What fond desire possessed you, drove you headlong
  Into such madness, wretched sinner, that

---

5. 5 [SD] **Panurgus** is a devil, appearing for the prosecution. **67. sovereigns** gold coins.

You set your God at naught? Took refuge in
My enemy's camp? What injury have I done you?   10
What favour has my enemy bestowed?
Let's draw the reckoning up, ungrateful wretch.
I gave you being when you were ashes, dust,
Were nothing, formed you to do all my bidding.
But, sinful, you preferred the baneful counsels   15
Of the arch enemy, ignoring mine.
Though spurned, I still remained your benefactor.
The more you hated me, the more my love
Grew for you, fearing I had done too little,
Unless I did too much. So I descended   20
From heaven that you might live in heaven; I lived
On earth to enable you to leave the earth.
Honours I scorned that, following my example,
You might scorn honours. For you I fasted, sorrowed,
For you I passed the sleepless nights in vigil,   25
Kept constant watch. And you were the lost sheep
I journeyed after, sought in all my labours.
Yet I, though everywhere, could find you nowhere.
For love of you I bore the wrongs, the affronts;
And shrank not from the hatred of the many   30
As long as I could count you my one love.
I suffered all the blows and scourging stripes
Upon my sinless body for sinful you.
Death and the cross I bore, freeing you from death.
By these my hands, my wounded, ravaged feet   35
I testify, these instruments and trophies,
Which you behold arrayed before you here.
Let the whole fabric of the earth proclaim,
And let the entire celestial host proclaim:
No greater services could I perform,   40
No more should I have needed to perform,
To bind you fast to me and me to you.
You turned from me the more, the more I loved you.
You vainly sought to equal all my blessings
Or to outdo them by repaying them   45
With frequent sinful deeds. Your arrogance

---

10. **camp** Ignatius's meditation on the Two Standards (i.e. ensigns) in *The Spiritual Exercises* depicts Christ and Satan as military opponents (see INSTRUCTIONS AND DEVOTIONS). **36. instruments and trophies** The material remains of Christ's passion—the cross, nails, spear, and sponge—are displayed on stage.

Defeated my humility, your pride
My candour, your hypocrisy my trust,
Your evil deeds my good. I did not suffer
The arrogance of angels unavenged;   50
Shall I now suffer yours? Then undergo
Your proper punishment: from age to age
To endure the flames prepared for the arch fiend.
Gnashing of teeth and wailing shall be heard
Perpetually; and no eternity   55
Shall snatch you from there.

SPIRIT OF CENODOXUS   Ah! Let mountains fall
And bury me.

JUDGES   Let him forever perish
Through God's just judgement.

PANURGUS   You're my captive, mine,
And shall be evermore.

SPIRIT OF CENODOXUS   Cursed be this day,
Accursed whoever made, whoever saw it.   [*Exeunt*]   60

5. 6 [*Cenodoxus' funeral*]

[*Enter* BRUNO, LAUDWINUS, HUGO, *and* OTHERS *to the corpse of* CENODOXUS]

BRUNO This corpse which I have left so often in fear
In fear I now return to.

LAUDWINUS   May a good ending
Attend these wondrous portents.

HUGO   May that be so.
But let the funeral rites proceed: God willing,
We'll pay the final honours to Cenodoxus.   5

CENODOXUS Ah me! Most wretched of all men!

ALL   O God!
O Christ!

CENODOXUS Leave off these funeral obsequies,
These prayers. They cannot help me any more.
Nothing you do can help. May she be cursed,
Be cursed, that ill-starred mother who brought me forth!   10
Ah, wretched me, most miserable of men!
BY GOD'S JUDGEMENT I AM ETERNALLY DAMNED.

56–7. **Let . . . me** Jesus prophesies to the weeping daughters of Jerusalem, 'Then shall they begin to say to the mountains, "Fall upon us", and to the hills, "Cover us"' (Luke 23: 30).

Ah, me, now I depart to suffer flames
And everlasting fires.

ALL   Have mercy, God.
Be sparing in your judgement.

LAUDWINUS   We all are doomed   15
Unless you judge the sins of men more mildly.

BRUNO What is the fate of the soul damned?

HUGO   And what
May sometime be my own unhappy fate?

LAUDWINUS My heart is faint with dread.

BRUNO   Both life and death
Appal me equally.

ALL   Where can we go?   20
What do?

BRUNO   Or how escape such dreadful judgements?

HUGO Tears, why so slow? Why not gush forth and soften
The judge's heart now?

LAUDWINUS   Let our cheeks grow moist,
Our hearts dissolve, suffused with copious weeping,
Our eyes, though worn with tears, not cease to flow,   25
If that most stern of judges but grant mercy.

BRUNO Burn, strike and lash, O God, and vent your wrath,
And spare no pain or torture in this world
That in the next we may be saved.

LAUDWINUS   How dark
God's judgements are. For who was ever thought   30
More saintly and innocent than Cenodoxus?
But this his sanctity and innocence
Before the judgement seat of that stern judge
Was neither sanctity nor innocence.

BRUNO I leave this ominous corpse; and being unable   35
To save another, seek my own salvation.

5. 7 [*Hell*]

[*Enter* PANURGUS, ASTEROTH, ASEMPHOLOTH HYPOCRISY, SELF-LOVE, *and*
SPIRIT OF CENODOXUS]

PANURGUS Ha, ha. Why shudder so? Do you imagine
You're among enemies? You're ours; we're yours.

5. 7 [SD] **Asteroth** and **Asempholoth** are devils.

SPIRIT OF CENODOXUS: You are my enemies.

ASTEROTH No, we're your hosts.

ASEMPHOLOTH Why now so fierce? You were calmer yesterday.   5

SPIRIT OF CENODOXUS You're a deceiver.

ASEMPHOLOTH   You knew that long ago.
    Why did you trust us then?

SPIRIT OF CENODOXUS   I won't in future.

ALL Hail, Cenodoxus.

SPIRIT OF CENODOXUS I'm no longer hale.
    I'm finished.

PANURGUS   You can't be finished.

SPIRIT OF CENODOXUS   I'm finished.

ASTEROTH   You're well,
    And will get better.

SPIRIT OF CENODOXUS I'm finished.

PANURGUS   I'll cure you quickly.   10
    You'll soon feel you're not finished. Drain this glass.

SPIRIT OF CENODOXUS I don't want any drink.

ALL   Ho, ho. You have
    To want our drinks.

PANURGUS [*forcing him to drink*] Now drink up; toss it back.

SPIRIT OF CENODOXUS A curse on all the human race. A curse
    On heaven and hell.

SELF-LOVE   Did it taste good, that drink?   15

SPIRIT OF CENODOXUS A curse on you, you plague, you ruined me.

HYPOCRISY Don't be so stubborn. I'm your Hypocrisy.
    Remember me?

SPIRIT OF CENODOXUS Be cursed. Self-Love, be cursed.
    A curse on both my parents. And let all things
    Be cursed.

ASTEROTH   What charming prayers indeed!

HYPOCRISY   Divine!   20
    But now he is divine.

PANURGUS   It's quite remarkable
    How he adapts his ways to ours.

ASTEROTH   Well done!
    You do learn quickly.

SELF-LOVE   Well, he was the ablest
    Of all the very wisest, cleverest men.

---

8. **hail...hale** An attempt to reproduce the wordplay on *salve* (Hello) and *salvus* (saved) in the original. 11. **this glass** probably a drink of sulphur and pitch.

HYPOCRISY The very fount of wisdom and of learning.   25
PANURGUS Why then, we'll make him Dean of Liberal Studies
   In fiery hell.

WILLIAM SHAKESPEARE

In every sense a special case, William Shakespeare (1563–1616) stands at the centre of the new early modern England that is emerging as a site of religious struggle and redefinition. While there is no conclusive evidence for Shakespeare's own religious convictions and practices, scholars now take more seriously Richard Davies' late 17th-c. comment, 'He died a papist', and recognize the circumstantial evidence in favour of Roman Catholicism. Stratford-upon-Avon remained partially loyal to Catholicism as, indeed, did Warwickshire, home to the Coventry mystery plays, an early dramatic influence on Shakespeare. Shakespeare's mother's family, the Ardens, were staunch recusants, one member, Edward Arden, suffering execution in 1583 for alleged complicity in the Sommerville plot. The poet's father, John Shakespeare, received two citations for recusancy (1591, 1592) and reportedly left behind a Catholic will and spiritual testament. The poet's daughter, Suzanna, also received a citation for recusancy in 1606. Some Stratford schoolteachers during Shakespeare's youth appear to have been Catholics, Simon Hunt and John Cottom, perhaps others. The Stratford Shakespeares certainly included Catholic families among their friends and acquaintances, notably the recusants Hamnet and Judith Sadler, as well as Thomas and Margaret Reynolds, whose son received a bequest in Shakespeare's will for a memorial ring. Shakespeare's early patrons were members of prominent Catholic families, Ferdinando Stanley, Lord Strange, and Henry Wriothesley, earl of Southampton. (Some also argue for Alexander de Hoghton.) And late in life, 1613, Shakespeare purchased the Blackfriars gatehouse, perhaps a centre of underground Catholic activity. Such evidence does not amount to anything like proof but, at least, to possibility.

What about Catholicism in Shakespeare's plays and poems? Unlike other poets, Dante, Spenser, and Milton, for example, Shakespeare provides in his work no clear window through which to look into his soul. Both Protestants and Catholics (and many others) find ample evidence there to claim him as their own. But since Shakespeare has been canonized for so long as the Protestant national poet, recognition of Catholic sympathies, reflexes, and perspectives has generated new understanding and interpretation. As the

---

26. Dean of Liberal Studies a witty translation of *antistes litteris* (master of letters).

selections below illustrate, the Catholicity of his works generally appears in four related and complicated manifestations: (1) a reverence for the 'bare-ruined choirs' (Sonnet 73) of the Catholic past, an admiration for its champions (Thomas More, Catherine of Aragon), and various disagreements with the judgements of Protestant historiography on central figures (King John, Oldcastle, and Henry VIII); (2) sympathetic reference to forbidden Catholic doctrines (miracles, purgatory, intercession) and practices (pilgrimage, exorcism); (3) balanced and often positive portrayal of Catholic religious (Friar Lawrence, Friar Francis), especially women (Abbess Emilia, Isabella, Thaisa), and mockery of Protestant counterparts such as Nathaniel or Oliver Martext and of Puritans; (4) an emphasis, particularly in the late plays, on penance, miracles, shrines, ceremonies, and theophany. Whether these manifestations issue from personal or artistic conviction, they draw on the rich traditions of Catholicism to create luminous and moving drama.

Hamlet, 1599–1601

[I. 5 *The battlements of the castle*]
Enter GHOST *and* HAMLET

HAMLET Whither wilt thou lead me. Speak, I'll go no further.
GHOST Mark me.
HAMLET   I will.
GHOST   My hour is almost come,
    When I to sulph'rous and tormenting flames
    Must render up myself.
HAMLET   Alas, poor ghost!
GHOST Pity me not, but lend thy serious hearing   5
    To what I shall unfold.
HAMLET Speak. I am bound to hear.
GHOST So art thou to revenge, when thou shalt hear.
HAMLET What?
GHOST I am thy father's spirit,   10
    Doomed for a certain term to walk the night,
    And for the day confined to fast in fires,
    Till the foul crimes done in my days of nature

HAMLET Among the mysteries of this inexhaustible play is the Ghost of Elder Hamlet, who appears to be part Senecan revenge spirit, part conventional stage spook, and part tormented soul from purgatory. Protestants, however, strictly maintained that 'the Romish doctrine concerning purgatory...is a fond thing, vainly invented, and grounded upon no warranty of scripture, but rather repugnant to the word of God' (*The Thirty-Nine Articles*, article 22). **3. sulph'rous** sulphurous, i.e. hot and hellish. **7. bound** obligated. **13. days of nature** time as a living human being.

Are burnt and purged away. But that I am forbid
To tell the secrets of my prison house,   15
I could a tale unfold whose lightest word
Would harrow up thy soul, freeze thy young blood,
Make thy two eyes like stars start from their spheres,
Thy knotted and combinèd locks to part,
And each particular hair to stand on end   20
Like quills upon the fearful porpentine.
But this eternal blazon must not be
To ears of flesh and blood. List, list, oh, list!
If thou didst ever thy dear father love—

HAMLET O God!   25

GHOST Revenge his foul and most unnatural murder.

HAMLET Murder?

GHOST Murder most foul, as in the best it is,
But this most foul, strange, and unnatural.

HAMLET Haste me to know 't that I, with wings as swift   30
As meditation or the thoughts of love,
May sweep to my revenge.

GHOST   I find thee apt;
And duller shouldst thou be than the fat weed
That roots itself in ease on Lethe wharf,
Wouldst thou not stir in this. Now, Hamlet, hear: 35
'Tis given out that, sleeping in my orchard,
A serpent stung me; so the whole ear of Denmark
Is by a forgèd process of my death
Rankly abused. But know, thou noble youth,
The serpent that did sting thy father's life   40
Now wears his crown.

HAMLET   Oh, my prophetic soul! My uncle?

GHOST Ay, that incestuous, that adulterate beast,
With witchcraft of his wit, with traitorous gifts—
Oh, wicked wit and gifts that have the power
So to seduce!—won to his shameful lust   45
The will of my most seeming-virtuous queen.
Oh, Hamlet, what a falling off was there!
From me, whose love was of that dignity

---

17. **harrow up** tear. 18. **spheres** sockets, here envisioned as the concentric, hollow spheres in which planets and stars moved. 19. **knotted and combinèd** fastened and arranged. 21. **porpentine** porcupine. 22. **eternal blazon** record of spiritual secrets. 23. **List** listen. 33. **fat** indolent. 34. **Lethe** river of forgetfulness in Hades. 36. **orchard** garden. 38. **process** account. 42. **adulterate** adulterous. 48. **dignity** worth.

That it went hand in hand even with the vow
I made to her in marriage, and to decline 50
Upon a wretch whose natural gifts were poor
To those of mine!
But virtue, as it never will be moved,
Though lewdness court it in a shape of heaven,
So lust, though to a radiant angel linked, 55
Will sate itself in a celestial bed
And prey on garbage.
But soft, methinks I scent the morning air.
Brief let me be. Sleeping within my orchard,
My custom always of the afternoon, 60
Upon my secure hour thy uncle stole,
With juice of cursèd hebona in a vial,
And in the porches of my ears did pour
The leprous distillment, whose effect
Holds such an enmity with blood of man 65
That swift as quicksilver it courses through
The natural gates and alleys of the body,
And with a sudden vigour it doth possess,
And curd like eager droppings into milk,
The thin and wholesome blood. So did it mine, 70
And a most instant tetter barked about,
Most lazar-like, with vile and loathsome crust,
All my smooth body.
Thus was I, sleeping, by a brother's hand
Of life, of crown, of queen at once dispatched, 75
Cut off even in the blossoms of my sin,
Unhouseled, disappointed, unaneled,
No reckoning made, but sent to my account
With all my imperfections on my head.
Oh, horrible! Oh, horrible, most horrible! 80
If thou hast nature in thee, bear it not.
Let not the royal bed of Denmark be
A couch for luxury and damnèd incest.

---

54. **shape of heaven** a beautiful appearance. 56. **sate...bed** cease to find sexual pleasure in a lawful marriage. 61. **secure** safe. 62. **hebona** poison. 63. **porches** entranceways. 64. **leprous distillment** distillation causing the symptoms of leprosy. 69. **eager** acid. 71. **instant...about** immediate eruption of scabs covered like bark. 72. **lazar** leper. 75. **dispatched** deprived. 77. **unhouseled** without reception of the Eucharist. **disappointed** unprepared. **unaneled** without having received extreme unction, the last anointing, a Catholic sacrament. 78. **account** judgement. 81. **nature** the natural feelings of a son. 83. **luxury** lust. **incest** Marriage to a sister-in-law was considered incestuous by many.

But, howsomever thou pursues this act,
Taint not thy mind nor let thy soul contrive   85
Against thy mother aught. Leave her to heaven
And to those thorns that in her bosom lodge
To prick and sting her. Fare thee well at once.
The glow-worm shows the matin to be near,
And 'gins to pale his uneffectual fire.   90
Adieu, adieu, adieu! Remember me.

Measure for Measure, 1603–4

[2. 4 Angelo's chambers]

ANGELO   Then I shall pose you quickly:
Which had you rather, that the most just law
Now took your brother's life, or, to redeem him,
Give up your body to such sweet uncleanness
As she that he hath stained?
ISABELLA   Sir, believe this,   5
I had rather give my body than my soul.
ANGELO I talk not of your soul. Our compelled sins
Stand more for number than for account.
ISABELLA   How say you?
ANGELO Nay, I'll not warrant that, for I can speak
Against the thing I say. Answer to this: 10
I, now the voice of the recorded law,
Pronounce a sentence on your brother's life;
Might there not be a charity in sin
To save this brother's life?
ISABELLA   Please you to do 't,
I'll take it as a peril to my soul;   15
It is no sin at all, but charity.
ANGELO Pleased you to do 't at peril of your soul

84. howsomever howsoever. 86. aught anything. 89. matin morning. 90. pale extinguish.

MEASURE FOR MEASURE Searching the paradoxes of law, justice, and mercy, this play (1604) features centrally Isabella, a novice in the Catholic order of Poor Clares, sister order to the Franciscans. Isabella finds herself desired by the corrupt magistrate Angelo, who offers a pardon for her condemned brother Claudio in exchange for sexual intercourse. The audience admires Isabella's indignant refusal of the indecent proposal but wonders at her moral logic, 'More than our brother is our chastity' (109). Shakespeare sympathetically presents this Catholic religious out of cloister and in the midst of the wrenching ethical and emotional conflicts of the fallen world. 1. pose place in difficulty with a question. 6. give i.e. to punishment; Isabella does not understand Angelo's question. 7–8. compelled...account Sins committed under compulsion may be numbered but not really considered in one's spiritual account. 9. warrant that guarantee that what I just said is true. 14. Please if it please. 17. do't i.e. have intercourse with me.

Were equal poise of sin and charity.

ISABELLA That I do beg his life, if it be sin,
    Heaven let me bear it! You granting of my suit,   20
    If that be sin, I'll make it my morn prayer
    To have it added to the faults of mine,
    And nothing of your answer.

ANGELO   Nay, but hear me.
    Your sense pursues not mine. Either you are ignorant
    Or seem so, crafty, and that's not good.   25

ISABELLA Let me be ignorant and in nothing good
    But graciously to know I am no better.

ANGELO Thus wisdom wishes to appear most bright
    When it doth tax itself, as these black masks
    Proclaim an enshield beauty ten times louder   30
    Than beauty could, displayed. But mark me.
    To be received plain, I'll speak more gross:
    Your brother is to die.

ISABELLA So.

ANGELO And his offence is so, as it appears,   35
    Accountant to the law upon that pain.

ISABELLA True.

ANGELO Admit no other way to save his life—
    As I subscribe not that, nor any other—
    But, in the loss of question, that you, his sister,   40
    Finding yourself desired of such a person
    Whose credit with the judge or own great place
    Could fetch your brother from the manacles
    Of the all-binding law, and that there were
    No earthly mean to save him but that either   45
    You must lay down the treasures of your body
    To this supposed, or else to let him suffer.
    What would you do?

ISABELLA As much for my poor brother as myself:
    That is, were I under the terms of death,   50
    Th'impression of keen whips I'd wear as rubies,
    And strip myself to death as to a bed
    That longing have been sick for, ere I'd yield
    My body up to shame.

---

18. **Were equal poise** there would be a balance. 23. **answer** responsibility. 27. **graciously** through grace. 29. **tax** accuse. 30. **enshield** enshielded, i.e. covered. 32. **gross** directly. 36. **Accountant . . . pain** accountable to the law for that penalty. 38. **Admit** suppose. 39. **As . . . other** Not that I actually allow this or any other way to save his life. 40. **loss of question** provided there is no dispute. 51. **impression** marks. 53. **longing . . . for** I had grown sick with longing for.

ANGELO Then must your brother die.   55

ISABELLA And 'twere the cheaper way.
  Better it were a brother died at once
  Than that a sister, by redeeming him,
  Should die forever.

ANGELO Were not you then as cruel as the sentence   60
  That you have slandered so?

ISABELLA Ignomy in ransom and free pardon
  Are of two houses. Lawful mercy
  Is nothing kin to foul redemption.

    .   .   .   .

ANGELO Plainly conceive, I love you.   65

ISABELLA My brother did love Juliet,
  And you tell me that he shall die for 't.

ANGELO He shall not, Isabel, if you give me love.

ISABELLA I know your virtue hath a license in 't,
  Which seems a little fouler than it is   70
  To pluck on others.

ANGELO   Believe me, on mine honour,
  My words express my purpose.

ISABELLA Ha! Little honour to be much believed,
  And most pernicious purpose! Seeming, seeming!
  I will proclaim thee, Angelo, look for 't!   75
  Sign me a present pardon for my brother,
  Or with an outstretched throat I'll tell the world aloud
  What man thou art!

ANGELO   Who will believe thee, Isabel?
  My unsoiled name, th' austereness of my life,
  My vouch against you, and my place i' the state   80
  Will so your accusation overweigh
  That you shall stifle in your own report
  And smell of calumny. I have begun,
  And now I give my sensual race the rein.
  Fit thy consent to my sharp appetite;   85
  Lay by all nicety and prolixious blushes
  That banish what they sue for. Redeem thy brother
  By yielding up thy body to my will,

---

57. **at once** (1) immediately; (2) one short time (as opposed to **forever**). 59. **die forever** suffer eternal damnation. 62. **Ignomy** ignominy. 65. **conceive** understand. 66. **Juliet** the pregnant fiancée of Isabella's brother, Claudio. He is condemned to death for having premarital intercourse. 71. **pluck on** test. 80. **vouch** testimony. 83. **calumny** slander. 84. **give ... rein** let loose my sensual desires. 86. **Lay by** set aside. **nicety** coyness. **prolixious** drawn-out. 87. **banish ... sue for** push away what they really desire.

Or else he must not only die the death,
But thy unkindness shall his death draw out   90
To ling'ring sufferance. Answer me tomorrow,
Or, by the affection that now guides me most,
I'll prove a tyrant to him. As for you,
Say what you can, my false o'erweighs your true.   *Exit*

ISABELLA To whom should I complain? Did I tell this,   95
Who would believe me? Oh, perilous mouths
That bear in them one and the self-same tongue,
Either of condemnation or approof,
Bidding the law make curtsy to their will,
Hooking both right and wrong to th' appetite,   100
To follow as it draws! I'll to my brother.
Though he hath fall'n by prompture of the blood,
Yet hath he in him such a mind of honour
That, had he twenty heads to tender down
On twenty bloody blocks, he'd yield them up   105
Before his sister should her body stoop
To such abhorred pollution.
Then, Isabel, live chaste, and, brother, die;
More than our brother is our chastity.
I'll tell him yet of Angelo's request,   110
And fit his mind to death for his soul's rest.   *Exit*

Pericles, 1606–8

[5. 1 *On Pericles' ship, outside Mytilene*]

DIANA [*appears to the sleeping Pericles*]

DIANA My temple stands in Ephesus. Hie thee thither
And do upon mine altar sacrifice.

91. sufferance torture. 92. affection passion. 95. Did If I did. 98. Either...approof Either to condemn or approve. 100. Hooking bending. 102. prompture impulse. 104. tender down lay down in payment.

PERICLES *Pericles* adapts Catholic miracle-play traditions into romance. It formed part of the repertory of Cholmeley's Players, a touring company which performed for Catholic households, and appeared on a book-list of mostly devotional and theological works from the Jesuit college at Saint-Omer, where it also may have been staged. At the end of the play (established as Shakespearean by B. Vickers, *Shakespeare, Co-Author*, 2002: 291–332), Pericles experiences a moving reunion with his daughter Marina, then sees in a dream the goddess Diana, who directs him to her 'altar' and 'maiden priests' at Ephesus, known in Shakespeare's time as a centre of Marian devotion. There he finds his long-lost wife Thaisa. The movement to a holy place for reconciliation rescripts the Catholic pilgrimage, just as Diana takes on some attributes of the Virgin Mary, complete with nuns as votaries. Catholic ritual animates the ancient pagan world. 5.1. [SD] *Mytilene* city on the island of Lesbos in the Aegean sea. [SD] Diana may descend from above the stage and exit by ascension. 1. temple originally a temple to mother goddesses, then to the Greek Artemis (Diana), and, in post-classical times, a celebrated shrine for the Virgin Mary.

There, when my maiden priests are met together
Before the people all,
Reveal how thou at sea didst lose thy wife.   5
To mourn thy crosses, with thy daughter's, call
And give them repetition to the life.
Or perform my bidding, or thou livest in woe;
Do't and happy, by my silver bow!
Awake, and tell thy dream!   [*She vanishes*]   10
PERICLES [*Awaking*] Celestial Dian, goddess argentine!
I will obey thee.—Helicanus!

[5. 3 *The temple of Diana at Ephesus*]

[*Enter* PERICLES, *his* TRAIN, LYSIMACHUS, HELICANUS, *and* MARINA *to* THAISA *in a
nun's habit*, CERIMON, *and other* EPHESIANS]

PERICLES Hail, Dian! To perform thy just command,
I here confess myself the King of Tyre,
Who, frighted from my country, did wed
At Pentapolis the fair Thaisa.
At sea in childbed died she, but brought forth   5
A maid child called Marina, who, O goddess,
Wears yet thy silver livery. She at Tarsus
Was nursed with Cleon, who at fourteen years
He sought to murder; but her better stars
Brought her to Mytilene, 'gainst whose shore   10
Riding, her fortunes brought the maid aboard us,
Where, by her own most clear remembrance, she
Made known herself my daughter.
THAISA   Voice and favour!
You are, you are—O royal Pericles! [*She faints.*]
PERICLES What means the nun? She dies! Help, gentlemen!   15
CERIMON Noble sir,
If you have told Diana's altar true,
This is your wife.
PERICLES   Reverent appearer, no.

---

6. **crosses** misfortunes. 7. **to the life** point by point. 8. **Or** either. 9. **happy** live happily. 11. **argentine** silvery.

5. 3. 2. **confess** proclaim. 4. **Pentapolis** a coastal group of cities in North Africa, which the play, however, depicts as a coastal city in Greece. 6. **maid** girl. 7. **Wears . . . livery** i.e. is still a virgin. 10–11. **'gainst . . . Riding** to which shore we came and set anchor. 13. **favour** appearance. 15. **nun** Shakespeare consistently imagines pagan votaries as Catholic nuns (cf. Emilia, also at the abbey in Ephesus, *The Comedy of Errors*). 16. **Cerimon** the magician-healer at Ephesus, who recovered and revived Thaisa. 18. **Reverent appearer** you who appear worthy of reverence.

I threw her overboard with these very arms.

CERIMON Upon this coast, I warrant you.

PERICLES   'Tis most certain.   20

CERIMON Look to the lady. Oh, she's but overjoyed.
  Early in blustering morn this lady was
  Thrown upon this shore. I oped the coffin,
  Found there rich jewels, recovered her, and placed her
  Here in Diana's temple.

PERICLES   May we see them.   25

CERIMON Great sir, they shall be brought you to my house,
  Whither I invite you. Look, Thaisa, is
  Recovered.

THAISA [rising] Oh, let me look!
  If he be none of mine, my sanctity   30
  Will to my sense bend no licentious ear,
  But curb it, spite of seeing.—O my lord,
  Are you not Pericles? Like him you spake,
  Like him you are. Did you not name a tempest,
  A birth, and death?

PERICLES   The voice of dead Thaisa!   35

THAISA That Thaisa am I, supposèd dead
  And drowned.

PERICLES Immortal Dian!

THAISA   Now I know you better.
  When we with tears parted Pentapolis,
  The King my father gave you such a ring. [She points to his ring.]   40

PERICLES This, this! No more, you gods! Your present kindness
  Make my past miseries sports! You shall do well
  That on the touching of her lips I may
  Melt and no more be seen.—Oh, come, be buried
  A second time within these arms! [They embrace.]

MARINA [kneeling]   My heart   45
  Leaps to be gone into my mother's bosom.

PERICLES Look who kneels here! Flesh of thy flesh, Thaisa,
  Thy burden at the sea, and called Marina
  For she was yielded there.

THAISA   Blest, and mine own! [They embrace.]

30–2. If...seeing If he is not my husband, my holiness will curb my longing for marriage, despite what I see. 39. parted left. 49. yielded born.

Henry VIII, 1613

[2. 4 *The royal court*]

[*The Queen rises from her chair and kneels before the King.*]

QUEEN Sir, I desire you do me right and justice,
And to bestow your pity on me; for
I am a most poor woman, and a stranger
Born out of your dominions, having here
No judge indifferent, nor no more assurance   5
Of equal friendship and proceeding. Alas, sir,
In what have I offended you? What cause
Hath my behaviour given to your displeasure
That thus you should proceed to put me off
And take your good grace from me? Heaven witness   10
I have been to you a true and humble wife,
At all times to your will conformable,
Ever in fear to kindle your dislike,
Yea, subject to your countenance—glad or sorry
As I saw it inclined. When was the hour   15
I ever contradicted your desire,
Or made it not mine too? Or which of your friends
Have I not strove to love, although I knew
He were mine enemy? What friend of mine
That had to him derived your anger did I   20
Continue in my liking, nay, gave notice
He was from thence discharged? Sir, call to mind
That I have been your wife in this obedience
Upward of twenty years, and have been blessed
With many children by you. If in the course   25
And process of this time you can report,
And prove it too, against mine honour aught—
My bond to wedlock or my love and duty—
Against your sacred person, in God's name

HENRY VIII Late in his career (1613), Shakespeare collaborated with John Fletcher to represent the reign of Henry VIII, the king revered by Protestants and reviled by Catholics for breaking with Rome. The play depicts Henry's reign in a curiously ambivalent light, featuring some stock anti-papal rhetoric and ending with a prophetic celebration of Elizabeth's birth, but avoiding throughout all serious engagement with the central religious issues. Shakespeare clearly adopts the view of Catholic historians such as Nicholas Sander (see HISTORIES) in his portrayal of Catherine of Aragon, Henry's discarded queen; she appears as a heroic figure, steadfast in faith, firm in virtue. In this scene (established as Shakespearean by Vickers, *Shakespeare Co-Author*, 333–402), Queen Catherine confronts those who would deny the validity of her marriage. **3. stranger** foreigner (from Spain). **5. indifferent** impartial. **6. equal** fair. **20. derived** aroused. **25. many** i.e. five, only one of whom (later Queen Mary) survived infancy. **27. aught** anything.

Turn me away, and let the foul'st contempt 30
Shut door upon me, and so give me up
To the sharp'st kind of justice. Please you, sir,
The King your father was reputed for
A prince most prudent, of an excellent
And unmatched wit and judgement. Ferdinand 35
My father, King of Spain, was reckoned one
The wisest prince that there had reigned by many
A year before. It is not to be questioned
That they had gathered a wise council to them
Of every realm that did debate this business, 40
Who deemed our marriage lawful. Wherefore I
Humbly beseech you, sir, to spare me till I may
Be by my friends in Spain advised, whose counsel
I will implore. If not, i'th' name of God,
Your pleasure be fulfilled! 45

    ·   ·   ·   ·   ·   ·   ·   ·

QUEEN   My lord, my lord,
I am a simple woman, much too weak
T'oppose your cunning. You're meek and humble-mouthed;
You sign your place and calling in full seeming,
With meekness and humility; but your heart 50
Is crammed with arrogancy, spleen, and pride.
You have, by fortune and His Highness' favours,
Gone slightly o'er low steps and now are mounted
Where pow'rs are your retainers, and your words,
Domestics to you, serve your will as 't please 55
Yourself pronounce their office. I must tell you,
You tender more your person's honour than
Your high profession spiritual; that again
I do refuse you for my judge; and here
Before you all appeal unto the pope, 60
To bring my whole cause 'fore His Holiness,
And to be judged by him.   *She curtsies to the King and offers to depart.*

---

33. **King your father** Henry VII (*r.* 1485–1509). 35. **wit** intelligence. **Ferdinand** Ferdinand II (*r.* 1479–1516). 36–7. **one The** the very. 41. **our marriage lawful** Henry claimed that scruples about marrying Catherine, his brother's widow, motivated his decision to divorce her. Catholics pointed to his infatuation with Anne Boleyn, whom he subsequently married. Earlier in the play Suffolk punctures the Protestant view of Henry's decision to divorce Catherine of Aragon with a very Catholic witticism: LORD CHAMBERLAIN: 'It seems the marriage with his brother's wife | Has crept too near his conscience.' SUFFOLK: 'No, his conscience | Has crept too near another lady' (2. 1. 16–18). 46. **lord** Cardinal Wolsey, worldly and arrogant, who dominated the reign from 1515 to 1529; his famous fall from power is depicted in the play. 49. **sign** show signs of. 53. **slightly** easily. 54. **pow'rs** powerful people. 55. **Domestics** servants. 55–6. **serve...office** Your words serve you in that they are obeyed as soon as you utter them. 57. **tender** value. 60. **pope** Clement VII (*r.* 1523–34).

BEN JONSON

Catholicism colours the work of Ben Jonson (1572–1637) early and late (see POETRY). *Sejanus* (1603–4) provoked Lord Henry Howard to summon Jonson before the Privy Council for 'popery and treason' (Jonson, *Informations*, ll. 325–7). Since no record of the session survives and since the extant play has been revised, we cannot know exactly what prompted the charges. But as it stands *Sejanus*, like the verse epistle to Lady Aubigny, reflects contemporary conflicts and mirrors the Catholic plight. The Roman government silences dissent, oppresses historians, burns books, falls prey to faction, and, most important, spies on and punishes its citizens. The Germanicans (here Silius, Sabinus, and Arruntius), like many English Catholics, look to the past nostalgically, suffer persecution, and debate the best course of action—patience or revolt. Jonson's Catholicism also fuels his satire against Puritans, whom he denounces generally in *Discoveries* thus, *Puritanus hypocrita est haereticus* (A Puritan is a heretical hypocrite, *Works*, 1641, sig. M2ᵛ). Moderate Protestants, of course, might well agree, but the charge of heresy pointedly echoes the Catholic brief against all Protestants. In *The Alchemist* (1610, excerpted below) two Puritans, Tribulation Wholesome and Ananias, seek power and wealth from the philosopher's stone. Railing against idols, traditions, and Rome, these fools, like their counterparts in *Bartholomew Fair* (1614), speak a particularly virulent and familiar anti-Catholic rhetoric, which, audiences may have uneasily realized, echoes the official convictions of the Church of England.

Sejanus, 1603–4

Act 1 [*Tiberius's court*]

> SILIUS Well, all is worthy of us, were it more,
>   Who with our riots, pride, and civil hate,
>   Have so provoked the justice of the gods—
>   We that within these fourscore years were born
>   Free, equal lords of the triumphèd world,   5

SEJANUS Drawn from Tacitus and other classical sources, this play dramatizes the fall of the corrupt Lucius Aelius Sejanus, who rose to power in the reign of Tiberius Claudius Nero (*r.* 14–37) and received condemnation in 31. It features also the family and friends of Germanicus (deceased military leader, Agrippina's husband) who oppose the regime.

ACT 1 1. **Silius** Caius Silius Caecina Largus (consul, 13), a general under Germanicus. **all . . . us** we deserve all the punishments of the time. **were** even if it were. **5. triumphèd** conquered.

And knew no masters but affections,
To which betraying first our liberties,
We since became the slaves to one man's lusts,
And now to many. Every minist'ring spy
That will accuse and swear is lord of you,   10
Of me, of all, our fortunes, and our lives.
Our looks are called to question, and our words,
How innocent soever, are made crimes.
We shall not shortly dare to tell our dreams,
Or think, but 'twill be treason.
SABINUS   Tyrants' arts   15
Are to give flatterers grace, accusers power,
That those may seem to kill whom they devour.

Act 3 [*At Silius's trial in the senate house*]

SILIUS   Ay, take part. Reveal yourselves.
Alas, I scent not your confederacies,
Your plots, and combinations? I not know
Minion Sejanus hates me, and that all
This boast of law and law is but a form,   5
A net of Vulcan's filing, a mere engine,
To take that life by a pretext of justice
Which you pursue in malice? I want brain
Or nostril to persuade me that your ends
And purposes are made to what they are,   10
Before my answer. O you equal gods,
Whose justice not a world of wolf-turned men
Shall make me to accuse, howe'er provoke,
Have I for this so oft engaged myself?

6. **affections** passions. 8. **one man** i.e. the emperor. Jonson, like Shakespeare, dates the change from republican to imperial government to the dictatorship of Julius Caesar (46 BC), some 'fourscore years' (4) before the events of the play. The first official emperor of Rome was Augustus Caesar (27 BC–AD 14). 9. **minist'ring** servile. 12–13. **Our looks . . . crimes** Jonson cites Tacitus: 'all the while Tiberius was distorting words and looks into crimes and storing them in his memory' (*Annals*, 1. 7); 'Tiberius and the informers showed no fatigue'; 'a charge of treason' was 'the complement now of all arraignments' (*Annals*, 3. 38); and Seneca: 'a universal frenzy for bringing charges of treason . . . seized upon the talk of drunkards, the frank words of jesters' (*On Benefits*, 3. 26) (*Sejanus*, ed. P. Ayres, 1990). 15. **Sabinus** Titius Sabinus, a knight, member of the Germanican faction. 17. **those . . . they** accusers . . . tyrants. The idea, marked in quotations in the quarto, is that tyrants, using accusers, kill whomever they wish.

ACT 3 Based on the historical trial in AD 24, Silius stands accused as an enemy of the state and commits suicide. His speech begins with indignant rhetorical questions. 1. **take part** play your role. 3. **combinations** alliances. 4. **Minion** obsequious favourite. 5–8. **This . . . malice** These lines echo protests against the execution of Catholics, purportedly for treason. 5. **form** show. 6. **filing** devising. The allusion is to the finely wrought net which Vulcan created to catch his wife Venus in adultery with Mars. **engine** trick. 8. **want** lack. 9. **nostril** perception. 9–11. **your . . . answer** you have already decided my fate before my defence. 11. **equal** just. 12. **wolf-turned men** an allusion to Lycaeus (Ovid, *Met.* 1. 198 ff.), whose impiety caused Jupiter to turn him into wolf and precipitated the destruction of the world for its wickedness. 13. **howe'er provoke** howsoever provoked.

Stood in the heat and fervour of a fight,   15
When Phoebus sooner hath forsook the day
Than I the field? Against the blue-eyed Gauls?
And crispèd Romans? When our Roman eagles
Have fanned the fire with their labouring wings,
And no blow dealt that left not death behind it?   20
When I have charged alone into the troops
Of curled Sicambrians, routed them, and came
Not off with backward ensigns of a slave,
But forward marks, wounds on my breast and face,
Were meant to thee, O Caesar, and thy Rome?   25
And have I this return? Did I for this
Perform so noble and so brave defeat
On Sacrovir? O Jove, let it become me
To boast my deeds when he whom they concern
Shall thus forget them!   30

Act 4 [*Inside Agrippina's house*]

LATIARIS It is a noble constancy you show
To this afflicted house, that not (like others,
The friends of season) you do follow fortune,
And in the winter of their fate forsake
The place whose glories warmed you. You are just,   5
And worthy such a princely patron's love,
As was the world's renowned Germanicus,
Whose ample merit when I call to thought,
And see the wife and issue objects made
To so much envy, jealousy, and hate,   10
It makes me ready to accuse the gods
Of negligence, as men of tyranny.
SABINUS They must be patient, so must we.
LATIARIS   O Jove!
What will become of us or of the times,
When to be high or noble are made crimes?   15
When land and treasure are most dangerous faults?

---

16. **Phoebus** Apollo, i.e. the sun. 18. **crispèd** with hair stiffly curled. 22. **Sicambrians** Jonson identifies these people as a Germanic tribe who wore their hair in a knot and lived in present-day Holland. 23. **backward ensigns** wounds on the back (from running away). 25. **Were meant to** which wounds were intended for. 28. **Sacrovir** Julius Sacrovir, Gallic leader who led a revolt in AD 21.

ACT 4 1. **Latiaris** Latinius Latiaris, an *agent provocateur*, who in this scene conceals spies (Rufius and Opsius) and entraps Sabinus in seditious talk; at the end of the scene the spies rush in and apprehend Sabinus. 2. **afflicted house** the house of Germanicus, consisting now of his wife Agrippina, and his sons, Nero, Drusus Jun., and Caligula. 3. **friends of season** fair-weather friends. 15–16. **When...faults** The lines echo complaints about government hostility to rich Catholics for mercenary rather than religious motives.

SABINUS Nay, when our table, yea, our bed, assaults
 Our peace and safety? When our writings are,
 By any envious instruments that dare
 Apply them to the guilty, made to speak   20
 What they will have to fit their tyrannous wreak?
 When ignorance is scarcely innocence,
 And knowledge made a capital offence?
 When not so much but the bare, empty shade
 Of liberty is reft us, and we made   25
 The prey to greedy vultures and vile spies
 That first transfix us with their murdering eyes?
LATIARIS Methinks the genius of the Roman race
 Should not be so extinct, but that bright flame
 Of liberty might be revived again,   30
 Which no good man but with his life should lose,
 And we not sit like spent and patient fools,
 Still puffing in the dark at one poor coal,
 Held on by hope till the last spark is out.
 The cause is public and the honour, name—   35
 The immortality of every soul
 That is not bastard or a slave in Rome—
 Therein concerned. Whereto, if men would change
 The wearied arm, and for the weighty shield
 So long sustained employ the facile sword,   40
 We might have some assurance of our vows.
 This ass's fortitude doth tire us all.
 It must be active valour must redeem
 Our loss, or none. The rock and our hard steel
 Should meet t'enforce those glorious fires again, 45
 Whose splendour cheered the world, and heat gave life
 No less than doth the sun's.
SABINUS   'Twere better stay
 In lasting darkness, and despair of day.
 No ill should force the subject undertake
 Against the sovereign, more than hell should make 50
 The gods do wrong. A good man should and must

---

17. **our bed** Jonson cites Tacitus (*Annals* 4. 60), who reports that even the nights were not safe for Nero because his wife reported his dreams and sighs to her mother Livia, and she, in turn, to Sejanus. 21. **they** the accusers. **wreak** vengeance. 25. **reft** taken from. 35. **name** reputation (which lives on after death). 40. **sustained** held up in defence. **facile** ready. 41. **vows** wishes. 42. **ass's fortitude** capacity to endure. 44. **rock...steel** The metaphor here is of striking fire from rock and steel, the latter a symbol for the sword. 49–52. Quotation marks in the quarto identify these lines as commonplaces.

Sit rather down with loss than rise unjust;
Though when the Romans first did yield themselves
To one man's power, they did not mean their lives,
Their fortunes, and their liberties should be   55
His absolute spoil, as purchased by the sword.

Act 4 [*Another scene*]

LEPIDUS   Arts, Arruntius?
None but the plain and passive fortitude
To suffer and be silent, never stretch
These arms against the torrent, live at home
With my own thoughts and innocence about me,   5
Not tempting the wolves' jaws; these are my arts.
ARRUNTIUS I would begin to study 'em if I thought
They would secure me. May I pray to Jove
In secret and be safe? Ay, or aloud?
With open wishes? So I do not mention   10
Tiberius or Sejanus? Yes, I must,
If I speak out. 'Tis hard, that. May I think
And not be racked? What danger is't to dream,
Talk in one's sleep, or cough? Who knows the law?
May I shake my head without a comment?   15
Say it rains or it holds up, and not be thrown
Upon the Gemonies? These now are the things
Whereon men's fortune, yea, their fate, depends.
Nothing hath privilege 'gainst the violent ear.
No place, no day, no hour we see is free—   20
Not our religious and most sacred times—
From some one kind of cruelty. All matter,
Nay, all occasion pleaseth. Madmen's rage,
The idleness of drunkards, women's nothing,
Jesters' simplicity—all, all is good   25
That can be catched at. Nor is now th'event
Of any person, or for any crime,
To be expected, for 'tis always one:
Death, with some little difference of place
Or time.   30

1. **Lepidus** Marcus Lepidus, a senator. **Arts** Arruntius, another senator, has just asked Lepidus what arts enabled him to reach old age. **10. So** so long as. **15. comment** i.e. someone else's comment. **17. Gemonies** steps on the Aventine hill, on which the bodies of executed criminals were dragged before being thrown into the river. **19. violent** malicious, perverting. **24. nothing** trivial chatter. **26. catched at** seized upon. **event** outcome. **28. expected** awaited.

The Alchemist, 1610

3. 1 [Outside Lovewit's house]

[Enter] TRIBULATION WHOLESOME, ANANIAS

TRIBULATION These chastisements are common to the saints,
  And such rebukes we of the Separation
  Must bear with willing shoulders, as the trials
  Sent forth to tempt our frailties.
ANANIAS   In pure zeal,
  I do not like the man. He is a heathen   5
  And speaks the language of Canaan, truly.
TRIBULATION I think him a profane person, indeed.
ANANIAS   He bears
  The visible mark of the Beast in his forehead.
  And for his stone, it is a work of darkness,
  And with philosophy blinds the eyes of man.   10
TRIBULATION Good brother, we must bend unto all means
  That may give furtherance to the holy cause.
ANANIAS Which his cannot; the sanctified cause
  Should have a sanctified course.
TRIBULATION   Not always necessary.
  The children of perdition are oft-times   15
  Made instruments even of the greatest works.
  Beside, we should give somewhat to man's nature—
  The place he lives in, still about the fire
  And fume of metals that intoxicate
  The brain of man and make him prone to passion.   20
  Where have you greater atheists than your cooks?
  Or more profane or choleric than your glassmen?
  More anti-Christian than your bell-founders?
  What makes the devil so devilish, I would ask you—

THE ALCHEMIST This play presents two schemers, Subtle and Face, who pretend to be alchemists in order to swindle various Londoners.

3. 1 [SD] *Lovewit* the absent master of Face. **1. saints** the Puritan elect. **2. we . . . Separation** (1) the elect, destined for salvation, as opposed to the reprobates; (2) Anabaptists (a radical Protestant sect), exiled from Germany and Holland. **4. zeal** standard term for Puritan dedication. **5. man** i.e. Subtle. **6. Canaan** Old Testament place of idolatry. **8. Beast** Antichrist (from the Apocalypse of St John), generally identified by Puritans as the Catholic Church. Those bearing the mark of the Beast are the damned (Apoc. 16: 2; 19: 20). **9. stone** the magical philosopher's stone, which could transform other metals to gold and silver, cure diseases, and effect other wonders. **10. philosophy** Ananias mistrusts all secular learning. **17. give somewhat** concede something. **18. still** ever. **22. glassmen** glass-blowers. **23. bell-founders** bell-casters.

Satan, our common enemy—but his being   25
Perpetually about the fire and boiling
Brimstone and ars'nic? We must give, I say,
Unto the motives and the stirrers-up
Of humours in the blood. It may be so.
Whenas the work is done, the stone is made,   30
This heat of his may turn into a zeal
And stand up for the beauteous discipline
Against the menstruous cloth and rag of Rome.
We must await his calling and the coming
Of the good spirit. You did fault t'upbraid him   35
With the Brethren's blessing of Heidelberg, weighing
What need we have to hasten on the work
For the restoring of the silenced saints,
Which ne'er will be but by the philosopher's stone.
And so a learned elder, one of Scotland,   40
Assured me, *aurum potabile* being
The only med'cine for the civil magistrate
T'incline him to a feeling of the cause,
And must be daily used in the disease.

ANANIAS I have not edified more, truly, by man,   45
Not since the beautiful light first shone on me;
And I am sad my zeal hath so offended.

TRIBULATION Let us call on him, then.

ANANIAS   The motion's good,
And of the spirit; I will knock first. [*Knocks*] Peace be within!

3. 2
[SUBTLE *opens the door; they enter*]

[SUBTLE] Oh, are you come? 'Twas time. Your threescore minutes
Were at the last thread, you see, and down had gone
Furnus acediae, turris circulatorius;

29. **humours** fluids that predominated in persons and determined personality. 30. **Whenas** at the time. 32. **beauteous discipline** a catchphrase for Puritanism. 33. **menstruous . . . Rome** Roman Catholicism, here depicted as a cloth stained with menstrual discharge. The metaphor derives from the common identification of Catholicism with the Whore of Babylon (Apoc. 17). 35. **You did fault** In 2. 5 Ananias asked to see results from the previous investments of the Heidelberg Brethren; Subtle angrily threatened to discontinue the alchemy and threw Ananias out. 38. **silenced saints** a contemporary reference to the Puritan clergy who were excommunicated for refusing to conform to the Hampton Court canons (1604). 41. *aurum potabile* 'drinkable gold', an alchemical elixir, here also meaning bribes. 43. **cause** law case. 45. **edified** profited spiritually (from my confrontation with Subtle). 46. **beautiful light** a metaphor for spiritual awakening by divine inspiration (see **revelation** below, 3. 2. 113). 48. **motion** impulse.

3. 2. 3 *Furnus acediae* 'furnace of sloth', i.e. a multiple furnace supplied by a single fire. *turris circulatorius* 'circulating tower', i.e. an apparatus for recirculating materials for further refinement. Throughout the play Subtle uses technical terms and Latinate mumbo-jumbo to dupe his victims.

Limbeck, bolt's head, retort, and pelican
Had all been cinders. Wicked Ananias! 5
Art thou returned? Nay, then, it goes down yet.
TRIBULATION Sir, be appeased; he is come to humble
Himself in spirit and to ask your patience
If too much zeal hath carried him aside
From the due path.
SUBTLE   Why, this doth qualify! 10
TRIBULATION The Brethren had no purpose, verily,
To give you the least grievance, but are ready
To lend their willing hands to any project
The spirit and you direct.
SUBTLE   This qualifies more!
TRIBULATION And for the orphans' goods, let them be valued, 15
Or what is needful else to the holy work,
It shall be numbered; here, by me, the saints
Throw down their purse before you.
SUBTLE   This qualifies most!
Why, thus it should be; now you understand.
Have I discoursed so unto you of our stone? 20
And of the good that it shall bring your cause?
Showed you—beside the main of hiring forces
Abroad, drawing the Hollanders, your friends,
From the Indies to serve you with all their fleet—
That even the med'cinal use shall make you a faction 25
And party in the realm? As, put the case,
That some great man in state, he have the gout;
Why, you but send three drops of your elixir,
You help him straight; there you have made a friend.
Another has the palsy or the dropsy, 30
He takes of your incombustible stuff,
He's young again; there you have made a friend.
A lady that is past the feat of body,
Though not of mind, and hath her face decayed
Beyond all cure of paintings, you restore 35

4. **Limbeck...pelican** Limbeck, an alembic (distilling mechanism). **bolt's head**, round flask. **retort**, glass with curved neck. **pelican**, vessel with a neck that curved and re-entered at the bottom. **10. qualify** dilute (an alchemical term), here, extenuate the offence. **15. orphans' goods** pewter, brass, and other metal objects that Subtle has collected from orphans and widows, purportedly to transform into gold. **17. numbered** paid for (by the Brethren). **22. main** principal objective. Jonson depicts the Puritans here as seditious supporters of foreign invasion, the usual charge against Catholics. **25. faction** political power. **26. put the case** for example. **27. state** high office. **30. palsy...dropsy** nervous dysfunction or paralysis...disease characterized by fluid retention and swelling. **31. incombustible** incapable of burning. **33–4. past... mind** too old to have sex but not too old to think about it. **35. paintings** cosmetics.

With the oil of talc; there you have made a friend,
And all her friends. A lord that is a leper,
A knight that has the bone-ache, or a squire
That hath both these, you make 'em smooth and sound
With a bare fricace of your med'cine; still   40
You increase your friends.

TRIBULATION   Ay, 'tis very pregnant.

SUBTLE And, then the turning of this lawyer's pewter
To plate at Christmas—

ANANIAS   Christ-tide, I pray you.

SUBTLE Yet, Ananias?

ANANIAS   I have done.

SUBTLE   —or changing
His parcel-gilt to massy gold. You cannot   45
But raise you friends withal, to be of power
To pay an army in the field, to buy
The king of France out of his realms or Spain
Out of his Indies. What can you not do
Against lords spiritual or temporal   50
That shall oppone you?

TRIBULATION   Verily, 'tis true.
We may be temporal lords ourselves, I take it.

SUBTLE You may be anything, and leave off to make
Long-winded exercises or suck up
Your 'ha' and 'hum' in a tune. I not deny   55
But such as are not gracèd in a state
May for their ends be adverse in religion,
And get a tune to call the flock together;
For, to say sooth, a tune does much with women,
And other phlegmatic people; it is your bell.   60

ANANIAS Bells are profane; a tune may be religious.

SUBTLE No warning with you? Then, farewell, my patience.
'Slight, it shall down! I will not be thus tortured.

TRIBULATION I pray you, sir.

---

36. **oil of talc** preparation from minerals, used as a cosmetic. 38. **bone-ache** syphilis. 40. **bare fricace** simple rubbing. 41. **pregnant** persuasive, filled with strong reasons. 43. **Christ-tide** 'Christ-time'. Puritans objected to 'Christmas' because it contained the word 'mass'. 45. **parcel-gilt** partially gilded ware. 46. **withal** in addition. 51. **oppone** oppose. 54. **exercises** prayers or sermons. 54–5. **suck…tune** Saying 'ha' or 'hum' was a mannerism of Puritan preaching, which here Subtle suggests can be arranged into a tune. 55–8. **I…together** I do not deny that those who are out of power may be irreligious and use Puritan mannerisms and even music to gather supporters. 59. **sooth** truth. 60. **phlegmatic** sluggish. **bell** summons. 63. **'Slight** by God's light (an oath). **it** the alchemical apparatus.

SUBTLE   All shall perish. I have spoke it.

TRIBULATION Let me find grace, sir, in your eyes; the man   65
   He stands corrected; neither did his zeal,
   But, as yourself, allow a tune somewhere,
   Which now, being toward the stone, we shall not need.

SUBTLE No, nor your holy vizard to win widows
   To give you legacies, or make zealous wives   70
   To rob their husbands for the 'common cause';
   Nor take the start of bonds, broke but one day,
   And say, 'they were forfeited by providence'.
   Nor shall you need o'er night to eat huge meals
   To celebrate your next day's fast the better,   75
   The whilst the Brethren and the Sisters, humbled,
   Abate the stiffness of the flesh. Nor cast
   Before your hungry hearers scrupulous bones
   As whether a Christian may hawk or hunt,
   Or whether matrons of the holy assembly   80
   May lay their hair out, or wear doublets,
   Or have that idol starch about their linen.

ANANIAS It is, indeed, an idol.

TRIBULATION   Mind him not, sir—
   I do command thee, spirit of zeal, but trouble,
   To peace within him!—Pray you, sir, go on.   85

SUBTLE. Nor shall you need to libel 'gainst the prelates,
   And shorten so your ears against the hearing
   Of the next wire-drawn grace. Nor of necessity
   Rail against plays to please the alderman,
   Whose daily custard you devour. Nor lie   90
   With zealous rage till you are hoarse. Not one
   Of these so singular arts. Nor call yourselves
   By names of Tribulation, Persecution,
   Restraint, Long-Patience, and such like, affected
   By the whole family or wood of you   95
   Only for glory, and to catch the ear

66–7. neither...allow in his zeal he, like you, only permitted. 68. toward near. 69. holy vizard pious facial expression. Subtle has accepted the apology and resumes listing practices that the Puritans will no longer need. 71. common cause i.e. the supposed good of the Puritan congregation. 72. Nor...day Nor collect the security on loans that are one day overdue. 77. stiffness resistance, with a bawdy pun that suggests copulation. 78. scrupulous bones fine moral problems to discuss. The following list suggests that the Puritans concern themselves with trivialities instead of theological or moral issues. 81–2. May...linen Contemporary female fashions included fancy hairdressing, the doublet (a man's sleeveless garment), and starched collars and handkerchiefs. 87. shorten...ears prepare to hear (perhaps with an allusion to the ear-cropping punishment sometimes inflicted on Puritans). 88. wire-drawn grace prolonged prayer. 89. alderman city magistrate (often depicted as fond of custard.) 92. singular unique. 95. wood collection.

Of the disciple.

TRIBULATION   Truly, sir, they are
    Ways that the godly Brethren have invented
    For propagation of the glorious cause,
    As very notable means, and whereby also   100
    Themselves grow soon and profitably famous.

SUBTLE Oh, but the stone, all's idle to it! Nothing!
    The art of angels, nature's miracle,
    The divine secret that doth fly in clouds
    From east to west, and whose tradition   105
    Is not from men but spirits.

ANANIAS   I hate traditions;
    I do not trust them,—

TRIBULATION   Peace!

ANANIAS   —they are popish, all.
    I will not peace, I will not—

TRIBULATION   Ananias!

ANANIAS—Please the profane to grieve the godly; I may not.

SUBTLE Well, Ananias, thou shalt overcome.   110

TRIBULATION It is an ignorant zeal that haunts him, sir,
    But truly, else, a very faithful Brother,
    A botcher, and a man by revelation
    That hath a competent knowledge of the truth.

SUBTLE Has he a competent sum there i' the bag   115
    To buy the goods within? I am made guardian,
    And must for charity and conscience's sake
    Now see the most be made for my poor orphans,
    Though I desire the Brethren too, good gainers.

    .   .   .   .

SUBTLE   I have trick   120
    To melt the pewter you shall buy now instantly,
    And with a tincture make you as good Dutch dollars,
    As any are in Holland.

TRIBULATION   Can you so?

SUBTLE Ay, and shall bide the third examination.

ANANIAS It will be joyful tidings to the Brethren.   125

SUBTLE But you must carry it secret.

---

106. **traditions** key term in contemporary religious polemic, representing the Church teaching that Puritans rejected. 113. **botcher** mender. **revelation** direct experience of God, as opposed to **traditions** (see also 3. 1. 46). 118. **orphans** Subtle pretends to be practising alchemy to help orphans. 119. **desire...gainers** also hope for the material prosperity of the Brethren. 122. **Dutch dollars** silver coins. 124. **third examination** most severe scrutiny.

TRIBULATION   Ay, but stay;
　This act of coining, is it lawful?
ANANIAS   Lawful?
　We know no magistrate. Or, if we did,
　This 's foreign coin.
SUBTLE   It is no coining, sir.
　It is but casting.
TRIBULATION   Ha? You distinguish well.   130
　Casting of money may be lawful.
ANANIAS   'Tis, sir.
TRIBULATION   Truly, I take it so.
SUBTLE   There is no scruple,
　Sir, to be made of it; believe Ananias.
　This case of conscience he is studied in.
TRIBULATION   I'll make a question of it to the Brethren.   135
ANANIAS   The Brethren shall approve it lawful, doubt not.
　Where shall't be done?
SUBTLE   For that we'll talk anon. (*Knock without*)
　There's some to speak with me. Go in, I pray you,
　And view the parcels. That's the inventory.
　I'll come to you straight.   [*Exeunt Tribulation and Ananias*]   140

PHILIP MASSINGER

Successor to William Shakespeare and John Fletcher as principal dramatist of the King's Men, Philip Massinger (1583–1640) wrote or collaborated on some fifty-five plays. Massinger may or may not have been a Catholic but at times he wrote like one. *The Maid of Honour* presents in the title-role Camiola, who climactically rejects her unworthy but hard-won paramour, Bertoldo, and chooses instead to enter a convent. *The Renegado*, excerpted below, defends the importance of good works as Satisfaction in Penance, the Real Presence of Christ in the Eucharist, and the validity of lay baptism. Moreover, after decades of fierce anti-Jesuit legislation and polemic, as well as recent satires such as Donne's *Ignatius his Conclave* (1611) and John Barclay's *Argenis* (1621, see FICTION), Massinger remarkably presents a Jesuit as his hero, Father Francisco, who kindly reclaims the sinners and devises a plot to rescue Christian captives from the cruel Turk.

---

128. know no magistrate recognize no civil authority in religious matters. The subsequent distinctions between foreign and local coin and between coining and casting illustrate self-serving Puritan casuistry.

The Renegado, 1624

4. 1 [*Outside in Tunis*]

Enter GRIMALDI *with a book*

GRIMALDI [*to himself*] For theft! He that restores treble the value
  Makes Satisfaction, and for want of means
  To do so as a slave must serve it out
  Till he hath made full payment. There's hope left here.
  Oh, with what willingness would I give up   5
  My liberty to those I have pillaged,
  And wish the numbers of my years, though wasted
  In the most sordid slavery, might equal
  The rapines I have made, till with one voice
  My patient sufferings might exact from my   10
  Most cruel creditors a full remission—
  An eye's loss with an eye, limbs with a limb—
  A sad account! Yet to find peace within here,
  Though all such as I have maimed and dismembered
  In drunken quarrels, or o'ercome with rage   15
  When they were giv'n up to my power stood here now
  And cried for restitution, to appease 'em
  I would do a bloody justice on myself—
  Pull out these eyes that guided me to ravish
  Their sight from others, lop these legs that bore me   20
  To barbarous violence, with this hand cut off
  This instrument of wrong till nought were left me
  But this poor, bleeding, limbless trunk, which gladly
  I would divide among them.

Enter FRANCISCO *in a cope like a bishop*

                Ha! What think I
  Of petty forfeitures? In this reverend habit   25
  (All that I am turned into eyes) I look on

---

4. 1 SD GRIMALDI is the titular *renegado*, a Christian who has profaned the Eucharist and turned against his faith to serve the Turk for money. Racked by his conscience, Grimaldi enters here to his former ship companions, the master and boatswain. *a book* perhaps the Bible (cf. Exod. 21, 22), or a Catholic book on penance. **2. Satisfaction** good works performed to remit the temporal penalty due to sin (according to Catholic teaching). **12. eye's ... eye** an echo of the *lex talionis*, the old law of retribution; cf. Exod. 21: 24; Matt. 5: 38. **22. This instrument** the other hand. **24. SD *cope*** ecclesiastical cloak. **26. All ... eyes** an extravagant figure to say that Grimaldi is looking on Francisco with his whole being.

A deed of mine so fiendlike that repentance,
Though with my tears I taught the sea new tides,
Can never wash off. All my thefts, my rapes
Are venial trespasses compared to what   30
I offered to that shape, and in a place too
Where I stood bound to kneel to't. *Kneels*

FRANCISCO   'Tis forgiven.
I with his tongue, whom in these sacred vestments
With impure hands thou didst offend, pronounce it.
I bring peace to thee. See that thou deserve it   35
In thy fair life hereafter.

GRIMALDI   Can it be?
Dare I believe this vision or hope
A pardon e'er may find me?

FRANCISCO   Purchase it
By zealous undertakings, and no more
'Twill be remembered.

GRIMALDI [*rising*]   What celestial balm   40
I feel now poured into my wounded conscience!
What penance is there I'll not undergo.
Though ne'er so sharp and rugged, with more pleasure
Than flesh and blood e'er tasted; show me true sorrow,
Armed with an iron whip, and I will meet   45
The stripes she brings along with her as if
They were the gentle touches of a hand
That comes to cure me. Can good deeds redeem me?
I will rise up a wonder to the world,
When I have given strong proofs how I am altered!   50
I that have sold such as professed the faith
That I was born in to captivity
Will make their number equal that I shall
Deliver from the oar, and win as many
By the clearness of my actions to look on   55
Their misbelief and loathe it. I will be
A convoy for all merchants, and thought worthy
To be reported to the world hereafter,
The child of your devotion, nursed up

27. **deed** While Francisco was celebrating mass, Grimaldi snatched the consecrated bread and wine and dashed them upon the pavement. 33. **I...tongue** an illustration of Catholic doctrines concerning Penance. Forgiveness is granted by God (**'Tis forgiven,** 32) and conveyed by the priest who gives absolution to the contrite sinner who makes a confession. 38–9. **Purchase...undertakings** another allusion to the doctrine of Satisfaction. 48. **Can...me** Protestants denied the salvific efficacy of good works. 54. **the oar** i.e. slavery. 57. **convoy** a protective escort (instead of a predator).

And made strong by your charity to break through 60
All dangers hell can bring forth to oppose me.
Nor am I—though my fortunes were thought desperate,
Now you have reconciled me to myself—
So void of worldly means, but in despite
Of the proud Viceroy's wrongs I can do something 65
To witness of my change. When you please, try me
And I will perfect what you shall enjoin me,
Or fall a joyful martyr.

FRANCISCO You will reap
The comfort of it. Live yet undiscovered,
And with your holy meditations strengthen 70
Your Christian resolution; ere long
You shall hear further from me.

GRIMALDI I'll attend
All your commands with patience. Come, my mates, *Exit Francisco*
I hitherto have lived an ill example,
And as your captain led you on to mischief, 75
But now will truly labour that good men
May say hereafter of me to my glory
(Let but my power and means stand with my will),
'His good endeavours did weigh down his ill.' *Exeunt Grimaldi, master, boatswain*

Enter FRANCISCO

FRANCISCO This penitence is not counterfeit; howsoever 80
Good actions are in themselves rewarded,
My travail's to meet with a double crown,
If that Vitelli come off safe and prove
Himself the master of his affections.

4. 3 [*The jail*]

Enter FRANCISCO, JAILER

FRANCISCO I come not empty handed. I will purchase
Your favour at what rate you please. There's gold. [*Gives gold*]

JAILER 'Tis the best oratory. I will hazard
A check for your content. [*He calls.*] Below, there!

VITELLI [*under the stage*] Welcome.

---

65. **Viceroy** Asambeg, ruler of Tunis, who has a captive Christian, Paulina. 67. **perfect** complete. 73. **mates** the master and boatswain on stage. 83. **Vitelli** Paulina's brother, seduced by the lascivious Turk Donusa, then caught, imprisoned, and sentenced to death.

4. 3. Francisco visits the repentant Vitelli, who seeks to die as a martyr for the Christian faith. 4. **check** rebuke.

Art thou the happy messenger that brings me 5
News of my death?
JAILER   Your hand. (VITELLI *plucked up*)
FRANCISCO   Now if you please,
A little privacy.
JAILER   You have bought it, sir.
Enjoy it freely.   *Exit Jailer*
FRANCISCO   Oh, my dearest pupil,
Witness these tears of joy. I never saw you
Till now look lovely; nor durst I e'er glory 10
In the mind of any man I had built up
With the hands of virtuous and religious precepts
Till this glad minute. Now you have made good
My expectation of you. By my order,
All Roman Caesars that led kings in chains, 15
Fast bound to their triumphant chariots, if
Compared with that true glory and full lustre
You now appear in, all their boasted honours,
Purchased with blood and wrong, would lose their names,
And be no more remembered.
VITELLI   This applause, 20
Confirmed in your allowance, joys me more
Than if a thousand full-crammed theatres
Should clap their eager hands to witness that
The scene I act did please, and they admire it.
But these are, father, but beginnings, not 25
The ends of my high aims. I grant to have mastered
The rebel appetite of flesh and blood
Was far above my strength, and still owe for it
To that great power that lent it. But when I
Shall make't apparent the grim looks of death 30
Affright me not, and that I can put off
The fond desire of life (that like a garment
Covers and clothes our frailty), hastening to
My martyrdom as to a heavenly banquet
To which I was a choice invited guest, 35
Then you may boldly say you did not plough
Or trust the barren and ungrateful sands
With the fruitful grain of your religious counsels.
FRANCISCO You do instruct your teacher. Let the sun

---

6. SD *plucked up* brought onstage through the trapdoor. **14. By my order** in my view. **21. allowance** praise. **28. owe** i.e. owe works of penance. **32. fond** foolish.

Of your clear life, that lends to good men light,   40
But set as gloriously as it did rise,
Though sometimes clouded, you may write *nil ultra*
To human wishes.
VITELLI   I have almost gained
The end of the race, and will not faint or tire now.

5. 1 [*The jail*]

Enter VITELLI, FRANCISCO

FRANCISCO You are wondrous brave and jocund.
VITELLI   Welcome, father.
Should I spare cost or not wear cheerful looks
Upon my wedding day, it were ominous
And showed I did repent it; which I dare not,
It being a marriage, howsoever sad   5
In the first ceremonies that confirm it,
That will forever arm me against fears,
Repentance, doubts, or jealousies, and bring
Perpetual comforts, peace of mind, and quiet
To the glad couple.
FRANCISCO   I well understand you,   10
And my full joy to see you so resolved
Weak words cannot express. What is the hour
Designed for this solemnity?
VITELLI   The sixth.
Something before the setting of the sun,
We take our last leave of his fading light,   15
And with our souls' eyes seek for beams eternal.
Yet there's one scruple with which I am much
Perplexed and troubled, which I know you can
Resolve me of.
FRANCISCO   What is't?
VITELLI   This, sir, my bride,
Whom I first courted and then won, not with   20
Loose lays, poor flatteries, apish compliments,

42. *nil ultra* 'nothing further' (Latin).

5. 1 Instead of converting to Islam to save his life, Vitelli converts Donusa to Christianity. They await their execution, which they consider to be their wedding. Sir Leslie Stephen (1877) adduced the dialogue of this scene as evidence of Massinger's Catholicism: '*The Renegado*, for example, not only shows that Massinger was, for dramatic purposes, at least, an ardent believer in baptismal regeneration, but includes—what one would scarcely have sought in such a place—a discussion as to the validity of lay-baptism' (*Massinger: The Critical Heritage*, ed. Martin Garrett, 1991: 189). **3. were** would be. **21. Loose lays** bawdy songs.

But sacred and religious zeal, yet wants
The holy badge that should proclaim her fit
For these celestial nuptials; willing she is,
I know, to wear it as the choicest jewel   25
On her fair forehead; but to you that well
Could do that work of grace, I know the Viceroy
Will never grant access. Now in a case
Of this necessity, I would gladly learn,
Whether in me, a layman without orders,   30
It may not be religious and lawful
As we go to our deaths to do that office?
FRANCISCO A question in itself with much ease answered:
Midwives upon necessity perform it,
And knights that in the Holy Land fought for   35
The freedom of Jerusalem, when full
Of sweat and enemies' blood, have made their helmets
The font out of which with their holy hands
They drew that heav'nly liquor; 'twas approved then
By the holy Church, nor must I think it now   40
In you a work less pious.
VITELLI   You confirm me.
I will find a way to do it. In the meantime
Your holy vows assist me.
FRANCISCO   They shall ever
Be present with you.
VITELLI   You shall see me act
This last scene to the life.
FRANCISCO   And though now fall,   45
Rise a blessed martyr.
VITELLI   That's my end, my all.   *Exeunt*

JAMES SHIRLEY

Massinger's successor in the King's Men, James Shirley (1596–1666) became a leading dramatist of the early and mid-seventeenth century, admired chiefly for his witty, satirical comedies. Ordained in the Church of England, Shirley may have become a Catholic around 1622; some of his thirty-seven plays and masques show marked sympathy for the Catholic faith. There is praise for the Benedictines throughout *The Grateful Servant* (1630)

23. **holy badge** i.e. baptism.

and reference to the blood of the dead working miracles (5. 2) in *The Doubtful Heir* (1640). *St Patrick for Ireland* (1639–40), Shirley's version of a medieval saint's play, depicts Saint Patrick's conversion of pagan Ireland to Christianity. A pivotal point of controversy, this conversion for Catholics demonstrated the papal origins of Irish Christianity, subordinated civil to clerical authority, and validated many doctrines rejected by Protestants. (See, for example, these polemical emphases in the source of the play, Jocelinus' *Life of St Patrick* as translated by B.B. in Alfonso de Villegas, *Lives of Saints*, 1628, 1636.) Producing the play for Protestant patrons at the new Werburgh Street Theatre in Dublin, however, Shirley suppresses all mention of papal mandate and steers clear of confessional controversy. He presents instead a ragbag of sensational incident, romantic plot, slapstick comedy, melodramatic villainy, and saintly heroism. This attempt at accommodationist Catholic drama apparently pleased neither Protestants nor Catholics: the projected second part never appeared and the play has never been revived after its first performance.

St Patrick for Ireland, 1639–40

5. 3 [*At Dichu's cave*]

PATRICK [*To Emeria*] You will be spouse to an eternal bridegroom,
    And lay the sweet foundation of a rule
    That after ages with devotion
    Shall praise and follow. [*To Conallus*] You are, sir, reserved
    To bless this kingdom with your pious government;   5
    Your crown shall flourish and your blood possess
    The throne you shall leave glorious. This nation
    Shall in a fair succession thrive and grow
    Up the world's academy, and disperse
    As the rich springs of human and divine   10
    Knowledge clear streams to water foreign kingdoms,
    Which shall be proud to owe what they possess
    In learning to this great all-nursing island.
CONALLUS May we be worthy of this prophecy.
PATRICK Discourse hath made the way less tedious.   15
    We have reached the cell already, which is much
    Too narrow to contain us; but beneath
    These trees, upon their cool and pleasing shades,
    You may sit down. I'll call upon my convert.

5.3. This climactic scene takes place outdoors at the cave of the hermit Dichu, formerly a nobleman. Saint Patrick approaches with his new flock of converts—the Queen, her son Prince Conallus, and Emeria, a victim of rape. Inside the cave Dichu's sons, Ferochus and Endarius, supposed dead, are taking refuge. **2. rule** order of nuns.

—Dichu, my penitent, come forth, I pray,   20
And entertain some guests I have brought hither
That deserve welcome—

Enter DICHU

DICHU   I obey that voice.
PATRICK—The Queen, and Prince, and Milcho's virtuous daughter,
  Gained to our holy faith.
DICHU [*kneeling*]   Let my knee speak
  My duty, though I want words for joy.   25
  Ten thousand welcomes! I have guests within too.
  You'll wonder to salute my sons, not dead,
  As we supposed, by heavenly providence,
  I hope, reserved to be made blest by you.
  They are here.

Enter FEROCHUS *and* ENDARIUS

              —Your duties to the Queen and Prince,   30
  Then to this man, next to our great preserver,
  The patron of us all.
PATRICK   A happy meeting!
  I must rejoice to see you safe and here.
  But tell us by what strange means all this while
  You have been preserved. Sit down. *Soft music*   35
CONALLUS What music's this?
QUEEN   'Tis heavenly.
PATRICK And a preface to some message
  Or will of heaven. Be silent and attend it.
  Such harmony as this did wait upon
  My angel Victor when he first appeared,   40
  And did reveal a treasure under ground,
  With which I bought my freedom when I kept
  Unhappy Milcho's swine. Heaven's will be done.
  What, all asleep already? Holy dreams
  Possess your fancy. I can wait no longer.   45

Enter VICTOR *and other* ANGELS
Song

VICTOR [and ANGELS] 'Down from the skies,
              Commanded by the power that ties
              The world and nature in a chain,

23. **Milcho** an officer, father of Emeria. **39–42.** There are several allusions to Patrick's former enslavement and miraculous ransom (e.g. 4. 1). His guardian angel Victor appears throughout the play. **45. wait** i.e. wait to sleep.

We come, we come, a glorious train,
　　To wait on thee,   50
And make thy person danger-free.
　　　Hark, whilst we sing,
And keep time with our golden wing,
To show how earth and heaven agree.
What echo rises to our harmony!'   55

VICTOR Holy Patrick, sleep in peace,
　Whilst I, thy guardian, with these
　My fellow angels, wait on thee,
　For thy defence. A troop I see
　Of serpents, vipers, and whate'er   60
　Doth carry killing poison, here
　Summoned by art and power of hell!
　But thou shalt soon their fury quell,
　And by the strength of thy command,
　These creatures shall forsake the land,   65
　And creep into the sea, no more
　To live upon the Irish shore.
　Once more then.

Song

'Patrick, sleep, oh, sleep a while,
And wake, the patron of this isle.'   70

Enter KING, ARCHIMAGUS, *and other* PRIESTS

ARCHIMAGUS [*to King*] Your person shall be safe. Fear not, great sir;
　I have directed all their stings and poison.
　See where he sleeps. If he escape this danger,
　Let my life with some horrid circumstance
　End in this place and carry all your curses.   75

Enter serpents, etc., creeping

What think you of these creeping executioners?
　Do they not move as if they knew their errand?
KING My queen, my son Conallus, Dichu! Ha!
　And the still-wand'ring ghosts of his two sons!
ARCHIMAGUS They are alive, sir.
KING　　　　　　　　　　　Ha, who dares abuse us?   80

---

71. SD King Leogarius. **Archimagus** chief magician and enemy of Patrick. **Priests** pagan magicians. **75. SD** Perhaps actors dressed as serpents, entering through the trapdoor.

PRIEST Will you not have compassion of the queen,
    And the prince, sir?
KING   How met they to converse?
ARCHIMAGUS They are all Christian.
KING   Let the serpent, then,
    Feed upon all, my powerful Archimagus.
PATRICK [*waking*] In vain is all your malice, art, and power   85
    Against their lives, whom the great hand of heaven
    Deigns to protect; like wolves you undertake
    A quarrel with the moon and waste your anger.
    Nay, all the shafts your wrath directeth hither
    Are shot against a brazen arch, whose vault   90
    Impenetrable sends the arrows back
    To print just wounds on your own guilty heads.
    These serpents—tame at first and innocent
    Until man's great revolt from grace released
    Their duty of creation—you have brought   95
    And armed against my life. All these can I
    Approach and without trembling walk upon,
    Play with their stings, which though to me not dangerous,
    I could to your destruction turn upon
    Yourselves, and punish with too late repentance.   100
    But you shall live, and what your malice meant,
    My ruin, I will turn to all your safeties.
    And you shall witness. [*To the serpents*] Hence, you frightful monsters,
    Go hide, and bury your deformèd heads
    Forever in the sea. From this time be   105
    This island free from beasts of venomous natures.
    The shepherd shall not be afraid hereafter
    To trust his eyes with sleep upon the hills;
    The traveller shall have no suspicion
    Or fear to measure with his weary limbs   110
    The silent shades, but walk through every brake
    Without more guard than his own innocence.
    The very earth and wood shall have this blessing
    (Above what other Christian nations boast):
    Although transported, where these serpents live   115
    And multiply, one touch shall soon destroy them.   *Exit serpents, etc.*

---

81. **of** on. **94–5. released . . . creation** cancelled their natural obligations to the Creator. **111. brake** thicket. **115. where** wherever.

KING See how they all obey him, Archimagus!
ARCHIMAGUS Confusion! All my art is trampled on!
   Can neither man, nor beast, nor devil hurt him?
   Support me, fellow priests! I sink, I feel   120
   The ground bends with my weight upon it, ha!
   The earth is loose in the foundation,
   And something heavy as the world doth hang
   Upon my feet, and weigh me to the centre!
   A fire, a dreadful fire is underneath me,   125
   And all those fiends that were my servants here
   Look like tormentors, and all seem to strive
   Who first shall catch my falling flesh upon
   Their burning pikes! There is a power above
   Our gods, I see too late. I fall, I fall,   130
   And in my last despair I curse you all! *Sinks*
KING Patrick, the king will kneel to thee. [*Kneels*]
PATRICK   Oh, rise,
   And pay to heaven that duty.
    KING [*Rising*]   Canst forgive?
   Let me embrace you all and freely give
   What I desire from this good man, a pardon.   135
   Thou shalt no more suspect me but possess
   All your desires. [*Aside*] The ground is shut again.
   Where now is Archimagus? How I shake,
   And court this Christian out of fear not love.
   [*To Patrick*] Once more visit our palace, holy father.   140
   [*To Dichu*] The story of your sons, and what concerns
   Your escape, madam, we will know hereafter.
   I'the meantime be secure.
ENDARIUS [AND] FEROCHUS We are your creatures.
ALL Our prayers and duty.
   PATRICK [*Aside*]   I suspect him still.
   But fear not; our good angels still are near us.   145
   Death at the last can but untie our frailty;
   'Twere happy for our holy faith to bleed.
   'The blood of martyrs is the Church's seed.'   *Exeunt all*

---

148. a proverb, originating in Tertullian (*semen est sanguis Christianorum* 'the blood of Christians is seed', *Apologeticus* 50. 13).

HISTORIES

At a dinner party in 1583, John Hardy cited a Latin passage in Eusebius which suggested the authority of the bishops over the emperor. Scenting non-conformity and a threat to the Elizabethan settlement, the preacher Peter German reported Hardy to the authorities, who interrogated and imprisoned him. At his hearing Hardy produced from his cloak the torn pages of Eusebius (*Unpublished Documents Relating to the English Martyrs*, ed. J. H. Pollen, 1908: 47–50). Clearly, reading or writing history in this period meant confronting the past directly, vitally, and consequentially. Demanding learning as well as a high tolerance for risk, this confrontation became charged with various political and theological significances.

Early modern Catholics read, translated, and wrote history. As we have seen, Thomas More, Edmund Campion, and other Catholics argued that the true Church descended visibly and continuously from Christ and the apostle Peter to the present day Roman Church and the pope. For them history functioned as the prime guarantor of their authenticity and sanctity. Hence the frequent appeals to Scripture, the Church Fathers, and Councils, the constant condemnation of Protestantism as heretical innovation, and the oft-repeated challenge, 'Where was your church before Luther?' Luther himself, of course, had begun to answer the question by depicting the true Church as receding into invisibility as the false Roman one emerged, steadily degenerating over time. Matthias Flacius massively documented the devolution in *Centuriae Magdeburgenses* ('The Magdeburg Centuries', 13 vols., 1559–74), which prompted rebuttals from many including Cardinal Baronius. With equal vehemence both sides claimed primacy and historical antecedence; both sides emphatically denied departure and innovation.

As John Hardy's trouble illustrates, the state-sponsored revolution in England fully participated in the great debate over the facts and meaning of the past. The Henrician Act of Appeals (1533), which first formally broke ties with Rome, invoked at the outset 'divers, sundry, old, authentic histories and chronicles', which bore witness to England's autonomy and the sovereignty of 'one supreme head and king' (*The Tudor Constitution*, ed. G. R. Elton, 1982: 353). Robert Barnes and John Bale led the charge. Barnes ransacked sources to demonstrate papal and clerical perfidy (*A Supplication unto … Henry VIII*, 1531) and to discredit current Roman practices (*Vitae Romanorum pontificum*, 1535). More scholarly though no less tendentious, John Bale traced the Church's deterioration from apostolic times to the present reign of Antichrist in dramas such as *King Johan* (1538–9), and polemical works such as *The Image of Both Churches* (1545) and *The Acts of English Votaries* (1546). According to his narrative the true Church lived for centuries in the hearts of the anti-Roman faithful and pure of heart, in such figures as Berengarius, who attacked the mass, Marsiglio of Padua, who opposed Roman claims to secular power, Wyclif, Hus, Luther, Calvin, and so on. This new view of salvation history naturally effected surprising re-evaluations of the local past. In the Tudor period the reviled King John was born again as an antipapal hero. The treasonous Sir John Oldcastle, executed for rebellion, found new life as a proto-Protestant martyr. (Shakespeare, by the way, fascinatingly declines to follow the Protestant line on both figures.) The missionary St Augustine of Canterbury became the papal legate who contaminated British Christianity with false doctrines. The revered St Thomas Becket, who chose death rather than assent to civil usurpation of Church prerogatives, suffered more public and dramatic devaluation: in 1538 the government revoked his status as saint and martyr, pronounced him a traitor, expunged his name from liturgical books, destroyed the shrine at Canterbury, and scattered his bones.

Officially endorsed by the government, John Foxe, the Marian exile and martyrologist, emerged as the most influential creator of Protestant English history. His popular *Acts and Monuments* (1563) begins by responding to the Catholic question, 'Where was your church before Luther?':

> First, we demand what they mean by this which they call *our* church? If they mean the ordinance and institution of doctrine and sacraments now received of us and differing from the church of Rome, we affirm and say that our church was when this church of theirs was not yet hatched out of the shell, nor did yet ever see any light. That is, in the time of the apostles, in the primitive age, in the time of Gregory I [*r*. 590–604], and the old Roman church, when as yet no universal pope was received publicly, but repelled in Rome, nor this fulness of plenary power yet known, nor this doctrine and abuse of sacraments yet heard of. In witness whereof we have the old acts and histories of ancient time to give testimony with us wherein we have sufficient matter for us to show that the same form, usage, and institution of this our present reformed church are not the beginning of any new church of our own, but the renewing of the old ancient church of Christ; and that they are not any swerving from the church of Rome but rather a reducing to the church of Rome (ed. G. Townsend, S. R. Cattley, 1837–41, rpt. 1965: i. 9).

Foxe tells the story of the English church from the founding mission of Joseph of Arimathea, through its deterioration, to the present restoration under the Tudors. In his narrative England emerges as the elect nation, the place where the flame of Christ, finally restored, blazes most truly and brightly. And the proof of Rome's apostasy and England's recovery, Foxe triumphantly demonstrates, resides in the history of English martyrs, that tragically glorious witness of Christ's body repeatedly crucified anew. The *Acts and Monuments* presents a new ecclesiastical calendar of saints and martyrs, featuring dissenters early and late as well as those who died for their faith, particularly in the reign of Queen Mary. Remembrance thus metamorphoses into practice, into the daily devotional and liturgical celebration of new saints and feast days. Revision of the past thus means redefinition of the present and the future.

In Latin as well as English Catholic writers and historians variously dissent. They recall three papal foundations of English Christianity: (1) that of St Peter, St Joseph of Arimathea, and Simon the Apostle (1st c.); (2) that of Fugatius and Damian, sent by Pope Eleutherius (*r.* 174–89) at the request of King Lucius; and, most important, (3) that of St Augustine of Canterbury, sent by Pope Gregory the Great (*r.* 590–604) to Saxon England (see Fig. 13). Translating Venerable Bede's *Ecclesiastica Historia* (1565), Thomas Stapleton recounts in detail St Augustine's conversion of Saxon pagans to Christianity to affirm the Roman Catholic nature and origins of British Christianity, recently led astray. Stapleton's preface and notes, moreover, point out the antiquity and, therefore, doctrinal validity of rejected practices and doctrines. Nicholas Sander rises to the Protestant challenge in several works, including *De visibili monarchia ecclesiae* (1571) and *De Origine ac progressu schismatis Anglicani* ('On the Origin and Progress of the Anglican Schism', 1585). Joining such works as *A Treatise of Treasons* (1572) and *Leicester's Commonwealth* (1584) in exposing the hidden secrets of the English 'Reformation', Sander's *De Origine* became the most widely read Catholic account of recent religious history. The titular 'schism' reveals the overarching moral framework as Sander focuses on the persons in the drama, both the sinners (Cardinal Wolsey, Henry VIII), and the saints (Catherine of Aragon, Thomas More) and rehearses all the scandalous gossip about Anne Boleyn. Marshalling various authorities, Robert Persons, SJ, publishes the weighty *A Treatise of Three Conversions of England* (3 vols., 1603–4). Here Persons denounces Foxe's history as inaccurate and heretical, devoting one famous chapter to the 'more than one hundred and twenty lies uttered by John Foxe in less than three leaves of his *Acts and Monuments*' (Bk. 3, ch. 19). Adducing the historical record and the adverse judgements of conflicting Protestant sects, Persons dismantles Foxe's calendar of saints one by one. In addition to these writers (excerpted below), other Catholics produced scholarly and polemical histories, notably Richard White, *Historiarum Brittanicae libri xi* (1597–1607), and the prolific

13. Giovanni Baptista de Cavalleriis, 'The Third Conversion of England', *Ecclesiae Anglicanae Trophaea*, 1584, pl. 10. The A section depicts St Gregory the Great returning to Rome from pagan England; B, the Pope commissioning Gregory for the mission to England; C, the baptism of St Ethelbert, king of England; D, the flight of St Germanus to Christian England.

Richard Broughton, *An Ecclesiastical Protestant History* (1624), and *The Ecclesiastical History of Great Britain* (1633).

Catholic historians, moreover, reflect the rise of antiquarianism and the new methods of historiography evident in the early seventeenth century. In *A Restitution of Decayed Intelligence* (1604) Richard Verstegan examines antiquities and uses comparative linguistics to advance the following argument: the English people descend from Saxon tribes; Saxon tribes became Christian in the sixth century through the missionary efforts of Pope Gregory the Great and St Augustine; ergo, Roman Catholicism is the original and authentic Christian religion of the English people. Following suit, William Blundell, an amateur Catholic historian in Little Crosby, studies a cache of Saxon coins found on his property in 1611. Poring over the physical evidence in the new manner of antiquaries such as Edward Bolton, Robert Cotton, Henry Spelman, and others, Blundell interprets the coins as evidence of the deep historical connection between Roman Catholicism and English, particularly Saxon, history, thus confirming Verstegan's historical and philological argument. Blundell's careful drawings of the coins furnish a later copperplate engraving (see Fig. 14).

Three additional historians featured below, Bartolomé de Las Casas, Philip O'Sullivan-Beare, and Elizabeth Cary, also write against prevalent orthodoxies and illustrate the diversity of the Catholic contribution. The Dominican Las Casas condemns Spanish cruelty and demands just treatment of the Indians in the new world. O'Sullivan Beare raises a powerful voice against English colonialism and oppression in Ireland; his narrative opposes the accounts of Edmund Spenser and Raphael Holinshed. The recusant Elizabeth Cary, perhaps the first English female historian (*The Tragedy of Mariam*) and the first English female historian, contributes an imaginative history of Edward II, remarkable for its dramatic portraits and sympathetic treatment of the papacy.

VENERABLE BEDE

Historian and Doctor of the Church, Venerable Bede (672–735) (*venerabilis* is an honorific title) lived as a monk at Wearmouth-Jarrow monastery. Consulting many ancient documents, Bede recounts the conversion of Great Britain to Christianity in his masterful *Historia Ecclesiastica Gentis Anglorum*. Thomas Stapleton, an exiled Catholic polemicist in Louvain, translated the Latin *Historia* in 1565 to show, as he says to the dedicatee, Queen Elizabeth, 'in how many and weighty points the pretended reformers of the Church in Your Grace's dominions have departed from the pattern of that sound and Catholic faith planted first among Englishmen by holy St Augustine [of Canterbury], our apostle' (sig. *3; see Fig. 14). After noting precedents for Catholic doctrines later denied by Protestants, Stapleton writes a Preface that emphasizes the role of the popes in the conversion of Britain and the confirming witness of many miracles and martyrs.

The History of the Church of England, tr. Thomas Stapleton, 1565

Differences between the primitive faith of England, continued almost these thousand years, and the late pretensed faith of Protestants

Our apostles said mass. In the first book, the twenty-fifth chapter, it is mentioned; *item*, of their successors in the fourth book, the fourteenth and twenty-second chapters. Nothing is more horrible in the sight of Protestants than mass. In the mass is an external sacrifice offered to God the Father, the blessed body and blood of Christ himself. In the fifth book, the twenty-second chapter, this doctrine is expressly reported. This seemeth   5 an extreme blasphemy to Protestants. This sacrifice is taught to be propitiatory in the fourth book, the twenty-second chapter. Protestants abhor utterly such doctrine.

Of confession of sins made to the priest, the fourth book doth witness in the twenty-fifth chapter and twenty-seventh chapter. This sacrament in the faith of Protestants of our country is abolished. Satisfaction and penance for sin enjoined appeareth in the   10 fourth book, the twenty-fifth chapter also; which in like manner the court of Protestants admitteth not. Merit of good works in this history is eftsoons justified in the fourth book, the fourteenth and fifteenth chapters. This doctrine seemeth to Protestants prejudicial (they say) to God's glory, but indeed to their licentious liberty.

Intercession of saints Protestants abhor. The practice thereof appeareth in this history   15 in the first book, the twentieth chapter, before we had the faith, and in the fourth book, the fourteenth chapter, after the faith received. The clergy of our primitive church after Holy Orders taken do not marry, in the first book, the twenty-seventh chapter. Now after Holy Orders and vow both to the contrary, priests do marry. In our primitive church the vow of chastity both of men and women was thought godly and practiced. See   20 the history, the third book, the eighth and twenty-seventh chapters, the fourth book, the twenty-third chapter, and in many other places. Such vows now are broken, are esteemed damnable, are not so much as allowed in such as would embrace that perfection commended in the Gospel and universally practised in the primitive church of the first five hundred years. Such monks and virgins lived in cloister, in obedience, in poverty. It   25 appeareth throughout all the last three books of the history, namely, the third book, the

---

pretensed pretended. **1.** *item* likewise, moreover. **12. eftsoons** again. **25. five hundred years** According to some Protestants, the true Church lasted six hundred years after Christ and became corrupt thereafter. In his famous sermon at Paul's Cross (26 November 1559) Bishop John Jewel challenged Catholics to justify their beliefs and practices by finding precedents for them in the first six centuries after Christ.

eighth chapter, and the fourth book, the sixth chapter. All such cloisters and orders the religion of Protestants hath overthrown as a state damnable and wicked.

Prayer for the dead, *Dirige* over night, and requiem mass on the morning was an accustomed matter in our primitive church. Witnesseth this history the third book and second chapter; *item*, in the fourth book, the twenty-first chapter. This devotion the sober faith of Protestants esteemeth as abomination before God. Reservation of the Blessed Sacrament thought no superstition in our primitive church or profanation of the sacrament, *lib. 4, cap. 24.*

[. . .]

Last of all, the final determination of spiritual causes in our primitive church rested in the See Apostolic of Rome. This practice appeareth in the second book, the fourth, the seventeenth, and the twentieth chapters; *item*, in the fifth book, the twentieth chapter. How far that See is now detested by the sober religion of Protestants all men do see.

To note how differently the Catholic faith of all Christendom was first planted in our country, and the parted faith of Protestants hath corrupted the same, the first difference is clear herein that our first Catholic faith we received of the See of Rome. This heresy hath begun by first departing from that See. The apostles of our faith came from Rome, the messengers of these schisms began first by scattering from the See Apostolic of Rome. How we received our faith of Rome the later chapters of the first book and the first of the second do testify.

Preface to the Reader

The author of this history being a man of such learning and virtue, a countryman of ours, one that writeth the history of things done at home, done in his lifetime, or in few years before, the memory of them being yet fresh and new, it shall not need, I trust, to persuade the reader in many words to give credit unto him in such things as he reporteth. Neither may I fear to prefer his authority before the authority or report of any man that now liveth. For beside his learning and virtue, it is to be considered that he lived in a quiet time, before these controversies which now so trouble Christendom were moved. He is an indifferent reporter. There is no suspicion of parts-taking, no prejudice of favouring either side, no fear of affection or misjudgement to be gathered upon him. We have good cause to suspect the reports of Bale, of Foxe, of Becon, and such other, which are known to maintain a faction and singular opinion lately sprung up, who report things passed many hundred years before their days. No such suspicion can be made of St Bede, who lived above eight hundred years past, and reporteth the planting of Christian religion among us Englishmen partly by that which he saw himself, partly by the report of such who either lived at the first coming in of Christendom to our country themselves or were

---

29. *Dirige* first word of the Latin antiphon 'Dirige, Domine, Deus meus, in conspectu tuo viam meam' (Direct, O Lord, my God, my way in thy sight, Ps. 5: 9), used as a prayer in the Office of the Dead. **32.** Reservation retaining of some part of the Eucharist for ministerial uses after the consecration. **36.** See seat. **52.** indifferent impartial. **54.** Bale . . . Becon All Protestant polemicists, John Bale (1495–1563) wrote dramas, satires, and attacks; John Foxe (1516–87) produced *Acts and Monuments*, the centrepiece of a national propaganda campaign; Thomas Becon (1512–67) wrote a catechism and many polemical and devotional works. **55.** singular separate.

scholars to such. Who also was no maintainer of any sect or faction, but lived and died in   60
the known common faith of Christendom, which then was and is now but one.

In this history, therefore, view and consider the coming in of Christian faith into our
country, the heavenly tidings brought to our land, the course, increase, and multiplying
thereof, the virtuous behaviour of our forefathers, the first Christian Englishmen. Peruse
and mark the faith which they believed, the hope wherein they continued, the charity   65
whereby they wrought. Their faith taught them to submit themselves to one supreme
head in Christ's Church, the apostolic pope of Rome, Peter's successor, to whom Holy
Scripture telleth us the keys of the kingdom of heaven were given (Matt. 16: 19). Their
faith taught them all such things as are now by Protestants denied, as for the more part
we have out of the history gathered by a number of differences placed in the second part   70
of the *Fortress*. Their hope and charity so wrought that our dear country of England hath
been more enriched with places erected to God's honour and to the free maintenance of
good learning than any one country in all Christendom beside.

Gather honey like bees out of this comfortable history of our country, not venom like
spiders. Read it with charitable simplicity not with suspicious curiosity, with virtuous   75
charity not with wicked malice. As, for example, the fact of Saint Gregory described in the
second book, the first chapter of this history, reporting how that holy man, seeing in Rome
certain of our countrymen set to be sold in the market, moved with their outward beauty,
began to pity and lament their inward foul infidelity, holy St Bede writeth diligently as an
argument of his great good zeal and tendering of Christ's religion, and construeth it to the   80
best, as no honest reader can otherwise do. But bawdy Bale, according to the cleanness of
his spirit and holy gospel, like a venomous spider being filthy and unclean himself, sucketh
out a poisoned sense and meaning, charging that holy man with a most outrageous vice
and not to be named. So, like another Nero (who, living in lewd lechery, would not be
persuaded that any was honest), this old ribald, as in other stories he practised, maketh this   85
history also, ministering no unhonest suspicion at all, nor giving any colour of unclean
surmising to serve his filthy appetite and beastly humour. It will better become the godly
reader and Christian heart to interpret all to the best. For indeed, none can think evil of
other which is not evil himself. 'Charity', saith St Paul, 'thinketh no evil, rejoiceth not of
iniquity, but is delighted in verity'(1 Cor. 13: 5–6). Such charity, if it had been in Bale and   90
his fellow Protestants, we should not now have had so many lewd lies and malicious
surmises upon the lives of holy men as are to be seen in the works of Bale, Foxe, and other.

In this history it shall be no lost time to peruse the learned, virtuous, and zealous
epistles of certain popes of Rome after St Gregory, as of Boniface, Honorius, Vitalian, and
other to the kings of our country, as well for the increasing of Christian faith as for the   95

---

60. **scholars** students. 71. *Fortress* Stapleton published another defence of Catholicism in 1565, *A Fortress of the Faith*
(Antwerp). 74. **comfortable** encouraging, fortifying. 81. **bawdy Bale** Bale told the story as a prime example of clerical
homosexuality and Catholic vice, supplying this gloss to the anecdote of Gregory's admiration for the English boys: 'See
how curious these fathers were in the well eyeing of their wares' (*The Acts of English Votaries*, Antwerp, 1546, sig. Cvi^v). See
Verstegan's account below. 84. **Nero** profligate Roman emperor (*r.* 54–68). 86. **ministering** checking. **giving...of**
providing any grounds for. 94. **St Gregory...Vitalian** St Gregory the Great (*r.* 590–604), St Boniface IV (*r.* 608–15),

extirping of Pelagians' heresy, for the due observation of Easter, which all Christendom hitherto keepeth, and other like matters. While ye peruse this ye may remember the lewd lies and slanderous reproaches of Protestants, daily preaching and writing that after St Gregory all faith was lost, God's honour was trod under foot, all right religion was overturned, and that by the popes themselves. Better to bestow idle hours in such virtuous lessons as this history giveth, and more charitable to note the godly writings of the popes here also comprised than to pry out with bawdy Bale the evil lives of our superiors. Who, were they as bad as the Pharisees or worse, yet they are to be obeyed by the commandment of our Saviour in such things as they say, though not to be followed in their doings. Truly, monasteries being now thrown down, no examples of virtue and perfection appearing in such as now preach and teach, all remembrance of Christian devotion would be forgotten if the help of stories were not.

As touching the manifold miracles mentioned in this history, note the person that reporteth them and the time they were done in, to wit, in the primitive church of the English nation. At the planting of a faith miracles are wrought of God by the hands of his faithful for more evidence thereof. Good life in such as newly receive the faith is more fervent. Visions and working of miracles accompany those as live in such fervent goodness and perfection. We have, therefore, rather more cause to lament the corrupt state of our time and the key-cold devotion of this age than to miscredit the perfect behaviour of our primitive church and the miracles wrought therein. 'Opera dei revelare et confiteri gloriosum est' (It is an honourable thing to reveal and confess the works of God) saith the angel to Tobias in Holy Scripture (Tob. 12: 7). Such, therefore, as will think the miracles of this history here reported either uncredible, either unprofitable, and such as might have been left out, truly either they must deny the author or envy at God's honour. Such as deny the author we will not force them to believe him. We make it not a matter of such necessity or importance. Yet, this I think I may be bold to require them, that they believe as far St Bede as they do the *Acts and Monuments* of Foxe, the story of Bale, and such other. I think it no sin to match Venerable Bede with any of them in any respect either of learning, honesty, or truth. It may rather savour of sin, or at least of wrong judgement and great partiality, to believe Bale and discredit Bede—the one being notoriously bent to one side, the other without all suspicion of favouring any side; the one a late-known naughty man, the other a confessed holy man of all the Latin Church; last of all, the one thought learned only of a few, the other accounted for excellently learned even of the Protestants themselves, namely those of Basel, who have most diligently and with much commendation published his works. But I may seem to do injury to that holy man to compare him with any of our days, glory he never so much of the spirit or of the Gospel. To return, therefore, to the matter: no indifferent reader hath

Honorius I (*r.* 625–38), and St Vitalian (*r.* 657–72). **96. Pelagians** followers of Pelagius (5th c.), who denied the doctrines of original sin and grace. **observation of Easter** Different ways of reckoning the date for Easter in a given year caused major controversy in the early Church. **114. miscredit** disbelieve. **129. those of Basel** Johann Herwagen published an eight-volume edition of Bede, *Opera Omnia* (Basel, 1563).

any cause to discredit the miracles reported in this history if he will have an eye to the person that writeth and to the time in which they were wrought. Nay, rather, it is no small argument for the confirmation of our Catholic faith, planted among us English-   135
men, that at the planting thereof such miracles were wrought.

The passion of St Alban and his fellows, which did shed their blood for Christ's sake

Among other suffered Saint Alban, of whom Fortunatus, priest, in the book he wrote in the praise of virgins, speaking of the martyrs which from all coasts of the world came unto God, saith, 'Albanum egregium faecunda Britannia profert' [*Carm.* 7. 3. 155] (the fertile land of batful Brittany, | Bringeth forth Alban, a martyr right worthy). This Alban,   140
being yet but a pagan when the cruel commandments of the wicked princes were set forth against the Christians, received into his house one of the clergy which had fled from the persecutors; whom he, perceiving both night and day to continue in praying and watching, being suddenly touched with the grace of God, began to follow the example of his faith and virtue, and by little and little instructed by his wholesome exhortations,   145
forsaking his blind idolatry, became Christian with his whole heart. At length, after the said person of the clergy had certain days tarried with him, it came to the ears of the prince that this holy confessor of Christ (whose time was not yet come that God appointed for him to suffer martyrdom) lay hid in Alban's house. Whereupon he commanded his soldiers to search his house with all diligence. Whither when they   150
were come, Saint Alban, apparelled in his guest's and master's garments, offered himself to the soldiers, and so was brought bound unto the judge. It chanced that the judge the same time was doing sacrifice unto the devils before the altars. And when he had seen Alban, being all chafed with anger for that he feared not voluntarily to offer himself unto the soldiers and peril of death for his guest whom he had harboured, he commanded him   155
to be brought before the idols of the devils, before whom he there stood. 'And for so much', quoth he, 'as thou hadst rather to convey away the rebel and traitor to our gods than deliver him up unto the soldiers that he might sustain due punishment for his blasphemous despising of the gods, look what pains he should have suffered if he had been taken; the same shalt thou suffer if thou refuse to practice the rites of our religion.'   160

But Saint Alban, which wilfully had before discovered himself to be a Christian, little heeded the menaces of the prince. But being thoroughly fenced with spiritual armour of grace, told him plainly to his face that he would not obey his commandment. Then said the judge, 'Of what house or stock art thou?' Alban answered, 'What is that to thee of what house I am? But if thou be desirous to know of what religion I am, be it known unto   165
thee that I am a Christian, and that I employ myself to Christian manners and exercises.' Then the judge demanded him his name. 'My parents', quoth he, 'nameth me Alban, and

---

ST ALBAN (d. 304), first martyr of Britain. **137. Fortunatus** Venantius Fortunatus (d. *c.*600), bishop of Poitiers, poet and hymnist. **140. batful** having good pasture lands. **148. confessor** proclaimer. **161. wilfully** freely.

I honour and worship the true and living God, which made all thing of nought.' Then the judge, being very wroth, said, 'If thou wilt enjoy long life, come off, and do sacrifice unto the great gods.' Alban answered, 'These sacrifices which you offer up unto the devils 170 neither help the offerers nor obtain them their desires, but rather purchase them for their reward eternal pains in hell fire.' The judge, hearing this, being in a rage, commanded the holy confessor of God to be all beaten of the tormentors, thinking his constancy would relent at stripes, which refused to yield to words. But he showed himself not only patient but also joyful in the middle of all his torments. 175

The judge, when he saw he could be neither won with words nor turned with torments from the religion of Christ's faith, commanded that he should be beheaded. In the way as he was led to his death, he came to a flood which with a very swift course ran betwixt him and the place where he should suffer. Now he saw a great company of all sexes, degrees, and ages going with him to the place of his execution, insomuch that it seemed the judge 180 was left alone at home without any to attend upon him. This company was so great and the bridge they had to pass over so little that it would be toward night ere they all could get over. Alban, longing much for his blessed death and hasting to his martyrdom, coming to the river's side and making there his prayer with lifting up his eyes and heart to heaven, saw forthwith the bottom to have been dried up and the water give place for him 185 and the people to pass over dry-shod, as it were, upon even ground. Which, when among other the executioner which should have beheaded him did see, he made haste to meet him at the place appointed for his death, and there (not without the holy inspiration of God) he fell down flat before his feet and, casting from him the sword which he held in his hand ready drawn, desired rather that he might be executed either for him or with 190 him, rather than to do execution upon him. Whereupon this man, being now made a fellow of that faith whereof before he was persecutor, and the sword lying in the ground before them, the other officers staggering and doubting all who might take it up and do the execution, the holy confessor of God with the people there assembled went unto a hill almost half a mile off from that place, beautifully garnished with divers herbs and 195 flowers, not rough or uneasy to climb but smooth, plain, and delectable, worthy and meet to be sanctified with the blood of the blessed martyr; unto the top whereof when he was ascended, he required of God to give him water.

And straight there arose a spring of fair water before his feet, whereby all might perceive that the river before was by his means dried. For he which left no water in the river would 200 not have required it in the top of the mountain but that it was so expedient for the glory of God in his holy martyr. For behold the river, having obeyed the martyr and served his devotion, leaving behind a testimony of duty and obedience, the martyr having now suffered, returned to his nature again. Here, therefore, this most valiant martyr being beheaded received the crown of life which God promiseth to them that love him. But he 205 which there took upon him to do that wicked execution had short joy of his naughty deed,

169. **wroth** angry. 183. **hasting** hastening. 190. **executioned** executed. 196. **delectable** delightful. 198. **required** asked.

for his eyes fell unto the ground with the head of the holy martyr. There also was beheaded the soldier which, being called of God, refused to strike the holy confessor of God, of whom it is open and plain that though he was not christened in the fount, yet he was baptized in the bath of his own blood and so made worthy to enter into the kingdom of heaven.   210

Now the judge, seeing so many strange and heavenly miracles wrought by this holy martyr, gave commandment that the persecution should cease, beginning to honour in the saints of God the constant and patient suffering of death, by the which he thought at first to bring them from the devotion of their faith. St Alban suffered his martyrdom the 20th day of June, nigh unto the city of Verulamium, where, after the Christian church   215 being quietly calmed and settled again, there was a temple builded of a marvellous rich work and worthy for such a martyrdom. In the which place truly even unto this day are sick persons cured and many miracles wrought. There suffered also about that time Aaron and Julius, town-dwellers of the city of the Leicester, and many other, both men and women, in sundry places, which after divers fell and cruel torments sustained in all   220 parts of their bodies, by perfect victory achieved by patience, yielded their souls unto the joys of heaven.

How that Augustine, coming into Britain, first preached unto the King of Kent in the Isle of Thanet, and so being licensed of him came after into Kent to preach

Augustine, being much encouraged with the comfort of St Gregory, returned to preach the word of God with the servants of Christ which were with him, and came into Britain. Ethelbert at that time was King of Kent, a man of great puissance, as the which had   225 enlarged the frontiers of his empire as far as the great flood Humber, by the which the south and north English are divided. At the east end of Kent there is the Isle of Thanet, 600 hides in compass, according to the estimation of English miles, which island is parted from the land by the flood Wantsum, which is of three furlongs breadth and in two places only passable, for both the heads of him runneth into the sea. In that island   230 was Augustine set on land and his fellows, to the number of almost forty persons. They took with them certain Frenchmen to be their interpreters, according as Gregory had commanded, and sending unto the King Ethelbert, they sent him word that they came from Rome, and that they brought him very good tidings, that is, to wit, that such as should follow and obey his doctrine, they should enjoy an everlasting kingdom in heaven   235 with the true and living God. Which, hearing this, commanded that they should tarry in

---

216. temple the Cathedral of St Alban, a holy shrine demolished at the dissolution, 1539, restored in the 19th c. and rededicated in 1993. **220. fell** cruel.

AUGUSTINE (Austin), Benedictine monk, apostle of the English, first archbishop of Canterbury (d. 604). Foxe takes a different view of Augustine as missionary, recalling his proud refusal, 'after the Romish manner', to give place in assembly to British bishops (ed. G. Townsend, S. R. Cattley, 1837–41, rpt. 1965: i. 338). **225. Ethelbert** King of Kent (560–616), issued the first Anglo-Saxon code of laws. **puissance** power. **226. flood** river. **228. hides** A *hide* or *familia* is the amount of land adequate to supply a household; the Isle of Thanet is presently 42 square miles. **229. flood** channel. **three furlongs** as reckoned in 1565, about 600 yards. **232. Frenchmen** These spoke some form of the Franconian dialect, probably similar to the Kentish dialect of the Old English. **236. Which** who (Ethelbert).

the said island, having all things necessary ministered unto them, until they should hear farther of his pleasure. For the bruit of Christian religion had come before unto him, as the which had married a Christian woman of the country of France named Bertha, whom he married with these conditions taken of her parents, that it should be lawful for her to keep unbroken the rites of her faith and religion with her bishop, Liudhard by name, whom they appointed her to assist and help her in matters of her faith. 240

Within few days hereof the king came unto the island and, sitting abroad, he bid Augustine with his fellows to come to common with him. He would not suffer him to come unto him into any house, lest if they were skilful in sorcery they might the rather 245 deceive him and prevail against him. But they came not armed with the force of the devil but endued with the strength of God, carrying before them in place of a banner a cross of silver and the image of our Saviour painted in a table and, singing the litanies, prayed both for themselves and also for them to whom and for whose sake they came thither. And when they, sitting down as the king did bid them, preached unto him the word of life and also to 250 all his household there present, he answered them saying, 'You give us very fair words and promises but yet for that they are strange and unknown unto me. I cannot rashly assent unto them, forsaking that ancient religion which this long both I and my people have observed. But for so much as you are come so far to the intent you might part unto us such knowledge as you take to be right true and good, we will not seek your trouble, but rather 255 with all courtesy receive you and minister you such things as are behoveful for your livelihood. Neither do we let but that you may win unto your profession with your preaching as many as you can.' He allowed them, therefore, a lodging in the city of Canterbury, which was the head city of his dominion and, as he promised, provided them of necessaries, and freely licensed them to preach. It is said that as they approached near the 260 city, having the cross and image of our King and Saviour Jesus Christ carried as their manner was before them, they sang all in one tune this litany following. 'We beseech thee, O Lord, for thy great mercy's sake that thy fury and thine anger may be taken from this city and from thy holy house because we have sinned. *Alleluia*.'

NICHOLAS SANDER

Louvain humanist and polemicist (see CONTROVERSIES), Nicholas Sander (1530–81) depicted the religious changes in England as heretical schism. Sander's *De Origine et Progressu schismatis Anglicani* (Rise and Growth of the Anglican Schism), revised by

238. **bruit** rumour. 239. **Bertha** daughter of Charibert, a Merovingian king of Paris. 243. **abroad** in an open place. 244. **common** converse. 248. **in a table** on a panel. 254. **part** impart. 256. **minister** provide. **behoveful** suitable. 257. **Neither ... that** Nor do we forbid but instead allow that.

Edward Rishton (Rheims, 1585) and later by Robert Persons, became the most popular Catholic account of English history in early modern Europe: translations and adaptations appeared in French, German, Spanish, and Italian. The work inspired a a history by the Dominican Girolamo Pollini, *L'Historia Ecclesiastica della Rivoluzion D'Inghilterra* (1591), and a Latin verse drama by Nicolaus Vernulaeus, *Henry VIII* (1624). Commissioned by Archbishop Whitgift, John Reynolds wrote a refutation, *Anti Sanderus* (1593). Drawing on fact as well as fiction, Sander vilifies Henry VIII, Anne Boleyn, and Elizabeth I (though Rishton apparently compiled this section from Sander's notes), and sanctifies Catherine of Aragon and Queen Mary I. He gives credence to the scandalous gossip about Anne Boleyn being Henry VIII's illegitimate daughter and blithely passes over Mary's many executions for heresy. Still, the history, like the accounts of fellow historian Nicholas Harpsfield, provides a counter-statement to prevailing Protestant histories and myths.

Rise and Growth of the Anglican Schism, 1585

[Catherine of Aragon and Henry VIII]

There was some difference in age between Henry and Catherine and a still greater difference in their lives. She was older than her husband in years, at the utmost five years, but more than a thousand years in character. Catherine used to rise at midnight in order to be present at matins sung by religious. At five o'clock she dressed herself, but as quickly as she could, saying that the only time wasted was the time spent in dressing. She 5 was a member of the Third Order of St Francis and wore the habit thereof under her royal robes. She fasted every Friday and Saturday and on bread and water on the eves of our Lady's feasts. She went to confession every Wednesday and Friday and on Sunday received communion. She said the office of our Lady daily and was present every morning in church for six hours together during the sacred offices. After dinner and in 10 the midst of her maids of honour she read the lives of saints for two hours. That done, she went to church and generally remained there till it was time for supper, which was with her a very scanty meal. She always prayed on her knees without a cushion or anything else between them and the pavement. Can anyone be astonished that so saintly a woman was to be tried in a greater fire of tribulation so that the fragrance of her goodness might be 15 the more scattered over the Christian world?

Meanwhile, Henry was giving the reins to his evil desires and living in sin, sometimes with two, sometimes with three, of the queen's maids of honour, one of whom, Elizabeth Blount, gave birth to a son, whom Henry made Duke of Richmond. The king, indeed,

---

4. matins morning prayers. **6. Third Order** an organization of men and women who remain in society but live by a religious rule. **9. office...Lady** prayers and Scripture readings at fixed hours of the day. **19. Duke of Richmond** Henry Fitzroy (1519–36), the only illegitimate child that Henry acknowledged.

admired the sanctity of his wife but followed evil counsels himself. His daughter Mary   20
was brought up in kingly splendour and made princess of the Britons or the Welsh, a
people by whom the island was first inhabited and who gave it the name of Britain. They
have a language of their own which hardly any Englishman understands.

[Catherine's Trial at Blackfriars, 1529]

Though the judges to please the king would not admit the appeal of Catherine,
nevertheless, because they would not pronounce the sentence of divorce, the king did   25
not think that they had done him any service. Accordingly, standing before the court
himself, he made a public declaration that in these proceedings he was not urged on by
any dislike of the queen but by scruples of conscience and the judgement of most learned
men. Though the cardinal of York was at hand, a legate *a latere*, to whom singly the
power of deciding the question might have been delegated, yet he, to avoid all occasions   30
of harsh judgements, had prevailed upon the Roman pontiff, the sovereign head of the
Church, to appoint judges to try the question, by whose decision, whatever it might be,
he called all men to witness he would abide.

When the king had spoken, the queen insisted on the allowance of her appeal. The
judges refused. Thereupon the queen, who was sitting on the left side of the court, rose   35
from her place and went up to the king, who was sitting under a canopy on the other
side. Falling upon her knees before him, she most humbly prayed him who was at home
in his own kingdom to allow her, a foreigner, to prosecute her appeal in Rome before the
common father of all Christians and also the judge whom the king himself acknowledged. The king rose from his seat and, looking at the queen with the utmost affection,   40
declared that he gave her leave. The people present in court, seeing the faces and the
demeanour of both husband and wife, could not refrain from weeping.

The queen thereupon went out of the court and immediately afterwards was told that
the judges and the king required her presence. 'I will obey my husband,' said the queen,
'but not the judges.' But her lawyers warned her that if she returned into court, her return   45
would be taken as a withdrawal of the appeal and damage her cause. She sent her excuses
to the king and returned to Castle Baynard, from which she had come to the court.
When she was at home, she said to her lawyers, 'Today, for the first time, not to damage
my cause, I disobeyed my lord the king; but the very next time I see him, I will go on my
knees and ask him to forgive my fault.' A woman worthy of a better husband! But it was   50
by persecution of this kind it pleased God to prepare for Catherine the crown of glory
that never fades.

---

20. **Mary** Mary Tudor, later Queen Mary I (*r.* 1553–8). **24 ff.** See Shakespeare's portrait of Catherine in *Henry VIII*, DRAMA. **27. public declaration** Foxe prints the king's oration with the following preface: 'This is certain, that it was not without the singular providence of God (whereby to bring greater things to pass) that the king's conscience herein seemed to be so troubled' (ed. G. Townsend, S. R. Cattley, 1837–41, rpt. 1965: v: 46). **29. legate *a latere*** representative 'from the side' (of the pope).

[Anne Boleyn]

Anne Boleyn was the daughter of Sir Thomas Boleyn's wife. I say of his wife because she could not have been the daughter of Sir Thomas, for she was born during his absence of two years in France on the king's affairs. Henry VIII sent him apparently on an honourable mission in order to conceal his own criminal conduct, but when Thomas Boleyn, on his return at the end of two years, saw that a child had been born in his house, he resolved, eager to punish the sin, to prosecute his wife before the delegates of the archbishop of Canterbury and obtain a separation from her. His wife informs the king, who sends the marquis of Dorset with an order to Thomas Boleyn to refrain from prosecuting his wife, to forgive her, and be reconciled to her.

Sir Thomas Boleyn saw that he must not provoke the king's wrath; nevertheless, he did not yield obedience to his orders before he learned from his wife that it was the king who had tempted her to sin and that the child Anne was the daughter of no other than Henry VIII. His wife then entreated him on her knees to forgive her, promising better behaviour in the future. The marquis of Dorset and other personages in their own and in the king's name made the same request, and then Sir Thomas Boleyn became reconciled to his wife and had Anne brought up as his own child.

But his wife had borne Sir Thomas another daughter before this one named Mary. Upon her the king had cast his eyes when he used to visit her mother, and now after the return of Sir Thomas he had her brought to the court and ruined her. The royal household consisted of men utterly abandoned—gamblers, adulterers, panders, swindlers, false swearers, blasphemers, extortioners, and even heretics. Among these was one distinguished profligate, Sir Francis Bryan, of the blood and race of the Boleyn. This man was once asked by the king to tell him what sort of a sin it was to ruin the mother and then the child. Bryan replied that it was a sin like that of eating a hen first and its chicken afterwards. The king burst forth into loud laughter and said to Bryan, 'Well, you certainly are my vicar of hell.' The man had been long ago called the vicar of hell on account of his notorious impiety; henceforth, he was called also the king's vicar of hell. The king, who had sinned before with the mother and the elder daughter, turned his thoughts now to the other daughter, Anne.

Anne Boleyn was rather tall of stature, with black hair and an oval face of a sallow complexion, as if troubled with jaundice. She had a projecting tooth under the upper lip and on her right hand six fingers. There was a large wen under her chin, and therefore to hide its ugliness she wore a high dress covering her throat. In this she was followed by the ladies of the court, who also wore high dresses, having before been in the habit of leaving

55

Six fingers.

54. she was born Arguments support a birth date of 1501 and 1507, a point of some significance for Sander's story of Henry's affair with her mother, as Henry was 10 years old in 1501 and 16 in 1507. **60. marquis of Dorset** Thomas Grey (d. 1530). **69. Mary** married to William Carey during the period of her affair with the king (the early and mid 1520s); Henry named one of his ships *Mary Boleyn* (see E. W. Ives, *Anne Boleyn*, 1986: 20). **74. Sir Francis Bryan** (1490–1549), gentleman of the privy chamber, later chief justice of Ireland. **84. six fingers...wen** The story of Mary's deformities (a **wen** is a tumour) is improbable, as Mary was certainly attractive to men. George Wyatt, a later source, more plausibly suggests a minor malformation of a fingertip and some facial moles (Ives, ibid. 50–1).

their necks and the upper portion of their persons uncovered. She was handsome to look at, with a pretty mouth, amusing in her ways, playing well on the lute, and was a good dancer. She was the model and the mirror of those who were at court for she was always well dressed and every day made some change in the fashion of her garments. But as to the disposition of her mind, she was full of pride, ambition, envy, and impurity.

At 15 she sinned first with her father's butler and then with his chaplain, and forthwith was sent to France, and placed at the expense of the king under the care of a certain nobleman not far from Brie. Soon afterwards she appeared at the French court, where she was called the English mare because of her shameless behaviour, and then the royal mule, when she became acquainted with the king of France. She embraced the heresy of Luther to make her life and opinions consistent but, nevertheless, did not cease to hear mass with the Catholics, for that was wrung from her by the custom of the king and the necessities of her own ambition.

On her return to England she was taken into the royal household and there easily saw that the king was tired of his wife. She also detected the aims of Wolsey, how much the king was in love with herself, and how quickly he changed in his lawless affections. Not to speak of strangers to her family, she saw how her mother first and then her sister had been discarded by the king. What was she, then, to hope for in the end if she did not take care of herself at first? She made up her mind what to do. The more the king sought her, the more she avoided him, sanctimoniously saying that nobody but her husband should find her alone. Nevertheless, she did not think there was any want of modesty in talking, playing, and even in dancing with the king. In this way she so fed the fires of the king's passion that he became more and more determined to put away Catherine, his wife, and to put a woman of such admirable modesty in her place. The news was carried over into France, and there it became a common report that the king of England was going to marry the mule of the king of France.
[...]

After this nothing more was wanting for the marriage of the king with Anne Boleyn but a public sentence of divorce, and the king had no expectation that the Roman pontiff would ever pronounce it. But he knew for certain that Cranmer, his tool, would shortly pronounce it, and then, lest he should be regarded as having made a person of low condition his wife, on the first day of September [1532] he created Anne Boleyn marchioness of Pembroke.

90. **every day...garments** After studying the size and splendour of Anne's wardrobe, Ives (ibid. 270–1) finds this story credible. **92. sinned first...chaplain** Modern historians have found no evidence to support these claims, or the claim of a subsequent affair with François I. **96. embraced...Luther** Anne much more actively promoted Protestantism than Sander notes: she campaigned for the break with Rome and royal supremacy; she supported Protestant clergy and educational institutions (Ives, ibid. 160 ff., 302–31). **101. Wolsey** Cardinal Thomas Wolsey (1475–1530), Lord Chancellor of England. **112. mule...France** Contrast Foxe's praise of Anne Boleyn's piety and charity and his final judgement: 'For the rare and singular gifts of her mind, so well instructed and given toward God, with such a fervent desire unto the truth and setting forth of sincere religion, joined with like gentleness, modesty, and pity toward all men, there have not many such queens before her borne the crown of England' (ed. G. Townsend, S. R. Cattley, 1837–41, rpt. 1965: v: 60–1, 135). **115. Cranmer** Thomas Cranmer (1489–1556), first Protestant archbishop of Canterbury (1533–56). **118. marchioness** the second rank of peerage (marquis), below a duke and above an earl.

The king, now impatient of further delay, though everything had not yet been duly prepared, determined to marry Anne Boleyn secretly on the fourteenth of the following 120 November. He must marry her for in no other way could he accomplish his will, and the marriage must be secret because he and Catherine had not been separated by any judicial decision. Accordingly, the king sent for Rowland Lee, then a priest, and whom afterwards he made bishop of Lichfield, and bade him say mass according to the Catholic and Roman rite. To him the king declared that at last sentence had been given in his favour in 125 Rome, and that it was lawful for him to take another wife. Lee, considering that it was not usual for kings to tell a lie, was at first silent; but immediately afterwards his conscience smote him and he said to the king, 'Your Majesty, I hope, has the pontifical brief.' The king made a sign to that effect, and the priest turned to the altar. Again the priest, being in doubt and afraid that he might be doing something that was wrong, said 130 to the king: 'The sacred canons require and it is of the utmost concern to us that the papal letters be read and published.' Thereupon the king asserted that he really had the papal brief but that it was in a very secret place, where he only could find it; it was not seemly that he should then go for it by himself for it was not yet daylight. Rowland Lee made no further resistance and, having said mass, gave Henry a second wife, the first 135 being not only still alive but not even divorced from him by any decision pronounced in any ecclesiastical court or anything of the kind whatsoever.

[Queen Mary I, 1553–8]

After a schism which lasted twenty years God gave the victory in a marvellous way to Mary, the Catholic princess, over almost all the nobles of the realm, and that without shedding one drop of blood. It was a manifest miracle wrought before all the world in 140 favour of the Catholic faith.

Mary, then, the daughter of Catherine, entered in triumph the city and Tower of London and at once restored to freedom and to their former rank, Edmund, bishop of London, Stephen, bishop of Winchester, Cuthbert, bishop of Durham, all the other Catholics who were in prison for the profession of the faith, together with Thomas, duke 145 of Norfolk, and William, earl of Devon. She rejected the title of the profane ecclesiastical supremacy and resolved to restore the ancient rights and reverence due to the Apostolic See, which she had always honoured even at the risk of her life in the days of her father and brother, and sent for Cardinal Pole.

She married Philip, son of the emperor Charles V. There were very grave reasons in 150 favour of that marriage, but the chief was this: the prince would be a help to her in bringing the kingdom back again to the faith and obedience of the Church.

119–37. The wedding probably took place in January 1533 and was, as Sander reports, a secret ceremony with few witnesses. Some sources identify the priest as George Brown. Ives argues that Sander's story of Henry's bullying dissimulation regarding the papal brief 'has a ring of truth about it' (211). **143–4. Edmund...Cuthbert** Edmund Bonner, Stephen Gardiner, Cuthbert Tunstall. **149. Cardinal Pole** (1500–58), scholar and theologian who oversaw the reclamation of England to Catholicism. **150. Philip** This future king of Spain (Philip II) married Queen Mary I of England on 25 July 1554.

Wyatt made a sedition in Kent for the purpose of thwarting the marriage and the reconciliation of the kingdom by renouncing heresy, but the queen overcame him not so much by the valour of her troops as by her own admirable faith.   155

The duke of Suffolk renewed the war, was taken prisoner and beheaded. The queen sent succours to her husband, who was laying siege to Saint-Quentin, and thereby lost Calais through the negligence or the treachery of her own subjects.

Cranmer, archbishop of Canterbury, who had pronounced sentence of divorce against her mother against all justice, was found guilty of high treason; the sentence was   160 confirmed in Parliament and by his own confession. In the hope of saving his life he pretended to be a Catholic and signed his recantations seventeen times with his own hand. In the end his hypocrisy was discovered, and certain bishops, having degraded him from all ecclesiastical rank, delivered him up to the secular arm, when he was burnt in Oxford by order of the queen.   165

The devotion, prudence, and firmness shown by the queen in the restoration of the Catholic religion throughout all her dominions ought not, I think, to be forgotten. They are matters that redound to the everlasting honour of that most saintly woman and to the shame and punishment of a sinful and unhappy people that afterwards returned so readily to its vomit.   170

[Queen Elizabeth I, 1558–85]

For a long time she retained the organs, the ecclesiastical chants, the crucifix, copes, candles, and principally for this reason, that the clergy in these garments might come forth in procession to receive her whenever either for business or pleasure she made her public entry into any city, as was her custom often to do. For the same reason too the bells were spared, that they might be rung whenever in her progress she passed by a church,   175 but principally on her birthday and on the day of her coronation, which days are kept with more solemnity throughout the kingdom than the festivals of Christ and of the saints. Indeed the Protestants were compelled by law to keep in some way or other almost all the ancient holy days of the Church, but they have shown their spite more especially against the feast of Corpus Christi, the Assumption, Nativity, and Conception of our   180 Lady, which they have utterly suppressed. And to show the greater contempt for our Blessed Lady, they keep the birthday of Queen Elizabeth in the most solemn way on the seventh day of September, which is the eve of the feast of the Mother of God, whose

153. **Wyatt** Thomas Wyatt (1521–54), son of the poet, marched on London early in 1554, surrendered, suffered trial, and was executed. 156. **duke of Suffolk** Henry Grey (c.1515–54). 157. **Saint-Quentin** town in northern France which Philip besieged in 1557. 158. **Calais** The Duc de Guise won Calais back for France in 1558, a humiliating defeat for the English. 159–65. Compare Sander's account of Cranmer's hypocrisy with Foxe's narration of his heroic end: 'His body did so abide the burning of the flame with such constancy and steadfastness, that standing always in one place without moving his body, he seemed to move no more than the stake to which he was bound; his eyes were lifted up into heaven, and oftentimes he repeated "his unworthy right hand" [which signed recantations], so long as his voice would suffer him; and using often the words of Stephen, "Lord Jesus, receive my spirit", in the greatness of the flame he gave up the ghost' (ed. G. Townsend, S. R. Cattley, 1837–41, rpt. 1965: viii: 90). For a balanced modern review see D. MacCullough, *Thomas Cranmer*, 1996: 587–605. 164. **secular arm** civil authorities, who levied the penalty for heresy. 166. **firmness** Sander makes no mention of the 300 people Mary executed for heresy. 171. **copes** vestments.

nativity they mark in their calendar in small and black letters, while that of Elizabeth
is marked in letters both large and red. And, what is hardly credible, in the Church of   185
St Paul, the chief church of London—whether elsewhere or not is more than I can tell—
the praises of Elizabeth are said to be sung at the end of the public prayers as the antiphon
of our Lady was sung in former days.

The Protestants are forced also somehow or other even now to keep the fast formerly
observed, though they do it very much against their will, for they complain loudly that   190
the ordering of matters of this sort is contrary to Scripture and the liberty of the gospel.
But the queen for the relief of their consciences herein makes a proclamation at the
beginning of Lent every year that the fast is ordered to be kept not for the sake of religion,
penance, or devotion, but simply for the good of the state, in order by the greater
consumption of fish to furnish the fishermen, a large class of men in the island, with a   195
livelihood, and to have during the rest of the year a more abundant supply of fleshmeat,
and in particular for the necessary provisioning of the fleet.

Not deeming the abstinence of Friday and Saturday to be a sufficient support of the
navy, the queen instituted a fast to be kept every Wednesday, now commonly known as
Cecil's fast, because it is regarded as his invention. Though the people who despise these   200
public fasts are liable to heavy fines, very few observe them, and certainly not the bishops
and the rest of the clergy who are very much ashamed to find themselves under the law of
fasting. But the queen herself easily grants a dispensation in writing upon cause assigned
to the lords, and others, and the archbishop of Canterbury also on the payment of fees.

In short, the queen lays down for her clergy a rule of life, outside of which they dare   205
not move, not only in those things which Protestants call indifferent, but in all matters of
faith, discipline, and doctrine in virtue of that supreme spiritual power with which she is
invested. She suspends her bishops when she pleases, she grants a licence to preach either
to those who are ordained according to her rite or to simple laymen, and in the same way
at her pleasure reduces whom she will to silence. To show her authority in these things   210
she occasionally from her closet addresses her preacher and interrupts him in the presence
of a large congregation in some such way as this: 'Master Doctor, you are wandering from
the text and talking nonsense; return to your subject.'

This, then, is the way in which religion is administered in England at this time. I will
now say nothing—for it must be reserved for another work and another occasion—of   215
civil affairs and the like, nor of the queen's suitors, foreign and domestic, whom she
encouraged, and who in their turn were masters in court and council; nothing of the
many noble personages—English, Scotch, Austrian, Swede, and French—whom she from
the very beginning of her reign to this day deluded, nor how both Houses of Parliament,
who often begged her for the sake of the succession and the safety of the realm to choose a   220
husband either among her own subjects or among strangers, were either satisfied or

187. **antiphon** responsorial prayer. 200. **Cecil's fast** named for William Cecil, 1st Baron Burlegh (1520–98),
Elizabeth's principal adviser. 203. **cause assigned** manufactured reason. 211. **closet** room in the palace for household
devotions.

mocked by her assertion that she was resolved to live and die a virgin; nor will I speak of the great scandal which she gave not only to Catholics but to the people of her own sect by this pretence of a single life, which was the ruin of the state, and by her ecclesiastical supremacy, which was the ruin of the Church.

But there is one thing, and it belongs in a special manner to the subject of my book, which ought not to be passed over in silence. The queen and her politicians understood at once as soon as their sect and religion had been set up that many of her subjects would be very much disturbed by the changes wrought in Church and state, that she would find a stern judge in the pope, and that the emperor and the most powerful Christian kings would withdraw from her. Then, being thus severed in faith and communion from the whole world, she would not be long safe against her own subjects or her neighbours. There was, therefore, no security for her but in inflicting a like calamity as soon as possible upon the neighbouring countries, France and Scotland and Flanders, that all the Catholic sovereigns, being fully occupied with their own affairs, might have no time to attend to those of others.

Accordingly, all the treaties between England and the great monarchs of Christendom were at once either openly violated or observed only in appearance; those of recent date, as well as the older treaties, were dealt with in the same way. Then, to the unutterable dishonour of England and to their everlasting shame, the queen and her councillors made a league with those who were in rebellion against all those sovereigns, with the men who were traitors to their country and plagues of the world. In Scotland they are the confederates of James the Bastard, Morton, and others against Queen Mary; in France they are leagued together with the admiral, and men of the same kind, most detestable tyrants, against the most Christian kings, three brothers in succession; in Flanders they ally themselves against the most mighty and just sovereign, Philip, with the scourge of God, the reprobate prince of Orange. In a word, they send troops into their countries, lay waste their borders, take their cities, plunder their treasuries; they send out pirates, who commit grievous depredations, and in every country urge the people into rebellion. By means of their barbarous religion, spreading like a pestilence, they have brought their neighbours the Scots to ruin, and their queen into that most miserable condition, utterly undeserved, in which we see her at this moment. In France they have been poison to unnumbered souls and brought kings still in their youth into extreme peril. Lastly, they have corrupted almost the whole of Belgium. They have made themselves the accomplices, the leaders, and the protectors of the seditious heretics in every nation to the end

225

230

235

240

245

250

255

234. **France . . . Flanders** Elizabeth gave some support to the Huguenots (French Calvinists), and to the Protestants in Scotland and Flanders (i.e. Holland and Belgium). 243. **James . . . Morton** James Stuart, earl of Moray (1531–70), illegitimate son of James V, and a leader of Protestants; James Douglas, earl of Morton (1516–81), Scottish noble instrumental in the overthrow of Mary, Queen of Scots. 244. **admiral** Gaspar de Coligny (1519–72), leader of Huguenots, killed in the St Bartholomew's Day massacre (1572). 245. **three brothers** Catholic French kings, François II (*r.* 1559–60), Charles IX (*r.* 1560–74), Henri III (*r.* 1574–89). 247. **prince of Orange** William of Orange (1533–84), leader of Protestant resistance against Spain in the Low Countries. 248. **pirates** Francis Drake (*c.*1540–96) and John Hawkins (1532–95), for example, slave-traders who preyed on Spanish merchant ships. 251. **queen** Mary, Queen of Scots, imprisoned for nearly two decades, executed in 1587.

that the disorder raging throughout Christendom might be made still greater. All this they did in order that, through the misfortunes of other sovereigns and other countries, they might themselves live in peace at home and by the scattering far and wide of the poison of their heretical corruption secure to themselves a longer continuance in their sect.

260

Bartolomé de Las Casas

Early in his life the Dominican priest, Bartolomé de Las Casas (1474–1566), received land and Indian slaves for participating in the conquest of Cuba. In 1514 he experienced the radical change of heart that initiated his life's work as an advocate for native peoples in present-day Mexico, Central and South America, and the Caribbean. Las Casas worked as a reformer and attorney, and as a writer reported the massacres perpetrated by the Spanish conquerors. His *Brevísima Relación de la Destrucción de las Indias* (1552) achieved translation into many European languages, becoming known in English as *The Spanish Colony* (1583) and *The Tears of the Indians* (1656).

Las Casas writes in the best tradition of the Roman Church that grants dignity to every human being as an image of Christ. He draws upon Pope Paul III's *Sublimis Deus* (1537), which affirmed the essential humanity of the natives, prohibited slavery, and encouraged conversion by the example of holy living. Unfortunately, other Catholic traditions were operative in Spain, some descending from Pope Alexander VI's *Inter caetera* (1493), which granted the settlement and conversion of the new world to the kingdom of Castile (see DOCUMENTS). Though *Inter caetera* calls for missionary work and conversion, later generations appropriated it to justify exploitation and murder. Modern historians have corrected some exaggerations in Las Casas's account, but it endures as an impassioned Catholic protest against the unjust exercise of power and as an affirmation of the rights and humanity of native peoples.

The Spanish Colony, 1583

God created all these innumerable multitudes in every sort,[1] very simple, without subtlety or craft, without malice, very obedient, and very faithful to their natural liege lords and to the Spaniards whom they serve, very humble, very patient, very desirous of peacemaking

---

1. **sort** kind.

and peaceful, without brawls and strugglings, without quarrels, without strife, without
rancour or hatred, by no means desirous of revengement.   5

They are also people very gentle and very tender and of an easy complexion, and which
can sustain no travail, and do die very soon of any disease whatsoever, in such sort as the
very children of princes and noblemen brought up amongst us in all commodities, ease,
and delicateness are not more soft than those of that country, yea, although they be the
children of labourers. They are also very poor folk, which possess little, neither yet do so   10
much as desire to have much worldly goods, and therefore neither are they proud,
ambitious, nor covetous. Their diet is such (as it seemeth) that of the holy Fathers in the
desert hath not been more scarce, nor more straight, nor less dainty, nor less sumptuous.
Their apparelling is commonly to go naked, all save their shamefast parts alone covered.
And when they be clothed, at the most it is but of a mantle of bombast of an ell and a half   15
or a two ells of linen square. Their lodging is upon a mat and those which have the best
sleep as it were upon a net fastened at the four corners, which they call in the language of
the Isle of Hispaniola, *hamasas*. They have their understanding very pure and quick,
being teachable and capable of all good learning, very apt to receive our holy Catholic
faith and to be instructed in good and virtuous manners, having less encumbrances and   20
disturbances to the attaining thereunto than all the folk of the world besides, and are so
inflamed, ardent, and importune to know and understand the matters of the faith after
they have but begun once to taste them, as likewise the exercise of the sacraments of the
Church and the divine service, that, in truth, the religious men have need of a singular
patience to support them. And to make an end, I have heard many Spaniards many times   25
hold this as assured and that which they could not deny, concerning the good nature
which they saw in them. Undoubtedly these folks should be the happiest in the world if
only they knew God.

Upon these lambs so meek, so qualified and endowed of their Maker and Creator as
hath been said, entered the Spanish, incontinent as they knew them as wolves, as lions,   30
and as tigers most cruel of long time famished, and have not done in those quarters these
forty years be past neither yet do at this present aught else save tear them in pieces, kill
them, martyr them, afflict them, torment them, and destroy them by strange sorts of
cruelties never neither seen, nor read, nor heard of the like (of the which some shall be set
down hereafter), so far forth that of above three millions of souls that were in the Isle of   35
Hispaniola and that we have seen, there are not now two hundred natives of the country.
The Isle of Cuba, the which is in length as far as from Valladolid until Rome, is at this
day, as it were, all waste. St John's Isle and that of Jamaica, both of them very great, very
fertile, and very fair, are desolate. Likewise the isles of Lucayos, near to the Isle of
Hispaniola and of the north side unto that of Cuba, in number being above threescore   40

8. **commodities** conveniences. 12. **that of** that the diet of. 14. **shamefast** shameful. 15. **bombast** cotton or cotton-wool.
ell measure equal to 45 inches. 18. **Hispaniola** 'Little Spain', i.e. present-day island that comprises the Republic of Haiti
and the Dominican Republic. 22. **importune** eager. 29. **so qualified** possessed of such qualities. 30. **incontinent**
unrestrained. 38. **St John's Isle** Puerto Rico, which used to go by the name of its principal city, San Juan. 39. **Lucayos**
part of the present-day Bahamas.

islands, together with those which they call the isles of Gigantes, one with another, great
and little, whereof the very worst is fertiler than the king's garden at Seville, and the
country the healthsomest in the world. There were in these same isles more than five
hundred thousand souls and at this day there is not one only creature. For they have been
all of them slain after that they had drawn them out from thence to labour in their   45
minerals in the Isle of Hispaniola, where there were no more left of the inborn natives of
that island. A ship riding for the space of three years betwixt all these islands to the end,
after the inning of this kind of vintage, to glean and cull the remainder of these folk (for
there was a good Christian moved with pity and compassion to convert and win unto
Christ such as might be found), there were not found but eleven persons which I saw.   50
Other isles more than thirty near to the isle of St John have likewise been dispeopled and
marred. All these isles contain above two thousand leagues of land and are all dispeopled
and laid waste.

Of the Isle of Hispaniola

In the Isle Hispaniola, which was the first, as we have said, where the Spaniards arrived,
began the great slaughters and spoils of people. The Spaniards, having begun to take their   55
wives and children of the Indies for to serve their turn and to use them ill, and having
begun to eat their victuals, gotten by their sweat and travail, not contenting themselves
with that which the Indians gave them of their own good will, every one after their
ability, the which is algates very small, forasmuch as they are accustomed to have no more
store than they have ordinarily need of, and that such as they get with little travail. And   60
that which might suffice for three households, reckoning ten persons for each household
for a month's space, one Spaniard would eat and destroy in a day.

　　Now after sundry other forces, violences, and torments which they wrought against
them, the Indians began to perceive that those were not men descended from heaven.
Some of them, therefore, hid their victuals; others hid their wives and children. Some   65
others fled into the mountains to separate themselves afar off from a nation of so hard-
natured and ghastly conversation. The Spaniards buffeted them with their fists and
bastonades, pressing also to lay hands upon the lords of the towns. And these cases
ended in so great an hazard and desperateness that a Spanish captain durst adventure to
ravish forcibly the wife of the greatest king and lord of this isle. Since which time the   70
Indians began to search means to cast the Spaniards out of their lands, and set themselves
in arms, but what kind of arms very feeble and weak to withstand or resist and of less
defence (wherefore all their wars are no more wars than the playings of children when as
they play at *Jogo di Canne* or *Reeds*). The Spaniards with their horses, their spears, and
lances began to commit murders and strange cruelties. They entered into towns,   75
boroughs, and villages, sparing neither children nor old men, neither women with
child, neither them that lay in, but that they ripped their bellies and cut them in pieces,

---

41. Gigantes part of the present-day Bahamas. **48. inning** gathering, harvesting. **49. good Christian** Pedro de Ysla, a
trader. **59. algates** always. **67. conversation** society. **68. bastonades** cudgels. **74. *Jogo* . . . *Reeds*** stick-fighting games.

as if they had been opening of lambs shut up in their fold. They laid wagers with such as with one thrust of a sword would paunch or bowel a man in the middest, or with one blow of a sword would most readily and most deliverly cut off his head, or that would 80 best pierce his entrails at one stroke. They took the little souls by the heels, ramping them from the mothers' dugs, and crushed their heads against the cliffs. Others they cast into the rivers, laughing and mocking, and when they tumbled into the water they said, 'Now shift for thyself such-a-one's corpse!' They put others, together with their mothers and all that they met, to the edge of the sword. They made certain gibbets long and low in such 85 sort that the feet of the hanged one touched in a manner the ground, every one enough for thirteen in the honour and worship of our Saviour and his twelve apostles (as they used to speak), and setting to fire, burned them all quick that were fastened. Unto all others whom they used to take and reserve alive, cutting off their two hands as near as might be, and so letting them hang, they said, 'Get you with these letters to carry tidings 90 to those which are fled by the mountains!' They murdered commonly the lords and nobility on this fashion: they made certain grates of perches laid on pickforks and made a little fire underneath to the intent that by little and little, yelling and despairing in these torments, they might give up the ghost.

One time I saw four or five of the principal lords roasted and broiled upon these 95 gridirons. Also I think that there were two or three of these gridirons, garnished with the like furniture, and for that they cried out piteously, which thing troubled the captain that he could not then sleep. He commanded to strangle them. The sergeant, which was worse than the hangman that burned them (I know his name and friends in Seville), would not have them strangled but himself putting bullets in their mouths to the end 100 that they should not cry, put to the fire until they were softly roasted after his desire. I have seen all the aforesaid things and others infinite. And forasmuch as all the people which could flee hid themselves in the mountains and, mounted on the tops of them, fled from the men so without all manhood, empty of all pity, behaving them as savage beasts, the slaughterers and deadly enemies of mankind. 105

[...]

After this I will rehearse another devilish part, the which I cannot tell whether it be less cruel and devoid of manhood than are those of savage beasts; that is, that the Spanish which are in the Indies do keep certain dogs most raging, taught and trained wholly to the purpose to kill and rend in pieces the Indians. That let all those that are true Christians, yea, and also those which are not so behold if ever there were the like thing 110 in the whole world: that is, to feed those dogs, they lead about with them wheresoever they go a great number of Indians in chains as if they were hogs and kill them, making a shambles of man's flesh. And the one of them will say to another, 'Lend me a quarter of

79. **paunch or bowel** cut open and eviscerate. 80. **deliverly** nimbly. 81. **ramping** snatching. 82. **dugs** breasts. 84. **shift for** take care of. 84. **such-a-one** The name of the victim would have been supplied. 85. **gibbets** gallows, i.e. upright structures for hanging people. 88. **quick** alive. 92. **perches...pickforks** rods laid on forked sticks to form a grid for the victims. 96. **gridirons** grills. 110. **behold** consider.

a villain to give my dogs some meat until I kill one next', altogether as if one should borrow a quarter of an hog or mutton. There be others which go forth a-hunting in the morning with their curs, the which being returned to eat, if another ask him, 'How have ye sped today?', they answer, 'Very well, for I have killed with my dogs today fifteen or twenty *viliacoes*.' All these diabolical doings with others like have been proved in the suits of law that the tyrants have had, one of them against another. Is there any case more ugly or unnatural?

I will here now deport me of this discourse until such time that there come other news of things in ungraciousness more notorious and remarkable (if it so be that there can be any more grievous) or until such time as we may return thither to behold them ourselves anew, as we behold them for the space of forty-two years continually with mine own eyes. Protesting in a good conscience before God that I do believe and I hold it for certain that the damages and losses are so great with the destructions and overthrows of cities, massacres, and murders, with the cruelties, horrible and ugly, with the ravins, iniquities, and robberies, all the which things have been executed amongst those people, and are yet daily committed in those quarters, that in all the things which I have spoken and deciphered as I was able the nearest to the truth, I have not said one of a thousand of that which hath been done and is daily a-doing at this present, be it that you consider the quality or be it that you consider the quantity.

And to the end that all Christians have the greater compassion of those poor innocents, and that they complain with me the more their perdition and destruction, and that they detest the greediness, loftiness, and fellness of the Spanish, that all do hold it for a most undoubted verity with all that hath been abovesaid that sithence the first discovery of the Indies until now, the Indians never did harm unto the Spanish in any place wheresoever until such time that they first received wrongs and injuries, being robbed and betrayed, but indeed did repute them to be immortal, supposing them to be descended from heaven, and they received them for such until such time as that they gave it forth manifestly to be known by their doings what they were and whereto they tended.

I will adjoin hereunto this that from the beginning unto this hour the Spaniards have had no more care to procure that unto those people should be preached the faith of Jesus Christ than as if they had been cur dogs or other beasts. But in lieu thereof, which is much worse, they have forbidden by express means the religious men to do it for because that that seemed unto them an hindrance likely to be to the getting of their gold and these riches which their avarice foreglutted in. And at this day there is no more knowledge of God throughout the Indies, to wit, whether he be of timber, of the air or the earth, than there was an hundred years ago, excepting New Spain, whither the religious men have gone, which is but a little corner of the Indies. And so are they perished and do perish all without faith and without sacraments.

---

118. *viliacoes* villains. 121. **deport me of** cease from. 127. **ravins** seizures. 130. **deciphered** revealed. 135. **fellness** cruelty. 136. **sithence** since. 147. **foreglutted** beforehand glutted itself. 149. **New Spain** present-day Mexico.

I, Brother Bartholomew de las Casas or Casans, religious of the order of St Dominic, which by the mercy of God am come into this court of Spain, to sue that the hell might be withdrawn from the Indies and that these innumerable souls, redeemed by the blood of Jesus Christ, should not perish forevermore without remedy, but that they might know   155
their Creator and be saved; also for the care and compassion that I have of my country, which is Castile, to the end that God destroy it not for the great sins thereof, committed against the faith and his honour and against our neighbours, for certain men's sakes, notably zealous of the glory of God, touched with compassion of the afflictions and calamities of others, followers of this court. Howbeit that I was purposed to do it, but   160
I could not so soon have done it because of my continual occupations, I achieved this treatise and summary at Valencia, the eighth of December, 1542, the force being mounted to the highest type of extremity, and all the violences, tyrannies, desolations, anguishes, and calamities abovesaid spread over all the Indies, where there are any Spaniards, although they be more cruel in one part than they be in another, and more savage and   165
more abominable.

Robert Persons

Eloquent, zealous, and prolific, Robert Persons (1546–1610) became a Jesuit in 1575, established seminaries abroad, and served as rector of the English College in Rome. Emerging as the leader of the English Mission (1579–81), he preached, administered sacraments, and set up a press which printed responses to attacks as well as Catholic offensives. Persons distinguished himself as a polemicist and as a devotional writer in works such as *Certain Reasons why Catholics Refuse to go to Church* (1580, see Langdale, CONTROVERSIES); the Ignatian *Book of the Christian Exercise* (1582, reprinted and revised forty times before 1640); and *A Treatise of Three Conversions* (1603–4), excerpted below, which presents a Catholic national history of England against the *Acts and Monuments* of John Foxe. Like William Allen, Persons advocated armed intervention in England and thus aroused the mistrust and hostility of most English Catholics.

The *Treatise* extends Stapleton's work on Augustine's conversion of England by documenting the two earlier conversions as well. Persons argues that the Roman Church has always been continuous and visible in England and elsewhere, despite repeated assaults by old heretics such as Wyclif or new ones such as Luther. He attacks Foxe's conception of martyrdom and new calendar of saints under eight separate headings, asserting that Foxe

153. **court of Spain** In 1542 Las Casas appeared in the court of Spain as an advocate for the Indians and read part of this work; the court passed the *Leges Nuevas* (New Laws) which forbade Indian slavery and sought to end the system of economic and political exploitation. 157. **Castile** region of central Spain. 160. **Howbeit that** although.

substitutes common thieves and traitors, some judged heretical by Protestants themselves, for figures of recognized holiness. Persons defends the horrific Marian executions for heresy. Despite his moral myopia in this matter, Persons provides a comprehensive Catholic response to regnant Protestant ideology and history.

A Treatise of Three Conversions of England, 1603–4

[Britain's three Roman conversions]

The purpose of this first part, gentle reader, is to declare by evident demonstration, both of histories, reasons, antiquities, and succession of times, and by confession and other testimonies of the adversaries themselves, that this our Isle of Britain and the people thereof, the Britons, Saxons, and English, have at three several times received Christian faith from Rome and by Romish preachers.   5

First under the apostles in the first age after Christ, and then under Pope Eleutherius in the second age, and thirdly under Pope Gregory in the beginning of the sixth age, and that this faith and religion was no other than the Roman Catholic faith, generally received over all Christendom in those days, and that it was one and the selfsame faith at all these three times, and that the same was continued and professed afterward in   10
England publicly for almost fourteen hundred years together, to wit, from the apostles' days unto the reign of King Henry the Eighth, under divers nations, states, governments, and variety of times by Britons, Saxons, Danes, Normans, and English, and that the selfsame faith continueth at this day in the Church of Rome and Christian Catholic world abroad without change or alteration of any one substantial article or point of   15
belief. And that all cavils and calumniations of heretics and sectaries in this behalf are vain and foolish and most manifestly here confuted. And, finally, a most clear, easy, evident, and infallible deduction visible to the eye and understanding of every mean intelligent reader is set down and brought from hand to hand without interruption from the first conversions of our realm unto this day, and this so perspicuously as no man that   20
will not wilfully shut his eyes can but see and behold the same, as by the chapters following, God willing, more particularly shall appear.

[Foxe's false history and false saints]

So seemed it not amiss for divers other considerations to offer this second book, concerning the examen of Foxe his new *Ecclesiastical Calendar* (being a part of the former argument and impugning the later part of his said *Acts*) unto the moderate and discreet   25

4. Britons . . . English Britons originally inhabited the south part of England; the Saxons were a Germanic tribe that settled in England in the 5th and 6th centuries; the English were the other inhabitants, composed of Angles, Jutes, Celtic, and Scandinavian tribes. several separate. 6. age century. Pope Eleutherius (r. 174–89). 7. Pope Gregory (r. 590–604); see Bede's account above. 16. sectaries members of sects. 18. mean average. 24. examen examination. 24–5. former argument i.e. that regarding the historical rise of Protestantism.

Protestant, thereby to let him see and consider how great a prejudice and dishonour both his cause and himself hath received by this work of Foxe pretended for his praise.

For first, touching the cause itself, whereas Foxe had promised in the title and forefront of his work and in the prefaces thereof to set down and prosecute the pedigree of his Protestant Church (different forsooth, as he will have it, from the Roman Chapel) and to deduce the same from her very offspring and beginning unto our days, first, he performeth nothing thereof at all for the space of above twelve hundred years together next after Christ but rather the quite contrary, laying down before his readers' eyes for all that space nothing else but the progress and gests of the said Roman Church or Chapel, spread over the world, without once naming any other visible church, chapel, congregation, or cottage of men, women, or children (out of the said Roman Church) to whom he durst betake himself, or to join fellowship in those days, or so much as to give to them the title or name of a Christian church, company, or society. So as during all these former ages by Foxe his own confession either the Protestants had no church or chapel at all (which were a pitiful matter and great disgrace indeed) or else it was the Roman Church, which perhaps to some would seem a greater disgrace. Of which point, for that I have treated largely in both parts of my former book or tome, I will say nothing here but refer thereunto the studious reader for his fuller information. And this shall suffice for the first point, concerning the disgrace which the common cause of Protestants receiveth from the former part of Foxe his *Acts and Monuments*, whereby it is convinced that for so many hundred years they had no church or chapel at all.

The second point is of personal disgrace received principally from the later part of the said *Acts and Monuments*, wherein John Foxe endeavoureth to frame unto his Protestants a visible new church, but of such people as their communion and association cannot be but most prejudicial and dishonourable unto them. For better understanding whereof and for more clear laying open this important point, it is to be considered that almighty God, having created man a sociable creature, hath placed the greatest part of his good or evil both for this life and the next in a certain communion, participation, society, fellowship, and communication with others.

[…]

And as this Communion of Saints and of good men is of so great estimation, honour, and benefit, so on the contrary side is the communion and participation with naughty people of singular hurt, dishonour, and danger to the participants. It was objected (as you know) by Isaiah the prophet to some men, that they were 'socii furum' (Isa. 1: 23, companions of thieves), and to others by another prophet, 'quod cum adulteris portionem suam ponerent' (Ps. 49: 18, that they did put their portion with adulterers and wicked men), which was a most grievous reproach. And, finally, when the Holy Scripture

27. **pretended** offered. 29. **prosecute** reveal in detail. 31. **deduce** trace. **offspring** origin. 34. **gests** deeds. 45. **convinced** proven. 55. **Communion of Saints** An article of the Apostle's Creed, the Communion of Saints is the spiritual union of the faithful on earth, the souls in purgatory, and the saints in heaven in the one mystical body of Christ. Members of this Communion confer upon each other spiritual benefits.

would lay before us the singular inconveniences, hurts, and calamities whereunto 'anima nequam' (a naughty soul and wicked spirit), by little and little draweth a man, after divers other evil effects recounted it addeth for the last and worst of all, 'quod deducet in sortem impiorum' Ecclus. 6: 4, that it will bring a man into the lot and portion of the wicked. 65 Which point, seemeth, may be rightly verified of Foxe in this place, who, being broken by heresy from the foresaid Communion of Saints in the Catholic Church and from their association and participation, hath brought himself and his Protestants that follow him into the communion and society of a most impious and infamous company of condemned heretics and wicked malefactors, some condemned for lewd life, conspiracies, 70 rebellion, and murder, some for atrocious demeanour in hurting and wounding quiet and innocent men, some for witchcraft, sorcery, and conjuring, even to the destroying of their prince's person, some for theft and manifest robberies, or rather, sacrilege, some for heresies confessed and detested by the Protestants themselves, some finally for open and flat denying of Christ himself, and other such like opprobrious enormities. 75

Eight Several Observations and Considerations
[concerning Foxe's saints and calendar]

[1.] But yet a far greater question it is, why the very first fathers and founders of Sacramentary religion itself are left out of this calendar, to wit Carlstadt, Oecolampadius, Zwingli, and Calvin, though for the first three that were immediate scholars of Luther and first brake from him to begin the Sacramentary sect, his severe sentence and condemnation of them, which we have set down before in the story of his life at large, 80 together with his detestation of their spirit (he being a saint himself also of this calendar [18 Feb.]) might perhaps detain John Foxe from canonizing them in this place. But of John Calvin some other reason must needs be, which I cannot imagine to be other but the notorious infamy of his life, as also the little liking which the state of England had of him and his actions as well for denying the supremacy ecclesiastical to temporal princes 85 (which is the chief wall of their religion) as also for setting up the dangerous plot of Puritanism, and spreading it from Geneva into England, Scotland, France, and other places, as you may see in the books of *Dangerous Positions, Survey of Disciplinary Doctrine*, and other such treatises written by our English Protestants against the Puritans. Wherein they are so far from making Calvin and Beza saints, as albeit for civility's sake they 90 give them the titles of Master Calvin and Master Beza, yet if you respect the substance of that they write against them, they do make them the most notablest deceivers and

---

77. **Sacramentary religion** Persons's term for the beliefs of those Protestants who, contradicting Luther, denied the real presence of Christ in the Eucharist. 77–8. **Carlstadt . . . Calvin** Andreas **Carlstadt** (1480–1541) was a professor at Wittenburg. John **Oecolampadius** (1482–1531) and Ulrich **Zwingli** (1484–1531) led the Protestants in Switzerland; Jean **Calvin** (1509–64) became a leading theologian and organizer of the movement in Europe. 81. **he** i.e. Luther. 88. *Dangerous . . . Doctrine* two anti-Puritan works, *Dangerous Positions and Proceedings* (1593) and *A Survey of the Pretended Holy Discipline* (1593), written by Richard Bancroft (1544–1610), later bishop of London and archbishop of Canterbury. 90. **Beza** Theodore Beza (1519–1605), author, translator, theologian, Calvin's successor at Geneva. 91. **respect** observe carefully.

cogging companions that ever were, and very knaves indeed, and firebrands of hell under the titles of masters.

[. . .]

[2.] And now as this first consideration hath been of them that have been left out, so may the next be of those that are put in, which is a point of more length than the former if we would prosecute the same. But I will only, as it were, with the finger point towards it and therewith leave it to the readers for their contemplation. It is then to be noted that in the calendar and story thereof are comprised all the heads of factions and sects that have been different from the known Catholic religion and opposite among themselves for these three or four last hundred years, as Waldo of Lyons and his Waldensians, the earl of Tholosa and his Albigensians, John Wyclif of England and his Wycliffians, John Huss of Bohemia and his Hussites, John Zisca of the same nation and his Thaborites, Walter Lollard in Germany and his Lollardians, and in our days Martin Luther and his Lutherans, both sects *molles* and *rigidi*, Ulrich Zwingli and his Zwinglians, John Calvin and his Calvinists, both mingled and puritans, and other the like. All which are allowed and commended by Foxe either in his calendar or history, though they did not a little disagree as well among themselves as with the Catholic Church both in words, actions, manner of life, preachings, and writings, as before hath been showed.

And whereas we that follow Catholic doctrine are so exact for holding union therein as we reject and hold for wicked (according to the Creed of St Athanasius and first Council of Nicaea) whosoever doth not believe inviolably the said Catholic faith wholly and entirely in every point, and do sometimes condemn even to death and burn some for dissenting in one only point of faith (as John Foxe himself hath divers times complained), how can it be that he and his church can gather up and tie together in one union of faith and communion of saints all these different and opposite heads together with their members and followers? Truly, no other way, but only as Sampson tied his foxes together by the tails [Judg. 15: 4 ff.], though their heads and faces were opposite and contrary, one to another, which served him not to plough or sow, plant or till, but only to set afire, waste, and destroy the corn which others had sowed before, which is the only office and peculiar work that these wrangling, opposite, heretical heads do bring forth in the Church of God, to wit, pull down, dig up, destroy, discredit, and disgrace that which

95
100
105
110
115
120

93. **cogging** cheating. 100. **opposite** conflicting. 101–4. **Waldo...Lollardians** Peter **Waldo**, a 12th-c. reformer who advocated poverty and simplicity and became identified with later Protestant movements in France; **Earl of Tholosa** (i.e. Toulouse), here associated with the Albigensian heresy of the 12th and 13th centuries, which believed in equal and opposed principles of good and evil. **John Wyclif** (1330–84) worked on translating the Bible into English and against papal temporal power and the doctrine of transubstantiation. **John Huss** (1370–1415), a Czech, followed Wyclif in advocating reform, predestination, and the primacy of Scripture over Church traditions. **John Zisca**, i.e. John de Trocznow, another Czech, sought the abolition of prayers for the dead, images, fasts, and clerical abuses; his followers called themselves **Thaborites** after the Biblical Mount Thabor in Palestine. **Walter Lollard**, burned in Cologne for heresy (1322), may be connected with the term Lollardians, which may also derive from *lollaert* ('mumbler'), and came to signify those who campaigned against clerical authority, transubstantiation, and Latin Scriptures. 105. *molles* **and** *rigidi* 'soft' and 'hard' varieties of Lutheranism. 106. **mingled and puritans** less and more severe varieties. 111–12. **Athanasius** (296–373) attended the **Council of Nicaea** (325) which formulated the Nicene Creed to combat the heresy of Arianism, denial of the full divinity of Christ. 121. **peculiar** particular.

was sown, planted, and established before them, and thereby to bring all to misdoubt, unbelief, and atheism. And so I leave them to John Foxe to be disposed of.

[3.] The third consideration may be of the different manner of proceeding in the   125
Catholic Church for declaring men's holiness from that which is used by heretics and sectaries. For as we, out of the common sense and reason of all men, do say and affirm that all are not of one holiness or merit of life in this world, so to publish or make declaration thereof after their death appertaineth rather to some public authority, which may ordain more certain and exact enquiry thereof, than to any particular man, who may   130
be carried away either with passion, or deceived by ignorance, or otherwise abused by false information more easily than a public magistrate. Whereupon it is seen that when among Catholics anyone is to be canonized, that is to say, to be declared for a holy man or woman, great and long search is made about the matter first, and many hundred persons examined; many records also are sought out of the life and actions of the person,   135
of his virtues and miracles, and such other points appertaining to sanctity.

And for so much as the public and highest ecclesiastical magistrate, in whose name and authority the examen is made, cannot be presumed to have interest or passion therein, it is evident that the matter must needs pass with far more indifferency, gravity, sincerity, and truth than if it passed upon the word, credit, or assertion of any one particular man,   140
as amongst heretics and sectaries it doth, where every man canonizeth or condemneth according to his own fancy. For that they, having no one general or supreme head acknowledged by all, do fall at division or strife among themselves, one part sanctifying and canonizing such for holy men and women as the other do commonly reject and condemn, as you have heard before in the stories of Luther, Zwingli, and Calvin, and other like. Yea,   145
some one man of a particular sect will presume to canonize sometime some for saints of his sect whom other of the very self-same sect will hold for wicked, as here in Foxe his calendar are many examples: as that of Cowbridge, who denied Christ; that of Collins,   ?
who held up the dog to be adored, and Foxe himself confesseth that he was mad; that of Flower, the apostate monk that wounded the priest at Westminster and said that it was   150
the spirit of God that had moved him thereunto; that of Roger Only, hanged for conjuring, and Eleanor Cobham, condemned for witchcraft; that of Oldcastle, Acton, and other rebels, hanged in St Giles' Fields for conspiring the death of King Henry the Fifth and his brethren; that of the famous ruffian and murderer Zisca; that of the three

139. indifferency impartiality. 148. Cowbridge . . . Collins executed 1538, in Foxe's calendar on 10 October. Persons quotes William Cowbridge's denials of Christ's divinity later (iii: sig. N4–N4ᵛ). Foxe calls Collins 'mad and distract of his perfect wits' (ed. Townsend, Cattley, 1843–9, rpt. 1965; v: 251). 150. Flower executed 1555, in Foxe's calendar on 9 April. Foxe remarks of William Flower, who repeatedly stabbed a priest distributing communion, 'he did not well nor evangelically' (Townsend, Cattley, vii: 69). 151–2. Roger Only . . . Eleanor Cobham executed 1441, in Foxe's calendar on 12 and 13 February. Persons later gives a detailed account of these two plotters against Henry VI (ii: sigs. R6–R8ᵛ). 152–3. Oldcastle . . . rebels Sir John Oldcastle was executed in 1418, Sir Roger Acton and others in 1413; in Foxe's calendar, 6 February, 7–10 January. Catholics such as Nicholas Harpsfield (*Dialogi sex*, 1566) and Persons view Oldcastle as a traitor; Protestants such as Bale and Foxe depict him as a proto-Protestant, condemned for Lollard heresy, 'the most valiant and worthy martyr of Christ' (Foxe in Townsend, Cattley, iii: 320). After condemnation for heresy, Oldcastle did participate in a revolt and plan to assassinate King Henry V. Sir Roger Acton was also condemned for treasonous conspiracy (Persons, ii. sig: N3). 154. Zisca executed 1416, in Foxe's calendar on 5 February. He led an armed revolt against

thieves, King, Debnam, and Marsh, hanged in chains by commandment of King Henry 155
the Eighth for robbing the church of Dovercourt in Kent. All these, I say, and other like
unholy saints, hallowed here and canonized by John Foxe for martyrs and confessors of
his church, I nothing doubt but will not be allowed for such by many of the discreeter
sort of Protestants in England, but rather rejected and thought fitter to be flung to the
dunghill than to be placed in an ecclesiastical calendar. And this is the good agreement 160
that sectaries can have among themselves in these points.

[4.] The fourth consideration may be what persons John Foxe hath put out of his
calendar that were in ours before, and what recompense he hath made for them by
putting in others in their places. For albeit he hath been so courteous as to let stand all the
apostles and some other old saints also, as St Mary Magdalen, St Mark, St Luke, and 165
some few others, yet doth he put out both St Barnabas, their equal, and all the doctors of
the ancient Church, Greek and Latin, with about two hundred martyrs and virgins, as
you may see in our calendar; and in place thereof hath put in such a multitude of
artificers, labourers, shearmen, weavers, cowherds, cobblers, tailors, smiths, and spinsters
as you may see in his calendar, who, as they could not be true martyrs for the reasons 170
before alleged, to wit, for dying for their own disagreeing fancies, so neither confessors,
partly for the same cause, and partly for that their lives were nothing eminent in virtue
above the common sort of men and women, by Foxe his own confession. For what
singular thing doth he commonly recite of any of these his confessors that exceeded the
vulgar sort of Christians? What extraordinary fasting, prayer, almsdeeds, mortification of 175
the flesh doth he allege in any of them? Nay, it is to be noted that scarce any one of them
all, man or woman, is recorded to have observed virginity or continent life! And yet will
not Foxe deny but that these things are great graces and gifts of God, which did shine
both in our Saviour, and his Blessed Mother, and in most of all Christian saints after
them. And yet that none of Foxe his saints should have this gift to contain but that all of 180
them yielded to the passion of the flesh is a very base matter if it be well considered, as it
is well worth the consideration.

But if we pass further yet and consider the rest also of their actions and compare them
with the lives and actions written and delivered unto us by antiquity of ancient saints, we
shall see the comparison so base and ridiculous as any modest Protestant himself would 185
blush to abide the trial. As, for example, he that should read the rare virtues of St Francis
(whose feast is upon the fourth of October), his prayers, his mortifications, his wonderful
miracles recorded by St Bonaventure, a saint also himself, and then shall come to Foxe his
calendar, and find him stricken out and one Catelle, a schoolmistress in France, put in his
place, who will not laugh or bite his lip thereat? And the like you shall find in hundreds 190
besides of no less indignity if you will go over the former calendar, as for example, the

the pope and Emperor Sigismond. **155. King…Marsh** Robert King, Robert Debnam, and Nicholas Marsh, executed
1532, in Foxe's calendar on 7, 8, 9 May. **166. St Barnabas** disciple of Jesus Christ and missionary. **171. confessors** ones who
profess faith. **180. to contain** to be continent. **189. Catelle** part of a dissenting group in Paris (Foxe in Townsend, Cattley,
iv: 396 ff.).

foresaid apostle St Barnabas, being stricken out upon the eleventh of June (for what cause God knoweth), Halliwell and Bowier are put in his place, the first a smith, the other a weaver. And what a change, think you, is this?

[. . .]

[5.] Wherefore the fifth consideration may be that John Foxe hath made the far greater   195
part of all his martyrs and saints in this calendar and throughout his whole volume (to wit, to the number of two hundred and sixty-eight, as before hath been noted) for denying the real presence of Christ's true body and blood in the Sacrament after the words of consecration. And for that they derided, scoffed at, and blasphemed the same, alleging always certain reasons of sense or human judgement against that most high   200
mystery of belief. In which such vain women and those that were most ignorant and unlearned of all others bear away the bell in that kind of contempt and railing, as before you have heard in the examen of all the twelve months. But now these saints of John Foxe, whom he confidently placeth in heaven and assureth us that they are partakers of God's everlasting bliss, 'exalted and enthroned', to use his phrase, 'in his eternal seat of   205
glory', these people, I say, dying for that cause cannot be saved except all the rest that held and defended the contrary be rejected and damned, who are first of all the holy Fathers, according as you heard confirmed before by Doctor Philip Melanchthon, a saint of this calendar [30 December], who gathered out their sayings and sentences about this article into a particular volume and affirmeth not only that all the said ancient Fathers believed   210
and taught the real presence of the very body of Christ in the Sacrament, but that himself would be content to die in defence of that belief against the Sacramentaries.

[. . .]

[6.] The sixth consideration may be how that all this notwithstanding, every one of John Foxe his saints (but especially those of the Zwinglian sect) did brag exceedingly of their peculiar spirit, of their election, predestination, and assurance they had thereof by   215
the inward testimony of the said spirit. Yea, many of them did insult and vaunt over their bishops and pastors and other ordinary judges for that they durst not assure themselves as these men did that they had the true spirit of God in them. As you have seen by many examples before, especially of Woodman the ironmaker, Allerton the tailor, John Fortune the smith, John Maundrell the cowherd, and many other, both men and women but   220
especially women, who, the less knowledge they had, the more obstinately did they rest themselves upon this persuasion of their inward spirit, which is the last refuge of any heretic whatsoever. For when once he condemneth the external authority of the visible Church and retireth himself to only Scriptures (for this is the first leap which commonly he maketh), and then, being pressed about the meaning or interpretation of Scriptures,   225

---

193. **Halliwell and Bowier** William Halliwell and Thomas Bowier, executed 1556 (actually in Foxe's calendar on 9, 10 June respectively).   202. **bear . . . bell** take away the prize.   208. **Philip Melanchthon** (1497–1560) humanist, educator, supporter of Luther.   219–20. **Woodman . . . Maundrell** Richard **Woodman**, executed 1557, in Foxe's calendar on 23 June; Rafe **Allerton**, executed 1557, in Foxe's calendar on 20 September; John **Fortune**, executed 1557, in Foxe's calendar on 30 September; John **Maundrell**, executed 1556, in Foxe's calendar on 27 March. Persons relates how Woodman claimed to be elect and to possess 'the spirit of God' (ii: sig. Kk1; see Foxe in Townsend, Cattley, xiii: 339–40).

he must presently, if he be unlearned and not able to stand in that combat, retire himself to the last hold of his own peculiar spirit; and if he be learned, though he wrangle for a time, yet this must needs be his last refuge and resolution, for that heresy, being novelty and singularity, cannot finally defend itself but by this only shift and deceit of the devil, which for the most part is so fortified by him as it is inexpugnable. For whatsoever you allege against them, either reason, authority, Scriptures, Fathers, or other persuasion, it is all rejected by this only persuasion of theirs, that they, being elect, their spirit and judgement cannot err. 230

[...]

[7.] There followeth the seventh consideration upon the premises, to wit, that supposing the former perversity of heretical people in England, and that they would 235 neither be instructed nor reduced themselves, nor cease from perverting of others, what should or could the pastors of England and such as had charge of conscience over their flock do in such a case? Foxe did everywhere exclaim and make fierce invectives against the bishops and clergy for punishing these people, condemning it (as you have heard) for barbarous cruelty, injustice, murder, and the like. For answering whereof it seemeth to 240 me that three points may be considered: first, whether the punishing of such as be condemned for heretics by the external and visible Christian Church of every age be lawful or not; and secondly, whether in Queen Mary's time and in the reigns of former Catholic English princes it were expedient to punish such people as they did, supposing it were lawful; and thirdly, whether the same were executed with cruelty or rather with 245 compassion upon necessity.

To the first: if we talk of matter of fact, there can be little controversy between English Protestants and us at this day, for that they do burn also Anabaptists, Arians, and other such like heretics, as is evident by Joan of Kent, and of George Paris, burned in King Edward's days, and divers others condemned to death by our Protestant bishops for 250 Anabaptism and burned for the same under Queen Elizabeth. And Michael Servetus was burned by the procurement of Calvin in Geneva; and Valentinus Gentilis was burned in like manner by the Protestant magistrates of Bern, which facts were not only allowed, but also highly commended both by Calvin and Beza, as conform to the word of God, which appeareth by their several books written of that matter (Calvin, *De supplicio Servet.*; Beza, 255 *De haeret.*).

[8.] But on the contrary side [to Foxe's invective against the Marian executions] is to be considered the charge of conscience that lay upon the bishops and pastors in those days for looking to their flock, whom every hour they perceived to be infected more and more by these heretical foxes and wolves. And if Christ our Saviour did condemn for hirelings 260

---

229. shift evasion. **230. inexpugnable** unassailable. **236. reduced** led back. **249. Joan of Kent ... George Paris** Edward VI executed Anabaptist Joan Boucher (Joan of Kent) in 1550, and, about the same time, George van Parre, who denied the divinity of Christ (Foxe in Townsend, Cattley, v: 704). **251. Michael Servetus** Spanish physician and theologian, infamously executed for heresy in 1553. **252. Valentinus Gentilis** executed for asserting that there were three separate divinities in the Trinity, Bern, 1566. **254. conform to** consistent with.

in the Gospel those pastors which did fly for fear of the wolf, to wit, when they saw the wolf strong, and potent, and armed with authority, against whom they should have spent their blood for preserving their flock [John 10: 11–15], what would he say of pastors that had authority on their side and power also to resist and punish the wolf? If these men, I say, not of fear (which is some excuse) but of negligence or of some compassion towards the wolves and foxes themselves should have permitted such noisome, wilful beasts to have lived freely among their flock, doing all hurts they could without restraint or punishment, what would our Saviour have said of such men? Truly, it is like he would not only have blamed them as hirelings but rather have condemned them as privy betrayers of his flock. And this was their case in Queen Mary's days, for that none of these wilful, ignorant people then burned could be brought either to revoke their heresies, or to keep them to themselves, or not to infect others, or any way to incline themselves to quietness.

Now, then, as to the last point, whether cruelty were used towards them or not, as everywhere John Foxe doth exclaim, the matter is easy to be judged by indifferent men. First, for that true justice lawfully administered cannot be called cruelty, and, secondly, much less where necessity standeth on the part of the magistrate and self-will on the behalf of the delinquent. Thirdly, if we consider the manner and circumstances of this execution used then against these heretics and sectaries, Foxe himself is forced to set down so many particularities everywhere of favour and compassion used towards them by the bishops and other ecclesiastical judges as do confound his own vain accusations of cruelty, showing somewhere that the said judges did weep when they gave sentence against them, considering their mad obstinacy; other, where that they entreated them, spoke them fair, reprieved them after their condemnation, delayed the execution, offered them pardon and remission, even at the very last cast, and the like.

RICHARD VERSTEGAN

Richard Verstegan (1548–1636) published poetry, horrific depictions of Catholic martyrdoms, an influential collection of Catholic prayers (see POETRY, Figs. 6, 9, INSTRUCTIONS AND DEVOTIONS), and an important historical work, *A Restitution of Decayed Intelligence in Antiquities* (1605). Eschewing the traditional adulation of Brut and primitive Britain,

268. **like** likely. 269. **privy** private, intimate. 276. **true justice** Speaking for many, Lord Burlegh disagreed in *The Execution of Justice in England* (1584). There he distinguished between Catholics Elizabeth executed for treason and the Protestants Mary executed for heresy: 'For though they which suffered in Queen Mary's time continued in the profession of the religion wherein they were christened, and as they were perpetually taught, yet they never at their death denied their lawful queen, nor maintained any of her open and foreign enemies, nor procured any rebellion or civil war, nor did sow any sedition in secret corners, nor withdrew any subjects from their obedience, as these sworn servants of the pope have continually done' (sig. Cii^v). 285. **cast** opportunity.

Verstegan demonstrates the Saxon origins of English people, language, and culture. Since Pope Gregory the Great and St Augustine converted the Saxons to Christianity in the sixth century, he argues, Roman Catholicism stands as the authentic Christian religion of England.

In the *Restitution* Verstegan innovatively treats language as historical artefact. The last section of the work traces the origins of English speech in the Saxon language. Verstegan thus belongs to the antiquarian movement of the early seventeenth century, which includes William Camden, Robert Cotton, John Selden, and Catholics such as William Blundell, who advanced the Saxon argument through numismatics (see Fig. 14). Verstegan and Blundell join forces with Thomas Stapleton (translator of Bede) and Robert Persons to demonstrate that to be English is 'to be Saxon, Catholic, and European, other historical traditions being founded in myth, mistake, and historical manipulation' (Donna B. Hamilton, 'Catholic Use of Anglo-Saxon Precedents', *Recusant History*, 27 (2003), 545).

A Restitution of Decayed Intelligence in Antiquities, 1605

[Saxon ancestry of the English]

Now albeit that these and many the like mistakings may unto some seem to be no matters of any moment yet are they surely of moment, for that such defect of due observing things anciently appertaining to nation and nation and language and language do breed much confusion, and are the occasion of involving things in such sort that oftentimes that which is attributed to one nation belongeth unto another. And by this 5 means cometh it to pass that we not only find Englishmen (and those no idiots neither) that cannot directly tell from whence Englishmen are descended and, chancing to speak of the Saxons, do rather seem to understand them for a kind of foreign people than as their own true and mere ancestors, but even among English writers themselves words divers times uttered that savour of reproach unto their own ancestors, the Saxons; for 10 Englishmen cannot but from Saxon original derive their descent and offspring, and can lack no honour to be descended of so honourable a race, and, therefore, are the more in honour obliged to know and acknowledge such their own honourable and true descent.
[. . .]

Having now, as I trust, given the reader sufficient satisfaction in this matter and left him to believe that our Saxon ancestors were merely and originally a people of Germany, 15 it followeth then to show what a highly renowned and most honourable nation the Germans have always been that thereby it may consequently appear how honourable it is

1. **these** confusions of primitive Britain with later England, the country which properly came into being with the Saxon invasion, *c.*AD 450. **4. sort** fashion. **9. mere** pure. **11. offspring** origin. **14. now** Verstegan has just outlined the history of the Saxons.

for Englishmen to be from them descended. For manifestation whereof I will first set down what things proper unto them do especially make them a most noble nation in the sight of all the world and then will I show the reports and testimonies which ancient authors of other nations do give them.

The first, therefore, and most memorable, and worthy of most renown and glory is that they have been the only and ever possessors of their country, to wit, the first people that ever inhabited it, no antiquity being able to tell us that ever any people have dwelt in Germany save only the Germans themselves, who yet unto this day do there hold their habitation.

Secondly, they were never subdued by any, for albeit that the Romans with exceeding great cost, loss, and long trouble might come to be the commanders of some part thereof, yet of the whole never, as of Gallia, Spain, and many other countries else they were.

Thirdly, they have ever kept themselves unmixed with foreign people, and their language without mixing it with any foreign tongue.

In all which three points of greatest national honour, I doubt whether any people else in the world can challenge to have equality with them.

And for their further honour it is to be considered that they have not only been the ever keepers of their own country (meanwhile so many other nations of the world have been transposed, and forced to fly from one region to another, and subjected to the irrecoverable loss of their national names, languages, and habitations), but many most warlike troops have gone out of Germany and taken possession in all the best countries of Europe, where their offspring even to this day remaineth. As first, for example's sake, to begin with the Saxons, the ancestors of our noble English nation, who came and took possession of Loegria, the best part of Britain, and left unto it the name of England, which unto this day with daily increase of honour it still enjoyeth.

[...]

And now touching their honesty of life, a rare thing among pagan people (for such they then were), Caesar himself reporteth that the youth of Germany were not given to the lusts of the flesh, the Germans accounting it a thing most beastly to have the company of any woman before she came to the age of 20 years. And Tacitus, showing their great continency, saith that matrimony is severely observed among them and that of all barbarous people they only did content themselves one man with one woman, except some very few which not for unruly lust but for their nobility's sake were sued unto for sundry marriages. Adultery is seldom committed in so populous a nation, and the punishment for it incontinently inflicted at the best liking of the husband, etc. It is very commendable among them that only virgins do marry, and that only once, and the man the like, contracting thus with the hope and desire of one wife, etc. No man

---

23. ever constant. 41. Loegria According to legend, Trojan Brut, descendant of Aeneas, founder of Britain, divided his kingdom into Loegria (England), Cambria (Wales), and Albania (Scotland). 44. Caesar Julius Caesar (100–44 BC) fought Germanic tribes in his conquest of Gaul (58–50) and recorded his observations in *Commentarii de bello Gallico*. 46. Tacitus a Roman historian (56–120) whose *Germania* supplies most of the information below about the qualities of the Saxons. 47. severely strictly. 51. incontinently immediately.

laugheth at vices. Good manners are of greater authority and force among them than elsewhere good laws. A rare commendation surely of such a people as the Germans then   55 were! I omit sundry other things very praiseworthy among them, and especially their most free and bountiful hospitality, the like whereof was nowhere else to be found. [...]

   And as touching the knowledge of the people, what learning or skill is there among men that they exceed not in? It is a mere imaginary supposal to think that the temperature of the air of any region doth make the inhabitants more or less learned or   60 ingenious, and such as so persuade themselves are therein undoubtedly deceived. I do confess that certain nations have certain virtues and vices more apparently proper to them than to others, but this is not to be understood otherwise to proceed than of some successive or heritable custom remaining among them, the case concerning learning and science being far different. For where was there ever more learning and science than in   65 Greece, and where is there now in the world more barbarism? What most excellently learned men and great doctors of the Church has Africa brought forth, as Tertullian, Optatus, Lactantius, St Cyprian, and St Augustine, and with what learned men is Africa in our time acquainted? Contrariwise, in the flourishing days of the Romans, how utterly without the knowledge of letters, sciences, and arts were the Germans, and how do the   70 Germans nowadays flourish in all learning and cunning—as in the well-speaking science of rhetoric, the truth-trying logic, the perfect arithmetic, the righteous geometry, the high-reaching astronomy, and the health-restoring physic, with all other most profound learning and excellent sciences. And in the knowledge of the imperial laws the Germans may rightly challenge the first place.   75

[Beginnings of Christianity among the Saxons]

Some few years before he received the said faith, it happened in the time that Aella reigned, king of Deira, sometime a part of the kingdom of the Northumbrians, that certain English children of that country (whether taken in war and so transported away by enemies, or that it were tolerable among pagan people sometimes to sell away their children) were brought to Rome to be sold (as captive heathen people are wont to be   80 among Christians) and standing there in the market. A certain reverend religious father named Gregory, being a man, as witnesseth Venerable Bede, of the greatest virtue and learning of his time, coming thither and beholding them to be of a very fair complexion, ruddy and white, with yellowish hair, demanded of the merchant that had them to sell of whence they were. Which being told him, he asked if they were christened; it was ans-   85 wered that they were not. Whereat, fetching a deep sigh, he said, 'Alas, that the author of

---

64. **successive or heritable** sequent or able to be inherited. 67–8. **Tertullian...Augustine** Tertullian (*c*.155–220), influential theologian; St **Optatus** of Milevis (4th c.), opponent of the Donatist schismatics; **Lactantius** (240–320), Christian apologist; St **Cyprian** (200–58), defender of the primacy of the Roman see and martyr; St **Augustine** of Hippo (354–430), great doctor of the Church. 71. **cunning** knowledge. 72. **truth-trying** truth-testing. **perfect** precise. **righteous** exact. 73. **physic** medicine. 76. **Aella** king of Deira in northern England (*r.* 559–588/90). 82. **Gregory** St Gregory the Great (540–604), pope and doctor of the Church. **Venerable Bede** (672–735), historian (for this incident, see above).

darkness should yet detain people of such bright countenances in his possession, and
that men of so fair faces should inwardly carry such foul souls.' Demanding by what
name this people were called, answer was made him that they were called Angles, or
rather (if it were pronounced as they then called themselves) 'Engelisce' that is to say, 90
'English'. The reverend father, perceiving this name to allude unto the name of *angeli* in
Latin, said, 'Verily, not without cause are they called Angles, for they have faces like
angels, and meet it were that such men were made partakers and co-heirs with the angels
in heaven.' Then demanded he the name of the province from whence they came, and it
was answered him they were of Deira. 'That is well,' quoth he, 'for they are to be 95
delivered *de ira Dei*, that is, 'from the ire of God', and called to the mercy of Christ.
What is the name', quoth he, 'of the king of that country?' It was answered that his name
was Aella. Unto which name also alluding, 'Alleluia', quoth he, 'must be founded in that
prince's dominions to the praise of almighty God, his creator.'

And being stricken with much compassion to behold that such angelical people in 100
respect of their great beauty and comeliness should continue the bondslaves of the foul
fiend of hell, he went unto Pelagius the Second, who then was pope, desiring of him that
some ministers of the word of God might be sent into Britain to preach unto the pagan
English people the faith of Jesus Christ, offering himself to be one of that number that
would in person undertake the journey, if so it pleased the pope to allow thereof. Some 105
that have written the life of St Gregory do report that he obtained of the pope this his
pious desire, and that he departed from Rome and was three days onward on his journey
toward Britain, and that the people of Rome, when they had gotten knowledge thereof,
were exceeding sorrowful, and went unto the pope, and in lamentable manner declared
how great a loss and detriment it would be unto the whole city to want the presence of so 110
worthy a person, and therefore besought him that this reverend father might be sent after
and called back again. The pope, considering their so earnest desire, he thereunto
condescended and, sending after him, caused him to return again to Rome. Venerable
Bede is herein somewhat brief and only showeth that, albeit the pope would have granted
him leave to have gone, yet would not the people suffer him to depart so far from their 115
city of Rome. But by this occasion the pope, now having the more knowledge of the life,
learning, and virtue of this good religious father, he soon thereupon advanced him to the
dignity of a cardinal and, himself not long after chancing to die, this cardinal was then
(though much against his own mind) chosen his next successor, and was the first in that
see of the name of Gregory, howbeit he became afterward more renowned by the name of 120
Gregory the Great, then of that name the first, and for his great learning and science
worthily reputed one of the four chief doctors of the Church.

Being now pope and mindful of the good work which before he purposed, moved
thereunto (as said Venerable Bede) by the inspiration of God, he sent St Augustine, and

93. **meet** fitting. 102. **Pelagius the Second** (*r.* 580–9). 122. **four chief doctors** The other three are St Ambrose,
St Augustine, and St Jerome.

with him certain other monks which feared God, to preach the word of God unto the   125
English nation.

Of the great antiquity of our ancient English tongue

Our ancient English-Saxon language is to be accounted the Teutonic tongue, and albeit
we have in later ages mixed it with many borrowed words, especially out of the Latin and
French, yet remaineth the Teutonic unto this day the ground of our speech, for no other
offspring hath our language originally had than that.   130

[Saxon vocabulary]

DEAD-BOOT: offices or service done for the dead. It is sometimes also used for penance.

DACGEF-FARE: a day's fare, a day's journey.

DEALE: a deal, a part or portion.

DEALD: divided, parted, dealt out.

DENE or DEN sometimes written DEANE and sometimes DENU: a valley, also a cave or   135
hollow place in the earth.

DEARE: grief, harm, or dolour.

DEMAN: a deputy, a substitute.

DEORWEORTH: dear worth, precious.

DIHT or DIGHT: metre or rhyme. Hereof cometh our name of 'ditties' for things that be   140
dighted, or made in metre. 'Dighting' or 'inditing' is also 'proof, set forth in exact
order'.

DOME: judgement; DOME-SETLE: a judgement seat, a tribunal.

DOMES-MAN: a judge.

DUVA also DUFA: a dove.   145

DUGUD or DOUGHT: virtue. We sometimes call a man of strength and valour 'a doughty man'.

[Saxon etymologies: names]

GODSCALK: *Scalk* is in our ancient language 'a servant', as *Theow* also is, etc. *Godscalk* is
servus Dei, 'the servant of God'.

GOSWINE: It should rightly be *Gods-wine*; *wine*, as hath been said, signifieth 'beloved',
and *Gods-wine*, 'the beloved of God'. It is now in the Netherlands vulgarly written   150
Gosen, as also *Goson*.

HARMAN: It should rightly be *Hartman*, to wit, 'a man of heart or courage'.

HELDEBRAND: *Held* in ancient Teutonic was written *haelt* and signifieth 'a stout or valiant
person', as a champion or suchlike, and because of the addition *brand*, it seemeth a
name or title given for service unto such as valiantly invading their enemies had   155
consumed and wasted their country by fire. *Heldebrand* is in Italian become *Aldo-
brando*.

127. Teutonic German.

HENRY or HENRYI: *Hen*, the first syllable hereof, was anciently written *han* and so was anciently used for 'have', as may appear in divers old English writings; and to this day in some parts of England they will say, 'Han you any?' for 'Have you any?' *Rye*   160
signifieth not only 'rich' but also 'possession and jurisdiction', so as *Hanrye*, which now we write 'Henry', importeth as much as a 'haver of wealth, possession, or jurisdiction', and so in likelihood a name given unto such as were the heirs unto some good estates of conditions of living.

[...]

[Saxon etymologies: surname terminations]

In BROOK: This, being the termination of divers names, as 'Brabrook' (more rightly as   165
I take it, 'Broadbrook'), etc., is the surname of an honourable and of sundry worshipful families. A *brook* we now take to be a small running water, but I find it in the Teutonic to be that which *palus* is in Latin, 'a waterish or moorish ground'. The city of Brussels took name of the brook-land or moorish ground lying on the north side thereof.

In BY: In this termination many of our ancient surnames do end as first, for example,   170
'Willoughby', the surname of honourable and worshipful families, also 'Kirkby', 'Holtby', and many others, the particle *by* serving to express near unto what thing of note the residence of such a family was when this their surname first began, as being near unto some noted willow tree, or by a church [*kirk*], or by a wood, for *holt* in our language is otherwise 'wood', etc.   175

In CASTER, CEASTER, and CHESTER, etc.: We have sundry terminations of places and, consequently, of surnames of men (taken from those places) which end in *caster, ceaster, cester, chester*, and *ceter*—all which do seem to me to have been but one, and not anciently coming from any Teutonic or Saxon word, but derived from *castrum* in Latin. And as we need not to doubt that the Romans in the many years that they bore sway in Britain did there make   180
divers fortifications which they called *castra* [camps], so may we think that our ancestors, the Saxons, finding these fortifications of the Romans, did imitate though corruptly (as all strangers are wont) their appellation, which in time grew more and more to vary, as first to become *caster* and *ceaster*, and afterward the 'c' to get an 'h' unto it, and so come to be *chester*. But this, as I take it, came through the orthography of the Normans and some, omitting in   185
pronunciation the 'h' as also the 's' in the midst of a word (as the French use to do) have made it *ceter*. Our Saxon ancestors coming into Britain after the Romans and to be the owners of such places so varied in denomination, they so came to be their surnames.

In CLIF: A *cliff* is a kind of rock on the seaside and, as it were, cleft or broken off. Divers of our surnames do therein end, as 'Radcliff', the surname of a right honourable family, also   190
'Whitcliff', and others. It may seem that 'Radcliff' was understood at the first for 'red cliff' as 'Whitcliff' for 'white cliff', both denoting the colour as other like names do the fashion or situation of their cliffs.

166. worshipful notable.

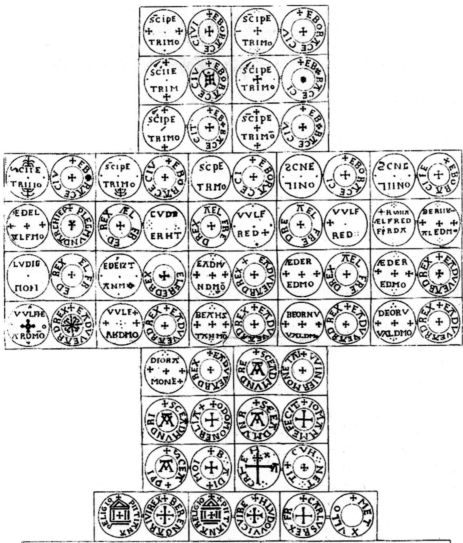

15. William Blundell, 'The Coins at Little Crosby'. The inscriptions of Cuthbert and Alfred Rex on two sides of a coin (5th row, 2nd column) recall St Cuthbert's appearence to the fugitive King Alfred (r. 871–900). Cuthbert tells Alfred that the English must suffer for their sins but that the glorious record of English assures their survival. Blundell's reading of such coins affirms the dependence of Saxon hegemony on Roman Catholic saints.

PHILIP O'SULLIVAN-BEARE

From County Cork, Philip O'Sullivan-Beare (1590?–1660?) studied at Compostella, served as a soldier, wrote saints' lives as well as his important *Historiae Catholicae Iberniae Compendium* ('History of Catholic Ireland', Lisbon, 1621). Like fellow countrymen Peter Lombard and David Rothe, O'Sullivan-Beare wrote his history in Latin for European audiences. The *Compendium* presents the complicated struggles of Ireland as a battle between heretical English invaders and native Irish Catholics. Though this approach simplifies the complex dynamics of the conflicts, it illuminates the fundamental tensions and historical realities largely invisible in such contemporary English accounts as Edmund Spenser's *A View of the State of Ireland* (1598, pub. 1633). Drawing on personal sources including his soldier father, Dermot, O'Sullivan-Beare dedicates his work to King Philip of Spain, who he hopes will deliver Ireland from 'the most violent fury of heresy' (p. xxiii).

The following selections from the *Compendium* protest the tyranny of Elizabeth's reign and describe the wars against England. O'Sullivan-Beare recounts the massacre at Smerwick (1580), perpetrated by the treacherous and brutal Lord Grey, whom Edmund Spenser later idealized as Artegall or Justice (*The Faerie Queene*, V). Spenser was probably present at the massacre, advocated the use of force on the primitive and rebellious Irish, and, in his role as colonizer, helped himself both to land and power in Ireland. O'Sullivan-Beare goes on to relate episodes of religious persecution in order to tell the tragic tale of Irish resistance, heroism, disunity, suffering, and, finally, defeat.

The History of Catholic Ireland, 1621

General sketch of the tyranny of Elizabeth and distractions of Ireland

Immediately on the death of the Catholic Queen Mary, she was succeeded by her sister Elizabeth, the daughter of Henry VIII and Anne Boleyn, and who became queen in the year of our Redeemer 1559. As soon as she wielded the sceptre, imitating her father, she excited the most violent and fierce storms against the professors of Christian truth. In England she nearly extinguished the Catholic faith and religion; then she set herself to   5 detach the Irish from the faith. The system of her persecutions has been given above and is here also repeated. The most blessed sacrament of the Eucharist, in which Christ our Lord is really and truly present, is removed from the churches and the eyes of the people; sacred images are burnt, priests banished, and the entire Catholic people groan under injustice.

3. **1559** Elizabeth ascended to the throne at the death of Queen Mary, 17 November 1558; she was officially crowned on 15 January 1559.

Churches are contaminated either by profane uses or execrable heretical superstitions. 10
Ecclesiastical revenues are bestowed on most abandoned heretics; all things established for
the honour of God are defiled. Catholic bishops, friars, priests, either in hiding or
disguised in secular apparel, scarcely dare to walk abroad. In their places Lutherans,
Calvinists, and other sects of heretics are supplied. The messenger of faith, religion, piety,
and virtue is banished; licentiousness, lust, crime, and heresy are hospitably received. The 15
queen is declared head of the Church in her own kingdoms, and all must admit her to be
head and attest the same by an oath. These ordinances began to be enforced by the royal
ministers and magistrates first in the queen's towns despite the greatest opposition and
firmness of the townsmen. Then they were carried into the territories of the Irish chiefs,
and here because the chieftains were no wise willing to conform, various artifices were 20
devised, by means of which they were despoiled of their property, gradually overthrown,
and punished with death. Hence the sword was drawn. The kingdom blazed, burned, and
perished with war, slaughter, and famine. As long as some of the Irish were in arms for the
liberty of the Catholic religion and of themselves, so long a cessation from persecution was
allowed to other chiefs and to the queen's towns until the defenders of liberty were 25
destroyed. Queen Elizabeth, the instigator of all these crimes, was not undeservedly
smitten with the sword of excommunication by Pope Pius V.

[The massacre at Smerwick]

These, embarking in six ships with a large commissariat, batteries, arms for four
thousand Irish, James, Cornelius, the bishop, and Doctor Sander, sailed from Spain
for Ireland, and after a prosperous voyage arrived in the harbour of Ardnacantus, which is 30
called Smerwick by the English, and is opposite the town of Dingle. There is in that port
rock, which the natives call the *Oilen-an-oir*, well fortified by nature, partly washed by the
tide, partly fenced by high rocks, and joined to the mainland by a wooden bridge. This
was in the charge of Peter Rusius, citizen of Dingle, who had there a guard of three or
four youths. James finds out where Peter is and, having seized him and bound him, 35
placed him on top of a siege engine, and by his soldiers pushes it towards the rock. Peter,
shouting out, orders his men to surrender the rock. James quickly threw into it six
hundred soldiers under command of Lieutenant Sebastian San Joseph. He fortified it
during six days of continuous work. Moreover, on the mainland in front of the rock he
constructed a trench and mound and stationed there cannons taken from the ships. It 40
was a very strong fortress, almost impregnable. He gathered from the neighbourhood
wine, oil, beer, sea-biscuits, and meat. He sent back the ships with the remaining two
hundred men.

27. **excommunication** by the infamous bull, *Regnans in excelsis* (1570) (see DOCUMENTS). 28. **These** a force returning to
Ireland from the Continent in 1579 with papal approval for rebellion against the English, led by James Fitzmaurice
Fitzgerald, leader of the Fitzgeralds of Munster. **commissariat** store of provisions. **batteries** military equipment for laying
siege, especially platforms and artillery. 29. **Doctor Sander** Nicholas Sander, exiled English Catholic scholar (see
above). 31. **Smerwick** port town in south-western Ireland, County Kerry.

In the meantime his cousin, John Fitzgerald, brother of Earl Gerald, and other noble youths joined him. To these he explained that he had been sent by the supreme pontiff to aid the Irish in asserting the rights and liberty of the Catholic Church against the heretics. On this account he carried the keys inscribed on his banners, because they were fighting for him who had the keys of the kingdom of heaven. He said, however, he would not be satisfied with John's fidelity until he had done some noble deed whereby he would provoke the anger and indignation of the heretics and show that he would be faithful to himself. Thereupon John, entering the town of Tralee, killed Davers, a magistrate, Arthur Carter, provost-marshal of Munster (both English heretics), Miach, a judge, Raymond the Black, and others. The rest of the Englishmen he drove out of the town. San Joseph was animated by James and encouraged to defend strenuously the fort, and he gave as interpreter an Irish gentleman of the Plunkett family. Cornelius the bishop and Doctor Sander were left with John to stir up and excite the good will of the men.

James himself set out with eight Irish horse and eighteen foot which Thady McCarthy had supplied in order to enlist in the war others with whom, before leaving Ireland, he had communicated the object of his journey. He met on the way Theobald Burke, lord of Castleconnell, with Richard and Ulick his brothers, and a number of cavalry and infantry greater than his own. These, although Irishmen, Catholics, and kinsmen of James, nevertheless swayed by an insane stupidity in order to prove their fidelity to the queen, fired on James from a distance. James now crossed the ford of the narrow pass (*Bealantha an Bhorin*) and the Burkes got to the same place. James was there struck by a bullet and, thereby roused to fury, he turned round his band. Both sides fought rather more bitterly than successfully. James, putting spurs to his horse, rushed into the tide at the ford, intrepidly followed by his horse and foot. He rushed on Theobald with drawn sword and struck him a great blow, splitting his skull in two through the helmet and scattering his blood and brains over his breast and shoulders. When Theobald fell dead from his horse, the Burkes yielded the ford; then James pushing forward, they took to flight, James following close on their heels. There perished of the Burkes with their leader Theobald, his brother. Richard, and William Burke, gentlemen; Ulick, also, the third brother, was mortally wounded. Edmund O'Ryan, gentleman, lost an eye, and several either fled wounded or were completely destroyed. On the other side, only James died within six hours of receiving his wound, having his sins first forgiven by a priest whom he had with him. Eighteen soldiers were wounded, of whom Gibbon Fitzgerald, surnamed the Black, stricken with eighteen wounds, was left hid in a hedge, where he was secretly nursed by a friend, a doctor. When the latter had left, a wolf coming out of the adjoining woods gnawed the old cast-off bandages tinged with pus and blood, but never attacked the abandoned sick man. The others, after they had buried at Cadmeus their leader, lost

45

50

55

60

65

70

75

80

---

45. pontiff Pope Gregory XIII (*r.* 1572–85). **47. keys** symbol of papal power, deriving from Matt. 16: 19: 'And I will give to thee the keys of the kingdom of heaven. And whatsoever thou shalt bind upon earth, it shall be bound also in heaven; and whatsoever thou shalt loose on earth, it shall be loosed also in heaven.' **52. Munster** (also, Munsters), a territory in south-west Ireland. **57. foot** foot soldiers.

in the engagement, returned to John Fitzgerald. The successor of the deceased lord of Castleconnell was created baron by the queen for this action.

The news of James's death having spread, the majority of the Irish participators in his plans lost hope and failed to take up arms. Sebastian San Joseph was privately alarmed. The English, on the other hand, plucked up spirit and applied for aid from England. The queen ordered an abatement of persecution. She sought to stir up the Irish. The earldom of Desmond is said to have been promised to Thomas Butler, earl of Ormond, if he would speedily bring the war to an end. She was afraid that Eugene O'Sullivan, chief of Beare, my kinsman, would join in the war, and so ordered him to be seized unexpectedly and put into prison; nor was he released until the war was over. A garrison under command of Fenton, an Englishman, was placed in Dunboy, the castle of his chieftaincy. With the earl of Ormond and other Irish troops, although they were Catholics, especially Anglo-Irish of Meath and their English followers, Grey, an Englishman, the viceroy of Ireland, got together about one thousand five hundred soldiers, forces very inadequate to storm such a fortification as the Golden Fort. Nevertheless, with these and two or three transport ships he blockaded Sebastian by land and sea with a double line and, having placed his cannon, made an attack. The assailed made small account of the attack, being not only well furnished with artillery and arms, but also thoroughly protected by the nature of the place. Already the heretic had for about forty days in vain plied his cannon on the fort, wasting his strength to no purpose. He was tried by the inclemency of winter at sea and in the open camp, where he was without houses, under shelter of a few camp tents; he was being deserted by the Irish, who were brought thither against their will; and he was losing some English troops, killed by the fire of the artillery, and amongst others John Shickius (*Shinkwin qy*), a man of great standing amongst them. However, not to abandon the enterprise which he could not achieve by force, he tried strategy. He sent a flag to demand a parley. Plunkett endeavoured to prevent a conference with the English, a callous and treacherous race of men, by whom Sebastian, a credulous and incautious man, might perhaps be deceived.

Sebastian, with whom the command rested, thought a conference should not be refused and so, having got a safe pass, he approached the viceroy in his camp with Plunkett as interpreter and, speaking with his head uncovered, showed himself a man of cringing disposition. The interpreter, however, kept himself covered. The viceroy and commandant proposed peace to each other. Plunkett interpreted their speeches opposite ways, making the commandant say to the viceroy that he would lose his life rather than surrender, and making the viceroy say to the commandant that he was determined to give no quarter to the besieged. The commandant, perceiving the false translations of the interpreter by the inconsistency of the viceroy's face, ordered Plunkett to be carried back

89. **Beare** territory including a small peninsula in south-west Ireland. 93. **Grey** Arthur Grey, fourteenth baron of Wilton (1536–93), Spenser's employer and a ruthless soldier who later boasted of killing in Ireland 1,500 gentleman and many churls, 'the account of which is beyond number' (PRO, SP 63/95/82, quoted in *The Spenser Encyclopedia*, 342). Spenser in the person of Irenaeus calls Grey 'gentle, affable, loving, and temperate' (*A View of the State of Ireland*, ed. Andrew Hadfield and Willy Maley, 1997: 103). 111. **head uncovered** a sign of respect.

to the fort and cast into prison, and negotiated with the viceroy through another interpreter. Then returning to his men, he informed them that he had obtained from the viceroy very fair terms of capitulation. Plunkett shouted from his chains that the pope's fort was perfidiously betrayed, that the viceroy would soon be forced by the winter's rigour to end the siege, that John Fitzgerald was coming to the rescue, that all the Irish would desert from the English if the commandant held the fort, that there was enough victuals for the besieged for many months, and, finally, that there was no trusting the heretics. To the same effect spoke the captains of the Cantabrians and Hercules Pisano, saying that they would not only defend the fort, but even engage the enemy in the open if necessary.

The commandant persuaded the soldiers to side with him and so through the cowardice of this timid general the valour of the others was overcome, and he who was more anxious to save his life than win glory lost both. He surrendered the fort in the month of December on the one condition, which was secured to the besieged by the oath of the viceroy, that he might march out safe with soldiers, arms, bag, and baggage. However, the heretical faithlessness held itself bound neither by honour, nor the sanctity of an oath, nor by the laws held inviolate amongst all people, civilized and barbarous. The fort being surrendered, the defenders were ordered to lay down their arms; deprived of which, they were slain by the English, except the commandant, who, being let off, is said to have gone to Italy. Plunkett was for a short time reserved for a more cruel death. Shortly afterwards he was put to death, having had his bones broken by a mallet. Hence 'Grey's faith' became a proverb for monstrous and inhuman perfidy.

Grey, returning thence to Dublin, placed garrisons in the Munster towns, and applied to the Irish and to England for aid against John Fitzgerald. He ordered his lieutenants to do their utmost to bring the war to a speedy termination, and not to rest until they either took or killed John. The earl of Ormond and other Irish nobles, hating the pride and power of the Fitzgeralds, were easily drawn to serve against them. John, with his brother James, his kinsmen and followers, the spirited young men of the MacSweenys (those who were cut off in McCarthy's war being sorely missed by the Fitzgeralds), Dermot O'Sullivan, my father, who led the infantry of Beare, and others, endeavoured to protect themselves, and at the same time harass the enemy.

An account of the fierce persecution started by the English against their faith

Whilst Ireland was thus pitifully ruined by the quarrels of the chiefs both between themselves and with the royal crown, and the blood of ecclesiastics was spilled by the

125. Cantabrians troops from a region in Spain. **135–6. deprived . . . English** The Latin is more graphic, 'nudi ab Anglis iugulantur' (naked, their throats were cut by the English). **139. inhuman perfidy** Modern historians confirm that Grey treacherously slaughtered some 600 soldiers (mostly Italian and Spanish), as well as some Irish men, women, and children. (See *A New History of Ireland*, iii. *Early Modern Ireland, 1534–1691*, ed. T. W. Moody *et al.*, 1976, corr. 1991: 105–8). Spenser defends the massacre in *A View*, denying any false promise of mercy and rehearsing Grey's argument that the victims were 'not any lawful enemies' but adventurers who could not, *ipso facto*, plead 'either custom of war and law of nations' (105). Spenser glorifies Grey further in *The Faerie Queene*, 5. 12. 25 ff., wherein Artegall or Justice attempts to 'reform that ragged commonweal' (5. 12. 26. 4), for which he is unfairly hounded by the hags, Envy and Detraction.

English, the chiefs (either worn out by their factions and now exhausted of their resources or hostages, many of them being in the hands of the English) seemed little likely to take up arms in defence of the Catholic religion. Hereupon a persecution broke out against the faith of Christ and the tyrant Queen Elizabeth ordered that all should entirely abandon the Catholic faith, forsake the priests, accept the teachings and doctrines of heretical ministers, embrace the queen's sect, and on holy days attend the services in the churches. And to this were they compelled by fear, terror, punishment, and violence.

This terrible attack on the Catholic faith was now the more severe and dangerous because just at this time, more than ever since the reception of the faith, were Irishmen ignorant of theology, philosophy, and jurisprudence, so that they were unprepared for controversy and for preserving the people in the true religion of Christ Jesus, because through factions, the confusion of affairs, and the barbarous fury of the heretics, their schools were gone to ruin and scarcely was there any one able to teach publicly the higher studies. The holy communities of friars were for the most part scattered and banished, and in many places priests could not easily be found to baptize infants. In many places the younger folk knew only so much of the faith as they had learned from their mothers and nurses, and some, indeed, were so ignorant of the evidences of the faith that they knew not how to prove or explain anything beyond that they themselves firmly believed whatever the Roman Catholic Church believed, that with it was the true doctrine of the Catholic faith, and that they had very little trust in the doctrines of the English, whom they believed to be ill-disposed to the faith. The royalist towns suffered more through this want of instruction and ignorance than the countries of the chiefs because the English used to congregate in royalist towns. And this is the reason why the herds and country people, not to mention the ancient and modern Irish chiefs, are more pure and enlightened in devotion to the Catholic faith than the Anglo-Irish who dwell in the royalist towns. In the depth of this darkness and ignorance there is no doubt but that the Irish providentially shunned, ridiculed, and despised the English preachers, and were saved from their errors by an unseen and secret light of faith, which, alone in a wonderful manner, guided many to follow the true faith of the supreme pontiff, from which the English had recently fallen away.

The Irish conquered not so much by the English as by one another

The Catholics might have been able to find a remedy for all these evils, had it not been that they were destroyed from within by another and greater internal disease. For most of the families, clans, and towns of the Catholic chiefs who took up the defence of the Catholic faith were divided into different factions, each having different leaders and following lords who were fighting for estates and chieftaincies. The less powerful of them joined the English party in the hope of gaining the chieftainship of their clans, if the existing chiefs were removed from their position and property, and the English craftily

181 ff. O'Sullivan-Beare has just given an account of the conflicts with England beginning in 1588 and extending through what modern historians call the Nine Years War (1594–1603), led by Hugh O'Neill, earl of Tyrone.

held out that hope to them. Thus, short-sighted men, putting their private affairs before the public defence of the holy faith, turned their allies, followers, and towns from the Catholic chiefs and transferred to the English great resources, but in the end did not   190
obtain what they wished for, but accomplished what they did not desire. For it was not they but the English who got the properties and rich patrimonies of the Catholic nobles and their kinsmen; and the holy faith of Christ Jesus, bereft of its defenders, lay open to the barbarous violence and lust of the heretics. There was one device by which the English were able to crush the forces of the Irish chiefs, namely, by promising their   195
honours and revenues to such of their own kinsmen as would seduce their followers and allies from them. But when the war was over the English did not keep these promises.

　　This hope turned Con and Henry, sons of the chief Shane O'Neill, and Art, son of Turlough, against O'Neill. The same greed for chieftaincy prompted Niall O'Donnell, surnamed Garve, to effect the destruction of Tyrconnell by levying war against O'Donnell.   200
The same envy drove Owen O'Sullivan against his cousin The O'Sullivan Beare. The same ambition set Thady O'Rourke against The O'Rourke, his brother. The same lust excited the English Maguire against The Maguire. Why should I narrate the dispute between Florence, Dermot, and Daniel as to the chieftaincy of Clancarty? Why should I recall how Earl James Fitzgerald was stripped of his resources by the faction of the other   205
James? Why repeat six hundred examples of the same thing? Assuredly, my countrymen, however high they may stand amongst the nations in the profession of and devotion to the Catholic faith and divine religion, yet during this war were far worse than Turks or heretics in faction, dissensions, ambition, and perfidiousness. Wherefore, it could not be otherwise than that by so many and so great distractions, Ireland should be utterly   210
destroyed, for as the holy Evangelist has it, 'Every kingdom divided against itself shall be destroyed' [Matt. 12: 25]. Indeed, my wonder is how it should have so long withstood so many divisions, so many wars, such incendiarism. And, indeed, had it not been accomplished by God, I do not think that the few Catholics could have so often overcome the multitude of Protestants and their allies; that half-armed soldiers could   215
have been able to defeat armies thoroughly equipped with all kinds of arms; that the attenuated resources of the Catholics could have withstood during fifteen years the wealth and power of the Queen of England; that from small beginnings a war should have beyond all expectation swelled to such dimensions that the heretics were nearly on the point of losing all Ireland.   220

What was the condition of Ireland after the war?

Thus the war was finished. Ireland was almost entirely laid waste and destroyed, and terrible want and famine oppressed all, so that many were forced to eat dogs and whelps;

---

198. Shane O'Neill Irish chief (1530–67) who rebelled against English rule and fought against Irish and Scottish chiefs. **222. famine** Cf. Spenser's famous description of the famine in Munster (*A View*, 101–2): 'Out of every corner of the woods and glens they came creeping forth upon their hands, for their legs could not bear them. They looked like anatomies of death; they spake like ghosts crying out of their graves; they did eat the dead carrions, happy where they could

many, not having even these, died. And not only men but even beasts were hungry. The wolves, coming out of the woods and mountains, attacked and tore to pieces men weak from want. The dogs rooted from the graves rotten carcasses, partly decomposed. And so   225 there was nought but abundance of misery and a faithful picture of ruined Troy as given by Vergil, Book 2, *Aeneid*:

> That night of slaughter and of gloom
> What pen can paint or tears atone?
> An ancient city meets its doom;   230
> Its rule of ages is undone.
> The streets are strewn with silent dead,
> E'en homes, aye God's abodes, are graves.
> Not only Trojan's blood is shed;
> The foeman's gore the streets belaves,   235
> And Trojan valour smites the Greeks.
> Around the cruel anguish spreads,
> And all with death and terror reeks.   [361–9]

As a result of this almost total destruction of Ireland, many Irishmen scattered themselves amongst foreign nations. A great number passed into France, and a far larger   240 number into Spain. The exiles were kindly and generously received by Catholics on account of their faith.

Elizabeth Cary

Elizabeth Cary (Tanfield), Viscountess Falkland (*c*.1585–1639), dramatist and historian, mastered Latin, Hebrew, and modern languages including Irish, and identified herself as 'a Catholic, and a woman' (*Reply*, 1630, sig. êi^v). After her conversion to Catholicism in 1626, her husband Henry Cary renounced her and forced separation from her children. Destitute, Elizabeth Cary performed charitable works and wrote translations, saints' lives, hymns to the Virgin, and the *History of Edward II* (1627), recounting the reign and assassination.

Like Christopher Marlowe, Cary conceives of Edward II's life as a tragedy, complete with prologue, acts, an interlude, actors, and morals, including the final lesson, 'had he

find them, yea, and one another soon after, insomuch as the very carcasses they spared not to scrape out of their graves. And if they found a plot of water-cresses or shamrocks, there they flocked as to a feast for the time, yet not able long to continue therewithal. That in short space there were none almost left, and a most populous and plentiful country suddenly left void of man and beast; yet sure in all that war there perished not many by the sword, but all by the extremity of famine, *which they themselves had wrought*' (italics mine). Since the English systematically burned crops and destroyed cattle, Spenser's blame of the Irish for their starvation reveals his own nation's myopia and brutality. **235. belaves** washes.

not, indeed, been a traitor to himself, they could not all have wronged him' (sig. Rr2^v). In the selections below Cary's dramatic skills enliven the narrative as she supplies speeches for the historical characters. Cary does not write polemical Catholic history in the manner of Robert Persons or Philip O'Sullivan-Beare, but instead shows her Catholicism in nostalgia for 'those religious times' and in the positive portrayal of Pope John XXII (*r.* 1316–34), as he intervenes in the temporal affairs of England, Scotland, and France. Focusing on a single reign, Cary draws morals, repeats saws and maxims, and creates dramatic orations, thus writing the kind of Tacitean 'politic' history evident elsewhere in the early seventeenth century, particularly in the work of John Hayward and Francis Bacon.

The Life, Reign, and Death of Edward II, 1627

[Pope John XXII's embassy and excommunication of Edward II]

The pope, who with a pious and a truly compassionate eye beheld the misery of this dissension and the unnatural effusion of so much Christian blood, seeks to reform it, and to this effect sends over two of his cardinals to mediate a peace and to compose, if it might be, the differences in question. They, being arrived in England, come down into the north to the king, by whom they are with great ceremony according to the fashion of   5 those religious times received and welcomed. They discourse to him the occasion of their employment and incline him with many excellent and virtuous motives to embrace a peace with Scotland. The greenness of the disgrace and the late wound yet bleeding new kept him in a long demurrer. Yet the holy and mild prosecution of these holy fathers won him at length to their mediation with a proviso that he were not too far prejudiced in   10 interest and honour. With this answer they take their leave and prosecute their journey for Scotland but, with an example full of barbarous inhumanity, they are in the way surprised and robbed. Infinitely is the king incensed with this audacious act, which threw so foul a stain upon the whole nation, which causeth a strict inquisition for the discovery of these malefactors, which are soon known and taken. Middleton and Selby, both   15 knights, expiate the offence with their shameful execution. The persons of ambassadors amongst the most savage nations are free from rapine, but being clothed in the habit of religion and such a greatness and going in a work so good and glorious, certainly it was an act deserved so severe a punishment.

Immediately at the heels of this follows another example, less infamous but far more   20 full of danger. Sir Josline Denville, having wasted his estate and not able to lessen the

---

1–2. **this dissension** the Scottish uprising in 1318. **3. compose** settle. **9. demurrer** indecision. **prosecution** persever-ance. **11. prosecute** undertake. **15. Middleton and Selby** Holinshed says that Gilbert Middleton robbed lands and proclaimed himself duke, for which he and his companion, Walter Selby, were executed; he considers the robbery of the cardinals as possible (*Chronicles*, 1587: 318). **20. another example** Holinshed describes this uprising of 1321 against Edward II (ibid. 325–7).

height of his former expenses, gets into his society a regiment of ruffians, terming themselves outlaws; with these he infests the north with many outrageous riots insomuch that no man that had anything to lose could be secure in his own house from murder, theft, and rapine. A little time had brought this little army, rolling like a snowball, to the number of two hundred; all the diseased flux of the corrupted humours of those parts fly to this imposthume. An attempt so impudent and daring flies swiftly to the king's knowledge. Report, that seldom lessens, makes the danger far greater than it deserved; the royal ear conceits it little better than a flat rebellion, whose apprehension felt itself guilty of matter enough to work on. This made an instant levy and as ready a dispatch for the suppression of the flame while it but burnt the suburbs. Experience soon returns; the fear is found greater than the cause; the principal heads and props of this commotion are surprised and fall under the severity of that law, whose protection they in this enterprise had absolutely disclaimed. Those that more narrowly examined the depth of this convention believed it but a mask for a design more perilous. The intemperate and indiscreet government had aliened the hearts of this people; there was a general face of discontent over the whole kingdom; the ulcers festered daily more and more; the Scottish disaster is ascribed to the regal weakness and all things seemed to tend to quick confusion. If this unadvised and ill-grounded disorder had tasted the general inclination in a more innocent and justifiable way, it was constantly believed the king had sooner felt the public revolt of the whole kingdom. But this work was reserved till a farther time and the operation of those that had the opportunity of effecting it with more power and a fairer pretence of justice. It is a very dangerous thing when the head is ill, and all the members suffer by his infirmity. Kings are but men, and man is prone to error; yet, if they manage their distempers with wisdom or discretion so that they lie not open to public view and censure, they may be counted faults but not predictions. But when the heart is gangrened and the world perceives it, it is the fatal mark of that infection which doth betoken ruin and destruction.

The cardinals are now come back; the hopes of peace are desperate; the Scots are on the sunny side of the hedge, and will have no conditions but such as may not be with honour granted. Edward, inflamed, will have no further treaty; this makes them take their leave and hasten homeward. Their losses liberally are requited and many goodly gifts bestowed at parting. Being come to Rome, they inform His Holiness of the success of their journey, who takes ill the contumacy of the perfidious Scots, and excommunicates both that king and kingdom. But this thunderbolt wrought a small effect: where honesty had so little an acquaintance, religion must needs be a great stranger.

---

26. **flux** discharge. **humours** essential bodily fluids that needed to be kept in proper balance. 27. **imposthume** swelling. The physiological imagery depicts rebellion as a disease in the body politic. 29. **conceits** imagines. 29–30. **whose...on** The ear's apprehension of the report made the king feel culpably responsible to attend to the matter. 30. **levy** raising of troops. 35. **convention** gathering (of rebels). 36. **aliened** alienated. 39. **tasted** tested. 46. **predictions** portents (of doom). 49–50. **on...hedge** in the better position. 52–6. Cary's supportive treatment of the 1320 excommunication contrasts with Holinshed's emphasis on the papacy's concern for lost revenues, the cost of the excommunication to the realm, and the subsequent oppression of the common people (ibid. 325).

[The deposition and death of Edward II]

But I will leave them to a reformation and proceed to the tragedy of this unfortunate king, who is now taken from the earl of Lancaster and delivered over by indenture to Sir Maurice Berkeley and Sir John Matrevis. They lead him back to the cage of his first imprisonment, carrying him closely and with a reserved secrecy lest his friends in the 60 knowledge of his remove might attempt his freedom. And to make his discovery more difficult, they disfigure him by cutting off his hair and shaving his beard. Edward, that had been formerly honourably used and tenderly served, is bitterly grieved with this indignity. And one day among the rest, when they came to shave him, which was attempted without fire and with a cold liquor, his eyes pour forth a stream of tears in 65 sense of his misfortune, which to the inquisitive actors gives this answer: 'He would have some warm water in spite of all their malice.' Another time, in the presence of two or three of those that were as well set to be spies over him as to guard him, in a deep, melancholy passion he thus discoursed his sorrow:

'Is mine offence', quoth he, 'so great and grievous that it deserves nor pity nor 70 assistance? Is Christian charity, all goodness, lost, and nothing left in subject, child, or servant that tastes of duty? Is wedlock-love forgotten so fully? All at once forsake me? Admit my errors fit for reformation (I will not justify myself, or censure others); is't not enough that it hath taken from me my crown, the glory of my former being, but it must leave me void of native comfort? I yet remain a father and a husband; a sovereign and a 75 master lost cannot deprive me of that which is mine own till death dissolve me. Where, then, is filial love? Where that affection that waits upon the laws of God and nature? My wretched cares have not so much transformed me that I am turned to basilisk or monster. What can they fear that they refuse to see me, unless they doubt mine eyes can dart destruction. I have no other weapons that may fright them and these (God wot) have 80 only tears to drown them. Can they believe or once suspect a danger in visit of a poor, distressed captive? Their hardened hearts I know are not so noble or apt to take a gentler, mild impression by seeing these poor ruins thus forsaken. What then occasions this so great a strangeness or makes them jealous of so poor a venture? Are they not yet content in the possession of all that once was mine, now theirs? But by what title their arms can 85 better tell than can their conscience. My misled, harmless children are not guilty; my wife betrays them and false Mortimer, who else I know would run to see their father. Justly I pay the price of former folly that let him scape to work mine own confusion. Had he had his desert, the price of treason, he had not lived to work me this dishonour. But time will come my wrongs will be revenged when he shall fall with his own weight unpitied. 90

57 ff. Queen Isabella, her lover Mortimer, and their forces landed in England 24 September 1326, executed Hugh de Spencer (the Younger), the king's lover, deposed Edward, and crowned his son in January 1327. Edward was murdered in September 1327. **58. earl of Lancaster** Henry of Lancaster, earl of Leicester. **indenture** contract. **58–9 Sir Maurice Berkeley** actually Thomas Berkeley, son of Maurice, whose life and lands had been taken by the Spencers. **59. Sir John Matrevis** another member of the queen's faction, related to the Berkeleys by marriage. **65. cold liquor** Marlowe expands upon this pathetic detail: his Edward cries out for water, is brought 'channel water' [i.e. water from the sewer] with which he is washed and shaved (5. 3). **66. sense** perception. **75–6. sovereign...lost** my lost state of sovereignty. **78. basilisk** mythical serpent with lethal breath and glance. **79. doubt** fear. **80. wot** knows.

Thou wretched state of greatness, painted glory, that falling findest thine own the most perfidious, must thou still live and yet not worthy of one poor look? It is a mere injustice. Would they would take my life; 'tis that they aim at. I will esteem it as an act of pity, that as I live but hate mine own condition.'

Here with a deep sigh of scalding passions, his tears break loose afresh to cool their 95 fury. All sadly silent while he rests perplexed, a stander-by makes this uncivil answer, whom Mortimer had placed to increase his sorrow. 'Most gracious sir, the queen, your wife, and children are justly jealous of your cruel nature. They know too well your heat and former fury to come too near so great and sure a danger; besides, they are assured that your intentions are bent to work them hurt or some foul mischief if they adventure 100 to approach your presence.'

'The queen, my wife,' quoth he, 'hath she that title while I that made her so am less than nothing? Alas, poor wretched woman, can her invention, apt for mischief, fashion no one excuse but this, so void of reason? Is there a possibility in her suspicion? Can I, being so resolved, act a murder, or can their false hearts dream me so ill-minded? I am, 105 thou seest, a poor, forsaken prisoner, as far from such a power as will to act it; they too well know it to suspect my nature. But let them wonder on and scorn my sorrow; I must endure and they will taste their error. But, fellow, thou that takest such saucy boldness to character and speak thy sovereign's errors, which thou shouldst cover not presume to question, know Edward's heart is as free from thine aspersions as thou or they from truth 110 or moral goodness.'

[. . .]

The fatal night in which he suffered shipwreck he eats a hearty supper but stays not to digest it; immediately he goes to bed with sorrow heavy. As soon he takes his rest and sleeps securely, not dreaming of his end so near approaching. Midnight, the patron of this horrid murder, being newly come, this crew of perjured traitors steal softly to his 115 chamber, finding him in a sweet and quiet sleep, taking away his life in that advantage.

The historians of these times differ both in the time, place, and manner of his death, yet all agree that he was foully and inhumanly murdered, yet so that there was no visible or apparent sign which way 'twas acted. A small tract of time discovers the actors and shows evidently that it was done by an extremity of violence. They long escape not, 120 though Mortimer's greatness for the present time keep them both from question and

92. **mere** pure. 93. **that** who. 98. **jealous** fearful. 109. **character** delineate. 112 ff. Cary passes over Hereford's famously ambiguous message, 'Edwardum occidere nolite timere bonum est', which can be construed 'Do not fear to kill Edward; it is good', or 'Do not kill Edward; to fear is good' (ibid. 341). 118. **foully . . . murdered** Unlike Cary, Holinshed does not omit the details: 'They came suddenly one night into the chamber where he lay in bed fast asleep and with heavy featherbeds or a table (as some write) being cast upon him, they kept him down and withal put into his fundament an horn, and through the same they thrust up into his body an hot spit, or (as other have) through the pipe of a trumpet a plumber's instrument of iron made very hot, the which, passing up into his entrails and being rolled to and fro, burnt the same, but so as no appearance of any wound or hurt outwardly might once be perceived' (ibid. 341). The staging of the assassination is not specified in Marlowe's play but Lightborne calls for a red-hot spit, a table, and a featherbed (5. 5. 28 ff.) before committing the murder.

punishment; yet by the divine justice they all meet with a miserable and unpitied death. And the master workman himself in a few years after suffered an ignominious execution.

The queen, who was guilty but in circumstance and but an accessory to the intention not the fact, tasted with a bitter time of repentance what it was but to be quoted in the margent of such a story. The several relations so variously expressed of their confessions that were the actors and consenters to this deed differ so mainly that it may be better passed over in silence than so much as touched. Especially since if it were in that cruel manner as is by the major part agreed on, it was one of the most inhuman and barbarous acts that ever fell within the expression of all our English stories, fitter rather to be passed over in silence than to be discoursed since it both dishonoureth our nation and is in the example so dangerous. It seems Mortimer was yet a novice to Spencer's art of that same Italian trick of poisoning, which questionless had wrought this work as surely with a less noise and fewer agents. It had been happy if such a villainy had never gained knowledge or imitation in the world; since it came to be entertained as a necessary servant of state, no man that runs in opposition or stands in the way of greatness is almost secure in his own house or among his friends or servants. I would to God we had not fresh in our memory so many bleeding examples, or that this diabolical practice might stop his career with the mischief it hath already done. But so long as the close conveyance is deemed a politic virtue, and the instruments by power and favour are protected, what can be expected but that in short time it must fall under the compass of a trade or mystery as fit for private murderers as statesmen?

But leaving the professors of this execrable practice to their deserts and that guilt which still torments them, thus fell that unfortunate King Edward the Second, who by the course of age and nature might have outrun many years, had not his own disorder, the infidelity of his subjects, and the treachery of those that had deprived him of his kingdom sent him to an untimely death and ruin. Many reasons are given, probable enough, to instance the necessity of his fall, which questionless may be the secondary means; but his doom was registered by the inscrutable providence of heaven.

125
130
135
140
145

---

123. **master workman** Mortimer, who was hanged for treason in 1530 and his estates forfeited to the crown. **126. margent** margin. **135. entertained** accepted. **139. close conveyance** secret murder. **141. mystery** occupation.

FICTION

Early modern Catholics wrote various fictions for various purposes, their works, consequently, comprising a miscellany rather than a free-standing genre. Individual pieces present exercises in well-known literary modes and types such as satire, devotional writing, and romance. Broader in perspective and less doctrinally contentious than other Catholic writing, Catholic fiction appealed to a broad range of readers. Erasmus's *Colloquies* (1526), for example, presented decadent Church practices in terms so acceptable to mainline Protestants that they repeatedly republished them. These dialogues wittily mock the superstitious invocation of saints for selfish ends as well as the manipulation of phoney relics for private profit. Erasmus lashes the conmen and hucksters who pretend to piety as well as their gullible victims, who, by light of reason, revelation, or Church doctrine, ought to know better.

Another moderate and widely popular Catholic fiction writer, Thomas Lodge, also writes satire in *Wit's Misery* (1596). Expressing sentiments found also in the works of the Protestant University Wits (George Peele, Thomas Nashe, and Robert Greene), Lodge generally excoriates vice and hypocrisy in the current London scene. His *Prosopopeia* (1596) deploys more specifically Catholic traditions to familiar devotional ends. This work varies the famous *Stabat mater* theme to give extended voice to the Virgin Mary as she laments the death of her son. Lodge employs baroque conceits to create a prose exercise in the Literature of Tears.

Some Catholics turned various historical narratives into romance—a capacious, flexible genre widely popular throughout Europe. Sir Philip Sidney's *Arcadia* provided the prototype for early modern romance—a complex, episodic narrative of love and adventure, featuring intrigues, disguises, battles, pirates, escapes, losses, exile, and, finally, reunion and restoration. Following Sidney, Robert Chambers presented Old and New Testament events as romance in *Palestina*, 1600. John Barclay wrote two Latin romances, *Euphormionis Lusinini Satyricon* (1605–7) and *Argenis* (1621), both avidly read and reprinted. Excerpted below in translation, *Argenis* transforms the French wars of religion into a complex, sprawling narrative, rich in sentiment and profuse in plot lines.

Two unusual pieces round out this sampling of Catholic fiction. Anthony Copley published a joke book, *Wits, Fits, and Fancies* (1595), which reflects, nonetheless, some serious religious issues. Elizabeth Southwell wrote a manuscript account of Queen Elizabeth's death and exploding body. Though fairly neutral itself, this account circulated as revisionist Catholic history, as an eyewitness report on divine punishment visited on the heretical Protestant queen.

DESIDERIUS ERASMUS

Dutch humanist, theologian, and scholar, Desiderius Erasmus (1459–1536, see CONTRO-VERSIES) also wrote fiction critical of the Church. *Julius exclusus* (1513), for example, depicts Pope Julius II denied admittance into heaven for his many crimes. The enormously popular *Familiarium colloquiorum formulae* (Colloquies, 1518, etc.), including *The Pilgrimage of Pure Devotion* below, satirizes superstitious practices and clerical profiteering while advocating true piety and service to the poor. Cuthbert Tunstall, bishop of London, rebuked Erasmus for his criticisms; the theology faculty at the University of Paris banned the book; the Church listed the *Colloquies* in its index of prohibited works. The Puritan William Burton published a translation of seven colloquies in 1606, claiming that they showed 'how little cause the papists have to boast of Erasmus as a man of their side' (sig. A6); another Protestant, Roger L'Estrange, published his translation in 1697. And yet, in notes, letters, and *De utilitate colloquiorum*, a formal defence first printed in the 1526 edition, Erasmus maintains that he attacks only excesses and abuses. He consistently defends the moderate and appropriate uses of relics, fasts, feasts, pilgrimages, invocations to saints, and veneration of the Virgin.

Colloquies, 1518

The Pilgrimage of True Devotion

OGYGIUS From that part toward the east there is a little chapel full of marvels and thither I went. There was I received of another of our Lady's chaplains. There we kneeled down to make our little prayers. By and by he brought forth the joint of a man's finger,

PILGRIMAGE This dialogue first appeared in 1526. 1. **Ogygius** (Primeval), the traveller who converses with **Menedemus** (Stay-at-Home). **little chapel** chapel of St Laurence, near the cathedral of St Thomas Becket.

the greatest of three, which I kissed and asked whose relics they were. He did say that they were St Peter's. 'What, the apostle?' said I. 'Yea,' said he. Then I did better behold the joint, which for his greatness might well have been a giant's joint rather than a man's. 'Then', said I, 'Saint Peter must needs be a great man of stature.' But at that word there was one of the gentlemen that stood by that could not forbear laughing, for the which I was very sorry. For if he had holden his peace, we had seen all the relics; yet, we meetly well pleased Master Sexton with giving him two or three groats. Before that chapel there was a little house, which he said once in wintertime, when that there was little room to cover the relics, that it was suddenly brought and set in that place. Under that house there was a couple of pits, both full of water to the brinks, and they say that the spring of those pits is dedicate to our Lady. That water is very cold and medicinable for the headache and that heartburning.

MENEDEMUS If that cold water will heal the pains in the head and stomach, then will oil put out fire from henceforth.

OGYGIUS It is a miracle that I tell, good sir, or else what marvel should it be that cold water should slake thirst?

MENEDEMUS This may well be one part of your tale.

OGYGIUS They say that the fountain did suddenly spring out of the earth at the commandment of our Lady and I, diligently examining all things, did ask him how many years it was sith that house was so suddenly brought hither. 'Many years agone,' saith he. 'Yet,' said I, 'the walls do not appear so old.' He did not deny it. 'No more these wooden pillars.' He could not deny but that they were set there not long ago, and also the matter did plainly testify the same. Afterward said I, 'This roof, which is all of reed, doth appear not to be very old.' And he granted also these great beams which lie overthwart and these rafters which hold up that house were not set long agone. He affirmed my saying. 'Well,' said I, 'seeing that no part of the house is left but all is new, how can you say that this is the house which was brought hither so long ago?'

MENEDEMUS I pray you, how did the housekeeper avoid himself from your argument?

OGYGIUS By and by he did show to us the matter by the skin of a bear which had hanged by the rafters a long season and did almost mock the simpleness of our wits that could not perceive so manifest an argument. We, being persuaded by this argument, asked pardon of our ignorance, and called into our communication the heavenly milk of our Lady.

---

10. meetly sufficiently. groats small coins. 12. suddenly...set an allusion to the legend that angels moved the Walsingham chapel to its present site. This legend echoes that of the Santa Casa in Loreto, Italy, believed to be Mary's original house in Nazareth likewise miraculously transported. 13. pits wells. 14. spring flow of water. 23. agone ago. 28. overthwart crosswise. 32. avoid himself escape. 33. skin...bear The exhibition of the bearskin, of course, provides no answer to Ogygius's question but is intended to confuse him into credulity. 36. pardon of pardon for. called...communication asked to see. milk The Virgin's milk, purportedly from Bethlehem, was a venerated relic at Walsingham since AD 1300.

MENEDEMUS Oh, how like to the son is the mother, for he hath left to us so much blood here in earth and she so much milk that a man will scarcely believe a woman to have so much milk of one child, in case the child should suck none at all. 40

OGYGIUS They say the same of the holy cross, which is showed in so many places both openly and privately that if the fragments were gathered upon one heap, they would appear to be a just freight for a ship, and yet Christ did bear all his cross himself.

MENEDEMUS But do not you marvel at this?

OGYGIUS It may well be a strange thing but no marvel, seeing that the Lord, which doth 45 increase this at his pleasure, is almighty.

MENEDEMUS It is very gently expounded but I am afraid that many of these be feigned for lucre.

OGYGIUS I suppose that God would not suffer himself to be deluded of such a fashion.

MENEDEMUS Yes, have not you seen that when both the mother, the Son, the Father, and 50 the Holy Ghost hath been robbed of these sacrilegious thieves, that they would not once move or stir neither with beck or crack whereby they might stay away the thieves? So great is the gentleness of God.

OGYGIUS So it is, but hear out my tale. This milk is kept upon the high altar and in the midst there is Christ with his mother upon his right hand for her honour's sake; the 55 milk doth represent the mother.

MENEDEMUS It may be seen, then?

OGYGIUS It is closed in crystal.

MENEDEMUS It is moist, then?

OGYGIUS What tell you me of moistness when it was milked more than a thousand and 60 five hundreth year agone? It is so congealed that a man would say that it were chalk tempered with the white of a egg.

MENEDEMUS Yea, but do they set it forth bare?

OGYGIUS No, lest so holy milk be defouled with the kissing of men.

MENEDEMUS You say well for I suppose that there be many that kiss it which be neither 65 clean-mouthed nor yet be pure virgins.

OGYGIUS When the sexton saw us, he did run to the altar and did put upon him his surplice and his stole about his neck, kneeled down religiously, and worshipped it, and straightforth did offer the milk to us to kiss. And at the end of the altar we kneeled down devoutly, and then first of all we saluted Christ, and then after we called upon 70 our Lady with this prayer, which we had made ready for the same purpose. 'O mother and maid, which did give suck with thy virgin's teats the Lord of heaven and earth, thy son, Jesus Christ, we, being purified through his precious blood, do desire that we may attain and come to that blessed infancy of thy columbine's meekness, which is immaculate without malice, fraud, or deceit, and with all affection of heart doth 75

---

40. **in case** even if.   49. **deluded of** lied about in.   52. **beck or crack** nod or sound (*nutu vel crepitu*).   **stay** keep.   68. **surplice** white, wide-sleeved linen vestment work over a cassock.   **stole** narrow strip of silk or linen worn over the shoulders.   74. **columbine's meekness** dove-like gentleness.

covet and study for the heavenly milk of the evangelical doctrine to go forth and increase with it into a perfect man, into the measure of the plentifulness of Christ, of whose company thou hast the fruition together with the Father and the Holy Ghost for evermore, so be it.'

MENEDEMUS Verily, this is a holy prayer. But what did she?   80

OGYGIUS They both becked at us, except my eyes wagged, and methought that the milk danced. In the mean season the sexton came to us without any words but he held out a table such as the Germans use to gather toll upon bridges.

MENEDEMUS By my troth, I have cursed very oft such craving boxes when I did ride through Germany.   85

OGYGIUS We did give him certain money, which he offered to our Lady. Then I asked by a certain young man that was well learned, which did expound and tell us the saying of the sexton (his name, as *fere* as I remember, was Robert Aldridge), by what tokens or arguments he did know that that it was the milk of our Lady. And that I very fain and for a good purpose desired to know, that I might stop the mouths of certain   90 newfangled fellows that be wonted to have such holy relics in derision and mockage. First of all, the sexton with a froward countenance would not tell, but I desired the young man to move him more instantly; but somewhat more gently he so courteously behaved himself that an he had prayed our Lady herself after that fashion, she would not have been displeased therewith. And then this mystical chaplain, as and if he had   95 been inspired with the Holy Ghost, casting at us a frowning look, as and if he would have shot at us the horrible thunderbolt of the great curse, 'What need you,' saith he, 'to move such questions when you see before your eyes so authentical and old a table?' And we were afraid lest that he would have cast us out of the church for heretics but that our money did temper his great fury.   100

MENEDEMUS What did you in the mean season?

OGYGIUS What suppose you? We were amazed as and if a man had struck us with a club or we had been slain with a thunderclap, and we very lowly asked pardon of our foolish boldness, and got us from thence.

[...]

OGYGIUS The church which is dedicate to St Thomas doth stretch up upon height so   105 gorgeously that it will move pilgrims to devotion afar off, and also with his brightness and shining he doth light his neighbours; and the old place, which was wonted to be

---

77. **perfect** perfected, i.e. according to the metaphor, fully nurtured on Gospel doctrine from spiritual infancy to mature Christian commitment. 81. **becked** nodded. **except...wagged** unless my eyes deceived me (*nisi me fallebant oculi*). 83. **table** collection plate (*tabellam*). 88. *fere* nearly (Latin). **Robert Aldridge** Cambridge scholar and friend of Erasmus. 89. **fain** eager. 92. **froward** ill-disposed, frowning. 93. **instantly** urgently. 94. **an...prayed** if...petitioned. 105. **St Thomas** Thomas Becket (1118?–1170), murdered in the cathedral of Canterbury for opposing King Henry II's attempts to appropriate traditional Church offices and privileges. In 1538 the government proclaimed Becket a traitor not a martyr and destroyed the shrine. 107. **the old place** monastery dedicated to St Augustine of Canterbury.

most holy, now in respect of it is but a dark hole and a little cottage. There be a couple of great high towers, which do seem to salute strangers afar off, and they do fill all the country about both far and near with the sound of great bells. In the front of the temple, which is upon the south side, there stand graven in a stone three armed men, which with their cruel hands did slay the most holy St Thomas, and there is written their surnames, Tracy, Breton, and Beryston.

MENEDEMUS I pray you, wherefore do they suffer those wicked knights be so had in honour?

OGYGIUS Even such honour is given to them as was given to Judas, Pilate, and Caiphas, and to the company of the wicked soldiers, as you may see painted in the tables that be set before altars. Their surnames be put to lest any man hereafter should usurp any cause of their praise. They be painted before men's eyes because that no courtier after this should lay violent hands other upon bishops or the church goods, for these three of this guard straight upon that wicked act went stark mad; nor they had never had their mind again but that they prayed to blessed St Thomas.

MENEDEMUS O blessed patience of such martyrs!

OGYGIUS At our entry in, Lord, what a princely place did appear unto us where as every man that will may go in!

MENEDEMUS Is there no marvel to be seen?

OGYGIUS Nothing but the great wideness of the place and a sort of books that be bound to pillars, wherein is the Gospel of Nicodemus, and I cannot tell whose sepulchre.

MENEDEMUS What then?

OGYGIUS They do so diligently watch lest any man should enter into the choir of iron that they will scarcely suffer a man to look upon it, which is betwixt the great church and the high choir, as they call it. A man that will go thither must climb up many stairs before, under the which there is a certain wicket with a bar that openeth the door upon the north side. There standeth forth a certain altar which is dedicate to our Lady; it is but a little one and, I suppose, set there for no other purpose but to be a old monument or sign that in those days there was no great superfluity. There they say that this blessed martyr said his last good night to our Lady when he should depart hence. In the altar is the point of the sword that stirred about the brains of this blessed martyr. And there lie his brains shed upon the earth, whereby you may well know that he was near dead. But the holy rust of this grate I devoutly kissed for love of the blessed martyr. From thence we went under the crowds, which is not without his chaplains,

---

108. **couple** three, actually, two at the west end and the great central tower. 113. **Tracy...Beryston** William de Tracy, Richard le Breton, and Reginald Fitzurse (in the Latin, fancifully, *Tusci, Fusci, Berri*). 118–19. **usurp...praise** find any reason to praise them. 121. **guard** group. 127. **sort** number. 128. **Gospel of Nicodemus** (*Acta Pilati*), an apocryphal Hebrew text popular in the sixteenth century, which described Christ's trial, resurrection, and descent into hell. 130. **choir of iron** the upper part of the choir, separated from the church by iron gates and grille. 133. **wicket** gate. The traveller now approaches the site of the murder in the north-west transept. 139–40. **whereby...dead** a mistranslation; the original reads, 'evidently so that death would come more quickly' (*videlicet quo mors esset praesentior*). 141. **under the crowds** into the crypt (*cryptoporticum*). **his chaplains** its custodians.

and there we saw the brain-pan of that holy martyr, which was thrust quite through; all
the other was covered with silver; the overpart of the brain-pan was bare to be kissed,
and there withal is set forth a certain leaden table, having graved in him a title of
St Thomas of Acres. There hang also the shirt of hair and his girdle with his hair   145
breeches, wherewith that noble champion chastened his body. They be horrible to
look upon and greatly reprove our delicate gorgeousness.

MENEDEMUS Yea, peradventure, so they do the monks' slothfulness.

OGYGIUS As for that matter, I cannot affirm nor yet deny; nor yet it is no point of my
charge.   150

MENEDEMUS Ye say truth.

OGYGIUS. From thence we returned into the choir, and upon the north side be the relics
showed, a wondrous thing to see! What a sort of bones be brought forth, skulls, jaws,
teeth, hands, fingers, whole arms! When we had worshipped them all, we kissed them
that I thought we should never have made an end but that my pilgrimage fellow, which   155
was an unmeet companion for such a business, prayed them to make an end of setting
forth their relics.

MENEDEMUS What fellow was that?

OGYGIUS. He was an Englishman called Gratian Colt, a man both virtuous and well
learned, but he had less affection toward pilgrimages than I would that he should have.   160

MENEDEMUS One of Wyclif's scholars, I warrant you.

OGYGIUS. I think not, although he had read his books; how he came by them I cannot tell.

MENEDEMUS He displeased Master Sexton grievously.

OGYGIUS. Then was there brought forth an arm which had yet the red flesh upon it; he
abhorred to kiss it. A man might see by his countenance that he was nothing well   165
pleased, and then by and by Master Sexton put up his relics. But then we looked upon
the table which was upon the altar, and all his gorgeousness, afterward those things
that were hid under the altar. There was nothing but riches exceeding; a man would
account both Midas and Croesus beggars in respect of those riches that there was set
abroad.   170

MENEDEMUS Was there no more kissing then?

OGYGIUS. No, but another affection and desire came upon me.

MENEDEMUS What was that?

OGYGIUS I sighed that I had no such relics at home.

MENEDEMUS Oh, a wicked desire and an evil thought!   175

OGYGIUS I grant, and therefore I asked forgiveness of St Thomas before I removed one
foot to depart out of the church. After this thus we were brought into the revestry. Oh,

---

142. brain-pan skull. **145. St Thomas of Acres** i.e. Thomas Becket. Acres is Akka, a town in Palestine, and a legend
identified Thomas's mother as a Saracen. **shirt of hair** rough fabric worn for mortification of the flesh. **159. Gratian
Colt** John Colet (1467–1519), scholar, theologian, educator, dean of St Paul's cathedral, and friend of Erasmus. **161. Wyclif**
14th-c. heretic who denied transubstantiation and campaigned for ecclesiastical poverty; adopted by later Protestants as a
proto-reformer. **169. Midas and Croesus** mythological figures of great wealth. **177. revestry** sacristy.

good Lord, what a goodly sight was there of vestments of velvet and cloth of gold!
What a sum of candlesticks of gold! We saw there St Thomas's cross staff. There was
seen also a reed overlaid with silver; it was but of a small weight, unwrought, nor no   180
longer than would reach unto a man's middle.

MENEDEMUS Was there no cross?

OGYGIUS I saw none at all. There was showed us a robe of silk, truly, but sewed with
coarse thread, garnished with neither gold nor stone. There was also a napkin full of
sweat bloody, wherewith St Thomas wiped both his nose and his face. These things as   185
monuments of ancient soberness we kissed gladly.

MENEDEMUS Be not these things showed to everybody?

OGYGIUS No, forsooth, good sir.

MENEDEMUS How happened it that you were in so good credence that no secret things
were hid from you?   190

OGYGIUS. I was well acquainted with the reverend father, William Warham the archbishop. He wrote two or three words in my favour.

MENEDEMUS I hear of many that he is a man of singular humanity.

OGYGIUS But rather thou wouldst call him humanity itself if thou didst well know him.
For there is in him such learning, so virtuous life, such pureness of manners that a man   195
could wish no gift of a perfect bishop in him that he hath not. From thence afterward
we were led to greater things. For behind the high altar we ascended, as it were, into
another new church; there was showed us in a chapel the face of the blessed man
overgilted and with many precious stones goodly garnished. A sudden chance here had
almost marred the matter and put us out of conceit.   200

MENEDEMUS I tarry to know what evil chance you will speak of.

OGYGIUS Here my companion, Gratian, got him little favour for he, after we had made
an end of praying, enquired of him that sat by the head: 'Hark,' he said, 'good father, is
it true that I hear, that St Thomas while he it lived was merciful toward the poor
people?' 'That is very true', saith he, and he began to tell greatly of his liberality and   205
compassion that he showed to the poor and the needy. Then said Gratian: 'I think that
affection and good mind in him not to be changed but that it is now much better.'
Unto this granted the keeper of the head. Again said he: 'Then, inasmuch as this holy
man was so gracious unto the poor when he was yet poor and he himself had need of
money for the necessaries of his body, think ye not that he would be content now that   210
he is so rich and also needeth nothing, that if a poor woman, having at home children
lacking meat and drink, or else daughters being in danger to lose their virginity for
default of their substance to marry them with, or having her husband sore sick and

---

179. **cross staff** ceremonial staff usually topped by a cross (*pedum*). 180. **reed** staff. 183. **robe of silk** shoulder garment which the pope gives to archbishops (*pallium*). 184. **napkin** linen worn around the neck to protect liturgical vestments (*sudarium*). 191. **William Warham** (1450–1532), archbishop of Canterbury, Lord Chancellor of England, one of Erasmus's patrons. 198. **face** bust that enclosed the remains of the martyr's head. 200. **put...conceit** disturbed our happiness. 204. **he it** he life. 213. **substance** means to provide a dowry.

destitute of all help, in case she asked licence and privily stole away a small portion of so great riches to succour her household, as and if she should have it of one that would other lend or give it to her?' And when he would not answer that kept the golden head, Gratian, as he is somewhat hasty: 'I,' saith he, 'do suppose plainly that this holy man would be glad if that he, now being dead, might sustain the necessity of poor people.' But there Master Parson began to frown and bite his lip, with his hollow eyes like to Gorgon the monster to look upon us. I do not doubt he would have cast us out of the temple and spit upon us but that he did know that we were commended of the archbishop. But I did somewhat mitigate the man's ire with my fair words, saying that Gratian did not speak as he thought but that he jested as he was wonted to do, and stopped his mouth with a few pence.

MENEDEMUS Truly, I do greatly allow your goodly fashion but oftentimes earnestly I consider by what means they may be accounted without fault and blame that bestow so much substance in building churches, in garnishing and enriching them without all measure. I think, as touching the holy vestments and the silver plate of the temple, there ought to be given to the solemn service his dignity and comeliness. I will also that the building of the church shall have his majesty decent and convenient. But to what purpose serveth so many holy water pots, so many candlesticks, so many images of gold? What need there so many pair of organs (as they call them), so costly and chargeable? For one pair cannot serve us. What profiteth that musical crying out in the temples that is so dearly bought and paid for, when in the mean season our brothers and sisters, the lively temples of Christ, living by the walls die for hunger and cold?

OGYGIUS There is no virtuous or wise man that would not desire a mean to be had in these things. But inasmuch as this evil is grown and sprung up of superstition beyond measure, yet may it better be suffered, specially when we consider on the other side the evil conscience and behaviour of them that rob the churches of whatsoever jewels there may be found. These riches were given in a manner great men and of princes, the which they would have bestowed upon a worse use, that is to say, other at the dice or in the wars. And if a man take anything from thence, first of all, it is taken sacrilege; then, they hold their hands that were accustomed to give; beside that, moreover, they be allured and moved to robbing and vaining. Therefore, these men be rather the keepers of these treasures than lords. And to speak a word for all, methinketh it is a better sight to behold a temple richly adorned, as there be some with bare walls, filthy, and evil-favoured, more meet for stables to put horses than churches for Christian people.

214. licence pardon (*veniam*). 215. as and if as if. 220. Gorgon mythical monster whose glance turned onlookers to stone. 225. allow...fashion approve your piety (*tuam pietatem...approbo*). 227–8. without all measure excessively. 229. will allow. 230–5. Echoing the protests of Luther, Calvin, and others, these questions drew censure from Catholic authorities. Elsewhere Erasmus objected to excessive attention to music in churches. 233. chargeable burdensome. crying out neighing (*hinnitus*). 236–47. Like Erasmus elsewhere, Ogygius speaks against excess and for the moderate, appropriate use of wealth and ceremony in churches. 240. in a manner from the class of. 244. vaining vain actions. 246–7. bare...evil-favoured Ogygius here voices contemporary Catholic criticism of Protestant churches.

ANTHONY COPLEY

A Catholic poet who responded to Spenser's *Faerie Queene* in *A Fig for Fortune* (1596, see POETRY), Anthony Copley (1567–1609?) also published a book of jests, *Wits, Fits, and Fancies* (1595). Largely translated from a Spanish work, *La floretta spagnola*, Copley published the book to 'minister content and merriment'(sig. A3) to readers. *Wits, Fits, and Fancies* displays the kinds of humour evident in the drama of the period, rich in puns, wordplay, and character stereotypes. Including jokes about doctors, worldly clerics, and famous church figures, the selections below also touch upon serious religious issues of the time, the persecution of Jews and the dissolution of the monasteries.

Wits, Fits, and Fancies, 1595

It was discoursed at the table of Pope Alexander the Sixth whether physicians were necessary in a commonwealth, yea or no, some affirming that Rome being six hundred years and odd without them, the citizens lived in good health and lusty all that while, and therefore a kind of cattle that might very well be spared in a commonwealth. 'Not so,' said the pope; 'rather are they right necessary in my opinion, for without them the world   5
would increase so fast that one could not live by another.'
[. . .]
    A cardinal complained unto Pope Clement the Seventh how one Michelangelo, his painter, in a picture which he had drawn of doomsday in St Peter's chapel at Rome had therein figured him in hell amongst the damned, beseeching him to bid it be altered to some other favour. Whereunto the pope answered, 'Well you wot I can release a soul out   10
of purgatory but not out of hell.'
[. . .]
The said cardinal [Don Pedro Gonzalez de Mendoza], seeing a priest carrying a cudgel under his gown, said unto him, 'It ill beseems your habit to bear a weapon about you.' Whereunto the priest answered and protested that he bare it not in quarrel against any Christian creature in the world but only to defend himself against the dogs of that town,   15
which he found to be fierce and angry curs.
    'Oh,' replied the cardinal, 'and wherefore, I pray you, then serves St John's Gospel?'

---

1. **Alexander the Sixth** (*r.* 1492–1503). 4. **kind of cattle** species of man. 7. **Clement the Seventh** (*r.* 1523–34). **Michelangelo** (1475–1564) painted the Last Judgement in the Sistine Chapel in the Vatican, not in St Peter's Cathedral. 10. **wot** know. The pope here refers to his capacity to issue indulgences, i.e. to remit the temporal punishment due to sin, and thus release souls from purgatory. 12. **Pedro Gonzalez de Mendoza** (1428–95) cardinal and chief bishop of Spain. 17. **St John's Gospel** a general reference to the Gospel's exhortation to love.

He answered, 'True, my lord, but these curs understand no Latin and therefore against them am I fain to bear this defence, as you see.'

[...]

A gentleman of Cardinal Wolsey, making way before his lord as he passed through the church and seeing a poor priest kneeling at his prayers in the way, raised him up, saying, 'Room for my Lord Cardinal's Grace.' Whereupon the priest rose up and said, 'Will His Grace, trow ye, supply my place?'

[...]

The archbishop of Cologne, riding along the plain, all rounded about with men of war, and himself most brightly glittering in arms, a swain ploughing thereabouts laughed to see him so. Which the prelate, perceiving, commanded him straight before him and asked him why he laughed so. 'Marry, I laugh,' answered the peasant, 'to see an archbishop so soldierly gallant.'

'Why, sirrah,' said the bishop, 'I am thus as a duke not as an archbishop or a priest.'

'Even so, sir,' replied the swain. 'Now I pray, then, crack me this nut: were my Lord Duke at the devil, where, trow ye, were my Lord Archbishop then?'

[...]

A Spanish bishop, riding on the way, saw a shepherd sunning himself under a bank and thus he bespake him: 'I marvel much, shepherd, that shepherds nowadays are not like as they were in times past, when there were of them great prophets and great kings in the world, and to them it was that the angel first denounced the nativity of our saviour Jesus Christ afore all others.'

'Oh, sir,' answered the shepherd, 'neither are bishops nowadays like to those good ones of old time, at divers of whose deaths the bells did ring of themselves, and now can scarce be made to toll but with many men's strength.'

[...]

Bishop Gardiner, being deprived of his bishopric, one thus saluted him in derision: 'Farewell, bishop *olim*.' He answered, 'Gramercy, knave *semper*.'

Lord Cromwell reproaching the Bishop Gardiner, being deprived of his bishopric by the king, said 'Where is now, Sir Bishop, all your *gloria patri* [glory to the Father] become?' He answered, 'Even as it hath pleased the King, my liege. Nevertheless, *sicut erat in principio* [as it was in the beginning], so am I still, my lord, as good a gentleman as yourself.'

[...]

---

19. **fain** willing. 20. **Cardinal Wolsey** (1475–1530) cardinal and statesman who dominated England during the reign of Henry VIII, a figure of worldly pride. 23. **trow** think. **supply** take. 25. **swain** farm labourer. 29. **sirrah** term of address to social inferiors. 31. **at the devil** in hell. 32. **under** on. 35. **denounced** announced. 40. **Bishop Gardiner** Stephen Gardiner (1482–1555), resisting nascent Protestantism, was deprived of the bishopric of Winchester in 1550. 41. *olim* formerly. **Gramercy** Thank you. *semper* always. 42. **Lord Cromwell** Thomas Cromwell (1485–1540), principal adviser to Henry VIII, an architect of the new state religion of Protestantism. 43. *gloria patri* The Latin selections here are from the *Gloria* prayer, 'Glory be to the Father, to the Son, and to the Holy Spirit, as it was in the beginning, is now, and ever shall be, world without end. Amen.'

Cardinal Medici, now Duke of Florence, seeing certain Jews walk sabbathly upon a Saturday in his fair garden on Mount Trinity in Rome, commanded them (in despite of such their Saturday sabbath) to be employed all that day in servile work in his said garden, and at night made them a liberal supper of good cheer. Amongst which he caused   50 minced pork to be set afore them so cunningly disguised and besauced that unwittingly they fell to it and eat thereof, contrary to their superstitious pork-opinion in that point, and after they had supped paid them a large day-wages, and so dismissed them.

They at parting, being told of the disguised pork they had eaten, were stark mad. And whereas before they held themselves guilty only of their servile labour that day (it being   55 their sabbath day), now were they outrageous testy at both together, and in a full stomach of detest flung down their wages, and would none of it. But to their synagogue they hied them, and there told their rabbi of all the premises. Whereupon he forthwith excommunicated the cardinal and deeply accursed him to the pit of hell in full congregation. Which he, understanding, went the next day to Pope Pius Quintus and in jest told him   60 all the story as aforesaid, concluding with the rabbi's excommunication and accurse against him, and withal merrily besought the pope to release him thereof. The pope took it in a far other sense and greatly rebuked the cardinal therefore, affirming that he had done a very scandalous act so to force the conscience of a Jew, they not being sheep of Christ's fold and therefore without the liberty of his crozier to pastorize much less to   65 enforce in matter of religion. So saying, he enjoined him a very severe penance, both personal and pecuniary.

[. . .]

A Dominican and a Franciscan friar, travelling together on the way, arrived at a brook, where the Dominican requested the Franciscan, inasmuch as he was barefoot, to carry him over the water on his back. The Franciscan was content and up he took him and into   70 the river he went. And being stepped into the channel, there he paused and said to the Dominican, 'Tell me, brother, have you any money about you?'

The Dominican, thinking that he aimed thereby at a consideration for his pains, answered, 'Yea, marry, have I a little, but not much.'

'Much or little then,' replied the Franciscan, 'well you wot my order allows me not to   75 carry any money about me, though well you may, and therefore—.'

And with that down he let slip the Dominican into the channel, where his money could not save him from being very well wet.

[. . .]

One in Queen Mary's days that had formerly under King Henry gotten much by the fall of the abbeys went about to build a chapel. Whereupon a gentleman, his neighbour,   80

---

47. **Cardinal Medici** Cosimo de Medici (1519–74), crowned grand duke of Tuscany by Pius V in 1570. **sabbathly** in a manner befitting the sabbath. **52. eat** ate. **56–7. full . . . detest** high rage. **57–8. hied them** hurried. **58. premises** previous circumstances. **58–9 excommunicated** cut off from all association. **60. he** Cardinal Medici. **Pope Pius Quintus** (r. 1566–72). **61. accurse** curse. **65. without . . . pastorize** outside his jurisdiction to act as pastor over. (A **crozier** is a bishop's staff.) **79. Queen Mary's days** 1553–8, when the queen unsuccessfully tried to return England to Catholicism. **King Henry** King Henry VIII, dissolving the abbeys in 1534, took all Church lands and possessions.

said that it was like as if one, having first ravished the mother, would afterward pay for the nursing of the child.

THOMAS LODGE

Having converted to Catholicism, probably during his youth (1581?), Thomas Lodge (1558–1625) studied law, sailed on expeditions, studied medicine, worked as a London doctor with a large Catholic practice, and suffered several indictments for recusancy. Among other works he translated the Dominican Luis de Granada, and wrote pamphlets, plays, and fiction (including the pastoral *Rosalynde*, a source for *As You Like It*). As a London author Lodge mainly shares the vision and artistic values of the Protestant University Wits, George Peele, Thomas Nashe, and Robert Greene. Anatomizing contemporary vice in the manner of their works, *Wit's Misery* (1596), for example, discovers in early modern London seven devils and their offspring, walking about as contemporary slanderers, fashion-mongers, actors, liars, and haters of virtue.

And yet, Lodge's Catholicism colours his fiction. As a loyalist, he decries the 'counterfeit Catholic' who hates the country 'wherein he was bred'. He endorses a decree of the Council of Trent on the proper use of stage plays. He ridicules the fraudulent use of relics and criticizes those who 'bring Christians and Catholic religion in hatred'. Lodge's *Prosopopeia: The Tears of Mary* (1596), an exercise in the Literature of Tears (see Southwell, Crashaw, POETRY), conjoins theological meditation, dramatic skill, and baroque ingenuity to present Mary *dolorosa*, lamenting the death of Christ, in order to move the reader to reformation: 'Briefly, our Lord, send a plentiful harvest of tears by this meditation, that the devout hereby may wax more confident, the incredulous, believing, the indifferent, more zealous' (sig. A7).

Wit's Misery, 1596

Scandal-and-Detraction

The next harpy of this breed is Scandal-and-Detraction. This is a right malcontent devil! You shall always find him, his hat without a band, his hose ungartered, his rapier *punto riverso*, his looks suspicious and heavy, his left hand continually on his dagger. If he walk

---

1. **harpy** legendary creature, half-bird, half woman. **this breed** offspring of Leviathan, the devil 'that tempteth with pride' (sig. B1ᵛ). 2. **hat . . . band** i.e. in disarray. 2–3. *punto riverso* in position for a backhand sword thrust from the left side (as opposed to the direct thrust).

Paul's, he skulks in the back aisles, and of all things loveth no societies. If at any time he
put on the habit of gravity, it is either to backbite his neighbour or to work mischief. Well   5
spoken he is, and hath some languages, and hath read over the conjuration of Machiavel.
In belief he is an atheist or a counterfeit Catholic, hating his country wherein he was
bred, his gracious prince under whom he liveth, those grave counsellors under whom the
state is directed, not for default either in government or policy, but of mere innated and
corrupt villainy and vain desire of innovation. He hath been a long traveller and seen   10
many countries, but as it is said of the toad that he sucketh up the corrupt humours of the
garden where he keepeth, so this wretch from all those provinces he hath visited bringeth
home nothing but the corruptions to disturb the peace of his country and destroy his
own body and soul. If he study, it is how to dispense and frustrate statutes and, being
grounded by ill counsel and prepared for mischief, he laboureth (as the legist saith) not to   15
avoid the sin but the penalty.

   This fellow spares neither nobility, clergy, nor laity, but, like that Roman emperor
unworthy the naming, desireth that the whole people and commonality had but one
head that he might cut it off at one stroke. Let him have no cause, he wisheth Vitellius's
misery to majesty and swears by no small bugs that all the world is imprudent that   20
employs him not. This is he that in privy conventicles draws discontented gentlemen to
conspiracies and, having brought them past the mercy of the law, he bewrays them first,
bringing them to a violent end and binding himself to perpetual prison. 'But woe be unto
him,' saith Christ, 'by whom the scandal and offence cometh. It were better for him that a
millstone hung about his neck and that he were cast into the bottom of the sea' (Matt. 18:   25
6). It is a position in the apophthegms of the rabbins that he that draweth many men to
sin can hardly settle himself to repentance. Then, in what miserable estate is this wretch
that delighteth in nought else but traitorous and devilish stratagems? His daily companion in walk, bed, and board is rebellion and disobedience. And of the seed of this serpent
are raised so many monsters that no city in Italy hath been unstained with them and no   30
kingdom in Europe unmolested by them. Ill would they observe that golden sentence of
Cornelius Tacitus registered by Machiavel, who saith that men ought to honour things
past and obey the present, desiring and wishing for good princes and howsoever they
prove to endure them. 'Ay, but,' answers Scandal, 'I never respect how things be, but how
I wish them to be.' Notwithstanding, Sir Devil, let this be your looking glass, that never   35
scandal or conspiracy hath been raised but the practiser hath at last rued it. The little
Spaniard that assailed Ferdinando, the wise king, with a knife, Dervis, the Turkish priest

4. **Paul's** St Paul's Cathedral in London, a popular place for meeting and worship. **societies** company. **5. habit**
appearance. **backbite** slander. **6. Machiavel** Niccolò Machiavelli (1469–1527), whose *Prince* gained him a reputation as
an amoral politician for whom the ends justified the means. **7. counterfeit Catholic** false seditious Catholic, as opposed to
the true ones who remain loyal to their country. **9. innated** innate. **15. legist** legal philosopher. **19. Let him have** even if
he has. **19–20. Vitellius's misery** In AD 19, after less than a year of rule, the Roman emperor Vitellius was murdered by his
own troops. **bugs** terrifying spirits, bogeymen. **21. privy conventicles** secret meetings. **22. bewrays** exposes. **26.
apophthegms…rabbins** Hebrew wisdom literature, i.e. the biblical books of Job, Proverbs, Ecclesiastes, Wisdom of
Solomon, and Ecclesiasticus. **32. Cornelius Tacitus** (55–120?) Roman historian. **35. looking glass** mirror. **37. Ferdinando**
Ferdinand II, King of Aragon and Castile, wounded in Barcelona, 1493.

that assaulted Bajazeth—what end came they to? Either their envy (to their shame) was discovered by their fear or drowned in their bloods. The schoolmaster that betrayed the Falerians' children—was he not whipped home by Camillus? Antigonus, Caesar, and all 40 these monarchs—have they not loved the treason but hated the traitor? Read all the annals and observations of antiquity, and there hath nothing begun in corruption but hath ended in mischief.

But for your detraction, Scandal, blush you not to use it? 'No,' say you, 'the devil delighteth in mischief.' Yet will I give Your Mastership short horns, since you are so 45 cursed a beast, that you may hurt no man. Your course is, you say, to backbite superiors, to scandal the fathers and governors of the Church, to bring Christians and Catholic religion in hatred. But wretch as thou art, know this, that he that toucheth the credit of the clergy toucheth 'the apple of God's eye' (Zach. 2: 8). And whoso loveth to detract is hateful to God. The wise man saith that the detractor is *abhominatio hominum* (the 50 abomination of men). And Gerson saith that detraction is grievouser than theft. This devil is fitly figured in that beast which Daniel saw, having three ranks of teeth, to whom it was said, 'Arise and eat much flesh' (Dan. 7: 5). These three orders of teeth are three manners of detraction. The first is to diminish or misinterpret the action of a man as if done under corrupt intention, or comparing one desert with another to show that the 55 action was not done so virtuously as it ought, neither so perfectly as it might have been. The second manner is under an intent of defamation to publish a man's hidden defects, which by the law of charity should be hidden and in reason may be winked at. The third manner is the most mischievous, which is to imagine treasons and impose them on innocents. These teeth Peter teacheth all Christians to beat out when he saith, 'Laying 60 apart all malice, and deceit, simulation, envy, and detraction, desire milk' (1 Pet. 2: 1–2). And what milk is this? Truly, sweet and charitable words, for it is the nature of the tongue to speak good and virtuous things. What otherwise it uttereth, it is but the corruptions of the heart. A detractor, as a Father saith, may rightly be compared to Cadmus of Greece, who sowed serpents' teeth on the earth, out of which arose men who slew one another 65 (Ovid, *Met.* 3. 104 ff.). So the detractor spreadeth nothing but corrupt and venomous seed, out of which spring contentions, wars, and dissensions among men. A detractor likewise, saith Holkot, is like a stinking sepulchre, for as out of the one issueth foul and poisonous savours, so out of the other's mouth cometh seditious and pernicious con- spiracies. It is a conclusion of Austin's that 'Qui negligit famam crudelis est' (He that 70 neglecteth his fame is cruel). And another philosopher witnesseth that he that loseth his

---

38. **Bajazeth** 15th-c. sultan of Turkey. 39–40. **schoolmaster...Camillus** Plutarch tells the story of the treacherous Falerian schoolmaster who delivered the children in his charge to the Roman general Camillus, who was besieging their city, Falerii; outraged, Camillus had the schoolmaster bound, whipped by his students, and returned home (*Parallel Lives*, 'Camil- lus'). 40. **Antigonus** Probably Antigonus II Gonatas (320–239 BC), who claimed Macedonia when Seleucus was murdered in 281. 51. **Gerson** Jean de Gerson (1363–1429), medieval theologian and mystic. 52. **beast** usually glossed as the Persian empire. 64. **Father** Church Father. 68. **Holkot** Robert Holkot, 14th-c. English Dominican philosopher. 70. **Austin** St Augustine. 71. **fame** reputation.

credit hath nought else to lose. Beware, therefore, of this devilish Scandal, Rebellion, and Detraction, and cross you from this devil lest he cross you in your walks.

Lying

Who is this with the Spanish hat, the Italian ruff, the French doublet, the Muff's cloak, the Toledo rapier, the German hose, the English stocking, and the Flemish shoe? Forsooth, a son of Mammon's that hath of long time been a traveller. His name is Lying, a devil at your commandment. If you talk with him of strange countries, why, you bring him a bed: he will hold you prattle from mornings very to candle lighting. He will tell you of monsters that have faces in their breasts and men that cover their bodies with their feet instead of a penthouse. He will tell you that a league from Poitiers near to Crontelles there is a family that by a special grace from the father to the son can heal the biting of mad dogs. And that there is another company and sort of people called Savveurs, that have St Catherine's wheel in the palate of their mouths, that can heal the stinging of serpents. He will tell you near Naples of miraculous wells, and of a stone in Calabria that fell from heaven and no sooner touched the earth but it became a fair chapel. If you put him to it, he will swear he hath taken St Thomas by the hand in his tomb. Nay, he will offer you the earth which our Lady sat on when Christ was born. He hath oil of St James, St Peter's forefinger, St Anne's skirt of her neckerchief, St Dunstan's walking staff, the stone the devil offered Christ to make bread on, the top of Longinus's spear, the bark of the Tree of Life in Paradise, a stone of Trajan's tomb, a piece of Caesar's chair wherein he was slain in the Senate house. Tell him of battles, it was he that first pulled off Francis the First his spur when he was taken up by the emperor, and in the battle of Lepanto he only gave Don John de Austria encouragement to charge afresh after the wind turned. At Boulogne he thrust three Switzers through the belly at one time with one partisan, and was at the hanging of that fellow that could drink up a whole barrel of beer without a breathing. At the battle of Cerisoles he will only tell you that he lent Marquis Guasto a horse when he fled from the duke of Anjou and retired to Alst, and that he healed his shot in the knee with only three dressings of his balsamo. There is no end of his falsehood except his tongue be cut out of his head. He will lie against God and misinterpret the Scriptures; he will falsify history and verify false miracles; he will swear

75

80

85

90

95

100

---

73. **cross you from** avoid. **cross** (1) meet; (2) cheat. 74. **Muff** resident of Switzerland or Germany. 76. **Mammon** devil who tempts by avarice, or immoderate desire for worldly wealth. 78. **hold you prattle** keep you in idle talk. **very** even. 80. **league from Poitiers** about 3 miles from a town in west central France. 83. **St Catherine's wheel** spiked wheel upon which St Catherine was tortured, here some unusual oral formation. 88. **skirt** edge. **St Dunstan** 10th-c. Benedictine, one of the most revered saints in England. 89. **stone...on** the first temptation of Christ in the desert (Matt. 4: 1–4). 89–90. **Longinus's spear** the weapon that pierced the side of the crucified Christ (John 19: 34). 90. **Tree of Life** a tree in paradise, representing God's blessings (Gen. 2: 9). **Trajan's tomb** The ashes of the Roman emperor Trajan (98–117) lie beneath the famous column bearing his name. 92. **pulled...spur** defeated. **Francis the First** François I of France (r. 1515–47), defeated by the Holy Roman Emperor Charles V at the battle of Pavia (1525) and subsequently imprisoned. 93. **battle of Lepanto** famous naval battle off the coast of Greece (7 Oct. 1571) in which the Christian forces under Don John of Austria defeated the Ottoman Turks. 94. **Boulogne** city in northern France captured by Henry VIII in 1544 against Swiss and German mercenaries. 95. **partisan** long-handled spear. 96. **Cerisoles** site of 1544 battle at which the French defeated the Imperial (Spanish and Italian) forces under Marquis del Vasto (**Guasto**, 97). 98. **balsamo** medicinal resin.

to any inconvenience to further his profit and ascribe honour to any man, let him but pay him for his commendations. He will testify a falsehood marvellous cunningly, and excuse a sin as smoothly as is possible. This is the likest devil to his father as any of his kindred for *Mammon mendax est* ['Mammon is a liar'] and so is he.

Player Devil

They say likewise there is a Player Devil, a handsome son of Mammon's, but yet I have   105
not seen him because he skulks in the country. If I chance to meet him against the next impression he shall shift very cunningly but I'll pleasantly conjure him, and though he hath a high hat to hide his huge horns, I'll have a wind of wit to blow it off speedily. For all of that sect I say thus much: If they use no other mirth but Eutrapelian urbanity and pleasure mixed with honesty, it is to be borne withal; but filthy speaking, scurrility unfit   110
for chaste ears—that I wish with the Apostle that it should not be named amongst Christians (Eph. 5: 4; cf. Arist. *Ethics*, 4). Again in stage plays to make use of historical Scripture, I hold it with the legists odious and, as the Council of Trent did (Sess. 4, *Fin.*), I condemn it. The conclusion shall be Tully's and, good fellows, mark it: 'Nihil est tam taetrum, nihil tam aspernandum, nihil homine indignius quam turpido' (*Tusculan*   115
Disputations 2. 46: There is nothing more vile, nothing more to be despised, nothing more unworthy a man than villainy and filthiness.) And if you will follow my counsel, therefore, write this over your theatres, 'Nil dictu foedum visuque haec limina tangat' (Juvenal, *Sat.* 14. 44: Let nought unfit to see or to be said | Be touched, or in these houses be bewrayed).   120

Prosopopeia: The Tears of Mary, 1596

I lift not up my voice with Esau to weep. He found a brother, I have lost a son. Jacob kissed Rachel and wept for joy to see her; I kiss the body of my son and weep because I see him not. Oh, would my Rachel might be his wounds, would my concubine were his

101. **let him** provided that he (the man). 105. **Player Devil** an actor. 106–7. **against ... impression** before the next onset (of a play). 107. **shift** evade (me). **conjure** summon. 109. **Eutrapelian** from the Greek *eutrapelia* (pleasant in conversation), considered a moral virtue by Aristotle. 113. **Council of Trent** nineteenth ecumenical council of the Church (1545–63), convened to combat Protestant heresies. Promulgating decrees concerning the publication and use of Scripture, Session IV (1556) concluded as follows: 'Besides the above, wishing to repress that temerity, by which the words and sentences of sacred Scripture are turned and twisted to all sorts of profane uses, to wit, to things scurrilous, fabulous, vain, to flatteries, detractions, superstitions, impious and diabolical incantations, sorceries, and defamatory libels; (the Synod) commands and enjoins, for the doing away with this kind of irreverence and contempt, and that no one may hence forth dare in any way to apply the words of sacred Scripture to these and such like purposes; that all men of this description, profaners and violators of the word of God, be by the bishops restrained by the penalties of law, and others of their own appointment' (*The Canons and Decrees of the Council of Trent*, tr. J. Waterworth, 1848: 20–1). 120. **bewrayed** revealed.

PROSOPOPEIA A **prosopopeia** is a fictional representation of a person speaking. 1. **Esau to weep** Esau wept upon being reunited with his brother Jacob after many years (Gen. 33: 4). 1–2. **Jacob ... wept** an allusion to the first meeting of Jacob and his future wife Rachel (Gen. 29: 11). 3. **would ... wounds** Would I might kiss his wounds as Jacob kissed Rachel. **concubine** lover.

cross, would his winding clothes were my wedding coats, and individed grave might bear two individed hearts. The daughters of Israel wept over Saul, and he a wicked king (2 Kgs. 1: 24). Oh, ye daughters of Jerusalem, weep, howl, and lament (Luke 23: 28)! A saviour is departed from you, a just king hath suffered. Let your faces be swollen with weeping for I will water my couch with tears. Let the voice of my mourning be heard in your streets for the noise of tribulation is harboured in my heart. Weep discomfortable tears, and I will mingle my drink with weeping (Ps. 101: 10). With weeping conduct that Lord to the grave who weepingly bewailed and bewailingly wept over your city. Enforce yourselves to weep whilst my eyes fail me through weeping (Jer. 14). Pour your tears on his heart whilst I feed on tears day and night. I will pour all my tears into his wounds; he will put all your tears into his bottle (Ps. 79: 6).

Let your tears run like a river, and let my tears be seas to suck them up. Only assist me in my strong weeping and tears, and he will wipe away all your tears. Why claim I partners in my grief who have no partners in my love? No creature loved thee dearer in thy life, and shall I seek associates in bewailing thee? Ah, my son, could aught but death depart thee and me? Nay, could there be one step betwixt me and death, who only in death may now seek thee?

Oh, Jesu, my father, my son, see here an indissoluble enigma: I, a virgin, had thee, a son; thou, a son, hadst me, a spouse; my son is my father, and I am the daughter of my son. I will then weep for thee as my father, sigh for thee as thy daughter, die for thee as thy spouse, and grieve for thee as thy mother. And as thou art wonderfully mine, so will I weep such a labyrinth of tears as no mortal mourner shall be able to track them. I will dissolve my relenting and yielding passions with all their fruits to lament thee as a son; I will put on the robes of dissolution to mourn thee as my spouse; I will gather and engross all grief to weep for thee as my father; and beginning where I end and ending where I began, I will make my tears famous in their continuance and my love more inflamed by thinking on thee.

I conjure you, ye daughters of Jerusalem, to look on me but weep no more with me. I lament a son lost to teach you to weep for the sorrows of your children to come. But if the entrails of your pity and springs of compassion must needs break out, weep you only his harms in life and let me bewail the loss of him by death. My confident mind and firm constancy, when the world was disturbed at his passion, made me peremptory. When the earth trembled, I was not troubled; when the pillars of heaven were shaken, I sounded not; they fell, I stood. Now am I drowned in the sea of bitterness. His eye of compassion (the pilot in those seas) hath left me; the helm of my hope is broken; the sun of my comfort is eclipsed. He hath passed the briary and thorny paths. The scourges hath registered his patience on his back; the nails have tied his triumphs, our sins his body, to

---

4. **winding clothes** burial cloths. The extravagant sexual and marital metaphors in this passage express Mary's ardent desire to be united with Christ in his suffering. **4–5. individed . . . individed** single . . . united. **19. depart** divide. **21. indissoluble enigma** *enigma inextricabile*, reads the marginal note, citing St Benedict, *Vita Mariae*. For similar paradoxes, see Southwell, POETRY. **35. peremptory** immovable. **36. sounded** cried out. **40. patience** suffering.

the cross. Injury hath spit her venom; infamy hath done his worst; justice hath ransacked his right. Wail this, ye daughters of Jerusalem, for your children shall wring for it. I only exclaim on death; death hath triumphed over life till glory overcome death. The holy one hath perished and seeth no corruption. One day's, one hour's, one minute's want of that I love makes every day an age, every hour a million of ages, every minute an eternity of 45 sorrow for that I want.

O you that pass this way and behold this body, you that look on these wounds and see these limbs, tell me, is not beauty oppressed, majesty embased, innocency martyred? Come near and judge if any grief may be compared with mine. The fairer children we have the dearer we love them; and should I, who bare the mirror of all 50 beauty in my womb, cease to weep for him? You men of Israel that behold this, be not amazed at my grief. My love was extreme, my grief must not be extenuate. The grace was great to bear Christ, the courage is as great to bewail him. His beauty was infinite, and shall my moans be definite? These thorns which martyrize his beauteous brows, this blood which bedeweth his bloodless face, these wounds that disgrace his blessed 55 body, this humility in so great and mighty a monarch are pricks and spurs to egg you unto repentance, springs to wash you from your wickedness, gates to bring you to glory. All these are but stings to stir you to love God, mirrors in which you see his beauty, books in which you read his wisdom, and preachers which teach you the way to heaven. O thou paschal lamb, whose blood hath been sprinkled on the timber of 60 the cross! O thou by whom men are delivered from the thraldom of Egypt and the captivity of the prince of this world, whose death killed their death, whose sacrifice satisfied for their sins, whose blood delivereth them from the chastising angel, whose meekness pacifieth the ire of the father, and whose innocency deserveth for them true security and justice! 65

ROBERT CHAMBERS

Originally from Yorkshire, Robert Chambers (1571–1628) studied at the English colleges at Rheims and Rome and received ordination as a Catholic priest in 1593. From 1599 to 1623 he served as confessor to the English Benedictine nuns in Brussels. Chambers wrote an account of the miracles performed by the Virgin Mary at Montaigu (1606) and a biblical romance, *Palestina* (1600), excerpted below. There the Emperor of the heavenly

48. embased debased. 52. extenuate lesser. 54. definite limited. martyrize wound. 60. paschal lamb the lamb sacrificed at the Jewish feast of Passover, whose blood sprinkled on the doorposts originally protected the families within. 61. thraldom captivity.

Jerusalem plans to defeat the Enchanter by sending the Prince, his only son, to die for our redemption.

Palestina, 1600

[Heaven and Earth, Fall and Redemption]

In the heavenly Jerusalem dwelleth an Emperor, so worthy and so wealthy as in his presence both the rarest majesty seemeth base and the richest monarch a beggar. The city wherein he abideth is so stately and so strong as neither Nineveh without a lipe, nor Babylon or Ecbatane may without a blush either be named or numbered with it. It is of a glass-like transparent but the purest-tried gold, that he resteth free from all doubt of ever having it wasted with fire, and void of all fear that it will not last forever. The streets of the cities are of the same gold. Through them runneth a river as clear as crystal; on either side of which groweth a tree, which for every of the twelve months giveth a several fruit and, according unto the effect it worketh, is called the Tree of Life. It is watered with the river, which is of no less virtue than the tree, and hath his first vent from under the Emperor his throne. The city is square, 375 miles as well in height as length and breadth; the compass is 1500 mile. About it is a wall 216 foot high, all of jasper stone, which, beside the firmness thereof, is of a most fresh and beautiful green colour that it moveth the beholders to wish as much as to wonder. The wall is built so low of purpose that the stateliness of the city may appear the better unto all passengers. The foundation of the wall is of twelve precious stones, the jasper, the sapphire, the chalcedony, the emerald, the sardonyx, the sardius, the chrysolite, the beryl, the topaz, the chrysoprase, the hyacinth, the amethyst. In this wall were twelve gates in all points correspondent unto the stateliness of the wall—three toward the east, as many toward the west, also three toward the north, and three toward the south. Every several gate is one of those twelve several precious stones, and no one of the gates without all the rest of the stones. But they are not so much beautified by them as by the presence of twelve princes, which stand in every of the twelve gates one, who seem there to abide only as allurements to their city, if any, being weary of the world's illusions, should endeavour to seek their safety; for neither have they any cause to look unto their gates, nor any custom to lock them.

And no worse than princes can stand at his gates, all whose household are princes, every one of them rich because they cannot enjoy more than they do, all happy because they cannot become less than they are, and only contend who shall to their power give him most praise, who hath filled their hearts with such joy as neither eye hath seen, ear

3. **Nineveh** wealthy capitol of ancient Assyria. **lipe** jerk (of embarrassment). 4. **Babylon** magnificent city of Mesopotamia, later capital of the Chaldee empire (7th–6th c. BC). **Ecbatane** capital of ancient Media, conquered by Persia. 9. **Tree of Life** See Gen. 2: 9. 10. **vent** source. 12. **compass** circumference. The figures do not make sense by earthly computation. 26. **all ... princes** in whose household all are princes. 29–30. **neither ... conceive** an echo of St Paul: 'eye

hath heard, nor heart (but their own) can conceive, and furnished all their senses with   30
such delight as still they covet but never want, still they taste but are never glutted,
because they no sooner wish than have, and every taste giveth a fresh appetite. If the very
pavement of their streets be of most pure gold and the foundation of their walls of most
precious stones, think what ornaments are those which are within their palaces. No night
succeedeth their day; no winter's cold nor summer's heat disturbeth that temperature   35
which an everlasting springtime maintaineth in lively vigour. One kingdom contenteth
them all, and because they all hold it of one in whom only they joy and by whom they
enjoy it, they know not how to live but as one. No one envieth at another's good, both
because every one hath what his heart can desire and also for that they all have one object,
which so mightily draweth all their powers to the continual love and, looking thereon as   40
they have neither power nor leisure to apply themselves to any other. More than that they
love each other in respect that every one loveth him, who, as each thinketh, cannot be
loved too much.

How daintily do they feed whose meat and drink is love! For if anything delight
without any likelihood of ever loathing it, it is his love; if anything do please without   45
danger of poison, it is his love; if anything be able to quicken what seemeth quite dead, it
is his love. Oh, how well did the poets aim at the truth when they said that love was a god
but shot much wide when they feigned that he was blinded, whose seeing only and being
seen is that which giveth life to all men; but never woundeth he any against their wills,
and whose heart he woundeth, he salveth with the joy of such a love as is far more noble   50
than themselves, and will not leave the least love unrequited.

This sovereign lord over so many happy princes, his estate is such as cannot by any art
be described; his glorious throne no eye is able to behold; his profound wisdom no
understanding is able to comprehend; his authority no power is able to resist. He liveth in
light inaccessible, he ruleth with majesty incomparable, and because his very name is   55
ineffable, too much presumption it were to attempt to set forth the worthiness of his
nature. In his works he hath shown himself so provident as all may justly admire him, so
good as all may above all love him, so sweet as all may joy sufficiently in him, but for any
inferior unto himself perfectly to know him were to limit his perfections, which are
beyond all bounds because they are infinite.   60

With this Emperor lived the above mentioned princes without any tediousness, desire
of change, or any kind of sorrow, being incapable of anything but happiness, until a
marvellous rare and rigorous seeming accident befell them. For their Emperor having
one only son, equal unto his father in power, might, and authority, and in no one point
of perfection degenerating from him, from both whom for the infinite likeness betwixt   65
them proceeded an infinite love, he deputed him to a public, shameful, and a painful
death, which did so amaze the princes attendant, whose love was no less unto him than

hath not seen, nor ear heard, neither hath it entered into the heart of man, what things God hath prepared for those that
love him' (I Cor. 2: 9). **46. quicken** enliven.

unto his father, that (might they have been suffered) they would all have sustained that punishment to have saved their prince; but their offer was refused for the sentence was irrevocable.   70

The motive of this unnatural seeming judgement was an exceeding great love which he bare unto a lady, his adopted daughter, who was so enchanted by her own folly, as of a most comely and beautiful creature she became so misshapen and so ugly that she was loathsome even unto herself. This enchantment was by eating an apple of which her father before had given her, warning she should not taste upon peril of that which should   75 ensue thereof. But her pride was so great that, ingrateful to so good a lord and disobedient to so careful a father, she followed the motion which was made unto her by a false though a fair-spoken enemy and eat thereof, contrary to her father his commandment.

The enchantment was so devised that, having taken effect, it should not be dissolved   80 but by the death of the only son of an emperor, who should exceed all the princes in the world in gifts both of body and mind. He should be peerless for his birth, riches, beauty, wisdom, and might, whose father should never know any woman, nor his mother any man, and should in the very self-same instant both have and want both father and mother. The liking by any such prince of such an unlovely lady being unlike, and the   85 birth of any such prince or other seeming impossible made the Enchanter secure that this his work should endure forever.

The Enchanter himself was one of more malice than might, but yet of more might than an unruly assailed could well resist. He was sometime a prince of the Emperor his court, and among princes a prince, being endowed with far more excellent gifts than any   90 his fellow princes, and exalted unto that honour as he was reputed the chiefest under his lord and master. But bearing himself so proudly against his maker, he found by too late an experience that he who bestowed those graces upon him could also again bereave him of them, and because he had once abused them with intolerable pride he should ever after be abridged of them to his eternal pain. To revenge which disgrace he assayed the lady,   95 the Emperor his daughter, and won her love so far forth as she gave more credit unto him than unto her father, and would do more at his request than at her father's commandment. For although she seemed at the first to have a small liking unto his motion, yet with fair promises and too far above his power to perform, in the end he made her give a consent unto her utter overthrow, had not the Emperor his son, being deputed by his   100 father thereunto, undertaken to release her by the loss of his own life.

The ransom being appointed to be disbursed infinitely exceeding that which was to be redeemed, too gracious for so ungracious a creature, and too bountiful for her who wilfully made herself bond-slave by selling outright a royal and real good for a proud, imaginative Godhead, a great difficulty arose in what manner it should be paid. For the   105 Prince, being of so excellent a nature that he was not capable of the smallest annoyance

72. **lady** Eve (and all humanity). 78. **eat** ate.

and in so strong a hold that he could not sustain the least harm, much less the loss of his life, it was needful he should both take upon him a nature and abide in such place as in which and where he might effect his desire.

Here love, which maketh everyone it possesseth to conform themselves unto their love, quickly determined what was in doubt and made this conclusion: that he should take upon him the same nature of which his sister was and, her perverseness only excepted, he should in all things be like unto her. Which conceit love made so conformable unto his former counsel as the more he thought upon it the fitter the means seemed to bring his purpose to a good pass. For first, he thought that hereby he might in a most lovely manner enjoy her company, whom he so entirely loved, without giving any cause of jealousy to her over diligent keeper. Secondly, he thought that the keeper, taking him for his captive, might the more easily be overtaken for his carelessness. Thirdly, he thought this nature fittest for his purpose, that she whom he loved, being of the same nature, might the better guess at the torture he should suffer for her sake (because by the shedding of his blood he was to work her safety), and fancy him the sooner who would adventure so far to win her love, who was not worthy of a good look.

ELIZABETH SOUTHWELL

In 1607 Elizabeth Southwell, a former royal maid who converted to Catholicism, wrote a manuscript account of Queen Elizabeth's sickness and death. Southwell gives an eyewitness report, rife with sensational incident: the receipt of a magic coin from Wales, supposed to preserve life; the discovery of a playing card nailed to the queen's chair as part of an evil spell; the appearance and disappearance of Elizabeth's ghost before her death; the sudden explosion of the dead queen's body in the coffin. Cecil appears throughout this account as presumptuous, untrustworthy, and menacing. Queen Elizabeth dismisses her Protestant divines as worthless and refuses to name James her successor.

Though Southwell refrains from editorializing, her narrative served to confirm Catholic views of the queen and her reign. Robert Persons, SJ, published Southwell's manuscript with embellishments to show that 'there may be a just fear of her [Queen Elizabeth's] everlasting damnation' for heresy (*A Discussion of the Answer of M. William Barlow*, 1612, sig. Ee4ᵛ). Persons reads the incident of the queen's exploding body as a fitting climax to her immoral life, an example of God's terrifying judgement. Though partisan in its emphases and unverified, Southwell's narrative contests the accepted narratives of Elizabeth's end, also to some degree partisan and unverified, which have passed as historical fact.

107. **hold** position. 113. **conceit** plan. 117. **keeper** i.e. the Enchanter.

The Sickness and Death of Queen Elizabeth, 1607

Her Majesty being in very good health, one day Sir John Stanhope, being the vice-chamberlain and Secretary Cecil's dependant and familiar, came and presented Her Majesty with a piece of gold of the bigness of an angel, full of characters, which he said a old woman in Wales bequeathed her on her deathbed. And thereupon he discoursed how the said old woman by virtue of the same lived to the age of one hundred   5 and twenty years, and being in that age, having all her body withered and consumed, and wanting nature to nourish, she died, commanding the said piece of gold to be carefully sent Her Majesty, alleging further that as long as the said old woman wore it upon her body, she could not die.

The queen upon the confidence she had hereof took the said gold and wore it about   10 her neck. Now though she fell not suddenly sick, yet daily decreased of her rest and feeding and within fifteen days fell downright sick. And the cause being wondered at by my Lady Scrope, with whom she was very private and confident, being her near kinswoman, Her Majesty told her, commanding her to conceal the same, she saw one night in her bed her body exceeding lean and fearful in a light of fire. For the which the   15 next day she desired to see a true looking glass, which in twenty years before she had not seen but only such a one which of purpose was made to deceive her sight. Which glass being brought her, she fell presently exclaiming at all those which had so much commended her, and took it so offensively that all those which had before flattered her durst not come in her sight.   20

Now falling into extremity, she sat two days and three nights upon her stool ready dressed and could never be brought by any of her Council to go to bed or eat or drink. Only my Lord Admiral one time persuaded her to drink some broth. For any of the rest she would not answer them to any question but said softly to my Lord Admiral's earnest persuasions that if he knew what she had seen in her bed, he would not persuade her as he   25 did. And Secretary Cecil, overhearing her, asked if Her Majesty had seen any spirits. To which she say she scorned to answer him to so idle a question. Then he told her how, to content the people, Her Majesty must go to bed. To which she smiled wonderfully, condemning him, saying that the word 'must' was not to be used to princes. Thereupon said, 'Little man, little man, if your father had lived, ye durst not have said so much; but   30 thou knowest I must die and that maketh thee so presumptuous.' And presently commanding him and the rest to depart her chamber, willing my Lord Admiral to

---

1. **John Stanhope** (1568?–1611).   1–2. **vice-chamberlain** an officer of the Royal Household.   2. **Secretary Cecil** Robert Cecil (1563–1612), secretary of state, succeeded his father, William Cecil, Lord Burlegh, as Elizabeth's chief minister.   3. **angel** a coin.   13. **Lady Scrope** Philadelphia Scrope (d. 1627), Southwell's great aunt, a lady of the bedchamber. **confident** trusting.   15. **in . . . fire** This vision of burning Persons amplifies, dating it from the queen's stay at Whitehall before the onset of sickness and recounting another conversation about it (*Discussion*, 1612, sig. Eei ᵛ).   21. **stool** privy stool (box for chamber utensils) or cushions.   23. **Lord Admiral** Charles Howard, earl of Nottingham (1536–1624).

stay, to whom she shook her head and with a pitiful voice said, 'My lord, I am tied with a chain of iron about my neck.' He, alleging her wonted courage to her, she replied 'I am tied and the case is altered with me.' Then two ladies waiting on her in her chamber 35 discovered in the bottom of her chair the queen of hearts with a nail of iron knocked through the forehead of it, the which the ladies durst not pull out, remembering that the like thing was used to the old Lady of Sussex, and proved afterwards for a witchcraft, for the which certain were hanged as instruments of the same.

The lady Elizabeth Guilford, then waiting on the queen and leaving her asleep in her 40 privy chamber, met her, as she thought, three or four chambers off; fearing she would ha'been displeased that she left her alone, came towards her to excuse herself, and she vanished away; and when she returned into the same chamber where she left her found her asleep as before. So growing past recovery, having kept her bed fifteen days, besides three days she sat upon her stool and one day, being pulled up by force, stood on her feet 45 fifteen hours, the Council sent to her the bishop of Canterbury and other of her prelates. Upon sight of whom she was much offended, cholerically rating them, bidding them be packing, saying she was no atheist, but knew full well that they were [illegible] hedge-priests, and took it for an indignity that they should speak to her.

Now being given over by all and at her last gasp, keeping still her sense in everything 50 and giving ever when she spake apt answers, though she spake very seldom, having then a sore throat, she desired to wash it that she might answer more freely to what the Council demanded, which was to know whom she would have king. But they, seeing her throat troubled her so much, desired her to hold up her finger when they named whom liked her. Whereupon they named the king of France, the king of Scotland, at which she never 55 stirred. They named my Lord Beauchamp, whereto she said, 'I will have no rascal's son in my seat but [illegible] one worthy to be a king.' Hereupon instantly she died.

Then the Council went forth and reported she meant the king of Scots, whereupon they went to London to proclaim him, leaving her body with charge not to be opened, such being her desire. But Cecil having given a secret warrant to the surgeons, they 60 opened her, which the rest of the Council afterwards passed it over though they meant it not so. Now her body, being seared up, was brought to Whitehall, where, being watched every night by six several ladies, myself that night there watching as one of them, being all

35. **case is altered** situation has changed. 36. **queen of hearts** The playing card is evidence of witchcraft used against Elizabeth, perhaps in conjunction with the gold coin. 42–3. **she vanished away** This story of Elizabeth's ghost reflects ironically on the queen's haughty dismissal of Cecil's question about spirits. 46. **bishop of Canterbury** John Whitgift (1530–1604). 48–9. **hedge-priests** uneducated, inferior clerics. Persons embellishes Southwell's account: Elizabeth complains that the archbishop of Canterbury pronounced the sentence of death upon her 'as if she had lived an atheist'; and no one prays in her presence until she is 'past sense and at the last gasp' (*Discussion*, 1612, sig. Ee2). The narratives of Southwell and Persons conflict with other accounts, wherein the prelates greatly comfort the dying queen. 54–5. **liked her** she liked. 55. **king of France** Henri IV (r. 1589–1610) **king of Scotland** James VI (r. 1567–1625), Elizabeth's successor, James I of England (r. 1603–25). 55–6 **she never stirred** In other accounts Elizabeth clearly indicates James. 56. **Lord Beauchamp** Henry Seymour Beauchamp (1561–1612), son of Catherine Grey (sister of Jane Grey, queen of England for nine days in 1553), and hence a claimant to the throne. The **rascal** (low or common sort) that Elizabeth refers to is Beauchamp's father, Edward Seymour Beauchamp who married Catherine Grey in secret. 60–1. **they opened her** Southwell alone asserts that Cecil defied the queen's orders and issued a secret warrant to open her body, i.e. to disembowel her. 62. **seared up** cauterized for burial. **Whitehall** a royal palace in London. 62–3 **watched every night** Southwell is the unique source for this vigil.

about the body which was fast nailed up in a board coffin with leaves of lead covered with velvet, her body and head brake with such a crack that splitted the wood, lead, and 65 cerecloth! Whereupon the next day she was fain to be new trimmed up. Whereupon they gave their verdicts that if she had not been opened, the breath of her body would ha'been much worse, but no man durst speak it publicly for displeasing Secretary Cecil.

Her Majesty understood that Secretary Cecil had given forth to the people that she was mad and, therefore, in her sickness did many times say to him, 'Cecil, know I am not 70 mad. You must not think to make Queen Jane of me.' And although many reports by Cecil's means were spread how she was distracted, myself nor any that were about her could ever perceive her speeches, so well applied, proceeded from a distracted mind.

JOHN BARCLAY

Scottish polemicist and writer, John Barclay (1582–1621), despite his Catholicism, found favour at the court of James I, doubtless through the influence of his father William, who had vigorously denied papal authority over kings (see Bellarmine, CONTROVERSIES). John Barclay held similar views and satirized the Jesuits but he defended the sacrament of the Eucharist, as well as the intercession of saints, miracles, and relics. Barclay wrote two Latin works of fiction that enjoyed enormous popularity in Europe, the satirical *Euphormionis Lusinini Satyricon* (1605–7) and *Argenis* (Paris, 1621), part historical *roman à clef*, part romance. Excerpted below, *Argenis* achieved over fifty editions in the next century and translation into every major European language, including a partial (now lost) English version by Ben Jonson, commissioned by King James I.

Argenis takes its name from the lead character, the daughter of Meleander, king of Sicily, who is pursued by four suitors. While Barclay maintains no exact parallels, the plot generally describes the conflicts over succession in late sixteenth-century France. Argenis represents true sovereignty and the hero Poliarchus, Henri of Navarre, who became King Henri IV (r. 1589–1610) and converted to Catholicism (1593). The wicked Selenissa represents Catherine de Médicis, who organized the St Bartholomew's Day Massacre of Protestants in 1572 (see Fig. 15). The first selection below analyses the phenomenon of Puritan violence, particularly

---

65. her...brake Other contemporary accounts do not mention this explosion of the queen's corpse; Persons adds the phrase 'to the terror and astonishment of all that were present' (*Discussion*, 1612, sig. Ee2). Some speculate that gases from the decomposing body could have caused this incident. 66. cerecloth linen coated with wax, used for wrapping corpses. 67. breath odour. 69–70. she was mad Along with other contemporary witnesses, Southwell attests that Elizabeth was not mad but *compos mentis* unto her death. 71. Queen Jane probably Jane Seymour (1509–32), third wife of Henry VIII, who suffered from delirium on her deathbed.

resonant to Stuart England, and counsels a *politique* gentleness of response; the second presents the romance reunion of Argenis and Poliarchus.

Argenis, 1629

[Hyperphanii or Puritans]

[Iburranes:] 'We have given this name to them of Hyperphanii out of the nature of their superstition; their faction, troublesome to princes, was in our days begun, having one Usimulca for their author. He, despising the religion which ever hath been professed in Sicily, was bold to bring in a new one and trouble the quiet of such minds as either pride or too much simplicity made fit for him to prey upon. Some, therefore, were ambitious   5
of dissenting with such a teacher from the belief of their ancestors; others were deceived by his eloquence, mingled with a show of piety. To these was added a furious love of novelty, so blinding their souls that the barbarous devices of Usimulca wanted not those that commended them, not out of the wild and furthest parts of the world but, which is to be admired, even of the foster children of Sicily. Although there be nothing more ugly   10
than those monsters with which he polluted his schools, I am ashamed to relate his madness, so full of contumely to the gods. He denied that any man commits a sin but he whom the gods compel to do it and have predestined him to the same; that howsoever thou strive against sin, be innocent in thy life among men and liberal in the service of the gods, he yet affirms that by this piety thou art made nothing the dearer to the gods. For   15
that all these are not the virtue that doth render men acceptable to the gods but only the signs of that virtue. Further, that there is no difference in sins but in them that commit them, for those with whom the gods were displeased, should they but steal a few pot-herbs, did deserve whatsoever the Furies, as the poets make them, could inflict; but the others, not with parricide nor with incest could slake the friendship which the gods had   20
contracted with them. So from this same mire of sin these to come out untouched, those polluted and filthy, as if thou dost thrust under water any kind of water fowl, thou mayst pull them out with dry feathers, where other birds in the same water and held there a less time do lose the fashion and use of their wings. Other frenzies of Usimulca I forbear to speak of; nor would these monstrous things have found followers any longer time, had   25
they not happened upon the infancy of our kings, in which for the most part those which are of turbulent humours can neither be kept from ill nor punished for it.

---

1. **Iburranes** Barberinus, i.e. Maffeo Barberini (1558–1644), in 1601 papal legate to France, in 1623 elected Pope Urban VIII. **Hyperphanii** 'super-appearing', i.e. Puritans. 3. **Usimulca** i.e. Jean Calvin (1509–64). 4. **Sicily** i.e. France. 10. **admired** wondered at. 12. **contumely** insolence. 12–13. **He . . . same** the Calvinist doctrine of predestination, positing that God predetermined the saved (the elect) and the damned (the reprobate) (see Erasmus, CONTROVERSIES). 13–16. **that . . . gods** the Calvinist denial of the salvific efficacy of good works. 19. **Furies** goddesses of retribution. 23. **where** whereas.

16. Giorgio Vasari, 'The Massacre of the Huguenots', Sala Regia, Vatican Palace, 1572–4. At the behest of Pope Gregory XIII, Vasari depicts the infamous St Bartholomew's Day Massacre (24 August 1572) as the prevention of a plot against the French royal family and as a divine triumph over seditious heretics.

'This disease was increased by the eagerness of the factions, and some of the nobility made themselves leaders of the Hyperphanii that then were in an uproar. But then in most woeful manner was Sicily, from the one end to the other plagued with civil arms; and as many as loved the licentiousness of rebellion revolted to the Hyperphanii, being bold also to bring their colours into the field against the kings themselves. Nothing then escaped their fury: the altars of the gods were trodden under foot, their temples razed, the towns defaced with fire, and the novelty of their doctrine consecrated to the Furies in the blood of their own countrymen. So many years being past since, thou mayst yet see the cities, as it were, mutilated, the roofs and pinnacles of the temples being broken down, which they have showed their rage upon. In those garboils they did so separate and in a sort divorce themselves from the other Sicilians that as making another country and another people; not in making of peace and leagues would they sincerely communicate with the rest of the nation and, being tossed by their unquiet disposition, they always either threaten war or fear it.

'Their minds thus affected, what free power of command dost thou think the kings could have over them? Cities, soldiers, haven, nay, almost whole provinces they possessed, out of which they disdainfully consult how much they may with their own conveniency spare the king, how far despise and refuse him. If either for his wars or other affairs they promise their assistance as meriting thanks, they brag of that fidelity, forgetting that of good subjects those covenants are not required, neither that they should need so often to renew them if once they were firm and stable. Far like confederates than subjects they aid, and are either friends to the king's designs or against them. Thus do they carry themselves as arbiters both of the kings and the gods, proportioning what they owe to either not by the laws and customs of their country but by their own humours. How great plagues this contagion doth threaten to Sicily, if no man should inform thee, thou wouldst easily see. For as those hatreds are most irreconcilable that burn out of the contentions of different religions, it is with reason to be feared that at one time or at other the Hyperphanii, what with their own forces they cannot, though with the destruction of their own country, will seek to obtain by inviting foreign nations and those that envy us, not more to the war than to the prey and, as it were, to the possession of Sicily. But if the gods, being more merciful, preserve us from that, yet how great are those which we both see and feel? If children be offended with their parents, if noblemen with the king, immediately they with a counterfeit profession throw themselves into the sect as a certain kind of enfranchisement, not being ignorant that therein they principally hurt themselves, but at so high a price they are content to buy the torturing of such as they malign. What should I speak of the vestal nuns? What of the priests? When they grow weary of living chaste, they presently renounce their religion and, hired with the reward of

---

32. colours flags, i.e. troops. **33 ff.** Iburranes describes the wars of religion in France (1562–98). **37. garboils** tumults. **38. in a sort** in some manner. **that as making** as if they made. **48. Far** more. **55–6. what . . . nations** what they cannot obtain with their own forces will seek to obtain by inviting foreign nations, to the destruction of their country. **57. prey** plunder. **61. enfranchisement** liberation. **64–5. hired . . . marriages** Catholic priests and nuns who became Protestant

incestuous marriages, betake themselves to the Hyperphanii. With these examples and 65
that liberty of disputing and living, the common sort are made to waver, that first what
gods there are or how to be worshipped they are in doubt, and straight with an ignorant
and wicked arrogance do hold nothing sacred, nothing certain of the gods. So by this
impiety the service of the gods doth suffer and withal it frets into the peace of the
commonwealth and wasteth the strength of diseased Sicily, which will never recover her 70
former vigour, except first the Hyperphanii, being restored to their right wits, this wound
be skinned.'

Then Archombrotus: 'But,' saith he, 'why do the Sicilians forbear with all their force at
once to smother this fire? Or why are they loath with full armies to cut off this imposture,
which with a most pernicious infection eats further into them? In truth, I that am a 75
stranger here do make offer of my hand and sword to the business. Neither will I believe
that I shall ever offer a more pleasing sacrifice than when I shall pour out their blood to
the gods or they through my wounds shall take assay of mine. It is reason that thou
shouldst speak this, Iburranes, to Meleander and, as thou canst, persuade him to this
war.' 80

Iburranes smiled. 'And I commend,' saith he, 'thy earnestness, kindled by thy young
fervour. In times past many have been of the same opinion until by the event of things it
appeared that as certain creatures are nourished with poison, so this sect grows stronger
with the public calamities, and is fatted with war and slaughter. That, therefore, thy
advice may be more mild, hear me a little, Archombrotus. Many do now favour 85
Usimulca slightly, who, if with force or menaces they shall be commanded to quit his
doctrine, will more straightly embrace that sect as oppressed. And then with a secret lust
of being free in their opinion and besides of being opposite to the laws of the land will
obstinately wed themselves to the faction. So with indignation and the tempest of
partaking they will indeed suck up that superstition into their minds, which, if no 90
man had pressed them, they would either careless have neglected or, looking quietly
upon it, of their own accord have condemned. That, as threads of themselves slender,
which when they are loose thou mayst easily break, but if with a violent wreathing thou
dost twine them together, the more hard thou strain them, the more strongly they hold
together and in the end become a cord which thou wilt never be able to break. So these in 95
their own nature more negligent of their own side and which with delay would become
more tractable to us, when they see the sword bent against their bosoms, enjoining them
to a forced, that is (as they account it) a shameful recantation, they furiously join
themselves to their own side and, tying themselves in a knot of conspiring, grow to the
strength of a whole nation, hardly to be resisted. For then the infection spreads itself 100
among more than can either be indicted as guilty or called to their trial by an officer.

renounced their vows of celibacy and were free to marry each other. **69. frets into** disturbs. **72. skinned** healed. **73.**
Archombrotus ('earthly ruler'), i.e. François D'Anjou, duke of Alençon (1554–84), son of Henri II (r. 1547–59) and
Catherine de Médicis, a moderate Catholic, suitor to Argenis. **74. imposture** deception. **78. take assay of** try. **79.**
Meleander ('sweet man'), i.e. Henri III (r. 1574–89), also a son of Henri II and Catherine de Médicis. **82. event** actual
occurrence. **97. tractable** manageable.

And, besides, this sect of the Hyperphanii not with suffering and obeying (as those best and primitive ones) doth seek to grow greater but, easily persuaded to stir and rise in rebellions, doth use to maintain and make good their mischiefs with no little effusion of blood. And Sicily is full of youth, which now levity, now want, now the love of arms doth   105
so transport that, not caring for right or their own honour, they will enrol themselves with the faction and bear arms with them, though against the gods and all mankind. In this sort many, while arms are stirring in hope of spoil, join themselves to the Hyper-phanii, who in peace would renounce them; and the kings, making war upon them, do create more new delinquents than they can cut off from the old number.'   110

'Must, then,' said Archombrotus, 'this bane of the kingdom be endured? And while the venom spreads itself must you stay till all the members of it be destroyed? At least in the physic, how dangerous so ever you make it, there can be nothing more grievous to be feared than this dead-killing delay.'

But Iburranes: 'There are,' said he, 'other devices, Archombrotus, and those more   115
certain, by which Sicily may be cleansed of this stain. But the destinies have given that ability of doing this cure only to kings; and we hope that the piety and care of Meleander will make the rage of this disease to abate so that these civil wars once come to an end, which have ever added much to the Hyperphanii. In the peace, quiet, and happy estate of the kingdom, they are to be tamed, in which time they have nothing which by robbing   120
the whole land they may give to their uncertain and seditious assistants. And that not being sharpened by the eagerness of their adversaries, their own is much lenified. And of the chief of them, many have their eyes bent upon the king, upon whose favour in that calm all things depend. But if he shall pursue their doctrine, not so much with hate as contempt, he shall by it more effectually than by any war bring the nobility to change   125
their minds, who, if with an unhappy bashfulness they be hindered from forsaking their sect, at least they will provide for their children and commit them to masters who shall instruct them after the ancient manner that they may live in the court in favour. For those which do prefer their stiff obstinacy before heaven, reason, and the constitutions of their ancestors, adhering to Usimulca, will be overcome, believe me, with this passage to   130
honours and the hope of the king's bounties being warily shut up; especially if these punishments be not inflicted upon them by public laws made against them (for that were enough to drive them, being madded with it, into complaints, conspiracies, and froward arms), but with a soft and gentle fashion of the prince, not giving them any part of the public benefits of the state, nor permitting them to stray beyond the liberty which the   135
laws do allow. In other things, let him be gentle to them and, using them familiarly sometimes, labour to appear to them such a one as is worthy to be pleased. For many of them, Archombrotus, do not err out of their own inclination, but by the fault of the sect and their bringing up, which, if it were not, are of an even disposition and not inferior to their ancestors. These remedies, however slow, will by little and little cut in sunder the   140

113. **physic** medicine. 121. **that** that cause. 122. **lenified** softened. 133. **froward** perverse.

sinews of the Hyperphanii; and they, which have under show of a higher understanding grown together, discovering also and condemning the abuses of that philosophy which at the first appeared so stately, will not with much difficulty be severed. But these are courses to be taken in a time of a more settled peace—which the powers above restore to Sicily and not permit the Hyperphanii to aid Lycogenes! For him, truly I do not believe that he will, whatsoever report doth brag, ever be of their religion, neither to make himself gracious with that faction that is with scarce the fortieth part of Sicily, that he will pull upon himself the hatred of all the rest.' 145

When Iburranes had thus spoken, he invited Archombrotus to supper, and did familiarly advise him also to use the Hyperphanii with all courtesy. For that they (as the state of Sicily then stood) were more to be reformed with fair usage, with example, and temperate disputation than with a professed and mutual loathing. 150

[Reunion of Argenis and Poliarchus]

'Do I see thee,' said she, 'my dearest? Or is it a dream that thus presents thee to me and brings a supposed joy to thy Argenis?' 'Thou seest me, lady,' replied he, 'who now with a fresh sensibleness of them do again feel my passed miseries, and by beholding thee am put in mind how great a calamity it was to me to have been so long absent from thee. But if the remembrance of it be not grievous to thee, give me leave to ask what thou thoughtest, what heart thou hadst in my dangers. How wert thou sorrowful? How often didst thou blame my absence?' 155

Then she, 'Too well, alas, thou mayst of thine own griefs collect how sad days I passed while thou wert absent. By so much also the more unhappy, Poliarchus, that I might not follow thee, that I know thou didst wander in the midst of dangers, finally, that there are some that dare hope I may prove inconstant. But tell me again, art thou indeed the same Poliarchus? Art thou returned into Sicily? Art thou in safety? Do I see thee here before me? But, alas, am not I, Poliarchus, the cause of this leanness which I see in thy face? Or must we not again run the same fortunes and thy banishment be renewed? Must we always love in fears and doubtfulness?' 160

165

He then compendiously acquainted her with all the accidents which had befallen him, how he was shipwrecked, how he overcame the pirates, how he had lien sick in the Numidian court. Argenis, on the other side, informed him (which did more concern them) in few words of the desires of Radirobanes. And that, indeed, she feared lest her father might be inclined to receive for his son-in-law a man which had well deserved of him. 'A mischief,' said she, 'if not hindered by thee, which I will prevent with my own death. But how miserable a thing dost thou think it is to be continually subject to the deadly stroke, which is no farther from me than the conclusion of this match, which the 170

175

145. **Lycogenes** ('wolf born'), i.e. Henri, duke of Guise, head of the militant Catholics, suitor to Argenis. **153 ff.** The union of the lovers represents the restoration of true sovereignty and peace to France. **168. compendiously** summarily. **169. lien** lain. **171. Radirobanes** Philip II of Spain (r. 1556–98), powerful Catholic, suitor to Argenis.

Sardinians do most earnestly press. To this is added that I am alone; I have none to comfort me or to whom I might impart my cares. I am afraid of Radirobanes, who hath armed forces. I am not assured of my father. Selenissa herself (oh, the wicked woman!) is revolted to my enemies.'

'And I,' said Poliarchus, 'have now a-good looked about for her. For this is the first   180
time that ever I spake with thee in her absence.'

'I will,' said Argenis, 'if I live, render her most miserable. She is for the king of Sardinia. Neither do I know why or how she came to be changed. But that thou mayst be out of doubt of her treachery, when we were in private she praised Radirobanes. Now was that enough, but she did further dare to persuade me that at least with a feigned   185
friendship I should show myself kind to him; that is, as with the turn of the tide I should by degrees fall off from thee. Now also that she might not know thou wert hers, I have given her leave to go to him. They both now in the garden do determine of my fate. But she shall not offend without her payment. If ever I be happy, she is ruined.'

176. **Sardinians** i.e. the Spanish. 178. **Selenissa** ('moon woman,' so called for her inconstancy), Catherine de Médicis (1519–89), wife of Henri II. 180. **a-good** thoroughly.

DOCUMENTS

Popes produced various legislative documents: *constitutions*, decisions on faith or discipline applying to all the faithful; *encyclicals*, letters to bishops; *decrees*, pronouncements relating to the general welfare of the Church; *decretals* or *rescripts*, replies to petitions; *privileges*, concessions or favours; and *briefs*, less formal papal letters. These documents were often called *bulls* (from *bulla*, or 'bubble'), a term that referred to the leaden seals which authenticated papal and royal documents. Whether promulgated in council or not, papal documents had binding authority and far-reaching, if often unintended, consequences.

The suppression of heresy by ecclesiastical and civil authority is as old as the Church but the Inquisition, a papal tribunal empowered to try offenders, originated in the thirteenth century. Its beginnings appear in the decrees of the Fourth Lateran Council (1215) and in those of Pope Gregory IX (1227–41), particularly his *Ille humani generis* (1231), excerpted below. This letter empowers Dominicans at Regensburg to form an inquisitorial tribunal that would cooperate with local bishops and the secular courts but remain directly answerable to the pope. Thus began one of the most notorious institutions in Church history, infamous for secret proceedings, the confiscations of property, the persecution of the rich and *conversos* (converted Jews or Muslims), the use of torture (authorized by Pope Innocent IV in *Ad extirpanda*, 1252), and the *auto da fé* (act of faith) or public execution by burning. Attempting to clarify the historical perspective, scholars point out that the Church only convicted or acquitted persons of heresy and that the state then subsequently determined and executed all punishments. Historians also cite the Protestant executions for heresy, the wars of religion, the polemical exaggeration and distortion of Inquisition proceedings. They demonstrate how the institution became appropriated by corrupt clerics and powerful kings, as well as by anti-Catholic propagandists. Still the appalling record of examinations, confiscations, and executions constitutes one of the most shameful chapters in Church history (see Fig. 17).

The next papal bull below, Pope Alexander VI's *Inter caetera* (4 May 1493), granted the settlement and conversion of the unclaimed new world to the kingdom of Castile (Spain), currently in dispute with a rival claimant, Portugal. Ceding to Castile all rights to unclaimed territories west of a meridian situated one hundred leagues west of the Azores and Cape Verde islands, this bull became a major legal document in the subsequent colonization of the Americas and Africa. Though *Inter caetera* calls for missionary work by 'honest, virtuous and learned men, such as fear God', subsequent generations appropriated it to justify plunder and massacre. Some Catholics protested, including Bartolomé de Las Casas (see HISTORIES) and Pope Paul III (1534–49), whose *Sublimus Dei* (1537) asserted the humanity of native peoples and prohibited the seizure of their property or persons. And yet, *Inter caetera* grandly disposes of whole continents and notes approvingly Columbus's building of a fortress 'with good munition' and the reputation of the new world for gold, spices, 'and many other precious things'. In 1997 indigenous rights activists gathered in Honolulu to burn the bull and call for its revocation.

In the fifth Lateran Council Pope Leo X promulgated the next bull reprinted below, *Inter sollicitudines* (1515), which required that all publication be subject to the examination and censorship of the Church. Secular and sacred powers, to be sure, had long assumed control over the circulation of seditious or morally harmful writing, often confiscating and burning offensive materials; but this decree formally recognized the power of print to spread heresy, set up the bishops and others as judges and censors, and established serious penalties for non-compliance and violation. The involvement of the Inquisition eventually led to the compilation of the *Index Librorum Prohibitorum* (1559, discontinued in 1966), which at one time or other condemned the works of Erasmus, Rabelais, Montaigne, Descartes, Milton, Swift, and many others.

Pope Pius V promulgated the last bull reprinted here, *Regnans in excelsis* (1570), which excommunicated and deposed Queen Elizabeth, and absolved her subjects from all obedience and fealty. There was precedent for his actions: Pope Innocent III (r. 1198–1216) had excommunicated and deposed King John for refusing to accept Stephen Langton as archbishop of Canterbury, entrusting King Philip of France to execute the sentence; King John capitulated. Pius V hoped that his bull would martial European political and economic might against the heretic nation and succour English Catholics. The bull failed disastrously on both counts. Angry at not being consulted beforehand, European leaders such as Philip of Spain ignored his pronouncement; and Catholics, torn by conflicting loyalties to their country and faith, suffered increased suspicion and persecution. For decades afterwards authorities seized upon the bull and tried Catholics by the 'bloody questions', which forced them to deny papal authority or declare themselves traitors (see Allen, CONTROVERSIES). Ironically, neither Catholics nor Protestants protested papal presumption and intervention in

17. Pedro Berruguete (1450–1504), 'Inquisition: Auto da fé and Pardon', Museo del Prado, Madrid. Berruguete depicts St Dominic (1170–1221), founder of the Order of Preachers, presiding over the Inquisition tribunal; he orders burning for two victims, tied by their throats to stakes, and a pardon for the penitent in the pointed hat.

temporal affairs at Lepanto, where Pius V organized a celebrated victory over the Turks the following year, 1571.

PAPAL BULLS

The Inquisition (Ille humani generis), 1231

Gregory, bishop, servant of the servants of God, to his beloved sons... Prior Burchard and Theoderic, brothers of the Order of Preachers in Regensburg, greetings and apostolic benediction.

That inveterate enemy of the human race, the instigator of all evils, whom his own pride drew down from the highest to the lowest state, not content that by his wicked deceptions he led mankind to the Fall and to the labours of wretchedness, craftily tries to ensnare mankind in his pestilential nets, artfully contriving against them that they may not reascend to obtain once again that height from which they once fell. In these recent times, perfidiously attempting to deprave the faith by his ministers, the workers of iniquity, he has spread deadly poison, scheming seditiously that enemies who appeared familiar might be efficacious at doing mankind injury. Exuding pleasant appearances, these sting with their tails like scorpions, and they would infuse their pestilential poison even into the golden chalice of Babylon.

Although the heretics have lain concealed for a long time, scuttling about in hiding like crabs and, like little foxes, attempting to destroy the vineyard of the Lord of Hosts, now, however, their sins leading them on, they rise up in the open like horses ready for battle and manifestly presume to rise up publicly, preaching in certain places, seeking food in the simple, and victims in those without learning. Wishing to entrap some of the faithful in their wiles, they have made themselves teachers of error, who once were students of truth.

Wherefore it is fitting that we rise up against them manfully so that the faith of Christ may flourish and this heresy of theirs be confounded, and that a crown should be the reward of those who resist temptation. Since, therefore, the faith has recently shone forth in Germany, and by it we desire to do battle with these poisonous animals lest perhaps the simple be seduced by their artful deceptions and the learned be deceived dangerously and led to the depth of evils by their depraved artifices, because these also attack the

---

1. Gregory Pope Gregory IX (*r.* 1227–41) supporter of the Franciscans and Dominicans, advocate of the Crusades. **9–10. workers of iniquity** heretics, including the French Albigensians, who asserted a dualism of good and evil while denying the divinity of Christ and the resurrection of the body. **13. Babylon** great ancient capital of the Chaldee empire and the mystical city of the apocalypse; here, figuratively, the Roman Catholic Church, without the pejorative connotations of later uses. **15. foxes** See Cant. 2: 15.   **Lord of Hosts** Lord of armies, an honorific title of God.

foundations of faith, we who are as a father constituted by the gospels, come into the vineyard of the Lord at the eleventh hour among the workers, or, rather more truly, above the workers, warned by the voice of the bridegroom to catch the little foxes who seek to destroy the vineyard of the Lord, stricken by grief of heart, unable to sustain such contempt of the Creator, and seeking to wipe out the danger of these beasts. 30

We seek, urge, and exhort your wisdom by apostolic letters sent to you under the apostolic seal that you be sent as judges into different districts to preach where it seems useful to you to the clergy and people assembled together, using for this purpose other discreet people known to you, and to seek out diligently those who are heretics or are infamed of heresy. If you should discover heretics or people infamed of heresy, unless they should be willing upon examination to obey the commands of the Church, you are to proceed against them according to our statutes against heresy recently promulgated, as well as against the receivers, defenders, and helpers of heretics, as the statutes state. If any heretic, having abjured, wishes to return to the unity of the Church, you may receive him according to the Church's formula of absolution and lay upon him the burden that it is customary to lay upon such people, paying very close attention to the possibility that someone may appear to revert and under the appearance of piety may commit impiety, and that the angel of Satan may transform himself into an angel of light, on account of which it has been ordained (as I have made to be promulgated by Brother Hugo, sent as preacher of the word of God in Germany) that you must investigate them thoroughly and the nature of their beliefs by the discretion given you by God. 35 40 45

You may exercise the office thus given to you freely and efficaciously concerning this and all of the things which we have mentioned above, and all in particular places who are swayed by your preaching [may be accepted thus back into the Church] within twenty days. We release from their penitence for three years by the power and mercy of almighty God and the blessed apostles Peter and Paul those who offer you help, advice, or favour against heretics or their helpers, receivers, or defenders in fortified places, castles, or other places against the rebels against the Church. And if any of these die in the active prosecution of this work, we grant them full forgiveness for all the sins for which they have been contrite in heart and confessed orally. And lest anyone be reluctant to aid you in the business mentioned above, in offering censure against those contradictors and rebels against the Church which we wield through your priesthood, we concede to them the free faculty of wielding the sword against the enemies of the faith. 50 55

We give you the permission to restrain those preachers and seekers of alms whose interest is chiefly charitable from the office of preacher of this business, which is none of their affair, so that if you are not able to interest all in involving themselves in the pursuit of this affair, the two of you may pursue it. 60

Given at Rieti, 10 kalends of December, in the fifth year of our pontificate.

---

29. bridegroom i.e. Jesus Christ (Matt. 9: 15). **36. infamed** accused. **45. Brother Hugo** Hugo of Saint-Cher (*c.*1200–63), a Dominican cardinal and papal legate. **64. 10 . . . December** i.e. 22 November.

The Colonization of the New World (Inter caetera), 1493

Alexander, bishop, the servant of the servants of God, to our most dear, beloved son in Christ, King Ferdinand, and to our dear, beloved daughter in Christ, Elizabeth, Queen of Castile, Leon, Aragon, Sicily, and Granada, most noble princes, greeting and apostolical benediction.

Among other works acceptable to the Divine Majesty and according to our hearts' 5 desire, this certainly is the chief, that the Catholic faith and Christian religion specially in this our time may in all places be exalted, amplified, and enlarged, whereby the health of souls may be procured and the barbarous nations subdued and brought to the faith. And, therefore, whereas by the favour of God's clemency (although not with equal deserts) we are called to this holy seat of Peter, and understanding you to be true Catholic princes, as 10 we have ever known you and as your noble and worthy facts have declared in manner to the whole world, in that with all your study, diligence, and industry you have spared no travails, charges, or perils, adventuring even the shedding of your own blood with applying your whole minds and endeavours hereunto; as your noble expeditions achieved in recovering the kingdom of Granada from the tyranny of the Saracens in these our days 15 do plainly declare your facts with so great glory of the divine name. For the which as we think you worthy so ought we of our own free will favourably to grant you all things whereby you may daily with more fervent minds to the honour of God and enlarging the Christian empire prosecute your devout and laudable purpose, most acceptable to the immortal God. 20

We are credibly informed that whereas of late you were determined to seek and find certain islands and firm lands far remote and unknown (and not heretofore found by any other) to the intent to bring the inhabitants of the same to honour our Redeemer and to profess the Catholic faith, you have hitherto been much occupied in the expugnation and recovery of the kingdom of Granada, by reason whereof you could not bring your 25 said laudable purpose to the end desired. Nevertheless, as it hath pleased almighty God, the foresaid kingdom being recovered, you, willing to accomplish your said desire not without great labour, perils, and charges, have appointed our well beloved son Christopher Columbus (a man certes well commended as most worthy and apt for so great a matter), well furnished with men and ships and other necessaries, to seek by the 30 sea where hitherto no man hath sailed such firm lands and islands far remote and hitherto unknown. Who, by God's help, making diligent search in the ocean sea, have found certain remote islands and firm lands which were not heretofore found by any other. In

1. **Alexander** Pope Alexander VI (r. 1492–1503), worldly and wealthy. 2. **Ferdinand...Elizabeth** Ferdinand of Aragon and Isabella of Castile, whose marriage in 1469 began the unification of their kingdoms into modern Spain. 11. **facts** deeds 15. **recovering...Granada** In 1492 Ferdinand and Isabella conquered Granada, the seat of the Moorish kingdom in Andalusia (southern Spain). 24. **expugnation** conquest. 29. **Christopher Columbus** (1451–1506), explorer whose voyages initiated the colonization and conquest of the Americas. **certes** certainly.

the which, as is said, many nations inhabit, living peaceably and going naked, not
accustomed to eat flesh.   35

And as far as your messengers can conjecture, the nations inhabiting the foresaid lands
and islands believe that there is one God, Creator in heaven, and seem apt to be brought
to the embracing of the Catholic faith and to be imbued with good manners; by reason
whereof we may hope that if they be well instructed, they may easily be induced to
receive the name of our saviour Jesu Christ. We are further advertised that the forenamed   40
Christopher hath now builded and erected a fortress with good munition in one of
the foresaid principal islands, in the which he hath placed a garrison of certain of the
Christian men that went thither with him, as well to the intent to defend the same as also
to search other islands and firm lands far remote and yet unknown. We also understand
that in these lands and islands lately found is great plenty of gold and spices, with divers   45
and many other precious things of sundry kinds and qualities. Therefore, all things
diligently considered, especially the amplifying and enlarging of the Catholic faith, as it
behoveth Catholic princes, following the examples of your noble progenitors of famous
memory, whereas you are determined by the favour of almighty God to subdue and bring
to the Catholic faith the inhabitants of the foresaid lands and islands.   50

We, greatly commending this your godly and laudable purpose in our Lord, and
desirous to have the same brought to a due end and the name of our Saviour to be known
in those parts, do exhort you in our Lord and by the receiving of your holy baptism
whereby you are bound to apostolical obedience, and earnestly require you by the bowels
of mercy of our Lord Jesu Christ that when you intend for the zeal of the Catholic faith   55
to prosecute the said expedition to reduce the people of the foresaid lands and islands to
the Christian religion, you shall spare no labours at any time or be deterred with any
perils, conceiving firm hope and confidence that the omnipotent God will give good
success to your godly attempts. And that, being authorized by the privilege of the
apostolical grace, you may the more freely and boldly take upon you the enterprise of   60
so great a matter, we of our own motion and not either at your request or at the instant
petition of any other person but of our own mere liberality and certain science and by the
fullness of apostolical power do give, grant, and assign to you, your heirs and successors,
all the firm lands or islands found or to be found, discovered or to be discovered, toward
the west and south, drawing a line from the pole Arctic to the pole Antarctic, that is, from   65
the north to the south, containing in this donation whatsoever firm lands or islands are
found or to be found toward India, or toward any other part whatsoever it be, being
distant from or without the foresaid line drawn a hundred leagues toward the west and
south from any of the islands which are commonly called *De los Azores* and *Cabo Verde*.

---

48. behoveth suits. **49. determined** appointed. **56. reduce** lead back. **61. of... motion** a technical phrase (*motu proprio*,
of his own accord) signifying that some action occurs through the pope's personal volition, not necessarily through the will
of the cardinals or other advisory bodies. **instant** pressing. **62. science** knowledge. **68. hundred leagues** about 320
miles. **69. *De los Azores... Verde*** The Azores are islands in the Atlantic; Cape Verde is a group of islands in the Atlantic,
west of Senegal.

All the islands, therefore, and firm lands found and to be found, discovered and to be 70
discovered, from the said line toward the west and south, such as have not actually been
heretofore possessed by any other Christian king or prince until the day of the nativity of
our Lord Jesu Christ last passed, from the which beginneth this present year, being the
year of our Lord one thousand four hundred and ninety-three, whensoever any such shall
be found by your messengers and captains. 75

We by the authority of almighty God granted unto us in St Peter and by the office
which we bear on the earth in the stead of Jesu Christ, do forever by the tenor of these
presents give, grant, assign unto you, your heirs and successors, the kings of Castile and
Leon, all those lands and islands with their dominions, territories, cities, castles, towers,
places, and villages with all the right and jurisdictions thereunto pertaining, constituting, 80
assigning, and deputing you, your heirs and successors, the lords thereof with full and
free power, authority, and jurisdiction. Decreeing, nevertheless, by this our donation,
grant, and assignation, that from no Christian prince which actually hath possessed the
foresaid islands and firm lands unto the day of the nativity of our Lord before said their
right obtained to be understood hereby to be taken away or that it ought to be taken 85
away.

Furthermore, we command you in the virtue of holy obedience (as you have promised
and as we doubt not you will do upon mere devotion and princely magnanimity) to send
to the said firm lands and islands honest, virtuous, and learned men, such as fear God
and art able to instruct the inhabitants in the Catholic faith and good manners, applying 90
all their possible diligence in the premises.

We, furthermore, straightly inhibit all manner of persons, of what state, degree, order,
or condition so ever they be, although of imperial and regal dignity, under the pain of the
sentence of excommunication which they shall incur if they do to the contrary, that they in
no case presume without special licence of you, your heirs and successors, to travel for 95
merchandise or for any other cause to the said lands or islands found or to be found,
discovered or to be discovered, toward the west and south, drawing a line from the pole
Arctic to the pole Antarctic, whether the firm lands and islands found and to be found be
situate toward India or toward any other part being distant from the line drawn a hundred
leagues toward the west from any of the islands commonly called *de los Azores* and *Cabo* 100
Verde, notwithstanding constitutions, decrees, and apostolical ordinances whatsoever they
are to the contrary, in Him from whom empires, dominions and all good things do
proceed. Trusting that almighty God directing your enterprises if you follow your godly
and laudable attempts, your labours and travails herein shall in short time obtain a happy
end with felicity and glory of all Christian people. But forasmuch as it should be a thing of 105
great difficulty these letters to be carried to all such places as should be expedient, we will
and of like motion and knowledge do decree that whithersoever the same shall be sent, or
wheresoever they shall be received with the subscription of a common notary thereunto

92. inhibit prohibit.

required, with the seal of any person constitute of ecclesiastical dignity, or such as are authorized by the ecclesiastical court, the same faith and credit to be given thereunto in   110 judgement or elsewhere as should be exhibited to these presents.

It shall, therefore, be lawful for no man to infringe or rashly to contrary this letter of our commendation, exhortation, request, donation, grant, assignation, constitution, deputation, decree, commandment, inhibition, and determination. And if any shall presume to attempt the same, he ought to know that he shall thereby incur the   115 indignation of almighty God and his holy apostles, Peter and Paul.

Given at Rome at St Peter's in the year of the incarnation of our Lord one thousand four hundred and ninety-three, the fourth day of the nones of May, the first year of our seat.

The Publication of Books (Inter sollicitudines), 1515

Leo, bishop, servant of the servants of God, for an everlasting record, with the approval of the sacred Council.

Among the cares weighing upon our shoulders we ponder with constant concern how we may lead back to the path of truth those who err and gain them for God by his grace operating in us. Truly, this is what we earnestly seek, and to this we carefully order the   5 disposition of our mind, and over this we watch with eager diligence.

It is surely permissible to obtain a knowledge of the arts and sciences easily through the reading of books. And the art of printing books, chiefly discovered or rather enlarged and perfected in our time by divine favour, has brought many benefits to mortals, since at small expense a great number of books can be had, in which minds can be exercised very   10 conveniently in the acquisition of knowledge; and men learned in every kind of language, especially those who are Catholics (whom we wish the Church to have in abundance), can easily arise, who can then identify unbelievers, instruct them in holy doctrines, and increase the flock of the faithful by the wholesome teaching of the Christian faith.

Nevertheless, since many complaints have come to our hearing and that of the   15 Apostolic See that some masters of this art of printing presume to print and sell publicly in different parts of the world books—some translated from the Greek, Hebrew, Arabic, and Chaldean languages into Latin as well as some edited in Latin and in a vernacular tongue—which contain errors in faith as well as pernicious teachings and things contrary to the Christian religion and damaging to the reputation of persons outstanding in   20 dignity and position. By the reading of such works not only are readers not edified but

118. fourth . . . May 4 May. 119. seat pontificate.

PUBLICATION 1. Leo Leo X (r. 1513–21), pope who excommunicated Luther, consolidated papal power, and built up Rome. 2. sacred Council The fifth Lateran Council (1512–17), which restored peace among warring Christian princes and affirmed the primacy of the pope over councils.

they fall into the gravest errors, as much in matters of faith as in life and morals, whence various scandals often have arisen (just as experience, instructor in all things, teaches), and even greater scandals are feared every day.

And, therefore, lest that which was invented healthfully for the glory of God and the advance of the faith and the increase of good arts be turned to contrary purposes and become an obstacle to the salvation of those faithful to Christ, we have judged that our care must be directed to the printing of books so that in the future thorns do not grow with good seeds nor poisons get mixed with medicines. We wish, therefore, to provide a suitable remedy to these dangers, with the approval of this sacred Council, in order that the business of printing books may thrive the more prosperously the more hereafter is applied greater supervision, with more diligence and caution. We, therefore, decree and ordain that for the rest of future times no one shall presume to print or have printed any book or other writing whatsoever in Rome or in whatever cities or dioceses unless first the writings have been carefully examined (1) by our vicar and the master of the sacred palace; (2) or in other cities and dioceses truly by the bishop or another experienced in the subject of the book and in the printing of such writing, having been assigned to this task by the same bishop; (3) or by the inquisitor of heresy for the city or diocese in which the printing of the book would occur. And, moreover, the books must be approved by a warrant, signed with their own hand, to be given freely and without delay under penalty of excommunication. Besides the seizure and public burning of the printed books, and the payment of a hundred ducats to the building of the Basilica of the Prince of the Apostles [St Peter's] in Rome without hope of remission, and the suspension of the business of printing for a whole year, he who presumes otherwise will incur the sentence of excommunication. Finally, if his obstinacy increases, the offender shall be punished by his bishop or by our vicar respectively with all the penalties of law in such a way that others, by his example, will not presume to try similar things.

The Excommunication of Elizabeth I (Regnans in excelsis), 1570

Pius, bishop, a servant of the servants of God, for the future memory of the business.

He that rules in the heavens above and to whom all power is given both in heaven and earth gave unto one only on earth, namely, to Peter, the chiefest amongst the apostles, and to the pope of Rome, Peter's successor, a holy, catholic, and apostolic church (without which there is no salvation), to govern it in the fullness of power. And this he ordained as chief above all nations and kingdoms to pull down, destroy, dissever, cast off, plant, and erect; to combine in the unity of spirit his faithful people, connected together

---

1. **Pius** Pius V (*r.* 1566–72). **5. without** outside.

through mutual charity, and present them whole and sound to his Saviour. Which charge we, who through the grace of God are thereunto called, submitting ourselves to the government of the same church, cease not with all our best labours and endeavours to   10 preserve this unity and Catholic religion, which He who was the author thereof so suffered to be encumbered for the trial of the faith of his and for our correction.

But the number of the ungodly is so great in power that there is not a corner left upon the whole earth now untainted with their wicked doctrines. Amongst which Elizabeth, pretended queen of England, is above all the shelter and refuge of error and most noisome   15 enemies. It is she who, after she had possessed the kingdom, usurping monster-like the place of the chief sovereign of the church in England and the principal jurisdiction and authority thereof, hath thrown into miserable ruin the whole kingdom when it was even brought to the Catholic faith and began to bring forth good fruits. For she with a powerful hand prohibiteth the exercise of true religion—which was heretofore overthrown by Henry   20 the Eighth, the forsaker thereof, and afterwards repaired with the help of this See by Marie, lawful queen of England, of famous memory—and embraceth the heresies of obscure persons; the royal council once composed of the English nobility she hath broken off; oppresseth such as made profession of and exercised the Catholic religion; re-established the wicked ministers and preachers of impiety; abolished the sacrifice of the mass, prayers,   25 fastings, the dividing of the meats, the celibate, and all Catholic ceremonies; sent books over her whole kingdom containing manifest heresies; commended to her subjects the profane mysteries and institutions which she had received and observed from the decree of Calvin; displaced the bishops, rectors, and Catholic priests from their churches and benefices and disposed of them to heretics; and is bold to take upon her to judge and   30 determine ecclesiastical affairs; forbade the prelates, the clergy, and people to acknowledge the Roman church or observe her commandments and canonical duties; enforced divers to swear obedience to her detestable ordinances, to renounce the authority due to the Roman dignity, and acknowledge her the only sovereign over temporal and spiritual things; imposed penalties and taxes upon such as were refractory to her injunctions; inflicted   35 punishments upon those who persisted in the unity of the faith and obedience; imprisoned the prelates and governors of the Catholic churches, where divers, being with a tedious and languishing sorrow, miserably finished their unhappy days. All which things, being thus evident and apparent to all nations and so manifestly proved by the grave testimony of divers, that there is no place left for any excuse, defence, or tergiversation.   40

We, perceiving that these impieties and mischiefs do still multiply one by another, and that the persecution of the faithful and the affliction of the church doth daily increase and wax more heavy and grievous, and finding that her heart is so obstinate and obdurate that she hath not only despised the wholesome prayers and admonitions which the Christian princes have made for her better health and conversion, but that she hath denied passage   45

15. **pretended** Judging the marriage between Henry VIII and Anne Boleyn to be invalid, the pope considered Elizabeth an illegitimate child and, hence, disqualified for succession to the crown. **22. Marie** Mary Tudor, queen of England (*r.* 1553–8). **26. dividing of** abstinence from, a dietary restriction.

to the nuncios who for this end were sent from this See into England, and being compelled to bear the arms of justice against her, we cannot moderate the punishment that we are bound to inflict upon her, whose ancestors merited so well of the Christian commonwealth. Being then supported by His authority who hath placed us upon the sovereign throne of justice, however incapable of so great a charge, out of the fullness of   50
our apostolic power do pronounce and declare the said Elizabeth an heretic and favourer of heretics, and those who adhere unto her in the foresaid things, have incurred the sentence of anathema, and are cut off from the unity of the body of Christ. That she is deprived of the right which she pretends to the foresaid kingdom and of all and every seignory, royalty, and privilege thereof; and the peers, subjects, and people of the said   55
kingdom, and all others upon what terms so ever sworn unto her freed from their oath and from all manner of duty, fidelity, and obedience. As we do free them by the authority of these presents and exclude the said Elizabeth from the right which she pretendeth to the said kingdom and the rest before mentioned. Commanding, moreover, and enjoining all and every the nobles as subjects, people, and others whatsoever, that they shall not   60
once dare to obey her or any her directions, laws, or commandments, binding under the same curse those who do anything to the contrary. And forasmuch as it may seem difficult for them to observe these presents in every place where they have occasion for them, our will is that copies hereof, being written by some public notary and sealed with the seal of some ecclesiastical prelate or of his court, shall be of as good effect through the   65
whole world as these presents might do if they were exhibited and represented.

    Given at Rome at St Peter's, the fifth of March in the year of our Incarnation of our Saviour one thousand five hundred and sixty-nine and of our pontificate the fifth.

---

46. nuncios ambassadors. **53. anathema** condemnation, i.e. consignment to damnation, a sentence reserved for heretics and the worst offenders. **68. one thousand five hundred and sixty-nine** i.e. 1570 (since the year was reckoned as starting on 25 March instead of 1 January).

FURTHER READING

INTRODUCTION

Reappraisals may begin with the research guide of John W. O'Malley, *Catholicism in Early Modern History* (1988), as well as his *The First Jesuits* (1993), and *Trent and all that* (2000). John C. Olin has documented reform movements in the Church in two collections, *The Catholic Reformation* (1969), and *Catholic Reform from Cardinal Ximenes to the Council of Trent, 1495–1563* (1990). Lucien Febvre has been translated into English, *A New Kind of History*, ed. Peter Burke (1973). Hubert Jedin's seminal essay on Catholic reform is also available in English, *The Counter-Reformation: The Essential Readings*, ed. David M. Luebke (1999), 21–45; so also is his study of the Council of Trent, tr. Ernest Graf, 2 vols. (1957–61).

Works that reassess European Catholicism in the period include Pierre Janelle, *The Catholic Reformation* (1949); Henri Daniel-Rops, *The Catholic Reformation* (tr. 1962); Carlos M. N. Eire, *War Against the Idols* (1986); Louis Châtellier, *The Europe of the Devout* (tr. 1989); R. Po-Chia Hsia, *The World of Catholic Renewal* (1998); Robert Bireley, *The Refashioning of Catholicism, 1450–1700* (1999). See also Emanuel Le Roy Ladurie's microhistory, *Montaillou* (tr. 1978). For Scotland see William Forbes-Leith, *Narratives of Scottish Catholics* (1875), and *Memoirs of Scottish Catholics*, 2 vols. (1909). For Wales see 'The Carols of Richard White', *Unpublished Documents Relating to the English Martyrs*, ed. J. H. Pollen (1908: 90–9); *Welsh Recusant Writings*, ed. Geraint Bowen (1999); the entry below on St Winifred (Robert, Prior of Shrewsbury, **Instructions and Devotions**). For Ireland see the entry below under O'Sullivan-Beare (**Histories**).

Re-evaluation of Catholicism in early modern England has begun with careful regional studies: J. C. H. Aveling on Yorkshire (1963, 1966, 1970); Roger B. Manning on Sussex (1969); K. R. Wark on Cheshire (1971); Christopher Haigh on Lancashire (1975); A. G. Petti on Staffordshire (1979); Margaret Bowker on the Diocese of Lincoln (1968, 1981). Dom Hugh Bowler has meticulously edited recusant rolls for the Catholic Record Society. (For Cornwall and some other counties see also *Collections*, ed. George Oliver, 1857.) Sometimes the focus has been familial: Robert Julian Stonor, *Stonor* (1951); Godfrey Anstruther, *Vaux of Harrowden* (1953); Michael C. Questier (on the Brownes), *Catholicism and Community in Early Modern England* (2006). Virginia C. Raguin, ed., has documented some material aspects of Catholic culture in the period, *Catholic Collecting* (2006).

Broader works on English Catholicism include John Bossy, 'The Character of Elizabethan Catholicism', *Past and Present*, 21 (1962), 39–59; Patrick McGrath, 'Elizabethan Catholicism: A Reconsideration', *Journal of Ecclesiastical History*, 35 (1984), 414–28; Caroline M. Hibbard, 'Early Stuart Catholicism: Revisions and Re-revisions', *Journal of Modern History*, 52 (1980), 1–34; J. J. Scarisbrick,

The Reformation and the English People (1984); Christopher Haigh's edited collection, *The English Reformation Revised* (1987), and his *English Reformations* (1993); Eamon Duffy, *The Stripping of the Altars* (1992), and his microhistory, *The Voices of Morebath* (2001); Anthony Milton, *Catholic and Reformed* (1995); Michael A. Mullett, *Catholics in Britain and Ireland, 1558–1829* (1998); Roland Connelly, *The Women of the Catholic Resistance in England 1540–1680* (1997); Marie B. Rowlands, 'Recusant Women 1560–1640', *Women in English Society 1500–1800*, ed. Mary Prior (1985), 149–80; Rowlands has also edited *English Catholics of Parish and Town 1558–1778* (1999). Peter Lake has written a series of provocative articles and books, including 'The Significance of the Elizabethan Identification of the Pope as Antichrist', *Journal of Ecclesiastical History*, 31 (1980), 161–78; 'Anti-Popery: the Structure of a Prejudice', *Conflict in Early Stuart England*, ed. Richard Cust and Ann Hughes (1989), 72–106; and (also with Michael Questier), *The Anti-Christ's Lewd Hat* (2002). Lisa McClain has studied the practical innovations of English Catholics in *Lest We Be Damned* (2004). Ethan Shagan has edited a collection of essays, *Catholics and the 'Protestant Nation'* (2005).

Studies of the English Catholic clergy include Godfrey Anstruther's dictionary, *The Seminary Priests*, 4 vols. (1968–77), and his *A Hundred Homeless Years: English Dominicans, 1558–1658* (1958); David Lunn, *The English Benedictines* (1980); and the works of Thomas M. McCoog, SJ, especially *English and Welsh Jesuits, 1555–1650*, 2 vols. (1994–5); *The Society of Jesus in Ireland, Scotland, and England* (1996). There are also two articles by Patrick McGrath and Joy Rowe, 'The Marian Priests under Elizabeth I', *Recusant History*, 17 (1984), 103–20; 'The Elizabethan Priests: Their Harbourers and Helpers', *Recusant History*, 19 (1989), 209–33. Alice Hogge has written a well researched and absorbing account of the English Mission up to the Gunpowder plot, *God's Secret Agents* (2005).

On manuscript production and distribution see H. R. Woudhuysen, *Sir Philip Sidney and the Circulation of Manuscripts 1558–1640* (1996), and Peter Beal, *In Praise of Scribes* (1998). On Catholic manuscripts see Nancy Pollard Brown, 'Paperchase: The Dissemination of Catholic Texts in Elizabethan England', *English Manuscript Studies, 1100–1700*, ed. Peter Beal and Jeremy Griffiths (1989), 120–43; Arthur F. Marotti, *Manuscript, Print and the English Renaissance Lyric* (1995); David Shorney, *Protestant Non-Conformity and Roman Catholicism: A Guide to Sources in the Public Record Office* (1996); Gerard Kilroy, *Edmund Campion: Memory and Transcription* (2005). Michael C. Questier has edited two volumes of Catholic newsletters, one from the archpresbyterate of George Birkhead (1609–14), the other from the Caroline court (1631–8) (1998, 2005).

On Catholic print publication see A. F. Allison, 'Franciscan Books in English, 1559–1640', *Recusant History*, 3 (1955), 16–65; T. A. Birrell, 'English Counter-Reformation Book Culture', *Recusant History*, 22 (1994), 113–22; and Alexandra Walsham's wide-ranging survey, ' "Domme Preachers"? Post-Reformation English Catholicism and the Culture of Print', *Past and Present*, 168 (2000), 72–123.

CONTROVERSIES

Peter Milward provides a lucid survey of the writers and printed sources in his *Religious Controversies of the Elizabethan Age* (1977) and *Religious Controversies of the Jacobean Age* (1978), as does, on a smaller scale, A. C. Southern, *Elizabethan Recusant Prose, 1559–1582* (1950). Helpful monographs include Thomas Clancy, *Papist Pamphleteers* (1964), and Peter Holmes, *Resistance and Compromise* (1982). *The Oxford Encyclopedia of the Reformation*, ed. Hans J. Hillerbrand, 4 vols. (1996), provides a good starting point for the Protestant controversialists, who have been generally better preserved. To place the controversies in wider political perspectives see J. W. Allen, *A History of Political Thought in the Sixteenth Century* (1941); Quentin Skinner, *The Foundations of Modern Political Thought*, 2 vols. (1978); J. H. Burns, ed., *The Cambridge History of Political Thought, 1450–1700* (1991); Vincent P. Carey, ed., *Voices for Toleration in an Age of Persecution* (2004).

Desiderius Erasmus speaks to modern students in English through the splendid Toronto edition, *Collected Works* (1974–). The debate with Luther on free will appears in volumes lxxvi and lxxvii (*Controversies*, 6, 7). On Erasmus's biblical scholarship see Jerry H. Bentley, *Humanists and Holy Writ* (1983), and Jaroslav Pelikan *The Reformation of the Bible/The Bible of the Reformation* (1996). Douglas H. Parker has edited William Roye's translation of the *Paraclesis* (2000). Robert Adams has translated *The Praise of Folly* and other writings, including prefaces from his New Testaments (1989). Important studies include M. M. Phillips, *Erasmus and the Northern Renaissance* (1949); Erika Rummel, *Erasmus as a Translator of the Classics* (1985); Cornelis Augustijn, *Erasmus, his Life, Works, and Influence*, tr. J. C. Grayson (1991); and accounts by James McConica (1991) and Léon-E. Halkin, tr. John Tonkin (1993). The large influence of Gregory Martin on the Authorized Version of the Bible is documented by James G. Carleton, *The Part of Rheims in the Making of the English Bible* (1902).

Erasmus's contemporary and friend, **Thomas More**, appears in the standard Yale edition of the *Complete Works*, 15 vols. in 20 (1963–97). Volume vi contains *A Dialogue Concerning Heresies*. Nicholas Harpsfield, Cresacre More, and William Roper contributed early biographies; Richard Marius attempted a psychological portrait (1984) and Peter Ackroyd (1998) has written a splendidly readable account. Richard Sylvester and G. P. Marc'hadour have edited *Essential Articles for the Study of Thomas More* (1977). See also Jackson Campbell Boswell, *Sir Thomas More in the English Renaissance: An Annotated Catalogue* (1994), and Albert J. Geritz, *Thomas More: An Annotated Bibliography of Criticism, 1935–1997* (1998).

Geoffrey de C. Parmiter has written a full account of **Edmund Plowden**, *Edmund Plowden: An Elizabethan Recusant Lawyer* (1987). See also Marie Axton, 'The Influence of Edmund Plowden's Succession Treatise', *Huntington Library Quarterly*, 37 (1974), 209–26; and for background, Ernst H. Kantorowicz, *The King's Two Bodies: A Study in Mediaeval Political Theology* (1957).

On **Nicholas Sander** see Thomas McNevin Veech, *Dr. Nicholas Sanders and the English Reformation, 1530–1581* (1935).

There are biographies of **Edmund Campion** by Richard Simpson (1867), Evelyn Waugh (1935), and Harold C. Gardiner (1957), and an important collection of essays edited by Thomas M. McCoog, *The Reckoned Expense: Edmund Campion and the Early English Jesuits* (1996). James V. Holleran has recently edited the Tower debates from the available manuscripts, *A Jesuit Challenge: Edmund Campion's Debates at the Tower of London in 1581* (1999). Gerard Kilroy has published some new materials in *Edmund Campion: Memory and Transcription* (2005).

Informative discussions of Robert Persons's conflict with **Alban Langdale** on external conformity appear in Peter Holmes, *Resistance and Compromise* (1982), and Alexandra Walsham, *Church Papists* (1993).

Martin Haile (1914) has written a biography of **William Allen** and P. Renold (1967) has edited correspondence. Robert M. Kingdon (1965) has edited Burlegh's *The Execution of Justice in England* together with Allen's response, *A True, Sincere, and Modest Defense of English Catholics*. Critical monographs include Thomas McElligott, *The Eucharistic Doctrine of Cardinal William Allen (1532–1594)* (1939), and Garrett Mattingly, *William Allen and Catholic Propaganda in England* (1957). Michael E. Williams explores Allen's dealings with Spain in *Recusant History* (22 (1994), 123–40) and Eamon Duffy has written an incisive reappraisal in the same journal (22 (1995), 265–90).

Philip Caraman has written two books on **Henry Garnet**: *Henry Garnet, 1555–1606, and the Gunpowder Plot* (1964); *A Study in Friendship: Saint Robert Southwell and Henry Garnet* (1995); see also A. E. Malloch, 'Father Henry Garnet's Treatise of Equivocation', *Recusant History*, 15 (1981), 387–95; Thomas M. McCoog, SJ, 'Remembering Henry Garnet, S. J.', *Archivum Historicum Societatis Iesu*, 75 (2006), 159–88.

George Albert Moore has edited and translated the *De rege et regis institutione* (1948) of **Juan de Mariana**; see also Guenter Lewy, *Constitutionalism and Statecraft during the Golden Age of Spain* (1960). He has also translated and edited the *Tractatus* on papal power by **Robert Bellarmine** as *The Power of the Pope in Temporal Affairs against William Barclay* (1949). See also Bellarmine's *The Louvain Lectures* (including an autograph copy of his 1616 declaration to Galileo), ed. Ugo Baldini and George V. Coyne (1984); *Spiritual Writings*, ed. John Patrick Donnelly and Roland J. Teske (1989). James Brodrick has written a biography (1961), and Peter Godman a monograph, *The Saint as Censor: Robert Bellarmine between Inquisition and Index* (2000).

Dorothy L. Latz has published a facsimile edition (2000) of **Jane Owen**, *An Antidote against Purgatory*; see also Donna B. Hamilton's edition in *Women Writers Online*.

LIVES AND DEATHS

The *Dictionary of National Biography*, now revised and online, remains the standard reference work. Despite the hagiographical slant and need for updating, there is still useful information in Richard Challoner, *Memoirs of the Missionary Priests*, ed. John Hungerford Pollen (1924); John Morris, ed., *The Troubles of our Catholic Forefathers Related by Themselves*, 3 vols. (1872–7); Henry Foley, *Records of the English Province of the Society of Jesus*, 7 vols. in 8 (1877–83); and Joseph Gillow, *A Literary and Biographical History*, 5 vols. (1885–1902). John Hungerford Pollen has made available some important material, *Unpublished Documents Relating to the English Martyrs*, i. *1584–1603* (1908), and ii (with W. MacMahon), *The Venerable Philip Howard, Earl of Arundel* (1919). He has also written an overview, *The English Catholics in the Reign of Elizabeth* (1920). The journal *Recusant History* and the volumes published by the Catholic Records Society provide much reliable biographical information. Michael Hodgetts has written the authoritative account of hides or 'priest-holes', *Secret Hiding-Places* (1989); and G. F. Nuttall has resurveyed the Catholic martyrs, 'The English Martyrs, 1535–1680: A Statistical Review', *Journal of Ecclesiastical History*, 22 (1971), 191–7.

The subject of martyrdom continues to inspire critical studies, among them, Diana Wood, ed., *Martyrs and Martyrologies* (1993); John R. Knott, *Discourses of Martyrdom in English Literature, 1563–1694* (1993); J. T. Rhodes, 'English Books of Martyrs and Saints of the Late Sixteenth and Early Seventeenth Centuries', *Recusant History*, 22 (1994), 7–25; Peter Lake and Michael Questier, 'Agency, Appropriation and Rhetoric under the Gallows: Puritans, Romanists and the State in Early Modern England', *Past and Present*, 153 (1996), 64–107; Brad S. Gregory, *Salvation at Stake: Christian Martyrdom in Early Modern Europe* (1999). Anne Dillon has written a lucid, wide-ranging, and learned study, *The Construction of Martyrdom in the English Catholic Community, 1535–1603* (2002); see also Susannah Brietz Monta, *Martyrdom and Literature in Early Modern England* (2005).

The Latin *Confessions* of **Augustine of Hippo** have recently been edited by James J. O'Donnell, 3 vols. (1992) and Books I–IV by Gillian Clark (1995). There are many modern translations, including those of R. S. Pine-Coffin (1988) and Henry Chadwick (1991). Henry Chadwick (1986) and Peter Brown (rev.

2000) have written biographies. R. A. Markus has edited a collection of critical essays, *Augustine* (1972), as have Eleonore Stump and Norman Kretzmann, *The Cambridge Companion to Augustine* (2001). See also *Augustine Through the Ages: An Encyclopedia*, ed. Allan Fitzgerald and John C. Cavadini (1999).

The *Works* of **Teresa of Ávila** have been edited and translated by E. Allison Peers (1946), and Kieran Kavanaugh and Otilio Rodriguez (1976–85). Stephen Clissold (1982), Victoria Lincoln (1984), and Cathleen Medwick (2000) have written biographies. Studies of the *Vida* include Alison Weber, *Teresa of Avila and the Rhetoric of Femininity* (1990), and Carole Slade, *St Teresa of Avila: Author of a Heroic Life* (1995). Other important studies include Robert T. Petersson, *The Art of Ecstasy: Teresa, Bernini, and Crashaw* (1970); Jodi Bilinkoff, *The Avila of Saint Teresa: Religious Reform in a Sixteenth-Century City* (1989); Carlos M. N. Eire, *From Madrid to Purgatory* (1995); Gillian T. W. Ahlgren, *Teresa of Avila and the Politics of Sanctity* (1996); and John Sullivan, ed., *Centenary of Saint Teresa* (1984).

On **Thomas More** and **Edmund Campion** see above under **Controversies**.

John Morris published some manuscript material concerning **Margaret Clitherow**, in *The Troubles of Our Catholic Forefathers*, vol. iii (1877); there is a biography by Katharine M. Longley, *Saint Margaret Clitherow* (1986). See also Claire Cross, 'An Elizabethan Martyrologist and his Martyr: John Mush and Margaret Clitherow', in Diana Wood, ed., *Martyrs and Martyrologies* (1993), 271–81; Dillon, *Construction*, 277–322.

The autobiography of Campion's fellow Jesuit, **William Weston**, has been edited and translated by Philip Caraman (1955), as has that of another Elizabethan Jesuit, John Gerard (1951). On possession and exorcism see Keith Thomas, *Religion and the Decline of Magic* (1971); D. P. Walker, *Unclean Spirits* (1981); F. W. Brownlow, *Shakespeare, Harsnett, and the Devils at Denham* (1993).

Richard Challoner provides an account of **Alexander Rawlins** and **Henry Walpole** in *Memoirs*, 217–27. See also 'Some Papers of Bl. Alexander Rawlins', *The Venerabile*, 8 (1937), 208–19. Augustus Jessopp has edited Walpole's letters (1873), and written a biography, *One Generation of a Norfolk House*, 3rd edn. (1914).

The life of **Toby Matthew** has attracted some modern attention: see A. H. Mathew, *A True Historical Relation of the Conversion of Sir Tobie Matthew* (1904); A. H. Mathew and Annette Calthrop, *The Life of Sir Tobie Mathew, Bacon's Alter Ego* (1907); and David Matthew. See also John P. Feil, 'Sir Tobie Matthew and his Collection of Letters' (University of Chicago Ph.D. thesis, 1962); Anthony G. Petti, 'Unknown Sonnets by Sir Toby Matthew', *Recusant History*, 9 (1967), 123–58.

The Institute of the Blessed Virgin Mary (now known as the Congregation of Jesus) has published numerous pamphlets on the life of its founder **Mary Ward**; there are also biographies by Mary Catherine Elizabeth Chambers, 2 vols. (1882, 1885), Mary Oliver (1959), and Henriette Peters, tr. Helen Butterworth (1994). M. Emmanuel Orchard presents her life story through her writings, *Till God Will* (1985); Jeanne Cover has studied her spirituality, *Love, The Driving Force* (1997). Laurence Lux-Sterritt has studied her order and the French Ursulines, *Redefining Female Religious Life* (2005).

POETRY

On Catholic poetry see Roman R. Dubinski, *English Religious Poetry Printed 1477–1640: A Chronological Bibliography with Indexes* (1996); Steven W. May and William A. Ringler, Jr.'s exhaustive *Elizabethan Poetry: A Bibliography and First-line Index of English Verse, 1559–1603*, 3 vols. (2004). Louise Imogen Guiney's *Recusant Poets* (1938) provides a good starting point for surveying Catholic poets of the period, though only volume i reached print (vol. ii remains in manuscript at Holy Cross College). A. D. Cousins, *The Catholic Religious Poets from Southwell to Crashaw* (1991), has attempted a critical assessment. After Louis L. Martz, *The Poetry of Meditation* (1954, rev. 1962), argued for the importance of Ignatian meditation to seventeenth-century poetry, theories about 'Protestant poetics' have long dominated the field: major studies include William H. Halewood, *The Poetry of Grace: Reformation Themes and Structures in English Seventeenth-Century Poetry* (1970); Barbara Kiefer Lewalski, *Protestant Poetics and the Seventeenth-Century Religious Lyric* (1979); John N. King, *English Reformation Literature: The Tudor Origins of the Protestant Tradition* (1982), and *Spenser's Poetry and the Reformation Tradition* (1990) (see also his bibliography, *English Literary Renaissance*, 21 (1991), 283–307). Among those who have reacted against this critical orthodoxy and demonstrated the vitality of Catholic traditions are Anthony Low, *Love's Architecture: Devotional Modes in Seventeenth-Century English Poetry* (1978), and *The Reinvention of Love: Poetry, Politics and Culture from Sidney to Milton* (1993); and R. V. Young, *Doctrine and Devotion in Seventeenth-Century Poetry* (2000).

For background to the 'Walsingham' **Lament** see H. M. Gillett, *Walsingham: The History of a Famous Shrine*, 2nd edn. (1950); for Catholic **Ballads** see Hyder Edward Rollins, ed., *Old English Ballads, 1553–1625, Chiefly from Manuscripts* (1920); Peter J. Seng, ed., *Tudor Songs and Ballads from MS Cotton Vespasian A-25* (1978). Phebe Jensen has written on the role of ballads in religious debate, 'Ballads and brags: free speech and recusant culture in Elizabethan England', *Criticism*, 40 (1998), 333–54.

Richard S. M. Hirsch has edited the works of **Chidiock Tichborne** in *English Literary Renaissance*, 16 (1986), 303–18 (see corrections in the same journal 17 (1987), interleaved after p. 276).

The life and works of **Francis Tregian** have been discussed by John Morris, ed., *The Troubles of our Catholic Forefathers*, i (1872), 59–140; see also Raymond Francis Trudgian, *Francis Tregian, 1548–1608, Elizabethan Recusant, A Truly Catholic Cornishman* (1998).

The challenge of **Thomas Pounde** appears reprinted in Robert Crowley's rebuttal, *An Answer to Six Reasons* (1581, STC 6075). Henry Foley published an account of the man and his work in *Records of the English Province of the Society of Jesus*, 7 vols. in 8 (1877–83).

Joan Grundy has edited the *Poems* of **Henry Constable** (1960); Patrick Cheney has written an introduction to a facsimile reprint of the 1594 edition of *Diana* (1973). See also John Bossy, 'A Propos of Henry Constable', *Recusant History*, 6 (1962), 228–37.

Pierre Janelle (1935), Christopher Devlin (1956), and F. W. Brownlow (1996) review the life and works of **Robert Southwell**. The prose has appeared in sporadic editions, including *The Triumphs over Death* and some letters, ed. John William Trotman (1914); *An Humble Supplication to her Majesty*, ed. R. C. Bald (1953); *Two Letters and Short Rules of a Good Life*, ed. Nancy Pollard Brown (1973); *An Epistle of Comfort* (facs. edn., 1974); *Mary Magdalen's Funeral Tears* (facs. edn., 1975). James H. McDonald and Nancy Pollard Brown (1967) have meticulously edited the English poetry. John N. King (*English Literary Renaissance*, 13 (1983), 221–7) and Vittorio Cavalli (*Recusant History*, 21 (1992), 297–304) review recent studies. Important critical investigations of the poetry include Louis Martz, *The Poetry of Meditation* (1954, rev. 1962); Nancy Pollard Brown, 'The Structure of "Saint Peter's Complaint"', *Modern Language Review*, 61 (1966), 3–11; and Scott R. Pilarz, *Robert Southwell and the Mission of Literature, 1561–1595: Writing Reconciliation* (2003).

The Spenser Society published *A Fig for Fortune* by **Anthony Copley** (1883, rpt. 1967). The poem has received critical attention from Frederick Padelford, *Modern Language Quarterly*, 3 (1942), 525–33; Alison Shell, *Catholicism, Controversy and the English Literary Imagination, 1558–1660* (1999); and Paul J. Voss,

Ben Jonson Journal, 7 (2000), 1–26. Some of Copley's prose works appear in the English Recusant Literature series, vols. 31 (1970) and 100 (1972).

Some idea of the life and varied career of **Richard Verstegan** may be gleaned from Anthony G. Petti's edition, *The Letters and Despatches of Richard Verstegan (c.1550–1640)* (1959), his bibliography of Verstegan's writing (*Recusant History*, 7 (1963), 82–103), and Paul Arblaster's illuminating *Antwerp & the World: Richard Verstegan and the International Culture of Catholic Reformation* (2004). Rivkah Zim discusses the translations of the psalms in *English Metrical Psalms: Poetry as Praise and Prayer 1535–1601* (1987), 129–32.

The works of **William Alabaster** have appeared in some recent editions: the sonnets, ed. G. M. Story and Helen Gardner (1959); the unfinished Latin epic, *Elisaeis*, ed. and tr. Michael O'Connell (1979); the Latin tragedy *Roxana*, edited in facsimile, John Coldewey and Brian F. Copenhaver (1987); poetry and prose, including Alabaster's account of his own conversion, ed. Dana F. Sutton (1997).

On **Toby Matthew** see above under **Lives and Deaths**.

Since H. J. C. Grierson's edition (1912), **John Donne** has received the attention due to a major literary and religious figure. His work appears, notably, in Helen Gardner's *The Divine Poems* (1952, rev. 1978) and in other Oxford editions; his sermons in the 10-volume edition of George Potter and Evelyn Simpson (1953–62). A *Donne Variorum* under the editorship of Gary Stringer has been producing volumes since 1995. Readers interested in Donne's complicated religious views may consult his anti-Jesuit satire, *Ignatius his Conclave*, ed. Timothy S. Healy (1969); his *Devotions upon Emergent Occasions*, ed. Anthony Raspa (1975); and his *Pseudo-Martyr*, ed. Antony Raspa (1993). R. C. Bald (1970) has written the standard biography; John Carey, *John Donne: Life, Mind, and Art* (1981) reads Donne as apostate from Catholicism; Arthur Marotti, *John Donne: Coterie Poet* (1986), locates him in specific cultural contexts; Dennis Flynn has investigated Donne's Catholic family background, *John Donne and the Ancient Catholic Nobility* (1995); John Stubbs argues that he aligned himself with the emerging nation rather than the Catholic Church, *John Donne: The Reformed Soul* (2006). See also M. Thomas Hester, *Kinde pitty and brave scorn: John Donne's Satyres* (1982); Anthony Raspa, *The Emotive Image: Jesuit Poetics in the English Renaissance* (1983); Theresa M. DiPasquale, *Literature & Sacrament: The Sacred and the Secular in John Donne* (1999); and collections edited by Raymond-Jean Frontain and Frances M. Malpezzi (1995), as well as Mary Arshagouni Papazian (2003). *The John Donne Journal* (1982–) is a goldmine of information as are the three annotated bibliographies of criticism by John R. Roberts (1973, 1982, 2004).

On **Ben Jonson** see the entry below under **Drama**. The poetry has been superbly edited by Ian Donaldson (1975); see also Paul Cubeta, 'Ben Jonson's Religious Lyrics', *Journal of English and Germanic Philology*, 62 (1963), 96–110,

The works of **John Beaumont** are available on a limited basis: *Poems*, ed. Alexander Grosart (1880, rpt. 1967); *The Metamorphoses of Tobacco* (facs. edn., 1971); the entertainment, *The Theatre of Apollo*, ed. W. W. Greg (1926); and *The Shorter Poems*, ed. Roger D. Sell, published in Abo, Finland (1974). B. H. Newdigate published some verses from Beaumont's *Crown of Thorns* (*Review of English Studies*, 18 (1942), 284–90); this unfortunately neglected poem received some attention from Ruth Wallerstein, 'Sir John Beaumont's "Crowne of Thornes": A Report', *Journal of English and Germanic Philology*, 53 (1954), 410–34.

The poetry of **William Habington** has been edited by Kenneth Allott (1948) and discussed by A. D. Cousins, *The Catholic Poets* (1991), 115–23.

Gertude More has been rediscovered by Dorothy L. Latz, 'The Mystical Poetry of Dame Gertrude More', *Mystics Quarterly*, 16 (1990), 66–82; and, also hers, *Neglected English Literature* (1997).

Standard editions of **Richard Crashaw** have been produced by L. C. Martin, 2nd edn. (1957) and George W. Williams (1970). Claes Schaar has published Marino's Italian *Sospetto d'Herode* and Crashaw's translation on facing pages, *Marino and Crashaw: Sospetto d'Herode: A Commentary* (1971). Critical studies include Ruth. C. Wallerstein, *Richard Crashaw: A Study in Style and Poetic Development* (1935); Austin Warren, *Richard Crashaw: A Study in Baroque Sensibility* (1939); Mario Praz, *The Flaming Heart* (1958); George Walton Williams, *Image and Symbol in the Sacred Poetry of Richard Crashaw* (1963); Marc F. Bertonasco, *Crashaw and the Baroque* (1971); R. V. Young, *Richard Crashaw and the Spanish Golden Age* (1982), and *Doctrine and Devotion in Seventeenth-Century Poetry* (2000). John R. Roberts has edited essays offering new perspectives (1990), and compiled an annotated bibliography (1985; supplement, *English Literary Renaissance*, 21 (1991), 425–45).

INSTRUCTIONS AND DEVOTIONS

The texts of Patristic writers, the Church Fathers, have been gathered by J.-P. Migne, *Patrologiae cursus completus* (1844–80): *Series graeca*, 161 volumes, and *Series latina*, 221 volumes (this latter available as an electronic database). Supplementing Migne's useful but dated collections are the *Corpus Christianorum: Series graeca* (1977–present) and the *Corpus Christianorum: Series latina* (1953–present); the *Sources chrétiennes* (1942–present), which includes texts and French translations. For English versions of the Church Fathers there are several major series: *The Ante-Nicene Fathers*, 10 vols. (1885–96, and reprinted); *A Select Library of Nicene and Post-Nicene Fathers of the Christian Church*, ed. Philip Schaff, 14 vols. (1886–90, and reprinted); *Ancient Christian Writers: The Works of the Fathers in Translation* (1946–present); *Church Fathers in English* at the *Christian Classics Ethereal Library* (online database).

John W. O'Malley's bibliography, *Catholicism in Early Modern History* (1988) has illuminating chapters on Catholic instructions and devotions as well as on individual religious orders. Helen C. White surveys Catholic and Protestant works in *English Devotional Literature, 1600–1640* (1931), *Tudor Books of Private Devotion* (1951), and *Tudor Books of Saints and Martyrs* (1963). For some Catholic writers see John R. Roberts, *A Critical Anthology of English Recusant Devotional Prose, 1558–1603* (1966). Jaroslav Pelikan has written two wide-ranging studies: *Jesus through the Centuries: His Place in the History of Culture* (1985); *Mary through the Centuries: Her Place in the History of Culture* (New Haven, 1996). On Mary there is also Marina Warner, *Alone of all her Sex: The Myth and the Cult of the Virgin Mary* (1976).

Two important reference works on **Prayers and Hymns** are Edgar Hoskins, *Horae Beatae Mariae Virginis, or Sarum and York Primers* (1901); and J. M. Blom, *The Post-Tridentine English Primer* (1982). Eamon Duffy discusses individual prayers and practices, *The Stripping of the Altars* (1992). See also the online database *Thesaurus Precum Latinarum*.

On saints see Peter Brown, *The Cult of the Saints* (1981); David Hugh Farmer, *The Oxford Dictionary of Saints*, 4th edn. (1997); Jacobus de Voragine, *The Golden Legend: Readings on the Saints*, tr. William Granger Ryan, 2 vols. (1993). On some regional saints, see *Nicholas Roscarrock's Lives of the Saints, Cornwall and Devon*, ed. Nicholas Orme (1992). Two medieval lives of **St Winifred** have been edited by Ronald E. Pepin and Catherine Hamaker (2000). There is a modern account by Thomas Meyrick (1996). The medieval cult of St Winifred appears often in Ellis Peters's popular Brother Cadfael series of novels, notably in *A Morbid Taste for Bones* (1977) and *The Holy Thief* (1994).

Translations of *The Imitation of Christ* by **Thomas à Kempis** abound, often with helpful background information, e.g. William C. Creasy (1989), Joseph N. Tylenda (1998), and Harold J. Chadwick (1999); on early English translations see B. J. H. Biggs's edition (1997), and (for Margaret Beaufort's translation) Lee Cullen Khanna's *Early Tudor Translators: Margaret Beaufort, Margaret More Roper, and Mary Bassett* (2001).

On **Ignatius Loyola** and the Society of Jesus, see John W. O'Malley, *The First Jesuits* (1993); *A Pilgrim's Journey: The Autobiography of Ignatius Loyola*, ed. Joseph N. Tylenda (2001); *The Spiritual Exercises of Saint Ignatius*, tr. and commentary, George E. Ganss (1992). The research centre for the order is the *Institutum Historicum Societatis Iesu*, which publishes important series including a journal, *Archivum Historicum Societatis Iesu*, and documents in the series *Monumenta Historicum Societatis Iesu*.

For further reading on **Consolations** see the individual authors here excerpted, **Thomas More** (above, **Controversies**) and **Robert Southwell** (above, **Poetry**). Cecilia A. Hatt has edited the *English Works* of **John Fisher** (2002); re-evaluations have been contributed by Brendan Bradshaw and Eamon Duffy, eds., *Humanism, Reform, and the Reformation: The Career of Bishop John Fisher* (1989); and Maria Dowling, *Fisher of Men: A Life of John Fisher, 1469–1535* (1999).

On Catholic **Meditations** see Helen C. White, *English Devotional Literature, 1600–1640* (1931); also her *Tudor Books of Private Devotion* (1951); and Louis Martz, *The Poetry of Meditation* (1954, rev. 1962). See also Anne Dillon, 'Praying by Number: The Confraternity of the Rosary and the English Catholic Community, *c*.1580–1700', *History*, 88 (2003), 451–71. The English Recusant Literature series has reprinted in facsimile works of **Luis de Granada** and **John Bucke**.

David Dymond and Clive Paine have carefully edited and annotated the memoir of **Roger Martin**, *The Spoil of Melford Church: The Reformation in a Suffolk Parish* (1989).

The music of **William Byrd** is readily available in numerous formats. The standard edition is *Works: The Byrd Edition*, ed. Phillip Brett, 17 vols. (1970–). For the biography see John Harley, *William Byrd: Gentleman of the Chapel Royal* (1997); critical studies appear in the memorial volume, *Byrd Studies*, ed. Alan Brown and Richard Turbet (1992). See also Joseph Kerman, 'William Byrd and the Catholics', *New York Review of Books*, 26 (17 May 1979), 32–6.

Modern editions and translations of **Francis de Sales** are readily available; see also A. Ravier's biography, tr. Joseph D. Bowler (1988).

Iain Fletcher (1950) has edited *Partheneia Sacra* by **Henry Hawkins** as has Karl Josef Höltgen (1993). Rosemary Freeman gives a good general account of Hawkins and emblems in *English Emblem Books* (1948). See also Mario Praz, *Studies in Seventeenth-Century Imagery*, 2 vols. (1939–47); Peter M. Daly, *Literature in Light of the Emblem*, 2nd edn. (1998).

Justin McCann has edited the Life of **Augustine Baker** by Peter Salvin and Serenus Cressy, as well as some memorials and historical documents (with R. Hugh Connolly, 1933). Antony Low (1970) has written a general account; see also James Gaffney, *Augustine Baker's Inner Light: A Study in English Recusant Spirituality* (1989), and Michael Woodward, ed., *That Mysterious Man: Essays on Augustine Baker* (2001).

DRAMA

Important studies of medieval antecedents include Karl Young, *The Drama of the Medieval Church* (1933); O. B. Hardison, Jr., *Christian Rite and Christian Drama in the Middle Ages* (1965); V. A. Kolve, *The Play Called Corpus Christi* (1966); Rosemary Woolf, *The English Mystery Plays* (1972); Robert Potter,

The English Morality Play (1975); Clifford Davidson, *The Saint Play in Medieval Europe* (1986); and Richard Beadle, ed., *The Cambridge Companion to Medieval English Theatre* (1994), which has an extensive bibliography of primary and secondary sources. On anti-Catholic drama see Rainer Pineas, *Tudor and Early Stuart Anti-Catholic Drama* (1972); Frances E. Dolan, *Whores of Babylon* (1999).

The plays of **John Heywood** have been edited by Richard Axton and Peter Happé (1991). Robert Johnson has written an overview, *John Heywood* (1970); Philip C. Kolin, a bibliography of criticism, *English Literary Renaissance*, 13 (1983), 113–23; Greg Walker, a critical discussion, *The Politics of Performance in Early Renaissance Drama* (1998).

For the Greek original of *Iphigeneia at Aulis* by **Jane Lumley**, see the Oxford Classical Text edition of Euripides by J. Diggle, vol. iii (1994); Erasmus's Latin adaptation appeared as *Hecvba et Iphigenia in Aulide Evripidis Tragoediae in Latinum Translatae Erasmo Roterodamo interprete* (Vienna, 1511). Diane Purkiss has published Lumley's play in *Three Tragedies by Renaissance Women* (1998). Feminist and critical appraisals have been contributed by Elaine V. Beilin, *Redeeming Eve* (1987), 151–7; Stephanie Hodgson-Wright, *Readings in Renaissance Women's Drama*, ed. S. P. Cerasano and Marion Wynne-Davies (1998), 129–41. See also articles by Diane Purkiss (*Women's Writing*, 6 (1999), 27–45) and Patricia Demers (*Renaissance & Reformation*, 23 (1999), 25–42).

Thomas W. Best (1975) has surveyed the life and works of **Jacob Bidermann**, whose collected plays appeared in a facsimile edition, *Ludi theatrales 1666*, ed. Rolf Tarot, 2 vols. (1967). D. G. Dyer and Cecily Longrigg have published the Latin *Cenodoxus* with facing English translation (1974). On the American production see Nicholas Varga, *Baltimore's Loyola/Loyola's Baltimore* (1990); see also Robert S. Miola's account in *Theatre and Religion: Lancastrian Shakespeare*, ed. Richard Dutton, *et al.* (2003), 71–87. For a helpful overview of Jesuit drama see William H. McCabe, SJ, *An Introduction to the Jesuit Theater* (1983); and Nigel Griffin, *Jesuit School Drama: A Checklist of Critical Literature* (1976, suppl. 1986). The work of an English Jesuit appears in *Jesuit Theater Englished: The Five Tragedies of Joseph Simons*, ed. Louis J. Oldani and Philip C. Fischer (1989).

Religion has always loomed large in the vast bibliography of works on **William Shakespeare**. In modern times arguments, often tendentious, for Shakespeare's Catholicism include John Henry de Groot, *The Shakespeares and 'The Old Faith'* (1946); H. Mutschmann and K. Wentersdorf, *Shakespeare and Catholicism* (1952). The most energetic recent proponent of Shakespeare as Catholic is Peter Milward, SJ, who has followed up his *Shakespeare's Religious Background* (1973) with a series of books and articles including *The Catholicism of Shakespeare's Plays* (1997), two studies of the great tragedies, *Shakespeare's Meta-drama* (both 2003), and *Shakespeare the Papist* (2005). Since E. A. J. Honigmann, *Shakespeare: The Lost Years* (1985, rev. 1998) resuscitated the theory that Shakespeare spent some of his youth in a Lancashire Catholic household, biographers have been more receptive to the possibility of Shakespeare's Catholicism, including Ian Wilson (1993), Park Honan (1998), Michael Wood (2003), and Stephen Greenblatt (2004). Robert Bearman, however, has cast a cold eye on the Lancashire theory (*Shakespeare Quarterly*, 53 (2002), 83–94) and on John Shakespeare's supposedly Catholic will (*Shakespeare Survey*, 56 (2003), 184–203). Other important discussions include Gary Taylor, 'Forms of Opposition: Shakespeare and Middleton', *English Literary Renaissance*, 24 (1994), 283–314; Richard Wilson, 'Shakespeare and the Jesuits', *Times Literary Supplement* (19 December 1997), 11–13; the essays in *Shakespeare Survey*, 54 (2001); *Shakespeare and the Culture of Christianity in Early Modern England*, ed. Dennis Taylor and David Beauregard (2003); Richard Dutton, Alison Findlay, and Richard Wilson's two volumes on *Lancastrian Shakespeare* (2003), one on theatre and religion, the other on region, religion, and patronage; John Finnis and Patrick Martin's reading of 'The Phoenix and the Turtle' as a tribute to

Anne Line, Catholic martyr, *Times Literary Supplement* (18 April 2003), 12–14. Studies of individual works can be located through the *Modern Language Association* and *Shakespeare Quarterly* bibliographies. Clare Asquith implausibly argues that Shakespeare's works contain a secret code that reveals his Catholicism, *Shadowplay* (2005). More substantial recent studies include Jean-Christophe Mayer *Shakespeare's Hybrid Faith* (2006), Beatrice Groves, *Texts and Traditions* (2007), and an overview by Alison Shell (forthcoming). Dennis Taylor at Boston University sponsors a number of helpful websites on Shakespeare and religion.

The New Cambridge Edition of **Ben Jonson** will soon replace the monumental edition of C. H. Herford and Percy and Evelyn Simpson, 11 vols. (1925–52). There are many well-annotated editions of individual plays, including *Sejanus*, ed. Philip J. Ayres (1990); *The Alchemist*, ed. F. H. Mares (1967), Alvin B. Kernan (1974), Elizabeth Cook (1991), and Simon Trussler (1996). David Riggs (1989) and W. David Kay (1995) have written biographies. The last decade has seen a renewed interest in Jonson's Catholicism: Ian Donaldson, 'Jonson's Duplicity', *Jonson's Magic Houses* (1997), 47–65; James P. Crowley, ' "He took his religion by trust": The Matter of Ben Jonson's Conversion', *Renaissance & Reformation*, 22 (1998), 53–70; Robert S. Miola, 'Ben Jonson, Catholic Poet', *Renaissance & Reformation*, 25 (2001), 101–15; Julie Maxwell, 'Ben Jonson among the Vicars: Cliché, Ecclesiastical Politics, and the Invention of Parish Comedy', *Ben Jonson Journal*, 9 (2002), 37–68; Peter Lake, 'From *Leicester his Commonwealth* to *Sejanus his Fall*: Ben Jonson and the Politics of Roman (Catholic) Virtue', *Catholics and the 'Protestant Nation'*, ed. Ethan Shagan (2005), 128–61.

The standard edition **Philip Massinger** is *Plays and Poems*, ed. Philip Edwards and Colin Gibson, 5 vols. (1976). See also essays gathered by Douglas Howard (1985); Martin Garrett, ed., *Massinger: The Critical Heritage* (1991).

The *Dramatic Works and Poems* of **James Shirley** are easily available only in a 1966 reprint of William Gifford and Alexander Dyce's 1833 edition. Many individual plays have been edited in modern times, however, including *St Patrick for Ireland* (1979) by John P. Turner, Jr. Religious issues have been treated cursorily by Stephen J. Radtke, *James Shirley: His Catholic Philosophy of Life* (1929), and Elbridge Colby, *English Catholic Poets* (1967).

HISTORIES

Helpful guides to early modern British history include John Morrill, *The Oxford Illustrated History of Tudor & Stuart Britain* (1996); and David Loades, *Politics and Nation: England 1450–1660*, 5th edn. (1999). These works contain detailed bibliographies on political, cultural, and religious history including standard works on the Protestant revolution by A. G. Dickens, Patrick Collinson, G. R. Elton, Diarmaid MacCulloch, Philip Hughes, Joyce A. Youings. There are also the relevant volumes of *The Oxford History of England* and *A History of the Modern British Isles*. Conyers Read published a bibliography of British history for the Tudor period (1959); Godfrey Davies, for the Stuart (2nd edn., Mary Frear Keeler, 1970). Two learned and sensible studies of historiography in the period are F. J. Levy, *Tudor Historical Thought* (1967), and D. R. Woolf, *The Idea of History in Early Stuart England: Erudition, Ideology, and 'The Light of Truth' from the Accession of James I to the Civil War* (1990); see also by Woolf, *The Social Circulation of the Past: English Historical Culture 1500–1730* (2003). John Vidmar has begun to analyse Catholic historiography, *English Catholic Historians and the English Reformation, 1585–1954* (2005), as has Arthur F. Marotti, though he is focused on discourses as well as on formal histories, *Religious Ideology and Cultural Fantasy* (2005).

The *Ecclesiastical History* of **Venerable Bede** has been edited by Bertram Colgrave and R. A. B. Mynors (1969, rpt. 1992); there is a good commentary by J. M. Wallace-Hadrill (1988); on Bede's translator see Marvin R. O'Connell, *Thomas Stapleton and the Counter-Reformation* (1964).

For **Nicholas Sander** see the bibliographical note under **Controversies**. Modern studies of individual figures treated in the *Anglican Schism* include Garrett Mattingly, *Catherine of Aragon* (1941); J. J. Scarisbrick, *Henry VIII* (1968); E. W. Ives, *Anne Boleyn* (1986); Diarmaid MacCulloch, *Thomas Cranmer: A Life* (1996); Jasper Ridley, *The Life and Times of Mary Tudor* (1973); Jennifer Loach, *Parliament and the Crown in the Reign of Mary Tudor* (1986); David Loades, *Mary Tudor: A Life* (1989); *The Church of Mary Tudor*, ed. Eamon Duffy and David Loades (2006). Studies of Elizabeth I and her reign continue to proliferate, including those by D. M. Palliser (1983), Christopher Haigh (1985, 2001), Jasper Ridley (1987), Wallace T. MacCaffrey (1992, 1993), David Loades (2003), and Susan Doran (1994, 2000, 2003).

The writings of **Bartolomé de Las Casas** on the Indians are available in modern translations by Nigel Griffin (1992), Stafford Poole (1992), Herma Briffault (intro. Bill M. Donovan) (1992), and Andrew Hurley (2003). Nigel Griffin has also translated and edited *Las Casas on Columbus* (1999).

The letters and memorials of **Robert Persons** appear in several Catholic Records Society volumes (2, 4, 39). Jos. Simons has published a useful book-length summary in translation of *Certamen Ecclesiae Anglicanae* (1965); William T. Costello, an edition of *The Judgement of a Catholic Englishman* (1957); and Victor Houliston, the first book of *The Christian Directory, 1582* (1998). Francis Edwards has written a biography (1995), and there are recent appraisals by Michael L. Carrafiello, *Robert Parsons and English Catholicism (1580–1610)* (1998); Malcolm H. South, *The Jesuits and the Joint Mission to England during 1580–1581* (1999); John Bossy, 'The Heart of Robert Persons', ed. T. McCoog, *The Reckoned Expense* (1996), 141–58; Victor Houliston, *Cathlic Resistance in England* (2007). On Persons's *Treatise* see Ceri Sullivan, '"Oppressed by the Force of Truth": Robert Persons edits John Foxe', in David Loades, ed., *John Foxe: An Historical Perspective* (1999), 154–66; Anne Dillon *The Construction of Martyrdom* (2002), 323–69.

For **Richard Verstegan** see the bibliographical note above under **Poetry**, as well as Donna B. Hamilton, who discusses Verstegan's *Restitution of Decayed Antiquities* in *Prose Studies*, 22 (1999), 1–39, and also in *Theatre and Religion: Lancastrian Shakespeare*, ed. Richard Dutton *et al.* (2003), 87–104.

William Blundell has been admirably analysed by D. R. Woolf, 'Little Crosby and the Horizons of Early Modern Historical Culture', *The Historical Imagination in Early Modern Britain*, ed. Donald R. Kelley and David Harris Sacks (1997), 93–132; and Margaret Sena, 'William Blundell and the Networks of Catholic Dissent in Early Modern England', *Communities in Early Modern England*, ed. Alexandra Shepard and Phil Withington (2000), 54–75.

The *Compendium* of **Philip O'Sullivan-Beare** appears in Matthew J. Byrne's partial translation as *Ireland under Elizabeth* (1903, rpt. 1970); see also *A New History of Ireland*, iii: *Early Modern Ireland, 1534–1691*, ed. T. W. Moody, *et al.* (1976, rev. 1991); *The Making of Modern Irish History*, ed. D. George Boyce and Alan O'Day (1996); Nicholas Canny, *Making Ireland British, 1580–1650* (2001). On Spenser and Elizabethan foreign policy see Patricia Coughlan, ed., *Spenser and Ireland: An Interdisciplinary Perspective* (1989); Andrew Hadfield, *Spenser's Irish Experience: Wilde Fruit and Salvage Soyl* (1997).

Elizabeth Cary has attracted much recent attention. David Lunn has written a biography (1977); Heather Wolfe has edited the *Life* and letters (2001). On *Edward II* see Donald A. Stauffer, 'A Deep and Sad Passion', *Essays in Dramatic Literature: The Parrott Presentation Volume*, ed. Hardin Craig (1935), 289–314; F. J. Levy, 'Hayward, Daniel, and the Beginnings of Politic History in England', *Huntington Library Quarterly*, 50 (1987); Jesse Swan, 'Contextual Materials', *Renaissance Women Online*.

FICTION

On **Desiderius Erasmus** see the entry under **Controversies**. The *Colloquies* have been translated by Craig. R. Thompson, *Collected Works of Erasmus*, vols. xxxix–xl (1997). Tudor translations of the *Colloquies* (1536–84) appear in facsimile, ed. Dickie A. Spurgeon (1972). Relevant critical works include Peter Iver Kaufman, *Augustinian Piety and Catholic Reform: Augustine, Colet, and Erasmus* (1982); Carlos M. N. Eire, *War against the Idols: The Reformation of Worship from Erasmus to Calvin* (1986); Richard L. DeMolen, *The Spirituality of Erasmus of Rotterdam* (1987); and Hilmar M. Pabel, ed., *Erasmus' Vision of the Church* (1995).

See the entry for **Anthony Copley** under **Poetry**.

A. F. Allison has compiled a bibliographical catalogue for **Thomas Lodge** (1973). There is a relatively accessible but unannotated *Complete Works* by the Hunterian Club, with an introduction by E. W. Gosse, 4 vols. (1883, rpt. 1963). Accounts of the life and work have been published by N. Burton Paradise (1931), Charles J. Sisson (1933), and Wesley D. Rae (1967). Kevin J. Donovan has assembled a bibliography, *English Literary Renaissance*, 23 (1993), 201–11. Charles W. Whitworth has analysed Thomas Lodge as an 'Elizabethan Pioneer', *Cahiers Elisabéthains*, 3 (1973), 5–15. Lodge's Catholicism has been the subject of recent enquiry: Erin E. Kelly, 'Jewish History, Catholic Argument: Thomas Lodge's Works of Josephus as a Catholic Text', *Sixteenth Century Journal*, 34 (2003), 993–1010; R. W. Maslen, 'Lodge's Glaucus and Scilla and the Conditions of Catholic Authorship in Elizabethan England', *EnterText*, 31 (2003), 59–100.

The writing of **Elizabeth Southwell** has been dismissed by J. E. Neale, 'The Sayings of Queen Elizabeth', *History*, 10 (1925), 212–33, and defended by Catherine Loomis, 'Elizabeth Southwell's Manuscript Account of the Death of Queen Elizabeth [with text]', *English Literary Renaissance*, 26 (1996), 482–509.

Good modern translations and editions of **John Barclay** have appeared: David A. Fleming, *Euphormionis Lusinini Satyricon (Euphormio's Satyricon) 1605–1607* (1973); Mark T. Riley and Dorothy Pritchard Huber, *Argenis* (2004).

DOCUMENTS

For background on **Papal Bulls** see J. N. D. Kelly, *The Oxford Dictionary of Popes* (1986); Eamon Duffy, *Saints and Sinners: A History of the Popes* (1997); Frank J. Coppa, ed., *Encyclopedia of the Vatican and Papacy* (1999); Philippe Levillain, ed., *The Papacy: An Encyclopedia* (2002). Among the useful online collections are *Papal Encyclicals Online* and *Vatican: The Holy See*. For Latin versions of papal bulls see *Bullarum Diplomatum et Privilegiorum Sanctorum Romanorum Pontificum Taurinensis Editio*, 25 vols. (1857–72).

ILLUSTRATIONS

Searches conducted under the individual artist's names will be most productive. In addition, see Tessa Watt's overview, *Cheap Print and Popular Piety, 1550–1640* (1991); Margaret Aston and Elizabeth Ingram, 'The Iconography of the *Acts and Monuments*', *John Foxe and the English Reformation*, ed. David Loades (1997), 66–142; Alexandra Walsham, ' "Domme Preachers"?' *Past and Present*, 168 (2000), 72–123 (for a section on Catholic illustrations); and Anne Dillon's study of the *Trophaea* and *Theatrum*, *The Construction of Martyrdom* (2002).

TEXTUAL NOTES

CONTROVERSIES

Desiderius Erasmus

Novum Instrumentum Omne, Basel, 1516, sigs. bbb1ᵛ–bbb2 [*Apologia, seq.*, n.p.]; *Paraclesis*, tr. William Roye, *An exhortation to the diligent studye of scripture*, Antwerp, 1529 (Short Title Catalogue (STC) 10493), first gathering, 5th leaf verso–A1; *De libero arbitrio, Collected Works of Erasmus*, vol. lxxvi: *Controversies*, ed. Charles Trinkaus, tr. Peter Macardle, annotated by Peter Macardle, Clarence H. Miller, and Charles Trinkaus (Toronto, 1999), 21, 36–8, 77–80. Reprinted with the permission of the University of Toronto Press.

On the New Testament
129 Lydians] lesbes

Thomas More

A dyaloge of syr Thomas More knyghte, London, 1530 (STC 18085), sigs. si–siii, ziiᵛ–ziii. [The title *A Dialogue Concerning Heresies* comes from the 1557 edition of More's works.]
13. a false] as false   141. easy] eth

Edmund Plowden

MS Rawlinson A 124, cap. 4.
22 fifth] first   66 I make] I make I make

Nicholas Sander

A Treatise of the Images of Christ, and of his Saints, Louvain, 1566 (STC 21696), sigs. Biiiᵛ–Biiiiᵛ, Giiiiᵛ–Gvii, Hviiᵛ–Hviiiᵛ, Kv–Kvi.
5 Lady's] Ladie   117 led] leaden

Edmund Campion

Letter, MS Harley 422, fos. 132–3; *Debates*, MS Harley 422, fos. 162–3.

Letter
19 voice] vysage   48 in] and

Alban Langdale

Alban Langdale, Public Records Office (PRO) 12/144/69 [see *Calendar of State Papers* (*CSP*) *Domestic 1547–1580*, 691 (31 Dec. 1580)].

19 novice-ship] novasship   25 idolaters and] Ido   29 prorsum] *proru*   47 were] was

William Allen

A Trve, Sincere, and Modest Defence of English Catholiques, Rouen, 1584 (STC 373), sigs. D7–D8; *A Declaration of the Sentence and deposition of Elizabeth, the vsurper and pretensed Quene of Englande*, Antwerp, 1588 (STC 22590).

Henry Garnet

Peter Canisius, *A Svmme of Christian Doctrine* [tr. Henry Garnet, with additions], London, 1592–6 (STC 4571.5), sigs. Rr7-Rr8, Tt1-Tt2, Vv1ᵛ–Vv2, Vv3ᵛ; *A Treatise of Equivocation*, ed. David Jardine, London, 1851, 8–11.

Of Indulgences
68 [. . .] *illegible*

Juan de Mariana

De Rege et Regis Institutione, Toledo, 1599, sigs. E5ᵛ–F1ᵛ. My translation.

Robert Bellarmine

Tractatus de Potestate Summi Pontificis adversus Gulielmum Barclajum, Variorum Operum . . . ad Fidei Controversias Spectantium Collectio, Tomus 5, Venice, 1721, sigs. E8–E8ᵛ. My translation.

Jane Owen

An Antidote against Pvrgatory, Saint-Omer, 1634 (STC 18984), sigs. D2ᵛ–D4ᵛ, D7–D8, I12ᵛ–K1ᵛ, K4–K5ᵛ, F9–G3.

LIVES AND DEATHS

Augustine of Hippo

The Confessions of the Incomparable Doctovr S. Avgvstine [tr. Toby Matthew], Saint-Omer, 1620 (STC 910), sigs. E1–E2, F1ᵛ–F2ᵛ, K3–K4, S3–S3ᵛ, S8ᵛ–T2, Aa3–Aa4ᵛ, Bb5ᵛ–Bb8, Gg4–Gg4ᵛ, Kk6–Kk6ᵛ.
24 were] was   24 full] full of   239 looking for] looking

Teresa of Ávila

The Lyf of the Mother Teresa of Iesus, tr. W. M. [Michael Walpole?], Antwerp, 1611 (STC 23948.5), sigs. Ff1–Gg1.
40 exorcized] exercised

Thomas More

William Roper, *The Lyfe of Sir Thomas Moore, knighte*, ed. Elsie Vaughan Hitchcock, *Early English Text Society*, 197 (London, 1935), 80–104. Reprinted with the permission of Oxford University Press.

Edmund Campion

William Allen, *A Briefe Historie of the Gloriovs Martrydom of XII. Reverend Priests*, Rheims, 1582 (STC 369.5), sigs. ev–evii; Thomas Alfield, *A true reporte of the death & martyrdome of M. Campion*, London, 1582 (STC 4537), sigs. A4–C2ᵛ.

Letter

23 go] to go   27 on] one   84–5 For...all.] *omitted*

Margaret Clitherow

John Mush, *An Abstracte of the Life and Martirdome of Mistres Margaret Clitherovve*, Mechlin, 1619 (STC 18316.7), sigs. A3–A6ᵛ, B1ᵛ–B2, B3–B4, B7–B7ᵛ, C, C3–C6ᵛ.

101 forth] for   103 backs] backe   112 God] Cod

William Weston

'Life of Father William Weston', in *The Troubles of our Catholic Forefathers*, ed. and tr. John Morris, ii (London, 1875), 100–3, 210–13.

77 they] it   125 or fornicated,] *omitted*

Alexander Rawlins and Henry Walpole

Venerable English College, MS Scritture 21. 2. 1. Reprinted with the permission of the Venerable English College.

23 took] taken   50 superna] supera

Toby Matthew

A True Historical Relation of the Conversion of Sir Tobie Matthew, ed. A. H. Mathew (London, 1904), 21–30, 134–7.

Mary Ward

First Letter of Instruction: *Autobiographical Fragments, Childhood and Youth of Mary Ward*, 8–10; *Second Letter of Instruction, Mary Ward's Autobiography, 1600–1609*, 18–19; *Letters*, no. 4, 7–8; Mary Poyntz and Winifred Wigmore, *The Brief Relation*, 23; transcriptions of these manuscripts were supplied by, and reprinted by permission of, the Institute of the Blessed Virgin Mary (now know as the Congregation of Jesus), Bar Convent, York. Institute of the Blessed Virgin Mary, ed., *The Mind and Maxims of Mary Ward* (London, 1959) [for the *Memorial* and *Conference*], 9–12, 24–6. These selections are reprinted by permission of The Continuum International Publishing Group.

Autobiography

26 appeared as a sign] appeared sign

Letter

2 send myself] send   18 in which] which   21 my] by

Conference

8 we love] love

Brief Relation

22 locked] lock   23 other] *omitted*   35 walls of] walls had of

POETRY

A Lament and Some Ballads

'Lament', Rawlinson Poet. MS 219, fos. 16–16ᵛ; 'Winter Cold', Additional MS 15,225, fos. 33ᵛ–35; 'Calvary Mount', Additional MS 15, 225, fos. 2ᵛ–3; 'Jerusalem', Additional MS 15,225, fos. 36ᵛ–37ᵛ.

'Calvary'

| 15 Pilate] Polat | 18 cursèd] cused | 43 bows] boes | 54 ere] or | 67 grace] gace |

'Jerusalem'

| 41 are] *omitted* | 66 choir] Queere | 72 about] above |

Chidiock Tichborne

Tanner MS 169, fo. 79.

Francis Tregian

The Troubles of our Catholic Forefathers, ed. John Morris, i (London, 1872), 125–30.

Thomas Pounde

'A Challenge unto Foxe', PRO 12/157/48, fos. 105–10ᵛ.

Henry Constable

Diana. The praises of his Mistres in certaine sweete Sonnets, London, 1592 (STC 5637), sigs. C2, D1, D2ᵛ; *The Spiritual Sonnets*, Harleian MS 7553, fos. 32, 33ᵛ, 36, 38ᵛ.

'Sweet Hand'

| 4 in] my | 14 Thy…thy] This…this |

'To God the Father'

| 10 whilst] wil'st | 13 'cense] sence |

'To our Blessed Lady'

10 Beauty's] beuty

Robert Southwell

'Christ's Bloody Sweat', lines 13–24, 'Decease Release', Additional MS 10422, fos. 12ᵛ–13, 31ᵛ–32; 'The Nativity of Christ', 'Saint Peter's Complaint', *Saint Peters Complaint, With other Poemes*, London, 1595 (STC 22955.7), sigs. G1ᵛ, A4, C1–C2, C3–C4; 'The Virgin's Salutation', 'Christ's Return out of Egypt', 'Christ's Bloody Sweat', lines 1–12, 'The Virgin Mary to Christ on the Cross', *Moeniae. Or, Certaine excellent Poems and spirituall Hymnes*, London, 1595 (STC 22955.5), sigs. B2ᵛ, C1ᵛ, C2, C3ᵛ; 'The Burning Babe', 'What Joy to Live', *Saint Peters Complaint. Newlie augmented With other Poems*, London, 1602 (STC 22960a), sigs. L4ᵛ, H4ᵛ–I.

'The Virgin's Salutation'

No stanza breaks   3] *line supplied by Additional MS 10422*

'Christ's Return out of Egypt'

No stanza breaks

'The Burning Babe'
No stanza breaks; in fourteen-syllable couplets   12 fed] bred

'Christ's Bloody Sweat'
No stanza breaks 1–12   2 pours] powers   7, 11 phoenix's] Phenix   13–24] *omitted;*
supplied by Additional MS 10422

'Decease Release'
23 in] in in

'What Joy to Live?'
17 meanness] meanes   21 sights] sighs   22 enchants] enchant   23 aim] avme

'The Virgin Mary to Christ on the Cross'
No stanza breaks; in sixteen-syllable couplets

'Saint Peter's Complaint'
39 aumbries] Ambrose   75 Lancing] Launching   105 vowed] vovde   110 rind] ryue
117 Inconsolable] In consolable

Anthony Copley
A Fig for Fortune, London, 1596 (STC 5737), sigs. I2ᵛ–I3ᵛ, K1–K3ᵛ.
12 solder] Sowder   14 emerald] Emeraud   16 jacinth] Iacent   31 a-mounting]
amounting

Richard Verstegan
Odes in Imitation of the Seaven Penitential Psalmes with Sundry other Poemes and ditties tending to
deuotion and pietie, Antwerp, 1601 (STC 21359), sigs. D4, B2–B3.

William Alabaster
'Over the brook' and ''Tis not enough', *Sonnets*, ed. G. M. Story and Helen Gardner (Oxford, 1959);
reprinted with the permission of Oxford University Press. MS Eng. Poet. e. 57, fos. 3–5, 11.

'Away, fear'
9 them] him

'A Preface'
11 takes] take

Toby Matthew
Huntington 198, fo. 95.

John Donne
Poems, London, 1633 (STC 7045), sigs. Pp1–Pp1ᵛ, I4ᵛ–K1ᵛ, E2ᵛ–E3, Z3ᵛ, Z1ᵛ–Z2; *An Anatomy of the*
World, London, 1611 (STC 7022), sigs. A5, A8–8ᵛ; *Poems*, London, 1635 (STC 7046), sigs. Bb8–Bb8ᵛ.

'Relic'
20 times] time

'Cross'
26 And] But   50 others] other   52 Points] Pants   55 thy] the   61 fruitfully]
faithfully   63 That] the

'Good Friday'
4 motions] motion

'Hymn'
5 now] here   12 their] those   20 Shem] *Sem*

Ben Jonson

B. Jon: His Part of King James his Royal and Magnificent Entertainment, London, 1604 (STC 14756), sig. E4ᵛ; *The Workes of Beniamin Ionson*, London, 1616 (STC 14751), sigs. Vuu4ᵛ–Vuu5, Xxx1ᵛ–Xxx2, Xxx4–Xxx4ᵛ, Aaaa4ᵛ–Aaaa5, Ttt3ᵛ; 'The Garland of the Blessed Virgin Mary', Anthony Stafford, *The femall glory: or, The life, and Death of our Blessed Lady*, London, 1635 (STC 23123), sigs. Cvii–Cviiiᵛ; *The VVorkes of Bejamin Jonson. The Second Volume*, London, 1640 for 1641 (STC 14754), sigs. Z2–Z2ᵛ.

'The New Cry'
14 twelve] twelves   17 locked] look'd

'Sinner's Sacrifice'
Stanzas are numbered.

John Beaumont

Bosvvorth-field: with a Taste of the Variety of Other Poems, London, 1629 (STC 1694), sigs. E5ᵛ–E6; 'Of the Assumption of our Blessed Lady', 'On the death of many good people slain by the fall of a floor at a Catholic sermon in Blackfriars', MS Stowe 960, fos. 8ᵛ–9, 10; *The Crown of Thorns*, Additional MS 33,392, fos. 1, 16, 47ᵛ–48, 48ᵛ–52, 143.

Crown
30 grow] grows

William Habington

Castara. The first part, London, 1634 (STC 12583), sigs. B1ᵛ–B2, C1ᵛ–C2. *Castara: The Third Edition, Corrected and Augmented*, London, 1640 (STC 12585), sigs. K3–K4.

'To Castara: A Vow'
9 cottage's view] cottage, view

'*Universum*'
Title *stratum*] *statum*   18 whither] whether

Gertrude More

The Spiritval Exercises of the most Vertvous and Religious D. Gertrvde More, Paris, 1658 (Wing M 2632), Preliminaries 1ᵛ (Frontispiece), sigs. Aiiiiᵛ–Av, Avii, C1ᵛ–Ciiᵛ, Lvii.

'*Cantum Cygnaeum*'
14 untie] vnity

'If we would die'
17–18 *lineation*] And . . . or | it desire,

'A Short Oblation'
1 My] MT   11 I'll] le

Richard Crashaw

'Upon the Ensuing Treatises', Robert Shelford, *Five Piovs and Learned Discourses*, Cambridge, 1635 (STC 22400), sigs. A1–A1ᵛ; *Carmen Deo Nostro*, Paris, 1652 (Wing C6830), sigs. Givᵛ–Hiii, Liii–Miiᵛ, Oi–Oii, Oiiiᵛ–Oivᵛ, Biii–Biiiᵛ, Ai–Bi.

'Pathetical Descant'
10 own] one   26 If . . . just] Is . . . soft

'Weeper'
26 vine] wine   46 your] their

'The Flaming Heart'
2 wounds] wound

'Hymn in the Holy Nativity'
13–30] *No stanza breaks*

'Name'
74 your] yours   87 lose] loose   93 aloud] loud   132 thy] thee

INSTRUCTIONS AND DEVOTIONS

Prayers and Hymns

The Primer, or Office of the Blessed Virgin Marie in Latin and English, tr. R[ichard] V[erstegan], Antwerp, 1599 (STC 16094), sigs. T11–V2, D4, V3–V5; 'The Fifteen Oes' from *Hor[a]e B[ea]te marie virginis ad usum Saru[m]*, Antwerp, 1525 (STC 15939), fos. cxlv–cxlix; 'The Litany of Loreto', appended to Lorenzo Scupoli, *The Spiritval Conflict*, tr. John Gerard, Rouen, 1613 (STC 22128), sigs. H5ᵛ–H6ᵛ. Luca Pinelli, SJ, *Breife Meditations of the Most Holy Sacrament* [tr. Henry Garnet?], London, 1600 (STC 19937), sigs. ¶2–¶3, ¶6ᵛ–¶8ᵛ; Richard Crashaw, *Carmen Deo Nostro*, Paris, 1652 (Wing C6830), sigs. Iiᵛ–Iiii. [In some prayers below I have silently modernized awkward second-person forms, e.g. 'suffered' for 'sufferedst'.]

'Fifteen Oes'
5 things] thing   8 *and elsewhere* and] et   21 vouchsafe] saufe   25 been] be
28 nor] ne by   30 marrow] mary   33 to thee that] tho the that

Lauda, Sion
No stanza breaks   18 prime] privy   36 effects] affects   56 in] *omitted*

Adoro te
33 my faith,] *omitted*   33–6] *printed as a separate stanza*

Robert, Prior of Shrewsbury

The Admirable Life of Saint Wenefride, Virgin, Martyr, Abesse, tr. I[ohn] F[alconer], Saint-Omer, 1635 (STC 21102), sigs. D3–D7, N4–N6.

Thomas à Kempis

The Folovving of Christ, trans. Richard Whitford, Rouen, 1585 (STC 23968), sigs. fii–fvi.
38 be come] become   112 conformed] confirmed

Ignatius Loyola

The Examen, Tomas de Villacastin, *A Manvall of Devout Meditations and Exercises, Instructing how to pray mentally. Drawne for the most part, out of the Spirituall Exercises of B. F. Ignatius* [tr. Henry More], Saint-Omer, 1618 (STC 16877), sigs. C4ᵛ–C6; *The Spiritual Exercises of St Ignatius Loyola, Spanish and English, with a Continuous Commentary*, ed. and tr. Joseph Rickaby, SJ (London, 1915), 18–19, 23–6, 68–71, 109–13, 208–10.

6 indifferent to] detached in regard of

Consolations

John Fisher, *A spirituall consolation*, London, 1578 (STC 10899), sigs. Avi–Avii; Thomas More, *The vvorkes of Sir Thomas More Knyght*, London, 1557 (STC 18076), sigs. Iiviii ᵛ–KKii ᵛ; Robert Southwell, *An Epistle of Comfort* [London], 1587–8 (STC 22946), sigs. F2–F3 ᵛ.

Consolation

15 gilt] gylted

Dialogue

4 *and elsewhere* one] tone   4 *and elsewhere* other] tother   39 Cam's] Canes   97 hovered
a-loose] hoved a loose   98 amid] amid mong

Epistle

10 losing] leasing

Meditations

Luis de Granada, *Of Prayer and Meditation* [tr. Richard Hopkins], Paris, 1582 (STC 16907), sigs. Kiii–Kvii; John Bucke, *Instrvctions for the vse of the beades*, Louvain, 1589 (STC 4000), sigs. Aviii–B1.

Of Prayer

102 Dalila] Dalida

Roger Martin

'The state of Melford Church and of our Lady's Chapel at the east end, as I, Roger Martin, did know it', *The History of Long Melford*, ed. Sir William Parker (London, 1873), 70–3.

William Byrd

Gradvalia, ac Cantiones Sacrae, London, 1610 (STC 4244), sigs. Eii, Eiii–Eiii ᵛ, Dii.

Francis de Sales

An Introdvction to a Devovte Life [tr. John Yaxley], Douai, 1613 (STC 11316.5), sigs. M10 ᵛ–N3.

67 coping] copning   76 forces] force

Henry Hawkins

Henry Hawkins, SJ, *Partheneia Sacra, or the Mysteriovs and Deliciovs Garden of the Sacred parthenes, Symbolically set forth and enriched with Piovs Devises and Emblemes*, Rouen, 1633 (STC 12958), sigs. Bvii–Civ.

20 cellar] cellarie   33 ails] ail   182 spineti] spinati

Augustine Baker

Sancta Sophia, or Directions for the Prayer of Contemplation, ed. Serenus Cressy, Douai, 1657 (Wing B480), sigs. Ff4–Gg3 ᵛ.

33 which] with   46 with] which   71 as] *omitted*   107 to] *omitted.*

DRAMA

John Heywood

A mery play betwene the pardoner and the frere, the curate and neybour Pratte, London, 1533 (STC 13299).
7 where] were   16 collation] colacyou   17 presence] prese   24SD *and elsewhere* be]
ben   24SD *whole*] hole   55 fault] faut   160 Jeez, I sha'] Jys I sh   171SP FRIAR]
pardo.   188SP PARSON] *omitted*

Jane Lumley

Iphigenia at Aulis Translated by Lady Lumley, ed. Harold H. Child, Malone Society Reprints (London,
1909), ll. 1023–411.
166, 169, 172SP MESSENGER] Nun.

Jacob Bidermann

Jacob Bidermann, *Cenodoxus*, trans. D. G. Dyer, Cecily Longrigg, *Edinburgh Bilingual Library*, 9
(Austin, Tex., 1974), 82–7, 181–9. Reprinted with the permission of Edinburgh University Press.

William Shakespeare

The Tragicall Historie of Hamlet, Prince of Denmarke, London, 1604 (STC 22276), sigs. D2–D3^v;
Measure for Measure, The Norton Facsimile: The First Folio of Shakespeare, ed. Charlton Hinman (New
York, 1968), Through Line Numbers (TLN) 1055–201; *The Late, and much admired Play, Called Pericles,
Prince of Tyre*, London, 1609 (STC 22334) sigs. I1^v–I3; *Henry VIII, The Norton Facsimile*, TLN 1363–410,
1464–80.

Hamlet
20 on] an   44 wit] wits   47 what a] what   55 lust] but   55 angel] Angle
56 sate] sort   58 scent] sent   67 alleys] allies

Measure for Measure
3 or] and   26 Let me be] Let be   44 all-binding] all-building

Pericles
The scenes in the quarto are largely in prose.
5. 1   7 life] like
5. 3   6 who] whom   15 nun] mum   37 Immortal] I mortall

Ben Jonson

Seianvs his Fall, London, 1605 (STC 14782), sigs. B1^v–B2, F3–F3^v, H3^v–H4, I2–I2^v; *The Workes of
Beniamin Jonson*, London, 1616 (STC 14751), sigs. Ggg6–Hhh2^v.

The Alchemist
3. 2   118 orphans] orphan

Philip Massinger

The Renegado, A Tragaecomedie, London, 1630 (STC 17641), sigs. H2^v–H4, I3^v–I4, K2–K3.
4. 1   24SD] *after* 32   78 stand] hand   82 travail's] trauailes

4.3   4 content. Below] content below
5.1   38 font] fount

James Shirley

St Patrick for Ireland. The first Part, London, 1640 (STC 22455), sigs. I1ᵛ–I4.

5. 3.   28 supposed] suppose   109 traveller] travellers   144 SP ALL] *Omnes*   148 SD *all*]
Omnes

HISTORIES

Venerable Bede

The History of the Chvrch of Englande, tr. Thomas Stapleton, Antwerp, 1565 (STC 1778), sigs. _4–||2,
A2ᵛ–A4ᵛ, E1–E3, H2ᵛ–H4.

93 lost] losse   149 Alban's] *Albanus*   227 south] west   228 hides] miles
238 bruit] brute   263 mercy's] mercy

Nicholas Sander

Rise and Growth of the Anglican Schism, tr. David Lewis (London, 1877), 7–8, 53–5, 23–6, 92–4, 221–3,
284–90.

Bartolomé de Las Casas

The Spanish Colonie, or Briefe Chronicle of the Acts and gestes of the Spaniardes in the West Indies, tr.
M.M.S., London, 1583 (STC 4739), sigs. A1–A4, M1ᵛ–M3.

46 inborn] inbornes   111 lead about with] led about w

Robert Persons

A Treatise of Three Conversions of England from Paganisme to Christian Religion, 3 vols., Saint-Omer,
1603–4 (STC 19416), i: sigs. A1–A1ᵛ; ii: sigs †2ᵛ–†8; iii: sigs. Z6–Bb6ᵛ.

103 Bohemia] *Bemeland*   112 Nicaea] Nice

Richard Verstegan

A Restitvtion of Decayed Intelligence In antiquities, Antwerp, 1605 (STC 21361), sigs. †4ᵛ–††, F1ᵛ–G2ᵛ,
S2ᵛ–S3ᵛ, Aa2ᵛ, Dd4ᵛ, Kk2ᵛ–Kk3, Nn2ᵛ–Nn3.

39 example's] example   49 nobility's] nobillitie   61 such] suck

Philip O'Sullivan-Beare

Historiae Catholicae Iberniae Compendium, Lisbon, 1621, partially translated, Matthew J. Byrne, *Ireland
under Elizabeth: Chapters towards A History of Ireland* (Dublin, 1903), 1–2, 21–5, 43–4, 57–8, 181. [I have
silently corrected Byrne's translation where I have judged it to be infelicitous or inaccurate.]

Elizabeth Cary

*The History of The Life, Reign, and Death of Edward II, King of England, and Lord of Ireland with The Rise
and Fall of his great favourites, Gaveston and the Spencers*, London, 1680 (Wing F313), 42–4, 147–56.

65 with] *omitted*

FICTION

Desiderius Erasmus

A dialoge . . . intituled the pylgremage of pure deuotyon, tr. anonymous, London, 1536 (STC 10454), sigs. Biii^v–Bviii, Diii–Ei^v.

6 *and elsewhere* been] be   54 my] me   55 honour's] honor   70 then] the
145 hair] heren   216 lend] leane

Anthony Copley

Wits Fittes and Fancies, London, 1595 (STC 5738), sigs. G1^v, G2^v–G3, G3^v, G4^v, H1, H2^v–H3, O3^v.

Thomas Lodge

VVits Miserie, and the VVorlds Madnesse: Discouering the Deuils Incarnat of this Age, London, 1596 (STC 16677), sigs. Di–Dii, Fii–Fii^v, Fiv^v; *Prosopopeia containing the teares of the holy, blessed, and sanctified Marie, Mother of God*, London, 1596 (STC 16662a), sigs. B5–B8^v.

Wit's Misery
78 mornings very] morningsberie   89 Longinus's] Lunges   115 taetrum] tetrum

Prosopopeia
5 two] to

Robert Chambers

Palestina, written by Mr R.C.P. and bachelor of Diuinitie [London], 1600 (STC 4954), sigs. A2–B1^v.
3 Nineveh] *Niniuie*   16 chalcedony] Calcedonicke   59 were] where   111 made] make

Elizabeth Southwell

Catherine Loomis, 'Elizabeth Southwell's Manuscript Account of the Death of Queen Elizabeth [with text]', *English Literary Renaissance*, 26 (1996), 482–509 [484–87]; I modernize Loomis's transcription of Stonyhurst Ang. iii.77, and reprint with the permission of the editors and author.

John Barclay

Iohn Barclay his Argenis, tr. Robert Le Grys and Thomas May, London, 1629 (STC 1394), sigs. G6^v–H1, Q8–Q8^v.
11 I] that I

DOCUMENTS

Papal Bulls

Ille humani generis, Edward Peters, ed., *Heresy and Authority in Medieval Europe: Documents in Translation* (London, 1980), 196–8, reprinted with the permission of Ashgate Press and Edward Peters; *Inter caetera*, Pietro Martire d'Anghiera, *The Decades of the newe worlde or west India*, tr. Richard Eden, London, 1555 (STC 647), sigs. Vviii–Xx1; *Inter sollicitudines*, Norman P. Tanner, SJ, ed., *Decrees of the Ecumenical Councils* (London, 1990), 2 vols, i. 632–3, my translation; *Regnans in excelsis*, William Camden, *Annales, the True and Royall history of the famous empresse Elizabeth Queene of England France and Ireland &c*, London, 1625 (STC 4497), sigs. Ii3–Ii4ᵛ. I have silently made minor adjustments to translations where they are misleading or infelicitous.

Colonization
9 with] without

Excommunication
47 See] siege

ILLUSTRATIONS

Durante Alberti, 'The Martyrs Picture', 1583. Reprinted with the permission of the Venerable English College, Rome.

Frederick Staphylus, 'A Show of the Protestants' Pedigree', *The Apology*, tr. Thomas Stapleton, 1565, between Gg4 and Hh1. Reprinted with the permission of the Folger Shakespeare Library.

Giacomo della Porta, Interior of the Gesù, Rome, 16th c. Photo credit: Scala/Art Resource, NY. Reprinted with the permission of Art Resource.

John Foxe, 'Edwardian Revolution: Iconoclasm and Purgation', *Acts and Monuments*, 1576, p. 1257. Reprinted with the permission of the Folger Shakespeare Library.

Sandro Botticelli (1444–1510), 'Dante's Purgatorio III: The Excommunicated'. Staatliche Museen zu Berlin. Photo Credit: Bildarchiv Preussicher Kulturbesitz/Art Resource, NY. Reprinted with the permission of Art Resource.

Richard Verstegan, 'The Execution of Mary, Queen of Scots', *Theatrum crudelitatum haereticorum*, 1587, sig. L3. Reprinted with the permission of the Rare Books division, The New York Public Library, Astor, Lenox and Tilden Foundations.

Gian Lorenzo Bernini, 'Ecstasy of St Teresa of Ávila', Coronaro Chapel, Santa Maria della Vittoria, Rome, 1645–52. Photo Credit: Alinari/Art Resource, NY. Reprinted with the permission of Art Resource.

Giovanni Baptista de Cavalleriis, 'The Martyrdom of Edmund Campion, Alexander Briant, and Ralph Sherwin', *Ecclesiae Anglicanae Trophaea*, 1584, pl. 33. Spencer Collection, New York Public Library, Astor, Lenox and Tilden Foundations. Reprinted with the permission of the New York Public Library.

Richard Verstegan, 'The Martyrdom of Margaret Clitherow', *Theatrum crudelitatum haereticorum*, 1587, sig. K3. Reprinted with the permission of the Rare Books division, The New York Public Library, Astor, Lenox and Tilden Foundations.

Richard Crashaw, 'Mary Magdalen, Weeping, with Flaming Heart', *Carmen Deo Nostro*, 1652, p. 85. Reprinted with the permission of the Folger Shakespeare Library.

Fra Angelico (1387–1455), 'The Annunciation', San Marco, Florence. Photo credit: Nimatalla/Art Resource, NY. Reprinted with the permission of Art Resource.

Henry Hawkins, [a] 'The Devise' and [b] 'The Emblem', *Partheneia Sacra*, 1633, pp. 17, 25. Reprinted with the permission of the Folger Shakespeare Library.

Giovanni Baptista de Cavalleriis, 'The Third Conversion of England', *Ecclesiae Anglicanae Trophaea*, 1584, pl. 10. Spencer Collection, New York Public Library, Astor, Lenox and Tilden Foundations. Reprinted with the permission of the New York Public Library.

Giorgio Vasari, 'The Massacre of the Huguenots,' Sala Regia, Vatican Palace, 1572–4. Photo Credit: Alinari/Art Resource, NY. Reprinted with the permission of Art Resource.

Pedro Berruguete (1450–1504), 'Inquisition: Auto da fé and Pardon', Museo del Prado, Madrid. Photo credit: Erich Lessing/Art Resource. Reprinted with the permission of Art Resource.

INDEX

A WINNING CASE

How to Use
Persuasive Communication Techniques
for Successful Trial Work

A WINNING CASE

How to Use
Persuasive Communication Techniques
for Successful Trial Work

Noelle C. Nelson, Ph.D.

PRENTICE HALL
Englewood Cliffs, New Jersey 07632

Prentice-Hall International (UK) Limited, *London*
Prentice-Hall of Australia Pty. Limited, *Sydney*
Prentice-Hall Canada, Inc., *Toronto*
Prentice-Hall Hispanoamericana, S.A., *Mexico*
Prentice-Hall of India Private Limited, *New Delhi*
Prentice-Hall of Japan, Inc., *Tokyo*
Simon & Schuster Asia Pte. Ltd., *Singapore*
Editora Prentice-Hall do Brasil, Ltda., *Rio de Janeiro*

© 1991 *by*

PRENTICE-HALL, Inc.

Englewood Cliffs, NJ

10 9 8 7 6 5 4 3 2 1

Library of Congress Cataloging-in-Publication Data

Nelson, Noelle C.
  A winning case : how to use persuasive communication
techniques for successful trial work / by Noelle C. Nelson
        p.   cm.

  Includes bibliographical references and index.
  ISBN 0-13-932278-7
  1. Trial practice—United States.   2. Jury—United States.
3. Forensic oratory.   4. Persuasion (Psychology)   I. Title.
KF8915.N45 1991
347.73'75—dc20   91-2651
[347.30775]   CIP

ISBN 0-13-932278-7

PRENTICE HALL
BUSINESS & PROFESSIONAL DIVISION
A division of Simon & Schuster
Englewood Cliffs, New Jersey 07632

PRINTED IN THE UNITED STATES OF AMERICA

Acknowledgments

For permission to quote copyrighted materials, I am grateful to the following: Section of Litigation, American Bar Association, for the quotations from *The Litigation Manual* (Section of Litigation, American Bar Association, 1983); Southern Illinois University Press, for the quotations from *Communication and Litigation* by Janice Schuetz and Kathryn H. Snedaker (Carbondale: Southern Illinois University Press, 1988); National Institute for Trial Advocacy, for the quotations from *The Master Advocates' Handbook*, edited by D. Lake Rumsey (St. Paul, Mn: National Institute for Trial Advocacy, 1986). I am also grateful for the excerpts from *On Trial* by Normal Sheresky, copyright © 1977 by Norman Sheresky, reprinted by permission of the publisher, Viking Penguin, a division of Penguin Books USA Inc.; for the excerpts from the book, *Women Trial Lawyers: How They Succeed in Practice and in the Courtroom*, edited by Janine N. Warsaw, 1987, used by permission of the publisher, Prentice-Hall, Inc., Englewood Cliffs, New Jersey; for the excerpts reprinted from *The Trial Lawyers*, by Emily Couric, © 1988 by Emily Couric, published by St. Martin's Press, reprinted by permission of the author.

Special thanks are due to Ellen Kadin, who first saw the potential of the manuscript and taught me much about transforming a manuscript into a viable book.

My heartfelt thanks go to Gerald Galbo of the Business & Professional Books Division at Prentice Hall, who painstakingly and with constant kindness, brought his excellent and incisive editor's skills to bear in shaping the book, giving me invaluable suggestions and much appreciated encouragement.

Sincere thanks then go to those attorneys and other professionals who gave so generously of their time and wisdom in helping me prepare this book, in particular Sally Allen, Peter Gellerman, Dave Glickman, Jim Gregory, Mimi Gramatky, Peg Morell, Robert Sapia, and Ed Steinbrecher, and of course to my illustrator, James Rumph, who magically transformed my feeble stick figures into enlightening drawings.

A special note of gratitude to Downey Grosenbaugh, past President of the Los Angeles Trial Lawyers Association and Fellow of the American College of Trial Lawyers, without whose unfailing support, ideas, and patient reading and rereading of the manuscript, this book would not have been possible, and finally, loving thanks to my husband, Dr. Joseph M. Fabricatore, for everything. This book is dedicated to my parents, Suzy and Frank Cross, with all my love.

NOTE: Throughout the text, the masculine pronouns "he," "his," and "him" are used purely as a matter of convenience, and should be considered as a short form of "he and/or she," "his and/or hers," "him and/or her."

What This Guide Will Do for You

Ten years ago, if an attorney hired a consultant to help him be more persuasive in front of a jury, he almost invariably kept a secret, for fear of seeming "weird," "insecure," or "conniving." Now, attorneys openly hire consultants of all kinds, from acting coaches to psychologists, to help them win their cases. This new development has assumed such importance that the *Los Angeles Times* ran a full front page feature on the subject in November of 1987, *Time* magazine ran a special article covering the same topic in August of 1988, as did CNN. In 1987 and 1988, the Lost Angeles Trial Lawyers Association included a section on persuasive communication skills as applied to trialwork in their annual convention, and the National Society of Trial Consultants, created in 1984, is booming. Times have changed, and with them, what it takes to be a successful trial attorney. Juror expectations have been forever altered by the impact of television; jury boredom in the increasing number of cases involving complex business matters is problematic; the stakes are ever higher for each case; the number of attorneys in practice grows each year. Legal expertise alone no longer suffices; an attorney must also be a skilled and persuasive communicator if he is to win his case.

A Winning Case provides you with a practical step-by-step guide to persuasive communication techniques specifically designed for contemporary trialwork. Each technique is explained in detail; worksheets, exercises, and checklists are included at the end of the relevant chapters in order to facilitate understanding and application. Some of these techniques are drawn from the field of acting, for example:

- how to project a charismatic presence
- how to use your voice to win the jury over emotionally
- how to use eye contact to discredit a witness
- how to use the pause to highlight an important point

All of the acting techniques have been selected to fit the specific demands of trialwork, and do not produce theatrical effects, which have little place in today's Courtroom.

Other techniques in *A Winning Case* are drawn from the fields of psychology and social psychology, for example:

- how to make an immediate convincing impression on the jurors
- how to get critical information from prospective jurors in *voir dire*
- how to get the jurors to trust and believe you
- how to maintain the jury's attention and interest

- how to get an uncooperative witness to cooperate
- how to throw a witness off balance

In addition, *A Winning Case* provides you with step-by-step instructions on how to design the presentation of the substantive issues so that your case has maximum impact. You will learn specific ways that, psychology has demonstrated, are most effective in getting your point across and other valuable techniques such as:

- how to make the most of the emotional and logical sides of the jurors' decision-making process
- how to keep the jury's focus exactly where you want it
- how to tap into powerful pre-existing sources of influence and persuasiveness to convince the jury

Once these techniques have been presented, *A Winning Case* takes you through the five major parts of trial, from *voir dire* to summation, and shows you in detail how to apply the techniques successfully and persuasively to each part. Throughout the book, *A Winning Case* gives you real-life examples of the techniques in action, examples taken from important cases of noted trial attorneys.

To ensure that you maximize the benefits to be gained from the skilled application of persuasive communication techniques, *A Winning Case* then shows you in practical step-by-step fashion:

- how to develop a dynamic Courtroom style, based on your own personality and tailored to fit the case at hand
- how to deal successfully with fears of failure and incompetence, thereby overcoming Courtroom anxiety
- how to coach your witnesses so that they present themselves effectively and persuasively

Finally, *A Winning Case* looks at a number of problem situations which commonly arise during the course of a trial, and uses the techniques demonstrated in the book in order to resolve these situations successfully.

A Winning Case will provide you with a wide range of persuasive Courtroom communication skills, and give you specific examples on how, when, and why to use them. *A Winning Case* does not propose to give you "one right way" to be a successful trial attorney, but rather shows you many ways to be successful depending on your personality, the nature of the case, and the nature of the specific jury, all of which are designed to give you the edge on the competition so that you may indeed—win your case.

Contents

How to Use Your Body Language to Win in Court 58

Step 1: How to Figure Out Your Current Body Language 58
Step 2: How to Use Your Body Language Skillfully to Communicate
  Most Effectively with the Jurors 59

The Five Basics of Persuasive Facial Expression and How to Use Them to Communicate Successfully with a Jury 60

How to Use the Basic Facial Expression of Serious Concern to Win the
  Jury's Trust 60
How to Convey Your Disapproval Subtly to the Jurors 60
How to Convey Your Approval Subtly to the Jurors 61
Smiles: A Warning 61
How to Use Your Brows to Communicate Interest or Distrust to the
  Jurors 61

How to Use Your Facial Expressions to Influence the Jurors 62

The Two Keys to Facial Expressions That Persuade Jurors 63
A Special Application of Facial Expressions: How to Use Eye Focus to
  Credit or Discredit a Witness 64

How to Develop Gestures That Clarify and Illustrate Important Points Convincingly 65

Don't Let Habitual Gestures Stand in the Way of Your
  Persuasiveness 65
How to Increase the Expressiveness of Your Gestures to Emphasize
  Your Points to a Jury 67
How to Time a Gesture to Maximize Its Impact with the Jurors 68

How Useless Mannerisms Damage Your Effectiveness in Communicating Your Points to the Jury 69

How to Get Rid of Useless Mannerisms 70

How to Use Movement Persuasively 71

How to Use Movement to Establish Control in the Courtroom 71
How Movement Persuades in the Courtroom 72
How to Use Movement to Persuade the Jurors 73
How to Use Movement to Create a Special Relationship with the
  Jury 74
How to Use Movement to Create a Special Relationship with Your
  Client During Trial 76

CHAPTER 1

Creating a Winning
First Impression

Within the first few moments that the jurors see you, they decide whether you are to be believed or not. Your initial physical presentation of yourself determines how the jurors view you, what they think of you and your client, and how they assess everything that is to follow: it is the background against which your every deed and word is evaluated. Your *first impression* with the jurors is the key to your credibility.

HOW TO ESTABLISH YOUR CREDIBILITY WITH A JURY

What is credibility? Credibility is your believability factor in front of a jury. Credibility is the jury's willingness to believe something is true because you say it is true. Credibility is what inspires confidence and influences decisions. Most attorneys take the notion of credibility very seriously—but only as pertains to the content of their case, to their witnesses, to the believability of their client. All too often, they ignore the most fundamental credibility of all—their own. Yet credibility is the very foundation of your success as a persuasive advocate, and because it is so important, it must be carefully established.

District Attorney Robert Morgenthau sums up the informed opinion of many outstanding trial lawyers when he states, "A lot of jurors make their decision not only on the evidence but on whether the lawyer is believable."[1] The worthiness of your client's cause is intimately related to your perceived worthiness. If the jury believes you are credible, it is willing to extend that credibility to your client and to your case. You are every bit as much on trial as is your client.

How to Recognize and Use the Two Basic Elements of Credibility

Credibility is composed of two basic elements:

1. *expertness*, the attorney's ability to make valid statements; and
2. *trustworthiness*, how fair and sincere is the attorney in making these statements.

Expertness

Expertness relates to how well you have prepared your case, how thorough you have been, how "professional." "Professional" is defined by jurors as "careful presentation of the evidence": the prototypical lawyer is one who is "meticulous and incisive."[2]

Trustworthiness

Trustworthiness includes "authoritative presentation" and the juror's perception of the attorney's "demonstrated allegiance and zeal for his client's cause."[3]

In assessing your credibility, the jurors look specifically at the following:

1. How well prepared are you?
2. How carefully do you present the evidence?
3. How sincere and fair are you?
4. Do you truly believe in your client's cause?

HOW THE JURORS FORM THEIR CRITICAL FIRST IMPRESSION OF YOU AND HOW TO TAKE ADVANTAGE OF IT

In their initial assessment of who you are, jurors rely on the most basic of decision making processes: gathering information, then assessing it. Scrutinizing the attorney, client, and witnesses for outward signs of worthiness and sincerity are significant parts of the information-gathering process; right from the start of trial, jurors often keep extensive notes of what attorneys do, including their personal grooming, habits, and gestures. Whether we like it or not, appearances do matter. They directly influence what the jurors think of you and therefore how they respond to you.

Since the jurors cannot ask questions, they must use what is going on in front of them as the sole source of the information that will go into their decision making. Consequently many behaviors which would in the course of daily life go unnoticed, and certainly unjudged, suddenly assume new and critical proportions.

CASE IN POINT

Situation 1:

An attorney gropes in his briefcase for a document

Jurors' Reaction:

Jury takes this observed behavior as evidence that the attorney is unprepared and therefore probably incompetent.

Situation 2:

A businessman gropes in his briefcase for a file

Associates' Reaction:

The businessman is looking for something.

Situation 3:

An attorney twists his wedding ring back and forth

Jurors' Reaction:

Jurors interpret this as nervousness and judge the attorney to be incompetent: if the attorney is nervous, he must be worried, so he must not be doing well, and he must be losing his case.

Situation 4:

A man is seen twisiting his wedding band while waiting for a bus

Onlookers' Reaction:

The ring-twisting goes unnoticed or is deemed a meaningless personal habit.

In sum, your perfectly innocuous personal habits and mannerisms are read as meaningful clues to your credibility, and take on a life of their own.

The Lasting Value of a First Impression

Not only is a first impression created almost instantaneously, but it is very difficult to alter once it has been created. Research demonstrates that people hold tenaciously to their first opinion, and will attempt to deny or devalue information which appears to contradict that first opinion.

CASE IN POINT

In rape cases in which the defendant is good-looking or handsome, women often ignore the facts pointing towards the guilt of the defendant, claiming that anyone who is that attractive has no need to rape in order to be sexually satisfied. The women prefer to trust their first opinion, based on the initial impression, "attractive, therefore not a rapist," to the facts of the case. A sobering thought.

Although it is very important that you maintain a favorable opinion of yourself with the jurors throughout the trial, the construction of their first opinion is the most important of all, because it is the most difficult to undo.

How Jurors Assess Your First Impression

The great trial lawyers truly believe in their client or their client's cause, and this belief shines through and informs their every word and action. It is this belief which convinces the jurors of their credibility. Now, you may have the same belief in your client and/or his cause, but if you do not express that belief both verbally and nonverbally in a way which the jurors *perceive* as sincere, that is to say credible, you will not be believed.

Jurors assess what they see by a process called "stereotyping," which then becomes the basis of their initial impression of you. Knowing how stereotyping works allows you to use it to your advantage in creating a credible first impression.

Stereotyping is the process which allows us to conduct our daily affairs with the speed and efficiency dictated by modern life. Stereotyping helps people figure out what to do with complex information by organizing and simplifying it; it enables us to categorize information virtually instantaneously so that we may react or respond appropriately.

CASE IN POINT

Situation 1:

A worried looking middle-aged woman, wearing a plain but clean house-dress, carrying a crying child in her arms asks you for help.

Stereotyped Interpretation:

Your instant stereotyped interpretation of the situation is: "Here is a concerned mother, the child is crying, he's probably sick."

Appropriate Response based on Stereotyped Interpretation:

You respond to her plea with compassion, and try to help her.

Situation 2:

A young man, long greasy looking hair flapping in the wind, dressed in torn leather with metal studs, tatoos adorning his naked chest, roars up on a motorcycle and asks you for help.

Stereotyped Interpretation:

Your instant stereotyped interpretation of the situation is: "This man looks like a Hell's Angel, his plea for help is undoubtedly just a way of getting me close enough to him so he can steal my wallet or knife me."

Appropriate Response based on Stereotyped Interpretation:

You pretend you never heard the man's plea, and duck into the nearest shop to avoid him.

Stereotyping helps us interpret and evaluate new information on the basis of what we already know, and thus helps us to make potentially meaningless situations, meaningful. Once an individual has made sense of a situation, he can anticipate future behavior or events based on the stereotype, and so is free to go on to deal with other matters.

CASE IN POINT

An attorney fidgets and keeps chewing on his mustache during opposing counsel's cross examination of his witness. The fidgeting and chewing are stereotyped as evidence of worry and anxiety. The jurors' assessment of such worry and anxiety is that the attorney must be ill-prepared and therefore unprofessional. With this frame of reference in mind, the jurors now know how to interpret anything the attorney does, and so are free to attend to other events occuring in the Courtroom.

You create an impression of yourself whether you do it on purpose or not. It doesn't make a bit of difference if you spend hours of thought, creativity and effort to create a given impression or don't spend a moment on it, the result is the same: people will respond to you on the basis of their perception of who you are.

Let me repeat that last statement because it is critical: you will be responded to in function of *how the jurors perceive you*, not in terms of who you really are. This is an important distinction. The worried woman in the example cited earlier could have been a kidnapper, the motorcycle rider could have been honestly in need of help. Most certainly, attractive looking men have been known to rape. These are realities. But all these people are responded to in function of how they are *perceived*, not in function of who they really are.

CASE IN POINT

In a study by Kraut & Poe[4], observers tried to determine, during the course of a customs interview, which airline travelers were smuggling contraband goods and which were not. Observers shared such a clear consensus about the stereotype of how a smuggler behaves, that they agreed to a striking degree as to which travelers were smugglers and which were not, yet in reality, the observers were almost always wrong in their perceptions. Regardless of the fact that the stereotype did not conform to the real behavior of smugglers, it was maintained as the guiding principle in "how to discern a smuggler."

The problem then is not, are you credible, but rather, *is that what comes across*? If you don't express yourself in ways which are stereotypically recognizable to the *jurors* as credible, you will not be perceived as such. Many attorneys are indeed trustworthy and highly professional, yet do not realize that their overt presentation of themselves goes directly against this inner reality. How then do you present yourself so that your inner trustworthiness and professionalism comes across as such?

Leave your habitual ways of expressing your persona at the door of the Courtroom, and attend to how you want to be perceived when you are in the Courtroom. What matters to your case is not who you know you are, but whom others perceive you to be. Hopefully, they will end up being one and the same. The inner sense you have of your own honesty, sincerity and worth will be translated into observable behaviors reflecting those qualities.

CAUTION Sincerity cannot truly be faked. It can be imitated perhaps for awhile, but it cannot be pretended for any length of time. Therefore, it goes without saying, that if you are not sincere in the representation of your client and his cause, no amount of communication skills training will somehow "give" you that sincerity. It is your first consideration, as an advocate, to be both trustworthy and expert, to be thoroughly grounded in the law and well prepared, to pursue your client's cause with "passion and zeal."

THE THREE WAYS TO CREATE A CREDIBLE FIRST IMPRESSION

The three ways to create an impression easily interpreted and accepted immediately by the jurors as credible are:

1. Look professional.
2. Appear self-assured and in control.
3. Respect the Judge, Court process, and Courtroom personnel.

1. Look Professional in Appearance

In Chapter 2, we discuss at length how to look professional. At this point, suffice it to say that a credible first impression is based on a neat, clean, attractive appearance.

2. Appear Self-Assured and in Control

There are three techniques which allow you to appear self-assured and in control:

1. Do things one thing at a time.
2. Be still.
3. Maintain direct and steady eye focus.

Technique 1: How to appear self-assured and in control by doing things one thing at a time

The first technique of appearing in control is based on doing things one thing at a time. Whenever you do two (or three or four . . .) things at the same time, you are splitting your focus. In other words, you are giving only a portion of your focus to each item. Some people are perfectly capable of doing five things at once and accomplishing each well, but since few people are capable of this, the stereotyped reaction to someone doing five things at once, is that some of those things are going to be poorly done. When people do things one thing at a time, the assumption is that they are attending to each thing carefully, and that each will therefore be properly accomplished.

Most rituals are executed with this principle in mind. An example is the Japanese ritual of the tea ceremony. Each step of the ritual is very carefully performed, with great attention given to every detail. Nothing is rushed, and the focus is total on whichever part of the ceremony is being performed at that moment. The impression conveyed is one of absolute mastery. Absolute mastery is power. So, for you to convey an impression of mastery, you must look like you are in complete control of what is going on, and one of the basic elements of that control, is doing things one thing at a time.

How to demonstrate self-assurance in entering the Courtroom

No matter how pressed for time or impatient you are, do not rush into the Courtroom, without looking where you're going or surveying what is going on, and slam yourself into your seat without further ado. Attend fully to each part of the process, albeit only for a moment. Professionalism, the meticulous attention brought to each point, the careful and thorough preparation of the case, is a trait highly valued by jurors. This impression is conveyed by a calm and confident manner, easily achieved by the simple physical expression of doing one thing at a time.

Regardless of how rushed you are, take a breath before you enter the Courtroom, make sure your clothes are in order, your hair is combed, your papers are neatly tucked away in your briefcase, and nothing is spilling out of your briefcase, pockets, or hands. Then walk in as if you had nothing more on your mind than going through that door (Illustration 1). At the door, take a moment to notice who is where, then look at your table, walk over to it, put your briefcase down, and then, sit. Once you've calmly seated yourself, open your briefcase, take out what you need, and only what you need. Then shut your briefcase, and put it aside on the floor, or wherever it won't be in the way.

1–1

Contrast the calm, self-assured impression conveyed by this entrance with the impression conveyed by a hurried entrance, where you rush in, papers in hand, slightly out of breath, hair mussed (Illustration 2). It literally takes only a few moments longer to complete a calm, doing-things-one-thing-at-a-time type entrance, than it does to effect a "rushed" approach. Yet in those few moments you will have projected an image of self-assuredness and of confidence which, properly maintained, can sustain you throughout the trial.

1–2

How to appear in control by being well-organized

Doing things one thing at a time also gives you the appearance of being well organized. Jury studies have demonstrated that an attorney who appears to be well organized impresses the jurors as being thorough and well prepared, and thereby increases his credibility, and by extension, his ability to persuade.

Take your papers and files out carefully, one at a time, put them in specific places on the table, attend carefully to what goes where. These are all behavioral expressions of the quality "well-organized." Neatness or tidiness also impress jurors as manifestations of "well-organized." Attorneys who somewhat frenetically search through a disorganized pile of papers are considered unprofessional. If you are not sure of where something is, it is better to take a little longer to look for it in systemized fashion by going through one file at a time, deliberately, than to try to speed up the process by rifling through your files. You lose credibility in the process.

A trial notebook can be extremely useful in helping to establish your credibility. If you have everything carefully catalogued in a trial notebook, you can easily look up things in organized one-thing-at-a-time manner. In addition to whatever substantive advantage such preparation affords you, you will certainly *look* more prepared, and therefore credible.

How to demonstrate self-assurance in handling evidence

Doing things one thing at a time is a principle which is applied in more general fashion throughout the trial. Whenever you want to give an impression of authority, of competence, simply slow yourself down, and do things one thing at a time.

For example, in making a point regarding a piece of evidence: walk over to the evidence, stop, look at it, then look up at the jury/witness/whomever you are addressing, and then say whatever it is you have to say.

How to demonstrate self-assurance in questioning a witness

In asking an important question of a witness: walk over to the witness (or wherever you choose to stand), stop, look at the witness, then ask your question. Your unflustered approach will convey an attitude of self-assurance and authority (Illustration 3)

1–3

It is said that Hemingway defined poise as "grace under pressure." The more hassled and harried you are in any given situation, and the less you let it show by trying to do five things at once, the less reactive you seem to be to the situation. The impression created is one of ability to cope in situations which would drive others mad, of not losing your control just because the *situation* is out of control.

What you are feeling inside is irrelevant. You may be feeling awful: panicked, scared, unsure. But people cannot crawl into your emotions and feel what is going on inside of you, and they will not find out unless you let your feelings show. So if you do things one thing at a time, which projects self-assurance and being in charge, people will assume that is how you feel and who you are, regardless of your inner reality, and your credibility is thereby enhanced.

No one likes to be guided by a fool. When jurors observe an attorney who is trying to do three things at once—take notes, whisper to co-counsel, and ask a question of the witness—they get the distinct impression that this attorney is ill-prepared, and the question becomes: "Does he know what he's doing? How can I rely on him to show me the way, when he doesn't seem to know what's important right now—taking notes, whispering, or questioning? Make up your mind!"

Whatever you focus on is automatically what the jurors will focus on. What you give importance to, by virtue of your attention, is what the jurors will attend to. If you attend to three things at once, the jurors get confused, and will turn to another source for guidance—opposing counsel.

Technique 2: How to appear self-assured and in control by being still

The second technique of appearing self-assured and in control is being still. When powerful people have something important to say, they start by holding perfectly still. Holding perfectly still is a great way of getting attention. It is also an important factor in the creation of focus. A soldier listening for the enemy doesn't move a muscle, his focus is completely on that not-yet-heard sound on which his very life depends. In a football game, no one moves until the ball has gone into play, then all heck breaks loose. Focus consists of keeping everything else still so you can give all your attention to what is going on in the present moment. Focus is what gives you the appearance of self-assurance.

People who are self-assured and in control have developed the art (naturally or otherwise) of standing perfectly still, not twitching or itching or anything else, when either saying something important, or listening to something important. More aptly stated, self-assured people make it *seem* they are listening to something important. You may be thinking of a thousand other things, but if you look like you are totally attentive, you will be effective. Have you ever noticed how when when you're talking to someone, and they're scribbling a note, drinking coffee, and tapping their feet under the desk at the same time, that you hardly feel listened to? That person may indeed have been listening to you and be able to repeat the conversation verbatim, but you didn't *perceive* the person as listening to you, and "perceive" is the operative word here.

This principle, however, is not to be interpreted as: just don't move and people will think you're in control. No, not quite. Just don't move and people are likely to think there's something wrong with you. Being still works specifically in two instances:

1. You want to get other people's attention, for example, before you say something particularly important, or to be sure they heard something you deem important.

2. You want to give an impression of complete and undivided attention; letting someone know by your stillness that *they* have your complete attention at that moment.

In both instances, the result is that you seem to be totally self-assured and in complete control of the situation.

How to show self-assurance when called to the bench

When the Judge calls you to the bench, for instance, walk up there, and be still. Don't fidget, scratch your earlobe, or play with your fingers. None of these actions conveys focus. Be still. By your physical attitude you are quite literally sending the nonverbal message, "I am ready to hear whatever you have to say. It is the single most important thing in my life at this moment. I therefore give you my undiluted, undivided, complete attention." That's power. And it is respected as such.

How to be in control of your questioning

Similarly, if you are ready to ask that one devastating question of your witness, start by quieting your body, by being completely still, then ask the question: "Did you kill your wife, Mr. Jones?" The stillness will alert the jury to pay attention, something of importance is about to happen.

How to be in control of an unpleasant situation

If opposing counsel, for example, has just made a particularly inappropriate or inept remark, simply be still for a moment, allow your stillness to signal to the jury that something of consequence has just happened.

CASE IN POINT

The following illustration is a classic example of being in control of an unpleasant situation:

An eminent trial attorney, who happens to be Jewish, was cross-examining a witness. During the course of the cross-examination, the witness made a very noticeable anti-Semitic comment. Rather than say anything, the attorney simply kept silent, stayed perfectly still, and allowed the jury to digest the full import of what had just happened. It worked. The attorney did win his case, and post-trial interviews with the jurors revealed that the way the attorney dealt with this unpleasant situation convinced the jurors of his integrity, and that the perception of the attorney as having integrity significantly influenced their favorable evaluation of his case.

Technique 3: How to appear self-assured and in control by maintaining direct and steady eye focus

The third technique involves your use of your eyes. Eye focus is tremendously powerful. With eye focus, we nonverbally tell people whether they are important or unimportant, to be respected or cast aside, to be valued or neglected. We are very susceptible to each other's eye focus: use that susceptibility to your advantage.

When people are unsure of themselves, their eyes wander, the focus is unsteady. How many times were you told as a child, "Look at me when you talk to me!" An unsteady gaze is considered indicative of deception, lying or insincerity. It is crucial to your credibility that you be perceived as sincere. Good eye focus is associated with calm, sanity, and forthrightness. In credible people, eye focus is direct, steady and level.

How to use the "fishhook" to master good eye focus

Good, steady eye focus is most effectively accomplished by a technique called the "fishhook." It is very difficult to look steadily into a person's eyes when you have two eyes to deal with; what usually ends up happening is a fixed stare. So rather than deal with two eyes, I suggest you only deal with one.

In order to do a "fishhook," send out your look just like a fisherman sends out a line, and "hook" the other person's diagonal eye with your look. In other words, look with your right eye at the person's right eye close to the bridge of the nose, not toward the temple, or with your left eye at the person's left eye (as in Illustration 4, but of course, facing each other). When you get tired of looking at one eye, simply switch to the other. If you are doing this properly:

1. Your look will be a gaze, not a stare, and therefore be respectful, not rude
2. It is much easier on you to maintain your gaze for long periods of time on one eye only
3. The other individual will have no idea that you are only looking at the one eye.

1–4

REMINDER *The "fishhook" may sound extremely artificial, and indeed, will take some practice before it feels natural, but remember, the only reason you are so comfortable with the way you presently express yourself is because you have been expressing yourself verbally and nonverbally the same way for a number of years. Any new behavior is going to feel foreign and artificial, especially a behavior that is as private and intimate as personal body language.*
Bear in mind that the purpose of the "fishhook" is to establish initial contact, or reestablish contact at important moments, it is not necessary to do it all the time. The discomfort the use of the "fishhook" may occasion is more than made up for by the rewards in terms of projection of self-assurance and control.

How to appear self-assured in voir dire

When you first address a prospective juror, in order to convey an impression of confidence, of knowing who you are and what you are doing, simply look the juror in the eye, using the "fishhook," and maintain that gaze through the introductions and the beginning of the interaction. Do not allow your gaze to wander away from the juror's eye during those first few moments. Nonverbally you are signaling to the juror two very important things:

1. that you are calm, confident and self-assured
2. that he is important, that he has your undivided attention.

Once these points are established, you can then allow your eyes to move naturally, but come back to the prospective juror's eyes every so often to re-establish self-assurance and focused attention.

How to appear self-assured in addressing the jury

In addressing the jury, look first at one member of the jury for a sentence or two, then at another for another couple of sentences, then focus on another member, and so on. Do not "pan" the jury with your eyes, letting the eyes just sweep over the members, this does not establish contact, and it is vital that you connect with the jury in order to establish your credibility.

Avoid a pattern of looking first at one juror, then at the juror directly next to the first juror, then at the juror directly next to the second juror, and so forth, rather allow your eyes to skip around and select jurors in different parts of the jury box, but be sure to look specifically and directly at each member of the jury in turn. Each member of the jury is important, and must be made to feel verbally and nonverbally that he is of value. Your calm gaze at the different members of the jury as you speak gives an unbeatable impression of self-assurance.

How to appear self-assured in addressing the Judge

When addressing the Judge, first look at him before speaking. Make sure your look actually connects before opening your mouth, even if it is only for a split second. This is a sign of respect.

The two ways of appearing in control with a witness

1. In control and **intimidating**

Let's say you want to put a witness on the spot during cross examination. Look at the witness, then absolutely do not let your look wander the whole time you are asking your question, while you wait for the witness's answer, and then through his answer. You will both appear totally in control and intimidating.

2. In control and **friendly**

Taking an example of the opposite situation: let's say you are questioning a friendly witness. Start by looking at the witness during your question. Then, as he answers, look at the witness during some of his answer, but take your eyes off of him and look thoughtfully a little to the side and down, still attentively listening, during some other parts of his answer. Be sure to get your eyes back up to the witness when he finishes. This is a more casual or interactive style; it allows the witness to relax, as it were, when you eyes are off him. The impression created is one of attentive warmth, self-assurance combined with friendliness.

Observe, in your daily life, how people use eye focus, and what it feels like to you, when people look at you attentively, or fail to do so. Experiment with taking your eye focus on and off people, and observe their reactions. Observation is a great teacher.

3. Gain Juror Approval by Expressing Your Respect toward the Judge, Courtroom Personnel, and the Court Process

When the jurors are ushered into the Courtroom, they are only certain of two things:

1. Court is a serious matter, and this is serious business.
2. The Judge is top man on the totem pole, he is Justice incarnate, whose function it is to be fair and impartial.

Jurors feel a bond between the Judge and themselves, they assimilate his role of fair and impartial observer to their role of fair and impartial decision makers. Jury studies have shown, time and time again, that jurors have high regard both for the Court process and for the Judge, and jury studies have also shown that jurors have considerably less high regard for attorneys.

This is not personal. Attorneys are, after all, advocates. They plead one side of a cause or the other. The jurors know perfectly well that if one side wins, the other side loses, and therefore attorneys are expected to be partial. Unfortunately attorneys have also been known to be underhanded, conniving and manipulative, and the stereotype of "attorney" does carry some of these connotations. Although some Judges may also have been underhanded, conniving and manipulative, the stereotype of "Judge" does not carry those connotations, and so the Judge is not saddled with an ambivalent or negative stereotype—the attorney is. It is therefore that much more critical that you create a winning first impression, and one of the components of that impression is how you, the attorney, treat the Judge and the Court.

CASE IN POINT

Given the high regard jurors have for the Judge, "It is beyond me," says Justice Patrick E. Higginbotham, "how, in the face of this reality, lawyers do other than treat judges with reverence in the presence of the jury. While I think that lawyers should be courteous to judges out of respect for the law, my point is the very practical one that you must do so to be successful."[5]

In reading studies and reports of how the great trial attorneys work, the words "polite" and "respectful" are repeatedly mentioned.

How to manifest your respect toward the Judge

Your attitude toward the Judge must be one of deference, of respectful looking at and listening to an esteemed authority. This tends to be especially important in how you *react* to what His Honor says. Never forget that the jury watches you constantly, and they see everything. If you are annoyed at the Judge's instruction, don't let it show by tapping your pencil against the table, or making a grimace. Blow up, if you wish, later in your office, but when you're in Court, never let your annoyance show. If you need to get a point across that may ruffle the Judge, do it with polite considerateness, always conveying your respect.

How to show respect toward Courtroom personnel

In addition, be polite and respectful to all Court personnel: bailiffs, court reporters, assistants, and colleagues. This is part of the "professionalism" that counts for so much in the juror's assessment of you. And of course, be polite with the jurors.

How to interact credibly with opposing counsel

As far as your dealings with opposing counsel go, again be polite, even when faced with opposing counsel who is rude. Hemingway's "grace under pressure" applies here too: if you are polite and courteous in the face of opposing counsel's rudeness, you score points. Be aware, that although jurors realize that attorneys know each other and are often friends out of the Courtroom, jurors do not appreciate it when you joke around or even strike up a friendly conversation with opposing counsel. This takes away, in their minds, from your appreciation of the seriousness of the event.

REMINDER *Be mindful that the jury evaluates your behavior at all times, not just in the Courtroom. You can demolish your credibility instantly by being respectful and courteous in the Courtroom, then dropping that behavior and being jocular, abrasive or rude in the hallway.*

How to demonstrate your respect for the Court process

Jurors expect you to take the case at hand as seriously as they do. Joking in the hall with opposing counsel does not reinforce their image of you as a serious, dedicated professional. Reading the newspaper on breaks makes them doubt your dedication to the case, as does discussing another case with co-counsel. You must, at all times, convey that the present case is serious business and has your complete attention. After all, if you don't care about your case to that degree, why should the jurors? To you, trial work may be just part of the job, to the jurors it is a huge and often frightening responsibility. In order to be successful, you must understand and respect their point of view.

SUMMARY

In the first four minutes the jurors see you, they form an initial lasting impression of you. Be in control of those first four minutes, use your knowledge of stereotyping to your advantage. Be aware of how you want to be perceived, and do not confuse reality with the perception of reality. Credible presence is a combination of different factors which all create focus: doing things one thing at a time, being still, creating and maintaining good eye focus. A professional appearance, and an attitude of respect and politeness towards the Judge, Courtroom personnel and Court process, reinforces that presence and underscores your professionalism. A winning first impression is crucial to your ability to persuade the jurors and win your case.

USING THE STEREOTYPES WORKSHEET

1. Increase your understanding of stereotypes by observing your own stereotyped
    and non-stereotyped interpretations of the following situations:

You see a person who is:	*Your stereotyped interpretation of the situation is:*	*Other possible interpretations are:*
flustered	_____	_____
	_____	_____
	_____	_____
	_____	_____
anxious	_____	_____
	_____	_____
	_____	_____
	_____	_____
neat	_____	_____
	_____	_____
	_____	_____
	_____	_____
unhurried	_____	_____
	_____	_____
	_____	_____
	_____	_____
giggly	_____	_____
	_____	_____
	_____	_____
	_____	_____
calm	_____	_____
	_____	_____
	_____	_____
	_____	_____

You see a person who is:	Your stereotyped interpretation of the situation is:	Other possible interpretations are:
running away	_____	_____
	_____	_____
	_____	_____
	_____	_____
dressed in rags	_____	_____
	_____	_____
	_____	_____
dressed in tails	_____	_____
	_____	_____
	_____	_____
	_____	_____
smiling	_____	_____
	_____	_____
	_____	_____
serious	_____	_____
	_____	_____
	_____	_____
frowning	_____	_____
	_____	_____
	_____	_____
gesticulating	_____	_____
	_____	_____
	_____	_____
	_____	_____

You see a person who is:	Your stereotyped interpretation of the situation is:	Other possible interpretations are:
swearing	_____	_____
	_____	_____
	_____	_____
	_____	_____
coughing	_____	_____
	_____	_____
	_____	_____
	_____	_____
standing stiffly	_____	_____
	_____	_____
	_____	_____
	_____	_____
smiling pleasantly	_____	_____
	_____	_____
	_____	_____
	_____	_____
muttering to himself	_____	_____
	_____	_____
	_____	_____
	_____	_____
crying	_____	_____
	_____	_____
	_____	_____
	_____	_____
wearing unmatched socks	_____	_____
	_____	_____
	_____	_____
	_____	_____

You see a person who is:	*Your stereotyped interpretation of the situation is:*	*Other possible interpretations are:*
staring off into space	_____	_____
	_____	_____
	_____	_____
	_____	_____

2. Observe how characters are interpreted on television programs and commercials. Many of these are stereotyped interpretations. Study them and use both these and your observations of your own interpretations to better your understanding of how the jurors perceive you and others.

Television Characters	*Stereotyped Interpretation*
1. _____	_____
_____	_____
_____	_____
2. _____	_____
_____	_____
_____	_____
3. _____	_____
_____	_____
_____	_____
4. _____	_____
_____	_____
_____	_____
5. _____	_____
_____	_____
_____	_____
6. _____	_____
_____	_____
_____	_____

Television Characters   *Stereotyped Interpretation*

7. _____   _____

    _____   _____

    _____   _____

8. _____   _____

    _____   _____

    _____   _____

9. _____   _____

    _____   _____

    _____   _____

DOING THINGS ONE THING AT A TIME WORKSHEET

Practice doing things one thing at a time. If you have access to a video-recorder, by all means, use it. Videotape provides excellent feedback which makes learning easy and quick.

Place a table and chair some distance in front of a doorway, replicating the position of your table and chair in Court, even if the distance is not accurately represented. Put the videocamera on a tripod in front of the table (Illustration #5). Once you have recorded the sequences described below, watch the playback of what you have done, being sure to take note of what you are doing well, before taking note of what needs to be corrected. If you don't have access to a videocamera, ask a friend or colleague to watch you in order to give you feedback.

Practice the following sequences, noting any problems as you see the playbacks, and repeating the sequences until you are able to execute them fluidly and easily.

1. Open the door, walk in, stop, look at who is in the room, go to your table, put your briefcase down, sit.

Problems:
Too rushed _____
One part of the sequence overlapping another _____
Unnaturally slow pace _____
Uneven pace _____
Other _____

2. From your seated position: open your briefcase, extract the necessary documents, close your briefcase, put it aside.

Problems:
Too rushed _____
One part of the sequence overlapping another _____
Unnaturally slow pace _____
Uneven pace _____
Other _____

3. From your seated position: Arrange your documents in organized fashion on the table.

Problems:
Too rushed _____
One part of the sequence overlapping another _____
Unnaturally slow pace _____
Uneven pace _____
Other _____

4. From your seated position: Practice finding something in your papers and files in unhurried systematic fashion.

Problems:
Too rushed _____
One part of the sequence overlapping another _____
Unnaturally slow pace _____
Uneven pace _____
Other _____

BEING STILL WORKSHEET

Learn how to be still in Court by practicing keeping your body perfectly still at different moments in your daily life. Note whatever problems you are having, and work towards correcting them as you repeatedly practice being still.

1. Be still when listening to a colleague. Keep your body totally quiet and really focus on what you are listening to.

Problems:
Body swaying _____
Shifting weight from one foot to the other _____
Head bobbing _____
Hands moving _____
Other _____

2. Still your body before making an important point or a statement. Let the quiet of your body provide an effective backdrop to the importance of your words.

Problems:
Body swaying _____
Shifting weight from one foot to the other _____
Head bobbing _____
Hands moving _____
Other _____

EYE FOCUS WORKSHEET

Practice eye focus as much as possible. When you speak with your spouse, your colleagues, your secretary, very deliberately train yourself to use the fishhook. Notice whatever problems you are having. Being aware of the problems you have in maintaining good eye focus enables you to correct them. Repeat whichever part of the sequence is difficult for you until it becomes easy. Then integrate the formerly problematic part back into the whole sequence and repeat the sequence until the whole is fluid. Practice the fishhook until it is easy for you to do, but do not expect it ever to become totally comfortable.

1. Practice looking diagonally into one eye, hold for a while, then look into the other eye. Hold for a moment.

Problems:
Difficulty in establishing original eye contact _____
Difficulty in maintaining eye contact _____
Eyes seem to have a life of their own: you can't keep them still: _____
Eyes glaze: focus is unnaturally held too long _____
Other _____

2. Practice looking into someone's eye, then looking off bringing your eyes slightly to the side and down, then bringing your eyes back to the person's eyes and re-establishing a fishhook. Practice this until you begin to feel a natural flow to looking, looking off, and looking back.

Problems:
Difficulty in establishing original eye contact _____
Difficulty in maintaining eye contact _____
Eyes seem to have a life of their own: you can't keep them still: _____
Eyes glaze: focus is unnaturally held too long _____
Other _____

RESPECT WORKSHEET

Observe your own behavior toward the Judge, Courtroom personnel, and the Court process. Be honest in your assessment. Only by accurately evaluating your behavior are you in a position to correct it.

Degree of respect shown

Judge

	minimal:	some of the time	_____
		most of the time	_____
		hardly ever	_____
	moderate:	some of the time	_____
		most of the time	_____
		hardly ever	_____
	100% respect:	some of the time	_____
		most of the time	_____
		hardly ever	_____

Courtroom Personnel:

Bailiffs

	minimal:	some of the time	_____
		most of the time	_____
		hardly ever	_____
	moderate:	some of the time	_____
		most of the time	_____
		hardly ever	_____
	100% respect:	some of the time	_____
		most of the time	_____
		hardly ever	_____

Court Reporters

	minimal:	some of the time	_____
		most of the time	_____
		hardly ever	_____
	moderate:	some of the time	_____
		most of the time	_____
		hardly ever	_____
	100% respect:	some of the time	_____
		most of the time	_____
		hardly ever	_____

Degree of respect shown

Assistants	minimal:	some of the time	_____
		most of the time	_____
		hardly ever	_____
	moderate:	some of the time	_____
		most of the time	_____
		hardly ever	_____
	100% respect:	some of the time	_____
		most of the time	_____
		hardly ever	_____
Colleagues	minimal:	some of the time	_____
		most of the time	_____
		hardly ever	_____
	moderate:	some of the time	_____
		most of the time	_____
		hardly ever	_____
	100% respect:	some of the time	_____
		most of the time	_____
		hardly ever	_____
Other: _____	minimal:	some of the time	_____
		most of the time	_____
		hardly ever	_____
	moderate:	some of the time	_____
		most of the time	_____
		hardly ever	_____
	100% respect:	some of the time	_____
		most of the time	_____
		hardly ever	_____

Degree of respect shown

Opposing Council	minimal:	some of the time	_____
		most of the time	_____
		hardly ever	_____
	moderate:	some of the time	_____
		most of the time	_____
		hardly ever	_____
	100% respect:	some of the time	_____
		most of the time	_____
		hardly ever	_____
Court Process	minimal:	some of the time	_____
		most of the time	_____
		hardly ever	_____
	moderate:	some of the time	_____
		most of the time	_____
		hardly ever	_____
	100% respect:	some of the time	_____
		most of the time	_____
		hardly ever	_____

CHAPTER 2

Using Body Language to Convince the Jurors of Your Credibility

Communication is how thought is expressed so that it can be understood by another. Communication is achieved via three channels:

1. your body
2. the actual words you say
3. the way you say those words.

In Court, you use all three channels at the same time. All three are important to the overall persuasiveness of your communication, but each has a different function relative to that persuasiveness.

CAUTION Your thoughts and ideas are the bottom line of your communication. If your case has no substantive value, your communication is worthless, regardless of how persuasively you use the three channels.

The content of your communication is not the purview of this book. That content relies solely on your legal expertise. However, how you *translate* that content into words, the intonations with which you speak those words, and how you convey that content through your body, are most definitely the concern of this book. This chapter is devoted to the practice of persuasive body language, Chapter 3 is devoted to vocal techniques of persuasion.

HOW TO COMMUNICATE CREDIBLY
WITH BODY LANGUAGE

Body language is the single most important communication channel. Communication research has demonstrated time and time again that when body language and the content of a communication are in disagreement, body language will always be believed over the words.

CASE IN POINT

You are in Court, concluding your opening statement.

Your words:

"And the evidence will show, ladies and gentlemen of the jury, that my client, Mr. Jones, is not guilty of negligence."

Your body language: You stand slump shouldered, both hands jammed in your pockets, your eyes darting about the jurors.

Result: The jurors believe your client is guilty.

Your body language belies your words. Your body language clearly states:

1. "I'm nervous, insecure, and unsure of myself." Slumped shoulders, eyes darting.

2. "Maybe I'm even hiding something." Eyes darting, hands jammed in pockets.

In this example, it hardly matters what you actually say, your body language is so strongly in contradiction to the content of your statement, that it completely overrides the effect of your words.

Your body language, then, is used by the jurors as a constant check on the veracity of your words. If your body language is consistent with what your are saying, your words will be believed, if it is inconsistent with what you are saying, your words will not be believed.

Use this awareness to your advantage. If you want your words to be believed, align your body language so that it is consistent with and supports those words. If you do not want your words to be believed, shape your body language so that it is in contradiction with, or to some degree invalidates, what you are saying.

CASE IN POINT

You are cross-examining a witness whom you are sure is lying. You can't say flat out "You're lying," but you want to let the jurors know you aren't buying his story, not at all.

1. Your words: ". . . and so you were simply out for a stroll, when you happened to see the gun, and pick it up."

2. Your body: Standing, your arms crossed in front of you, your head level or slightly down (Illustration 1).

3. The witness's words: "Yes."

4. Your body: Drop your head down just a little, and cock it to one side just a little (Illustration 2).

2–1   2–2

Your words communicate one message; however, your body is communicating quite a different message. Your body is saying the following:

1. Arms crossed in front, head level or slightly down.

"I am defending myself against what you are saying, I am not receptive to it, I do not believe it."

2. Head dropped slightly down.

"Now I'm really closing off to you."

3. Head a little cocked to one side.

"I'm curious, I wonder what you're up to."

The jurors will inevitably read your body language, recognize the contradiction with your words, and believe your body. You have made a important point in subtle yet highly persuasive fashion.

Specific body postures and gestures are understood in certain very defined stereotypical ways. In the absence of any other yardstick by which to measure you, the jury will rely on those stereotypes. As mentioned in Chapter 1, do not confuse reality with the perception of reality. It is irrelevant, for example, that you cross your arms only because it is more comfortable for you, and in no way expresses defensiveness. Crossed arms are stereotypically read as indicative of defensiveness and will be read as such regardless. As with the stereotypes connoting credibility, an awareness of body language stereotypes can be used entirely to your advantage.

CAUTION There is no such thing as the "right" body language. There is only the body language which will effectively enhance or support your message to the jurors.

Knowing this, you can use your body to say what your mouth cannot. As you read this chapter then, absorb the information given not as "the way to do things," but rather as a number of alternative ways of doing things depending on your purpose at any given point in time.

Successful use of body language demands that you learn a second "language" to be used harmoniously with the language of your intent. Your first task is to learn this second language in all its diversity; your second, to learn to use it to persuade.

HOW TO USE THE FIVE BASICS OF EFFECTIVE BODY LANGUAGE TO GAIN THE JURORS' CONFIDENCE AND GUIDE THEM TO YOUR INTERPRETATION OF THE FACTS

Your Posture: Confidence-Maker or Confidence-Breaker?

All good trial lawyers are self-confident, or, put more accurately, exude self-confidence. Posture is critical in expressing self-confidence.

1. Good posture implies *strength:*

The world can literally sit on your square shoulders. You seem able to handle whatever may come your way, your back is strong and will not yield to every knock and blow. It is hardly coincidental that armies all over the world demand that their soldiers demonstrate erect posture: it symbolizes force and resilience in the face of adversity.

2. Good posture implies *energy:*

Your good posture is the mark of an energized person, you not only can but want to take on responsibilities, you are not only willing but eager to demonstrate your competance. Good posture signals readiness, the energy to get things done now, rather than put them off to another day.

How to express self-confidence with your posture

The placement of your back

Good posture is basically erect posture. Stand with your spine straight, not curved in either direction (Illustration 3). If your spine is curved forward, you seem old and without energy (Illustration 4). If you stand so erect that your back is arched, curving backwards, your posture suggests a military background or rigidity (Illustration 5).

Use this dancer's trick to help you stand erect: stand with your feet about 8 inches apart, hands at your side. In your imagination, run a cord from the base of your spine, through your spine, up through your neck, and out the top of your head (Illustration 6). Then pull the imaginary cord upwards. Feel your spine straighten as you do this.

If you are unsure as to whether or not you are achieving good posture, consult a trainer in a gym, a physical therapist, or other qualified professional.

> *CAUTION* It should not cause you any pain to achieve good posture. If it does, or if any of the other body language positions described in "A Winning Case" are painful, discontinue them at once, and consult your physician.

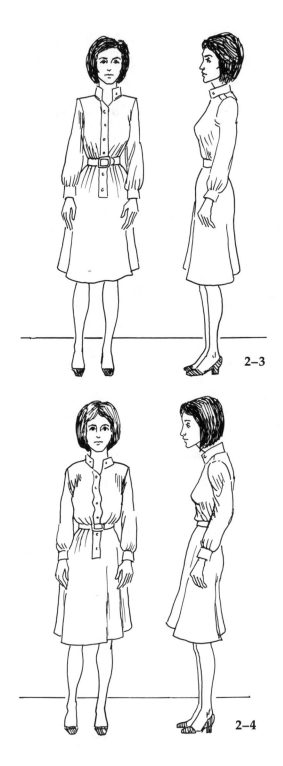

2–3

2–4

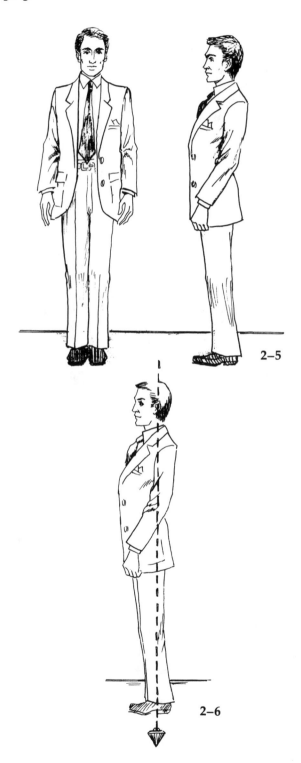

2–5

2–6

The placement of your shoulders

In good posture, the shoulders are "square," that is to say, level (Illustration 7). Stand with your shoulders comfortably in line with your straight spine. Do not slump your shoulders forward, this makes you seem weak or insipid. Do not tilt your shoulders downwards either to the right or to the left, this makes you seem unwilling to carry your load (Illustration 8).

2–7   2–8

Your Stance: How to Create a Sure Foundation

Your posture symbolically represents your ability to carry the weight of the world—or your portion thereof—on your shoulders. Your stance is the foundation which enables you to carry that weight. How you stand lets the observer know whether or not you have what it takes to fulfill your responsibilities.

The "neutral stance": How to establish self-confidence and reliability

The neutral stance is a solid stance which expresses confidence and reliability, without appearing aggressive or belligerent. It is achieved by standing with your feet slightly apart. "Slightly" means the following:

1. Stand with your feet apart, and find the top of your pelvic bone, just under your waist and in front of your hip (Illustration 9). If you were to drop an imaginary plumb line from the top of your pelvic bone on either side straight down, it should hit the top of your toes (Illustration 10).

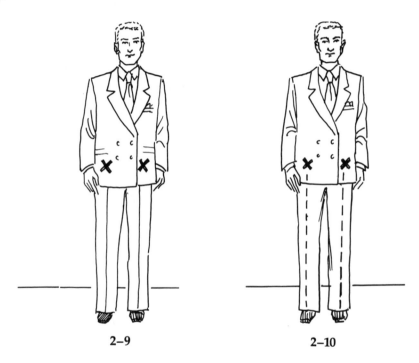

2-9   2-10

2. Your knees should be straight but not stiff, and your arms loosely by your sides, hands relaxed and easy.

When you first try the neutral stance, you will probably find it quite awkward and uncomfortable. Yet the neutral stance looks terrific: it gives you an appearance of self-confidence, energy and readiness, as well as sure-footed dependability. The neutral stance feels awkward to you when you first try it simply because you are not used to standing that way. Most of us have very sloppy standing habits, and have had these habits for many years. Changing anything as intimate as personal stance is undoubtedly uncomfortable, but the rewards in presentational effectiveness are well worth it.

The neutral stance is effective by virtue of its balanced nature. Be sure your feet are equi-distant and only the distance apart described above. Do not stand with your feet close together, you can be pushed over quite easily, both physically and symbolically. If your feet are further apart, you are certainly very solid and can not be pushed over easily (Illustration 11A), but the width of your stance conveys belligerence, an attitude which is usually too strong for the Courtroom (Illustration 11B). The neutral stance is "balanced"; you're not a push-over, but you're not pushing for war, either.

2–11 A   2–11 B

How to use a wide neutral stance to show determination

There are probably no situations in which you wish to be seen as a "pushover," but there may very well be occasions in which you do not want to give verbal utterance to your willingness to go to war, but may wish to transmit that message with body language. In order to do so, use the wide neutral stance, which is the non-verbal equivalent of "Don't mess with me, I won't let you push me or my client around." The jurors will quite clearly read your message regardless of how gently and calmly you speak your words.

REMINDER There is no one "right" way to design your body language: the "right" way is whichever suits your purpose.

How to use the neutral stance as a safety mechanism when in trouble or in doubt

The neutral stance is your "safe stance." Anytime you want to project an image of self confidence and reliability, simply go to your neutral stance. Anytime you've been thrown for a loop, but don't want it to show, resume your neutral stance. When in doubt as to how to communicate a point effectively non-verbally, go back to your neutral stance. At the worst, you'll be expressing poise and self-assuredness. This, of course, is assuming your posture is erect, as discussed previously. If you lack good posture, your stance is meaningless. If the foundation is excellent, but the house is shoddy and collapsing—who cares? Build a good foundation and have it support a solid structure.

"Sitting on a hip": How to appear casual and relaxed

A more casual stance may be assumed as an alternative to the neutral stance, this is known as "sitting on a hip." In this stance, your weight is slightly more on one leg, with your hip jutting out in the direction of the leg you're standing on, and the other leg is somewhat bent (Illustration 12). There are several variations on this stance, but they all share a more relaxed, more intimate feel than the neutral stance.

2–12

When sitting on a hip is effective and when not

For that reason, "sitting on a hip" should not be used with the Judge, as it is less formal (and by extension, less respectful), nor should it be used with the jury until you have had a chance to get to know the jurors, and they you, at which point a more relaxed stance is indeed appropriate. However, even when you know the jury well, when you have something very important to say "sitting on a hip" is not advised, as the casualness of your stance negates the seriousness of your message.

How to vary sitting on a hip according to what you want to express to the jurors

The variations on the "sitting on a hip" stance have to do with the degree to which the hip is jutted out, and the way the feet are placed. The rule of thumb is, the more your hip is jutted out, the more the non-verbal message is one of indifference, or cockiness (Illustration 13). If your feet are very close together, the message is of snobbiness, if your feet are very far apart, you appear arrogant. In general, therefore, in order to convey simple relaxation, only moderately jut your hip out, and keep your feet slightly apart. For most people, this is a very comfortable and easy position.

2–13

In other variations of sitting on a hip, your foot may be crossed in front of your supporting foot (Illustration 14A), or behind it (Illustration 14B). These are somewhat ambivalent foot positions, which are read by some people as denoting irritation or restlessness, an unwillingness to "stand one's own ground," and by others as indifference or boredom. Be mindful of these interpretations if you choose to use these variations.

2–14 A   2–14 B

CAUTION Sitting on a hip is not a good position to use at the beginning of trial in establishing a first impression, as it does not convey self-confidence and reliability in the same way as does the neutral stance, nor by the same token, is it a good stance to assume throughout. It must be judiciously used at those times when your message is a more relaxed and friendly one. Use the neutral stance in all important moments.

What to Do with All Those Arms and Hands

Attorneys often feel at a loss as to what to do with their arms and hands, and so end up doing all sorts of strange things, without realizing the interpretations to which their arm and hand positions are subject. The placement of your arms and hands indeed affects how your body language is read.

The "neutral arm" position: How to express openness and non-defensiveness

The neutral position for arms is arms hanging loosely by your sides, hands relaxed, palms facing your legs (Illustration 15). This position conveys nondefensiveness, a relaxed openness and willingness to deal with whatever happens. As with the neutral stance, the neutral arm position is a "safe" position. When in doubt as to what to do with your arms, return to this position. Because it is so open and non-defended, this position is highly uncomfortable for many people and must be practiced often in order to feel even somewhat comfortable. Don't be surprised by the discomfort, it's normal and will disappear as the neutral arm position becomes more familiar.

2–15

How fists and crossed arms negate the neutral arm position

The open and non-defended aspect of this position will be destroyed immediately, however, if you fist your hand (Illustration 16). Fists convey hostility, and are to be avoided. Fists with the fingers curled around the thumb convey angry powerlessness and are equally to be avoided (Illustration 17). Arms crossed in front of the body at chest level project defensiveness, a closing off (Illustration 18). As with the other body expressions of anger, crossed arms need to be used with caution. Anger tends to alienate others unless you have a truly valid reason to be angry.

Arm-holding positions to avoid: Don't convey fear and worry

If you hold onto your arms with your hands in an across the chest position, you are literally "holding onto yourself," which conveys fear and worry (Illustration 19). Similarly, if you cross one arm chest height across your body and hold the other arm, you express insecurity or fear (Illustration 20). Neither of the arm-holding positions are advisable, as they undermine a position of self-confidence and self-assurance.

2–16   2–17

2–18   2–19   2–20

Arms akimbo: How to express readiness or confrontation

Both arms akimbo, hands on hips, suggests readiness, interest and energy (Illustration 21). If, however, the body is pitched forward somewhat and your facial expression is very serious, you will be perceived as belligerent and confrontational. Women need to be especially careful of the arms akimbo position, as it will be interpreted as confrontational even without the body pitched forward (Illustration 22). Women are better advised to use the one arm akimbo, hand on hip position, with erect posture, which will be understood as conveying determination, readiness and some degree of confrontation (Illustration 23). Do bear in mind, however, that for women, arms akimbo (whether one or both arms), have a "fish-wife" connotation, and should be used sparingly. For men, a one arm akimbo, hand on hip, is interpreted as a milder version of both arms akimbo (Illustration 24).

2–22

2–21

2–23 2–24

2–25 2–26

Arms in front of the body: How to avoid conveying insecurity or submissiveness

The stereotypical understanding of other arm and hand positions are also sex-related. Arms in front of the body, hands clasped low, is more acceptable for women than for men (Illustration 25). In men, it is called the "fig-leaf" position and is highly protective, implying insecurity and fear of harm. In women, it does not have that connotation, although it is often perceived as indicative of submissiveness. Hands clasped at the waist for women express a spinsterish or teacher attitude and may be very useful when you wish to instruct (Illustration 26). On men, however, the same position tends to be seen as "prissy."

Arms behind the back: How to express authority and avoid victimhood

Arms behind the back, hands clasped low, on men conveys an authoritative, quasi-military attitude, especially if the stance is wide (Illustration 27). On women, hands clasped behind the back tend to accentuate a "victim" or prisoner facet, and as such are rarely effective in Court (Illustration 28).

Hands hidden from view: How to maintain a conventional male stance and avoid conveying deceptiveness

Hands hidden from view in any fashion—behind your back, in your pockets, and so forth—are often interpreted as secretive, as expressing a need to deceive or dissimulate. The exception to this is the conventional male stance with one hand in pants pocket (Illustration 29). Be aware,

2–27   2–28   2–29

however, that this is a casual relaxed position and should not be used in serious or formal moments. Also, if you favor this hand position, do not mess with your keys, change, or other contents of your pocket, as this is very distracting.

How to Affect the Jurors' Perception of You and Convey Your Opinions with the Effective Placement of Your Head

The position of your head will also affect how you are perceived.

"Neutral head" position: How to express self-confidence and forthrightness

Neutral position for the head is straight ahead, with your chin level, neither tilted up nor down (Illustration 30). As with the neutral stance and arm positions, the neutral head position is your "safe" head position, and will always stand you in good stead. A straight level head position projects self-confidence, forthrightness, and trustworthiness.

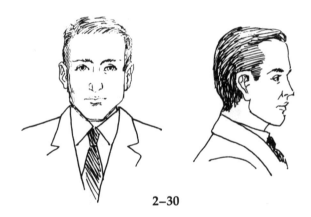

2–30

Chin tilts: How to avoid arrogance and express strength or belligerence

If you tilt your chin skyward, you project arrogance or aloofness, you are literally "looking down your nose" at other people (Illustration 31). If you tilt your chin a little in and down toward your neck ("tucking" the chin), the interpretations of your body language vary according to the angle of the tilt. A slight downward tilt is very effective and conveys determination, strength, and a no-nonsense attitude (Illustration 32). A greater degree of tilt conveys stubbornness or belligerence and is to be used cautiously (Illustration 33).

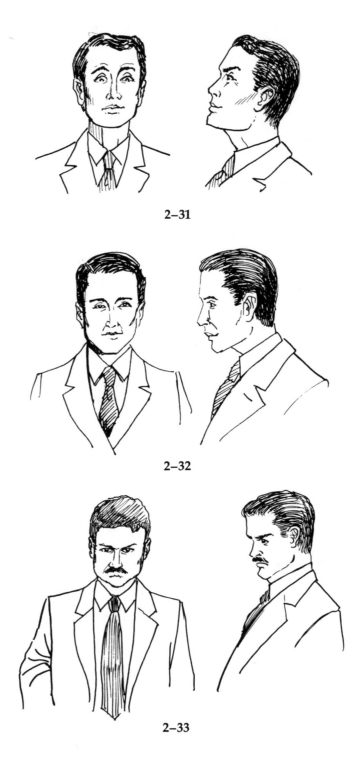

2–31

2–32

2–33

Cocking the head: How to convey interest and good listening

If you tilt your head to either side ("cocking" the head), you convey interest, curiosity, or inquisitiveness. This is a good listening position to alternate with the neutral head position. Be careful, however, that you do not cock the head too much, which will make you seem insecure or weak (Illustration 34). Women, in particular, need to be careful not to overdo the degree to which the head is cocked.

Side head position: How to express distrust and disbelief

If you turn your head to one side, but keep your eyes facing forward, you convey an impression of distrust, disbelief or suspiciousness (Illustration 35).

2–34

2–35

"Dropped head" position: How to convey thoughtfulness and turn potential disaster into an advantage

If you wish to convey thoughtfulness, simply drop your head down somewhat and let your eyes go slightly to the side (Illustration 36). This is a highly useful position. If, for example, a witness has suddenly revealed something unexpected during cross-examination, rather than letting your body give away your surprise and momentary panic, simply drop your head down and let your eyes go to the side, as if deep in thought.

Jurors are unfavorably impressed by attorneys' reactions of surprise: they feel an attorney should know everything about the case if he is truly well-prepared and they evaluate surprise as unprofessional. Dropping your head down will give you the time to collect your thoughts and figure out what to do next without your body language betraying your discomfiture. Whenever you want to buy time for any reason, simply drop your head down in thoughtfulness. The jurors will wait the few moments it takes, and will respect the serious consideration of the matter at hand that your body language conveys. Be careful not to drop your head too far down, however, as a bowed head is commonly interpreted as a sign of depression, grief, or despair (Illustration 37).

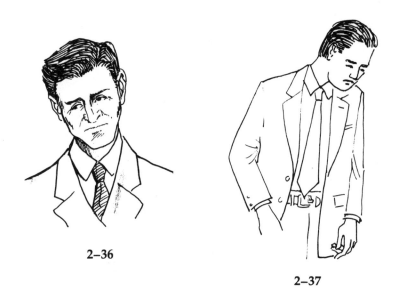

2–36

2–37

How to Use Body Language Convincingly from a Seated Position

The position of your head will be understood the same whether you are standing or sitting. When sitting however, there are some specific body language signals which need to be mentioned.

The "body shift": How to express involvement or hostility

The first and most important of these is the body shift. Whenever your body as a whole is leaning somewhat forward, you are expressing interest, energy, and involvement. This is an active position which is very favorably perceived (Illustration 38). As you shift your body back, you express a more passive and receptive orientation which can be interpreted on a gamut from simple listening to indifference to boredom to outright hostility (Illustrations 39 and 40).

Because the leaning back position can be so variously interpreted, the easiest way to know how to use body shifts is to lean your body forward anytime you wish to express interest in the proceedings (Illustration 41), and lean back anytime you wish to express disinterest or dislike.

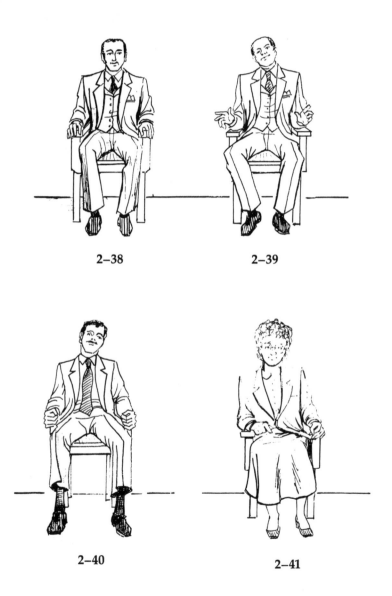

2–38   2–39

2–40   2–41

Feet and legs: appropriate positions for men and women

For men, your feet should be flat on the floor when seated—this is the seated equivalent of a neutral stance (Illustration 42). The "four-square" position (Illustration 43) often adopted by men is too relaxed given the formality assigned by jurors to a Courtroom, and the crossed-legs position (Illustration 44) is too easily interpreted as a sign of defensiveness. In addition, the feet-on-the-floor position is a very easy one from which to rise, and gives you an air of readiness associated with energy and purpose.

2–42   2–43   2–44

For women, feet flat on the floor, or legs crossed at the ankles are the best seated positions (Illustrations 45 and 46). If you cross your legs, it may take you too long to uncross them in order to rise. However, if you know you won't need to get up for a long period of time, the crossed legs position is perfectly acceptable, as long as you resist any foot swaying, which projects insecurity or boredom (Illustration 47).

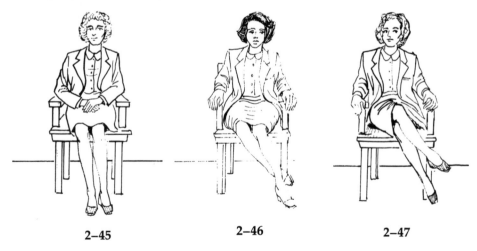

2–45   2–46   2–47

How to avoid arm positions that diminish your persuasiveness

As far as arm positions are concerned, you can keep both arms on the table if desired, hands clasped or open (Illustration 48). Hands clasped on the table is a mildly defensive posture and may convey some protectiveness, but not nearly as much as arms crossed over chest. The great temptations to be avoided when seated at a table are:

1. running your hands over your face (Illustration 49)
2. putting your hands in front of your face, as both of these are very distracting (Illustration 50)
3. holding your head up with your arm, which causes you to slump and look fatigued and defeated (Illustration 51)
4. fidgeting and moving around unnecessarily in your chair, which makes you seem anxious
5. changing whole body positions, which again, makes you seem insecure

2–48

2–49   2–50   2–51

How to seat yourself to convey confidence and self-assurance

The great temptation to avoid when actually sitting down is plopping yourself down in your chair with an "oof" of relief. You will seem like a tired old hound, and will impress no one favorably. Regardless of how tired you feel, seat yourself in your chair with energy and purpose, in order to convey an attitude of confident self-assurance.

HOW TO USE YOUR BODY LANGUAGE TO WIN IN COURT

Before we go on to discuss the specifics of how to use your expressiveness in Court, that is to say, your facial expression and gestures, let's first consider how you can use the body language stereotypes described above to your maximum advantage.

Step 1: How to Figure Out Your Current Body Language

In order to effectively implement these stereotypes, first you need to figure out what you are already doing.

1. Stand the way you usually stand and check yourself out in a mirror. Be honest with yourself. How is your posture? What kind of foundation are you creating with your stance? How do you hold your head? Where are your arms? Use the worksheets provided at the end of the chapter to help you assess yourself.

2. Then ask yourself, what are the comments people have made over the years about the way you express yourself physically? Have people commented on your good posture, or have they asked you often if you're having a bad day when you're not (maybe you slump), or have they commented that you always seem to be going 50 places at once (maybe you fidget)? Use the worksheets provided at the end of the chapter to help you.

3. Look at pictures taken of yourself over the past few years, preferably candid. What do you see? What is your predominant expression? How do you stand, sit? Where are your arms? Again, use the worksheets provided.

4. For a week or so, simply observe your own body positions. Notice how you prefer to stand and sit naturally, what is the habitual position of your head? Don't try to change your body language in any way, just observe it. Use the worksheets provided.

Most of us take our bodies so much for granted, we never stop to attend to what our bodies might be expressing, we think, "Well, that's just the way I am." No. That's the way you are *given 20 or more years of habit formation,* it is certainly not "just the way you are." Unless you are unfortunately heir to a body in some way damaged or deformed, your posture, stance and expressiveness are in large part the result of your upbringing and environment, and as such, are highly changeable.

Step 2: How to Use Your Body Language Skillfully to Communicate Most Effectively with the Jurors

Once you know how you are currently expressing yourself with your body, you can choose those aspects you wish to keep, those you wish to change, and which you simply wish to practice so as to have available as desired, but not as a regular part of your body language repertoire. In this way, you will be really using your body effectively as a communication channel; you can then make deliberate choices which will enhance and support your primary message to the jurors.

CASE IN POINT

For example, from your personal observation of yourself, of your photographs, and taking into account what others say of you, you conclude that you tend to slump, that you often fold your arms across your chest, and have a habit of cocking your head.

Given this information, you decide to make the following changes in how you communicate with the jurors:

1. you decide to correct your posture and make that a permanent change, in order to express self-confidence and energy to the jurors at all times,

2. you decide to use the arm-across-the-chest position deliberately and only at certain moments to express hostility or disagreement with what's going on to the jurors,

3. the head cock appears to be an effective listening position and you decide to use it for that purpose, both in voir dire and with witnesses.

Your awareness of how different body language postures are interpreted, and what your specific postures are, allows you now to use your body language skillfully to communicate, rather than letting it distract from or distort your primary message.

THE FIVE BASICS OF PERSUASIVE FACIAL EXPRESSION AND HOW TO USE THEM TO COMMUNICATE SUCCESSFULLY WITH A JURY

How to Use the Basic Facial Expression of Serious Concern to Win the Jury's Trust

Adopt, as your basic facial expression, an expression of serious involved concern. You will thus be conveying a very professional and trustworthy attitude, which is highly desirable (Illustration 52).

How to Convey Your Disapproval Subtly to the Jurors

You hear opposing counsel say something you do not like, and you want to make sure the jurors realize you don't like it, do not look over at them with a "see what the idiot is doing now" expression (Illustration 52A); simply frown, and hold the frown as you listen (Illustration 53). Your non-verbal message will be clear.

2–52

2–52 A   2–53

How to Convey Your Approval Subtly to the Jurors

A witness says something helpful to your case: allow your face to relax somewhat from its normal serious cast to let the jury know you like what you hear, and perhaps allow a slight smile to cross your face (Illustration 54).

Smiles: A Warning

Smiles are to be used with great care, as jurors do not feel Court is a lighthearted experience, and if not used judiciously, may make you appear smug. Smile if it is appropriate, for example, if a witness blurts out something obviously funny, and let the size of your smile vary according to the degree of humor expressed. All-teeth-out smiles (ie. a full Colgate commercial-type smile) are generally to be avoided.

How to Use Your Brows to Communicate Interest or Distrust to the Jurors

Raised brows are useful for indicating overt interest or curiosity (Illustration 55), they make your face look alert and alive. This is a good listening position when you want it known that what you are listening to is relevant and worth hearing. Be careful, however, that your brows are not raised too high, which conveys great surprise or shock (Illustration 56), unless of course that is your intent.

2–54

2–55

2–56

One brow raised by itself conveys suspiciousness or distrust, and can be used to great effect (Illustration 57). Practice different brow positions in the mirror until you are comfortable with them. Figure out, for example, just how much you need to raise your brows to express simple interest, and how much is too much.

2–57

HOW TO USE YOUR FACIAL EXPRESSIONS TO INFLUENCE THE JURORS

How do you use your facial expressions to influence the jury? You start with a basic expression which projects serious involved concern, and then allow your face to *react* as a function of what's going on in the Courtroom.

Your primary facial reactions are as follows:

1. *frown* when worried, concerned, or upset;
2. *raise both brows* when interested or curious;
3. *raise one brow* when suspicious or distrustful;
4. allow your face to *relax* when pleased, with possible addition of different degrees of smile when appropriate.

The jury will follow your version of the case by following your face and body *reactions* to the proceedings. This is how you let the jurors know how you feel about what is going on.

To learn more complex facial expressions in addition to the primary ones listed above, watch a good television program or movie with the sound turned off. Watch how good contemporary actors express themselves both in body and face, and practice the facial expressions and body language you think would be useful to you in Court.

CAUTION Bear in mind that you are not trying to become an actor, simply learning a broader range of reactions than you currently have available to you.

The Two Keys to Facial Expressions that Persuade Jurors

There are two keys to the persuasive use of facial expressions:

1. Know what your face is currently expressing.
2. Be congruent.

The first key: Know what your face is currently expressing

Start with a clean slate. If you don't know what your habitual facial expression is, you cannot change it to something more effective.

Figure out your habitual facial expressions as follows:

1. Ask close friends or family how they perceive you: does your facial expression usually connote sadness, happiness, anger, worry? You'd be surprised how often people are not aware of the impression their faces give. You may feel like a happy-go-lucky person, but others may perceive you as serious: why? Is it because your forehead is permanently creased in a frown? Or do the corners of your mouth naturally turn down? What specific aspects of your face create this impression? Use the worksheets at the end of the chapter to help you.

2. Sit down in front of a mirror and deliberately set your face in the expression others say is your habitual expression. Often the lines in your face will give you a clue as to how you ordinarily express yourself. A deep line set vertically between the eyes, for example, is generally the result of a habitual frown (Illustration 58). Look

2–58

in the mirror at how your face expresses now, and then figure out what you have to change to help your face express what you want it to express, not what it expresses as a matter of habit. Use the worksheet provided at the end of the chapter.

The second key: Be congruent

When you speak, make sure your facial expressions are congruent with what you are saying. If you're commenting on a sad state of affairs, don't smile. If you smile while commenting on a sad state of affairs, you convey sarcasm. You should only convey sarcasm if that is what you wish to convey. Know your intent and let it guide you. If you're describing how nice things were for the plaintiff before that awful car crash, allow your face to soften and warm up at the niceness. This will provide an excellent contrast for you when you later speak with heavy frown about the crash itself. Each part of your speech will have been congruent, your non-verbal communication supporting and enhancing your verbal message.

People are more believable when they are congruent. If you say you're sorry, and you look sad, people are more likely to believe you than if you say you're sorry, but smile fully. Trustworthiness is one of the fundamental traits an attorney must express if he is to be successful with the jury. Keeping your facial expressions and body language congruent with your words adds greatly to the perception of your trustworthiness.

> *CAUTION In using your facial expressions to influence the jury, be subtle—very, very subtle. Remember that out of 12 jurors, at least one (and probably more) member of the jury is watching you intently at any given point in time, and given the fact that jurors may not discuss the case until they deliberate, a favorite topic of conversation throughout the trial is you, every little thing about you. You are virtually under a microscope at all times, you are always "on." If you grimace, or overdo a facial expression, it will be tremendously obvious at once, given the intense focus you're subject to, and the jurors will promptly react to you as you do to a bad actor: you will not be believed, you will be perceived as manipulative and "phony," the jurors will not like you.*

A Special Application of Facial Expressions:
How to Use Eye Focus to Credit or Discredit a Witness

In Chapter 1, we discussed how to use eye focus to establish credibility. We also mentioned that maintaining eye focus on an individual signifies that you value that person. As part of your use of facial expressions to guide the jurors, make and maintain good eye focus whenever you wish to indicate that you approve of a witness or opposing counsel or what he is saying.

Let's say, however, that you don't want to value the witness, on the contrary, let's say that you wish to discredit the witness. Then don't even attempt direct eye focus. Simply glance over at the witness, letting your look hit wherever it wants, preferably not looking at the individual's eyes or face, just looking in a vague general way at him, and quickly at that. The nonverbal statement is that this person barely exists for you; you disassociate yourself from him in any meaningful way. The implication is that this witness's opinion is valueless and not to be taken into account.

CAUTION Eye focus is powerful, and withholding it must only be done with good reason. Jurors highly value respect, and not looking at someone implies disrespect.

HOW TO DEVELOP GESTURES THAT CLARIFY AND ILLUSTRATE IMPORTANT POINTS CONVINCINGLY

In addition to body language positions and facial expressions, we also communicate non-verbally by the use of gestures. Gestures are hand, arm, shoulder and head movements which are used to clarify or illustrate a point. If body language and facial expression can be said to enhance and support your message, gestures accent it, they provide the spice, as it were.

Gestures, although highly personal in the sense that people will tend to express themselves repeatedly through certain gestures and not others, are amenable to stereotyping, and each culture recognizes a stereotypical meaning to specific gestures. For example, shrugging the shoulders is interpreted as "I don't know" or "So what?"; pushing the hands down and away from your body means "Stop" or "Stay away"; bringing the hands up, palms up connotes innocence (Illustration 59); nodding the head means "Yes," shaking it means "No" (Illustration 60). There are far too many gestures to be able to list all of them here; our purpose is rather to help you learn how to use gesture effectively.

Don't Let Habitual Gestures Stand in the Way of Your Persuasiveness

Know what your habitual gestures are. How do you illustrate a point? Do you use few gestures, many gestures, and what are they? A practical way to observe your habitual gestures is to videotape yourself in two conditions:

2–59

2–60

1. Have a conversation with a good friend, making sure to spend some of the time standing, and some sitting.
2. Give a "speech" directly to the camera, an opening statement, for example.

Use the worksheet at the end of the chapter to help with this exercise.

Persuasive individuals use many illustrative gestures, for example, indicating with the hand that something is far away (Illustration 61A), shaking the head with dismay over an unfortunate event (Illustration 61B). Nonpersuasive individuals use either too few or too many gestures, but most importantly, non-persuasive individuals use gestures which do not illustrate anything. Nonpersuasive individuals use gestures haphazardly and give the appearance of movement for movement's sake, rather than that of motivated movement.

2-61A

2-61B

Notice your use of gestures when you watch the replay of your conversations on the videotape. If you turned the sound off, would you know *from your gestures*, what was happening? Would you be able to estimate, with considerable accuracy, not so much the content of the conversation, but how you felt about the different points, what your opinion was? If your gestures have no apparent relationship to the conversation, if they do not in some way *comment* on the content, then they are not illustrative.

How to Increase the Expressiveness of Your Gestures to Emphasize Your Points to a Jury

If you find that your gestures are not illustrative, or they are, but your repertoire is restricted, then, once again, watch a good television program or movie with the sound turned off. Imitate and practice the gestures you see that feel comfortable to you and which seem to illustrate a point clearly. Then practice, practice, practice until those gestures are truly yours; comfortable, fluid, and second nature.

Most gestures are persuasive as long as they illustrate a point and are appropriate to the Courtroom. The single exception is pointing your finger. Pointing is highly useful as long as it is not done in someone's face. You can very effectively point in the direction of a piece of evidence, a visual aid, or to identify someone in the Courtroom. It is not wise, however, to point your finger at someone directly in front of you, and certainly never directly at the jurors.

Pointing is experienced as intrusive and threatening, it carries too many memories of domineering third grade teachers, and makes people feel powerless and intimidated. Even if you want a witness to feel powerless and intimidated, pointing your finger is far too aggressive a gesture to use. The jurors will immediately identify with the person being pointed at, and feel compassion for that person. This is hardly your intent! Equally problematic is shaking your finger in front of someone's face. This too is experienced as invasive, and is best avoided.

How to Time a Gesture to Maximize Its Impact with the Jurors

Timing is very important in the effectiveness of a gesture. Gestures are most persuasive when made before or after a verbal point; *before* if you wish to set up your point, *after* if you wish to pride a reaction to that point. For example, let's say your verbal position is "My client is innocent." You could set that up nonverbally by opening your arms, palms up, a gesture which conveys innocence, and then say "My client is innocent" (Illustration 62). Or, let's say you want to negate something opposing

2–62

counsel said: you start off by saying, "My learned colleague says his client is innocent," then shake your head. Nonverbally you're contradicting the former statement. Then go on to say "We will show this is not the case." The gesture illustrates and accents your point clearly. This is the purpose of timing. If you use gestures right on top of your spoken message, you're likely to blur the message rather than illustrate it. It is far better to develop a few clear, direct, easily understood gestures and use them sparingly but well, than to develop a whole collection of gestures you simply throw out at random. This would defeat the very purpose of gesturing.

HOW USELESS MANNERISMS DAMAGE YOUR EFFECTIVENESS IN COMMUNICATING YOUR POINTS TO THE JURY

Gestures must be distinguished from mannerisms. Gestures are socially shared movements, movements which illustrate a point in a way which is similarly understood by members of a given culture. Mannerisms are quite different. Mannerisms are personalized gestures performed repetitively by a given individual. For example, you may rub your chin when thinking, or tug at your earlobe, or twist the ring on your finger (Illustration 63). Your mannerisms are uniquely yours; they convey messages which others only figure out over time, as they get to know you.

2–63

The jurors, however, have not had the advantage of a long personal acquaintanceship with you, and since mannerisms are not on the whole available to a stereotyped definition, they tend to distract from the more important part of your message, as the jurors try to interpret the significance of your ring-twisting, ear-lobe-pulling, etc., and in the process, ignore some (often much) of what you are saying. Often, mannerisms hardly seem worth trying to figure out at all, they are so distracting and annoying. Watching an attorney constantly stroke his beard as he sits listening to opposing counsel, watching an attorney chew busily away at a hangnail, watch another twirl his pencil obsessively between his fingers, can be most irritating.

These are all examples of mannerisms that get in the way of your effectiveness. They each project an impression of split focus, thereby diminishing your personal power, your credibility, as well as the perception of your professionalism. Persuasive people are persuasive because they are single-mindedly devoted to the task at hand, unselfconscious, self-assured and calm. Learn to quiet your body so it does not detract from your essential message, but rather adds to the perception of your professionalism.

How to Get Rid of Useless Mannerisms

1. Observe your habitual mannerisms

Become aware of your mannerisms. Most of us have no idea what are our personal tics and twitches, until they are pointed out to us, and then we are often quite distressed: "What, I gnaw my lower lip to death? Never!" Ask your friends and family what your mannerisms are, or ask a friend to mimic you. He will undoubtedly exagerate your mannerisms (much to your horror), which will make it much easier for you to see them and realize the effect they have. Use the worksheets provided at the end of the chapter.

2. Observe your mannerisms under stress

Find out if you have some mannerisms which only show up in stressful conditions. Again, appeal to friends and family for help, or, if possible, have someone videotape you when you are in a stressful situation.

Some people unconsciously lose all sense of social decorum under stress and find themselves indulging in mannerisms (pulling at nose hairs, paring fingernails, scratching near the groin) they are appalled to discover they've been doing in public. Still others have very mild, almost unobtrusive mannerisms until they are nervous, at which point they turn into churning windmills. An occasional licking of dry lips, in itself quite acceptable, becomes a constant and obtrusive licking, an occasional rubbing together of the hands becomes, under stress, a hand wringing marathon.

3. Awareness: a simple solution

Once you are aware of what your mannerisms are, quieting them becomes simply a matter of reminding yourself that they are useless, and not doing them. Awareness is the key.

HOW TO USE MOVEMENT PERSUASIVELY

How to Use Movement to Establish Control in the Courtroom

Preparation: Before the trial

The first and most critical use of movement in the Courtroom consists of movement the jurors will never see. Before you ever go into the Courtroom to try your case, make that Courtroom yours. Make it familiar to you, so that you move within it as easily and as confidently as you do within your own home. This will give you an aura of belonging there, which will make you seem in charge and in control. You will exude the confidence that comes naturally with a feeling of belongingness, in addition to which, you will actually feel more confident and secure from having made friends with what up to then was alien territory.

If at all possible, visit the Courtroom prior to the actual trial date, when no one is there. Walk all through the Courtroom, stand in various places, sit at your table, in the jury box, in the audience, walk the room thoroughly, until you really feel like you know it. Then sit quietly a moment, with eyes closed, and recreate the room in your mind. Look and see if you were accurate in your mental reconstruction, make any necessary adjustments. Now you will be able to actually see yourself in the Courtroom as you prepare various parts of the trial, this will help you prepare more effectively.

If you cannot visit the Courtroom prior to the trial at a time when no one is in it, visit it anyway, sit in the audience, and let your eyes walk for you. Let your eyes explore every area, mentally try to feel what it is like to stand or sit in the various places. Then on the day of the actual trial, get there early, before anyone is present, and walk the Courtroom so as to get comfortable in it.

Execution: During the trial

During the trial itself, use the Courtroom to the extent the Judge allows. If you can move freely in the Courtroom, be sure you do so, so that the jurors feel your comfort and ease in the Courtroom. You will give an appearance of being in charge and in control. Even if you are restricted to a podium, having explored the space will make you more comfortable and relaxed, and you will not tiptoe between podium and table, but rather stride comfortably, having walked this same passage many times before.

How Movement Persuades in the Courtroom

How movement attracts the jurors' attention

Sometimes this attention is negative, such as the attention a hyperactive child receives by running erratically around the house driving everyone nuts. Well-timed and well-executed movement, however, attracts great praise. A flawlessly executed dance movement or ski slalom is marvelous to behold. Well timed and well executed movement in the Courtroom has the same effect.

How movement keeps the jurors awake

Movement has a special function in the Courtroom: it wakes people up (including you). This may seem like a strange consideration, until you take into account that the average adult attention span is only 18 minutes. A trial lasts a good deal longer than that. Breaking up the constant flow of verbal communication with movement helps keep the jurors' interest and attention.

How movement keeps the jurors alert

This comes from our basic survival mechanism. If something moves, you may be in danger, so whenever something moves, you will pay attention. Do not misunderstand, however: movement is not a cue for danger. Movement simply signals us to be alert, in case there is danger, movement cues alertness. Movement, however, does not equate with nervousness. Fidgeting and shuffling do not constitute persuasive movement.

Movement, in order to be persuasive, is motivated, purposeful, and appropriate. Pacing may be motivated and purposeful, but it is not appropriate in a Courtroom. Why? Pacing is motivated by worry, and a professional attorney is one who knows what to do, who therefore might be serious and concerned, but will not worry. You can endanger your credibility by simply pacing.

How to Use Movement to Persuade the Jurors

How and when to move

The guideline for movement, in addition to appropriateness, is that it should not be accidental. You only move when you have a *reason* to do so, and the most common motivator of movement is the need for a *transition*.

Movement is a way of nonverbally stating, "I have finished with thought one, I am now going to move on to thought two."

CASE IN POINT

Let's suppose you are questioning a witness. You start by facing the witness and stating, "What you are saying then, is that you did not see your wife before you left the house that night" . . . then you turn and take a few steps away from the witness, and then stop, turn back toward the witness and say "Would you say that your marriage was a happy one, Mr. Jones?"

The brief walk allows the jury to digest the first bit of information, lets them know nonverbally you are on to something new, and wakes them up to be ready to hear the next bit.

This way of using movement is especially useful when you must ask a series of questions during which the jury may get confused or tend to blur all the answers together. Taking a few steps breaks up that rhythm, and helps the jury know when you have finished with one subject and are on to a new subject.

Movement must be well-timed in order to be effective. If you move all the time, people will react to you just as they do to a hyper-active child: negatively. If, however, you only move when you have a reason for doing so, your movement will be persuasive.

How to use movement to give a point maximum impact

Aside from moving in order to change the subject, what are some of the other reasons for moving? Movement can be used as a signal to indicate you are thinking something over; when you come to your conclusion, the point you want to drive home, you stop.

CASE IN POINT

Let's say the above sentence, "What you are saying then, is that you did not see your wife before you left the house that night" was in fact the conclusion to a logical sequence of question-answer, and let's see how movement can help you give your point maximum impact.

Attorney: "Did you see your wife when you came home from work?"

Witness: "No."

Attorney: "Did you see your wife when your brother-in-law came over?"

Witness: "No."

Attorney: "Did you see your wife during the time your brother-in-law was visiting?"

Witness: "No."

. . . Then you would walk a few steps, as if thinking this over, then stop and say,

Attorney: "What you are saying then, is that you did not see your wife before you left the house that night."

The reason for the movement and the final stop is to draw the jury's attention to the last sentence, which is in fact the one sentence you really want them to notice. The walk alerted their attention, they know something's coming, the stop before you spoke was an application of the principle of holding-still-when-you-have-something-important-to-say, which we discussed in Chapter 1. The interjection of movement set your last sentence apart from the rest of the sequence, pointing out its special importance.

How to Use Movement to Create a Special Relationship with the Jury

Another way movement is used to persuade the jury is in the creation of a special relationship with the jury. We will discuss the subject of "rapport" in detail in Chapter 4, at this point let's look at how movement is used to create rapport.

The science called "proxemics" studies the use of space. There are well-established rules which govern the normative use of space in our culture. Simply put, the farther away you stand from someone, the less intimate your interaction. Mother and child are closely intertwined, friends stand side by side easily and comfortably, strangers respect a certain distance.

When you first interact with the jurors, stand a certain distance away, anywhere from four to seven feet away. Slowly, as you get acquainted with the jury, allow yourself to stand a little closer (Illustration 64). Standing too close to someone too fast will scare them away—respect that.

Do not touch the jury rail in the beginning of trial. Think of the jury rail as the arms of the jury. Would you put your arm around the shoulder of a total stranger? If you did, he's likely to think you're a used car salesman trying to make a sale. Rather approach the rail gradually over time, allowing the jurors and yourself to mellow into a relationship, not push into it. You might simply touch it briefly at first, then leave your hand on it a moment, and so forth. Make friends with the jurors as you would with a new person in your life. Respect the protective boundary the jury rail represents.

2–64

How to Use Movement to Create a Special Relationship with Your Client During Trial

Proxemics apply also to how the jury perceives the relationship between yourself and your client. If you sit fairly close to your client, the jurors will assume a friendly relationship between you. If you are credible, that fact that you are willing to stand or sit near your client implies that he and/or his cause is also credible. Similarly, if you occasionally touch your client on the arm, a certain friendliness will be assumed.

How to Use Movement to Distract or Discredit a Witness

Movement can also be used to distract or discredit. Let's say you don't want the jury to focus on something the witness is going to say. Then while the witness is talking, walk away, or take a few steps to the side. Movement always takes precedence over words, and the jury by watching your movement, will be distracted from hearing what the witness is saying.

Walking away when someone is speaking to you is considered rude: doing such discredits the witness by taking respect away from him, it connotes that the witness, or what the witness is saying, is not worthy of ordinary considerateness. You can minimize the rudeness of your movement so as not to alienate the jurors by doing it quite slowly, or not going too far, for example only moving a few steps away.

> *CAUTION Moving away from someone while he is talking is a powerful communication: be sure you know what the effect will be before you decide to use it.*

Coordinating Movement with Gestures, Facial Expressions, and Eye Focus to Maximize Your Persuasiveness

Movement is used in conjunction with gestures, facial expressions, and everything we have covered so far, to create the desired effect. Learning how to make it all come together is a little like learning how to juggle. First you learn to use eye focus, then you learn body positions, then you learn how to use eye focus and body positions together; then you add gestures, and so on until you can work all the techniques together.

The easiest way to master these skills is to practice each of the techniques separately, get comfortable with each on its own, before you try to put them together. It's also in your best interest to work on these techniques *outside* of the Courtroom, so that you feel totally comfortable before using the techniques in a trial situation. You have enough to worry about during a trial without giving yourself the extra stress of the first-time tryout of a whole new set of nonverbal communication techniques!

HOW TO MAKE A PODIUM WORK FOR YOU
DURING A TRIAL RATHER THAN AGAINST YOU

A podium reduces your ability to express by limiting your movement, so if at all possible, work to one side of the podium or ignore it and work mostly in front of it. There are, however, situations in which you must stand behind the podium and stay there; in most federal courts, for example. In that case, rest your hands lightly on the podium, stand straight and true, and follow the guidelines for effective body language given previously. Remember, the only difference between being behind a podium and standing without one is that we don't see your body from mid-chest down. We still see all the rest, so head positions, gestures, and posture are as important as ever. This is how you make a podium work for you.

A podium will work against you as soon as you treat it as a prop or a crutch. You then cease to convey an impression of self-confidence and assurance, and rather convey an impression of fear and insecurity. So do not, under any conditions, *grip* the podium, which makes you look terribly out of control ("drowning rat clings desperately to sinking ship"), and do not lean heavily upon it. The jurors' perception of your ability to stand on your own two feet is seriously impaired if they observe you hanging all over the podium for support.

Even though the jurors can't see your bottom half when you're behind a podium, it's advisable to use a neutral stance. A neutral stance gives firm support to your erect posture and helps avoid any involuntary compensatory head angles (Illustration 65). In addition, you can "root" your body firmly with the neutral stance, since swaying from side to side, and shifting weight from one foot to the other, are both to be avoided.

2–65

HOW TO SELECT YOUR DRESS, MAKE-UP AND HAIR STYLE TO ENHANCE YOUR CREDIBILITY WITH THE JURY

Social psychologists have demonstrated time and again that attractive people are viewed more favorably and are automatically granted more credibility. Does this mean you must undergo extensive plastic surgery in order to be successful if you weren't born looking like Robert Redford or Bo Derek? Certainly not.

"Attractive" is a much broader concept than "beautiful" or "handsome." To be attractive means to have the power to draw people to you, to be pleasing and inviting. "Attractive" has a great deal more to do with how you present your physical person than it does with the sheer beauty of your person. A clean, well-groomed man, with a trim, fit body, whose hair style is properly cut to set off his features to their best advantage, whose clothes fit well and are of good cloth, free of spots or wrinkles, whose nails are clean and well-tended, whose smile is wholesome because he takes good care of his teeth is enormously attractive, able to draw people easily, regardless of the actual beauty of his features or body. In contrast, a man who is devastatingly handsome, but who has dirty ill-kempt hair, whose clothes are ill-fitting and soiled, who smells like yesterday's fish, and whose nails are black and jagged will not be attractive regardless of the incomparable beauty of his face.

How to Use the Four Elements of Attractiveness to Establish Yourself Favorably with the Jurors

The four elements of attractiveness are available to everyone and consist of the following:

Cleanliness

Cleanliness may or may not be next to Godliness, but it is certainly next to successfulness. Cleanliness means clean hair, body, face, and hands, and well taken care of teeth. It is easy to forget hands, yet clean nails are important. What is your instant opinion of a professional with dirty nails? Cleanliness also means clean clothes, no spots on ties or blouses; wrinkle free clothes, freshly pressed.

Remember, jurors notice everything. What seems like an insignificant spot to you may assume gigantic proportions when someone has nothing better to do than to stare at you. And there are long periods during trial when the jurors really have little to absorb their attention.

Good grooming

Good grooming means your choice of clothing, how you cut your hair and nails, how your makeup is applied. All is predicated on what fits and suits you well. This means you choose clothes which fit you well, and are of good cloth. You cannot "get away" with slightly frayed cuffs, an outdated tie, or a scraggly hem. Your shoes must be shined, your stockings run-free. Your hair and make up should be carefully chosen to best suit your face, not according to what is the latest fad.

There are many excellent consultants who can help you groom yourself; color consultants, hair stylists, personal wardrobe consultants, and so forth. Shop around, find out who is good, and consult. It will be worth the fee to look really professional and thereby enhance your credibility.

Appropriate accessories

The rule of thumb is: less is more. When in doubt, under-accessorize rather than over. We tend to dress and accessorize to express our personalities. As an attorney you need also to pay attention to what non-verbal message your accessories are conveying. You may have a special fondness for earrings, but it would be highly inadvisable to wear your favorite razzmatazz-and-all-that-jazz earrings in Court, for the simple reason that more attention will be paid to your ears than to what you are saying.

Accessories such as jewelry, glasses, hair clips, and so forth, are so much a part of us we forget to take a look and see what function they may or may not be performing. Your glasses may obscure your look: is the frame too heavy or too dark? Might you be better off with contact lenses? On the contrary, do your contact lenses make you blink all the time and tear: might you be better off with glasses? Is your jewelry more interesting than you are? Take a good look at yourself in the mirror and start questioning every one of your ordinary accessories, be sure they enhance and support your credibility rather than detract from it.

Being in shape

An out of shape tired body is not attractive. No, you don't need to turn into Jack LaLanne, but you do need to recognize that you're hardly going to project a confident energized image if you're drastically out of shape. Being in shape doesn't necessarily mean going on a diet. Weight isn't everything. People can be somewhat overweight, but if they keep up a decent regimen of exercise, their bodies will be toned and thus the impression of positive self-assurance will radiate forth. If you're reasonably in shape you will stand straight more easily, your movements will be more fluid, your gestures will have more life to them.

SUMMARY

How you present yourself physically is very important. Be sure your body is conveying the message you want it to convey. The tools you have to work with are the way you stand, your posture, your arm and head positions, your facial expressions, your gestures, and the way you move. Special circumstances such as being seated, and using a podium require specific attention. Do not overlook how you are dressed, the colors you wear, accessories you choose, and how you style your hair and do your makeup. All of these elements should add up to a credible and persuasive physical presentation which solidly enhances and supports your message.

BODY LANGUAGE WORKSHEET: HOW TO FIGURE OUT YOUR CURRENT BODY LANGUAGE

As you evaluate your body language according to this checklist, be honest in your assessment. The more accurate your observations, the more easily you can shape your body language so that you communicate effectively.

1. Your assessment of your habitual way of standing:
   (Looking at yourself standing in front of a mirror)

   Posture: erect ____   curved forward ____

                     arched ____

   Shoulders: square ____   slumped forward ____

                     tilted ____

   Stance: feet appropriate distance apart ____

                     feet too close together ____

                     feet too wide apart ____

   Knees: relaxed ____   stiff ____

   Hands: relaxed ____   hands fisted ____

                     hands fidgeting ____

   Head placement: level ____   tilted skywards ____

                     tilted down ____ cocked ____

   Face placement: face straight ahead ____

                     face slightly turned to either side ____

2. Comments others have made about how you express yourself physically:

   _____

   _____

   _____

   _____

   _____

3. Assessment of recent candid photographs:
   Note the number of times you adopt a certain way of standing, holding your shoulders, and so forth. For example, taking the category of "posture", from a total of 20 photographs, you stand erect in 18 of them, curved forward in 2. This gives a very different assessment than if out of 20, you are curved forward in 18 of the photographs, and standing erect in 2.

   Posture: erect ____   curved forward ____   arched ____

   Shoulders: square ____   slumped forward ____   tilted ____

   Stance: feet appropriate distance apart ____

                     feet too close together ____

                     feet too wide apart ____

                     sitting on a hip ____

                     with feet close together ____

                     with feet too far apart ____

   Knees: relaxed ____   stiff ____

   Arms: hanging relaxed at sides ____

                     crossed in front of you ____

                     crossed in back of you ____

                     one arm holding the other ____

                     both arms holding on ____

                     one arm akimbo ____

                     both arms akimbo ____

                     other _____

   Hands: relaxed ____   hands fisted ____

                     hands fidgeting ____

                     one hand hidden from view ____

                     both hands hidden from view ____

                     other _____

Head placement: level ____   tilted skywards ____

                        tilted down ____ cocked ____

Face placement: face straight ahead ____

                        face slightly turned to either side ____

4. Your overall assessment of your body language taking into account the information from the above three categories:
   Note here the adjustments you need to make so that your body language expresses confidence and self-assurance.

Posture _____

_____

_____

_____

Shoulders _____

_____

_____

Stance _____

_____

_____

_____

Knees _____

_____

_____

_____

Arms _____

_____

_____

_____

Hands _____

_____

_____

_____

Head placement _____

_____

_____

_____

Face placement _____

_____

_____

FACIAL EXPRESSIONS WORKSHEET: HOW TO FIGURE OUT YOUR HABITUAL FACIAL EXPRESSIONS

1. Comments friends and family have made about your facial expressions: You usually look:

sad ____	cheerful ____
depressed ____	surprised ____
anxious ____	vexed ____
worried ____	irritated ____
suspicious ____	spaced out ____
wired ____	puzzled ____
guilty ____	curious ____
upset ____	bored ____
hostile ____	expressionless ____
intrigued ____	excited ____
other _____	

_____

_____

2. Your assessment of your facial expressions:

Look at recent candid photographs of yourself. Be as objective as possible in evaluating your facial expressions. Note how many times you look a certain way. For example, out of 20 photographs, note that you look anxious 15 times, intrigued 3 times, and puzzled twice.

sad ____	cheerful ____
depressed ____	surprised ____
anxious ____	vexed ____
worried ____	irritated ____
suspicious ____	spaced out ____
wired ____	puzzled ____
guilty ____	curious ____
upset ____	bored ____
hostile ____	expressionless ____
intrigued ____	excited ____
other _____	

_____

_____

3. Look at yourself in a mirror. Notice the lines in your face, they accent the habitual cast of your face. Think about what your lines say about you.

> Do the crow's feet around your eyes
>> go up ____   or go down ____?

> What is the usual position of your mouth?
>> lips curved up ____   lips curved down ____
>>
>> lips pursed ____   lips relaxed ___
>>
>> mouth slightly open ____
>>
>> mouth tightly shut ____
>>
>> mouth shut but relaxed ____

> What is the usual position of your brows?
>> held straight across ____
>>
>> held slightly up ____
>>
>> furrowed together ____
>>
>> one brow held up, the other level ____

> How do the lines on your forehead go?
>> horizontal frown lines ____
>>
>> 1 vertical line between your brows ____
>>
>> 2 vertical lines between your brows ____

4. Practice the four basic facial expressions so that you can use them deliberately and at will, according to your purpose:

> a) frown (brows furrowed)
> a little
> a little more
> brows furrowed together as tightly as possible

> b) raise both brows
> a little
> a little more
> as high as you can

> c) raise one brow leaving the other level
> (people differ as to which brow raises most easily: experiment until you figure out which one raises most easily for you)
> a little
> a little more
> as high as you can

> d) face relaxed

GESTURES WORKSHEET:
HOW TO FIGURE OUT YOUR GESTURES

Videotape yourself in 2 conditions:

1. Non-stressed condition: having a casual conversation with a friend

2. In a stressed condition: presenting a mock opening statement directly to the camera.

   Then observe your gestures in each condition, and assess them according to the following guidelines:

   1. Non-stressed condition:
      Gestures: few ____   a moderate number ____   many ____

   What are your habitual gestures?

   _____

   _____

   Are your gestures:
      illustrative ____   non-illustrative ____

   Do you point your finger and/or shake it?
      point ____   shake ____

   2. Stressed condition:
      Gestures: few ____   a moderate number ____   many ____

   What are your gestures under stress?

   _____

   _____

   Are your gestures:
      illustrative ____   non-illustrative ____

   Do you point your finger and/or shake it?
      point ____   shake ____

3. Given the above observations, what adjustments would you like to make so that your gestures are persuasive?

   _____

   _____

MANNERISMS WORKSHEET:
HOW TO FIGURE OUT YOUR MANNERISMS

Using the same videotape that you made for the preceding gestures work-sheet, assess your mannerisms, both in non-stressed and stressed conditions. Then ask your family and friends what they think are your mannerisms, both when you are under stress and when you are not.

1. Self-observation:

Mannerisms in non-stressed condition: _____

_____

_____

_____

_____

Mannerisms in stressed condition: _____

_____

_____

_____

_____

2. Observations of friends and family:

Mannerisms in non-stressed condition: _____

_____

_____

_____

_____

Mannerisms in stressed condition: _____

_____

_____

_____

_____

3. Given the above observations, what adjustments would you like to make so that you avoid any distracting mannerisms?

_____

_____

_____

_____

_____

_____

CHAPTER 3

Using Vocal Persuasion to Win the Jurors Over to Your Interpretation of the Facts

"The judicial process and the rules of evidence which govern it are not tailored to minds honed by the information explosion of our media-dominated society. The facts come in through the slow, orderly, drip, drip, drip of testimony from the witness stand. If it were a TV show on the same subject, what takes two hours of Court time would be concentrated in a 30 second sound bite. The time spent/information received ratio of the Courtroom is way out of whack with the pace of our lives in the outside world. Even though this was an interesting, exciting case which was tried efficiently before an experienced judge, I found myself fighting off boredom at times. But I kept reminding myself of the gravity of the charge, not to mention how bad it would look for the only lawyer on the jury to doze off."[1]

"Imagine, for a moment, nine disembodied brains hovering over the chairs in the jury box. One brain is wondering if it's still snowing so he can run his plows that night; another brain is thinking of what the substitute teacher should be working on with her second graders. Another is confused over the matter of $56.64 void on the cash register that the defense lawyer keeps going over; two brains are fighting sleep and another is trying to decide whether one of the lawyers wears a hairpiece. That leaves three minds following the proceedings, and they may not agree on the point being made. One day we each took eight-minute periods to pay attention so that at least one person was alert during the afternoon."[2]

HOW A PERSUASIVE VOICE CAN WIN YOUR CASE

The above paragraphs were not written by uncaring jurists, resentful of their duty. They were written by individuals honored by the opportunity to participate in the trial process, individuals who were deeply concerned that their determinations of guilt or innocence would be accurate. Yet even these highly motivated jurists found themselves fighting boredom and the intrusion of unwanted thoughts. The boredom was not the result of boring substantive issues. The boredom was the inevitable outgrowth of how our judicial system operates—slowly. The problem is, no matter how exciting and stimulating your substantive issues, no matter how motivated the jurors, if your *delivery* does not command the jurors' attention, you will not be persuasive.

How to Go Beyond the Simple Presentation of Your Case to Dynamic Persuasion of the Jurors

There is nothing you can do to speed up the "drip, drip, drip" of testimony, but there is much you can do vocally to transform it into a far more interesting process. Your voice is a powerful instrument, your voice can profoundly move people or it can put them to sleep. Why do you think, for example, it is so difficult to drum up an audience for a lecture on theology, yet so easy to get thousands of people spellbound by TV preachers? The very word "lecture" conjures up yawns and sighs: you may love or hate TV preachers, but they are never boring. What is the difference? The content of the lecture is in all likelihood more intellectually stimulating, the message preached on television tends to be more simplistic and repetitious, so it's not a question of intellectual challenge. No, the main difference between a lecturer and a TV preacher is that the TV preacher is sincerely dedicated to persuading people to join his flock, the lecturer is presenting his point of view as the correct one.

There is a world of difference between *presenting* and *persuading*. Too often attorneys get caught up in presenting their cases when they need to be persuading jurors. TV preachers, who have minimal interest in presenting and whose main thrust is persuasion, use the full range of their voices, vary the volume, pitch, and pace to keep that audience listening with both ears, ready and willing to hear more, then they use emotional techniques and skills to make sure their audience is truly convinced. And it works. Granted, TV preachers have a *style* of vocal delivery which is inappropriate for the Courtroom, but the basic *skills* are the same. I use TV preachers as an example because their passionate commitment to getting their message across is absolute: it is that passionate commitment which leads them to use persuasive vocal techniques a less zealous individual might overlook.

If people are to be persuaded, first they must be awake. This may seem like a truism, but apparently it is not, for far too many attorneys forget this basic rule of verbal persuasion. In addition, your voice must be easy and interesting to listen to, and reflect your credibility. Our first concern, then, will be how to use your voice to keep the jury *attentive,* to make it easy and desirable for the jurors to listen to you. Only after that will we discuss specific techniques of vocal *persuasion.*

FOUR VOCAL TECHNIQUES GUARANTEED TO KEEP THE JURORS ATTENTIVE AND LISTENING

The voice is truly a magical instrument: it can enchant, delight, and captivate. Unfortunately, as with all magic, there's also a dark side: a voice can distract, annoy, and bore. As with body language, there are stereotypes for voices, and these will work for or against you. Most people do not know how their voice comes across, and so are unable to really use their voices as instruments. As an attorney, it is critical that you become aware of how you sound, and then be able to use your voice for specific purposes.

Technique 1: Vary Pace to Keep Jurors Awake and Interested

Pace refers to how quickly you speak. If you speak too quickly, the jurors will have trouble following you, and eventually will stop trying. If you speak too slowly, everyone will fall asleep. What is desirable, then, is a basic pace which is easy for people to follow, but quick enough to remain interesting.

Use pace to reflect good energy

Good pace reflects good energy, which as we have seen, is one of the components of competence and "professionalism." Good energy induces good energy in others. Have you ever noticed that if you sit around with a group of people who are feeling blah and out of sorts, you end up feeling equally blah and out of sorts, whereas if you're with a group of people laughing and singing and dancing, how your own energy comes up to theirs? If you maintain good vocal energy, the vocal equivalent of walking at a brisk pace, you will induce good energy in the jurors. Similarly, if you allow your pace to drag, the jurors' energy will begin to wear down.

Use pace to express confidence

Good energy also reflects confidence. When you know a subject well, you speak more quickly, whereas when you're unsure about an issue, your pace slows down, reflecting your internal search for ideas and words. Your basic pace, therefore, should be, as mentioned above, easy for people to follow but quick enough to be interesting. You then vary that pace according to your different purposes.

When to slow down or speed up your pace

Anything done the same way for long periods of time becomes monotonous. If you speak at a good pace, but never vary that pace, eventually your good pace becomes boring. To counteract boredom, use your basic pace most of the time, and vary it in two ways from time to time.

1. *Slow your pace down* when you wish to appear *thoughtful*, or when you want to give the jurors the impression that you are working through a process of induction or deduction even as you are speaking. Slow your pace down when you have something particularly *important* or serious to say, slow your pace down when you wish to show great *respect*.

2. *Speed up your basic pace* (but *not* so much that you become impossible to follow or difficult to understand) when you are *reviewing* information you have given before, or when you wish to make something seem *unimportant*. You can also speed up your pace somewhat when you're driving a point home, but be careful to go back to your basic pace when you get to the point itself.

How to determine your natural pace

In order to use the above techniques, you first need to determine your natural pace. What comments have people made over the years? Have you often been asked, "Could you slow down, please?" or do people say to you, "All right, so get to the point already." These are clues to your pace. Tape record the voice of a television personality whose pace you think reflects good energy and self-confidence, then tape record your own voice during two or three informal conversations. Compare the two voices. If you find that your voice is hard to follow, that you seem to be going at 90 mph all the time, slow yourself down. If, on the contrary, you make John Wayne sound like a speed freak, you need to speak more quickly. Then, it's just a question of practice.

Establish your basic pace first, then learn to vary it by speeding up a little, or slowing down a little. Deliberately use speeding up or slowing down according to the guidelines given above, so that the variation is motivated. The change in pace must reflect a thought change, it should not be gratuitous. If you simply vary your pace for the sake of varying your pace, you are likely to sound slightly crazy, which is not consistent with the image of the competent attorney.

How to cope with the effects of stress on pace

Be aware that pace is significantly affected by nerves. Most people "rush" when nervous, that is to say, speed up their rate of speech. If you know this is what happens to you, compensate for it. When you're in an anxiety provoking situation, deliberately speak more slowly than you usually would, and that will correct your "rushing." If the opposite is true for you, that under stressful conditions you suddenly develop a voice reminiscent of trudging through swamps, compensate by increasing your pace.

Technique 2: Use Pitch to Create an Impression of Authority and Strength

In our culture, deeper voices convey an impression of authority and strength, for both men and women. In addition, a deeper voice is considered more sincere, a reflection of that person's trustworthiness. The "depth" of your voice is created by the pitch of your voice. The pitch is basically where your voice is placed on a musical scale. If you talk up where the high notes are, your voice is high-pitched; if your voice resonates to the frequency of the low notes, your voice is low-pitched. A high-pitched voice is stereotypically considered weak, somewhat irritating, and is often associated with flaky personalities or "airheads." A voice lower in pitch is considered knowledgeable, indicative of self-assurance, and authoritative, and is often associated with people in power. This holds true for women as well as men.

In order to convey vocally the self-assurance and self-confidence which is the foundation of your credibility in the Courtroom, you need to have or develop a deep enough voice. This does not mean you need to develop a basso profundo if you've been a soprano all your life. It does mean you need to broaden the range of your voice *as it exists* on the low end of the musical scale.

How to determine your natural pitch

Your first task then is to determine whether your voice is high pitched, low pitched, or somewhere in the middle. An easy way to do this is, again, to tape a television personality's voice that you find appealing and can identify as low pitched, and then tape your own voice. Be sure to tape your own voice as it really is. You can accomplish this by simply leaving the tape recorder on during a breakfast conversation at home, or other such candid moment. Then compare your voice with the television personality's voice. This should give you a good of idea of your own pitch. If your pitch is already on the low end, great, if not, your pitch can be lowered.

How your pitch gets too high

Unless there are medical complications, such as a problem with your palate, or placement of your jaw, etc., high pitch is usually a function of poor breathing, habit, and nerves. In general, correcting your breathing will automatically lower your pitch to a more assured level. Proper breathing is diaphragmatic breathing, as is taught in LaMaze for childbirth. The principle behind proper breathing is that you allow your belly to do the work. Improper breathing is breathing from the chest, where the chest heaves in order to allow the passage of air. When you make your chest do all the work, you don't fill your lungs fully with air, and so there is very little air to support your words. The tightness or constriction this creates makes your voice tight and constricted, and by extension, high-pitched.

CAUTION You can learn to breathe properly on your own, as is demonstrated in the following exercise. However, **DO NOT DO THIS EXERCISE IF IT IS THE LEAST BIT PAINFUL OR ANX-IETY-MAKING.** *There are excellent vocal coaches and singing teachers who are trained to teach proper breathing and who can supervise you as you learn if this process is even remotely stressful. Just look in the telephone directory or ask friends in the entertainment business for a reference, and tell the instructor your specific need to learn proper breathing.*

How to use breath to lower your pitch

The exercise you can do on your own is as follows: sit in a straight backed chair with both feet flat on the floor. Place one hand on your belly and one hand on your chest (Illustration 1). Now breathe in through your nose, allowing your belly to swell out to a bit of a pot-belly. You should feel this movement with the hand that is on your belly (Illustration 2). Then breathe out through your mouth, letting your tummy help by pushing the air out gently (Illustration 3). Your chest should not move at all during this, and the hand you placed on your chest should help you keep it still. This exercise should be accomplished without strain in your throat. If you find yourself straining with your throat, stop at once. Do the exercise slowly, taking about four counts to inhale, hold your breath two to four counts, then exhale in four counts. This will help you develop strength and flexibility in your diaphragm and belly. Do the inhale-hold-exhale sequence about six times, then stop and rest a moment. Then repeat the sequence. Do this for about ten minutes total, then before you get up from your chair, sit still a moment before you attempt to rise, as you may feel slightly dizzy if you're unaccustomed to getting all that oxygen.

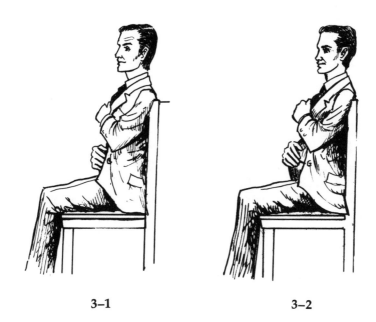

3–1 3–2

3–3

Another exercise which helps broaden your range and deepen the voice, is to sing along with the radio, one octave down. What I mean by this is sing along with the singer, but one octave down from where he/she is singing (two octaves down, if it's Michael Jackson). This is going to sound very peculiar and feel strange, but it will get you accustomed to working with a deeper voice. It's also more fun than practicing scales.

How nervousness affects your pitch

You may find that in general your voice is deep enough to convey authority and strength, but that when you get nervous or have to be "on," it suddenly flies up in pitch and you start sounding distinctly pre-pubertal. Nervousness and anxiety are major determinants of high pitch. When you are nervous, you unconsciously contract your muscles, ready for fight or flight. But when your stomach and chest muscles are tight, you do not enough air to properly support your voice, and you get the same tightness and constriction I spoke of earlier in reference to improper breathing, with the same results: a tight, constricted and therefore high-pitched voice. In addition, when you are nervous, you tighten the throat muscles, which further constricts your voice.

How to use breath to counteract the effects of nervousness

Proper breathing will help you relax, and consequently, lower your pitch back down to its normal level. When you feel yourself getting nervous, take a few deep breaths, from the belly as described above, then say inside yourself the word "Now." If "Now" feels like it's at your normal pitch, say a few more words to yourself to be sure your pitch is where you want it, then you can speak out loud with confidence that your voice will be where you want it, and not high and squeaky. If "Now" isn't hitting the desired pitch, simply take a few more deep breaths and try again. Once your voice has internally settled down, it will be in the right place for all to hear.

Getting past the pitch habit

Habit plays a large part in how we speak. You learned to speak from your parents, teachers, and peers, and once you learned a certain way of speaking, it became yours, you have spoken that way ever since. Your pitch is as much a part of you as how you walk. You probably have never questioned it until now. Don't be surprised then, if you decided your pitch is too high, and are working to change it, how uncomfortable it may be to do so. You will probably sound very strange to yourself. This is normal. You have been sounding one way for your entire adult life, any change is going to feel uncomfortable until it becomes the new habit. It should *not*, however, feel painful. If working to lower your pitch feels painful in any way, stop, and consult a speech therapist.

A special note for women regarding pitch

Women are caught in a bind regarding pitch. Culturally, women's voices are encouraged to be higher in pitch, in order to express greater vulnerability or delicacy. Many women learn therefore to speak in high, almost wispy voices, and feel very threatened in their femininity when it is suggested they allow their voices to drop down in pitch. However, the business of lawyering demands that a woman appear confident, strong, and in control. A high wispy voice does not express these characteristics.

If you fear that you will become unfeminine by lowering your pitch, I suggest that you allow your pitch to lower just a little, speak like that a while and take the time to really get comfortable with the slightly lower pitch, then lower it again just a little, and so on, until you have achieved the voice you desire.

Technique 3: Project Confidence and Competence by Using Articulation

If pitch is the vocal tool which gives you an impression of authority and strength, articulation is the primary vocal tool which allows you to be perceived as confident and competent. Stereotypically, poor articulation is associated with lack of education, mental retardation, laziness, and nervousness. None of these project confidence and competence. If you are a successful lawyer, a credible and professional one, you are expected to be well educated, endowed with a higher than average IQ, energetic, and sure of yourself. In addition, good articulation produces clear crisp language which is easy to follow. If you make it easy for people to listen, they are more likely to pay attention. If you make it easy for people to understand you, they are more likely to get your point.

How poor articulation loses jurors

Poor articulation has no redeeming virtues. It is never effective as a communications device. Poor articulation just makes other people say "What?" a lot. As a matter of fact, one way to find out if you are a mumbler, is to notice if people say "What?" a lot to you. Either your volume is way down, or you mumble. The jurors are at a distinct disadvantage in this respect. They cannot say "What?" The result is, *anything the jurors cannot understand does not exist for them.* You may make a vital statement, outline the very heart of your argument, if the jurors can't figure out what you're saying, it's as good as unsaid. And since the jurors can't say "What?" you never even know that your very important point just got lost.

Most people, as long as they are fairly easily understood by those around them, don't make efforts to produce clear speech. What you don't realize, is that most people around you have become used to the way you speak, and in a sense "interpret" your mumbles. If you're speaking with a stranger, he'll make efforts to understand what you are saying, or not care enough to do so and simply let the not understood parts stay that way, or will ask for clarification. The jurors will not do that. The jurors cannot ask for clarification, and if they are willing to make efforts to understand you in the beginning, will eventually tire and not be able to maintain that degree of constant attention. The jurors will not conclude, from their difficulty at attending to and understanding your speech, that their hearing is impaired; they will conclude that you are incompetent or insecure. Neither conclusion is desirable.

How to determine your articulation

You can figure out whether or not your articulation is good in the same way you figured out your pace and pitch: tape record your voice and compare it to that of a television personality whose voice seems clear and easy to understand. Ask your friends and family if you speak clearly most of the time. If your articulation is poor, much can be done to improve it.

> *CAUTION In some cases, poor articulation is due to a physical impairment, such as misaligned teeth, or a slight deformity of the palate, or placement of the tongue. If you have such an impairment, consult a speech therapist, usually your speech can be significantly ameliorated.*

How a lazy tongue impedes articulation

With the exception of certain physical impairments, poor articulation is caused by a lazy tongue. A lazy tongue is simply a tongue that doesn't work hard enough. The tongue is a muscle, and needs to be treated as such. An under-developed muscle does not have the strength to permit control of movement. You can't play tennis well if you are completely out of shape: you won't be able to control the position of your tennis racket. Similarly, if your tongue isn't developed, you cannot control how you shape words, and it is difficult to speak clearly and vigorously.

Tongue twisters: the cure for a lazy tongue

If your articulation is poor, the easiest way to improve it is to do tongue twisters. However, rather than going for speed in doing the tongue twisters, as you may have learned to do in school, aim for muscular development. In other words, the tongue twisters need to be done as isometric exercises for the tongue and lips rather than as mental gymnastics. Granted, as your muscular development increases, you will be able to impress friends and family as you whip off the tongue twisters with amazing speed, but that is not your primary objective.

You will find a set of tongue twisters to practice at the end of this chapter. Read them aloud very slowly, pressing your lips tightly together for the m, b, p sounds, pushing your tongue hard against the roof of your mouth for the n, ng sounds, hard against the back of your front teeth for the th sounds, really feel the sides of your tongue against your back teeth for the k, y and ch sounds. Don't concern yourself with the vowel sounds, those are open sounds and do not build up the tongue. Concentrate on making the consonants firm. Really exaggerate. Remember you are pressing against yourself (i.e., tongue against roof of mouth) to get the necessary resistance which creates muscular development. Focus on treating your tongue as a muscle, and don't worry about making the words sound right. They won't. This exercise, by the way, is an updated and less strenuous version of Demosthanes's projecting his voice across the ocean with a mouthful of marbles. The principle is the same: the marbles provided resistance the tongue had to work around. Tongue twisters are a lot easier, and do achieve the necessary effect. Mercifully, a Courtroom isn't an ocean.

Once you've done your tongue twisters slowly and laboriously for about 10 minutes, read some of them just naturally, without effort, and you'll notice that your speech is already clearer. This is a momentary improvement, which will only last as you strengthen your tongue over time, but nonetheless, it's amazing how quickly articulation improves.

CAUTION DO NOT STRAIN YOUR THROAT OR JAW WHILE DOING THIS EXERCISE. *Doing tongue twisters should not cause any pain at all, simply some muscular effort from your tongue.* IF YOU FEEL ANY STRAIN OR PAIN, STOP AT ONCE, AND CONSULT YOUR DOCTOR OR A SPEECH THERAPIST. *You're either doing the exercise incorrectly, or you have a physical impairment of some kind.*

You will find that some of the tongue twisters are more difficult for you to do than others—do those more, they are pointing up a problem area for you. Since tongue twisters require no thought, you can do them in the car, and take advantage of time otherwise wasted in traffic jams, at red lights, etc. Do them in five to ten minute sessions, for a total of 20 to 30 minutes, with rest periods in between. Articulation should be something you never think about, so good articulation must become second nature, as comfortable and automatic for you as walking.

Do not fall into the error of over-articulation. Although you should exaggerate in practicing your tongue twisters, you should not exaggerate in speaking. The tongue twisters will develop your muscles on their own, for the rest, just speak naturally, and as your muscles tone, your daily speech will automatically become clearer and more articulate, thereby reinforcing your image of a competent and confident attorney.

Technique 4: Regulate Your Volume for Maximum Impact

Once you have worked with pitch, to create an impression of authority and strength, reinforced the jury's impression of your confidence and competence with your clear articulation, and learned to vary your pace to keep the jury interested in what you have to say, it's time to learn how to use volume to achieve impact.

In order to have impact, your voice must first of all be easily and comfortably heard. If you speak too loudly, the jurors will become annoyed and irritated. Overly loud voices literally give people headaches. You are not very likely to convince someone who is suffering pain on your account. If you speak too softly, the jurors will try to listen to you at first, but eventually the effort will become too great, and they'll just give up. So before we can discuss using volume for impact, we must consider appropriate volume.

How to determine your natural volume

Tape record your voice in a number of different situations, through a variety of conversations, and compare your voice to the other speakers' voices. Is your voice significantly louder or softer than other people's? Do you find that your volume gets much louder when you're intense about something, or perhaps much softer when you get nervous about something?

Changes in volume are dead giveaways to people's emotions. When people are angry, they raise their volume, when they're embarrassed or anxious, their volume dies down. Ask friends and family their opinion on the loudness or softness of your voice, then use those opinions in conjunction with the tape recordings you have made to figure out just what your basic volume is, and how that volume changes in function of different emotional states.

How to regulate your volume for emotional effectiveness

Then all you need to do is practice raising or lowering your volume, so that you develop an appropriate easily heard basic volume, and practice compensating for the changes emotions create in your volume.

You must be in control of your vocal changes. Your voice is an instrument, and should express what you wish it to express, not simply what happens to be going on with you at the time. Do not misunderstand: certainly your voice must be an expression of yourself, but in the Courtroom, where your business is persuasion, your voice is at the service of that persuasion, and therefore must be controlled to be effective. You need to have worked sufficiently with your voice so that it does not express emotions you don't want made known to the jurors.

CASE IN POINT

If you are nervous about what your star witness might unexpectedly divulge, don't tip off the jury to your nervousness by unconsciously lowering your voice.

If opposing counsel has just infuriated you by some comment, but it would be inappropriate to express your anger at that time, don't give it away by suddenly speaking more loudly. Learn to use volume *deliberately*, for impact.

How to lower your volume for impact

Interestingly enough, raising volume for impact is rarely effective. It is the least subtle way of emphasizing a point, and has been so overused that it has just about lost all its power. Once in a while, strategically placed, raised volume can be very powerful, but it really should be reserved for special cases, and more subtle alternatives carefully considered. What is very effective, however, is *lowering* volume for emphasis: "Speak softly and carry a big stick." People who do not raise their voices in emotional moments are considered more steady and reliable, more competent and capable of dealing with crisis. Use lowered volume to capture the jury's attention, either to set up an important point, or to bring one home. This is especially effective in an emotional moment.

Bear in mind, though, you must still be heard easily and comfortably, so don't lower your voice too much. It is best to practice lowering volume for impact with the help of a tape recorder. Practice an opening statement, for example, using a basic comfortable volume for the most part, then lower your volume in very specific places to get maximum impact. Listen to the recording, figure out when it was effective to lower your volume, and when it wasn't, and do it again.

SIX POWERFUL VOCAL TECHNIQUES TO PERSUADE THE JURY

In the first part of this chapter, we looked at vocal techniques to keep the jurors attentive and interested in what you are saying, as well as impressed with your credibility and professionalism. In this section, we will discuss techniques of vocal persuasion. These, however, will only be effective if you add them to the first set of techniques. Bear in mind that you cannot be persuasive if you have not created a background of competence and self-confidence, and even less so, if you have put the jurors to sleep.

"The ability to handle language effectively is absolutely essential to success in Court. It is the trial lawyer's ultimate tool."[3] Again and again, master advocates emphasize the role of language in the Courtroom. It is imperative that you handle language with ease, grace and power if you are to succeed as a trial attorney. But how? Too often the importance of language is underscored, but the specific techniques that allow you to use it persuasively are insufficiently elaborated.

Technique 1: Use Phrasing to Make Sure the Jurors Get Your Point

Because, as an attorney, you must weigh the value of the *content* of your words so heavily, you forget that the *expression* of that content must be such that the content itself can be readily understood and appreciated in the way you want it to be. Spoken language is not the same as written language. The juror cannot, if he's missed a point, "read that last paragraph over again." If a juror has missed a point, he will in all likelihood miss the next three because he is worrying about the original point he missed.

Spoken language then, must be organized differently than written language. It must be managed so it does not come out as unintelligible gobbledy-gook. In addition, the juror does not have the same familiarity with the material as you do, and points which may be very obvious to you may not be at all obvious to the juror. You must design your delivery so that the points which *you* deem important are those perceived as important by the *jurors*.

How to phrase to get your meaning across

Phrasing is a primary way of assuring that the jurors will hear what you want them to hear. Phrasing is a way of grouping words together in logical fashion, with slight pauses on either side of the phrase, so that your thought can be easily grasped. Phrasing is how you make sense out of what you're saying.

When you are dealing with spoken language, think in terms of phrases, not sentences. Sentences are often too long to be easily understood; sentences can run whole paragraphs, whereas a phrase is usually only five to seven words long. Most importantly, a phrase represents a single thought. It is much easier to be persuasive if you are expressing one thought at a time. The jurors can then follow your thinking with minimal effort and better absorb your point.

CASE IN POINT

Let's look at the following statement:

"Shortly after he'd been examined by Doctor Searle in the emergency room Jack did regain consciousness although exhibiting many of the symptoms associated with brain concussion."

Said all together without a pause, this statement is difficult to digest, yet it is a relatively simple sentence. With the addition of pauses (/), it becomes easy to follow:

"Shortly after he'd been examined/ by Dr. Searle/ in the emergency room/ Jack did regain consciousness/ although exhibiting many of the symptoms/ associated with brain concussion."

How to use the pause to appear in charge and in control

A word of warning: these are *pauses*, not stops. A pause is just what it sounds like, a momentary phenomenon. It is not to be confused with an ending (a stop). It's the difference between slightly letting your foot ease up on the accelerator (pausing), and putting it on the brakes (stopping). Pauses, then, are the tool which allows you to phrase, and you phrase according to thought.

Notice how each of the phrases in the Case in Point above contains only one thought. The placement of the pause is not absolute, there are other ways to phrase the above sentence, the important point is that you restructure written language so it is easily and effectively understood as spoken language. When you phrase, you appear to be in command of language: this is actually the vocal equivalent of "doing things one thing at a time" we discussed in the context of creating charisma. By expressing one thought at a time, you appear to be in charge and in control, the very basis of power.

At the end of this chapter is an exercise to help you learn to use phrasing effectively and naturally. When you do the phrasing exercise, be sure you do it out loud. This holds true for all the vocal exercises in this chapter. Your voice as you hear it inside your head is not the same as your voice when it is heard out loud. As with the techniques given throughout this book, practice is of the essence. With practice, these skills become second nature and powerful, without practice, they are useless. I encourage you to practice the skills in your daily life so that they become easy to manipulate, and that you become expert at them.

Technique 2: Use the Pause to Highlight Important Points for the Jurors

The pause is not only useful in making language intelligible, it also is a prime way of highlighting important points. The days of histrionic oratory are long gone; contemporary speech must use subtle means of emphasis and persuasion. The pause is a wonderfully subtle technique. Judicious use of the pause provides you with the ability to make a point crystal clear, to give it maximum significance, with very little effort, and no histrionics.

CASE IN POINT

For example, in the following statement: "The car was going 80 mph when it hit the child," let's say you want to emphasize the *speed* of the car. Rather than using the pause simply to phrase your statement, use the pause both to phrase the statement for clear meaning *and* to emphasize your point.

The result is as follows: "The car was going// 80 miles per hour/ when it hit the child." The longer pause (//) is really unnecessary in terms of clarifying meaning, but it brings attention to the speed of the car very effectively.

How to use the pause subtly to emphasize important points

The pause-for-emphasis is a set up: it is the nonverbal communication of "Are you ready, folks? Something important is coming." The pause has tremendous power. It is the vocal equivalent of stillness, and stillness pulls attention. It is important NOT to "punch" or emphasize with *volume* the "80 miles per hour" that follows the pause: this is overkill and will sound melodramatic. It is critical that the words following the pause are not said in a louder voice, or a different voice, than those preceding it, or you will lose the subtlety of your effect.

How to change the placement of the pause to emphasize an important point

By simply maneuvering the placement of the pause, you can change the point you wish to emphasize.

CASE IN POINT

Taking the previous example, let's say, for instance, that you want *the child* who was hit to be the focus of the jury's attention.

Change the placement of the pause:

"The car was going 80 mph when it hit// the child."

Try the sentence out loud with this new pause. Now the important point is the child.

If you want to emphasize that the car *hit* the child, simply move the pause over:

"The car was going 80 miles per hour when it// hit the child."

The guideline for effective use of the pause is to pause *in front of* the point you wish to emphasize. Don't pause three words away from your point, pause right in front of *the* critical word.

How to use pitch skillfully in conjunction with the pause for effective emphasis of a point

Be careful that your voice does not pitch down right before the pause. Pitching your voice down undermines the value of the pause. Bear in mind that the pause used to highlight a point is essentially setting up that point: if your voice pitches down, you won't set up your point, you will shoot it down. Your pitch should remain level or even go a little up to set up a point, but never down. The pause is a powerful tool and should only be used for important points. Don't pause for every point, your speech will become choppy; reserve it for your main point.

How to use the pause to minimize the importance of a point made by a witness or opposing counsel

If pausing highlights a point, then taking out the pause will diminish its importance. For example, if you restate something opposing counsel said that you wish to devalue, restating it without any pauses will make opposing counsel's point seem less important.

CASE IN POINT

Opposing counsel announces that:

"The// bloodstains/ on the carpet were of// human origin."

The emphasis is on "bloodstains" and "human origin." You can reduce the impact opposing counsel achieved with his pauses by removing them. Upon repetition, your version becomes:

"The bloodstains on the carpet were of human origin."

No one word is pointed up more than any other, the overall statement is rendered monotonous and thus loses impact.

You can also change the *emphasis* opposing counsel made by changing the placement of the pause.

CASE IN POINT

Using the same example, opposing counsel states:

"The// bloodstains/ on the carpet were of// human origin."

Opposing counsel's emphasis is still on "bloodstains" and "human origin." Your re-interpretation might be:

"The bloodstains on the// carpet were of human origin."

You have non-verbally denied the importance of "bloodstains" and "human origin," and shifted attention to "carpet," a relatively innocuous word.

The pause is an excellent example of how it really isn't just what you say, but how you say it that makes all the difference.

The exercise on pauses at the end of the chapter will help you develop the ability to use the pause naturally and persuasively. The pause is a very powerful tool. The more you work with it, the more you will come to appreciate just how powerful it is. Be sure to practice out loud.

Technique 3: Make Dull Testimony Come to Life Using "Color," "Peaks," and "Valleys"

Phrasing and pausing are techniques to help you make your words make sense, and call the juror's attention to certain points: "color," "peaks," and "valleys" are designed to help you make your words interesting. If your language is not interesting, you will not be persuasive. After all, you must talk for long periods of time in front of the jurors, who, try as they might, may not find the substantive issues as compelling as you do. You must engage the jurors interest regardless of the sometimes dull and uninteresting nature of the issues, and over longer periods of time than most of us listen to anything. "Color," "peaks," and "valleys" are ways of making what you're saying exciting, so that the jurors want to continue listening to *your* point of view, not opposing counsel's.

How to create a compelling vicarious experience for the jurors by using "color"

In addition to making otherwise uninspiring testimony inspiring, color brings an event right into the Courtroom, through the power of the voice. When the jurors are in the jury box, they cannot see the event you are describing, they cannot experience that awful/triumphant/heartbreaking moment, unless you make that moment happen for them. Only if you make that moment real for them, will you be persuasive. Color is how to bring a moment to life, vocally. Color is literally, painting pictures with your voice.

How to manipulate words in order to create color

How is this accomplished? You give life to a word by making it sound like what it *means*. As Oliver Wendell Holmes so beautifully put it: "A word is the skin of a living thought and may vary greatly in color and content according to the circumstances and time in which it is used." Attending to the meaning, the thought, which the word represents is how you give a word *power*.

Technically, color is achieved by either stretching the word (lengthening it), or shortening the word. Words such as "hit" or "kick" are shortened, to give a vocal rendition of a blow, words such as "lonely" or "painful" are stretched, lengthened to give them an aspect of suffering. The word must not simply be lengthened or shortened, however, you must try to put into the word what its value is. How boring can you make the word "boring" sound? How hurt can you make the word "hurt" sound? If you really *think* about what you are saying, you'll find you do this quite naturally. It is only when we speak without truly attending to our choice of words that we lose the dimension of color.

CASE IN POINT

Let's take the following sentence as an example:

"John's headaches have been going on a long, long time."

Try stretching the word "long" by stretching the "ng" sound. Make the word "long" sound long. Now say "long" in the context of the sentence, taking care only to stretch the first "long," leaving the second one alone. Do this out loud.

If you absolutely do not raise your volume when you color the word "long," you will very effectively have brought the sentence to life *without* resorting to melodramatic effect. You will have helped the jury feel just what is going on with John in a sincere and believable way.

CAUTION Do not stretch the vowel sounds (a,e,i,o,u) when lengthening a word. Stretching vowel sounds is what you do when you sing, and singing is inappropriate for a Courtroom. Work the consonants, consonants are the meat of the word, consonants are what give a word texture and definition.

How to use color to get the jurors to react emotionally to a point

Color is a useful alternative to the pause in emphasizing a point, especially when you have several important elements in one sentence. You can use the pause to emphasize some points, and color to emphasize others. The rule of thumb as to when to choose color rather than the pause to emphasize, is as follows:

Use color when the emphasis is a more emotional one, when you want the jurors to react emotionally to a point, use the pause when you are looking for a more cerebral or logical reaction.

CASE IN POINT

Let's go back to our earlier example:

"The car was going 80 miles per hour when it hit the child."

You can make the word "hit" sound like a blow, by shortening the word, and giving the final "t" emphasis. Now, phrase the statement, and use color on the word "hit":

"The car was going 80 mph/ when it **hit** the child."

You can almost feel the impact.

As you develop your case, as you think about how you want to present your case to the jury, think in terms of coloring words, of really giving words their true value, so as to make your speech more alive, more exciting.

How to practice using color

In addition to the color worksheet included at the end of the chapter, an easy way to practice coloring is to work with a romance or adventure novel. Romance and adventure novels are loaded with "color" words, since their very goal is to bring an adventure to life with words. Very deliberately, and with exaggeration, make as many of the words from the novel sound like what they mean as you possibly can. Do this out loud, one word at a time. Then, once you've practised in exaggerated fashion for about ten to fifteen minutes, forget about it.

As you do this exercise on a daily basis, you'll find your everyday speech becoming more interesting, richer, more varied, *without your making any special effort.* You are training yourself in a general fashion to attend to the value of words, to color, and this will quite naturally find its way into your daily speech. So although you practice in exaggerated fashion, you end up coloring subtly.

How to keep the jurors interested and attentive by using "peaks" and "valleys"

There is nothing worse than trying to listen to someone speaking in a monotone. Even if the content of your speech is riveting, it is very difficult to stay tuned into, and attentive to a monotonous voice. You must keep the jurors interested and attentive if you are to persuade them. Simply put, a monotonous voice is death to your argument. In addition, you are faced with an inescapable reality: the shortness of adult attention. You may be fascinated and wide awake for hours on end as you speak, but that's no guarantee the jurors are. Vocal variety is a constant challenge.

How to create peaks and valleys that work

Peaks and valleys are important ways of keeping people listening to you. Peaks and valleys are slight changes in your basic pitch. In other words, you have a basic pitch level, with which you are comfortable, but within that level, you need variety. In order to accomplish this, you raise some words up a bit ("peaks"), and drop others down a bit ("valleys"). "A bit" here means about a one-note value on a musical scale (Illustration 4).

The peak has a dual function: it both keeps the jurors attentive by the simple fact of pitch variety, and brings attention to a word in the same way a pause or coloring do. It is the vocal equivalent of underlining a word in red.

3–4

CASE IN POINT

Going back to an earlier example: "The car was going 80 mph when it hit the child," let's say that the speed of the car has already been established, so now you just want to remind the jurors of that fact.

Simply raise the "80 mph" in this case:

"The car was going '80 mph' when it hit the child."

You have brought attention to the relevant point, but in subtle fashion (Illustration 5).

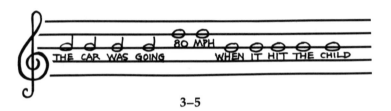

3–5

Be careful to drop back down to your basic pitch; don't allow the peak to seduce you into a higher-than-normal-pitch once the word has been said.

"Valleys" are roughly one-note *drops* of a word or a phrase. Valleys are often used with personal comments or information deemed important but not crucial.

CASE IN POINT

Let's look at the statement:

"This photograph, as a matter of fact, was added to the evidence just today."

The phrase "as a matter of fact" represents a personal comment, and as such, would be dropped slightly in pitch.

Taking a different example:

"This photograph, already entered in evidence, shows John on April 2, 1979."

Since the entire phrase "already entered in evidence" represents information already noted, and not crucial at the moment, it is dropped slightly in pitch (Illustration 6).

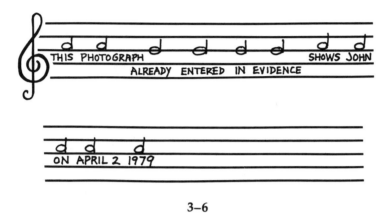

3–6

Peaks and valleys, in order to become a natural part of your speech, must be practiced. The worksheets at the end of the chapter provide you with sentences which are best practiced out loud. Use a tape recorder to help you determine when you are truly raising a word, or lowering your pitch. Although it takes patience and practice, vocal variety is well worth the effort. There's nothing quite as reassuring as an awake, alert jury, attentive to your every word.

Technique 4: Use the Five Senses to Recreate a Scene Vividly and Persuasively for the Jury

Bringing a scene to life relies not only on the use of color, as described above, but also on your choice of words. For the jurors to be persuaded, they must be moved, as we shall see in detail in Chapter 7, and in order to be moved by a scene, they must experience it. The jurors must experience the event as if they were there, feel your client's suffering as if it were their own, his outrage as if it were theirs.

How do we experience an event? Through our five senses. "Experiencing an event" is actually the synthesis of how we see, hear, touch, taste and smell that event. Depending on the event, some of the senses are more prominent than others: sight, hearing and touch are almost always included. When you describe an event, then, deliberately choose words and phrases which engage the senses.

How to choose words and phrases that powerfully engage the jurors' senses

---

CASE IN POINT

Let's say that the information you need to convey about your client is as follows:

"John lies in his hospital bed, paralyzed from the neck down."

It may be intellectually sufficient to give the jurors the information in such a straightforward unembellished statement, but it does not allow the jurors to experience the truth of John's life as he lives it.

Choose words and phrases to engage the senses, such as:

"John lies in his hospital bed very still, a fly buzzes in front of his face, but he cannot shoo it away, despite the annoying sound; the sun pours brightly onto his bed, he can see it and the sight warms his heart, but it does not warm his body, because he cannot feel it; the phone rings beside his bed, John looks longingly at the phone, but he cannot pick up the receiver: John can't do a lot of things we all take for granted. John is paralyzed from the neck down."

Certainly, engaging the senses takes a good deal more work and effort than simple sharing of information. However, information in and of itself is rarely persuasive, and if you are to win, you must persuade.

Practice describing events to friends and family using all five senses. You will undoubtedly find that you use some of the senses to the exclusion of others. Try to work with all the senses, so that you can make an experience as rich as possible for the listener. Bear in mind that by engaging the senses, you not only make it easier for yourself to persuade, you also are more interesting to listen to, and if the jurors are attentive, they are much more likely to get your point.

Technique 5: Use Emotions Appropriately In Order to Sway the Jurors

Emotions: properly used, they are a primary tool of persuasion; improperly used, they are a primary tool of dissuasion. If you don't convey feeling in your arguments, you appear robot-like, unconnected to the rest of the human race, more importantly, unconnected to the world as the jurors know it. If you use emotions melodramatically, you come across as insincere, phony, and the jurors won't believe you. Emotions must be used with care, but must be used. Emotion, as we will see in Chapter 7, is critical to the jurors' decision-making process, and therefore critical to your ability to persuade.

How to choose specific emotions to convince the jurors of your point

The first step in using emotion is to determine which emotion it is that you want the listener to feel. If you want the listener to feel outrage, then **you** must sound outraged; if you want the listener to feel pleased, then **you** must sound pleased.

CASE IN POINT

Let's look at which emotions would be appropriate in the previously used example:

"John lies in his hospital bed very still, a fly buzzes in front of his face, but he cannot shoo it away, despite the annoying sound; the sun pours brightly onto his bed, he can see it and the sight warms his heart, but it does not warm his body, because he cannot feel it; the phone rings beside his bed, John looks longingly at the phone, but he cannot pick up the receiver: John can't do a lot of things we all take for granted. John is paralyzed from the neck down."

There are several emotions here to choose. For example, you could use *annoyance* through the phrase "a fly buzzes in front of his face," feelings of *contented pleasure* through the phrase "he can see it and the sight warms his heart," and *longing* through the phrase "John looks longingly at the phone." These emotions will help the jurors connect to John's experience.

Notice that I did not choose to convey emotion through the whole statement. A little emotion goes a long way. Specifically, avoid putting emotions on phrases which are already highly emotional, just by virtue of their content. I deliberately did not put emotion through the phrases "but he cannot shoo it away," "because he cannot feel it," "but he cannot pick up the receiver," because these phrases already have plenty of emotional impact purely on an information level.

How to use your voice to convey emotion persuasively to the jurors

Emotion must not only be chosen properly, it must also be carried through your voice. In other words, the jurors must perceive the emotion *you* wish them to perceive, and not something else. In order to find out if you are indeed conveying the emotion you wish to convey, practice saying phrases with different choices of emotion into a tape recorder, then play back the tape: were you successful? Can you recognize in your voice the emotions you chose? This is a skill which takes some time to develop, but which is wonderfully effective.

Keep talking into the tape recorder and listening to the feedback until you are easily able to express the emotion of your choice. A list of different emotions is given at the end of the chapter. This is by no means a list of all emotions, but has been included to give you an idea of the diversity of emotions available to you, which you may want to consider using. Some emotions will be more difficult for you to convey than others, these require more practise.

How to avoid losing your case by being melodramatic

Emotion only becomes melodrama when it is inappropriately used. Unfortunately, emotion is inappropriately used a great deal. For example, a broken leg is cause for annoyance, irritation, certainly frustration, but it is not cause for heartrending grief. So if in speaking of your client's broken leg, you adopt a tone of profound grief, you will be misusing emotion in the worst way, and succumbing to excesses of melodrama. On the other hand, if you rattle off a child's death deliberately caused by a sadistic killer as if you were measuring out oatmeal for breakfast, you also misuse emotion in the worst way; by not using it.

The use of emotion is very simply governed by *appropriateness*. All you need to do to avoid melodrama is choose the emotion which fits your content; if anything, underplay a little, choose an emotion slightly less powerful, if you are afraid of becoming melodramatic. Do, however, use emotion. Just because it must be used cautiously does not mean you should avoid it. On the contrary, the fact that emotion must be used cautiously reflects its enormous power, and you should avail yourself of that power.

Technique 6: The Build-Drop: A Master Technique for Creating Dramatic Effect to Emphasize a Major Point *without* Appearing Theatrical

There is no place in today's Courtroom for rhetorical flights of fancy. If you wish to create dramatic effect, you must somehow do that subtly. Any effect that smacks of theatricality will also smack of phony, and must be avoided. The build-drop is a very effective technique which without seeming dramatic, has a very dramatic effect.

How to create a build-drop

The build-drop consists of a set-up, and the point you want to get across. The set-up is whatever information leads up to your important point, and is delivered with consistently rising pitch. The point you want to get across is delivered with a drop in pitch.

CASE IN POINT

Let's do a build-drop using the statement:

"John can't do a lot of things we all take for granted. John is paralyzed from the neck down."

Your *set up* would be "John can't do a lot of things we all take for granted": your *important point* would be "John is paralyzed from the neck down."

The build-drop would be said like this: (Illustration 7).

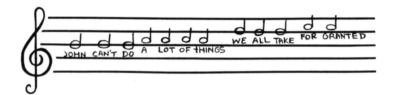

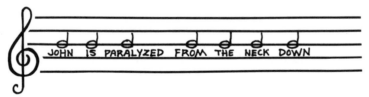

3–7

The set up is *built up* in pitch, then there is a *pause*, then the important point is *dropped down* in pitch.

Let's take another example, this time within a single sentence:

"John is paralyzed from the neck down."

Here the *set up* is "John is paralyzed," then comes your pause, then the *important point* "from the neck down" (Illustration 8).

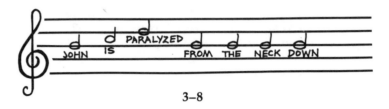

3–8

In delivering a build-drop, *do not* alter your volume for the important point, or you will lose all subtlety.

How to use the build-drop in a question/answer format

The build-drop is often effectively used with a question answer format: "Did Mary run from the scene of the crime? No." The set up is the entire question, then comes the pause, then the word "no" (Illustration 9).

As long as you don't alter your volume, you will have created dramatic

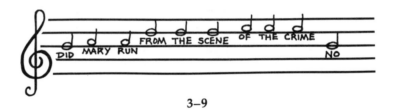

3–9

effect with great subtlety and persuasiveness. Bear in mind that because the build-drop is dramatic, it must not be overused. Reserve it for statements which really need to be delivered with maximum impact.

SUMMARY

There is nothing worse than having to strain to understand or hear someone. Curing your mumbles will guarantee that you will be easily and effectively heard. Correcting your speech for pitch, pace, volume and articulation is a necessary first step. Using pauses, phrasing, color, peaks and valleys will further the effectiveness of your speech. Using *emotion* will then make your words truly persuasive.

TONGUE TWISTERS WORKSHEET

Do the following tongue twisters as described in the text, going for the muscular development of your lips and tongue, rather than for speed.

Bim comes, Ben comes, Bim brings Ben's broom, Ben brings Bim's broom, Ben bends Bim's broom, Bim bends Ben's broom, Bim and Ben's broom bends, Ben's bent broom breaks, Bim's bent broom breaks, Ben's broom is broke, Bim's broom is broke, both brooms are broke.

When beetles fight these battles with their paddles in a bottle and the bottle's on a poodle and the poodle's eating noodles they call this muddlepuddle tweedle poodle beatle noodle battle paddle bottle.

A maid in Grathum mum once played the national anthem mum and broke a chrysanthemum mum.

Which is the witch that wished the wicked wish?

If a doctor doctored another doctor would the doctor doing the doctoring doctor the other doctor in the way the doctored doctor wanted to be doctored?

A tooter who tooted a flute tried to tutor two tooters to toot. Said the two to the tooter is it harder to toot or to tutor two tooters to toot?

Leith listlessly lisps and lips lots of lengthy lectures.

Never need nine of nothing not new nor old.

If Roland Reynolds rolled a round roll round a round room, where is the round roll which Roland Reynolds rolled round the room?

Whether the weather be fine or whether the weather be not, whether the weather be cold or whether the weather be hot, well we'll go whatever the weather, whether we like it or not.

Freshly fried flesh of fresh fried fishes is fine for fat folk.

Gailey gathered the gleaners the glossy golden grain and garned it gladly in granny's great grainery in Godfrey's green grassy glen.

The monk's monkey got in the ink, the monk's monkey drank it. The monk woke up his uncle. He thought it was a prank, ink the monkey drank.

One violet winkle veering west was Worthington went working around Vermont.

Triangular tangle gangs that wangle anger Tommy Prangle, they're from a jungle Prangle says, but not to be outfangled.

Who sews crows clothes, Sue sews crows clothes, Slow Joe Crow sews who's clothes, Sue's clothes, Sue sews socks of fox-in-socks, now Slow Joe Crow sews socks of fox-in-socks, now Sue sews roses on Slow Joe Crow's clothes.

PAUSES WORKSHEET

Try pausing at different places in the sentences below, and see how you vary the importance of what you are saying according to where you have placed your pause. Remember a pause brings attention to what **follows** it.

1. Was the speed of the vehicle excessive?

2. Mr. Smith was traveling at 95 mph.

3. This is a dangerous stretch of road.

4. Mr. Smith hit the child at that speed.

5. Mrs. Jones only visited her doctor twice.

6. The impact could not have caused that much damage.

7. Was Mrs. Jones in danger?

8. Whose handwriting is that, Doctor?

9. Mr. Smith was driving 75 mph at the time but he was not drunk.

10. There was kind of a bump in the road.

PHRASING WORKSHEET

Try phrasing the sentences below so that you really make sense of what you are saying. Experiment with different choices of phrasing until you are satisfied.

1. How could Mrs. Smith forget to get her brakes fixed?

2. According to Dr. Jones, Mr. Smith's injuries are minimal.

3. Mr. Jones attempted a right hand turn from the left hand lane.

4. We do not know just when Mrs. Smith arrived on the scene.

5. So whatever information the doctor gets is from the patient himself if he is able to talk?

6. Was Mr. Smith driving erratically at the time or did he swerve to avoid the child?

7. Mr. Smith did not have time to come to an appropriate stop or he wasn't paying attention.

8. Was he speeding when he hit the side of the barn?

9. You stated in your deposition that you had brought the documents to Mr. Jones before the meeting June 8th is that correct?

10. You stated previously that you were in the vicinity of the plant at approximately 9:15 am which was the time of the explosion did you not?

COLOR WORKSHEET

Make the words you want to emphasize in the following sentences sound like what they mean. For example: make the word "pain" sound **painful**. Be careful not to use volume to do this.

1. At this particular area, there are no curves in the road, it is relatively flat: is that correct?

2. Then you weren't speeding at the time, you were paying attention to your driving.

3. And were there any complications on this repair job?

4. There were treatments given in an effort to strengthen the leg and restore proper motion.

5. The headaches occur daily, the duration being as long as an hour or two.

6. Mrs. Jones has noticed that her husband, previously a happy, thoughtful man, is now nervous and preoccupied.

7. The photographs will show the severity of the impact.

8. It was a clear, bright day: driving conditions were excellent.

9. There was never any discussion as to the implications of the new will.

10. The head trauma was severe, no doubt, however I am not convinced that Mr. Jones's distress is solely a consequence of that injury.

PEAKS AND VALLEYS WORKSHEET

Find as many *peaks* (raising a given word) and *valleys* (dropping a word or phrase down in pitch) as you can in the following sentences. Have fun with this exercise, exaggerate to get the feel of peaks and valleys.

1. Ladies and gentlemen, the evidence shows that my client did not embezzle the funds.

2. Mr. Smith will never walk properly again.

3. Dr. Beck is a highly reputable physician, whose standing in the medical community is well known.

4. Mrs. Jones sustained severe injuries and is still under medical supervision.

5. Is it your opinion that Mr. Jones was traveling in a reasonable manner?

6. You wouldn't know whether Mrs. Smith stopped at the stop sign, would you?

7. I am confident that the evidence will show Mr. Jones did sustain a bump on the head and was rendered unconscious because of it.

8. There is nothing in the evidence to substantiate Mrs. Herbert's claim.

9. Late in the afternoon of May 30, Mr. Jones was seen talking with Mr. Ames, which needless to say put him in a very embarrassing position with his own department.

10. There is no excuse, ladies and gentlemen of the jury, for the shabby treatment my client has endured in the course of this trial.

EMOTIONS LIST

The following is a list of emotions for you to work with in the Emotions Worksheet, and when practicing with romance and/or adventure novels. It is not a complete list of all emotions, simply a list to give you an idea of the emotional range available to you in your work.

happy	serene	at peace
wonderful	indifferent	bored
depressed	disappointed	anxious
nervous	uneasy	scared
angry	hostile	embarrassed
heartbroken	distressed	pessimistic
confused	troubled	helpless
hopeless	ridiculed	criticized
belittled	devastated	trapped
jittery	awkward	outraged
concerned	worried	desperate
annoyed	irritated	puzzled

EMOTIONS WORKSHEET

Select an emotion from the "Emotions List," and say one of the sentences below deliberately making your voice carry the emotion you chose. Tape record yourself and listen carefully when you play back the recording: does your voice indeed convey the emotion you chose? If not, try again. Then pick a different emotion from the "Emotions List," and say the same sentence as before, but with your voice carrying the new emotion. Tape record yourself again, and listen. Do you hear a distinct difference? Were you able to clearly convey the second emotion you picked? If so, great. If not, try again. Then pick a third emotion and repeat the exercise. When you have run as many emotions as you want through a sentence, go on to another sentence and follow the same procedure.

Patience and persistence are the key to learning how to persuade with your voice. So, practice! You'll be impressed with the results.

1. The impact was very minor.

2. To put it another way, 4-year-old children are simply not responsible.

3. Doctor, would you describe the results of your operation as a failure?

4. Now do you remember these questions being asked of you and the answers given?

5. The facts of the case are relatively uncomplicated.

6. Maybe Mr. Smith was drunk at the time.

7. He impacted the car because he was traveling 45 mph in a 15 mph zone.

8. Mr. Smith was drunk at the time and he was speeding.

9. Mrs. Smith did hit the side of the barn but she was not speeding.

10. Perhaps Mr. Jones was careless in forgetting to turn his lights on.

CHAPTER 4

Creating Rapport to Get the Jurors' Approval and Cooperation

Twelve blank faces stare out at you, waiting to hear what you have to say, waiting to see how you measure up, if you're any better than the attorney representing the other side. Twelve strangers, whom you must convince to adopt your point of view rather than opposing counsel's. But how are you going to do it? How are you going to persuade these 12 unknowns, that you're right and he's wrong? The truth of the matter is, if they remain strangers, you will not succeed. Persuasion is based on trust, and people trust those who are familiar to them. If you are to succeed, then you must start, not by trying to convince the jury of your version of the facts of the case, but by becoming familiar to the jurors, by winning the jury's trust.

Whom do we trust? We trust people we know and feel comfortable with, those with whom we have "rapport." Rapport means relationship: the creation of rapport means entering into a "sympathetic relationship"[1] with an individual. When we say so-and-so has "good rapport" with a person, we mean he relates easily with that person, seems to understand the person, gets along well with the person. When you create rapport, what you are doing in essence is establishing trust. Without trust, there can be no persuasion.

CASE IN POINT

All those bad jokes about the stereotypical used car salesman are really reflections of the used car salesman's failure to create rapport. The salesman is trying to get you to trust him regarding the worth of a car (and

127

therefore persuade you of the purchase) before any rapport has been developed. That's virtually impossible. There is no relationship, how can there possibly be any trust?

Usually, the tighter the relationship, the greater the degree of trust. The closer you are to someone, the more likely you are to trust him. And in turn, the more you trust someone, the more likely you are to allow yourself to be persuaded by that person. Your best friend, for example, has a great deal more influence on you than the checker at the grocery store. Your first task, then, is not to persuade the jury of anything, but to enter into a sympathetic relationship with the jurors which will, in turn, engender their trust.

You do not, however, have unlimited time or situations in which to do this. The friendship you have with your best friend probably took years to develop and grew out of the many experiences you shared together; you don't have the benefit of pre-trial years with the jurors, and you'll only be seeing them in Court. You cannot therefore expect rapport to manifest itself spontaneously with the jurors in the way it did with your best friend. You must rely on other ways of developing a close and trusting relationship. This chapter is devoted to how to create a relationship with the jurors similar in persuasive power to that you have with your best friend, given the structural and time limitations of the Courtroom.

HOW TO GET THE JURORS ON YOUR SIDE BY CREATING COMMON GROUND

People relate best and most easily to that which is familiar to them.

CASE IN POINT

The secretary you've had for ten years is familiar to you, you know how she works, you can depend on her to do certain things consistently very well, and you can equally depend on her to do certain things not so well. You may or may not like her, but you know her. Ever noticed how your life changes when your secretary is on vacation and you hire temporary help? The temp may be a lovely person, but she's an unfamiliar entity, and you don't know whether she will file things in the right places, and type briefs on time, much less with what degree of accuracy. Anything she does differently from your regular secretary will make you uncomfortable. You feel like there's a guest in the office, not a team-mate.

Novelty causes uncertainty and conflict, which may be stimulating in certain situations, but not in the already anxiety producing situation jurors find themselves in. There, the unfamiliar will only cause discomfort.

If people relate comfortably to that which is familiar to them, what does that imply? That people relate best to that which is *similar* to themselves, because they know themselves better than anything or anyone else.

CASE IN POINT

If you like baseball, and you find yourself among a group of people all enthusiastically talking baseball, you'll feel right at home, and decide that these are terrific people you could easily become friends with, after all, you have a lot in common. If, on the other hand, you find yourself with a group of people raving about soccer, who don't say anything against baseball, but are completely indifferent to your baseball enthusiasm, you probably won't stick around, you'll find it difficult to relate to them, you have nothing in common.

This ties in with a very interesting result from communications research: when people don't know you, if in the beginning you clearly indicate that your own position is in accord with theirs, people are more likely to accept your message, *even if your message actually ends up being quite different from that original position.*

Aligning your initial position with that of those you wish to influence is known as "establishing common ground." It puts you on their side, you become one of them, thus more acceptable. Once you've established common ground, you can lead people to your point of view with far greater ease and effectiveness. Persuasion, then, can be thought of as a process, which starts from the establishment of common ground (similarities), which creates familiarity, which facilitates rapport (relationship), which engenders trust, which is the precursor to persuasion. Bear in mind, however, that this is an additive process. The psychological aspects of persuasion will only be effective if you've established your credibility and expertness as described in the previous chapters, but if those *have* been established, then the psychological dimension will greatly enhance your persuasive power.

CASE IN POINT

Let me share with you a particularly brilliant example of how a trial attorney established common ground. Norman H. Sheresky relates how: "Once, during the course of a trial in New York City during early summer, Bruno Schachner, an old and respected trial warrior, arose and suggested to the court that the jury would be more comfortable if they were permitted to remove their jackets. The trial judge became infuriated and told the jury that the suggestion was improper; that Mr. Schachner could not care less if the jurors fried in hell, and that he was only trying to solicit their favor.

"The tirade was so stern," recounts Sheresky, "that I, as associate counsel, felt the perspiration pouring down my sleeves. Schachner replied, 'Your Honor, I had no idea that my suggestion would be considered improper, but if it was, I most respectfully apologize to you and particularly to the jury.' Upon which he sat down and whispered in my ear, 'Screw him, look at the jury; they love me.'" [2]

The jury loved Schachner because he had definitively sided with them. He had established common ground, "it's hot, I'm hot, you must be hot," and by doing so made himself one of them.

HOW TO INCREASE YOUR PERSUASIVENESS BY TREATING THE JURORS AS EQUALS

Let's look for a moment at the level of relationship you must create in order to be persuasive. Rapport implies mutuality. A sympathetic relationship is one that goes both ways. Research in the area of social power has demonstrated that your ability to persuade someone is far more effective when the acceptance is reciprocal, in other words, when you accept the jurors as much as they accept you. The jurors must feel that you are *with* them, that you are working side by side with them, guiding them through your version of the facts. Notice I did not say teaching them, or instructing them. Most adults do not like to be told what to do, it damages our self-esteem. We like to think we are reasonably intelligent, and given a little supportive assistance, can understand enough to make up our own minds. The Judge can get away with telling the jurors what to do, in their eyes, he's anointed, but you can't, you've not been conferred such an honor. If you are to persuade the jurors, you must treat them as equals, and you must treat them with respect.

If you respect the jurors, they will respect you, it's that simple. If you talk down to the jurors, a common attorney trait, the jurors will rebel by not attending to you. Jurors interviewed in jury studies often complain of being treated as if they were stupid or retarded. Treat the jurors like idiots, and they will promptly turn toward someone who treats them better. Validate their self-worth by treating them as equals, and they will reward you with trust and acceptance.

HOW TO CREATE RAPPORT BY EMPHASIZING SIMILARITIES BETWEEN YOURSELF AND THE JURORS

Once your jury has been selected, tailor the presentation of your case to that very specific jury. Do not assume even if the selection process has yielded a jury basically favorable to your client, that you can stop there. On the contrary, your work has only just begun.

Rapport is not a generic concept; rapport must be created differently for every case, because every jury is different. Create rapport with the jurors by emphasizing the similarities between yourself and them, both verbally and non-verbally.

We all have different aspects to our personalities. There are times when you are more formal than others, times when you are willing to unwind and act silly, times when you're quiet and reflective. In order to emphasize the similarities between yourself and the jurors, express the facet of your personality that is most like the dominant personality of the jury as a whole. You are not being someone you are not, adopting a phony persona for the benefit of the trial, that would be virtually impossible, and quite frankly, ineffective unless you are a actor on a par with Dustin Hoffman. You are simply choosing to express that part of yourself which most closely resembles the character of the jury. This will make the jury feel more comfortable with you, you will be like them, and they will be more open to your arguments.

CASE IN POINT

William P. Allison of Lynch, Zimmerman, White & Allison in Austin, Texas, gives an excellent example of what happens when you ignore this precept: "The out-of-town defense lawyers walked into the modest West Texas courtroom dressed in their finest, most expensive apparel. The jurors came from the community, and they wore calico and overalls. The case was the corruption trial of the Speaker of the Texas House of Representatives, but because of the environment of the trial, it became the case of the Brooks Brothers lawyers versus the Sears, Roebuck jurors. The well-dressed defense lawyers lost, and so did the Speaker of the House." [3]

The point is not that the defense attorneys should have come in wearing overalls and affecting a West Texas dialect, this would have been imitation, not identification. Rather the defense attorneys should have recognized the less formal, down to earth character of the jury as a whole, and emphasized their own less formal, down to earth side. By choosing to ignore the issue of rapport and failing to make the jurors comfortable by emphasizing the similarities between the jurors and themselves, the defense lawyers lost.

How to Win the Jurors' Favor by "Mirroring"

How could these defense lawyers have emphasized the similarities between themselves and the jurors? By a process called "mirroring." Mirroring is a technique whereby you reflect physically and vocally another individual's physical attitudes and vocal characteristics. The four main areas where mirroring is used are dress, body language, voice, and vocabulary.

How to use dress to emphasize similarities between yourself and the jurors

Since Mr. Allison focused on dress in his comments, let's first take a look at how mirroring would apply to the defense attorneys' dress. The jury panel was down to earth, wearing overalls and calico. Reflecting the simple homespun quality of this style, the defense attorneys could have worn a suit without the vest, leaving the jacket unbuttoned, a suit appropriate to the local weather both in cloth and color. This attire would have reflected or "mirrored" the jurors' values.

The operative word here is reflect, not imitate. People are highly offended by imitation of themselves; too often imitation feels like mockery and it is invariably phony. When, however, you reflect the predominant tone of body language, dress and voice, you point out in nonverbal fashion the likenesses between you and the jury, making yourself easier for the jurors to identify with, without denying your own personality.

The process is as follows:

1. Research the jurors' background

Do your research, figure out how the jury is likely to dress given the community, time of year, and socio-economic background of the jurors.

2. Select your wardrobe appropriately for mirroring

Select from your wardrobe clothes which express the side of you that is more like the jury, still staying appropriately dressed as an attorney. Vary your dress according to your jury: ask yourself, "How can I dress to make this jury feel I am one of them, while retaining my professionalism?" The above example illustrates how a male attorney can dress more casually, yet still be appropriately professional. For a female attorney, a homespun quality could be reflected in a suit or dress of simple design and color: this would not be the time to make a fashion statement. Jewelry would be kept to a minimum and be simple, hair and make-up would be traditional and conservative. If you are a male attorney working with a more urban, upper socio-economic, corporate type of jury panel, for example, a three-piece suit is appropriate, in dark grey or dark blue.

3. Adjust your wardrobe to your specific jury

If you thought, based on your research, that the jurors would be conservatively dressed, but in their Sunday best, and when you walked in, dressed in your best three-piece going-to-meeting suit, they were in jeans, plaid shirts, and cowboy boots—adjust. Unbutton your jacket for now, and tomorrow, show up in a suit without the vest, maybe of a lighter color. In addition, bear in mind that the jurors start out as 12 strangers, but end up as a close-knit group. In the beginning, rely on your research for appropriate dress, but as the trial continues, notice how the jurors will start to dress in similar fashion amongst themselves, and start adapting your wardrobe to what is now a group norm. Stay flexible and use your common sense.

How to mirror with body language to create a relationship of acceptance and trust with the jurors

Dress is the easiest way to mirror, and certainly contributes importantly to the jurors' first impression of you. It is however, generic, in the sense that you're stuck with mirroring the jury as a whole, and cannot really use the mirroring to more specific ends. Mirroring body language and voice, however, is very different, as body language and voice mirrors can be used to achieve particular objectives.

Mirroring body language is based on the same principle as mirroring dress: reflection, not imitation. If, for example, you wish to facilitate a prospective juror's cooperation in voir dire, start by mirroring his body language. First, notice if his body is shifted forward or back. Reflect that position. Notice the placement of his head, arms and legs, and allow your body position to suggest similar placement. Do not copy the exact body position. That will look stupid and be resented. Take your time in fitting your body language to his. Start with the overall body shift, then, for example, let the head be placed, then the arms. Don't try to mirror a whole body posture all it once, it doesn't work. Mirrors are highly effective nonverbal tools but they must be created with subtlety in order to be successful. Illustrations 1 through 3 demonstrate how to accomplish a successful mirror, with the female attorney mirroring the male witness.

Mirrors do more than emphasize the similarities between yourself and the person you are mirroring. Mirrors are a tremendously, tremendously powerful way of establishing your acceptance of an individual. In Chapter 2, it was pointed out that body language is believed over words: whenever there is a discrepancy between your stated message and your

4–1

4–2

4–3

body language, your body language will be believed, not your statement. By adopting an individual's body language, you have nonverbally stated, "Mr. Jones, whoever you are is fine by me. I accept you exactly as you are, and show my acceptance of your present being by conforming to your physical attitudes and postures." Because the communication is nonverbal, it will be believed.

There's nothing quite like acceptance to make people feel worthy. Total acceptance is the very essence of unconditional love. Think what power unconditional love has: using the same principle uses the same power, albeit to a different degree. When you mirror your prospective juror, you nonverbally validate him as he is, and this acceptance encourages him to be open to you, to give you what you want. If, as you go along questioning him, his body language changes, you can continue mirroring the changes if you wish to solidify rapport. Mirroring is most important, however, at the beginning of the interaction, to establish acceptance and rapport initially.

CAUTION Be careful to mirror changes slowly, and with somewhat of a lag. If the juror puts his hand on his chest and you instantly let your hand fly to your chest, the juror is going to know something fishy is going on. You are communicating acceptance, not playing "monkey-see, monkey-do." The distinction is important.

Anytime you wish to establish rapport, you can do so with mirroring body language. This applies to witnesses as well as jurors.

1. How to use body language mirroring to obtain cooperation from an uncooperative witness

What do you do, however, when faced with an uncooperative witness? Proceed no differently: mirror. This may sound very strange, but it works. If the witness sits there, shifted somewhat back in his chair, holding onto the chair arms defensively, a dour expression on his face, do not attempt to warm him up by smiling and opening up your arms, he'll trust you even less. No, rather adopt his body language, shift your body back, maybe cross your arms to suggest the defensiveness of his chair-arm grip, and allow your face to assume a serious concerned look. At least you're now playing in the same ball park. You're not rejecting his unhappiness, you're accepting it, and continuing nonetheless.

CASE IN POINT

Think how awful it feels when someone comes up to you when you're depressed, and claps you on the back, saying with a great big smile "Cheer up, old boy, things can't be that bad!" Oh, yes they can. And the last thing you will feel like doing is opening up to this fellow who obviously doesn't understand anything. If, on the other hand, someone comes up to you quietly, standing a little stooped, just as you are, and says, with a serious and concerned look on his face in a gentle way, "Cheer up, old boy, things can't be that bad," you'll probably open right up, and say "Oh yes they can." The message is the same, but the body language of the second person gave you permission to be you, and so you are willing to open up (Illustration 4).

4–4

Try this on friends and family before taking it out to the courtroom, you'll be surprised at how effective the technique is.

2. How to use reverse body language mirroring to make a witness anxious and uneasy

If mirroring an individual's body language implies acceptance, then not mirroring an individual's body language implies rejection, and can be used as such. Let's say you want to make a witness anxious and uneasy. Simply fail to mirror his body language. Reverse it, as it were. If the witness is sitting comfortably shifted back, relaxed, arms simply resting on the chair arms, shift your body forward, cross your arms, tense your body overall somewhat. The witness won't know what is going on, but he won't feel accepted, and not knowing why he's being nonverbally rejected, he'll get uneasy.

Anytime you need to close someone off, or reject them, remember the power of body language. Countering someone's body language is a far more subtle and effective rejection technique than raising your voice or resorting to rudeness.

3. How to use mirroring to convince a whole jury

If you wish to create rapport, when addressing the jury as a whole, adopt a physical posture which reflects the predominant physical attitudes of the jurors. You'll find that the jurors as a whole are either relaxed and casual, or uptight and somewhat rigid, and so forth. Use the techniques given in Chapter 2 to shape your body language to suggest that same attitude, so as to create a nonverbal bond between yourself and the jurors.

Similarly, when listening to someone, if you want to create the feeling that you and the jury are listening together, that you are a unit, conform your body language to the predominant posture of the jurors. Anytime you wish to create, reinforce, or express the bond between yourself and the jurors, reflect their overall physical attitudes.

How to mirror a jury vocally to establish rapport

Mirroring is done with the voice just as it is done with the body. In order to create rapport with the jury as a whole, find out what the vocal pace of the community is. For example, urban dwellers often speak more quickly than country folk, take this into consideration if you were raised in the country and trying a case in a large city. Do not, however, affect an accent or dialect that is not your own. You are likely to sound fake and thus untrustworthy.

With an individual witness or juror, use vocal mirroring to establish rapport, and reverse vocal mirroring to prevent it.

CASE IN POINT

For example, if you wish to create rapport with your witness, an anxious middle-aged woman, who speaks in a quiet voice with many pauses because of her anxiety, then take more pauses when you speak, and ask your questions in a somewhat softer voice, to make her feel at ease and accepted.

If you wish to discomfit a witness, reverse the mirror. The same anxious witness can be easily rattled by your asking questions at a good clip, without many pauses, in a normal volume firm voice. This will be subtle enough not to be felt as abrasive by the jurors, but rejecting enough to produce further anxiety in the witness.

How to emphasize similarities with a jury by using a common vocabulary

Your training as an attorney is very literate. You are highly educated, and are used to words. You read and write more than almost any other profession. You deal in complex concepts all day long, and discuss your cases primarily with colleagues who are familiar with the same concepts. You tend, therefore to forget that the majority of Americans are not as well educated as you, and do not have the benefit of constant communion with higher level concepts and vocabulary.

I am not only referring to the use of "legalese." It is undoubtedly already clear to you that the use of professional jargon puts people seriously off. It makes you seem aloof and "better than": jurors don't warm up to the condescending attitude implied by the use of legalese. I am more specifically referring to your overall level of vocabulary, which by virtue of your education and work, is significantly more developed than that of the vast majority of your fellow-citizens. Furthermore, not all regions of the country employ the same expressions. Your usual mode of speech may include phrases which are not easily understood outside of your community. If you mirror the vocabulary level of the jury panel rather than expressing yourself with your habitual vocabulary, and monitor your expressions so they fit the community you're working in, you will accomplish three important objectives:

1. The jurors will have the energy to follow your argument

If the jurors are expending energy trying to understand your words or expressions, they will have very little energy left with which to understand your arguments. If your choice of vocabulary becomes too difficult for the jurors to follow, they will eventually give up. In addition, if a juror hears a word he doesn't understand, he will stay stuck on that word, trying to figure it out, and thus is likely to miss your next point. Be aware of the educational level and occupational status of the jurors and address yourself to them at that level: do not use expressions that may be unfamiliar to the jurors.

2. *The jurors will feel you are treating them with respect*

Respect, as we discussed earlier, reinforces acceptance. By using a vocabulary level and expressions readily accessible to the jurors, you are treating them as equals. You do not imply, by your language, that they are somehow inferior.

3. *You solidify the feeling that you are working with the jurors, that you are "one of them"*

The more the jurors feel you are their guide, working *with* them to understand the case, rather than manipulating them into a favorable decision, the stronger the rapport, and the better your ability to persuade. Speaking in words and expressions already familiar to the jurors makes them feel comfortable, makes you more acceptable to them, makes them more available to your point of view.

Part of your initial research on the community from which the jury panel will be selected should include research on the vocabulary and expressions indigenous to the area. Listen, during voir dire, to the actual words and expressions used by the prospective jurors. Tune into their level of understanding and get used to thinking at that level. Bear in mind that some juries will be highly literate, and so it is not an matter of scaling your vocabulary down, but rather attending to what is the *jury's* level, and addressing that level specifically.

CAUTION Both body language mirroring and vocal mirroring are very powerful communication techniques, and should not be dealt with lightly. Dress and vocabulary mirroring can be planned ahead and simply presented, body language and vocal mirroring must be performed in the heat of the moment. If your mirroring is clumsy, it will not enhance your persuasiveness. It is critical then, that you practice body language and vocal mirroring ahead of time. Worksheets are provided at the end of this chapter to help you. Practice mirroring with your family, friends, colleagues, and as many other people as possible before you start using it as a persuasion technique in court. With practice however, mirroring becomes second nature, and then is wonderfully effective. Practice is the key.

THE POWER OF "PERCEPTUAL MODES": HOW TO WIN THE JURORS' TRUST BY PERCEIVING THE WORLD THE SAME WAY THEY DO

The stronger the "kinship" you create between yourself and the jurors, the more easily they will allow themselves to be persuaded by you. It is therefore in your best interest to use every possible means of creating rapport. Remember that people relate best and most easily to that which is familiar to them. Well, communications research has recently demonstrated the power of the familiar in a most surprising context: "perceptual modes."

Perceptual modes are how we perceive the world; your perceptual mode determines the specific way you perceive the world. It seems we do not all perceive the world similarly. Of the three basic ways in which to perceive the world, people tend to favor one: we either see the world, hear it, or feel it. This is not to say that people who favor a visual mode, for example, only experience the world through their eyes, just that they first and predominantly experience the world in visual terms. Visually oriented persons certainly make use of the auditory and feeling modes, but only secondarily.

CASE IN POINT

If you went to Greece, for example, and wanted to persuade a Greek of something, you would attempt to speak in Greek. Trying to get the Greek to change over to English so that you could persuade him of whatever it is you had on your mind would be three times more work, and in all likelihood unsuccessful. The very idea seems foolish, yet we ignore each other's perceptual modes blithely, disregarding that they represent our internal language.

What does this imply in the Courtroom? If, for example, you address a prospective juror using the perceptual mode you know to be his, he will get the impression that you really understand him, after all, you view the world in the same way he does. You will be experienced by the witness as comfortable and familiar because, in a very profound sense, you are truly speaking the language that he speaks. This automatically makes him more trusting and accepting of you, more willing to cooperate. Attending to the juror's perceptual mode is a far more effective technique than remaining closed to it and relating to the witness via *your* perceptual mode regardless of whether it is the same as his or not.

How to Recognize the Jurors' Perception of the World

In order to effectively use perceptual modes in the Courtroom, you must first be able to recognize them. You can learn to do this quite easily, simply by listening to the words an individual chooses to express himself.

Recognizing visually oriented people

Visually oriented people perceive the world mainly through their eyes. They understand the world by how it *looks* to them. Visually oriented people use phrases such as:

I *see* what you mean

I'm *clear* on that

How does that *look* to you

I can't *picture* it

I need to get a better *perspective*

and so on. Visually oriented people tend to notice color and shape, and mention these when asked to describe something.

Recognizing auditory people

Auditory people perceive the world mainly through their ears. They understand the world in terms of how it *sounds*, and what its rhythms are. Auditory people use phrases such as:

I *hear* you (for "I understand you")

That *sounds* good to me

Let's *talk* about it

That *struck a chord* for me

It doesn't *ring a bell*

I didn't miss *a beat*

and so on. An auditory person comments on whether a person had a loud or soft voice, if a room is quiet or noisy, and is sensitive to such small auditory disturbances as noisy air conditioning units, or street noises.

Recognizing kinesthetic people

Kinesthetically oriented people perceive the world mainly through their *feelings*, through both the actual physical sense of touch and their internal feelings or emotions. A kinesthetic person speaks primarily in terms of how things feel to him, both on a tactile level and at an internal emotional level. Kinesthetic people will say:

I understand how you *feel*
That's a *heavy* problem
That's a *hot* idea
I'll be *in touch* with you
I want to *get a handle* on it
It's not *comfortable* for me

and so on. Kinesthetic people mention texture often, and include how they feel about something when describing it.

An awareness of perceptual modes allows you to avoid the kinds of communication difficulties that prevent the development of rapport.

CASE IN POINT

For example, think of what happens when a visually oriented attorney is valiantly trying to explain to a kinesthetically oriented juror how something looks, while the kinesthetically oriented juror is trying to figure out from how it looks, how it must feel. Under these conditions, rapport is difficult at best.

How to Use a Prospective Juror's Perceptual Mode Advantageously in Voir Dire

Now that you can easily recognize a perceptual mode, let's look at how to apply that knowledge in an area of concern to many attorneys, voir dire. Voir dire is the prospective juror's only dialogue with you, it is your one opportunity to speak with what may end up being a juror, on a one-to-one basis. Take advantage of this opportunity to build rapport.

In questioning a prospective juror, first of all, listen carefully to how he responds: if at all possible, ask a question which does not imply any particular perceptual mode, and pay attention to how he answers. If opposing counsel is questioning a juror, listen equally carefully. Then design your questions using the juror's perceptual mode. If he's visual, ask him how a given position "looks" to him: if auditory, how it "sounds" to him: if kinesthetic, how it "feels" to him. If you find, over the course of the next few questions, that you were off base, simply change to what now appears to be the correct choice of modes, and design the ensuing questions accordingly.

You can proceed in the same fashion with each prospective juror. The process is so subtle, that none of the other jurors listening will be aware of what is going on, yet you will be very effective. You can adopt a similar strategy with witnesses. Listen to determine the correct mode, then speak in that mode, make changes when necessary.

> *CAUTION A perceptual mode cannot necessarily be determined by the first few sentences out of someone's mouth. Listen for a while before you decide on which is the predominant mode. Be careful not to ask questions which slant the person's answer in a pre-determined perceptual mode. If you ask, for example, "Did you see the girl sitting in the car, Mr. Kane?" regardless of his orientation, Mr. Kane will reply in visual terms. Notice rather how he expresses himself in more open-ended questions, which do not imply any particular perceptual mode, and notice his word-preference over a period of time.*

In order to benefit from the rapport-building power of perceptual modes, you must be able to speak in all three of the modes easily and at will. This is accomplished only through diligent practice. Use the worksheets at the end of this chapter to help you. As you become facile with recognizing people's perceptual modes, practice conversing with them in those modes. Practice especially those modes which are not your own.

CASE IN POINT

If, for example, your primary mode is visual, pretend you can no longer use sight, but must relate to something purely through the sounds and rhythms of it. This may seem difficult at first, but will get easier as you enlarge your perceptual vocabulary to include auditory type words. Then, pretend you can only relate to things and people through feelings and the sense of touch. Figure out how to communicate via a kinesthetic mode to the exclusion of the others. The key to this process is incorporating feeling type words to your habitual way of expressing yourself.

In Chapter 3, we discussed the different ways to use your voice persuasively in the Courtroom. Learning how to speak in a visual mode uses the skill described in that chapter as "coloring"; painting pictures with your voice. You use words to create a vivid visual rendition of the event you are describing. When you color, you also make words sound like what they mean. This automatically accesses the auditory mode. Learning to "color," then, not only has a useful function in alleviating vocal monotony, but also allows you to access both the visual and auditory modes simultaneously. In addition, learning to use emotion as described in Chapter 3 will help you to access the kinesthetic mode. The different skills and techniques set forth in this book all work together to help you become truly persuasive.

How to Use Perceptual Modes Persuasively in Your Opening Statement

A jury will inevitably be composed of people of all three perceptual modes. Bearing this in mind, use words and phrases from all three modes in addressing the jury. This will give jurors of each perceptual type an opportunity to feel comfortable and at ease with you. If you make an effort to express yourself in all three modes, you will insure that you are truly heard by all the jurors, in a perceptual language they can each understand. This is where a knowledge of your own mode comes in particularly handy. If you are primarily visual, for example, then be sure you include auditory and kinesthetic words as you speak: if you are auditory, you must not ignore the visual and kinesthetic modes: if you are kinesthetic, learn to incorporate visual and auditory words.

Men tend to be primarily visual, and women tend to be primarily kinesthetic. There are fewer auditory types and these tend to be fairly evenly divided by gender. Do not misunderstand, there are certainly men who are kinesthetic and women who are visual. However, if your jury is primarily composed of women, then you might want to stress the kinesthetic expression; if your jury is primarily composed of men, pay more attention to the visual.

How to Use Perceptual Modes to Obtain Cooperation from a Difficult Witness

An awareness of perceptual modes can help you obtain information from a difficult witness. If you seem to be having trouble eliciting what you want from a witness, notice his perceptual mode, and then start speaking in that mode. For example, if the witness says, "I don't see how I can answer that," you might come back with, "Well, let me see if I can clarify it for you," and respond to him in visual terms. Or if he says "I don't remember exactly what happened, it just didn't feel right to me," you might well be able to jog his memory by prompting with a question composed in the same perceptual mode (kinesthetic): "I can understand that, I mean it must have been a pretty rough moment; just how did it feel to you?" You will be surprised how much more cooperative a witness can become as you speak in his perceptual mode.

How to Use Conflicting Perceptual Modes to Throw a Witness Off Balance

Let's look at another possible use of perceptual modes. Let's say that you want to confuse a witness, or discredit an expert. You can use your understanding of perceptual modes to do just that. Once you have determined in the case of the expert witness, for example, that the expert's mode is visual, start speaking in that mode, which will create rapport and lull the witness into feeling comfortable and secure. When you are ready to throw the expert off balance, start speaking to him purely in auditory or kinesthetic terms. He will now feel very uncomfortable, although he won't know why, because a change of perceptual modes is an extremely subtle technique. The jurors, in turn, will attribute the expert's discomfiture to the expert himself, to his insecurity, or ineptness, but not to anything you have done.

You see, unless someone is deliberately looking for it, it's just about impossible to pinpoint what the source of the discomfort is. People don't walk around looking for shifts in perceptual mode: quite frankly, 99% of the population doesn't even know what a perceptual mode is. Yet the result is highly desirable: you have created the desired confusion and discomfort without seeming to do anything at all.

The rule of thumb is the same as with mirroring: if you want to create rapport, create similarities. If you want to disrupt rapport, create dissimilarities. The use of perceptual modes is very powerful. Practice it until you've mastered it, it's well worth the effort.

SUMMARY

Science continues to provide us with clearer and clearer understandings of how humans communicate. A skilled use of mirroring and perceptual modes develops the necessary foundation of trust and acceptance which will most effectively support your persuasiveness.

BODY LANGUAGE
MIRRORING WORKSHEET

1. Videotape yourself in a brief (5 minute) conversation with a friend, with both of you seated.

2. During the conversation, practice mirroring your friend's body language to the best of your ability.

3. Watch the replay of the videotape and assess your mirroring skills using the following guidelines. Rank how well you are mirroring in terms of percentages, ie., you are able to pick up on body shifts well 70% of the time, fair 10% of the time, poorly 20% of the time.

	Good	Fair	Poor
Ability to pick up on friend's body shifts:	⸻	⸻	⸻
Ability to mirror specific movements: arms head legs	⸻ ⸻ ⸻	⸻ ⸻ ⸻	⸻ ⸻ ⸻
Ability to mirror subtly:	⸻	⸻	⸻
Appropriate timing in accomplishing mirrors:	⸻	⸻	⸻
Main problem in timing: Moving too quickly: ___ Moving too slowly: ___			

4. Given the above assessment, indicate the corrections you feel are needed to improve your mirroring skills:

_____

_____

_____

_____

_____

5. Work on the corrections you have noted, then do another videotape session, and observe your progress.

6. Now videotape yourself in conversation with a friend, only this time ask your friend to vary his position, so that some of the time he is seated, and some of the time he is standing. Repeat the assessment process as described above, using the following guidelines:

	Good	Fair	Poor
Ability to pick up on friend's body shifts:	——	——	——

Ability to mirror specific movements:
               stance
               arms
               shoulders
               head
               legs
	——
	——
	——
	——
	——
		——
		——
		——
		——
		——
			——
			——
			——
			——
			——

Ability to mirror subtly:	——	——	——
Appropriate timing in accomplishing mirrors:	——	——	——
Main problem in timing: Moving too quickly: ___ Moving too slowly: ___			

7. Given the above assessment, indicate the corrections you feel are needed to improve your mirroring skills:

_____

_____

_____

_____

_____

_____

8. Work on the corrections you have noted, then do another videotape session, and observe your progress.

VOCAL AND VOCABULARY MIRRORING

1. Audiotape or videotape yourself in a 15 minute conversation with a friend.

2. Mirror your friend's pitch, volume and pace.

3. Listen to the replay of the audiotape or videotape and assess your mirroring skills using the following guidelines. Rank how well you are mirroring in terms of percentages, ie., you are able to mirror pitch well 70% of the time, fair 10% of the time, poorly 20% of the time.

	Good	Fair	Poor
Ability to mirror pitch:	____	____	____
Ability to mirror volume:	____	____	____
Ability to mirror pace:	____	____	____
Ability to mirror subtly:	____	____	____
Appropriate timing in accomplishing mirrors:	____	____	____
Main problem in timing: Mirroring too quickly: ___ Mirroring too slowly: ___			

4. Given the above assessment, indicate the corrections you feel are needed to improve your mirroring skills:

_____

_____

_____

_____

_____

_____

5. Work on the corrections you have noted, then do another audiotape or videotape session, and observe your progress.

6. Audiotape or videotape another 15 minute conversation with your friend, only this time attend only to his vocabulary.

7. Mirror the level of vocabulary and type of words used by your friend, and then assess your mirroring skills as described above, based on the following guidelines:

	Good	Fair	Poor
Ability to mirror level of vocabulary:	____	____	____
Ability to mirror types of words:	____	____	____
Ability to mirror subtly:	____	____	____
Appropriate timing in accomplishing mirrors:	____	____	____
Main problem in timing: Mirroring too quickly: ___ Mirroring too slowly: ___			

8. Given the above assessment, indicate the corrections you feel are needed to improve your mirroring skills:

_____

_____

_____

_____

_____

_____

9. Work on the corrections you have noted, then do another audiotape or videotape session, and observe your progress.

COMPLETE MIRRORING WORKSHEET:
BODY LANGUAGE AND VOCAL MIRRORING COMBINED

1. Once you feel you can comfortably and easily mirror body language and voice separately, work on mirroring them both at the same time.

2. Videotape yourself in a 15 minute conversation with a friend and mirror both his body language and vocal qualities.

3. Watch the replay of the videotape and assess your mirroring skills using the following guidelines. Rank how well you are mirroring in terms of percentages, ie., you are able to pick up on head positions well 70% of the time, fair 10% of the time, poorly 20% of the time.

Body Language Assessment	Good	Fair	Poor
Ability to pick up on friend's body shifts:	___	___	___
Ability to mirror specific movements:			
stance	___	___	___
arms	___	___	___
shoulders	___	___	___
head	___	___	___
legs	___	___	___
Ability to mirror body language subtly:	___	___	___
Appropriate timing in accomplishing language mirrors:	___	___	___
Main problem in body language timing: Moving too quickly: ___ Moving too slowly: ___			
Vocal Assessment:	Good	Fair	Poor
Ability to mirror pitch:	___	___	___
Ability to mirror volume:	___	___	___
Ability to mirror pace:	___	___	___
Ability to mirror level of vocabulary:	___	___	___
Ability to mirror types of words:	___	___	___
Ability to mirror subtly:	___	___	___
Appropriate timing in accomplishing mirrors:	___	___	___
Main problem in body language timing: Mirroring too quickly: ___ Mirroring too slowly: ___			

7. Given the above assessment, indicate the corrections you feel are needed to improve your mirroring skills:

_____

_____

_____

_____

_____

_____

8. Work on the corrections you have noted, then do another videotape session, and observe your progress.

PERCEPTUAL MODES WORKSHEET

1. Listen carefully to yourself. What types of words do you use to convey your experience of life? Do you primarily see things, hear them or feel them? Determine your own perceptual mode, then determine that of different friends and colleagues.

	Visual	Auditory	Kinesthetique
Your perceptual mode:	——	——	——
Friend #1:	——	——	——
Friend #2:	——	——	——
Friend #3:	——	——	——
Friend #4:	——	——	——
Friend #5:	——	——	——
Friend #6:	——	——	——
Friend #7:	——	——	——
Friend #8:	——	——	——
Friend #9:	——	——	——
Friend #10:	——	——	——

2. Now that you can easily recognize another's perceptual mode, practice communicating in that mode. Audiotape or videotape yourself in conversation with a friend. Then listen to the replay of the conversation and observe whether or not you are accurately using your friend's perceptual mode. Rank your skills in terms of good, fair or poor.

Accurate use of friend's perceptual mode:	Good	Fair	Poor
Conversation #1:	——	——	——
Conversation #2:	——	——	——
Conversation #3:	——	——	——
Conversation #4:	——	——	——
Conversation #5:	——	——	——

3. Note which perceptual mode is most difficult for you to use easily, and practice it until you express yourself comfortably and with equal facility in all 3 modes.

CHAPTER 5

Using Creative
Listening to Get
the Advantage to Win
Your Case

When you drive your car, you don't simply put your foot on the accelerator and drive without paying attention to what is going on around you, on the contrary, you are attentive to the other drivers; you vary your speed, your turning angles, and so forth according to your observations of the other drivers' behavior, you take into account the *interplay* of your actions and their reactions. Effective communication is very similar to good driving; it requires the *interplay* of what you are expressing and others' reaction to it.

Communication is not a one way street, although many of us behave as if it were. All too often, attorneys are so focused on pursuing a line of questioning, they ignore the other half of communication: listening.

CASE IN POINT

"I have seen very competent people," says noted trial attorney Richard "Racehorse" Haynes, "have an idea of the questions they want to ask, then mechanically go through asking those questions without really listening carefully to what is being said. If you only listen partially, you do not catch the nuances that suggest to a seasoned practitioner that this witness is not telling the truth . . ."[1]

Communication, in order to be effective, must consist both of persuasive expression of your thought, and discriminating listening for the impact of that thought.

HOW GOOD LISTENING INCREASES YOUR ABILITY TO DISCERN WEAKNESSES AND STRENGTHENS YOUR CASE

Good listening is what distinguishes an ordinary trial lawyer from a great trial lawyer.

CASE IN POINT

"What is it then which sets the winners apart? Why is it, since we all work in the same forum and under the same rules, that some are consistently successful while others are less so? . . . Consistently successful trial lawyers, in addition to properly preparing their cases, make maximum use of physical traits possessed by all of us in order to gain the edge. These traits are the senses of sight and hearing. The exceptional trial lawyers seem to possess that rare ability to press an advantage at the proper time; to find, through persistent and knowledgeable probing, the weakness in the armour of key witnesses; and to exploit those weaknesses with the explosiveness and decisiveness of Patton on the attack." [2]

As the Honorable Earl Strayhorn so accurately states, sight is every bit as important as hearing. Listening is done at least as much with the eyes as with the ears. Why is that? The "weaknesses" Judge Strayhorn speaks of are those inconsistencies of content, vocal tone, and body language which point up an area of vulnerability. You use your ears to determine inconsistencies of content and vocal tone, and your eyes to read inconsistencies of body language.

How Pretrial Preparation Increases Your Ability to Listen Effectively

This is where solid, thorough pretrial preparation really pays off. If you are still formulating your arguments, racking your memory for some important point, searching your files for a misplaced document, you are not free to really listen. Of course you will hear the main information being given, but you will not hear and see the nuances that will give you the edge you need in order to win.

The better prepared you are, the more you can filter what you hear through your prior knowledge of the facts, then you can quickly catch when something doesn't sound quite right, doesn't ring true. The better prepared you are, the more energy you have available to really watch the witness or juror, and be attuned to slight changes in body posture or expression.

HOW TO ACQUIRE INFORMATION THAT CAN WIN YOUR CASE BY LISTENING FOR WITNESS/JUROR/OPPOSING COUNSEL INCONSISTENCIES

What are you listening for, specifically? Lack of congruence. This is the true definition of an inconsistency. In Chapter 2, when we discussed body language, we defined congruence as a harmonious interaction of body language and content: for example, if as you speak angry words, your fists are clenched and you are frowning, you are displaying congruence. All parts of your communication are going in the same direction, expressing the same idea; your communication is therefore believable. When you observe a witness or juror for possible weaknesses, watch and listen for lack of congruence, for moments where one part of the individual's communication conflicts with another part.

Let's take each of the main areas one at a time to see how this works in practice.

How to Recognize the Three Key Verbal Inconsistencies and How to Use Them to Your Advantage

There are three ways verbal content may be incongruent: content clashing with content, content conflicting with emotional tone, and content conflicting with body language.

1. Content that clashes with content

This is the first and most obvious way to listen for inconsistencies. The witness will answer one way to a question on Day 1, and differently to the same or a similar question on Day 2. Although such an inconsistency may happen in obvious fashion, more often it is not so obvious, and may make all the difference to your case. If you are not truly alert and listening, you might miss a vital point.

CASE IN POINT

An excellent example is provided by a case in which David M. Harney, an eminent trial attorney from Los Angeles, California, was cross-examining an expert witness for the defense. The case involved a boy's cancerous condition. The cancer specialist, Ian Macdonald, " . . . offered as a basis for his expertise his observations of a man with a similar cancer in his arm at the New York Sloan-Kettering Hospital in the 1930's. This man's cancer, said Macdonald was extremely slow-growing; he observed its slow growth because the patient refused surgery. But later in his testimony Macdonald—to support his opinion that the growth rates of this cancer are 'variable'—said he had seen one 'fast-growing' cancer, and he described the patient as a man in New York in 1936 with a cancer in his arm. When Harney cross-examined Macdonald and asked him to describe more fully the 'slow-growing' cancer he had mentioned earlier, the doctor referred to the very same man in New York. Through his sharp listening skills, Harney had caught the redundancy in the examples and pointed out the doctor's mistake. Thus Harney completely discredited Macdonald as an expert witness."[3]

Once the discrepancy is pointed out, it becomes very noticeable. If, however, you are too focused on the questions you wish to ask down the line, and not listening attentively enough to the answers you are getting in the moment, you can easily miss such a valuable point altogether. Review past trial transcripts and carefully read the witnesses' answers to your questions. Are there subtleties you missed? Were there contradictions in the testimony you ignored at the time? If you find that your listening skills are deficient, you can readily improve them by simply clearing your mind of extraneous thoughts, and focusing on what you are hearing.

Practice this in your daily life. It may take a while before you are able to stay focused on what you're listening to, but it is a skill well worth developing. A worksheet is provided at the end of the chapter to help you improve these skills.

2. Content that conflicts with emotional tone

Listen for incongruence between the content of the communication and the underlying emotional tone. If the witness says how upset he was, but his tone is calm, or even somewhat pleasant, something is wrong. If a prospective juror says he accepts a certain idea, but he sounds nervous and uneasy, something is wrong. An incongruity between content and underlying emotional tone will not tell you what specifically is wrong; it operates rather like a red flag, warning you to pay attention, things are not what they seem to be. It indicates an area where you should probe.

3. Content that conflicts with body language

Similarly to content conflicting with emotional tone, assess the difference between what is said, and what the person's body is expressing. This is where listening is done primarily with the eyes. There is incongruence when an expert witness states he is sure of a fact, but he is picking at his fingers, or nervously adjusts his clothing. There is incongruence when a white prospective juror states he would consider a black defendant's testimony no differently than that of a white defendant's, but his arms are crossed tightly over his chest. As with content conflicting with emotional tone, the discrepancy between body language and verbal content will not necessarily tell you specifically what is amiss, but it does serve as a clear warning signal, that here is fertile ground for probing.

How to Recognize the Three Key Nonverbal Inconsistencies and How to Use Them to Your Advantage

1. Variations in vocal tone

Content provides a very specific way to look for inconsistencies. You screen for direct contradictions to the content in emotion or body language. Other ways of spotting inconsistencies are not as direct, but equally fruitful. Vocal inconsistencies, for example, can tell you a great deal about the "truth" of a statement. For example, let's say that during a witness's testimony, his voice rises somewhat in pitch, or that his pace increases. A rise in pitch or increase in pace is indicative of nervousness, so ask yourself; "Why would he be nervous right now? Is he lying? Was there something about how I phrased the question that struck a sensitive spot? Is he worried about my present line of questioning?" Then probe in function of your questions.

2. Overly frequent pauses and "uh" sounds

On the other hand, the witness's speech may be full of "uh" sounds and pauses in between every word or two: such hesitation is a typical sign of anxiety. Ask yourself: "What is causing him such anxiety? Does he reply like this to every question? Is it just courtroom anxiety? Or is it this question? What about my question might make him anxious?"

3. Inconsistencies in vocabulary

Listen for inconsistencies in vocabulary: if all of a sudden a witness uses words and phrases that seem too formal or too educated (given his prior responses) in response to a question, he may very well have been coached in that response (and badly at that): here is a weak spot to probe.

HOW TO ACQUIRE INFORMATION THAT CAN WIN YOUR CASE BY OBSERVING BODY LANGUAGE CUES

Just as the jurors (and others) can read your body language, so can you read theirs. The difference, however, is that your reading must be accurate if it is to be useful, and so cannot be based on purely stereotypical interpretations. As we have seen, stereotypical interpretations may be widely accepted, but not necessarily accurate.

How to Interpret a Juror's Body Language Cues Accurately

If you are to correctly interpret body language, you must read it in a *context*.

CASE IN POINT

Just because a prospective juror is sitting very straight in his chair, gripping the arms of the chair for dear life, does not necessarily mean he's a hostile angry person who would be death on the jury panel. He may be, but he may also simply be very intimidated by the trial process. Observe him *for a period of time*, notice whether his position shifts in response to various questions, how he sits when he's not the object of questioning. Notice if he adopts other postures congruent with a hostile attitude, or if, on the contrary, he adopts postures more indicative of anxiety.

Read the juror's basic position in the context of his overall body language, and your interpretation will be accurate and therefore useful.

How to Use Body Language Cues to Evaluate Your Impact on the Witness

Body language is particularly useful in helping you determine the impact of your (or opposing counsel's) words. Watch for shifts in body position, changes in body language in response to a given question: these will tell you what is really going on with the witness. Does he begin to fidget, or shift in his seat, which would indicate nervousness? Does he suddenly sit up much straighter, which might indicate defensiveness, as would crossing his arms over his chest? Does his foot begin to tap or move repetitively, which indicates annoyance or anxiety? Does his body shift into a more relaxed slumped mood, did you just let him off the hook? Do his eyes narrow or his lips tighten, which may indicate suspiciousness or defensiveness? Do his hands fist, or curl tightly around the arms of the chair: he's probably angry. The witness's body language will serve as a guide to your questioning: as you learn to read it, you will be able to figure out quite readily whether you're on the right track and really onto something, or barking up the wrong tree.

How to Use Jurors' Body Language Cues to Guide You in the Successful Development of Your Case

Watch just as attentively when the witness is responding to opposing counsel, or the prospective juror is being questioned by opposing counsel: you can get valuable cues from these interactions. Pay attention to the jury, observe their reactions, both to your own and opposing counsel's statements. Notice in particular the shifts in their facial expressions as well as major body shifts: look for signs of approval and disapproval, belief or disbelief. Remember that the jurors are mute during the trial; since the only avenue of expression available to them is their body language, they are likely to use it. Make adjustments to the presentation of your case in function of the jurors' reactions. Bear in mind the idea of interplay: take into account how the *jurors* are affected by your questioning and arguments and make changes accordingly.

HOW TO USE EYE CONTACT TO MAKE A JUROR/WITNESS FEEL LISTENED TO AND CREDIBLE

Although the ears are the sensory receptors for sound, if the eyes are not also "listening," we do not *feel* heard. Try the following experiment. You'll need a friend's cooperation: be sure to warn him first of the experimental nature of the experience. Ask the friend to talk to you, about anything—the content is irrelevant. As your friend is speaking, simply look away from him, without moving your head or body, just look over to the side (Illustration 1). Keep listening very attentively, however. Do this for a minute or so. Then stop your friend, and ask him how it felt when you looked away. You'll find, that although you could probably repeat the minute conversation verbatim, your friend *did not feel listened to at all* when your eyes were off him.

Then, ask your friend once again to talk to you. This time, keep your eyes on him steadily throughout his "speech," and nod your head occasionally. Do not, however, listen to him at all. Think about an upcoming case, reminisce about last night's party, do your grocery list in your head,

5–1

but do not listen. Just keep looking at him and nodding from time to time. After about a minute of this, stop your friend, and ask him how he felt. You'll find that this time, he *felt* listened to, even though you weren't listening at all. The eyes then are far more critical in the *perception* of being heard than are the ears.

What does this tell you? That the easiest way to make a prospective juror feel listened to, feel that his words are credible and valued, is simply to look at him the whole time he is speaking. Wait until he is finished with his entire answer before you look down at your notes. Similarly, to make a witness feel secure and comfortable, look at him the whole time he is talking. If a witness is giving a particularly long piece of testimony, start by looking at him to ensure his security and comfort, then you can look down or slightly to the side, as if thinking, but be sure to look back up at him whenever you want to underline the importance of something he is saying, or to reassure him of his value to you.

REMINDER Bear in mind that the jurors are staring at you all the time. You are permanently on stage. If you look at the witness while he is talking, that is a cue to the jury that the witness is important, or that what he has to say is valuable. They will in a sense—follow your eyes—to know what is meaningful and what is not.

How to Use Deliberate Avoidance of Eye Contact to Discredit a Witness's Testimony

If looking at an individual makes him feel worthy and valued, then not looking at a person who is talking makes him feel worthless and his words empty. You can easily make a witness feel highly uncomfortable simply by not looking at him while he is answering.

Ask your question, then right away take your eyes off the witness, then drop your head slightly into "thoughtful" position (see Chapter 2, Illustration 36). Do not let your eyes flit about the room, however, this would be interpreted as disrespect by the jurors, and jurors don't like disrespectful attorneys. Simply keep your eyes down or slightly to the side, as if in thought: this is not interpreted as disrespect, but is highly discomfiting to the witness. If the witness you are deliberately seeking to unsettle suddenly says something you *do* want the jurors to notice, simply bring your head up and stare at him for a moment, then go back to your "thoughtful" position. Your change in eye focus will signal to the jury that here is something worth listening to.

CAUTION Be subtle in using eye focus to discredit. Bear in mind that the jurors are wary of any manipulations you may display, and are usually more on the side of the witness than on yours.

HOW TO USE YOUR BODY TO BRING THE JURY'S ATTENTION TO A POINT

In addition to your eyes, your body can be used to signal whether or not you value a witness's statements. If you want to assure that the jurors will listen fully to a witness in order to absorb a given point, you must yourself listen fully to that witness. Your body language must project to the jurors what the witness is saying is important. Face the witness square on, keep your face and body still, do not take notes, do not gesture. Lean your body in slightly if standing, a bit more if seated (Illustration 2). Watch the witness as he speaks, keeping your eye focus steady.

This body posture will accomplish two things:

5-2

5-3

1. it will signal to the jurors to pay close attention to the witness
2. it will make the witness feel valued and important.

Anytime you wish to bring attention to a point, use this position of attentive listening.

How to Use your Body to Distract the Jury's Attention from a Point

The opposite is of course equally true. If you want to distract from the witness, and thereby devalue what he is saying, do not face the witness when he is talking, move around or do something physical (take notes, clean your glasses), lean back or away from the witness, and do not maintain good steady eye focus (Illustration 3).

Your lack of stillness and eye focus will accomplish two things:

1. since movement pulls attention to itself, the jurors' focus will be split between you and the witness
2. your lack of stillness will project the message that what this witness has to say is not very important, certainly not worth being still for.

HOW TO USE ACKNOWLEDGEMENT TO GAIN THE WITNESS'S COOPERATION

Effective listening consists of more than simply staring at the witness, you must acknowledge what you hear as well. Acknowledging is accomplished in two basic ways: by head nodding and by saying "uh-huh." Nodding your head every so often lets the witness know that you are following what he is saying. It is a non-verbal signal indicating: "I'm with you, I understand, keep going." Saying "uh-huh" or any equivalent thereof, even as a murmur, serves the same function. Doing neither one of these will generally lead an individual to believe that he is not understood, perhaps not even heard, and can be very distressing.

An experiment similar to the one described above will demonstrate this point forcefully. Ask a friend to talk to you, and as he speaks, look at him with good eye focus, holding still, but do not nod, change your facial expression, or give him any verbal acknowledgements. Chances are your friend will complain that you were being very cold, and may even have perceived you as critical. Ask him to talk to you once more, but this time, although you maintain good eye focus and a still body, nod every so often, allow your facial expressions to vary in function of your reaction to what you hear, and/or make acknowledgement noises, such as "uh-huh." This time he will perceive you as warm, and will feel listened to, and understood. It is very important, then, to add acknowledgements to your listening skills, and use them in conjunction with the other techniques described above, whenever you want to project that a person or statement is significant.

Making acknowledgement nods and sounds is important in the development of rapport, and should be used early on with the jurors, in voir dire, as well as throughout the trial, with witnesses, as you feel the need to connect with them. Acknowledgement encourages the witness to continue, makes him feel valued and worthy, and thereby more willing to cooperate with you.

How to Withhold Acknowledgement to Discomfit a Witness

The converse is equally true. Attentively listening to a witness with eyes and body language, but withholding all acknowledgment has a truly disconcerting effect. The witness will feel riveted, impaled on your look, and will react by either physically or mentally "squirming." Meanwhile, the jury will have no idea what you're doing, because your body position and eye focus are signaling "look here, something important is happening." And indeed it is, your unhappy witness is projecting nervousness all over the place. Creating such distress can rapidly lead a witness to discredit himself.

HOW TO USE REACTIONS TO INFLUENCE THE JURORS' THOUGHT PROCESS TO YOUR ADVANTAGE

Reacting is a more complex process than simple acknowledgment. Reacting consists of listening to and acknowledging the speaker, ingesting what you have just heard, connecting it up to your own thought, and then nonverbally communicating a response, in such a fashion that it can be easily and accurately interpreted by an observer. Although this sounds complicated, it is a process we perform quite unconsciously continually throughout our day. For example, someone says something that makes us happy, we smile, someone says something that saddens us, we sigh. The difference with reacting naturally and reacting in the context of a Courtroom is that in a Courtroom, you design your reactions so that they have a *specific and predetermined effect*. What is usually an automatic and unconscious process must therefore become conscious.

Reactions can be skillfully used in the Courtroom to let the jurors know how you feel about what is going on.

CASE IN POINT

For example, let's take a cross examination. You question the witness, listening effectively, nodding, and then, after the witness has answered your question, you give a reaction to what you've just heard: you cock your head and give a quizzical look. The jury, by watching your reaction (cocking your head, giving a quizzical look), observes that there was something about the witness's answer that bothered you. The jury, at this point, may not know *why* the witness's answer bothered you, but from having watched your reaction to the witness's answer, now knows that *something* indeed does disturb you about that witness's answer. The jurors will be attentive, from this point on, to what it might be about that witness's statement that bothers you.

By letting the jurors know how you feel about the witness's answer, you guide their thought along the lines you want. You lead them to discover *with* you the conclusion you'll eventually reveal. By their participation in your thought process, the jurors are more readily influenced by your conclusion. They see how you got there. This is a far more effective persuasion technique than announcing a conclusion the jurors had no part in discovering.

If you don't react, the jurors don't know how you feel, and will allow themselves to be guided by other influences, such as opposing counsel, regarding how they are to interpret the witness's response. The more you help the jury evaluate the case the way *you* want the case evaluated, the better your chances of winning. In addition, since your reactions are not aimed directly at the jury, but rather are aimed at the person to whom you are responding, reactions are an indirect way of communicating your feelings to the jurors, and therefore are more subtle and more effective than any direct expression to the jury would be.

How to Design Your Reactions to Purposefully Guide the Jurors to Your Interpretation of the Facts

Whether you realize it or not, you are reacting all of the time. The jurors pick up on those reactions and use them to better understand your communication. Rather than leave this understanding up to chance, design your reactions on purpose, so that the jurors understand your communication as *you* want it understood.

Reactions are expressed through body language, gestures, and facial expressions. Reactions range from the very subtle, expressed with a simple change of the brow, to the very obvious, expressed through a major body shift with gesture. Use stereotypical definitions of the various body language postures and facial expressions, as given in Chapter 2, to guide you in creating desired reactions. Bear in mind that reactions must be easily read: mannerisms are not a good choice as their meaning is too personal. Practice various reactions either in front of a mirror or with a videocamera until they become natural and easy.

How to Know When to Use Reactions to Influence the Jurors

Reactions should be used every time you want to convey your opinion on a behavior or a point to the jury, regardless of whether your opinion pertains to opposing counsel's behavior or the veracity of a witness's statement. For example, you can express approval or disapproval, belief or disbelief, satisfaction or dissatisfaction with reactions. You are only limited in your choice of reactions by the limits of your imagination.

HOW TO USE THE TECHNIQUE OF "OVERHEARD CONVERSATIONS" TO GET YOUR POINT ACROSS TO THE JURORS

Some years ago, social psychologists undertook interesting research which showed that when people think a person trying to influence them has an ulterior motive, they are more convinced by a conversation they overhear involving that person, than by a direct communication from the person. In other words, when people suspect you are directly trying to win them over because you have something to gain by it, they are not very open to you. When however, people overhear you talking to someone from whom you have nothing to gain, they are far more likely to be convinced by you.

What does this mean to you? That the conversations you have in and around the Courtroom should be conducted with this knowledge in mind. Your "casual" conversations anywhere within earshot of the jurors should be in no way "casual." These are golden opportunities to convince the jurors of your arguments. Be aware that the jurors are not only watching you all the time, they are listening to you all the time as well. The discussions you have with co-counsel, the times when you explain to your assistants how you want visual aids displayed and why, what you say to a colleague who stops you in the Hall and asks "How's it going?", all these are opportunities to give information which, overheard by a juror, will lead to a favorable assessment of you and your case.

The reverse is also true. If a juror overhears you being disrespectful of the Judge in talking to a colleague, he will believe that statement more than he will believe your appropriately respectful behavior when in the Courtroom. If he overhears you denigrating your client in an aside to co-counsel, your credibility just plummeted. Anything overheard will be believed more than anything you say in the Courtroom. Knowing this gives you added power: use the knowledge well and to your advantage.

SUMMARY

Listening constitutes half of all communicating. Listen with your ears, your eyes, your whole body. Listen actively, scanning for inconsistencies on many levels: content, vocal, body language and emotional levels. Acknowledge and react: these are valuable tools too often ignored. Use them, and you'll come out a winner.

ATTENTIVE LISTENING WORKSHEET

1. Audiotape or videotape a 15 minute conversation with a friend.

2. Whenever your friend speaks, clear your mind of all other thoughts, including formulating your reply, and focus all your attention on listening.

3. Respond when appropriate.

4. Listen to the replay of the audiotape or videotape, and assess your listening skills using the following guidelines:

	Seldom	Frequently	Occasionally
Do you have difficulty clearing your mind and focusing?	——	——	——
Do you interrupt your friend?	——	——	——
Do your responses incorporate what your friend just said?	——	——	——
Do you ignore what your friend says and just stay with your own thought?	——	——	——

5. If you find you have difficulty clearing your mind and focusing, learn the "back pocket" technique. Create an imaginary back pocket, where you put all extraneous thoughts, to be pulled out and looked at later, when it is appropriate. Then, when in conversation, try to focus on what your friend is saying. Whenever an extraneous thought goes through your mind, send it to your "back pocket" where it belongs.

   If you still have great difficulty clearing your mind and focusing, learn meditation techniques. These are very helpful in quieting an overactive mind.

6. If you find that you often interrupt and ignore your friend's input, use clarification and reflection to improve your listening skills.

   These consist of carefully listening to your friend, and then asking him:
   "If I understand you correctly, what you mean is ..." or
   "So what you mean is ..."or
   "Then the way you see the situation is ..."

   Reflect and clarify before you go on to your own response. This way you insure that you do not interrupt and have indeed included your friend's input in your response.

VERBAL INCONSISTENCIES WORKSHEET

1. Videotape a television program, preferably a straight dramatic show. Watch several short segments, from 3 to 5 minutes in length, one at a time and ask yourself the following of each segment:

	Yes	No

Segment #1

Does content conflict with content? _____ _____

If yes, how? _____

_____

_____

_____

Does content conflict with emotion? _____ _____

If yes, how? _____

_____

_____

_____

Does content conflict with body language? _____ _____

If yes, how? _____

_____

_____

_____

Segment #2

Does content conflict with content? _____ _____

If yes, how? _____

_____

_____

_____

	Yes	No
Does content conflict with emotion?	____	____

If yes, how? _____

_____

_____

_____

Does content conflict with body language?   ____   ____

If yes, how? _____

_____

_____

_____

Segment #3

Does content conflict with content?   ____   ____

If yes, how? _____

_____

_____

_____

Does content conflict with emotion?   ____   ____

If yes, how? _____

_____

_____

_____

Does content conflict with body language?   ____   ____

If yes, how? _____

_____

_____

_____

	Yes	No

Segment #4

Does content conflict with content? ____ ____

If yes, how? _____

_____

_____

_____

Does content conflict with emotion? ____ ____

If yes, how? _____

_____

_____

_____

Does content conflict with body language? ____ ____

If yes, how? _____

_____

_____

_____

Segment #5

Does content conflict with content? ____ ____

If yes, how? _____

_____

_____

_____

	Yes	No
Does content conflict with emotion?	____	____

If yes, how? _____

_____

_____

_____

	Yes	No
Does content conflict with body language?	____	____

If yes, how? _____

_____

_____

_____

2. Then replay each segment and observe how accurately or inaccurately you observed inconsistencies. Repeat the exercise until you can easily and comfortably spot verbal inconsistencies.

NONVERBAL INCONSISTENCIES WORKSHEET

1. Television is truly a wonderous self-teaching tool. Teach yourself to notice nonverbal inconsistencies by watching characters on your favorite programs, and observing the following:

   sudden or unexpected rises in pitch

   increases or decreases in pace

   increased frequency of "uh"s

   pausing between every word

   inconsistencies of vocabulary

2. Then ask yourself: what is motivating these nonverbal changes? Why, for example, would an otherwise strong and authoritative man, start to say "uh" every three words?

3. Once you have a feel for inconsistencies via your television set, attune yourself to those inconsistencies as they occur in the people (including yourself) in your daily life.

BODY LANGUAGE CUES WORKSHEET

1. Become more sensitive and receptive to body language cues using the following
   exercise:

   Observe the people around you, at work or at play. Note your first impression
   based on their body language, then note your impression after observing them
   for 10 minutes, taking the context into account. The more you learn to take
   context into account, the more accurate your reading of body language cues.

Person's body language	*First impression of what this body language means*	*Impression after 10 minutes of what this body language means*
#1 _____	_____	_____
_____	_____	_____
_____	_____	_____
_____	_____	_____
_____	_____	_____
#2 _____	_____	_____
_____	_____	_____
_____	_____	_____
_____	_____	_____
_____	_____	_____
#3 _____	_____	_____
_____	_____	_____
_____	_____	_____
_____	_____	_____
_____	_____	_____
#4 _____	_____	_____
_____	_____	_____
_____	_____	_____
_____	_____	_____
_____	_____	_____

Person's body language	First impression of what this body language means	Impression after 10 minutes of what this body language means
#5 _____	_____	_____
_____	_____	_____
_____	_____	_____
_____	_____	_____
_____	_____	_____
#6 _____	_____	_____
_____	_____	_____
_____	_____	_____
_____	_____	_____
_____	_____	_____

2. Videotape a 20 minute conversation with a friend. Watch the replay of the conversation, and observe what body language cues your friend is giving you as to the *impact* of what you are saying. Notice in particular the following:

> Your friend's body shifts
> > eye positions
> > arm movements
> > leg changes
> > head movements

See if you can accurately pinpoint which comment of yours provoked which element of body language. Practice this exercise until you can comfortably and easily pinpoint body language reactions to your statements.

Statement	Body language elicited
#1 _____	_____
_____	_____
#2 _____	_____
_____	_____
#3 _____	_____
_____	_____

Statement	*Body language elicited*
#4 _____	_____
_____	_____
#5 _____	_____
_____	_____
#6 _____	_____
_____	_____
#7 _____	_____
_____	_____
#8 _____	_____
_____	_____
#9 _____	_____
_____	_____
#10 _____	_____
_____	_____

EFFECTIVE LISTENING WITH THE BODY WORKSHEET

1. Videotape yourself in conversation with a friend. Observe your body language as you listen to him. Note the following:

When listening:	Sometimes	Occasionally	Rarely
Is your body square?	____	____	____
Is your body still?	____	____	____
Is your head still?	____	____	____
Are you gesturing?	____	____	____
Is your body slightly leaning forward?	____	____	____
Is your eye focus steady?	____	____	____

2. Based on the above observations, note the corrections you need to make so that your body listens effectively:

_____

_____

_____

_____

_____

_____

ACKNOWLEDGMENTS WORKSHEET

1. Videotape yourself in a 20 minute conversation with a friend. Observe how you acknowledge him when he is speaking, and note the following:

	Sometimes	Occasionally	Rarely
Do you maintain steady eye focus?	——	——	——
Do you nod your head?	——	——	——
Do your facial expressions vary in function of what you are hearing?	——	——	——
Do you make "uh-huh" or similar acknowledgement sounds?	——	——	——

2. Based on the above observations, note the corrections you need to make so that you acknowledge effectively:

_____

_____

_____

_____

_____

_____

REACTIONS WORKSHEET

1. Watch people as you go about your daily life, and watch actors on television. Observe how people react to different situations. What do their faces and bodies do specifically to express different reactions? Use your understanding of stereotypes as outlines in Chapter 2 to help you figure this out.

Observe people in various situations and note the following:

In reacting to a situation, people feel:	*This is expressed in facial expressions and body language as:*
disappointed	_____
	_____
	_____
	_____
disapproving	_____
	_____
	_____
	_____
disgusted	_____
	_____
	_____
	_____
sad	_____
	_____
	_____
	_____
interested	_____
	_____
	_____
	_____

In reacting to a situation, people feel:	*This is expressed in facial expressions and body language as:*
intrigued	_____
	_____
	_____
	_____
curious	_____
	_____
	_____
	_____
suspicious	_____
	_____
	_____
	_____
annoyed	_____
	_____
	_____
	_____
righteously indignant	_____
	_____
	_____
	_____
determined	_____
	_____
	_____
	_____

In reacting to a situation, people feel:	*This is expressed in facial expressions and body language as:*
inspired	_____
	_____
	_____
	_____
approving	_____
	_____
	_____
	_____
satisfied	_____
	_____
	_____
	_____
(other)	_____
	_____
	_____
	_____
(other)	_____
	_____
	_____
	_____

2. Different people express their reactions differently, however, there are usually 2 or 3 main ways of expressing a reaction in any given culture. Look for the *main ways* reactions are commonly expressed, always bearing in mind the individual peculiarities of each of us.

3. Taking the same list of emotions, videotape yourself reacting to an imaginary person who is evoking that particular emotion. Observe whether or not your facial expressions and body language do indeed express the reaction you want them to express. Adjust your expressions and body language until you are confident of the effectiveness of your own reactions.

In reacting to a situation, you feel:	*Adjustments you need to make to your facial expressions and body language to effectively communicate this reaction:*
disappointed	_____
	_____
	_____
	_____
disapproving	_____
	_____
	_____
	_____
disgusted	_____
	_____
	_____
	_____
sad	_____
	_____
	_____
	_____
interested	_____
	_____
	_____
	_____
intrigued	_____
	_____
	_____
	_____

In reacting to a situation, you feel:	*Adjustments you need to make to your facial expressions and body language to effectively communicate this reaction:*
curious	_____
	_____
	_____
	_____
suspicious	_____
	_____
	_____
	_____
annoyed	_____
	_____
	_____
	_____
righteously indignant	_____
	_____
	_____
	_____
determined	_____
	_____
	_____
	_____
inspired	_____
	_____
	_____
	_____

In reacting to a situation, you feel:	*Adjustments you need to make to your facial expressions and body language to effectively communicate this reaction:*
approving	_____ _____ _____ _____
satisfied	_____ _____ _____ _____
_____ (other)	_____ _____ _____
_____ (other)	_____ _____ _____

CHAPTER 6

How to Satisfy the Jurors' Need for Logic

Emotions and logic seem to be antithical forces: when you're being emotional, logic flies out the window, when you're being logical, you appear cold and unfeeling. Yet despite their apparently conflictual nature, emotions and logic are *both* essential to the decision-making process, and your persuasiveness with the jurors relies greatly on your ability to use each appropriately.

HOW LOGIC AND EMOTION INFLUENCE THE JURORS' DECISION-MAKING PROCESS

Research in social psychology has clearly demonstrated that decisions are made at an emotional or "gut" level, and are then backed up at the level of the mind. If the jurors are wonderfully swayed at the level of their emotions, but cannot, in deliberation come up with logical reasons why that emotional reaction is legitimate, they will reject your argument. We are very uncomfortable when we cannot justify our "gut" feelings, especially in a professional atmosphere such as a Courtroom. Ours is not an intuitively based culture: we like to have sound arguments and reasons for our feelings. It won't do you any good to have a juror say of you during deliberation; "I think he ought to win because it feels right" and leave it at that, the juror must be able to say; "I think he ought to win because of points one, two, and three." On the other hand, if the jurors can enumerate logical reasons supporting your argument, but have no feeling for your client or your cause, they are likely to gravitate toward a more emotionally appealing client or cause. You cannot win on the basis of logic alone or on the basis of emotions alone; they are interdependent forces and the decision-making process requires both.

How to Use Logic and Emotions Respectively to Most Effectively Impact the Jurors' Decision-making Process

How then can you use each appropriately? It seems impossible to be both logical and emotional at the same time, and yet, in reality it can be done. The relationship between emotions and logic is very much like that between skeleton and flesh in the human body. If I asked you, "Is the human body hard?," you'd say, "Well, sort of, but not really," and if I asked you, "Is the human body soft," you'd also say "Well, sort of, but not really." If, exasperated, I then asked, "Well then, which is it?," you would explain to me how some of it—the skeleton—is hard, and how some of it—the flesh—is soft. So it is with decision making. Logic is the skeleton of decision making: it is the core, the basis, the underlying structure and foundation. Emotions are the muscles and skin of decision making: they provide the allure, the pizzazz, the cosmetic overlay.

CASE IN POINT

We rarely say of a beautiful woman, "What a terrific skeleton," but we do say, "She has good bones." We recognize that her beauty is supported by a well-defined structure. Her beauty, however, the part which attracts our attention and our appreciation, lies in her flesh: the shape of her lips, the color of her eyes.

Emotions persuade, but without strong underlying logic, that persuasiveness is momentary and does not lead to action. Combine emotions with logic, and action—a vote cast in your favor—follows.

In the following chapter, we will discuss the many techniques available to you in creating the emotional flesh of your case: this chapter is devoted to the creation of a solid foundation through logic.

CAUTION The "logic" referred to in this chapter is the logic of psychology, not the logic of law. Throughout this book, I am discussing psychological and social psychological techniques as they apply to the presentation of your case, not the correct development of the substantive issues, or the content of your case. Please bear in mind that you and you alone are the expert on legal matters: my goal is to help you convey and communicate that expertise as persuasively as possible.

How to Use Structure to Promote Juror Acceptance of Your Interpretation of the Facts

Appealing to the logical mind basically relies on the use of structure. The logical mind needs structure in order to function, and if not provided with structure, will seek to create its own. We need structure to categorize and catalogue, to label and define. It is the only way we can create order out of chaos, meaning out of senselessness. What is your object? You want the jurors to see the case the way you do, to interpret the facts the way *you* want the facts of the case interpreted, not haphazardly, nor according to opposing counsel's point of view. It is up to you, then, to provide the jurors with the structure which will enable them to adopt *your* version of "order" and "meaning." Bear in mind that if your structure is not clear and easy to grasp, the jurors will turn toward opposing counsel rather than develop their own. Most of us suffer from mental inertia, and will follow what is available rather than develop something new. The following techniques will help you structure your content so that your particular interpretation is accepted.

HOW TO USE A CASE THEME TO STRUCTURE YOUR CASE CONVINCINGLY

A skeleton has a distinct shape, and that shape is defined by clearly articulated elements which fit together coherently. So too does a case have a distinct shape, and that shape is equally defined by clearly articulated elements which fit together coherently. Your first task, in creating a solid structure for your case, is to define the overall shape of your case. This is your case theme. You then organize the facts of your case so that they fit together coherently in the service of that theme.

CASE IN POINT

An example of a particularly brilliant case theme is that developed by criminal defense attorney James F. Neal, in defending Dr. George Nichopoulos, accused of contributing to Elvis Presley's death by the criminal prescription of drugs. Originally, it looked like there was no defense. What case theme could be developed given that the medical review board had indeed suspended Dr. Nichopoulos for overprescribing drugs, prescribing them too frequently and for too long? But what Neal found, in examining the facts of the case more closely, was that Dr. Nichopoulos was in fact dealing with a number of addicted patients who were difficult and desperate, and that he was in effect attempting to wean them off drugs in controlled fashion, rather than cutting off their supply entirely, and having them resort to possibly criminal means of feeding their addictions.

Out of these facts, Neal developed his defense, and the theme of the "Good Samaritan" became his case theme. "Neal told the jury that Nichopoulos jeopardized his medical license to help all his addicted patients [including Presley] diminish their supply of drugs and cure their addictions. He did this when many other doctors turned these people away, explained Neal. Nichopoulos was the man who would take a chance and even practiced in what other doctors would see as an unorthodox way if he believed it would help—rather than turning his back and passing on, leaving these victims to the mercy of the street peddlers."[1] Neal then proceeded to present his facts so that they would support this one over-riding case theme.

The Five Ways a Case Theme Contributes to Your Courtroom Success

1. You control the definition of your case

First of all, and most importantly, by creating a case theme, you control the definition of your case. You do not allow opposing counsel to define it for you, because they are not going to define it in a way favorable to you. By controlling the definition of your case, you take charge, you are powerful.

CASE IN POINT

An historic example of what can happen when you don't develop a case theme is the trial of Bruno Hauptmann, accused of kidnapping the Lindbergh baby in 1932. The defense did not have a theme: the defense simply denied that Hauptmann committed the crime. Despite the moving emotional outcries of both Hauptmann and his wife throughout the trial, the defense lost, in large part because they abdicated control of their case by ignoring the critical importance of defining a case theme.[2]

2. You provide a mental handle for the jurors

A case theme gives the jurors a mental handle with which to understand the case. This is the first element of structure. If you don't provide the jurors with a convenient mental handle, they will either provide their own, over which you have no control, or lean toward that of opposing counsel. If I don't provide a mass of flesh with a skeleton, all there is is a blob. Did you ever try to hold onto a blob? A case without a theme is too difficult for the jury to make sense of, they need something definite, something concrete to make order out of that chaos. A case theme gives the jurors a central concept to grab onto, a generalizing principle around which they can organize the information given during the trial.

3. You provide a mental handle for yourself

In the same fashion as a case theme gives the jurors a generalizing principle around which information can be organized, so too does it give you one. The great trial lawyers emphasize the need for an overall strategy as well as day to day tactics. Too often, you become so caught up in the daily details of your case, you lose sight of the overall thrust of the case. The case theme embodies your overall strategy in nutshell and helps you organize your case so that you keep yourself on target.

Every point you make should be made with one directive in mind: Does it advance my case theme? Does this point fit coherently with other points, reinforcing my theme, or is it extraneous and therefore unimportant?

If your skeleton is in the shape of a man, don't elaborate points that distort that shape: a foot that grows out of a man's thigh does not clarify the shape of the man, it confuses.

4. You provide guidance for the jurors throughout the trial

Think what it must be like to sit in the jury box, listening day after to day to subject matter with which you're rarely conversant (even the simplest cases now are involved and complex), listening to innumerable witnesses, told to take note of innumerable documents, not allowed to talk about the case, or study the case at night, nor even discuss the case with your fellow jurors, and then suddenly, it's over, and you have to make a decision. If you haven't been provided with some kind of guidance, your decision will not be well informed. You will look for guidance, and take it wherever you can get it.

The successful trial attorney gives the jurors that guidance, right from the beginning of the trial and all through the trial, in the form of the case theme. If you have created a good case theme, and organized your case succinctly and consistently around that theme, you have given the jurors an excellent guide through the informational jungle which is a trial. If they cannot follow you, they cannot be on your side, regardless of the strength of your substantive issues.

5. You enhance your professionalism

You are the attorney, you are supposed to know what the case is about. The jurors look to you for expertise. By establishing a case theme, you let the jury know that you see the case in a very specific way, which lends credence to your professionalism and competence. Successful trial lawyers are never wishy-washy.

The Psychological Advantage of the "Rule of Threes" in Substantiating Your Case Theme

Once you've established your case theme, select no more than three main points or issues to substantiate it. Although psychological research has not yet understood the reasons behind this mechanism, it seems that information is most compelling when it is grouped in sets of three: three points, three arguments, three phrases.

CASE IN POINT

For example, notice the difference in impact between the following two different presentations of the same facts:

Poor Presentation:

> Jane is a hardworking person. She is a real "winner," dedicated to the principles of the firm.

Good Presentation:

> Jane is hardworking.
>
> Jane is dedicated.
>
> Jane is a winner.

The facts are identical in the two formats, but the three-point structure makes the second presentation truly dynamic. By structuring your case in terms of three main points, you access a powerful, albeit not-well-understood phenomenon of the human mind.

How to Use the "Rule of Threes" Persuasively to Support Your Case Theme

In addition to the psychological impact of a set of three points, three seems to be the number of points the mind can absorb and manipulate easily. The jurors must not only retain the points you make, they must also be able to manipulate them mentally: that is to say, compare them with opposing counsel's points and weigh their relative merit. If you attempt to present more than three issues, you will in all likelihood confuse the jurors and lose your case. Be picky, choose those issues which most clearly focus the facts and evidence in support of your case theme. Then use a diagrammatic format to help you organize your facts around the three issues you've chosen:

(Case Theme)		
(Point 1)	(Point 2)	(Point 3)
Facts supporting	Facts supporting	Facts supporting
Point 1	Point 2	Point 3

If you organize your facts in this fashion, you give the jurors—and yourself—clear guidelines by which to evaluate your case. Refute opposing counsel's arguments by reference to your structure. Do not allow opposing counsel to panic you into distorting your original case theme and three points: if your case theme is strong, and your three points logically support and enhance it, you have a winning structure, stick to it. When a lawyer changes his case theme or main issues mid-trial, it's usually lethal.

CASE IN POINT

Let's look at an example of how a case theme and three-point argument structure works in an actual trial. Fred H. Bartlit, Jr., was asked to defend Dun & Bradstreet in a major antitrust law suit brought against it by National Business Lists. In a nutshell, National Business Lists, whose business is mailing lists, accused Dun & Bradstreet of monopolizing the information needed for those lists. Rather than elaborating a defense which consisted of denying or in some way defending against the antitrust charges, Bartlit developed a totally different and original case theme, which he then proceeded to uphold. His theme, repeated over and over again, was that National Business Lists was essentially getting a "free ride" by copying information Dun & Bradstreet worked hard to obtain. Here's how he elaborated his three points during his opening statement to the jury:

"Now, what is the believable evidence going to show in this case? Well, there are three important things.

The first important thing is that Mr. Gans, who is sitting over there on the end in the first row, he is the man who runs National Business Lists. He will be the first witness. He started his business from the first day under false pretenses.

The second important point is that for twenty-five years, twenty-five years, he has run his business with a free ride because these names you have heard about, an awful lot of them were copies from Dun and Bradstreet, just copied. We got the names, not him, and he copied them.

And the third point is that even after we told him in 1975 to stop copying because it is illegal, he just ignored that and kept right on."[3]

Notice how clearly Bartlit elaborates his three points. He even says, right at the beginning, "there are three important things," and then enumerates them: "The first important thing . . . the second important point . . . and the third point . . ." You cannot get lost in such a clear concise framework. The jurors can easily remember and refer to those three points throughout the trial, as can Bartlit himself. The points are readily understandable, easy to follow, and directly relate to the case theme. From then on, Bartlit organized the evidence and facts around those three points in defense of his case theme, in consistent and repetitive fashion. Structure that strong is virtually unbeatable.

How to verify the clarity of your case theme and three points

A good way to find out if your case theme and points are solid, clear, and easy to follow, is to present them to a lay person. The worst thing you can do is run your case theme and points by a fellow attorney. Things which make sense to other attorneys can be complete gobbledy-gook to a person outside the profession. Frankly, a relatively intelligent 15 year old should be able to understand your case theme and points, and agree that your points fit coherently with and support that theme. This is not to say that the jurors will have the mentality of 15 year olds, only that given everything else going on in a trial, your case theme and points must be that clear and accessible for your foundation to be a good one.

HOW TO USE SIMPLE LANGUAGE AND PHRASING TO ENHANCE YOUR ARGUMENTS

Logic has to do with reasoning: logic is the domain of the mind or of thinking. Anything which supports or enhances clear thinking, then, contributes to the logic of your case. Stated simply: you can't persuade the jurors if they are confused. Aristotle's recommendation is worth noting: "Think as wise men do, but speak as the common people do." Verbosity, complex expressions, indirect questioning, are all confusing to a juror. The more direct your speech, the clearer it is, the more powerful it will be.

Bear in mind that a trial is presented *orally*. Too many attorneys speak like they write. Understanding written text and spoken speech have little in common. You can look up words you don't understand in a text, you can reread complex passages and phrases until you understand them. You can even choose to ignore the parts you don't understand and move on to the next passage. What happens in speech is totally different. A juror can't ask you to stop and explain a word or a passage, and if he didn't understand something, he's likely to get stuck on the not-understood word or concept and not hear the next three things you say.

Five Techniques to Insure that Your Use of Language Helps Rather than Hurts Your Case

1. Speak everyday language

Use simple language, the language of everyday conversation. Use real words, not the language of police reports. Ordinary people don't "alight from a motor vehicle," they get out of a car. We don't say of someone, "Subsequently, he left the premises"; we say "Then, he left the restaurant."

2. Avoid jargon or legalese

Using jargon makes the jurors feel like outcasts, they're not part of the "in-group." Your whole object in relating to the jury is in making yourself familiar to them, don't destroy that with legal-ese. Most legal terms can be expressed in layman's language with a minimum of effort.

When it comes to the necessary explanation of technical terms, do so as simply as possible, without talking down to the jurors. Your attitude in describing technical terms should be; "Here's how I came to understand it myself, and now I'm sharing that understanding with you." Not: "OK, you dodos, listen up."

3. Phrase for clarity of thought

Phrasing can help you greatly in achieving clarity of thought. Phrase your ideas one thought at a time (as described in Chapter 3), pausing often between phrases if you're explaining a complicated concept. When you ask questions, be careful to ask only one item per question. A witness cannot respond properly if you ask: "Did you take that route on a regular basis and were you driving it that Tuesday, June 10?" More importantly, the jurors wonder exactly what it is you are trying to get at. Are you attempting to determine whether this route is a regular one, and therefore a familiar one, or do you want to know where the gentleman was that Tuesday? You don't seem to know. Ask one question at a time; you'll seem more professional, and the jurors won't be confused.

4. Get to the point

Don't ask; "Would it be fair to say, perhaps, that you were on good terms with the deceased at the time?" Ask simply: "Did you get along well with Mr. Jones?" "Did you consider him a friend?" Speak a language all the jurors can understand, not the one or two who went to graduate school. It's difficult enough to uncover the facts of the case and construct a good defense: It's tragic to lose a valid case simply because you are not understood.

5. Check your speech

Practice an opening statement using a tape recorder; then enlist the help of a friend and tape record yourself conducting mock direct and cross examinations. Listen closely to the playbacks. Is your choice of vocabulary clear and easy to understand? Are you phrasing for sense or nonsense? Get a non-attorney friend to listen to the tapes and see if he has any difficulty understanding you. Ask him to be specific in his comments; is your word choice faulty? Are your sentences too long, containing too many thoughts? Do your thoughts follow logically? Use the opening statement practice worksheet at the end of this chapter to help you with your opening. You can significantly increase your chances of winning your jury trials simply by clarifying your speech.

HOW TO ORDER YOUR POINTS SO THAT YOU ARE MOST PERSUASIVE

The simplicity and clarity of your thought contribute greatly to your persuasiveness, so too does the *order* of your thought.

How to Enhance the Impact of a Point with the "Law of Primacy" and the "Law of Recency"

The "Law of Primacy" and the "Law of Recency," as defined by communications research, state that what you say first will be remembered best, what you say last will be remembered second best, and what you say in the middle will be remembered least well. Whether you are designing your opening statement, or deciding the order in which your witnesses are to appear, the psychological effect of order must be a primary consideration. Be careful not to bury an important point in the middle of your opening statement, or an important witness in the middle of a long string of witnesses.

How to Diminish the Impact of a Point

If order can be used to strengthen the impact of an idea, then so too can order be used to weaken the impact of an idea. If opposing counsel has called certain witnesses first and last, thereby making their testimony valuable, and you wish to diminish the impact of that testimony, call your witnesses in a different order, one that supports your case theme.

CASE IN POINT

In the Hauptmann case, mentioned earlier, a critical analysis by communication scholars Schuetz and Snedaker revealed that the defense not only failed to put forth a case theme, but also lacked coherent order in their presentation of witnesses.[4] The defense did not order witnesses so they corroborated Hauptmann's story, but rather skipped around from one set of evidence to another, without regard to a logical sequencing of witnesses, much less with regard to the rules of primacy and recency. Schuetz and Snedaker concluded that; "Reclustering and reordering of the witnesses could have produced a more coherent order and hence a more persuasive defense narrative."[5]

A VALUABLE TECHNIQUE TO FAVORABLY PREDISPOSE THE JURORS' MINDS TO YOUR POINT OF VIEW: THE "UMBRELLA STATEMENT"

There is a concept in acting called a "beat." A beat is the organization of thoughts around one idea. A new beat begins every time you introduce a new idea, and the beat ends when you've exhausted your thought, for the moment at least, on that idea. In a trial, you have new beats constantly. You introduce new evidence, witnesses, concepts and exhibits throughout the trial. The jurors need some kind of structure to help them assimilate this new information in a way that is both comprehensible to them and compatible with your definition of the case. That structure is the "umbrella statement."

How to Use the Umbrella Statement to Provide an Initial Overview for the Jurors

The umbrella statement is a statement which gives an overview of what's coming, a preview of sorts which allows the juror to adjust his mind set so that it is receptive to the information about to come. Without the help of this overview, the juror does not know where you are headed, and, since the mind seeks structure when it is not provided, focuses his energies on trying to figure out where you are going. The result is his attention is not on the point you are making, but on his quest for a structure that will allow him to organize the information. The juror may miss your substantive issue entirely until such time as he has accomplished this task.

Let me give you an everyday example of what this is like: you're in a restaurant and you overhear a conversation at the next table. Notice how you listen for a while to figure out what the people at the neighboring table are talking about exactly, and during that time, notice how your mind is actively searching for a context, some structure with which to make sense of the information you are overhearing. The mind cannot deal with disjointed facts.

CASE IN POINT

For example, in the case previously cited in which James F. Neal defended Dr. Nichopoulos, Neal used an umbrella statement in beginning his cross-examination of a witness: "I want to take you back to the life of Elvis Presley. Do you agree that you had conversations with Dr. Nichopoulos in which Dr. Nichopoulos referred to Elvis Presley as a problem patient?" [6] The sentence "I want to take you back to the life of Elvis Presley" is an umbrella statement which told the jurors to ready themselves for information regarding Presley's life, rather than information regarding Nichopoulos's reputation, for example. Well provided with structure, the jurors could attend to what was most important: Neal's interpretation of the facts of the case.

How to Use the Umbrella Statement to Re-introduce a Topic During Trial

An umbrella statement is also useful when you need to re-introduce an old beat, for example to further develop a subject, or add new information. It helps the juror place the new information in an already existing framework, and frequently serves to remind them in brief of what had already been discussed.

CASE IN POINT

Howard L. Weitzman, defending John DeLorean, used an umbrella statement in this fashion in cross-examining a witness:

Weitzman: "Mr. Tisa, we were discussing I think October the nineteenth a little earlier this morning. The decision was made that John should be arrested before he came to Los Angeles, correct?"

Tisa: "Yes."

Once Weitzman had thus oriented the jurors, he proceeded with the substantive issue he wanted to develop:

Weitzman: "When was that decision made?"

Tisa: "Sometime right just prior to the—I guess the eighteenth or nineteenth . . ."

Weitzman: "You had already concluded that he had been involved in and committed a crime, correct?"

Tisa: "Yes . . ."

Weitzman: "You will agree with me, won't you, that Mr. DeLorean did not know the cocaine was going to be in the room?"

Tisa: "Yes . . ."

Weitzman: "Regardless of how he reacted, he was going to be arrested anyway, wasn't he?"

Tisa: "Yes . . ."[7]

The jurors could very easily follow Mr. Weitzman's line of questioning; consequently, his point was clearly and forcefully made. Good structure is truly the foundation for persuasiveness.

HOW TO INOCULATE THE JURORS AGAINST OPPOSING COUNSEL'S ARGUMENTS BY ADMITTING YOUR WEAKNESSES

It is tempting to present only your side of the case: to pride yourself on the strength of your arguments and be convinced that once they have heard your argument, the jurors will be inevitably swayed by their brilliance and dismiss opposing counsel's as a sham. Tempting indeed, but fatal. Social psychologists have clearly demonstrated that a convincing one-sided communication presenting only positive arguments will indeed sway people toward the communicator's point of view, however, when the same people hear an opposing point of view, also supported by what seem to be valid arguments, they will now be influenced in the opposing direction. This is not beneficial to you. You need the jurors to be swayed by your argument in such a fashion that they stay swayed by your argument, *regardless* of what opposing counsel has to say. One way to accomplish this is through "inoculation."

How to Admit Weaknesses In a Way that Strengthens Your Case

Inoculating a jury is similar to being inoculated against a disease: you present the jurors with the weaknesses in your case, and those of opposing counsel's arguments you believe potentially damaging to your case, *and you lead the jurors nonetheless to your conclusion.* You have now given the jurors a way to ignore or discount opposing counsel's arguments; they have already heard them and been provided with reasons to dismiss them, thus "inoculated" the jurors are much more likely to retain your interpretation of the facts.

CASE IN POINT

A classic example of the value of inoculation, is found in the Julius and Ethel Rosenberg case. In his critical analysis of why the prosecuting attorney gave the better (and winning!) argument, noted professor, author and trial attorney J. Alexander Tanford shows how the prosecutor used admission of weaknesses to strengthen his case: "One example [of using two-sided communication admitting weaknesses] was his recognition that his witnesses were spies and traitors who were cooperating out of self-interest, but then using that to his advantage by comparing their apparent repentance and attempt to 'make amends for the hurt which has been done to our nation', to the Rosenbergs' compounding of their betrayal with lies and deception. The defense used only one-sided communication, never admitting any weaknesses and addressing only the favorable evidence."[8]

How to Disclose Weaknesses to Increase Your Trustworthiness

Your trustworthiness also increases as you show yourself willing to disclose weaknesses. As defense counsel, for example, rather than adamantly rebut every one of opposing counsel's arguments, admit that opposing counsel has some good points, and then go on to show how your conclusion is valid anyway. There is something in all of us that loves a confession. You will be perceived as fair and honest by the jurors, and your interpretation of the facts more readily accepted because of your "honesty."

CASE IN POINT

Edward Bennett Williams, considered one of the "greats" by his trial lawyer peers, spoke of how disclosure of weaknesses enhances trustworthiness in his discussions with Norman Sheresky: "Such a quality [the ability to seem sincere or truthful to a court or jury] requires the advocate to avoid overstating, and sometimes it requires him to do or say things that seem counterproductive to his interests. He has to tell the jury about the weaknesses of his case as well as the strength: [quoting Williams] 'You have to have all of the cosmetics of fair play, and I have found over a quarter of a century that, certainly, the best way to have all the cosmetics of fair play is to do fair play.' The jury will love you for it."[9]

HOW TO USE AN EXPLICIT CONCLUSION TO SWAY THE JURORS

Logic is an attempt to bring order out of chaos. The more concrete and specific you are in your thinking, the easier it is to bring order out of chaos. It may seem elegant to argue a convincing case, and then leave the conclusion up to the jury so as not to browbeat them or be heavy-handed, however, communications research shows, that it is far more effective to state conclusions explicitly. Stay concrete and specific in your thinking right through to the end.

Don't confuse the jurors by suddenly leaving *your* thinking up to *them* to do. At the end of your opening statement, for example, don't say something to the effect of: "Listen and keep your minds open," or "Listen and do justice." The jurors are thereby left without guidance: how are they supposed to translate "keep your minds open" and what does "do justice" mean? These categories are far too broad. After all, in a general sense opposing counsel wants the same thing. Rather, tell the jurors directly what you want: "guilty" or "not guilty." Give them a concrete and specific outcome to focus on, one that can help them structure their thinking. You are much more likely to get it.

SUMMARY

A thorough knowledge of communication principles will greatly facilitate your work. Understanding how both logic and emotion are necessary to the decision-making process will help you structure your arguments so that you win your case. Techniques used in the service of logic are the case theme, the three point argument, order, the laws of primacy and recency, simplicity and clarity of speech, umbrella statements, and inoculation. Once your substantive issues are structured such that your case has a solid logical foundation, the emotional appeals you make will have validity. This is truly a winning combination.

LOGIC AND STRUCTURE WORKSHEET:
Checklist of Psychological and Social-Psychological Techniques
Designed to Increase the Persuasiveness of Your Case

Use this checklist to help you incorporate the techniques discussed in this chapter.

CAUTION   *Remember, your case is only as good as your expert legal handling of the substantive issues. Presentation does not replace content, it enhances it.*

1. What is your case theme? _____

_____

_____

2. What are the three points supporting your case theme?

    1. _____

    _____

    2. _____

    _____

    3. _____

    _____

3. What are the facts supporting each of your three points?

    Point #1: _____

    _____

    _____

    Point #2: _____

    _____

    _____

    Point #3: _____

    _____

    _____

4. Observe your use of language:

    1. Is it everyday language?
    2. Is there any jargon?
    3. Do you clearly and simply explain technical terms?

    Technical terms: *Explanation:*

    #1 _____   _____
                                        _____
                                        _____

    #2 _____   _____
                                        _____
                                        _____

    #3 _____   _____
                                        _____
                                        _____

    #4 _____   _____
                                        _____
                                        _____

    #5 _____   _____
                                        _____
                                        _____

5. Observe your use of phrasing:

    1. Do you express one thought per phrase?
    2. Are your phrases to the point?
    3. Are your phrases clear and easy to understand?
    4. Do your thoughts follow logically?

6. Are your points ordered for effect? How? _____

    _____

    _____

    _____

7. Are your witnesses ordered for effect? How?

_____

_____

_____

_____

8. Have you provided umbrella statements to introduce topics? What are they?

_____

_____

_____

_____

_____

9. Have you provided umbrella statements to re-introduce topics? What are they?

_____

_____

_____

_____

_____

10. Have you inoculated the jurors against opposing counsel's arguments? What weaknesses have you disclosed?

_____

_____

_____

_____

11. Is your conclusion explicit? What is it?

_____

_____

_____

LOGIC AND STRUCTURE PRACTICE WORKSHEET

Videotape or audiotape your opening statement. Then listen to the replay of your statement, and use the following checklist to assess the persuasiveness of your presentation.

1. Do you have a case theme?   Yes ____   No ____

2. Are there 3 points supporting your case theme? Yes ____ No ____

3. Are there facts supporting each of your 3 points?

   Point #1: Yes ____   No ____   Not enough ____

   Point #2: Yes ____   No ____   Not enough ____

   Point #3: Yes ____   No ____   Not enough ____

4. Observe your use of language:

   a. Is it everyday language? Yes ___   No ___ Some ___

   b. Is there any jargon?   Yes ___   No ___ Some ___

   c. Do you clearly and simply explain technical terms?

                    Yes ___   No___ Sometimes ___

5. Observe your use of phrasing:

   a. Do you express one thought per phrase?

                    Yes ____   No ___ Sometimes ____

   b. Are your phrases to the point? Yes ____ No ___ Sometimes ____

   c. Are your phrases clear and easy to understand?

                    Yes ____   No ___ Sometimes ____

   d. Do your thoughts follow logically? Yes ____ No ____ Sometimes ____

6. Are your points ordered for effect?   Yes ____ No ____ Some ____

7. Are your witnesses ordered for effect? Yes ____ No ____ Some ____

8. Have you provided umbrella statements to introduce topics?

                    Yes ____   No ___ Some ____

9. Have you provided umbrella statements to re-introduce topics?

                    Yes ____   No ___ Some ____

10. Have you inoculated the jurors against opposing counsel's arguments?

   Disclosed weaknesses? Yes ____ No ___ Some ____

11. Is your conclusion explicit? Yes ____   No ____

   With the above observations in mind, note the corrections you feel are necessary to improve your use of logic and structure to persuade. Use the logic and structure techniques checklist to help you figure out how to make the necessary corrections.

CHAPTER 7

Using Emotions to Win Juror Belief

Logic is the language of the conscious mind, whereas emotions are the language of the unconscious mind. Emotions do not follow the laws of logic, emotions are predicated on subjective experiencing. Although subjective experiencing does not lend itself to reasoning, it is susceptible to a reliable set of techniques. These techniques facilitate the jury's subjective association with your client's or a witness's experience either by directly or indirectly engaging the jurors' own emotions. If you can get the juror to feel the witness's pain as his own pain, the witness's outrage as his own outrage, then you can convince the juror of the rightness of your position. If you do not engage the juror's emotions, the juror can easily remain uninvolved with your client's plight and therefore susceptible to opposing counsel's arguments.

Emotion, which comes from the Latin emovere, means to move away, or to move greatly. Given that decisions are first made emotionally, then backed up logically, your primary objective in Court is to literally move the jurors away from their present point of view over to your point of view. To accomplish that, you must indeed move them greatly.

A SPECIAL APPLICATION: HOW TO USE EMOTIONS TO PERSUADE IN A BUSINESS CASE

It is easy to see how emotions are important and can be used effectively in a personal injury case or a wrongful death action. A doctor mistakenly removing a healthy kidney from a man's body rather than the cancerous kidney evokes an immediate emotional reaction. A juror can easily relate to and understand the man's distress. The importance of emotions and how to use them effectively is much less obvious in a case involving complex business law, a battle say between two corporations

205

over a copyright infringement which involves millions of dollars, but leaves the average juror cold. And that is indeed a problem. Leaving the juror cold will lose your case. It is in the business case and similar seemingly non-emotional type cases that the use of emotions is the most crucial, because only by using emotions will you get the juror to relate to your case in a meaningful way.

CASE IN POINT

Fred H. Bartlit, Jr., representing Dun & Bradstreet, Inc. in the previously mentioned antitrust lawsuit initiated by National Business Lists, gave a brilliant demonstration of the use of emotions in a business case. The antitrust arguments revolved around such issues as the definition of a competitive market in the areas of credit information and business lists. These are not areas which have emotional appeal for the vast majority of jurors.

Rather than argue the case in terms of such impersonal economic issues, Bartlit redefined this very complex case into a simple formula with direct emotional appeal: that National Business Lists, had in fact been operating their business since its inception 25 years ago on information stolen from Dun & Bradstreet. The emotional message Bartlit reinforced over and over was:

"So they've [National Business Lists] been stealing from us all these years and now they turn around and accuse us of being the bad guys? No way!" [1]

A jury can easily identify with the outrage of being unjustly accused. It's happened to each and every one of us at some point in our lives. Very few jurors, however, can relate in any meaningful way to 2 major corporations battling over an antitrust issue. It is just too far away from the juror's daily cares and personal concerns. And if the jurors remain uninvolved and emotionally distanced from the issues in the case, it will be extremely difficult for you to convince them. That is why no matter how difficult it may be to translate business cases into terms that can be subjectively experienced by the jury, it is vital to do so.

Emotions, then, basically operate in two ways in trial work: they gain sympathy for your client and/or his cause, and they enable the juror to experience the case in subjective fashion.

CAUTION *Note that "sympathy" in this context does not mean "feel sorry for," rather that "sympathy" means to support, be in accord with, to approve of a person or his cause. Making the jurors feel pity for your client is not an effective persuasive technique: getting them to approve of your client is.*

HOW TO USE EMOTION TO FOCUS THE JURORS' ATTENTION ON YOUR INTERPRETATION OF THE FACTS

Emotions focus attention onto specific aspects of a situation rather than others: emotions determine what is taken into account, and what is ignored.

CASE IN POINT

If you like someone, for example, you notice his good points: how handsome he is, how intelligent, how witty. If you don't like someone, those good points may exist, but your attention is focused so that it is congruent with your emotion; you are aware of his dishonesty and his aggressiveness, for example, and are quite oblivious to his looks, intelligence and wit.

Emotions make some facts more salient than others. If the jurors relate emotionally to your client or his cause, and are sympathetic to him, then they will notice those facts and arguments which tend to support their positive feeling about the client, and dismiss those which are contrary to that feeling. If, however, the jurors do not relate in sympathetic fashion to your client or his cause, then they will tend to notice arguments which support their negative feelings—and opposing counsel will win. The importance of an emotional appeal in the decision making process then is clear: the jurors must be convinced on an emotional level for your substantive issues to be persuasive.

By using emotions, you enable the jurors to focus on your interpretation of the case, and be amenable to persuasion.

HOW TO USE EMOTIONS TO GAIN JUROR SYMPATHY FOR YOUR CLIENT'S CAUSE

If you are to win the jury's approval of your client's cause, then *you* must approve of it. Jury studies have clearly demonstrated that the most effective position for an advocate to demonstrate is allegiance and zeal for his client's cause. Jurors are favorably impressed by an attorney who is "demonstrably enthusiastic"[2]: you cannot be lukewarm about your case, if you are, the jurors will be too. Passionate belief in your client's cause inspires others to believe: studies in social power conclude that a person's ability to influence others increases with his increasing certainty in his own opinion.[3]

How to Express Sincerity to Influence the Jurors Favorably

There is a catch, however. The jurors must perceive your belief in your client's cause as *sincere*. This is why a blatant emotional appeal does not work: it is not perceived as sincere. Times have changed; dramatic gestures and expressions of passionate belief are no longer accepted as sincere, largely due to the changes in the media. Film and television require more subdued playing than does theater, due to the size of the images on the screen, and the use of microphones. We have become accustomed to more restrained expression of emotion, and are likely to be uncomfortable with grand gestures.

CASE IN POINT

Although F. Lee Bailey has certainly done very well as a trial lawyer, his style may not be as persuasive now as it has been in the past: the jurors in the Patty Hearst trial (1976) "reported great displeasure with the dramatic and overbearing deportment of her attorney, F. Lee Bailey; in the end, Patty Hearst did not fare well in their verdicts."[4]

You must walk a fine line: on the one hand, jurors do not approve of a reserved, passive approach, but nor do they appreciate it if you express your commitment to your client in overly dramatic fashion. Sincerity is largely a matter of suiting the emotion to the deed, as we described in Chapter 3, in order to avoid melodrama, and having an attitude of dedication and commitment to your client's cause. Exaggeration of your client's case is to be avoided: sincere people do not exaggerate. If you are to err, err on the side of understatement, you can always flesh out and strengthen your case as the facts substantiate your claim. It is almost impossible to undo the damage wrought by exaggeration.

How to Use Positive Emotions to Win the Jurors' Approbation

Positive emotions are much more attractive to a jury than negative emotions. You can effectively engender sympathetic feelings for your client and/or his cause by appealing to positive emotions such as love, pride, or devotion to an ideal. Appealing to negative or hostile emotions by attacking opposing counsel or his client, trying to convince the jury to hate the other party for his crime, or sarcastically ripping to shreds opposing counsel's case do not engender sympathy for your client. Jury studies systematically show that jurors tend to be highly critical and disapproving of attorneys who indulge in such disparagement. Over-aggressiveness has been repeatedly pointed out as the advocate's most common flaw.

This suggests a dangerous misunderstanding of the effect of negative emotions. Negative emotions rarely persuade, rather negative emotions make people uncomfortable and they tend to avoid them, especially when the negativity seems disproportionate. This is not to say, however, that you cannot have, for example, a moment of honest anger during a trial, or that you cannot indulge in an occasional sarcastic comment. Both these and other negative emotions can be very persuasive, but they should not constitute the main emotional thrust of your argument.

THE POWER OF SHARED EXPERIENCE: HOW TO CREATE EMOTIONAL RAPPORT WITH THE JURORS AS A BASIS FOR PERSUASION

Rapport must not only be established through body language, voice, and mirroring, rapport must also be established emotionally. It is very important to create an emotional alignment between your client and/or his cause and the jurors; the jurors must be able to empathize with your client's plight if they are to be receptive to your arguments on his behalf. The question then is not whether it is necessary to create emotional rapport in trial work, the question is rather, how do you do it? Emotional rapport is created in much the same way that you created non-verbal rapport, by emphasizing similarities between yourself and the jurors. Remember the sequence: similarity—familiarity—rapport—trust. Emphasize the similarities between your case and what goes on in the jurors' daily lives, between your client's concerns and their own concerns. People like what is similar to themselves, people feel comfortable with *what is familiar to them*. Speak to the jury of shared experience.

CASE IN POINT

Arthur L. Liman, for example, representing the New York City Transit Authority in their and the City of New York's action against Pullman Incorporated and Rockwell International Corporation over the purchase of defective subway cars, spoke of shared experience in explaining breach of warranty:

"Now, this is a case, as the court indicated, of breach of contract and breach of warranty. *The term 'warranty' is familiar to anyone who has ever bought a refrigerator or a television set.* Here we are dealing with warranties on a different type of product and a different consumer. Here the consumer was the City of New York and the Transit Authority, and the product was subway cars."[5]

By defining "warranty" in terms of refrigerators and television sets, Liman established the commonality between his client's concern and the jurors' daily concerns, he paved the way for a bond between his client and the jurors. The emotional bond is developed roughly as follows: the juror thinks, "I got it; it's like when I buy a TV set, brand new, and it falls apart, and the guy won't fix it—even though I've got a warranty. OK, I know what that feels like—it feels like I've just been ripped off, I hate it. So this guy's subway cars broke, and the manufacturer won't fix them, even though he's got a warranty—that's awful!" Now you have emotional rapport, based simply on shared experience.

Although it is especially critical to establish emotional rapport in an opening statement, the use of shared experiences is invaluable throughout the trial, both to keep the jurors reminded of their emotional tie to your client or his cause, and to get them back over to your side anytime you feel you've "lost" them. After all, if opposing counsel is good, the jurors may drift away from you. Use the technique of shared experiences anytime you need to hook the jury back in emotionally. If you give the jurors an emotional basis for relating to your client, you'll find they are much more willing to let themselves be convinced by you.

HOW TO USE STORY TELLING TO PERSUADE THE JURORS

Story telling is mentioned repeatedly by the great trial lawyers as a reliable and necessary technique to get the jurors on your side. But why? What is it that you can accomplish so successfully through story telling?

Capture the Jurors' Attention

First of all, a story gets the jurors' attention. We all love a story; jurors are no exception. People are far more likely to sit up and listen to a story than to a Spartan listing of the facts. A story is simply more interesting. Story telling, which is an ancient art, has been reinforced significantly in this century by the media. Both television and film use story telling extensively as a way of communicating ideas. Jurors are thus highly familiar with and accepting of the story format. Although story telling is used in its most elaborate form in opening statements, story telling can be used throughout the trial, in encapsulated form, whenever you feel the jurors' attention wandering.

Organize the Facts in an Emotionally Meaningful Way

Secondly, telling a story is a way of organizing material so that the jurors can make an emotional connection to it. Material which is not organized into story format is difficult to experience emotionally. For example, many people find avant garde music or art disconcerting because these mediums do not tell a story. They find it hard to enjoy these art forms because they cannot connect to them on a feeling level. In the courtroom, there is a good deal more at stake than enjoyment. Much of the jury's decision will be based on purely emotional considerations, so it is critical that the jurors be able to connect easily with your client and his cause. In order to help the jury make that emotional connection, organize the facts into a story.

CASE IN POINT

A good example of organizing facts into a meaningful emotional framework is to be found in one of Philip H. Corboy's opening statements. Corboy was representing Danny Schaffner, a young man who was permanently mentally and physically disabled as a result of a fall from a bicycle, in a suit against the Schwinn Bicycle Company and a railroad, the Chicago and North Western Transportation Company. The facts Corboy was presenting were that as Danny and his friends pedaled over a bumpy railroad crossing with which they were very familiar, the front wheel of Danny's bike came off, he flew off his bike and hit the pavement, and as a result was crippled for life. Here's how Corboy presented those facts:

> "This is the story of a typical family, had its ups and had its downs, had its heartbreaks, it's had its good times, and had its bad times. But it was a normal everyday American, mid-American type of family. Perry and Jean Schaffner met sometime before 1953 where they both lived in Chicago, both attended high school in Chicago. They fell in love, got married in 1953, and they started to raise a family. They moved in 1960 out to a far north suburb, as a matter of fact, even into a different county called Lake County, where they began to raise their children in Highland Park, Illinois. There were three children born of that marriage. Terry was born in 1956. James was born in 1958. And Daniel, the boy who has been injured was born in 1961, approximately a year after they moved out into the suburb."

Corboy continued, detailing the ordinary events of Danny's young life, until he got to the day of the fall. He told the jury in vivid and specific detail every moment of that day, taking them with him through his description down every street and through every turn the boys made as they bicycled along on their way to a Saturday afternoon movie, creating a virtual imaginary re-enactment of that ride. Finally Corboy's story led him to the crucial moments:

> "As Danny got on to these tracks [at the railroad crossing], he started bouncing and his bike went out of control. All of a sudden he was bouncing and he eventually got to the other side of the tracks, and he was completely off the tracks when his bike disassembled and his bike came apart and he fell to the ground. When he fell to the ground it was immediately apparent to his pals who came up to him that he was hurt, and his pals asked him what had happened, and he does not respond as to what occurred on the crossing because he does not know. But he did say, 'My shoulder hurts,' and he said it loudly, and he was crying, and then he said, 'My shoulder hurts,' and it was lighter, and then he didn't talk anymore. He went into a coma."[6]

Corboy skillfully organized the facts into a story framework with which the jurors could easily connect. He even stated right at the outset that this was a story, the story of an average American family. Notice how Danny's physical and mental condition assumes much more emotional relevance when it is described within the context of his life story. The jurors can readily identify with a young boy's growing up in normal suburbia, and feel the impact of his sudden impairment more vividly, placed as it is against the backdrop of that environment, than they could simply hearing it described in and of itself. Either way the event is tragic, but Danny's fall is more *moving*, therefore more persuasive, when it is woven into a story format.

Facilitate the Jurors' Vivid Vicarious Experiencing of an Event

The third function of story-telling in the Courtroom is to create a reenactment of any given event so rich in sensory detail, that the jury literally sees, hears and feels that event. Your goal is to make your description so vivid, that the jurors feel your client's distress as their own, and are moved by it. How do you do this? By addressing the senses. The senses, as we discussed in Chapter 3, are the gateway to the emotions. Story telling provides you with an excellent vehicle for accessing the emotions via the senses. Talk in terms of how things *feel*. What was your client's experience like? Was it warm, cold, soft, hard, calm, excited, dark, light? Was it sudden, slow, tearing, searing, harsh? What did it feel like, look like, taste like, smell like, sound like? Use the color words described in Chapter 3 to express how things feel.

CASE IN POINT

For example, let's take the following facts:

"Dr. Peters, a 32 year old pediatrician, was run over and killed by a yellow Pontiac in the parking lot of the local hospital."

In and of themselves, the facts are sad, a life was lost, but they are not particularly heartrending. After all, we all have to die sometime. Now, let's reorganize the facts into a story, using descriptive words to appeal to the senses, and see what happens.

"Dr. Peters, a 32 year old pediatrician, leaves her office, as usual, around 6:00 pm Friday evening. She strolls through the near empty parking lot, pleased with the way her day has gone—her 7-year-old patient on Ward III is responding nicely to the new leukemia medication. Dr. Peters stops for a moment to chat with a colleague about the new medical center that's soon to be built, and then continues to walk toward her car, feeling good, tired but happy, enjoying the warm August sun of late afternoon, when all of a sudden, seemingly out of nowhere, a yellow Pontiac comes hurtling straight at her and—that's all. No more Dr. Peters. Just a limp lifeless body lying bloody on the hard concrete of a parking lot."

That's a story. It has the emotional impact you need. You have used descriptive words to engage the jurors emotions via their senses, so that they feel Dr. Peter's experience, vicariously relive it, and are thus receptive to your interpretation of the facts. Facts in and of themselves rarely win anything. An emotional presentation of the facts does.

The more concrete and specific your descriptive details, the more persuasive your story telling. People connect much more easily with concrete and specific details: such details give immediacy and reality to your description.

CASE IN POINT

A good example of this is to be found in Edward Williams' opening statement in the 1956 U.S. v. Icardi case. In a nutshell, Lieutenant Aldo Icardi was accused of killing a Major William Holohan: both men were volunteers parachuted, with others, behind enemy lines in Italy during World War II on a special mission, called the "Chrysler Mission." In defending Icardi, Williams used story telling extensively. Notice the use of concrete specific detail in the following passage, taken from the opening statement in which Williams is describing the events leading up to the time of Major Holohan's death:

"... The next day they [the members of the Chrysler Mission] rowed back to the western shore of Lake Orta, because it had been shown to them that this was not a safe hiding place. They went up into the mountains and lay there one whole night in a driving torrential mountain rain. On November 1 they abandoned the mountains. They went to the city of Grassona and there one of the same priests hid them again. This time he hid them in his church in a small hole in the roof underneath the ceiling. After they were hidden some Nazi troops came into Grassona. They searched every nook and cranny, and forty of them lived in the church underneath the Americans for five days and five nights ... "[7]

Williams' use of specific detail pulls the listener into the story, making it real, making it believable. He doesn't just say "the shore of Lake Orta," it's the *western* shore." The rain is not simply "torrential," it's *"driving torrential mountain* rain." The members of the mission were not simply "hidden in a church," they were hidden *"in a small hole in the roof underneath the ceiling."* They didn't live over the very heads of the Nazi troops for "about a week," they lived there for *"five days and five nights."* All these details make it much easier for the jurors to create the visual and sensory experience in their imaginations, allowing them to experience the event as if they had been there, as if it had happened to them. Such powerful emotional identification is truly persuasive.

Use Well-known Myths and Stories with Built-in Emotional Appeal

You can organize a set of facts in an emotionally significant and meaningful way by placing those facts within the larger context of an individual's life, as in the examples given above, or you can organize a set of facts to the same effect by casting them in the familiar and recognizable lines of a classic story or character. Classic stories or characters, such as David and Goliath, Cinderella, Beauty and the Beast, the story of Cain and Abel, for example, are stories common to our culture, stories we grew up with and understand. On a deeper level, these stories and characters are archetypal; they represent prototypical experiences common to all humans and are to be found across cultures and across epochs. They tap a profound emotional dimension we respond to almost instinctively. We know, when we hear such a story, who is the good guy and who is the bad guy, the moral of the story is built-in, as it were. By structuring your story so that it suggests archetypal characters or story lines, you identify your client's cause with that of the "good guys," and the justification for that definition is inherent to the story.

CASE IN POINT

For example, James F. Neal's defense of Dr. George Nichopoulous, cited earlier, was based on the archetypal story of the Good Samaritan. By defining his case along archetypal story lines, Neal took advantage of already existing powerful emotional triggers.

The Good Samaritan is a culturally and societally accepted "good guy"; Dr. Nichopolous became a "good guy" by association.

CASE IN POINT

Melvin Belli, in his defense of Jack Ruby, also used a classic character. Although Belli lost the case for many reasons, his use of an archetype was innovative and skillful: "Ah, what great sport to have in our community 'the character.' In the old days we used to call him the 'village clown,' 'the village idiot.' There's a chained wolf to be tormented, there's the hunchback of Notre Dame, there's our own Emperor Norton in San Francisco, the old humpty-dumpty who, for fifty cents, would bend over and allow people to hit him on his backside with a board. Ah, what great sport for this . . . troubled human being we're trying, until something goes wrong. There's trouble. Then the cry goes out, 'Who do you suspect the most, who would do an unusual thing like that?' The answer: 'The village idiot.' You substitute the village clown, the village idiot—Jack Ruby!"[8]

What Belli was attempting to achieve was the emotional association between Jack Ruby and the classic character of the village idiot, a character we all accept as a mentally impaired person not responsible for his actions.

CAUTION *Bear in mind that emotional association is a potent mechanism and must be used with care. If you cannot back up your definition of a case along a particular story line substantively, opposing counsel will demolish your definition and make it very difficult for you to regain rapport.*

HOW TO GET YOUR POINT ACROSS SUCCESSFULLY BY USING ANALOGIES AND SIMILES THAT TIE INTO THE JURORS' LIFE EXPERIENCE

Analogies and similes are ways of creating links between an idea you want to get across, and the jurors' life experience. Analogies compare ideas or situations which are identical in some ways but not in others; for example, cooperation on a surgical team may be compared to that on a baseball team. Most people are familiar with baseball, few are intimate with the details of surgery. The comparison between the familiar and the unfamiliar allows the unfamiliar to be understood, at least in terms of what is identical to the two situations, in this example—cooperation.

Similes liken one thing to another using a comparative word such as "like" or "as." For example, a common simile for psychotherapy is: "Psychotherapy is like a bridge between where you are and where you want to be." Not many people have personal knowledge of psychotherapy, but just about everybody knows what a bridge is. By comparing therapy to a bridge, the therapist ties into common experience (the bridge) and makes it easier for the lay person to understand an otherwise very complex idea (psychotherapy).

We use analogies and similes constantly in our daily life without thinking about them as specific communicative tools. All you have to do in order to use analogies and similes powerfully is use them deliberately. How? Simply take something from common experience and compare your specific fact to that common experience. For example, imagine your specific fact is represented by the word "it" in the following statements: "It's like pearls before swine," "It's the difference between night and day," "It's clear as day," "She took to it like a fish to water," "It's like a dog barking up the wrong tree" and so forth.

How to Use Analogies and Similes to Get the Jurors to Relate Emotionally to Your Point

Analogies and similes are critical to trialwork for the simple reason that jurors come from a variety of life situations and may or may not have had any experience with the issues in the case. Analogies and similes, by comparing the legal issue to something commonly understood and experienced, allow the jurors to relate and connect emotionally to the issue.

CASE IN POINT

Terry Hallinan, one of San Francisco's most venerable trial lawyers, used an elaborate and compelling analogy in order to explain to the jury how to evaluate the conflicting contentions of eyewitnesses for the defense. Hallinan was representing the plaintiff, his son, in *Terence Hallinan v. Michael J. Brady*, City and County of San Francisco, and Norbert Butierrez:

> "Some years ago I was in another city and a friend took me to an establishment that he deemed would be interesting. We walked down a curious kind of street with old-fashioned houses on each side and strange-looking, almost artificial-looking trees, and there was no life to it, no traffic along a cobbled street. No birds sang in the trees. There was no sound or sign of life behind the windows. And then we came to one of the houses about a block and a half down, and the door was open and behind it were struts, two-by-fours, holding up the wall. It wasn't a house at all. It was the facade of a house, a moving picture set. We were on a Hollywood lot. I didn't have to go back to the other houses to find out that they were facades, too. And you don't have to go back and examine everything that these men said to convince yourself that you can't put a moment's reliance on any single thing that they uttered."[9]

The comparison between a facade masquerading as a house, and a verbal front masquerading as truth is a powerful one.

How to Use Analogies and Similes to Give Focus and Impact to an Issue

In addition, analogies and similes enable you to focus the issue strongly so that your point is communicated effectively.

CASE IN POINT

For example, District Attorney Linda Fairstein, in prosecuting Marvin Teicher, a dentist accused of making a number of his women patients engage in sexual contact with him when they were in a helpless anesthesia-related drugged state, compared Dr. Teicher's actions to those of a necrophiliac—with the difference that in Dr. Teicher's case, the bodies were still warm.[10] The idea of necrophilia is horrific to most people. With this simple analogy, Ms. Fairstein was able to galvanize the jurors' emotions by connecting Dr. Teicher's behavior to something already established as nefarious in our culture. Her point was communicated most effectively.

When you use an analogy to help the jurors identify with a point, in a sense, the analogy does the work of persuasion for you. People already have feelings hooked into the analogy: necrophiliacs are sick or bad people, houses on a movie set are without substance and therefore useless in the real world. Those feelings are transferred to your point, as long as your analogy is an accurate one.

How to Select Analogies and Similes that Have Emotional Appeal for Your Specific Jury

Selecting appropriate analogies and similes can be delicate, especially when dealing with highly complicated technical issues.

CASE IN POINT

Arthur L. Liman, in the previously cited case of the New York City Transit Authority against Rockwell International Corporation, for example, chose his analogies and similes skillfully when he compared subway cars provided by Rockwell, which the Transit Authority claimed were defective, to Edsels:

"To give you the case in a nutshell, the proof here will show that when the defendants were selling and promoting the R-46 [subway car] to the city, they promoted it as if it were a Rolls Royce of the subway industry, fast, safe, quiet, and long-lasting. We will show you that they didn't deliver a Rolls Royce. They delivered an Edsel, a lemon, a car whose undercarriage is disintegrating, literally."[11]

Not only were the engineering matters discussed in regard to the subway cars difficult to understand, they were virtually impossible for the average person to connect to *emotionally*. How many of us can relate on a feeling level to a discussion of cracks in the transom arms of subway cars? The Rolls Royce and the Edsel however are commonly held cultural symbols of excellence and failure, respectively. Excellence and failure are easy to relate to on an emotional level.

CASE IN POINT

Later during the course of his closing argument for this case, Liman, who uses analogy and simile masterfully, compared the defenses given by Rockwell's attorneys to mechanical rabbits:

"I call them rabbits because they remind me of the mechanical rabbits that they have in tracks where they have dog races, and the dogs are let loose and they chase after the mechanical rabbit and they expend a lot of energy, and of course, they never catch it, and they come away very,

very confused. And they have set a lot of rabbits loose in this courtroom and I intend now to deal with them and show that they are nothing more than that. They are nothing but phony alibis."[12]

The analogy of mechanical rabbits is wonderfully vivid and readily engages the senses. Because it refers to something most people in our culture understand and relate to, it gives emotional focus to the jurors as they deliberate, a focus directed by Liman himself. This is a sterling technique and one well worth developing.

How to Avoid the Problems Inherent in Using Analogies

However, there are problems in using analogies and these must be addressed.

1. Make sure your analogy is accurate

First of all, if your analogy isn't 100% accurate, opposing counsel can take your analogy and turn it against you. Be sure you turn your analogy inside out before using it, verifying that no matter how it's turned around, it still works for you. A movie set can be nothing more than a facade, for example, no matter how you look at it. There are no redeeming aspects to an Edsel. These are good analogies given the context of the cases.

2. Avoid overstatement

Secondly, be careful not to overstate or overemotionalize your case with your analogy, you are giving ammunition to opposing counsel. Be sure you can back your analogy up with a detailed factual argument. A phony emotional hook is deadly.

3. Be sure your analogy suits your jury

Thirdly, suit the analogy both to your jury. If your jury is quite young, analogies from the Depression may have little impact; if your jury is primarily female, sports-oriented analogies may be worthless. Think carefully about what the life-experience of your jurors has been, and choose analogies and similes from that life-experience.

4. Choose analogies from your own experience

Last of all, choose analogies that make sense to *you*. You cannot be persuasive discussing something you know nothing about. Be sure the analogy is one you thoroughly understand and relate to. Don't use an analogy from baseball, for example, if you know nothing about the game. Bear in mind that your sincerity is a prime persuasive tool, and you must sincerely believe in the value of your analogy for it to be effective.

HOW TO USE REPETITION AND CATCH PHRASES TO REINFORCE YOUR INTERPRETATION OF THE FACTS

How to Use Repetition to Advance Your Case

Repetition may seem like a simplistic technique, but it is a surprisingly effective one. Sheer repetition creates familiarity with an idea or event, and that familiarity leads to liking. We tend to interact often with people and situations we like, and avoid those people and situations we dislike. Use repetition then throughout trialwork; repetition of themes, of points, of key arguments, and repetition of *catch phrases.*

How to Use Catch Phrases to Define a Point to Your Advantage

Catch phrases are phrases designed to capture the essence of an idea. They are then used over and over again. Frankly, we are a nation of catch phrases. We tend to speak a great deal in catch phrases:

"We're Number 1"

"The Pepsi Generation"

"We shall overcome"

"Blondes have more fun"

"Buy now, pay later"

"The antidote to civilization"

and so on. It is no accident that advertisers use catch phrases as extensively as they do. Their research has shown how easily we respond to catch phrases, and how well we remember a product when it is attached to a catch phrase. Catch phrases have a decidedly useful function: once defined, everyone knows what they mean, and they can be repeated endlessly to reinforce an idea.

When you refer to your client as "the victim," you are using this very technique. Repeated identification of your client as "the victim" will lead the jury to define your client, Mr. Smith, not as a whole person with a multitude of other roles (father, brother, banker, softball fanatic), but as one thing only: "the victim."

Catch phrases are essentially a way of labeling someone or something with a particular emotional bias so that the jurors will come to perceive it in the same way. In the above example, you label your client "the victim" very deliberately because you want the jury to dwell on the *victimhood* of your client, not on his success as a banker or his reputation as a womanizer.

Catch phrases can be developed out of the story you tell in your opening statement to reinforce that story as the trial goes on, or out of an analogy to reinforce the analogy.

CASE IN POINT

Every time Ms. Fairstein, in the previously cited case, referred to Mr. Teicher's sexual activities as "necrophilia," she reminded the jurors of the emotional bias with which she had tagged the sexual activity: completely unacceptable and nefarious. Eventually, it becomes difficult to separate the thing or behavior from the bias of the label.

The persuasiveness of this technique, however, relies on an accurate assessment of a what might be a valid catch phrase. You can label to your heart's content: if there isn't enough documentation to substantiate the bias, the catch phrase either won't take hold or will work against you. We are not talking about inventing a catch phrase to somehow change things in the case to your advantage, but rather using the catch phrase as a way of expressing an emotional truth inherent to the behavior or thing being described.

How to Use a Case Theme to Reinforce Your Point of View

The *case theme* can be thought of as a special kind of catch phrase. It is a catch phrase or slogan used over and over again which sums up what is going on in your case; "The Good Samaritan," "the village idiot." If you accurately capture the essence of your case in your case theme and repeat it often, the jury will come to see the case as you do, just by the familiarity you have thereby created.

HOW TO USE "MONEY WORDS" TO TAKE ADVANTAGE OF IDEAS THAT ALREADY INFLUENCE JURORS

In their research, in addition to the idea of catch phrases, advertisers have come up with a concept called "money words." A "money word" is a word that represents something of value for people in a given culture and which is therefore emotionally loaded. It is no accident, for example, that a recently created credit card is called "Discovery." "Discover" is a money word; discovering things and ideas has great meaning for Americans, we pride ourselves on discovering frontiers and miracle cures, great ballplayers and missing children. People pay particular attention to money words, a money word alerts them to a situation or event which has emotional relevance for them.

The money words useful to the attorney are: discover, health, easy, proven, results, safety, love. Whenever it is possible for you to use one of these words rather than another similar word, use it. You are taking advantage of a word which already has intrinsic power, and you can make that power work in your favor.

HOW TO USE PERSONALIZATIONS TO GET A JUROR OR WITNESS TO RELATE SUBJECTIVELY TO A POINT

The most valuable money words of all are "you," and a person's name. There really is no better attention-getter than a person's name. Try this around the office. Insert the other party's name every so often in the course of a conversation, and notice how the person with whom you are conversing seems to perk up at those moments and pay more attention. Notice how *you* instantly perk up and pay attention when you hear your name called. The word "you" serves a similar function.

The word "you" or your name symbolizes yourself, your very being. The mention of either one of them demands attention, if only on a survival level. When you use the word "you" or a person's name, you are personalizing the discussion, you are making the discussion more immediate, more relevant to that person. You are in a sense, forcing the person to assess not whether X statement is true for others (a thought which may or may not be of interest to him), but to assess whether statement X applies directly to him. For example, in questioning a prospective juror, saying "People often feel hesitant about discussing such things" is much less effective than saying "You may feel hesitant about discussing such things— people often do." In the latter format, you've still taken the juror off the hook by generalizing his feeling to a lot of people, but you've made your statement powerful by addressing yourself specifically and directly to the juror. He cannot escape considering the issue since it is now directly aimed at him.

The word "you" is used most effectively when you want the jurors to relate vividly and directly to your client's experience, as if it were their own. This is a very powerful technique, which should be reserved for occasions when you believe it is essential that the jury get maximum emotional impact from the experience. Rather than relate your client's experience in the third person, relate the event as if it were happening to the jurors themselves.

CASE IN POINT

For instance, using our previous example of Dr. Peters, the fictitious 32 year old pediatrician killed by a yellow Pontiac in the parking lot of the local hospital, let's say that Dr. Peters was maimed for life, rather than killed, and restate it in "you" form:

"Let's say you're going for a walk, oh at around 6:00 pm on a Friday evening. You're pleased with the way your day went—one of those days when everything seemed to go right. Along your way you stroll through an almost empty parking lot, you stop for a moment to chat with a neighbor about a new building that's soon to be built in the neighborhood, and then continue to walk feeling good, tired but happy, enjoying the warm August sun of late afternoon, when all of a sudden, seemingly out of nowhere, a yellow Pontiac comes barreling straight at you and—that's all. That's it. That's all you remember until you wake up in a hospital room, confused and in pain, and you try to get up, and then you realize you can't, you have no legs. And you have no idea how that happened. All you know is one moment you were a healthy functioning human being, and now something is terribly wrong. . . . That, ladies and gentlemen of the jury, is Dr. Peters' experience. And that is why we are here today."

The word "you" puts the jurors on the spot. It forces them to identify directly with what is going on. It takes an active effort of will not to identify with "you" statements, and most people will not choose to exert that effort. Because the word "you" puts people on the spot and obliges them to identify with what is going on, it must not be used lightly. As with the other techniques taught throughout this book, use the word "you" in accord with your overall strategy, not haphazardly, and be well aware of its power when you do so.

How to Personalize Experiences to Give Your Point Maximum Impact

The more directly an individual has experienced an event or situation, the more meaning it has for him. People who lived through and suffered the effects of the concentration camps in World War II relate emotionally to the experience in a way no twenty-year old ever could. Your client is the only person who can truly relate to the situation which has brought him to court, he is the only one who truly feels the despair, distress, rage or hopelessness of his condition. The closer you can get the jurors to feeling the client's distress (or the righteousness of his cause) as he does, the more persuasive you will be.

Role-play is the single most powerful way to induce attitude change through vicarious experiencing. In an experiment designed to convince people to stop cigarette smoking, noted social psychologist Irving Janis had cigarette smokers role-play having lung cancer. The smokers playacted reviewing X-rays, receiving the news that they had cancer, discussing the operation with the Doctor, having the operation, and so forth. The number of smokers who stopped smoking following the experiment was significantly greater than those in a control group who had not participated in the role play, and, more importantly for our purposes, the more intensely the smokers participated in the role play, the greater the likelihood that they would stop smoking.[13] You cannot, in a Courtroom, get the jurors to role-play an event, but the closer you can get to role-play, the better your chances of persuading the jurors.

Engage the jurors vigorously in the process of vicarious experiencing by personalizing events and situations. There are two ways to do this:

1. Directly engage them with the "you" format, recasting the event in personalized terms
2. Translate the event or situation into terms directly taken from the jurors' personal experience.

Get the jurors directly engaged with the "you" format

CASE IN POINT

An excellent example of this approach is to be found in Clarence Darrow's (1926) brilliant defense of Henry Sweet, one of eleven blacks arrested and charged with first-degree murder, shortly after Sweet and his family had moved into an all-white neighborhood in Detroit, Michigan:

"Ten colored men and one woman are in this indictment, tried by twelve jurors, gentlemen. Every one of you is white. At least you all think so. We haven't one colored man on this jury. We couldn't get one. One was called and he was disqualified. You twelve men are trying a colored man on race prejudice. . . . You don't want him. Perhaps you don't want him next to you. *Suppose you were colored. Did any of you ever wake up out of a nightmare dreaming that you were colored? Would you be willing to have my client's skin? Why? Just because somebody is prejudiced! Imagine yourself colored, gentlemen. Imagine yourselves back in the Sweet house on that fatal night.* That is the only right way to treat this case, and the court will tell you so."[14]

The italicized phrases represent those which challenge the jurors to relate to the experience directly and personally. Darrow took the alien experience of being black in 1926 and recast it in terms the jurors could relate to from intimate details of their own experience: what would it be like to have a different color of skin? Undoubtedly some of the jurors had nightmares of being colored. By asking such direct, pointed questions, Darrow forced the jurors to put themselves in Sweet's shoes; this is a highly effective form of mental role-playing.

Translate the event or situation into terms taken from the jurors' personal experience

Situations which are clearly meaningful to an attorney often leave a juror emotionally cold, and therefore unpersuadable. The net result is, opposing counsel thinks you have a heck of a good point, but the jurors could care less. This does not advance your cause.

CASE IN POINT

Rikki Klieman gives an example worth noting. She takes the statement "It was a coerced confession," which is certainly significant to an attorney, but has little *emotional* impact on a jury, and translates it into relevant personal terms as follows:

"They brought him into the room at four o'clock in the morning. The room was eight by ten. It was like a large closet at best. It had one light bulb. He asked for something to eat. They didn't give him anything. They kept talking to him for hours and hours. He kept saying that he didn't know anything. He asked for something to drink. The temperature kept going down and they wouldn't give him a coat when he asked for a coat. In fact, later on, they told him to remove his sweater and next to remove his shirt. He had to remove his socks and his shoes. He was freezing."[15]

Klieman is in a sense obliging the jurors to experience the event from the client's point of view by reframing it in terms that the jurors can identify with. An abstract notion "coerced confession" has been made real by translating it into actual sensory details, with which the members of the jury can identify from their own experiencing. Bear in mind, at all times, that the emotions are accessed through the senses. Ask yourself, "What did this experience *feel* like" and then ask yourself, "How do I have to describe this so the jurors feel it that way too?" Don't simply state, for example, that your client suffers pain from his injury, translate that pain into personal details the jurors can experience vicariously; talk about how your client has to get up an hour and a half earlier now to get to work on time, because it takes him 20 minutes to button his shirt, the pain is so bad in his damaged hands, and how it takes forever for him to work a zipper, it hurts so for him to put his fingers together to hold the zipper, and so on.

Medical and technical terms obviously need translation into reality: a "tri-malleolar" fracture may mean a lot to a doctor, but little to a juror. "There are three bones in the ankle. He broke all three bones. These bones connect the foot and the ankle. Now the foot and ankle are disconnected."[16] These statements give reality to the "tri-malleolar fracture"; the jurors can relate to their own feet and ankles and to how awful it must be to have those disconnected.

What is less obvious is that terms not generally thought of as technical, such as distance expressed in feet, or temperature expressed in degrees, are not emotionally effective. Few people think in terms of "12 feet away," or "9 inches apart." Make these concepts real either by showing them on a diagram, by pacing the distance off in the Courtroom, or by showing what the distance is with your hands: do whatever you have to do to translate the distance into experiential rather than conceptual terms. Don't talk about the plant workers "having to deal with 102 degree heat"; talk about it being "so hot you can't breathe, and your sweat keeps dropping in your eyes." In a word, make it real. It's the only way you'll have impact.

CHOOSE A CASE THEME THAT SELLS

How do the jurors select which version of the case, yours or opposing counsel's, that they are going to believe? They select that version which interprets the facts in a way that is most consistent with the jurors' knowledge and experience of human behavior, which fits in with their understanding of the way the world works. Respect the fact that a basic human urge is to protect the weak against the strong, that jurors tend to do what is morally right, rather than what is technically correct. Choose a case theme that addresses these concerns; choose a case theme that sells.

CASE IN POINT

A good choice of case theme is given by Barney Sears in his prosecution of seven police officers from the Summerdale District of the Chicago Police Department, charged with conspiracy to commit burglary and receiving stolen property.[17] Sears defined the conspiracy as a violation of public trust, and made the moral reprehensibility of such an act his case theme: in so doing, he appealed strongly and convincingly to the jurors' desire to do what is morally right.

How to Win by Elevating Your Case Theme to a Higher Cause

Often, in order to formulate a case theme that will be both meaningful to a given jury, and persuasive, you must elevate your theme to a higher cause. You will not engage a jury emotionally, for example, by simply arguing the details of whose car hit whose in an automobile personal injury case; raise the theme to a larger issue, that of irresponsible drivers, for example, or of the state of automobile safety, issues with which the jurors can connect emotionally. Open to the jurors the possibility of making their community safer for other drivers, of preventing many needless deaths, give them the opportunity to right some fundamental wrong. These are moving issues, persuasive issues, issues to which people can commit on a feeling level.

CASE IN POINT

An unexpected and spectacular elevation of a case theme was demonstrated by Philip Corboy, defending a well-off couple, the Kluczynskis, who had been bumped from a Delta Airlines flight, and thus inconvenienced on their way to a social weekend with friends. The suit was for $100,000. No one thought Corboy would win. His clients had been, at the most, slightly inconvenienced, and by an average citizen's definition, hardly inconvenienced at that.

Corboy raised the theme of the case to an unexpected level, that of the need to deter airlines from dealing lightly with people, pointing out how people miss important moments in their lives: marriages and funerals, business meetings and long-awaited encounters, reunions with loved ones, due to the irreverent attitude of airlines toward their patrons. By elevating the theme to this level, Corboy allowed the jurors to relate emotionally to the Kluczynskis' experience in terms that had meaning in their personal lives, and appealed to the jurors' basic human desire to right a moral wrong. The jury not only returned a verdict in favor of the Kluczynskis, but awarded them twice the amount which had been asked for. [18]

It is especially important to raise your case theme to a higher level when you know your client's position is counter-normative, that is to say, goes against the prevailing norms in the community. The farther away your client's position is from those norms, the more difficult it will be for you to persuade the jurors. You must all the more carefully therefore select your case theme in order to guide the jurors in a direction they will find acceptable.

CASE IN POINT

It is counter-normative to approve of a Doctor who encourages and supports a patient's drug addiction: James Neal was perfectly aware of this when called upon to defend Dr. Nichopoulos in the case cited previously. Mr. Neal chose, therefore, to raise the case theme to a higher level, that of the moral issue of doing whatever it takes to help someone, even if how you do it is unpopular and may be to your own detriment.

The theme of the Good Samaritan was very effective. The jurors were able to set aside conventional ways of dealing with the case, and focus rather on the moral issues involved, guided as they were by Neal's case theme.

HOW TO USE THE PRESENT TENSE TO ENGAGE THE JURORS' EMOTIONS

When describing to the jurors the events and circumstances relevant to your client's presence in Court, in order to have the jurors connect effectively emotionally to those circumstances, you must move them across space and time. You must somehow make the jurors feel that the event is happening *now*, not at some time in the remote past, because the farther away an event is in time, the less urgency is felt around its occurrence. The song "Time Heals Everything" is apt. For most people, time indeed is a great healer. Time puts things in perspective, time cushions the raw feelings which erupt at the time of a traumatic event. But what you need is for the jury to experience something which happened to someone else in the past with the same intensity as if it were happening to them, personally, in the present. The use of the word "you" and personalization, as described above, is a way of getting the jurors to identify emotionally with your client's circumstances as if they were the jurors' circumstances. The use of the present tense in describing the circumstances is how to get the jurors to feel the event as if it were happening *now*.

The present tense should be used any time you want the jurors to "feel it now."

CASE IN POINT

Attorney David M. Harney's direct examination of an expert witness, Dr. John S. Wilson, provides a very clear example. Mr. Harney represented Harry

Jordan in a suit brought against the Long Beach Community Hospital, and all the doctors involved, for removing Mr. Jordan's healthy right kidney, rather than his cancerous left kidney, which was the kidney targeted for surgery, leaving Mr. Jordan in very poor health with multiple physical and financial problems. Part of Mr. Harney's direct examination went as follows:

". . . In other words, doing an X-ray review for impending major surgery with the urologist, without talking to a radiologist who is within a few feet of this box, within a few feet, and he doesn't talk to the radiologist. He spends five to fifteen seconds talking to a urologist who has the films in backwards, where he, Dr. Waters himself, has them in backward. Now, is that below the standard?"[19]

Let's restate that passage in the past tense, which would be more accurate in terms of reality, and see what it does to the intensity of the experience:

". . . In other words, having done an X-ray review for impending major surgery with the urologist, without having talked to a radiologist who was within a few feet of this box, within a few feet, and he didn't talk to the radiologist. He spent five to fifteen seconds talking to a urologist who had the films in backwards, where he, Dr. Waters himself, had them in backward. Now, was that below the standard?"

Notice how, stated in the past tense, the experience does not have the same vividness as when the experience is stated in the present tense, and vividness is what appeals to the *emotions*. The experience has been made more comfortable, more removed, and therefore less intense. But for the jurors to really identify with Mr. Harney's point, the substandard level of care, they must feel that lack of care now, feel outraged here in the present moment, not comfortably removed from the experience at some distant point in the past. The principle then, is as follows: any time you want to recreate an event or situation vividly and emotionally for the jurors, state it in the present tense.

How to Use the Past Tense to Distance the Jurors Emotionally from an Event

This principle also works in reverse. In other words, if you want an event to seem less immediate, less important, put it in the past tense. When you talk about the opposition's distress, put it in the past tense, it won't seem quite so real. Distance the jury from the experience by recasting it as something that happened in a dim and less important past. You will lessen the impact of the event very subtly and effectively.

HOW TO KEEP THE JURORS' FOCUS WHERE YOU WANT IT BY USING THE POSITIVE FORM OF SPEECH

The positive and negative forms of speech are little recognized but very powerful techniques of influence. You can easily keep the jury's attention on a certain point simply by stating the point in the positive, and distract attention by stating the point in the negative.

For example, if someone says "Don't think of a pink elephant," 99% of you will immediately think of a pink elephant. The mind does not distinguish between "do" and "do not," as it sorts through your memory to bring all relevant material to your attention. Your mind simply attempts to bring to consciousness *all* elements included in the statement. If you say, "I want this meeting to run smoothly and well," chances are everyone will simply think "OK" internally. The mind simply picks up information pertaining to "meeting run smoothly and well." If however, you say "I don't want this meeting to get out of control," the mind picks up information on "meeting go out of control" and you have just unwittingly introduced the possibility that the meeting could get out of control.

If you want to keep a juror's or witness's mind attending to certain issues and not others, bear the following principle in mind when phrasing your comments: phrase your statement positively to keep the person's mind on a certain track, phrase the statement negatively if your purpose is to introduce an element of doubt.

CASE IN POINT

In the course of voir dire, for example, if you say: "Is there any reason why, if *you* were on trial, you would not want eight jurors just like yourself?" the prospective juror's mind will immediately come up with 20 reasons why he would not want eight jurors just like himself. If this is not the desired result, then phrase the question positively: "Would you, if *you* were on trial, be satisfied with eight jurors just like yourself?" Phrased like this, the mind will not hunt for negatives. It will simply "go with the flow" and respond "yes"; it will stay on that positive track unless you are really off base in your questioning, and the answer is an obvious "no."

How to Sow Doubt by Using the Negative Form of Speech

The reverse, of course, is equally true. If you *want* the prospective juror to come up with twenty reasons why he should not want a juror such as himself on the jury, phrase your question negatively.

CASE IN POINT

To get an idea of how this works, let's take Mr. Harney's direct examination of the expert witness in the above mentioned case against Long Beach Community Hospital once more as an example: ". . . In other words, doing an X-ray review for impending major surgery with the urologist, *without talking* to a radiologist who is within a few feet of this box, within a few feet, and he *doesn't talk* to the radiologist. He spends five to fifteen seconds talking to a urologist who has the films in backwards, where he, Dr. Waters himself, has them in backward. Now, is that below the standard?" The underlined phrases are in the negative form.

Confronted with "without talking," the mind immediately jumps to "should have talked," "why didn't he talk," "could have talked," and so forth. Similarly, faced with "doesn't talk," the mind instantly asks "why not?" This is the very effect Mr. Harney desired. Now, let's look at what happens when the same question is posed in positive form:

". . . In other words, a radiologist is within a few feet of this box, within a few feet, doing an X-ray review for impending major surgery, *he talks only with* the urologist. He spends five to fifteen seconds talking to a urologist who has the films in backwards, where he, Dr. Waters himself, has them in backward. Now, is that below the standard?"

Notice how using the positive form greatly dilutes the emotional impact of what happened, and yet emotional impact is what you need in order to persuade the jury, as Mr. Harney did, of the outrageousness of the substandard care.

Why is this? Well, in the positive form, the mind does not instantly pose probing questions. The positiveness of a statement puts the mind on a comfortable emotional track, it lulls the mind into emotional comfort, which then makes the mind slower to probe for the possible negatives in the situation. It requires mental effort for the mind to pick up on the incongruity of the Doctor speaking only with the urologist in a situation where speaking with the radiologist would be most effective. We are generally unwilling to make that kind of an effort unless we are suffering from some sort of discomfort. Phrasing ideas in the negative is an excellent way to generate the emotional discomfort necessary to lead us to probe and question.

HOW TO CHOOSE YOUR WORDS TO INFLUENCE THE JURORS' THINKING

Words have great impact. Words not only communicate meaning, words also have emotional connotations. People relate to different words differently. Saying of your client that he suffers from whiplash is not as powerful as saying he is a "neck cripple." An "accident" elicits a much different emotional reaction than does a "wreck," "pile-up," or "smash." To appeal to the jurors' emotional level, make your choices as vivid as possible. Do not fall into melodrama, which can be avoided simply by making word choices which reflect the reality of the situation and can be substantiated (for a discussion of inappropriate choices, see Chapter 3), but do use words with enough impact to get your idea across clearly and effectively.

CASE IN POINT

Two of the cases cited earlier illustrate this point particularly well.

Ms. Fairstein's choice of the word "necrophilia" in her analogy characterizing Dr. Teicher's sexual behavior in the case cited earlier, is an excellent example of the power of appropriate word choice. Dr. Teicher was interacting sexually with non-consenting women in a drugged condition; non-consenting and drugged is very close to dead, when it comes to sexual relations. The word "necrophilia" was thus appropriate. The power of the word is clear: most people have a powerful emotional revulsion to sexual relations with a dead body.

Mr. Liman's choices of "Rolls Royce" and "Edsel" in the New York City Transit Authority case are equally powerful. "Cadillac" and "Pinto" would not have had the same impact. "Rolls Royce" has come to be culturally defined as the summum of automobiles, and although the "Pinto" has had problems, it does not have the generally recognized association with total debacle that "Edsel" has.

How to Relabel Opposing Counsel's Terms to Diminish His Impact on the Jurors

The reverse of the above principle is of course also true. If opposing counsel persists in labeling his client's broken leg "a mangled limb," you can call him on it, and relabel the leg as merely broken. If he refers to the accident as a "wreck," you can relabel it an "accident." This will greatly diminish the impact of his terms. However, you will only be successful in relabeling opposing counsel's terms if he has made inappropriate, that is to say basically exaggerated or overstated, terms. Since opposing counsel can obviously turn around and do the same to you, be careful that your word choices do reflect the facts of the case accurately and simply express the reality vividly, not in overstated fashion.

HOW TO INFLUENCE WITNESSES' ANSWERS WITHOUT LEADING

Word choice is not only important in persuading the jurors, it is also critical to directing witnesses' answers in a direction favorable to you. How you design your questions has a great deal to do with how they are answered. Psychological research has clearly demonstrated that people respond very differently, for example, when asked to estimate a person's height depending on whether the question asked is "How tall is he?" versus "How short is he?" When asked the height of a basketball player, those asked "How tall?" answered, on the average, 79 inches. When the question posed was "How short is he?" of the same player, subjects answered, on the average, 69 inches. That's a difference of almost a foot![20]

Carefully choosing words such as "fast" to suggest speed, "far" to suggest distance, "tall" to emphasize height, "short" to minimize it, will not, except in rare circumstances, be held against you as "leading" the witness. They will, however, have a definite effect on how the witness responds. "How fast was the car going?" suggests high speed; "At what speed was the car traveling?" suggests more moderate speed. "How far was the intersection?" suggests that the intersection was far away; "How near was the intersection?" suggests the opposite. Choose the word which presupposes your desired answer. If you want the intersection to have been closer, use "How near?"; if you want the intersection to have been farther away, use "How far?"

Be aware of the differential meanings of such words as "a" and "the." "A" and "the" may seem interchangeable, but they are not, they imply very different things. "A" refers generically to an undefined object. "The" refers specifically to a defined object. "Did you see *a* man with *a* limp?" does not focus a person's attention in the same way as "Did you see *the* man with *the* limp?" does. The use of "the" presupposes that the man exists, the limp exists, and that the only question is whether or not the witness saw the man. Thus the witness will search his memory more assiduously given the unconscious message that the man with limp exists, than if asked whether he saw "a man with a limp" which contains no such presupposition.

Similarly, notice the different impact of such words as "frequently," "occasionally," "sometimes," "often." Subjects in the research cited above, when asked if they had headaches "frequently" and how often, replied on the average, having had 2.2 headaches per week. Subjects asked if they had headaches "occasionally," stated, on the average, that they suffered from headaches 0.7 times per week. The power of such words to elicit different responses is considerable. Don't throw this power away by using words in haphazard fashion. Choose those words which reveal most clearly your interpretation of the facts.

FIVE SPECIFIC WAYS YOU CAN USE VISUAL AIDS TO ENHANCE YOUR PERSUASIVENESS WITH THE JURORS

The choice to use visual aids is predicated on many factors, including appropriateness to the case, personal preference, availability, and so forth. In this section, we'll look at how visual aids can assist you in creating the necessary emotional impact on the jurors.

1. Use Visual Aids to Keep Jurors Awake and Interested

First and foremost, visual aids help keep the jury awake and interested in the proceedings. They break up the monotony of words. I do not mean to imply that your words are monotonous, only that any experience repeated over long periods of time becomes monotonous. You may be the most dynamic attorney in the Courts, there are still many long tedious moments in a trial. Bear in mind that the adult attention span is only 18 minutes long. Visual aids are very useful in providing a different stimulus every so often to keep the proceedings lively. Jurors can be emotionally swayed much more easily if they alert and interested in what is going on.

2. Use Visual Aids to Focus Jurors' Attention

Nonetheless, there will be moments when the jurors are distracted or bored. Their attention will inevitably wander at different points during the trial, and visual aids can then be useful to encourage the jurors to be distracted in a way useful to you. If, for example, you have various visual displays in the Courtroom, the jurors will naturally tend to look at those displays during those times that their attention is wandering. In this way, you are directing their attention even when the jurors are seemingly distracted.

3. Use Visual Aids to Access the Visual Perceptual Mode

Visual aids are also useful in accessing the visual mode of perception we discussed in Chapter 4. Since many people are highly visual, illustrating important points or explaining complex points with the use of visual aids can make a significant difference to your ability to communicate those points. The use of different colors in graphics permits the influence of those colors at an unconscious level, and again, serves to liven things up.

4. Use Visual Aids to Get the Jurors to Experience Events and Concepts as Real

Using visual aids makes things more real. The old saying "A picture is worth a thousand words" truly applies. A photograph of the accident damages, a blowup of a document with a contested signature on it, these are infinitely more effective than the *telling* of the incident. Remember that we are a visual generation. Television and film have largely replaced the written word for most people as a mode of communication. We are used to *seeing* events more than we are to simply hearing about them. Use this reality to your advantage in order to influence the jurors through a medium that they are used to and which is familiar to them.

CASE IN POINT

For example, have your witnesses work with your charts. Have a diagram of the location of an incident drawn up, for instance, and then have your witness go over and mark where what happened. Having the witness go over to the chart and mark on it, "This is where I stood, this is where my car was, this is where the man was when he threw the bottle at me, this is where I fell" is far more tangible and more emotionally relevant than having the witness simply state, "He threw the bottle at me from 10 feet away."

Be careful though that your witnesses are well rehearsed if you use this technique, otherwise opposing counsel can come in and demolish your effect by questions designed to confuse your witness.

Documents and photographs are always more effective blown up. It makes them seem more important, and they stick out in the jurors' minds. Be careful of using blackboards: opposing counsel can easily erase your diagram and draw their own. You are safer using charts and transparencies.

5. Use Visual Aids to Reinforce Your Point Emotionally

Perhaps the most critical effect of visual aids, however, is to reinforce your point in a highly charged emotional way. This is particularly true of still photographs or actual pieces of evidence.

CASE IN POINT

For example, in the previously cited case, in which Philip H. Corboy represented Danny Schaffner, the 15 year old boy crippled as the result of a bicycle mishap, Corboy entered the broken bike as his first exhibit. That broken bicycle remained in the Courtroom for the duration of the trial, an immensely powerful silent witness to the drama of this boy's life.

The emotional impact of that bicycle was tremendous. Clearly, it is not always possible to bring in a physical piece of evidence as compelling. However, still photographs of shocking events or important pieces of evidence have a similar effect. The still photograph allows the juror's imagination to wander, to try to figure out what must have happened before or after; it draws the juror's attention back to a certain moment or situation again and again, reinforcing the emotional impact. Thus still photographs are best left in Court as long as possible to have the desired emotional effect.

HOW TO INFLUENCE JURORS BY THE WAY YOU HANDLE EVIDENCE

How you handle evidence, physically, is just as important as *what* evidence you introduce. Think of physical evidence as props, physical elements designed to enhance your interpretation of the facts, just as stage props enhance the reality of a performance. If you want a piece of evidence to seem abhorrent, for example, handle it gingerly and with some measure of distaste, your body language will express your feelings more effectively than words ever could.

CASE IN POINT

A good example of how physical handling of evidence can affect the meaning attributed to that evidence is given by Rikki Klieman, in her defense of a man charged with manslaughter:

"In Michael's case, the .357 Magnum, an incredibly powerful gun, will be treated by the prosecutor (if he or she is good) as if it were a cannon. I once saw a prosecutor literally put a pen through the part where the trigger was and hold it by the pen as if he were afraid of the gun. That gun became huge. . . . I used the gun in my opening and treated it like a Roy Rogers or Dale Evans pistol. I played with it so that it looked like a cap gun. No matter how many times the government tried to portray it as the 'third most powerful handgun in the world,' somehow my picture, because I am a small woman, created a different image."[21]

By handling the gun as if it were a toy, Klieman diminished the emotional impact attempted by the prosecution of "third most powerful handgun in the world." Don't ignore the effect your handling of exhibits has on the jurors; *everything* you do in a Courtroom adds up to either increase or diminish your persuasiveness.

HOW TO CONVINCE JURORS
OF YOUR INTERPRETATION OF THE FACTS
BY PHYSICALLY DEMONSTRATING YOUR POINT

Earlier in this chapter, I discussed how role play is the single most effective way to accomplish attitude change. The closer you can get to role play, the better your chances of persuasion. Actually handling evidence encourages the jurors to identify with you, and to mentally handle the evidence themselves. The clearer your body language is in handling evidence, the more accurately it expresses how you feel about that evidence, the easier it is for the jurors to emotionally connect with you and experience the evidence in a similar way. Illustrating a point physically is effective for the same reason.

CASE IN POINT

An excellent example of this is to be found in David Harney's cross-examination of an expert witness during his defense of Harry Jordan, whose healthy kidney had been removed by mistake, rather than his diseased cancerous kidney:

Harney: And how could he [the operating surgeon] ever get a game plan [for surgery] if he never found out which side the tumor was on?

Karlan: He was told which side the tumor was on.

Harney: [holding a ball in his right hand and showing it to Karlan] Which hand is this ball in?

Karlan: Mr. Harney, if you told me that ball was in your left hand, I would have the utmost respect for you and say it is in your left hand.

Harney: Sir, which hand has the ball in it?[22]

The expert witness could repeat all day how the assistant surgeon must respect what the head surgeon says is truth, the jurors are going to be swayed by that very common-sense demonstration. Physically demonstrating a point is always more powerful than simply verbally explaining the same point.

The use and format of visual aids in the Courtroom is only limited by your ingenuity. Judges are generally willing, if asked in advance, to allow all sorts of visual aids. I encourage you to take advantage of their liberality.

SUMMARY

Accessing the unconscious allows you to influence the decision making process where it starts—at the emotional level. Through this chapter, we've looked at a number of ways to do that. By using the techniques of instant rapport, story telling, analogies and similes, catch phrases and repetition, money words, personalization, present tense and positivity, word choice and visual aids, you will be able to speak directly to the emotions, where you can be most persuasive.

EMOTIONS WORKSHEET:
Checklist of Psychological and Social Psychological Techniques Designed to Increase Your Persuasiveness

This checklist may be thought of as a "think list." It is designed to encourage you to actively *think* about how to be emotionally persuasive in some very specific ways. You may choose, in function of your legal expertise, to use all, some, or none of the items in this checklist, but the important part is that you know *why* you choose to include or discard any of the items listed.

1. Are you sincere in your presentation? Yes ____ No ____

    If "No", what can you do to increase the sincerity of your presentation?

    _____

    _____

2. Do you emphasize the positive emotions in your presentation?

    If yes, which ones? If no, why not? _____

    _____

    _____

    _____

    _____

3. Have you created emotional rapport with the jurors? Have you spoken to them of shared experience?

    If yes, how? If no, why not? _____

    _____

    _____

    _____

    _____

4. Have you organized the facts of the case into a story?

    If yes, how? If no, why not? _____

    _____

    _____

    _____

5. Is your story telling descriptive and rich in sensory detail?

   If yes, how? If no, why not? _____

   _____

   _____

   _____

   _____

6. Are you availing yourself of the power of emotional archtypes?

   If yes, how? If no, why not? _____

   _____

   _____

   _____

   _____

7. Have you included analogies and similes in your presentation to help the jurors relate emotionally to your points?

   If yes, how? If no, why not? _____

   _____

   _____

   _____

   _____

8. Are your analogies and similes accurate?

   If yes, how? If no, why not? _____

   _____

   _____

   _____

   _____

9. Do you avoid overstatement?

   If yes, how? If no, why not? _____

   _____

   _____

   _____

   _____

10. Are your analogies and similes from your own experience?

If yes, how? If no, why not? _____

_____

_____

_____

_____

_____

11. Do you use repetition for effect?

If yes, how? If no, why not? _____

_____

_____

_____

_____

_____

12. Have you included catch phrases in your presentation?

If yes, how? If no, why not? _____

_____

_____

_____

_____

_____

13. Have you included "money words" in your presentation?

If yes, how? If no, why not? _____

_____

_____

_____

_____

_____

14. Have you used personalizations to get the jurors to relate directly to events? If yes, how? If no, why not? _____

_____

_____

_____

_____

_____

15. Have you translated events and situations into terms directly taken from the jurors' personal experience?

If yes, how? If no, why not? _____

_____

_____

_____

_____

_____

16. Does your case theme sell?

If yes, how? If no, why not? _____

_____

_____

_____

_____

_____

17. Would it be useful to elevate your case theme to a higher cause?

If so, how would you do it? _____

_____

_____

_____

_____

18. Have you used the present tense when you want to make an experience immediate and vivid?

   If yes, how? If no, why not? _____

   _____

   _____

   _____

   _____

19. Have you used the past tense when you want to diminish the impact of an experience?

   If yes, how? If no, why not? _____

   _____

   _____

   _____

   _____

20. Have you used the positive form of speech when you want to keep the jurors on a certain track?

   If yes, how? If no, why not? _____

   _____

   _____

   _____

   _____

21. Have you used the negative form of speech when you want to sow doubt in the jurors' minds?

   If yes, how? If no, why not? _____

   _____

   _____

   _____

   _____

22. Have you carefully chosen your words for maximum effect?

    If yes, how? If no, why not? _____

    _____

    _____

    _____

    _____

    _____

23. Have you relabeled opposing counsel's terms to diminish their impact?

    If yes, how? If no, why not? _____

    _____

    _____

    _____

    _____

    _____

24. Have you included the use of visual aids as an emotional hook for the jurors?

    If yes, how? If no, why not? _____

    _____

    _____

    _____

    _____

    _____

25. Have you considered how you will handle the physical evidence so that you give the evidence certain distinct emotional connotations?

    If yes, how? If no, why not? _____

    _____

    _____

    _____

    _____

    _____

26. Have you considered how to demonstrate certain points physically in order to get the jurors to connect emotionally to those points?

    If yes, how? If no, why not? _____

    _____

    _____

    _____

    _____

    _____

CHAPTER 8

Applying the Techniques of Persuasion to Each Part of a Trial

So far, we've looked at persuasive communication techniques individually, analyzing and discussing how each one of them works, how each can be used in trial work, and how to acquire those techniques. Now we'll look at the five main parts of a trial—voir dire, opening statement, direct examination, cross examination, closing argument—and see how the techniques are integrated into each of these parts for maximum persuasiveness.

CAUTION As before, bear in mind that these techniques are psychological and social psychological techniques designed to enhance and augment the persuasiveness of your legal expertise, not replace it. Always develop your case to the best of your lawyering abilities first, and then incorporate those of the techniques of persuasion presented in this book that you believe, given your knowledge of legal procedure, are appropriate to your case and will help you win.

HOW TO MAKE *VOIR DIRE* WORK TO YOUR MAXIMUM ADVANTAGE

This discussion of voir dire is not designed to teach you how to select a jury: there are entire books and seminars devoted to this subject alone. Rather, my purpose is to help you use the process of voir dire from a presentational standpoint to accomplish, through the process of voir dire, two critical objectives:

1. *a winning first impression* that will predispose the selected jurors favorably to you, and by extension, to your client's cause,
2. *good rapport* with the prospective jurors which will make them receptive to you, and therefore open to being persuaded by you.

Create a Winning First Impression

A winning first impression is one which conveys credibility, that is to say professionalism and trustworthiness. Given that the eventual jurors' first look at you is during the course of voir dire, voir dire is *the* situation in which to establish your credibility in front of the jurors. The importance of voir dire from this point of view cannot be over-emphasized. How then do you create a credible first impression in voir dire?

Establish your professionalism

Your professionalism relies greatly on looking like you know what you're doing. If you don't look like you know what you're doing, you may be a brilliant attorney, but that will not be the prospective jurors' perception. Knowing what you're doing means, for example, that you don't turn to the Judge the first day of voir dire, and ask if he wants you to sit or stand. The jurors' internal reaction to that one is, "Doesn't he know? What is this, his first trial?" The jurors don't know that every trial judge has his peculiarities, and you certainly cannot preface your question to the Judge with, "Oh, by the way, prospective jury members, all judges have different ways of proceeding, so I have to ask some procedural questions now." All the jurors see is that apparently you don't know what to do in a Courtroom, and if you don't know something that basic, how can you possibly be a good lawyer?

Know your Courtroom, and know your Judge. How is the Courtroom physically laid out? How much room do you have in which to move around? Does this Judge allow moving around or does he require a lectern? What are the acoustics like? Find out ahead of time how the Judge presiding over your trial likes to conduct voir dire. Find out all the details: does he prefer the attorneys to stand or sit, what kind of questions does he allow, does the judge like to give the jury the preliminary instructions or does he leave this up to the attorneys, and so on. The more you know ahead of time, the more professional you will seem.

Your professionalism is supported by how you are dressed and groomed. Clean, neat, appropriate dress and grooming are the bottom line. Your briefcase and files should be tidy and organized, be sure you can easily locate your pens and pencils.

Strive to be not only credible as a professional, but charismatic as well. Do things one thing at a time, do not rush, give your complete focus to whatever you are attending to at that moment. Remember you are being observed at all times. Don't let that intimidate you, use it to your advantage. Show the jurors what you want them to see.

Establish your trustworthiness

Having established your professionalism, how do you establish your trustworthiness in voir dire? By an attitude of sincerity and dedication to the case. Your attitude should be pleasant but serious: justice is a serious matter to the jurors, it should be to you also. When you are not either questioning prospective jurors or listening while they are being questioned by opposing counsel, take notes, appear to be reviewing the case. Show that you care. Leave your newspaper at home. Do not attend to matters extraneous to the case at hand in the presence of the jurors. Maintain an attitude of polite civility toward opposing counsel, do not crack jokes or appear over friendly toward opposing counsel in the presence of the jurors even if he is your best buddy. Treat the members of the Court, especially the Judge, with respect and politeness at all times.

Create Good Rapport with the Prospective Jurors

Let's now consider the second major objective of voir dire from a presentational point of view: the creation of good rapport. Remember that rapport is the development of relationship, and good rapport is the development of a relationship that allows you to persuade the jurors. Start voir dire with an attitude of empathy toward the jurors. Be aware that this is a frightening and novel experience for them; as you gather the necessary information from the prospective jurors, you must also put them at ease, and make them feel comfortable and secure with you. Only if jurors feel comfortable and secure with you will they allow you to be their guide through the trial.

Emphasize similarities with the jurors

Bear in mind that we are all most comfortable with that which is familiar to us. Before your first day of voir dire, gather as much relevant information as you can on the community from which the jurors are to be drawn. Then emphasize aspects of your dress, body language, and choice of vocabulary which accord with the basic tendencies of that community. At this stage of trial, you will only be able to connect on very broad levels: urban versus rural, suburban versus sophisticated, ethnically mixed versus a common ethnicity, and so on. Once the jury has been selected, you will be able to refine those broad choices to more specific ones, but you will have already, from the outset, established some degree of similarity, which works in your favor.

Treat the jurors as equals and with respect

When you interact with the jurors, talk with them, not at them. Think in terms of working with the jurors, of sharing information, rather than imparting it. Talk to the jurors as if you were speaking informally with a group of friends about some important subject. Don't cross-examine the prospective jurors. An aggressive probing attitude puts most people on the defensive; it definitely alienates jurors. Be firm but polite. Maintain a friendly, interested attitude throughout. Remember the power of good eye focus. Whether you are questioning a prospective juror, or listening to his response, look at him. It is vital to the development of rapport that you look at the jurors anytime you talk with them. Note-taking splits your attention and makes it difficult for you to do this. Assign to co-counsel or an assistant the task of taking down responses and making notes.

Design your questions to build rapport with the jurors as well as gather information

When you ask questions of the prospective jurors, be sure to ask the kinds of questions that build rapport as well as reveal information. Ask questions that invite dialogue, rather than "yes" "no" type answers. For example, asking a generic question such as: "Have any of you read any magazine articles, or newspapers about personal injury cases involving airlines?," will give you a "yes" "no" response, and leave the juror quite cold. Such a format does not personalize the interaction, allowing relationship to develop. It simply asks for factual information. A more personalized approach would be, for example, "What type of magazine articles or newspapers have you read regarding personal injury cases involving airlines?" "What are your feelings about cases involving these types of injuries?" Asking the prospective jurors about their *feelings* regarding any given point will both elicit more information regarding their biases and attitudes, and give the jurors the impression that you care about how they think and feel, that it matters to you. People like people who care about them.

Don't overlook the value of questions regarding hobbies, what organizations the prospective juror belongs to, volunteer activities and so forth. What an individual does with his leisure time often tells you more about his personal biases and attitudes than does his job. Vary your questions: don't ask for the same information in the same way juror after juror after juror. Repetition is only valuable as a persuasive technique if it is done deliberately, for impact. Otherwise, it is just plain boring, and you hardly want to *start* trying your case by boring the jurors.

Avoid embarrassing or indiscreet questions

Don't ask more personal questions than you absolutely need to for the case. Speak clearly, using simple language everyone can understand. If, for any reason, a prospective juror does get confused by one of your questions, immediately take the blame for this yourself. Take the juror off the hook by saying, for example, in a warm friendly way: "I'm sorry, my question was unclear: let me put it to you another way," and start over again. Use the juror's name in speaking with him: remember how powerful is the insertion of person's name in any given communication.

Remember jurors' names

Make it a point to remember names and pronounce them properly, the jurors will be impressed by your doing so, it makes it seem that you *care*. If you're not sure how to pronounce a name, ask for the correct pronunciation the first time you ask the juror's name, then write the name down in such a way that you will remember the correct pronunciation. An easy way to remember names, and other important information about the prospective jurors, is to have your assistant create a seating chart of the jury panel, with the relevant information marked at that person's place. You can easily refer to the chart discretely as needed.

Listen attentively to the jurors

When you've asked a question, be sure to listen to the answer. Listen not just for the factual information you need, but also for hesitancies, inconsistencies, emotional undertone. Make sure you acknowledge answers by nodding or making "uh-huh" type sounds. Acknowledgement goes a long way in creating rapport.

Pay attention to juror body language cues

Listen also with your eyes: observe the prospective jurors as you speak with them, pay attention to what they wear, how they sit, what their body language suggests. Have co-counsel or your assistant observe also, and make notes of those observations. Have them especially observe what the prospective jurors do when they're not actually interacting with an attorney. How do they relate to each other? What do they do during recess? Do they read, knit, stare into space? All these things are little bits of information which add up to your really *knowing* your jury, and thus being able to address your case specifically to the jury *actually trying your case*, and not to some generic jury composed of faceless strangers. Strangers are much harder to convince.

HOW TO CREATE A COMPELLING *OPENING STATEMENT*

The value of a compelling and persuasive opening statement is now established beyond any doubt. Whether the jurors actually *finalize* their decision at the end of the opening statements, as some studies have shown, or hold their decision in abeyance until the end of closing arguments, as other studies suggest, jury studies have clearly demonstrated that the verdict jurors give at the end of the trial is almost invariably identical to their feelings at the end of the opening statements.

An opening statement can be considered in two phases: its preparation and its presentation.

Preparation of Your Opening Statement

Although you have undoubtedly been preparing your opening statement all along, do not finish it until after your jury has been selected. To be most effective, your opening statement must incorporate the values and life-style of your jurors, and you cannot know these prior to selection. The careful observations you and co-counsel made during voir dire as to the jurors' dress, body language, vocabulary level, habits, sex, age, ethnicity, education, religion, employment, hobbies, and so forth now are put to good use.

Choose an effective case theme

Choose a case theme which makes sense to the specific jury you are now addressing, be sure it is one the jurors can all understand and relate to. Your case theme should be drawn from the jurors' life experience, taking into account the values and norms of their community. Make sure your case theme also accurately reflects your interpretation of the facts and can be substantiated by those facts.

Back your theme up with three major points

At this stage of the trial, the jurors need a map, not the entire territory described in encyclopedic detail. The detail will come later, as you bring forth the evidence and witnesses. The purpose of an opening is to provide the jurors with a framework which will allow them to see the case through your eyes, a blueprint, if you will, of the trial. Keep it simple. If you attempt to bring forth more than 3 points, the jurors will only get confused and lost. Bear in mind the laws of primacy and recency: be sure your first point is the most important.

Create a story

Weave your points into your story, the story of the events leading up to this trial. The case theme defines the heart of the story, the "moral" as it were, the story itself is the narrative of how your client got there. Your points need to be clearly stated as such, but their placement in your story is a matter of personal preference. As long as you have created an umbrella statement in the beginning of the opening which orients the jurors as to the nature of the story being told, the jurors will be able to fit your points into the logic of your story.

Choose the most dynamic story telling style for your specific case

A story is just that—a story. There are two basic ways to tell a story: start with the peak moment, then go back to the starting point in time and then tell the story in chronological sequence, or start back in time at the starting point and continue in chronological sequence up to the peak moment. Both are effective, your choice depends on your purpose. Starting with the peak moment tends to "grab" an audience more quickly and emphasizes the *event* itself, working your way through a simple chronology emphasizes the *context* of the event rather than the event itself. Choose the story-telling style that fits best with your interpretation of the facts.

Personalize your client's experience for the jurors

Personalize your client's experience as you tell the story either by directly engaging the jurors with the "you" format, or translating the experience, if not immediately meaningful, into terms the jurors can easily relate to. Be sure to call your client by name, so that the jurors can relate to him as a living breathing human being. If your client is a corporation, find a way to humanize the corporation so that the jurors can connect to the corporation emotionally (see Chapter 12). Make sure as you go along, that you include moments of shared experience so that you continue to create rapport with the jurors. Continue developing rapport also by using your knowledge of the jurors to include vocabulary, analogies and examples which are from their world and thus are easily accessible and familiar to them. Be careful to try out your analogies in every possible way so that you don't mistakenly choose one opposing counsel can turn against you.

Engage the jurors' emotions

Tell your story with lots of descriptive words accessing all three perceptual modes. Include plenty of color words to connect with the jurors at an emotional level. Remember the power of word choice: select words and catch phrases for impact. Use repetition judiciously, not as filler, but for its persuasive value. When you get to the peaks of your story, use the present tense to make your client's experience more real to the jurors. Be careful to use the positive form of speech when you want to keep the jurors' thoughts on one track, and the negative when you want them to question or doubt something.

Expose the weaknesses in your case

Inoculate the jurors so that opposing counsel's attempt to tear down your interpretation of the facts will lack impact. If you are second in line, do not attack opposing counsel directly, simply acknowledge his interpretation, and then go on to present yours.

Give the jurors an explicit conclusion

Be sure to include a summary of your case theme and three points at the end of your opening, then tell the jurors explicitly what you want from them: certainly, you want "justice," but what else?

Check the clarity of your opening

Then read your finished opening statement to a lay person—or two or three—and see if they can easily understand your language and follow your points. If so, you're ready for the next step, presentation.

Presentation of Your Opening Statement

Practice using an outline

Before you go into Court with your opening, rehearse it as many times as you can in front of a lay person, in front of a videocamera, and just on your own. Do not have the opening written out in full in front of you and attempt to memorize it. This is guaranteed to cause you anxiety and heartache. Rather transform your full opening statement into an outline with which you are extremely familiar, and serves to remind you of the major points you wish to cover.

Know your Courtroom setup

Find out whether the Judge prefers a lectern, or allows you to move around, find out what visual aids will be allowed in the opening.

Use visual aids

Design visual aids to enhance and reinforce your points, and practice with the visual aids until they become a natural extension of yourself. Be sure to have the visual aids placed where they are easy for you to get hold of and work with. Remember that blackboards can all too easily be erased and used by opposing counsel to his benefit. Do not overwhelm your opening with visual aids: visual aids should *enhance* your opening, not *be* your opening.

Design your personal presentation to mirror the jurors' style

Now that your jury has been selected, you can refine your choices of dress, body language, and vocal pace to mirror that specific jury. Keep within your personal style, however, as is explained in Chapter 9.

Be well groomed and comfortable

Be sure, in addition to being impeccably groomed, that your clothes are comfortable to wear. This is not the time to try out those new shoes you love which also happen to pinch your feet to death. Any personal discomfort will take away from your ability to totally focus on your case.

Be clearly focused before speaking

When you are ready to start your opening, stand, avert your eyes for a moment and "center" yourself. "Centering" means to take a breath, clear your mind of all thought, and focus within for a moment. It is easiest to do with your eyes averted (as in the "thoughtful" position). Then look up, look at the person you will address first, then silently inside yourself, say "now," then open your mouth and start. Eye focus is vital. Look first at one juror, then at another, do not "pan" the jury, but look at each one of them in scattered fashion as you speak. Keep your eyes on the jurors as much as possible throughout the opening in order to engage them directly.

Attend to your pitch, pace, volume, and articulation

Remember to use a clear, articulate voice, appropriate volume and pitch, and a pace which lightly mirrors that of the jurors.

Use good pauses and phrasing

Use frequent pauses, phrase your thoughts carefully so you express one thought at a time. Let the pauses be the time to let a point or a peak moment sink in.

Cover your mistakes gracefully

If you get flustered or lose your place in your opening, simply stop talking a moment, avert your eyes, collect your thoughts, lift your head, and start in again. If you don't make a big deal of your mishap, no one else will.

Mirror the jury's overall body language

Your body language should reflect that of the jurors: if the panel is basically casual and relaxed, don't stand like a ramrod with your hands behind your back.

Respect the jury rail

Be aware, however, that too much casualness implies disrespect, don't lean all over the lectern or the jury rail. The jury rail is the symbolic arm of the jurors. During the opening, maintain enough distance from the jury box—6 to 9 feet—so as not to be felt as intrusive or invasive by the jurors. It is much too early in the trial to actually go over and touch the rail.

Use motivated movement

If the Judge allows movement, then by all means move. Remember that motivated movement in the Courtroom implies that you are at home in this environment, that it belongs to you. This adds to the jurors' impression of you as a competent professional. Bear in mind the word "motivated" movement: don't pace, or move simply out of frustration or anxiety. Move in order to make a point, not just because you feel like moving.

Use stillness for effect

Bear in mind that stillness is very effective: when you have something particularly important to say, keep absolutely still, and let the words stand out against the backdrop of your stillness.

Illustrate your story with gestures

Use gestures that illustrate your story. If you are stuck behind a lectern, remember that your top half is still visible, use gestures as best you can given this limitation. Be sure that your body language and facial expressions are congruent with what you are saying: it is best to practice your opening full out, with gestures and movement, in order to assure congruence.

Choose appropriate emotions

You basic emotional tone should be one of sincerity and deep concern for your client's cause. If you are describing a violent or upsetting event, allow your voice to express the corresponding emotion, but be careful not to go overboard and drop into melodrama. When in doubt, simply express deep concern. Be positive, upbeat and passionately convinced of the rightness of your client's cause. This is most often expressed through the case theme.

Keep track of the jurors' reactions

Have co-counsel note the jurors' nonverbal reactions during your opening. The easiest way for him to do this, is for you to give co-counsel a copy of your outline, with lots of room beneath each heading. Under each heading, co-counsel can jot down any observations of jurors' reactions, and you will then at least have a rough idea of what provoked those reactions. Observe the jurors during opposing counsel's opening statement, and make similar notations.

HOW TO CONDUCT A PERSUASIVE *DIRECT EXAMINATION*

The purpose of direct examination is to flesh out and substantiate the story you told the jurors in your opening statement.

Order the Sequence of Your Witnesses for Effect

Sequence your witnesses, then, so that the order of their appearance helps tell the story, and bear in mind the laws of primacy and recency. Be sure you start off each day with an important (and preferably interesting) witness, and try to end your direct with a similar witness.

Ask Clear and Direct Questions

Your questions should be simple and clear; do not ask two different things in the context of a single question. You will confuse your witness, and he will not respond effectively. Make sure your questions follow in a logical sequence which makes it easy for the jurors to understand the unfolding of the story. The last question you ask of any given witness should elicit a strong answer that vigorously upholds your interpretation of the facts. If you get a particularly good piece of testimony toward the end of your planned questions, you may even choose to stop questioning right there, and leave the jurors with the effect of that testimony, rather than risk the possibility of diluting it by going on.

Have Your Witness Handle Visual Aids

Help your witnesses tell the story by using visual aids and props where appropriate. Bear in mind the value of the emotional hook provided by significant exhibits—blown up photographs, actual physical evidence, and so forth—and figure out exactly when it would be most effective to introduce them. Mark your exhibits ahead of time so that they are ready to be used at the specific moment you choose. The jurors identify with the witnesses far more readily than they do with you: the witnesses are more likely to be people like them.

Have the witnesses, then, participate in showing the exhibits. Have the witness go up to a chart and indicate where the event took place, have the witness illustrate how something works using props as needed. The jurors will vicariously participate in the explanation through the witness's participation: remember that the closer you can get to role-playing, the more likely you are to influence a person's decision.

Personalize Experiences for the Jurors

Sometimes a witness's description of an event or a situation will lack obvious relevance to the jurors' lives: personalize that experience so that the jurors can connect emotionally to it. Keep using analogies and examples from the jurors' world, and make sure your language is vivid and descriptive; keep using words from all three perceptual modes.

Avoid Boredom

If a witness's testimony is boring, see if you can rephrase what he just said to make it more interesting, under the guise of summarizing or ensuring clarity. A similar tack can be used to emphasize an important point: remember the value of repetition. Avoid boring the jurors by varying the way you ask questions; have a half-a-dozen ways of asking the same question memorized so you can pull them out at any time. Keep your pace moving. Ask your questions in a firm energized manner and don't drag in between.

Maintain Your Professionalism and Trustworthiness

In addition to keeping the process of direct examination interesting for the jurors, asking questions in firm energized fashion adds to the impression of your professionalism. Be aware that throughout the trial you either increase or diminish the assessment of your credibility. Everything you do goes into reinforcing or damaging that first impression. Your professionalism is enhanced if you are well-organized; if you ask your questions in logical order, know where your exhibits are, have your questions ready for each witness, and so forth. Your competence is enhanced if your attitude is confident, energized, and conveys the impression that all is going well, regardless of how the trial is actually going. Your trustworthiness and sincerity are enhanced as you treat the questioning process with care and serious concern, and as you treat the witnesses with respect.

Be Empathic and Respectful Toward Your Witness

Respect for your witness starts with an attitude of empathy toward the unfamiliar and somewhat frightening situation he finds himself in. Let your manner be friendly, albeit serious, and give the witness a few moments to get comfortable, to settle in, as it were. Help the witness do this by mirroring his body language, tone, and pace, and be sure to mirror *subtly*. Use a gentle tone to start your questioning, especially if faced with a frightened witness. Use the witness's name, and use it often. Be sure to face the witness squarely as much as possible, to show interest and respect (Illustration 1). Establish good solid eye focus with the witness, and keep it there. Let your eyes be the life-line the witness can cling to.

8–1

Position yourself physically to best guide and support your witness

Stand at the far end of the jury box so that the witness will be addressing the jury directly even as he looks at you for support and encouragement. As the trial progresses, you can get closer to the symbolic "arm" of the jury, the jury rail, and eventually can touch it, or occasionally place a document there momentarily. Do not, however, lean all over the rail, regardless of how cozy you feel with the jurors: this is experienced as inappropriate and distasteful. Also, show your respect for the jurors by never turning your back to them; arrange your exhibits and work your visual aids with this in mind (Illustration 2).

8–2

Listen to and acknowledge your witness

Show your respect for the witness by keeping still during his testimony; don't read notes, shuffle, pace, take notes, or do anything else that might be distracting. Listen carefully to the witness and *acknowledge* his responses by head nods or slight "uh-huh" type sounds. Don't interrupt the witness unless it is absolutely necessary, and when you do, do so politely.

Follow carefully your witness's testimony

Be careful to really listen to the witness's testimony: jury studies show that jurors consistently are annoyed with attorneys who don't take into account the witness's response in asking their next question. It makes you look like you're really not listening, which seriously damages your credibility. Don't be so wedded to your specific questions that you are inflexible and neglect to incorporate pertinent aspects of the witness's testimony into questions following that testimony.

Rescue your witness when necessary

Remember that the jurors identify more with the witness than they do with you, if the witness is in trouble, find a way to graciously get him out of it. Take the witness off the hook: if the witness is confused, or answers a question that clearly shows he didn't understand it, don't blame him for it. Either rephrase your question, or find a way to ask the next question so that you now elicit the necessary testimony.

Guide the Jurors with Your Reactions

React subtly to the witness's testimony, allow your facial expressions to discretely convey the emotions appropriate to the information revealed in the testimony. Your facial expressions will guide the jurors as to how to feel about the testimony, and are therefore very important, but they must be discretely manifested, or you will not be perceived as sincere.

Do not, however, at any cost, react with distress or surprise at a heretofore unknown bit of information or potentially damaging testimony. Keep your facial expression confident and interested, as if all was going well. If you react as if "that's it, it's all over," the jurors will attach enormous significance to the testimony, having been so guided by your reaction. If you don't tip nonverbally that you've just been mortally wounded, the jurors will assume that everything is still pretty much all right, and will attach less significance to the testimony.

HOW TO *CROSS-EXAMINE* EFFECTIVELY

Pay Attention to Opposing Counsel's Direct Examination

Cross-examination is a delicate art, one which requires great skill and expertise. It is where your thorough grounding in the facts of the case is most valuable. Cross-examination cannot be "winged," it must be prepared with deliberation and forethought. Much of the information you gather for cross-examination is from opposing counsel's direct examination.

Listen to the witness for inconsistencies

As you listen to opposing counsel's direct, listen not only for factual inconsistencies and lacks, listen for nonverbal signs of possible weakness, anxiety or confusion. Listen for hesitancies in speech, sudden changes in pitch or pace, shifts in volume. Listen for emotional undertones, incongruencies between verbal content and facial expression.

Watch the witness's body language for clues to weaknesses

Notice whether the witness appears perfectly relaxed, or seems to tense up at certain moments. Does he fidget? Does he start picking at his clothes? If so, when? Does he maintain good eye focus, or do his eyes wander? Does he avert his eyes at a certain moment? Allow the witness's nonverbal behavior to cue you as to fruitful areas to probe. Learn to take notes in an almost shorthand fashion, and quickly, so that your eyes can be observing the witness as much as humanly possible. Have co-counsel make notes of his observations also; anything you miss he will probably pick up.

Conduct Your Cross Examination to Advance Your Story

In cross examination, you get the opportunity to re-establish your interpretation of the facts so that your story is the one the jurors accept. Everything you do in cross, then, must be designed with this purpose in mind: the advancement of your story.

Include your case theme

Work your case theme into your cross examination, keep the jurors on track.

Use clear, focused questions

When you cross-examine a witness, start with a clear focused question and proceed with your questions in logical sequence so that the jury can easily follow you.

End your cross examination like a winner

Be sure to end on a favorable note, that is to say, after the witness has said something which advances your cause. No matter what happens during cross, look like you got what you wanted. Under no circumstances (unless the witness literally drops dead on the stand) should you seem flustered, angry, disappointed or disheartened when you sit down at the end of cross-examining the witness. Sit down like a winner. The jurors will associate your radiant confidence and poise with the foregoing testimony and assume your story is coming out on top.

Win Jury Votes with Politeness

Your basic attitude toward all witnesses should initially be one of respect and politeness. With lay witnesses, your attitude should deviate as little as possible from that stance, with expert witnesses, you can deviate considerably.

As mentioned previously jurors identify with witnesses, in particular with lay witnesses. If you are polite and respectful to the lay witness, you enhance your "good guy" image with the jurors: you are treating the witness as the jurors would like to be treated. If you light into a lay witness aggressively during the course of cross-examination, the jurors instinctively want to protect this poor helpless witness trapped on the stand, subject to your cruel and vicious pummeling.

We tend to side with the weak against the strong, and any direct attack on a witness is going to turn the jurors against you. Certainly you can attack the witness and/or his testimony, but you must do so from a respectful and polite point of view. Use your "confusion" and "lack of understanding" as the springboards to your questioning, use attempts to "clarify" as the way to expose inconsistencies, and so forth. Take a courteous attitude of "trying to understand" as your basic posture; this approach will allow you to accomplish your objective in cross, and still retain the jurors' favorable evaluation of you.

Treat the expert witness with authority

Your approach to expert witnesses can be quite different. Jurors do not identify in the same way with expert witnesses, especially not with expert witnesses who testify for a living. Although you should still start with a respectful polite approach, you can allow yourself more vigorous questioning than you would with a lay witness. Try to stay away from aggressive frontal attacks, however; confrontation should be firm but not vicious. Sometimes sarcasm, disappointment, irritation or a stunned silence can be used for effect, just be aware of their import and don't get melodramatic (inappropriate choices).

One of the most effective ways to persuade the jurors in cross-examining an expert witness is to know more than he does. Since you will be questioning the witness on a narrow range of knowledge you can in most cases gain that knowledge fairly easily. Your best source of that knowledge and how to gain it is your own expert witness. If you can draw a medical diagram, for example, quickly, simply and accurately, and stump a medical expert by being more precise and explicit than he can, you score points with the jury.

Use Your Body Language to Subtly Discomfit Witnesses

Since it offends the jurors if you are overtly aggressive, learn the covert tactics body language affords you. In conducting direct examination, you need to put your witness at ease, and so you mirror his body language and general manner. In cross, you have the opposite need; you want the witness to be as uncomfortable as possible. Why? Because the more uncomfortable the witness is, the more likely he is to confound himself, and the more likely he is to seem anxious or nervous. The jurors will attribute his seeming anxiety or nervousness to his dishonesty, not to anything you are doing, since overtly you are being polite and respectful.

How do you accomplish this? Simply use reverse mirroring: make the witness uncomfortable by reflecting the opposite of his body language and vocal tone. If he's relaxed, stand up straight, if he's poised and glacial, be more casual. If his pace is slow, pick yours up, if his is fast, slow down a bit. The witness won't know why he is uncomfortable, because you're not doing anything obvious, he just is.

Don't maintain good eye focus with the witness; look directly at him, but maintain your focus ever so slightly off his eyes—at his forehead perhaps. This is truly disconcerting and yet will go unnoticed by the jurors. Even the witness will not be able to put his finger on why he's so uncomfortable.

Use contrary perceptual modes to make a witness uncomfortable

Use a perceptual mode which is not his: observe during direct what his primary mode is, and then, don't use it in questioning him. If he's primarily visual, for example, use auditory formulations. Again, this is an eminently subtle way of making the witness uncomfortable, and therefore vulnerable, which the jurors will not perceive because it's so subliminal.

Use mirror switches to throw the witness off balance

All the above tactics can be used in a slightly different format equally effectively. Start by mirroring the witness *accurately*. Put him totally at ease by your body language and manner. Then, when you get to *the* crucial question, reverse the mirroring, and switch perceptual modes. The witness, up to now lulled into the comfort of familiarity, will suddenly find himself out in the cold, as it were. This will catch him off guard and disorient him. The jurors will attribute the witness's discomfort to distress over your question, not to a shift in mirroring, and will doubt the veracity of his reply.

Diminish the Impact of Witness Testimony

Take advantage of cross examination to minimize the impact of a witness's previous testimony by restating it in the past tense, without using descriptive language, and distance the experience from the jurors by expressing it in third person terms. Ask your questions in a way designed to encourage an answer using the past tense and third person. Use the negative form to suggest doubt in the jurors' minds.

Reduce the impact of opposing counsel's terms

Relabel opposing counsel's terms in less picturesque ways: for example, substitute "neck spasm" for opposing counsel's "neck cripple."

Handle Evidence to Reinforce Your Story

Handle the evidence in a way directly relevant to your story. Counter opposing counsel's gingerly handling of a knife for example, with a calm firm handling of the knife; transform it by your body language from a weapon of death to an ordinary utensil used to slice bread.

Bear in mind at all times that your job is to persuade the *jurors* of your point of view, not opposing counsel's witnesses. If you can accomplish your purpose by simply revealing an inconsistency, or disconcerting the witness, leave it at that. You don't have to convince the witness of anything.

HOW TO CREATE A COMMANDING FINISH
WITH YOUR *CLOSING ARGUMENT*

A winning close proceeds from a good strong opening. The more carefully you choose your case theme and develop your story to yield a plausible interpretation of the facts in your opening statement, the easier it is for you to create a persuasive closing argument. This is because in closing you are in essence coming full circle: in the opening you said you would show X, then through direct and cross examinations you showed X, and now in the closing argument you tell how you showed X. If you have indeed accomplished these three objectives, then the inescapable conclusion should be a verdict in your favor. This is perhaps why jury studies show that jurors rarely change their mind from their original impression after opening statements: if your closing argument is the logical outgrowth and conclusion of what you promised in your opening, the jurors' opinion will be the same at both points in the trial. If, however, you have neglected to create an opening statement with a solid case theme, and have been slipshod in fashioning your story, you will have great difficulty recouping with your closing argument.

Review Your Version of the Case

Your first task in closing argument, given that you established a solid case theme and story right from the beginning, is essentially to review who did what to whom and why. In reviewing who did what to whom, organize references to witnesses, testimony and evidence so that they fit neatly into your story. You will thus fulfill your original promise to the jury, "and we will show that," which both strengthens the power of your arguments and enhances your credibility. The purpose of this review is to arm the jurors already favorably disposed to you with facts, explanations and arguments (reasons) with which they can in turn convince those jurors who are unsure or not already favorably disposed to you. Logic, then, is extremely important in closing argument. Although jurors make their decisions at an emotional level, they must be able to back those decisions up at a logical level, and closing argument is your best opportunity to provide the jurors with that logic.

Get down to the facts of the case, go over important testimony thoroughly and in sufficient detail. Jurors do like to be reminded of important points. Since, however, this can be a tedious process for the jurors, given that they have already heard the information, vary how you present the testimony. Rather than repeating verbatim what a witness said, since the jurors already heard it in that format, tell the jury what that statement meant, comment on it, place it in the context of your story. Save verbatim repetition of a witness's words for some truly sterling revelation, and be sure the moment is worth it. Remind the jurors of how a witness looked, or behaved, when he testified. Present the testimony on a chart. Be sure to organize your references to testimony and evidence in orderly, step by step fashion, so that the way they fit into your story is clear and easy to follow.

In reviewing why things happened as they did in the case being tried, explain motive in reference to your case theme, and elaborate any discussion of motive with reference to your three points. Keep the jurors clearly on track. Be sure your explanation of the motive is plausible, and fits in with the current norms and mores of the community. If the jurors can't understand the motive, they won't accept it. Since one of the most important functions of the case theme is to provide an acceptable and persuasive rationale for the actions of your client, be sure to think in terms of motive when you first create your case theme. You can't afford to have your case theme fall apart at the end; you won't have a case.

Give the Jurors Solid Reasons to Vote in Your Favor

Your second task in closing argument is to give the jurors a reason why they should return the verdict you want. Don't leave the specifics of that verdict up to the jurors' imaginations, tell them explicitly what you want; you'll vastly increase your chances of getting it. Then ask yourself: Why is returning a verdict in your favor desirable? How does it insure that the jurors "did the right thing"? How does it further the cause of America, peace, mankind, our way of life, for example? Does it make the world a better place? What will be the effect or consequences of their decision? Spell the impact of their verdict out in detail for the jurors: give them a compelling reason for deciding in your favor. The jurors need to feel good in leaving the Courthouse, they need to feel that they were on the side of justice, part of the "good guys." Help them feel that way by making the ramifications and implications of their decision clear.

It is a waste of time to tell the jurors in great detail why opposing counsel should lose. Save your energies for explaining why you should win. Your case theme gives you a specific positive focus for your closing argument, keep it that way. You can acknowledge opposing counsel's argument if you wish, but keep it down to a minimum and spend your time and energy on promoting your own argument. Certainly admit weaknesses, bearing in mind the value of a two-sided communication, but don't belabor the point. You want to appear fair and just, not weak-kneed. The opposite extreme is not desirable either: don't attack opposing counsel. Jurors find it highly distasteful for you to attack opposing counsel, and don't like it much better if you attack his case—both stratagems are best avoided. Your most successful strategy is to focus on your positive reasons why your client's cause is just.

Integrate Jury Instructions by Giving Concrete Real-Life Applications

How you integrate jury instructions affects the way you support your claim that a verdict in your favor is the appropriate one. Anticipate how the judge will instruct the jurors, review those instructions for the jurors, especially those important to your case, and define for the jurors the concrete applications of those instructions to the facts in your case. As much as possible, use real-life examples and analogies to help the jurors understand the instructions and their applications. Realize that the judge's instructions are often in abstract form and difficult for the jurors to apply without further explication: your desire to help them understand enhances your credibility. When the jurors then hear the instructions from the Judge, they will remember your using the same words, and they will take your explanation all the more seriously.

Bear in mind how venerated the judge is in the jurors' minds; when you both expound the same matter, you become respected by association. The respect accorded the judge has another implication: jury studies demonstrate that juries are significantly impressed by closing arguments which integrate and analyze the evidence according to the judge's instructions. Attorneys who failed to observe these instructions are noticed and not appreciated. Use the respect automatically accorded the judge to work in your favor: structure your closing according to his instructions, and make it clear to the jury how you have done this.

Present Your Close in an Emotionally Effective Way

Having discussed what needs to be covered in your closing argument, let's look at how to present that information. Successful presentation uses those techniques and approaches which affect decision-making by accessing the emotional level. Your tone and manner of delivery should be one of profound sincerity and conviction. You must convey that you believe in the absolute rightness of your client's cause. Keep your emotional tone appropriate to the issue you are discussing, do not lapse into melodrama. Rely on vivid, descriptive words and examples to access the emotions, rather than a tone of emotional excess. Analogies are excellent in a closing argument, with the same caveat as before: work them in every possible direction to be sure opposing counsel won't turn them against you.

As is true in delivering your opening statement, use clear articulate speech, good phrasing, pauses; maintain good eye focus looking at the different members of the jury; use illustrative gestures and motivated movement.

Keep your pace moving, to keep both yourself and the jurors alert. Remember the short attention span we all suffer from, and break up your close with visual aids of different kinds. Refer to exhibits, illustrate with charts and diagrams, show blown up photographs. Plan the use and sequence of your visual aids, rehearse them so they are well integrated into your closing argument; visual aids should flow naturally from your comments, not stick out like a sore thumb.

Invite Juror Participation with Visual Aids

Besides keeping jurors awake, interspersed visual aids have other benefits. In addition to the fact that most people are primarily visual, thus the importance of accessing the visual mode, visual aids require that the jurors participate in the process. Showing someone something requires more involvement out of them than does the more passive act of hearing, and the more involved the jurors are in the decision making process, the more they will hold to that decision.

Involve the jurors through visual aids, analogies (which require them to compare other experiences to the one you are describing, an active process), and questions, rhetorical and otherwise. Questions require activity; you have to go internally and figure out the answer. Give the jurors the opportunity to participate in the decision-making process by involving them actively in your closing argument; they will then have persuaded themselves.

Engage the Jurors' Sympathy by Reaffirming Rapport

Closing argument represents your last opportunity to create rapport with the jurors. Re-establish feelings of similarity and familiarity, especially at the beginning of your closing argument. Make notes throughout the trial of unusual or interesting things that happened, and reiterate some of those shared experiences during the close. Speak in a conversational tone, don't lecture the jurors. Stay *with* them throughout this very important moment in the trial, don't distance yourself by all of a sudden turning "preacher" on them. You have been their guide through this strange and unfamiliar territory, now you are relating for the benefit of them all, the wondrous adventure you've been through *together.*

In addition, don't suddenly turn into a formal stranger by thanking the jurors in unctuous terms. Be sincere, state your appreciation in brief, simple manner, compatible with the rapport you have developed throughout the trial. End on a positive note of firm resolve, preferably well planned. Although the rest of your closing argument should, like your opening, be delivered spontaneously with the help of an outline, your opening and closing sentences should be very well thought out, although not necessarily memorized.

Check Your Closing Argument for Clarity

As with your opening statement, practice your closing argument in front of a lay person—or 2 or 3. Get his (or their) opinion as to how logical your arguments are, whether you reviewed the evidence clearly and thoroughly, how you covered the jury instructions. If the lay person is confused or unconvinced, the jurors will be confused or unconvinced.

Rehearse Your Closing Thoroughly

Rehearse your closing argument until you can do it in your sleep. Then put it aside for a couple of days, and simply review it the night before it is to be presented. This will insure a fresh and spontaneous delivery. Then simply say what you mean, and mean what you say. There is nothing more convincing than passionate sincerity.

SUMMARY

This chapter brings together all the elements discussed in previous chapters in direct application to the major parts of a trial. It serves as a guide to enable you to use the techniques in the reality of the Courtroom.

CHAPTER 9

How to Develop
a Dynamic Courtroom Style

The successful trial lawyer is a breed apart. The successful trial lawyer not only knows the law and can work with it masterfully, the successful trial lawyer knows *himself* and can present *himself* masterfully: the successful trial lawyer has a dynamic Courtroom style. There is nothing uncertain or vague about top attorneys; their way of being in a Courtroom is well-defined and clear. They are eminently recognizable persons; they do not, under any circumstances, fade into a crowd of anonymous others. Yet the top trial lawyers are very different from each other, their styles have little in common. Richard "Racehorse" Haynes, for example, has an emphatic, emotional style, combined with a willingness to be very personal and intense. Arthur L. Liman is reputed to combine considerateness and kindness with great strength. Edward Bennett Williams, who is known for having command over any Courtroom, emphasizes politeness, pleasantness, and civility in his presentation. Julius LeVonne Chambers has a very quiet style, based on serious concern and thoughtfulness.

HOW A DYNAMIC COURTROOM STYLE CONTRIBUTES TO YOUR SUCCESS

These are obviously very different styles, yet they all work beautifully. Why? For three distinct reasons:

1. As different as these styles are, they all incorporate and emphasize aspects that support the attorneys' credibility, and forego aspects that would damage that credibility.
2. Winning personal styles are invariably based on competence, which is expressed as confidence, and a genuine caring for people and their distress, which is expressed as sincerity.

3. Each attorney's style is based on himself, on the development of his strengths and transformation of his weaknesses, not on the slavish copying of some idealized other.

Becoming a successful trial attorney, one of the "greats," is no different from becoming a great ball player. To become a top ball player, you find out what attributes it takes, and then you develop those attributes *from what you already have.* If you're not very tall, but you can run, you become good by learning to run very very fast. Certainly you enhance your strength, but you don't try to beef up to develop the world's best arms. Best arms aren't your forte, speed is. Similarly, if you're tall and well muscled, but not very fast, you develop your strength and power, and although you jog enough to make sure you can run decently and acceptably, you don't try to turn yourself into a jackrabbit.

To become a top litigator, you must be yourself. You cannot become powerful and dynamic by being somebody else. You can, however, emphasize some traits, and work with others. Some attributes are useful to lawyering, others are best left at home. But all of them must be first and foremost, yours. This chapter, then, is devoted to helping you take those traits you have which are well-suited to a dynamic personal Courtroom style and developing them to their fullest, and taking those traits which are less well-suited and transforming them so that they too, contribute to your success.

IDENTIFYING YOUR PERSONAL STYLE

Your first task, in constructing a winning personal style, is to identify your strong points and your weak points. Modesty, at this time, is not helpful, "Oh, well, I'm just an ordinary Joe, nothing special about me," nor is blind positivism, "Me? I'm terrific, I'm great—nothing wrong with me!" Realism is. We all have our strong points, our assets, and our weak points, those traits we'd rather dispense with. Your job is to figure out just what those are.

How to Determine Your Strengths and Weaknesses

Your strong and weak points exist on three different levels: physical, mental, and emotional. Take a good look at each. Use the worksheets at the end of the chapter to help you with your assessment.

Physical strengths and weaknesses

What do you like about your physical being? What would you consider your strong points? Be specific. First consider general characteristics such as height, weight, and overall shape. What are the good parts and what are the not-so-hot aspects? Be objective, look at yourself as if you were looking at a colleague: what would you think of a colleague of this particular height, weight and shape? Then, starting with the top of your head, with your hair, and working your way down to your feet, specifically note what you like about your physical being, and don't like. Do you like your hair, the color of your eyes, what about your smile? Do you like your hands, what do you think about the strength of your arms, do you stand firmly and squarely on your feet? Do you approve of your body tone, does your skin look healthy? Are you happy with the way you move, what do you think of your posture?

Once you've inventoried your body, repeat the process, only this time examining yourself when dressed in one of your trial outfits. Do you like the way you put colors together, do you like the way your clothes fit on you, what do you think of your choice of jewelry?

Then reflect on what people have commented on about your physical being: do people tell you what a winsome smile you have, or how well you dress, or ask how you manage to keep in such great shape despite your hectic schedule? Ask a couple of good friends to tell you what their impression of your physical persona is. Request that they be as specific as possible. Often what other people tell you is a more accurate rendition of your own qualities than your personal evaluation. We tend to overvalue or underrate our own characteristics.

From this detailed consideration of your physical being, coming both from your friends and yourself, come up with a list of physical strengths and weak points. Now go on to a consideration of your mental attributes.

Mental strengths and weaknesses

Take inventory of your mental faculties. Are you a quick thinker, or does it take time for you to figure out things? Are you extremely bright, very bright, or about average? Are you good with details, or do these frustrate you? Are you methodical and orderly, preferring to attend to tasks one at a time, or do you like to juggle 20 things at once? Do you prefer analyzing things, figuring them out, or are you better at pulling things together, synthesizing? Do you have a vivid imagination, or are you more practical and concrete? Is your memory clear and sharp, or do you get muddled? What have you always prided yourself on mentally?

What was school like for you: college and then law school? What was easy and what was hard? Were you better at writing term papers than you were at presenting in the classroom or vice versa? Did you prepare for your exams throughout the year, or did you cram? Were you always good at English Literature and terrible at math? Or were you the whiz in physics who couldn't write a poem to save his soul?

What have people commented on over the years? Which of these aspects do you consider strengths and which weaknesses? Again, ask your friends what they think of your mental abilities. Then come up with a combined list which specifies your mental strengths and weaknesses.

Emotional strengths and weaknesses

Are you generally in a good mood? Are you pleasant and easy to get along with? Or are you moody, your feelings depending on what's going on in your day? Are you overall a happy person, or an unhappy person? Are you slow to anger, but then you really explode, or are you easily angry, but it wears off fast? Are you energetic? Enthusiastic? Or are you more lethargic, happier with a mellower pace? Are you shy and insecure, finding it difficult to talk easily to people you don't know, or are you a true "people person," who finds it easy to relate to just about anybody? Are you a warm person, who likes affection, dogs, children, or are you a cooler sort, preferring the quiet company of books and a good game of chess?

Are you mild-mannered and rather calm, or are you exuberant and boisterous? Are you a humorous sort, readily finding the funny side of any given situation, or are you more serious, inclined to thoughtfulness and concern? Are you arrogant or modest? Are you easily affected by others' experience, and find yourself sad for someone's distress, or do you distance yourself, keeping your emotions deep within you? Are you more passive, preferring that others take the initiative, or are you assertive, eager to take up a new challenge? Do you do things spontaneously and impulsively, or do you prefer to have things planned well in advance? Would you consider yourself rigid, preferring a set way of doing things, or are you flexible, do you find it easy to incorporate changes? Are you honest and straightforward, or do you tend to hold back and wait to see what the other side is going to do?

What do you like about yourself, emotionally? What would you say is unique about yourself? Ask your friends to make a list of your emotional assets and liabilities, then ask them to sum up your personality in a nutshell. What makes you a good friend? What do they think is unique about you? If they were trying to describe you to a Martian, what would they come up with? Once you've sorted out your list of emotional strengths and weaknesses, take both lists, yours and your friends, and combine them, as before.

HOW TO BUILD FROM YOUR PERSONAL STYLE TO A POWERFUL COURTROOM STYLE

You should now have three lists from which to work: a list of physical strengths and weaknesses, a list of mental strengths and weaknesses, and a list of emotional strengths and weaknesses. Take just the strengths and study them. Your strengths are going to become the anchor of your Courtroom style. Your assets are those attributes you *like* about yourself, they comprise what is special about you. You must have the courage to express that specialness in a Courtroom.

CASE IN POINT

Let's say, for example, that physically you like your eyes and you're happy with your overall shape; mentally you're a quick thinker, very bright, and prefer analyzing to synthesizing; emotionally you're on the mellow side and warm. What your friends value about you and consider your uniqueness is your considerateness.

Now, let's translate these *personal* strengths—regardless of whatever weaknesses you might have—into *Courtroom* assets:

1. *Considerateness* has a high value with jurors, be aware that you are blessed with that gift, and use it fully with witnesses, the judge, and opposing counsel.

2. You like your *eyes*, terrific, use them! Eye focus is a powerful nonverbal tool, let your eyes work at their true value.

3. You are happy with your *overall shape*, wear clothes which enhance it, staying of course within the bounds of appropriateness for the Courtroom. Let your appreciation of your overall shape be what gives you good posture, which impresses jurors as a reflection of your credibility.

4. You're a *quick thinker*, very bright and prefer *analysis* to synthesis: your ability to figure out what is really going on in a case is then your strong suit, you are also well equipped to spot logical inconsistencies and flaws in witnesses' testimony, which will make your cross-examinations effective.

5. You are on the *mellow* side; your manner will lend calm and stability to a Courtroom. Your warmth will make it easier for jurors to relate to you, and witnesses to cooperate.

Knowing that you have these qualities, and working to express them fully in the Courtroom, will do wonders for your self-confidence. Self-confidence is based on two main factors: feelings of self worth and competence. If you know who you are, and value your strengths at their just worth, then you walk in with true self-esteem. Competence is derived from excellent preparation and well-honed skills. If you know you can do the job, and you can do it well, you will feel very good about yourself.

A dynamic Courtroom style, then, is built from a knowledge of your personal style, and a willingness to adapt and express that style so that it wins in the Courtroom.

HOW TO WEED OUT WHAT WILL AND WON'T WORK IN COURT

Identifying your strengths gives you the foundation of your personal style. Other factors must then be taken into account since there are definitely attributes which do and do not contribute to persuading a jury. Let's look at what does and doesn't work.

People are persuaded most easily by others who are "extroverted, involved, positive, and moderately relaxed."[1]

Focus Out Toward People Instead of Focusing on Yourself

"Extroverted" does not, contrary to popular belief, mean ebullient or flamboyant. "Extroverted" means: "One whose attention and interest are directed chiefly toward other people and the external world rather than toward himself."[2] You must have a genuine liking of people, a willingness to go toward them, if you are to succeed as a trial lawyer. You are in the people business, and cannot ignore this very important factor. People who are shy are in fact preoccupied with what others will think of them: learning to go toward other people is often learning to switch your focus from what others think of you, to how you can help them. If you are shy, remind yourself of your competence as an attorney, and what you have to offer others, it will help you take your focus off yourself.

Be Dedicated and Committed Instead of Distant and Aloof

"Involved" means dedicated and committed to your case. You cannot remain distant from it, allow yourself to become intrigued, fascinated, wrapped up in it. This will give you the passionate conviction in your client's cause so appreciated by jurors.

Have a Positive Focus Instead of a Negative One

"Positive" means you see the upside, look for the pluses, look for the way forward. You do not indulge in disappointment, disheartened feelings, you do not give up. Certainly, you may feel these emotions from time to time, the difference is, you do not wallow in them. You assume, regardless of how the case is going, that you will win, and your attitude constantly reinforces that assumption.

This is not to be confused with arrogance. Arrogance has no basis in fact. An arrogant person assumes he will be victorious just by virtue of being. He makes no efforts to support that conviction by dealing with reality. If you are positive, you strive to create a winning case in terms of your facts, evidence, witnesses and arguments at all times, and keep working to make your assumption of victory real.

Being Moderately Relaxed Instead of Overly Anxious or Asleep

"Moderately relaxed" means you are comfortable with yourself and your case, so you are relaxed, but not so relaxed that you are overly casual or asleep. A certain degree of tension is necessary in the maintenance of alert attention. A certain degree of relaxation reassures the jurors that you know what you are doing, too much relaxation makes them think you don't care.

If your personal style then has elements that are contrary to these: for example, you are often of a pessimistic frame of mind and by nature an anxious person, you need to do something about it. These traits will not allow you to develop a winning personal style regardless of your assets. Being aware of your weaknesses is what will enable you to work with them; refer to your lists of strengths and weaknesses and identify those weaknesses which impede the development of extraversion, involvement, positive attitude, or moderate relaxation, and work to correct those either on your own, or with the help of a competent professional.

Do What It Takes to Enhance Your Credibility

The other elements which go into a winning Courtroom style are the same as those which make up a winning first impression: you must be credible. You must be professional and trustworthy regardless of the specifics of your style. The elements which make up charisma—good eye focus, stillness, doing things one-thing-at-a-time—can be incorporated into any personal style. Good posture, cleanliness and good grooming are easily integrated into all styles. Sloppiness, slovenliness, mumbled speech and slouched shoulders never made a winner, certainly not a winning trial lawyer.

Review the first three chapters of this book, and check to see if your list of weaknesses includes any elements which would prevent your coming across professional, trustworthy and charismatic. If so, work on correcting these either by yourself, with the help of a videocamera if possible, or with an appropriate professional.

HOW TO EXPRESS YOUR PERSONAL STYLE PHYSICALLY FOR MAXIMUM IMPACT IN COURT

Once you have defined your personal style in terms of your strengths and uniqueness, and have eliminated any aspects that might diminish your credibility, you are well on your way to having a winning Courtroom style. That style, in order to be truly effective, however, must be expressed through your voice, body language and dress.

CASE IN POINT

Let's say you like your smile, others have found it winsome, and you like your stature, you're a tall man. You are thoughtful and serious, careful and methodical, bright but not quick. Emotionally you are warm, empathic, and enjoy people although you're not very outgoing. Your friends say your uniqueness is that you're steady as a rock; you can always be counted on in a rough moment.

Your voice, body language, and dress must express these characteristics, and express them congruently, if your presentation of yourself is to be believed and perceived as sincere. Each aspect of your presentation must support and enhance the other for your style to be persuasive and dynamic.

Given the above attributes, for example:

1. Your voice should be low in pitch, the pace moderate, with frequent pauses to allow you to collect your thoughts

2. Your face should reflect your serious concern for others, but in a pleasant way, not dour, so as to reflect your warmth and appreciation of others. Be aware that others find your smile winsome, use it occasionally, especially to soothe a nervous witness, once in a while with the jurors

3. You like your height, so standing tall should be easy for you. Let your stature be comforting, recognize its symbolic protective value, it contributes to your "steady as a rock" uniqueness

4. Your gestures and movement should be calm and steady, and reinforce your "steady as a rock" quality

5. Your clothes should be well cut and simple, again supporting your uniqueness, the fabrics pleasing to the touch (even if no one touches you, this quality is also evident to the eye) to accent your empathic and warm quality. You would wear little jewelry, and in general keep your clothes and manner simple, so that your "steady as a rock" quality is most evident, uncluttered by superficial distractors.

Figure out specifically what kind of voice, body language and dress would most effectively convey your personal style and uniqueness, using the guidelines given in Chapters 1, 2, and 3, and the worksheet provided at the end of the chapter. Study candid photographs of yourself, listen to recorded conversations, videotape yourself having an informal conversation, or conducting a mock cross-examination, or giving a closing argument.

Ask yourself: objectively, am I conveying what I know to be my assets and my uniqueness? What would I need to sound like, look like, and move like to make that happen? Ask yourself who you know, or who you can observe (on television, for example), who conveys those qualities dynamically. Use these examples as role models, observe how these people are able to convey powerfully whatever aspect you are interested in, and see if their approach works for you. If it does, great, if not, it may give you some ideas on what approach will work for you.

Generally you will find that getting your personal style to be expressed persuasively through your voice, body language, and dress, is a matter of a few simple adjustments. Often, just being *aware* of what your personal style actually is, and emphasizing those traits in your speech, dress, and movement will create the necessary adjustments.

HOW TO TAILOR YOUR STYLE TO DIFFERENT COURTROOM CIRCUMSTANCES

Once you have determined your personal Courtroom style, pick an approach which will suit your case. Four matters must be taken into consideration:

1. The nature of the jury
2. The range afforded you by your personal style
3. Your case theme
4. Opposing counsel's personal style

Take Into Account the Nature of the Jury

The nature of the jury will affect how you present yourself.

CASE IN POINT

For example, let's say that your style is highly professional, somber, relying heavily on intellectual skills. You find yourself in front of a jury that is down-home and folksy. Well, it would be foolish to attempt to extensively mirror this jury and turn yourself into a folksy type, that just isn't you. However, we all have different facets to our being, a range of behaviors which goes from very formal and proper to relaxed and casual. The range is different for each one of us, but we each have a range. Faced with a down-home, folksy jury, mirror that jury *to the extent that your range easily and comfortably permits.*

Using the chapter on rapport as a guide, mirror those aspects of the jury which you can mirror without feeling like you're turning yourself inside out.

Incorporate Your Case Theme Into Your Approach

Incorporate the nature of your case theme when deciding which approach would be most persuasive. Is your case theme best presented in a thoughtful manner? Or more emotionally? Would you get your point across more successfully taking a straight-ahead factual approach? Or should you be more philosophical? Let your case theme determine the *overall* approach you take to the case, an approach you reinforce every time you repeat your case theme. Then react realistically to the events as they unfold in the Courtroom: this determines your *moment-to-moment* approach.

Take Into Account the Range of Your Personal Style: Don't Go Against Your Nature

Your approach is influenced by the range made available by your personal style. If you are very emotional by nature, and value that emotionality as an asset, but have in a particular case determined that a thoughtful, more factual approach would be more successful, then simply tone your emotionality down somewhat. Choose to emphasize the rational, considered side of yourself rather than your emotionality. Do not deny your emotionality or attempt to take it out of yourself—that's impossible. Simply choose not to use it actively as a tool, and lean toward the more factual side of your range.

In this way you are, at all times, yourself. Sometimes you are more one side of yourself than the other, but you are at no time pretending a portion of you does not exist. In this way, you will always project sincerity and be credible, the very basis of successful trial lawyering.

Take Into Account Opposing Counsel's Style

One last matter must be considered before you launch into the Courtroom ready for battle: opposing counsel. Know your opposition. The more you know about opposing counsel and his style, the better you can choose your approach. If you can't find out anything about him before trial, observe opposing counsel carefully during voir dire. It is rarely advisable to fight fire with fire. If opposing counsel, for example, is emphatic, emotional and a bit on the dramatic side, then let your more factual, calm, and steady side come forth. Persuade the jurors by providing solidity and quiet strength in contrast to opposing counsel's emotionality.

The one exception to this is if opposing counsel is soft-spoken, considerate and kind. You cannot go against this and be loud, rude and mean. Be equally considerate and kind, but attend then to what possible approaches opposing counsel is using mentally: is he relying on detailed analysis, is he perhaps overly meticulous and a little monotonous? Then counter by incorporating synthesis, make sure your speech is vivid and descriptive, make your pace a little more vigorous. A case is tried on many levels: let your dynamic personal Courtroom style support and reinforce your legal expertise.

SUMMARY

You are, and can only be, yourself. But you can be yourself persuasively, dynamically, powerfully. Creating and presenting a strong personal Courtroom style relies on a specific understanding of who you are, your strengths and weaknesses, your uniqueness, and a willingness to work with these characteristics so that they are transformed into Courtroom assets.

IDENTIFYING YOUR PHYSICAL STRENGTHS AND
WEAKNESSES WORKSHEET

1. Check off which of your physical attributes you consider strengths and which you consider weaknesses. Briefly indicate the reason you do or do not like each attribute. Be objective. The more honest your assessment, the great its value.

Attribute	*Strength*	*Weakness*	*Reason*
Height	____	____	_____
			_____
Weight	____	____	_____
			_____
Overall shape	____	____	_____
			_____
Hair; color	____	____	_____
			_____
Hair; texture	____	____	_____
			_____
Face	____	____	_____
			_____
Eyes; color	____	____	_____
			_____
Eyes; shape	____	____	_____
			_____
Mouth; shape	____	____	_____
			_____
Mouth; smile	____	____	_____
			_____
Nose	____	____	_____
			_____
Chin	____	____	_____
			_____

Attribute	Strength	Weakness	Reason
Neck	____	____	_____ _____
Shoulders	____	____	_____ _____
Arms	____	____	_____ _____
Hands	____	____	_____ _____
Torso	____	____	_____ _____
Legs	____	____	_____ _____
Feet	____	____	_____ _____
Skin	____	____	_____ _____
Body tone	____	____	_____ _____
Posture	____	____	_____ _____
Stance	____	____	_____ _____
Ease of movement	____	____	_____ _____

2. Wearing one of your trial outfits, look at yourself critically in a mirror. Figure out which are your strengths and weaknesses and indicate the reasons for each.

Aspect of Dress	Strength	Weakness	Reason
Appropriateness of outfit	____	____	_____ _____

Aspect of Dress	Strength	Weakness	Reason
Fit of clothes	____	____	_____
			_____
Choice of colors	____	____	_____
			_____
Choice of accessories	____	____	_____
			_____
Hair style	____	____	_____
			_____
Make up	____	____	_____
			_____
Grooming of hands and nails	____	____	_____
			_____
General neatness	____	____	_____
			_____
Cleanliness	____	____	_____
			_____
Other _____	____	____	_____
			_____

3. Think back to what people have said of your physical persona over the years. What kind of comments have you received? _____

_____

_____

_____

4. Ask some friends to give you specific input as to how they perceive your physical persona:

_____

_____

_____

5. Now, taking all of the above information into account, create a composite list of your physical strengths and weaknesses:

    Strengths   *Weaknesses*

_____   _____

_____   _____

_____   _____

_____   _____

_____   _____

_____   _____

_____   _____

_____   _____

_____   _____

_____   _____

_____   _____

_____   _____

_____   _____

_____   _____

_____   _____

_____   _____

_____   _____

_____   _____

_____   _____

_____   _____

IDENTIFYING YOUR MENTAL
STRENGTHS AND WEAKNESSES WORKSHEET

1. Check off what you think are your strengths and weaknesses in the following mental categories. For example, under "intelligence", if you are bright and think that is a strength, mark "S" after the word "bright". Then note briefly why you think a given attribute is either a strength or a weakness.

Attribute	*Assessment*		*Reason*
Style of thought	quick__	slow__	_____
Intelligence	very bright___		_____
	bright___		_____
	average___		_____
Detail oriented	yes___	no ___	_____
Methodical	yes___	no ___	_____
Juggle many things at once	yes___	no ___	_____
Analysis	yes___	no ___	_____
Synthesis	yes___	no ___	_____
Vivid imagination	yes___	no ___	_____
Practical and concrete approach	yes___	no ___	_____
Good memory	yes___	no ___	_____
other_____	yes___	no ___	_____
other_____	yes___	no ___	_____
other_____	yes___	no ___	_____
other_____	yes___	no ___	_____

2. Reflect on your schooling. Note what was easy for you at each stage of your education, and what was difficult:

High school: _____

_____

_____

_____

_____

_____

_____

College (undergrad): _____

_____

_____

_____

_____

_____

_____

Law School: _____

_____

_____

_____

_____

_____

_____

Other:_____

_____

_____

_____

_____

_____

_____

3. Reflect on people's comments over the years. What have they said of your mental attributes?

   Ask your friends to comment on your mental strengths and weaknesses:

   _____

   _____

   _____

   _____

   _____

4. Now, taking all of the above information into account, create a composite list of your mental strengths and weaknesses:

Strengths	*Weaknesses*

IDENTIFYING YOUR EMOTIONAL STRENGTHS AND WEAKNESSES WORKSHEET

1. Check off the emotional attributes you feel represent your strengths and weaknesses. Briefly indicate the reason why you feel any given attribute is either a strength or a weakness.

Attribute	*Strength*	*Weakness*	*Reason*
Generally in a good mood	—	—	_____ _____
Pleasant	—	—	_____ _____
Easy to get along with	—	—	_____ _____
Moody	—	—	_____ _____
Basically happy	—	—	_____ _____
Basically unhappy	—	—	_____ _____
Slow to anger	—	—	_____ _____
Quick to anger	—	—	_____ _____
Energetic	—	—	_____ _____
Lethargic	—	—	_____ _____
Shy, insecure	—	—	_____ _____
People person	—	—	_____ _____
Warm	—	—	_____ _____

Attribute	*Strength*	*Weakness*	*Reason*
Affectionate	—	—	_____ _____
Cool	—	—	_____ _____
Calm	—	—	_____ _____
Mild mannered	—	—	_____ _____
Exuberant	—	—	_____ _____
Good sense of humor	—	—	_____ _____
Serious	—	—	_____ _____
Thoughtful	—	—	_____ _____
Arrogant	—	—	_____ _____
Modest	—	—	_____ _____
Empathic	—	—	_____ _____
Withdrawing	—	—	_____ _____
Assertive	—	—	_____ _____
Passive	—	—	_____ _____
Impulsive	—	—	_____ _____

Attribute	Strength	Weakness	Reason
Planner	—	—	_____
			_____
Rigid	—	—	_____
			_____
Flexible	—	—	_____
			_____
Honest	—	—	_____
			_____
Direct	—	—	_____
			_____
Cautious	—	—	_____
			_____
Other _____	—	—	_____
			_____
Other _____	—	—	_____
			_____
Other _____	—	—	_____
			_____
Other _____	—	—	_____
			_____

2. Think about what people have said of your emotional way of being. Ask friends to describe your emotional attributes: _____

_____

_____

_____

_____

_____

_____

3. Now, taking all of the above information into account, create a composite list of your emotional strengths and weaknesses:

Strengths	*Weaknesses*
_____	_____
_____	_____
_____	_____
_____	_____
_____	_____
_____	_____
_____	_____
_____	_____
_____	_____
_____	_____
_____	_____
_____	_____
_____	_____
_____	_____
_____	_____
_____	_____
_____	_____

4. What is your uniqueness? Think about yourself: what do you value most about yourself emotionally, what makes you distinctly you? Think about what friends and others have said about your uniqueness over the years, ask your friends directly for their input:

_____

_____

_____

_____

_____

IDENTIFYING WHAT WILL AND WON'T
WORK IN COURT WORKSHEET

Ask yourself if you have the following attributes, and if not, what must be done to develop them.

1. Are you focused outward towards people? Yes ___ No ___

   If not, what can you do to become more of a people person? _____

   _____

   _____

   _____

   _____

   _____

   _____

2. Are you consistently dedicated and committed to your client's cause? Yes ___ No ___

   If not, what can you do to increase the level of your commitment? _____

   _____

   _____

   _____

   _____

   _____

   _____

3. Do you maintain a positive orientation? Yes ___ No ___

   If not, what can you do to help yourself be and stay more positive? _____

   _____

   _____

   _____

   _____

   _____

   _____

4. Are you comfortable with yourself and your case so that you are moderately relaxed? Yes ___ No ___

   If not, what can you do to increase your degree of comfort? _____

   _____

   _____

   _____

   _____

5. Are you credible? Do you strive to maintain your professionalism and trustworthiness? Yes ___ No ___

   If no, what can you do specifically to increase your credibility? _____

   _____

   _____

   _____

   _____

CHECKLIST OF ELEMENTS TO CONSIDER
IN TAILORING YOUR PERSONAL STYLE TO DIFFERENT
COURTROOM CIRCUMSTANCES

1. What is the nature of the jury? _____

   _____

   _____

2. What do you need to do to specifically adjust your personal style to create rapport with this jury? _____

   _____

   _____

3. What is your case theme? _____

   _____

4. How do you need to adjust your personal style to deliver that case theme most credibly and persuasively? _____

   _____

   _____

5. What is the best approach to take to win this case? _____

   _____

   _____

6. Which side of yourself is best suited to fit with this approach? _____

   _____

   _____

7. What is opposing counsel's style? _____

   _____

8. How do you need to adjust your personal style so that you are most effective, given opposing counsel's style? _____

   _____

   _____

CHAPTER 10

How to Deal
Successfully with
Courtroom Anxiety

The responsibility you hold as a trial attorney is considerable—a client's cause, his financial status, sometimes his life—but this is no different than the responsibility held by a surgeon, yet the anxiety you experience is very different. The tremendous anxiety experienced by the vast majority of attorneys when facing a trial date is due not so much to the responsibility of the task, but to the public nature of the work.

It is said that the fear of public speaking is second only to the fear of death. In fact, the popular *Book of Lists* notes that *more* people are afraid of speaking before a group than are afraid of dying. Anxiety is much less prevalent in situations in which attorneys primarily interact in private with their peers, such as during settlement conferences, than when faced with a jury. If, however, you are one of the lucky few who do not suffer from Courtroom anxiety, feel free to skip this chapter, otherwise, read on.

HOW TO RECOGNIZE YOUR INTERNAL AND EXTERNAL RESPONSES TO COURTROOM ANXIETY

Your subconscious mind interprets the responsibility and public pressure to perform of the Courtroom situation as a life and death matter, and it responds with one of four basic survival modes: flight, fight, freeze or faint. You experience these responses on two different levels: internally as *fears* and externally as *symptoms*.

1. Fears are the internal *feelings* that are generated: You may experience these as anxiety, panic, feelings of "out of control," memory gaps, or blanking out.

2. Symptoms are the external *behaviors* that result from the feelings: You may manifest such symptoms as dry mouth, breaking out in a cold sweat, feeling nauseous, shaking, having your voice go up significantly in pitch, your speech "rush," your shoulders tense, or your hands unconsciously "fist," among others.

All of these are simply manifestations of your subconscious attempt to help yourself survive by either fleeing, fighting, freezing, or fainting. Unfortunately, as helpful as those tactics might have been to our Neanderthal forebears, they are of minimal use in a Courtroom. Your task, then, is to find a conscious and deliberate way of dealing with Courtroom anxiety so that your subconscious doesn't have to resort to fears and symptoms which distress you.

Bear in mind that you will probably never get to a point where you experience no symptoms or fears. Frankly, your fears have an important function: they support your cautiousness and thoroughness, traits which are vital to the success of your case. The idea, then, is not to remove all fear, which is not only virtually impossible but fundamentally undesirable, but to *reduce* your fears to a helpful and constructive level, which in turn will reduce the external symptoms of those fears to a *manageable* level.

Be aware that sometimes internal fears and external symptoms are deeply rooted and indicative of a serious ailment, and as such require medical or psychological attention. Try working with your own awareness, and the ideas set forth in this chapter, but if the fears and symptoms persist, consult a qualified professional. Fears and symptoms should not be allowed to become an impediment to the successful development of your practice.

THE FIVE STEPS TO CONQUERING COURTROOM ANXIETY

1. Acknowledge Your Fear

The first step in conquering Courtroom anxiety is to acknowledge it. The more you attempt to deny the very real terror you feel, the more your subconscious will attempt to protect you by manifesting one or another of the survival modes with increased vigor. Don't try to intellectualize your fear by telling yourself that this is silly, it's only a Courtroom, you'll be fine. Your subconscious does not distinguish between a pouncing tiger and a jury. If you are experiencing the internal or external symptoms described above, despite your excellent rationalizations, you are scared and you help yourself most by admitting it.

Talk to yourself. Confess your fears to yourself out loud. Don't brush aside fears that seem trivial or insignificant, a fear is a fear, regardless of your intellectual assessment. Really allowing yourself to know, in private conversation with yourself, that this trial is scary, and that you have a lot of fears about it, will enable you to face those fears and work constructively to abate them. You cannot fight what you cannot see.

2. How to Identify Your Internal Fears

The second step in conquering Courtroom anxiety is to identify your *specific* internal fears so that you can counteract them.

The most common internal fears in Courtroom anxiety are fears of being embarrassed or humiliated. You feel the constant scrutiny by both jurors and the Court, you are aware of the intimate and unrelenting evaluation you are subjected to, and you fear that under such scrutiny, you will be found wanting. You anguish over doing or saying something "stupid," and your anxiety may be such that you feel panic just at the thought of an upcoming trial.

Identify exactly what you are afraid that you might do or say that will embarrass or humiliate you. Make a detailed list of those specific situations.

CASE IN POINT

Common trial fears:

1. I'll go blank in the middle of my opening statement and the jurors will think I'm an idiot.

2. I'll drop the documents I'm handling, and feel like a fool picking them up.

3. I'll forget the next question I wanted to ask the witness and have to stand there stupidly for 5 minutes before I remember it.

4. My witness will say the opposite of what he's supposed to say and I'm going to look like a fool.

5. I'll have forgotten to bring an important document to trial and have to ask for a recess to have it brought over: the jurors will think I'm incompetent.

---

3. How to Counteract Your Internal Fears with Powerful Antidotes

Make your list of internal fears as complete as possible. Go through the entire sequence of a trial and try to pinpoint every possible embarrassment or humiliation. Then counter each fear with an "antidote." Figure out, using the principles described in the previous chapters, exactly how to look and behave, so that even if your worse fears come true and you do go blank, drop something, and so forth, you *appear* confident and competent, and if need be, buy yourself the time to remedy the situation in a manner that impresses the jury as professional and responsible. Knowing that you have an "antidote," a strategy to counteract every eventuality, will considerably diminish your anxiety. You are no longer dealing with an amorphous and generalized fear, but rather with a specific set of problems and preplanned solutions to correct them.

Six common internal fears and their antidotes

Fear 1: "I'll go blank in the middle of my opening statement and the jurors will think I'm an idiot."

Antidote: Learn how to create body language that will allow you to go blank *without* looking like an idiot.

Create a brief and concise outline of your opening statement. Rehearse your opening statement using the outline until you can do it in your sleep. When it comes time to present your opening, take the outline with you, holding it comfortably and easily, or place it where it is easy to look at, at your table. Then, if you should go blank in the middle of your opening, simply drop your head down a little, somewhat to the side *as if in thought*, look at your outline (walking over to it if necessary), and once you're ready to go again, take a deep breath, look up, and begin by saying something to the effect of "in other words . . ." or "now . . ." and then go on.

The jurors will respect your "think time." They have no idea it's really your "help, I'm lost time," your body language makes it look just like you are simply thinking. Thought is respected in our culture. If you don't tip the jurors by your body language that something is desperately wrong, they won't know it. Keep your body still and composed, avert your eyes, take your time to get back on track. Although it may feel like it takes an inordinate amount of time to accomplish this process, in fact, only a few seconds will have passed. Knowing you have a way to deal with "going blank" will considerably diminish the probability of your actually doing so, or of panicking if you should do so.

Fear 2: "I'll drop the documents I'm handling, and feel like a fool picking them up."

Antidote: Learn how to drop things and pick them up with *poise.*

Poise is defined as grace under pressure. Poise is maintaining the ability to do things one-thing-at-a-time when the heat is on. When you drop something, the trick is not to get flustered. Don't make a big deal out of it. Everybody drops something sometime. Once you've dropped the item, do not allow your facial expression to change, keep it calm and composed. Simply look at the item, squat down to retrieve it, get up, put it back in order if need be, take a deep breath, and resume your argument.

If you act as if it is perfectly acceptable to drop something, and retrieve the item with grace, then the jurors will think it's perfectly acceptable also, and will respect you for keeping your cool during the retrieval.

If you are concerned with dropping things, then practice dropping them and retrieving them gracefully. Videotape yourself doing so until you are satisfied that you routinely react without loss of composure and know how to squat appropriately, pick up your document, and go on.

In the performing arts, the art is not in learning how not to make mistakes. After all, we are human and the very nature of our imperfect being makes mistakes unavoidable. The art is in learning how to make mistakes look wonderful.

CASE IN POINT

During Olympic meets, when an ice skater falls, the crowd doesn't send him to the showers. The crowd waits with bated breath to see how he is going to recover from the fall, and when the skater picks himself up, head high, and goes on valiantly with his routine, the crowd cheers.

It is no different for you. Accept that you will occasionally trip, stumble, or drop something and that the drop is not the important part: it is your courage to recover with poise which will win you the jury's favor.

Fear 3: "I'll forget the next question I wanted to ask the witness and have to stand there stupidly for five minutes before I remember it."

Antidote: Learn to rely heavily on prior preparation. Learn to cover your blanks with effective body language and use specific visualization techniques. Prior preparation will always stand you in good stead. It is one of the surest antidotes to anxiety.

For direct examination: create an outline of the questions you want to ask the witness and go over it until you are thoroughly familiar with it. Design the order of your questions so that they are in logical sequence: this will help you stay on track as well as help the jurors follow your train of thought. Then leave the outline on your table (if you choose to stand and walk around) where it can be easily seen if you need to refer to it discretely. Just knowing that your outline is accessible will considerably diminish your fear and thereby diminish the likelihood that you will actually need it.

In addition to creating an outline and familiarizing yourself thoroughly with it, *listen* to your witness. If you have designed your questions logically, then his answers will logically inspire your next question. Also, listening carefully to your witness will remove some of your focus off yourself. You can't hold two thoughts in your mind at the exact same time: if you are truly attending to what your witness is saying and how he is saying it, you cannot simultaneously be worrying about whether or not you'll forget your next question. Simply listen to the witness, if you have gone over your outline sufficiently, his answer will cue the next question, and if you draw a total blank, you can always walk calmly over to the table as if in deep thought, and glance at your outline to see what your next question is. Notice the use of the words "calmly" and "as if in deep thought." This is a reiteration of the principle given in the antidote to Fear 1: jurors respect thought. If you appear to be thinking something over, you can take the few moments you need to get past a "blank." The trick is again in not letting on that anything is wrong; just keep your facial expression neutral and your body language composed.

For cross examination: take notes during opposing counsel's direct so that you know what you want to ask the witness. Put the three or four key words that will cue you as to the questions you want to ask on a paper that you can see easily at your table, just as you did for direct examination. Bear in mind, however, that the piece of paper is an emergency measure. It is there in case of need, but it is not, and should not be used as, a crutch. The paper is the equivalent of a trapeze artist's net: wonderful in case of emergency, but not a normal part of the act.

As in direct examination, be sure to listen to the witness. Often his answer will automatically cue your next question.

Fear 4: "My witness will say the opposite of what he's supposed to say and I'm going to look like a fool."

Antidote: Prior preparation of your witness, and learn how to control your facial expressions and body language.

This is where preparation of your witness is invaluable. If you coach your witness as described in Chapter 11, the likelihood of his saying the opposite of what he is supposed to say is virtually nil. However, should this untoward event happen, don't let the jurors know it. Keep your facial expression and body language calm and composed, react as if you got precisely what you wanted. If you don't react as if anything awful is going on, chances are excellent that the jurors will think that you have everything under control and that all is going in your favor. You will not look like a fool.

Bear in mind that jury studies have demonstrated that jurors react most unfavorably to attorney's surprise. A reaction of surprise indicates that you don't have matters well in hand, and are therefore less than competent. Your calm, composed body language and facial expression will counteract the potentially damaging effect of your witness's answer. Then you have a choice: either drop the issue, or rephrase your question, depending on which strategy you think is most beneficial.

Fear 5: "I'll have forgotten to bring an important document to trial and have to ask for a recess to have it brought over: the jurors will think I'm incompetent."

Antidote: Prior preparation and review lists.

Prepare a list ahead of time of all documents and exhibits needed each day. Review the list the night before each trial day and make sure you have everything you need. When you get to the Courthouse in the morning, get there a little early, leave yourself some extra time to go over your list, verifying that you do indeed have all the documents and exhibits you need that day. If not, send someone right away to get the item, don't wait on the off chance you might not need it.

Fear 6: "I'm afraid my mind will go blank, particularly at a crucial moment."

Antidote: Visualize your way out of memory gaps

If you are afraid of going blank, or having memory gaps, use the following memory trick:

Figure out the key words which represent the issues you wish to cover, during your opening, direct, cross or closing, and list them in the correct sequence. Then create an image which corresponds to each word.

CASE IN POINT

Let's say you have four key words for the four main areas you want to explore during cross examination: "road," "key," "knife" and "time." Then "place" those key word-images in a strategic location. For example, before beginning cross-examination, stare at the witness box for a moment, visualizing each of the words at a different place on the witness box. For "road," visualize a winding strip of road on the left side of the witness box; for "key," a key balancing on the edge of the box in front of the witness; for "knife," a knife balancing next to the key; and for "time," an alarm clock going off to the right of the witness. When you look at those areas of the witness box, the images you have visualized will pop up in your mind, and cue you to your next issue (Illustration 1).

This technique works most effectively if there is some *movement* associated with the image, as shown in Illustration 1. That's why in the images created above, the road was "winding," the key and knife were "balancing," and the alarm clock was "going off." However, you cannot wait until the day of the trial and expect this technique to work magically first time out. Practice it in different situations at work or around the house, so that it becomes easy to summon up clear moving images quickly and efficiently. Learn to rely on this technique to remember your errands and you'll naturally progress to using it to remember points for cross examination.

10–1

The secret to conquering internal fears

Being well prepared is the secret to allaying fears of being embarrassed and humiliated. This applies to all areas of trialwork: being well prepared in terms of knowing your case and your primary witnesses inside out; in terms of preparing your opening statement, direct and cross examination, and closing argument with skill and care and rehearsing them over and over and over; being well prepared in terms of having documents and exhibits ready ahead of time rather than waiting until the last minute; in terms of coaching your witnesses in plenty of time so they can digest and rehearse the necessary information; being well prepared in terms of having corrected those verbal and non-verbal aspects of your personal presentation that mar your full effectiveness as an advocate and diminish your charisma.

The better prepared you are in all these areas, the more confident you will feel, and the better you will perform in Court. The fear of being embarrassed and humiliated will be reduced to a minor case of butterflies, easily controlled with a couple of deep breaths, and your focus will be first and foremost on the excitement of the challenge ahead.

4. How to Identify Your External Symptoms

External symptoms are the outward manifestations of internal fears. Once you have dealt with your internal fears as described above, you will find that your external symptoms decrease accordingly. However, you will undoubtedly still experience some symptoms, and these must be dealt with.

Identify your external symptoms specifically. Think about the ways in which anxiety manifests itself physically for you: pinpoint each one in detail, just as you did with your internal fears.

CASE IN POINT

Common External Symptoms

1. You open your mouth to speak, and find there's not enough saliva to get the words out properly: you're suffering from dry mouth or "cotton" mouth.

2. You break out in a cold sweat or perspire excessively when nervous.

3. Your hands tremble when you are nervous, your knees shake.

4. When you open your mouth to speak, you suddenly discover your pitch is up an entire octave from its usual placement: you sound squeaky or whiney.

5. You feel all bunched up: your shoulders and neck hurt terribly after a day at Court.

6. You feel nauseous and queasy; you're afraid you may throw up.

---

5. How to Counteract Your External Symptoms with Powerful Antidotes

Although external symptoms have an internal source, your fears, they still are external manifestations, and as such, are susceptible to external correction. The antidotes to the most common external symptoms are described below.

CAUTION Bear in mind, that both the internal and external aspects of anxiety must be dealt with if you are to successfully reduce your Courtroom anxiety. Attempting to deal with your external symptoms without addressing your internal fears will not work, nor will simply addressing your internal fears successfully eradicate your external symptoms.

Six common external symptoms and their antidotes

External symptom 1: You open your mouth to speak, and find there's not enough saliva to get the words out properly: you're suffering from dry mouth or "cotton" mouth.

Antidote: When you arrive at the Courthouse, before going into the Courtroom, go to the restroom and gargle with a solution of warm water and glycerine. A few drops of glycerine, easily available over the counter at any pharmacy, in about half a glass of warm water should suffice. There is no need to swallow the glycerine; just spit it out and don't rinse your mouth out after the gargle. This will lubricate your mouth to help you past the first few minutes when your own saliva is stopped by anxiety. If you let the glycerine facilitate your speech, and simply ignore the feeling of "cotton mouth," you will find that after the first few minutes your anxiety will diminish and your own saliva will start to flow appropriately. If you need to, simply repeat the gargle at several points throughout your day.

Avoid foods and beverages which dry up your system. All dairy products create mucous, which can make speaking more difficult.

CASE IN POINT

Singers notoriously avoid cream in their coffee, yoghurt, cheese, ice cream and all other dairy products the day before a performance.

Decongestants unfortunately also tend to dry one up, as do many antihistamines. If you need to take this sort of medication during a trial, tell your doctor you suffer from dry mouth and ask him to recommend the least dehydrating medication possible. Some people find tea dehydrating, certainly diuretics are dehydrating. Be aware of your daily intake, food and medication, and be sure you are not accentuating your dry mouth unnecessarily.

External symptom 2: You break out in a cold sweat or perspire excessively when nervous.

Antidote: Test out different anti-perspirants and use the one which keeps you driest. Wear clothes which are not tight or binding, and which will not show excessive perspiration. For men, this often means wearing an undershirt, for women, the use of shields. Keep a clean folded handkerchief in your pocket and when you need to wipe your brow, do so. Do so, however, as if everyone wipes their brow upon occasion, with calm and composure, as if it were the most natural thing in the world. As long as you do not give away in your body language or facial expression the distress you are feeling, no one will know you are feeling it.

Have enough clean folded handkerchiefs on hand so that the one you are currently using never appears wet or crumpled. Pat your brow, don't scrub away at it. Do not use paper tissue, they tend to come apart. A handkerchief is much classier. Stay with white: a colored handkerchief draws too much attention.

CAUTION Be careful not to eat spicy foods or very hot beverages during trial, these encourage perspiration.

External symptom 3: Your hands tremble when you are nervous, your knees shake.

Antidote: Take a deep breath. Shaking is often minimized, as are many other external symptoms, with the intake of a deep breath.

When you are gesturing, no one will notice that your hands are shaking. If you are at the table, simply keep them lightly on the table. If at a podium, rest them lightly on the podium. Be careful, the operative word is "lightly." If you grip the table, the podium, or anything else to minimize the trembling, you'll only make it worse. If you need to hold a document or exhibit, hold it with both hands to help you control your shaking. Keep taking deep breaths to help you relax.

If your knees shake, take a good solid neutral stance to help yourself feel grounded, and again, breathe. Bear in mind, with regard to either your hands or knees shaking, that the symptom is much more obvious to you than it is to the jurors. If you do not draw attention to the trembling by looking distressed, but simply carry on as if nothing untoward were happening, the jurors won't notice anything. Take it in stride, as if it were but a minor, hardly worth noticing, inconvenience. Your attitude will make it so.

External symptom 4: When you open your mouth to speak, you suddenly discover your pitch is up an entire octave from its usual placement: you sound squeaky or whiney.

Antidote: In order to correct an undesired rise in pitch, start by taking a couple of deep breaths. Consciously relax your neck and throat. Before you actually speak out loud, say the word "now" to yourself several times. Once you hear the word "now" at the proper pitch inside yourself, it is safe to open your mouth and speak. Every so often, take a deep breath and say "now" internally to reposition your voice.

Similarly, if you find yourself "rushing" (speaking too quickly) when anxious, counteract that tendency by taking a deep breath and deliberately slowing your pace down for the first few sentences. Then, as you get more comfortable and settle into speaking, you will find that your pace settles down on its own. Every so often, take a deep breath just to keep yourself on track.

External symptom 5: You feel all bunched up: your shoulders and neck hurt terribly after a day at Court.

Antidote: This is a very common symptom, and is easily corrected with awareness and breathing. Whenever you think of it, check to see if your shoulders are somewhere around your ears. If so, take a deep breath and consciously relax them. Check at the same time and notice if your hands are making fists: if so, allow your fingers to relax and stay loose. Then throughout the day, check periodically to see if any part of your body is particularly tense, take a deep breath and deliberately relax that area.

External symptom 6: You feel nauseous and queasy; you're afraid you may throw up.

Antidote: Congratulations! You've just joined the ranks of some of the world's most prestigious performers. Nausea is a common manifestation of stagefright, and unfortunately, one of the most uncomfortable. First of all, be sure that you eat lightly before trial, and eat only foods that have a history of being comfortably and well digested by you. Your physician can provide guidance in this area if you are in doubt. Secondly, be sure you take enough *time* to eat, chewing well, eating slowly, so that your over-anxious system has its best chances of properly digesting your food.

Having taken these precautions, when you feel nauseous, remind yourself you haven't eaten anything likely to cause you problems, and take a few deep breaths. If you really and truly feel that you need to throw up, just before trial, go to the restroom and do so. You'll be in good company. Many actors do the same before walking on stage opening night. However, if the nausea persists, and you find yourself throwing up more than once during a trial, consult your physician. Never ignore a persistent physical symptom, even if you're convinced it's "just nerves."

The secret to coping with external symptoms

In order to cope with external symptoms, become aware of what symptoms exactly you manifest when anxious, and plan ahead of time what to do about those symptoms. Bear in mind that if you don't let on that you are nervous, very few people will even notice. Remember that your shaking, sweaty palms, or dry mouth are always much more obvious to you than they are to any one else. Don't allow your nerves to run the show, be in control of your nerves. The jurors will remain oblivious to your symptoms, or discount them as irrelevant, unless you bring attention to your symptoms by reacting with distress or not knowing how to counteract them.

Be aware that most nervous symptoms die down between 5 and 20 minutes after onset, at least enough for you to be able to function comfortably. Follow the guidelines given above, be aware that most symptoms will dissipate within a short time, and as you interact with the Judge, opposing counsel and jurors, behave as if everything is fine. Soon, it will be.

HOW TO VISUALIZE YOUR WAY TO SUCCESS

Over the past few years, psychologists have become increasingly aware of the powerful influence mind has over emotions and body. For example, physicians and psychologists have had remarkable success using mental techniques, in particular visualizations and mental imagery, to contain such life threatening conditions as cancer. Other psychologists, intrigued by the power of thought, have explored further applications of the mind-body connection; sports psychologists, for example, have made visualizations an integral part of Olympic training.

CASE IN POINT

The visualizations used by Olympic athletes may be thought of as a sort of *mental rehearsal* of the event for which the athlete is preparing.

How is this visualization accomplished? An Olympic runner, for example, as a regular part of his training regimen, sets aside some time each day during which he first gets himself into a relaxed condition, and then mentally visualizes his whole race, exactly as it will take place the day of the competition. He mentally sees, hears and feels himself going through the entire race, starting from the time he gets dressed in the locker room, to placing himself in the correct position at the starting line, through intensely feeling the crowd in the stands, hearing them cheer him, hearing the starter gun, to actually running the race, feeling his muscles obeying him perfectly, seeing himself passing the other athletes one by one, hearing the roar of the crowd as he runs free, to breaking the ribbon at the finish line, and all this accompanied with the sights, sounds and emotions of successfully winning the race.

By doing all this, the runner is priming himself to win. He is readying his subconscious for success. The daily repetition of these success visualizations gear his emotions and body up to win, and help counteract any fears or negative thoughts the athlete might have.

How to Create a Winning Courtroom Visualization

Running a race or hurling a javelin is no different in essence to conducting a trial. Everything is riding on this moment, and you must perform at peak level. Mental rehearsal can help you considerably in this endeavor.

Create your visualization in the following manner: about three weeks before your trial date, set aside some time to develop the mental imagery of your visualization. Sit or lie down in a quiet spot, where you will not be interrupted, but be careful not to go to sleep. You need to be relaxed and comfortable, but not unconscious. Loosen any clothes which are tight, take off your glasses, your watch, make yourself pleasantly comfortable. Once you are comfortable, close your eyes, take a few deep breaths, and then proceed to relax all your muscles. This is most easily accomplished by first tensing all your muscles from the feet up to the top of your head, one muscle group at a time, tensing first your feet, then your calves, your thighs, buttocks, abdomen, chest, shoulders, arms and hands, neck, jaw and face, and once you've tensed all your muscles, holding the tension a moment, then relaxing all your muscles in the same sequence, but reversing it so you start by relaxing from the top of your head down, relaxing first your face and jaw, then your neck, arms and hands, shoulders, chest, abdomen, buttocks, thighs, calves, and feet.

> *CAUTION If progressively tensing and then relaxing your body causes you any discomfort, discontinue the exercise immediately and consult your physician. This should feel very good, not bad.*

Repeat the process of first tensing all your muscles, then relaxing all your muscles. You should feel very relaxed. Do it one more time if you wish, then take a deep breath. Now start to visualize the trial.

Visualize yourself the first day of the trial, before going into the courtroom, make a mental image of yourself calm and happy, feeling good about the work done so far, feeling terrific about your preparation. Feel yourself strongly self-confident, excited about the trial, see yourself talking to your assistants and colleagues in a firm and positive manner. See them responding to you with equal positiveness and enthusiasm.

> *REMINDER It is very important that during the entire visualization you really feel the attendant emotions vividly, otherwise the visualization will be ineffective.*

Then see yourself walking into the courtroom, looking and feeling confident, competent and highly professional. Then visualize yourself throughout the specific moments of the trial. Create a mental image of yourself doing a dynamic opening statement, successfully conducting direct and cross examination, dealing with all exhibits and visual aids wonderfully, dealing with objections masterfully, delivering a closing argument that is terrific, and feel all the feelings of power and success that come from being effective and persuasive.

See yourself as powerful and charismatic, and impressing the jurors with your sincerity, your trustworthiness and your competence. Visualize the jury on your side, responding to you, accepting what you have to say, being convinced by your excellent advocacy. Visualize the judge and opposing counsel responding to you as you wish them to respond. Visualize the decision being handed down in your favor, feel the wonderful feelings of joy and success that come with winning your case. See opposing counsel deflated by his loss but impressed by your advocacy. See your colleagues crowding around you back at the office, wanting all the details on how you won that fantastic judgement. Hear your best friend or spouse calling you up on the phone, congratulating you on your success. Feel the happiness and joy of success flood your whole being.

You can vary this visualization any way you want to, in accord with your own personality and goals. Just make sure you really feel the feelings, and that you do put in all the elements necessary for your success. If there is something particularly difficult for you to do during the course of the trial, such as handling a particular exhibit, see yourself doing that very task easily and successfully. Be as thorough as possible in creating the visualization.

Set aside time every day during the three weeks before the trial date to first get comfortable, progressively tense and relax your muscles, and then do your visualization. If your time is too limited to visualize the entire trial in full detail every day, create a shortened version of your visualization, emphasizing those aspects about which you have the most concern, and do that every day. The day before the trial itself, however, do the full length version and really be there emotionally.

> **REMINDER** *The more important and complex the trail, the more days before the trial date you should do the visualizations, and the more you should use the full length version.*

Continue to do the visualization on a regular basis throughout the trial, especially if you feel discouraged or dismayed by the way the trial is going.

Visualization can make the difference between feeling deep down like you know what you're doing, and being insecure about the chances of your success. It reinforces your qualities and strong points, boosts your self-confidence and self-esteem, and helps you think creatively in a positive mode. Visualizing, with all the attendant emotions, helps keep all parts of yourself on the same track by focusing your thoughts and emotions on one dimension only—success. Lawyering is a difficult business; the more you can help yourself be successful, the better off you will be.

> *CAUTION The magic of visualization is not to be substituted for thorough preparation and legal skills. Mental rehearsal cannot invent what is not there: if you have not prepared an excellent "show," there is nothing to rehearse.*

SUMMARY

It does not serve you to have a wonderful set of techniques and skills beautifully rehearsed and learned if you are too nervous to use them when the time comes. This chapter is dedicated to helping you cope with anxiety, from explaining the source of your nervous symptoms to giving you some very practical ways to deal with these. In addition, we described a way that you can "go for the gold" by using visualizations in mental rehearsal, a truly Olympic way to win.

Use the worksheets at the end of this chapter to help you plot your internal fears and external symptoms and their different antidotes. You will also find a worksheet to help you design a visualization for success.

INTERNAL FEARS AND ANTIDOTES WORKSHEET

List your specific internal fears in the left hand column, then figure out the most powerful antidotes in the right hand column, using the examples given in the chapter to guide your thinking:

Fears   *Antidotes*

#1_____   _____

                  _____

                  _____

                  _____

                  _____

                  _____

#2_____   _____

                  _____

                  _____

                  _____

                  _____

#3_____   _____

                  _____

                  _____

                  _____

                  _____

#4_____   _____

                  _____

                  _____

                  _____

                  _____

Fears	Antidotes
#5_____	_____
	_____
	_____
	_____
	_____
	_____
#6_____	_____
	_____
	_____
	_____
	_____
	_____

EXTERNAL SYMPTOMS AND ANTIDOTES WORKSHEET

List your specific external symptoms in the left hand column, then figure out the most powerful antidotes in the right hand column, using the examples given in the chapter to guide your thinking:

Symptoms   *Antidotes*

#1_____   _____

                        _____

                        _____

                        _____

                        _____

                        _____

#2_____   _____

                        _____

                        _____

                        _____

                        _____

                        _____

#3_____   _____

                        _____

                        _____

                        _____

                        _____

                        _____

#4_____   _____

                        _____

                        _____

                        _____

                        _____

                        _____

Symptoms	*Antidotes*
#5_____	_____
	_____
	_____
	_____
	_____
	_____
#6_____	_____
	_____
	_____
	_____
	_____
	_____

VISUALIZATION WORKSHEET

1. Think about the upcoming trial. Think about each part of the trial specifically, and note what are the points which concern you most about each part. Then note how you want that point to turn out, what is the *best* case scenario. Your mental images of the trial are built out of what is most desirable, what would constitute maximum success. Use your best case scenarios as the basis of your visualization, placing each point in context within the overall trial.

Points of Concern   *Best Case Scenarios*

1. Voir Dire

_____   _____

_____   _____

_____   _____

_____   _____

_____   _____

_____   _____

2. Opening Statement

_____   _____

_____   _____

_____   _____

_____   _____

_____   _____

3. Direct Examination

_____   _____

_____   _____

_____   _____

_____   _____

_____   _____

Points of Concern   *Best Case Scenarios*

4. Cross Examination

_____   _____

_____   _____

_____   _____

_____   _____

_____   _____

_____

5. Making and Answering Objections

_____   _____

_____   _____

_____   _____

_____   _____

_____   _____

_____

6. Closing Argument

_____   _____

_____   _____

_____   _____

_____   _____

_____   _____

7. Relationship with Jurors

_____   _____

_____   _____

_____   _____

_____   _____

_____   _____

_____   _____

Points of Concern	*Best Case Scenarios*

8. Relationship with Judge

_____ _____

_____ _____

_____ _____

_____ _____

_____ _____

_____

9. Opposing Counsel

_____ _____

_____ _____

_____ _____

_____ _____

_____

10. Self-Presentation

_____ _____

_____ _____

_____ _____

_____ _____

_____

11. Visual Aids

_____ _____

_____ _____

_____ _____

_____ _____

_____ _____

Points of Concern   *Best Case Scenarios*

12. Handling Evidence and Exhibits

_____   _____

_____   _____

_____   _____

_____   _____

_____   _____

_____   _____

13. Witnesses

_____   _____

_____   _____

_____   _____

_____   _____

_____   _____

_____   _____

14. Client

_____   _____

_____   _____

_____   _____

_____   _____

_____   _____

_____   _____

15. Other

_____   _____

_____   _____

_____   _____

_____   _____

_____   _____

_____   _____

CHAPTER 11

How to Coach Your Witness for Effective Presentation in Court

To a greater or lesser degree, all witnesses, including your client (whether he testifies in Court or not), must be prepared. Failure to prepare your witnesses properly invites disaster. Clearly, the more important the witness, the more time and effort must be spent preparing him. In this chapter, we focus on how to prepare an important witness. The same guidelines apply to preparing less important witnesses, the time and energy spent in so doing will, however, be correspondingly less. Please note that throughout this chapter, the generic term "witness" includes lay witnesses, expert witnesses, and your client, unless otherwise specified.

HOW YOUR WITNESS'S CREDIBILITY WITH THE JURORS DEPENDS ON HIS SELF-PRESENTATION

The validity of your case rests to a large extent on the credibility of your witnesses, since a witness's credibility profoundly affects the way the jurors evaluate his testimony. If your witnesses are perceived as trustworthy and sincere, their testimony will be considered valid. If your witnesses aren't perceived as credible, their testimony is worthless, if not downright damaging. Anything your witness says is automatically assessed against the backdrop of his presentation of self. If his presentation of self is credible, the veracity of his testimony will be upheld. This process is identical to that by which your credibility affects the jurors' willingness to believe your statements. A witness's credibility, however, has another, quite different, effect on the way the jurors perceive his testimony.

HOW YOUR WITNESS'S CREDIBILITY
AFFECTS THE JURORS'
ATTRIBUTION OF RESPONSIBILITY

If your witness appears credible, then any disreputable activity will to a significant degree, if not totally, be attributed to the *situation* the witness found himself in at the time, rather than to the witness himself. The witness is, in a sense, absolved of full responsibility for his acts; the role of mitigating factors, unusual circumstances, and so forth, will be willingly taken into account. Why? Because it just doesn't make sense, according to ordinary logic, for an apparently sincere, upright citizen, a credible person, to do such an awful thing or tell such a terrible lie. It defies our normal understanding of how the world works, and our minds resist incongruent information. If, on the other hand, your witness does not appear credible, then any disreputable activity will be considered a direct and logical consequence of the witness's basic personality, and he will be held wholly responsible. Other factors will be discounted or considered irrelevant.

CASE IN POINT

Two men are accused of aggravated assault: a surly man, with mean and shifty eyes, who sits sloppily in his chair, hostile and sarcastic in his replies, and a middle-aged, good-looking stockbroker, whose manner is forthright and courteous, whose posture is good and whose expression is concerned but pleasant. The surly man is automatically more likely to be thought inherently capable of, and therefore guilty of, aggravated assault, than the stockbroker.

Aggravated assault is, according to a common sense understanding of the world, consistent with the surly man's presentation of himself, and *inconsistent* with the stockbroker's self-presentation. The jurors will therefore be more receptive to the possibility of error, or of mitigating circumstances, in evaluating the stockbroker's case. Your witness's credibility, then, has ramifications which go way beyond supporting the veracity of his testimony. A witness's credibility or lack thereof may change the very nature of your case.

Just as your credibility had to be explored and developed, in order to be perceived by the jury, so too does your witness's credibility. You cannot take your witness's credibility for granted, you must help him present and express himself in credible manner.

A FIVE-PART STRATEGY FOR SUCCESSFUL WITNESS PREPARATION

Your witness's credibility is the end result of his successful preparation as a witness. This preparation consists of five parts:

1. getting to know your witness and using that knowledge to help your witness present himself credibly;
2. evaluating your witness's verbal and non-verbal behavior and correcting any elements which interfere with your witness's credibility;
3. helping your witness make appropriate and persuasive emotional choices;
4. role-playing direct and cross examination with your witness;
5. building your witness's confidence.

1. Ensure Your Witness's Credible Self-Presentation

Getting to know your witness gives you the information you need to lay the foundation for his credibility. Specifically, you need three kinds of information about your witness:

1. what will make him sympathetic to the jurors
2. what his fears are
3. how he will react under pressure

In order to get this information, start by developing rapport.

How to develop rapport to win your witness's trust and cooperation

The creation of rapport is important to the success of your case in all areas, including witness preparation. Rapport, as you will recall from Chapter 4, is the basis of trust. The more your witness trusts you, the better he will be able to do whatever it is you need him to do. He will disclose information he may only know at a subliminal level, he will be willing to discuss sensitive and painful facts, he will be more responsive to your guidance and coaching: all in all, he will make a far better witness than the individual with whom you have no rapport. There are, however, specific barriers to the creation of rapport with the witness, with which you should be familiar.

Many witnesses are in awe of "the attorney." Don't forget you have many more years of education than the average person, make a great deal more money than many people, and occupy a higher social status than most people. These are intimidating factors for many witnesses. For other people, the image of "the attorney" is tainted with overtones of manipulativeness, slickness, and "anything for a buck" type behavior. "The attorney" is seen as conniving, ruthless, and powerful. These are not traits which lead normally to the development of trust. Somehow you must help the witness past these barriers so that you can effectively work with him. How?

Get to know the witness as a person

To develop rapport with your witness, first get to know him as a person. Depending on the importance of the witness, this may take 20 minutes or 20 hours. Use the techniques of mirroring and perceptual modes as described in Chapter 4 to establish familiarity quickly and efficiently, and to get past the barriers of higher education and socio-economic status. Demonstrate sincere interest in the witness by maintaining good eye focus, and by nodding acknowledgement. Don't be too eager to focus strictly on the information you need, let the witness talk about himself, let him relate the incident as he wishes, stressing what is important to *him*, get a feel for the witness as a human being before you zero in on the facts you need to know. You may wish to tape record these sessions, rather than take notes, in order to facilitate rapport.

In addition to helping your witness feel comfortable with you and therefore trusting, endeavor to make your witness feel valuable and important. Gratitude and appreciation go a long way toward making a witness willing to cooperate with you. Maintain the same politeness and respect that is your bottom line behavior in the Courtroom. Put your phones on hold for the first "getting to know you" session, and do so in front of the witness. Impress him with your willingness to devote your entire attention to him.

Explain your view of the case to the witness

Once you have a feel for the witness as a person, explain your concept of the case to him. Witnesses cooperate more freely and totally when they understand what is going on. Explain your concept of the case to your witness, as well as your overall approach and strategy. Give more elaborate details and specifics in function of the importance of the witness. Then explain to your witness how he fits in, what is his importance to the case, and why you are asking him to look, sound and behave a certain way. This will counteract the image of "the attorney" as slick and conniving. Knowing why you are approaching the case a certain way, what role you expect the witness to play and why, gives your witness an understanding of how you operate, so that your behavior is perceived as tactical, part of a winning "strategy," rather than the "slick and conniving" ways of an underhanded lawyer.

How to make your witness sympathetic to the jurors

As you get to know your witness, note your impressions of him: what is there about this particular witness or about his situation, that a juror might find sympathetic? The more you let your witness talk, about himself, his life both in terms of work and family, the case, how the case affects his life, his hobbies, his passions, his pursuits, his dreams, where he came from, how he got where he is now, and so forth, the better you get to know him. The better you get to know him, the more likely you are to find out things about the witness that a jury will find sympathetic. The more important the witness, the more time and effort you devote to this process.

Do not assume, before meeting your witness, that you know what will make him sympathetic. Certainly, there are some basics of verbal and non-verbal presentation discussed in the next sections which enhance a witness's sympathetic presentation of self, but beyond these very basic tenants, there are specific elements and attributes about this particular witness or his situation which will make him sympathetic to the jury. These must be uncovered and explored. This is especially important when you are dealing with an obviously unsympathetic client.

CASE IN POINT

Rikki J. Klieman describes how she defended her client, accused of killing a young man with a .357 Magnum. This client presented highly unsympathetically: Klieman describes him as falling into the "Hell's Angels" category. The community in which the crime happened, and from which the jury was drawn, was composed of white Irish Catholics, certainly not a population favoring Hell's Angels type individuals. There was no way Klienman could present her client as an innocent lamb, he would have been totally unbelievable as such. Instead, she found elements in his life which would make him sympathetic to the jury.

She discovered that he was not from that neighborhood, that he was there that day because of the St. Patrick's Day parade and party, which he had attended with his wife. His wife, Klieman found out, is a very tiny woman, of whom her client was very protective. Klieman discovered that her client was familiar with guns, his hobby from childhood being collecting guns and hunting. With this information, carefully gleaned from her "getting to know you" sessions with her client, Klieman was able to construct a winning case: ". . . some sense of Michael's [the client's] position. He's an outsider. He's in a neighborhood that is not his own. There are bottles and crates and objects being thrown around him. He is good enough to fire a warning shot. He's protective of his wife. The dinner and the parade set a different scene and a different picture from that of a 'bikey' coming into town with his .357 Magnum, which is no small pistol indeed [which was the picture painted by the prosecutor]."[1]

Had Klieman not spent the necessary time and energy really getting to know her client, she would have been stuck with an unsympathetic client in an unsympathetic situation. Gathering information on his life, his feelings, and his background allowed Klieman to transform a losing case to a winning one.

Gathering information of this nature is also what allows you to transform a corporate client, with whom few jurors can identify, into a real human being or group of individuals, with whom the jurors can readily identify.

CASE IN POINT

In a case previously cited, in which Liman sued Rockwell on behalf of the New York Transit Authority, Liman could have used high-ranking and sophisticated professionals to testify on the Transit Authority's behalf. Instead, he chose to use those with whom the jury could identify, using as one of his primary witnesses, for example, a middle-aged, mid-level Transit Authority manager. The end result was that Liman "made it appear to the jury that it was a case of the Transit Authority engineer, on a civil service salary, trying to do his job. All he needed was equipment that would work."[2]

Liman could not have accomplished such a feat had he not taken the time to thoroughly research the corporation, thus giving him the wherewithal to transform the corporation into living, breathing people sympathetic to a jury. Getting to know your witness, whether we're talking about an individual witness, or a corporate entity, is critical to the success of your case.

How to discover and diminish your witness's fears

Find out how your witness feels about himself, about the case. Few are totally self-confident, convinced of the rightness of their position and articulate about it. Most witnesses are, to a greater or lesser degree, personally insecure, unsure of the rightness of their position or their ability to articulate it, or frightened of the Court process. If you don't know what your witness's fears and worries are concerning his presentation of himself or his performance in Court, you cannot effectively prepare him to do well. You are leaving him vulnerable to opposing counsel's attack. Therefore, explore the witness's feelings about these areas. Bolster his self-confidence by describing to him how you will help prepare him for the Court experience.

We fear most the unknown: realize most witnesses have no real knowledge of the trial process. Their impressions are for the most part garnered through television, movies, and accounts heard from friends. These impressions represent highly distorted versions of reality. Allay your witness's anxieties by giving him accurate, real-life information. Diminish his fear by explaining to him exactly how the Court process works, what he can expect, and precisely how you will help him through it successfully. The more familiar the witness is with the Court process and his role in it, the more self-confident he will be, and the more credible his presentation.

How to help your witness react effectively under pressure

Psychologists say that the best predictor of future behavior is past behavior. The best assessment of how your witness is going to stand up to the rigors of Court is to find out how he has coped with major stressors in the past. To any but the most experienced expert witness, being in Court, even when the witness is not testifying (i.e., your client does not take the stand), is a major stressor. Ask your witness to describe a stressful experience in his life: his very choice of what he defines as stressful will help you evaluate how he will do in Court. If your witness, for example, describes an unpleasant encounter with a rude waitress as a major stressful experience, then you know you have a lot of work to do if you want him to successfully withstand the cross examination of opposing counsel. Ask him what kind of stresses he has on the job, and how he copes with them.

Then ask your witness what he expects might be stressful in Court. Ask him to imagine he's being cross examined and ask him how he thinks he might react. Be on the lookout for over-confident as well as under-confident responses. Witnesses who say they absolutely will not flinch, ever, and are totally secure, are in all likelihood simply denying their fear. Once you feel you have an estimate of how the witness will hold up in Court, explain to him what may happen (in terms of stressors), and explain to him how you will prepare him for such eventualities.

CASE IN POINT

You are suing a truck company on behalf of your witness who is still in pain from injuries suffered as a result of the incident that occurred four years ago: the poorly maintained brakes on a truck failed, and the truck rammed into your client at 40 mph. Your client believes the truck company is entirely at fault, he is frustrated over the slowness of the judicial process, and his finances are suffering. He gets irritated during your "getting to know you" sessions when he talks about the incident, and he reports that he often flares up over small conflicts on the job.

You realize that he will probably flare up a good deal when cross-examined by opposing counsel, and his petulant irritation will not win him points with the jury. You explain to him, therefore, that opposing counsel will sense that your client's reaction to pressure is to flare up, and that opposing counsel will do everything in his power to get your client to flare up at precisely the moment when it will create the worst impression on the jurors. Then explain to your witness that in your "working sessions" (described in the following section) you will role-play cross examination with him and help him learn alternate reactions to high-pressure situations.

Just knowing that you are not simply throwing him to the wolves, vulnerable and exposed, significantly helps the witness deal with the pressures of the trial. The later role-play sessions give him the practical tools to react effectively when the time comes.

Knowing how your witness reacts under pressure gives you the means to counteract his natural mode of reaction if it interferes with his credibility. In the absence of such knowledge, you leave yourself open to some unpleasant surprises in the Courtroom.

2. Help Your Witness Speak and Behave Credibly

Once you feel you have gathered as much information as you need, begin "working sessions" with your witness. These "working sessions" are designed to help your witness eliminate any verbal or non-verbal behaviors which interfere with the witness's ability to express himself credibly and effectively, and must be explained to your witness as such. "Working sessions" are not to be confused with information-gathering sessions, and are most effective if they are conducted in a practical, problem-solving manner. Be sure, however, that you always take the time to explain to your witness why you are asking him to make the changes you request.

It is highly advantageous to videotape these sessions, as your witness can more easily understand (and therefore accept) behavior that is not working in his favor if he can actually see and hear it. Most of us are remarkably unconscious of how we appear to others. In addition, it is important to let the witness know that you are not trying to change him:

you are not attempting to turn him into some other person. You are simply helping him express himself in a way that is readily understood and believed by those observing and listening to him.

How to correct faulty speech

Pay attention to your witness's articulation, pace, volume, and pitch

First attend to how your witness presents vocally. Note his articulation, pace, volume, and pitch. His articulation should be clear; don't let him mumble. His pace should be such that it is easily listened to: if he speaks so quickly he cannot be understood, point that out. His volume should be such that he can be easily heard: people who speak too softly do not convey conviction and are less believed. His pitch is only a concern as to what happens to it when he gets nervous. With most people, pitch goes up when nervous; instruct your witness to take a deep breath when he gets nervous—this will correct his pitch sufficiently for trial.

Work with your witness directly, showing him what you mean by clearer articulation, deep breathing, and so forth. Go over whatever vocal corrections you want enough so that you are sure the witness understands what you want and how to achieve it. Then schedule another working session about a week later, and see how he is doing. Be sure to tell your witness to practice between sessions.

Pay attention to ineffective speech patterns and habits

Next, listen to how your witness expresses himself verbally. The easiest way to do this is to ask him to talk about the case, or answer a question regarding the case, and video or audiotape the response. Then listen to the playback with your witness, and listen for verbal patterns and habits which interfere with his effectiveness. If he does not already do so, encourage him to speak in short sentences. Teach him to use the pause, to speak in meaningful phrases, one thought at a time. Help your witness learn to get to the point and to speak directly. If you notice any "kind of," "sort of," "well I think that perhaps maybe," and other such phrases which dilute the impact of what the witness is trying to say, point these out to him. They detract from his persuasiveness.

Many people repeat a phrase habitually, such as "you know" before every sentence. Listen for such habits and eliminate them. Pay attention to the presence of "Uh" or "Um" sounds, these occur especially when people are nervous. It is better to stay silent a moment, than to say "Uh, Um . . . Uh" before speaking. Too often, these sounds are associated with lying or "hedging," neither of which increase your witness's believability.

Help your witness speak in specifics. Saying "it took a really long time" is meaningless: teach him to give the specifics—are we talking about 10 minutes, three hours, a whole day? "Between 10 and 15 minutes" carries more conviction than, "well, I don't know, about 10 minutes or so."

Teach your witness to listen

Teach your witness to listen carefully. Help him to resist answering the question in his mind before the whole of the question has been asked: he may miss the most important part of the question. Practice asking him questions and then asking him what he thinks you're asking him: ask him to paraphrase your question. You will be surprised how often the two versions differ. Teach your witness the critical value of thinking before he speaks. Tell him that he can take his time before he opens his mouth, not to be frightened or intimidated into blurting something out just to provide an answer.

Help your witness organize his thoughts with a timetable and a "fact-diagram"

Witnesses often have difficulty answering questions because their thoughts lack an organizational framework. Witnesses are used to telling their story a certain way, and can be easily thrown by a question requesting that they approach their story differently. Encourage your witness to write down a timetable of the events leading up to and associated with the facts of the case, and to thoroughly familiarize himself with that timetable, so he knows exactly where each event fits in the overall sequence of events, and is not confused by a question addressing one of those out of context.

Help your witness to create a fact-diagram, which places facts into categories which the witness can easily refer to mentally when asked a question.

CASE IN POINT

Your witness suffers pain related to a car accident. When you first meet with the witness, you ask him "How has this incident affected your life?," the witness gives you a very rambling answer, which certainly brings out an impression of pain and suffering, but few specifics. In preparing your witness for testimony therefore, help your witness create the following "fact-diagram":

Pain and Suffering				
	Physical	*Emotional*	*Social*	*Work*
At time of incident	1.Intense; surgery	1.Scared; fear of death	1.Cut off from family	1.Had to quit
Between time of incident and last few months/year	1.Intense; poor recovery 2.Painful physical therapy 3.More surgery	1.Angry 2.Depressed 3.Withdraws 4.Consults psychiatrist; shame	1.Fights 2.Spouse leaves 3.Difficulty in relating to children	1.Can't work 2.Loss of income 3.Difficulty in retraining
Presently	1.Limps 2.Moderate to severe pain	1.Bitter 2.Chronic depression 3.Anxious	1.Few friends 2.Difficulty relating to people	1.Part-time, low paying job

Once this fact-diagram is created, and the witness has gone over it many times, he can answer questions specifically and with the confidence that knowing what you are talking about brings. The answer to "How has this incident affected your life?" now becomes something along the lines of "Well, it's affected my life in a number of ways. Back then, when I was actually thrown from the car, I was in terrible pain, my leg was smashed, I had to have surgery right away, which meant I couldn't work, and I was real scared . . . " and so on. The witness is answering the question bearing in mind a time slot, "back then" as opposed to "now," for example, and is answering bearing in mind the categories, "physical, emotional, social, work," in which he has been affected. Each time the witness is called upon to answer a question relating to a different aspect of his pain and suffering, he mentally refers to the appropriate category, and answers using the elements contained within that category.

CAUTION The above fact-diagram is over-simplified, and to be used only as a guide to the kinds of information which are to be included. The more specific and detailed the fact-diagram, the more easily your witness can organize his thought and consequently reply appropriately and thoroughly to any question asked.

Help your witness create "emergency" phrase

Develop "emergency" phrases with your witness, pat phrases to help him out if he's in trouble. *Do not* make the mistake of simply giving your witness a list of stock pat phrases to memorize. People are rarely effective using language that is not their own: it takes actors years to develop that skill. Rather, take the time to develop with your witness phrases that feel comfortable to him. Certainly, you can use stock phrases as a starting point, just don't stop there.

Phrases which come in handy are those created to deal with situations in which your witness can't remember something, or doesn't know the answer to a question, or doesn't hear or understand a question. Knowing that he has a familiar and comfortable repertoire of phrases to draw from when confronted with such anxiety provoking situations helps your witness stay calm and present himself credibly during trial.

Make sure your witness avoids slang and profanity

Although your witness should in general use his own vocabulary, slang and swear words are to be avoided. Slang is not necessarily understood by those outside the group which uses it as a matter of course, and the slang which is understood commonly is usually considered too casual a language for the formality and seriousness of a Courtroom. Help your witness understand that it is important he be readily understood by a jury who may differ from him in many ways, and thus must express himself in a language common to all members of the community, and a language which befits the nature of a trial. Profanity is not considered appropriate and is frowned upon by the jurors.

How to correct noncredible behavior

Your witness's body language is as important as your own. His body language must be consistent with his presentation of himself as a sincere, credible individual. Videotape the witness as he replies to a series of questions, then watch the playback with the witness and point out to him those aspects of body language that interfere with his presentation of himself as sincere and credible.

Encourage good eye focus and a steady head position

First and foremost, watch how your witness holds his head and what he does with his eyes. Your witness's head should be up: when people are scared, their heads often drop down, which unfortunately conveys an impression of shiftiness or avoidance (Illustration 1). Help your witness learn how to maintain steady eye focus (Illustration 2): teach him to look directly at people, and not avoid their gaze, which is often what happens

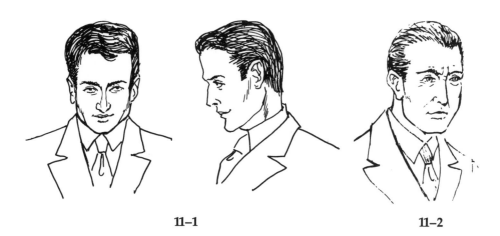

11-1   11-2

when people are anxious. Tell the witness when you want him to look at you, and when you want him to look at the jurors. Don't rely on his ability to discern when he should look where. Help him feel confident about his presentation by giving him specific direction. Teach your witness how to look at the different jurors in the same way you do, looking from one to the other.

Pay attention to your witness's posture, mannerisms and gestures

Encourage your witness to have good posture, and not slouch or slump in his chair. Use the guidelines given in Chapter 2 to notice and correct ineffective body language, such as chin cocked skyward (arrogance) or arms crossed over chest (defensiveness). Watch for mannerisms and habits such as foot tapping, foot swinging, nail biting, playing with fingers, pulling at hair. All of these distract from the witness's ability to present himself well. Be careful that the witness does not hide any part of his face with his hand: hand over mouth, over cheek, holding forehead. Such gestures too easily convey deceptiveness and avoidance.

Encourage consistency in your witness's self-presentation

Be sure your witness realizes fully that he is being scrutinized the entire time he is in the Courtroom, not just when he is on the stand, or even if he never is put on the stand. He must, therefore, be consistent in his presentation of himself. If your witness maintains that his disability prevents him from picking up a pen off the floor, then he'd better never, ever, do that, or a similar act, in the possible presence of a juror. That means in the cafeteria, restroom, hall, parking lot, and so forth. If your witness maintains that he is afflicted with a limp and must always be supported in order to walk properly, then this is not the time to be brave and try to forego his cane. He will destroy his credibility in one instant, as well as your whole case, if he presents himself inconsistently.

The rule of consistency applies to every aspect of the witness's verbal and nonverbal behavior. For example, your witness cannot present himself as speaking properly and respectfully on the stand, and then lapse into swear words and slang in the restroom. All it takes is for one juror to overhear him swearing to demolish the credible impression he had made earlier. Impress upon the witness that he is "on show" the whole time he is anywhere near the Courtroom: tell him specifically what you mean by that and be sure he has understood you and can behave consistently.

Practice with visual aids

If you intend to use visual aids with your witness, make absolutely sure he has plenty of practice time working with those visual aids. If, for example, you want to use a diagram, where you point at various parts and ask him to identify them, rehearse that procedure with your witness. Don't assume "it's easy, he'll be fine." Assuming "it's easy, he'll be fine" is begging for trouble. If you want the witness to draw a graph or demonstrate something, be sure to rehearse it over and over again with him. The more familiar the visual aids are to your witness, the more comfortable he is with them, the more persuasive he will be in dealing with them in the Courtroom.

After your initial working session or sessions, leave a few days or a week in between, then have another session or series of sessions. This will enable you to see what "sticks": which aspects your witness has truly understood, rehearsed, and made his own, and which need more work. The better prepared your witness, the better his performance in Court. It's that simple.

Review all aspects of dress, hair, and make-up with your witness

Be sure to review your witness's dress, hair, and, when appropriate, use of makeup. The bottom line here is cleanliness and neatness. Do not attempt to make the witness someone he is not. Ask your witness to wear to your office what he thinks would be appropriate to wear in Court, and then correct from there. Take into account the community and what is familiar and acceptable to the jurors, given community standards. For men, for example, this generally means a jacket and tie. But it does not mean that a witness who has never worn a three piece suit should suddenly be stuffed into an Armani or Pierre Cardin corporate style grey suit. If your witness shows up at your office in his version of Court wear, for example, a sportscoat, flashy tie, and slacks, you might want to suggest a more conservative tie depending on your take on the jurors, and just assure yourself that his clothes are clean and pressed. That's it. That's enough.

For ladies, dresses or suits are generally best; conservative is generally more appropriate than flashy, but again, cleanliness and neatness are the bottom line. For both sexes, hair should be trimmed, clean and neat. Make-up is best kept to a minimum. Jewelry should be simple and not distracting. Be realistic. Don't ask the widow of the victim to wear black day in, day out, when her husband's death occurred seven years ago. Subdued colors, yes, black every day, no. The jurors won't buy it. Similarly, don't have a witness wear the same outfit everyday to show his poverty. Even very poor people change clothes occasionally.

3. Help Your Witness Make Appropriate and Persuasive Emotional Choices

Once you have corrected any aspects of your witness's verbal and non-verbal behavior that might interfere with his credibility, turn your attention to how he expresses his feelings. The basic attitude your witness should impart is one of sincerity, conviction, and willingness. Review his videotaped question-answer session with you, and assess with him the nature of his attitudes. Help him express himself so he conveys sincerity, conviction and willingness. Show him specifically what he is doing that either enhances or detracts from these winning attitudes. Sarcastic or "smartass" attitudes are to be avoided at all costs. Nothing alienates a jury faster than disrespect and put-downs. Openness, a willingness to respond, to cooperate, are all winning attitudes.

It is important to show your witness what he is doing right, what is working to his advantage, so he can increase those behaviors. Too often attorneys only criticize their witness's behavior, and point out the negatives. It's difficult to develop winning behaviors when the only thing pointed out to you are your flaws. With expert witnesses, humility is key. Help your experts share their knowledge rather than impose it.

Histrionic displays of emotion are rarely effective. They tend to embarrass the jurors, and interfere with the witness's ability to tell a coherent story. Help your witness tell his story with sincerity, letting the pain or anger show somewhat, if those are his real emotions which he feels he must express, but not so much that it overwhelms his testimony. Remember also that everyone loves a winner. It is more effective for the witness to demonstrate how, for example, despite the depth of his tragedy, he is going on with his life, than it is for him to indulge in an endless "woe is me" which alienates the jurors. Feeling sorry for oneself is not a highly valued attitude in our society.

CASE IN POINT

A good example of how this works was demonstrated by David Harney when he represented a race car driver who had crashed into a guard rail, resulting in the loss of both his legs. Mr. Harney argued that the guardrail was defective, and he was suing the raceway: "When the client [the race car driver] took the stand at the end of the trial, Harney refused to let him elaborate on how terrible it was to have no legs. Harney simply asked the young man about the race and how the crash happened. Then Harney asked the young man, 'How are you doing now?' 'I'm doing great, Mr. Harney,' the former racer replied in an upbeat voice."[3]

The jurors can easily figure out what life is like without legs; during the course of expert testimony, that has in addition been made abundantly clear. How much more affecting, then, to show how your client is brave in the face of such adversity, rather than allowing him to wallow in it, moaning and groaning. The case was settled in the race car driver's favor for a substantial sum of money.

Use your expert judgement to help your witness determine which emotional choices will be most effective, given the specifics of your case. There is no one emotional choice which works in all cases. There is only the emotional choice which best advances your client's cause. Do not, however, leave these choices up to your witness, or up to chance. Figure them out, deliberately, explain to the witness your rationale for these choices, then have your witness rehearse his testimony repeatedly, using those choices.

4. Use Role Play to Help Your Witness Present Credibly Under Pressure

Once you've coached your witness on his verbal and non-verbal behavior, and gone over his attitudes and emotional choices, it's time to role play the witness's experience in Court. In the case of a client whom you decide not to put on the stand, you only need to role play his walking into Court, how he is to behave when seated next to you, where he is to look, and his general demeanor and deportment. With all witnesses who are to testify, however, role play is much more complex.

Make the role play as close to the real thing as possible. Begin by having your witness role play walking over to the "witness stand" and swearing in. Then take him through direct and cross examinations with zeal and vigor. Teach him how to hold up under pressure. Ask him to tell his story as many different ways as you can think of, always in his own words. Have him tell it from many different angles, deliberately poke holes in it, try to stump him, make it difficult for him. Keep changing how you ask him questions, so he doesn't get used to replying by rote, whether on direct or cross. Make him tell it until his story holds under any circumstances, until he can respond with conviction and sincerity regardless of how you lambast him. Explain to your witness how this present torture will not only prevent future agony on the stand, but will significantly increase the client's chances of success.

Teach your witness to stay cool under fire, teach him to keep his brains in gear and his gut under control. Help him not to take insinuations, or attacks personally by telling him how opposing counsel is simply trying to do his job, and shaking the witness up is an expected part of the game. Get colleagues to take your witness through direct and cross for a number of sessions so that the witness doesn't get too used to your style, and is thereby lulled into a false sense of security.

Make it as hard as you can for the witness during these practice sessions, keep telling him how this will save him much grief later. Videotape these sessions, and go over them with the witness. Help him see and hear where he presents effectively and persuasively, and where he falls down. Show him what to do to correct his mistakes, and then take him through it again. Do this until you are secure in the knowledge that your witness can cope with all the dangers you can think of, then practice some more.

5. Reduce Your Witness's Courtroom Anxiety and Increase His Self-Confidence

Once you've taken your witness through rigorous role play, build his confidence by reassuring him that he is now well and truly prepared to deal with just about anything that can happen in the Courtroom. In addition, use the visualization techniques described in Chapter 10 to reduce any anxiety the witness might have about the actual appearance in Court. Bear in mind that fear of public speaking is one of the most common phobias, and almost all of us fear it to some degree. In addition to excellent preparation, then, take specific steps to allay the witness's fears.

Give your witness a pretrial introduction to the Courtroom

If at all possible, start by taking your witness to the Courtroom ahead of time, or a Courtroom similar to the one in which the trial will occur, show him where everything is located (where the jury sits, where you sit, etc.) and show him what he will be expected to do: where he will walk, sit, and so forth. If it is not possible to take your witness to the actual Courtroom, then draw for him a layout of the Courtroom, and show him where everything will take place.

Explain the technique of visualization and its benefits to your witness

Tell your witness exactly what the technique consists of, how it will help him be less nervous and therefore present himself persuasively in Court, and how you will go about doing the visualization. During your "getting to know you" sessions with your witness, you explored his fears and how he is likely to react under pressure. Use this information now to help you build a successful visualization.

Create a visualization audiotape with your witness

Then begin the actual visualization technique. Have the witness sit comfortably, relax, close his eyes and proceed to take him through his portion of the trial, just as you took yourself through the whole trial in your visualization. Make sure you use highly descriptive words, including what your witness will see, hear, and experience, and create a positive winning version of what is to happen. Keep the visualization in the present tense, for example: "You feel calm and in control, you speak easily and clearly, you find it easy to answer the questions asked."

CASE IN POINT

Your client, Jane, is to testify regarding her injuries, and the pain and suffering she has incurred as a result of the rape she was a victim of two years ago: she is no longer able to have children. This is a very emotional issue for her, and she is afraid of getting hysterical and out of control during cross examination.

Once your witness is comfortably seated, have her take a few deep breaths, and then ask her to listen to the sound of your voice, really seeing, hearing, and feeling everything you talk about.

Start the visualization off by stating your intent: "Jane, the purpose of this visualization is to help you experience the upcoming trial in a positive fashion, so that it is as comfortable as possible for you. Simply follow the sound of my voice as I take you through the trial in your imagination."

Then go through the different aspects of the trial: "As we walk into the Courtroom Tuesday morning, Jane, you are calm and positive. You are a little nervous, which is normal, after all this is a new experience for you, but you feel confident and in control. When it is your turn to testify, you walk calmly to the witness stand, just as you did when we visited the Courtroom a few days ago, and swear in. You answer my questions easily and calmly, you feel comfortable and self-assured. When Mr. Jones gets up to cross-examine you, you remain calm and self-assured. You answer him clearly, calmly, staying in control at all times.

When you feel yourself getting too emotional and are afraid of going out of
control, you simply take a deep breath, wait a moment, and then start answering
again. You handle yourself well throughout the trial, and find that it is all much
easier than you had feared. See yourself impressing the jury favorably, feel them
really on your side."

Include in the visualization any reminders you may wish to give
your witness, such as reminders about posture, eye focus and so forth.
The visualization can be as detailed as you like, but should not run more
than about 20 minutes, or else it will be too long for your witness to do
on a regular basis.

Audiotape the visualization session, and give your witness the tape
to listen to at home, every day, for two to three weeks preceding the trial.
Unconsciously, he will be preparing himself for success, and you will
have a terrific witness.

HOW YOUR CREDIBILITY HELPS ESTABLISH
YOUR WITNESS'S CREDIBILITY

Once you have worked with your witness in the five part strategy
described above to present and express himself in credible manner, one
last element remains to assure his credibility with the jurors: your relationship with him. If you have established *yourself* as credible, then you
can transfer that credibility to your witness by the nature of your relationship to that witness.

If you, a credible attorney, are seen to relate with kindness, courtesy
and warmth or concern to your witness on a consistent basis, then the
jurors will come to see your witness and someone worthy of such consideration. The jurors figure that if you, a credible person, value the witness, then there must be something worthwhile about him and the jurors
will be receptive to accepting the witness as credible also. Your credibility
interacts with that of your witness, and lends credence to his trustworthiness and sincerity.

SUMMARY

Solid preparation of the witness is critical to your case. Tailor the
time and energy you devote per witness in function of each one's relative
importance, but prepare all of your witnesses, even the minor ones. Even
the most experienced sometimes find themselves awkward and uncon-
vincing. Prepare your witnesses well, and it will pay off a hundredfold.

WITNESS INFORMATION WORKSHEET

1. "Sympathetic" information:

_____

_____

_____

_____

_____

_____

_____

Ideas on how to use this information in trial:

_____

_____

_____

_____

_____

_____

2. Witness's fears:

   a. Fears I observe: _____

   _____

   _____

   _____

   _____

   b. Fears witness expresses: _____

   _____

   _____

   _____

   _____

3. Reactions under pressure:

   a. Reactions I observe:_____

   _____

   _____

   _____

   b. Reactions witness reports:_____

   _____

   _____

   _____

"WORKING SESSIONS" WORKSHEET

1. Verbal Behavior:

	Problems	*Corrections*
a. articulation, pace volume, pitch	_____	_____
	_____	_____
	_____	_____
	_____	_____
	_____	_____
	_____	_____
	_____	_____
	_____	_____
	_____	_____
b. ineffective verbal patterns	_____	_____
	_____	_____
	_____	_____
	_____	_____
	_____	_____
	_____	_____
	_____	_____
c. listening skills	_____	_____
	_____	_____
	_____	_____
	_____	_____
	_____	_____
	_____	_____
	_____	_____

	Problems	Corrections
d. "emergency phrases"	_____	_____
	_____	_____
	_____	_____
	_____	_____
	_____	_____
	_____	_____
	_____	_____
	_____	_____
	_____	_____
e. slang and profanity	_____	_____
	_____	_____
	_____	_____
	_____	_____
	_____	_____
	_____	_____
	_____	_____
	_____	_____

2. Non-Verbal Behavior:

   a. eye focus and head position

	Problems	Corrections
b. posture, mannerisms and gestures	_____	_____
	_____	_____
	_____	_____
	_____	_____
	_____	_____
	_____	_____
	_____	_____
	_____	_____
	_____	_____
c. consistency of presentation	_____	_____
	_____	_____
	_____	_____
	_____	_____
	_____	_____
	_____	_____
	_____	_____
	_____	_____
d. visual aids	_____	_____
	_____	_____
	_____	_____
	_____	_____
	_____	_____
	_____	_____
	_____	_____

	Problems	Corrections
e. dress, hair, and make-up	_____	_____
	_____	_____
	_____	_____
	_____	_____
	_____	_____
	_____	_____
	_____	_____
	_____	_____
	_____	_____

TIME-TABLE AND FACT-DIAGRAM WORKSHEET

1. Ask your witness to write out a time-table which includes all the important facts of the case, in sequential order and with the appropriate dates and times noted. Review the time-table with the witness to make sure nothing has been omitted, then help your witness familiarize himself thoroughly with the time-table by asking him questions randomly from different points on that time-table.

2. Review with the witness the important facts of the case. Then help him write out a fact-diagram, as described earlier, for each important fact. Then ask him questions approaching the same facts from different angles, so that he gets used to referring mentally to the appropriate categories on the fact-diagram, and thus remains clear and focused at all times during questioning.

WITNESS VISUALIZATION WORKSHEET

1. Review your witness's "Witness Information Worksheet". Note the fears and reactions to pressure you noted, both your own observations and your witness's reported fears and reactions. Jot down those you want to counteract in the visualization:

_____

_____

_____

_____

_____

_____

2. Make a note of any reminders you want to include regarding your witness's verbal and non-verbal behavior:

_____

_____

_____

_____

_____

_____

3. Make a note of the "emergency" phrases you want your witness to use and when those are to be used:

_____

_____

_____

_____

_____

_____

4. Make a note of the appropriate emotional choices and attitudes you want the witness to make:

_____

_____

_____

_____

_____

_____

5. Using the above information, create an outline of the visualization as you will say it to your witness, being sure to include overall confidence building statements. Keep the visualization postive, highly descriptive, and in the present tense:

_____

_____

_____

_____

_____

_____

_____

_____

_____

_____

_____

_____

_____

_____

_____

_____

_____

CHAPTER 12

Questions and Answers: A Trial Sampler

During the course of my work with attorneys, we discuss how some of the specific problems encountered in trialwork can be alleviated through the use of communication principles. This chapter is devoted to a question and answer sampler of these problems, which are representative of many of the concerns attorneys have expressed. The suggested solutions will show you how some of the techniques described throughout the book are used in specific situations. The suggested solutions, of course, only represent one way of handling these problems, but should help you better understand the direct application of communication principles.

REMINDER "A Winning Case" pertains only to the application of communication principles to the resolution of problems: the substantive aspect of that resolution relies wholly on your legal expertise.

HOW TO DEAL WITH DISTRACTING COUNSEL

Question:

How do I handle distracting conduct of opposing counsel when I or my witness is speaking? For example, opposing counsel shuffles papers, talks to his client or uses other body language showing that what is being said by myself or my client should be ignored or devalued.

Answer:

Notice that opposing counsel is using movement as a distractor, and that it is effective. To counter this, if you yourself are talking, pause a moment, look quizzically at opposing counsel without any anger, not even a trace of it, crossing your face, as if to say "Is there something I can do for you?" If opposing counsel stops, then simply continue your discussion in a calm, sincere tone of voice. If, however, opposing counsel continues, glance briefly at the jury, with a slight smile, as if to say "Gee, some people are really rude, please forgive them," and continue your discussion.

If opposing counsel is carrying on while your witness is speaking, do all of the above, except you obviously do not pause mid-discussion, since you're not talking. In either case, keep a look of absolute innocence on your face, as if you really could not comprehend how someone could do something like that; that opposing counsel must be ill or distracted or just plain old rude, and a subject of pity, not anger.

Anger is not an attractive emotion, and is best used when in the service of righteous indignation, for something really important, and when you are sure the forces of good are on your side. Otherwise it tends to scare people. Showing your exasperation with opposing counsel may only focus attention on the interaction with opposing counsel, and not on your client, where it belongs.

HOW TO MINIMIZE A NEGATIVE SITUATION

Question:

I represent a private bus company. The bus dragged a passenger for two blocks: the person was hanging out of a back door of the bus. How can I minimize the recklessness and inattention of the bus driver?

Answer:

Often, the best defense is a good offense. Assuming there really was recklessness and inattention, then your best bet is to defuse the whole situation by talking up front about the recklessness and inattention; getting to it, in other words, before opposing counsel does, so that you can take the sting out of it. You would therefore admit to the recklessness and inattention—yes there was recklessness, yes there was inattention, but then bring up a list of mitigating factors. Perhaps the bus driver was very ill, or suddenly had migraine, or feared that the bus was going out of control etc..

Use the past tense to distance the experience emotionally from the jury ("there was recklessness, there was inattention"). Don't use color on the words "recklessness" or "inattention," let them be relatively flat. Then, when you talk about the mitigating factors, put these in present tense, and relate them in story format, with lots of color, to make these as vivid and real to the jury as possible.

HOW TO REDEFINE AN ISSUE TO YOUR ADVANTAGE

Question:

I need to show a jury that X Chemical Company's discharge of a hazardous waste into domestic drinking water supplies is insignificant and poses no threat to the environment. What are the elements of courtroom communication that will help me accomplish this task?

Answer:

The power of words is tremendous. The words "hazardous waste" are loaded with emotional connotations, so the first thing to do would be to try to redefine "hazardous waste" into terms which are less emotionally damaging.

Domestic drinking water is composed of many different elements: a chart drawn to visually express the insignificance of this particular element might be useful.

Present yourself as an ordinary "nice guy," not a corporate hireling. Use a tone of warm sincerity, some informality in your speech, wear clothes which are not too formal, nor too stark in color. If you can, personalize your argument. Make analogies to everyday life that the jurors can easily relate to. Stay away from technical terms as much as possible. Making yourself as warmly human as possible will help project the image of Company X as warmly human, and thus unlikely to do anything which would endanger the environment.

HOW TO DEAL WITH ANNOYING COUNSEL

Question:

What do I do when opposing counsel makes noises or gestures after my questions as if to say "That was a dumb question," or "You don't know what you're asking," or inferring my client is lying?

Answer:

Opposing counsel is using body language reactions to "speak" when he really can't speak. If he did it a little more subtly, it would have its effect on the jury without your being able to do much of anything. Fortunately for you in this case, opposing counsel's use of reacting is overt and therefore can be countered.

There are two basic ways of getting ahead in almost any situation: rising above the situation, or chopping off heads. Opposing counsel's method is chopping off heads. You can't beat him at that game without getting dirty yourself, so your best bet is to do the opposite: rise above. Use that same innocent quizzical look at opposing counsel that was suggested above in the answer to the first question, and stay very very cool. Ask your questions in a firm confident manner, with warmth and sincerity. It will be difficult for opposing counsel to effectively imply you don't know what you are doing or that your client is lying, if your manner is one of confidence and warm sincerity.

HOW TO CONDUCT AN IMPROMPTU ORAL ARGUMENT

Question:

What do I do once I've responded adequately to questions by the Judge, but find then that I am suddenly apparently supposed to conduct an oral argument on the spot, and I have no point of reference?

Answer:

First of all, if you've responded adequately, be quiet. You have no more to say. If, however, you feel the need to further explain something, or you feel that it is expected of you to go on, rather than talk without a point of reference, look down a moment (buy yourself some private "think" time), collect your thoughts, then look up and talk. Don't attempt to open your mouth before you are sure of what you have to say.

When in trouble, you're always better off saying less, but having what you say be meaningful.

HOW TO DEAL WITH FRIVOLOUS OBJECTIONS

Question:

Is there a way to subtly express my exasperation to the jury when opposing counsel makes one too many frivolous objections?

Answer:

Yes. Be quiet a moment, look down at the table, close your eyes a second as if it were just too much to bear, but don't make a gesture with your mouth or anything else. Be careful to keep your body language subtle. All eyes are on you so you don't need to do much. Then look up, and in a calm, confident, sincere voice, continue.

The jury is not stupid. They too can hear that the objections are frivolous. If you don't let that throw you, they will be impressed by your ability to "rise above."

HOW TO DEAL WITH AGGRESSIVE COUNSEL

Question:

What do I do when I am faced with more aggressive opposing attorneys who seem to establish a rapport with the Judge and then, go on talking until they've convinced the Judge and before I can object?

Answer:

Those opposing attorneys are communication-smart. Establishing rapport with the Judge and taking advantage of that rapport are good communication tactics. How can you counter these tactics? By developing some of your own, in particular, by developing your assertiveness.

You can develop your assertiveness by taking assertiveness classes, or working with a psychologist, or you can teach yourself with the aid of tapes and books. I highly recommend a book by Manuel J. Smith, Ph.D., called *When I Say No, I Feel Guilty* which gives you many excellent and very practical ways to be more assertive verbally without becoming obnoxious.

While you're building up your assertiveness skills in more general fashion, so *you* can be the one to establish rapport and keep talking, rather than opposing counsel, you need to be able to object. Thinking that you can't is detrimental. Simply say "Excuse me, Your Honor" clearly and in a firm confident voice, and walk forward two steps, then stop. If need be, repeat again "Excuse me, Your Honor" politely and clearly, with a little more volume, then wait.

The two steps forward you took represent a "body break," which will disrupt the current situation with body language in an extremely subtle way, and throw everyone a little off balance so you can be heard. You obviously were not being heard previously. A body break can be used anytime you need to disrupt ongoing proceedings, and may be as overt or subtle as you think is necessary.

HOW TO RELOCATE YOUR FOCUS TO CONTROL YOUR NERVOUSNESS

Question:

What do I do about my shaky voice and my inability to make my mind work while I'm the focus of attention?

Answer:

Take the focus off yourself. You have work to do. If your voice quavers and your mind blocks, for example, during your opening statement, then concentrate on mirroring different members of the jury as you talk, concentrate on putting the appropriate emotion through your voice at the appropriate moments. If it happens when you're doing your cross-examination, focus in on creating rapport with the witness.

Whenever you feel on the spot, that all eyes are on you, judging you, *immediately* focus out and onto someone other than yourself. Your symptoms will fade quite rapidly. Remember, however, that your voice sounds shakiest to yourself. Remember also that anytime you can't think, simply drop your head down a moment, collect your thoughts, raise your head, and speak. It usually only takes a few seconds to collect your thoughts, and people will wait.

Before the trial, work on the techniques given for reducing Courtroom anxiety. Be sure to include in your visualization of the trial, the optimum solution and ways of dealing with your shaky voice and blocking mind, so that you will be very prepared on a conscious as well as a subconscious level to deal with the situation when the time comes.

HOW TO HUMANIZE A CORPORATE CLIENT

Question:

I would like to get the jury's sympathy for my subcontractor *corporation*, having been cheated by the general contractor, an *individual*. How do I accomplish this?

Answer:

The jury's stereotype of a corporation is of an impersonal, inhuman entity which has no concern for human values. So what you need to do is humanize, personalize the corporation. Present yourself as a warm kind human being. Dress in a way which is not overly formal, wear colors which suggest warmth. Use a moderately casual vocabulary and delivery, steer clear of pedantic terms or anything too formal.

If at all possible, talk about your corporate client in terms of the people it is composed of. Make this a story about *people* just like the jurors, who in this instance are getting hurt, just as undoubtedly members of the jury at one time or another have been hurt. This will enable to jurors to identify with, and therefore empathize with, the corporation. They can't do that with a nameless and faceless corporate entity.

HOW TO PREVENT YOUR PERSONAL DISLIKE OF A CLIENT FROM ADVERSELY AFFECTING THE JURORS

Question:

My client is a brilliant man, and undoubtedly has the law on his side in this case, but he is rude beyond belief, an intolerable cur. I am afraid that my personal distaste for my client will bleed off into the jury and damage my case. How can I prevent that?

Answer:

You are quite right, you cannot allow your personal dislike of a client to stand in the way of the success of your case. First of all, see if you can work with your client to demonstrate to him that his rudeness is easily perceived by the jurors, and can affect his case adversely. Appeal to his self-interest. Secondly, with your body language, transfer your credibility to your client. Whenever you're in view of the jurors, sit reasonably close to your client, listen attentively when he speaks, smile at him occasionally (slight smile, not all teeth), occasionally touch his arm or shoulder when speaking to him.

If he hasn't changed his behavior much, the jurors may still perceive your client as rude, but the effect will be attenuated by your considerate treatment of him. After all, if he is acceptable to you, a credible person, then by inference there must be something worthy about him.

HOW TO KEEP TALKING WHEN TOLD BY THE JUDGE TO STOP

Question:

What do I do when the Judge, who has too many cases to hear and wants to get on with it, tells me to stop when I'm in the middle of my argument, and have some very legitimate points still to make? I have the right to present my case as I wish, and an obligation to my client to get all my points across.

Answer:

Yes, you do have both the right and responsibility to present your case as you wish, but the Judge is Lord and Master of the Courtroom. What he says, goes. Therefore, adopt a two-step solution. First of all, show respect to the Judge, acknowledge his concerns. This generally consists of repeating in somewhat different words whatever the Judge gave as reasons for wanting you to stop: "Your Honor, I understand that you feel I have sufficiently addressed . . . " Secondly, find a way to *continue* rather than trying to violate the Judge's order. Don't say "But I just have one more point," rather ask the Judge to allow you to *finish* your point, "Please just let me finish my point." Rarely will he deny you this, but if he does, accept the order graciously.

Don't let your displeasure with the Judge show in words, tone, or body language. Remember that juries venerate Judges, and whatever he says is "right." By your respect and deference to the Judge, gain points with the jurors, even if you are unhappy with the Judge's order.

HOW TO CURTAIL YOUR WITNESS'S VERBOSITY DURING CROSS-EXAMINATION

Question:

Sometimes my witness wants to be really helpful, or wants to make absolutely sure he gets his story across, or is uncertain as to how much he should say, and so he just keeps going on and on, and ends up giving opposing counsel all sorts of information I would rather he didn't have. How do I keep my witness from talking too much during cross-examination?

Answer:

First of all, impress upon your witness the substantive importance of answering only the question that is asked him, and that as simply and directly as possible. Secondly, help your witness in his moments of doubt by giving him appropriate body language and facial expressions. Tell your witness that if you feel it is in his best interests to keep talking, you will be looking at him in an open and encouraging way, and show him what you mean. If, on the contrary, you feel he could damage his case by continuing, you will be looking down or away.

In other words, teach your witness to work cooperatively with you when he is on the stand. Let him know that he is not alone, that you are there to support and guide him as he goes through cross examination.

HOW TO CURTAIL AN ADVERSE WITNESS'S VERBOSITY

Question:

What do I do when an adverse witness starts talking a mile a minute and I am afraid of appearing rude or obnoxious by interrupting him?

Answer:

Don't try to interrupt him. Let him talk. Let him, as Mr. David R. Glickman puts it succinctly: " . . . talk all he wants. The more an adverse witness talks, the more his mouth is open. The more his mouth is open, the more room there is to stick his foot in, and the more frequently your opponent's case dies of foot-in-mouth disease."[1]

There is no need for you to appear rude or obnoxious. Simply hear the witness out, make mental notes as to all the new information you now possess that can be useful to you, and go on once he's done.

HOW TO GAIN JUROR SYMPATHY FOR PERPETRATORS OF HEINOUS CRIMES

Question:

I am a criminal defendant, and as such, often represent people who have committed really heinous crimes. How do I present such a person to the jurors in a way that will win over their sympathy for my client?

Answer:

Get to know your client. Find out everything you can about him, and as you sift through the information you've received, start off by looking for the little bit of good there is in him. Proceed, however Pollyannaish it may seem, on the assumption that there is a little bit of good in every one, and look for that good. When you find that bit of good, use it to try to convince the jury that this person's life is worth saving.

Secondly, sift through the same information looking for reasons why the person committed this heinous crime. It is highly unusual for a person to be evil from birth, just on his own, in the complete absence of contributing factors. Look for those contributing factors: was your client abused as a child, did he have an alcoholic father, was he born of a chronically depressed and dysfunctional mother? Help the jurors to understand these factors. Remember that we all want to live in a world that makes sense. If you can present your client's crime in such a way that, no matter how hideous it is, it is a logical outgrowth of certain conditions, you have better chances of gaining the jurors' sympathy.

HOW TO GET COOPERATION FROM DIFFICULT OR NONTRUSTING CLIENTS

Question:

As public defendant, I am often faced with clients who come from totally different worlds from mine: they don't like me, don't trust me, and are difficult to work with, even though I am convinced they know it is in their best interest to cooperate with me. How do I get them to be more cooperative?

Answer:

Spend some time with your clients. Find out what their world is like, find out what is interesting to them. Mr. Jim Gregory, an eminent Los Angeles–based criminal attorney, cites two specific examples which illustrate this point well. He was defending a 60-year-old man in a child-shooting case, and having difficulty working with the man. He found out his client loved to read, and so he sent him books while the man was in jail awaiting trial. Mr. Gregory succeeded in building rapport, and its natural consequence—cooperation—by attending to what his client liked. Similarly, in the course of defending a gang member, Mr. Gregory became interested in Los Angeles gangs in general, and was able to speak knowledgeably with his client about the local gangs. In this way he established communication with his client, which in turn generated the rapport and cooperation he needed in order to conduct a persuasive defense.

HOW TO USE A DEPOSITION TO YOUR BEST ADVANTAGE

Question:

I've heard conflicting opinions on the usefulness of taking depositions myself, as opposed to letting a junior associate handle it, or sending a written interrogatory. Do you feel depositions are useful for the presentational aspects of trial or not?

Answer:

Depositions are very useful for the presentational aspects of trial. Depositions are your opportunity to explore a witness's general appearance, mannerisms, body language and posture, emotional reactivity, attitude of sincerity and conviction, how the witness expresses himself, how he perceives things, how he is likely to respond under pressure, and so forth, all adding up to how the witness is likely to impress a jury. Armed with such vital prior knowledge, think how much more successfully you can build your case.

Contrast the wealth of information so obtained with what you get from a written interrogatory. A written interrogatory only gives you facts, information of use to the substantive dimension of your case, whereas a deposition gives you both the substantive information and information for the presentational dimension of trial. This is why it is highly advisable to take the deposition of a defendant even when there is no question as to liability.

As to the matter of whether or not a junior associate should be the one to take depositions, the answer would be: only if you have trained him well as to what to look for. If you don't have someone that well trained on your staff, then absolutely, take the deposition yourself.

SUMMARY

Communication techniques are practical techniques. A thorough knowledge of the techniques and principles presented in *A Winning Case* will help you handle situations which otherwise might seriously hamper the success your expertise warrants.

References

CHAPTER 1

1. Couric, Emily, *The Trial Lawyers*. New York: St. Martin's Press, 1988, p. 43.
2. Cramer, M. Michael, "A View from the Jury Box," *The Litigation Manual*. Section of litigation, American Bar Association (1983), pp. 145-47.
3. *Ibid*.
4. Sears, David O., Jonathan L. Freedman, and Letitia A. Peplau, *Social Psychology*. Englewood Cliffs, NJ: Prentice-Hall, 1985.
5. Higginbotham, Patrick E. (1983). "How to Try a Jury Case: A Judge's View," *The Litigation Manual*. Section of litigation, American Bar Association, p. 133.

CHAPTER 3

1. Bailey, William S., "A Lawyer Looks at Jury Duty." *The Docket*, Winter 1989, pp. 9–15.
2. Gamblee, Joanne D., "What It's Like to Serve on a Jury." *Barrister*, 1979, Vol.6 (3), pp. 16–20.
3. Hanley, Robert F., "The Importance of Being Yourself." *The Docket*, Fall 1985, pp. 12–13.

CHAPTER 4

1. *Doubleday Dictionary*. New York: Doubleday, 1985.
2. Sheresky, Norman, *On Trial*. New York: Viking Press, 1977, pp. 12–13.
3. Allison, William P., "The Environment of the Trial," in D. Lake Rumsey (Ed.), *Master Advocates' Handbook*. St. Paul, MN: National Institute for Trial Advocacy, 1986, p. 24.

CHAPTER 5

1. Couric, Emily, *The Trial Lawyers*. New York: St. Martin's Press, 1988, p. 319.
2. Strayhorn, Honorable E., "The Importance Of Watching and Listening," in D. Lake Rumsey (Ed.), *Master Advocates' Handbook*. St. Paul, MN: National Institute for Trial Advocacy, 1986, p. 14.
3. Couric, Emily, *The Trial Lawyers*. New York: St. Martin's Press, 1988, p. 137.

CHAPTER 6

1. Couric, Emily, *The Trial Lawyers*. New York: St. Martin's Press, 1988, p. 207.
2. Schuetz, Janice and Kathryn H. Snedaker, *Communication and Litigation*. Carbondale and Edwardsville: Southern Illinois University Press, 1988, p. 82.
3. Couric, Emily, *The Trial Lawyers*. New York: St. Martin's Press, 1988, pp. 27–28.
4. Adapted from Janice Schuetz and Kathryn H. Snedaker, *Communication and Litigation*. Carbondale and Edwardsville: Southern Illinois University Press, 1988.
5. Schuetz, Janice and Kathryn H. Snedaker, *Communication and Litigation*. Carbondale and Edwardsville: Southern Illinois University Press, 1988, p. 84.
6. Couric, Emily, *The Trial Lawyers*. New York: St. Martin's Press, 1988, p. 209.
7. Couric, Emily, *The Trial Lawyers*. New York: St. Martin's Press, 1988, pp. 107–8.
8. Schuetz, Janice and Kathryn H. Snedaker, *Communication and Litigation*. Carbondale and Edwardsville: Southern Illinois University Press, 1988, p. 175.
9. Sheresky, Norman, *On Trial*. New York: Viking Press, 1977, p. 24.

CHAPTER 7

1. Couric, Emily, *The Trial Lawyers*. New York: St. Martin's Press, 1988, pp. 1–39.
2. Cramer, M. Michael. "A View from the Jury Box," *The Litigation Manual*. Section of litigation, American Bar Association, 1983, p. 146.
3. Cartwright, Dorwin (Ed.), *Studies in Social Power*. Ann Arbor: University of Michigan, 1959, p. 147.

4. Kerr, Robert L. and Robert M. Bray (Eds.), *Psychology of the Courtroom*. New York: Academic Press, 1982, p. 203.

5. Couric, Emily, *The Trial Lawyers*. New York: St. Martin's Press, 1988, p. 162.

6. Couric, Emily, *The Trial Lawyers*. New York: St. Martin's Press, 1988, pp. 243–44.

7. Sheresky, Norman, *On Trial*. New York: Viking Press, 1977, p. 43.

8. Sheresky, Norman, *On Trial*. New York: Viking Press, 1977, pp. 206–18.

9. Sheresky, Norman. *On Trial*. New York: Viking Press, 1977, pp. 68–76.

10. Couric, Emily, *The Trial Lawyers*. New York: St. Martin's Press, 1988, pp. 49–54.

11. Couric, Emily, *The Trial Lawyers*. New York: St. Martin's Press, 1988, p. 162.

12. Couric, Emily, *The Trial Lawyers*. New York: St. Martin's Press, 1988, pp. 180–81.

13. Sears, David O., Jonathan L. Freedman, and Letitia A. Peplau, *Social Psychology*. Englewood Cliffs, NJ: Prentice-Hall, 1985, p. 154.

14. Sheresky, Norman, *On Trial*. New York: Viking Press, 1977, pp. 2–3.

15. Klieman, Rikki J., "How To Deliver a Convincing and Winning Opening Statement in a Criminal Defense," in Janine N. Warsaw (Ed.), *Women Trial Lawyers: How They Succeed in Practice and in the Courtroom*. Englewood Cliffs, NJ: Prentice-Hall, 1987, p. 282.

16. Lambert, Marie, "How to Improve Your Courtroom Appearance," in Janine N. Warsaw (Ed.), *Women Trial Lawyers: How They Succeed in Practice and in the Courtroom*. Englewood Cliffs, NJ: Prentice-Hall, 1987, p. 97.

17. Sheresky, Norman, *On Trial*. New York: Viking Press, 1977, pp. 110–20.

18. Touhy, James, "Effective Final Argument for the Plaintiff," *The Litigation Manual*. Section of litigation, American Bar Association, 1983, pp. 168–71.

19. Couric, Emily, *The Trial Lawyers*. New York: St. Martin's Press, 1988, p. 143.

20. Loftus, E., "Reconstructing Memory: The Incredible Eyewitness" *Psychology Today*, 1974, Vol.8 (1), p. 116.

21. Klieman, Rikki J., "How To Deliver a Convincing and Winning Opening Statement in a Criminal Defense," in Janine N. Warsaw (Ed.), *Women Trial Lawyers: How They Succeed in Practice and in the Courtroom*. Englewood Cliffs, NJ: Prentice-Hall, 1987, pp. 284–85.

22. Couric, Emily, *The Trial Lawyers*. New York: St. Martin's Press, 1988, p. 140.

CHAPTER 9

1. Kerr, Robert L. and Robert M. Bray (Eds.), *Psychology of the Courtroom*. New York: Academic Press, 1982, p. 175.
2. *Doubleday Dictionary*. New York: Doubleday, 1975.

CHAPTER 11

1. Klieman, Rikki J., "How to Deliver a Convincing and Winning Opening Statement in a Criminal Defense," in Janine N. Warsaw (Ed.), *Women Trial Lawyers: How They Succeed in Practice and in the Courtroom*. Englewood Cliffs, NJ: Prentice-Hall, 1987, p. 281.
2. Couric, Emily, *The Trial Lawyers*. New York: St. Martin's Press, 1988, p. 164.
3. Couric, Emily, *The Trial Lawyers*. New York: St. Martin's Press, 1988, p. 121.

CHAPTER 12

1. Quote taken from an interview with Mr. Dave Glickman, by the author, on January 19, 1990.

Index